Second Edition

RACE AND ETHNICITY

THE UNITED STATES AND THE WORLD

edited by

Raymond Scupin

Lindenwood University

PEARSON

Boston   Columbus   Indianapolis   New York   San Francisco   Upper Saddle River
Amsterdam   Cape Town   Dubai   London   Madrid   Milan   Munich   Paris   Montreal   Toronto
Delhi   Mexico City   Sao Paulo   Sydney   Hong Kong   Seoul   Singapore   Taipei   Tokyo

Editorial Director: Craig Campanella
Editor in Chief: Dickson Musslewhite
Publisher: Nancy Roberts
Project Manager, Editorial: Nicole Conforti
Editorial Assistant: Nart Varoqua
Director of Marketing: Brandy Dawson
Senior Marketing Manager: Laura Lee Manley
Managing Editor: Maureen Richardson
Project Manager, Production: Shelly Kupperman
Senior Operations Supervisor: Mary Fischer

Senior Operations Specialist: Sherry Lewis
Director, Cover Design: Jayne Conte
Cover Designer: Bruce Kenselaar
Cover Art: ©Blend Images/Alamy
Digital Media Editor: Rachel Comerford
Full-Service Project Management and Composition:
  Integra Software Services Private Ltd.
Printer/Binder: R.R. Donnelley & Sons
Cover Printer: R.R. Donnelley & Sons

Credits and acknowledgments borrowed from other sources and reproduced, with permission, in this textbook appear on page 461 within text.

Library of Congress Cataloging-in-Publication Data
Raymond Scupin,
  Race and Ethnicity: the United States and the World/edited by Raymond Scupin.—2nd ed.
    p. cm.
  ISBN-13: 978-0-205-06447-2 (alk. paper)
  ISBN-10: 0-205-06447-7 (alk. paper)
  1. Race.   2. Ethnicity.   I. Scupin, Raymond.
  GN269.R325 2012
  305.8—dc22

                                        2010050447

10 9 8 7 6 5 4 3 2 1

ISBN 13: 978-0-205-06447-2
ISBN 10:   0-205-06447-7

CONTENTS

Part II   Race and Ethnicity in the United States

Chapter 11 ASIAN AMERICANS 246

Janet E. Benson, Kansas State University

PREFACE

Ethnic unrest and tension are prevalent in the contemporary world. Newspapers and television news are rife with stories about ethnic violence among the peoples of the former Soviet Union and Eastern Europe, Africa, Sri Lanka, India, Ireland, the Middle East, and the United States. Thus, as globalization rapidly expands and both undermines and strengthens ethnic and national identities, an understanding of race and of ethnicity issues becomes more pertinent.

This book is an introductory survey of the basic concepts and research in the field of anthropology and sociology on race and ethnicity in the United States and throughout the world. Both sociologists and anthropologists have been doing research on race and ethnicity for more than a hundred years and have developed a profound understanding of race and ethnicity issues. However, these sociological and anthropological insights have not been communicated widely. Race and ethnicity issues have had immense effects on both U.S. and global political trends and have created innumerable tensions and misunderstandings among different groups. An anthropological and sociological understanding of race and ethnicity has clarified some of these misconceptions and may help relieve some of these tensions.

One of the major objectives of both sociology and anthropology is to comprehend both the differences and the similarities among different groups of humans throughout the world. A major lesson derived from anthropological and sociological research is that as different groups learn about each other's cultural values, norms, behaviors, goals, and aspirations, the less likely they are to maintain rigid stereotypes and misconceptions about one another. Thus, one of the practical results of anthropological and sociological research is a reduction in racism, ethnocentrism, and animosities and tensions. As students learn to discern what sociologists and anthropologists have learned about race and ethnicity issues, they are more likely to be able to adjust and become more productive citizens in an increasingly multicultural and globally integrated world. A comprehensive understanding of race and ethnicity issues is a fundamental aspect of a well-rounded liberal arts education.

WHAT'S NEW TO THIS EDITION

- We have re-emphasized both the anthropological and sociological approaches to race and ethnicity issues to incorporate both disciplines throughout the textbook.
- We have condensed the chapter on the History of "Scientific" Racialism and incorporated the most recent findings on the controversial IQ and race issues debunking the *Bell Curve* and Phillipe Rushton's racialistic conceptions.
- We have updated the most recent findings regarding the genetic and paleoanthropological data that highlight the misconceptions of a simplistic typological view of race, emphasizing the social construction of the race concept.
- We have added a discussion of David Berreby's book *Us and Them* within the chapter by Donald E. Brown dealing with the universals of ethnocentrism and ethnicity.
- We have updated all the census and demographic data regarding all the different ethnic groups in U.S. society.
- Ellen Bigler has added a critique of Samuel Huntington's book *Who Are We?* and his simplistic approach in understanding Hispanic/Latino Americans.
- We have added more recent materials on the current issues that have an impact on Arab Americans since 9/11 in the chapter on Arab Americans.

- We have included new materials on race and ethnicity in the chapters on Latin America and the Caribbean, Africa, the Middle East, and Asia.
- Norman Buchignani reconstructed and updated the discussion of multiculturalism in Canada.
- Pamela Ballinger has added new materials on the current issues of immigration along with new discussions of ethnic issues that have influenced Europe.

The editor would like to thank all of the contributors, who provided excellent chapters representing the most recent anthropological research on the various aspects of race and ethnicity. Unfortunately the author of Chapter 2, Leonard Lieberman, passed away in February 2007. As a physical anthropologist, Leonard Lieberman had made tremendous contributions in understanding both historical and contemporary race issues. In this second edition of the textbook we have modified and updated his chapter in honor of his contributions. All of the contributors have reviewed and suggested revisions for the chapters written by the editor. The editor, and the contributors, would also like to thank Bernard Bernier, University of Montreal; John J. Bukowczyk, Wayne State University; Martin Cohen, California State University, Fullerton; Pamela A. DeVoe, St. Louis Community College, Meramec; Dru Gladney, Pomona College; Robert M. Hayden, University of Pittsburgh; Sharlotte Neely, Northern Kentucky University; Mary O'Connor, University of California, Santa Barbara; Susana Sawyer, University of California, Davis; Robert Sussman, Washington University; and William C. Young, Yarmouk University, Irbid, Jordan, for reviewing the chapters. We would also like to thank David Berreby of *Us and Them* fame for his excellent suggestions for Donald E. Brown's Chapter 5 on the naturalness of ethnocentrism and ethnicity.

Our thanks go to Nancy Roberts, Publisher for Social Science, for recommending this textbook for publication, Nicole Conforti and Shelly Kupperman for managing this project, and Shiny Rajesh at Integra for keeping this textbook on deadline.

Ray Scupin

1

■ ■ ■

Race and Ethnicity: Anthropological and Sociological Perspectives

Raymond Scupin, *Lindenwood University*

In 1999, 21-year-old Benjamin Smith spent the July 4th weekend cruising in his car in Chicago and central Indiana areas shooting at African Americans, Orthodox Jews, and Asians. In this three-day shooting spree, two were killed and nine were wounded before Smith shot and killed himself during a police chase. The African American killed was Rick Birdsong, a former basketball coach at Northwestern University. He was jogging with his children when he was shot in the back. Won Joined Soon, a Korean graduate student at Indiana University, was killed outside of a Korean church.

Benjamin Smith was a former member of the World Church of the Creator, which is currently led by Matt Hale of East Peoria, Illinois. Hale refers to himself as Pontifex Maximus and teaches that only white Anglo-Saxons are true human beings, descendants of Adam and Eve. Jews are believed to be illegitimate offspring of Eve and Satan, and African Americans and other people of color are descendants of inferior non-Adamite anthropoids called "mud people." The church believes that the United States should be "cleansed" of all Jews and nonwhites. The church's Web site features a discussion of the mental inferiority of African Americans, with a reference to Canadian psychologist Philippe Rushton's "scientific" research confirming this view.

Although groups such as the World Church of the Creator are small, with only a few thousand members, their influence seems to be on the rise. For many years, most social scientists believed that racism and ethnic conflict were going to decline. However, the Southern Poverty Law Center (splcenter.org), a group that has been a leading authority on reporting hate groups, indicates that since 2000 there are a record number of 926 hate groups in the United States, an increase of more than 50 percent. These hate groups include Klu Klux Klan cells, Neo-Nazi sects, white nationalists, racist skinheads, and other merchants of hate. Despite the fact that the current U.S. president is an African American and the United States has politicians who are

Jewish, Muslim, and Hispanic, hate groups and racism are still a reality in U.S. society and the world.

Some commentators have suggested that since Obama was elected as president, the United States has become a *post-racial* society. In one major interpretation of this *post-racial* phenomenon, Obama represents the fulfillment of Dr. Martin Luther King Jr.'s famed "I Have a Dream" speech in 1963 in which he suggested a future U.S. society where all humans would be judged by the content of their character, rather than the color of their skin. This interpretation of *post-racial* suggests that President Obama's election has ended prejudice and discrimination based on skin color or ethnicity and the reduction of inequality in income, education, and political power. However, as the various chapters in this textbook will indicate, the term *post-racial* appears to be a greatly exaggerated interpretation of Barack Obama's 2008 election. Racial prejudice

President Barack Obama.

and discrimination persists in U.S. society (and elsewhere throughout the world). The claim that race or ethnicity does not matter any longer in the United States or elsewhere has to be viewed with a great deal of skepticism.

And in other parts of the world, extremist racist and ethnic groups have emerged within the past two decades. For example, in the former East Germany there has been a rise of a neo-Nazi movement among German youth who resent the immigration of nonwhites into their society. Ethnic extremism among the Hutu and Tutsi peoples in Central Africa has resulted in tragic genocidal policies. Conflicts among Serbs, Croatians, and Bosnians in Yugoslavia, Tamils and Sinhalese in Sri Lanka, Jews and Arabs in Israel, and so-called "white Europeans" and "people of color" in the United States are ongoing. Everywhere one looks, ethnic conflict seems to be emerging worldwide. Although the causes of these conflicts are very complex, ethnic and race conflicts remain a continuing global problem in the twenty-first century.

Currently, we live in societies that are becoming more globalized, with more extensive contact among peoples of different ethnic backgrounds and cultures. Globalization refers to the expansion and interlinking of the world's economy through the spread of market capitalism, communications technology, and industrialization and their consequences. One of the results of globalization has been the transfer of capital, technology, labor, and media throughout the world. Global migration trends have been radically transformed since the 1950s. Immigration from Latin America and the Caribbean, Asia, Africa, and the Middle East—the so-called Third World—to the industrial societies of Europe, the United States, Australia, and Canada has increased substantially. For example, England and France have growing numbers of immigrants from their former colonies in Africa and Asia. Furthermore, the societies in the Third World are also being transformed by new trends in immigration. Refugees and migrants are becoming increasingly mobile throughout the world.

Societies that may have been very homogeneous or ethnically similar in the past are now facing questions about their increasing multicultural and multiethnic differences.

As we will see in later chapters, U.S. society in the nineteenth and early twentieth centuries faced similar issues. Immigrants flowed into the United States from many areas of the world. Currently, the United States is again encountering the challenge of multiculturalism. For example, a typical elementary school in Los Angeles may have as many as 20 different native languages spoken by members of the school population. In 2000, California became the first U.S. state where the white ethnic population became a minority. Due to the increase of Hispanic and Asian populations, the white ethnic population was 49.9 percent. Event calendars in daily newspapers announce ethnic festivals in major U.S. cities that originated in many nations. All of these changes have resulted in some reservations regarding the new ethnic patterns and multiculturalism in the United States. In 1991, the distinguished historian Arthur Schlesinger wrote a book entitled *The Disuniting of America,* which argued that ethnic and racial separatism was the major obstacle for a truly integrated multicultural society in the United States. Schlesinger believes that extreme versions of multicultural education and what he terms the "cult of ethnicity" are tearing apart the U.S. social and political fabric. He suggests that the growing emphasis on multicultural heritage exalts racial and ethnic pride at the expense of social and political cohesion. On the other hand, other scholars, such as Nathan Glazer in his book *We Are All Multiculturalists Now,* argue that all children should be taught mutual tolerance and respect for all of the various ethnic groups in U.S. society.

As societies become more multicultural and multiethnic, they confront new challenges. In many circumstances, ethnic groups may be in competition with each other over political and economic resources. In other cases, they may be at odds over religious or other cultural differences. Conversely, some people are benefiting from the multicultural trends in their society by learning from one another's cultures, thereby discovering that multicultural environments can enrich one's experience and be extremely rewarding.

In any case, many people are seeking answers to basic questions regarding these new changes in race and ethnic trends within their societies in the twenty-first century. What are the reasons for these continuing race and ethnic conflicts and problems? Do the claims of people like Matt Hale and the World Church about superior and inferior racial groups have any scientific validity? What are the significant distinctions among the races? What is the difference between race and ethnicity? What is the basis of one's ethnic identity? Why do some societies and countries have less race and ethnic conflict than others? Why has there been a recent increase in racial and ethnic conflict around the globe? Have these racial and ethnic conflicts always existed? Under what conditions do increases in race and ethnic conflict occur? Under what societal conditions do race and ethnic prejudice and discrimination develop? In what interracial and interethnic situations can race and ethnic prejudice be reduced? Under what conditions do different ethnic groups live peaceably together and benefit from each other's experience?

Sociologists and anthropologists are currently engaged in major research efforts in an attempt to answer some of these questions. In fact, both disciplines have an intimate acquaintanceship with questions about race and ethnicity issues. Anthropology was the first field devoted to systematic scientific investigations into questions about race and ethnicity. These questions persist as one of the fundamental priorities within the research efforts of contemporary anthropologists.

This textbook will cover some of the most important research on race and ethnicity by both sociologists and anthropologists. Although the authors of the various chapters are anthropologists, most of them have drawn from sociological studies, too. But, first, we will discuss the interrelationship between these questions about race and ethnicity and the discipline of anthropology.

ANTHROPOLOGY: THE FOUR FIELDS AND RACE AND ETHNICITY ISSUES

The word *anthropology* stems from the Greek words *anthropo,* meaning "human beings" or "humankind," and *logia,* translated as "knowledge of" or "the study of." Thus, we can define anthropology as the systematic study of humankind. The field of anthropology emerged in Western society in an attempt to understand non-Western peoples. Europeans, including Christopher Columbus, had been exploring and colonizing the world since the fifteenth century. They had encounters with non-Western peoples in the Americas, Africa, the Middle East, and Asia. Various European travelers, missionaries, and government officials had described some of these non-Western societies, cultures, and races. By the nineteenth century, anthropology had developed into the primary discipline and science for understanding these non-Western societies, races, and cultures. The major questions that these early nineteenth-century anthropologists grappled with had to do with the basic differences and similarities of human societies, cultures, and races throughout the world.

The predominant explanation that nineteenth-century anthropologists offered to explain the differences and similarities among human societies, cultures, and races became known as *unilineal evolution.* Charles Darwin had developed his theory regarding the evolution of life in 1859, with the publication of his book *On the Origin of Species.* Many anthropologists of the nineteenth century were influenced by Darwin's thesis, and attempted to apply these evolutionary concepts to the study of human societies, cultures, and races. These early anthropologists took the descriptions of early historians, archaeologists, classical scholars, travelers, missionaries, and colonial officials for their basic data. Based on these data, they proposed that all societies and cultures had developed from early, original "savage" stages through a stage of "barbarianism," and eventually some evolved into "civilized" stages. Thus, these early anthropologists developed models of the stages of humankind's universal history using the concept of unilineal evolution.[1] They constructed a model of a hierarchy of societies that could be ranked from savage to civilized based on differences in society, culture, technology, and race.

Since the nineteenth century, anthropology as a field has continued its research efforts of different societies, cultures, and "races." However, beginning in the twentieth century, many of the ideas of nineteenth-century theorists were thoroughly criticized and debunked through systematic and scientific research techniques. The efforts of nineteenth-century anthropologists need to be understood within their own historical setting. These early anthropologists did not have a very precise understanding of the concept of "culture," nor did they comprehend the roles of genetics and heredity. The development of a more thorough concept of culture and a scientific understanding of heredity and genetics did not develop until the twentieth century. Because of their limited understanding of culture and heredity, they labored under many misconceptions about non-Western societies, cultures, and races. One of the basic underlying assumptions was that their own society and culture were superior to those of any other. This is an example of what is known as *ethnocentrism,* the belief that one's own society and culture are superior to any other. In addition, during the nineteenth century, most of these early anthropologists were convinced that their own so-called "race" was superior to that of any other "race." This is known as *racism,* the belief that there are distinctive biological "races" and that one can rank and categorize superior and inferior biological "races" within the human species.

It was only after twentieth-century anthropologists absorbed the new findings of genetics and heredity, developed a more sophisticated comprehension of the concept of culture, and had a better appreciation of concepts of "race" and "ethnicity" that these earlier views could be criticized exhaustively. One of the major anthropological projects that critiqued these early views was associated with the efforts of Franz Boas (1858–1942). Boas had been born, educated, and trained in physics in Germany. Later, he became interested in geography and culture and did research among the Eskimo in the Canadian Arctic. Through these experiences he turned to the study of anthropology, immigrated to the United States, and taught for many years at Columbia University. While at Columbia, Boas and his students carried out extensive research in physical anthropology, archaeology, linguistics, and cultural anthropology (or ethnology), providing the contemporary foundations for the systematic investigation of such topics as race, culture, and ethnicity (Degler 1991; Stocking 1968). One of the primary aspects of research that Boas emphasized was the "fieldwork" experience in anthropology. Instead of speculating on various theories about the evolution of culture based on written materials, anthropologists had to go into the "field" and do empirical research among the people in different societies.

In the United States, Boas's research activities developed into what has become known as the "four-field approach" within anthropology. Most U.S. anthropology programs feature four subdisciplines, or subfields, that bridge the natural sciences, the social sciences, and the humanities. These four subdisciplines—physical anthropology, archaeology, linguistic anthropology, and ethnology—give anthropologists a broad, holistic approach to the study of humanity through space and time. In addition, all four of these fields have enabled contemporary anthropologists to contribute significantly toward the study of race and ethnicity. Though these four subfields demarcate the fields within which most anthropological research is conducted, we need to emphasize that within these four fields anthropologists draw on the findings of many other disciplines, such as biology, history, psychology, economics, sociology, and political science, to examine race and ethnic relations. These four fields, however, offer anthropologists a unique perspective for assessing questions of race and ethnicity.

Physical Anthropology

Physical anthropology (or biological anthropology) is the branch of anthropology most closely related to the natural sciences. Physical anthropologists conduct research in two major areas: human evolution and human variation. The majority of physical anthropologists focus on human evolution. Some investigate fossils, the preserved remains of bones and living materials from earlier periods, to reconstruct the evolution and anatomical characteristics of early human ancestors. The study of human evolution through analysis of fossils is called *paleoanthropology* (the prefix *paleo* means "old" or "prehistoric"). Paleoanthropologists use a variety of sophisticated scientific techniques to date, classify, and compare fossil bones in order to determine the links between modern humans and their biological ancestors. For example, paleoanthropologists are studying the relationship of early populations of *Homo erectus* and Neandertals to determine their precise connections with modern humans.

As we will see in Chapter 3, on race, paleoanthropologists have been doing basic research on the evolution of physical characteristics of ancestral populations in all parts of the world. Paleoanthropologists have developed elaborate techniques to measure observable physical characteristics of humans based on their fossil remains, primarily fossil bones and teeth. Early paleoanthropologists tried to establish clear-cut criteria for distinguishing the evolution of various "races" in different regions of the world. However, modern paleoanthropologists have concluded that these early attempts were based on simplistic categories of racial differences. Today, paleoanthropologists have much more sophisticated methods and techniques for differentiating ancestral human populations, and they exercise extreme caution when evaluating the evolution of different races.

Another group of physical anthropologists focuses their research on the range of physical variation within and among different "modern" human populations. These physical anthropologists study human variation by measuring physical characteristics such as body size, by comparing blood types, and by examining differences in skin color or hair texture. *Human osteology* is the particular area of specialization within physical anthropology dealing with the comparative study of the human skeleton and teeth. Physical anthropologists are also interested in evaluating how disparate physical characteristics reflect evolutionary adaptations to different environmental conditions, thus shedding light on why human populations vary. Noting how specific physical traits have enabled these populations to adapt to different geographic environments, these anthropologists reveal how human populations have developed. Early physical anthropologists wanted to use biological attributes to classify various living populations throughout the world into distinctive "races." Eventually, however, physical anthropologists developed advanced research techniques and methods that led to the abandonment of simplistic constructions of "race" among human populations. As physical anthropologists have learned more about physical variation among human populations, they became more aware of how difficult it was to classify humans into distinguishable "racial" populations. They discovered that traditional biological characteristics such as skin color did not necessarily correlate with other physical characteristics that demarcate one "race" from another. In fact, the vast majority of anthropologists have rejected the concept of "race" as a useful scientific concept. Thus, today, physical anthropologists have learned to be extremely careful with their assessment procedures in attempting to study biological characteristics and classifications among human populations.

An increasingly important area of research for some physical anthropologists is genetics, the study of the biological "blueprints" that dictate the inheritance of physical characteristics. Research on genetics examines a wide variety of questions. It has, for example, been important in identifying the genetic sources of some diseases such as sickle-cell anemia, cystic fibrosis, and Tay-Sachs disease. Genetics has also become an increasingly important complement to paleoanthropological research. Through the study of the genetic makeup of modern humans, geneticists have been working on calculating the genetic distance among modern humans, thus providing a possible means of inferring evolutionary relationships within the species. For example, genetic studies have been used to determine the physical and evolutionary connections between Native American Indians and Asian peoples.

Archaeology

Through *archaeology,* the branch of anthropology that seeks out and examines the artifacts of past societies, we learn much about the lifestyles, history, and evolution of those societies. *Artifacts,* the material remains of former societies, provide tangible clues to the lifestyle, environments, and political economies of extinct societies. Some archaeologists investigate past societies that did not have written documents through which to leave a record of their past. Known as *prehistoric archaeologists,* these researchers study the artifacts of groups such as Native Americans to understand how these people lived. Other archaeologists, called *classical archaeologists,* conduct research on ancient civilizations, such as Egyptian, Greek, and Roman, in collaboration with historians and linguists. Another group of archaeologists, known as *historical archaeologists,* pursue research with historians and investigate the artifacts of societies of the more recent past. For example, many historical archaeologists are probing the remains of plantations in the southern United States to gain an understanding of the lifestyles of slaves and slave owners during the nineteenth century.

Only after intensive analysis do archaeologists cautiously interpret the data they have collected and begin to generalize about a past society. Unlike the glorified adventures of fictional archaeologists, the real-world field of archaeology thrives on the intellectually challenging adventure of careful, systematic, detail-oriented scientific research that enhances our understanding of past societies.

Modern archaeologists have developed a greater in-depth understanding of past societies in various parts of the world, and have shown how environmental circumstances and prehistoric or historic conditions have influenced the societal development of human populations in different regions. They have illuminated through careful research how nineteenth-century archaeologists were misled by their simplistic categorizations, and racist and ethnocentric beliefs, in assessing the societal developments of other cultures. Thus, recent archaeological research has refuted racist and ethnocentric views about non-European or non-Western societies.

Linguistic Anthropology

Linguistics, the study of language, has a long history that dovetails with the discipline of philosophy, but it is also one of the integral subfields of anthropology. *Linguistic anthropology* focuses on the relationship between language and culture, how language is used within society, and how the human brain acquires and uses language. Franz Boas was the founder of linguistic anthropology in North America, and his pioneering linguistic research revolutionized the study of language, culture, and ethnicity.

As do researchers in other fields within anthropology, linguistic anthropologists seek to discover the ways in which languages are different from each other as well as how they are similar. Two wide-ranging areas of research in linguistic anthropology are *structural linguistics* and *historical linguistics*. Structural linguistics explores how language works. Structural linguists compare grammatical patterns and other linguistic elements to learn how contemporary languages mirror and differ from one another. Structural linguistics has uncovered some intriguing relationships between language and thought patterns among different groups of people. Do people who speak different languages with different grammatical structures think and perceive the world differently from each other? For instance, do native Chinese speakers think or view the world and life experiences differently from native English speakers? This is just one of the questions that structural linguists attempt to answer. Such questions bear on the relationship among language, culture, and ethnicity.

Linguistic anthropologists also examine the connections between language and social behavior in different cultures. This specialty, called *sociolinguistics,* focuses on both how language is used to define social groups and how belonging to particular groups leads to specialized language use. For example, a number of linguists have been doing research on Ebonics, a distinctive variety of American English spoken by some African Americans. The term *Ebonics* is derived from the words "ebony" and "phonics," meaning "black speech sounds" (Rickford 1997). These linguistic anthropologists find that Ebonics is no more a lazy form of English than Italian is a lazy form of Latin. Instead, Ebonics is a different language with systematically ordered grammar and pronunciation usages. Linguistic research such as this has helped to undo racist and ethnocentric assumptions about various ethnic minorities.

Another area of research of interest to linguistic anthropologists is historical linguistics. *Historical linguistics* concentrates on the comparison and classification of different languages to discern their historical links. By examining and analyzing grammatical structures and sounds of languages, researchers are able to discover rules for how languages change over time, as well as which languages are related to each other historically. This type of historical linguistic research is particularly useful in tracing the migration routes of various groups through time, confirming archaeological and paleoanthropological data gathered independently. For example, historical linguistics has been used to confirm the migration of the Navajo Native American Indians from Canada down into the southwest region of the United States.

Cultural Anthropology

Cultural anthropology is the subfield of anthropology that examines contemporary societies. Contemporary cultural anthropologists do fieldwork in all parts of the world, from the tropical rain forests of Africa and Latin America to the Arctic regions of Canada, from the deserts of the Middle East to the urban areas of China. Until recently, most cultural anthropologists conducted research on non-Western or remote cultures in Africa, Asia, the Middle East, Latin America, and the Pacific Islands, and on the Native American populations in the United States. Today, however, many anthropologists are doing research on their own cultures in order to gain a better understanding of their institutions and cultural values. In fact, as will be seen in chapters in Part II, which focuses on the United States, ethnographers have been actively engaged in research on ethnic groups in the United States for decades.

Cultural anthropologists use a unique research strategy in conducting their fieldwork in different settings. Unlike the early nineteenth-century "armchair" anthropologists, contemporary ethnologists live for an extended amount of time within the societies that they study. The American Franz Boas and the Polish-born British Bronislaw Malinowski are two examples of those who used this important research strategy in twentieth-century anthropology. They knew that the early studies relied too heavily on superficial, nonquantifiable descriptions and comparisons from classical scholars, travelers, missionaries, and colonial government officials.

Boas and Malinowski promoted and institutionalized the practice of doing intensive fieldwork in the various societies around the world—a research strategy called *participant observation,* which involves learning the language and culture of the group being studied by participating in the group's daily activities. Through this intensive participation, the ethnologist becomes deeply familiar with the group and can understand and explain the society and culture of the group as an insider. Presently, many anthropologists use the term *etic* to refer to the description of the culture by the anthropologist, and *emic* to refer to the natives' point of view of their culture.[2]

The results of the fieldwork of the cultural anthropologists are written up as an *ethnography,* a description of a society. The typical ethnography describes the environmental setting, economic patterns, social organization, political system, and religious rituals and beliefs of the society under study. However, some ethnographies concentrate on particular areas such as religious beliefs and practices, whereas others may focus on environmental conditions or political institutions. The description of a society is based on what anthropologists call *ethnographic data.* The gathering of ethnographic data in a systematic manner is the specific research goal of the ethnologist or cultural anthropologist. Some anthropologists use ethnographic data to do comparative cross-cultural studies of different societies. These comparative studies are extremely important in discovering both differences and similarities among people throughout the world—one of the major objectives of the anthropological project.

Most contemporary cultural anthropologists do their research in a much more different manner than Boas or Malinowski did in the beginning of the twentieth century. Today, in the twenty-first century, many of the so-called natives with whom ethnographers interact are combining their traditional understanding of their own culture with formal education, and some are even choosing to become anthropologists themselves. Thus, cultural anthropologists are becoming more like colleagues with the people they are studying, collaborating on research projects together. Instead of the "lone ranger" cultural anthropologist doing research alone on an island among isolated tribal populations, contemporary anthropologists are more likely to reside in urban areas and work with teams of people from the native population to comprehend the effects of globalization and related processes and change within local regions of the world. And, as we will see in this text, many present-day cultural anthropologists are working with ethnic groups within their own society and collaborating on research projects to gain insights into ethnic interaction and cultural change within multicultural societies.

Most U.S. anthropologists are exposed to all four subfields of anthropology in their education. Because of all the research being done in these different fields, however, with more than 300 journals and 100 of books published every year dealing with anthropological research, no one individual can keep abreast of all the developments across the discipline's full spectrum. Consequently, anthropologists usually specialize in one of the four subfields. Though the four-field approach tends to be an ideal for anthropology in this age of proliferating information and research data, the research in these different disciplines has been important in establishing basic conclusions regarding race, culture, and ethnicity.

As emphasized earlier, anthropology does not limit itself to its own four subfields to realize its research agenda. Although it stands as a distinct discipline, anthropology is interdisciplinary and has strong links to other fields of study. Cultural anthropology, for instance, is closely related to the fields of history, cultural studies, and in particular sociology. In the past, cultural anthropologists examined traditional, whereas sociologists focused on modern societies. Today, cultural anthropologists and sociologists explore many of the same societies using similar research approaches. For example, both rely on statistical and nonstatistical data whenever appropriate in their studies of different types of societies. In later chapters, we will see how basic sociological research has informed ethnographic studies of ethnicity. A recent, allied field that has influenced anthropology is cultural studies, which combines a number of disciplines with the concept of culture to do research on a number of topics related to ethnic and race relations. Likewise, anthropology dovetails considerably with the field of history, which, like anthropology, encompasses a broad range of events. Studies of ethnicity could not be conducted without a comprehensive historical perspective. These fields, as well as others, which will become evident throughout this textbook, have contributed to the anthropological perspective on race and ethnic relations.

Through their interdisciplinary approach, sociologists and anthropologists have emphasized both a *holistic* and a *global* perspective. The holistic and global perspectives enable sociologists and anthropologists to consider the biological, environmental, psychological, economic, historical, social, and cultural conditions of humans at all times and in all places. Sociologists and anthropologists do not limit themselves to understanding a particular ethnic group or set of societies but, rather, they attempt to demonstrate the interconnections among different societies. This combined holistic and global perspective is used throughout this text to demonstrate how different ethnic groups have developed unique interrelationships and patterns throughout the world.

In this age of rapid communication, worldwide travel, and increasing economic interconnections, young people preparing for careers in the twenty-first century must recognize and be able to deal with the cultural and ethnic differences that exist among peoples while also understanding the fundamental similarities that make us all distinctly human. In this age of cultural diversity and increasing internationalization, sustaining this dual perception, of underlying similar human characteristics and outward cultural differences, has both practical and moral benefits. Although nationalistic, ethnic, and racial bigotry are rife in many parts of the world, our continuing survival and successful adaptation depend on greater mutual understanding and cooperation. Anthropology promotes a cross-cultural perspective that allows us to see ourselves as part of one human family in the midst of tremendous diversity. Our society needs citizens that have skills in empathy, tolerance of others, and an understanding of a complex interlocking world. We need world citizens who can function in inescapably multicultural and multinational environments to work cooperatively and become productive citizens, as well as helping to solve humanity's pressing problems of bigotry, poverty, and violence.

Notes

1. The British Edward B. Tylor (1832–1917) is one of the best-known nineteenth-century anthropologists. Tylor's major anthropological and theoretical works are *Primitive Culture,* 2 vols (volume 2 is titled *Religion in Primitive Culture,* part II of *Primitive Culture,* Harper Torchbooks, 1871/1958); *Researches into the Early History of Mankind and the Development of Civilization*

(John Murray, 1881); and *Anthropology: An Introduction to the Study of Man* (D. Appleton, 1881/1898). The other well-known nineteenth-century anthropologist is the American Lewis Henry Morgan (1818–1881). Morgan did an early anthropological work entitled *League of the Ho-De-No-Sau-Nee or Iroquois* (2 vols, New York), a detailed description of one group of Seneca Indians living in upstate New York. Morgan's later work included a cross-cultural analysis text called *Ancient Society* (1877), which had an enormous influence on nineteenth-century thought.

2. The terms *etic* and *emic* are derived from the words "phonetic" and "phonemic," as used in linguistics. Phonetics refers to the different types of sound units in languages. Thus, there is an International Phonetic Alphabet used to designate various sound units of languages throughout the world. In contrast, a phoneme is a sound unit that is understood to have a meaning within a particular language. Phonemics refers to the sound units understood by the native speaker of a specific language.

References Cited

DEGLER, CARL N. 1991. *In Search of Human Nature: The Decline and the Revival of Darwinism in American Social Thought.* Oxford: Oxford University Press.

RICKFORD, JOHN R. 1997. Suite for ebony and phonics. *Discovery* 18(2):82–87.

STOCKING, JR., GEORGE W. 1982 [1968]. *Race, Culture, and Evolution: Essays in the History of Anthropology.* Chicago, IL: University of Chicago Press.

2

...

A History of "Scientific" Racialism

Leonard Lieberman, *Central Michigan University*
Raymond Scupin, *Lindenwood University*

Have you heard statements like these?

- Blacks excel in athletics because of their race.
- The black race has lower intelligence.
- Intermarriage between blacks and whites results in degeneracy.
- The black race is closer to the apes.
- Proof of the superiority of whites is seen in their conquest of Africa, the Americas, and much of Asia.
- African cultures are simpler, therefore, inferior.

They are examples of widespread, everyday (folk) racialism. These and related stereotypes are directly or indirectly supported by "scientific" racialism.

SO WHAT IS "SCIENTIFIC" RACIALISM?

Embedded in this question are several others. What is science? What is race? What is racism? "Race" is the belief that the human species is divided into biological subdivisions thought to be easily identified by the similarity of their biological characteristics so that populations can easily be sorted into white, yellow, and black or Caucasoid, Mongoloid, and Negroid. However, as we will see in Chapter 3, contemporary physical anthropologists emphasize that humans vary biologically across geographic regions, and they do so in gradations (clines) that do not match the idea of separate populations with homogeneous biological features.

 Racialism can become an ideology or doctrine, a set of beliefs suggesting that "races" exist and that there are significant differences among them (Dikötter 2008; Todorov 1993). One dimension of racialism in Europe and the United States has been the ideology (beliefs) that Caucasians are biologically superior and that most people of color, especially blacks, have an inferior culture determined by their "race." Ideological racialism assumes a causal link between biological "race" characteristics and cultural behavior. Ideological racialism is far from harmless. They seriously injure the populations they target by depriving them of self-respect, by defining them as the inferior "other," and by appearing to justify and encourage acts of racism.

In this chapter, we will examine the extent of "scientific" racialism in psychology and anthropology. However, there are, and have been, many varieties of "scientific" racialism in the many branches of biology and medicine. Why has "scientific" racialism been widely believed and so long-enduring? A first reason is because it presents a naturalistic explanation for its insistence that "races" differ in their behavior (Blakey 1998). In this case, naturalistic means that behavior is said to be determined by the inherited biology of each "race." Second, a biological explanation sounds more authoritative than do those based on social influences. Third, it explains social problems by reference to biological factors that seem to provide a persuasive causal explanation. Fourth, it is assumed that these biological functions cannot be significantly altered, avoiding the necessity of studying and considering changes in the environment, including social institutions and policy, thereby supporting the status quo (maintaining things as they are in a society). Fifth, they combine with, reinforce, and receive strength from the prevailing belief in the biological inferiority of people of color.

We have placed quotation marks around "scientific" in "scientific" racialism because in their writing and publication most of its practitioners use scientific concepts and measuring procedures but miss the essential character of science, which requires testing alternative concepts or hypotheses in a way in which they can be disproven if invalid.

On first encountering "scientific" racialism a person might ponder this question: If scientists were wrong in the past, how are we to know whether they are right or wrong now? Isn't it just one person's opinion against another? There are several guidelines to follow: First, what *evidence* does the author present? Evaluate that evidence, especially following the information presented

later in this chapter. Second, what counterevidence does the author present against his or her own position? Third, does the author give an accurate and fair presentation of the evidence against racial hierarchies? Fourth, does the author really reply to that counterevidence? Fifth, does the author allow for significant and varying environmental interaction with heredity, or merely give it lip service?

ORIGINS OF RACE AND RACISM

Have the Ideas of "Race" and Racialism Always Been Present in Human Cultures?

Humans are a classifying species and they classify each other on the basis of whatever seems different. Ancient Egyptian wall paintings show individuals of different skin color. But we do not know if they conceptualized these as representing distinct and homogeneous "races," or merely differences in color and a few other traits. To ancient Athenians of 400 B.C.E., other people were automatically inferior by comparison to their own culture, a phenomenon that anthropologists refer to as *ethnocentrism.* But were these other people "races"? In translating from the ancient Greek, the noun *genos* is erroneously translated as "race," but the prime meaning of *genos* has to do with those who are bound together in families, clans, and tribes over generations (Hannaford 1996:220). The other peoples were designated *barbaros* or barbarians.

Hippocrates (460–370 B.C.), the Greek physician known as the father of Western medicine, believed that the natural world was made up of four elements (water, air, fire, and earth) and the human body consisted of different mixtures of these elements to form four basic humors (phlegm, blood, yellow bile or choler, and black bile). These humors were influenced by both climate, environment, diet, and physiology to produce different types of humans. Thus, Hippocrates helped provide the Greek notion that humans were naturally disposed because of inherent, essentialist characteristics. Yet, he emphasized that these essential characteristics could be shaped by climate, diet, and the environment (Wade 2002).

While the idea of "race" was not available to be used by the Athenians to create and justify a social hierarchy, there were other ways to achieve that end. As Plato told the story, Socrates, in the tale of the metals, advised that a stable society required three classes. Those whose souls corresponded with gold shall be the rulers, those corresponding to silver will be administrators and officials, and those corresponding to brass and iron shall be husbandmen (e.g., farmers and craftsmen). These will all be carefully taught that they "must keep to their proper place in society for when a man of brass or iron guards the State, it will be destroyed." The tale justifies a rank order on the basis of alleged biological inheritance (Gould 1996:51–52).

Socrates' tale omits slaves, one order of society lower than that of the husbandman. Aristotle justified slavery as necessary because he believed humans were innately unequal (Chase 1975). Ironically, many of these slaves were captured in warfare from other Mediterranean and Greek city-states and were not different in biological appearance from the Athenians. The significant difference between the conquered and the Athenians was that one group had power over the other; once enslaved, the "others" were defined as innately inferior and were required to dress and act in ways that reflected their lack of access to the dominant culture; therefore, they were perceived as inferior to the classes above.

In medieval times, St. Thomas Aquinas synthesized the religious beliefs of Christianity and the philosophical traditions of the Greeks into what became known as the "Great Chain of Being" that justified the rank order in society as part of the divine plan. In the Christian tradition, the rank of slavery was justified by reference to the Bible and the story of Noah's son, Ham. Having seen his father naked in a drunken sleep, Ham was cursed and sent off in exile to become father of black people, who were seen as biblically justified servants of white men (Braude 1997; Davis 1997; Leach 1988).

When Did "Race" and "Scientific" Racialism Originate?

The two ideas developed together. In the eighteenth century, a "scientific" concept of race and "scientific" racialism began to replace the medieval religious justifications of hierarchies. In 1758, Carolus Linnaeus, a Swedish scientist, developed a classification that placed *Homo sapiens* among the primates in the animal kingdom. *Homo sapiens* were divided into four varieties or "subspecies," or "races," different in biological traits, including skin color: white, red, yellow, and black; surprisingly, behavioral characteristics were included as part of each "race." Linnaeus described *Homo Sapiens Europaeu* as gentle and governed by laws, *Homo Sapiens Asiaticus* as haughty and governed by opinions, *Homo Sapiens Americanus* as choleric (short-tempered) and regulated by customs, and *Homo Sapiens Afer* as indolent and governed by caprice (whim). Thus Linnaeus presented a hierarchy ranging from superior laws to customs, to opinions, to the most inferior, caprice. The stature of Linnaeus as a botanist and taxonomist lent the aura of validity to his hierarchy. It was a taxonomy of superiority–inferiority that reflected the politically correct views of his time. It was a way of thinking that would prevail, with few exceptions, for the next 300 years (Marks 2007).

One such exception was Johann Blumenbach, a German physician, anatomist, and anthropologist and a student of Linnaeus, who also classified humans into different races, but

Carolus Linnaeus. Swedish Naturalist (1707–1778).

believed that "it is very clear they are all related, or only differ from each other in degree" (Montagu 1942:15). Blumenbach saw the "Caucasoid race" as beautiful, naming it after an ancient crania (skull) excavated from the Caucasus Mountains. He argued that the high brows of the Caucasian race made them intellectually loftier than other races and more generous in spirit. Blumenbach proposed five major races (Caucasoid, Mongoloid, Malayan, American (red), and Negroid) the other four resulting from degeneration from the perfection of the Caucasoid (Spencer 1997:184). Blumenbach lived in an era of assumed European superiority and seemed unaware of the contradiction between his egalitarian belief and his idea of degeneration.

The nineteenth century saw the crystallizing of a core of racialist ideas that would persist into the twentieth. Prior to that century and in that century a number of scientists held blacks to be inferior to whites.[1] Charles Darwin (1809–1882), who originated the idea of natural selection as the mechanism by which evolution occurred (1859), was skeptical of efforts to identify the number of races and denied that evolution had a progressive direction; yet he followed the thinking of his time by writing that women were in some respects like the lesser "races" of mankind. Lacking fossil evidence for evolution, he saw the lesser races as a stage linking humans and apes. While Darwin and many of the scientists of the time made contributions in their special areas, they also expressed the racialism of their day. They were operating from the European ethnocentric sense of superiority and the ideas that measurements led to knowledge and that "races" were biological realities. They did not seek to create racist inequalities, but in presenting a "scientific" explanation for them, they provided a set of ideas that justified and perpetuated those inequalities. To his credit, Darwin raised the question of whether the situation of the poor was due to nature or institutions: "If the misery of our poor be caused not by the laws of nature, but by our institutions, great is our sin" (*Voyage of the Beagle,* quoted by Gould 1996). But this sentence did not appear in Darwin's major books. This,

and the other voices of doubt about hereditary biological inferiority, constituted no more than a whisper.

Racialism received a powerful stimulus from nineteenth-century Darwinian theory in what came to be called *Social Darwinism* associated with the British sociologist Herbert Spencer. Spencer held that the superior biological "races" triumph over the inferior. The theory seemed to be confirmed by the European colonial conquest of the Western Hemisphere, Africa, and parts of Asia. The need to justify that conquest coincided with "scientific" racialism involving the use of apparently scientific techniques to measure brain sizes is an attempt to demonstrate hereditary superiority for the Causasoid "race" (Dennis 1996).

Some earlier work was drawn upon to provide evidence for this social Darwinist racialist perspective. The early nineteenth-century research of Samuel G. Morton provided measurements to support the C>M>N (Caucasoid, Mongoloid, Negroid) hierarchy that many others espoused during the nineteenth century and into the next. Morton, a Philadelphia physician, collected and measured the volume of over 600 human skulls from around the world and produced the figures that he believed certified that "races" varied in the average cranial volume in a hierarchical pattern. Morton's works on "race" were *Crania Americana* (1839) and *Crania Aegyptiaca* (1849). He shared in the prevailing outlook that some "races" were superior and that the greatest among these was "Caucasoid," followed by the "Mongoloid" and then the "Negroid" (C>M>N).

Morton's numbers indicated that "Caucasians" had a mean brain size of 87 cubic inches, whereas "Mongolians" and American Indians measured 83 and 82, respectively, and "Ethiopians" 78. Stephen J. Gould (1981:54) explains the serious sampling errors that resulted in "Caucasoids" being ranked first. Only three Hindu skulls were admitted to Morton's "Caucasian" sample because, as Morton explicitly states, "the skulls of these people are probably smaller than those of any other existing nation"

(1839:261). If more Hindu skulls had been used, the average cranial size for "Caucasoids" would have been lower. Morton's sample of Native American Indians is also biased by overrepresentation of smaller Inca/Peruvian crania, whereas only three large-brained Iroquois skulls were included. Gould (1981:60) suggests that the difference in cranial size between "Caucasian" and "Ethiopian" is because half of Morton's "Caucasian" sample is male and probably only one-third the "Ethiopian" sample is male. Male cranial size is around 10 percent larger than that of females. Morton seemed unaware of this sampling error, since he explicitly described his procedure. It is indicative of the power of folk beliefs about blacks that they were placed last in hierarchies of the nineteenth century (Marks 2008).

J. C. Nott and George Gliddon used Morton's data in their book *Types of Mankind* (1854:454). Gliddon was an amateur Egyptologist who used Morton's method to support the claim that the pharaohs were "Caucasoids," the only race then thought to be capable of high civilization (Molnar 1992:16). Morton, Nott, and Gliddon came to be regarded as the nucleus of the American school of anthropology, noted for *polygenesis,* the idea that races had separate origins and that some were created inferior (Erickson 1997a:65). Nott and Gliddon presented Morton's research to the American South, hoping thereby to justify slavery (Brace 1997:865). Southerners accepted the skull measurements that seemed to prove black inferiority, but rejected the polygenic idea because it conflicted with the Genesis view of one and only one creation, that of Adam and Eve.

The works of Morton were read in France and Germany. Morton's procedures and conclusions, however erroneous, were widely cited as the alleged scientific foundation for proving that "races" were unequal. In *Essai sur l'inégalité des races humaines* (*Essays on the Inequality of Human Races*) (1854:111), Joseph-Arthur Comte de Gobineau presented a summary table of Morton's measurements to support his view that "Nordics" were superior to all other races, having created "high" civilizations (Molnar 1992:258).

Gobineau has been nominated "grandfather" of academic racialism for his work of 1853–1855. He held that all high human achievements were the work of the Aryan superrace, who created the civilizations of the Hindus, Egyptians, Assyrians, and Europeans. According to Gobineau, the Aryan superrace declined because of interbreeding with other "races."

Later, these views would influence Adolf Hitler and the Nazi program that justified the program of "race purification" by mass extermination in order to eliminate non-Aryans from the German gene pool during the 1940s.

How and Why Did Racialism Originate?

The uniform support for the C>M>N hierarchy coincides with a century in which Europe had achieved dominance over most of the world's people with darker skin. From the 1830s on, the expansion of the power and territories of the United States was advocated as an expression of "manifest destiny." In the second half of the century, evolutionary ideas emerged and evolutionists would interpret the difference among "races" and their cultures as stages of evolution. Anthropology emerged in the nineteenth century as the study of evolution from primitive barbarism to advanced civilization. It was a point of view that assumed the superiority of Europe and the "Caucasoid" race. This paradigm of linked biological and cultural evolution supported the hierarchical ordering of the races in much of the nineteenth and early twentieth centuries.

Racialism, like the idea of races, can be traced to the attempt to justify European colonization of much of the world, the rise of European capitalism, and the slave trade (Dennis 1996:715). Colonization, although a highly varied process, in general involved entry of a militarily powerful society into the territory of a weaker one for purposes of forcefully extracting valuable resources. In order to justify the cruelties that were practiced, the colonized peoples were portrayed as inferior dark-skinned "races."

Ethnocentrism laid the foundations for racialism by regarding people of different cultures as inferior, but racialism adds a seemingly persuasive biological dimension in which the "others" look different and therefore behave differently. We have seen that European and American scientists such as Linnaeus were building the idea of race in the eighteenth century, stimulated by the diversity of peoples in the New World. Scientists, scholars, and theologians were also confronted with explaining the origin of these "races." The only possible explanation in a pre-Darwinian era had to be consistent with the biblical teaching of creation by God. The two schools of thought that debated how this came about were monogenism and polygenism. Monogenists held that "races" were all part of one recently created species. As we discussed, Blumenbach (1795) held that racial differences arose because of degeneration from the original creation. The polygenists contended that the "races" were different species created at different times. The monogenic view was strongly supported by Catholic theologians and most scholars of the sixteenth and seventeenth centuries, the first two centuries of colonialism. The Catholic church and Queen Isabella of Spain insisted that all the peoples of the New World had souls that missionaries could save.

Polygenism became the predominant view in the first half of the nineteenth century, supported by a multitude of cranial measurements initiated by Morton, by Paul Broca in Paris, and by others in England and Germany (Erickson 1997b; Lieberman 2001; Marks 2008). Polygenism and cranial measurements provided the scientific support for the alleged inferiority of the dark "races" that was intended to justify their exploitation, especially in the eighteenth and nineteenth centuries. Those who supported slavery and religiously held to monogenism could reject the idea of multiple creations but could take comfort in Morton's cranial measurements. For scientists, it would appear that polygenism was contradicted by Darwin's *On the Origin of Species,* published in 1859. But few scientists understood how Darwin's natural selection related to evolution, and polygenism

remained an influential theory (Erickson 1997b). In the first three decades of the twentieth century, in the context of the ideas of polygenism and racial hierarchy, IQ tests provided a new method of measuring individuals and comparing "races." Those decades from 1900 to 1930 were part of a terminal phase of colonialism, in which 40 million Europeans came to the United States from 1880 to 1920. They encountered other Europeans already there, rather than Native Americans who could be shunted aside. After 1900, they were arriving when the idea of eugenics was developing across Europe and the United States.

Eugenics and Scientific Racialism

The term *eugenics* was invented in the 1880s by Frances Galton,[2] a wealthy Englishman and a first cousin and contemporary of Charles Darwin, who assessed the number of great men in different "races" and concluded the British to be superior. Galton claimed that he was able to trace his ancestry (and Darwin's) back through 12 centuries of Norman dukes as well as Anglo-Saxon and French kings (Tucker 1994:39). Galton was much concerned that the better classes of society would decline in numbers and the lesser classes increase. He used the term *eugenics* to designate the science of improving the human species. In 1901, Galton's lecture to the British Anthropological Institute ignited interest and activity in England, the United States, and Germany. In Britain, prominent scientists and intellectuals, some of them socialists, who supported eugenics included Sir Ronald Fisher, J. B. S. Haldane, Julian Huxley, H. J. Muller, H. G. Wells, and George Bernard Shaw (Kevles 1985). The social movement that developed expressed fear of the expansion of the poor and the inferior "races," and zealously advocated sterilization (Tucker 1994).

Eugenicists came to focus upon hereditary social traits, and under the influence of the genetic principles of Mendel, rediscovered in 1900, assumed that these traits were controlled by one or two Mendelian factors (genes) operating in a simple dominant–recessive pattern. The social traits included pauperism, manic depression, scholastic ability, feeblemindedness, epilepsy, and criminality (Allen 1999). These traits were attributed to the poor, blacks, and immigrants, making it possible to mobilize public interest in eugenics. Scientists and the public also supported eugenics because of the popularity of the social Darwinism of Herbert Spencer and the American sociologist William Sumner, with its emphasis on the survival of the fittest, those possessing superior qualities, which purportedly led to some races, nations, classes, and the male gender having more wealth, power, and status as a product of evolution. Therefore, attempts at social welfare for the poor were held to defy laws of nature and enable the unfit to multiply (van den Berghe 1996).

Over the first decades of the twentieth century, prominent citizens became interested in eugenics and formed associations dedicated to improving their "race." Exhibits were displayed at county fairs. High school and college courses included eugenics as a topic. The pioneer scientist and eugenicist in the United States was Charles B. Davenport, a biologist, who organized the Eugenics Record Office (ERO) in Long Island in 1904. There he gathered family histories and trained eugenic fieldworkers. Davenport and Harry H. Laughlin, supervisor at the ERO, were especially interested in crime, tracing it primarily to inherited temperamental instability. Laughlin presented data showing that Negroes, Mexicans, and Puerto Ricans were overrepresented in prison populations, and he believed it was not because of slums or economic stress. Laughlin gave testimony for two days before the congressional committee that wrote the 1924 Johnson Act severely restricting immigration from southern and eastern Europe, including Catholics and Jews, most of whom were believed to be biologically inferior and prone to criminal behavior.

Eugenicists also urged sterilization of the unfit. Laughlin prepared a model sterilization law for introduction to various state legislatures. Laughlin and his coworkers argued for what they termed "progressive" legislation, and by 1935, 30 states had adopted similar legislation. Over 60,000 persons had been sterilized before the repeal of most of those laws in the 1970s (Allen 1999). The eugenic movement was international, with sterilization laws passed in Denmark (1929), Norway (1934), Sweden (1935), Finland (1935), Estonia (1936), and Iceland (1938), and in one Swiss canton (1928). Also included were Cuba, Czechoslovakia, Yugoslavia, Lithuania, Latvia, Hungary, and Turkey. In the first decades of the twentieth century, various German sources praised the American sterilization laws and the immigration restriction law. Widely read were translations of American eugenic books such as Madison Grant's *Passing of the Great Race* (1916), as well as H. H. Goddard's (1912) study of the Kallikaks. Under the Nazis, Germany's eugenics law, modeled after those in the United States, used tubal ligation for women and vasectomy for men. In the first four years of the law over 50,000 persons were sterilized per year in Germany (Proctor 1988). In Germany, scientists in the universities and physicians strongly supported eugenics, as did scientists and physicians in other nations.

We have seen that the history of racism is not confined to any one nation. Eugenics was an international movement supported by scientists and essayists.

Was Racialism in the Humanities and Sciences in the United States a Minority View?

The major Enlightenment philosophers of Europe who influenced U.S. political leaders and others such as Thomas Jefferson and Benjamin Franklin held "racialistic" views. For example, Immanuel Kant wrote scientific treatises on how the African race (and others) were retarded and incapable of rational thought compared to the Europeans. In his 1775 essay "Of the Different Human Races," Kant relied on his close colleague, anthropologist Ernst Haeckel, biblical teachings regarding the sons of Ham, and other European philosophers and scientists such as Comte de Buffon to perpetuate the views of innate racial inequalities in intelligence and also that different races could not and should not reproduce with one another (Bernasconi 2001). Of course, these ideas of race influenced Thomas Jefferson and other leaders who participated in the drafting of the U.S. Declaration of Independence and the U.S. Constitution that emphasized the "Equality of Man." These American leaders were excluding populations such as African slaves that many of them owned, and Native American Indians.

By the end of the nineteenth century, most of the world was under European control, and the acceptance of "scientific" racialism meant that few scientific or humanitarian objections were likely to be raised:

> In the United States during the latter portion of the 19th century the inequality of races was the predominant view of scientists and intellectuals. American thought from 1880 to 1920 "generally lacks any perception of the Negro as a human being with potentialities for improvement." Most of the people who wrote about Negroes were firmly in the grip of the idea that intelligence and temperament are racially determined and unalterable. [Gossett 1965:286]

In literary circles, the list of those believing in the inequality of "races" included James Fenimore Cooper, Henry Adams, Frank Norris, Jack London, Owen Wister, and Henry James (Gossett 1965:198). In Europe, a comparable group of writers included Rudyard Kipling and Sir Walter Scott, whose *Ivanhoe* converted a feudal class struggle into an affair of "self-conscious racial conflict" between Saxon and Norman (MacRae 1960:80). The majority of intellectuals and scientists had beliefs that helped give racism respectable veneer. But there were some intellectuals who did not support racism: George Washington Cable, Winslow Homer, Mark Twain, Stephen Crane, and J. S. Mill. Among scientists there were a few men who were generally not racist in their thinking. The list includes Adolf Bastian, Rudolph Virchow, William Ripley,

Theodore Waitz, Friedrich Ratzel, Henry Rowe Schoolcraft, and John Wesley Powell (Gossett: 245). They were forerunners of a reformed view of "race," generally believing that "races" differed only in minor respects (Lieberman 1968:134–135).

A REVOLUTION IN SCIENCE

How Could an Accurate View Replace the "Scientific" Racialism That Prevailed in the Nineteenth Century?

The debate over the inequality of races was largely one-sided until the 1920s. The historian Gossett writes that the stemming of the tide of inequality was the work of "one man, Franz Boas, who was an authority on several fields which had been the strongest sources of racism" (1965:429–430). Boas asked for proof that race determines mentality and temperament. From then on, "it would be the racists who were increasingly on the defensive . . . it was clearly Boas who led the attack." In 1912, Boas published evidence demonstrating changes in head shape in children of Italian and Jewish immigrants. It weakened both the older concept of the fixity of race (Shapiro 1969:376) and the implication that mental ability was racially determined.

Boas was most influential through his leadership in cultural anthropology. According to Gossett, the ethnographic work his students began "had the utmost importance for race theory because the close and detailed knowledge of . . . primitive peoples showed how directly ideas and customs are interrelated and how fallacious is the idea that any society can be meaningfully interpreted in terms of its racial inheritance" (1965:416). Gossett holds that what was needed to break through the dominant misconceptions was a way to explain character as an outcome of institutions, history, and environment. Boas and his students did that by building the idea of culture, by developing the relativistic approach to cultural differences, and by insisting on masses of evidence.

Boas's influence on his students helps explain the spread of his views in anthropology. One of his most prominent students was Alfred Kroeber, whose 1917 article, "The Superorganic," was one of the influential statements calling for a sociocultural rather than a biological interpretation of human societies. Among the students of Boas were a number of women who became pioneer anthropologists and who combated racialism and racism through their teaching and research publications. They included Ruth Benedict, Katherine Dunham, Zora Neale Hurston, Margaret Mead, Elsie Clews Parsons, Ruth Underhill, and Gene Weltfish. Benedict's *Patterns of Culture* (1934) was widely influential in popularizing the idea of culture, thereby providing a nonracial and nonracist explanation of human societies (Lieberman 1997).

Until about 1940, mainstream science was consistent about the reality of race and the inferiority of blacks. Almost all physical anthropologists utilized the typology of three major races and thereby indirectly gave support to the inferiority of the "other" species. There were two exceptions. One was, as discussed, the Boasian school, which had its beginning in those early decades. The second was "in the writings of those [African Americans] stereotyped by the sciences of the day" (Stepan and Gilman 1993:170). It is a measure of the power of "scientific" and everyday racialism that these authors are still too little known and seldom quoted. Among them was Frederick Douglass, a former slave, who in 1854 presented an audience with anatomical and cranial similarities of blacks and whites that outweighed the differences; therefore, he asserted that the Negro was entitled to full membership in the human species (Stepan and Gilman 1993:175).

W. E. B. Du Bois is another example of a neglected critic of racialism and racism. He was born in Massachusetts of African American and European American ancestry, and earned his Ph.D. from Harvard in 1895. In sociology, Du Bois was the leading spokesman for liberal reform and against Social Darwinism, just as Franz Boas was in anthropology (Baker 1998:99).

W.E.B. DuBois (1868–1963) First African American PhD.

Early in his career, Du Bois argued that the color line of segregation in all walks of life prevented Negroes from progressing and that the inequality of the black "race" was due to the heritage of slavery, not biology (Baker 1998:111). He held that the color line was the central problem of the twentieth century.

Eventually, social scientists, including psychologists, began to reassess their perspectives on "race." Otto Klineberg (1935) was one psychologist who had contact with Boas and his students. He later gathered evidence in support of environmental influences through his work identifying the rising IQ scores of Negro children who had moved from southern to northern schools. In sociology, the same trend occurred but under differing influences.

What numerous social scientists had done was to respond to racialism with a scientific rebuttal. Scientific antiracialism came to be the accepted position in the social sciences and among intellectuals. The idea was soon to spread and become a popular ideology partly replacing racialism and competing with it. But a set of ideas does not become an accepted ideology simply because it is soundly scientific. It spreads when cultural conditions are appropriate. The earlier ideas ran against the tide of social conditions supporting racialism. But in the 1940s, a social base for antiracialism was emerging.

Gossett comments: "We owe something to impersonal forces in the decline of [racialism], but the trouble with impersonal forces is that they can as easily work one way as another. We owe far more to the people and the organizations motivated by a concern for equality for all" (1965:445). Gossett's position seems to be that of the historian and humanist: people and ideas make history. The view that must be added is that individuals also can as easily work one way or another; who succeeds often depends on the influence of social and cultural conditions. Boas's ideas could spread only when the social structure was ready. Individual humans may make history, but they do not do so under circumstances of their own choosing.

In the twentieth century, the forces for antiracialism began to develop in the United States through the emergence of the social sciences as organized disciplines and through their influence on education. To these must be added the transcendent influence of World War II. The propaganda developed during the war was based on the fact that Nazi Germany was totalitarian, racialist in ideology, and racist in practice. Since the enemy was racialist and racist, America had to proclaim itself antiracialist despite its history of slavery and continuing practice of segregation. The massive antiracialist propaganda and the racist policies of the enemy silenced the racialist groups in the United States that had been so vocal in the 1930s.

Beginning in 1942, anthropologist Ashley Montagu published the first of six editions of *Man's Most Dangerous Myth: The Fallacy of Race.* It reached a large popular audience with scientific

evidence that the "race" concept was invalid and was inextricably tied to racialism and racism. Other scientists in the United States and in Great Britain began to see the need to combat racialism within science itself (Stepan 1982:160). The decline of racism among policymakers was clearly evident in the 1954 U.S. Supreme Court rejection of the established rationale of "separate but equal" and in the Court's mandating of desegregated schools. More than that, what the Court did was to accept the statements of social scientists concerning the belief that a number of alleged "racial" behaviors were not hereditary but were, in fact, a product of environment and learning (Barkan 1987:3).

In the 1950s, scientists from several disciplines began to issue statements about "race" and racialism that marked the beginning of the end of "scientific" racism as the majority belief among scientists. Several statements on race were issued by the United Nations Education, Scientific, and Cultural Organization (UNESCO) and by professional organizations of scientists. Four statements were issued by UNESCO from 1950 to 1967, formulated by committees whose members were drawn from a number of scientific disciplines. The first statement, published in 1950, was "Statement by Experts on Race Problems" (Montagu 1972). It was five years after the end of World War II, and during the still-growing awareness of the 6 million Jews, Gypsies, and Poles killed in Nazi death camps and with the assumption that behavior is racially determined. One passage from the 1950 statement declares that:

> So far as temperament is concerned, there is
> no definite evidence that there exist inborn
> differences between human groups. There
> is evidence that whatever group differences
> of the kind there might be are greatly over-
> ridden by the individual differences, and by
> the differences springing from environmen-
> tal factors. [quoted in Montagu 1972:10]

Similar statements appeared in the other three declarations.

THREE PEAKS OF IQ–"RACE" CONTROVERSY: THE IQ CENTURY

Why Is "Scientific" Racialism Reborn Again and Again?

Early in the twentieth century, at about the time that Boas and his colleagues were developing the concept of culture, a new way to measure intelligence was being introduced. This new method used pencil and paper tests to measure what has come to be called the *intelligence quotient,* or IQ. Three times in the twentieth century IQ test scores were used in an attempt to demonstrate racial inferiority. Stephen Jay Gould, a paleontologist and a specialist in the history of science, refers to these episodes as racial backlashes. Each was followed by research and debate among scientists disproving the racialist claims. Early in the century these episodes were reactions against the increasing numbers of immigrants. In the 1960s, the reactions followed the claims for equal rights in the civil rights movement led by Martin Luther King Jr. In the 1990s, a third backlash criticized government social programs with emphasis on welfare.[3] These three episodes are examples of how racialist ideas are used to justify racism in practice. In the following section, we will present the characteristics of "scientific" racialism in these three phases. We will follow each of these characteristics with examples of the evidence that contradicts and disproves the assumptions of race–IQ determinism.

The "Race" and IQ Tradition Begins

The nineteenth-century reliance on skull sizes was largely replaced when Alfred Binet (1903), a French psychologist, presented his method of mental testing involving analogies and reasoning skills. Before that, for three years beginning in 1898, Binet had measured the heads of students identified as the best and the worst. The differences he found were extremely small, and Binet wrote of resisting his own temptation to magnify those differences (Gould 1981:147).

Binet had been commissioned by the Ministry of Public Education in France to develop a procedure for identifying pupils in need of special instruction. His test consisted of a diverse set of tasks relating to everyday problems requiring basic reasoning processes of logic and ordering, rather than skills learned through direct teaching such as reading. Binet avoided reducing intelligence down to a specific number suitable for linear ranking, and rejected distinguishing between acquired and genetic causes. His goal was not to label but to improve (Gould 1981).

In the first decade of the twentieth century our story shifts to Henry H. Goddard, who introduced the Binet IQ tests to the United States. Goddard was director of the New Jersey Institute for the Feebleminded. He had Binet's 1908 test translated into English, with minor adjustments. He tested it on 400 inmates and published the results in 1910. He also administered his test to 2,000 public school students in Vineland, New Jersey, and claimed to distinguish normal from feebleminded children. Later, he assigned labels to mental age: including idiots through 2 years of age, imbeciles through 7 years, and morons through 12 years, and always with a hereditarian assumption. His books, *The Kallikak Family* (1912) and *Feeblemindedness: Its Causes and Consequences* (1914), claimed that inherited mental deficiency is the source of delinquency, crime, promiscuity, disease, drunkenness, illegitimacy, and pauperism. Goddard strongly supported eugenics, attributed inferiority to the "black race," and alleged that most social problems were caused by the feebleminded.

The IQ testing process took another step in 1913 when Goddard sent research assistants to Ellis Island. In two and a half months, they were to identify the feebleminded (below age 12) by sight (Gould 1981:165). They tested 35 Jews, 22 Hungarians, 50 Italians, and 45 Russians. The results were frightening: some 83 percent of Jews were said to be feebleminded, as were 80 percent of Hungarians, 79 percent of Italians, and 87 percent of Russians. Gould explains that the tests were administered to "a group of frightened men and women who spoke no English and had just endured an oceanic voyage in steerage. Most are poor and have never gone to school; many have never held a pencil or pen in their hand" (p. 166). By 1928, Goddard later recanted his thinking to the extent that he acknowledged that only a small proportion of those who tested 12 years or less were feeble-minded, and regardless of their mental age most could be trained to be useful citizens. Goddard concluded that feeblemindedness could be cured and that most of the feebleminded need not be institutionalized (1928:225).

Lewis M. Terman (1916), a professor of psychology at Stanford, would take IQ testing onto the national stage. He was not the first to utilize the Binet tests, but his predecessors had only translated the test or partly modified it. Terman undertook a thorough revision of the Binet tests. He was concerned with racial variations in intelligence.

It was Robert M. Yerkes who initiated the testing of World War I army recruits. Yerkes, aware of preparations for the war, conceived of a grand foundation for a "scientific" psychology. He proposed that all recruits into the army be tested. As Colonel Yerkes, he would be commanding a select cadre of psychologists and would train those who would administer the tests to 1,750,000 recruits. Yerkes assembled the premier psychometricians to write the tests. And so Yerkes, Terman, Goddard, and their colleagues designed the largest program of mental measurement the world had seen.

The army made only casual use of the scores. Their impact arose from the attention given in the press to summary data, which reported three startling conclusions. First, the average mental age of white American adults stood just at 13, slightly above the level of "morons" (8–12 years). Second, the people of southern and eastern Europe were less intelligent than those of northwestern European nations. Third, the Negro scored at the lowest portion of the scale. Although thoroughly criticized by the

journalist Walter Lippmann (1922), the new "scientific" racialism had been established and would reappear in both the United States and Great Britain.

The role played by Terman and Yerkes in the United States had its parallel in Great Britain in the work of Cyril Burt. Study of separated identical twins provided the evidence that Burt and others used to support their hereditarian beliefs. Since they were identical in their genes, the degree of twins' similarity in intelligence was presented as proof that IQ was highly heritable. Eventually Burt reported on 53 pairs of identical twins and correlated their IQ scores. He claimed 80 percent heritability for intelligence. His research was emulated by others, Burt's achievements praised, and he became Sir Cyril Burt. Burt's data were the keystone for the assertion that IQ was highly heritable, and was relied upon by later IQ researchers (Lewontin et al. 1993:155). However, studies by Burt finding high correlations of .94 for the IQ of identical twins in the same household did not allow for their very similar environments (Kamin 1974:38). Therefore, Burt used identical twins reared in separate households, and reported correlations of .77. These studies further supported the claim for high heritability, since the environments in the two households were said to be different. However, Kamin (1974) reanalyzed the data and found that the separate households were very similar, such as one twin reared by the mother, the other by her cousin in the same English village. Correlations of the IQ scores of separated twins were .5, indicating that both heredity and environment were important.

One discovery in particular brought Burt's research to public attention. Oliver Gillie, a journalist for the London *Sunday Times*, was unable to locate Burt's research coworkers, a Miss Conway and a Miss Howard. They had published papers in a journal Burt edited, but they had never been seen by any of Burt's other coworkers and could not be located. Gradually and grudgingly it was acknowledged that Burt had committed fraud. Yet his defenders said there was still much merit in his research. One reviewer of Burt's work concluded:

> I do believe that Burt made things up about the twins, about factor analysis, and about the parent-child data used in his "social mobility" study. Having analyzed Burt's many publications, I find too many omissions in his references, too many inconsistencies among different articles, and definitely some clear contradictions between what he had written at one time, and what thirty years later he claimed to have written earlier— although he may not be unique in doing so. [Samelson 1992:231]

Can scientific conclusions sometimes be influenced by the social context? Comparison of the British and American hereditarians illustrates that these scientists may have been strongly influenced by their own national cultures. The British strand of mental testing, pioneered by Burt and actively supported by others, focused attention on social class (the poor) and its relation to IQ and education. In the United States, the focus has had three concerns: race, immigrants, and the poor. Each nation has been obsessed with its own historical tensions. The British were justifying their class system. The Americans had to reconcile (or ignore) a history of slavery and discrimination, anti-immigrant feelings, and inequality between rich and poor with a tradition that proclaimed equality of opportunity. Furthermore, in the United States the three periods of controversy over race and IQ in the twentieth century occurred not merely because of developments in the discipline of psychology but because of the context of social events. The nineteenth century was the last opportunity to build empires. It was a time to defend subjugation of peoples with darker skins by supposedly superior races. If there had been no IQ tests, it is likely that some other scientific-appearing way of asserting biological differences would have been used. Of this, the nineteenth-century studies of cranial size contains abundant evidence.

The Second Phase of the IQ Century: The 1960s and 1970s

Beginning in the 1960s, a revival of "scientific" racialism began. For example, the journal *Mankind Quarterly* was sponsored by the Pioneer Fund, which supports and finances much "scientific" racialism. The historian who has thoroughly studied this phenomenon is Barry Mehler (1989). Mehler reports that the Pioneer Fund was endowed by Wickcliffe Draper, a textile manufacturer, and incorporated in 1937 by Harry Laughlin and Frederick Osborne. The year before the journal's founding, Laughlin had received an honorary degree from Heidelberg University for his contributions to Nazi eugenics, and in 1937, Osborne wrote that the Nazi sterilization law was the most exciting experiment that had ever been tried.

The fund was based on the Nazi "breeding program," and its purposes were, first, to "encourage the propagation of those 'descended predominantly from white persons who settle in the original 13 states prior to the adoption of the Constitution of the United States and/or from related stocks, or to classes of children, the majority of whom are deemed to be so descended.' The second purpose was to support academic research and the dissemination of information about problems of heredity and eugenics and the problems of race betterment" (Mehler 1989:21). In short it was a program of positive and negative eugenics, increasing those descendants of colonial stock and providing information that would lead to reducing those not of that origin. Harry Laughlin, one of the founding directors of the Pioneer Fund, was influential with the congressional committee that passed the 1924 immigration law. A second director was Frederick Osborne, secretary of the American Eugenics Society and an admirer of the Nazi eugenic sterilization laws (Sedgwick 1994:234).

According to the grants the fund has awarded, it is interested in "limiting immigration, stopping busing, reversing integration, and ending affirmative action" (Sedgwick 1994:234). In other words, back to Jim Crow segregation plus even more limited immigration. Mehler (p. 21) reports on one of the fund's projects in 1937 in which plans were made for the distribution of two films to high schools, colleges, and churches. The films were Nazi propaganda for eugenics showing luxury living for defectives, and poverty conditions for people of Aryan stock. In the years following the U.S. Supreme Court's *Brown vs. Board of Education* desegregation decision, the fund was allied with those opposed to that decision. Over the years, the Pioneer Fund has provided millions in funding research that supports "scientific racialist research."

The reader should be reminded that we are looking at those periods during which considerable controversy developed. Published early in the 1960s was anthropologist Carleton Coon's *Origin of Races* (1962), which attempted to use fossils to support a racial hierarchy. He presented the idea that *Homo erectus* evolved into *Homo sapiens* five times as each of five "races" passed a threshold from one species into the other. Caucasoid was first at 250,000 years ago, Mongoloid passed over at 150,000, Australoid at 40,000, and African at 40,000 years ago. Of these transitions Coon wrote:

> It is fair inference . . . that the subspecies that crossed the evolutionary threshold into the category of *Homo sapiens* the earliest have evolved the most, and that the obvious correlation between the length of time a subspecies has been in the *sapiens* state and the levels of civilization attained by some of its populations may be related phenomenon (pp. ix–x). [If Africa was the cradle of mankind] it was only an indifferent kindergarten. Europe and Asia were our principal schools. [p. 656]

Coon's views were met by vigorous critical opposition from anthropologists and book reviewers concerning his Eurocentric bias against Africans and his failure to explain societal differences using cultural and environmental history.

During the 1960s, the controversy was also ignited by an article by psychologist Arthur Jensen, with much advanced publicity, published in the 1969 *Harvard Educational Review* by the title "How Much Can We Boost IQ and Scholastic Achievement?" The article began with a statement that would infuriate the environmentally inclined: "Compensatory education has been tried and it apparently has failed." The paper that followed was 123 pages long and presented many of the elements of "scientific" racialism. There were no new breakthroughs, but it stimulated a large number of research studies that refuted its claims (Block and Dworkin 1976; Montagu 1975).

The Third Phase of the IQ Century

The third phase of the IQ century began with the publication of *The Bell Curve* in 1994, coauthored by psychologist Richard Herrnstein and political scientist Charles Murray. In brief, *The Bell Curve* claimed, as had earlier practitioners of "scientific" racism, that (1) IQ tests measure intelligence, an abstract mental property called "g" (p. 22); (2) IQ tests show a large gap between those at the bottom of society and those above; (3) similarly, there is a gap of 10–15 points between the African American race and whites (p. 276); (4) 40–80 percent of this gap is due to heredity (pp. 23, 298); (5) remedial environmental efforts, such as Head Start, can do little to improve IQs because heredity is so strong (p. 389); (6) poverty, crime, illegitimacy, and welfare dependency are associated with low IQ (pp. 127, 235, 167, 191); and (7) we are moving toward a two-caste society with a cognitive elite upper level and an expanding cognitively deprived lower level (p. 509).

The argument in *The Bell Curve* and in all the studies of "race" and IQ are based on two false foundations. First, the race concept lacks supporting research because of the greater variation within traditional "races" than among them, as well as other evidence stated earlier. Second, as will be shown below, IQ tests really measure scholastic learning, not a hereditary essence in the brain. The general assumption that IQ tests measure an abstract ability called "g" led to the reductionist idea that intelligence was one uniform entity in the brain. This view has been successfully refuted by psychologist Howard Gardner (1985) using cross-cultural data, and the observation available to everyone that individuals vary in their aptitudes for mathematics, music, spatial perception, and interpersonal interpretation. Intelligence is a combination of many different mental potentials. IQ tests do not measure these multiple intelligences.

What IQ tests do measure is reflected in their predictive validity through correlations: .80 with scholastic achievement, .50–.70 with occupational status, .35 with income, and .20–.25 with actual performance on the job (Flynn 1980). Earlier we stated that IQ tests are said to measure what is called "g," which has to do with problem solving, abstract reasoning, generalizing from specifics, and perceiving abstract relationships. These skills are closely related to scholastic achievement, but because of low correlation with income and actual performance on the job, there are dimensions of important life chances poorly predicted by IQ tests.

In the context of evolutionary biology, we have evolved to manipulate and survive in a variety of changing situations, and test taking relates to that process only in the narrower scholastic sense measured by IQ tests devised for modern industrial society (Patterson 1995). An ethnic group may have a lower mean IQ score because the test reflects skills at participating in a society that prevents that ethnic group from the full participation that would equalize IQ scores (Chidley 1994). Examples are endless: Catholics in Northern Ireland score lower than Protestants; blacks in South Africa score lower than "colored" people (from India or mixed marriages), who score lower than whites under apartheid; blacks in the U.S. South score lower than blacks in the North; and Jews entering Ellis Island in the early 1900s scored lower than Jews today. "George DeVos studied IQ scores of a Japanese minority caste, the Burakumin, thought traditionally to be 'unclean' because they worked as tanners. In Japan their test scores reflected their disadvantaged social-economic position, the gap between their scores and those of Japanese children was similar to the gap between Africans and whites in the U.S. But Burakumin children whose families migrated to the U.S. achieved scores identical to other Japanese-American children (5–11 points higher than average white scores)" (from Bates and Fratkin 1999:30, citing Goleman 1988). Put differently, "Racial differences in average IQ scores are simply one measure of the impact of racism and racial inequality" (Hudson 1995:6).

It is possible to test claims of Herrnstein and Murray and others that so-called races as biological entities differ significantly from each other in intelligence due to heredity. If the authors of *The Bell Curve* are correct, then African Americans who have more European and less African ancestry should have higher IQs. One study that directly tested this proposition was by psychologist Sandra Scarr (Scarr et al. 1977). Restated, the proposition was that the higher the proportion of European ancestry, the higher should be the IQ of African Americans. They gave an IQ test to a sample of 350 African American schoolchildren in the Philadelphia area. They estimated each person's degree of African and European ancestry from blood samples, in which they could identify serum proteins indicating 12 hereditary traits that were more likely to have either African or European ancestry. These results were supported by the degree of skin color and were similar for siblings. According to Scarr and Weinberg:

> The results were unequivocal. Blacks who had a large number of European ancestors did no better or worse on the tests than blacks of almost total African ancestry. These studies dispute the hypothesis that IQ differences between blacks and whites are in large part the result of genetic differences. [1978:32]

In the language of correlations, they found zero correlations between degrees of "race" and test scores. It is difficult to correlate "race" and "g," two phenomena that do not exist. Herrnstein and Murray do not refer to this study in the 552 pages of their main text, presenting only a brief footnote on page 729 (following appendix 7).

The claim made by Herrnstein and Murray in 1994 and Jensen in 1969 is that remedial environmental programs can do little because heredity is so strong. We have already cited a crucial study that contradicts that biological determinism (Scarr et al. 1977). We have also cited comparative cultural studies showing the power of the environment. Illustration of the positive effects of an environmental program is provided by the Abecedarian project in North Carolina. Parents of the children in the project had low IQs and minimal family income. A large minority of the children were African Americans. The program provided enriched educational day care outside the home every weekday starting at three months of age until they entered public school. Children participated in baking projects requiring measuring amounts, group chats, and games involving diverse experiences. By age three, the toddlers averaged an IQ of 101, a huge 17 points over the control group. The results were lasting; a decade later, at age 15, children from the intervention group had maintained an average of 5 points over controls (97.7 vs. 92.6). The greatest improvements were shown by children of mothers with IQs below 70 (Wickelgren 1999). After the publication of *The Bell Curve,* the Science Directorate of the American Psychological Association issued a "media advisory" that "there is a wealth of research evidence showing that early educational interventions are effective in raising performance and achievement levels for disadvantaged groups" (Duster 1995:160).

According to *The Bell Curve,* those at the bottom of society are there because of low IQ, and since they have larger families, the intelligence of Americans overall will decline. The prediction was frequently made early in the century in reaction to the flood of European immigrants. That the United States would become a nation of imbeciles has been disproved by James Flynn (1987), who discovered that IQ tests move the norm to 100 every 15–25 years. The Wechsler test was first normed in 1953 and again in 1978. In 1981, a group of people took both tests and scored 7.5 points higher on the older test. Given the 25 years between the two standardizations, the gain was 3 points per decade (Neisser 1998:12). This same rising curve has been found in 20 nations (Flynn 1984, 1987; Wickelgren 1999). At the same time, the gap in scores between blacks and whites has narrowed, leaving a difference of only 7 IQ points on the Ravens Progressive Matrices Test (Nisbett 1995:50). These changes may be because the average number of years of schooling has increased from 8 in the 1920s to over 13 in the 1990s. Also, more parents are better educated, and home environments are more enriched (Wickelgren 1999).

In the most recent evaluation of the question of IQ, race, and the environment, psychologist Richard Nisbett of the University of Michigan relies on numerous studies—statistical, historical, and experimental—to refute the notion that IQ is deeply encoded in our genes (2009). In his book *Intelligence and How to Get It* (2009), Nisbett writes about how class differences are much more important than race or heredity in influencing IQ scores. When poor children are adopted into upper class homes, their IQ scores rise by 12–18 points. Nisbett suggests that IQ scores are expandable depending on the enrichment of children's environments. He records an enormous amount of data demonstrating the rapid trend in upward IQ scores. The average score of an IQ test in 1917 would amount to only 73 on today's IQ test and half the population would be considered mentally retarded by today's measurements. IQ scores have risen remarkably over time, indicating that environmental and educational factors are much more important than heredity in determining intelligence.

This rapid trend toward upward test scores cannot be explained by genetic evolution, which occurs over a much longer span of time. Rather, it is a powerful veto to the argument that "race" determines IQ. Environment is not a minor factor influencing IQ; it is a major factor enhancing the chances for success of individuals and groups. IQ is not a fixed or hereditary entity; it can change significantly over time. Remedial social programs are not unproductive; if the environment is enriched and sustained, performance increases proportionately. Insofar as IQ scores are important, their increase indicates that America is not dumbing down. With the publication of *The Bell Curve* in 1994, it appeared that "scientific" racialism had acquired a new focus of controversy. However, that controversy obscured the appearance in the 1980s of the more explicit and extreme voice of J. Philippe Rushton, to which we now turn.

What More Could Be Said about "Race" and IQ? The Excesses of J. Philippe Rushton

Rushton is a psychologist at Western Ontario University in Canada and current director of the Pioneer Fund. He is dedicated to proving that there is a "racial" hierarchy that determines cultural differences in which blacks are inferior in almost every way. He draws upon scientific concepts and data in his attempt to support that racial hierarchy. He is unique in using both brain weight and/or cranial size and correlating it with IQ scores. In other words, he uses data from the nineteenth and twentieth centuries that have been discredited as sources of information about intelligence of "races." He has modified the nineteenth-century hierarchy by moving "Mongoloids," or Asians, to the top, while "Negroids" stay on the bottom, and "Caucasoids" are in the middle but close to Mongoloids. Rushton's promotion of Asians to the top coincided with the enormous economic prosperity occurring in Asia beginning in the 1970s, an example of one more environmental influence on a supposedly gene-based theory (Lieberman 2001).

"Race" is a pivotal concept for Rushton, yet most anthropologists have discarded the concept because there is more variation within "races" than among them, clear boundaries do not exist, "races" lack biological uniformity, and all of this

stems from migration, the flow of genes through mating, and the operation of varying intensity of natural selection across geographic regions without respect to boundary lines (see Chapter 3). Yet Rushton uses the concept of "race" without precisely defining the term beyond referring briefly to skin color and a few facial features, and stating that they are biological and that the three "races" are in Asia, Africa, Europe, and the Near East. More abstractly, and without providing specifics for each population, he states that "races are recognized by a combination of geographic, educational, and morphological factors and gene frequencies of biochemical components."

Rushton asserts that "races" merge, that there are three major "races," and that there are varieties of minor races within them (1995:96). These assertions lump together within each "race" an enormous range of biological variation. Rushton justifies this by using what he calls the principle of aggregation. In other words, he claims that by combining and averaging the cranial sizes of many populations within each "race," any variations in the accuracy of particular research studies will be averaged out and that the resulting correlations will be higher as well. However, his low correlations do not support that claim. Rushton "explains" variation in cultural achievement leading up to "civilization" with the claim that "Mongoloids" have the largest mean brain size and "Negroids" have the smallest, while "Caucasoids" are intermediate. We wish to place this brain-size explanation in several comparative contexts that demonstrate its scientific insignificance.

IQ IN CONTEXT 1: THE NORMAL RANGE IN CRANIAL SIZE FROM 1,000 TO 2,000 CC. The question of which "race" has the largest cranial size and intelligence is devoid of merit because it rests on the invalid race concept, on aggregating diverse populations into the three race boxes, and on the dubious claims that IQ tests measure a hereditary essence in the brain. It is necessary to examine the mean measurements reported by Rushton (1995:130): M = 1,364 cc, C = 1,327, and N = 1,267. The range between these means is

97 cc. Normal cranial size for *Homo sapiens* varies from 1,000 to 2,000 cc. The range of normal variation for modern *H. sapiens* is about 1,000 cc; therefore, a range of 97 cc between means is very small and cannot represent a causally significant difference. Normal human populations can appear anywhere along this continuum.

CONTEXTS 2 AND 3: CULTURES CHANGE DESPITE EVOLUTION OF SMALLER BRAINS. These concern the variation in cranial volume from Neandertal, at about 1,550 cc, to present-day *Homo sapiens* in Europe, at about 1,350 cc. The decrease was part of the skeleton becoming lighter, a process called gracilization, and marking the shift during the Paleolithic (about 100,000 to 35,000 years ago) to modern *H. sapiens*. Despite this decrease in absolute cranial size, culture changed dramatically from the Mousterian to the period of the Neolithic, and then to the scientific and industrial revolutions. If larger brains are smarter, as Rushton repeatedly tells us (often without correcting for body size or height), why did so many scientific and technological developments occur during the period when cranial head size had grown smaller by 100 cc—about the same amount that lies between the alleged means of Asians and Africans? Or can we assert that smaller brains are smarter? When challenged on these small differences in mean brain size, Rushton states that billions of neurons are involved in a 97 cc difference. There are also the multitude of dendrites connecting neurons. But the crucial point is that a greater number of neurons and dendrites can be packed into a smaller brain space. Holloway (1968) has reported that the packing distance between neurons decreases as the brain increases. It has also been demonstrated that women have 4,000 more neurons per cubic millimeter in their smaller cerebral cortex.

CONTEXT 4: FEMALES HAVE SMALLER BRAINS BUT THEIR IQ SCORES ARE NOT LOWER THAN THOSE OF MALES.   This represents height and sexual dimorphism. Brain weight varies significantly with body height. Females have about 10 percent smaller brains than men, an example of sexual dimorphism. Yet this difference disappears when corrected for height. Most importantly, no major sex differences exist in general mental ability, and mean IQ scores of males and females are very much the same (Jensen 1980, cited by Ankney 1992). Since the alleged difference in mean cranial size between blacks and whites is about the same as the average difference between sexes, we once again see that cranial size does not determine intelligence.

There is nothing to be gained by debating Rushton. He contends that opposition stems from "political correctness." The likely audience for pseudo-scientific racialism is not social scientists but policymakers and those either leaning toward ideas of racial inferiority or already committed to racialism and racism. Rushton thus joins that century-long network of race–IQ determinists for whom it matters little whether Europeans or Asians are on top. The major consequence of such "racial" hierarchies is to justify discrimination against those on the bottom. The further consequence is that such biodeterminism can be taken by policymakers to justify worldwide benign neglect of those living in poverty, including one in five of American children.

CONCLUSION

Yali's Question

In his 1999 condensation of his earlier book of 1995, Rushton has an added section entitled "Yali's Question and Marco's Answer." "Yali's Question" appeared in a book by Jared Diamond (1997), a UCLA biologist. Yali is a public official in New Guinea who asks Diamond, "Why is it that you white people developed so much cargo and brought it to New Guinea, but we black people had little cargo of our own?" (p. 14). "Cargo" refers to all the manufactured products that Europeans brought to New Guinea. Yali had earlier been a leader in founding cargo cults. These cults viewed cargo as a product of the spiritual world and prayed that the spirits would bring cargo to the black people of New Guinea (Worsley 1957).

What would be Rushton's answer to Yali's question? Consider Rushton's racialist theory: "race" determines that blacks shall have the worst or least of everything, "orientals" the most, with whites a close second. Thus blacks will have the smallest brains, lowest intelligence scores, lowest cultural achievements, highest intercourse frequency and most sexually transmitted diseases, most aggressiveness and impulsivity, least marital stability and least law abidingness, least administrative capacity, and so on (Rushton 1995:5). It is a truly comprehensive list in which blacks can do nothing right, according to Rushton. The one phrase, "cultural achievements," embraces a multitude of possible behaviors. So why those alleged differences? Rushton's answer to Yali is provided by Marco Polo, who after his time in China in the thirteenth century is alleged to have written: "Surely there is no more intelligent race on earth than the Chinese" (no source is given). The answer is consistent with Rushton's race–IQ determinism.

Jared Diamond (1997) gives a vastly different answer. He explains that the answer is not "race." He asks why the Aztecs did not bring guns, germs, and steel to Europe? If the Aztecs or the Africans had lived in the area of the Fertile Crescent then they would have invaded and conquered the rest of the world. Guns, germs, and steel were proximate causes, but the ultimate causes lie in a pattern of history in which by chance most of those plants and large mammals that could be domesticated existed in the area of the Fertile Crescent of southwest Asia where the Tigris and Euphrates join.

Over thousands of years in the Fertile Crescent hunting and gathering was gradually replaced by farming. Harvests became abundant and farm animals provided plentiful protein, droppings for fertilizer, and power for plowing and transportation. Population grew, and small cities developed with stratified specializations in crafts, religion, and government. In such settings innovations were more likely, including writing. Centuries later there had accumulated the technological knowledge and power to conquer others. Germs to help conquer the Americas were present

in the Europeans because they had acquired them through contact with their domesticated animals. They evolved resistance and developed immunity. The inhabitants of the New World had few animals, and did not develop the resistance needed and therefore suffered a massive loss of life after first contact with Europeans and their diseases such as smallpox. Diamond also adds that the processes of developing agriculture were easier in Eurasia because it is a continent along a horizontal axis in which the same latitudes allow for easy dispersal of plants and animals over wide geographic areas. By contrast, the Western Hemisphere and Africa are situated along a north–south axis that includes latitudes with very different climates that are barriers to plants and animals. In addition there were geographic barriers such as the Sahara Desert and tsetse flies in Africa, and in the Americas the greater distance, lack of animals for transportation, and the narrow isthmus of Panama with its tropical rain forest.

Diamond's explanation parallels what anthropologists have long argued: that the differences between cultures are not due to race but to geographic location and environmental resources (ecology), cultural history, and cultural contact. The nations and kingdoms of the Egyptians, Greeks, Romans, Spanish, British, Aztecs, Incas, Chinese, Ghanaians, and Malians rose and fell independent of the "race" of their inhabitants. However, Yali's question about cargo is not fully answered. There is a gap in Diamond's explanation following the beginning of complex cities in the Fertile Crescent, and also following the time when European expansion began after Columbus's voyages of exploration and exploitation. The latter gap is the time in which European growth occurred in population, capitalism, science, and industrialization, accompanied and stimulated by the colonization and globalization of the rest of the world—all of which could have originated in Eurasia regardless of what "race" occupied Europe and the Fertile Crescent.

Rushton ignores how contemporary anthropologists have devoted themselves to explaining differences among societies using historical, cultural, and ecologically based ethnographies.

Within the disciplines of psychology and anthropology, there are vigorous critics of past "scientific" racism and of its contemporary manifestations. In both disciplines too little attention is paid to informing future scientists of that history and its present manifestations. In this history we have attempted to trace the consistent theme that the practitioners of "scientific" racialism present. Using the techniques but not the essence of science, they have claimed that there is a racial hierarchy in which blacks are always at the bottom. The consequences of such a contention is to justify the inferior and exploited position of people of color. We have presented the research of a number of those who developed such ideas over

past centuries, as well as some of the counterevidence from almost a century of research and debate. The strongest evidence for an interaction of heredity and environment does not support the notion of biologically determined "race" differences in intelligence. The ultimate test for "race" differences in intelligence can only occur in a society where equal access to cultural resources is available to all. Yet it is precisely that access that is opposed, in one way or another, by "scientific" racialism. The differences among human populations and societies are best explained by examination of their different ecology, geography, demography, and contacts with other societies—in short, their different cultural histories.

Notes

1. Among these seventeenth- and eighteenth-century scientists were (1) Franz Gall (1758–1828), a physician, who studied the bumps on the human cranium and linked such bumps to intellect and morality, thereby reflecting and reinforcing the biological explanation of behavior; (2) Georges Cuvier (1769–1832), founder of paleontology, who traced the "races" to Adam, and viewed blacks as the most inferior of all "races"; (3) Paul Broca (1824–1880), who specialized in neuroanatomy and physical anthropology, developed many new tools for measuring the cranium, and asserted that mixed "races" were inferior in almost every way; (4) Ernst Haeckel (1834–1919), a specialist in embryology, who enthusiastically adopted Darwin's ideas but differed from Darwin by viewing evolution as progressive, with inferior "races" eventually being eliminated, a view that would become state policy under Adolf Hitler in the 1940s; and (5) Louis Agassiz (1835–1910), a zoologist, who was an influential antievolutionist, and a strong supporter of the inferiority of blacks and the idea that the "races" had been created separately (polygenic) and were different species.

2. In *Hereditary Genius* (1869), Galton was among the first to apply to mental phenomena the prin-

ciple of deviation from the average. He divided the normal curve of ability into classes A through C although he did not have a procedure for assigning individuals to these categories (Tucker 1994). Galton also developed a calculus for the correlation coefficient, percentile ranking, regression to the mean, and the distinction between general mental ability (intelligence) and special abilities (particular aptitudes), and he advocated twin studies (Evans and Waites 1981:36). Galton was certainly not an egalitarian, and although he was opposed to hereditary aristocracy, he favored meritocracy based on purported mental abilities. "Galton achieved a synthesis of liberal individualism with Darwinism which offered a rationale for a class-stratified but socially mobile society" (Evans and Waites 1981:38). It was a line of reasoning still evident in the latter-day hereditarians, Jensen, Herrnstein and Murray, and others.

3. Stephen J. Gould interprets these phases in relation to their social context: the reasons for recurrence are sociopolitical, and not far to seek; resurgence in biological determinism correlates with episodes of political retrenchment, particularly with campaigns for reduced government spending on social programs, or at times of fear among ruling elites when disadvantaged groups

sow serious social unrest or even threaten to usurp power. What argument against social change could be more chillingly effective than the claim that established orders, with some groups on top and others at the bottom, exist as an accurate reflection of the innate and unchangeable intellectual capacities of people so ranked (Gould 1996:28)?

References Cited

ALLEN, GARLAND. 1999. Modern biological determinism. In *The Biological Basis of Human Behavior.* Robert W. Sussman, ed. Pp. 294–304. Upper Saddle River, NJ: Prentice Hall.

ANKNEY, C. DAVISON. 1992. Sex differences in relative brain size: The mismeasure of women, too? *Intelligence* 16:329–336.

BAKER, LEE D. 1998. *From Savage to Negro: Anthropology and the Construction of Race, 1896–1954.* Berkeley, CA: University of California Press.

BARKAN, ELAZAR. 1987. From Race to Ethnicity: Changing Concepts of Race in England and the United States between the Two World Wars. Ph.D. dissertation, Brandeis University.

BATES, DANIEL G., and ELLIOT FRATKIN. 1999. *Cultural Anthropology.* 2nd edition. Boston, MA: Allyn & Bacon.

BENEDICT, RUTH. 1934. *Patterns of Culture.* Boston, MA: Houghton Mifflin.

BERNASCONI, ROBERT, ed. 2001. *Race.* Maden, MA: Blackwell Publishers, Inc.

BINET, ALFRED. 1903 [1973]. *Les Idées Modernes sur les Enfants.* Paris: Flammarion.

BLAKEY, MICHAEL. 1998. Beyond European Enlightenment: Toward a critical and humanistic human biology. In *Building a New Biocultural Synthesis.* Alan H. Goodman and Thomas L. Leatherman, eds. Pp. 379–406. Ann Arbor, MI: University of Michigan Press.

BLOCK, NED J., and GERALD DWORKIN. EDS. 1976. *The IQ Controversy: Critical Readings.* New York: Random House.

BLUMENBACH, JOHANN FRIEDRICH. 1795. *On the Natural Varieties of Mankind.* Thomas Bedyshe, trans. New York: Bergman.

BOAS, FRANZ. 1912. *Report on Changes in the Bodily Form of Descendants of Immigrants.* New York: Columbia University Press.

BRACE, C. LORING. 1997. Race. In *The History of Physical Anthropology.* Frank Spencer, ed. Pp. 861–867. New York: Garland.

BRAUDE, BENJAMIN. 1997. The sons of Noah and the construction of ethnic and geographical identities in the medieval and early modern periods. *William and Mary Quarterly: A Magazine of Early American History and Culture* 54(1):103–142.

CHASE, ALLAN. 1975. *The Legacy of Malthus: The Social Costs of the New Scientific Racism.* New York: Knopf.

CHIDLEY, JOE. 1994. The brain strain. *Maclean's* 107:72–73.

COON, CARLETON. 1962. *The Origin of Races.* New York: Knopf.

DARWIN, CHARLES. 1859 [1968]. *The Origin of Species.* Harmondsworth: Penguin.

DAVIS, DAVID BRION. 1997. Constructing Race: A Reflection. *William and Mary Quarterly: A Magazine of Early American History and Culture* 54(1):7–18.

DENNIS, RUTLEDGE M. 1996. Racism. In *The Social Science Encyclopedia.* Adam Kuper and Jessica Ruper, eds. Pp. 715–717. London: Routledge.

DIAMOND, JARED. 1997. *Genes, Germs, and Steel: The Fates of Human Societies.* New York: Norton.

DIKÖTTER, FRANK. 2008. The racialization of the globe: An interactive interpretation. *Ethnic and Racial Studies* 28(4):1–19.

DUSTER, TROY. 1995. What's new in the IQ debate. *Black Scholar* 25:25–31.

ERICKSON, PAUL A. 1997a. American school of anthropology. In *The History of Physical Anthropology.* Frank Spencer, ed. Pp. 65–66. New York: Garland.

———. 1997b. Polygenism. In *The History of Physical Anthropology.* Frank Spencer, ed. Pp. 832–833. New York: Garland.

EVANS, BRIAN, and BERNARD WAITES. 1981. *IQ and Mental Testing: An Unnatural Science and Its Social History.* Atlantic Highlands, NJ: Humanities Press.

FLYNN, JAMES R. 1980. *Race, IQ and Jensen.* London: Routledge and Kegan Paul.

———. 1984. The mean IQ of Americans: Massive gains, 1932 to 1978. *Psychological Bulletin* 95:29–51.

————. 1987. Massive IQ gains in 14 nations. What IQ tests really measure. *Psychological Bulletin* 101:171–191.

GALTON, FRANCIS. 1869. *Hereditary Genius.* New York: Appleton.

GARDNER, HOWARD. 1985. *The Mind's New Science.* New York: Basic Books.

GOBINEAU, JOSEPH-ARTHUR. 1854 [1966]. *Essays on the Inequality of Human Races.* Adrian Collins, trans. Los Angeles, CA: Noontide Press.

GODDARD, HENRY H. 1912. *The Kallikak Family: A Study of the Heredity of Feeble-Mindedness.* New York: Macmillan.

————. 1914. *Feeble-Mindedness: Its Causes and Consequences.* New York: Macmillan.

————. 1928. Feeble-Mindedness: A question of definition. *Journal of Psycho-Asthenics* 33:219–227.

GOLEMAN, DANIEL. 1988. An emerging theory on blacks' IQ scores. *New York Times,* Education Supplement, April 10, pp. 22–24.

GOSSETT, THOMAS F. 1965. *Race: The History of an Idea in America.* New York: Schocken Books.

GOULD, STEPHEN J. 1981. *The Mismeasure of Man.* New York: Norton.

————. 1996. *Mismeasure of Man.* Revised and expanded. New York: Norton.

GRANT, MADISON. 1916. *The Passing of the Great Race.* New York: Charles Scribner's Sons.

HANNAFORD, IVAN. 1996. *Race: The History of an Idea in the West.* Baltimore, MD: Johns Hopkins University Press.

HERRNSTEIN, RICHARD J., and CHARLES MURRAY. 1994. *The Bell Curve, Intelligence and Class Structure in American Life.* New York: Free Press.

HOLLOWAY, RALPH L. 1968. Cranial capacity and the evolution of the human brain. In *Culture: Man's Adaptive Dimension.* Ashley Montagu, ed. Pp. 170–196. New York: Oxford University Press.

HUDSON, J. BLAINE. 1995. Scientific racism: The politics of tests, race, and genetics. *Black Scholar* 25:3–20.

JENSEN, ARTHUR R. 1980. *Bias in Mental Testing.* New York: Free Press.

KAMIN, LEON J. 1974. *The Science and Politics of IQ.* Potomac, MD: Erlbaum.

KEVLES, DANIEL J. 1985. *In the Name of Eugenics.* Berkeley, CA: University of California Press.

KLINEBERG, OTTO. 1935. *Negro Intelligence and Selective Migration.* Westport, CT: Greenwood.

KROEBER, ALFRED L. 1917. The superorganic. *American Anthropologist* 70:163–213.

LEACH, EDMUND. 1988. Noah's second son. *Anthropology Today* 4(4):2–5.

LEWONTIN, R. C., STEVEN ROSE, and LEON J. KAMIN. 1993 [1984]. IQ: The rank ordering of the world. In *The "Racial" Economy of Science: Toward a Democratic Future.* Sandra Harding, ed. Pp. 142–160. Bloomington, IN: Indiana University Press.

LIEBERMAN, LEONARD. 1968. The debate over race: A study in the sociology of knowledge. *Phylon* 39:127–141.

————. 1997. Gender and the deconstruction of the race concept. *American Anthropologist* 99: 545–558.

————. 2001. How Caucasoids got such big crania and why they shrank: From Morton to Rushton. *Current Anthropology* 42:69–95.

LIPPMANN, WALTER. 1922. The mental age of Americans, October 25. The mystery of the "A" men, November 1. The reliability of intelligence tests, November 8. The abuse of tests, November 5. Tests of hereditary intelligence, November 22. A future for the tests, November 29. *New Republic.* Reprinted in Block and Dworkin, ibid.

MACRAE, DUNCAN. 1960. Race and sociology in history and theory. In *Man, Race and Darwin.* Phillip Mason, ed. Pp. 76–86. London: Oxford University Press.

MARKS, JONATHAN. 2007. Long shadow of Linneaus's taxonomy. *Nature* 447:28.

————. 2008. History of scientific racism. In *The Encyclopedia of Race and Racism*, Volume 3. John H. Moore, ed. Pp. 1–16. Detroit, MI: MacMillan Reference USA.

MEHLER, BARRY. 1989. Foundation for fascism: The new eugenics movement in the United States. *Patterns of Prejudice* 23:17–25.

MOLNAR, STEPHEN. 1992. *Human Variation: Races, Topics, and Ethnic Groups.* 3rd edition. Englewood Cliffs, NJ: Prentice Hall.

MONTAGU, ASHLEY. 1942. *Man's Most Dangerous Myth: The Fallacy of Race.* New York: Columbia University Press.

————. 1972. *Statement on Race.* 3rd edition. New York: Oxford University Press.

————. 1975. *Race and IQ.* New York: Oxford University Press.

MORTON, SAMUEL GEORGE. 1839. *Crania Americana.* Philadelphia, PA: John Pennington.

————. 1849. *Crania Aegyptiaca.* Philadelphia, PA: John Pennington.

NEISSER, UBRIC, ed. 1998. *The Rising Curve: Long-Term Gains in IQ and Related Measures.* Washington, DC: American Psychological Association.

NISBETT, RICHARD. 1995. Race, IQ and scientism. In *The Bell Curve Wars: Race, Intelligence and the*

Future of America. Steven Fraser, ed. Pp. 36–57. New York: Basic Books.

———. 2009. *Intelligence and How to Get It: Why Schools and Culture Count.* New York: W.W. Norton & Co.

NOTT, JOSIAH C., and GEORGE R. GLIDDON. 1854. *Types of Mankind.* Philadelphia, PA: Lippincott, Grambo.

PATTERSON, ORLANDO. 1995. For whom the bell curves. In *The Bell Curve Wars: Race, Intelligence, and the Future of America.* Steven Fraser, ed. Pp. 187–213. New York: Basic Books.

PROCTOR, ROBERT N. 1988. *Racial Hygiene, Medicine under the Nazis.* Cambridge, MA: Harvard University Press.

———. 1995. *Race, Evolution, and Behavior: A Life History Perspective.* New Brunswick, NJ: Transaction.

SAMELSON, FRANZ. 1992. Rescuing the Reputation of Sir Cyril Burt. *Journal of the History of the Behavioral Sciences* 28:221–233.

SCARR, SANDRA, ANDREW PAKSTIS, SOLOMON H. KATZ, and WILLIAM B. BARKER. 1977. The absence of a relationship between degree of white ancestry and intellectual skills within the black population. *Human Genetics* 39:69–86.

SCARR, SANDRA, and RICHARD W. WEINBERG. 1978. Attitudes, interests, and IQ. *Human Nature* 1: 29–36.

SEDGWICK, JOHN. 1994. The mentality bunker. *IQ* 64:228–236.

SHAPIRO, HARRY R. 1969. The history and development of physical anthropology. *American Anthropologist* 67:376.

SPENCER, FRANK. 1997. Johann Friedrich Blumenbach. *History of Physical Anthropology* 1:183–186.

STEPAN, NANCY. 1982. *The Idea of Race in Science, Great Britain 1800–1960.* Hampton, CT: Shoestring Press.

STEPAN, NANCY, and SANDER L. GILMAN. 1993. Appropriating the idioms of science: The rejection of scientific racism. In *The "Racial" Economy of Science.* Sandra Harding, ed. Pp. 170–193. Bloomington, IN: Indiana University Press.

TERMAN, LEWIS M. 1916. *The Measurement of Intelligence.* Boston, MA: Houghton Mifflin.

TODOROV, TZVETAN. 1993. *On Human Diversity.* Cambridge, MA: Harvard University Press.

TUCKER, WILLIAM H. 1994. *The Science and Politics of Racial Research.* Urbana, IL: University of Illinois Press.

VAN DEN BERGHE, PIERRE. 1996. Social Darwinism. In *The Social Science Encyclopedia.* Adam Kuper and Jessica Kuper, eds. Pp. 783–784. London: Routledge.

WADE, PETER. 2002. *Race, Nature, and Culture: An Anthropological Perspective.* London: Pluto Press.

WICKELGREN, INGRID. 1999. Nurture helps mold able minds. *Science* 283:1832–1834.

WORSLEY, PETER. 1957. *The Trumpet Shall Sound.* New York: Schocken Books.

3

■ ■ ■

The Concept of Race in Contemporary Anthropology

Scott MacEachern, *Bowdoin College*

INTRODUCTION

What is race? First of all, "race" is a word, and like many words it has a variety of meanings. Some of these occur frequently in everyday life, as we talk about "the human race" or about American "race relations." Other meanings are used in government offices and forms, as when Americans note which of a number of races they belong to for the Census. Yet other meanings of the term "race" are more technical, when, for example, a biologist talks about different races of a particular species of plant or animal. The meanings attached to this word "race" are different in all of these contexts, sometimes very different, but in everyday use we continually blur the differences between these meanings. This would be a recipe for confusion in any case but, given the history of this term "race" in the United States, the potentials for uncertainty and discord are especially great in this country. "Race" is a loaded word in part because people use that word in very different ways but assume that they are talking about the same thing.

Anthropologists often use the word "race," as well. One of the most important tasks of anthropologists is the examination of the biological and cultural variability that exists within humanity. We look at the customs of societies in different parts of the world, seeking to find the common elements that define our shared existence and the differences that lend variety to our lives. We study the biological characteristics of different human populations, our relations with our relatives—the apes and monkeys, and the evolutionary history of our species. We use archaeology to examine human prehistory. We examine the role that language plays in helping us define our worlds—and we try to put all of this knowledge to use in the wider world around us.

Every human occupies a position in a complex of groups with different sizes, constructions, and purposes. These groups can include families, bands, villages, religious organizations, fraternities, tribes, companies, and nations. Our membership in these different sorts of groups adds a vital structure to our lives, allowing us to learn how to be human and placing us in a dense web of relationships with family, work-mates, friends, strangers, and enemies. Anthropologists study, among other things, how humans create these groups. Questions of racial identification are extremely important in these interactions, and are especially significant in modern, multicultural societies. Given these investigations into the nature of human groups, we could expect that anthropologists would have a lot to say about race as it applies to human beings. After all, we might argue that races are among the largest and most inclusive of such human groups, and many people seem to base expectations of other people's behavior on their racial identities.

The study of human races has been an important part of anthropology since its origin as a professional discipline in the nineteenth century (see Chapter 1). Physical anthropologists have in the past studied the physical characteristics of members of different races; archaeologists and paleoanthropologists have studied human evolution with the goal of identifying the origins of these races; and cultural anthropologists have studied the ways that people use racial identifications to control social interactions around the world. Anthropologists have certainly had a lot to say about human races, and the results of our research sometimes reflect—and sometimes challenge—the various meanings given to this word "race" by nonanthropologists in the United States.

This chapter will summarize some of the conclusions of anthropological research on human races—on their origins, on the ways in which people have been identified with different races, and on the ways in which race can affect interactions between individuals and groups. Anthropologists working within the different subfields of our discipline have different conceptions of race and the meaning of racial identifications, and like nonanthropologists they sometimes use the term without specifying exactly what they mean. Among the questions that this chapter seeks to answer then are: What are anthropologists talking about when they talk about race, and are they always talking about the

same thing? Are there common elements in all anthropological usages of the term *race*, or are these usages sometimes contradictory? Perhaps most important, what are human races, and how do they originate and function? This chapter will focus on the biological concepts associated with race, and especially on the relationship between biological and cultural definitions of human races.

BIOLOGY AND CULTURE

Anthropologists consider the meaning of the word "race" in two different ways. First, physical anthropologists look at the *biological* characteristics of human populations in different areas of the world. They compare these populations to one another, with the goal of understanding the patterning of human biological variation. In the nineteenth century, anthropologists studied the external features of people: their skin color, the color and configuration of their hair, the proportions of their limbs, the features of their faces and bodies. In the twentieth century, studies of more subtle variation—of blood groups and antibody types, and most recently and more fundamentally, of genetic material—has added new levels of detail and complexity to that research. Physical anthropologists talk about the scales at which this human physical variation exists, from tiny, local communities to groups found across whole continents. Race for these anthropologists implies the existence of a number of fundamental biological populations into which all humans can be sorted. This concept was a central part of studies of humanity from their beginning almost two centuries ago. The question before anthropologists in this case is: do human races exist as *biological* groupings, and if so what are their characteristics?

Other anthropologists, in their study of human cultures and behavior, look at race from an entirely different perspective. In this case, the emphasis is not on the biological characteristics of human populations, but rather on the ways in which people divide their *social* worlds into various groups of humans. In Europe and North

America, these divisions have often used language that focused on physical and geographical differences: "Black," "White," "Nordic," "African," and so on. Anthropologists have established that ingrained prejudices have often had far more to do with these racial definitions than have the real physical characteristics of people. "Race" in these investigations by cultural anthropologists is conceived of as a *cultural* construction, not a biological fact. It is in reality a kind of *ideology*, a way of thinking about, speaking about, and organizing relationships among human groups: Who is your friend, or enemy? Who is a neighbor, or a foreigner? This ideological understanding of race may use the *language* of physical features when talking about group differences, but biology is not fundamentally important to the ways that these groups are defined. The question before anthropologists in this case is: how and why do people use *cultural* criteria to define human races, and how have these definitions changed through time?

These two ways of thinking are obviously very different. If race is examined as a *biological* concept, then we must think about the physical features of humans, the external ones that we all can see as well as our internal biological and genetic makeup. We would probably examine biological races by seeking to trace their evolutionary history over long periods of time, using data from genetics, from physical anthropology, and from archaeology. If race is examined as a *cultural* concept, then we must think about attitudes and cultural categories, ideas that exist within people's minds and that are acted upon in the real world. These attitudes and ideas can change very quickly indeed, so that we can probably trace the evolution of cultural categories of race over much shorter time periods—centuries, or perhaps even decades. Our data will mostly be derived from cultural anthropology and historical research.

It is important to remember that the objects of study—*biologically defined races* of humans and *culturally defined racial categories* of humans—are not the same in these different approaches. This means that the existence of one kind of race does not necessarily imply the existence of the other. Biological races might exist among humans, without having any cultural significance: if, for example, people were settled in one place and only saw neighbors who looked just like them, then their definitions of social groups would probably not include a racial component. (This is a hard situation for us to imagine today, where we constantly see people from all around the world.) Similarly, people may use language that talks about physical features to divide people up into races, but that does not mean that membership in those races are necessarily based on those physical features. We can see this in the United States by thinking about how many "whites" and "blacks" actually have skin that is white or black in color. *The fact that people talk about "race relations" in the United States today does not imply that those races are real biological units, any more than the fact that people tell ghost stories implies that ghosts really exist.*

For the most part, anthropologists examine race from one or the other of these two perspectives, and only quite rarely do they mix them up. One important exception involves forensic anthropologists, who study human skeletal remains in order to provide information for legal proceedings—the sort of work we might watch on *CSI* or similar shows. These anthropologists examine skeletal remains carefully, gathering data on age at death, sex, stature, population affiliations, and a number of other possible characteristics of the individual(s) who died. However, for that information to be *used*, they then have to translate this information into the racial categories that are used by the police, the legal system, and by members of the general public. As we will see, this raises interesting question of the relations between biological and cultural conceptions of race. In the rest of this chapter, I will examine some of the evidence for these different kinds of races, seeking to answer a number of the questions that have been posed above. I will pay particular attention to biological concepts of race, because much of the evidence for race as a cultural concept will be examined in other chapters of this textbook.

BACKGROUND OF THE TERM

The precise origin of the word "race" is unknown, but it seems to originate in a Latin root, *ratio*, with a meaning similar to terms like "species" or "kind" (of thing) (Smedley 2007:37–41). Five hundred years ago, "race" was occasionally used in English to designate groups of humans marked by their common origins or shared characteristics, physical or otherwise. Over the next 200 years, the word was increasingly used in English in ways similar to words like "group," "nation," "people," and so on. This general meaning of the word "race" is more or less obsolete today. We still talk about "the human race," but we almost never encounter people using terms like "the race of Smith's" or "the race of baseball players," although such uses were fairly common 150 years ago.

Over the last two centuries, a more restricted meaning of the word "race" has become common in English. In this case, a race designates one of a number of fundamental divisions within the human species. These races are usually described in *biological* terms, although people have most often claimed that *behavioral* and *cultural* differences between races exist as well. The number of races identified according to this meaning of the term has varied, but Europe, Africa, and Asia are often identified as the homelands of three of these races, and people talk about "Europeans" (or "Caucasoids"), "Africans" (or "Negroids"), and "Asians" (or "Mongoloids") as if those three groups constitute fundamental units of humanity.

In North America today, this is the meaning that the general public usually associates with the word "race":

a. human races are extraordinarily *important*;
b. they are based on *biological* differences;
c. they are ancient and (relatively) *unchanging*; and
d. they are *easily distinguishable* from one another.

Scientists, including anthropologists, contributed a great deal to the popularization of this idea of human races through the nineteenth and early twentieth centuries. These scientists gathered a great deal of data on human physical diversity and on the cultures of societies around the world, but their interpretations were very much colored by their own prejudices. They furnished what appeared to be support to these biological models of human races but, as a variety of scholars have noted (Baker 1998; Barkan 1992; Hannaford 1996; Jahoda 1998; Smedley 2007), these researchers were themselves very much influenced by stereotypes of different groups and the relations between these groups that were pervasive in their own societies.

The history of scientific racism has been covered in Chapter 2, but two things should be made clear at this point. First, through much of the history of anthropological studies of human races, such studies were concerned with *hierarchy* and not only with classification. Scientists who compared human populations from different areas of the world were trying to distinguish such populations from one another, but they usually *ranked* these groups with reference to one another as well. Such rankings might be based on notions of intellectual superiority and inferiority, of savagery and civilization, of greater and lesser degrees of evolution, but they have almost always placed Europeans (almost always upper- and middle-class European males) at the pinnacle of human development. Africans, Asians, Native Americans, and other people had to be content with lower rankings, at varying distances from those "superior" specimens of humanity.

Many of these scientists had never had any contact with the people who they described in their writings and when they did, these people from other parts of the world were most often servants, slaves, or objects of curiosity. Perhaps the ultimate expression of these prejudices was the concept of *polygenesis*, which held that the human races actually had originated and evolved separately from one another—that Africans, Europeans, and Asians were, in fact, separate species. Such a theory seems absurd to us today, with so much more known about human evolution and with the concept of a species as a biological population that can interbreed accepted as commonplace. At a time when evolution was not well understood and when bigotry against non-Europeans was nearly universal, polygenesis seemed a reasonable theory of human origins and development.

These studies frequently mixed up *biological, behavioral,* and *cultural* characteristics when defining human races, just as nonscientists continue to do today. In the middle of the eighteenth century, Carolus Linnaeus defined the different races not only upon their *physical* features (skin and eye color, type of hair, and so on) and their *temperaments* (melancholy, lazy, timid, and so on), but also by the type of *clothes* they wore and the characteristics of their *governments*. The latter are cultural characteristics, and—as we know—very subject to change. Such an approach can cause people to mistake more or less transitory cultural influences, characteristics that exist for a short period because of the environment that people are brought up in, for permanent biological characteristics.

We may, for example, laugh at Linnaeus for trying to define races based on whether people wear loose or tight clothing. However, we run the same risk today when, for example, we think of people of African descent as "natural athletes." A century ago, Africans and African Americans were excluded from many athletic competitions and considered simply incapable of playing many sports; today, the grandchildren and great-grandchildren of these people excel in sports around the world. There is nothing "natural"—that is, biological—in the cultural changes that have accompanied this transformation in athletic success. We have to try and keep biological and cultural influences entirely separate when we evaluate whether such population units exist.

BIOLOGICAL RACES

Advocates of "scientific" racialism sometimes claim that questioning the existence of biological races is the same as denying the existence of biological variation among human beings. This is nonsense. Everyone, including anthropologists, knows that biological variation exists. I resemble my brothers and sister in some ways, but there are many physical features that distinguish us. Males and females, and old people and young people, differ physically in a variety of very significant characteristics—and these differences are predictable. We can make a reasonable guess about whether someone we see in the street comes from Norway or Italy, or whether they are Moroccan or Senegalese, although there is often a good chance of making a mistake in such cases. We recognize that populations of Nuer people from the Sudan are on average much taller than are Mayan people from Guatemala. No one would argue that each of 6.5 billion human beings is a member of his or her own private race, or that I belong to a different race than does my daughter because I am 48 and male and she is 16 and female, or that 6-footers belong to a different race than do people who are 5 feet tall. If the term "race" is to have any meaning within anthropology at all, it must involve something more exact than just physical difference.

The primary questions remain, then: *how do physical anthropologists define races*, and what criteria have they used to define them? How many human races have been defined? What are the origins of such human races?

The answers to these questions depend very much on the definitions of "race" that researchers have used when investigating human biological differences. This is a difficult problem, because races are not precisely defined within biology as a whole. The *species* is the fundamental unit of evolution, characterized by the ability of members of one species to successfully interbreed and thus to share genetic innovations and adaptations. There are, however, no such clearly defined units below the level of the species, and it is unclear how researchers should divide species up into subunits—including races. Thus, Ernst Mayr (1963:453–460) notes that a whole variety of different kinds of biological populations have been identified as races, and that these different kinds of populations vary considerably in their characteristics.

There have been approximately as many *anthropological definitions of races* as there have been physical anthropologists who have studied the question, but we can divide such definitions up into three types, one of which is now entirely obsolete. Polygenicists thought of populations originating in different areas of the world—Africans, Europeans, Asians, and so on—as different *species* of humanity, each with their own origins and with limited abilities to interbreed. Africans and Native Americans were even at various times described as species intermediate between "real" humans and apes (Jahoda 1998:75–76). This claim stemmed in great part from the vicious bigotry toward these other people that many Europeans and European Americans held in the nineteenth and twentieth centuries. It would be comforting if we could dismiss polygenesis as a fantasy of the nineteenth century, but the well-known British geneticist and racist Reginald Ruggles Gates (1948:366) still claimed that Africans, Asians, and Europeans were different species in a book published just after World War II. Traces of polygenesis are still to be found in the writings of racist organizations today, but no reputable anthropologist believes that such theories have any connection with reality at all.

More recently anthropologists have conceived of human race in one of two different ways. Some researchers have conceived of biological races as well-defined, stable *types of human beings*—real biological groups in and of themselves. We could also call this a *subspecies* model, because it implies that races in humans are what we would call subspecies among animals: populations that are isolated from one another and somewhat different, but not so much so that they have lost the capability to interbreed (Futuyama 1986:107–109). Other physical anthropologists, in contrast, have conceived of races as simple expressions of difference in the *physical features of different populations* of people. In this case, *any* group of humans that can be differentiated from other groups based on some physical characteristic or characteristics can be considered a race. A possible alternative term for this second definition

would be a *statistical* model of human races, because it depends on the statistical distribution of physical features within and between different human groupings. There is no expectation of isolation or significant difference between these populations in this case.

The difference between these two concepts is one of degree, not of kind. At the same time, these *typological* and *population* models tend to yield different views of human biological variability, and they are subject to different sorts of criticisms.

Races as Types

> ... A race is a great division of mankind, the members of which, though individually varying, are characterized as a group by a certain combination of morphological and metrical features ... which have been derived from their common descent ... [Hooton 1946:446]

Many anthropologists have in the past claimed that there exist (or existed) a limited number of geographically distinct groupings of humans, each of these groups possessing a more or less well-defined set of physical characteristics, and have called these types *human races*. These races are often linked with a particular continent, although their territories are not in fact contiguous with continents. These researchers have believed that these human races occupied different parts of the world through very long periods of time, and that they evolved their unique physical characteristics as adaptations to the particular environments of these regions. Thus, "Negroids" evolved in sub-Saharan Africa, and a number of physical features—dark skin, everted lips, tightly curled hair, a long skull, and so on—are characteristic of Negroid populations and adaptations to African environments. Similarly, "Caucasoids" (Europeans, but also people living in North Africa, the Middle East, and parts of Asia) evolved somewhere in Eurasia and a limited number of physical features—light-colored skin, noneverted lips, straight or curled hair, a narrow nose, and so on—are both characteristic of "Caucasoid" populations and adaptations to the environments where the "Caucasoid" race evolved (wherever that might have been). The same would be the case for "Mongoloid" populations, supposedly associated with Asia and sometimes with the Americas.

There are two important characteristics of this model, and these two characteristics are closely related. First, this model is *geographical*. Each race is associated with a particular region of the world, where it is supposed to have developed in relative isolation and in adaptation to the particular environments of that region. Geographical isolation is often important in biological definitions of *subspecies*, populations of a single biological species that have been isolated from one another by some geographical barrier that prevents interbreeding. This genetic isolation might eventually lead to the separation of the two subspecies into separate species. This has not, of course, happened with humans.

Second, this model of human races views such races as real biological *types*. As noted, these different fundamental types of humanity are held to have evolved over very long times in the geographical heartlands of each race. Thus, each race is relatively stable and long-lived, with boundaries that were in ancient times comparatively easy to define—although they may have become rather more blurred in recent times. Each race also has a set of distinctive and essential characteristics, physical adaptations to the particular environments of the regions where that race evolved. The humans belonging to any particular race share this set of characteristics, although they may be expressed differently in each individual. The racial identity of every human is then supposed to be detectable through an examination of these characteristics. More generally, the different features of humans within one race are supposed to occur together: we may think of a race as a well-defined group of people sharing a well-defined group of traits.

In the most extreme of these typological theories, race is conceived almost as a substance, the *essence* of a group of people, which in pure form or when intermixed determines the characteristics of any individual. Joseph Deniker (1912:8) writes of race as " . . . once met with in a real union of individuals, now scattered in fragments of varying proportions among several ethnic groups, from which it can no longer be differentiated except through a process of delicate analysis." This view often led anthropologists to the conclusion that "pure races" had existed in the past, but that the migrations, conquests, and colonizations that we know of through recorded history had resulted in the disappearance of these "pure races" through admixture. Biological race is then an almost purely abstract concept, and has very little to do with the actual physical characteristics of humans.

Human races conceived of as subspecies would have a number of specific features, and we can look for those features as we try to decide whether these models are realistic. First, if races developed more or less in isolation, then the boundaries between those races will be relatively clear-cut and generally will fall along the obstacles (deserts, oceans, mountain ranges, and so on) that divide them. It is of course possible that more recent population movements would have obscured such clear boundaries. Second, the essential characteristics of each race would be widely shared, because these characteristics would be adaptive responses to the environmental conditions within which each race evolved. Third, we would expect that the processes of isolation, adaptation, and differentiation that generate races would yield a fairly consistent hierarchy of such races through time. If human races are essentially subspecies, we could expect that races are relatively well-defined, stable entities, and that their definition and analysis should be a fairly straightforward process.

How well do these implications match up against real human variability? We can draw on data from physical anthropology, genetics, geography, and archaeology to look at this issue. What we find is just the opposite of this well-ordered model. We find that the populations identified by researchers as human races have been extremely variable, that there is a huge amount of disagreement about their characteristics, and that even their associations with particular regions and sorts of environments are often quite weak.

Perhaps the most basic question that we can ask is simply: *how many human races are there?* Answers to this question have been very diverse indeed. Many researchers have identified three primary human races—the "Negroid," "Caucasoid," and "Mongoloid" races noted above—although sometimes using different and/or overlapping terms (see, for example, Hooton 1946:569; Bean 1926; von Eickstedt 1950:496). This definition seems to originate in the popular typologies of race that have been established in Europe and North America since the nineteenth century. As European and American knowledge of other parts of the world grew, other populations were either fit into one of these three categories, or put forward as independent races. Thus, a variety of aboriginal peoples living in South and Southeast Asia were lumped together as "Negritos" and classified either as part of the "Negroid" race (which assumes that they came there from Africa at some time in the past) or as a separate "Negrito" race. Australian Aboriginal people were frequently classified as a separate race ("Australoids"), sometimes alongside populations from New Guinea and sometimes not. Pacific Island groups were sometimes classified as "Mongoloids," sometimes as "Australoids," and sometimes as their own race. Anthropologists established a bewildering variety of classification systems in order to divide humanity into races and subraces, major and minor races, and so on. Hooton (1946:575–650), for example, identified three "primary" and about 20 "secondary" races of different sorts. The geneticist William Boyd identified six races in *Genetics and the Races of Man* (Boyd 1950), but increased this number to 13 some years later (Boyd 1968). Keith (1948:235–244) identified two basic human groups, races in all but name. In 1950, three other well-known researchers (Coon et al. 1950) identified 30 human races. Coon (1965:7) himself later identified " . . . five full-sized subspecies and . . . two dwarfed subspecies" of modern humans, and

called these "subspecies" races. Different researchers have at one point or another identified between 2 and 200 of these "fundamental" human groups (Garn and Coon 1968:9). Not only that, these elaborate classifications conflict with one another, in the number of races identified, in the characteristics of particular races, and in the racial affiliations of particular peoples.

Paralleling this question of race number is a question of geography: *do the boundaries between races correlate with barriers to human interaction*, which might isolate them? In fact, in many cases there is no correlation between race and geographical boundaries. Perhaps the most striking example is on the continents of Europe and Asia, where the two races known as Mongoloids and Caucasoids are supposed to have evolved. The boundary between Europe and Asia is more or less theoretical, since both continents are part of a single landmass, usually called Eurasia. No substantial barrier to human interaction exists between Europe and Asia, as we can see from the ancient presence in Central Asia of people speaking Tocharian languages, related to English and other Indo-European languages (Adams 1984), and of Asian genetic contributions to populations in Northwestern Europe (Zerjal et al. 1997). If "Caucasoids" and "Mongoloids" really evolved in isolation, what factors were enforcing that isolation between them?

The geographical origin of the "Negroid race" may seem more clear-cut: after all, Africa is a continent mostly surrounded by oceans and seas. However, northern Africa is inhabited by people traditionally referred to as "Caucasoids" (like Europeans), but "Caucasoids" indigenous to Africa. These are primarily Berber-speaking peoples. The geographical factor enforcing isolation in the African case is supposed to be the Sahara Desert, and "Negroids" are supposed to have evolved in the tropical lands south of the Sahara. Yet, even this is not as clear-cut as we might think, because the Sahara is not a permanent feature of the African landscape. Eighteen thousand years ago, it was larger and drier than it is now, but by 9,000 years ago the desert had disappeared, replaced by grasslands and inhabited by large numbers of people. At that point, it was a fertile corridor between the Mediterranean and equatorial Africa, not a barrier to interaction. Such conditions had existed in earlier times, as well, as did corridors along the Nile Valley (van Peer 1998) and between Ethiopia and Arabia.

The isolation mechanisms associated with races in other areas of the world are equally obscure. We might think about Australian Aboriginal people as isolated on that island continent, but with the drastically lowered sea levels of the last Ice Age Australia and New Guinea were one landmass, called Sahul. This island continent was separated from mainland Asia by quite narrow areas of open water, and Australia was settled by at least 35,000 years ago. The first unequivocal evidence of open-ocean voyaging, from about 25,000 years ago, comes from the Solomon Islands off the east coast of New Guinea (Wickler and Spriggs 1988). Such seafaring culminated in the expansion of Austronesian populations to occupy islands as far apart as Madagascar and Hawaii over the last few thousand years. Further to the north, peoples from Asia entered the Americas at some point during the last Ice Age. The processes by which the ancestors of Native Americans occupied the New World are not well understood today, but there is some evidence for multiple immigrations into (and possible out of) the continent over the last 10,000 years (Greenberg et al. 1986; Kozintsev et al. 1999; Starikovskaya et al. 1998). Alaska and Siberia are not, after all, very far apart.

In all of these cases, we could probably come up with some sort of speculations about ancient populations being isolated at particular times and evolving into the ancestors of modern races. However, we would have to test such speculations, and no one has ever confirmed any such ideas about how races were formed. When examination of skeletons more than a few thousand years old is undertaken, what we often see is that the characteristics of such skeletons do not fit *any* modern race, that they are in fact sometimes subtly and sometimes drastically dissimilar to the skeletons of modern peoples (see, e.g., Henneberg 1988; Ozolins et al. 1997; Powell and Rose 1999). This indicates that, skeletally at least, the modern races that researchers have talked about are not ancient subdivisions of humanity, but rather fairly recent configurations of the human body in response to changing selection pressures, which can be environmental and/or cultural.

More generally, the archaeological information we have all points to one overriding fact: *human beings are travelers, and we have been so for a long time.* Our ancestors could not jump on an airplane and travel thousands of miles in a day, but over centuries and millennia they gradually changed their territories, they encountered new peoples, and sometimes they went on voyages of exploration and migration that covered substantial distances. They moved around a lot, over longer distances than we often think, and they developed the technologies necessary for such movement further back in prehistory than we sometimes expect. If that is the case, then where would the isolation necessary for race development take place? We do know of a very few populations that seem to have been isolated for long periods of time. Tasmanian Aboriginal people seem to have been isolated on that island through most of the last 10,000 years, for example (Pardoe 1991), but such small groups are usually not considered as separate races of humans. Some supporters of typological race models recognized that the geographical isolation demanded by these models did not exist in the past (see, e.g., Coon 1965:29–30) and instead invoke cultural barriers to such contact between human communities. This explanation is even less convincing than that of geographical barriers: what kind of differences in culture would isolate people from their neighbors for not merely centuries, but thousands of years?

This constant human movement has left its traces in one fundamental element of our physical beings: our genes. Humans are quite homogeneous genetically, which is certainly due in great part to the constant interaction between populations in different regions. All six and a half billion of us, spread across the continents and islands of the entire world, contain within ourselves somewhat less genetic variation than do small populations of chimpanzees living in different parts of Central Africa (Becquet et al. 2007). Genetic diversity between human populations is low compared to that of other large mammal species that are spread over large areas of the world, or indeed compared to those found in quite small areas (Templeton 1999:182). When we compare the genetic variability among human populations to that of subspecies in many other large mammal species, we see again that these animal subspecies are more different from one another than are the most distant of human groups.

These genetic studies have also substantiated earlier work on human populations, which indicated that the biological characteristics of racial groups do not covary. Recall that if races originated in the adaptation of isolated human populations to particular environments, we would expect to see a set of characteristics shared by members of that particular race but considerably more rare outside of that group. These traits would derive from varying combinations of adaptations to those environments, descent from common ancestors, and/or mutations that appeared in the isolated racial group. Biologically, members of a particular race would, in that case, share a fairly well-defined bundle of biological traits, both externally visible and invisible. These might include combinations of traits for particular skin color, hair type, facial features, blood types, genetic markers, and so on. The boundaries of that race's territory would be comparatively abrupt, although possibly somewhat blurred by interactions and exchange of genetic material with neighboring communities of other races.

This is not what we see when we examine human groups. The various characteristics of human populations do not form such nicely defined sets, and that characteristics that we think of as limited to one race are often far more widely shared. Thus, dark skin color is not only often taken as distinctive of "Negroid" peoples originating in Africa, but is also found among "Caucasoid"

populations in South Asia and "Mongoloid" and "Australoid" groups in the Pacific. Recent, large-scale surveys of the genetic characteristics of human populations in different parts of the world showed a very complex set of relationships, probably traceable to many episodes of long-distance migration and more local population mixture—but no evidence for continental human races (Hunley et al. 2009; Tishkoff and Kidd 2004). Furthermore, the distributions of these genetic characteristics are not very concordant: knowing the distribution of one feature tells researchers quite little about the distributions of others. We see an extraordinary variety in biological features among populations grouped together in particular races, and significant similarities between neighboring populations across what are supposed to be racial boundaries.

As C. Loring Brace (2000) has noted, our perceptions of human racial variation is conditioned by the ways we see people in different parts of the world. Today, we can look at pictures of people from Stockholm, Lagos, and Bangkok, and we see that they tend to be physically very different. Centuries ago, European explorers and merchants sailed around the world, but the encounters they had with different populations were in many ways similar to our modern, electronic voyages; they simply took more time to move from port to port. However, the very fact that such voyages move from one point to a distant point means that travelers do not see the gradients of difference that separate these places. If a person could *walk* from Lagos to Stockholm, or to Bangkok, they would see a progressively shifting spectrum of physical characteristics, reflecting the constant interactions between neighboring communities through many thousands of years. These interactions yield biological relationships between populations that are complex, and that are often *clinal* (Livingstone 1962; Serre and Paabo 2004): that is, there is a gradual transition in characteristics between the groups involved, not any sort of sudden racial boundary between them.

If our hypothetical traveler could look beneath the skin of the people she met, at their blood types, at the forms that their proteins take, and at their genetic material itself, the situation would become even more complex. Humans have historically grouped people into races on the basis of visible characteristics, but of course there is no reason to exclude these other, invisible but equally fundamental traits when we think about dividing humans into groups. Human groups defined on the basis of these invisible traits in many cases do not, however, resemble races defined on the basis of external characteristics. Plots of the frequencies of blood types will in some cases group particular populations of Native Americans with Australian Aborigines, and sub-Saharan Africans with Central Asians. Similar plots for particular variants of the Rh blood system will group Africans with Southeast Asians, with Native Americans intermediate. The gene for lactose absorption links Europeans with African pastoral groups, while the hemoglobin S mutation is found in West and Central Africa, Saudi Arabia, and South Asia (Cavalli-Sforza et al. 1994). Other examples of such connections and similarities across traditional racial boundaries are very common. Furthermore, the level of distinction at which humans are classified into different groups, racial or otherwise, is arbitrary (Cavalli-Sforza et al. 1994:19). We could, using the same genetic data, claim that there are 2, or 3, or 5, or 9, or 21 "races"—and none of those reconstructions would be more or less valid than any others. The authors of this research are not, needless to say, believers in the reality of human races.

The conclusion seems obvious. Whatever races might be, they are not fundamental biological types of humanity. The clinal nature of human biological traits, the relative genetic homogeneity of humans, and the archaeological evidence for ancient human population contacts do not reflect the existence of ancient population isolates over the periods when races were supposedly developing. The lack of concordance of human biological characteristics does not indicate long-term adaptation of such isolated racial groups to particular original environments. We should remember that *this is not a denial that human biological variation exists*: it obviously does. However, the scope of human physical variation is far too complex to be accommodated within simplistic typological race models.

Races as Populations

A race is: a division of a species which differs from other divisions by the frequency with which certain hereditary traits appear among its members. [Brues 1977:1]

Typological models of race are still common in the United States, but anthropologists have developed more sophisticated models of human biological variation. In some cases, however, the term "race" is still used for these systems. Such models define human races as groups of humans that can be distinguished from other groups *based on the frequency of some heritable characteristic(s)*—as distinct biological *populations*. For example, elevated frequencies of red hair, fair skin, and freckles (if such exist) might allow anthropologists to define an "Irish race"; short stature, epicanthic folds, extreme hair curvature, and steatopygia might allow the definition of a "Khoisan race"; and straight dark hair, dark eyes, epicanthic folds, and comparatively short arm and leg length might allow the definition of an "Eskimo race." A huge number of such populations might exist, and the features used to define them do not have to be externally visible. The elevated frequency of Tays-Sachs Syndrome and Gaucher's disease among Ashkenazi Jewish populations (O'Brien 1999), or of the MNS*M, HLAB*18 and b^{39}-thalassemia alleles (Cavalli-Sforza et al. 1994:274) among Sardinians, would help define those populations as a "Jewish race" and a "Sardinian race," respectively. The suntans found among Australians of European descent are the result of particular behaviors, not heredity, and so we could not define an "Australian race" on that basis—at least until such behaviors have resulted in natural selection for resistance to skin cancer on that continent.

This is a very different concept of human races than that seen in the typological models discussed above. It does not involve assumptions about the origins of races in isolated ancestral populations, or about the stability, age, and internal homogeneity of those groups. Stanley Garn (1971:6) notes that "A race is a race whether it goes back unchanged for six millennia or whether it resulted from admixture after 1850." Population models of racial variability locate the definition of races primarily in the perceptions and goals of the observer: what is the *purpose* of looking for "race," and what choice of characteristics will best suit that purpose? For this reason, research can be undertaken at many different levels of detail, and a single biological characteristic might be used to define different races for different purposes! In general, advocates of population models of race are less interested in detecting primordial types of humans than they are in examining the processes by which human populations become different from or assimilated to one another.

The definition of human races in population models is to some degree *instrumental*: one defines races in order to do things. (Of course, people have often identified typological races in order to do things as well—to study human variability or to justify racism, for example—but the assumption in those cases was that the races under study were primordial.) Researchers examine human variability in order to investigate particular phylogenetic, biological, historical, or even medical problems. Why do Basque populations have very unusual Rh blood group distributions and somewhat unusual head shapes? What accounts for the elevated levels of breast cancer among some Jewish populations, and how might knowledge of that fact be used in early detection and treatment? Why do Inuit and Nilotic peoples have proportionally different limb lengths? Why do African American men tend to have greater frequencies of high blood pressure? The varying questions asked by researchers will drastically affect both the level of detail of the racial definition and the characteristics under examination.

Garn (1971:15–26) and Brues (1977:2), two of the most influential American advocates of population models of races, have both emphasized

the hierarchical nature of their race definitions: researchers can define racial groupings at a variety of population levels, from the most general and widespread to the most specific and localized, depending on the goals of their work. An anthropologist might in some cases study "Caucasoids" as a major race, but could also subdivide that grouping and compare "European" and "South Asian" races, and in still other research might look within Europe at the differences between, perhaps, "Italian" and "Polish" races. Garn (1971) makes this hierarchy very explicit. He identified nine "geographical races," including "Amerindian," "African," "Melanesian-Papuan," and "European," each of which is found over a significant area of the Earth. Within each "geographical race" is a number of "local races," including, "Northwest European," "Northeast European," "Alpine," and "Mediterranean" groups within Europe. Garn (1971:168) claims that these "local races" are true units of evolutionary change, and that *thousands* of "local races" exist. Within each "local race" are again many "micro-races," which correspond essentially to any communities between which physical and/or genetic difference can be detected. There would presumably be *tens or hundreds of thousands* of such "micro-races" in the world today.

Population definitions of race escape many of the criticisms that can be directed at typological definitions of race. They make no assumptions about the primordial nature of human races, or about the degree of their isolation from one another, or about the limited set of essential characteristics that typological definitions of race require. Races are conceived of simply as the continuing results of population interaction, gene flow and interruption of gene flow, and adaptation, rather than as distillations of ancient racial essences. Disagreements between racial identifications made by different researchers are less important, if those identifications are made only in order to do particular kinds of research.

At the same time, there are different problems associated with population models of race, and these need to be examined. First, the relationships between different levels of the racial hierarchies in population models are often not particularly clear. According to Garn's definitions, "local races" are true units of evolutionary change, corresponding to human breeding populations. In that case, it becomes difficult to say exactly what kind of units "geographical races" and "micro-races" actually are. "Geographical races" correspond to the major continents and island chains (Garn 1971:18), and their distinctiveness is supposed to be caused by geographical barriers to gene flow between human communities. At the same time, four of the nine "geographical races" (the "Asian," "Polynesian," "Melanesian-Papuan," and "Micronesian" races) are scattered across island chains, which is itself evidence of the human ability to cross geographical barriers. Garn's "geographical races" seem to be little more than relics of earlier typological classification systems. "Micro-races" would presumably be the result of restrictions in gene flow within "local races," which calls into question the status of the latter as fundamental evolutionary units.

Second, the characteristics used to define races are frequently difficult to determine. Population models of race tend to rely on a restricted list of traits for the definition of each racial unit, just as typological models do. Why choose those particular traits instead of the many other traits that each of us humans possesses? As I said, these traits can indeed be chosen according to the objectives of a particular research project—sickle-cell trait when looking at adaptations to malaria, limb length and cold adaptations, and so on—but the racial models advanced by Garn, Brues, and other anthropologists are supposed to be general descriptions of human variability. There is little discussion in these works about the reasons for giving priority to some traits and not others when defining races, especially at large geographical scales. Garn (1971:169–178) gives examples of a variety of "large local races" that are defined according to a stew of physical, genetic, linguistic, religious, regional, and traditional criteria, with no real indication of why these definitions are most important.

Third, definitions of "race" that just call for the presence of some difference in trait frequencies between human groups also risk extending the race concept to impossibly local levels. In principle, races would be identifiable in any cases where any differences in biological characteristics—even extremely minor changes in gene frequencies—exist between any groups of people. We can easily imagine a situation where people living in a particular district or neighborhood might display very minor differences in trait frequencies, and so would be called a separate "race." Such minor differences are also the basis of many folk typologies. These are informal classification systems used in various parts of the world to assign people to particular groups. Thus, in the Cape Verde Islands off the west coast of Africa, a complex folk classification links particular islands and their traditions of European contact with particular physical and behavioral characteristics (L. De Andrade, personal communication, 2000). The people of Sao Vincente, for example, are believed to have dark skin, black and very straight hair, and sharp facial features, as a result of the intermarriage of West Africans with people from Portugal and England, while people from Brava are ruddy-skinned and fair-haired because of French settlement on that island. At the most detailed levels of analysis, the boundary between "micro-races" and such folk typologies begin to blur: if "races" are to be defined on the basis of their detectability, then are such folk typologies supposed to define races as well?

Populational models of race can designate any biological population, from continental to local, as races. However, this definition of "race" is so far from common understandings and from earlier anthropological definitions of the term that it risks causing a great deal of confusion. The idea that people living in a single neighborhood of a single town might be defined as a "race" implies that hundreds of thousands (or millions) of other "races" exist in the world today. As we have seen, previous anthropological usage, and continuing popular use in North America, involves typological definitions of "race" that are very different indeed from these definitions that designate any distinct human population as a separate race—so should we use the same word "race" for both definitions? The precision required of scientific research demands the use of correspondingly precise terminologies. From this point of view, anthropologists should not use the term "race" as a synonym for biological populations.

INTERSECTIONS OF RACE, CULTURE, AND HISTORY

Biological variability among humans certainly exists, as anyone can see. Peoples in different areas of the world differ in vastly different ways. Moreover, anthropologists and biologists can group humans into populations on the basis of a variety of physical and genetic features. On the other hand, *no rule says that we have to call such populations "races,"* or that we have to use the term "race" at all in any biological sense. The history of science is full of terms that have become obsolete, because the theories behind them were proven false. Three centuries ago, chemists wrote about "phlogiston," which was thought to be a kind of essence of fire, contained within all substances that burn and released upon burning. Researchers eventually learned that no such substance existed, and they stopped using the term "phlogiston." A century ago, physicists used the term "aether" to denote a substance that permeated the entire universe and provided the medium through which light waves propagated, much as sound waves move through air or water. Researchers eventually learned that this was an inaccurate explanation of the properties of space, and they stopped using the term "aether." Sentimental attachment to an ancient term did not save either "phlogiston" or "aether," and so these terms were not reused to describe the scientific concepts that eventually replaced them. From a biological point of view, "race" appears to be another one of those terms whose time has passed, ripe for replacement by words that carry less, and less pernicious, historical baggage. In fact, one researcher, Ashley Montagu (1969:xii), called the race concept " . . . the Phlogiston of our times . . . "

If this is the case, why does the term "race" continue to be used by anthropologists? Anthropologists continue to talk about race because their study is human culture in general, and because in different areas of the world people talk in the language of physical characteristics and geographical origins when they are dividing other humans up into social groups. In the United States, this is done in the course of everyday social interaction, when terms like "black," "white," "Asian," and so on are used to describe a whole range of people who are, in fact, Americans. Bureaucracies like the Census use a complex terminology (e.g., *American Indian/ Alaska Native, Asian, black/African American, Native Hawaiian/Other Pacific Islander,* and *white and Hispanic*) that mixes ethnic affiliation, supposed physical characteristics, and geography when defining race and ethnicity for governmental purposes.

These classifications have little to do with real biological characteristics, or human origins. Traditionally, racial identification through most of the United States was defined according to a hypodescent, or "one-drop" rule, where a mixed race child was identified with the racial grouping of the lower status parent—in the American case, almost always an African or African American woman. Furthermore, the degree of racial admixture is more or less irrelevant; "one drop" of African blood was enough to identify a person as black. This has nothing to do with actual ancestry or biological characteristics of a human being. It was simply a way of enforcing racial hierarchies in the United States, and the "one-drop" rule was a part of American legal systems until the middle of the twentieth century. In parts of Central Africa, populations are referred to as being "black" or "white," exactly the terms used in North America. All of those people are Africans, however, coming from the same area of the continent. The distinction between them is made on religious and cultural, not physical, grounds: people who are Muslim (or, increasingly, Christian) call themselves "whites" and call nonbelievers "blacks." In some countries in South America, racial identity is based in part on socioeconomic status, and may vary from person to person depending on how well-off they are (da Costa 1977:297–298).

Anthropologists study the ways in which these classification systems work within cultural systems, as we will see throughout the other chapters in this book. The situation is even more complicated than this, however, because of the ways in which biological and cultural notions of race are intertwined even beyond explicit systems of classification. Anthropologists are no more immune to confusion about these questions than are other people. To illustrate the complexity of some of these issues, I want to turn to some examples of the difficulties that we may encounter in distinguishing biological and cultural concepts of race.

Race in Forensic Anthropology

Many of us have at one point or another watched TV shows like the *CSI* series or read novels about forensic anthropologists, where experts are able to tell a great deal about a dead person from the characteristics of his or her skeleton: his or her sex, age at death, stature, physical condition, and sometimes even the person's occupation or the diseases and chronic conditions that he or she had endured during life. It always seems very impressive, an illustration of the power and sophistication of research techniques. Very often, such analysis will include determination of the race of that individual, as well. Prominent forensic specialists, physical anthropologists who study human skeletal remains in order to provide information for legal proceedings, have affirmed that human biological races exist, and stated that the race concept is fundamental to their research (see, e.g., Gill [1990, 1998]). Surely such experts must be taken at their word?

In fact, the circumstances in which race is identified in forensic research are very complex. Forensic anthropologists, more than most other practitioners of anthropology, function in cooperation with nonspecialists: law enforcement officers, legal specialists, and members of juries. These people for the most part do not have a background in anthropology, and so their views of biological variation tend to be those of the North American public—they accept traditional racial divisions, and they hold typological views of race. Forensic anthropologists must report their results in terms that are meaningful to their nonanthropological audience, and they have adopted traditional race categories as the most effective way of doing that. As Gill (1990:viii) says, "Providing answers for the attribution of race solves cases just as much as providing a useful age bracket or living stature for the individual. Law enforcement agencies know this, and request simple, straight answers. Any anthropologist who contends that races do not exist and provides a vague answer as to ancestry of an unidentified skeleton, or launches into a discourse on 'ethnic groups,' will likely never be called upon again to assist in solving a case." A major reason for the use of racial categories by American forensic anthropologists is thus pragmatic: their target audience wants to hear about race.

Forensic anthropologists in other countries do not seem to feel the same need to talk about "race," and to avoid mentioning "ethnic groups" in forensics (see, e.g., Evison 1999). The author of an important British textbook on the analysis of the human skeleton (Mays 1998) managed to go through the whole book without referring to race once; he wrote about human populations instead. Even some American forensic anthropologists seem less than committed to the concept (Kennedy 1995; Sauer 1992). More to the point, the "races" that forensic anthropologists identify vary according to local demographic and social conditions. Thus, in the southwestern United States a great deal of attention has been given to distinguishing the skeletons of Native American people from those of people of European descent, while in the southeast differentiation of Americans of African descent is at least as important. Among southwestern American samples that include people of European descent, Rhine (1990) distinguishes between "Anglo" skeletons and those of "Hispanics." That distinction might well be of importance to law enforcement and other government agencies in that area, concerned with the accurate identification of local people in terms that local people recognize—but no physical anthropologist would argue that "Anglos" and "Hispanics" are separate biological races.

Similarly, forensic anthropologists try to distinguish skeletons from Southeast Asian, East Indian, and Nubian populations, not because these groups are ancient "races" but because modern North American urban populations include people from these groups (Brooks et al. 1990:45). In other cases, the variability in skeletons of particular races (Native American peoples, for example) has confounded attempts by forensic anthropologists to develop techniques for archaeological identification (Fisher and Gill 1990). In Britain, forensic anthropologists work at differentiating people of Western European descent from South Asians, while in France the forensic identification of peoples of Western European, North African, and Southeast Asian descent might attract comparable amounts of attention. In all of these areas, investigators are concerned that the increasing mobility and multiethnic backgrounds of peoples from all over the world will make their job more complex.

Forensic anthropologists examine the skeletal variability of different human populations. They investigate a variety of traits, recognizing that not all of these characteristics are distributed in the same way through the different populations under study, and that the reliability of their results may vary drastically depending on the relations between those populations and available comparative samples. These different identifications are not made because these groups are fundamental biological types of humans (Relethford 2009). They are made because human populations are physically variable in all kinds of detectable ways, because the remains that are found often reflect the makeup of local populations, and because both law enforcement agencies and communities at large need to know the identities of the dead. We might argue that forensic anthropologists should be trying to educate their clients about the complexities of human physical variation and

the difficulties of grouping humans into well-defined populations, but they in turn could (and do) as well argue that the necessity of providing well-understood information to everyone from local sheriffs to war-crimes tribunals takes precedence. Far from substantiating a view of human races as important biological groupings, as the claims of some researchers would imply (Gill 1998, 2000), the work of forensic anthropologists actually testifies to the complexity and range of variation in human populations—and to the important ways in which social classifications and social pressures can mold the outcomes of scientific enquiries.

Race and Running

The United States is a nation obsessed by sports, as well as by race, and it is no surprise that race relations in this country have often been played out in the arenas of amateur and professional athletics. International sport has equally acted as a field for competition between societies, nations, and political systems. (The constant sports metaphors—e.g., "played out" and "field of competition"—demonstrate just how much sport pervades our everyday life.) Probably any of us can think of famous images and slogans that have brought race into athletics, and athletics into race: Jesse Owens at the Berlin Olympics in 1936, Jackie Robinson as the first black player in major league baseball, "white men can't jump." In all of these cases, and many others, people make assumptions about the physical and intellectual abilities of the athletes in competition, and by extension about the communities that these athletes come from. Some of these—like the early twentieth-century idea that Jewish people are "natural" basketball players and boxers—are quite unfamiliar to us today, while others—the idea that black American men do not have the intellectual ability to play quarterback in football, for example—are more recent.

We can look at some of these issues through the lens of a book published some years ago, Jon Entine's (2000) *Taboo*, which examines the relations between race and athletic success around

Jesse Owens. Four Gold Medals, Olympics 1936, Berlin, Germany.

the world today. The book is a controversial one: Entine takes the stance that race is a biological reality, that biological differences between races are reflected in differential success in particular sports, but that many Americans do not talk about these differences because they fear a slippery slope down to the vicious racism that has bedeviled so much of the history of the United States. The book is also a polemic, examining the issue from just one point of view; the author begins it convinced of the existence and importance of biological races, discounts any arguments made against the concept, and ends the book with, again, the conclusion that white men (and so presumably white boys) can't jump. At the same time, *Taboo* is somewhat different from many of the works written on the topic from earlier in this century. Entine devotes a good deal of attention to the pernicious effects of traditional

racist thought, in sports and in society in general, and he also rejects the widespread assumption that athletic and intellectual ability are inversely related to one another—a destructive idea that has particularly followed people of African descent.

The usage of race language in the book is, however, quite interesting. Entine (2000:341) writes about "black athletic superiority," but it seems that this superiority is actually a very complicated phenomenon. In the first place, it essentially encompasses two different sets of abilities. Entine claims that West Africans are good at sprinting and, it appears, at a variety of professional sports that use similar abilities, while East Africans are good at middle- and long-distance running. These appear to call for quite different forms of musculature and cardiovascular development, so the idea of one unitary kind of athletic superiority seems to be wrong. Neither of those geographical terms is entirely accurate, either. "West African" in this case encompasses not for the most part people from West Africa, but instead anyone born in the New World or Europe who has any noticeable African descent, on the assumption that all of their enslaved ancestors must have been from West Africa.

In fact, *West Africans themselves* have not been notably successful in Olympic sprinting and related sports, even though the population of that area is about the same as that of the entire United States. Ironically enough, although Entine and similar authors claim a "West African" biological superiority in sprinting and related sports, their only explanation for the lack of success of West Africans is cultural: people from West African countries have not had the benefits of the training and coaching that would allow them to excel. In Entine's (2000:241) book, the best-known "West African" sprinter actually from Africa is Frankie Fredericks, who has won a number of Olympic medals and run the 100 m dash in less than 10 seconds 27 times. However, Fredericks is from Namibia. Namibia shares a border with the Republic of South Africa, and both countries are—unsurprisingly—in southern Africa. Namibian populations, environments, and economies are very different from those found in the countries of West Africa. One might equally call Moroccan or Egyptian runners "West Africans." All of the intervening countries of Central Africa appear to have been eliminated, perhaps because they do not appear to have produced any elite track-and-field athletes.

Similarly, most East Africans are not champion distance runners. Success at middle- and long-distance running is concentrated in two countries, Kenya and Ethiopia, and among particular ethnic groups. In Kenya, Kalenjin cattle pastoralist populations are especially well represented among elite distance runners, although Kikuyu, Kamba, and Kisii runners are also significant. Ethiopian runners have come from a variety of different populations, with, for example, a number of successful Amhara runners. Of these particular communities, the Kalenjin peoples—among whom distance-running success has been most marked—have only been considered a distinct ethnic group since the 1940s; before that, and still today, the term "Kalenjin" referred to a group of related languages. (The distinction is important, equivalent to that between "the English" as a population and "English-speakers" as a population. The fact that a Sri Lankan, a Nigerian, and a Scotsman all speak English does not mean that they are members of one ethnic group.)

Entine (2000:47–50, 285–286) uses Kalenjin running success as a central argument for the existence of black athletic superiority, and thus for the reality of biological differences between racial groups as traditionally conceived of in North America. He argues that Kalenjin domination of distance running is so great that it cannot be completely explained by environmental factors: the availability of good coaches and good training, cultural practices that encourage young people to run a lot, the example of earlier runners, and so on. Instead, running success among Kalenjin speakers is supposed to be due to some genetic advantage, possibly related to selection for speed on foot when engaged in cattle raiding, or to the altitude at which Kalenjin people run. As with West Africa, cultural factors can be kept in reserve, however; Entine (2000:325–326) uses

such factors to help account for the lack of domination of *women's* distance running by Kenyans.

These explanations seem, on the face of it, rather unlikely. There are a number of other groups of people in East Africa who engaged in cattle raiding, but who have not generated champion runners. Kalenjin-speaking communities are known to have exchanged group members, through migration and intermarriage, with many surrounding, non-Kalenjin populations; we would expect this to disperse any "genes for running" over neighboring areas in Kenya, but so far this does not appear to have happened to any great extent. More than that, other Kenyan peoples who have had success in international distance running—the Kikuyu and Kamba, for example—are Bantu-speaking farmers, not Kalenjin-speaking cattle pastoralists, and they live some distance away from the latter group. To the degree to which East African running success is concentrated among Kalenjin-speaking people, it is probably most realistic to think of it as the results of cultural factors. The specific biological adaptations that are supposed to contribute to "West African" sprinting success are never really addressed at all.

That being said, there is no reason to think that biological differences between populations could not contribute to success (or failure) in particular sports. At the extremes, this is obvious. It is not likely that people from groups with a short average height, like Guatemalan Maya or Aka people from southern Cameroon, would succeed as professional basketball players; people from populations that are on average very tall, like the Dinka of Sudan, are more likely to do so. (Manute Bol, former center for the Washington Bullets, is a Dinka.) Anthropologists have documented a huge variety of physical differences between populations in different parts of the world, and it is quite conceivable that the height of Nilotic peoples like the Dinka, or the oxygen uptake capacities of some Tibetan populations, might have implications for athletic success. The likelihood of more subtle effects may be even greater, especially given that extremely minor differences in performance can spell success or failure in elite athletics—but such effects must be demonstrated to exist, not merely assumed. It may be that at some point some such biological adaptations will be proven to have a genetic basis among Kalenjin people (Larsen 2003; Saltin 1996)—although this has not happened to date.

The question remains: what does all this have to do with race? The scale of human groups under analysis shifts back and forth constantly in Entine's book, from "black athletic superiority" at the most general level to "West" (in fact, mostly African American) and East African abilities in a variety of sports, to the tremendous successes of Kalenjin runners. But does one of these imply the others? Can we say that, because Kalenjin are very successful marathoners, all East Africans will be very successful marathoners, or all Africans? Of course not. These are very different kinds of human groupings—yet all of this variability is supposed to be simply biological, and each level is supposed to imply the others. No one would seriously claim that the Kalenjin comprise a separate race from other East Africans, and the particular kinds of athletic success that Entine examines are in fact very unevenly distributed among populations of African descent, within and outside of the continent (Entine 2000, Figure 4.1). Entine gives no explanation for "black athletic superiority," apart perhaps from some fairly vague musings on the history of hunting and cattle herding on that continent—much of which is simply proof that the geneticists that Entine uses as sources are not very well-informed historians. Success in particular athletic events is associated with fairly specific groups of people, and it appears to be traditional, typological views of race that lead Entine to generalize innate athleticism to all Africans and all people of African descent. Unfortunately, this view can lead to a lack of interest in the conscious commitment and planning that play a central role in so much of elite athletics. Chapter titles in *Taboo* like "Nature's experiment: the 'Kenyan miracle'" and "Winning the genetic lottery" illustrate this danger, with their implication—consciously made or not—that African athletic success is not due to the efforts of athletes themselves but to some unearned genetic legacy.

Anthropology and the Politics of Race

In the early twenty-first century, the concept of race retains its central place among American preoccupations, in society at large, and in anthropology more particularly. Publication of controversial books like *The Bell Curve* (Herrnstein and Murray 1994) and *Race, Evolution and Behavior* (Rushton 1995) has focused renewed attention on questions of race in America, and fuelled debates about the biological and cultural meanings of the word. These books attempt to resurrect the race hierarchies of the nineteenth and early twentieth centuries, primarily through varying claims that Africans and especially African Americans are on average less intelligent, more violent, and generally less civilized than people from Europe or Asia. At the same time, some anthropologists continue to argue that biological races are real and important entities, usually claiming that disbelief in the existence of such biological units amounts to nothing more than "political correctness." "Political correctness" is rarely defined in such claims, but one of two general meanings is usually implied. It means either an inappropriate interest in the experiences of women, people of color, and the disadvantaged or an inappropriate wariness about the objectivity of certain kinds of scientific research.

Recently, a well-known anthropologist and a journalist published a book entitled *Race: The Reality of Human Differences* (Sarich and Miele 2004), one that linked these two threads of debate in ways that illustrate some of the complexities touched upon in this chapter. The authors argue that races are real biological entities, designating them as " . . . populations, or groups of populations, within a species, that are separated geographically from other such populations or groups of populations, and distinguishable from them on the basis of heritable features" (Sarich and Miele 2004:207). They note the multilevel nature of this definition: races are "fuzzy sets," and the exact number of races defined depends on the level of detail into which individuals and groups are sorted, and the goals of the sorting exercise (pp. 209–211). This is, of course, a quite conventional populational definition of biological race, similar to those put forward by Garn and Brues (see above). Fair enough, so far.

The question becomes, however, what do the authors actually do with that unexceptionable definition of race? In fact, the treatment of race in the modern world throughout the rest of the book is almost entirely typological. John Entine is quoted approvingly on race and sports—and so again Kalenjin people from Kenya become bearers of the "racial essence" of African running ability (Sarich and Miele 2004:174–184). Kalenjin people win marathons; Kalenjin people live in Africa; therefore, Africans are natural athletes. This is a logical fallacy, and a pretty straightforward one. Similarly, the authors' primary sources on race and behavior are academics like Philippe Rushton and Richard Lynn, both of whom have married denigrating images of Africans and African Americans with entirely typological models of race. The last half of the book deals with modern racial characteristics, and in that section the conventional, continental racial types—Asians, Europeans, and Africans—are treated as homogeneous units of human evolution. Historical sources are quoted to claim that these continental racial types are primordial (Sarich and Miele 2004:34–56), as if we would not expect that ancient peoples would be as likely to note any kinds of physical difference as we are, and ignoring the fact that—usually negative—descriptions of all sorts of foreigners are common in such texts. The Sahara is supposed to be a "geographical filter," an "ancient boundary," between "Caucasians and Negroes" (pp. 209–210)—even though the authors themselves note that it was in the relatively recent past fertile, and inhabited by large game and humans (p. 56).

This seems perplexing: why do we find a *populational* definition of race in this book, accompanied by an entirely *typological* description of variation between races? In fact, the explanation for this is quite straightforward. It is hard to see how the sorts of disparities in ability

and intelligence that the authors claim exist could have arisen without recourse to highly typological, differentiated racial groupings, evolving in relative isolation from one another over extended periods of time—no "fuzzy sets" here, in practice. If brain size, intelligence, and athletic ability vary among modern human races according to the cultural and environmental backgrounds within which these races evolved, and if the difference in these factors is as great as the authors claim, then presumably those races are supposed to have evolved in very different environments and in considerable isolation from one another. As we have seen in Chapter 2, however, claims that these differences exist are not well supported by the data.

Thus, the segue from populational definition to typological treatment is necessary for the authors' broader argument. On the one hand, research has demonstrated that human biological variability is clinal and multivariate, with a substantial lack of concordance between a variety of biological characteristics. On the other hand, traditional concepts of race hierarchy in the United States require that races be relatively well differentiated from one another, so that they can be talked about, compared, and used as a foundation for political action essentially as monolithic, homogeneous things. In *Race: The Reality of Human Differences*, the authors' political agenda becomes evident at the end of the book, when they discuss the policy implications of their understandings of race—taking the American situation as representative of the whole world as they do so (Sarich and Miele 2004:233–262). They claim that three possible approaches to public policy concerning race exist: a future meritocracy, where people are judged as individuals—and individuals and groups "find their place" in social and economic hierarchies; a future of race quotas and "levelling down," as governments try to boost the fortunes of inferior groups; and a future of resegregation. Unsurprisingly, given their thesis, the authors prefer the first of these visions of the future.

Central to all of these scenarios is the *assumption* that race is fundamental to all aspects of human interaction, with the characteristics of different groups permanent for the long term. If, however, it turns out that many of the differences between racial groups listed by Sarich and Miele are rooted in historical circumstance and modern environments—as many examples from this book suggest that they are—and *not* in inevitable biology, then a different set of imperatives suggest themselves. A claim that all is biology—Sarich and Miele's ultimate thesis—is an excellent crutch for people who would prefer not to occupy themselves with the plight of people who are poor, powerless, and disadvantaged. If we admit the likelihood that people often find themselves in such circumstances because of transitory conditions in the modern world, then it becomes incumbent upon us to change those conditions for the better.

CONCLUSION

"Race" is, as I noted at the beginning of this essay, a word, and it is a word that admits of a wide variety of meanings. The history of the United States of America has meant that some of these meanings of "race" are laden with an immense significance. This perhaps masks the fact that American definitions and American relations of race are not necessarily universal—although the power of the United States today means that social and cultural debates about race around the world are increasingly debated using American meanings. The continuing American preoccupation with and debate about race and race relations is in some ways a testament to the ideals of the Republic, implying at least a theoretical commitment to the equality of all its citizens. Americans may disagree vigorously on whether such equality has been substantially attained—as a noncitizen, my outsider's perspective is that it has not—but there is broad agreement that the question itself is important. This has not been the case in all of the countries where important issues of race relations exist.

One central element in these debates involves decisions about when "race" is a useful and appropriate concept to be used in particular kinds of analysis, and when it is not. To what degree can differences in educational attainment between different groups in the United States be ascribed to racial discrimination? Are there significant differences in the way elections are handled in predominantly black and predominantly white districts across the country, and is this due to these variations in population? Is race or socioeconomic status a better proxy for student needs in affirmative action programs? Active argument surrounds all of these issues, and hinges on the meaning, scope, and utility of social concepts of race, and on the relations of those concepts to other ways of characterizing American society.

The same situation holds in anthropology: we can (and must) investigate the various dimensions of race, describing and critiquing the concept as we do so. This involves, among other things, examining whether biological race concepts are appropriate models for investigating variability among human beings. This has been one preoccupation of physical and biological anthropology for more than a century now, and it appears that the answer to this question is "No." The typological race models that had held sway in anthropology through most of the existence of the discipline are not good descriptions of how human biological variability works. The implications of populational models, on the other hand, are so far removed from popular understandings of the term "race"—with hundreds of thousands or perhaps millions of "micro-races" dotted around the globe—that use of the term in such cases does nothing more than risk needless confusion. Science is not an exercise in nostalgia: when a term progresses from being burnished by long use to being made obsolete by increasing knowledge, it needs to be discarded. The concept of biological race in anthropology is at that point.

This does not mean that anthropologists will stop studying human biological variability, either in individual or populational terms. Such research will obviously continue, benefiting especially from the extraordinary advances in genetic research that have taken place over the last two decades and that seem to accelerate in pace every day. There is, however, no reason for such research to be hobbled by terminology that sows confusion rather than illuminate the real world. It is unlikely that people, in America and elsewhere, will stop using physical characteristics as representations for social difference. Such preoccupations are very deeply ingrained within human societies around the world, and they would not be easily given up. It remains, however, for both anthropologists and people in society in general to be continually conscious of the origins of such practices, and of the nature of human biological and cultural variability.

References Cited

ADAMS, DOUGLAS. 1984. Towards a history of PIE n-stems in Tocharian. *Journal of the American Oriental Society* 100:439–443.

BAKER, LEE. 1998. *From Savage to Negro: Anthropology and the Construction of Race, 1896–1954.* Berkeley, CA: University of California Press.

BARKAN, ELAZAR. 1992. *Retreat of Scientific Racism: Changing Concepts of Race in Britain and the United States Between the World Wars.* Cambridge: Cambridge University Press.

BEAN, R. BEAN. 1926. Human types. *Quarterly Review of Biology* 1:360–392.

BECQUET, CELINE, NICK PATTERSON, ANNE C. STONE, MOLLY PRZEWORSKI, and DAVID REICH. 2007. Genetic structure of chimpanzee populations. *PLoS Genetics* 3:e66 (http://www.plosgenetics.org/article/info%3Adoi%2F10.1371%2Fjournal.pgen.0030066).

BOYD, WILLIAM C. 1950. *Genetics and the Races of Man: An Introduction to Modern Physical Anthropology.* Boston, MA: Little, Brown and Company.

———. 1968. Genetics and the races of man. In *Readings on Race.* S. Garn, ed. Pp. 17–27. Springfield, IL: Charles C. Thomas.

BRACE, C. LORING. 2000. Does race exist? An anagonist's perspective. *Nova Online* (http://www.pbs.org/wgbh/nova/first/brace.html).

BROOKS, SHEILAGH, RICHARD BROOKS, and DIANE FRANCE. 1990. Alveolar prognathism contour, an aspect of racial identification. In *Skeletal Attribution of Race.* G. Gill and S. Rhine, eds. Pp. 41–46. Maxwell Museum of Anthropology, Anthropological Papers 4. Albuquerque, NM: University of New Mexico.

BRUES, ALICE. 1977. *People and Races.* New York: Macmillan.

CAVALLI-SFORZA, L. LUCA, PAOLO MENOZZI, and ALBERTO PIAZZA. 1994. *The History and Geography of Human Genes.* Princeton, NJ: Princeton University Press.

COON, CARLETON. 1965. *The Living Races of Man.* New York: Alfred A. Knopf.

COON, CARLETON, STANLEY GARN, and JOSEPH B. BIRDSELL. 1950. *Races.* Springfield, IL: Thomas.

DA COSTA, EMILIA. 1977. Slave images and realities. *Proceedings of the New York Academy of Sciences* 292:293–310.

DENIKER, JOSEPH. 1912. *The Races of Man: An Outline of Anthropology and Ethnography.* New York: Charles Scribner's Sons.

ENTINE, JON. 2000. *Taboo: Why Black Athletes Dominate Sports and Why We Are Afraid to Talk about It.* New York: Public Affairs.

EVISON, MARTIN. 1999. Computerised 3-D facial mapping. Paper presented at the First International Conference on Forensic Human Identification, London, October 23–26.

FISHER, THOMAS, and GEORGE GILL. 1990. Application of the Giles and Elliot discriminant function formulae to a cranial sample of northwestern Plains Indians. In *Skeletal Attribution of Race.* G. Gill and S. Rhine, eds. Pp. 59–64. Maxwell Museum of Anthropology, Anthropological Papers 4. Albuquerque, NM: University of New Mexico.

FUTUYAMA, DOUGLAS J. 1986. *Evolutionary Biology.* Sunderland, MA: Sinauer.

GARN, STANLEY. 1971. *Human Races.* 3rd edition. Springfield, IL: Charles C. Thomas.

GARN, STANLEY, and CARLETON COON. 1968. On the number of races of mankind. In *Readings on Race.* S. Garn, ed. Pp. 9–16. Springfield, IL: Charles C. Thomas.

GILL, G. 1990. Introduction. In *Skeletal Attribution of Race.* G. Gill and S. Rhine, eds. Pp. vii–xii. Maxwell Museum of Anthropology, Anthropological Papers 4. Albuquerque, NM: University of New Mexico.

———. 1998. The beauty of race and races. *Anthropology Newsletter* 39(3):1, 4–5.

————. 2000. Does race exist? A proponent's perspective. *Nova Online* (http://www.pbs.org/wgbh/nova/first/gill.html).

GREENBERG, JOSEPH, CHRISTY Turner II, and STEPHEN ZEGURA. 1986. The settlement of the Americas: A comparison of the linguistic, dental, and genetic evidence. *Current Anthropology* 27:477–97.

HANNAFORD, IVAN. 1996. *Race: The History of an Idea in the West*. Washington, DC: Woodrow Wilson Center Press.

HENNEBERG, MACIEJ. 1988. Decrease of human skull size in the Holocene. *Human Biology* 60(3):395–405.

HERRNSTEIN, RICHARD, and CHARLES MURRAY. 1994. *The Bell Curve: Intelligence and Class Structure in American Life*. New York: Free Press.

HOOTON, EARNEST ALBERT. 1946. *Up from the Ape*. New York: The Macmillan Company.

HUNLEY, KEITH L., MEGHAN E. Healy, and JEFFREY C. Long. 2009. The global pattern of gene identity variation reveals a history of long-range migrations, bottlenecks, and local mate exchange: Implications for biological race. *American Journal of Physical Anthropology* 139:35–46.

JAHODA, GUSTAV. 1998. *Images of Savages: Ancient Roots of Modern Prejudice in Western Cultures*. London: Routledge.

KEITH, ARTHUR. 1948. *A New Theory of Human Evolution*. London: Watts.

KENNEDY, KENNETH R. 1995. But Professor, why teach race identification if races don't exist? *Journal of Forensic Science* 40:797–800.

KOZINTSEV, ALEXANDER, ANDREI GROMOV, and VYACHESLAV MOISEYEV. 1999. Collateral relatives of American Indians among the Bronze Age populations of Siberia? *American Journal of Physical Anthropology* 108(2):193–204.

LARSEN, HENRIK B. 2003. Kenyan dominance in distance running. *Comparative Biochemistry and Physiology. Part A, Molecular & Integrative Physiology* 136:161–70.

LIVINGSTONE, FRANK B. 1962. On the non-existence of human races. *Current Anthropology* 3(3):279–281.

MAYR, ERNST. 1963. *Animal Species and Evolution*. Cambridge, MA: Belknap Press.

MAYS, SIMON. 1998. *The Archaeology of Human Bones*. London: Routledge.

MONTAGU, ASHLEY, ed. 1969. *The Concept of Race*. London: Collier-Macmillan.

O'BRIEN, STEPHEN J. 1999. Ghetto legacy. In *The Biological Basis of Human Behavior: A Critical Review*. R. Sussman, ed. Pp. 59–62. Advances in Human Evolution Series. Upper Saddle River, NJ: Prentice Hall.

OZOLINS, ERIK, VINCENT H. STEFAN, M. RHOADS, and JOSEPH F. POWELL. 1997. Craniofacial morphometric similarities between modern and Late Pleistocene human populations. *American Journal of Physical Anthropology* 24(Supp.):182–183.

PARDOE, COLIN. 1991. Isolation and evolution in Tasmania. *Current Anthropology* 32(1):1–21.

POWELL, JOSEPH, and JEROME ROSE. 1999. Report on the osteological assessment of the "Kennewick Man" skeleton (CENWW.97.Kennewick). In Report on the non-destructive examination, description, and analysis of the human remains from Columbia Park, Kennewick, Washington [October 1999] (http://www.cr.nps.gov/aad/kennewick/powell_rose.htm).

RELETHFORD, JOHN H. 2009. Race and global patterns of phenotypic variation. *American Journal of Physical Anthropology* 139:16–22.

RHINE, S. 1990. Non-metric skull racing. In *Skeletal Attribution of Race*. G. Gill and S. Rhine, eds. Pp. 9–21. Maxwell Museum of Anthropology, Anthropological Papers 4. Albuquerque, NM: University of New Mexico.

RUGGLES GATES, R. 1948. *Human Ancestry from a Genetical Point of View*. Cambridge: Harvard University Press.

RUSHTON, J. PHILIPPE. 1995. *Race, Evolution, and Behavior: A Life History Perspective*. New Brunswick, NJ: Transaction Publishers.

SALTIN, BENGT. 1996. Exercise and the environment: Focus on altitude. *Research Quarterly for Exercise and Sport* 67(3):S1–S10.

SARICH, VINCENT, and FRANK MIELE. 2004. *Race: The Reality of Human Differences*. Boulder, CO: Westview Press.

SAUER, NORMAN. J. 1992. Forensic anthropology and the concept of race: If races don't exist, why are forensic anthropologists so good at identifying them? *Social Science and Medicine* 34: 107–111.

SERRE, DAVID, and SVANTE PAABO. 2004. Evidence for gradients of human genetic diversity within and among continents. *Genome Research* 14:1679–1685.

SMEDLEY, AUDREY. 2007. *Race in North America: Origin and Evolution of a Worldview*. 3rd edition. Boulder, CO: Westview Press.

STARIKOVSKAYA, YELENA, REM SUKERNIK, THEODORE SCHURR, ANDREAS KOGELNIK, and DOUGLAS WALLACE. 1998. MtDNA diversity in Chukchi and Siberian Eskimos: Implications for the genetic history of ancient Beringia and the peopling of the New World. *American Journal of Human Genetics* 63(5):1473–1491.

TEMPLETON, ALAN. 1999. Human races: A genetic and evolutionary perspective. In *The Biological Basis of Human Behavior: A Critical Review*. R. Sussman, ed. Pp. 180–192. Advances in Human Evolution Series. Upper Saddle River, NJ: Prentice Hall.

TISHKOFF, SARAH, and KENNETH KIDD. 2004. Implications of biogeography of human populations for "race" and medicine. *Nature Genetics* 36:S21–S27.

VAN PEER, PHILIP. 1998. The Nile corridor and the out-of-Africa model. *Current Anthropology* 39: 115–140.

VON EICKSTEDT, EGON F. 1950. The science and history of the human races. In *This is Race*. E. W. Counts, ed. Pp. 489–514. New York: Henry Schuman.

WICKLER, STEPHEN, and MATTHEW SPRIGGS. 1988. Pleistocene occupation of the Solomons. *Antiquity* 62(237):703–707.

ZERJAL, TATIANA, BUMBEIN DASHNYAM, ARPITA PANDYA, MANFRED KAYSER, LUTZ ROEWER, FABRICIO SANTOS, and WULF SCHIEFENHOVEL. 1997. Genetic relationships of Asians and northern Europeans, revealed by Y-chromosomal DNA analysis. *American Journal of Human Genetics* 60:1174–1183.

4

···

Ethnicity

Raymond Scupin, *Lindenwood University*

Ethnicity is based on a conception of a shared cultural heritage. An *ethnic group* is a collectivity of people who believe they share a common history, culture, or ancestry. However, the terms *ethnicity* and *ethnic group* have had a long history of misinterpretations in Western culture. For example, anthropologist David Maybury-Lewis noted that "ethnicity has a will-o'-the-wisp quality that makes it extremely hard to analyze and not much easier to discuss" (1997:59). He goes on to say that everyone knows that ethnicity has something to do with a kind of fellow-feeling that binds people together and makes them feel distinct from others. Yet, it is difficult, if not impossible, he says, to say precisely what kind of feeling it is, and why and when people will be affected by it. Under some circumstances, some people are willing to die on behalf of their ethnic group, whereas other people are not strongly preoccupied by their ethnicity in their everyday lives. In some circumstances, people will be classified as a particular ethnic group without feeling it or recognizing it themselves. Maybury-Lewis refers to the example of Native Americans, who were a diverse group of people before receiving that ethnic label "Indians" from Europeans. Also, the criteria for distinguishing ethnic groups require a complex interpretive process. At times, an ethnic group may be distinguished by language, in other cases by religion, in still other situations by skin color or by a shared historical past. But it is also recognized that an ethnic group's shared past is open to reconstruction and reinterpretation in a variety of ways. This chapter will introduce the conceptions of ethnicity that have driven anthropological research and have led to a variety of insights into these complex questions.

As is evident in Chapters 1–3, one of the fundamental misconceptions in early Western perspectives on race and culture, and in later "scientific" racist views, was the confusion between "race" and "culture." Purported racial characteristics, such as skin color or nose shape, were associated with particular "essences" that determined behavior and cultural attributes. These misunderstandings were also prevalent in the early usages of the word *ethnicity*. The Greek term *ethnos* (derived from *ethnikos*) was used to refer to non-Greeks, or to *other* peoples who shared some biological and cultural characteristics and a common way of life. The Greeks tended to refer to non-Greeks as peripheral, foreign barbarians, or *ethnea,* and referred to themselves as civilized peoples, *genos Hellenon* (Hutchinson and Smith 1996). Later, the word *ethnos,* as used in the Greek New Testament, was associated with non-Jewish and non-Christian peoples and nations that were referred to as pagans, heathens, and idolaters (Simpson and Weiner 1989). Eventually, in various European languages ethnic, ethnical, ethnicity, *ethnique,* and *ethnie* corresponded to an association with "race" (Simpson and Weiner 1989). As the field of anthropology, including the subdisciplines of cultural anthropology and ethnology, developed in the nineteenth century, the usage of ethnology or ethnicity also became associated with "race." Thus, ethnological studies focused on the scientific investigation of the different "races of mankind." Race, language, and religion were perceived as a fusion of physical and cultural traits by the Western scientists and anthropologists of the nineteenth century.

However, as emphasized in earlier chapters, one of the basic findings of the research of Franz Boas and later anthropologists is that the physical characteristics of a specific group of people are not associated with any particular behavior or culture or language. In other words, one's language or culture is not inherited through biological transmission or genetics. Boas stressed that culture was far more involved in explaining how people in different ethnic groups behaved than any biological factors. One acquires his or her language and culture through *enculturation,* by learning the language and various symbols, values, norms, and beliefs in the environment to which one is exposed. Since the 1960s, anthropologists and other social scientists have generally used the term *ethnicity* or *ethnic group* to refer to an individual's cultural heritage, separate from one's physical characteristics.

In the modern definition, we emphasize both the objective and subjective aspects of ethnicity. The objective aspect is the observable culture and shared symbols of a particular group. It may involve a specific language or religious tradition that is maintained within the group, or it may be particular clothing, hairstyles, preferences in food, or other conspicuous characteristics. The subjective aspect involves the internal beliefs of the people regarding their shared ancestry. They may believe that their ethnic group has a shared origin, or family ancestry, or a common homeland. In some cases, they may believe that their ethnicity has specific physical characteristics in common. This subjective aspect of ethnicity entails a "we-feeling" and a sense of

community or oneness, or a distinction between one's own "in-group" versus an "out-group." It doesn't matter whether these beliefs are historically or scientifically accurate, genuine, or fictional. This subjective identification of individuals with an ideology of a (at least imagined) shared history, unique past, and symbolic attachment to a homeland are often the most important expressions of ethnicity (Smith 1986).

Thus, one's ethnicity is not innately determined by biology or purported racial characteristics. Despite early classifications of the European "race" or the English, German, French, or Polish "races," these differences among Europeans were not based on physical characteristics, but rather on linguistic and cultural variation. Likewise, there is no African "race." Rather, Africa is a continent of the world where hundreds of different ethnic groups reside that vary from region to region. The descendants of African slaves residing in the United States have a very different ethnicity than descendants of African slaves who live in the Caribbean. In Asia, the differences among the Chinese, Japanese, Koreans, Thais, Indonesians, Vietnamese, Cambodians, and Laotians are not based on racial differences but on ethnic differences. Though there may be some minor genetic differences among these populations, they are slight and do not result in distinctive "races." These ethnic groups have different languages, histories, and cultural traditions that create variation among them.

Since ethnicity is based on cultural characteristics, it is much more variable, modifiable, changeable, and, as we will see, more situational than an identity based on physical characteristics. But before we begin an analysis of ethnicity, we need to comprehend the importance of culture as it is employed by anthropologists to understand ethnic identity issues.

THE CONCEPT OF CULTURE

Culture is a fundamental concept within the discipline of anthropology. In everyday usage, many Americans refer to culture as "high culture"—Shakespeare's works, Beethoven's symphonies, Michelangelo's sculptures, gourmet cooking, imported wines, and so on. Anthropologists, however, use the term in a much broader sense to refer to all of the learned and shared ideas and products of a society.[1] E. B. Tylor, a British anthropologist, proposed a definition of culture in the nineteenth century that includes much of human experience: "Culture . . . is that complex whole which includes knowledge, belief, arts, morals, law, custom, and any other capabilities and habits acquired by man[kind] as a member of society" (1871:1). This view suggests that culture includes tools, weapons, fire, agriculture, animal domestication, metallurgy, writing, the steam engine, glasses, airplanes, computers, penicillin, nuclear power, rock-and-roll, video games, designer jeans, religion, political systems, subsistence patterns, science, sports, and social organizations. In Tylor's view, culture includes all aspects of human activity, from the fine arts to popular entertainment, from everyday behavior to the development of sophisticated technology. It contains the plans, rules, techniques, designs, norms, and policies for living.

Nineteenth-century theorists tended to link biological traits with cultural characteristics. It was not until the twentieth century, when anthropologists such as Franz Boas began to use systematic scientific research techniques to demonstrate that there was no causal link between biological ancestry and possession of a particular culture, that scientists, including anthropologists, gained a better understanding of genetics, heredity, and the roles of environment and culture. Biological traits are passed to individuals through genes, whereas culture is transmitted to individuals through learning or what anthropologists refer to as *enculturation*. Most anthropologists today would accept a broad conception of culture as a shared way of life that includes values, beliefs, and norms transmitted within a particular society from generation to generation.

Notice that this definition includes the term *society*. In general, society refers to a particular group of humans within a specific territory. In particular, it refers to the patterns of relationships among the distinct social statuses and roles within this definite territory. In the past, anthropologists attempted to make a simple distinction between culture and society. Society was said to consist of the patterns of relationships among people within a specified territory, and culture was viewed as the by-products of those relationships. This view of society as distinguishable from culture was derived from ethnographic studies of small-scale societies. In such societies, people within a specific territory usually share a common culture. However, as we will see, in most countries where modern anthropologists conduct ethnographic research, societies are multicultural and multiethnic and consist of ethnic groups that maintain some commonalities in cultural tradition, but also may have very little commitment to many of these common aspects of the larger culture.

Symbols, Language, and Culture

The human capacity for culture is based in part on our linguistic and cognitive ability to *symbolize. Symbols* are abstract ideas that are embodied within language. *Language* is the standardized system of symbols that allows people to communicate with one another. Language ensures the continuity of a cultural heritage. As human children learn their language, symbols and culture are transmitted from generation to generation. One recognized aspect of language is that humans can speak using complicated phonological and syntactical and grammatical rules, without ever being conscious of those rules. Speakers and listeners of a particular language cannot consciously express those complicated rules. Obviously, some aspects of human culture are also unconscious. As humans learn their language, both consciously and unconsciously, they learn how to subsist, how to interact, how to govern their society, and what gods to worship. Culture is the transmission of learned knowledge. A group of people who share knowledge of this sort to a greater degree than they share it with others can be considered an ethnic group. Culture is the historical accumulation of learned symbolic knowledge that is shared by an ethnic group. This symbolic knowledge is transmitted through enculturation, and it can change rapidly from one generation to the next. Generally, however, most people go to great lengths to conserve their cultural and symbolic traditions. As we will see in later chapters, the persistence of cultural and symbolic traditions, the basis of ethnic identity, is as widespread as cultural and ethnic change.

We noted that culture consists of the shared practices and understandings within a society. To some degree, culture is based on shared meanings that are to some extent "public" and thus beyond the mind of any individual. Culture exists before the birth of an individual into the society, and it will continue (in some form) beyond the death of any particular individual. These publicly shared meanings provide designs or recipes for surviving and contributing to the society. On the other hand, culture exists within the mind of individuals. For example, a particular ethnic group learns the symbolic meanings of their own group by observing practices and learning a language. However, the child is not just a passive receptor of that cultural knowledge; rather, the child uses that knowledge to make decisions and develop strategies for interacting with others. Cognitive anthropologists emphasize *schemas,* or cultural models that are internalized by individuals and influence decision making and behavior. Culture is acquired by and modeled as schema within individual minds, which can motivate, shape, and transform these symbols and meanings (D'Andrade and Strauss 1992; Quinn and Holland 1987).

In addition, culture has some influence on people's emotions. Cultural symbols, both implicit and explicit, can appeal to people in almost a physical way. People do not merely think about symbols, they feel and experience them emotionally. Anthropologists often discuss how culture and cultural symbols become *naturalized* within a particular society. The symbols become so natural to people that they cannot conceive of doing, feeling, or thinking in any other way. For some people, a particular ethnicity feels "biological" or "innate" or "natural." To be an Italian American, a Native American, an African American, an Igbo from Nigeria, a Fijian, or Irish may feel emotionally rooted within the self of an individual. On the other hand, depending on their experience, some people may not have deep emotional attachments to any specific ethnicity.

It is apparent that cultural understandings are not shared equally by all members of a society. Even in small-scale societies, culture is shared differently by males and females, rich and poor, young and old. Some individuals in these societies have a great deal of knowledge regarding agriculture, medical practices, or religious beliefs, while others have less. In a complex industrialized society such as the United States, culture consists of a tremendous amount of information and knowledge regarding technology and other aspects of society. Different people learn different aspects of this culture, such as repairing cars or television sets, understanding nuclear physics or federal tax regulations, or composing music. Hence, to some extent, culture varies from person to person, region to region, class to class, age to age grouping, and gender to gender. As will be discussed later, anthropologists who conduct research on ethnic groups within multicultural and multiethnic societies find diverse configurations of shared culture and practices. There may be some overlap in shared practices and culture among these different ethnic groups, but there are various degrees of commitment to particular aspects of a "common" culture. In many cases, the so-called common culture may be contested and struggled against. The extent to which an individual or an ethnic group shares a particular culture is an empirical question that the anthropologist has to investigate.

The concept of culture has two dimensions that are sometimes distinguished by anthropologists: material and nonmaterial culture. *Material culture* consists of the physical products of human society (ranging from clothing styles to housing and building types to technologies of transportation). Material culture often constitutes important ethnic boundary markers, which are used to differentiate one group from another. Clothing styles are often used to demarcate one ethnic group from another. *Nonmaterial culture* refers to the intangible products of human society (e.g., symbols and language, values, beliefs, and norms). *Values* are the abstract standards by which members of an ethnic group define what is good or bad, holy or unholy, beautiful or ugly. They are assumptions that are shared within the ethnic group. Values are the abstract generalizations that underlie beliefs and practices. All ethnic groups have *beliefs*, which are cultural conventions that concern true or false assumptions, including specific descriptions of the nature of the universe and one's place in it.

When discussing culture, many anthropologists refer to the worldview of a particular ethnic group. A *worldview* consists of various beliefs about the nature of reality and provides a particular ethnic group with a more or less consistent orientation toward the world. Some beliefs may be combined into an ideology. An *ideology* consists of cultural symbols and beliefs that reflect and support the interests of specific ethnic groups or subgroups within an ethnic group. Particular ethnic groups promote ideologies for their own ends as a means of maintaining and justifying economic and political authority.

In some societies, especially complex societies with different ethnic groups, sociopolitical and ethnic configurations of power relations may produce *cultural hegemony,* or *ethnic hegemony,* the ideological control by one dominant ethnic group over beliefs and values. One ethnic group that has political power may impose its cultural beliefs on other subordinate ethnic groups. As we will see in later chapters, for a long historical period the dominant ethnic group in early U.S. history, white Anglo-Saxon Protestants, was able to impose its language, cultural beliefs, and practices on other ethnic groups in society. Likewise in Russian society, many ethnic minorities had to learn the culture and language of the dominant Russian majority. In many areas of the world, ethnic minorities were often forced to accept the ideologies of the politically dominant group.

Norms are an ethnic group's rules of right and wrong behavior. They are like the traffic regulations of behavior within an ethnic group. *Norms* are shared rules or guidelines that define how members of an ethnic group "ought" to behave under certain circumstances. Norms are generally connected to the values, beliefs, worldviews, and ideologies of an ethnic group. Some anthropologists use the term *ethos* to refer to the socially acceptable norms within an ethnic group. Norms guiding ordinary usages and conventions of everyday life are known as *folkways.* Thus, among different ethnic groups there are a variety of rules for greeting people, gift exchanges, table manners, and innumerable other social occasions. *Mores,* or morality norms, have much stronger sanctions than folkway or etiquette norms. Members of ethnic groups believe that their mores are crucial for the maintenance of a decent and orderly way of life. People who violate mores are usually severely punished, though punishment for the violation of mores varies from one ethnic group to another. It may take the form of ostracism, vicious gossip, public ridicule, exile, dismissal from one's job, physical beating, imprisonment, commitment to a mental hospital, or even execution.

When discussing values, beliefs, and norms, ethnologists often distinguish between ideal culture and real culture. *Ideal culture* consists of what people within an ethnic group say they do or should do, whereas *real culture* refers to their actual behaviors. Ethnologists have discovered that the ideal culture frequently contrasts with people's actual behavior. For instance, a Chinese anthropologist may learn that people in the United States cherish the value of equal opportunity, yet in observing U.S. culture, the anthropologist might encounter many cases in which people from different racial and ethnic backgrounds are treated in a highly unequal manner. This difference between ideal and real culture is an important distinction for anthropologists in assessing race and ethnic relations. Various patterns of prejudice and stereotypes regarding ethnic and race relations may not be expressed within the ideal culture, but may be an aspect of the real culture. Anthropologists find that there are differences between the ideal and real cultural practices of individuals in all societies.

The terms for nonmaterial culture, including values, beliefs, norms, ideologies, ethos, and worldviews are used by many anthropologists in their research on ethnic groups. However, not all anthropologists agree with concise, clear-cut distinctions among these terms. Instead, these terms are based on the models that anthropologists build on when studying and interpreting other cultures. Terms such as values, beliefs, norms, or worldviews are used as heuristic devices and research aids to help explain behavior and understand the complex symbols shared by ethnic groups. Contemporary anthropologists recognize that these models are only partial solutions to explaining and understanding the empirical and existential realities of ethnicity and culture.

Additionally, anthropologists differ in respect to how culture should be understood and analyzed. They advance different methodological and analytical approaches that may result in variant understandings of the term *culture*. Some anthropologists view culture as an indirect reflection of the material aspects of a society. In other words, the environmental and technological factors within a society produce a specific form of culture. That is, culture is a by-product of the material conditions within a particular society (Harris 1979, 1999). These anthropologists maintain that certain types of economic, social, political, or other institutions develop in relation to specific ecological conditions and technological changes. Therefore, "culture" is part of an adaptive mechanism that corresponds to the material conditions within the society. Thus, an ethnic group's culture and behavior are indirectly produced by the technological and ecological conditions that are available to the group. Other anthropologists emphasize how "culture" is an indirect reflection of the organization of political and economic interests within a society. In this view "culture" is used, shaped, modified, and changed to correspond to specific social, economic, or political interests of groups and individuals. Whether focusing on environmental or technological features, or economic and political phenomena, these anthropologists attempt to offer explanations for human behavior, ethnicity, and cultural characteristics.

Some anthropologists, however, refer to "culture" as a set of linguistic symbols that have to be treated and interpreted like a "text" (Geertz 1963) or "code" (Sahlins 1976). As these anthropologists conceptualize the cultural text or code, they focus on the highly symbolic and nonmaterial aspects of a society. They are not concerned with the question of why particular institutions or ethnic patterns develop but, rather, how to make sense of institutions and ethnicity in relation to specific cultural values, beliefs, norms, and practices. These symbolic anthropologists attempt to interpret the meaningfulness of cultural symbols within the ethnic groups that they study. In their view, humans are meaning-seeking creatures that need to maintain an identity and purpose in their lives. These meaningful symbols or codes are shared by ethnic groups and provide coherent frameworks for interpreting the world. Anthropologists who rely on the symbolic approach tend to offer interpretations of culture and human behavior rather than explanations of these phenomena.[2]

Another type of materialist approach to the understanding of culture is referred to as the "epidemiological perspective," pioneered by Dan Sperber and his colleagues (Ross 2004; Sperber 1996; Sperber and Hirschfeld 1999). These anthropologists draw on the fields of cognitive science and cognitive psychology to discuss how culture propagates like a contagious disease from one person to another. Thus, religious beliefs, cooking recipes, folktales, and even scientific hypotheses are ideas or representations within the human mind that spread among people in a shared environment. Chains of communication propagate these beliefs or cultural representations within a population. As in the spread of a contagious disease, some representations take hold and are maintained in particular populations, while other beliefs or representations do not resonate with specific groups and become extinct. Also, some beliefs or representations spread more easily and are retained more easily within a population because they are more easily acquired than other beliefs.

As will be seen, anthropologists differ with each other on how culture and ethnicity ought to be understood based on whether they focus on material/political interests or symbolic-interpretive frameworks. The materialist perspective is viewed by some critics as overlooking the symbolic significance and meaning of culture for ethnic groups, and they argue that these important symbols and meanings cannot be reduced to adaptive mechanisms. These critics also express their skepticism about whether culture and ethnicity can be reduced to political dynamics and interests within a society. On the other hand, the symbolic approach is criticized for not grappling with the dimensions of power, politics, and material factors and the roles they play in ethnic relations.

Although recognizing that the differences and divisions in anthropology between those who prefer materialist or political explanations and those who prefer textual or symbolic interpretive understandings of culture have had their effects on analyzing ethnicity and ethnic relations, every society must confront the problem of adjusting to the practical circumstances of life. People need food, shelter, clothing, and the necessary technology and energy for survival. The material component of culture is related to a group's survival. There is also the nonmaterial aspect of culture: norms, values, beliefs, ideologies, and symbols. These cultural norms and symbols have emotional significance and are meaningful. Symbols may not be directly related to the practical circumstances of life; instead, they may indicate some aesthetic or moral values that are not directly related to the material conditions of society. Thus, most anthropologists admit that both the material and nonmaterial dimensions of culture are fundamentally important in comprehending ethnicity and ethnic relations.

THE CULTURAL SIGNIFICANCE OF RACE AS ETHNICITY

As we have emphasized, ethnicity is based on cultural characteristics, including language and other learned and shared values, beliefs, and norms. Our ethnicity is not transmitted to us biologically. And, as we have seen in the chapters on race and "scientific" racism, the notion of race as a biologically meaningful scientific concept is highly questionable. Anthropologists find, however, beliefs about "purported races" that are culturally constructed in many societies throughout the world. In other words, though the scientific meaning of a distinctive "race" or separate "races" is questionable, people in different societies have "folk categories" of "race" that are based on phenotypic differences, such as skin color, hair color and texture, nose shape, and other physical characteristics that become embedded within the culture.

These folk categories of race are perpetuated and become cultural models for how ethnic identities are understood by outsiders and sometimes by the people themselves. In some cases, physical traits become both objective and subjective ethnic boundary markers. They are used to designate the ethnic identity of individuals. And the people designated as belonging to a specific identity may come to believe that these physical traits are an aspect of their ethnicity. In many societies, these invented folk categories are extremely powerful and are used by government agencies to classify people according to highly arbitrary racial classifications. These racial classifications become culturally meaningful and become the basis for social interaction within many societies. Thus, "race," as well as language, religion, and beliefs about an ancestral homeland, is used to demarcate the boundaries of ethnic groups.

Since the nineteenth century in the United States, a system termed the *hypodescent concept* of racial classification has been used in cases of racial mixture whereby the offspring of the parents have the race of the parent with the lowest racial status. Since black Americans were considered to be a lower-status "race," a person is considered black if he or she has a black ancestor anywhere in the family history. This is known as the "one-drop rule" of racial classification because it is based on the myth that one drop of "black blood" is sufficient to determine racial blackness. Thus, Americans with both white and black ancestry are usually classified as black and often encouraged to identify as black in personal and social contexts. In contrast, a person is classified as white if he or she has no black ancestry anywhere in the family history. This means that in order to be white, a person has to prove a negative, the absence of black ancestors. Other racial categories such as mulatto (half black and half white), quadroon (one-quarter black and three-quarters white), and octoroon (one-eighth black and seven-eighths white) were developed as an extension of the one-drop rule. Until the 1950s in Louisiana, it was illegal for a doctor to give a blood transfusion from a black person to a white person. Despite the fact that this notion of the one-drop rule is mythical and is based on false notions of "racial essences," these ideas still persist in some circles.

Anthropologist Virginia Dominguez (1986) did research on a legal case involving race classification used in Louisiana in the 1980s. In 1982–1983, a Louisiana woman, Susie Guillory Phipps, contested the state's classification of her as a "black" and claimed that she had a white racial identity. She sued the Louisiana Bureau of Vital Records to change her racial classification from black to white. As a descendant of an eighteenth-century white plantation owner and a black slave, Phipps was designated "black" on her birth certificate. A 1970 state law declared anyone with at least one-thirty-second "Negro blood" to be black. This was a clear manifestation of the hypodescent rule or the one-drop rule. Phipps's attorney argued that the racial categories assigned on a birth certificate were unconstitutional, and that the one-thirty-second designation was inaccurate. The woman lost her case in Louisiana, and the court upheld the state law that quantified racial identity and classification. Eventually, the law was declared unconstitutional and was repealed. Nevertheless, the case illustrates how the concept of race is culturally constructed and employed for social, legal, and political purposes.

In contrast to the one-drop rule, Native American Indians in the United States are treated differently. Because Native Americans have entitlements based on legislation, the U.S. federal government has sometimes imposed blood quanta rules of at least 50 percent ancestry from a particular tribe in order to be classified as a Native American Indian. This has created considerable confusion both legally and socially for many Native American Indian peoples. The one-drop rule and blood quanta tests emphasize that the mythical ideas of racial essences are deeply embedded within the folk culture of U.S. society. Socially, legally, and politically these U.S. folk racial distinctions trump other ethnic cultural characteristics. A group's physical traits have become a significant impermeable boundary that separates European "white" Americans from people of color, including Native Americans, African Americans, Hispanic Americans, Asian Americans, and Arab Americans.

Similar folk conceptions are held about race in other societies. In Northern Ireland, some Protestants and Catholics believe that they can identify members of the other group based on physical differences, despite their obvious physical similarities. In South Africa, the government categorized different populations as "white," "coloured" (a mixture of different "races"), "Asian" (which includes Chinese and Indians but not Japanese, who were considered honorary "whites"), and "black." The South African government used this classification scheme based on highly arbitrary racial categories for social, legal, and political purposes. In Puerto Rico, an island colonized by the Spanish and later by the United States, racial classifications are used to categorize people by skin color. Puerto Ricans use *blanco* to refer to whites, *prieto* to refer to blacks, and *trigueño* to refer to tan-skinned people. In Brazil, a complex racial classification exists that uses different criteria with which to categorize people from those in the United States. An individual categorized as "black" in the United States might be categorized as "white" in Brazil (Harris 1964).

As we will see in later chapters, in countries such as Puerto Rico, Brazil, China, and Japan folk categories of race were historically important in classifying various peoples. Anthropologists have recognized that although these folk conceptions of race are based on subjective, arbitrary categories, they have a profound social and cultural significance in many societies. So, when assessing race and ethnicity issues, we find that folk beliefs about race are sometimes embedded within the ethnicity of a particular group of people.

ETHNICITY: MAJOR ANTHROPOLOGICAL PERSPECTIVES

Anthropologists have employed a number of different theoretical strategies to study ethnic groups and processes of ethnicity. One early model developed in the 1960s is known as the *primordialist model.* The primordialist model of ethnicity is associated with anthropologist Clifford Geertz, who suggested this view of ethnic identity in an essay entitled "The Integrative Revolution: Primordial Sentiments and Civil Politics in the New States" (1963). Geertz attempted to describe how many Third World countries were trying to build nations and integrate their political institutions based on a "civil order," a political system based on democratic representation processes rather than traditional ties of kinship or religion. However, as he indicates in the essay, this new civil order clashed with older traditional or "primordial" aspects of kinship, race, ethnicity, language, and religion.[3]

Geertz suggests that ethnic attachments based on assumed kinship and other social ties and religious traditions are deeply rooted within the individual through the enculturation process. He maintains that ethnic affiliation persists because it is fundamental to a person's identity. In this view, as people are enculturated into a particular ethnic group, they form deep emotional attachments to it. These emotional sentiments are sometimes evident through *ethnic boundary markers,* which distinguish one ethnic group from another. These ethnic boundary markers include religion, dress, language or dialect, and other visible symbols. But Geertz tends to focus on the intense internal aspects of ethnicity and the deep subjective "feeling of belonging" to a particular ethnic group. This is one of the strengths of the primordialist perspective on ethnicity. It

emphasizes the meaning and significance that people invest in their ethnic attachments. Geertz emphasizes how the "assumed givens" are subjective perceptions of attributes such as blood ties and ancestry, which may or may not coincide with the actual circumstances of one's birth.[4] Geertz goes on to say that the primordial ties are experienced by the people of these new nations, and that despite the introduction of new forms of civil political institutions and ideologies, these ethnic attachments endure, and are at times obstacles as new nations attempt to integrate their societies based on a new civil political order. He suggests that there is a basic conflict between the modern state and one's personal identity based on these primordial ties.

Another proponent of the primordialist model is Joshua Fishman. In an essay entitled "Social Theory and Ethnography," Fishman describes how ethnicity is intuitively defined and experienced as part of an actor's "being" (as distinct from his "doing" and "knowing").

In his discussion, Fishman emphasizes the interrelationship between language, symbols, and ethnicity. He describes ethnicity as a *Weltanschauung* (worldview) that provides explanations for origins and other meaningful questions. As Fishman describes, the "blood, bones, and flesh" of ethnicity become symbolic metaphors in the language of the ethnic groups. They are not based on scientifically based biological realities but on symbolic metaphors that are deeply rooted both consciously and unconsciously within the emotions of individuals. Fishman indicates that the language of ethnicity is the language of kinship. Kinship is the basis of one's felt bond to one's own kind. It is the basis of one's solidarity with others in times of stress. It is the basis of one's right to rely upon them in times of need; it is the basis of one's dependency, sociability, and intimacy with others as a matter of course. Various songs, chants, sayings, prayers, rites, jokes, and riddles are aspects of the language of ethnic expression and identification. They are symbols of ancestral patrimony that Fishman refers to as the "corpus mysticum."

For example, a small ethnic group known as the Old Order Amish maintains very strong ethnic boundary markers in U.S. society (Hostetler 1980; Kephart and Zellner 1994). They emphasize their ethnic difference through language by speaking a German dialect among themselves. The Amish dress in a traditional manner similar to the cultural codes of the 1600s. Men wear hats and long beards, women wear long hair, which is always covered by a hat in public. Based on their interpretation of the Bible, the Amish strive to maintain a conservative, traditional way of life that does not allow the adoption of modern technology such as electricity, automobiles, and television. They do not allow their children to be educated beyond the eighth grade so that they are not exposed to modern U.S. culture. The Amish have a deeply emotional attachment to their ethnicity and culture. These primordial sentiments are deeply rooted within Amish culture and are evident in the *ethnic boundary markers*—such as language, dress, and a traditional lifestyle—that distinguish them from other North Americans.

One of the criticisms of the primordialist model of ethnicity is that it appears to be based on what Geertz refers to as "ineffable" givens or spiritual traditions, or what Fishman refers to as "mystical" concepts. Some anthropologists have suggested that Geertz reduced primordial attachments to innate, fixed, unchangeable, unmodifiable, and unanalyzable characteristics (Eller and Coughlan 1993). It is not surprising that most of the anthropologists who have utilized the primordialist approach tend to be symbolic anthropologists who interpret culture as a "text" or "code." These texts or codes are deeply rooted within the emotional characteristics of the individual through enculturation. However, Geertz does emphasize how historical and political processes play a role in exacerbating or reducing primordial ethnic tensions. He says that as newly modernizing states attempt to repress ethnic attachments and construct new arrangements based on a somewhat alien order, people risk losing their personal identity, and in many cases end up being dominated by some other rival ethnic group (1963:258–259). Thus, to some extent, these primordial identities or "assumed givens" are produced by concrete historical processes that vary from person to person, from time to time, and from society to society. Also, as Geertz pointed out, individuals differ in respect to how much attention they pay to these primordial attachments.

The Circumstantialist Model

Another model of ethnicity began to surface within anthropology during the 1960s based on research within multiethnic societies. Michael Moerman, in a classic essay entitled "Who Are the Lue?" (1965), had intimated that ethnicity was more problematic than anthropologists had assumed. The Lue were a group of people in northern Thailand who lived among other ethnic groups, and Moerman was attempting to describe their ethnicity. But when he asked them to identify their cultural traits, such as language, culture, political organization, and religion, he found that they often mentioned cultural traits that they shared with other ethnic groups in the region. In addition, individuals differed with respect to the cultural traits that they listed as criteria for their ethnic group.

Moerman concluded that being "Lue" was not based on any objectively identifiable traits but, rather, stemmed from a completely subjectively defined and variable identity. In fact, he states that the Lue cannot define themselves ethnically without referring to other ethnic groups. The Lue did not make up a discretely bounded ethnic community but, rather, a more diffuse and situationally defined community. Instead of clear-cut objective categories, Moerman points to a more *emic* ("the native's point of view") understanding of their ethnic boundaries. In other words, anthropologists cannot use a "cookie-cutter" notion of culture, or a coherent-bounded homogeneous unit, to analyze ethnic groups. Ethnic groups in multicultural societies are not simplistic, easily identifiable culture units. Instead, they are overlapping groups that encompass other ethnic groups.

These problematic issues were clarified with the publication of anthropologist Fredrik

Barth's *Ethnic Groups and Boundaries* (1969). In a number of case studies in this book, Barth noted the fluidity of ethnic relations in different types of multiethnic societies. Although ethnic groups maintain boundaries such as language to mark their identity, people may modify and shift their language and ethnic identity in different types of social interaction. He criticized a view of culture based on earlier anthropological research in small-scale societies that tended to treat ethnic groups as having discrete, impermeable boundaries. Barth emphasized the interaction between ethnic groups and how people identify with different elements of their own ethnicity and express or repress those elements and characteristics in different circumstances for economic, political, or other practical interests. This model is sometimes referred to as an *instrumentalist* approach to ethnicity but has become known widely in anthropology as the *circumstantialist* model of ethnicity.

In the circumstantialist approach, Barth emphasizes how ethnic boundary markers, such as language, clothing, and other cultural traits, are not based on deeply rooted, enduring aspects of ethnicity. Ethnic boundaries are continually being revised, negotiated, and redefined according to the practical interests of the actors. Ethnic boundaries are generated by the varying contexts and circumstances in which people find themselves. For example, in the United States, people of German descent may refer to themselves as "German Americans" to distinguish themselves from "Irish Americans" or "Italian Americans." Should they happen to be among Europeans, however, these same people might refer to themselves simply as "Americans." The circumstantialist model explains how people draw on their ethnic identity for specific economic, social, and political purposes. People strategically use their ethnic affiliations as the basis for collective political mobilization or to enhance their economic interests. Barth showed how some people modify and change their ethnic identity when it is perceived to be advantageous for their own interests. They may emphasize the ethnic or racial identities of others or establish boundaries between themselves and others in order to interact with others for political or economic purposes. Thus, in Barth's view, ethnicity is not fixed and unchanging but is, instead, fluid and contingent, as people strategically use, define, and redefine their ethnicity to respond to their immediate basic needs.

Anthropologist Abner Cohen's approach to ethnicity is an example of the circumstantialist view. Cohen views ethnic collectivities as types of political organizations that are mobilized for different purposes. He notes that ethnic group organizations have two distinctive dimensions. They provide a symbolic meaningful framework for people, but they also have potential as political networks and associations. The symbolic framework offers people answers to the basic questions of life concerning ancestral origins and destiny, whereas the political aspect furnishes people with organizations to accomplish practical goals.

In a classic ethnography in West Africa, in the country of Nigeria, Cohen analyzed the relationship among various ethnic groups. He focused on the interrelationship between the people known as the Hausa and the Yoruba in Ibadan, a city dominated by the Yoruba. Cohen (1969, 1974) described how ethnic distinctions between the Hausa and Yoruba became the basis of political and economic competition over various resources. Hausa migrants had entered the city and became very successful in monopolizing the cattle trade in a short period of time. Cohen used the term *retribalization* to refer to the Hausa strategy of using ethnic affiliations as an informal network for economic and political purposes. The Hausa drew on their shared culture and ethnicity, including their Islamic religious tradition, to strengthen their group solidarity and political networks. These networks were, in turn, used to extend and coordinate Hausa cattle-trading activities in Ibadan. Cohen demonstrated how ethnic processes and the meaningful cultural symbols used by ethnic groups can mobilize political and economic behavior. Ethnicity, in Cohen's view, is an idiom and mechanism for producing political alignments, which are strategically used for practical ends. Thus, ethnic continuity or revival can be found in almost all societies, both developed and undeveloped.

Cohen's ethnography illustrates how individuals within ethnic groups that adapt to specific types of economic and political circumstances in a multiethnic society may emphasize their shared identity as a means of enhancing cooperation with other members of the group. Throughout the world, individuals migrating to different areas often use ethnic ties as a means of social adjustment. Individuals may pursue political interests through ethnic allegiances. In numerous situations, people may manipulate ethnic traditions and symbols to their advantage.

This circumstantialist view of ethnicity also asserts that ethnicity will be displayed to a different degree by various ethnic groups. Ethnic traits will vary from one historical time to another, and group identity may shift from one generation to another. Ethnic groups are not stable collective entities. They may appear and vanish within or less than a generation. Ethnic groups will come into being during different historical periods. *Ethnogenesis* refers to the origins of an ethnic group. Ethnogenesis has taken place throughout the world in many different historical circumstances. For example, the Amish ethnicity described earlier originated in Switzerland during the sixteenth century. The Amish descend from a group of Anabaptists who split off with their own leadership during the Protestant Reformation. After this split, the Amish began to define themselves as different from other Anabaptists, Protestants, and Catholics, and they faced a great deal of persecution from the religious authorities (Kephart and Zellner 1994). This new definition of themselves resulted in ethnogenesis. Eventually, the Amish fled to the United States in the 1700s, settling first in Lancaster, Pennsylvania. From there, they have grown in size, and live in 20 different states. The Amish population is more than 200,000 today. There are no longer any Amish in Europe. Ethnogenesis is a continual, ongoing sociocultural and political process that began in prehistory and continues today for many people.

There have been many criticisms of the instrumental or circumstantialist view of ethnicity. The strength of this approach is to demonstrate how fluid and contingent ethnic boundaries

and the cultural criteria defining them are supposed to be. These theorists emphasize how ethnicity is not "static," but a highly dynamic aspect of human behavior. Most of the anthropologists who employ this circumstantialist approach tend to view "culture" as an indirect reflection of politics, economics, and other materialist factors. Ethnicity is a process that is activated and cultivated for strategic purposes in different contexts. The major criticism of this circumstantialist view, however, is that at times ethnicity does appear to endure and persist despite changes in historical, economic, and political change. Critics suggest that the circumstantialist view does not account for the fact that ethnicity is not highly mutable or changeable for some people. Some groups are not as able to free themselves from their ethnic attachments as others. Under some conditions, groups cannot jettison, negotiate, or manipulate their ethnic identity to pursue particular interests. Another criticism suggests that the circumstantialist view assumes that the individual is a completely "autonomous," "rational," "calculating" actor in social interaction. This assumption has been questioned by many anthropologists, who emphasize that "culture" plays a much more important part in human decision making and strategic interaction than the circumstantialist theorists admit.

As a result of the criticisms of both the primordialist and circumstantialist models, most contemporary anthropologists have drawn from both perspectives to explain or interpret ethnicity. As anthropologist Stanley Tambiah suggests, ethnic identity is a combination of the "semantics of primordial claims" and "the pragmatics of calculated choices" in the contexts of political-economic competition among differing interests groups (1989:336). Both models of ethnicity have helped illustrate the nuances of ethnic identity throughout the world. The primordialist model has been extremely useful in substantiating the persistence of ethnicity, whereas the circumstantialist model has helped demonstrate how ethnic identity can be altered and constructed in various economic and political conditions.

Presently, many contemporary anthropologists occupy a middle ground between these positions as they pay close attention to the detailed manner in which ethnicity may be both primordial and manipulable. As seen in the example of the Amish in U.S. society, both the primordial and circumstantialist views were useful in explaining and understanding different aspects of ethnicity.

Anthropologists today investigate how societal conditions may impinge on how people define themselves ethnically. What are the ethnic categories that have enduring meaningfulness and purpose for people, and under what circumstances are those categories asserted, negotiated, reaffirmed, or repressed? Also, to what extent and to what ends are the elements of ethnicity "invented" and "imagined" by ethnic groups? Anthropologists have to provide a detailed understanding of the ethnogenesis of a particular ethnic group. How does an ethnic group come to construct a shared sense of identity? What are the particulars of this ethnic identity? Is most of the ethnicity tied to religion? Or is it based on common ancestors or shared myths of common history and territory? Furthermore, anthropologists find it necessary to understand the global and local economic and political dynamics and processes that affect ethnic relations in continually changing societies. Globalization, government policies, the labor market, urbanization, and other aspects of the political economy have a profound influence on how ethnicity is expressed in different societies.

PATTERNS OF ETHNIC RELATIONS

Pluralism

To analyze ethnic relations within a single nation, the concept of the plural society was elaborated by the late anthropologist M. G. Smith. In his book *Pluralism in Africa* (1969), edited with the late anthropologist Leo Kuper, Smith describes a plural society as one in which different groups are internally distinguished from each other by institutional and cultural differences. Instead of one overarching homogeneous identical system of institutions shared within a society, a plural society consists of ethnic groups that differ in social organization, beliefs, norms, and ideals. Building on this framework, anthropologists have utilized the phrase *cultural pluralism* to describe how various ethnic groups maintain diverse cultures within one society. The example of the Amish in U.S. society would exemplify cultural pluralism. In contrast, *institutional pluralism* is the phrase used to refer to how different ethnic groups may have a similar culture but maintain separate institutions, including schools, churches, businesses, and other organizations, within a society. These ethnic groups may share the same language and dietary practices, and subscribe to the same values and beliefs, but they have minimal social interaction with other ethnic groups. In the United States, the Mormon religious community exemplifies this type of institutional pluralism.

Smith and Kuper classify different forms of plural societies based on the political order and legal institutions (1969). In some forms of plural societies, ethnic groups are not only divided culturally and structurally but are also organized in highly unequal political relationships. They term such societies as "radically plural" societies. In these radically plural societies, a minority ethnic group rules other ethnic groups through coercion. The state or government rules as an agent to protect the interests of the dominant ethnic group. The subordinate ethnic groups are treated as "subjects" rather than "citizens." This results in an ethnic hierarchy with the dominant ethnic group in control of the political, economic, and prestigious social positions within the society. Some radically plural societies evolved in early ancient agricultural civilizations. However, Smith and Kuper note how these forms of radically plural societies developed in more recent times with European colonialism in many parts of Latin America, the Caribbean, Africa, the Middle East, and Asia. These radically plural societies had a European elite that ruled through the control of the political economy and the legal institutions within these colonized regions. Typically, these inegalitarian plural societies usually result in divisive ethnic conflict and strained ethnic relationships.

Other forms of plural societies, sometimes referred to as *consociational plural societies,* are based on more egalitarian relationships among ethnic groups. In these plural societies, the government protects the structural and cultural differences among the ethnic groups. These ethnic groups are formally recognized by the state and legal institutions to allocate political rights and economic opportunities proportionally. Each ethnic group has a great deal of political autonomy, and, in theory, there is no politically dominant ethnic group. In Europe, Switzerland is often cited as an example of a plural society where different ethnic groups have distinctive cultures but have parity or equality with each other. Switzerland consists of French, Italian, German, and Romansh ethnic groups, and they all have relatively similar political and economic opportunities. Another European country, Belgium, is also known as an egalitarian plural society in which the population is divided into two major ethnic groups: the Dutch-speaking Flemish and the French-speaking Walloons. In such plural societies, ethnic groups have the legal and political right to maintain their own language, educational systems, and culture. A balance of power is often reached among the different ethnic groups according to a political formula that grants each group a proportional representation of the multiethnic population. As expected, cultural pluralism endures and remains stable in these ethnically egalitarian societies, resulting in relatively amicable relationships.

Many plural societies today fall between the inegalitarian radically plural and egalitarian consociational forms. Following decolonization in most of the countries of Latin America, Africa, the Middle East, and Asia, the radically plural forms of society were dislodged. The European elites were replaced by indigenous

elites in these postcolonial societies. However, as will be seen in later chapters, these societies remained pluralistic, as they were composed of many different ethnic groups. In some cases, the indigenous elites represented one particular ethnic group and perpetuated a continuation of radically plural politics. In other situations, new indigenous-based governments developed policies to manage competition and rivalry among different ethnic groups. This resulted, under some conditions, in another form and pattern of interethnic relations known as assimilation.

Assimilation

Another pattern of ethnic relations and interaction within many societies described by anthropologists is often referred to as assimilation. *Assimilation* is a process of ethnic boundary reduction that may come about when two or more ethnic groups come into contact with each other. One or more ethnic groups adopt the culture, values, beliefs, and norms of another ethnic group. The process of assimilation results in the similarity of culture and homogeneity among ethnic groups. As would be expected, assimilation occurs more easily when the physical and cultural characteristics of the different ethnic groups are more similar from the beginnings of contact.

Pierre van den Berghe has indicated a number of general factors that favor assimilation (1981). He notes that when ethnic groups are very different physically and culturally from one another, assimilation takes place at a slower pace, if at all. Also, if ethnic groups are dispersed within a territory they tend to assimilate more quickly. For example, if ethnic groups are residing in different cities or rural areas throughout a particular country, they would assimilate at a rapid pace. A corollary of this is that if a specific ethnic group is located within a specified region with ties to the territory, the pace of assimilation would be very slow. In addition, if the ethnic group is a small minority and dependent on a larger ethnic population for vital economic resources, assimilation is likely to be rapid. Also, low-status groups usually assimilate more readily than do high-status groups, and immigrants are more likely to assimilate than the native resident population, because of economic and political pressures.

Anthropologists have been engaged in research to determine whether these general factors are valid in different societal and cultural contexts. But in order to refine their research, they distinguish different forms of assimilation: cultural assimilation, structural assimilation, and biological assimilation.

Cultural assimilation involves one ethnic group's adoption of the cultural traits, including language, religion, clothing styles, diet, and other norms, values, and beliefs, of another group. Anthropologists such as Robert Redfield and Melville Herskovits in the 1930s used the term *acculturation* to refer to the tendency of distinct cultural groups to borrow words, technology, clothing styles, foods, values, norms, and behavior from each other (1936). Generally, cultural assimilation and acculturation have slightly different meanings to anthropologists. Cultural assimilation involves a subordinate ethnic minority adopting some of the culture of another ethnic group, whereas acculturation refers to the overall adjustment and adaptation of the group to the dominant ethnic group. Obviously, the process of cultural assimilation or acculturation has been going on since the earliest days of humanity and continues today.

As groups came in contact with one another, they borrowed from each other's cultures. Anthropologists, however, find that cultural assimilation and acculturation can be a very complex process for many ethnic groups. These processes may vary, depending on government policies and other societal conditions. For example, some cultural assimilation may be voluntary, wherein a particular ethnic group may choose to embrace the culture of another group. Many ethnic groups who immigrate into a particular society adopt the culture of the ethnically dominant group to secure their political rights and economic prospects. In some societies, government and educational policies may encourage groups to assimilate the culture of the dominant ethnic

group. During different historical periods, the policies of many governments, such as the U.S., French, Mexican, Nigerian, Israeli, and Chinese, have promoted cultural assimilation on a voluntary basis within their societies.

Conversely, under some historical conditions, governments may require nonvoluntary or *forced cultural assimilation.* This is where the government forces ethnic groups to take on the culture of the dominant ethnic group of the society. Sometimes, anthropologists refer to forced cultural assimilation as *ethnocide,* which implies the killing of the "culture" of a particular ethnic group. Ethnocide demands an ethnic group to abandon their language, religion, and other cultural norms, values, and beliefs and to adopt the culture of the dominant group. This process of ethnocide developed in various ancient agricultural civilizations such as Egypt, India, China, Rome, and the Aztec. As these agricultural civilizations expanded and conquered territories and other ethnic groups, at times they forced these other ethnic groups to assimilate and adopt the culture of the dominant ethnic group. This pattern of induced ethnocide was also prevalent during more modern forms of colonialism. For example, as Europeans colonized areas of Latin America, or as the Japanese colonized areas in Asia such as Taiwan, or as the United States colonized the region of North America, indigenous peoples were often forced to assimilate. This type of forced assimilation is usually extremely difficult for individuals. They have to forsake their own language and cultural traits to become a part of a different, often antagonistic set of values and beliefs. As will be seen in later chapters, forced cultural assimilation, or ethnocide, continues to influence many contemporary patterns of ethnic relations.

Structural assimilation, or *integration,* is the process by which ethnic groups not only adopt the culture of another ethnic group but also become participants within the basic institutions in the society. In other words, an ethnic group increases their social interaction with members of the other ethnic group within neighborhoods, schools, businesses, clubs, churches, and other organizations within the society. It would also include intermarriage among the different ethnic groups. The degree of structural assimilation within the society depends on the accessibility for ethnic groups to "integrate" within a particular society. In some societies, there may be obstacles for structural assimilation for specific ethnic groups. Racism, ethnocentrism, prejudice, and discrimination may play a role in the access of some groups to structural assimilation. Despite the cultural assimilation of some ethnic groups, there may not be opportunities for structural assimilation for these groups. In other cases, ethnic groups may become both culturally and structurally assimilated, which entails the complete eradication of their status as "another" ethnic group. At that point, in some circumstances, whatever minority status they may have had is completely eliminated.

One pattern of assimilation identified by researchers on ethnic relations has been referred to as *segmented assimilation* (Portes and Zhou 1994). Segmented assimilation combines some elements of assimilationist and pluralist tendencies in ethnic relations. In most cases of cultural assimilation, ethnic minorities adopt much of the culture of the dominant ethnic group. In some situations, however, some of these ethnic minorities are believed to be so different from the dominant ethnic group that their structural assimilation is obstructed. Physical characteristics, language, or religion may inhibit some groups from being completely assimilated within the society. Consequently, the children of these ethnic minorities may be encouraged to retain some of their ethnic group's culture while at the same time to adopt the majority ethnic group's culture in a piecemeal fashion. Under some conditions, an ethnic minority group may become economically successful but intentionally try to conserve some of their basic cultural traditions, thus advocating assimilationist and pluralist strategies.

Biological assimilation refers to the process of intermarriage and reproduction among different ethnic groups resulting in a new ethnic group. This is also known as *amalgamation,* or the biological merging of formerly distinct ethnic groups. The process of biological assimilation has been taking place for thousands of years as different groups began intermarrying and reproducing with each other. Usually intermarriage among ethnic groups occurs after a great deal of cultural and structural assimilation following extensive interethnic contact. Thus, usually ethnic boundaries have been extensively reduced, if not eliminated, when intermarriage takes place. The degree of biological assimilation may range from a society where there are no longer any cultural and biological distinctions among the population to societies where new forms of ethnicity develop. Historically, in the United States intermarriage among different European Americans (descendants of English, Irish, Germans, Italians, Polish, etc.) has reduced most meaningful ethnic boundaries. On the other hand, as will be seen in the chapter on Latin America and the Caribbean, new forms of ethnicity emerged as intermarriage took place among Europeans, native populations, and African slaves.

Contemporary anthropologists who study ethnicity have become extremely cautious about utilizing the concepts of pluralism and assimilation in making generalizations about different types of ethnic relations. They find that these models may simplify or exaggerate tendencies found in different societies. One way they have tried to overcome the simplicity of these models is to differentiate between group and individual behavioral tendencies. Thus, in some cases, pluralist or assimilationist patterns may not affect whole ethnic groups within a society; rather, some individuals may define their ethnic identity in pluralistic terms, or adopt the culture of the dominant ethnic group, or intermarry within another ethnic group. In these situations, one will have difficulty specifying the pluralistic or assimilationist trends for the entire society and different ethnic groups. Anthropologists have learned to distinguish between group and individual levels of behavior in assessing pluralist and assimilationist patterns. The patterns of pluralism and assimilation are to be understood as models that allow anthropologists to focus on the outcome of processes that effect ethnic relations.

Ethnic Violence

Three other patterns of ethnic interaction have been identified by anthropologists and other social scientists. One is *segregation,* or the physical and social separation of categories of people. Segregation was the policy of many southern states in the United States following the abolition of slavery until the civil rights movements of the 1950s and 1960s. Jim Crow laws were developed which resulted in the creation of separate facilities and institutions for African Americans and white Americans. There were segregated schools, restaurants, drinking fountains, restrooms, parks, neighborhoods, and other areas. Until recently, the South African government had developed similar laws to segregate the "races" and ethnic groups within its legal constitution.

Another pattern of ethnic interaction is *ethnic cleansing,* the attempt to remove an ethnic group from its location and territory within a society. Recently, the Serbs have attempted to bring about ethnic cleansing and remove ethnic groups such as the Bosnians from regions within the former country of Yugoslavia. In East Africa, the former ruler Idi Amin expelled East Indian immigrants from Uganda for economic and political reasons. Following the Vietnam War in 1975, the Vietnamese government encouraged the migration of more than 1 million ethnic Chinese from their country. These people were abruptly eliminated as an ethnic minority, despite the fact that many had assimilated into Vietnamese society. In the past, the U.S. government removed Native American Indians from their territories, a process of ethnic cleansing that resulted in reservation life for these ethnic groups.

Finally, the third pattern of ethnic interaction is known as *genocide,* the systematic attempt to kill and eliminate a particular ethnic group. Genocide may overlap with ethnic cleansing.

In both the cases of the U.S. government and Native American Indians and the Serbs and the Bosnians, removal policies were often combined with more deadly policies of genocide. When the British colonized the area of Australia, native populations such as the Tasmanians were exterminated. There were 5,000 Tasmanians in 1800, but as a result of being attacked by the British, the last full-blooded Tasmanian died in 1876. In the settling of South Africa by the Dutch, indigenous populations such as the Hottentots were systematically killed off. In the twentieth century, the most horrific forms of genocide befell European Jews and other ethnic groups under Adolf Hitler's reign of terror. The Nazi party murdered over 6 million Jews and millions of others of different ethnic groups, including European Gypsies. In Cambodia, the Communist ruler Pol Pot killed as many as 2 million people (one-fourth of the population) in what has become known as the "killing fields." Ethnic minorities such as people with Chinese ancestry or Muslims were favored targets in this genocidal campaign (Kiernan 1988). In 1994, in the country of Rwanda in Central Africa, the majority ethnic group (the Hutus) slaughtered some half-million ethnic Tutsis within a few weeks. Though genocidal policies have been condemned by recognized moral standards throughout the world, they have occurred time and again in human history.

ETHNICITY AND NATIONALISM

Another important aspect of ethnic relations examined by anthropologists is how nationalism influences ethnicity, and how ethnicity has an impact on nationalism. *Nationalism* is a set of symbols and beliefs providing the sense of belonging to a single political community. *Nationalism* involves a strong sense of loyalty, ideological commitment, and feelings of identification with a distinctive sovereign nation-state or country. A *nation-state* is a centralized political entity, exercising the legal authority to collect taxes, rule over a specific territory, and employ military force. The "classical" form of nationalism is a relatively new development, emerging in eighteenth- and nineteenth-century Europe and areas influenced by Europe. Before the development of this classical form of nationalism, the primary focus of loyalty was to the local community, a particular ruler, ethnicity, religion, and the family (Anderson 1991; Eriksen 2010; Gellner 1983). For example, in the agricultural states of Europe, most peasants rarely identified with the entire population within a specific territory. However, as industrialization uprooted many peoples from their traditional communities, and peasants moved from rural areas to large cities for employment, new forms of loyalty were demanded.

In industrializing states, with increases in literacy and mass education, nationalism became a unifying force of political expression. Print technology was particularly important because it helped to create what political scientist Benedict Anderson (1991) refers to as "imagined communities," an allegiance to a nation-state that is often far removed from everyday family or local concerns. As a literate populace began to read about their history and culture in their own language, they embarked on a new self-identification. In most cases, a particular language had to be legitimized by the government to serve as the basis of nationality. But eventually people began to express a source of pride in and loyalty to these newly defined countries. Anderson, though, is not suggesting that nationalism is just "invented," but holds that people who begin to define themselves as members of a nation will never know most of their fellow members, meet them, or even hear of them. He notes that the fact that people are willing to give up their lives for their nation or country means that nationalism has a powerful influence on people's emotions and sentiments.

Unlike nation-states, ethnic communities are as old as human prehistory, and ethnicity did not disappear with the development of nationalism. Some theorists argue that there is no radical break between the prenation ethnic communities and the evolution of nation-states. For example, Anthony

Smith proposes that most nations were fundamental continuities of earlier ethnic communities or revitalized ethnic communities (1981, 2009). He endorses the view that early ethnic communities used their myths of common ancestry, religion, and other cultural symbols to unify themselves and develop their nation-states around ethnicity. When one examines the development of classical nationalism in Europe (e.g., England, France, and Germany), Asia (e.g., Japan, China, and Korea), or other areas of the world, ethnicity does appear to play a significant role in the development of this form of classical nationalism.

The late anthropologists Clifford Geertz (1963) and Ernest Gellner (1991) distinguished two forms of nation-states in the contemporary world that draw on different forms of nationalism: civic and ethnic. Civic polities or nation-states attempt to unify a population on "universalistic criteria," regardless of their ethnicity, race, language, and religion. These civic polities try to gain allegiance and loyalty through a political creed that gives people equal political and social rights based on their individual choice. This political creed is usually a constitution or other political and legal documents that offer universal justice and equality to all of its citizens. In contrast, ethnic polities maintain that a citizen's allegiance and loyalty are based on their ethnicity into which they have been born or assigned to by the nation-state. In other words, their national loyalty overlaps considerably with their ethnicity and "particularistic features," which are transmitted and inherited through their cultural and symbolic traditions. As we will see in later chapters, as many parts of the world have become more ethnically diverse through globalization processes, many ethnically based polities are attempting to transform their states into civic polities. Nationmaking based on a political creed rather than ethnicity is a major phenomenon in many multiethnic societies.

Conversely, globalization has also resulted in the fragmentation of nation-states into smaller ethnic groups, which combine ethnicity and nationalism. In some cases, these ethnic groups may be minorities who perceive the "universalistic criteria" or the political creed–based political, legal, and social rights of civic polities as a *particularistic* expression of a dominant ethnic group. They view the imposition of language, culture, and the political creed of the dominant ethnic group as a form of cultural hegemony. To contest and resist this cultural hegemony, these ethnic groups may want to secede and develop their own ethnically based nation-states. Such ethnic secessionist developments are often called *ethnonationalist* movements. One question that arises is, how can these ethnic groups be nationalistic, when they really do not have their own nation-state? It would appear that these ethnonationalist movements are slightly different than the classical forms of nationalism. In some cases, the sentiments and emotions of nationalism may be "prior" to the actual formation of a nation-state. Obviously, these nationalist sentiments are indirectly influenced by the cultural milieu of nationalism expressed by the countries in which these ethnic groups are minorities. In Canada, for example, the Native American Indian peoples refer to themselves as "First Nations." Subsequently, as a way of expressing its sympathy with Native American Indian nationalist sentiments, the Canadian government uses the term *First Nation* as a label for Native American Indian communities. Many other indigenous people and ethnic minorities have expressed their identity in nationalistic terms, without actually having an existing nation-state.

Many ethnonationalist movements emerged in areas of the world that were once colonized by Europeans. Ethnonationalist movements played a role in the struggle against European colonialism. Leaders such as Mohandas Gandhi in India, Jomo Kenyatta in East Africa, and Simon Bolívar in Latin America mobilized new forms of ethnonationalism in order to free themselves from European colonialism. After independence, these new postcolonial societies had to form nation-states that incorporated disparate ethnic communities and cultures. In some instances, during the colonial period some ethnic groups had prospered more than others and this often resulted in postcolonial states in which ethnic

and cultural hegemony was prescribed by the dominant ethnic group. As yet, many of these postcolonial states have a very weakly developed sense of nationalism because ethnic minorities perceive their own local interests and culture as being undermined by the dominant ethnic group.

Another variation on the postcolonial ethnonationalist movements occurred with the downfall of the former Soviet Union and its satellite countries in Eastern Europe. Various ethnic minorities, such as the Latvians, Estonians, Lithuanians, Belorussians, Ukrainians, Georgians, Turkmens, Uzbeks, Azeris, Tajiks, and others, began to stress their ethnic identities and regional nationalism as the Soviet Empire began to collapse in the late 1980s. Historically, the Soviet Union was administered by 15 Soviet Socialist Republics that contained Autonomous Republics that were defined by ethnic groups or nationalities. However, under the orthodox Marxist ideology that provided the foundations for Soviet political policies, ethnic groups, or "ethnos," were supposed to "wither away" and be replaced by a Soviet "super-ethnicity." This was an attempt by the Soviet political elite to use its own version of nationalism, based on a political creed, to produce a civil polity (Banks 1996; Gellner 1988). In reality, none of these autonomous regions were allowed political rights, and they were strictly controlled by Soviet authorities in Moscow. Members of ethnic groups were subject to deportation or exile, and their boundaries were manipulated by the Soviet state.

In most cases, contrary to Marxist dogma, the various ethnic minorities did not abandon their cultural, linguistic, and religious traditions as expected. As the Soviet system began to disintegrate, a variety of ethnonationalist movements developed throughout the empire. In the aftermath of the dissolution of the Soviet Union, these ethnonationalist aspirations resulted in myriad newly independent countries. In Eastern Europe, as the communists lost their authority over Hungary, Czechoslovakia, Bulgaria, Romania, Poland, Yugoslavia, and East Germany, ethnonationalist movements materialized, which have had major consequences for these regions. For example, deep tensions between the ethnic Czechs and Slovaks led to the division of the former Czechoslovakia. Much more tragic results transpired in Yugoslavia, which will be discussed later in this text.

In general, globalization processes have been a major factor in the appearance of ethnonationalist movements (Friedman 1994, 2003). At times, regional and ethnic identities are intensified in a response to and as a defense against the growing impact of the wider world on their lives. Globalization processes usually result in the production of uniform forms of culture and identity that are imposed on local regions and ethnic groups. The communications media, including television, film, and the Internet, are diffusing particular forms of culture as globalization has an impact on all areas of the world. Some theorists have referred to this globalization process as the "McWorld tendency"—the proliferation of McDonalds, MacIntosh computers, and Mickey Mouse throughout the world (Barber and Schulz 1996). One response to these globalizing trends is a reassertion and revitalization of one's own ethnic and local identity leading to ethnonationalist movements. Many ethnic groups view these globalizing trends as a menacing process that tends to obliterate their own cultural traditions. Today, as a result, ethnonationalist movements include Scottish and Welsh nationalism in the United Kingdom, Catalan and Basque nationalism in Spain, Igbo nationalism in Nigeria, Kurdish nationalism in the Middle East, Quebecois nationalism in Canada, Sikh nationalism in India, and Native Hawaiian nationalism in the United States. These and many others will be discussed in later chapters.

CONCLUSION

Anthropological research on ethnicity has established that ethnicity is not simply an "innately based" propensity for human beings to bond together (Maybury-Lewis 1997). Instead, ethnicity is altered, modified, and asserted in differing historical, social, political, and cultural contexts. The centrality of culture, consisting of symbols, language, values, beliefs,

worldviews, myths, ideologies, and norms, has enabled anthropologists to understand and explain ethnic processes in many different societies. Anthropologists examine questions such as why and under what conditions ethnic groups develop cordial and peaceable relationships, and when and how ethnic conflict erupts.

One of the problems that anthropological studies of ethnicity have highlighted is that of stereotyping, or making generalizations about various ethnic groups. This problem is frequently referred to as essentialism. *Essentialism* is the tendency to reify a "culture" or an "ethnicity" as a separate totalistic entity and emphasize the boundedness and immutability of this entity. This was a deficiency of most early anthropological research on ethnicity. Early anthropologists overemphasized the boundedness of a particular ethnic group and its specific distinctiveness (Eriksen 2010). Thus, various peoples were categorized as Germans, Irish, Italians, British, Hispanics, Chinese, and so on. Anthropologists today view this as an abuse of the concept of culture. It reduces the complex behavior of people to the embodied creators and bearers of stereotyped ethnic traditions. This essentialist strategy usually exaggerated the internal homogeneity of the particular ethnic group and its manifest culture (Turner 1993). Contemporary anthropologists have been extremely wary of any totalistic generalizations about "races" or "ethnic groups." To combat these essentialist notions, anthropologists have to do deep, rich, fine-grained investigative research to illuminate the external and internal relations in ethnic processes.

This problem of essentialism is not just a challenge for anthropologists; it is a challenge for everyone. All humans classify the world and the people within the world into general categories. These general categories result in simplistic stereotypes and folk beliefs about "races" and "ethnic groups." These racial and ethnic mental images and stereotypes can become the foundations for *prejudice,* arbitrary beliefs and feelings toward an entire group of people. In some cases, essentialism also results in *discrimination,* the active denial of members of "racial" or "ethnic groups" the opportunity to enjoy equal access to human rights. Serious forms of prejudice and discrimination can create violence directed at an individual, or in extreme cases the annihilation of an entire group of people. Essentialism can be overcome by recognizing the complexities of ethnicity and realizing that these stereotypes and generalizations about "races" and "ethnic groups" do not stand up when subjected to empirical studies, critical thought, and analysis. The various studies by anthropologists, taken up in subsequent chapters, will enable you to perceive the inadequacies of essentialism and the dangers of stereotyping ethnic processes and interactions.

Notes

1. There were different understandings of the term *culture* in various European societies. In the nineteenth century, the French term *culture* was identified with "civilization," and represented the culmination of a progressive evolution of French civilization. The German word *kultur* was used by nineteenth-century intellectuals to refer to a romantic, emotional passionate feeling about one's language and nationality (Herder 1800). Like the French usage of *culture,* the British in the nineteenth century used culture to refer to civilization, and usually to indicate a superior form of European "British" civilization (Arnold 1873).

2. Some anthropologists attempt to mediate between the more material perspectives on human behavior and culture and the symbolic interpretive approach. For example, Dan Sperber (1996) advocates a theoretical program that begins with interpretation of symbolic representations, but suggests that anthropologists can complement this interpretive approach with explanations of human behavior and culture. In a book illustrating complementary approaches between the explanatory and interpretive approaches, James Peacock uses metaphors from photography (1986). Peacock refers to the anthropological lens that consists of "harsh light" and "soft focus." The "harsh light" concerns the basic realities of the human condition, including biological realities, whereas "soft focus" is the attempt to interpret the symbolic interconnections of human affairs.

3. The primordial tradition of ethnicity is an outgrowth of earlier sociological theories such as the distinction between *Gemeinschaft* and *Gesellschaft* developed by such German theorists as Ferdinand Toennies (1963). Geertz's perspective on ethnicity drew on the ideas of sociologist Edward Shils (1957).

4. Another version of the primordialist perspective is that of Pierre Van den Berghe, who takes a sociobiological view of ethnicity. In his book *The Ethnic Phenomenon* (1981), Van den Berghe suggests that family and kinship relations are the biological basis of ethnicity, and that humans are naturally motivated to aid in the reproduction of their own ethnic group. He believes that these biological ties are deep-seated and genetically based. Ultimately, these primordially based biological ties result in ethnic and racial competition throughout the world among different ethnic groups, resulting in slavery, colonialism, warfare, and the like. This biological version of primordialism has been criticized by many anthropologists, sociologists, and sociobiologists who refer to this view as "pop sociobiology." The most extensive review and critique of Van den Berghe's view is by anthropologist Richard Thompson in his *Theories of Ethnicity* (1989), chapter 2.

References Cited

ANDERSON, BENEDICT. 1991 [1983]. *Imagined Communities: Reflections on the Origins and Spread of Nationalism.* 2nd edition. London: Verso.

ARNOLD, MATTHEW. 1873. *Literature and Dogma.* London: Macmillan.

BANKS, MARCUS. 1996. *Ethnicity: Anthropological Constructions.* London: Routledge.

BARBER, BENJAMIN, and ANDREA SCHULZ, eds. 1996. *Jihad vs. McWorld: How Globalism and Tribalism Are Reshaping the World.* New York: Ballantine.

BARTH, FREDRIK, ed. 1998 [1969]. *Ethnic Groups and Boundaries: The Social Organization of Culture Difference.* Prospect Heights, IL: Waveland Press.

COHEN, ABNER. 1969. *Custom and Politics in Urban Africa.* London: Routledge.

———. 1974. *Two-Dimensional Man.* London: Tavistock.

D'ANDRADE, ROY, and CLAUDIA STRAUSS, eds. 1992. *Human Motives and Cultural Models.* New York: Cambridge University Press.

DOMINGUEZ, VIRGINIA R. 1986. *White by Definition: Social Classification in Creole Louisiana.* New Brunswick, NJ: Rutgers University Press.

ELLER, JACK, and REED COUGHLAN. 1993. The poverty of primordialism: The demystification of ethnic attachments. *Ethnic and Racial Studies* 16(2):183–202.

ERIKSEN, THOMAS HYLLAND. 2010. *Ethnicity and Nationalism: Anthropological Perspectives.* 3rd edition. London: Pluto Press.

FISHMAN, JOSHUA. 1980. Social theory and ethnography. In *Ethnic Diversity and Conflict in Eastern Europe.* Peter Sugar, ed. Pp. 84–97. Santa Barbara, CA: ABC-Clio.

FRIEDMAN, JONATHAN. 1994. *Cultural Identity and Global Process.* London: Sage.

———, ed. 2003. *Globalization, the State, and Violence.* Walnut Creek, CA: AltaMira Press.

GEERTZ, CLIFFORD. 1963 [1973]. The integrative revolution: Primordial sentiments and civil politics in the new states. In *The Interpretation of Cultures.* Clifford Geertz, ed. Pp. 255–310. New York: Basic Books.

GELLNER, ERNEST. 1983. *Nations and Nationalism.* Oxford: Oxford University Press.

———, ed. 1988 [1977]. *State and Society in Soviet Thought.* Oxford: Blackwell.

———. 1991. *Plough, Sword, and Book: The Structure of Human History.* London: Paladin.

HARRIS, MARVIN. 1964. *Patterns of Race in the Americas.* New York: Norton.

———. 1979. *Cultural Materialism: The Struggle for a Science of Culture.* New York: Random House.

———. 1999. *Theories of Culture in Postmodern Times.* Walnut Creek, CA: Altamira Press.

HERDER, JOHANN GOTTFRIED. 1967 [1800]. *Outlines of a Philosophy of the History of Man.* T. O. Churchill, trans. London: Luke Hansard.

HOSTETLER, JOHN A. 1980. *Amish Society.* 3rd edition. Baltimore, MD: Johns Hopkins University Press.

HUTCHINSON, JOHN, and ANTHONY D. SMITH, eds. 1996. *Ethnicity.* Oxford: Oxford: University Press.

KEPHART, WILLIAM M., and WILLIAM ZELLNER. 1994. *Extraordinary Groups: The Sociology of Unconventional Life Styles.* 4th edition. New York: St. Martin's.

KIERNAN, BEN. 1988. Orphans of genocide: The Cham Muslims of Kampuchea under Pol Pot. *Bulletin of Concerned Asian Scholars* 20(4):2–33.

KUPER, LEO, and M. G. SMITH, eds. 1969. *Pluralism in Africa.* Los Angeles, CA: University of California Press.

MAYBURY-LEWIS, DAVID. 1997. *Indigenous Peoples, Ethnic Groups, and the State.* Boston, MA: Allyn & Bacon.

MOERMAN, MICHAEL. 1965. Who are the Lue? Ethnic identification in a complex civilization. *American Anthropologist* 67:1215–1229.

PEACOCK, JAMES L. 1986. *The Anthropological Lens: Harsh Light, Soft Focus.* Cambridge: Cambridge University Press.

PORTES, ALEJANDRO, and MIN ZHOU. 1994. The new second generation: Segmented assimilation and its variants. *Annals of the American Academy of Political and Social Science* 530:74–96.

QUINN, NAOMI, and DOROTHY HOLLAND, eds. 1987. *Cultural Models in Language and Thought.* Cambridge: Cambridge University Press.

REDFIELD, ROBERT, and MELVILLE HERSKOVITS. 1936. Memorandum on the study of acculturation. *American Anthropologist* 38:149–152.

ROSS, NORBERT. 2004. *Culture and Cognition: Implications for Theory and Method.* Thousand Oaks, CA: Sage Publications.

SAHLINS, MARSHALL. 1976. *Culture and Practical Reason.* Chicago, IL: University of Chicago Press.

SHILS, EDWARD. 1957. Primordial, personal, sacred and civil ties. *British Journal of Sociology* 7:113–145.

SIMPSON, JOHN A., and EDMUND S. C. WEINER. 1989. *Ethnic.* vol. 5. *Oxford English Dictionary.* 2nd edition. Oxford: Clarendon Press.

SMITH, ANTHONY. 1981. *The Ethnic Revival in the Modern World.* Cambridge: Cambridge University Press.

———. 1986. *The Ethnic Origins of Nations.* Oxford: Blackwell.

———. 2009. *Ethno-symbolism and Nationalism: A Cultural Approach.* London: Routledge.

SPERBER, DAN. 1996. *Explaining Culture: A Naturalistic Approach.* Oxford, England: Blackwell Publishers.

SPERBER, DAN and LAWRENCE HIRSCHFELD. 1999. Evolution, cognition, and culture. In *MIT Encyclopedia of the Cognitive Sciences.* Frank Kiel and Robert Wilson, eds. Cambridge, MA: MIT Press.

TAMBIAH, STANLEY. 1989. Ethnic Conflict in the World Today. *American Ethnologist* 16(2):335–349.

THOMPSON, RICHARD H. 1989. *Theories of Ethnicity: A Critical Appraisal.* New York: Greenwood Press.

TOENNIES, FERDINAND. 1963 [1887]. *Community and Society (Gemeinschaft and Gesellschaft).* New York: Harper & Row.

TURNER, TERENCE. 1993. Anthropology and multiculturalism: What is anthropology that multiculturalists should be mindful of it? *Cultural Anthropology* 8(4):411–429.

TYLOR, EDWARD. 1958 [1871]. *Primitive Cultures.* 2 vols. London: Torchbooks.

VAN DEN BERGHE, Pierre L. 1981. *The Ethnic Phenomenon.* New York: Elsevier.

5

Ethnicity and Ethnocentrism: Are They Natural?

Donald E. Brown, *University of California, Santa Barbara*

Ethnocentrism—a preference for one's own kind and their ways—is a pervasive, and often profoundly unfortunate, feature of present-day life. But it is nothing new, and there is little reason to think that it flourishes more today than in the historic past. Ethnocentrism is such a robust phenomenon that it was recognized as a human universal well over 2,000 years ago. The ancient Greek historian and traveler Herodotus tells the story of King Darius noting the mutual horror expressed by certain Greeks and Indians when they were called before the king and told how each treated the bodies of their deceased fathers. Herodotus concluded that all peoples were "convinced that their own usages far surpass those of all others" (*Persian Wars,* Book III, 38).

The universality of ethnocentrism remains almost entirely unquestioned to this day.[1] William Graham Sumner (1906), who coined the term *ethnocentrism,* assigned it a highly important role in shaping both the relationships between peoples and many of the internal dynamics of their societies. Sumner argued, for example, that ethnocentrism served to strengthen respect for a society's customs and usages, and that conflict with outsiders would typically result in a strengthening of this tendency. Sumner, like Herodotus, put stress on the preference for the ways or customs of one's own kind. But it is important to note that the preference for one's own kind—one's own people—is as much a part of ethnocentrism as the preference for their ways or customs.

Note: Earlier versions of this chapter were given at Arizona State University, at the University of Michigan, at a 1996 conference in Stockholm on Human Behavior and Evolutionary Biology sponsored by the Royal Swedish Academy of Sciences, and at the 68th annual meeting of the Southwestern Anthropological Association (Brown 1997). The author received valuable comments from attendees at all those occasions, as well as from David Berreby, Francisco Gil-White, and Raymond Scupin on this version.

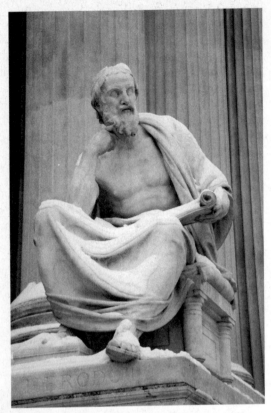

Herodotus (Greek historian, 484 – 425 B.C.).

Equally important is that from Sumner's writing onward "ethnocentrism" has been something of a misnomer, as it has not been confined to ethnic settings:

Ethnocentrism is by no means confined to tribes and nations. It manifests itself in social groups of all kinds—families, . . . local communities, classes, castes, sects, races, etc.—and assumes such diverse and developed forms as nationalism, patriotism and chauvinism, family pride, class consciousness, sectionalism, religious intolerance and race prejudice. [Sumner 1906:613]

Although Sumner envisaged ethnocentrism as having evolved in the context of intersocietal relations among hunters and gatherers, he was very much concerned with its manifestations, by extension, in all sorts of intergroup settings within modern societies and among the nation-states of the modern world (where he saw it as sometimes giving rise to dire consequences). Thus, Sumner also coined the terms *in-group* or *we-group* and *out-group* or *others-group* as settings for what might be called a generic we-centrism that occurs even in nonethnic settings. The phrase *in-group bias* has come to designate this generic phenomenon. Thus, when referring to interethnic relations, in-group bias and ethnocentrism are simply synonyms. Studies of the various components of ethnocentrism have often been conducted in the more generic settings of in-group bias. Some of the illustrations given in this chapter are from the generic settings.[2]

Twenty-five years after Sumner's writings, an influential encyclopedia entry on ethnocentrism (Murdock 1931) expanded both on its complexity and the extent to which its basic elements are not confined to ethnic contexts. Much later, in an exhaustive survey of the concept of ethnocentrism, Le Vine and Campbell (1971) formulated what they called the "the universal syndrome of ethnocentrism," a set of features that either define ethnocentrism or are closely related to it in all societies.

A revised version of the syndrome will be presented here, but I will substitute "complex" for "syndrome." "Complex" denotes an objectively observed set of co-occurring traits, not necessarily negative or abnormal. Two qualifications to this revision should be noted. One is that toward the end of the description of the complex a few features will be included that are not universal in the usual sense of that term. The reasons for their inclusion will be explained at that time. The other is that, for reasons that will be given later, the existence of its universal complex suggests the possibility that ethnocentrism—and ethnicity, too—might be fundamentally natural rather than cultural. This possibility and its implications will be discussed after the complex is described.

The list of elements in the complex begins at the very basic level of group formation, which, like in-group bias, includes but is not confined to, ethnic settings.[3]

THE ETHNOCENTRIC COMPLEX

1. *Group thinking, collective thinking (the reification or entification of collectivities when physically all we have is individuals).* In the United States one talks and thinks about blacks, Asian Americans, Anglos, and many, many more groups and categories (that even include such entities as General Motors, or Amazon.com, or California, or the United Kingdom) as though they were entities or actors in our social order. Similarly, in Rwanda one might hear that "both the Tutsi and Hutu look down on the Twa" or in Malaysia that "the Chinese control the economy." The extent to which the members of any imagined entity of this sort really do act in concert or get treated as a unit is highly variable. Nonetheless, peoples everywhere assume that individuals do coalesce into social entities (some of the general issues are summarized in Brown [1976]; studies of the cognitive means by which humans create and perceive ethnicity are summarized in Brubaker et al. [2004]; see also item 30 below).

2. *Individuals identifying with collectivities, and assuming or projecting such identifications on the part of others.* Asian Americans or Native Americans, Germans or Russians, Hutu or Tutsi, along with many other human groupings—ethnic and nonethnic—are, in important senses, only imaginary entities, made real ("entified") by the individuals who share in the imagination and act accordingly. Cross-culturally, the strength, exclusivity, and permanence of such identifications are quite variable—giving way to the great fluidity of many modern societies, in which ethnic identities overlap, nest inside one another, are created anew, are falsely claimed, and allow individuals to shift their sense of ethnic identity from moment to moment depending on context (see, e.g., Berreby 2005; Haley and Wilcoxon 2005; Keyes 1981; Waters 1990).

3. *Division into in-group and out-group members, we–they, we–others.* Whereas "we" can be an ethny,4 a race, or a nationality, it can also be a family, a group of friends, a village, a nation, or myriad other entities.

4. *Endowing collectivities with continuity/ perpetuity, so that past actions are relevant to the present.* Americans have no difficulty in imagining that Native Americans regret "their" losses to settlers, mostly of European origin, who founded, peopled, and expanded the United States. And yet the regret is felt now, while the loss occurred generations ago, to persons long deceased. Similarly, the modern state of Israel was founded by persons many of whose ancestors had not lived in Israel for many, many generations but who had millennia-old claims upon the land. In all such cases, living individuals identify with and are identified by others as having a tie with long-deceased members of a category or group of people that persists as an actor among the social entities of human imagination.

5. *In-group badging.* Whether it is a distinct language or dialect, a tribal hairstyle, a taste in food or music, the business suit, the jargon of a profession or occupation, or a multitude of other such patterns, people everywhere have characteristics that mark who is in their category or group and by which they are set off from outsiders.

6. *Stranger-recognition mechanisms.* By failing to exhibit the appropriate in-group "badges"—for example, by having a different accent or language, different means of deporting oneself, and different tastes and habits—individuals are identified as being strangers, others, not members of one's in-group(s).

7. *Marked sensitivity to out-group markers.* Not only do humans notice differences of accent, gait, and the like, but they are very sensitive to them—seemingly without any special instruction. It appears to be the case that humans cannot train themselves to not notice accents different from their own.

8. *(Relative) peace (cooperation) inside, conflict (noncooperation) outside.* Within any particular group, there is greater willingness to cooperate and to resolve conflict than there is with strangers or outsiders.

9. *Greater empathy with members of the in-group.* Humans are more concerned with what happens to their fellows, the persons of their kind, than with what happens to strangers. This pattern is found even among those societies with universalistic ethics. Thus, Christians are generally more concerned with the welfare of other Christians than with non-Christians. The saying that "charity begins at home" expresses this idea. "Germany for Germans" is the slogan for those opposed to recent immigration trends in Germany.

10. *Lack of empathy, or a heightened threshold for empathy, for outsiders.* From chuckles over the misfortunes of rivals, or the ready thought that "they had it coming to them," this is very much a part of everyday life. In extreme forms it is pleasure in out-group misfortunes, even of the most tragic sort. In his seminal work on the (ethnically) plural society, J. S. Furnivall (1956:150, 306, 308) identified the absence or weakness of a "common social will" as one of its distinctive features. That absence resulted from the diminished concern the members of each ethnic segment of the society had for the welfare of their fellow humans in the other segments. (See also item 28 below.)

11. *Mistrust of those in the out-group.* This is one of the most frequently reported elements in the complex. In its stronger forms, it becomes fear or even a sort of paranoia. Among the numerous examples is the suspicion among some African Americans that AIDS is a disease designed by white scientists to wipe them out, or the fear of villagers in various places that outsiders will kidnap their children to harvest their organs for transplants. In an early twentieth-century collection of stereotypical sayings about the members of various castes in India, which were and are envisaged by many Hindus as distinct races (Béteille 1967), mistrust was one of the commonest themes. Among the sayings about Brahmans, for example, was "Trust a pariah [outcaste] in ten things, a Brahman in none" (Risley 1915:306). In its consequences, Adolf Hitler's paranoid fear of Jews is surely the most horrendous case we know of (Herf 2006). Political fear mongering derives its potency from this propensity to mistrust the out-group.

12. *Assuming the worst of out-group members; giving the benefit of a doubt to in-group members.* In spite of the commonplace belief that there are two sides to every story, humans more readily accept the stories told by those in their in-group and are more likely to doubt the stories told by those in out-groups.

13. *The out-group's saints/heroes are the in-group's devils.* In part, this is perhaps an exaggerated form of the preceding item. Examples can be read in our newspapers on almost any day, as in the vilification of Saddam Hussein, Fidel Castro, and many others who, to many of their countrymen, were or are heroes. As one writer to a newspaper put it, "The Palestinian terrorists . . . are considered heroes by the Palestinians; we think of them as criminals."

14. *Ethical dualism.* As in our own society, it is almost always wrong to kill within the group—for that is murder—but glory may be achieved by killing out-group members, even in great numbers. (If not glory, then greater or lesser degrees of indifference.) Similar attitudes and practices prevail with respect to lying to or stealing from out-group members. Sasanka Perera captured the issues in the attitudes of many Buddhist Sinhalese of Sri Lanka:

> Here we are faced with a contradiction in terms of Buddhist ethics and common sense: it is barbaric for Tamil militants to kill defenseless Sinhalese civilians, but it is not barbaric for the military to massacre Tamil civilians in the guise of anti-terrorist operations. The [Sinhalese] head of the household who recounted the many massacres of Sinhalese peasants was genuinely grieving and angry about the incidents. He made the following statement in the same conversation:
>
> "One of my friends in the army told me that when they move through a village in the north not even a cat is left alive. That is the way these Tamils should be treated. They are getting too big for their boots." [1991:94–95]

15. *Loss/absence of objectivity.* While this is fundamental to ethnocentrism or in-group bias, it probably takes various distinct forms. It is acknowledged in phrases like "the first casualty when war comes is truth." It drives home the point that ethnocentrism is a state of mind, in its extreme forms almost like an altered state of consciousness, in that the ethnocentric mind processes everyday information in a distinctly distorted manner. This feature deserves more extended discussion.

The cognitive distortions that result from in-group bias are so obvious that already in the fourteenth century the Arab historian ibn Khaldun identified a form of this bias as the first among his reasons for why falsehoods are so common in the historical record:

> If the soul is infected with partisanship for a particular opinion or sect, it accepts without a moment's hesitation the information that is agreeable to it. Prejudice and partisanship obscure the critical faculty and preclude critical investigation. The result is that false-hoods are accepted and transmitted. [1958:71]

However, as perceptive as ibn Khaldun's observation is, it understates the problem. It is not only in the transmission of information that bias occurs; it occurs, too, in the perceptions of eyewitnesses. Two extraordinary studies are particularly revelatory of the phenomenon. The first study (Hastorf and Cantril 1954) revealed the sharply divergent perceptions reported by the supporters of Princeton and Dartmouth at an unusually rough football game. It was the last game of the season for both teams. Princeton was unbeaten and its star player had just appeared on the cover of *Time* magazine. The game took a nasty turn early on, and many penalties were called. Princeton's star was removed from the game with a broken nose and mild concussion, and a Dartmouth player suffered a broken leg. Reports and analyses in the press conflicted wildly.

Hastorf and Cantril conducted a follow-up study, in which some of their subjects were

eyewitnesses to the game and others only saw a movie of the game. Disagreements about what happened in the game, and how to characterize those happenings, were substantial. Even on more objective matters—such as the number of infractions and characterizations of their severity—supporters of the two sides who viewed the same movie differed sharply. Hastorf and Cantril concluded that "the 'same' sensory impingements emanating from the football field, transmitted through the visual mechanism to the brain, . . . gave rise to different experiences in different people" (1954:132).

The second study, and one more directly related to ethnicity, demonstrated the same phenomenon but under more controlled conditions in which supporters of Israel and of the Palestinian Arabs watched the same television news reports of the 1982 Beirut massacre, and then judged the extent to which the news reports were biased (Vallone et al. 1985). The partisans of each side found that the reports were so (intentionally!) biased against their side that they felt that neutral observers seeing the same news reports would come away with a more unfavorable view of their side. On a seemingly objective task—counting the negative and positive statements about Israel in the reports—the supporters of each side arrived at sharply contrasting numbers.

The authors of the study concluded that basic cognitive and perceptual mechanisms seemed to be involved, so that the disagreements between the two sets of partisans were not just over evaluation of what they had seen but over the very content of what was seen. A particularly depressing finding of the study was that those subjects who judged themselves to be more knowledgeable about Near Eastern affairs tended to arrive at the stronger perceptions of bias against their side. So, too, did those who judged themselves most emotionally involved in the issues.

The authors noted that what they examined experimentally is in fact an everyday observation: that partisans regularly find strong support for their positions in what neutrals see as ambiguous. What should be stressed is that the observers on both sides in cases like this very often consider their assessments to have been "obvious," which is evidence that their minds have tricked them, so to say, and that they are not intentionally trying to deceive.

The implications of these findings for ethnic relations are sobering indeed. They suggest, for example, that even mutually fair treatment may be perceived—by each party to a conflict or competition—as systematically biased against them.

16. *Certitude, moral certitude.* The normal skepticism that we might exercise in our everyday affairs is regularly suspended when judgments cross the boundary between in-group and out-group. The judgments we make about our heroes and their devils, who is the victim, who the most unfair, and so on appear to be "obviously" true.

17. *Degrading or dehumanizing the out-group.* Outsiders are often seen as deficient in morality, decency, or intelligence, with the extreme lying in a denial of the humanity of the out-group. Certain untouchable, outcaste groups among the Japanese (described in De Vos and Wagatsuma 1967) were so despised that they were referred to with an extended hand, thumb folded under the palm, with the four fingers hanging down like the legs of an animal—to symbolize their animality. In Rwanda, Tutsi and Hutu alike referred "half-jokingly" to the very small minority of pygmoid Twa among them as "more akin to monkeys than to human beings" (Maquet 1961:10).

18. *In-group pride.* The emotional side of ethnocentrism must not be ignored (see, e.g., Scheff 1994). Building pride in an organized group—whether an army, a school, a nationality, or an ethnic or racial group—is a serious business everywhere. Ethnic pride and shame are significant concerns in present-day polyethnic states, where perceptions of shame often lead easily to rage. Humans can be very sensitive to possible insult, as when individuals find jokes about their ethny less funny than others do. (See also item 26 below.)

19. *Discrimination.* This term refers to the very wide range of actions taken on the basis of ethnocentrism, as when persons of a particular race or national origin are not allowed to hold certain occupations or live in certain areas, or are denied education, or are denied voting rights—to give but a few examples from modern societies. Discrimination may be unconscious as well as conscious.

20. *Stereotyping.* This consists of two elements: simplification, such that a few traits come to stand for the full complexity that collections of individuals everywhere possess; and the generalization of those few traits to all members of the category being stereotyped (i.e., ignoring the individuality of out-group members). Stereotypes are attached to all sorts of groups, and in some cases provide the ideological underpinning for social order. Thus stereotypes between northerners and southerners are as vigorous in Italy (Romanucci-Ross 1975) as in the United States; and stereotypes are a central feature of the racially conceptualized caste system of Hindu India (see, e.g., Sinha and Sinha 1967).

21. *Ignoring or downplaying others in myth-history while focusing on the in-group.* In modern societies, such as the United States, this tendency is now countered by attempts to produce more "inclusive" histories. In many other societies, out-groups are just not mentioned. In the myth-histories of yet other societies, out-groups are singled out for vilification, as was the case for Jews in many European images of the past.

22. *Judging others in the in-group's terms.* Familiar examples abound, as when the haves and have-nots, or men and women, or capitalists and socialists each employ their own perspectives, values, and insights to assess those whose experiences have been so different. Interethnically, this item in the complex may be an inevitable effect of linguistic and cultural differences, which pose particular difficulties in grasping other peoples' perspectives and worldviews. The relativistic attitude and the development of the intellectual tools required to grasp other people's perspectives have been rare accomplishments in human history.

23. *Scapegoating, and a generalized tone of praise and blame in discussions of inter-group relations.*   Scapegoating consists of blaming the out-group for one's problems. A familiar example is the blame put on Jews in Nazi Germany. In a striking example from Sri Lanka, Perera found a consensus even among high school teachers that "all our problems are the result of terrorism by Tamil guerrillas and the separatist demand by the Tamil United Liberation Front" (1991:152).

24. *Endogamy.*   Probably most individuals everywhere tend to marry within their own ethny, and among many peoples it is a conscious or cultural preference. But it may also be an accidental tendency resulting from such underlying factors as a general tendency to marry persons nearby or to more easily establish amicable relations with persons of similar culture and language. Moreover, there are clear exceptions to endogamy, as when individuals in relatively small minority groups, scattered throughout a larger population, find themselves more frequently marrying outside their group—as is true today among Japanese Americans and Jewish Americans. Yet even in these cases, the tendency toward endogamy may still result in statistically disproportionate tendencies to marry one's own kind.[5]

25. *Intensification of ethnocentric tendencies in times of internal crises.*   During economic downturns, for example, existing tensions between groups intensify. One manifestation is the rise and fall of hostility to immigrants in U.S. history: when times are good, immigrants are more welcome; when times are bad, they are less welcome. (On the other hand, it should be noted that existing tensions within a society may be muted to meet with greater unanimity an external crisis—for example, conflict with parties who are even more outsiders.)

26. *Some sort of vicious cycle or "feeling trap."*   An example of a feeling trap occurs when one is embarrassed, notes that others have sensed the embarrassment, and then feels all the

more embarrassed; the others note the deeper confusion, which is yet further embarrassing, and on and on (Scheff and Retzinger 1991:104). The sociologist Thomas Scheff (1994) has argued that feeling traps of spiraling shame and rage figure importantly in ethnocentrism and large-scale intergroup violence. The phrase "cycle of violence," often applied to situations such as that between Palestinians and Jews in Israel, or between the Tamils and Sinhalese in Sri Lanka (Tambiah 1986), refers to conditions that are at least partly set or kept in motion by feeling traps.

27. *Sensitivity to out-group coalitional tendencies.*   This is not documented in all societies but in enough to suggest that it is probably a near-universal. It is often expressed as a dislike of clannishness. The Sinhalese of Sri Lanka, for example, have "the strong impression that the Tamils are 'clannish,' 'communal-minded,' and motivated to form strong networks to protect and promote their interests" (Tambiah 1986:105). Perera quotes a Sinhalese college student claiming that the Tamils "always stick together" (1991:97).

28. *Ignoring the concerns of subordinate out-groups.*   This trait logically follows, and is an implication of, item 10 above. But as familiar as it may be in modern settings, it applies only in plural societies. Hence it is a "conditional universal": given a specified condition (in this case the condition is ethnic plurality), it always appears.

29. *Ghettoization, niche-exploiting.*   This is another conditional universal, occurring regularly in the context of plural societies. It refers to the tendency of members of specific ethnies to be confined to particular locations and/or particular occupations, professions, or other economic specializations. Where it is imposed upon groups, ghettoization seems the better term. Where it is more a matter of choice, niche-exploiting seems appropriate. Many cases may, of course, straddle the boundary.

Among the numerous striking examples was the sudden dominance of immigrant Cambodians in doughnut retail shops in California (Akst 1993) and the dominance of

Koreans in shops in African American inner-city neighborhoods, a pattern that developed initially from Korean domination of the wig industry that sprang up to provide Afro wigs (Yoon 1991:165–169). In the old capital of Brunei (a Malay sultanate in northwest Borneo), its various wards were economically specialized, and each ward claimed a distinctive origin, virtually a distinct ethnic identity (Brown 1976:157–158). South of Brunei, in Kuching, Sarawak (now a part of Malaysia), the various Chinese subethnies (Cantonese, Hokkien, etc.) specialized in and sometimes monopolized one or another occupation or craft (Brown 1976:152–157). The caste system of Hindu India, in which each caste was associated with particular occupations, is among the many other examples.

30. *The essentialization of ethnies.*   This item might more properly be called a hypothesized innate universal. What is meant by this is that the members of particular ethnies are conceived as having an inner essence that makes them what they are. Because they are "essentialized," ethnies are perceived as distinct human "kinds," analogous to species (Gil-White 2001; Hirschfeld 1996). In the modern world, the essentialization of ethnies is more unambiguous in racial than in ethnic classifications, but there is little doubt that throughout the world a great many peoples conceive of what we would call ethnic differences as very much like racial differences.

DISCUSSION

Although the list of elements in the universal complex of ethnocentrism raises numerous issues, only two will be addressed here. One is a cautionary statement concerning the sorts of refinements the list requires. The other is the large issue of whether the complex is natural or cultural, and what the implications of this would be.

Clearly, the list needs more specification of the kinds and ranges of conditions that elicit each item and the ranges or variant forms that responses

take. For example, in item 7, I noted that detecting accents is obligate; one cannot turn off that feature of the mind. By contrast, stereotyping, discriminating, and other elements of the complex are more optional or open-ended in nature and more variable in their range of intensity (even though they occur in all societies and probably in all individuals). More needs to be said (or known) about the conditions that elicit those responses. Fortunately, these are topics of considerable ongoing research.

Another refinement concerns ordering the items in relation to each other. Some may be core features, some more peripheral; some may be preconditions to others, and surely there are other forms of interaction between the items. It is tempting to think, for example, that identification of an individual as either a member of the in-group or out-group (by noting badges or their absence) in some fundamental sense "frames" the subsequent processing of information on him or her and thus switches one's mind-set and behaviors between those designed for the in-group and those designed for out-groups. A *frame,* which is a term derived from cognitive science, must be built into any computational system (as in a computer or a mind) to guide the processing of what would otherwise be overly cumbersome masses of informational input (Tooby and Cosmides 1989:34).

A study by Warnecke et al. (1992) gives intriguing clues about how such a framing process works. In this study, American subjects watched (without accompanying audio) unidentified televised leaders from France, Germany, and the United States. The subjects felt more negatively toward the foreigners, but this effect disappeared when the images were accompanied by audio. Apparently, the subjects detected differences in facial expressions and deportment in the foreign leaders and thus saw them as strangers, perhaps not to be trusted. But when sound was added, the foreigners, though still different, could be identified as friendly—the allies of Americans—and the wariness or mistrust of strangers declined. Thus the different sets of badges or markers to be scanned triggered two different frames: one for strangers, another for allies.

In spite of the tasks that remain to refine the description of the ethnocentric complex, enough is already known to emphatically raise the question of whether it—including ethnicity itself—is natural, whether it is a feature (or set of features) of human nature. This possibility is suggested by the universality and complexity of the complex and by other evidence, too. Let us explore some of the issues.

To begin, why does a universal complex suggest nature instead of culture? Much of the explanation can be found in conventional anthropological thought. Cultural anthropologists have often assumed that if a phenomenon is universal—that is, is found among all peoples, past as well as present—then there is some likelihood that in some direct manner it must reflect human nature rather than environmental circumstances.[6] This is because our humanity goes with us everywhere, whereas most environmental influences on human life—whether physical or sociocultural—vary considerably from place to place and time to time. That the ethnocentric complex is complex, as well as universal, even more strongly suggests that human nature is involved, since its complexity makes ethnocentrism even less likely to have developed everywhere in the same form either by accident or through the usually highly variable forms of cultural development.

Beyond its universality and complexity, the principal lines of evidence that ethnocentrism, including ethnicity, is natural consist of signs of psychological preparedness in humans. "Preparedness" refers to a capacity to learn something relatively easily. For example, humans are innately prepared to learn language (Pinker 1994) but not to memorize strings of random numbers (computers are roughly the opposite). Often, preparedness manifests itself in a particular period of maturation of the individual, called a "critical" or "sensitive period" (see Seligman and Hager 1972 for a general review of these matters).

Lawrence Hirschfeld's *Race in the Making* (1996) provides highly relevant evidence for preparedness. Although an anthropologist, his work is rooted in experimental psychology and an approach to discovering features of human nature by exploring child development to determine whether the mind seems specially prepared to think about particular topics in particular ways. Hirschfeld found that very young children acquire racial conceptions so easily and, in the earliest ages, in theory-like forms sufficiently unlikely to have been learned from their elders, that one must conclude that the human mind is innately prepared to think about "human kinds."[7] "Theory-like" means that children have certain assumptions or expectations about human kinds. The *specific* kinds—Swede, American, Navajo, Yanomamo, Malay, Chicano, Korean, black, white, and so on—that we classify under the heading of "ethnic" or "racial" kinds are *not* given in nature and, typically, are appropriately analyzed in terms of social, cultural, political, economic, and historical factors.

Hirschfeld's findings suggest that humans have a functionally specialized mental faculty—a "mental module"[8]—for thinking about human kinds. The specific set of ethnic or racial categories found among particular peoples results from an *interaction* between this module and its propensities, on the one hand, and the specific social, cultural, political, economic, and historical setting of those peoples, on the other. This formulation goes a long way toward resolving the uncertainty among social scientists as to whether ethnicity, including racial thinking, is a product of time and place or is something "primordial." In very important senses it is both (see also Gil-White 1999).

It is important to stress that Hirschfeld is *not* arguing that specifically *racial* thinking is natural in the sense that it is an evolved characteristic, an adaptation. On the contrary, it is an "effect," which is a by-product of one or more other adaptations.[9] As Hirschfeld (1996:13) correctly notes, whatever the reality of racial differences they would have been very rarely observed in the environments in which humans evolved: during nearly all of human evolution, humans did not have the ability to travel the distances required for anything approaching common observation of racial differences.[10] And unless the differences were recurrently observed, there would be little likelihood of any evolutionary adaptation to them. Thus, Hirschfeld argues that racial thinking "parasitizes" our adaptation to think about, perceive, and pay attention to human kinds.

What Hirschfeld means by this is, first, that the human mind is functionally specialized (and presumably adapted) to readily distinguish children from adults or male from female, and to be attuned to the differences between peoples. Such differences might include the culturally variable styles of dress, ornament, and deportment from one society to another, but might also include reputed differences that are not readily observed. Second, this specialization to detect different human kinds works just as well—and hence is parasitized—to detect racial differences. It is as if the racial differences so readily observed in the modern world mimic the cultural differences that humans had observed for hundreds of thousands of years.[11]

Note that some evidence concerning the theory-like way that humans innately think about human kinds suggests that it is quite close to racial thinking as indicated in item 30 of the ethnocentric complex. According to Hirschfeld's findings, humans tend to naturalize human kinds—that is, to consider them as "naturally" occurring and possessing an inner *essence* that distinguishes them from other kinds (see also Gil-White 2001). Racial thinking is one means of doing this. That human kinds are natural is the "theory" (or default assumption, so to say) that human minds tend to impose upon their perceptions of human kinds.

As Hirschfeld summarizes the evidence, humans are psychologically prepared to conceptualize, perceive, and reason about human kinds, which include what he calls "ethnoraces" (1996:20–21). What this term indicates, apparently, is the tendency of the human mind to impose upon the ethnies it perceives or imagines a "theory" that treats them much like races.

The other line of evidence for preparedness is related to in-group bias and is shown by an extensive body of data that refers to what are called "minimal-group" studies. These consist of attempts to discover how little it takes to make individuals think in terms of we–they and to prefer the we. *Very* little is required:

In numerous experiments by Henri Tajfel and other social psychologists, people are divided into two groups, actually at random but ostensibly by some trivial criterion such as whether they underestimate or overestimate the number of dots on a screen or whether they prefer the paintings of Klee or Kandinsky. The people in each group instantly dislike and think worse of the people in the other group, and act to withhold rewards from them even if doing so is costly to their own group. This instant ethnocentrism can be evoked even if the experimenter drops the charade with the dots or paintings and divides people into groups by flipping a coin before their eyes! The behavioral consequences are by no means minor. In a classic experiment, the social psychologist Muzafir Sherif carefully selected a group of well-adjusted, middle-class American boys for a summer camp, and randomly divided them into two groups which then competed in sports and skits. Within days the groups were brutalizing and raiding each other with sticks, bats, and rocks in socks, forcing the experimenters to intervene for the boys' safety. [Pinker 1997:513–514, with references on 586; for a lengthier summary, see Rabbie 1992; for a caveat, see Mummendey et al. 1992]

Not only does in-group bias appear to be something for which we humans are strongly prepared, there is even reason to think that this preparedness has truly ancient roots. Since coalitional behavior occurs among chimpanzees (deWaal 1982) and other species (Harcourt and de Waal 1992), it is entirely possible—indeed, likely—that in-group bias in some form predates the formation of ethnies, which are uniquely human (Kurzban, Tooby, and Cosmides 2001).

In sum, there is indeed evidence beyond its universality to suggest that ethnicity/ethnocentrism is natural. Although evidence on behalf of this proposition falls short of a conclusive demonstration that it is in fact correct, it is sufficient to justify continued research and thinking to explore the issues further.

Such research and thinking is two-pronged. On the one hand, research looks for causes. These are both ultimate causes—which are illuminated by looking toward the ancient past to ask how ethnocentrism evolved, how it came to be what it is—and proximate causes, which are to be found in the human mind and brain. The literature on these matters is relatively small but still too large, speculative, and contentious to be summarized here.[12] In the course of determining these causes, the ethnocentric complex will be better understood, we will have greater insight into ourselves, and—one hopes—thereby be better able to manage our personal and civic affairs.

On the other hand, research issues lie in tracing the workings of ethnicity/ethnocentrism—and all their components—in our present-day or historically recorded lives.[13] Here, the literature and the opportunities for observation and experimentation are vast, because the issues are so large and so pervasive in human affairs. But large as the issues are they will be better understood if the underlying psychodynamics—the way the human mind produces and reacts to ethnocentrism and

ethnicity—are well understood. The ethnocentric complex is both a central part of those dynamics and a manifestation of them.

In pursuing both lines of research, and in thinking through their implications, it certainly must be borne in mind that *natural* implies neither good (the "naturalistic fallacy") nor bad. Ethnocentrism may be either or both, depending on circumstance and point of view. Perhaps it goes without saying that we must also bear in mind that if ethnocentrism is in any way natural it is nonetheless changeable. Some parts of the ethnocentric complex, such as detecting accents, may not readily change. Similarly, one should probably not hope that stereotyping will easily disappear from our lives. But stereotypes can and do change; with time and effort they probably can *be* changed. In very large measure the social sciences, certainly anthropology, took as a central mission the task of understanding ethnocentrism so that its unfortunate aspects can better be ameliorated if not eliminated. Much of the methodology of anthropology, for example, is specifically designed to circumvent the effects of researchers' own in-group biases and thus allow more objective analyses of the peoples of the world, including ourselves. An objective understanding is a crucial step toward that end.

The clearer our understanding of ethnocentrism, the more enabled we will be to curb its excesses. There is no shortage of materials to study, and ample reason to give the subject high priority.

Notes

1. Certain exceptions or qualifications should be noted. For example, Swartz (1961) cites Pacific Islanders who considered their society or culture inferior to that of the United States. However, Swartz noted that the Islanders did not cease to consider themselves superior to neighboring peoples. And he explained the apparent exception away by arguing that the Islanders considered themselves and Americans to be essentially the same people. Sometimes individuals find the

exotic attractive, and the evidence is overwhelming that many individuals voluntarily leave their own societies to become members of others. The latter does not entail an immediate and full defection from one's ethnic affiliation, but it often leads in that direction. Limited as these exceptions may be, they should figure into any careful understanding of ethnocentrism.

2. One should not conclude, however, that in-group bias is aroused with equal ease or inten-

sity in all contexts. Hirschfeld (1996:61) notes that humans find ethnicity or race more salient and/or easier to think about than class, and he suggests that class often transmutes itself into race (imagined "race," of course) because the latter is so much easier to think about. A corollary of this, I would suggest, is that where class (or any other analogous social structural principle) comes to resemble ethnicity—as when it results in distinct accents, apparel, or deportment—it becomes more salient, more meaningful to people.

3. Although it has its origin in Le Vine and Campbell's (1971) list, the list given here has been considerably revised in the light of further research, and is subject to further refinement. Some elements could probably be combined; others could probably be split up. Given further evidence, some items may be dropped from the list and others added.

4. The term is van den Berghe's (1987), and it has the advantage of referring both to an ethnic group and an ethnic category. Generally in the social sciences a "group" has some degree of organization as a unit, while a "category" does not. It is unfortunate that the term *ethnic group* tends, misleadingly, to be used for both of these conditions.

5. Gil-White (2001) considers endogamy to be one of the necessary and sufficient conditions of an ethny; that is, an ethny will be perceived as such to the extent that it is perceived as biologically self-reproducing, like a species.

6. Nonetheless, *cultural* universals do exist. Generally they are very ancient and very useful—like the use of fire or cooking food—or they are in some way reflections or responses to universal conditions; kinship terminologies are an example (Brown 1991).

7. For Hirschfeld, human kinds include not only ethnic and racial kinds ("ethnoraces"), but also occupational kinds, kin, the two sexes, and unspecified other kinds. But compare Gil-White (2001),

who argues for a more specific adaptation for thinking about ethnicity, per se. Berreby (2005) applies the notion of human kinds to a very wide range of us-and-them situations.

8. See discussions of mental modularity in Barkow et al. (1992) and Hirschfeld and Gelman (1994).

9. That human ears can hold up glasses is an effect or by-product of the adaptive design of the outer ear, which functions to channel sound waves to the eardrum. Kurzban et al. (2001) report experimental findings consistent with the proposition that racial thinking is an effect of a fundamental adaptation to coalitional thinking in general.

10. Paleontological findings indicating that Neandertals and *Homo sapiens* overlapped in time and space (or, much earlier, that other species of hominids may also have coexisted) might force a rethinking of this statement.

11. As Hirschfeld notes, "Costume, clothing, and ornaments were surely the most marked physical differences that our ancestral populations encountered" to distinguish human kinds (1996:107). Interestingly, Hirschfeld found that the present-day markers of occupation, just like racial differences, seem to trigger human-kinds thinking in children, so that they imagine occupations to be similar to races. Equally interesting is that although children exhibit a considerable interest in human kinds, they are not quick to learn how to identify persons by race. Children may, for example, absorb racial stereotypes without realizing that their very playmates are of the race or races being stereotyped (Hirschfeld 1996).

12. But see, for example, van den Berghe (1987), Reynolds et al. (1987), and Gil-White (2001). For theoretical guidance on the evolution of human nature, see Barkow et al. (1992). On mind and brain, see, for example, Brubaker et al. (2004) and Van Bavel et al. (2008).

13. For the role of history in discovering human nature and tracing its effects, see Brown (1999).

References Cited

AKST, DANIEL. 1993. Cruller fates. *Los Angeles Times*, March 9, pp. D1, D6.

BARKOW, JEROME H., LEDA COSMIDES, and JOHN TOOBY, eds. 1992. *The Adapted Mind: Evolutionary Psychology and the Generation of Culture*. New York: Oxford University Press.

BERREBY, DAVID. 2005. *Us and Them: Understanding Your Tribal Mind*. New York: Little, Brown and Company.

BÉTEILLE, ANDRÉ. 1967. Race and descent as social categories in India. *Daedalus* 96:444–463.

BROWN, D. E. 1976. *Principles of Social Structure: Southeast Asia*. London: Duckworth.

———. 1991. *Human Universals.* New York/Philadelphia: McGraw-Hill/Temple University Press.

———. 1997. Are ethnicity and ethnocentrism natural? *Southwestern Anthropological Association Newsletter* 38(1):1, 4, 6, 9–10, 16–17, 19.

———. 1999. Human nature and history. *History and Theory* 38:138–157.

BRUBAKER, ROGERS, MARA LOVEMAN, and PETER STAMATOV. 2004. Ethnicity as cognition. *Theory and Society* 33:31–64.

DE VOS, GEORGE, and HIROSHI WAGATSUMA, eds. 1967. *Japan's Invisible Race: Caste in Culture and Personality.* Berkeley, CA: University of California Press.

DeWAAL, FRANS. 1982. *Chimpanzee Politics: Power & Sex among Apes.* New York: Harper & Row.

FURNIVALL, JOHN S. 1956. *Colonial Policy and Practice: A Comparative Study of Burma and Netherlands India.* New York: New York University Press.

GIL-WHITE, FRANCISCO. 1999. How thick is blood? The plot thickens . . . : If ethnic actors are primordialists, what remains of the circumstantialist/primordialist controversy? *Ethnic and Racial Studies* 22(5):789–820.

———. 2001. Are ethnic groups biological "species" to the human brain? Essentialism in our cognition of some social categories. *Current Anthropology* 42(4):515–554.

HALEY, BRIAN D., and LARRY R. WILCOXON. 2005. How Spaniards became Chumash and other tales of ethnogenesis. *American Anthropologist* 107:432–445.

HARCOURT, ALEXANDER H., and FRANS B. M. DE WAAL, eds. 1992. *Coalitions and Alliances in Humans and Other Animals.* Oxford: Oxford University Press.

HASTORF, ALBERT H., and HADLEY CANTRIL. 1954. They saw a game: A case study. *Journal of Abnormal and Social Psychology* 49:129–134.

HERF, JEFFREY. 2006. *The Jewish Enemy: Nazi Propaganda during World War II and the Holocaust.* Cambridge, MA: Belknap Press.

HERODOTUS. 5th century b.c. *The Persian Wars.* Various editions.

HIRSCHFELD, LAWRENCE A. 1996. *Race in the Making: Cognition, Culture, and the Child's Construction of Human Kinds.* Cambridge, MA: MIT Press.

HIRSCHFELD, LAWRENCE A., and SUSAN GELMAN, eds. 1994. *Mapping the Mind: Domain Specificity in Cognition and Culture.* Cambridge: Cambridge University Press.

IBN KHALDUN. 1958. *The Muqaddimah: An Introduction to History,* vol. I. Franz Rosenthal, trans. Princeton, NJ: Princeton University Press.

KEYES, CHARLES F. 1981. *Ethnic Change.* Seattle, WA: University of Washington Press.

KURZBAN, ROBERT, JOHN TOOBY, and LEDA COSMIDES. 2001. Can race be erased? Coalitional computation and social categorization. *Proceedings of the National Academy of Sciences* 98:15387–15392.

LE VINE, ROBERT A., and DONALD T. CAMPBELL. 1971. *Ethnocentrism: Theories of Conflict, Ethnic Attitudes, and Group Behavior.* New York: Wiley.

MAQUET, JACQUES J. 1961. *The Premise of Inequality in Ruanda: A Study of Political Relations in a Central African Kingdom.* London: Oxford University Press.

MUMMENDEY, AMÉLIE, et al. 1992. Categorization is not enough: Intergroup discrimination in negative outcome allocation. *Journal of Experimental Social Psychology* 28:125–144.

MURDOCK, GEORGE PETER. 1931. Ethnocentrism. In *Encyclopaedia of the Social Sciences*, vol. 5. Pp. 613–614. New York: Macmillan.

PERERA, SASANKA. 1991. Teaching and learning hatred: The role of education and socialization in Sri Lankan ethnic conflict. Ph.D. dissertation, University of California, Santa Barbara.

PINKER, STEVEN. 1994. *The Language Instinct: How the Mind Creates Language.* New York: Morrow.

———. 1997. *How the Mind Works.* New York: Norton.

RABBIE, JACOB. 1992. The effects of intragroup cooperation and intergroup competition on in-group cohesion and out-group hostility. In *Coalitions and Alliances in Humans and Other Animals.* Alexander H. Harcourt and Frans B. M. de Waal, eds. Pp. 175–205. Oxford: Oxford University Press.

REYNOLDS, VERNON, VINCENT FALGER, and IAN VINE, eds. 1987. *The Sociobiology of Ethnocentrism: Evolutionary Dimensions of Xenophobia, Discrimination, Racism and Nationalism.* London: Croom Helm.

RISLEY, HERBERT. 1915. *The People of India.* London: W. Thacker & Co. (See Appendix I, "Caste in Proverbs and Popular Sayings.")

ROMANUCCI-ROSS, LOLA. 1975. Italian ethnic identity and its transformations. In *Ethnic Identity: Cultural Continuities and Change.* George De Vos and Lola Romanucci-Ross, eds. Pp. 198–226. Chicago, IL: University of Chicago Press.

SCHEFF, THOMAS J. 1994. *Bloody Revenge: Emotions, Nationalism, and War.* Boulder, CO: Westview Press.

SCHEFF, THOMAS J., and Suzanne M. Retzinger. 1991. *Emotions and Violence: Shame and Rage in Destructive Conflicts.* Lexington, MA: Lexington Books.

SELIGMAN, MARTIN E. P., and JOANNE L. HAGER. 1972. *Biological Boundaries of Learning.* New York: Appleton-Century-Crofts.

SINHA, GOPAL SHARAN, and RAMESH CHANDRA SINHA. 1967. Exploration in caste stereotypes. *Social Forces* 46:42–47.

SUMNER, WILLIAM GRAHAM. 1906. *Folkways: A Study of the Sociological Importance of Usages, Manners, Customs, Mores, and Morals.* Boston, MA: Ginn.

SWARTZ, M. J. 1961. Negative ethnocentrism. *Journal of Conflict Resolution* 5(1):75–81.

TAMBIAH, S. J. 1986. *Sri Lanka: Ethnic Fratricide and the Dismantling of Democracy.* Chicago, IL: University of Chicago Press.

TOOBY, JOHN, and LEDA COSMIDES. 1989. Evolutionary psychology and the generation of culture: Part I: Theoretical Considerations. *Ethology and Sociobiology* 10:29–49.

VALLONE, ROBERT P., LEE ROSS, and MARK R. LEPPER. 1985. The hostile media phenomenon: Biased perception and perceptions of media bias in coverage of the Beirut massacre. *Journal of Personality and Social Psychology* 49:577–585.

VAN BAVEL, JAY J., DOMINIC J. PACKER, and WILLIAM A. CUNNINGHAM. 2008. The neural substrates of -in-group bias: A functional magnetic resonance imaging investigation. *Psychological Science* 19:1130–1138.

VAN DEN BERGHE, PIERRE. 1987. *The Ethnic Phenomenon.* New York: Praeger.

WARNECKE, A. MICHAEL, ROGER D. MASTERS, and GUIDO KEMPTER. 1992. The roots of nationalism: Nonverbal behavior and xenophobia. *Ethology and Sociobiology* 13:267–282.

WATERS, MARY C. 1990. *Ethnic Options: Choosing Identities in America.* Berkeley, CA: University of California Press.

YOON, IN-JIN. 1991. Self-employment in business: Chinese-, Japanese-, Korean-American, black, and white. Ph.D. dissertation, University of Chicago.

6

■ ■ ■

American Indians

Rachel A. Bonney, *University of North Carolina at Charlotte*
Raymond Scupin, *Lindenwood University*

*One can make the case that the Native people of the United States are
perhaps the most studied and least understood of all those who make up
the tapestry of American life.*

[HIRSCHFELDER AND DE MONTAÑO 1991:IX]

American Indians can be distinguished from other American ethnic groups in several ways: they have been in America longer than any other ethnic group; they are the only ethnic groups whose ancestors did not emigrate to North America voluntarily—and as the descendants of once-independent societies, they are the only ethnic groups to have treaty rights; and, as a group, they are so diverse that they are not one single ethnic group as much as a number of distinct groups. Technically, until the "discovery" of the "New World" by Europeans, "American Indians" did not exist; more than 500 distinct named ethnic groups inhabited North America. Columbus, thinking he had found the East Indies, erroneously termed the peoples he encountered "Indians," a categorization that has had repercussions throughout history as first Europeans and then Euro-Americans treated "Indians" as a single cultural unit with a common language and culture. Nothing could be farther from the truth. American Indians were and continue to be distinct cultural, political, and ethnic groups, despite strong efforts to assimilate them into the mainstream of American society.

Contemporary definitions of "Indians" are imprecise. The federal government has no legal or consistent definition of Indian established by either Congress or the courts, although to be eligible for federal services, individuals must be members of federally recognized tribes or groups. Eligibility to receive federal services from the Bureau of Indian Affairs requires a folk-based "blood quantum" (or proportion of "pure Indian blood," such as one-quarter or one-eighth), while census figures are based on self-ascription or identification. "Recognized" or "acknowledged" Indians usually have reservations—lands reserved or set aside for exclusive Indian use and held in trust by the federal government—where government agencies provide educational, health, economic, and social services to registered tribal members. Each tribe has its own folk-based criteria for membership, usually based on a "blood quantum" of varying degrees of ancestry. Indians lacking federal recognition may have state recognition and/or state reservations, but they do not receive services or financial assistance from the federal government through the Bureau of Indian Affairs; also, they are ineligible for a variety of federal programs and may not have gaming operations in their communities. Unofficial folk-based criteria of Indianness include purported genetic characteristics or physical appearance, membership in specific families, participation in viable Indian cultural systems, belief and participation in a native religion, speaking a native language, and living on a reservation or in an Indian community or enclave—resulting in more diversity among Indians than most non-Indians realize.

This chapter will examine the American Indians as peoples who have maintained cultural and, sometimes, linguistic integrity and a sense of Indian identity, despite pressures for assimilation. Fredrik Barth, in the introduction to *Ethnic Groups and Boundaries* (1969), examined the persistence of ethnic groups in larger societies through "boundary-maintaining mechanisms" that separate ethnic groups from each other as well as from the dominant society: overt signs or signals—language, style of clothing, house form, and so on—or general lifestyle and basic value orientations. Boundary maintenance is based on identity systems and personal affiliation with certain shared symbols: artifacts, words, role behaviors, or ritual acts, as well as commonly shared cultural traditions and historical events. In "Persistent Cultural Systems" (1971), Edward H. Spicer (1971:795) focused on the "oppositional process" as a primary boundary-maintaining mechanism in the historical continuity of ethnic groups that have been absorbed into larger political entities—as, for example, African nations incorporated into the British Empire or Indian tribes under the jurisdiction of the United States.

Despite changed political systems, these groups have persisted because of collective identity systems grounded in shared symbols—flags, leaders, a series of past (historical) events, and so on. One common feature Spicer identified in the 10 cases of persistent cultural systems he investigated was "a continued conflict between these peoples and the controllers of the surrounding state apparatus" (1971:797); he saw this continued opposition as the "essential factor in the formation and development of the persistent identity system" maintained through linguistic communication, shared moral values, and a political organization to achieve group objectives.

For over 400 years Indians have survived as distinct ethnic groups, despite efforts to annihilate them, assimilate them, or legislate them out of existence. They must operate in a variety of arenas and interact with a wide range of persons while retaining their sense of Indianness. Their separate and collective experiences have strengthened an identity that has persisted and maintained the boundaries separating them from other ethnic groups and from the dominant society, although tribal identities may be superseded by a situational "Indian" identity. To understand who the American Indians are today, one must understand where they started and what experiences they have undergone. The following cultural descriptions are, of necessity, brief. For more detailed discussions of tribal cultures, see Hodge (1981), Hudson (1976), Josephy (1991), Kehoe (2006), and Sutton (2008).

PREHISTORY

Long before the arrival of the first Europeans in the "New World," the Americas were inhabited by populations of Asian ancestry which had migrated into the Americas by way of a land bridge connecting North America and Siberia at the Bering Straits some 30,000 years ago during the Pleistocene (glacial) age. Small nomadic bands hunted Pleistocene megafauna such as bison and mammoth using stone-tipped spears. With the recession of the glaciers at the end of the Pleistocene, the resulting climatic shifts created a variety of ecological zones in North America, triggering changes in human subsistence and lifestyles as populations adapted to new flora and fauna, which, in turn, created the diversity of cultural types encountered by the Europeans (Fagan 2005; Kehoe 2006; Sutton 2008).

During the Archaic period, beginning about 7000 or 8000 B.C., hunting was supplemented by increased reliance on wild plant foods that were ground into meal. Ground stone axes and adzes in the East indicate a shift to a forested environment, and the *atlatl*, or spear-thrower, improved hunting efficiency. In the Great Basin, Plateau, and Plains, the Archaic persisted to historic times; in the Southwest, it was replaced by the Anasazi, Mogollon, and Hohokam traditions, (A.D. 1–1541), and in the East by the Woodland tradition (1000 B.C.–A.D. 700). In both areas these cultures were transitional between hunting-gathering and farming economies. Domestication of plants (corn, beans, squash) provided the food surplus that permitted sedentary village settlement patterns; technological innovations included bows and arrows tipped with small stemmed or triangular points, tapered axes or celts, stone pipes, basketry, and ceramics.

The cultural traditions encountered by the Europeans were the Mississippian (A.D. 500–1600) in the Southeast, the Anasazi on the Colorado Plateau (A.D. 1 to modern times), and the Hohokam in the Sonoran Desert (A.D. 900–1450) in the Southwest, all with similarities to Mesoamerican civilizations. All were characterized by a farming economy supporting town life, complex political and religious organization, and elaborate material cultures with distinctive ceramic styles. The largest urban center was the Mississippian site of Cahokia, near East St. Louis on the Mississippi River; the Anasazi perhaps are best known for the "cliff dwellings" of Mesa Verde and large fortified towns such as Pueblo Bonito in New Mexico's Chaco Canyon; the best-preserved Hohokam site is Casa Grande in Arizona. For more complete descriptions of North American prehistory, see Fagan (2005).

THE AMERICAN INDIANS AT FIRST CONTACT

Although Columbus mistakenly identified the first natives he encountered as "Indians," the North America population consisted of distinct cultural groups in what anthropologists call "culture areas," geographic areas characterized by distinctive cultural types: the Northeastern and Southeastern Woodlands, the Great Plains, the Southwest, the Northwest Coast, the Great Basin-Plateau, California, the Subarctic, and the Arctic. Cultural descriptions of these areas usually are based on the "pre-contact" cultures immediately prior to or at the time of the arrival of the first Europeans. Population estimates of pre-contact Native American Indian populations range from 8 to 18 million people (Sutton 2008).

Despite the diversity of pre-contact cultures, similarities existed. Kinship was important in economic, political, religious, and social life; family heads represented their kinsmen on village or tribal councils or acted as judges to settle disputes. Spirituality was reflected in the integration of religious, ritual, and supernatural beliefs into all aspects of daily life. Many beliefs revolved around nature and natural phenomena and the belief that humans are part of the natural scheme of life. The importance of religion and ritual also is reflected in mythology, art forms, dance, music, and, in some cases, games.

The Southeast

The rich fertile soils, long growing season, and heavy precipitation evenly distributed throughout the year made the Southeastern Woodlands— southern Virginia to the Gulf of Mexico, the Atlantic coast to eastern Texas—attractive to both pre-Columbian and European farmers. The area was dominated by the Five Civilized Tribes—the Cherokee, Choctaw, Chickasaw, Creek, and Seminole (a Creek offshoot). Some are gone—the Timucua and Calusa and Natchez—and others survive as small remnant populations—the Catawba, Caddo, and Chitimacha, for example.

Southeastern culture in the sixteenth century was based on the Mississippian pattern.

Sedentary farmers lived in fortified towns on watercourses near cities or ceremonial centers such as Cahokia and Etowah, and supported complex sociopolitical and religious organization. Fortified towns were supported by crops grown in fields located around the houses or outside the palisade. Chiefs' houses, council houses, and ceremonial grounds were built on earth mounds facing central plazas. Towns, some belonging to confederations, could be ceremonial centers where political and ceremonial leaders lived and ritual and political activities were held.

The basis of the farming economy was corn, beans, and squash, although tobacco, sunflowers, and gourds also were raised. Although men assisted in clearing and harvesting of fields, farming was the women's responsibility. Cultivated foods were supplemented by wild foods gathered by the women and by meat provided by male hunting and fishing. With the exception of the priest-chiefs, full-time specialists were unknown.

The important social unit, the matrilineal family, determined descent and inheritance; membership in matrilineal clans, named after animals or plants, crosscut town lines and determined social position, political roles, place of residence, and choice of marriage partners. A town's peace chief, whose position was based on his clan affiliation, was assisted in decision making and sometimes dispute settlement by a war chief and an all-male council. Towns often were allied in confederacies for mutual aid and defense; warfare was frequent, ritualized, and a source of male prestige.

Religion played an integral part in virtually all aspects of life, from individual prayers to the spirits of animals killed in the hunt to elaborate group rituals, such as the annual "Green Corn" (or "busk") ceremonies. The latter was both a harvest or first-fruits ceremony and a new year renewal of the world and of life involving a ritual cleansing and purification, a time when houses were cleaned out, utensils were replaced, new fires were started from the central sacred fire, all offenses but murder were forgiven, and individuals were cleansed internally (taking an emetic known

as the "black drink") and externally (sweat baths). Prayers, singing, dancing, and feasting were all part of the ritual, which lasted several days (Sutton 2008).

The Northeastern Woodlands

The environmental diversity of the Northern Woodlands (extending from the Atlantic Ocean to the Mississippi River and from the Ohio River north to western Ontario and Manitoba) is reflected in its cultural diversity: north-central tribes relied on wild rice as their staple food, coastal hunting-and-gathering tribes also farmed, and the Iroquois and the Huron supplemented farming with hunting and gathering.

THE IROQUOIS.   The Iroquois, an intrusive linguistic wedge extending north into an otherwise all-Algonkian-speaking area along the eastern Lower Great Lakes, were culturally like their southern relatives. A matrilineal farming people living in palisaded villages of approximately 50 longhouses, they were united in a political confederation of five separate tribes (six with the addition of the Tuscarora in 1760) known as the League of the Ho-de-no-sau-nee, or "Longhouse People": the Seneca, Cayuga, Onondaga, Oneida, and Mohawk. Originally established for mutual protection by culture heroes Deganawidah and Hiawatha, the confederacy expanded through force and cajolery, incorporating smaller tribes into the alliance; the "protected" or "conquered" smaller tribes were denied the rights and privileges accorded to the five founding tribes.

The distinctive Iroquois democratic political structure grew out of their kinship system. A League council of 50 sachems (peace chiefs elected by the women of their clans to lifelong positions; hereditary in certain matrilineal clans) handled only external relations with other tribes and, later, with the Europeans; it had no voice in local town or tribal matters. The sachems' votes represented the opinions and wishes of their tribes/clans, which could remove them from office for unsatisfactory performance of duties.

Iroquois Indian in traditional dress.

In historic times, the French, who did not understand the Iroquois political system, preferred to deal with the "Pine Tree Chiefs," men, usually war chiefs, and sometimes women, rewarded for meritorious service by the tribal and League councils. The numbers of these nontransferable and nonhereditary titles increased during times of war, and over time the title did become hereditary; today, individuals with the greatest amount of power tend to be descendants of famous Pine Tree Chiefs (Kehoe 2006; Sutton 2008).

ALGONKIANS. Northeastern Algonkian-speaking tribes in New England's North Atlantic slope, a zone transitional between farming/hunting and fishing, were marginal maize farmers; in the subarctic areas south of Hudson Bay, hunting and fishing supported small tribes spread over large territories; and in the Upper Great Lakes wild rice supplemented hunting and fishing. Despite regional or tribal variations, all the northeastern Algonkian groups were hunters of big game and smaller fur-bearing animals; men also fished, and women gathered wild plant foods in season.

Their dependence on food collecting in a boreal environment of scarce resources necessitated a lifestyle of independence and autonomy, isolation, nomadism or seminomadism, and seasonal shifting of bands. Households, scattered and isolated during the winter, came together in summer villages for communal subsistence activities, games, and ceremonies. Recognized band territories could be subdivided into smaller family units. Ojibwa men had clearly marked hunting territories that even wives and children were forbidden to use without permission. Winter fishing grounds were owned individually, summer fishing grounds were communal property, and game was regarded as private property to be turned over to the women for distribution. The division of labor was gender based: men hunted and went to battle, and women did everything else, including collecting maple sugar from individually owned sugar maple trees (women owned the vats and the sap, which they collected and boiled cooperatively).

Life and activities corresponded to the shifting seasons. The Ojibwa spring began in March at the maple syrup camps and ended in May, when 3–15 related families moved to the summer villages. Summer activities—berrying, fishing, and trapping small game—lasted until the August move to the wild rice beds for the communal wild rice harvest. By November, the wild rice beds were abandoned as the groups broke up into small family units to winter in the deeper and more protected areas of the forests.

The pattern of shifting settlement affected social organization. The largest units, patrilineal bands rarely numbering more than 200 persons, were groups of nuclear families. No overall political or tribal organization existed, and bands never came together to take tribal actions. The headman, spokesman for the band, held his position by virtue of his skill and prestige as a hunter. Since political control was in the hands of a council of elders, he had little real authority.

Algonkians tended to emphasize individual achievements and dependence on one's own survival skills over collective and group concerns. Male success in life depended on lifelong supernatural aid obtained through the vision quest at puberty. Young men spent four or five days in isolation, without food or water, praying and sometimes inflicting wounds to bring the visions that put them in contact with their supernatural guardian spirits. Leadership of war parties also

depended on visions, and visions brought supernatural powers that could be used for curing illness caused by evil spirits or sorcery. Control of supernatural powers was regarded as personal property, and possession of such power was a source of influence and prestige (Kehoe 2006; Sutton 2008).

The Great Plains

For most modern-day Americans, "Indians" lived on the Plains, wore warbonnets, rode horses, lived in tipis, and hunted buffalo. Since the Plains Indians have been depicted most frequently (often inaccurately) in Hollywood and TV westerns, because they were among the last to succumb to white political domination, and because Buffalo Bill Cody's Wild West Shows put Plains Indians on display, such a stereotype is not surprising. However, the Plains culture was a historical development made possible by the introduction of the horse and the gun, and the "typical" Plains tribes (Cheyenne, Comanche, Kiowa, and Dakota or Sioux) were comparative newcomers to the Plains. In pre-contact times, small foraging bands roamed the High Plains, and sedentary farmers lived along the major rivers.

The large, treeless, subhumid or semiarid Plains extend from the Rockies to the Mississippi River and from Alberta and Saskatchewan south almost to the Rio Grande and Mexican border. The hot summers and cold winters of this harsh climate are intensified by relentless wind. Native grasses supported large herds of bison, pronghorn antelope, and other nomadic herd animals, and deer, elk, and small animals could be found in the well-forested river valleys.

CLASSIC/NOMADIC BUFFALO HUNTERS. The introduction of horses and guns into the Plains coincided with white expansion in the East, displacing and forcing tribes onto the Plains. The nomadic hunting, gathering, and pastoral culture that emerged was necessitated by the reliance on nomadic herd animals for food and was facilitated by the use of the horse in hunting and moving material possessions (by means of the *travois,* a hoop with a rawhide net attached to two tipi poles dragged behind the horse).

Although elk, antelope, and smaller animals were hunted, the bison, or American buffalo, was the primary source of food, shelter (tipi covers), sleeping robes, tools (made from bones and horns), and cooking containers (made from the stomachs). Human settlement followed the bisons' movements: small herds of the winter months, when forage was scarce, came together in immense herds in the late summer. Small groups hunted during the winter, but the most important economic event was the communal cooperative summer bison hunt, when the entire tribe gathered to try to kill enough animals to provide food to last all winter. Everyone participated in the hunt, including women and children, and before the hunt military societies maintained rigid control over all hunters; anyone trying to hunt prematurely was punished severely. The remainder of the summer was spent curing the meat for use in the winter and participating in communal rituals such as the Sun Dance.

Most nomadic Plains tribes traced descent bilaterally, and most had bilateral kin groups responsible for social control within the band, groups of related families or bands that camped together in the protected river bottoms during the winter. The larger social and political unit, the tribe, came together in the summer for the communal hunt, rituals, and political gatherings. Both men and women also belonged to voluntary associations connected to warfare, the men's military fraternities and the women's auxiliaries.

Warfare was the mechanism by which men earned honor and prestige in an otherwise egalitarian society. Warfare was both defensive—defense of camps under attack or pursuit of small enemy parties that had driven off horses or taken scalps—and offensive, to redress a wrong or for booty. New war parties were formed each time they went to war, under the leadership of proven warriors whose visions promised success. Men achieved status and prestige through war honors earned by counting coup, taking something (e.g., guns, scalps, horses, and lives) from the enemy. Coup was counted by touching a portion of the enemy's body with the hand or with a coup stick, actions honored because of the danger overcome by the warrior or because of the conditions under which it was accomplished. Coup, graded according to the order in which it was counted or the degree of danger involved, encouraged hand-to-hand combat in front of witnesses. War honors also included capturing a gun, weapon, shield, or horse belonging to an enemy, and leading war parties. A man's claim to war honors was validated by his comrades in victory celebrations, often dramatic reenactments of battles. For each war honor performed, a man also earned the feathers that could be made into his warbonnet by the members of his military society. Thus the warbonnets, worn only on ceremonial occasions, were a kind of honorary degree indicating a man's status as warrior and bestowed by his comrades (Kehoe 2006; Sutton 2008).

The guardian spirits that brought hunters and warriors success were acquired through the vision quest. Men unsuccessful in this quest could assume the alternative role of *berdache*, or "man-woman." The berdache wore women's clothing, performed women's tasks, and was believed to possess strong supernatural powers to aid young men in courtship or bring good fortune to war parties.

One common communal ceremony of the Plains was the Sun Dance, held annually midsummer as a world renewal ceremony to ensure the perpetuation of the supernatural world. Men pledged to participate in the piercing of the ceremony—attaching themselves to thongs fastened to a pole by a skewer piercing the pectoral muscles and dancing around the pole for 24 hours or until they went into a trance. Women, having proved their ability to bear pain in childbirth, did not have to participate in the ceremony (Kehoe 2006; Sutton 2008).

SEDENTARY PLAINS TRIBES. Located along the alluvial floodplains of the Missouri River drainage were the sedentary farming tribes: Mandan and Hidatsa of North Dakota (who merged their villages in 1835); the Arikara on the Missouri River in the Dakotas; the Omaha, on the west side of the Missouri River in Nebraska; the Iowa on the eastern side of the Missouri River; the Oto, Kansa, and Missouri; and the southernmost tribes, the Osage and the Wichita.

The sedentary tribes, whose origins can be traced to the prehistoric Upper Republican culture, lived in semisubterranean earth lodges in villages on terraces above streams. Stockades protected villages from marauding nomadic tribes, and most towns had enormous ceremonial lodges for winter and communal events. Between 70 and 80 percent of their food came from farming, but the diet was supplemented by the communal bison hunt held every summer, an event in which all able-bodied people participated.

Descent was unilineal, patrilineal among the southern tribes (Omaha, Ponca, Iowa, and Missouri), and matrilineal in the north (Mandan, Hidatsa, and Arikara); lineages were strong corporate landowning units. Military fraternities also were found among the sedentary Plains tribes, but, unlike those of the nomadic tribes, they were age-graded, so that a group of males progressed from one level to the next, purchasing the paraphernalia associated with each grade from the group preceding them.

Religion focused on farming, maize cultivation, and weather control and incorporated such Southwestern elements as shrines, sand paintings, clowns, and certain deities. The pre-eminent supernatural beings were the Sun, related to the eagle, whose feathers were sacred ritual objects, and the Moon, a female deity associated with fertility and maize. Unique to this area, and found primarily among the Pawnee, was the morning star ceremony in which a female virgin was sacrificed to Venus each year (Kehoe 2006; Sutton 2008).

The Southwest

As both a geographic and culture area, the Southwest—present-day Arizona, New Mexico, southwestern Colorado, southern Utah, eastern Texas, and northwestern Sonora—is far more heterogeneous than any other area of North America. The major unifying feature of the area is its aridity. The mesas and mountain ranges of the Colorado Plateau in the north, with elevations of 5,000–11,000 feet, are drained by the Colorado River system. A climatic drying cycle, compounded by overgrazing by livestock, has caused the thick grasslands of the past to be replaced by scrub vegetation mixed with piñon, mesquite, and cactus. The Colorado Plateau ends abruptly in the Mogollon Rim, a sharp escarpment dropping 1,000 feet to the Sonoran Desert of southwestern Arizona and northern Sonora. Here the basin and range topography is drained by the Gila and Salt River systems, and desert vegetation mixes with a variety of trees wherever water is found.

The plant and animal life of the Southwestern desert were sufficient to support hunting and gathering economies, while floodwater farming, irrigation, and drought-resistant varieties of corn made farming possible along the rivers. Subsistence for most societies was farming, ranging from the irrigation farming of the Eastern Pueblos on the Rio Grande and the Pima along the Salt and Gila rivers to the floodwater farming of the Tohono O'odham to their west to the dry farming of the Hopi and Zuni on the Colorado Plateau. While the Navajo and Apache, newcomers to the Southwest, also farmed, the Apaches were primarily hunters and gatherers, and the Navajo became pastoralists with the Spanish introduction of sheep and goats after 1540. The Colorado River tribes also farmed, and all tribes in the Southwest supplemented their farming with hunting and gathering, some placing more reliance on food collecting than others (Kehoe 2006; Sutton 2008).

ANASAZI/PUEBLO. The Spanish called the descendants of the Anasazi the Pueblo because they lived in *pueblos*, the Spanish word for *towns*. Anthropological distinctions between Eastern and Western Pueblos are based on differences in kinship, political and ritual organizations, languages, and farming technologies. The small Eastern Pueblos, along the Rio Grande from Albuquerque north through Santa Fe to the Colorado border, have been occupied since at least 1700. The Western Pueblos are the Hopi on Black Mesa in north-central Arizona; the Zuni, located 30 miles south of Gallup, New Mexico; and the Laguna and Acoma in north-central New Mexico.

Hopi female.

Pueblo villages were permanent compact clusters of multistoried, terraced houses inhabited by multiple families. Each village also had underground ceremonial structures, *kivas*, which also served as men's clubhouses in the west. Spanish-introduced crops of wheat, alfalfa, and fruit trees were added to aboriginal crops of maize, beans, squash, cotton, and tobacco. Because the Western Pueblos relied on rainfall to water their drought-resistant varieties of crops, their religious rituals stressed weather control more than those of the Eastern Pueblos, who were able to irrigate their fields. Villages or clans owned the land, which was worked by the men, who also hunted, built the houses, and wove the fabrics for their clothing.

Among the Western Pueblos kinship was based on exogamous matrilineal clans; the bilateral extended family was the primary social unit among the Eastern Pueblos. Villages in both the

east and west were autonomous. The Western Pueblo village chief came from a specific clan and held his position for life; a council composed of clan or association heads assisted with his political and ceremonial responsibilities. Eastern Pueblo political organization also dealt with both religious and secular issues but was based on a dual organization: political and ceremonial responsibilities alternated between two chiefs who were equal in status and authority.

Religion and ritual permeated all aspects of Pueblo life, which they saw as interrelated, balanced, and based on interdependent and reciprocal relationships between humans and nature. Disruption of the equilibrium by human thoughts, words, and deeds caused illness, disasters, and drought, but it could be restored and maintained through ceremony. Western Pueblo ritual focused on weather control, manifested in the Kachina cult, whose masked dancers impersonated the kachina spirits who brought the rains. Eastern Pueblo religion was centered on both weather control and on health. In both the and Western Pueblos, "clowns" maintai control during the public dances. Ritu also included warfare (Eastern war control of flora and fauna (hur associations), and village harmon Sutton 2008).

SOUTHERN ATHABASCANS.

ers to the Southwest, the simila Athabascan-speaking Navajo and Apache in their common origins. Both moved into the Southwest from the Subarctic about 800 years ago, the Navajo settling along the San Juan drainage on the Colorado Plateau as neighbors of the Pueblos, and the Apache moving to the Mogollon Rim. Initially, both groups were nomadic hunters and gatherers, but the Navajo borrowed farming (and other cultural elements) from the Pueblos and, later, horses, sheep, and goats from the Spanish. They became seminomadic pastoralists dependent on livestock for food, clothing, and cash. Weaving, also learned from the Pueblos, became a source of cash income in historic times as Navajo women became as well known for their woven rugs and saddle blankets as the men were for their silver and turquoise jewelry. The Apache relied on hunting and gathering and later raiding (primarily Piman groups in the Sonoran Desert) for subsistence, supplemented by some farming done by the women.

Both the Navajo and Apache had matrilineal clans and matrilocal residence. The largest political unit was the band; neither had a tribal-wide political structure until the twentieth century. The Navajo "outfit" was an extended kinship unit headed by an older man, a *Nataani* or "peace chief," responsible for maintaining diplomatic external relations. Apache bands were broken into family groups or outfits led by headmen chosen by the entire group for their wisdom and generosity.

The focus of religious ceremonies was health and curing to restore the harmony or balance of good and evil in the universe. Both groups had female puberty rituals, held shortly after a girl's first menses. Rituals in both tribes often involved masked dancers who impersonated the Holy People (the Navajo *Yeibechei* and the Apache *Ghaan* or Mountain Spirits). The primary deity for both tribes was Changing Woman, who gave birth to the War Twins (fathered by the Sun), Child of the Waters and Monster Slayer. Also significant were the Sun, First Man and First Woman, and a number of animal spirits.

THE PIMANS. Culturally, the Sonoran Desert was dominated by the Piman-speaking Pima and Tohono O'odham (Papago), believed to be descendants of the prehistoric Hohokam tradition, with its Mesoamerican traits of ball courts, temple mounds, ceramic styles, and irrigation. Pima (O'odham) settlements were located along Sonoran rivers from the Gila in Arizona to the Altar in Mexico, while the Tohono O'odham inhabited the more arid country west of the Pima.

Both the Pima and Tohono O'odham were farmers, depending on maize, beans, and pumpkins. Pima irrigation of their fields with waters from the Salt and Gila rivers made permanent village life possible. The Tohono O'odham relied on flooding from the summer rains to water their fields, located on the floodplains of dry washes

and impermanent streams; summer camps were located near their fields, their winter camps near permanent sources of water. Although both Pima and Tohono O'odham women gathered wild plant foods to supplement the diet, food collection was more important to the Tohono O'odham. All parts of a variety of cactus were used, but the fruits of the prickly pear, called "tunas," and the saguaro cactus were of particular importance. Saguaro fruits were made into a fermented wine consumed ceremonially to usher in the new year and to ensure the coming of the late summer rains. Men hunted deer, antelope, and jackrabbits communally during the winter, an activity less important to the Pima, who usually had a food surplus, than to the Tohono O'odham, whose professional deer hunters were exempt from farming responsibilities.

Villages usually were made up of patrilineal extended families or clans presided over by headmen and councils. Originally both tribes had dual headmen to oversee peace and war, as well as a moral leader known as the "Keeper of the Smoke." Continual Apache raids on Pima villages eventually made war leaders more powerful. Lifelong leadership positions were based on charisma among the Tohono O'odham and were hereditary in the patrilineal line among the Pima. All decisions of the village council, composed of all the adult men, had to be unanimous or consensual.

Of the religious ceremonies focused on crops and rain, the July saguaro (rain) ceremony was the most important. The harvest ceremony, held about November every four years, was essentially a world-renewal ceremony. Rituals, including hunting ceremonies, girls' puberty rituals, and purification rituals for warriors (requiring 16 days of isolation outside the village) involved recitation of the accounts of *Iotoy*, "Elder Brother" (a helpful supernatural being who had killed the monsters in the mythical past), songs, and offerings. Shamans, whose powers came from dreams, directed rituals to diagnose and cure diseases caused by witchcraft. "Curing singers" acquired their powers in dreams from the animal spirits that caused the diseases (Kozak 2008).

RANCHERIAS. The farming village settlement pattern of tribes along the Colorado River (Hualapai, Yavapai, Havasupai, Mojave, and Quechan/Yuma) gives them the name *rancheria* people. All practiced a mixed economy of hunting, gathering, fishing, and farming, depending on location and water supply. Most were patrilineal, and the Mojave and Yuma also had totemic patrilineal clans. The responsibilities of political leaders, whose positions were hereditary in certain families or clans, revolved around warfare, mediation of disputes, organization of communal hunts, and the care of the sick and elderly. Tribal councils composed of headmen from villages or clusters of villages and war leaders whose positions were based on their reputations as warriors and on having had special dreams were found in some tribes.

The rancheria peoples believed they had little control over the supernatural. Dreams were important sources of knowledge and ritual competence, and ritual leaders were usually shamans who had acquired their powers through a vision experience, sometimes expedited by the use of jimson weed (*datura*). Shamans cured illness caused by witchcraft, violation of taboos, or contact with enemies. The Keruk was a major annual communal ritual to commemorate the dead. All tribes had a girls' puberty ritual.

California–Great Basin–Plateau

Three culture areas that had similar subsistence activities were California, the Great Basin or desert country, and the Plateau. In all three areas subsistence was based on food collection—gathering, marginal hunting, and fishing—and their material cultures and social structures reflected this subsistence orientation.

THE GREAT BASIN. The combination of semi-desert and true desert of the Great Basin, part of Utah and Nevada between the Wasatch and the Sierra Nevada mountain ranges and the Snake River in Idaho and the Colorado River and Grand Canyon, is caused by low precipitation and high evaporation rates, creating an arid climate with high daytime temperatures and rapid nighttime

cooling. Although much of the vegetation, adapted to minimal water requirements, can be eaten by humans as seeds, fruits, or bulbs, it does not support large game animals. The principal large game was a scattered, sparse, and unreliable food source, necessitating reliance on smaller animals and a variety of plant foods. The basic food in the higher elevations was piñon nuts; roots, bulbs, and deer were more abundant in the piñon-juniper belt. At elevations over 8,000 feet, mountain sheep were hunted for food.

Population density along the Snake and Colorado rivers and in the piñon-fir-aspen zones of the lower slopes of the Sierras varied with the food supply and the ecology of the area. These tribes relied on the rich and nourishing piñon nut and almost 100 other kinds of plants. Rabbits and antelope, though hunted, were less important than all the other animal foods combined, including rodents, reptiles, and insects. Whenever antelope and rabbits were sufficiently plentiful, communal hunts were organized under the control and direction of the shaman.

The scattered and sparse availability of food resulted in a nomadic settlement pattern of small groups roaming over large territories according to season. Poorly built temporary shelters consisted of arbors or windbreaks in warm weather; caves and rock shelters also were utilized whenever possible. Sweat houses were used for sweat baths and as meeting places for the men. The material culture of the Basin tribes was meager, limited to what could be carried from camp to camp.

With a gender-based division of labor, men hunted—a time-consuming, arduous, and often unrewarding task—and women gathered wild plant foods, prepared the food, cared for the children, did camp chores, and wove fabric for clothing. Children assisted the parent of their sex and assumed adult roles at an early age.

The primary social unit of the Great Basin was the family—a man, his wife or wives, their children, and often several other relatives—moved wherever food was available. Individual families might camp alone for several days at a time, and families came together for collective or communal hunts directed by the "rabbit boss," an experienced older man, and in years of good piñon harvests. Marital rather than political ties linked different groups. Infrequent warfare was usually sporadic feuds caused by suspected witchcraft or disputes over women.

Individualistic supernatural beliefs focused on supernatural powers that came from dreams and vision experiences, welcome but not deliberately sought. Shamans who acquired supernatural powers through visions not only earned prestige and honor as curers but also were feared lest they use their supernatural powers to harm through witchcraft (Sutton 2008).

THE PLATEAU. The Plateau, more a geographic than a culture area in eastern Washington, Oregon, and western Idaho, ranges from sagebrush and juniper flats to meadows and prairies to volcanic wastelands, rugged canyons, and heavily forested mountains. The Rocky Mountains protect the region from the harsh winter storms of the Plains, contributing to the area's mild climate. Rainfall amounts vary; the south is warm and arid, and the north is cool and humid with more than 25 inches of annual precipitation. The Fraser and Columbia rivers provided both a reliable and easily accessible food supply and avenues of communication and transportation.

The cultural diversity of the area reflects environmental and cultural influences, the latter from tribes in neighboring culture areas. Marginal Northwest Coast traits are seen in northern tribes (Lillooets and Klikitats); Plains influences among the Kutenais, Flatheads, and Nez Percé; and California elements in tribes in the central portion of the area. Tribes uninfluenced by outside areas fit more closely with the food-collecting patterns already described.

Fish, particularly salmon, were a source of protein for tribes along the Fraser and Columbia rivers and their tributaries; bulbs were important to the Nez Percé. Despite the variety of game animals on the Plateau, their numbers were not great enough for them to be a major source of food. Some large animals were hunted communally under the direction of qualified leaders.

Small semipermanent villages located along the rivers and streams of the salmon runs ranged in size from hamlets of five families to villages with populations up to 400 in areas where fishing was particularly good. The larger circular semisubterranean earth lodges usually were multiple family dwellings. Although the autonomous villages controlled nearby fishing stations, berry patches, and camas meadows, this control was not exclusive. Villages were free to make use of resources near other villages, and residents were free to move from one permanent village to another. The village headman's primary duties were to maintain internal peace and to settle disputes, sometimes assisted by subchiefs and councils. No overall tribal organization existed, although neighboring villages shared kinship ties from frequent intermarriage and a common language and culture, and met for social and ceremonial activities. Disputes were settled without violence or warfare, although sporadic small-scale raids sometimes occurred.

Nuclear families or several related nuclear families made up the households. Bilateral descent emphasized the patrilineal line. Women were important in all aspects of life, including political and religious, and they also had puberty rituals. The male ritual tended to be longer and more vigorous than that of the females and culminated in a mandatory vision quest.

Religious focus was individual. The world was believed to be filled with a variety of spirits and supernatural forces that could be either helpful or dangerous; vision quests by both sexes revealed a guardian spirit(s) that guaranteed success in life. Those with particularly strong guardian spirits were likely to become shamans, each directing activities related to his animal guardian. Shamans also cured illness attributed to witchcraft or soul loss (Kehoe 2006; Sutton 2008).

CALIFORNIA. Most of the present state of California, from the western slopes of the Sierra Nevada to the Pacific Ocean and from the deserts of southern California to the area of Mount Shasta, is isolated from the rest of North America by rugged mountain ranges. Dominated by the vast interior valley drained by the San Joaquin and

Sacramento River systems, the diverse region of narrow coastal plains, warm interior valleys, and mountain systems stretches for almost a thousand miles along the Pacific. The diversity in natural resources is reflected in the diversity of tribes, languages, and subsistence modes, although most groups depended on acorns as their staple food. Regional variations included the southern Mojave and Yuma farmers, similar to their Southwestern neighbors, and the northern Yurok and Hupa, with their Northwest Coast traits.

In addition to acorns, California tribes depended on a variety of foods: shellfish, saltwater fish, and salmon, while groups near inland lakes relied heavily on fish and waterfowl. The maritime hunters of Santa Monica Bay and along the channel islands took advantage of stranded whales and used Northwest Coast–style plank canoes to fish and to hunt sea lions and sea otters (Glassow 1996). The abundant and regular food supply made permanent village life possible. Single or extended families lived in circular or oval houses and used temporary brush shelters away from the villages. All villages had semisubterranean sweat lodges used daily by the men, and larger villages had large circular dance lodges.

The patrilineal or bilateral nuclear family was the basic social and economic unit of California societies. No overall tribal organization existed; the primary territorial units were primary villages with several lesser settlements, occupied continuously over several generations. Boundaries of village-owned territories of approximately 100–150 miles were known and respected. Political leadership was in the hands of councils made up of all the adult males of the local community. Hereditary headmen were more ceremonial than political; they were respected and wealthier than others in the village but had little authority, other than settling disputes.

Warfare was usually infrequent, motivated by unauthorized trespass on a village's territory or to avenge a death attributed to enemy warfare. Individuals of skill and courage led war parties in surprise attacks and brief skirmishes. Scalps were taken, and captured women and children usually were adopted into the tribe.

Annual and semiannual ceremonies helped to ensure the continuity of the food supply and to ward off disasters. The Kuksu cults of the interior valley were secret societies into which all men were initiated during the male puberty ritual. In curing ceremonies, shamans cured diseases caused by foreign objects shot into a victim's body by dancing, singing, and smoking, followed by the removal of the foreign object by sucking it from the patient's body (Kehoe 2006; Sutton 2008).

The Northwest Coast

The heterogeneous environment of the Northwest Coast, a narrow coastal strip extending 1,500 miles from northern California to southeastern Alaska between the mountains and the Pacific Ocean, shifts gradually from a maritime boreal zone in the north (where the cultures were the most highly developed) to the marginal areas of northern California. Although Northwest Coast tribes were hunters and gatherers, the richness of natural resources and the resulting food surpluses made possible cultural patterns normally associated with farming economies: village life, elaborate material cultures, and social stratification.

The moderate climate and heavy rainfall of the Northwest Coast produce a heavy temperate rain forest, abundant and diverse shrubs and bushes for a range of edible berries and roots, and a plentiful animal life. Most food came from the Pacific Ocean and the rivers flowing into it. Fish, particularly salmon, were an important part of the tribes' diet, but the coastal waters also were rich in shellfish and marine mammals, such as seals, sea lions, porpoises, sea otters, and whales.

Settlements scattered along narrow coastal beaches, usually near the mouths of rivers, in coves, on islands, and in river valleys, were made up of large, rectangular red cedar plank houses—multiple family dwellings—with gabled roofs. Round or oval doors in the gabled end faced the sea and beach. A series of steps or benches led down to fire pits in the center of the house; family sleeping compartments, sometimes miniature duplications of the house itself, were located along the outer walls of the house.

The food surplus supported a complex social organization and an elaborate material culture. Autonomous local groups were based on kinship ties, each with its own chiefs, ceremonies and ceremonial rites, and crests. Local groups were drawn together into economic cooperation and temporary military alliances by combinations of extended unilineal kin groups, called moieties, and clans and the related mutual obligations and reciprocal duties. No overall political linkages existed, however.

The stratified Northwest Coast society was not a typical class system of nobles, commoners, and slaves. Two classes existed, "freemen" and "slaves." The class of "freemen" was a ranking of social positions, nobles (whose parents had given a potlatch) and commoners (whose parents had not). High-status individuals were granted greater deference and more prerogatives and rights than those of lower status, but no formal dividing line separated high-ranked individuals from those of low rank, other than the potlatch. Upward and downward mobility also was common, a result of the potlatch. Because the class of "slaves" was not involved directly in the potlatch cycle, they did not belong to the class system characterized by upward and downward mobility.

Persons born to their ranks did not automatically assume them; claims to high status had to be validated through *potlatches*, ceremonies in which valuable material goods—food, blankets, and copper (shieldlike sheets of hammered native copper)—were given away. Funeral potlatches validated the inheritance of one's status; house-building potlatches validated a man's status as "house chief"; mourning potlatches were held at the death of a chief; and vengeance potlatches redressed grievances. In order to hold high status, one's parents had to have hosted a potlatch. Potlatches reinforced group solidarity and cohesiveness: all members of the kinship group participated by helping collect the goods for distribution and by dancing and singing during the celebrations, and all benefited in sharing the prestige accrued from the display and dispersal of their wealth, for the honors and titles were bestowed on family members who had contributed. Potlatches also provided an economically important means for redistribution of economic goods throughout the society (Kehoe 2006; Sutton 2008).

Northwest Coast art was distinctive and is well known, particularly woodworking, wood carving, and basket making. Wood-carving skills are evident in ceremonial masks, many of which had movable parts; in sculptured food dishes and bowls; and in red cedar boxes, containers, and canoes. Huge oceangoing canoes used in hunting and warfare, sometimes more than 50 feet long and 7–8 feet wide, were decorated with carved or painted family crests. The best-known art form is probably the totem poles, which have come to be almost as symbolic (or stereotypic) of American Indians as are the Plains Indians' tipis and warbonnets. Totem poles were narrative family histories, originally erected at or near the graves of persons to be honored and commemorated. During the nineteenth century these poles were greatly elaborated as corner and doorposts in houses and as mortuary poles and became symbols of status and privilege.

The distinctive decorative arts are characterized by highly conventionalized and stylized heraldic art showing ancestry and glorifying individual and family status. Animals were the most common motif in the two-dimensional caricature-like representations, identifiable by ears and distinctive attributes: the killer whale's exaggerated blowhole and dorsal fin, the beaver's tail and teeth, the bear's claws and canine teeth, and the shark's dorsal fin and teeth. This art differs from European art in its emphasis on symmetry, splitting and spreading animals out in ways that are strange to outsiders, and in filling all blank spaces with interlocked and intertwined figures. Decorative arts could be found on the painted exterior walls of houses; on carved doors and corner posts of houses; on canoes, boxes, and eating utensils; and on ceremonial objects (Kehoe 2006; Sutton 2008).

The Subarctic

A wide belt of coniferous forest extending across North America from central Alaska and the Canadian Rockies to Hudson Bay, Labrador, and

Newfoundland, the Subarctic is rugged and wild. Mountains, streams, lakes, and large expanses of muskeg and spruce stands are interspersed with balsam fir and deciduous trees. In the past, wildlife included large herds of caribou—the primary game animal—and musk ox, many smaller mammals, fish in the glacial lakes and rivers, and waterfowl and birds.

Because of the remoteness of the area and the early decimation of the tribes and cultures, Subarctic cultures have not been well studied or described. Local adaptations to environmental conditions accounted for regional cultural variations. Two linguistic groups predominated: the small, constantly shifting Athabascans—the Koyukons, Hares, Slaves, Yellowknives, and Beavers—in the west, and a small number of Algonkian speakers in the east—the Naskapi, Montaignais, Cree, and Ojibwa-Ottawa.

Subarctic subsistence was based on nomadic hunting and fishing; hunting small mammals and birds and gathering berries and other wild plants were of secondary economic importance. On the tundra, the large barren ground, caribou was the primary animal hunted; other groups fished and hunted animals such as moose. Athabascan groups along western streams took advantage of the annual salmon runs; because of the richness of this food supply and the Athabascans' proximity to the Northwest Coast, their culture was more elaborate than those of other Subarctic tribes. The one universal of Subarctic subsistence was that it was precarious, and during historic times periods of starvation seem to have been common.

Material culture was limited by and adapted to the environment. Snowshoes and toboggans were Subarctic inventions to facilitate travel during the winter; in the summer, transportation was usually by bark canoes on the lakes and streams. The most common type of dwelling was the conical tipi, its framework covered with brush or bark or with hides. Some groups, such as the Slave, made small gabled earth-covered log houses for winter stays of fairly long duration.

The nomadic lifestyle contributed to the simple and largely unstructured social organization known as "composite bands," amorphous and leaderless groups of often unrelated families. Nuclear or extended families hunted and camped together; bands were formed when they were joined by other, similar family groups. Membership in the ephemeral bands was fluid; headmen were skilled hunters who sometimes possessed special supernatural powers but had no real authority. No political units existed beyond the band, although bands might speak the same language or similar dialects, share a common culture and lifestyle, and occupy adjoining territories.

Puberty for boys was marked by a vision quest, a period of fasting and isolation to acquire "power" or "medicine." Because menstruating women were considered dangerous—they could deprive men of their strength and supernatural powers—and a source of potential contamination, they were isolated and had to observe taboos and restrictions, particularly in relation to men. Both senilicide (killing of the elderly) and cannibalism appear to have existed during times of starvation, more commonly among the Algonkians and the Cree than others. Because of the social stigma attached to cannibalism, individuals who craved human flesh were considered to be possessed by the cannibalistic supernatural monster Windigo or Witiko spirit.

The Athabascans attributed illness and death to sorcery or other supernatural causes, and ghosts and death were so feared that lodges in which people died were abandoned and the dead were buried immediately. Algonkians expressed grief through self-mutilation and held annual feasts for the dead. Supernatural beliefs and rituals appear to have been individualistic—informal, unstructured vision quests seeking the guardian spirits, who were more important than a creator god, to help in times of crises and for protection from harmful spirits. Other beliefs and rituals centered around the hunt. The belief that animals allowed themselves to be caught and killed meant that violation of the taboos or inappropriate behavior could offend the spirits of the animals, who would withhold themselves from the hunters.

Shamans were men who possessed special supernatural powers and who could deal with the supernatural world to determine the cause and cure of illness and, in some groups, to determine why game was scarce or absent and to foretell the future. Shamanistic rituals were held to prevent illness and to ward off disease-causing evil spirits. Although shamans could use their powers for witchcraft, generally they believed that sorcery was caused by witches outside one's own social group (Kehoe 2006; Sutton 2008).

The Arctic

A vast, treeless arctic desert stretching across northern North America, from Siberia to Greenland, from the rocky islands and flat barren lands of the Canadian Arctic Plains and Alaska to the cold glacial fjords of Greenland, the Arctic is characterized by a range of topography and land form, climate, vegetation, and fish and game. The Arctic is a desert of cold with surprisingly little precipitation, as little as four inches of snow annually. Freshwater sources include streams (which freeze in the winter), brackish stagnant water that collects in shallow depressions of the tundra bottomlands, and the summits of ocean ice along the winter shore. This seemingly inhospitable tundra supported an aboriginal population of approximately 100,000 people calling themselves Inuit ("humans" or "men") or Yuit. Physically, culturally, and linguistically, they were different from the Athabaskan Indian populations to the south, who called them Eskimo ("raw meat eaters").

Arctic life was affected by the two seasons, summer light and winter darkness. During the short summers, from June to Fall, temperatures rise above freezing and the sun shines for 24 hours; water travel is facilitated by the melting of streams, and the breakup of ocean ice opens expanses of sea for hunting walrus and whales. Swampy conditions created by the melting of the tundra to the permafrost level make land travel difficult. The first severe freeze, in November, marks the onset of winter, which lasts until the spring equinox. Temperatures are cold, averaging 30 degrees below zero (Fahrenheit) on the coast and 65 degrees below zero in the interior, and the wind chill of the cold, gale-force winds lowers coastal temperatures dramatically. During the long, dark winters, the people returned to permanent villages and campsites with the food collected during the summer; summer tents were replaced by winter houses, and boats were exchanged for travel by dogsleds.

While all native Arctic dialects are mutually intelligible, no tribal units were recognized. The Copper Eskimo, the Greenland Eskimo, the Caribou Eskimo, and the Netsilik and Iglulik Eskimo of the central Arctic refer to geographic rather than political groups. Some scholars base their division of the eastern and western Inuit on how they exploited sea mammals, but essentially Arctic culture was characterized by a common shared base of hunting with similar tools and weapons.

Arctic natives relied almost entirely on animals for their food. The seal, found in all areas of the Arctic, was the primary source of food, clothing, and oil for cooking and lighting. Whales and walrus were hunted in Pacific waters; the pelts of polar bears were particularly prized; caribou were hunted; and wolves, wolverines, and fox were hunted for their pelts. Fish and birds were of secondary importance in the Inuit diet.

Summer camps were moved frequently in search of game, but winter base camps were fairly permanent. The stereotypical igloos, or snow houses, were used when hunting seals away from the winter base camps, but they were not the primary winter habitation except in the Canadian Arctic, where nomadism was common even during the winter. Winter houses in the east were made of sod and stone, and in the west of sod; summer shelters were easily transported tents.

Hunting techniques varied according to region and the type of animal being hunted. Seal hunting tended to be individual endeavors or the efforts of fathers and sons, and large game—whale or caribou—was hunted in cooperative groups in which each hunter had an assigned task. Large-game hunting involved careful adherence to ritual to ensure successful hunts and to avoid insulting the spirits of the animals.

Arctic transportation was distinctive. During the winter, dogs hitched in fanwise traces pulled sleds with wooden or bone runners, and in the summer travel was usually by water in light-weight boats with wooden or bone frames covered with skins. The kayak was used by single hunters, using double-bladed paddles, seated in the middle of the vessel and protected by skin coverings that laced around the hunter's waist. The larger umiak was used for whale hunting and for transporting freight and families from one camp to another.

Social structure revolved around the economic and subsistence activities of the household, a kinship unit consisting of a nuclear family and additional relatives led by the head of the family. Marriage ties were economically and socially important, reflecting the cooperative relationship between men and women necessary for both survival and for prestige and status. Preferred marriage partners were those with whom no kinship bonds of support, assistance, or mutual aid already existed. Legally, marriage was defined as continuous cohabitation, but marriages were considered stable and binding only when children were born. Ties between nonkin were established through economic and social partnerships involving friendship, hospitality, and social interaction, consummated by wife-lending or reciprocal wife exchange (such exchanges were not viewed as adultery).

Religious beliefs centered around the special relations between humans and animals, reflected in food taboos, songs, and charms. Animals had to be cajoled, coerced, or placated into letting themselves be caught. Fresh water had to be offered to all sea animals, which allowed themselves to be caught because they were thirsty. Special care had to be taken with bones and waste so as not to offend the animals' spirits, which were released at death. Offended spirits could communicate with other spirits, and all animals then would withhold themselves from humans, causing starvation. Some religious rituals or festivals involved masked impersonations of animals and animal spirits; through dancing, singing, and drumming hunters attempted to exercise some control over the animal spirits. Animals also were the source of the mana-like power of successful hunters, lovers, and shamans. Shamans' spirit helpers usually were associated with land animals; brown bear, wolf, and fox power were highly valued, bear power because it was valuable in curing (Kehoe 2006; Sutton 2008).

HISTORIC RELATIONSHIPS

Although a number of European nations explored the "New World" in the fourteenth through the sixteenth centuries, American Indian cultures were affected most by the French, Spanish, and English. Of these, the fledgling American nation based its practices on established English policies. European attitudes and treatment of the natives depended on their reasons for coming to the New World at a time when European politics were in turmoil. With the Spanish expulsion of the Moors from Spain and the imposition of the Inquisition, the Spanish Crown had to fulfill its promise to provide land to the men who had fought the Moors. Northern Europe was in the midst of social reform, the beginning of industrialism, the rise of the middle classes and decline of the landed aristocracy, and the Protestant Reformation. France, involved in the Huguenot wars, sought trade routes to the Orient, while in England, after Oliver Cromwell's "Roundheads" (Puritans) gained and then lost power, a number of them fled first to Holland and then to the New World, seeking religious freedom. The changes in the sociocultural environment resulting from the European presence in the Americas also led to changes in the Indian cultures.

Early European Contacts and Policies

Initially, neither the French nor the Spanish came to the New World as colonists. While the Spanish came for gold, to save souls, and for land for the veterans of the Holy Wars, the French sought the Northwest Passage or northern waterway to the Orient and commerce in the fur trade. Because neither included women or children in their expeditions, both not only permitted but also encouraged intermarriage between Indian women and European men. The French, who respected Indian customs, also tried to learn the native languages. Both regarded the Indians as human beings, albeit innocent, who were capable and deserving of civilization, which, to them, was conversion to Christianity. Both groups needed peaceful contacts with the Indians (the French need for tribal alliances to facilitate the fur trade led to an avoidance of tribal displacements or annihilations as they moved to the interior of the continent). The Spanish *encomienda* system, which gave Spanish landowners the right to the labor of the natives living on their land grants and which became a form of slavery in some areas, was the result of the need for Indian laborers in the mines and on the estates (Kehoe 2006; Sutton 2008).

The English goal, however, was settlement—establishing homes in the New World where they could own land and raise families. Indians were seen as inferior heathens with whom intermarriage was sinful and for whom conversion to Christianity was inappropriate. English colonial policy was based on commerce. Because the Protestant English colonists did not consider hard work degrading, they had no need for serfs or slaves, and no legal mechanisms were developed to exploit Indian labor. Most conflicts were over land caused by different value systems and perceptions: to the English, land was a commodity to be owned, purchased, and fenced off; to the Indians, land was something shared and used but not owned.

By the time of the American Revolution, the English had established a number of policies that the Americans adopted and that are still in place today. Compensable Indian title to the land, an important principle underlying the Indian Claims Commission cases of the mid-twentieth century, was established in colonial America in the early seventeenth century with laws requiring whites to *buy* Indian lands. This concept had no legal precedents in British law; the colonists used the Bible as their authority. The policy of "reserving" protected lands (reservations) for the Indians also was established in the colonial period, and by the

1750s most New England legislatures had established guardianship over Indians and their lands. "Plantations," or Indian communities, in Massachusetts, for example, were governed by three guardians who had the power to allot land, to rent or lease remaining lands to "suitable" non-Indian persons, to prevent trespass on Indian lands, and to approve sales or leases of land between Indians, all basic tenets of later reservation policy.

Colonial governments controlled Indian trade, requiring licenses for traders going into Indian Country (lands west of the frontier); prohibited the sale of alcohol and firearms to Indians; made the Indians "protected" wards of the federal government; negotiated treaties; and appointed superintendents to regulate trade and negotiate acquisitions of Indian land. A boundary drawn in the Proclamation of 1763 between Indian Country and the colonies, west of the Appalachians from the tidelands of eastern Florida into Canada, was the basis of twentieth-century suits of tribes seeking compensation for lands lost to whites through the Indian Claims Court. Eligibility depended on location west of that boundary line; most tribes to the east were considered to have lost their lands prior to the establishment of the United States (Kehoe 2006; Sutton 2008).

Early American Policies

The American Revolution marked a turning point in Indian–white relations and in Indian cultures: Indian power and independence were undermined by alliances with the European powers who lost the battles for white supremacy in the New World. The French defeat in the French and Indian War left Indians in the interior with no European ally to protect them from English advances. Which side Indian nations had taken in the American Revolution also affected how they were treated in the following years. For example, the Iroquois Indians who were allied with the British were punished and persecuted by the Americans after the revolution.

Indian affairs were of concern to white Americans, and in 1775 the Second Continental

Congress established an Indian Department and appointed commissioners to deal with Indian nations. The policy of the Continental Congress was to treat Indians as dependent internal nations with whom legal treaties concerning land use were made. The seeds of paternalism can be seen in the policy prohibiting Indians in Indian Country from selling land without congressional consent. The Constitution of the United States granted Congress plenary, or supreme, power over Indian affairs in trade, treaty, warfare, and welfare and the power to take Indian land for public purposes as long as just compensation was paid. While a number of American policies were intended to further Indian assimilation, many, in fact, intensified Indian isolation and strengthened ethnic ties and identities.

Following the Revolution, the main American concern was economic—getting Indian trade. The Indian Trade and Intercourse Act was passed in 1790, and between 1790 and 1834 all Indian legislation came under this heading, including licensing of traders in Indian Country; requiring treaties to purchase Indian land; determining the penalties for murder of Indians by non-Indians in Indian Country; appointing agents in Indian Country; defining Indian Country; and prohibiting the sale of alcohol to Indians. Much legislation dealt with land issues, which continued to be the primary source of conflict between Indians and whites. As settlers pushed into Indian Country, the question became one of accommodation or extinction of the Indian peoples. Treaties established boundaries in the belief that Indians would be absorbed slowly into American society and would be willing to sell their lands; when this did not happen, pressures were applied to Indian tribes to cede their lands and move west to Indian Territory (present-day Oklahoma). In 1875, for example, the Shawnee cession of a small amount of land in Pennsylvania was supposed to guarantee their protection; between the Revolutionary and Civil wars, 11 treaties of cession were signed in exchange for protection by the government.

Biological Impact of European Contact

As mentioned above, the pre-contact population of Native American Indians has been estimated between 8 and 18 million people. By 1900 the population had declined to 375,000 (Stannard 1992). Warfare and enforced slavery led to much of the depopulation. However, epidemic diseases introduced by Europeans devastated much of the native population. American Indians did not have the built-up immunities to diseases such as small-pox, measles, influenza, malaria, typhus, bubonic plague, whooping cough, tuberculosis, diphtheria, yellow fever, cholera, and typhoid fever. European populations had developed immunities to these diseases over time because of long-term contact and domestication of various animal species such as cattle, pigs, sheep, horses, and chickens. These animals did not exist in the Americas for the native Indians. Therefore, the Indians did not develop immunological resistance to these new diseases. In some areas, 95 percent of the native population died as a result of these epidemic diseases (Diamond 1992).

THE INDIAN REMOVAL ACT. Despite treaties of cession and appropriation of federal monies to pay southeastern tribes to move to Indian Territory and the newly acquired Louisiana Purchase, Indians were reluctant to leave their homelands. White pressure to remove Indians from the East led to the passage of the Indian Removal Act on May 20, 1830, setting up districts in Indian Territory to accept the eastern tribes. Indians could choose to be under federal jurisdiction or have title to the land and be free of the U.S. government. One-half million dollars was appropriated in compensation for improve-ments on their land, to support them for one year, and to protect them.

Despite Indian resistance to removal, the process could not be stopped, and during the 1830s and 1840s most Indians east of the Mississippi were moved to Oklahoma, overseen in part by the government agency responsible for Indian Affairs created in 1834 and placed in the

War Department. At the same time Congress redefined Indian Country and trader policy and established the basic structure of Indian administration. General superintendents were appointed for designated areas of Indian Country, with subagencies and agents responsible to the superintendents. The position of Indian Commissioner was authorized by Congress in 1832, and in 1849 control over Indian Affairs was shifted from the War Department to the Department of the Interior. During the eighteenth and nineteenth centuries, most European Americans believed that the Indians needed to be civilized or eliminated (Sutton 2008). However, despite the fact that some groups such as the Cherokee had become "civilized" they were ruthlessly uprooted from the Southeast region to be forced-marched to Indian territory in Oklahoma with many thousands dying on what is known as "The Trail of Tears."

During the 1850s and 1860s, the attention of the federal government was on the South and the Civil War, but after the war, attention shifted to the West (Plains) and the Southwest (acquired through the Gadsden Purchase in 1853), where continued pressures for Indian lands and Indian military reactions led to the Indian Wars of the 1860s and 1870s. Defeated Indians were forced onto reservations in an effort to eradicate Indian cultures and assimilate them into American culture: nomadic hunters and gatherers were taught to farm; traditional ritual practices of most tribes were prohibited; polygynous marriages were prohibited; and schools were established or children were removed from reservation communities, sometimes forcibly, to attend all-Indian boarding schools, where they would learn white ways. Children often were not allowed to go home for visits lest they "backslide" (Kehoe 2006; Sutton 2008).

Exploitation of Indians by agents, politicians, missionaries, and military personnel was typical of this period. Missionary and military pressures led to congressional investigations of Indian affairs in 1865. In response to an 1867 report, which described drastic population decline, violation of reservation boundaries,

intolerable reservation conditions, and rampant disease and starvation, proposals suggested turning Indian matters over to missionaries, relocating Indians in the Dakotas and Oklahoma, and dividing the Rockies into districts. By 1873, reservations had been divided among missionary groups, whose presence did lead to some improvement, although exploitation of the Indians continued.

DAWES SEVERALTY ACT (THE ALLOTMENT ACT).

During the 1870s, settlers pushing into "protected" Indian lands and, violating reservation boundaries, pressured for termination of Indian title. As the government's long-range goal always had been assimilation of the Indians, a policy of "allotment"—the individualization of Indian lands—seemed a practical way to accomplish both purposes. Communal ownership and civilization were considered incompatible. Indians farming individually owned plots of land would become self-sufficient and independent of the federal government's support; they would own their land and be able to sell it—to non-Indians—if they wished.[1]

Despite the fact that Indians usually lost fee simple lands, in the 1860s efforts to pass allotment legislation began. Advocates of allotment claimed that Indian tribes threatened with extinction would become self-supporting and would be protected from the loss of reservation lands; domination by certain families would be avoided, and allotment ultimately would lead to assimilation. Opponents to allotment argued that allotment would lead to the alienation of Indian lands, that tribes to be allotted had a nonagricultural orientation, and that the concept of land as private property was alien to Indians. But the majority of Americans believed that the Indians need to be forced to assimilate to the "white American way of life."

Allotment bills introduced in 1878 and 1880 failed; the Indian Homestead Act of 1884 gave Indians restricted title to land that could not be sold for 25 years and could not be taxed. Allotment proponents won with the passage of the General Allotment Act in 1887 (Dawes Severalty Act), which required all tribal lands to be surveyed and divided among members according to the formula of the Omaha Treaty of 1854: 80 acres to single persons, 160 acres to married couples, and 320 acres to families of five or more. A provision to sell surplus lands at public auctions was not mandatory but usually was invoked. Lands would be held in trust for 25 years, after which trust patents would be issued and the Indians would become U.S. citizens under state jurisdiction. The Curtis Act of 1898 extended allotment to the Five Civilized Tribes of Oklahoma, effectively ending their tribal government and education systems, and in 1906 the Burke Act waived the 25-year waiting period for issuance of fee simple title, depending on the competency of the Indian owner.

The most significant long-range result of allotment, which ended in the 1930s, was the loss of approximately 100 million acres of land, most through the sale of surplus lands on large reservations owned by small tribes. "Checkerboarding," when Indians and non-Indians own adjoining tracts of land, made development of allotments and governing of Indian lands impossible, and factionalism, lack of political unity, and little or no social or economic progress resulted. Traditional settlement patterns and social organization were disrupted among some tribes, such as the Pima of Arizona, when individuals left traditional agricultural villages to live on their allotments. Ultimately, allotment increased rather than decreased Indian dependency (Kehoe 2006; Sutton 2008).

INDIAN RESPONSES TO EUROPEAN AND AMERICAN CONTACTS. Indian tribes were autonomous sovereign ethnic groups in control of their own territories and destinies when the Europeans arrived in the fifteenth century. Intertribal contacts were based on economic trade networks or military or political alliances. Initially, some tribes that shared cultural traditions and, sometimes, language reacted to the European presence by strengthening intertribal alliances—the New England Algonkian confederacies: the Abenaki, Wampanoag, Delaware, and Massachusetts confederacies (Underhill

1953:80–81). Several Caddoan confederacies were located in what is now Texas, Louisiana, and Oklahoma (Swanton 1952), but among the better-known alliances are the Powhatan Confederacy (Lurie 1971) in tidewater Virginia (perhaps best known for Powhatan's daughter Pocahontas), the Creek Confederacy of Muskogean speakers incipient in the Southeast at the time of Hernando de Soto's arrival (Swanton 1928, 1952), and the Iroquois Confederacy of the Lower Great Lakes region (Wallace 1970). The only early western alliance led the Pueblo Revolt of 1680 in New Mexico, when autonomous Pueblo villages allied themselves temporarily to drive out the Spanish, if only for a brief time. Such alliances intensified with increased European threats to Indian lands and sovereignty. Indian political and military organization remained strong, their cultures continued to be based on traditional social and belief systems, and they believed themselves, if not superior to, at least equal to the whites and able to deal with them on even terms.

Indian perceptions of their situation changed over time. Increased white settlements encroached on their territory; treaties were violated; efforts of Christian missionaries and white educators intensified; and the ravages of illness and warfare caused the decline in Indian populations. No longer could they vanquish the whites through military force and political unity alone; supernatural assistance was necessary and took the form of revitalization movements (Wallace 1956)—efforts to restore balance in the face of cultural loss resulting from intense acculturation. Nativistic or millenarian movements attempted to return to a "golden age" of past culture, often through a cataclysmic event brought about by supernatural intervention. Such movements were revolutionary and openly hostile to whites:

> The religious trend reflects the yearnings of the Indians for the recovery of their own culture, which was rapidly declining. Such movements . . . sought to salvage and renovate a culture already in crisis by rejecting the white man and his civilization. This

trend is retrospective; for in these movements it is the past that offers the way to salvation. [Lanternari 1963:114–115]

Approximately 20 such nativistic or messianic movements appeared in the United States prior to 1890 (Barber 1941:475–476). Their doctrines were similar, attributing the problems and suffering of the Indians to the coming of the whites and to the Indians' rejection of traditional ways and acceptance of white customs. If the Indians returned to their traditional or aboriginal ways of life, rejected foreign traits and customs, and participated in special ritual practices, the Great Spirit and his emissary would intervene to transform the world into a utopian paradise of eternal happiness and no sickness or death. The essentially peaceful doctrines excluded whites and those Indians who had taken up the white way of life.

During the eighteenth century, just before the forced removal of some northeastern Algonkians from their homelands, several messianic movements provided mythical justification for and reinforcement of military confederacies. The first was the 1760s "conspiracy" of the Ottawa chief Pontiac, based on the teachings of the Delaware Prophet (Hunter 1971; Spicer 1969); the second appeared about 40 years later among the Shawnee, led by Tecumseh and his prophet brother, Tenskwatawa (Eggleston 1878; Mooney 1896; Spicer 1969). The military alliances of Pontiac and Tecumseh tried to drive the English from their lands; both efforts failed. In the Pacific Northwest, the "Dream" religion of the prophet Smohalla provided the justification for the 1877 Nez Percé "uprising" led by Chief Joseph. All these movements were nativistic, advocating a return to the old ways, yet also representing a syncretism of both traditional Indian religions and Christianity. However, the nativistic emphasis on a return to the old ways meant that they could use only native weapons such as bows and arrows, no European firearms, which contributed to their failure; the numbers of Europeans moving into Indian territories continued to increase.

The most widespread messianic movement among western tribes was the Ghost Dance religion of the 1870s and 1890s. The 1890 movement grew out of the earlier 1870 movement, led by the Paiute prophet Wodziwob (Lanternari 1963:131). By the 1870s, the peaceful hunting and gathering Paiutes were losing their hunting grounds to white ranches and were forced to take whatever wage work they could find in the white settlements (Spicer 1969:90). Wodziwob taught that a major cataclysm would shake the world and swallow the whites, but the whites' buildings, goods, and tools would remain behind for the use of the Indians and their dead ancestors, who would return in a railroad train. With the establishment of this heavenly era, the Great Spirit would come to live among them, and they would live in prosperity and immunity to sickness and death (Wax 1971:138). The early movement died out, to be revived about 20 years later by the prophet Wovoka at a time when all western Indians faced drastically altered conditions: restrictive reservation life, military defeat, extinction of the buffalo, and increased dependence on the Bureau of Indian Affairs for food and clothing (Spicer 1969:91). Faced with the threat of starvation and the loss of the old way of life, the message of Wovoka provided hope for salvation and a restoration of the old ways (Barber 1941:476).

In a vision in 1890, during a solar eclipse, in which he believed he died, Wovoka was taken to the "other world" where he saw God and the old people who had died long ago and where he was given God's message and dance to take back to his people. By dancing at intervals for five consecutive days, they could hasten the return of the old ways and the elimination of the whites: "The time will come when the whole Indian race, living and dead, will be reunited upon a regenerated earth, to live a life of aboriginal happiness forever free from death, disease, and misery" (Mooney 1896:19). The fact that there was no place for whites in the utopian world probably contributed to the widespread popularity of the movement. Whites and all things that served a temporary purpose would be removed by supernatural means; Indians only had to observe certain rituals and behaviors. Wovoka's teachings included ritual, a mythology, and a moral code that involved changes in Plains behavior patterns unacceptable to the whites. Although Wovoka stressed peaceful coexistence with whites and obedience to authority until the millennium arrived, as Spicer points out, "It was nevertheless a teaching opposed to the acceptance of White values and way of life. It rested on the belief that Indian ways were good and could be restored" (1969:90).

The original date for the millennium was the spring of 1891; when it failed to materialize, advanced dates were set, until finally the date was left open for sometime in the unknown future. The Ghost Dance spread rapidly among western, particularly Plains, tribes and Sitting Bull introduced it to the Dakota, who gave it a more warlike interpretation. The Indian agent on the Pine Ridge reservation, who did not understand the significance of the Ghost Dance and feared it was an uprising, banned the dance, and asked for—and received—additional soldiers. Confiscation of Indian guns left them with no means for hunting, threatening them with starvation and leading to the "uprising" at Wounded Knee in 1890, precipitated by the murder of Sitting Bull as he was being taken into custody. Some of Sitting Bull's followers joined the band of Big Foot as they were going to a Ghost Dance celebration. All 300 men, women, and children were massacred by white soldiers, who left the bodies to freeze where they lay. The religion spread to other tribes both east and west of the Rockies, with less tragic results.

Although the massacre at Wounded Knee in 1890 represented the end of the Ghost Dance, this revitalization movement and its relationship to the massacre has remained as a vital sacred metaphor and memory for many of the Plains Indians. The Ghost Dance songs and dances are still heard among the native Americans up to the present. For example, in February 1973, Wounded Knee once again became the site for a violent confrontation between the Plains Indians and the U.S. military forces. Led by leaders such as the Lakota Indians, Russel Means, and spiritual leader Leonard Crow Dog, the organization

known as AIM, the American Indian Movement, took over the Pine Ridge Indian reservation at Wounded Knee. AIM accused the tribal government leaders of political and economic corruption, and demanded justice and civil rights for all Native Americans. Leonard Crow Dog led a Ghost Dance ritual during the 70-day occupation in order to create solidarity and spiritual renewal among the Sioux at Wounded Knee. (In addition, the Sun Dance ritual was also conducted at Pine Ridge in 1973.) Firefights between AIM and the FBI and U.S. forces were common throughout the longest siege in American history since the Civil War. The Wounded Knee of 1973 represented the frustration and resentment of many Native Americans regarding their conditions after a century of subordination by the U.S. government. The Ghost Dance led by Leonard Crow Dog symbolized the spiritual resurgence and religious renewal of contemporary Native Americans on the Plains (Scupin 2008).

Not all revitalization movements stressed a return to the old ways; several were "adaptive," combining elements of native concepts with Christianity and stressing accommodation to and acceptance of the changed conditions under which they lived. Although these religions were messianic in origin, because they stressed adaptation rather than a millennium, several of them emerged as fully fledged religions and continue to function in supratribal contexts.

The earliest adaptive movement was the Handsome Lake religion of the Seneca, which developed at the same time that the Shawnee Prophet and Tecumseh were advocating a return to the old ways. Handsome Lake's teachings spread to all the Six Nations and became the religion known as the Long House religion, which still functions on the Six Nations Reserve in Canada. After the Revolution, the unity of the Iroquois League was broken, and its members suffered destruction, illness, population decline, alcoholism, and social pathology. Wallace (1970:194–201) refers to the conditions on the Seneca reservation after the Revolution as "slum conditions." Added to disease, population decline, and starvation during the harsh winters was the American policy of waging "total war" against the Iroquois, which included destruction of complete settlements and the loss of confidence in their ability to survive as a people.

Handsome Lake (Ganeodiyo), half-brother of Seneca chief Cornplanter, was an alcoholic who suffered from ill health, which culminated in a trance in June 1799, during which he was believed to have died. During his vision he was visited by four supernatural beings who gave him the *Gaiwiio*, or "Good Message," from the Creator. Three more visions gave him his gospel of three interrelated themes: the imminent destruction of the world by a great fire that would destroy the wicked; sin, the most serious of which was the failure to believe in the Good Message; and salvation through belief in the Good Message and adherence to its teachings and practices. Subsequent visions gave Handsome Lake a social or moral code that stressed temperance, peace, retention of tribal lands, selective acculturation, and domestic morality in daily life. Handsome Lake's teachings represented an adaptive syncretistic movement that utilized elements of both traditional Iroquois culture and Quaker elements of white culture, creating a new social system and a new religion that was adopted by all the Iroquois. After Handsome Lake's death, the Good Message was written down in the Code, which continues to be recited to the adherents of the religion and is still practiced by the tradition-oriented Iroquois on the Six Nations Reserve (Kehoe 2006; Sutton 2008).

Another syncretism of native and Christian (Roman Catholic) elements was the Indian "Shaker" religion of the Pacific Northwest, so-called because of the bodily shaking of the head and arms during worship. Like Handsome Lake, the prophet John Slocum, a Squaxin Indian from the Puget Sound area, had turned to alcohol and gambling as an escape from reservation conditions in the late nineteenth century.

At the same time that the Ghost Dance was spreading through the western Plains, another religious movement was beginning. Although messianic, it also stressed adaptation to the changed cultural conditions of the Plains tribes and eventually evolved into a fully established religion, the American Indian Church, which involves the ingestion of peyote as a sacrament.

The small cactus peyote grows in the Rio Grande valley of Texas and farther south into Mexico. Ingestion results in sensory alterations, such as sensations of levitation, visions of brilliantly colored images, and enhanced perception of sounds and shapes to the point of hallucinations, with occasional nausea as the only negative side effect. The button is neither deleterious nor habit-forming (LaBarre 1959:7). The use of peyote by American Indians has been recorded among the Aztecs but is probably older. Before its introduction into the Plains area, peyote was used by tribes of northwestern Mexico; the Huichol and Tarahumara used it in a first-fruits ceremony in conjunction with shamanism. Its ritual use spread north to the Mescalero Apache in the 1870s where it was incorporated into the individualistic Apache search for power through visions. By the mid-1870s, peyote had reached the southern Plains Comanche and Kiowa, where it emerged as a collective syncretistic cult utilizing the therapeutic properties of peyote but stressing "the problems engendered by the relationship between the Indians and the whites" (Bee 1965:23). By the 1880s, the religion had begun its rapid diffusion throughout the Plains and eastern areas, where the degraded and deprived conditions of Indians made it a hope of adjustment to and acceptance of their changed circumstances.

The man credited with being the founder and chief promoter of the peyote religion was John Wilson, an Anadarko, Oklahoma, native of mixed Delaware, Caddo, and French ancestry (Hertzberg 1971:243–245; Lanternari 1963:69–72). Introduced to peyote in 1890 while attending a Ghost Dance at Darlington, Oklahoma, Wilson went into seclusion to study its effects on him and to analyze the revelations he experienced. During his visions, Wilson was taken to heaven, where he saw representations of different events in the life of Christ and the home of traditional Delaware beings; he also saw the "Peyote Road," a road leading from the open grave of Christ to the moon over which Christ had walked in order to reach his Father. By following the Peyote Road in their lives, believers could increase their knowledge until they reached the end of the journey—death—bringing them into the presence of Peyote and Christ. At the same time, Wilson received a body of moral and religious teachings, details of the ceremonial procedures to be followed, detailed instructions on the construction of the Peyote altar (crescent moon), paraphernalia to be used in the rituals, and the songs to be sung during the rituals (Aberle 1965:12–13; Lanternari 1963:69–71). Because Indians were not responsible for Christ's crucifixion, they did not need the Bible to receive God's truth but would receive it directly from the Peyote Spirit. The fact that peyotism was exclusively for Indians was an important factor in Indian opposition to whites and white policies (Lanternari 1963:71). The moral code was supported by supernatural sanctions. Those who followed the Peyote Road would find tranquillity in life and material goods and bliss in the next life; those who lapsed morally would suffer in the peyote meetings, both spiritually and physically, in the form of nausea (Aberle 1965:13).

As the religion spread, prophets appeared in other tribes, and the doctrine underwent modification in keeping with individual tribal traditions. Between 1900 and 1910, the religion had spread throughout the Plains, the Southwest, and the northern Woodland tribes. By 1918, when the peyote religion was incorporated as the American Indian Church, there were approximately 12,000 members. Today those numbers are greatly increased. Although the peyote religion originated in the Plains and contains many elements of Plains traditions, its spread can be attributed to a number of factors: it is a compromise between the old and the new; it is an "Indian" religion expressing the concept of brotherhood; the prohibition of alcohol cured many Indians of alcoholism; peyote was regarded as a panacea or "cure-all" for many things (one purpose of peyote meetings was curing); and the hallucinatory vision experienced by eating peyote was in keeping with the Plains tradition of vision quests for spirit helpers (Hertzberg 1971:280–282; Sutton 2008).

TWENTIETH-CENTURY POLICIES

Twentieth-century federal Indian policy has fluctuated from efforts to assimilate Indian tribes to programs stressing Indian self-determination and some degree of autonomy. The lack of consistency in policy has contributed to a continuing sense of tribal and supratribal or "Indian" ethnic identity. In the early twentieth century, the disorganization in Indian communities could be attributed to such federal policies as allotment, forced school attendance, mandatory adherence to federal regulations, and prohibition of tribal ceremonies (Pueblos who held Kachina ceremonies were tried by a Court of Religious Offenses). The corruption, mismanagement, and prejudice typical of the Bureau of Indian Affairs, and Indian reactions to the loss of civil rights, prompted investigations by the government and private organizations. The 1922 Red Cross investigations of reservation health conditions and health care delivery revealed shocking conditions: death rates double those of the rest of the country and excessively high rates of diseases such as trachoma and tuberculosis. Additional investigations were triggered by the failed Indian Omnibus Bill in 1923, which focused on individualization of all remaining tribal lands and the withdrawal of all federal responsibility from Indian reservations. In 1924, legislation gave full citizenship to all Indians born in the United States, although some civil rights were withheld (Arizona Indians were denied the right to vote until 1948).

THE INDIAN REORGANIZATION ACT. The Roosevelt administration of the 1930s has been referred to as the "New Deal" for Indians. Directed by Commissioner of Indian Affairs and anthropologist John Collier, new policies and "new deals" resulted in legislation affecting education and tribal government. The 1934 Johnson-O'Malley Act allowed the federal government to contract with individual states to provide services to Indians, such as education (federal funds were given to individual school districts to take over Indian education), social welfare, health, and agricultural assistance. The most significant and far-reaching legislation of this era was the Indian Reorganization Act (Wheeler-Howard Bill), also passed in 1934, which was designed to stop the alienation (loss) of Indian lands, to authorize tribal organization, and to develop modern business opportunities, credit, and scholarships. Eventually all provisions of the act were extended to all tribes, including those in Alaska and Oklahoma.

THE INDIAN CLAIMS COMMISSION. In 1946, Congress created the Indian Claims Commission, which permitted Indian tribes to sue the federal government for a series of grievances, most of which concerned lands and treaty violations. Tribes had five years to file their claims, and over a period of 10–15 years more than 800 separate causes of action were filed with about $400 million awarded in settlement. The government saw the court-type proceedings as final justification for withdrawal from "the Indian business" and termination of tribes.

RELOCATION. Included in the government's efforts to "get out of the Indian business" was the Voluntary Relocation Program, intended to ease economic pressures and unemployment on reservations (created by returning World War II veterans and defense workers) by relocating Indians and their families in major urban centers. After initial assistance in finding housing and jobs and providing financial assistance until the first paycheck, the Indians were on their own. Later, vocational training and social and welfare services were added to the program. Although relocation was not part of the termination policy, the two programs were linked in the minds of the Indian people.

TERMINATION. U.S. government policy has always encouraged Indians to assimilate into the dominant society. Eventually long-lasting hostilities and resentments led the government to realize that assimilation could not be legislated, and the Indian Reorganization Act was passed in hopes that Indians could be assimilated by letting them use their own cultures as springboards and bases of integration into the dominant society. The

1940s and 1950s saw an emphasis on policies intended to end the federal government's responsibilities to Indian tribes through "termination," a policy that can be interpreted several ways. One branch of the federal government can turn its responsibilities over to another (transfer of the Bureau of Indian Affairs Division of Health to the U.S. Public Health Service); the Bureau of Indian Affairs may relinquish certain responsibilities to tribes; the Bureau may withdraw certain services usually provided to tribes; or states may be given authority to extend civil and criminal laws to reservations (Public Law 280), depriving the tribes of the powers of self-government. What usually is meant, though, is legislation severing the historic relationships between the federal government and the tribes, abolishing tribal governments, and placing tribal affairs and resources under state control.

The termination act, House Concurrent Resolution No. 108, was passed in 1953 for the "rapid freeing" of Indians from federal support and dependency. Each tribe to be terminated required special legislation. The first to be terminated were the Menominee of Wisconsin in 1954, and others followed: the Klamath in Oregon, smaller Oregon tribes, a mixed-blood Ute settlement, small Paiute bands in Utah, the Wyandotte, Peoria, Ottawa, California rancherias, the Catawba (South Carolina), and the Alabama-Coushatta of Texas. Termination was not a success. For example, conversion of the 234,000-acre Menominee reservation into a county meant that the Indians were responsible for road maintenance, utilities, sewer and water plants, and schools. Children were bused to white community schools, the Public Health Service hospital was closed, and all roads and utilities had to be improved to meet state standards. Because their one economic endeavor, a local sawmill operation, could not support the community and its people, the Menominee were forced to convert part of their land and lake area into a resort community, which was sold to whites. Still they were unable to meet all state requirements, and a grass-roots effort, supported by the state government and congressional representatives, actively sought restoration to tribal and reservation status. The Menominee Restoration Act was signed into law in October 1973, a landmark event reversing the termination policy that had been promoted so enthusiastically 20 years earlier. In 1992, the Catawba of South Carolina also were restored to federally recognized status.

Other legislation in the 1950s was intended to promote termination: Public Law 280 transferred civil jurisdiction to Minnesota, Nebraska, Oregon, Wisconsin, and California; the Indian Health Service Branch was transferred to the U.S. Public Health Service in 1954; and 1953 legislation allowed state laws and tribal organizations to regulate the sale of liquor on reservations in conformity with state law. By removing federal funds from the reservations, termination policies resulted in unemployment, declining health, and poverty for Native American Indians.

TRIBAL DEVELOPMENT. Although Congress did not recognize the failure of termination officially until 1973, the procedure ended as an official policy between 1960 and 1966 under Commissioner of Indian Affairs Phileo Nash, an anthropologist whose policies stressed economic and political development, relocation, education, and on-the-job training programs; many of these programs have been carried out by his successors, most of whom have been Indians. Tribal development focused on enhancing existing resources, tourism, and industry, and by 1965 approximately 56 industrial plants were located on or near reservations. Tourism was promoted among the North Carolina Cherokee and the White Mountain Apaches of Arizona, and mineral and timber operations have been significant among the Navajo, Laguna Pueblo, Klamath, and Red Lake Chippewa. Tribal farming and ranching and arts and crafts have been promoted among some tribes, and during the 1990s gaming became an important source of revenue for a number of tribes.

LATE TWENTIETH-CENTURY LEGISLATION/ POLICY. During the administration of Lyndon Johnson, federal policy shifted from termination,

officially repealed in 1988, to self-determination, a policy that has continued to the present, particularly evident in such late twentieth-century legislation as the Indian Self-Determination and Education Assistance Act (1975), which permitted tribes to administer their own federal programs if they desired. The American Indian Religious Freedom Act of 1978 was intended to provide constitutional protection of religious freedom under the First Amendment. But because the legislation failed to give Indians rights that could be enforced legally, this act is regarded as a policy statement. Passage of the Indian Child Welfare Act in 1978 ended the practice of placing Indian children in non-Indian homes for foster care, or adoption. In 1982, the Indian Tribal Governmental Status Act permitted tribal governments to issue bonds, and the 1990 American Indian Language Act reversed policies suppressing and exterminating Indian languages and cultures (Hirschfelder and de Montaño 1992).

Some legislation involved the settlement of land claims against the government: the Alaska Native Claims Settlement Act, passed in 1971 and amended in 1988; and the 1978 Maine Indian Claims Settlement Act, which also confirmed the recognition of the Passamaquoddy, Penobscot, and Houlton Band of Maliseet. Several tribes that were terminated in the 1950s were restored to federally recognized status. In 1983, the U.S. Seventh District Court of Appeals recognized the hunting, fishing, trapping, and gathering rights of the Lac Courte Oreilles Band of Chippewa Indians (Wisconsin), guaranteed in treaties in 1837, 1842, and 1854. Other acts restored sacred lands, objects, or treaty rights to tribes: in 1970, Blue Lake was returned to the Taos Pueblo; Mount Adams was returned to the Yakima of Washington in 1972; and in 1974, treaty-guaranteed fishing rights were returned to 14 tribes in Washington, including the right to fish in off-reservation waters. In 1991, after passage of legislation in 1989 creating the Museum of the American Indian as part of the Smithsonian Institution (which also required the Smithsonian to return human remains to tribes requesting them), sacred objects taken from the Omaha in

1898 were returned by the Smithsonian and by the Peabody Museum of Harvard University, and the Smithsonian returned the skeletal remains of 756 Kodiak Islanders for reburial.

Of particular importance to a number of tribes were the 1988 Indian Gaming Regulatory Act and the Native American Indian Graves Protection and Repatriation Act (NAGPRA) passed in 1990. The Gaming Act created opportunities for economic development by permitting gaming on reservations of federally recognized tribes, especially important after budget cuts reduced tribal revenues. By 2001, at least 200 tribes had some 320 gaming facilities in 29 states and in 2005 they took in more than 23 billion dollars (Sutton 2008). The largest Indian gaming operation in the United States is the Mashuntucket Pequots' Foxwoods High Stakes Bingo and Casino in Ledyard, Connecticut. It grosses over a billion dollars a year with 75 million going to the state of Connecticut (Sutton 2008). The Pequot have used these revenues to establish educational, health, and police services, and a museum.

Under NAGPRA, museums or agencies receiving federal funding are required to inventory collections of Indian human remains, mortuary objects, sacred items, and materials of "cultural patrimony" and to return them to tribes requesting them (which had to prove tribal ownership). As tribes have reclaimed items of "cultural patrimony," a number of tribal museums have been developed to house them.

AMERICAN INDIAN ACTIVISM

Some of the policies of the latter part of the twentieth century have their roots in the activism of the late 1960s and early 1970s (Bonney 1975; Day 1972; Steiner 1968). Beginning in 1958, armed Lumbees in Robeson County, North Carolina, broke up a Ku Klux Klan rally. In 1961, Indian leaders at the American Indian Chicago Conference, organized by anthropologist Sol Tax, created a "Declaration of Indian Purpose," a statement of Indian intent to retain spiritual and cultural values and to promote self-determination. A group of Indian college students, uninvited and excluded from the conference proceedings and frustrated with Bureau of Indian Affairs policies and the caution of the "Uncle Tomahawks" (tribal councils and other Indian leaders), met and formed the National Indian Youth Council at the Gallup Intertribal Ceremonial in 1961. Their policy of "red nationalism" and their tactics of direct action and civil disobedience emulated the sit-ins of the black civil rights movement, as did Iroquois Wallace "Mad Bear" Anderson, who took over the Six Nations' council house to protest the construction of a dam on the Tuscarora Reserve. Using revolution to accomplish their goals, they initiated a series of "fish-ins" protesting the violation of treaties signed by several Washington tribes that had ceded tribal lands in exchange for the right to fish in traditional, off-reservation fishing grounds.

The success of the Washington fish-ins and the sympathy of the dominant society set the stage for other "red power" actions (associated with Indian militants). The Mohawk demanded, and won, free admission to the 1964 New York World Fair in Flushing Meadows, New York, on the basis of their treaty of cession of that land in 1684; Isleta Pueblo in New Mexico evicted a Catholic priest in 1965 for interfering with and ridiculing traditional Pueblo practices; the Mohawk blocked the International Bridge between New York and Canada under the leadership of "Mad Bear" Anderson in 1965; and in 1967, Red Lake Chippewa Tribal Chairman Roger Jourdain protested a General Electric advertisement in *The Saturday Evening Post* saying, "When you decide to shoot wild Indians, you can't afford to miss." The Passamaquoddy in Maine stopped logging operations of the Georgia Pacific Company in 1968, and in 1969 set up a roadblock on U.S. Highway 1 protesting the state legislature's failure to provide funds for child welfare; the Quinault tribe closed 25 miles of their beaches in Washington to whites in protest of abuses of beach-use privileges; and the Fort Yuma Quechan seized Bureau of Reclamations equipment to regain lands.

Attention in the 1960s was focused on the seizure of the former federal penitentiary

Alcatraz, in California, by a group of Indian students calling itself "Indians of All Tribes," under the 1868 Fort Laramie Sioux Treaty, which called for surplus federal lands to be returned to the Indians. They intended to create an Indian Cultural Center, Institute of American Indian Studies, research center, medical center, and a museum. The occupation ended in 1971 with the removal of the 15 Indians remaining on "the Rock" by armed federal marshals.

The American Indian Movement (AIM), founded in 1968 in Minneapolis, Minnesota, by young urban Ojibwa and Sioux, probably is the best-known red power organization. Initial concerns focused on local issues—discrimination against and harassment of Indian peoples and negative stereotypes. By 1970, however, membership had become national, drawing primarily from urban and disenfranchised rural communities, and the issues of Indian sovereignty and broken treaties became the focal point of AIM's efforts. The group's tactic of direct confrontation was first seen in sit-ins at Mount Rushmore in 1971 and 1972 and the seizure of the Chippewa Dam at Winter, Wisconsin, by the Lac Courte Oreilles Chippewa Band. National attention was drawn to AIM with the "Trail of Broken Treaties" and the occupation of the Bureau of Indian Affairs building in Washington, D.C., in November 1972, and with the 77-day occupation of the Pine Ridge Sioux community of Wounded Knee, South Dakota.

Wounded Knee was an expression of AIM's concern over Indian sovereignty and the validity of traditional forms of tribal government rather than those imposed by the Indian Reorganization Act. Originally, AIM members were invited to an open meeting at Wounded Knee to discuss tribal government and the Bureau by the Pine Ridge Civil Rights Organization, Sioux traditionalists who rejected official tribal government and protested the administration of tribal chairman Richard Wilson. Within hours, the village was barricaded by police roadblocks and cordons, but the seizure and occupation of the village by AIM was triggered by a beating of AIM leader Russell Means and AIM's desire to fight for the rights of all Indians. Wounded Knee, the site of a massacre in 1890, became the symbol of white injustice to Indians. After a 77-day siege, AIM leaders and federal officials signed an agreement to end the occupation; Wounded Knee defendants were indicted on a number of felony charges, and most defendants, tried in Sioux Falls, South Dakota, were convicted. The trials of seven AIM leaders, indicted on 11 charges, were held in Federal District Court in St. Paul, Minnesota, beginning in January 1974. AIM leaders Russell Means, Dennis Banks, and Clyde Bellecourt were acquitted. Since that time, AIM has concentrated on legal actions, including efforts to gain freedom for Leonard Peltier, convicted of the murder of two FBI agents in a shoot-out with Indians on the Pine Ridge Sioux reservation in 1975. Although AIM declined in membership during the 1980s, beginning in the 1990s they have been trying to revitalize this pan-Indian organization (Sutton 2008).

AMERICAN INDIANS TODAY

In the twenty-first century, Indian ethnic identity appears to be stronger than ever, usually focused on specific tribal identities reinforced by legislation, shared historical events and relationships, and participation in both traditional and pan-Indian organizations and activities. The definition of "Indian" is not precise. Dictionary definitions usually refer to aboriginal inhabitants of the New World based on European explorers' beliefs that they had found Asia or the Indies; census definitions tend to be based on self-ascription rather than biological or genetic determination. Persons who are less than one-fourth "Indian"—the usual "blood" requirement—must be accepted as "Indians" by the community. Mixed stock refers to the non-Indian parent as white; mixed Indian and black generally are considered black unless Indian characteristics predominate or they are accepted as Indians by the Indian community.

Eligibility for Bureau of Indian Affairs services requires residence within or adjacent to reservations or trust or restricted lands receiving *direct* Bureau services. Membership in federally recognized tribes—those with reservations and receiving federal services—requires one-fourth degree of Indian ancestry. Tribal rules for inclusion on tribal rolls vary, from one-sixteenth degree of Indian ancestry among the Cherokee to tribes requiring one Indian parent (one-half degree). Most "recognized" or "federal" Indians are in the West, where first European contacts were sporadic and later in time than those in the East, where they were able to maintain their territorial base and their languages. Acculturation and cultural borrowing were selective, usually connected to material culture and economy. Recognized Indians receive federal services through the Bureau of Indian Affairs, the branch of government within the Department of the Interior responsible for carrying out federal programs authorized by Congress, acting as trustee for Indian lands and resources, and creating a climate in which Indian groups can operate by and for themselves. The commissioner of Indian Affairs, a presidential political appointment confirmed by the Senate, oversees all Bureau functions, including education, welfare programs, employment, tribal development, and financial assistance.

During the nineteenth century Indian education was in the hands of missionary groups that received federal money to run the Indian schools with the long-range goal of assimilation. The first off-reservation government-run Indian schools were opened, reinforcing policies of allotment and assimilation; the military academy atmosphere of Carlisle Institute in Pennsylvania served as a model for Indian education of the time. From 1890 to the 1930s, on-reservation boarding and day schools continued to strive for assimilation, hiring non-Indian teachers who conducted all classes in English. The National Study of Indian Education (1955), under the direction of Estelle Fuchs and Robert Havighurst, investigated conditions in seven categories of Indian schools and resulted in the passage of the Indian Education Act of 1972. This act was not only to improve educational opportunities and programs on reservations but to make federal money available for special programs for nonreservation and "unrec-

ognized" Indian children in public school systems, as well as for adult education in both on- and off-reservation communities.

The latter part of the twentieth century saw an increase in Indian control over the education of their children through Indian-controlled school boards (the Navajo Nation's Rough Rock Demonstration School teaches a curriculum chosen by the community in both English and Navajo), the growth of a number of Indian magnet schools that focus on multicultural education, and of tribal colleges, such as Navajo Community College and Sint'e Gleska University at Rosebud, South Dakota. These schools stress native values and ways of learning rather than the competition and individualism of the public school systems.

Members of recognized tribes also receive medical care through the Indian Health Service, which was transferred to the U.S. Public Health Service in the 1950s. Reservations clinics, health stations, or hospitals provide medical care to reservation Indians that is unavailable to urban Indians. Although health care has improved since the 1960s, Indian life expectancy tends to be below the national average. While they no longer suffer from some of the epidemics of the past (influenza, measles, whooping cough, diphtheria, and tuberculosis, one of the major killers), Indian health problems reflect social and economic conditions, especially alcohol and drug abuse. Primary causes of death include heart disease and cancer (both have increased since the 1960s), diabetes, influenza, pneumonia, and cirrhosis (high in the past and remaining high), as well as accidents (often related to alcohol), suicide, and homicide. The incidence of disease depends on environmental conditions, economic status, educational level, and traditional attitudes, all of which contribute to practices related to nutrition, cleanliness, health consciousness, and the availability of and demand for medical services. Medical facilities are not available to geographically isolated communities; few medical care providers are Indian, speak Indian languages, or understand Indian cultures and values. Most doctors stay for only a brief time, so there is little continuity.

Also, Western medicine is not the holistic medicine to which Indians are accustomed.

"Unrecognized" Indians include those who relinquished their rights to government services and their reservations, such as urban Indians, and terminated Indians, but the term usually refers to tribes, primarily along the eastern seaboard, who have never been under Bureau control but who have maintained Indian and tribal identities and, sometimes, ceremonies. Among such groups are the Lumbee, Coharie, Haliwa, and Tuscarora of North Carolina, the Narragansett of New England, small enclaves in Virginia, and the Houma of Louisiana. Early European contact led to loss of land, intermarriage, acculturation, mixed ancestry, and rural enclavement as they sought to retain their Indian identity. Many of their ancestors fought in the Revolution and are referred to in the 1790 census as "free persons of color," distinguishing them from black slaves. Until the 1830s they could own property, vote, serve in the militia, and, in the South, own slaves. But then they were disenfranchised. Denied the right to self-government, and segregated and discriminated against as "colored," and despite the loss of cultures, languages, religions, and social organizations, they retained a sense of "Indian" identity, separate from blacks and whites. For many, one of the primary boundary-maintaining mechanisms was education: denied the right to attend white schools and the right to "Indian" schools, they were forced to send their children to black ("colored") schools. Opposed to ascription of a "colored" identity, they chose not to send their children to public school and attempted to open "Indian" schools. The University of North Carolina at Pembroke began as the Lumbee Indian Normal School in 1887.

Many of the unrecognized groups have sought or are seeking recognition or acknowledgment through the Bureau of Indian Affairs. Between 1830 and 1970, recognition required the tribe to have existed as a "distinct political community"— a social group distinct from non-Indians—and that the federal government had taken actions acknowledging the political relationship with and responsibility for the tribe (Roth 2001).

Many of the unrecognized Indians in urban areas had left the reservations to improve their economic situations. As early as 1928, Indians were recognized as living in urban areas and were covered in a special chapter of the Meriam Report. Many of these early migrants to urban centers were assimilated into the dominant society as they internalized its values. Their descendants often do not identify themselves as "Indians," nor are they considered such by reservation Indians. The first government effort to relocate Indians in urban areas occurred after World War II when about 75,000 Navajos and Hopis who had served in the armed forces or had been employed in off-reservation war industries returned to their reservations and were unable to find jobs.

In 1952, the program, now called the Voluntary Relocation Program, was expanded to include other tribes. Intended to teach Indians to be self-sufficient in urban areas, the program provided a range of services for relocatees and their families, including selection of the relocation point, finding temporary and permanent housing for the applicant and his family, financial assistance for transportation and subsistence en route to the destination and until the relocatee received his first paycheck, and follow-up services to relocatees and their families. Major relocation points included Chicago, Los Angeles, Denver, San Francisco, St. Louis, Oakland, and Dallas.

Though the program ended in 1980, the number of Indians living in urban centers in some cases exceeds that of Indians on reservations; more than 50 percent of the total Indian population today is urban. Adjustment to urban life was difficult for a tradition- and kin-oriented people, and problems such as returning to home communities (and losing jobs) and alcohol abuse were pervasive in some urban communities (Graves 1970; Price 1968; Sutton 2008). Urban Indian centers were established to provide services—economic, social, educational, and recreational—to relocated Indians. Powwows became an important feature of many urban Indian centers as a way of allowing Indians to express and reaffirm their ethnic identity.

Originally the word *powwow* was used to refer to New England Algonkian community gatherings for political deliberations and feasting around large fires (Wissler 1954:62–63). Today it refers to secular intertribal gatherings found across the country, ranging from large intertribal ceremonies, sometimes organized by chambers of commerce as tourist attractions (the Gallup, New Mexico, Intertribal Ceremonial) or by mixed Indian and non-Indian committees (All American Indian Days at Sheridan, Wyoming), to small annual reservation or community social events held in the summer and urban center powwows. The latter may be held monthly throughout the year, though they tend to be more common during the winter months when there are no reservation powwows to attend.

Modern powwows evolved out of the early Plains reservation culture as Indians attempted to reorganize and stabilize community life by providing opportunities for socializing and singing and dancing in the old "Indian" style—reasserting their Indianness—as well as escaping temporarily from acculturation pressures. The modern focus on such Plains traits as singing, dancing, and regalia is a result of the Wild West and Indian medicine shows, which usually featured Plains Indians. Powwows focus on competitive dancing, the primary form being the "war dance," an amalgamation of northern and southern tribal styles (Powers 1968). Underlying the "fast" or "fancy" war dance, performed by young men, with its fancy footwork, abrupt posture changes, and quick spins and dips, is an older form dating to the 1870s, referred to as the "classic" style and usually danced by older men. Dance styles continually evolve and spread throughout Indian Country, including the newer "jingle dancing" from the northern Plains and the women's shawl dance, which involves intricate footwork similar to that of the men's fast war dance.

Although there are regional variations, certain features are central to powwows: dancers, regalia, singers and drummers, competitions (a way to win honor and recognition), dances honoring veterans and other individuals,

give-aways, tipi encampments, feasting, and social dances in which everyone may participate. Although non-Indians may participate in powwows if they are dressed in the appropriate regalia, powwows are primarily an Indian activity (Sutton 2008).

CONCLUSION

Instead of being assimilated into the mainstream of U.S. culture, today the American Indians seem to be in a strong position of ethnic survival, their ethnic identity strengthened by the very policies intended to assimilate them by placing them in positions where they were forced to resist and to oppose the federal government and its policies. Reservation and removal policies reinforced geographic isolation, and their status as wards of a paternalistic government enhanced social isolation and dependency, further separating them from the mainstream of American culture. The lack of consistency in federal policy has increased their resistance to assimilation, and recent legislation only reinforces their separate ethnic identity. The Indian Arts and Crafts Bill, NAGPRA, Indian gaming—all make Indian identity something to be desired, whether on a tribal (federally recognized) or individual level.

Despite different tribal backgrounds, most American Indians share common historical experiences that bind them together in a shared identity of "Indian," a situational supratribal identity that supersedes tribal identities. Milton Gordon, in *Assimilation in American Life* (1964), referred to identity systems as a series of concentric rings around a person's "core" identity. For Indians, this can be a layered identity encompassing core identity to kinship to tribal to Indian to American. Within the tribal community, identity is based on kinship connections; in a supratribal situation, identity may be tribal, but in the larger outside world, where tribal distinctions are not recognized by the general public, an Indian identity is assumed—always a distinct identity separate from mainstream America. For many the important part of that identity is "Indian"; one AIM leader said he preferred to be called an "Indian American" than an "American Indian." The important part of his identity was the Indian component, not the American.

Ethnic awareness and pride are expressed in the revival of traditional arts and crafts, participation in supratribal events such as powwows or in "Indian" religions, such as the American Indian Church, and identification with "Indian" symbols. This awareness and pride are evident in the increased efforts of a number of eastern tribes to gain acknowledgment. As tribal or ethnic groups, American Indians have resisted assimilation for 400 years, and, though statistically a small percentage of the overall population, they remain strong—at least 500 distinct ethnic groups (Sutton 2008).

Notes

1. Indian lands are held in three types of title: *fee simple* (the full range of landownership giving individuals full title to the land, which can be sold or willed to others); *trust* (the land is held in trust for the Indians, who use it in perpetuity and must be compensated if it is taken away; lands cannot be taxed, sold, mortgaged, or leased without government consent); and *restricted* (may be subject to taxation but cannot be sold or leased without federal permission). Although individual Indians own land in all three classes, most prefer trust status, which provides the most protection.

References Cited

ABERLE, DAVID. 1965. The peyote religion among the Navajo. *Viking Fund Publications in Anthropology*, no. 42.

BARBER, BERNARD. 1941. Acculturation and messianic movements. *American Sociological Review* 6:662–667. Reprinted in William A. Lessa and Evon Z. Vogt, eds., *Reader in Comparative Religion*. Pp. 474–477. Evanston, IL: Row, Peterson, 1958.

BARTH, FREDRIK. 1969. *Ethnic Groups and Boundaries: The Social Organization of Culture Difference*. Boston, MA: Little, Brown.

BEE, ROBERT L. 1965. Peyotism in North American Indian groups. *Transactions of the Kansas Academy of Science* 68(1):13–61.

BONNEY, RACHEL A. 1975. Forms of supratribal Indian interaction in the United States. Ph.D. dissertation, University of Arizona, Tucson.

DAY, ROBERT C. 1972. The emergence of activism as a social movement. In *American Indians Today: Sociological Perspectives*. Howard M. Bahr, Bruce A. Chardwick, and Robert C. Day, eds. Pp. 506–532. New York: Harper & Row.

DIAMOND, JARED. 1992. The arrow of disease. *Discover* 13(October): 64–73.

EGGLESTON, EDWARD. 1878. *Tecumseh and the Shawnee Prophet*. New York: Dodd, Mead.

FAGAN, BRIAN M. 2005. *Ancient North America: The Archaeology of a Continent*. 4th edition. New York: Thames and Hudson.

GLASSOW, MICHAEL A. 1996. *Purisimeño Chumash Prehistory: Maritime Adaptations along the Southern California Coast*. Fort Worth: Harcourt Brace.

GORDON, MILTON M. 1964. *Assimilation in American Life: The Role of Race, Religion, and National Origins*. New York: Oxford University Press.

GRAVES, THEODORE D. 1970. The personal adjustment of Navajo Indian migrants to Denver, Colorado. *American Anthropologist* 72(1):35–54.

HERTZBERG, HAZEL. 1971. *The Search for an American Indian Identity: Modern Pan-Indian Movements*. Syracuse, NY: Syracuse University Press.

HIRSCHFELDER, ARLENE, and MARTHA KREIPE DE MONTAÑO. 1992. *The American Indian Almanac: A Portrait of Native America Today*. New York: Macmillan.

HODGE, WILLIAM H. 1981. *The First Americans: Then and Now*. New York: Holt, Rinehart, & Winston.

HUDSON, CHARLES E. 1976. *The Southeastern Indians*. Knoxville, TN: University of Tennessee Press.

HUNTER, CHARLES E. 1971. The Delaware nativist revival of the mid-eighteenth century. *Ethnohistory* 18(1):39–49.

JOSEPHY, ALVIN M., JR. 1991. *The Indian Heritage of America.* Boston, MA: Houghton Mifflin.

KEHOE, ALICE B. 2006. *North American Indians: A Comprehensive Account.* 3rd edition. Upper Saddle River, NJ: Prentice Hall Press.

KOZAK, DAVID. 2008. Shamanisms: Past and present. In *Religion and Culture: An Anthropological Focus.* Scupin, Raymond, ed. 2nd edition. Upper Saddle River, NJ: Prentice Hall Press.

LABARRE, WESTON. 1959. The peyote cult. *Yale University Publications in Anthropology,* no. 16. New Haven, CT: Yale University Press.

LANTERNARI, VITTORIO. 1963. *The Religions of the Oppressed: A Study of Modern Messianic Cults.* New York: Knopf.

LURIE, NANCY O. 1971. Indian cultural adjustment to European civilization. In *The American Indian: Past and Present.* Roger L. Nichols and George R. Adams, eds. Pp. 42–60. Waltham, MA: Xerox College Publishing.

MOONEY, JAMES. 1896. The Ghost Dance religion and the Sioux outbreak of 1890. *14th Annual Report, Bureau of American Ethnology.* Pp. 666–667. Washington, DC. Abridged edition, Anthony F. C. Wallace, ed. Chicago, IL: University of Chicago Press, 1965.

POWERS, WILLIAM K. 1968. Diffusion of the Plains war dance. *Powwow Trails* 5(6):68–72.

PRICE, JOHN A. 1968. The migration and adaptation of American Indians to Los Angeles. *Human Organization* 27(2):168–175.

ROTH, GEORGE. 2001. Law and the Southeastern Indians. In *Anthropologists and Indians in the New South.* Rachel A. Bonney and J. Anthony Paredes, eds. Tuscaloosa, AL: University of Alabama Press.

SCUPIN, RAYMOND. 2008. *Cultural Anthropology: A Global Perspective.* 7th edition. Upper Saddle River, NJ: Prentice Hall Press.

SPICER, EDWARD H. 1969. *A Short History of the Indians of the United States.* New York: Van Nostrand Reinhold.

———. 1971. Persistent cultural systems. *Science* 174:795–800.

STANNARD, DAVID E. 1992. *American Holocaust: Columbus and the Conquest of the New World.* Oxford: Oxford University Press.

STEINER, STAN. 1968. *The New Indians.* New York: Harper & Row.

SUTTON, MARK Q. 2008. *An Introduction to Native North America.* 3rd edition. Boston, MA: Allyn and Bacon.

SWANTON, JOHN R. 1928. Social organization and social usages of the Indians of the Creek Confederacy. *Bureau of American Ethnology Annual Report 42.* Pp. 23–472. Washington, DC: Smithsonian Institution.

———. 1952. The Indian tribes of North America. *Bureau of American Ethnology Bulletin 145.* Washington, DC: Smithsonian Institution.

UNDERHILL, RUTH. 1953. *Red Man's America.* Chicago, IL: University of Chicago Press.

WALLACE, ANTHONY F .C. 1956. Revitalization movements. *American Anthropologist* 58:264–281.

———. 1970. *The Death and Rebirth of the Seneca.* New York: Knopf.

WAX, MURRAY L. 1971. *Indian Americans: Unity and Diversity.* Englewood Cliffs, NJ: Prentice Hall.

WISSLER, CLARK. 1954. *Indians of the United States: Four Centuries of Their History and Culture.* Garden City, NY: Doubleday.

7

U.S. Ethnic Relations: Anglos and the "White Ethnics"

Raymond Scupin, *Lindenwood University*

The purpose of this chapter is to set the stage for an understanding of race and ethnic issues in U.S. society. Subsequent chapters discuss African Americans, Hispanic Americans, Jewish Americans, Asian Americans, and Arab Americans. These more specialized chapters were written by anthropologists who concentrate on the study of different ethnic groups in the United States. In order to form some basis for understanding these various ethnic groups, we need some background on the establishment of patterns of ethnicity and race relations by the European settlers in America. We begin the chapter with an overview of the early English settlers, the so-called WASP ethnic group, which provided the basic cultural heritage for U.S. society. In addition, we examine the patterns of non-WASP immigration from Europe in the nineteenth century and the consequences of this immigration for U.S. society. In order to grasp the complexities of this process, we focus on the early trends of immigration from northwest Europe by examining the experience of the German and Irish ethnic immigrants. To investigate later trends of immigration from southern and eastern Europe in the nineteenth century, we concentrate on the experience of the Italian and Polish ethnic groups. Finally, we address the various policies of assimilation and pluralism in U.S. society and how these so-called "white ethnics" have influenced these policies.

WASP DOMINANCE

The early European colonization of what was to become the United States begins with the so-called WASP, or white Anglo-Saxon Protestants. In actuality, the term *Anglo-Saxon* is a bit of a misnomer. The phrase is derived from the northern European ethnic groups, the Saxons and Angles, who invaded England during the fourth and sixth centuries A.D., displacing other ethnic groups such as the Celts and Romans, who had come from Europe in earlier centuries. Eventually, the Normans invaded England from France to intermingle with these other ethnic groups. Thus, the English settlers who came to settle the New England colonies were a product of a long history of the merging of different ethnic cultures. The acronym WASP was not actually popularized until the publication of a book in 1964 called *The Protestant Establishment* by sociologist E. Digby Baltzell (Christopher 1989). The term *WASP* has come to denote a northern European ethnic group with a particular cultural and institutional complex that dominated U.S. society for generations. The British settlers were able to overcome their rivals, the French, Spanish, and Dutch in colonial America, and were free to develop their own form of culture. With the exception of Native American Indians and enslaved African Americans, four out of five colonial settlers in America were British Protestant. Smaller groups of settlers, including Scots and Welsh, as well as Scotch-Irish (Protestants from Northern Ireland), Dutch, Germans, and Scandinavians, were present in early America. Yet, by the end of the seventeenth century, these early non-Anglo settlers assimilated, culturally and structurally, becoming part of the core WASP ethnic group that became dominant.

WASP ethnicity became preeminent in the United States through the establishment of its language, symbols, and culture. The English language was the fundamental underpinning of the cultural legacy that was bestowed by the WASPs on American society. It became the acceptable written and spoken language for the building of the nation-state and country, and it represented the standard for creating ethnic identity in colonial America. English was the institutional language of education and religion among the WASPs. Prior to the American Revolution, education was private and only accessible to affluent WASP citizens. The educational system was founded largely on the tenets of primarily Anglican and Calvinist-Puritan forms of the English Protestant traditions. Later, groups of Baptists and Methodists (and smaller groups of Lutherans and Quakers) influenced WASP religious culture. The cultural values of these religious traditions were transmitted through the English language. English-language facility was necessary for any type of education in early American society. Other early immigrant groups such as the Germans, Scandinavians, and Dutch were expected to readily adopt the English language or suffer the consequences if they did not.

Xenophobic attitudes (fears of foreigners) were expressed by some of the early English settlers when faced with ethnic groups who did not speak English. For example, Benjamin Franklin was extremely wary of German immigrants who were coming into America speaking another language and maintaining another culture. He said, "Should the Palatine Boors [Germans] be suffered to swarm into our settlements and by herding together establish their language and manners to the exclusion of ours? Why should Pennsylvania, founded by the English, become a colony of aliens who will shortly be so numerous as to Germanize us instead of our Anglifying them, and [who] will never adopt our Language or Customs" (Christopher 1989; Kamphoefner 1996:152). From the early establishment of WASP culture, the expectation held that any subsequent ethnic groups that came to America would have to learn the English language. This was the first stage of what has sometimes been referred to as "Anglo-conformity."

Along with the English language, the WASPs brought their basic fabric of the economic, legal, and political institutional framework for U.S. society. One of the primary reasons for colonization of North America by the British was to extract raw materials and to produce new markets for England. The English Crown chartered companies and granted territory for these companies to develop commercial capitalism in America. The ideals of commercial capitalism, including the right to own private property, were brought to America by the English settlers. The initiatives for taking land from Native American Indians, for developing European forms of agriculture including the importation of slaves, and for sending raw materials across the Atlantic were all aspects of the market-oriented capitalism that was transported from England to America. Following the American Revolution, this market-oriented capitalism became the cornerstone of the expansion of the Industrial Revolution in the United States. As the principal ethnic group that was engaged in the development of commercial capitalism and the industrial revolution, the WASPs were able to dominate and manage the major economic capitalist institutions within U.S. society.

Both the legal and political institutions of what was to become U.S. society emerged as a combination of early British and eighteenth-century French philosophy. The substance of the early laws enacted by the WASPs in the colonies was English in origin. Rights of property holders, contracts, equality before the law, and representative government had been institutionalized by the British government and were espoused by English philosophers such as John Locke (1632–1704). The English colonists' conceptions of a decentralized form of political process based on town meetings and participatory democracy were developed in early America. Broader philosophical and political beliefs that expressed ideals of equality, freedom, justice, individual rights, anti-aristocratic values, and checks and balances among separate divisions of government authority were adopted by leaders such as Thomas Jefferson and Benjamin Franklin from such French philosophers as Montesquieu (1689–1755) and Jean-Jacques Rousseau (1712–1778). These cultural ideals became the basis of the American Revolution and the fashioning of the new nation-state. Constitutional government and abstract principles of equality, justice, freedom, and political autonomy were promoted through this political creed and cultural ideals.

One of the questions that arises when discussing U.S. history after the American Revolution is to what extent the political leaders were intent on fashioning a nation-state that was based on Anglo ethnicity or whether they were trying to develop a civic polity based on a more universal basis. On the one hand, in *The Federalist Papers* (1787–1788), the political documents that provided the foundation for the U.S. Constitution, John Jay describes the American people as "descended from the same ancestors, speaking the same language, professing the same religion, attached to the same principles of government, very similar in their manners and customs. Surely, a band of brethren so united should never be split into a number of unsocial, jealous, and alien sovereignties" (cited in Walzer 1997). Thomas Jefferson developed an obsessive interest in beliefs of the superiority of the Anglo-Saxon race, and actually tried to learn the ancient language itself (Smedley 2007). These beliefs suggest that an "Anglo-WASP" ethnicity should (would) be the basis for the new American nation.

Conversely, it would appear that as the revolutionaries were forging a new nation-state, a number of the leaders were also fashioning the notion of a new form of identity for the nation, an "American" identity and nationality. With the Revolution, many U.S. citizens developed "Anglophobia" and hostility toward the British. In order to distinguish themselves from their European predecessors, including their British ancestors, some of the early leaders emphasized "American ideals," which were embodied in the political documents of the Revolution. It appears that some were trying to establish a civic polity rather than an ethnically based polity (Gleason 1980). In this view, ideally, to become an American, individuals did not have to be of any particular national or ethnic background. All they had to do was to subscribe to the political and cultural ideals of liberty, equality, and constitutional government. However, the *ideal culture* of the United States differed substantially from the *real culture*. For example, many of the revolutionary leaders perpetuated the slavery of Africans and the appropriation of land from Native Americans. It appeared that "whiteness" was the primary criterion for distinguishing different identities. European descent and "whiteness" were inextricably linked to create a divide among different groups of Americans. Thus, despite the attempt to be as inclusive as possible, the "American identity," which referred to all "men" or "mankind" in the various political documents, remained fairly exclusive. So, the question as to what extent the new "American identity" converged with or diverged from an Anglo-WASP identity has remained significant for many people throughout different periods of U.S. history.

NEW ETHNIC CHALLENGES FOR U.S. SOCIETY

It is necessary to reiterate one of the themes of this textbook at this juncture. The WASP or Anglo ethnic group, like any other ethnic group, exhibited a great deal of internal diversity and variation regarding socioeconomic status and cultural traditions. For example, in his book *Albion's Seed: Four British Folkways in America* (1989), David Hackett Fischer identifies four distinct peoples that represent British culture in early America: the English Puritans of New England, the southern planter culture of Virginia, the Quakers of Pennsylvania, and others who settled in the backcountry of Appalachia. However, as the economic and political institutions developed along with the Industrial Revolution in the United States, only a comparatively small number of persons within these different Anglo populations became part of the dominant elite. This political and economic elite, however, was able to maintain its political hegemony over other ethnic groups for a substantial period of U.S. history.

No one can question the reality that the language, cultural values, and practices of the descendants of the English settlers disproportionately influenced the institutional framework of the United States for generations. As we will see, in respect to later-arriving ethnic minorities, the WASP elite controlled the playing field for assimilation into U.S. society. Because they did not have many non-Anglo ethnic groups with economic or political power to compete with for resources or power, the WASPs had definite advantages in establishing their dominance. Historically, the significant rules for cultural and structural assimilation were established by the WASPs through immigration policies, laws regarding segregation or integration, removal policies, voting restrictions, and a number of other measures aimed at ethnic minorities.

Most sociologists and historians agree that the descendants of this WASP ethnic group still maintain an enormous and disproportionate amount of economic and political influence in U.S. society. For example, Arthur Schlesinger states, "For better or worse, the white Anglo-Saxon Protestant tradition was for two centuries, and in crucial respects still is, the dominant influence on American culture and society. This tradition provided the standard to which other immigrant nationalities were expected to conform, the matrix into which they would be assimilated" (1992:28).

The nineteenth century, however, was to see an enormous number of non-Anglos flowing in from other parts of the world who would begin to challenge Anglo dominance. More than 30 million non-Anglo European immigrants would come to the United States in the nineteenth century. Typically, sociologists and historians classify this immigration from Europe in the nineteenth century into two distinctive historical periods. The period from 1820 to 1880 is the first era of non-Anglo immigration and is sometimes called the "Old Immigration" period. The period from 1880 to 1920 is referred to as the "New Immigration."[1] The Old Immigration period is associated with immigrants from northwest Europe, including the Irish, Germans, and Scandinavians from Norway and Sweden. The New Immigration era is identified with southern and eastern European immigrants, including Italian, Polish, Greek, Russian, and Jewish groups. All of these European populations were considerably different ethnically from the WASPs. Many were non-Protestant, maintaining either Catholic or Jewish religious traditions. In addition, especially in respect to those ethnic groups from southern and eastern Europe, these people had different languages that were historically far removed from the developments of the English language. To illustrate the patterns of ethnicity in the United States, we will focus on the German and Irish immigrants to examine the early period of European immigration from northwest Europe. Later we will focus on the Italian and Polish immigrants to illustrate how U.S. society regards these people from southern and eastern Europe.

GERMAN AMERICANS

Since the seventeenth century, approximately 7 million people born in the area now known as Germany settled in North America. Currently, more Americans trace their ancestry to Germany than any other country. Although it is difficult to assess these numbers precisely, some 50–60 million Americans are descendants of Germans (Adams 1993).[2] One group of the earliest German immigrants arrived in 1683 in Philadelphia and settled nearby in an area that became known as Germantown. These immigrants were mostly religious Quakers and Mennonites, and Pennsylvania provided a tolerant atmosphere for them. In the first American census of 1790, the population of the city of Germantown was 225,000, about a third of the citizens in Pennsylvania. Most of these Germantown residents were weavers, merchants, or artisans. Other early German immigrants settled in the English colonies of New York, New Jersey, Maryland, Virginia, and South Carolina. The population of Germans in the colonies at the time of the American Revolution was approximately nine percent of the total. These early German settlers came to America primarily in search of a better standard of living and to escape the extremes of the class structures, which limited economic opportunities in German society. Political and religious freedom and the threat of military induction motivated others to immigrate from Germany. Many early German settlers were "chain migrants" who followed relatives and friends into the colonies (Adams 1993; Kamphoefner 1987). These friends and relatives helped provide aid and comfort for these new immigrants. Early German immigrants were very diverse, divided by class, education, religion, and dialect. Most of the residents of Germantown anglicized their names, quickly learned English, and began to intermarry outside of their group. On the other hand, some of the German settlers were threatened by the WASP ethnic dominance, and were fearful of language loss and culture (Conzen 1980).

Later, in the nineteenth century, largely because of failed political reforms and revolutions, crop failures, and the lack of economic opportunities in Germany, German immigrants flowed into the United States. These German immigrants represented different religious traditions—Protestant, Catholic, and Jewish. (See Chapter 8 on Jewish Americans.) Some of these migrants came as "indentured servants." As indentured servants, they signed a contract with a ship's captain who had the right to sell the passenger, along with his family, into a form of servitude for three to four years in order to pay their passage (Adams 1993). More than 220,000 Germans arrived in the year 1854.

Up until the twentieth century, when Germany was able to industrialize enough to absorb its rural population into its labor force, German immigrants continued to choose the United States for settlement. Over 5 million German immigrants came to the United States in the nineteenth century (see Table 7-1). Unlike earlier German immigrants, who began to assimilate swiftly, generally the migrants of the nineteenth century began to move to areas where there were substantial German settlements. Many of the Germans with rural backgrounds sought out reasonably priced farmland in areas where German schools and German-language churches already existed (Adams 1993; Kamphoefner 1987). Those from the same villages in Germany would follow each other into rural America. The chain migration continued to form significant German communities throughout the Mid-Atlantic states. Most of the rurally based German populace settled along the waterways of the Great Lakes or the Ohio, Missouri, and Mississippi rivers.

Many of the German immigrants entering the United States were urban-based people skilled in crafts, trades, or professional occupations. The booming cities of Cincinnati, St. Louis, Chicago, Pittsburgh, Milwaukee, Indianapolis, and Louisville, located along waterways or railways, were attractive sites for Germans with urban skills. Breweries, bakeries, distilleries, flour millers, tailor shops, print shops, surveying businesses, and plumbing stores were established by these immigrants. A number of well-educated immigrants who had fled Germany for political

TABLE 7-1 Germans in the U.S. population, 1850–1970		
Year	Number	Percent of Foreign-Born
1850	583,774	26.0
1860	1,276,075	30.8
1870	1,690,533	30.4
1880	1,966,742	29.4
1890	2,784,894	30.1
1900	2,663,418	25.8
1910	2,311,237	17.1
1920	1,686,108	12.1
1930	1,608,814	11.3
1940	1,237,772	10.7
1950	991,321	9.5
1960	989,815	10.2
1970	832,965	8.7

Source: U.S. Bureau of the Census, *Historical Statistics of the United States, Colonial Times to 1970* (Washington, DC, 1975), Series C, pp. 195–227, 286–295.

reasons became important political activists and officials within the U.S. government. Thus, nineteenth-century German American ethnic communities included both skilled and unskilled laborers. Because of their numbers and the occupational diversity of their population, German Americans could develop extremely self-sufficient communities. By 1900, one-third of Wisconsin's population was German, and Minnesota and Illinois had more than one-fifth from Germany (Adams 1993).

As the numbers of immigrants from Germany increased, rather than assimilate quickly into U.S. society, many attempted to retain their ethnic identity, including their language, culture, and religious traditions. As in other areas of Europe, the Industrial Revolution in Germany engendered nationalist movements. These nationalist movements began to draw together disparate peoples throughout Germany into a perceived unified ethnicity and identity, and these movements affected the migrants entering the United States as well. Many of these German immigrants wanted to conserve

their ethnic and nationalist identity within the United States. Aside from German-language schools and churches, they began to establish ethnically based organizations such as music societies, theater clubs, beer halls, lodges, and political clubs. In particular, the institution known as the *Turnvereings* ("Turner Clubs"), which emphasized physical body-building through gymnastics and calisthenics, as well as German nationalistic, intellectual, and artistic culture, were sites for emphasizing ethnic expression and Germanness. The Turner Clubs provided German-language instruction and adult classes in German history, politics, and philosophy. Through these organizations and institutions, as well as the private schools and churches within specific neighborhoods, various "Little Germanies" emerged throughout major cities such as St. Louis, Cincinnati, and Milwaukee. The endeavor to preserve German culture in the United States even led to a proposal to establish an exclusive German state in the Union (Adams 1993; Cornell and Hartmann 1998).

The German language was prevalent in the schools and churches within the German American communities throughout most of the nineteenth century. German was spoken by about 9 million people in the United States as late as 1910 (Adams 1993). Most of the private schools in the German American neighborhoods taught exclusively in German, and for some time states like Pennsylvania and Ohio allowed German as an alternate language to English in the public schools. German Americans struggled politically with the public school systems to allow for bilingual education so that children would not forget their native tongue. German-language books, magazines, and newspapers were published and circulated widely within these communities. By the late nineteenth century, the largest non-English-speaking ethnic group were the Germans, who chose to differentiate themselves ethnically from the WASP majority by maintaining their language and culture. To a great extent, the Germans and non-Germans maintained separate communities, which were institutionally apart, the hallmark of what is known as a plural society.

As seen earlier in the remarks of Benjamin Franklin, some of the WASPs were concerned about ethnic Germanness and its impact on U.S. society. Eventually, in the 1850s, these latent xenophobic feelings led to an open nativistic political movement aimed at Germans and other immigrants. A political party known as the Know-Nothings developed. The Know-Nothing program aimed to elect only WASPs to political office, to fight against Roman Catholicism, and to restrict citizenship and voting rights to immigrants who had resided in the United States 21 years instead of the 5 years required by law. (They were known as Know-Nothings because party members were instructed to divulge nothing about their political program and to say they knew nothing about it.) However, it was not until World War I and then World War II that extensive anti-German prejudice emerged within U.S. society. As the United States entered World War I against Germany and Italy, the ethnic German American status became endangered. The excessive nationalistic tendencies in World War I Europe were countered by an intensive "Anglo-American nationalism" in the United States.

During the war, U.S. newspapers were filled with anti-German hysteria. Numerous political cartoons characterized the German American community as a perceived threat to U.S. society. The German language was no longer taught in public schools, and public libraries removed German-language books and magazines from their shelves. Wartime hysteria even led to the banning of the use of the German translation of the Bible in Lutheran churches. As a reaction to these anti-German sentiments, rapid cultural assimilation began to dominate within the German American communities. For example, German surnames and German business names were Anglicized.

World War II and the horrors of Nazism sealed the fate of ethnic Germanness in U.S. society. The aftermath of the wars resulted in most German Americans adopting and assimilating to Anglo culture as quickly as possible. Typically, the use of the German language was thoroughly abandoned in advertising and in the teaching of history and religion. German parents no longer taught their children German. In addition, there was a high rate of intermarriage among German

Benjamin Franklin.

Americans and other ethnic groups. Most German Americans had been successful in adjusting economically, socially, and politically in American society. Large numbers of them had achieved equality with WASPs in terms of education, income, and occupation. And, in reality, ethnic German culture had a major impact on the culture of the WASPs. The national diet, work habits, intellectual culture, educational system, and political and religious traditions were influenced widely by German cultural traditions. But, following the world wars, ethnic Germans did not want to forsake their overall success in the United States by emphasizing their Germanness. They did not want to be a target of persecution, discrimination, and prejudice. Consequently, cultural and structural assimilation became their predominant ethnic strategy. Only small groups such as the Old Order Amish (see Chapter 4) and other smaller religious communities retained the German language and culture in order to preserve a separate ethnic identity.

IRISH AMERICANS

Immigrants from Ireland began to enter colonial America during the 1600s. Most of these early immigrants were the so-called Scotch-Irish who had earlier immigrated to Northern Ireland from England after England conquered Ireland in the twelfth century. Most of the Scotch-Irish were Protestants, of the Anglican or Calvinist (Presbyterian) religious traditions, along with smaller numbers of Methodists, Baptists, and Quakers. However, about one-third of these early immigrants were Irish from southern Ireland, who had been Catholic but most of whom converted to Protestantism. Since there were few Catholic institutions such as churches and priests at the time in colonial America, most early Irish immigrants became Baptists or other kinds of Protestants (Byron 1999). It is estimated that some 40 percent of George Washington's revolutionary army were Irish (Christopher 1989). An Irishman, John Barry (1745–1803), became the "father of the United States Navy" (Blessing 1980). At the end of the American Revolution, the

Irish made up about 10 percent of the U.S. population.

The major influx of Irish immigrants into the United States, however, came during the nineteenth century. Over 4 million Irish settled in the United States during the 1800s (see Table 7-2). Today, some 40 million Americans trace their ancestry to Ireland. A variety of factors led to the flood of Irish immigrants in the 1800s. Like Germany, Ireland lacked a sufficient industrial base to absorb the increasing population of rural laborers. As a result of British policies in Ireland, there were enormous numbers of rural Irish who were landless or who held marginally small landholdings. The constant pressure of population on the resources of the Emerald Isle resulted in heavy emigration. And most importantly, the well-known Great Famine of the 1840s was a traumatic ecological and economic disaster that resulted in large-scale immigration. Most of the

TABLE 7-2	Irish immigration to the United States, 1820–1975
Years	Number of Immigrants
1820–1830	54,338
1831–1840	207,381
1841–1850	780,719
1851–1860	914,119
1861–1870	435,778
1871–1880	436,871
1881–1890	655,482
1891–1900	388,416
1901–1910	339,065
1911–1920	146,181
1921–1930	220,591
1931–1940	13,167
1941–1950	26,967
1951–1960	57,332
1961–1970	37,461

Source: U.S. Immigration and Naturalization Service, *Annual Report, 1975* (Washington, DC, 1976), pp. 62–64.

rural Irish subsisted on the potato crop. In 1845, a fungal potato blight resulted in 80 percent of the harvest being destroyed. Approximately 90,000 people starved to death because of nutritional deficiencies and other related physical problems (Blessing 1980; Byron 1999). The potato famine resulted in at least a million Irish immigrating to the United States between 1847 and 1854. The severe persecution of the poor Irish by British landlords and political authorities in southern Ireland was another significant factor in driving immigration. An intensive ethnonationalist movement based on Irish Catholic ethnicity had developed in Ireland, and a number of politically active Irish were attempting to revolt against the British authorities. One response of the British authorities was to promote immigration as a solution to the "Irish troubles" (Miller 1985). Thus, both economic and political factors "pushed" Irish immigration and led to the arrival of many Irish to U.S. shores in the mid-nineteenth century.

The Irish immigrants in the United States represented diverse peoples from different regions of Ireland. Like the German immigrants, many of the Irish came as chain migrants who relied on networks of relatives and friends to help them settle. In particular, kinship networks and people sharing a surname aided each other in the settlement process. Also, many employers sent money to Ireland to pay the passage of the cheap labor they wanted. There were rural laborers and also urban workers from cities like Dublin, Belfast, and Cork. Some people from the middle stratum of Irish society could pay their own passage and had education, skills, and capital to make a start in the United States. Others, fewer in number, were from more remote and distressed famine areas of Ireland. They were the poorest immigrants and lacked education, skills, and capital. Many of them had to come as indentured servants. The better-off immigrants spoke English (and many may have resided in Britain for some time before moving to the United States), while fewer in number, the poorest rural Irish from remote areas spoke only Irish (Gaelic, the ancient Celtic language of Ireland), while many other Irish were bilingual. On the whole, the majority

of the Irish were English-speaking immigrants, albeit, there were a number of Anglo-Irish dialects that were (and still are) often identified as the "brogue" (Byron 1999). And though the vast majority of these Irish immigrants were Catholics, smaller numbers were Protestants.

As the Irish Catholics settled in the United States, they adapted within many different types of occupations, skilled and professional. Many of the immigrants with education, capital, and skills were able to establish their own businesses in the booming economies of nineteenth-century America. Some of them became the leaders of major enterprises. Other white-collar workers were clerks, clergy, or teachers. However, the many Irish who came with little education and capital were forced to take the lowest-paying jobs in factories, mines, mills, construction, and other unskilled occupations. For example, large numbers of Irish workers were involved in the construction of the Erie Canal in New York State. Later, Irish labor was used to build the intercontinental railroad across the country. Others worked in foundries, railway locomotive factories and repair shops, furniture factories, boat-building shops, breweries, and other unskilled industries. Many of the Irish women began to work as domestic servants for WASP households, or in the textile mills and factories in eastern cities such as New York and Boston. In large cities like New York and Boston the Irish crowded into tenements, at times 20 or more families within a house. The press referred to these Irish tenements as "human rookeries." The availability of both Irish skilled and unskilled labor was instrumental in transforming the United States into a powerful industrial economy.

As Irish (and German) immigration increased in the nineteenth century, xenophobic sentiments (fears of foreigners) helped usher in nativistic movements among the WASP. In particular, Roman Catholicism, associated with the Irish, was perceived to be untrustworthy. Anti-Catholicism had originated in Europe and was brought to colonial America by the early WASP immigrants. Part of this anti-Catholic sentiment was the fear of the Pope taking control of various institutions and religious traditions. But the cry against "popery" and Catholicism increased as Irish immigrants flooded into the United States. As mentioned earlier, the Know-Nothing Party, the nativist political organization, was directed at prohibiting non-WASP and Catholics from participating in American social and political life. Much of the party's activity was aimed at the Irish, who were unwelcome because they were non-WASP and Roman Catholic. The Irish Catholics were beginning to bring their priests, religious institutions, and schools with them to America, and this reawakened old European religious hatreds. Like the Germans, the Irish Catholics reestablished these institutions as a means of retaining their Irish Catholic ethnicity. They formed societies such as the Hibernians, an organization linked to the Catholic Church, which promoted Irish ethnicity. But these activities resulted in the Irish feeling the sting of prejudice and discrimination from the WASP majority.

Other conceptions of Irish Catholic immigrants began to circulate among many WASPs. The Irish Catholics were perceived to be a "separate race" and were purported to have a distinctive biology that made them different from the WASPs. This construction of "race" was associated with prevalent stereotypes and generalizations about the Irish Catholics. Of course, this was at the time when "race" was confused with "ethnicity." The Irish "race" was perceived by the WASPs as undesirables who were immoral, unintelligent, uncouth, dirty, lazy, ignorant, temperamental, hostile, and addicted to alcohol. Some of these stereotypes and prejudices held by the WASPs had emerged in England and were imported into America. But in America these racially based stereotypes became vicious caricatures that were used to discriminate against the Irish. Underlying these stereotypes were the anti-Catholic prejudices, the extreme poverty associated with Irish immigrants, and their willingness to work for lower wages than other Americans. This resulted in some WASP employers blatantly refusing to hire the Irish. In cities such as Boston and New York, there were signs in storefronts, housing complexes, and factories saying, "No Irish Need Apply."

Unlike the German Americans, many of the Irish resisted their secondary status in WASP America by utilizing economic and political strategies. For example, many of the Irish involved themselves in early labor organizations to challenge their employers. The Irish workers frequently found themselves in bad working conditions and shameless exploitation. In addition, they faced the nativist WASP Americans who resented them because of their competition in the labor market. Wages were extremely low, ranging from 82¢ to $1.25 per day, and some of the Irish workers were paid in whiskey or "credit" in company stores, which charged high prices. To counter these conditions, Irish workers began to organize themselves. In the anthracite coal mines of Pennsylvania, the Irish formed the Molly Maguires, an organized union group that fought for better working conditions. The Mollies had actually started in Ireland but was transported to the United States (Kenny 1998). They used strikes and sometimes threats of violence, and actual violence, arson, and sabotage in order to struggle against coal company bosses who wanted to squelch their union. It is generally acknowledged that the Molly Maguires' struggle was the embryo of the organized labor movement in the United States. Irish workers continued their organized labor activities and eventually came to dominate many local unions. George Meany (1894–1979), a grandson of an Irish refugee from the Great Famine, became president of a major American union, the AFL-CIO. This union activity enabled the Irish to overcome some of the discrimination directed at them, and thereby become more economically successful in U.S. society.

Another means of success for the Irish in the United States was the employment of political strategies. The historical experience in Ireland and the struggle with the British pre-adapted the Irish for American politics. In the large cities, the Irish were adept at learning the political game that developed in nineteenth-century America. In particular, the Irish became associated with the Democratic Party in U.S. politics. Big-city political machines were often created and controlled by the Irish immigrants. Through the political process the large numbers of immigrants were able to elect their own Irish representatives. As soon as new immigrants landed in New York or Boston, they were drilled by Irish voters and representatives about the political issues that affected them. Irish ethnic unity was cultivated by anti-WASP attitudes. The Irish political ward bosses frequently provided government jobs for their own group, and city contracts were given to Irish-owned private businesses. These political machines also furnished needed services such as better housing, food, coal, and other amenities to poor immigrants. The infamous Tammany Hall political machine in New York City in the early 1800s was controlled by Irish political bosses. Though there were many political scandals that developed based on graft and corruption at this time in U.S. society, these Irish-dominated political machines created opportunities for the Irish in the large cities to move upward to challenge the WASP political hierarchy. Overall, this tradition of Irish American politics and its affiliation with the Democratic Party left a legacy that eventually resulted in the accomplishments of the descendants of the Irish such as the Kennedy family in Massachusetts.

Anthropologist Reginald Byron's (1999) in-depth ethnographic and historical study of the Irish in Albany, New York, suggests that the experience of the Irish in the cities of New York and Boston do not tell the complete story of the Irish in the United States.[3] Indeed, only about 10–15 percent of the Irish stayed in the large cities. Most of them settled in small cities, towns, villages, and rural communities throughout the United States. In order to gain an understanding of the more typical Irish American experience, Byron concentrates his ethnographic work on Albany, a town where many Irish immigrants settled. His ethnographic study on what it means to be Irish in the United States reveals complex phenomena that counter any simplifications or generalizations. He suggests that many of the generalities about the Irish American are based on the historian's interpretations of newspapers, church records, government reports, and other documents that are associated with the Irish in the large cities. By focusing his ethnographic study on a medium-sized city with a substantial Irish immigrant population, Byron was able to investigate another side of the Irish American experience. Instead of finding people who were clinging to a "primordial" ethnic identity in distinctive neighborhoods, like the portrayal of the Irish in Boston or New York, he discovered that the descendants of the Irish immigrants in Albany have a highly abbreviated "Irishness." They have very vague recollections of their ancestral history, and overall, Irish ethnic identity does not have much resonance beyond participating in the St. Patrick's Day parade.

St. Patrick's Day Parade.

ITALIAN AMERICANS

During the second major period of immigration (the so-called "New Immigration," 1880–1920), many southern and eastern European ethnic groups entered the United States: Greeks, Italians, Serbians, Hungarians, Bulgarians, Russians, Ukrainians, and Poles. The United States was undergoing an unprecedented economic and industrial transformation that demanded large reservoirs of labor. Industrial expansion in the garment industries, food processing, mining, construction, and other manufacturing and services offered opportunities for people in southern and eastern Europe. Approximately two-thirds of the foreign-born population that came into the United States during this period were from these regions. Unlike the northern European groups, such as the German, Dutch, and Irish, these new immigrants had languages and cultures that were far and away much different from those of earlier immigrants.

A small number of northern Italians had settled in colonial America during the seventeenth century. Later, during the mid-1800s, other northern Italians came to California for the gold rush, and stayed to work as merchants, grape growers, wine makers, storekeepers, and truck farmers. But most of the Italians, over 4 million, primarily from southern Italy, came to the United States between 1880 and 1920 (see Table 7-3). Some of these southern Italians only stayed for a short time before returning home; however, the vast majority remained. Presently, over 15 million Americans trace their ancestry to Italy. In the nineteenth century, regions like Naples and Sicily in southern Italy were the most undeveloped parts of the country. An oppressive feudal agricultural system dominated by absentee landlords, and discrimination in trade, industry, and education by northern Italians drove emigration from southern Italy. Although some southern Italians immigrated to North Africa and South America to work in agriculture, the wages and opportunities of the U.S. industrial economy were strong attractions for these people. In contrast to the northern Italians, these new immigrants tended to be

TABLE 7-3 Italian immigration to the United States, 1820–1970

Years	Number of Immigrants
1820–1830	439
1831–1840	2,253
1841–1850	1,870
1851–1860	9,231
1861–1870	11,725
1871–1880	55,759
1881–1890	307,309
1891–1900	651,893
1901–1910	2,045,877
1911–1920	1,109,524
1921–1930	455,315
1931–1940	68,028
1941–1950	57,661
1951–1960	185,491
1961–1970	214,111

Source: U.S. Bureau of the Census, *Historical Statistics of the United States: Colonial Times to 1970* (Washington, DC, 1975), pp. 1, 105–106.

poor, uneducated, and less skilled. Thus, most of them entered the labor force at the lowest end of the unskilled jobs (Lopreato 1970).

In the nineteenth century, Italy itself was in the process of creating its own nationalism out of its many different ethnic groups. It was the American experience that helped forge ties of ethnic identity among Italians. As these different ethnic groups from Italy arrived, they were classified by the U.S. government officials as "Italian." And, as 90 percent of these "Italians" settled in urban areas, and founded communities, they came to recognize their similarity of tastes and preferences for food, dress, and other cultural traditions. Different ethnic groups such as the Neapolitans and Sicilians came together to assist one another in their settlements in the U.S. urban environments. Many of the early immigrants had come through a form of indentured labor known as the "padrone system." A *padrone*, or boss, would recruit laborers in Italy, pay for their passage to the United States, and arrange work for them, mostly in construction. Other padrones recruited immigrant labor at the port of entry. The worker was obligated to pay a commission to the padrone for his services. Other Italian immigrants came through "chain migration," relying on kinship networks. As Roman Catholics, they used church organizations and other voluntary mutual aid societies to help them adapt to the new conditions in the United States. Because of these ties, eventually, these immigrants began to perceive themselves as having a common identity as "Italian Americans" (Alba 1985). This new identity created the foundation for the "Little Italys" in urban areas such as New York, Boston, Chicago, and St. Louis.

By the twentieth century, Italian Americans had adapted to a variety of professions, trades, and occupations in U.S. society. Many of the unskilled laborers had started as stone workers, cement workers, dock workers, luggage makers, and railroad workers. A number of Italian Americans had established major businesses such as the Planter Peanut Company, cigar companies, real estate and building companies, and banks. Italian women were working in the garment industries, as well as in candy, paper, and cigar companies within the larger cities such as New York and Chicago (Nelli 1980). Like the Irish, many Italians organized and joined unions to help them to move ahead economically in the United States. The founder of the amalgamated Clothing Workers of America, a labor union representing garment workers in Chicago, was an Italian American. Eventually, both Italian men and women joined unions to improve working conditions for their communities.

Italians also used the political process and the big-city political machines to gain advantages in the United States. In the Italian wards, the political bosses tended to be of Irish ethnicity. The Irish political bosses hired Italian men to organize the voters and lead their communities to the polls. The Italians provided votes that retained ward bosses and political machines in operation in exchange for jobs and contracts for Italian American businesses. Numerous Italian Americans sought public employment within the cities for a steady income and job security. As the Irish had developed connections within the Democratic Party and controlled the political machines, so the Italian Americans became associated with the same political party. In some instances, a few Italian Americans anglicized their names and ran for political office. For example, Paolo Antonio Vaccarelli, born in Naples, took the name Paul Kelly and became an influential politician in the Democratic political machine in New York (Nelli 1980).

As Italians were adjusting to U.S. society, Italian-language newspapers and the Roman Catholic Church served as integral aspects of their ethnicity and culture. The Italian-language newspapers provided a mechanism for communication in the neighborhoods for the first generation of immigrants. They allowed these immigrants to voice their grievances and complaints about the new society in which they found themselves. It also enabled Italians to maintain their ethnic cohesiveness in the early years of immigration. Like the political machines, the Roman Catholic Church in the United States was controlled and staffed by the Irish. Italian Catholicism was culturally different from that of the Irish austere form of Catholicism. The Italian Catholics emphasized the images, processions, colorful festivals, and other rituals that were not part of the Irish tradition (Nelli 1980). Therefore, many of the first-generation Italians felt alienated from the Church. Eventually, the Church in the United States began to develop "national parishes" to serve the needs of the Italian and other non-English-speaking immigrants. These national parishes were another means of consolidating an Italian ethnicity for the peoples from different locales in this first generation of immigrants.

Italian Americans confronted a number of problems that were similar to, but different from, those of other earlier immigrants. Like the Irish, the Italians were categorized by many WASPs as a different "race" that was inferior intellectually and morally to that of the Anglo-Saxons. But this construction of an "Italian race" was even more severely restrictive than that applied to the Irish. An "Anglo-Saxon based racialism," which was linked to "scientific racism" in the 1880s and 1890s, grew in the United States as a reaction to the immigration of southern and eastern European peoples (see Chapter 2). The "Italian race," as well as other Mediterranean and eastern European "races," was classified as inferior, in contrast to the northern European "races." IQ tests and literacy tests were given to these early Italian Americans, and as expected, they scored lower than the "average" American. These IQ and literacy tests were purported scientific proof of these new immigrants' inferior intellect (Kamin 1974). These racist beliefs were promoted by the media and other "scientific" works of the time. Anglo-Saxon Americans were warned not to intermarry with Italians because it would cause the degeneration of the "race." The "Italian race" was identified with such characteristics as jealousy, overly emotional, rough, mean, dirty, lazy, and other negativities (Roediger 2005).

Anti-Catholic prejudices and other stereotypes were also directed toward the early Italian immigrants, as many WASPs saw these immigrants bringing in non-Protestant beliefs and traditions. These anti-Catholic sentiments developed into stereotypes about how Italians (or the more pejorative labels of "wops" or "dagos") were superstitious, ignorant, and could not become Americanized. Since the Russian Revolution developed during this period of massive immigration, working-class Italians, especially those involved with unions, were sometimes identified with radical revolutionary movements.[4] In addition, along with Italian immigration, the organized criminal system known as the "Mafia" was modified and adapted to America by some Sicilians. Although until the time of prohibition, most of the crime syndicates in the United States were controlled by the Irish, Jews, and other groups, in the minds and stereotypes of many Americans, the Italian Mafia was associated with most organized crime. Crime was a means of upward mobility for many new immigrants in U.S. society, including the Italians. However, despite the fact that very few Italians in the United States have been associated with the Mafia, the stereotype endures. The film and television industries continue to perpetuate and reinforce these stereotypes.

Most of the sociological evidence suggests that in spite of the problems that Italian Americans had in adjusting to U.S. society, by the second and third generations, assimilation, both culturally and structurally, had taken place. Sociologist Herbert Gans (1982) wrote a classic study of the Italian Americans in Boston's West End. He found that by the second generation, Italian Americans had no strong loyalty to their traditional culture or language. The children of the first generation began to learn English and abandoned Italian. The children did not read the Italian newspapers that their parents had relied upon for their ethnic identity, and they no longer spoke Italian with each other. Although they tended to follow the food preferences of their parents, Gans found that there was very little visible about traditional ethnicity for these second-generation Italian Americans. And, as many of the third generation of Italian Americans have continued to move upward from the working class into the middle class in U.S. society, their ethnic status as Italian Americans has dissolved. For the most part, friendship, work connections, and interests are not based on Italian American ethnicity but on educational and class-based preferences (Alba 1995; Waters 1990).

POLISH AMERICANS

Like many others from Europe, people from Poland were pushed and pulled by economic, political, and religious factors that influenced their decision to emigrate. Poland, a Roman Catholic nation founded by the Western Slavs in the tenth century A.D., became a large empire in the sixteenth century. At that time Poland was a large agricultural civilization known as the granary of Europe, and it was the most powerful country in Europe. The 1500s were known as the "Golden Century" to Polish historians

(Bukowczyk 1987). In the 1600s, other countries, such as Sweden to the north, launched a series of invasions into Poland, and gradually, the Polish state began to decline. The Polish empire was surrounded by the newly centralized states of Prussia (later Germany), Russia, and Austria in Eastern Europe. Internal economic and political weaknesses led to the partitioning of Poland by these stronger states in the eighteenth century. Russia seized the largest part of Poland, and Prussia and Austria divided up the rest until after World War I. The Poles, most of whom were peasant laborers on outmoded feudal estates, were at the mercy of these invading empires. Although Polish resistance leaders attempted to challenge these larger empires, Poland as a country disappeared from the map of Europe. During the partitioning, these larger empires attempted to suppress the language and cultural heritage of the Polish people. Various insurrections and uprisings by Polish nationalist and religious leaders in the foreign-occupied Polish partitions were crushed by these large powerful empires.

Poland, like most other European states, consisted of a feudal agrarian economy during the period of partition. During the nineteenth century, however, while it was under the control of these other empires, early stages of industrialization, commercialization, and mechanization of agriculture were transforming the feudal economy. Rural peasants were displaced from their traditional livelihood as serfs on the feudal estates and became a large surplus class of impoverished, landless peoples (Bukowczyk 1987). Some of this displaced labor moved into the cities and industrializing centers in different areas of Europe, but many of the Polish peasants (together with some members of the Polish middle class and intelligentsia) began to seek a new way of life in the United States. Letters from relatives and friends in America advertised high wages and employment opportunities there. In addition, class, political, and religious oppression from the occupying rulers propelled Polish emigration. Poles with sufficient funds could buy transatlantic tickets, and others depended on their relatives to provide kinship connections in the process of chain migration for their resettlement in the United States.

Small numbers of Polish immigrants arrived in the eighteenth and early nineteenth centuries and settled in farming communities in the midwestern and southern regions of the United States. The major migration of Poles took place between 1890 and 1920, when approximately 2 million moved to the United States. Although about 3 of every 10 migrants returned to Poland, about 9 million Americans trace their descent to Polish ancestry. Many of the early Polish immigrants came through Ellis Island in New York harbor and were interrogated by U.S. immigration officials. Like the Italian immigrants, many were approached by labor recruiters, who would take them by train or rail to their new destinations (Bukowczyk 1987). Many went to coal-mining towns like Scranton, Wilkes-Barre, Windber, and Hazelton in Pennsylvania or to steel-manufacturing cities such as Pittsburgh and Cleveland. Midwestern cities like Toledo, Milwaukee, Minneapolis, St. Louis, Chicago, and Detroit attracted Poles who were seeking work in the mills, slaughterhouses, foundries, refineries, and factories. In 1920, Chicago had 400,000 Poles, New York 200,000, Pittsburgh 200,000, Buffalo 100,000, Milwaukee 100,000, and Detroit 100,000 (Greene 1980). Within these towns and cities, Polish immigrants founded neighborhoods and communities known individually and collectively as "Polonia" (Latin for Poland).

One of the first studies of the Polish immigrant communities in the United States was carried out by sociologists William Thomas and Florian Znaniecki in the 1910s. In their five-volume work called *The Polish Peasant in Europe and America*, they used quantitative data, newspapers, books, letters, autobiographies, and extensive interviews to provide insight into Polonia communities. They conducted research in Poland in order to gain background on the conditions and factors that had an effect on these immigrants. This cross-national research enabled them to understand that the Polish immigrants were not just replicating an ethnic identity that was found in Poland but were constructing a new Polish

American ethnic identity in the United States. This new identity was formed by a combination of elements and experiences in Poland and the new environment and conditions within the United States. The researchers concluded that the Polish American ethnic communities suffered from "social disorganization," and were in a state of decline. They predicted the dissolution of Polish American ethnicity very quickly in U.S. society. Contemporary scholars, however, have debunked their portrayal of this ethnic dissolution and find that they failed to take into account the signs of Polish culture in America (Lopata 1994; Pula 1995).

Like the Italian immigrants, the Poles drew on their connections with relatives, voluntary organizations, small businesses, Polish-language newspapers, and, most importantly, the Catholic Church to develop their ethnic communities in Polonia. Voluntary organizations were developed by both men and women to serve the community. Similar to the German American Turner Clubs, the Poles established the "Polish Falcons," a nationalist organization that promoted the culture and traditions of Poland, and other large fraternal associations like the Polish National Alliance and the Polish Women's Alliance. Mutual funds were established in the neighborhoods and churches to aid families through crises, such as sickness, accident, or death. Eventually, these evolved into extensive insurance businesses to serve the Polonia communities. Building and loan associations were set up to help each other to buy homes and businesses, and bakeries, butcher shops, saloons, restaurants, print shops, funeral parlors, and other businesses were started. These businesses promoted their own enterprises within the Polonia communities through slogans such as "Buy Polish" or "Patronize Your Own" (Bukowczyk 1987). As these businesses flourished, they gave money to Polish charities to help the poor, jobless, or other indigent community members. The Polish-language newspapers flourished and featured news stories on politics in Poland, as well as problems that the Polish encountered in America. Chicago's *Gazeta Polska* ("Polish Gazette"), Buffalo's *Polak w Ameryce*

("Pole in America"), and other influential newspapers served to reinforce ties of Polish American ethnicity (Pula 1995).

The most important institution that maintained Polish American ethnicity was the Roman Catholic Church. Similar to that of Italian Americans, the experience of Polish Americans with the Catholic Church was difficult at first. In partitioned Poland, the Church was administered by the Polish clergy and was the basis of their nationalism and ethnicity. However, in the United States the Church was controlled primarily by a German and Irish hierarchy. The Polish immigrants' religious traditions, which focused on a variety of rituals and the veneration of symbols such as the "Black Madonna," the Blessed Virgin Mary who protected Poland, differed from American forms. At first, the Poles (like the Italians) were treated as second-class citizens by Church authorities. In the German-dominated churches, the Poles had to sit in segregated pews. Eventually, as Polish immigration increased, the American Catholic bishops saw that they needed to do something to retain the loyalty of the Polish community. Some of the immigrants had begun to build their own independent churches outside of the Catholic hierarchy. Therefore, ethnically based Roman Catholic parishes were established for the Polish communities to ensure their loyalty and to protect them from the independent churches or Protestant denominations. Polish American churches were developed along with parochial schools, which enrolled about two-thirds of the children of Polonia (Bukowczyk 1987; Pula 1995). The Church was the fundamental institution that transmitted the language, culture, and ethnicity of the Polish American communities.

With unprecedented immigration from southern and eastern Europe in the first two decades of the twentieth century into the United States, the Poles were subjected to severe discrimination and prejudice from many Americans. As we saw earlier, nativistic movements and the beliefs of the superiority of the WASPs and anti-Catholicism were developing at this time. The Poles were considered to be of the "Slavic race" and supposedly inferior to the "Anglo-Saxon race." Like the Italians, the Poles were given IQ tests when they entered the United States through Ellis Island, which were used to "assert" their supposed mental inferiority. The nativist movement ideology proposed that Polish immigrants were diluting the superior Anglo-American racial stock (see Chapter 2). The Poles were viewed as "noisome and repulsive," "the beaten members of beaten breeds" (Bukowczyk 1987). Also, according to the nativist, like other eastern Europeans, many of the working-class Polish immigrants were associated with the Bolshevik revolution in Russia and other radical social movements. It was believed that these working-class Poles were going to create revolutions and disrupt U.S. society.

Despite the racial prejudice and discrimination they faced, the Polish American communities were able to adjust to their circumstances through organized efforts in economic and political activities. For example, working-class Poles became very active in union organization and participation. Poles working in the coal mines of eastern Pennsylvania organized unions. In Milwaukee, Polish men and women organized unions to fight sweatshop conditions in the textile factories. Thousands of Polish workers participated in the sit-down strikes at the Hamtramck Dodge plant in Detroit, which eventually led to the increase in strength of the United Automobile Workers union. Solid union towns in Pittsburgh, Chicago, and Detroit were developed by working-class Polish Americans.

In politics, like other immigrants, many Polish Americans began to become involved in the Democratic Party. Unlike the Irish, generally the Poles did not run for office themselves, but they enthusiastically supported Democratic candidates, and they participated in machine politics in cities such as Chicago. Like other ethnics, the Polonia communities were rewarded with a considerable share of patronage, jobs, and a sense of control over their neighborhoods. Eventually, because of their links with the Democratic Party, the Poles turned out majority votes within their communities for Al Smith, the first Roman Catholic to run for president, and later Franklin D. Roosevelt. Both union and political activities provided the foundations for improvement in living standards and upward mobility for Polish Americans.

The second and third generation of Polish Americans began to assimilate culturally and structurally into U.S. society. Despite a resurgence of Polish American ethnicity during World War II, when the Nazis invaded Poland the new younger generation of Polish Americans began to lose the "Polish" side of their identity. The younger generation began to move into white-collar and skilled occupations and moved out of the older urban Polonia communities, going to the suburban regions that developed after World War II. Intermarriage between Polish Americans and other ethnic groups led to persistent patterns of assimilation. Urban renewal in the major cities destroyed the housing and residential areas of Polonia communities throughout the United States. Reindustrialization and the shutdown of steel and auto plants led to the demise of many working-class jobs for Polish Americans. These economic and demographic changes resulted in the erosion of most of the urban Polish communities. By the 1970s, the Polish parish churches and parochial schools began to use English in sermons and education and reached out to recruit other ethnic groups (Pula 1995). Polish-language newspapers began to have English sections. Although this represented the final blow to the coherent Polonia urban communities in the United States, and in due time they resembled "deserted cities," eventually the Polish American community began to reorganize itself, based on new professional networks and organizations. Instead of an urban-based ethnic form of "Polonia," these new Polish organizations represent nationally based professional associations with their own Polish-language newspapers and foundations.

THE MELTING POT: ASSIMILATION OR PLURALISM?

As we discussed, U.S. society was challenged dramatically by the massive immigration of non-Anglo populations in the nineteenth and early twentieth centuries. Questions were raised about whether German, Irish, Italian, and Polish immigrants could really become "Americans." Nativistic groups such as the American Protective Association directed prejudice and discrimination toward these immigrants. Prejudice against Catholicism and other ethnic traits, including language and purported "race," eventually resulted in restrictive immigration policies. In 1921, legislation was passed to limit the number of immigrants from southern and eastern Europe to 155,000, while permitting about 200,000 from northwestern Europe. In 1924, further legislation limited the annual number of immigrants to 164,667. This 1924 legislation stated that the number of visas allocated for each European nation should correlate to 2 percent of that nation's immigrants already residing in the United States as of 1890 (Adams 1993). With these new quota laws, the unlimited immigration for most Europeans, the age of the open doors, had come to an end. During this same period, state and local authorities began to restrict the use of languages other than English in schools and to require all teachers to be U.S. citizens. Government policies tried to promote the use of the public school system to "Americanize" and assimilate the various non-Anglo immigrants.

One of the popular manifestations of these policies of assimilation was the concept of "the melting pot," which became the popular symbol of ethnic interaction in the United States during the early twentieth century. The term *melting pot* was associated with a play by a Jewish immigrant Israel Zangwill called *The Melting Pot*, which had a long run in New York in 1909. Zangwill's play focused on the life of a Jewish immigrant who believed that the Old World nationalities and languages ought to be forgotten in the United States and that all ethnic elements should fuse together in the creation of a new and superior American nationality and ethnicity (Gleason 1980). This was not a new idea, but it was popularized at the time as a response to anti-immigration and antiforeign attitudes of the nativist movements. The melting pot ideal implied that the new "American" ethnicity would represent only the

best qualities and attributes of the different cultures contributing to U.S. society. It became a plea for toleration of the different immigrants as they poured into American society. It was assumed that the American ideals of equality and opportunity for material improvement would automatically transform foreigners into Americans. It also suggested that the Anglo or WASP ethnicity was itself being transformed into a more comprehensive global type of an "American" ethnic identity.

Despite the tolerant tone, universal appeal, and openness of the metaphor of the melting pot, it was still an emphasis on assimilation. The belief that immigrants must shed their ethnic identity and Americanize and adopt a "Yankee" ethnic identity was at the heart of this concept. As we have seen, for one reason or another, most of the descendants of the Germans, Irish, Italians, and Poles began to adopt the English language and American culture surrounding them. World Wars I and II compelled German Americans to abandon their language and traditions very rapidly. The second generation of Irish, Italians, and Poles also tended to assimilate into the Anglo-American culture of the majority. Economic, social, and political benefits accrued to these "white ethnics" upon assimilation. Economically, union participation for working-class immigrants tied different ethnic groups together. As the United Mine Workers, the United Automobile Workers, and the CIO unions emerged, there were separate groups of Irish workers, Italian workers, and Polish workers. Ultimately, these working-class ethnics recognized that they were *all* workers, regardless of their ethnicity, fighting for better working conditions and human rights. To pursue the American Dream, the "white ethnics" assimilated culturally and structurally into the fabric of U.S. society. As older ethnic neighborhoods and communities began to decline, most of the "white ethnics" abandoned their traditional languages and cultures. The metaphor of the melting pot appeared to have some validity, at least for most of these "white ethnics."

Along with this assimilationist trend in U.S. society, the crystallization of the race concept of "whiteness" was reinforced. Eventually, the people who came from Ireland, Germany, Italy, Poland, and other European countries became "white Caucasians," in contrast to other ethnic minorities (Jacobson 1998; Roediger 2005). For many Americans, "whiteness" became a new socially constructed category of race that differentiated these Europeans from non-Europeans in the United States. Native American Indians, African Americans, Hispanic Americans, and Asian Americans were nonwhites, and thereby excluded from the institutional benefits and privileges of the people with white identities. Although there were some who still referred to the Anglo-WASP racial category, the enlarged category of a "white identity" assigned to Europeans tended to become part of the racial consciousness of U.S. society.

Cultural Pluralism

Beginning in the late 1950s and 1960s, the melting pot metaphor was being challenged by many non-European ethnic groups. As we will see in later chapters, African Americans, Hispanic Americans, Asian Americans, and other non-European ethnic groups demanded equal rights and opportunities for their communities. Non-European ethnic groups asserted that because of their skin color and other cultural elements, they were not as "meltable" as the European ethnic groups. Some civil rights leaders such as Martin Luther King, Jr., rejected the assimilationist policies of U.S. society and called for a "plural" society, where different ethnic groups could retain their culture and heritage but have equal rights and opportunities like other Americans. The demand for cultural pluralism became a dominant trend within ethnic relations in the 1960s in U.S. society.[5] Various non-European ethnic groups emphasized a pride in their own unique history, experience, and culture. "Black Power" among African Americans, "Brown Power" among Hispanic Americans, and "Red Power" among Native American Indians became the rallying anthems for cultural pluralism in America. Rather than emphasizing the melting pot as an ideal, these

groups suggested that the United States should be a "salad bowl" or, better yet, a "stir fry," which implied that each group could maintain its own distinctive culture and ethnicity (ingredients) and still contribute to U.S. society.

The developments of the civil rights movement in the 1960s, and the call for cultural pluralism, resulted in a heightened sense of ethnic awareness for many Americans. Many of the third- and fourth-generation "white ethnics" were influenced by these new ethnic trends. Sociologists Nathan Glazer and Daniel Moynihan, in *Beyond the Melting Pot* (1963), emphasized that many of the immigrants such as the Italians and Irish had not really assimilated into the melting pot but rather had transformed their ethnicity. They argued that as these "white ethnics" had moved out of their former ethnic neighborhoods they now articulated and revitalized new forms of ethnicity based on their traditional attachments with each other. They emphasized that these ethnic identities were not "survivals" from the age of mass immigration but were newfound social identities. Later, in 1972, another book, *Rise of the Unmeltable Ethnics*, by Michael Novak, a descendant of Slovak immigrants, reinforced similar themes. It appeared that there was an ethnic resurgence for the "white ethnics." The first generation of these groups had maintained their culture, the second generation had become assimilated, and then in the 1960s and 1970s, the third and fourth generations were beginning to reassert their hyphenated ethnic identity. Bumper stickers and political slogans emphasizing "Italian American Power," "Polish Americans Are Beautiful," and ethnic festivals such as Octoberfest for German Americans were proliferating throughout U.S. society.

One of the questions regarding this ethnic resurgence for anthropologists and other social scientists is the degree to which ethnic resurgence among the "white ethnics" was based on the "primordial attachments" that people feel toward their history, culture, and language, or whether this revitalization was merely a "circumstantial" or situational adjustment to the civil rights and cultural pluralist movements of non-European ethnic groups. A number of sociologists, such as Herbert Gans, Richard Alba, Mary Waters, and Stanley Lieberson, have investigated this issue.[6] For example, Gans, in his study on Italian Americans, introduces the concept of "symbolic ethnicity." Symbolic ethnicity refers to a type of ethnicity that is individualistic in nature and does not have any real cost for individuals. Gans suggests that among the middle-class third and fourth generations of the "white ethnics," symbolic ethnicity developed as a means of individual satisfaction. These identity needs are met by visiting an ethnic restaurant, participating in an ethnic festival, or having pride in an ethnic politician, artist, or entertainer. Sociologists agree that white Americans have a great deal of individual choice in terms of their ethnic identities. Individuals within one family may choose to identify with their hyphenated ethnicity, or choose to be just "white" or "American," or choose to switch back and forth in different social contexts and situations. As Mary Waters emphasizes, "The option of choosing among different ethnicities in their family backgrounds exists because the degree of discrimination and social distance attached to specific European backgrounds has diminished over time" (1998:404).

Sociologists, however, also agree that these particular forms of symbolic ethnicity do not exist at present for African Americans, Hispanic Americans, Asian Americans, Native American Indians, or other non-European ethnic groups. As we will see in later chapters in this section of the textbook, the non-European racial and ethnic minorities have had a much different experience in U.S. society.

MULTICULTURALISM IN U.S. SOCIETY

In the 1950s during the cold war, the United States opened its doors to political refugees from Communist countries, such as Hungary and Cuba. Later, during the civil rights movement, and because of the demands for more cultural pluralism in the United States, a new immigration law in 1965 opened the doors again to other areas of the world. During the past 40 years there has been a significant growth in the population of peoples of non-European ancestry. A decline in the birth rate of the majority of the white population of European descent, coupled with new trends in immigration and higher birth rates of ethnic minorities, is changing the ethnic landscape of U.S. society.

As indicated in Figure 7-1, recent immigration from Europe to the United States represents a tiny fraction compared with that from Latin America and Asia. The ethnic diversity of non-European immigrants is remarkable. Among the Asians are Filipinos, Koreans, Chinese, Japanese, Vietnamese, Laotians, Cambodians, Thais, Indians, and Pakistanis. From South and Central America are people from El Salvador, Guatemala, Mexico, and other countries. And from the Middle East and Africa have come Palestinians, Iraqis, Iranians, Lebanese, Syrians, Israelis, Nigerians, and Egyptians. Like the nineteenth-century immigrants from Europe, the majority of these immigrants have come to the United States seeking economic opportunities, political freedom, and improved social conditions. The United States has truly become much more of a multicultural society. A movement known as *multiculturalism* developed as an extension of the demand for cultural pluralism in U.S. society. As a result of this multiculturalist movement, federal, state, and local governments have encouraged the development of educational programs to prepare people to live in this new type of society.

Multiculturalism led to revisions of the curricula in educational programs throughout the United States. Instead of focusing narrowly on a Eurocentric or an Anglo-centric version of history, texts were revised to include discussions of non-European ethnic groups and their contributions to U.S. history. Bilingual education was developed to extend equal education to those students not proficient in English. The ongoing multicultural movement emphasizes that there is no one model type of "American." Cultural pluralism is endorsed fully, and the multiculturalist movement tends to

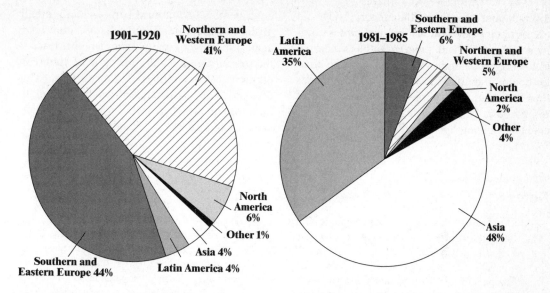

FIGURE 7-1 Legal Immigrants Admitted to the United States by Region of Birth.
Sources: From "Immigration to the U.S.: The Unfinished Story" by Leon F. Bauvier and Robert W. Gardner.
Copyright © 1986 by the Population Reference Bureau. Reprinted by permission; and U.S. Census Bureau,
Statistical Abstract of the United States, 1998.

suggest that there are no significant costs for retaining one's ethnic heritage. The movement for multiculturalism views cultural and ethnic differences as positive. It downplays any kind of competition or conflict among ethnic groups. Rather, the emphasis is on encouraging tolerance and cooperation among different ethnic groups. The hope is that as students become more ethnically literate, and more educated about ethnic groups, they will be able to appreciate and tolerate other people from different ethnic backgrounds. In addition, they will be able to make personal decisions, which would affect public policy promoting a more harmonious form of ethnic and race relations in the United States.

Although the goals and objectives of the multiculturalist movement are laudatory, some anthropologists have expressed reservations about this development. Terence Turner argues that the multiculturalist movement has become a form of identity politics, which is fraught with both theoretical and practical dangers (1993). He suggests that multiculturalism risks reduc-

ing race and ethnic groups and cultures to essentialist, stereotypical constructions and images. Cultures are not just collections of facts, vocabularies, assorted histories, and other elements. When these elements are taken out of their original cultural context and then reassembled into packaged curricula for educational programs, they are unlikely to reflect the complexities, nuances, inequalities, pride, and difficulties of race and ethnic groups. Multiculturalism can result in extreme revisionist forms of history and identity politics that do not have any critical basis.

Turner differentiates two forms of multiculturalism, *difference multiculturalism* and *critical multiculturalism*. Difference multiculturalism tends to become obsessed with "otherness" and ethnic identity, and it gives license to separatist tendencies and balkanization. This fixation on ethnic difference and identity politics tends to inhibit social relationships among groups. On the other hand, Turner emphasizes, "Critical multiculturalism seeks to use cultural diversity as a basis for challenging, revising, and relativizing basic notions and principles common to dominant and minority cultures alike, so as to construct a more vital, open, and democratic common culture" (1993:413). He proposes that anthropologists adopt this critical form of multiculturalism, which can only be done by extensive ethnographic studies to recognize the complexities of cultures, races, and ethnic groups. Critical multiculturalism should warn against the type of multiculturalism that leads to the romanticization and reification of culture or ethnicity (Eller 1997; Turner 1993). This textbook is devoted to this critical form of multiculturalism, which results in a deeper understanding of race and ethnic relations.

Notes

1. In actuality, this division between the Old Immigration period and the New Immigration period is artificial. For example, substantial numbers of Germans were coming from Europe in the 1880s (see Table 7-1). However, this divide between northwest European immigrants and southern and eastern European immigrants is useful as a historical narrative device for describing the different streams of Europeans.

2. The statistics for current numbers of ethnic groups in U.S. society have been drawn from the U.S. census. In the 1990 census figures, reported in the *Statistical Abstract of the United States, 1995*, the number of people identifying themselves as having German ancestry was 57,947,374. However, these figures are only rough approximations of ethnicity. Many of these people claim a mixed ethnicity, that is, they may claim themselves as German and English, or German and Irish, or a mixture of different ethnicities. This needs to be understood with respect to all of the various white ethnic groups in the United States.

3. Reginald Byron is a fourth-generation American and a descendant of the Irish immigrants of the nineteenth century. His family settled in Albany, New York. However, Byron moved to England as a graduate student in anthropology, and then moved to Northern Ireland, where he teaches at Queens University in Belfast in the department of social anthropology. He began to do his ethnographic project on Irish America in 1991 and continued his work on this project along with some research assistants through 1997.

4. The most well-known linkage between Italian Americans and radical politics was the Sacco and Vanzetti trial in 1927. Nicola Sacco and Bartolomeo Vanzetti, two Italian immigrants, were allegedly involved in an armed robbery in Massachusetts. Despite contradictory evidence and eyewitnesses who attested to their innocence, these individuals were found guilty. Following a number of appeals, Sacco and Vanzetti were executed. Supposedly, the two immigrants were members of an anarchist group. Anti-immigration and anti-union attitudes were elements that played a role in the trial. In 1977, after a review of the trial and evidence, the state of Massachusetts declared the trial unfair (Monroe 2000).

5. Cultural pluralism had been advocated earlier in the twentieth century by people like Horace Kallen. Kallen had argued against the "melting pot," viewing it as an extension of Anglo-Saxon ethnic hegemony. His views, however, were confused and undeveloped and never reached a substantial audience within U.S. society (Gleason 1980).

6. The sociological literature on the "white ethnic" revival is enormous. Some of the most important references include Mary Waters, *Ethnic Options: Choosing Identities in America* (Berkeley, CA: University of California Press, 1990); Richard D. Alba, *Ethnic Identity: The Transformation of White America* (New Haven, CT: Yale University Press, 1990); and Stanley Lieberson and Mary Waters, *From Many Strands: Ethnic and Racial Groups in Contemporary America* (New York: Russell Sage Foundation, 1988).

References Cited

ADAMS, WILLI PAUL. 1993. *The German Americans: An Ethnic Experience.* LaVern J. Rippley and Eberhard Reichmann, trans. Indianapolis, IN: Indiana University–Purdue University at Indianapolis.

ALBA, RICHARD. 1985. *Italian Americans: Into the Twilight of Ethnicity.* Englewood Cliffs, NJ: Prentice Hall.

———. 1995. Assimilation's quiet tide. *The Public Interest* (Spring):3–18.

BLESSING, PATRICK J. 1980. Irish. In *Harvard Encyclopedia of American Ethnic Groups.* Stephan Thernstrom, ed. Pp. 524–545. Cambridge, MA: Harvard University Press.

BUKOWCZYK, JOHN J. 1987. *And My Children Did Not Know Me: A History of the Polish-Americans.* Bloomington, IN: Indiana University Press.

BYRON, REGINALD. 1999. *Irish America.* Oxford: Clarendon Press.

CHRISTOPHER, ROBERT C. 1989. *Crashing the Gates: The De-Wasping of America's Power Elite.* New York: Simon & Schuster.

CONZEN, KATHLEEN NEILS. 1980. Germans. In *Harvard Encyclopedia of American Ethnic Groups.* Stephan Thernstrom, ed. Pp. 405–425. Cambridge, MA: Harvard University Press.

CORNELL, STEPHAN, and DOUGLAS HARTMANN. 1998. *Ethnicity and Race: Making Identities in a Changing World.* Thousand Oaks, CA: Pine Forge Press.

ELLER, JACK DAVID. 1997. Anti-Anti-Multiculturalism. *American Anthropologist* 99(2):249–260.

FISCHER, DAVID HACKETT. 1989. *Albion's Seed: Four British Folkways in America.* Oxford: Oxford University Press.

GANS, HERBERT. 1982 [1962]. *The Urban Villagers: Group and Class in the Life of Italian Americans.* New York: Free Press.

GLAZER, NATHAN, and DANIEL MOYNIHAN. 1963. *Beyond the Melting Pot: The Negroes, Puerto Ricans, Jews, Italians, and Irish of New York City.* Cambridge, MA: MIT Press.

GLEASON, PHILIP. 1980. American identity and Americanization. In *Harvard Encyclopedia of American Ethnic Groups.* Stephan Thernstrom, ed. Pp. 31–59. Cambridge, MA: Harvard University Press.

GREENE, VICTOR. 1980. Poles. In *Harvard Encyclopedia of American Ethnic Groups.* Stephan Thernstrom, ed. Pp. 787–803. Cambridge, MA: Harvard University Press.

JACOBSON, MATTHEW FRYE. 1998. *Whiteness of Different Color: European Immigrants and the Alchemy of Race.* Cambridge, MA: Harvard University Press.

KAMIN, LEON. 1974. *The Science and Politics of I.Q.* New York: Wiley.

KAMPHOEFNER, WALTER D. 1987. *The Westfalians: From Germany to Missouri.* Princeton, NJ: Princeton University Press.

———. 1996. German Americans: Paradoxes of a "model minority." In *Origins and Destinies: Immigration, Race and Ethnicity in America.* Sylvia Padraza and Ruben Rumbant, eds. Pp. 152–160. New York: Wadsworth.

KENNY, KEVIN. 1998. *Making Sense of the Molly Maguires.* Oxford: Oxford University Press.

LOPATA, HELENA ZNANIECKA. 1994. *Polish Americans.* 2nd revised edition. New Brunswick, NJ: Transaction.

LOPREATO, JOSEPH. 1970. *Italian Americans.* New York: Random House.

MILLER, KERBY. 1985. *Emigrants and Exiles: Ireland and the Irish Exodus to North America.* New York: Oxford University Press.

MONROE, JUDY. 2000. *The Sacco and Vanzetti Controversial Murder Trial: A Headline Court Case.* New York: Enslow.

NELLI, HUMBERT S. 1980. Italians. In *Harvard Encyclopedia of American Ethnic Groups.* Stephan Thernstrom, ed. Pp. 545–560. Cambridge, MA: Harvard University Press.

NOVAK, MICHAEL. 1972. *The Rise of the Unmeltable Ethnics: Politics and Culture in the Seventies.* New York: Macmillan.

PULA, JAMES S. 1995. *Polish Americans: An Ethnic Community.* New York: Twayne.

ROEDIGER, DAVID. 2005. *Working Toward Whiteness: How America's Immigrants Became White.* New York: Basic Books.

SCHLESINGER, ARTHUR M., JR. 1992. *The Disuniting of America: Reflections on a Multicultural Society.* New York: Norton.

SMEDLEY, AUDREY. 2007. *Race in North America: Origin and Evolution of a Worldview.* 3rd edition Boulder, CO: Westview Press.

THOMAS, WILLIAM I., and FLORIAN ZNANIECKI. 1918. *The Polish Peasant in Europe and America.* New York: Knopf.

TURNER, TERENCE. 1993. Anthropology and multiculturalism: What is anthropology that multiculturalists should be mindful of it? *Cultural Anthropology* 8(4):411–429.

U.S. BUREAU OF THE CENSUS. 1995. *Statistical Abstract of the United States, 1995.* Washington, DC: U.S. Government Printing Office.

WALZER, MICHAEL. 1997. *On Toleration.* New Haven, CT: Yale University Press.

WATERS, MARY. 1990. *Ethnic Options: Choosing Identities in America.* Berkeley, CA: University of California Press.

———. 1998. Optional ethnicities: For whites only? In *Race, Class and Gender: An Anthology.* M. L. Andersen and Patricia Hill Collins, eds. Pp. 403–412. Belmont, CA: Wadsworth.

8

...

Jewish Americans

Jack Glazier, *Oberlin College*

Even before the founding of the United States, Jews were living in North America. The first Jewish residents of the New World were Spanish speakers, and, indeed, Columbus's crew on his first voyage to the Western Hemisphere in all likelihood included a few Sephardic Jews (Jews of Spanish origin). Sephardim were the predominant Jewish group in the colonial era and in the early years of American independence. Although tracing their origins to Spain, many arrived in the New World by way of Holland and England, where their forbears settled following the Jewish expulsion from Spain in 1492. Since the 1970s, a large immigration of Jews from the former Soviet Union, as well as a smaller number of arrivals from Asia and the Middle East, has added to the diverse mix of Jewish Americans. During the intervening centuries, Jews from many places, but especially Germany, Russia, Poland, and other countries of Central and Eastern Europe, settled in the United States. Jewish ethnicity represents a dynamic phenomenon, changing its character with each Jewish immigrant accretion and altering again as each immigrant stream adjusted to life in the new country.

Across the diverse spectrum of Jewish immigrant groups to the United States, few people returned to the places of their birth. The precarious status of Jews in their European countries of origin explains to a considerable extent the low rates of Jewish reverse migration. As a case in point, Eastern European Jews, known as Ashkenazic Jews, were for centuries a particularly visible minority without civil rights, and therefore vulnerable to official and unofficial discrimination. They were subject to anti-Semitic decrees and policies restricting them to particular locales and limiting their ability to earn a living. The anti-Semitic climate also encouraged periodic mob attacks against Jewish life and property. By the 1880s, these factors set in motion a large Jewish immigration to the United States that continued until the mid-1920s. During those four decades, approximately 2.5 million Jews from Eastern Europe settled in the United States (Goldscheider and Zuckerman 1984:162).

The circumstances of Jewish life in Eastern Europe did not encourage the kinds of nationalistic or political ties to the old country that the descendants of Polish, Serbian, Greek, Hungarian, or other Eastern and Central European immigrants embrace. Despite some strong cultural attachments to their communities of origin, Jewish immigrants cast their lot irrevocably with America. Their one-way immigration pattern also typified the experience of Jewish immigrants during the American colonial period, the movement of German-speaking Jews in the mid-nineteenth century, the arrival of Sephardic Jews from the Balkans in the early twentieth century, and, most recently, the immigration of Russian Jews over the last three decades.

The Jewish population of the United States numbered approximately 5.9 million people in the early 1990s (Kosmin and Scheckner 1995:171). In 2008, the Jewish population was 6,489,110, an increase of approximately a half million people, constituting some 2.2 percent of the total U.S. population (Sheskin and Dashefsky 2008:156). Despite the increase, demographers consider the Jewish population of the United States to be fairly stable, with births and deaths nearly balanced. Immigration in the 1990s, predominantly from the former Soviet Union, constituted an important factor in Jewish population increase. Without the addition of immigrants, Jewish American demography trends toward zero or even negative population growth. In addition, strong tendencies within Jewish communities to assimilate into American society diminish, but do not obliterate, the distinctiveness of Jewish Americans and present some of the multiple methodological problems in enumerating the population. Overall, it can be said that the percentage of Jews in the American population has declined over the decades. Seventy-five years ago, for example, the Jewish population of the United States represented some 3.7 percent of the total. In terms of the numbers alone, American Jewish communities are looking toward a very dark twenty-first century horizon. Goldscheider, however, argues in a hopeful vein that the American Jewish future will pivot on the quality of Jewish life rather than on the size of the Jewish population (2004:71). It is not an argument that has effectively allayed Jewish communal concerns.

Religiously endogamous for most of their history—that is, a community that emphasized marriage within the group—Jews of America are now marrying exogamously (outside of the group) in record numbers, and there is no indication that these figures will decline. Reporting on marriages between 1985 and 1990, a large national survey found that approximately 52 percent of Jewish Americans were marrying non-Jewish people

(Kosmin et al. 1991:14). The majority of the children of these unions in all probability will maintain only the weakest bonds to Jewish life. These factors, as well as other assimilative tendencies that diminish the religious and ethnic distinctiveness of Jewish communities, raise questions about the Jewish future in the United States. Seymour Lipset and Earl Rabb observe that "current evidence suggests that group identity and cohesiveness are severely eroding for the large majority" (1995:47).

Throughout the twentieth century, when some 40 million newcomers arrived in the United States, immigrants actively struggled to synthesize new identities out of diverse cultural elements of the old and new countries. How could it be otherwise? The decision to emigrate, and especially, to settle permanently in a new country, is momentous. One enters a novel social and linguistic world. Familiar patterns of life and networks of social and economic support can be found only among other immigrants from one's homeland. Additionally, immigrant communities have received as much criticism as praise from the host society. Such processes can only bring turmoil in a person's self-concept and sense of tradition as he or she tries to negotiate a psychological and social place in the new society.

Ethnic culture, therefore, changes in accord with the strategies an immigrant group utilizes to adapt themselves to vastly new circumstances. These strategies, in turn, depend on how the host society views the persistence of immigrant cultures in its midst. Until the 1960s, American society took a dim view of ethnic communities seeking to maintain their cultural traditions and, instead, exhorted them to conform to the cultural mainstream, as the "melting pot" metaphor suggests. Relatedly, the prior experience of co-ethnics or coreligionists in the new country also influences accommodation strategies. The millions of Jewish immigrants arriving in the four decades after 1881 had before them relatively successful models of assimilation; these were the German American Jews, who had immigrated in the mid-nineteenth century. Their ideology of cultural assimilation into American society as well as their economic achievements accorded well with American values and set the stage for the next wave of Jewish immigrants.

Jewish immigrants as a whole identified closely with the new country, and hence the stakes were extraordinarily high in their effort to reach some accommodation and a reformulated identity. There was simply no going back. By contrast, some immigrant groups of the time—Italians for example—included many people who were "birds of passage," that is, temporary sojourners planning ultimately to return to the old country. Less consumed by identity conflicts, they were also impervious to pressures to learn English or to adopt American cultural patterns. The "birds of passage" aimed to work for a while and then return to Europe with money far beyond their potential earnings in Italy. In some years, the Italian rate of return was over 50 percent, while the Jewish return averaged about 8 percent (Glazier 1998:83).

Although there was not a single mode of Jewish immigrant adjustment to America a century ago, one way dominated. I refer here to *assimilation*, a process fully in keeping with the mainstream discourse about how to be an American. In the course of the immigrant experience, identities were largely reformulated in a complex process that alienated many of the newcomers, and especially their children, from old country traditions. The immigrants were, after all, faced with two mutually exclusive but very uneven choices—to be culturally different or to be equal. To remain different was to spurn the widely endorsed process of assimilation, or Americanization, as it was sometimes designated; immigrants would thereby lose the respect of their American neighbors and forgo the possibility of social and economic mobility. During the years of immigration, there was little discussion of how the country at large might adjust to the newcomers. Rather, the adjustment was conceived in the popular view as a one-way street bearing only immigrant traffic en route to assimilation. Still, assimilation is not a simple process; it has affected Judaism and Jewish culture somewhat differently.

The public discourse exhorted the immigrants to throw off ethnic practices in favor of conformity to more "American" styles. Such conformity occurred in many ways, large and small, including a turning away from ethnic vernaculars in favor of English and spurning ethnic-sounding names in favor of names that would not betray one's cultural origins. Jewish name-changing abounded among ordinary people and celebrities alike, including popular actors and entertainers such as John Garfield (Julius Garfinkel), Tony Curtis (Bernie Schwartz), Doris Day (Doris Kapplehoff), Kirk Douglas (Issur Danielovitch), and Bob Dylan (Robert Zimmerman). Of course these patterns were not limited to Jewish immigrants and their children; all Eastern and Southern European immigrant groups were subject to the same pressures toward Anglo conformity.

Along with other ethnic groups, Jewish immigrants had great difficulty sustaining themselves in a manner approximating their life in the old country. Moreover, repudiating cultural assimilation was unpatriotic. Until the 1960s, many Americans believed that a healthy, functioning democracy required cultural homogeneity, and hence the commitment of immigrants to the United States was in part measured by their progress in learning English and adopting American values and behaviors.

Jewish immigrants and others certainly experienced enormous prejudice and bigotry in the early 1900s. Often cast in racial terms, anti-Jewish and anti-immigrant sentiment in some ways paralleled the racism suffered by African Americans. Yet without the visible marker of skin color, the European immigrants endured the most overt and destructive forms of bigotry for only a generation, and it did not impede economic mobility over the long term. In effect, Jews, along with other European groups, "became white" (Brodkin 1998).

Collectively, Jewish Americans, whatever their immigrant origins, have achieved extraordinary success by virtually any measure. But that record is by no means universal among Jewish Americans. National statistics on Jewish success obscure the Jewish poor, who can usually avoid public relief and welfare rolls. Jewish communal organizations care for the poor across the country and, because they are private, manage to keep Jewish dependency from public view. Nevertheless, pockets of Jewish poverty occur, particularly among the elderly (Myerhoff 1979). But many Jewish immigrants from the former Soviet Union also require the assistance of Jewish organizations as well as federal supports available to refugees. An estimate from several years ago indicated that one-quarter of the Jewish population of New York City was near or below the poverty level (*Cleveland Plain Dealer* 2000). Based on the National Jewish Population Survey of 2000–2001, a study of economic marginality among Jews begins:

> Economic vulnerability remains a significant cause for concern in the American Jewish community. About 7% of American Jewish households have incomes that fall below the federal government's official poverty line, and double that proportion, 14%, have incomes that place them in a category that can be considered "low income." [United Jewish Communities Report Series 2004:3]

Conventionally, social scientists utilize data on income, occupation, and education as indices of class. Among all ethnic groups in the United States, Jews have reached some of the highest rankings. Family incomes are far above the American average, and Jewish representation in the professions, business, and the arts is well in excess of their numbers in the general population. Strong values on learning and scholarship combined with economic success have enabled the majority of Jewish Americans to send their children to college. Jewish Americans have thus attained a remarkably high educational level. They hold a wide range of elected and appointed political offices at the federal, state, and local levels; judicial posts, including U.S. Supreme Court judgeships; and advisory positions at the highest echelons of government.

These patterns clearly indicate that widespread anti-Semitism withered over the course of the twentieth century. Virulent anti-Semitism is now the province of only the most fringe elements of American society, although an active presence on the Internet has enhanced their visibility. No one can inject any obvious form of anti-Semitism into the public discourse without the severest opprobrium and condemnation. Still, coded expressions in the discourse on ethnicity, race, and immigration attest to the lingering sentiments that were once more vocal and public. Nonetheless, Jewish Americans have achieved equality in American life, and, as they have done so, cultural differences between themselves and their fellow citizens have atrophied.

The force of assimilation has resulted in the cultural convergence of several different streams of Jewish immigration. Although of diverse European origin, the Jewish American population has grown more uniform through its upward economic and social mobility and its entry into the American cultural mainstream. What were once cultural or ethnic differences among several Jewish immigrant groups—German and Eastern European Ashkenazic Jews and Sephardic Jews from the Balkans—have attenuated in the course of two generations. Now, the grandchildren of the Jewish immigrants arriving from Russia in 1910 and the grandchildren of Jewish immigrants arriving from Serbia at the same period share more in common culturally than they do with their respective grandparents. While ethnicity is not obliterated by the openness and opportunities of American society, it has certainly been fundamentally transformed in the experience of Jews and other European-derived groups.

RELIGION, RACE, ETHNICITY

Whereas Judaism constitutes a universally recognized world religion, the status of Jews as an ethnic category apart from their religious affiliation has been much less apparent. In the matter of "race," the same confusion consistently attaching to that term points up the error of considering Jews as a distinct biological group. Many years ago, Franz Boas, the most influential American anthropologist of the twentieth century, exposed the fallacies of the race concept. Writing in 1938, he observed that

> The term race, as applied to human types, is vague. It can have a biological significance only when a race represents a uniform, closely inbred group, in which all family lines are alike—as in pure breeds of domesticated animals. These conditions are never realized in human types and impossible in large populations. [1938:227]

He also pointed out the inadequacy of race as a scientific tool for understanding culture, or shared and learned human behaviors. Yet the resurgence in recent years of racialized explanations of culture in the face of definitive evidence to the contrary gives Boas's viewpoint great contemporary relevance. His caution about race applies no less to Jews than to others. The Jewish people do not collectively constitute a "uniform, closely inbred group."

Boas also strenuously argued that no necessary or causal relationship linked biology and culture. The twentieth century bore grim witness to the baleful consequences of asserting such connections. Prior to the realization of its worst manifestations, Boas exposed the fallacy of Nazi racial ideology, explaining that in the Nazi view, "every person is supposed to have a definite, unalterable character according to his racial descent and this determines his political and social status" (1938:226). Likewise, he also criticized the attribution of many negative qualities to black people, whose actions were erroneously portrayed as "racially determined, unescapable [sic] qualities" (p. 22). Consequently, false assumptions about unalterable patterns of behavior stemming from biology have profoundly impeded the life chances of African Americans. When clothed in the language of science, such racial explanations of human behavior have been particularly pernicious, for they have provided the authority and rationale for justifying the suppression or even the killing of minority populations.

Race is more properly regarded as a social and political invention, rather than an objective biological category. Cultural learning, not genetics or race, is the wellspring of human thought and behavior.

Unlike the explanatory dead end of race, the concept of "ethnicity" advances our understanding of the shape and diversity of cultural experience. Anthropologists regard ethnicity as a set of cultural features marking a distinctive community of descent, that is, a community of common cultural origin that continues through many generations. The cultural features that define an ethnic group are manifold and include shared language and religion. These, in turn, stem from a mutual history. Additionally, people of a single ethnic group have in common a broad range of cultural practices and beliefs that mark the group as distinct and delineate the group's social and cultural boundaries. These shared cultural features include dress, food, music and dance, humor, ceremonies, family dynamics, folklore, and a host of other traits. The cultural markers of an ethnic group represent the outward symbols of personal and collective identity and at the same time enable outsiders to distinguish it from other ethnic groups.

Individuals acquire the behavioral features characteristic of their ethnic groups through enculturation, or socialization, from earliest childhood. Ethnic affiliation is thus very much a matter of birth rather than choice. Yet a word of caution is necessary: one is born into an ethnic group, but ethnicity is acquired through the medium of culture rather than biology, no matter how deeply rooted, primordial, or "natural" ethnic patterns of behavior may appear. It is, therefore, erroneous to "racialize" ethnicity, for the latter is a dynamic phenomenon, shifting over time and subject to cultural influences from other traditions.

In considering Jewish ethnicity, the first task is to differentiate it from Judaism as a religion. The set of rituals, practices, beliefs, and sacred symbols constituting Judaism can be compared to those of Catholicism, Protestantism, Islam, and other world religions. But, in addition, Jewish ethnic affiliation is comparable to Polish, Italian, or Irish ethnic identity, apart from the Catholicism that these three groups share. The distinction between the religious and ethnic, or cultural, dimensions of the Jewish experience helps to make intelligible the segmentation characterizing the lives of many Jewish Americans. However paradoxical, they may identify closely with the distinctive cultural characteristics of their communities and forthrightly affirm a Jewish identity while also insisting that they are agnostics or even atheists.

To sort through the religious as opposed to the ethnic dimension of Jewish life, the anthropological distinction between the Great Tradition and the Little Tradition is particularly helpful (Redfield 1956). The *Great Tradition* refers to the sectors of culture that are codified or systematized by a literate elite. They are the authorities on the "official" version of the religion. In Judaism, the Great Tradition includes a body of sacred texts, prayers, liturgy, rituals, and a cycle of holy day observances determined by a lunar calendar. The Hebrew language serves as the medium of religious practice. Transcending place and time, these features with some variation define Jewish religious life throughout the world, although particular Jewish communities may otherwise differ culturally and linguistically. The rituals for any particular Jewish observance will thus be similar across the spectrum of the world's Jewish communities.

Until the eighteenth century, the range of variation in rabbinic understandings and interpretations of the Great Tradition was limited by the prevailing orthodoxy of Jewish communities and their religious leadership. Controversial tendencies toward liberalization in belief and practice then emerged. Some communities abandoned the dietary laws or utilized languages other than Hebrew in the religious service. Support of tradition or a move toward change or innovation hinged on whether one believed that customary beliefs must adjust to the realities of a modern scientific world.

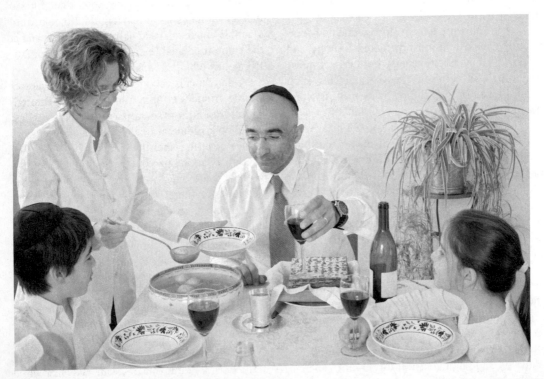

Jewish American family celebrating Passover ritual meal.

Complementing the Great Tradition is the *Little Tradition*, where ethnic features of community life independent of religion are paramount. The Little Tradition springs from the experience of daily living. It includes an entire cultural complex of activities and outlooks within a community. The languages of the Little Tradition, as well as the cultural practices, vary considerably in the Jewish communities in North America, South America, Europe, and Asia. The Little Tradition varies much more than the Great Tradition. In effect, it is appropriate to identify several Little Traditions, or ethnicities, within Judaism.

The intensity or significance of ethnic affiliation can vary over time. In keeping with its place as a cultural phenomenon, ethnicity is always fluid, changing gradually or, sometimes, dramatically, as exemplified by the Jews of America. Change in ethnic consciousness is particularly apparent in regard to the idea of the melting pot.

Prior to the 1960s, for example, many native-born Americans embraced the melting pot metaphor. That is, old bonds, loyalties, and cultural patterns were to be left behind in the old country in favor of a new, American identity. In this view, the distinctions and boundaries among various ethnic groupings would dissolve as the children of immigrants would come to share more with each other than they did with their immigrant parents and grandparents. They would simply be "Americans" rather than German Americans, Italian Americans, Polish Americans, or some other hyphenated identity. The process of "melting" began among the immigrants and accelerated in the second generation as ethnic groups rejected hyphenated identities. They sought instead to enter the mainstream only as "Americans" without a qualifying designation.

A telling illustration of the hold that the melting pot metaphor had on the American imagination is its literalization at the Ford Motor Company. Between 1914 and 1921, Ford offered its workers a profit-sharing plan if they would join the Ford English School, "to impress these men that they are, or should be, Americans, and that their former racial, national and linguistic

differences are to be forgotten." As described by the historian Lawrence Levine,

> Commencement exercises were held in a large hall. On the stage in front of a model of an immigrant ship stood a huge pot, seven and a half feet high and fifteen feet in diameter. The graduating members of the class, dressed in clothes representative of the nations from which they had come and carrying the types of luggage they had brought with them when they first arrived in the United States, marched down the gangplank from the ship and disappeared into the pot. Six of their teachers then stirred the pot with ten-foot-long ladles. When the pot began to "boil over," the workers emerged, . . . dressed in their best American clothes and waving American flags. [1996:111]

While the Ford English School commencement was unusually heavy-handed in conveying its cultural message, melting pot values in one form or another were ubiquitous in American society.

The power of the melting pot metaphor has greatly diminished in recent decades, and various Americans of European origin are now seeking to rediscover their immigrant and ethnic roots. Jewish Americans, as well as other groups, realize that the changes wrought in their ethnic communities over the course of the twentieth century have been extraordinary; various projects in cultural reclamation attest to the strong contemporary interest in asserting and demonstrating an ethnic heritage.

SEPHARDIC JEWS IN THE COLONIAL ERA

Until the eighteenth century, most of the early Jewish settlements in North America were composed of Sephardim—descendants of the Jews of Spain. Under the Spanish Inquisition, the latter had suffered expulsion from their homeland, beginning in the year of Columbus's westward voyage. Later, Jewish expulsions also occurred in Portugal. After 1492, Spanish Jewish refugees managed to find safe haven in a few places, including the Ottoman Empire, Holland, and the settlements in the Americas. The first documented arrival of Sephardic Jews in colonial America occurred in 1654, when 23 Jews arrived in New York following their banishment from Brazil. Dutch settlements in Brazil had provided a relatively safe haven for Jews, but the Portuguese conquest of these settlements imperiled the Jewish settlers. Mostly merchants and tradesmen, Sephardic Jews in the early days of the United States very successfully accommodated themselves to their new communities. In Spain, they were a generally prosperous, cosmopolitan minority, respected by their neighbors and unconfined to ghettos or other restricted areas. They mingled easily with the Christian majority in a social pattern that would eventually be duplicated in America. By the early nineteenth century, many Sephardic Jews had converted to Christianity or else married Christians in such large proportions that their descendants were eventually absorbed into the majority population.

GERMAN JEWS

Beginning in the late 1700s, other European Jews immigrated to America and eventually outnumbered the Sephardic settlers. Known collectively as Ashkenazic Jews, they originated in Central Europe and the German states, where Jews had lived since Roman times. After the First Crusade, anti-Jewish sentiment increased. The Jews then endured centuries of subjugation and periodic violence. By the 1300s, some Jews moved eastward into Poland and other parts of Central Europe. These Yiddish-speaking communities were the forbears of the wave of Jewish immigrants who began arriving in the United States in the 1880s.

The civil status of Jews in the German states and in parts of Western Europe greatly improved by the early nineteenth century after they were granted citizenship. Jews gained many of the social and political rights enjoyed by the Christian majority. They were thus able to participate in the Christian world on a more equal footing than at any time in the past. As a consequence of greater contact beyond the Jewish community, the process of linguistic and cultural assimilation gained momentum. Jewish communities came to utilize German more than Yiddish as other social differences between Jews and their neighbors eroded. At the same time, currents of religious change brought about a liberalization of Jewish belief and practice in some communities.

By the 1820s, economic decline and periodic outbreaks of anti-Semitism spurred many Jews in Central Europe, including the German states and Austria–Hungary, to seek refuge and commercial opportunities in the United States. This process continued over the next 30 years, increasing the Jewish population of the United States from roughly 1,200 in the late eighteenth century to approximately 50,000 in 1850 (Goldscheider and Zuckerman 1984:158). The German-speaking Jews were part of a much larger German immigration arriving over the course of several decades but particularly during the 1830s and 1840s.

Although German Jewish immigrants plied several trades, they were mostly merchants and itinerant peddlers. Quickly distributing themselves throughout the country, they took advantage of the opportunities for trade and commerce created by the movement westward. They were eager to make a new life where Jewishness would not narrow their opportunities. Settling in towns and cities, they also ventured into frontier settlements as shopkeepers or itinerant peddlers. Many contemporary American Jewish communities thus trace their origins to these German Jewish merchants. Until the 1880s, German Jews defined the ethnic and religious character of American Jewish life.

With little reservation, German Jews in America embraced assimilation and Reform Judaism, a very liberal version of their faith that accorded well with their goal of blending into the new country. Reform Judaism rejected many traditional beliefs and practices that were believed to be unenlightened and irrational in a scientific age. The traditional dietary laws about kosher food, the exclusive use of Hebrew rather than German or English in religious services, and the separation of men and women in synagogues were some of the traditions regarded as outdated and retrograde. German Jews wanted to obliterate the cultural differences between themselves and their non-Jewish neighbors. Only religion should distinguish Jews from non-Jews, but even on this point, religious differences were reduced since Reform Judaism was purging itself of many ancient and medieval religious practices.

A particularly dramatic declaration of independence from traditional practice occurred in Cincinnati on July 11, 1883. A banquet celebrating the tenth anniversary of the Union of American Hebrew Congregations (a federation of Reform temples) and the first graduates of the Hebrew Union College (a Reform seminary) featured various "abominations of Leviticus," foods prohibited in the Bible to the followers of Moses (Douglas 1966:54–72). The food prohibitions in Leviticus were in part the basis of the ancient kosher laws of Judaism. The banquet menu included clams, crabs, shrimp, and frog legs; additionally nonkosher beef appeared on the table, as well as cheese and ice cream, which, as dairy products, should never be served with meat. This subversion of Jewish religious symbolism provoked Orthodox guests at the banquet to exit en masse.

Cultural assimilation represented a strong value for Reform Jews. They believed their future lay in social integration in the United States rather than social separation. Because such Orthodox practices as strict dietary laws drew sharp boundaries around the faithful, thereby estranging them from non-Jews, the assimilationist-minded German Jews rejected them as added barriers to association and social exchange with other communities. The dietary laws in particular presented a salient object of Reform redefinitions of Judaism, in both its religious and social dimensions. Dispensing with the kosher laws and conventional meanings surrounding food symbolism not only struck a blow for rationality but also celebrated the erosion of social distinctions that

had historically alienated Jews from the Christian world. The banquet of 1883 dramatically illustrates how symbols can convey social messages about community boundaries; the messages may be about closure and exclusion or openness and incorporation (Glazier 1993:18–21). In other words, symbolic representations tell us something about a community's attitude toward acculturation and assimilation.

EASTERN EUROPEAN JEWS

The assassination of Czar Alexander II in 1881 set in motion the largest and most consequential Jewish immigration to the United States. Predicting a peasant revolution to topple the Russian monarchy, the assailants instead incited officially supported peasant violence and retaliation against Russian Jewish communities. Known as *pogroms*, these attacks included murder, rape, and the destruction of Jewish property and institutions. The government also enacted the notorious May Laws of 1882, severely curtailing the rights of Jews to gain an education, to live in particular places, to earn a living, or, in short, to eke out even the most meager existence. The bleakness of the Jewish future in Russia was apparent, as periodic violence and official repression continued into the twentieth century. These events triggered the massive Jewish immigration to the United States that continued for approximately four decades.

After some 600 years in Eastern Europe, the Ashkenazic Jewish communities of Imperial Russia were in turmoil. For centuries they had withstood periodic violence and other state-sponsored repression before embarking on a great exodus to America. On the eve of this momentous immigration, the American Jewish population numbered approximately 250,000. In 1900, 1 million Jews lived in the United States, and by 1924, the American Jewish population had reached 4 million (Goldscheider and Zuckerman 1984:158). This massive movement of Russian Jews—the largest Jewish migration in modern history—established the United States, along with Eastern Europe, as a center of Jewish life. Relatedly, because Russian Jews differed significantly in terms of culture and religion from the American Jewish population of German background, the mass immigration altered the demographic profile and the cultural content of Jewish communal life. Of the approximately 6.5 million Jews now in the United States, the overwhelming majority are the descendants of the immigrants from Russia and Eastern Europe.

While the popular view of the Eastern European Jewish newcomers emphasizes their religious orthodoxy, this picture is incomplete. Indeed, it has been argued that the most religiously observant Jews remained in Europe because they considered America a godless land where people might well lose their faith. To the extent that some Jewish Americans emphasize the ethnic rather than the religious side of their Jewishness, such fears were prescient. The stereotypic view of the deeply religious Jewish immigrant also resolutely ignores the participation of some Jewish immigrants in organized crime.

The new immigrants shared the Yiddish language and the associated Little Tradition culture known as *yidishkayt*. In Eastern Europe, they had also faced widespread intolerance and violence at the hands of the peasantry. Their precarious social and political status provided no reliable protection for themselves or their property. They differed, however, in their religiosity. Some newcomers were Orthodox adherents to Jewish law and custom, while others were secular critics of tradition and rabbinical authority. The latter were often animated by socialist ideals and a general skepticism about all religion. Many were activists in the labor movement and mobilized against the horrific, exploitative conditions in sweatshops. Once in the United States, all the newcomers sought an end to their historic vulnerabilities in order to live on much the same terms as other American citizens. In religion and culture, the Russian Jews collectively were culturally distinct from the established American Jewish population of German background and were accustomed to living in a world suffused by Jewish tradition. Moreover, the religiously observant could not easily disentangle the cultural and religious strands of their lives.

Because German American Jews emphasized cultural assimilation and wanted to guard their own economic and social success, they were apprehensive about the consequences of a rapidly increasing population of Eastern European Jews. They believed that the new immigrants, so unlike themselves in language, values, class, and culture, might provoke anti-Semitism and thus jeopardize the position and security of the established Jewish population. Accordingly, German American Jews appealed to the newcomers to set aside those behaviors marking their peculiar immigrant status—whether it was radical politics or stubborn adherence to traditional religious practices that did not seem to fit well into the new country. Many immigrants, however, resented efforts to transform them culturally; they considered the German American Jews snobbish and condescending, hardly different from Christians. A recurring theme in twentieth-century American Jewish history is the antagonism between the Eastern European Jews and the German Jews over the question of how to reconcile a religious and/or ethnic Jewish identity to American life and citizenship.

Ironically, the apprehension of German American Jews about the capacity or willingness of the Russian Jewish immigrants to adjust to their new country was misplaced. Many of the newcomers from Eastern Europe were not against accommodation and cultural change but, rather, resented the paternalism of German American Jews in promoting assimilation. The newcomers adapted rapidly to American life, but they also wanted to exercise some control over that accommodation. They did not want the German American Jews to define its terms. Many Russian Jews, like earlier Jewish immigrants, went into business. In addition, the children of the Russian Jews attended college and university in steadily increasing numbers. Consequently, a large proportion of immigrant families achieved a rapid economic and social mobility, with accompanying cultural changes, in a relatively short period of time.

Jewish immigrants, often before they left their European homes, knew that they would face great pressures to accommodate themselves to an American life based on some approximation of Anglo conformity. They quickly learned the meaning of "greenhorn," a derisive term applied to immigrants who were either fresh off the boat or slow to adopt "superior" American ways.

Mary Antin, born in Plotzk in Russian-controlled Poland, arrived in Boston in 1897 with her mother and three siblings to join her father. An immigrant's celebration of America, her 1912 volume, *The Promised Land*, details her life in Poland, the six-week journey to the New World, and her rebirth, so to speak, in the United States. From her very first day in Boston, she learns the importance of quickly putting the world of Plotzk behind her. On the ride from the pier to the small apartment Mary's father has set up, he instructs the children "not to lean out the windows, not to point and explained the word 'greenhorn.' We did not want to be 'greenhorns' and gave the strictest attention to my father's instructions" (p. 185). Soon after, they were taken to a department store, "where we exchanged our hateful homemade European costumes, which pointed us out as 'greenhorns,' to the children on the street, for real American machine-made garments." The process continued, as the children also shed their "impossible Hebrew names," for American versions (p. 187).

Even if one were less sensitive than Mary Antin's father to the greenhorn characterization, changes in most traditional lives inevitably came about simply because of economic necessity. The rhythm of the American workweek, for example, immediately created a predicament for the most religious of the Jewish immigrants. Saturday, the Jewish Sabbath, was inviolate, a sacred day requiring the observance of ancient strictures. The suspension of work was essential, but the immigrants soon found out that Saturday was a workday in the United States. They faced the wrenching choice of observing the Sabbath or keeping a job that was essential to the survival of their families. Economic necessity usually won out over spiritual fidelity. It was little comfort to the immigrants that their employers were sometimes Eastern European Jewish immigrants or German Jews who had immigrated a generation before.

The following brief account indicates in very human terms the work pressures facing many immigrants. Set in New York City in 1912, the narrative begins with a Jewish immigrant's desperate inquiry about employment.

> "Mister," he whispers insinuatingly, "Have you a job?"
> "What kind of a job?" we ask him.
> "I don't know," he answers.
> "What is your trade?" we ask.
> "I'm just a common laborer."
> "A laborer?" we ask in distrust, scanning his wispy body. He shoves out a grimy, hairy hand, the hand of a Volga boatman, hard as a nail. "Where did you work?"

The job seeker then describes a harrowing experience in the West, where he was severely exploited on a labor gang,

> "Do you have a job? But I don't work on the Sabbath. I never work on the Sabbath."
> We explained the difficulty of finding him a job under that condition. He remained rooted to the ground, looked wistful, concentrated his face as though studying a riddle and went away. That afternoon he returned. . . . With him he brought his wife, a little woman, plaintive, battered by life, but with pleasant kindly features.
> "Mister," she said, "I will let my husband work on the Sabbath," and then gulping hard, "I will take the sin upon myself." [IRO Publications 1914:5]

This vignette is typical of many such dilemmas faced by Jewish newcomers. The painful decision to accept a job in violation of religious beliefs represented the beginning of a longer term process of economic acculturation and assimilation.

SEPHARDIC JEWS: THE EARLY TWENTIETH-CENTURY IMMIGRATION

Although Sephardic Jews were the largest Jewish group in the early years of the United States, their community was steadily absorbed into the dominant society through intermarriage and conversion to Christianity. A new Sephardic immigration occurred in the early twentieth century when economic disruption, political conflict, and warfare in the Balkans drove 25,000 Sephardim to the United States. However, this number was only a small percentage of the Eastern European Jewish immigration, numbering annually in the tens of thousands. The Jewish immigrants from the Balkans were descendants of those Jews expelled from Spain by order of the Inquisition. As Columbus sailed westward from the port of Cadiz in 1492 with Sephardic Jewish sailors on board, other Sephardic Jews sailed eastward from that port. They were heading to the areas controlled by the sultan of the Ottoman Empire, who had promised them a refuge following the Spanish edict of expulsion. Eager to enlarge commerce and trade throughout his territories, the sultan believed that the refugees from Spain would serve his purpose. For nearly 500 years, their descendants flourished in the towns and cities of what would become Turkey, Greece, Bulgaria, and Yugoslavia.

Sephardic Jews constituted a Jewish ethnicity quite distinct from that of the Eastern European Jewish immigrants. Sephardic Jews spoke Ladino, or Judeo-Spanish, rather than Yiddish; like Yiddish, it is written in Hebrew script. They also maintained cultural practices and beliefs that clearly separated them from the Yiddish speakers. Modern American Sephardic communities emerged in New York, Los Angeles, Atlanta, Seattle, Rochester, and Indianapolis. That these communities are so little known tells us something about the character of Jewish American ethnicity. In popular thinking, Jewish life in the United States is defined overwhelmingly in terms of the Yiddish-speaking Eastern European Jews and their descendants. Constituting by far the largest Jewish ethnicity in the United States, this group has, accordingly,

attracted the most attention and shapes the popular profile of Jewish American life.

A common, although not monolithic, religious heritage joined Sephardic and Ashkenazic Jews in the Great Tradition; indeed, among the immigrants, Sephardic Jews were often more religiously minded than some of the Eastern European newcomers. But for each group, their ethnic and linguistic characteristics were as salient as religion in their self-definition as well as in the way they regarded each other.

While many of the immigrant generation of Sephardim were multilingual, their first language was Ladino. It is a vernacular built on the fifteenth-century Spanish spoken by Sephardic Jews when they arrived in the eastern Mediterranean. Like culture, language never remains static, and over the centuries the Ladino lexicon absorbed words from other languages, reflecting the experience of its speakers as they came into social and commercial contact with Turks, Serbs, Greeks, and others. Yet once in America, the legitimacy of their Judaism was disputed by the Ashkenazic majority because the Sephardim did not speak Yiddish, or "Jewish" (Glazier 1988:51; Zenner 1990:233–234). A legacy of rancor against those who were skeptical about their Jewishness is still recalled among older Sephardic Jews.

Beyond language differences, other cultural features defined each ethnic group, further distinguishing their respective immigrant generations. For example, Sephardic and Ashkenazic patterns of naming children contrast in important ways. Neither mode of naming is religiously sanctioned; they are simply ethnic variations, and, like the use of Yiddish or Ladino, did not make people more or less Jewish in religious terms. Still, Sephardic ethnic patterns were mistakenly interpreted by the Yiddish-speaking majority as indicators of inauthentic Judaism.

Among Ashkenazic Jews, parents name their children after the dead, usually kinsmen. Naming a child after a living person is portentous, for it connects the living person to the world of the dead. It may even imply his or her imminent death. Founded in the folk traditions of Eastern European Jews, the naming pattern commemorates and honors the dead but does so without biblical or other sacred textual authority. If that authority existed, Sephardic Jews would also honor the same religious tradition. Sephardic Jews, by contrast, pay tribute to the living by naming children after them. Derived from two distinct Little Traditions, naming patterns among Sephardic and Askenazic Jews nonetheless resulted in cultural misunderstandings between the immigrant generations.

Cuisine likewise separated Ashkenazic and Sephardic Jews. Food, along with other shared tastes, beliefs, and behaviors represents an important symbol of the ethnic community. Like linguistic and naming distinctions, dissimilar cuisines are an index of social distance and contrast. What are now taken to be conventional Jewish foods—bagels, blintzes, knishes, pickled herring, and so forth—were the particular foods of the Eastern European Jewish majority. They were quite foreign to the tastes of Sephardic Jews, whose cuisine closely resembled that of their Turkish and Balkan neighbors and included *borekas, boyos*, and *bulemas* (three varieties of pastries cooked with meat, vegetable, or cheese fillings), *quajados* (fritadas or soufflés), *yaprak* (stuffed grape leaves), and so on.

While these characteristic cuisines still grace the tables of Ashkenazic and Sephardic Jews, they do so now in a non-exclusive way and are not the singular preserve of either group. Ethnic cuisines continue to be durable cultural symbols, but they have diffused outward from their ethnic origins to the rest of contemporary America (Gans 1979). Bagels, for example, are so widely available in grocery stores that most people are probably unaware of their origin among Eastern European Jews. They are now simply one more item in the American pantry.

ETHNIC CONTINUITY AND DISCONTINUITY AMONG ASHKENAZIC AND SEPHARDIC JEWS

Immigration to America profoundly affected various European ethnicities, for it ruptured continuity with the old country in a mere two generations. The United States certainly offered great economic opportunity and personal security to people whose lives had undergone severe dislocation as a result of the political and economic turmoil in their homelands. But each group incurred major cultural costs in exchange for the benefits of living in America. The Jewish immigrant experience should thus be seen as part of a much larger process of acculturation and assimilation, including the movements promoting a revival of ethnic consciousness in the late 1960s and early 1970s (Glazer and Moynihan 1970; Novak 1971).

Sephardic and Ashkenazic Jews alike have prospered, and certainly Jewish Americans collectively rank among the most upwardly mobile and successful ethnic groups in the United States. No longer self-governing as they were under the Ottomans, the Sephardic Jews in their new American communities found themselves in a novel sociopolitical circumstance. Formal self-governance of ethnic communities was alien to the American political scene. The absence of a political boundary between their ethnic community and others was symptomatic of the weakening of other barriers—social and economic—that had once clearly defined and helped to perpetuate Sephardic communities in Europe. Cultural distinctiveness diminished as well. Likewise, the cultural distance between Ashkenazic Jews and their various neighbors shrank as they came to realize altogether new economic possibilities in the United States. The immigrants no longer faced the kind of legal restrictions that for centuries had narrowly specified Jewish vocations or places of residence.

At the same time, precipitous linguistic shifts in the course of a generation substituted English for Yiddish and Ladino among the second generation. The fate of these two languages in the United States is a telling barometer of acculturative change since the early 1900s. In other words, Jewish American life has undergone a major transformation in conjunction with the decline in the number of speakers of the ethnic vernaculars. Language codifies a culture and embodies its fundamental systems of classification and nuances of meaning.

Linguistic shifts, then, are interconnected to cultural changes. Few children of the Jewish immigrants, and especially their grandchildren, speak Yiddish or Ladino (Fishman 1966, 1985; Malinowski 1983). Indeed, a sharp decline in native language fluency in a single generation was the norm among European-derived ethnic groups.

The social and cultural divisions that at one time clearly circumscribed Ashkenazic and Sephardic ethnicities are now much diminished. Likewise, the porous borders of each community admit many mainstream cultural currents. American social life has ensured that the ethnic community, unless it made concerted efforts to keep the outside world at bay, could not successfully reproduce itself in ways characteristic of the European experience. European Jewish communities, Ashkenazic and Sephardic, of course, were not static. They had steadily evolved and absorbed various cultural influences from their neighbors. But the changes they underwent were contained by the political and social restrictions imposed upon them. These restrictions effectively negated the possibilities of their cultural absorption into the host society.

In the United States, assimilative changes coursing through the Sephardic Jewish community—numerically small to begin with—have prompted predictions of the imminent disappearance of that community (Angel 1974:136). Preservation efforts are thus underway and include academic and public programs, college courses, and museum exhibits that aim to revitalize Sephardic Jewish culture. Like other third- and fourth-generation Americans, some Sephardic Jews are actively researching their ethnic history. While such efforts are hopeful, they are simultaneously the worrisome symptom of the rapid cultural changes that sparked the revival in the first place. One must then ask if a culture, preserved primarily through formal institutions, holds the same significance it once did for the immigrants. For them, it was distinctly unself-conscious and an organic part of community living that pervaded every aspect of their experience. For the fourth generation, whose decisions about

everything from marriage partners to career choices to place of residence are not dictated by ethnic considerations, it is very doubtful that ethnicity will regain the same influence it once exercised.

The case of the third and fourth generations of Ashkenazic Jews closely parallels that of their Sephardic counterparts. Although much larger, the Ashkenazic generations also are little constrained by ethnic bonds and allegiances. High rates of intermarriage diminish the concentration of speakers of Yiddish that might occasion systematic use of the language and provide the setting in which children could learn it (Alba 1990:100). Likewise, continuity in ethnic culture is ruptured in the same way. Above all, the American embrace of personal freedom and choice works against a sense of social obligation and the authority of an ethnic or religious tradition. Individualism as a fundamental American value is played out in the wide range of options a person can choose from, but it can quite easily act at cross-purposes with the sense of common aims and shared goals that help to perpetuate an ethnic or religious community (Itoh and Plotnicov 1999).

Nevertheless, a minority of Ashkenazic Jews is also attempting to reclaim their ethnic and religious heritage. Part of the revival focuses on the Yiddish language; indeed, many Jewish community centers and other institutions sponsor adult classes in Yiddish. The preservation of books written in Yiddish is also occurring. Interest in Yiddish folklore and culture, including particularly the distinctive music of Eastern Europe's Jews, known as *klezmer*, is widespread. The development of Jewish studies programs offering courses on Eastern European Jewry in many colleges and universities is yet another indicator of cultural concern. But, as in the Sephardic case, these are not spontaneous community developments but, rather, self-conscious attempts by a relatively small number of people to revive and to nurture traditions that once pervaded Jewish communal life.

In the religious sphere, a return to orthodoxy represents a sincere attempt to renew faith and belief while establishing a connection to past generations, but this religious revitalization engages the interest of only a fraction of Jewish Americans. Moreover, Judaism in the United States is very fractious, reflecting a high level of internal diversity ranging from strict religious observance to liberal, modernist practices. Various contentious issues such as conversion, ritual innovation, feminism, homosexuality, intermarriage, and even the adoption of Buddhist or New Age beliefs also divide Jewish Americans.

Encompassing the movement broadly labeled "multicultural," many American Jews, no less than other communities of descent, have had to adapt to empowering efforts toward greater inclusion and tolerance regarding religious, ethnic, and racial and gender minorities. Inevitably, that adjustment has forced new ways of thinking about Jewish communal life and creating spaces for these minorities, who also happened to be Jewish. To take but one telling example, Alysa Stanton recently was a candidate for ordination at the Hebrew Union College-Jewish Institute of Religion in Cincinnati. A Jewish congregation in Greenville, North Carolina, has hired her as its spiritual leader. Rabbi Stanton is the first African American to receive ordination from an American Jewish Seminary and will be the first African American woman to lead a synagogue (Yarrow 2009).

HASIDIC JEWS

Hasidic Jews are an ultraorthodox segment of the American Jewish population. They number more than 200,000 people, the majority of whom live in New York State. Their communities derive from the settlement of Holocaust survivors from Eastern Europe in the years immediately after World War II. They are easily identifiable by their characteristic dress and appearance. The men are bearded and have earlocks. Their clothing includes black suits and hats. The women must

A Hasidic Jewish man and child.

always appear in modest attire, including head coverings and long dresses with sleeves over the entire arm. Hasidic Jews represent a particularly notable exception to the pattern of cultural and linguistic assimilation that has dominated the Jewish American experience. Thus, among this Ashkenazic group, marriages are endogamous and often arranged, gender role separation and hierarchy are normative, and mystical religious beliefs and practices that arose in eighteenth-century Poland flourish. The Yiddish language is thriving, if not the many associated secular features of Yiddish culture such as literature. Hasidic communities are led by charismatic rabbis believed capable of performing miracles.

The Hasidic Jews manage to be "in the world but not of the world." That is, they are not sealed off from their surroundings, and indeed must deal with the realities of living in densely populated urban environments, such as Brooklyn, which has brought about some political involvement. However, Hasidic communities very closely control the kinds of cultural influences that reach them, maintaining formidable social and cultural boundaries around their communities. Consequently, the rigorous culturally self-protective strategies of the Hasidic Jews have ensured a remarkable degree of religious and ethnic continuity compared to that of other segments of the Jewish American population.

RUSSIAN JEWS IN AMERICA SINCE 1975

Unlike the large-scale immigration of Eastern European Jews a century ago, the Russian Jewish immigration over the last 35 years or so has been linked to American foreign policy concerns. The cold war and the plight of minorities under Communist regimes created sympathetic American immigration and refugee policies—policies much less attentive to ethnic minorities suppressed by governments friendly to the United States. With the end of the cold war, Russian Jewish immigration to the United States has continued. Numbering some 350,000, the Russian Jewish community now represents the single largest refugee group in the United States. Russian Jews have established themselves in several large metropolitan areas including New York, Los Angeles, San Francisco, Boston, and Chicago, as well as in smaller cities.

The experience of Jews in Russia was conditioned by the Soviet goals of collective absorption into Russian national culture. Relentlessly assimilationist, state policy actively discouraged or punished ethnic and religious activity. Consequently, many Russian Jewish newcomers to the United States have little knowledge of Yiddish or of Jewish cultural or religious traditions. They often lack any prior experience in observing Jewish holidays or rituals.

There is, however, some variation among Russian Jewish immigrants depending on age. The oldest immigrants recall the early years of the Soviet Union, prior to the Stalinist repression of religious and cultural groups. They were socialized by parents into the culture, religion, and Yiddish language of Eastern European Jewry. The next generation came of age when Stalinism was fully entrenched, and they learned little of their ethnic or religious heritage. In accordance with state policy, they aimed to assimilate into Russian society; whatever success they gained in the Soviet Union depended on their ability to distance themselves as completely as possible from their ethnic background and to immerse themselves in Russian national culture. Even if they were inclined, they could not with impunity openly affirm or practice Judaism. The liberalization of Russian society in the late 1980s and the eventual collapse of Communism, however, enabled young people to study Judaism openly in Russia, although anti-Semitism did not suddenly dissipate. Many continued their involvement in Jewish education after immigration to the United States (Gold 1995:7–9).

Russian Jews have encountered many of the same problems that earlier Jewish immigrants confronted in trying to find a place for themselves in a new society and in redefining their identity. Language problems remain formidable, and current immigrant frustrations may be greater than a century ago when very few newcomers were from the professional ranks. Many Russian Jewish physicians, engineers, chemists, and so on work in modest, low-wage jobs because they lack adequate English-language skills to practice their professions. Although some immigrants thus become downwardly mobile, others manage to get good jobs or to start their own businesses.

The adaptation of the new immigrants, like that of their predecessors, also depends on attitudes of the host society as well as their established co-ethnics and coreligionists. In some respects, Jewish American organizations of assistance and support for the Russian Jews reproduce the patron–client relationship between German American Jews and the Russian Jewish immigrants of a century ago. Current Russian Jewish immigrants thus find some of the same condescending attitudes directed toward them. But, unlike the earlier immigrants for whom the national cultures of Eastern Europe held no value, today's Russian Jewish newcomers often have

positive feelings toward many aspects of Russian national culture, including its social intensity and the richness of intellectual life among many ordinary people.

Jewish Americans often have difficulty understanding why the newcomers do not want to jettison cultural values and attitudes rooted in Russia. Still, American society as a whole is now more sympathetic than ever before to ethnic groups joining the mainstream while preserving their cultural heritage. Indeed, many Russian Jewish immigrants are attempting to steer this middle course (Gold 1995:120). They hope to shape the terms of their accommodation to the new country. Still, the experience of Jewish immigrants of a century ago may model the future. If that is the case, then the blandishments of American society will further loosen the hold of the ethnic community, thus promoting a cultural convergence between the children of the latest Jewish newcomers and the descendants of other immigrants.

References Cited

ALBA, RICHARD. 1990. *Ethnic Identity: The Transformation of White America*. New Haven, CT: Yale University Press.

ANGEL, MARC. 1974. *The Sephardim of the United States: An Exploratory Study*. New York: Union of Sephardic Congregations.

ANTIN, MARY. 1912. *The Promised Land*. Boston, MA: Houghton Mifflin.

BOAS, FRANZ. 1938. *The Mind of Primitive Man*. New York: Macmillan.

BRODKIN, KAREN. 1998. *How Jews Became White Folks and What That Says about Race in America*. New Brunswick, NJ: Rutgers University Press.

CLEVELAND PLAIN DEALER. 2000. Jewish refugees in NYC put new face on poverty, July 16.

DOUGLAS, MARY. 1966. *Purity and Danger: An Analysis of Concepts of Pollution and Taboo*. London: Routledge & Kegan Paul.

FISHMAN, JOSHUA. 1966. *Language Loyalty in the United States*. The Hague: Mouton.

———. 1985. Mother-tongue claiming since 1960: Trends and correlates. In *The Rise and Fall of the Ethnic Revival: Perspectives on Language and Ethnicity*. Joshua A. Fishman, Michael H. Gertner, Esther G. Lowy, and William G. Milan, eds. Amsterdam: Mouton.

GANS, HERBERT. 1979. Symbolic ethnicity: The future of ethnic groups and cultures in America. *Ethnic and Racial Studies* 2(1):1–19.

GLAZER, NATHAN, and DANIEL PATRICK MOYNIHAN. 1970. *Beyond the Melting Pot*. Cambridge, MA: MIT Press.

GLAZIER, JACK. 1988. Stigma, identity, and Sephardic-Ashkenazic relations in Indianapolis. In *Persistence and Flexibility: Anthropological Perspectives on the American Jewish Experience*. Walter P. Zenner, ed. Albany, NM: State University of New York Press.

———. 1993. Subversive Food. Paper presented before Central States Anthropological Society, Beloit, WI.

———. 1998. *Dispersing the Ghetto: The Relocation of Jewish Immigrants across America*. Ithaca, NY: Cornell University Press.

GOLD, STEVEN J. 1995. *From the Workers' State to the Golden State: Jews from the Former Soviet Union in California*. Boston, MA: Allyn & Bacon.

GOLDSCHEIDER, CALVIN. 2004. *Studying the Jewish Future*. Seattle, WA: University of Washington Press.

GOLDSCHEIDER, CALVIN, and ALAN S. ZUCKERMAN. 1984. *The Transformation of the Jews*. Chicago, IL: University of Chicago Press.

IRO PUBLICATIONS. 1914. In our application rooms. *Distribution Monthly Bulletin of the Industrial Removal Office* 1(6):5.

ITOH, REIKO, and LEONARD PLOTNICOV. 1999. The Saturday morning informal service: Community and identity in a Reform congregation. *Ethnology* 38(1):1–19.

KOSMIN, BARRY A., SIDNEY GOLDSTEIN, JOSEPH WAKSBERG, NAVA LERER, ARIELLA KEYSAR, and JEFFREY SCHECKNER. 1991. *Highlights of the CFC 1990 National Jewish Population Survey*. New York: Council of Jewish Federations.

KOSMIN, BARRY A., and JEFFREY SCHECKNER. 1995. Jewish population in the United States, 1995. In *American Jewish Yearbook*, 1996. David Singer, ed. New York: American Jewish Committee.

LEVINE, LAWRENCE W. 1996. *The Opening of the American Mind: Canons, Culture and History*. Boston, MA: Beacon Press.

LIPSET, SEYMOUR MARTIN, and EARL RABB. 1995. *Jews and the New American Scene*. Cambridge, MA: Harvard University Press.

MALINOWSKI, ARLENE. 1983. Judeo-Spanish language-maintenance efforts in the United States. *International Journal of the Sociology of Language* 44:137–151.

MYERHOFF, BARBARA. 1979. *Number Our Days*. New York: Dutton.

NOVAK, MICHAEL. 1971. *The Rise of the Unmeltable Ethnics*. New York: Macmillan.

REDFIELD, ROBERT. 1956. *Peasant Society and Culture*. Chicago, IL: University of Chicago Press.

SHESKIN, IRA M., and AARON DASHEFSKY. 2008. Jewish Population of the United States, 2008. In *American Jewish Yearbook, 2008*. David Singer and Lawrence Grossman, eds. New York: American Jewish Committee.

UNITED JEWISH COMMUNITIES REPORT SERIES ON THE NJPS, 2001FV01. 2004. Economic Vulnerability in the American Jewish Population. Report 5. http://www. jewishfederations.org/page.aspx?id= 67288

YARROW, ALLISON G. 2009. Shalom Y'all: New Rabbi Lights Up Southern Town. *The Jewish Daily Forward*, November 11, 2009.

ZENNER, WALTER P. 1990. Chicago's Sephardim. *American Jewish History* 79(2):221–241.

9

■ ■ ■

African Americans

Susan Love Brown, *Florida Atlantic University*

This chapter will explore the development of African American culture within the context of American history. African Americans constitute about 13.5 percent of the population of the United States, or about 40.7 million people, making them the second largest minority group in the country and the largest minority in 24 states. Contrary to general perceptions fostered by the media, most African Americans are working class and middle class; however, around 24.5 percent of all African Americans do live below the poverty level (U.S. Census Bureau 2008).

People of African descent have been involved in the discovery, peopling, and building of civilization in North America for as long as Europeans, and although most of them are the descendants of slaves and have suffered many indignities in the course of their history, they have also left a legacy of fighting for civil rights and achievements in all areas of life. African Americans have been major contributors to American culture through their labor, language, and artistic creations, all of which had roots in African culture. However, because of the particular power of racism in North America, African Americans have often been misrepresented and misunderstood (see Smedley 2007).

African American ethnicity involves a great deal of diversity, for people of African descent continue to immigrate to the United States from countries in Africa, the West Indies, and South America. And from the beginning, African Americans have interacted with people from Spain, England, Holland, and France, as well as many Native American groups, and in doing so have created new cultural features. If we look at the beliefs, values, and norms that broadly define African American culture, we find that the focus is on the importance of family, the centrality of religious beliefs, and the struggle for freedom. However, these and other African American cultural assumptions have been fashioned by particular physical environments, social circumstance, and experiences.

African Americans were the only people brought to the North American continent unwillingly in large numbers, subsequently enslaved for 200 years, and then subjected to a state-imposed system of racial apartheid that effectively deprived them of all their civil liberties and set up a racial caste system that still affects American society today. These circumstances must be taken into consideration in any attempt to understand African American ethnicity.

THE GREAT DEBATE OVER THE PAST OF AFRICAN AMERICANS

For a long time people did not recognize any contributions from African culture at all, either to African American culture specifically or to American culture generally. In fact, African Americans were considered an inferior caste, not simply because they were slaves from "uncivilized" societies, but because whites and some blacks believed they had been deprived of any culture of their own and had had to adopt an ill-fitting European culture, making them less than adequate as people. This, however, turned out to be a false assumption.

Melville Herskovits, an anthropologist and a student of Franz Boas, referred to these beliefs as "the myth of the Negro past," embodying five points that seemed to support the case for Negro inferiority:

1. Blacks were childlike and adaptable to many situations, including slavery.
2. Those Africans enslaved were the less intelligent members of the community—those unclever enough to get caught.
3. The regional diversity of slaves meant that there was no common cultural background among them.
4. Any residual African traits would have been so inferior that the slaves would have given them up in favor of superior European customs.
5. "The Negro is thus a man without a past."[1]

Herskovits set out to systematically disprove these contentions by bringing to bear his knowledge of African culture and its retention by people of African descent in the United States. The claims of Herskovits brought him into direct opposition to sociologist E. Franklin Frazier, who, following an assimilationist model, contended that hardly any African culture remained, a condition that strongly disadvantaged blacks in the United States. For example, in his *The Negro Family in the United States*, originally published in 1939, Frazier wrote,

Probably never before in history has a people been so nearly completely stripped of its social heritage as the Negroes who were brought to America. Other conquered races have continued to worship their household gods within the intimate circle of their kinsmen. But American slavery destroyed household gods and dissolved the bonds of sympathy and affection between men of the same blood and household. Old men and women might have brooded over memories of their African homeland, but they could not change the world about them. Through force of circumstances, they had to acquire a new language, adopt new habits of labor, and take over, however imperfectly, the folkways of the American environment. Their children, who knew only the American environment, soon forgot the few memories that had been passed on to them and developed motivations and modes of behavior in harmony with the New World. . . . But, of the habits and customs as well as the hopes and fears that characterized the life of their forebearers in Africa, nothing remains. [1966:15]

Frazier's erroneous conclusions were a consequence of not understanding the nature of culture and its durability (see Strauss and Quinn 1997) and his lack of familiarity with the depth of African culture and the way in which culture is transmitted. In *The Myth of the Negro Past*, originally published in 1941, Herskovits presented detailed evidence demonstrating the presence of African cultural features among Americans of African descent, including retentions in music, dancing, and religious beliefs and practices. For example, West African cultures contributed musical elements that resulted in the creation of jazz, an African American musical form (Maultsby 1990), and the East African bardic tradition became the origin of the blues (Ottenheimer 1992).

Herskovits was not the only scholar to take issue with the myth. African American scholars, such as Carter G. Woodson and W. E. B. Du Bois, wrote books challenging the myth. Woodson, who was the first descendant of a slave to receive a Ph.D. in 1912 and also the founder of the Association for the Study of Negro Life and History and the originator of Black History Week (the precursor of Black History Month), wrote in *The African Background Outlined*,

> This elementary treatment of the African background of the Negro, together with brief outlines for the study of the race in the modern world, is intended to stimulate greater interest in this field. Hitherto most Europeans and practically all Americans have regarded the Negro merely as an undesirable—an undeveloped person constituting a problem in not being able to keep pace with others. The facts herein presented will show that the Negro has achieved much in various spheres, and to know the possibilities of the race a scientific appraisal of its past is necessary. The author considers the Negro as human—responding very much as others do to the same stimuli, advancing when free to go forward and lagging behind when hindered by obstacles not encountered by others. [1936:v]

W. E. B. Du Bois, the first African American to receive a Ph.D., wrote *Black Folk: Then and Now* in 1939, in which he also attempted to give depth to African and African American history. All three of these scholars spoke of the African cultural heritage of African Americans at a time when such a heritage was denied.

Herskovits, who had done fieldwork in Africa, the Caribbean, and the United States, was in a position to have seen the cultural similarities among peoples of African descent in Africa and the Americas, and was able to establish that African culture had not been lost, although it had been many times transformed. In North America, where Africans were in the minority (unlike many Caribbean societies), it often appeared that African culture had disappeared and been replaced by European culture. But it is wise to remember that even European cultures were transformed in the new environment (e.g., see Sobel 1987).

Today, we would not assume that a people moving from one area to another as adults had lost their culture. It is not easy to divest a people of their culture, which is largely unconscious and very persistent and tends to reassert itself in form if not in content (Strauss and Quinn 1997). In fact, many elements of African cultures have worked their way into mainstream American culture but go largely unnoticed (Philips 1990; Thompson 1990). Nor would we assume that cultures remain unchanged in new environments. Just as Europeans became various kinds of Americans, so did African Americans. To what degree aspects of African culture have been retained, either in form or substance, is a matter for empirical study. But what is certain is that people from Africa forged and continued to forge new cultures in America (Mintz and Price 1976). It is these diverse cultures, bound together by the common experience of slavery and the struggle for freedom, that define African American ethnicity.

This chapter will explore the development of African American culture within the American racial context and the diversity within that experience. We can think of the formation of African American culture as the result of a three-step process that involved (1) the adaptation of Africans from different groups to each other, (2) the adaptation of African cultural understandings to a new environment, and (3) the interaction of these understandings with those of other groups in North America, including Europeans and Native Americans. These factors varied greatly across geography and time, which makes African American culture exceedingly diverse.

Like that of most American ethnic groups, the story of African Americans begins elsewhere. We, therefore, begin in Africa, the point of origin of all human life and peoples, examining the specific areas from which most Africans came. Since it is not possible to give a full accounting in the space allowed, we will broadly sketch the origins of Africans coming to North America.

THE AFRICAN ROOTS OF AFRICAN AMERICAN CULTURE

From the beginning of the slave trade to the end, approximately 10–12 million men, women, and children were taken from the continent of Africa to the Americas. Of these, approximately a half a million ended up on the North American continent in what was to become the United States. The most immediate history and culture can be traced primarily to West Africa and Central Africa with minor populations from East Africa as well. Joseph Holloway notes that "although the West Africans arrived in North America in greater numbers, the Bantu of Central Africa had the largest homogeneous culture among the imported Africans and the strongest impact on the development of African-American culture" (1990:1–2).

Slaves destined for the New World came from settlements near the Atlantic coast of Africa, primarily from areas today known as Guinea-Bissau, Gambia, Senegal, Sierra Leone, Liberia, Ivory Coast, Ghana, Togo, Benin, and Nigeria in West Africa and from the Congo and Angola in Central Africa (Curtin 1969). It is important to remember that each of these areas encompassed multiple ethnic groups; however, many of these groups had some common cultural features, so that in spite of the diversity of African slaves, they also had a common cultural background.

Africans emphasized the extended family based on lineage systems in which either the father's line (patrilineal) or mother's line (matrilineal) was recognized, along with the preeminence of the mother–child bond and sibling bonds. Women often ruled beside men as queen mothers in West African societies and were skilled farmers. They also ran West African local markets, while men handled long-distance trade. Thus, African women were full participants in economic life. Africans had well-developed oral and storytelling traditions different from those of Europeans, and these would form the basis of a new folklore in North America. African education emphasized the use of memory, and Africans had developed sophisticated political and religious systems, as well as elaborate musical traditions and instruments.

The people of West Africa and Central Africa were experienced farmers and cattle herders. In fact, Leonard Liggio (1976) has argued that African slaves were sought specifically for their agricultural expertise. Africans brought to America included those skilled at iron smelting (blacksmithing) and textile manufacture (e.g., cotton). There were also skilled artisans who worked in gold and silver and carvers of wood, who participated in elaborate markets on a regular basis. The peoples of sub-Saharan Africa had long engaged in trade and cultural exchange with those from North Africa, the Middle East, Europe, and Asia. They were not the primitive peoples that many early scholars portrayed. In fact, Africans had been present in Europe, especially Spain, for a long time when colonization of the Americas began.

PEOPLE OF AFRICAN DESCENT IN THE COLONIES

Africans accompanied various European expeditions to the New World, coming initially from Europe. For example, in 1492 Pedro Alonzo Nino, believed to have been of African descent, accompanied Christopher Columbus on his first voyage to the Americas, as did Juan las Canarias, who traveled on the *Santa Maria*. Balboa, during his discovery of the Pacific, had 30 men of African descent with him. Another black, Estevanico, explored the southwestern part of the North American continent from Mexico to Arizona in 1538. Thus, people of African descent were always present (albeit sometimes in small numbers) as both slave and free persons (see Deagan and MacMahon 1995:9; Mabunda 1997:3; Singleton and Bograd 1995:5).

Slavery had existed in Spain and Portugal long before exploration of the Americas began, but it did not generate the kind of racism that was to arise in North America (see Smedley 2007). The decision to import slave labor to the New World came at the impetus of Bartolomé de Las Casas, who felt sorry for the Native American populations devastated because of their lack of immunity to Old World diseases. He recommended to Charles V, king of Spain, that Africans be used as slaves. Africans had been exposed to the same diseases as

Europeans and were experienced farmers. Thus, African populations became the basis for the plantation agriculture that flourished in North and South America and the Caribbean.

In 1526, the first Africans who arrived on the shores of what was to become the United States were brought by Spanish explorers to settle the area. According to Deagan and MacMahon (1995:16), they accompanied Vásquez de Allyón to what today is Georgia. The 100 black laborers rebelled and many joined Native Americans, abandoning the unsuccessful attempt to colonize North America. In 1528, Esteban, "gunbearer, scout, slave and soldier," made his way to Florida but died 10 years later in the southwest of the North American continent. At least three Africans accompanied Coronado to the New World in 1540, one of whom was a free person who acted as an interpreter (Deagan and MacMahon 1995:12). Blacks from the West Indies, South America, and Africa peopled Spanish Florida, where the oldest North American city, St. Augustine, was home to both slaves and free blacks. Kathleen Deagan and Darcie MacMahon estimate that they accounted for 10 percent of the population there (1995:16). Indeed, the first legally established African American town, Fort Mosé, was founded in 1738 in Florida.

In 1619, the Dutch brought 20 indentured servants of African descent to Jamestown, Virginia. Although indenture is a temporary state of servitude, it represented the beginnings of the slave trade in what was to become the United States. Most scholars agree that slavery came gradually upon the colonies as more and more restrictions were visited upon black indentured servants, separating them from their white counterparts, lengthening their terms of service, and extending the conditions to their offspring.

SLAVE AND FREE: THE FORMATION OF AFRICAN AMERICAN CULTURE, 1619–1863

Slavery was practiced throughout the colonies before the American Revolution, even in the North, largely due to a shortage of white laborers.

Slaves were imported into the New England colonies throughout the seventeenth century by English settlers, but the first colony to legalize slavery was Massachusetts in 1641. Maryland passed a law in 1663 making all imported Africans slaves. In 1670, Virginia passed a law denying the right to vote to freed slaves and indentured servants and designated all imported persons permanent slaves (Mabunda 1997:4, 5; Quarles 1964:33–38; Singleton and Bograd 1995:7–8).

In spite of the presence of slavery in all of the colonies, there were those who disapproved of the institution. The first antislavery resolution in North America was signed in 1688 by Mennonites in Germantown, Pennsylvania. The Quakers, another religious sect in Pennsylvania, also objected to slavery and threatened to expel any of their members who were found importing slaves. In fact, Pennsylvania actually moved to forbid slavery in that colony but was prevented from doing so by the English government (Mabunda 1997:5).

By 1700, about 28,000 slaves were in the colonies, about 5,000 in the North and 23,000 in the South, and many colonies had passed fugitive slave laws and other laws, more clearly defining the role of slaves in society. New York had more slaves than any other colony but South Carolina, and slaves were responsible for building much of New York City. African Americans recovered from a burial ground uncovered in the late twentieth century and studied by biological anthropologist Michael Blakey and his team at Howard University revealed much about the status of those blacks. Likewise, it has come to light recently that blacks, both slave and free, participated in the design of the District of Columbia (Washington, D.C.) and even the building of the Capitol. By 1714, the number of slaves in the colonies had multiplied to 59,000, growing to around 263,000 in 1754. This growth was spurred by the development of tobacco and rice agriculture and the continuing need for laborers. At the beginning of the Revolutionary War, more than half the slaves in the colonies were located in Virginia (Norton, Gutman, and Berlin 1983).

There were also eighteenth-century slave rebellions, and these led to repressive laws that affected both slaves and free people of color. For example, in 1723 Virginia denied free blacks the right to vote or carry weapons, and in 1740 South Carolina passed codes that prevented African Americans from owning and raising livestock. On the other hand, colonies also enacted laws to protect slaves from ill-treatment. There were even attempts at emancipation in the South as, for instance, when Thomas Jefferson attempted to enact a law for the emancipation of slaves in 1769 in the Virginia House of Burgesses.

In 1775, on the eve of the American Revolution, the Continental Congress barred blacks from participating in the army at the same time that the first abolitionist society was founded. On the other hand, Lord Dunmore, the royal governor of Virginia, offered freedom to those slaves who fought for the English, forcing General George Washington to change his mind and recruit blacks for service on his side (Mabunda 1997:6–7). Thus, before the American Revolution, the institution of slavery was still in its founding stages and attitudes toward blacks were ambivalent, even in the North.

In spite of their lofty ideals founded on individual liberty, the men who wrote the Constitution founding the United States of America did not resolve the contradiction that slavery presented them. Instead, they allowed the institution to prevail, setting up the conditions for a century of racial strife, including a devastating civil war and a racial ideology set deeply into American culture (see Smedley 2007). With the invention of the cotton gin in 1793 and the growing market for cotton, the economic incentive to maintain the institution of slavery was redoubled.

By 1804, all of the northern states had taken steps to eliminate slavery, and it remained a thriving legal entity only in the southern states (Nash 1983). By 1807, the slave trade had been prohibited in the United States, although not slavery itself, and much illegal importation of slaves took place. Benjamin Quarles estimated that as many as 5,000 slaves per year were illegally imported (1964:64). From this point on, the North and

South would take divergent paths with regard to African Americans, but the ongoing racial ideology in the South would affect the general reception of African Americans within U.S. society as a whole.

The defense of slavery and of the white, southern way of life became the basis of American racism and the foundation for "the myth of the Negro past." As Audrey Smedley (1999) has pointed out, the racial caste system first characterized by slavery and then by racial segregation laws was unique to North America. Southern whites developed an elaborate justification for the institution, reinforced by federal, state, and local laws. Slavery was an inhumane and immoral system that contradicted the very basis upon which the United States of America had been founded, but its edicts became deeply ingrained in the American consciousness as a consequence, and many persist to this day.

Even so, it is useful in understanding African American culture if we look at enslaved blacks as real people with everyday lives, as members of families, as laborers and producers, as people with creative faculties like any other people, and as problem solvers. While slavery generally left little latitude for blacks, it nevertheless offered some choice in its varied environments and conditions, and blacks often created more choice than circumstances seemed to allow. Thus, slaves exercised a certain amount of self-determination and were active agents in their own lives.

For example, in the North before the Revolutionary War many slaves were skilled craftsmen, often acquiring the ability to read and write in order to work as clerks or in the printing industry. And Quakers, through the administration of religious education, constituted a major source of learning for blacks. Reading and writing were considered prerequisites to freedom. Rhode Island, which had more slaves than any other New England colony, required the children of slaves to learn to read and write (Quarles 1964:41–43). In the South, blacks constituted about 80 percent of the skilled labor and even developed a "vernacular architecture" based on designs from Africa and used in various plantation buildings, including smokehouses, icehouses, and other structures such as shotgun houses (Deetz 1996:212–252; Jones 1985:200–207).

Living conditions for slaves varied according to crops and locations and the attitudes of the slave owners. Contrary to popular belief, plantation slavery was not typical in North America. According to Philip D. Curtin, the American South came to plantation life only in the eighteenth century and varied considerably from its Caribbean counterparts (see also Morgan 1998; Singleton 1985). Whereas the lucrative sugar plantations of the Caribbean had majorities that were black (both slave and free), southern plantations (with the exception of South Carolina) had majorities that were white who worked side by side with blacks. Curtin also noted that "even in the 1850s, when slavery reached its fullest development, fewer than half of the slaves belonged to planters who owned 30 or more" (1990:108).

Slavery in the American South differed from slave systems in other parts of the New World in that slaves experienced a natural increase in number rather than the frequent deaths known elsewhere, due largely to a healthier physical environment with fewer epidemic diseases and "a more even sex ratio in the slave population at an early date, which, in turn, may reflect the greater variety of tasks and smaller size of the American slave plantation" (Curtin 1990:109). Slavery required fairly close contact between owners and slaves, and most slaveowners on small farms or large plantations knew the names of all their slaves. Eugene D. Genovese, speaking of the kind of life lived on small farms, noted,

> Farms of ten slaves or less did not develop an extensive division of labor. The white farmer and his wife divided chores, but the extent of specialization among the slaves rarely went beyond the assignment of one or two women to house work, and even they had to work in the fields when needed. A common effort by master and slave at work together produced an easy familiarity, reinforced by living arrangements. The mistress or perhaps a female slave cooked for all at the same time and in the same way. Only segregation at table drew a caste line. The slaves either slept in one small house with the master's family or in a cabin that faced on the same yard. Slave and free, black and white, lived close to one another, and their relationship led to a widespread reputation for "better treatment." [1974:8–9]

Slaves who lived on larger plantations were part of a paternalistic world in which the slave owner ruled over them, his wife, and his children and any other dependents. According to Genovese, most slaves lived on farms (small or large) with the owner in residence, and "no more than one-third and possibly only one-fourth of the rural slaves worked under overseers, and many of these either worked under an overseer and a resident planter simultaneously or under an overseer who was a relative of the planter" (1974:13).

Many scholars believe that slavery constituted the beginning of the disruption of the black family and the pathology that followed it. But there is ample evidence that both the meaning of family to African Americans and the actual facts concerning black families during slavery were greatly misunderstood. In his book *The Black Family in Slavery and Freedom*, Herbert G. Gutman presents evidence that, in spite of the nature of slavery and the power of the owners over the fate of slaves and their family members, slaves were family oriented, and some scholars "underestimated the adaptive capacities of the enslaved and those born to them and to their children" (1976:21). Gutman found evidence that two-parent households and enduring unions characterized black families even in slavery and directly following emancipation.

Although it was true that children were often sold away from parents and spouses from one another, the importance of family to slaves manifested itself in efforts taken to keep track of family members and to find them following the war.

In the United States, a highly graded system based on color never developed as it did in the Caribbean and South America, largely because

Americans practiced what is called *hypodescent*, a form of racism in which the race of the child is determined by the lower caste parent (see Chapter 4). Because of laws and customs that declared as Negro any person with African heritage, no formal mulatto class developed as it did, for example, in Haiti. Although color consciousness did develop among American blacks, and slaveowners were more likely to free their own children, this system tended to create a solidarity among all people of African descent in the United States.

Nor did slavery manage to deprive Africans of their deep spirituality. According to W. E. B. Du Bois,

> In Africa the Negro had learned that there is in Heaven the God that made everything; but, diverging from the Europeanized creed of the Orient, the Negro believed that this God after creating things went so far off and became so unmindful of man that there was no necessity for man to concern himself about his divinity. What man needed to do, as the African understood it, was to appease the spirits of the millions of things organic and inorganic in which the spirit of this divinity is manifested. Such Christianity as the Negro conceived in his beginning in America was influenced by this African animism. [1970:358]

Slaves, in their roles as forced laborers, were nevertheless productive members of society, and often accomplished feats barely acknowledged. Let us use the example of the rice cultivators of South Carolina, descendants of peoples from Sierra Leone, a country on the west coast of Africa known for its rice cultivation techniques. South Carolina had a slave population larger than that of any other state, and blacks outnumbered whites two to one. Although slaveowners originally preferred Africans from the Congo and Angola, "in 1739, when African-born Angolans rose up against Carolina masters, slaves from this region were no longer so desirable" (Creel 1990:69). Instead, Africans from West Africa, namely, present-day

Sierra Leone and Liberia—peoples called the Gola and Kissi, among others—were preferred. On the coast of South Carolina, because of its isolation and because of the cultural similarity and numbers, Africans retained much of their culture, which they adapted to the new environment.

According to Margaret Creel, "Africans from Upper Guinea (Gola, Vai, Mende, Kissi, Kpelle, and so on) shared a common socioreligious bond that provided a certain cultural uniformity through mandatory secret societies. Names related to these societies appear in Gullah Creole" (p. 70). These slaves created a whole new language based on their African languages, which became known as Gullah Creole. This language is still spoken by some African Americans today and is related to the Krio language of Sierra Leone (Asante 1990).

These slaves, who cultivated rice and indigo, had done so in their native lands. Archaeologists who have studied the landscape of South Carolina coastal areas have discovered that the slaves engaged in massive work projects, moving earth in order to prepare the land for rice cultivation, actually moved as much earth as the slaves who built the pyramids of Egypt thousands of years before. In the course of transforming the face of the South Carolina and Georgia seacoast, they also created a distinctly African American culture, manifested in their own language, their own approach to religion, and their own attitudes toward life (Creel 1990:69–97).

It is worth noting that not all slaves were agricultural laborers or lived on plantations. Many lived in urban areas. For example, Loren Schweninger points out that many slaves worked in coastal areas "employed as shipwrights, ropemakers, and coopers," and others were "gold beaters, silversmiths, and cabinetmakers" (1990:80). Female slaves often resumed their role as market women, acquiring "control over much of the marketing network, selling slave-grown produce along the docks or through the streets of port cities" (ibid.). Urban opportunities for labor sometimes provided slaves with the means of obtaining their freedom, working for hire to pay their masters in return for their emancipation.

There was always a population of free blacks in the United States. In 1790, there were 59,557 free blacks (about 7.9 percent of the black population). In 1860, on the eve of the Civil War, there were 488,070 free blacks (11 percent of all blacks), more than half of whom lived in the South (Quarles 1964:83). The origin of free blacks was as varied as that of slaves, but they tended to live in urban areas. They were the descendants of indentured servants, runaways, those who had been freed after military service in the Revolutionary War, those who came from new territories, those who purchased their own freedom through their labor, and those freed by owners (especially those who were the children of unions between slaves and slaveowners). Quarles points out that by 1850 "the proportion of mulattos was 581 to every 1,000 blacks in the free Negro group, whereas it was only 83 mulattos to every 1,000 blacks in the slave population" (p. 84).

In the North, free blacks had fewer constraints because of antislavery sentiments, although they still were often subject to racial discrimination. Black males could vote in Massachusetts, Maine, New Hampshire, and Vermont, and even in New York if they owned $250 worth of property (an unlikely occurrence). In a number of states—California, Illinois, Indiana, Iowa, Ohio—blacks could not testify against whites. And in some cases, blacks could not serve on juries. As a rule, blacks were restricted to menial jobs, even when they had the qualifications for skilled labor, and blacks were not admitted to labor unions, because they were seen as competitors for jobs, especially as white immigrants increased in number (Quarles 1964:92–93).

In the North, free blacks founded the first independent black churches: the St. Thomas Protestant Episcopal Church, by Absalom Jones, and the Bethel African Methodist Episcopal Church, by Richard Allen. Both denominations founded in 1794 in Philadelphia spread throughout the North (Quarles 1964:99–100). These congregations played an important role in unifying African Americans and providing centers for social life. Blacks also founded mutual aid societies and library companies and joined abolitionist societies.

Free blacks in the South had special problems, because they represented a threat to the institution of slavery and often faced restrictive legislation that curtailed their rights. Free blacks were always required to prove their free status, usually by producing papers to that effect, and they seldom enjoyed the right to vote, hold office, testify in court, bear firearms, or assemble freely. They could, however, make contracts and acquire property (Quarles 1964:86–89).

Thus, African American culture was forged in both slavery and freedom, in rural and urban areas, in the North and the South, by both women and men, and within the context of an active spirituality and a continuing support of family.

While many scholars concede too quickly that blacks who lived in close proximity to whites retained less of their African culture than those who did not, they also fail to see culture as flowing in both directions or to see European culture changing as well in a new environment. Although it is generally agreed that African culture was more widely diffused among blacks in North America than elsewhere in the Western Hemisphere, this also resulted in this culture permeating the white community. "Cultural traits of African origin can be found in the white community, as well as the black, and in new forms that have continued to evolve in the United States—forms as various as jazz, southern cooking, and expected behavior in church" (Curtin 1990:110).

Early on, the diffusion of African cultural features into the general American culture was invisible, so that today many Americans are unaware that the banjo, many folk songs, certain foods and style of preparation (okra, black-eyed peas, fish stews, deep fat frying, etc.), many words (*okay, tote*), and even cattle herding techniques used by cowboys in the West originated in African cultures (Philips 1990:225–239; see also Morgan 1998 and Sobel 1987).

Anthropologists have known for some time that *acculturation*—the forceful imposition of the culture of a dominant group on a subordinate group—is a tenuous process and a two-way street. That is, a subordinate group will only accept from a dominant culture that which interfaces with its own culture in some meaningful way, a subordinate group often accepts the dominant culture by using it in a superficial way to disguise its own cultural features, and the dominant culture at some point begins to absorb features of the subordinate culture through prolonged contact and interaction. John Philips concludes that "when social scientists and historians begin to investigate systematically the survival of African culture among European-Americans they will discover that as much African culture survives now among whites as among blacks in the United States" (p. 227).

RESISTANCE TO SLAVERY

While most states had a variety of laws designed to limit the ill-treatment of slaves by their masters and overseers, slaves had no real legal recourse in the American South under slavery. Slaves were vulnerable to the whims of their masters, although in extreme cases masters could be punished for the mistreatment of slaves. But slaves did not enjoy their bondage. The stories, songs, and hymns of African Americans embody a passionate desire for freedom, an abiding and pervasive theme. Thus, the history of slavery is also the history of resistance to slavery and outright rebellion. Although in many respects blacks in North America had a more difficult time than their counterparts in the West Indies and South America with their black majorities and large maroon communities, slaveowners recognized the constant possibility of rebellion, feared it, and took steps to prevent it.

Resistance to slavery began in Africa and continued during the "Middle Passage"—the name given to the trip from Africa to the Americas—and continued once blacks were settled into their new lives. Throughout the course of slavery in North America, slaves engaged in various forms of resistance, including rebellions and escape. And although many southern whites from colonial days to the days of Jim Crow tried to convince themselves that blacks were content with their lives, their actions to prevent blacks from escaping those lives speak to the opposite reality.

Everyday resistance to slavery took the form of working more slowly and mishandling or destroying the master's property by breaking things or setting fires, pretending to be sick, self-mutilation, and mocking slaveowners in stories or songs (Quarles 1964:75–76). At times, slaves attempted to harm their owners through poisonings or beatings and other acts of "open defiance." According to John Hope Franklin and Loren Schweninger, "Nearly every year, in virtually every state in the South, slaves were indicted for killing their owners" (1999:78).

Throughout the eighteenth century, slaves revolted in different parts of the colonies. As early as 1712 in New York City, a slave revolt ended in the execution of 21 slaves, who had killed at least 9 whites (Mabunda 1997:5). In 1739, in South Carolina, several slave revolts took the lives of at least 81 whites and the lives of even more blacks. The Revolutionary War was itself a stimulus to black rebellion. Blacks had a vested interest in liberty, and Crispus Attucks was one of the first to fall in the battles that led to the struggle with England for independence.

In 1800, a slave named Gabriel Prosser conspired to lead a slave attack on Richmond, Virginia. The plan did not succeed, and the insurrectionists were captured and hanged. In 1822, in Charleston, South Carolina, Denmark Vesey planned a revolt that also failed, but the extensiveness of the conspiracy led to the establishment of laws that limited the mobility of both free blacks and slaves. In the end, Vesey and 36 co-conspirators were hanged, but 130 blacks and 4 whites were also arrested.

In this same year, blacks from the United States founded the African nation of Liberia. Repatriation of blacks to Africa was a constant theme among both blacks and whites, who saw it as a solution to the problem of slavery. Thomas Jefferson considered it a viable alternative to blacks and whites living together. Believing that blacks and whites were too different to live together, Jefferson believed that all parties would best be served if blacks simply left America. The American Society for Colonizing the Free People of Color of the United States (referred to as the

American Colonization Society) was founded in 1816 mostly by slaveholders to remove free blacks (whose freedom they considered a threat to their ownership of slaves) from the United States. Liberia also became a repository for Africans from liberated slave ships and freed slaves. The federal government supplied some of the money for this venture, and the capital of Liberia, Monrovia, was actually named after American President James Monroe. Liberia became an independent nation in 1847.

Because southern whites feared the influence of free people of African descent, both for the effect they might have on slaves and for the possibility of miscegenation, many of them supported this effort. However, in the long run, the movement removed relatively few blacks from the United States—around 15,000 in all, a number in any case offset by the continuing smuggling in of new slaves to the United States. Furthermore, the American Colonization Society was not popular in the Deep South, where black slave labor was in high demand. Nevertheless, return to Africa was a continuing, if unsuccessful, alternative to slavery into the early twentieth century.

The most famous slave revolt in the history of the United States was the Nat Turner Rebellion in 1831 in Southhampton County, Virginia. Turner, a preacher, led a group of slaves in rebellion. They killed 60 whites. Turner was hanged after being caught, leaving behind his famous *Confessions*. Southern whites responded to these rebellions by passing laws forbidding the education of blacks, forcing free blacks to leave the state, and limiting emancipation. In the long run, while slave rebellions occurred, they did not succeed in freeing the slaves. Nor did the growing protests of whites in the North and the abolitionist movements in which both whites and blacks participated.

Protests against slavery went as far back as the 1688 declaration signed by Mennonites in Germantown, Pennsylvania (Mabunda 1997:5). These protests spread to the Quaker population and gradually picked up adherents throughout the eighteenth century, taking the form of antislavery

societies and participation in the Underground Railroad, the name given to the series of groups of people who hid runaway slaves.

The New England Anti-Slavery Society was founded in 1832 by whites meeting at the African Baptist Church in Boston. Blacks and whites together established the American Anti-Slavery Society in 1833 in Philadelphia. Besides publishing antislavery tracts and sponsoring lectures, these societies also sometimes purchased the freedom of slaves. Presumably, their agitation had a certain effectiveness, especially in the wake of the British emancipation of all slaves in 1834, because President Andrew Jackson tried to prohibit the mailing of their tracts to the southern states. Congress also attempted to silence the abolitionists by disallowing the consideration of any legislation pertaining to antislavery. In 1839 in Warsaw, New York, the Liberty Party, an antislavery political organization, was founded and began to encourage boycotts of southern products (Mabunda 1997:14).

Fugitive slave laws had been on the books in some states since the seventeenth century, testifying to the fact that escape was a problem from the beginning of the slave trade. Slaves ran away because of harsh punishments and poor treatment, because their family members had been sold away, or because they simply had the desire for freedom. While some women plotted their escapes, the majority of runaways were male. Frederick Douglass, an escaped slave who fled North and then to England, was an active abolitionist, returning to the United States once his freedom had been purchased by his fellow abolitionists. Douglass escaped to the North from Maryland by borrowing the papers of a free black sailor and using them to take a train north. Harriet Tubman, the most famous "conductor" on the Underground Railroad, known to her people as "Moses," was herself a runaway slave.

But other slaves were too far south to head toward "the Promised Land" in the North, and many opted to get lost in a nearby city or to flee to the West or even further south. Some blacks went to Florida and lived among the Native Americans there, the Seminole, and became known as the

Black Seminoles.[2] Some of these were former members of the Spanish military who remained behind and settled among the Seminole, while others were escaped slaves from South Carolina and Georgia. Others were actually slaves purchased by the Seminole (Lower Creeks) from the English. These slaves lived a much different life from their counterparts in other states, because the Seminole gave them tools and land and corn to plant. The slaves gave some of their crops to their masters and kept the rest. As the word of these conditions spread, slaves sought out the Seminole, who let them live in their own villages and carry weapons. According to Kenneth W. Porter (1996:6), there was "basically no personal inequality between the two groups," and blacks served as interpreters of English, Spanish, and Muskogean and became advisers, eventually intermarrying with the Seminole.

AFRICAN AMERICANS AND RECONSTRUCTION, 1863–1877

Inevitably, the contradiction that slavery constituted in a nation founded on the principle of individual liberty and the economic and political conflicts between the North and the South led to violence, when the Confederacy attacked Fort Sumter in 1861, and the Civil War began. African Americans fought on both sides, with both slaves and free blacks recruited for the Confederate army. There were 4,441,830 slaves in the United States when the Civil War began. In 1863, Abraham Lincoln signed the Emancipation Proclamation, freeing all slaves in the Confederacy, but with no effect on slaves in those southern states that had not seceded or were under Union control (Delaware, West Virginia, Kentucky, Maryland, Tennessee, Louisiana, and Missouri). Nevertheless, the proclamation was inspirational, and many African American communities would hold emancipation celebrations.

Eventually, with the passage of the Thirteenth Amendment to the Constitution of the United States, adopted on December 18, 1865, slavery was abolished in the entire country. The Fourteenth Amendment, adopted on July 28,

1868, made all people born or naturalized in the United States citizens. The Fifteenth Amendment, adopted on March 30, 1870, guaranteed every citizen the vote regardless of race and previous status as a slave. However, it was black men who achieved the full status, while black women, along with white women in most states, though citizens, were still prevented from voting. Thus, following the Civil War, blacks gained equal status with whites in the eyes of the law for the first time in history, although exercising those rights would take a monumental struggle that would last well into the middle of the twentieth century, another hundred years.

Following the Civil War, various measures were taken to bring the Confederate states back into the Union. The attempt on the part of those in southern states to enact "black codes" to control the newly freed black population resulted in federal military occupation of the South largely for the purpose of drafting new state laws that recognized the rights of blacks. This period, from 1863 to 1877, was called Reconstruction.[3] It was a traumatic time for the United States, a time in which former slaves exercised their power as citizens but also had to face what W. E. B. Du Bois called "a reign of terror" in the form of the newly organized Ku Klux Klan, which used violence to keep newly freed blacks in their "proper place" as people subservient to whites (1970:209).

Although the experience was different in each of the southern states, the period was characterized by race riots in which whites assaulted blacks, who had little or no protection from either local law enforcement officials (who were often involved themselves) or the Union troops stationed in the states. It also exposed the effects of class difference between middle-class, educated blacks and those rural, often newly freed blacks. Nevertheless, African Americans made strides during this period.

The black leadership that developed during Reconstruction rose from the ranks of the black middle class, mostly men who had been free before the Civil War. According to Du Bois, these politicians accomplished three goals: (1) they established democratic government in the South following the war; (2) they established free public schools, thus affording education to those who had previously gone without it; and (3) they introduced a variety of social legislation that stayed on the books into the twentieth century (p. 210).

As part of Reconstruction in the South, state and local governments began to include African Americans as well as whites, yielding a democratic system for the first time. Many southern blacks were elected to political office during this period, and their efforts changed the face of the South. For example, between 1867 and 1876, 487 men were elected to state office in South Carolina, half of whom were black (Holt 1977:1). The first black to serve in the U.S. Senate was Hiram Revels of Mississippi in 1870. Blacks held offices as governor (Louisiana), lieutenant governor (Louisiana, Mississippi, and South Carolina), treasurer (Louisiana and South Carolina), superintendent of education (Arkansas, Florida, Louisiana, and Mississippi), and secretary of state (Florida, Mississippi, and South Carolina) during Reconstruction (Foner 1988:353). In addition, many blacks became policemen and even chiefs of police in municipalities across the South, and they also served in a number of other offices, such as magistrates and jury members (Foner 1988:362–363).

The struggle for education in the postwar South was notable as well. Because there had been no universal system of education for blacks or whites prior to the Civil War, the beginnings of universal education began after the war with efforts to set up a total public school system in the South as a basis for an egalitarian society (Foner 1988:366). Blacks were eager for education, and former slaves pushed for "universal, state-supported public education," in direct opposition to the planter elite who believed that education was not the business of the state (Anderson 1988:4).

African Americans also wanted to control their own schools, and the

> values of self-help and self-determination underlay the ex-slaves educational movement. To be sure, they accepted support from northern missionary societies, the Freedmen's Bureau, and some southern whites, but their own action—class self

> activity informed by an ethic of mutuality— was the primary force that brought schools to the children of freed men and women. [Anderson 1988:5].

Blacks resisted control of their educational institutions by others and had gone a long way toward establishing schools, even before missionaries came down from the North.

James D. Anderson tells of a case in Louisiana in which a well-established school system, supported by federal money and property taxes, was shut down by officials of the Freedman's Bureau. The freed slaves whose children attended these schools immediately offered to pay the entire tax burden in order to have the schools reopened. Anderson attributes the establishment of universal education largely to the efforts of freed slaves: "Ex-slaves used their resources first in a grass-roots movement to build, fund, and staff schools as a practical right; then they joined with Republicans to incorporate the idea into southern state constitutional law. With these actions they revolutionized the South's position regarding the role of universal public education in society" (1988:19–20).

During this time, we can see the rise of sharecropping as a way of life for many African Americans in the South. This system, which involved renting land from an owner, farming the land, and sharing the results with the owner, eventually developed into a "system of tenantry" in which former plantations in 40–80-acre pieces were parceled out. This system ultimately sustained the control of the white owners and placed black farmers under their economic control by establishing indebtedness that could never be paid off (Du Bois 1970:211–212).

Part of the failure of Reconstruction to realize total liberties for African Americans lay in the pervasive racial model that dominated American culture in both the North and the South. The lack of enthusiasm for bringing blacks into the fold of American citizenship ultimately led to failure in the South. Free blacks in the North had faced special problems with discrimination with the sudden influx of European immigrants, who competed with them for jobs and other resources. Many of these immigrants received special help from the government in the form of land grants in new territories that blacks did not share. White control of legislatures meant the continuing threat of disenfranchisement for blacks even in their own towns. Southern whites, who had created a unique and pervasive caste system based on race, tried to restore the order to their racial hierarchy by using city ordinances, state statutes, and federal court decisions to limit the freedom of African Americans and confine them to the lower economic level. The end of Reconstruction and the withdrawal of federal troops from the South introduced a new era in the struggle of African Americans to exercise the equal rights and citizenship they had been granted in the Constitution. The new era, coming gradually, was known as the Jim Crow era.

THE JIM CROW ERA: RACIAL APARTHEID IN THE AMERICAN SOUTH

Any gains that African Americans made during Reconstruction were short-lived. Little by little southern states began to disenfranchise blacks legally by passing state statutes and local ordinances that prevented blacks from voting, denied them easy access to education, limited their participation in business, and restricted their movement and safety within southern society as a whole. Racial segregation in the South was an attempt to reestablish white control by reinventing the social caste system that had prevailed during slavery. Although the laws that established legal segregation were only gradually enacted, they were finally in place by the first half of the twentieth century.

Segregation constituted a major impediment to the realization of true American citizenship that other peoples came to take for granted. It introduced a whole host of evils and troubles for blacks: the attenuation of political power, lack of or inferior education, limitations on the creation of black businesses, and stifling of meaningful

employment and competition. This era would lead directly to many of the problems in the black community identified by social scientists later in the twentieth century.

It is important to realize that racial discrimination had been a part of American life in both the North and the South from the beginning. In spite of the fact that northern communities had abolished slavery, the political and economic aspects of many of them were segregated, although sometimes casually so. The same was true in the South following the Civil War. A variety of practices on the part of private businesses continued racial discrimination. Hotels, restaurants, stores, and theaters often excluded blacks altogether or created separate or special accommodations for them. Railroads were also segregated. The difference between the North and the South, then, was relative but significant in terms of the economic opportunities provided in the industrial North compared to the rural South.

Blacks were affected by the reform movements that seized the United States in response to its rapid urbanization and industrialization in the nineteenth century. However, they were often forced to the periphery of these great issues due to the racial discrimination in labor unions and other key institutions that were the focus of reforms, or they were used as obstacles (as strikebreakers, for example) that management could call upon to frustrate the demands of white workers. Thus, blacks were in a political, economic, and educational no-man's-land in both the North and the South. But since the majority of them were located in the South, the system of legal segregation affected them more.

Nevertheless, the system of racial segregation did not eclipse the freedom of African Americans all at once. Some believe that the rise of poor whites to economic power and the competition over resources were responsible for the institution of segregation laws (Cashman 1991:7). It at once allowed poor whites to prove their superiority and at the same time to quash economic competition. But this racial caste system was not new, merely a transformation of the old set of relationships from slave days into a new set—this time equally supported by the government through an extensive network of laws. Blacks had to develop their own institutions—churches, schools, businesses, burial societies, social clubs—in order to survive, and these became an important locus of solidarity within African American communities. However, black institutional development was always limited by the laws that privileged white citizens over blacks in every phase of life.

The gradual achievement of segregation took between 30 and 50 years after the Civil War:

Thus South Carolina segregated the races in successive stages, beginning with trains (1898) and moving to streetcars (1905), train depots and restaurants (1906), textile plants (1915 and 1916), circuses (1917), pool halls (1924), and beaches and recreation centers (1934). Georgia began with railroads and prisons (1891) and moved to sleeping cars (1899) and, finally pool halls (1925), but refused to segregate places of public accommodation until 1954. . . . Mississippi was the first state effectively to disfranchise African-American citizens by a constitutional convention in 1890. It was followed by South Carolina in 1895, Louisiana in 1898, North Carolina (by amendment in 1900), Alabama in 1901, Virginia in 1901 and 1902, Georgia (by amendment) in 1908, and the new state of Oklahoma in 1910. Four more states achieved the same ends without amending their constitutions: Tennessee, Florida, Arkansas, and Texas. [Cashman 1991:7]

Southern states used poll taxes, literacy requirements, grandfather clauses, and gerrymandering to prevent African Americans from registering to vote. Thus, the black vote diminished as the nineteenth turned into the twentieth century. Without recourse to political power, blacks were vulnerable on every front.

A series of U.S. Supreme Court cases solidified the actions of the states. In 1896, the case of *Plessy v. Ferguson* upheld the right of Louisiana to provide "separate but equal" accommodations for whites and blacks on public transportation. In 1898, the case of *Williams v. Mississippi* upheld literacy tests for voters. The loss of civil rights that occurred during this period would have a number of effects: (1) it led to the formation of many black institutions, solidifying the centrality of the church in African American life; (2) it led to the formation of national rights organizations and the rise of a new black nationalism; (3) it led eventually to the modern civil rights movement that dismantled this system.

As the nineteenth century came to a close and the twentieth century opened, two views of what course blacks should take came forth from two different men: one was a former slave, Booker T. Washington, who grew up in the South; the other was the first African American to earn a doctoral degree from Harvard University, W. E. B. Du Bois, who grew up in the North. Their opposing views would define different courses of action for African Americans for decades to come and in many ways dramatized the different environments of the North and the South but also the schizophrenic nature of racial oppression.

Booker T. Washington, born into slavery in 1856 in Virginia, advanced what came to be known as "gradualism." Washington was a graduate of Hampton Institute in Virginia, and he started the Normal and Industrial Institute for Negroes in 1881 in Tuskegee, Alabama. He wrote his autobiography, *Up from Slavery*, and founded the National Negro Business League, which encouraged entrepreneurial activity among African Americans. At the Cotton States and International Exposition in Atlanta, Georgia, on September 18, 1895, Washington gave a talk that came to be known as the "Atlanta Compromise." In his speech, Washington emphasized the importance of increasing economic opportunities for blacks through training in industrial skills rather than through social equality. "In all things social we can be as separate as the fingers, yet one as the hand in all things essential to mutual progress" (cited in Cashman 1991:13–14).

In assuring whites that African Americans were not going to push for immediate social equality but work hard to better their lot, he removed some of the threat that blacks presented. Washington was successful in courting white philanthropists and getting them to support his various educational enterprises, and he was even invited to the White House by President Theodore Roosevelt. Having grown up in the South and understanding firsthand the violence possible against blacks by whites, Washington took a pragmatic approach to black progress (Cashman 1991:16).

William Edward Burghardt Du Bois, born in 1868 in Massachusetts, was a graduate of Fisk University and Harvard. A sociologist, Du Bois published *The Souls of Black Folk* in 1903, and his perspective was that of a northerner. While Du Bois was in favor of black laborers developing skills, he saw Washington's objectives as missing the point that white capital used "race prejudice and rivalry" within industry and white labor movements. Du Bois thought that education based on specific skills was pointless in view of developing "mass production" that would make them "obsolete in a generation or even in a day" (Du Bois 1970:213–214).

Blacks were usually left out of the union and populist movements of the day, so Du Bois did not hold out much hope for the Washington approach and disliked the seeming acceptance of racial inferiority in the equivocation about social equality. Du Bois advocated a broader educational program for African Americans, and he himself taught at the university level, eventually ending up at Atlanta University. He authored a number of significant works in the field of sociology, but *The Souls of Black Folk* remains the classic among his efforts.

In 1905, Du Bois was among a group of blacks and whites concerned about racial justice, who embarked upon a new approach at the Niagara Conference, which eventually led to the formation of the National Association for the Advancement of Colored People (NAACP) in 1910. This organization would be at the forefront of the civil rights movement, becoming known for its legal approach to the eradication of black inequality. For example, it was the NAACP that filed suit against election officials in Oklahoma who instituted a grandfather clause—one that stated that you could not vote unless your grandfather had voted in a previous election, which eliminated most blacks from the electoral process. In *Guinn v. United States* in 1915, the Supreme Court declared this tactic unconstitutional (Cashman 1991:22–23).

Du Bois believed that socialism was the answer to racial discrimination in the United States, a view that the majority of blacks never really agreed with. Eventually, Du Bois became disillusioned with American socialists, who failed to condemn both lynching and segregation. In his later years, Du Bois left the United States and moved to Africa, away from the racism that had plagued him throughout his life.

In 1911, the Urban League was founded in New York. Its main objective was to address social welfare issues. As more and more blacks migrated to the major cities of the North, its focus on the problems of poverty and ultimately institutional discrimination accounted for its longevity. Like the NAACP, the Urban League made slow progress but some inroads against the problems of urban blacks, which would become much more important later in the twentieth century when the modern civil rights movement, begun as a protest against legalized segregation, called attention to the plight of blacks in northern and western urban areas as well.

Meanwhile, in the United States generally and the South particularly, violence was getting out of hand. In 1892 alone, 235 lynchings occurred. Between 1882 and 1927, almost 5,000 persons were lynched, 3,500 of whom were African Americans (Du Bois 1970:214). Lynchings usually occurred because of alleged crimes by blacks against whites. Well into the twentieth century (between 1900 and 1960), 196 whites and 1,796 blacks were lynched, and the perpetrators of those killings were rarely, if ever, prosecuted. Southern whites defended lynching as a form of social control "as an indirect act of self-defence against the Negro criminal as a race" (Winfield H. Collins, cited in Cashman 1991:34). Southerners fought attempts to enact federal legislation against lynching, and lynchings were often social events in which whole families witnessed the violence as a form of entertainment, thus by reinforcing further the erroneous racial biases reinforced by the poor economic conditions that plagued the South—economic conditions generated by the interests of elite landowners who controlled political and economic power in the South.

Thirty Years of Lynching, 1889–1918 was published by the NAACP as part of a larger project seeking a federal antilynching law. Although southern senators managed to keep antilynching legislation from passing, the publicity created by the NAACP embarrassed the region, and eventually the number of lynchings decreased as southerners began to consider their actions more carefully and police themselves (Cashman 1991:34–35).

An equally difficult problem was posed by the rise of the Ku Klux Klan once again. Originally, the Klan was formed by elite southerners and manned by those who were disenfranchised after the Civil War because they had been officers in the Confederate army or complicit in the war in some other way. Under the pretense of protecting themselves and their society from dishonest and criminalistic former slaves, they used direct violence to terrorize former slaves and to keep them from exercising their right to vote. The reinstitution of the Klan in the twentieth century (1915–1944) found it largely changed in composition, no longer dominated by elite southern whites (many of whom joined White Citizens Councils). It consisted of those who felt displaced because of economic depressions, competition over resources due to immigration, and other social dislocations occurring during the period. While a central motive of the Klan was to keep blacks in line, it also discriminated against Jews, Catholics, and foreigners generally. The Klan decreased in influence and effectiveness as many of the country's problems were solved by economic improvements, assimilation, and legal suits. But strains of the Klan persist even to this day.

The gradual divestment of rights that African Americans had gained directly after the Civil War, the increasing violence used by whites to force blacks to conform to a social order in which they were the low caste, and the rise of repressive systems of labor in the form of sharecropping to replace slave labor, combined with changes in the world at large—and especially labor shortages in the urban North caused by growing businesses and the curtailment of immigration—led to a massive movement of African American people that became known as the Great Migration.

THE NEW CENTURY AND THE GREAT MIGRATION OF AFRICAN AMERICANS, 1910–1940S

The twentieth century began with the consolidation of racial attitudes in the United States as well as concerted efforts to oppose those attitudes. In the early decades of the twentieth century, anthropology became an organized discipline within academia, and Franz Boas became one of its key figures. The work of Gregor Mendel in genetics had been rediscovered in 1900, and this led not only to scientific advancements but also to the rise of scientific racism in the form of the eugenics movement, which sought to improve humanity through genetic selection, and these presuppositions were imbued with deeply ingrained social attitudes toward race.

Because Boas recognized that many of the traits assumed to be biological were learned (and that there was a general confusion about the relationship among race, language, and culture), he found it necessary to separate the edicts of the physical anthropology of the time from the study of culture, thus becoming the founder of American cultural anthropology. But, more importantly, Boas and his students were true public intellectuals. They carried out a concerted effort to educate the general public, both through their scientific studies and their writings in the popular newspapers and magazines of the day. Boas corresponded with Booker T. Washington and also knew W. E. B. Du Bois, who eventually invited him to give the graduation address at Atlanta University, during which Boas expounded on the marvels of African civilization, which were then generally unknown. But such enlightenment and such efforts to redirect the attention of scholars from race to culture did not bear fruit for a long time. Although Boas and his students provided the scientific underpinnings for the assumption of human equality, they were acting against the culturally ingrained attitudes toward race that had been 200 years in the making.

After a decade into the twentieth century, a great migration of African Americans took place, beginning prior to World War I, when the need for workers stimulated the recruitment of African Americans from the southern states, and continuing well into the 1940s. In 1900, there were approximately 8,834,000 African Americans in the United States, constituting 11.6 percent of the total population, most of whom lived in the southern states. The movement out of the South to the urban areas of the North changed the composition of the country's population and set the historical background for future problems for blacks living in cities across America (see Henri 1976; Lemann 1991; Marks 1989; Trotter 1991).

Although there are many theories that attempt to explain this phenomenon, it is clear that many blacks stood to benefit from higher wages and better jobs in the industrial North. "Emigrant agents," better known as labor recruiters, went south expressly for the purpose of urging blacks to move north. Their inducements included information on available employment in distant places, financial assistance in moving through the provision of train tickets, and even payment of debts. But blacks didn't need to be too deeply induced, because picking up and leaving was "a form of political protest," emigrant agents provided a means of escaping natural disasters that would have

otherwise left many African Americans destitute, and the ability to absent themselves from the scene encouraged whites to treat them better (Bernstein 1998:782–783).

In fact, as David Bernstein points out, southern whites attempted to control the black labor force by interfering with developing labor markets after the Civil War. The agents who came south to steal away the members of this labor force constituted a threat to southerners and their way of life. Therefore, the planters used licensing laws and other devices to penalize the agents (Bernstein 1998:785). Not only does this indicate the degree to which government action was involved with the repression of civil rights, according to Bernstein, but it also indicates how deeply committed to a racial caste system southern whites were, and how willing they were to use their political power to maintain it (p. 785).

However, whites did respond to the great migration of blacks away from the South by engaging in some reforms, such as providing better schools for black children. As James Anderson notes, "Public elementary schools became available to the majority of southern black children during the first third of the twentieth century, long after common schools had become universal for other American schoolchildren" (1988:148). Slaves had made the first push for universal education, while the second push came as an attempt to induce blacks to remain in the South. At the turn of the century, in the 16 southern states, out of a total of 1,120,683 black children, ages 5–9 years old, only 246,273, or 22 percent, attended elementary school (compared to 37 percent of white children). For children 10–14 years of age, the percentage attending school was 52 percent, compared to 76 percent of white children (Anderson 1988:151).

By 1940, 66 percent of black children ages 5–9 attended school (compared to 65 percent of white children), and 90 percent of black children ages 10–14 attended school (compared to 91 percent of white children) (p. 182). Thus, the impetus to improve black education that came from the migration of blacks from the South resulted in universal education for African Americans. While it was true that much of that education was in a segregated environment—a problem that would be addressed in the second half of the century—it was, nevertheless, an improvement.

In spite of efforts to keep blacks in the South, their "escape" was made easier by the existence of railroads. "In sum, the South lost 323,000 African-Americans in the 1910s and 615,000 in the 1920s—about 8.2 per cent of its African-American population" (Cashman 1991:26). The twentieth century would see some of the worst repression, and some of the greatest successes, for African Americans in the history of the country. The New York City African American community of Harlem and the city of Chicago became focal points for African American struggles and achievement (see Henri 1976; Lemann 1991; Marks 1989; Trotter 1991).

In 1914, a Jamaican-born printer named Marcus Moziah Garvey founded the Universal Negro Improvement and Conservation Association (UNIA) in Harlem for the purpose of bringing together peoples of African descent. In 1921, the UNIA had more than a million members. While black leaders such as Du Bois advocated integration of blacks into U.S. society, Garvey encouraged separatism, and his movement became one of the earliest expressions of black nationalism in the new century. Defined by Wilson Jeremiah Moses as "the effort of African Americans to create a sovereign nation-state and formulate an ideological basis for a concept of national culture" (1996:2), nationalistic feelings among blacks can be traced as far back as the American Revolution.

Garvey's organization set up the Black Star Steamship Line with an eye toward repatriating blacks to Africa. "It also petitioned the League of Nations to transfer the former German colonies in Africa, South West Africa and German East Africa, held as mandates by South Africa and Britain, respectively, to Garvey's control. In 1922 Garvey designated

himself president of a new African republic" (Cashman 1991:38). Garvey's contemptuous attitude toward many African American leaders led him into many ideological disputes. Garvey and Du Bois came to verbal and written blows over ideology, and in the end the UNIA itself was plagued with the problem of integrationism versus separatism, which eventually led to the killing of a former member of Garvey's camp and the indictment of Garvey himself for mail fraud in 1923. He was later deported from the United States. But the amount of support he gained from blacks in New York was indicative of the desire of those same blacks to find a solution to their many problems and made his movement the most successful black nationalist movement in history to that time (Moses 1996:241).

Harlem was also the site of the Harlem Renaissance, an efflorescence of black culture that emerged in the 1920s. The Renaissance was the product of the Great Migration and its effects on prosperity in Harlem. Such writers as Claude McKay, Zora Neale Hurston, Langston Hughes, Jean Toomer, Countee Cullen, Nella Larsen, Alain Locke, Jessie Redmond Fauset, and James Weldon Johnson made their names during this era. Many of these writers published their poems and fiction in *Crisis*, the magazine of the NAACP, and other, similar publications. Their books were published by mainstream publishers and read by whites as well as blacks. At the same time, black artists, musicians, and performers were busy creating new art forms, and their work was in much demand. Thus, the Great Migration shifted populations from rural areas to urban areas and brought together a critical mass of black talent such as had never been seen before. Although much of the achievement of the Harlem Renaissance was eclipsed by the Great Depression, which began in 1929, it stands out as a period of extreme creativity and cultural success in African American history.

Those who remained in the South had to live in a racially divided society in which they had very little political power. In her ethnographic study, *After Freedom: A Cultural Study in the Deep South* originally published in 1939, anthropologist Hortense Powdermaker captured the lives and interactions of blacks and whites in a Mississippi town she called Cottonville, a commercial hub of a cotton-farming community.

She found a town in which virtually all of the whites belonged to families that had been in the South "for three generations," and they were all born in the town in which they lived. They were divided into an upper class of plantation owners; a middle class of small farmers and those who actually managed the plantations, craftsmen, and merchants; and poor whites. The white section of town was beautifully land-scaped and with no hint of "slums," because all of the poor white people lived outside of town, as did the large landowners (1993:14).

Blacks were located literally "across the tracks" from the white part of town or nearby the farms on which they worked. Their neighborhood did not display a uniform level of economic well-being, but "runs the gamut of possibilities from comfort and poverty" (p. 12). Blacks patronized mostly white businesses, the exception being a black-owned grocery store, restaurant, doctor, and dentist. Many of the blacks moved between the country and the town.

Powdermaker describes a situation in which the physical separation of blacks and whites symbolized the social separation of the two groups. And while whites had negative stereotyped ideas about blacks, most of them thought themselves virtuous in their treatment of blacks; poor whites, however, resented blacks, who competed with them for employment. On the other hand, blacks were not allowed to ride in the best cars in trains or eat in white restaurants; and they were called by their first names or "Aunty" or "Uncle" while being required to address whites as "Mr." or "Mrs." Powdermaker also found that when whites talked among themselves, they almost always referred to blacks as "niggers" or "darkies." There was a taboo against blacks and whites eating together. Blacks were required to enter white homes through the back door (pp. 43–55).

Beyond these social constraints, African Americans in Cottonville also suffered from political and economic constraints, sometimes due to the uncertainty surrounding single-crop agriculture but also because of the pure lack of power. In Cottonville, only 39 percent of the full owners of farms were black (181 blacks to 467 whites), 30 percent of the part owners, and 2 percent of the managers, but 81 percent of the tenant farmers were black. "One fear of the Whites has always been that their labor supply would be taken from them. In the boom years there was intense feeling against northern agents who came to entice Negro workers up north, and every effort was made to oppose them" (p. 81).

Thus, Powdermaker substantiated through fieldwork in 1931 the reality of the fear of black migration, as well as the reasons why blacks might want to leave. Given these facts, the continuing migration of blacks to the North between the world wars is no surprise.

In 1945, St. Clair Drake and Horace R. Cayton published a landmark study of African Americans, *Black Metropolis: A Study of Negro Life in a Northern City*. This study is special because it attempts to look at an African American community as a whole. It captures not only the history of African Americans in the city of Chicago but also the diversity and complexity of their culture. The authors combined sociological and anthropological techniques in collecting the data for their study, and the book stands as one of the most comprehensive treatments of a black community. In a city founded in 1790 by a man of African descent, Jean Baptiste du Sable, the struggle of African Americans is rendered in microcosm, capturing the escape to freedom and the assumption of employment with economic possibilities and political participation, along with the blatant racism that resulted in riots, discrimination, and a vicious policy of housing segregation. The black community in Chicago was second in population only to that of Harlem.

In 1890, the population of Chicago consisted of 58 percent native whites, 41 percent foreign-born whites, and 1.3 percent African Americans. By 1944, the composition of Chicago's population was 73 percent native whites, 17 percent foreign-born whites, and 9 percent African Americans. In terms of actual population, in 1900 out of a total population of 1,698,575 people, 1,081,720 were native whites, 586,705 were foreign-born whites, and 30,150 were blacks. By 1944, out of a total population of 3,600,000, native-born whites were 2,642,000, foreign-born whites 621,000, and blacks 337,000 (Drake and Cayton 1945:8–9).

As African Americans arrived in greater and greater numbers in Chicago, they found their way to the center of the city—"poverty clusters near the center of the city" (p. 13). Foreign-born whites tended to move into colonies of like people, and as people became assimilated to American culture, they gradually moved toward the outer parts of the city. As immigrants moved into Chicago, they took on the unskilled jobs, allowing the native-born whites to move up to more skilled (and more highly paid) employment. In the meantime, their children became better educated than their parents and moved out of the poorest neighborhoods, becoming part of the native-white groups. However, "Negroes have replaced immigrants as the primary source of unskilled and menial labor," since World War I, constituting "the bottom of the social and economic pyramid and have inherited the slums" (p. 18).

Because of its centrality to the Midwest and its farm equipment and meat-packing industries, Chicago became a center of management–labor disputes, subject to violent outbreaks as the stresses, both economic and social, grew from time to time. Recurrent riots over labor practices and racism became part and parcel of Chicago's character as a city. Nevertheless, Chicago became a "refuge" for blacks escaping from the South before the Civil War where, after the passage of fugitive slave acts, they were protected by resident blacks, who formed a Liberty Association expressly to fight off the slave catchers and local magistrates who often kidnapped members of the free black population. It was also a destination after the war for those who wished to escape the increasingly repressive political and economic environment in southern states in hopes of freedom and a living wage (p. 34).

Any economic progress that blacks made in Chicago after the migration was eventually cut short by the Great Depression in 1929, but between "1930 and 1940 the Negro population increased by more than 43,000. With the collapse of cotton tenancy in the South, and because of discrimination in the dispensing of relief and emergency employment, thousands of Negroes set out for Chicago" (p. 88). This exacerbated an already difficult economic situation in which "four out of every ten persons on relief were Negroes" (ibid.) and increased the tension between blacks and whites in Chicago.

"The Great Migration created the 'Negro Problem,'" said Drake and Cayton (p. 733), bringing into direct contact whites with blacks and into specific relief the racial problems endemic to American culture. This problem would be addressed directly following World War II.

WORLD WAR II AND THE RISE OF AMERICAN POWER AND AFFLUENCE

World War II brought about many changes in U.S. society that laid the foundation and cleared away some obstacles for the start of the modern civil rights movement that began in the 1950s. First of all, World War II brought American hypocrisy to the foreground. While fighting against Hitler and the racism of the Nazi regime in Germany, the United States did so with a segregated army and with rights for blacks sharply curtailed by legal segregation and institutional racism at home.

A. Philip Randolph (1889–1979) decided that a "march on Washington" to protest the discriminatory treatment of blacks in defense industries would be a good idea. He and other leaders (among them Walter White, Mary McLeod Bethune, and Lester Grange of the Urban League) planned a march for July 1, 1941. However, because the march threatened President Franklin D. Roosevelt's own political agenda, Roosevelt took steps to prevent it by issuing an executive order that desegregated all training programs and defense industries on June 18, 1941. He also created the Fair Employment Practices Committee (FEPC) to enforce his order, but the organization lasted only for the duration of the war (Cashman 1991:73–74). With the increase in jobs brought about by the war industries, black migration to the North began again.

African Americans had participated in all of America's wars, and World War II was no exception. More than a million blacks joined the segregated armed forces where they continued to be subjected to unequal treatment and menial jobs. "Experiments," such as training almost 1,000 black pilots at Tuskegee, Alabama (later called the Tuskegee Airmen), for service in the army air force, provided evidence of black competence, but it was not until 1948 under President Harry Truman that the armed services were finally desegregated.

Following the war, the United States embarked on an unprecedented economic boom as it began its move to the status of world power, and its economy became a corporate one. The middle class grew from 13 to 46 percent of the population, due to government incentives, which offered education and housing to former GIs. As Americans became economically better off, so did African Americans, but not to the extent that they wished. For example, unemployment among whites in 1950 was 4.9 percent; it was 9.0 percent among blacks. The following year, unemployment had fallen to 5.3 percent among blacks and 3.1 percent among whites. However, whites still made more than twice as much as nonwhites: in 1950, whites had a median income of $7,057, whereas nonwhites had a median income of $3,828 (Cashman 1991:104, 109).

When black veterans returned home, open hostilities toward them from whites who feared the push for equality called attention to the fact that racial problems persisted. President Truman issued executive orders to eliminate racial discrimination in civil service hiring and in the military. Black migration to northern cities put pressure on politicians to respond to the growing number of votes coming from the black community. But the South was changing too, becoming more urbanized and more industrialized. Merchants in large southern cities often depended on black consumers for their profits.

The African American community was poised for the push that would succeed in desegregating the South and bringing the rights of American citizenship, including the right to vote, finally into their grasp. The push would begin in the South, where the violation of these rights was most egregious and the opposition to the violation most dangerous. However, the repercussions of these early struggles would be felt in African American communities all over the country. Each area had its own special problems to solve, but in every case African Americans drew on their own cultural understandings in deciding just how this battle had to be fought in their own backyards. And as they went about their protests, using their nonviolent strategies, millions of Americans watched on television as southern whites did become violent.

THE RISE OF THE MODERN CIVIL RIGHTS MOVEMENT

The NAACP had been sporadically successful in prosecuting cases of discrimination here and there before the war, signaling a change in the attitude of the U.S. Supreme Court, which in the past had upheld many laws imposing legal segregation or abridging the voting rights of blacks. NAACP lawyers decided to make an even more extensive bid against segregation by continuing to employ a legal strategy of bringing suits in court, getting a positive decision from the Supreme Court, and then acting on that positive outcome to bring about change. When the moment came, blacks would call upon the institutions established under segregation, their solidarity, and their emotional resources to guide them.

In 1954, the Supreme Court, by a unanimous vote in *Brown v. Board of Education of Topeka, Kansas*, found that separate educational facilities were inherently unequal. This case was one of many that had been filed by Thurgood Marshall, head of the NAACP Legal Defense

Fund. Eighty percent of southern whites polled were against school desegregation, and it was not supported by President Dwight D. Eisenhower or Congress. Many forms of obstruction were employed to prevent blacks from acting on the Court's decision, and the NAACP itself was the subject of skillful political maneuverings on the part of southern politicians who passed laws requiring the organization to disclose its membership (a very unsafe thing in many southern towns), prevented municipal or state employees from belonging, and engaged in acts of violence.

Most people date the formal beginning of the modern civil rights movement to the day when Rosa Parks, a seamstress in Montgomery, Alabama, refused to yield her seat on the bus to allow a white person to sit down on December 1, 1955, and was arrested. This case is particularly instructive, because it illustrates the way in which African Americans drew on their cultural and social strengths in order to participate in a contest that they would ultimately win, but not without great cost.

The city of Montgomery had at one time been the capital of the Confederacy, but its segregated bus system was different from most segregated systems in the South, including other parts of Alabama. Ralph Abernathy, in his autobiography, *And the Walls Came Tumbling Down*, explained,

Rosa Parks (1913–2005).

Throughout most of the South, the law prescribed that blacks begin seating from the rear forward and whites from the front backward. Under this arrangement, on a predominantly black route our people might well occupy all the seats on the bus or, if there were a few whites aboard, almost all. On the other hand, on a predominantly white route, blacks might be found only on the back row. The boundary would be established by the proportion of blacks to whites and by who got on first. This method was used in several Alabama cities, including Mobile.

In Montgomery, however, the first ten seats were reserved for whites only—whether or not there were any white riders on the bus. This meant that blacks could not sit in the three-seat benches in the front that faced each other or in the four first-row seats. So Mrs. Parks was acting within the law when she sat down in an outside seat in the eleventh row, with a black man to her right (next to the window) and two black women across the aisle. [1989:133]

The arrest of Rosa Parks became the deciding factor in the decision of African Americans in Montgomery to launch their bus boycott. Blacks had had problems with bus seating for years, and in this instance bus drivers had police powers and could forcibly remove blacks from the buses. Many black men chose to walk rather than suffer the humiliation of getting on the front of the bus to pay their fare and then walking to the back of the bus to get on, especially since blacks who had paid were sometimes left standing outside as the bus pulled away. Other people had been arrested not long before the Parks incident, but Rosa Parks was an upstanding member of the community around whom everyone could rally (see Abernathy 1989:131–134; Robinson 1987:19–22).

It was the Women's Political Council (WPC) that served as the liaison between the black community and the city officials when it came to complaints about the treatment of blacks on the buses (Robinson 1987:23). This organization had already mapped out its plans for integration in Montgomery, although it did not do so openly. Its chapters, which covered all parts of the city, also constituted an efficient means of communicating information about the boycott to all parties. Jo Ann Gibson Robinson, its president at the time of the boycott, had already met with the mayor and other city officials, and WPC members regularly attended city meetings until the boycott began. Other black organizations were also in place to help deal with complaints and other political issues that affected blacks and had met with bus company officials before to discuss problems. The 68 black organizations in the community meant that a network of both communication and action was in place when the decision to engage in a boycott was reached (pp. 27–39).

The plans for a bus boycott came to fruition on December 5, 1955, the Monday for which Rosa Parks's trial was set. Initially, the boycott was to last only one day. Robinson drafted the notice of the boycott and ran it off on the mimeograph machine at her college, making thousands of copies with the help of her students. The network of organizations aided in the distribution of the notices to all parts of the community. Because African Americans constituted three-quarters of the customers who rode the bus, a successful boycott would get the attention of the bus company (pp. 45–47).

Because the ministers were the leaders of the community and the churches were natural meeting places, and because the issue was an important one, the ministers rallied together "for the first time in the history of Montgomery," regardless of their denominations or the kinds of congregations they had. On the Friday evening before the boycott, a meeting was called at the Dexter Avenue Baptist Church (the church at which Martin Luther King, Jr., had just become pastor) at which all community leaders— ministers, presidents of organizations, and others—were present. They decided to call for a mass meeting at the Holt Street Baptist Church for Monday night.

Although members of the white community had found out about the boycott, and police officers accompanied the buses on Monday, the boycott was a total success. Black riders walked to work or took black taxicabs for a reduced rate. White passengers had also avoided the buses, some out of support for the boycott. Rosa Parks was tried and found guilty and fined. That afternoon Ralph Abernathy and Martin Luther King, Jr., gathered with other ministers to form the Montgomery Improvement Association. King was elected president. It was that evening at the Holt Street Baptist Church that King introduced the principles of nonviolent protest—an old strategy of earlier civil rights actions.

The boycott began as a one-day event for the purpose of gaining better treatment for blacks on the buses. However, due to the failure of city officials to yield on any points, blacks decided to continue the boycott and to push for total desegregation of the bus system. Whites formed White Citizens Councils and enlisted the aid of the chief of police. Houses and churches of blacks were bombed, and other acts of intimidation practiced. The movement, however, did not flag. With nightly church rallies, the boycott was maintained until 1957, when the federal courts declared segregated seating unconstitutional. The African Americans of

Montgomery, Alabama—ordinary women and men—had succeeded in their attempt to desegregate buses by calling upon their institutions, their discipline in applying nonviolence, and their fortitude in maintaining their resolve in the face of overt violence on the part of both private individuals and government officials. The boycott had lasted a total of 381 days.

The bus boycott ignited a number of other movements throughout the South and set the civil rights movement into full sway. The Civil Rights Act of 1957 created the infrastructure in the Department of Justice to handle civil rights issues and prohibited interference with voting, allowing the attorney general to handle such actions in district courts (Cashman 1991:136).

Martin Luther King, Jr., rose to national prominence as a result of his leadership during the boycott, and he and Ralph Abernathy, along with others, formed the Southern Christian Leadership Conference (SCLC) to encourage the continuation of activism. There followed a number of protests in various southern cities with different degrees of results. Americans watched on television as African Americans, practicing nonviolence, were confronted by jeering crowds of angry whites during attempts to desegregate Central High School in Little Rock, Arkansas, and as policemen arrested protesters in Birmingham, Alabama, intimidating them with dogs and water hoses.

Of particular significance was the beginning of student protest in the form of sit-ins at lunch counters in segregated restaurants. Four students from North Carolina Agricultural and Technical College were refused service at a Woolworth's lunch counter in Greensboro, North Carolina, on February 1, 1960, setting off spontaneous lunch counter sit-ins across the South. This led to the formation of SNCC, the Student Nonviolent Coordinating Committee, the brainchild of Ella Baker, a former executive director of SCLC, who wanted to make sure that sit-ins were coordinated and their participants trained in nonviolent protest. SCLC held a conference at Shaw University during an April weekend in 1960 for student leaders of sit-ins and northern whites who

had begun to lend their support to the movement (Stoper 1989:6–7).

Because lunch counters had been successfully desegregated the previous summer, in May 1961, SNCC members began their attempts to desegregate interstate transportation by taking "freedom rides" on interstate buses. Those riding from Washington, D.C., to Louisiana were attacked in Birmingham and arrested in Florida. In 1964, SNCC sponsored a "Freedom Summer" during which 700 students from the North went to Mississippi. Three of those participants were murdered (Stoper 1989:13). But 1964 also saw civil rights activist Fannie Lou Hamer of Mississippi challenge the right of white Democratic delegates to seats at the Democratic convention. Although Hamer's contingent was not seated, segregated delegations became unacceptable after that year.

The previous year had seen four momentous events: the murder of NAACP officer Medgar Evers on June 12, 1963; the gathering of 250,000 people at the March on Washington where Martin Luther King, Jr., delivered his famous "I Have a Dream" speech (on August 28, 1963); the bombing on September 15, 1963, of a Birmingham, Alabama, black church in which four young girls attending Sunday school were killed; and the assassination of President John Fitzgerald Kennedy on November 22, 1963, in Dallas, Texas.

An ever growing amount of federal legislation and executive orders led to the effective end of legal segregation in the South. In 1962, President Kennedy had issued an executive order ending segregation in federally assisted housing. The Civil Rights Act of 1964, passed during the administration of President Lyndon Johnson and supported by 152 Democrats and 138 Republicans, prohibited discrimination in public accommodations, businesses, and trade unions. The 1965 Voting Rights Act allowed federal agents to register blacks denied this right.

The civil rights movement begun in Montgomery, led by ministers, and participated in by the rank and file dealt with the problem of

Martin Luther King, Jr. (1929–1968).

segregation in the South. The movement captured the attention of blacks all over the United States, especially those in urban areas who faced different kinds of problems that required different tactics. Some of these blacks did not think of integration as an appropriate goal, and some sought a separate nation altogether. Following in a tradition of black nationalism that stemmed from revolutionary days, a group that had been around for many decades, the Nation of Islam, produced a leader who captured the imaginations of the impoverished in northern ghettos. His name was Malcolm X.

BLACK NATIONALISM: MALCOLM X AND THE NATION OF ISLAM

Black nationalism, the idea of a separate black state, had been a strain of thought among African Americans from the revolutionary era onward (Moses 1996). The Nation of Islam was a religious movement that had started in 1931 in Detroit, Michigan, primarily among poor and

unemployed blacks, probably in response to the Great Depression. Its founder, W. D. Fard, originally called it the Temple of Islam. By the time the modern civil rights movement began, the Nation was led by Elijah Muhammed (1897–1975), who held that leadership for 41 years until his death. Openly nationalistic and hostile to whites, the Nation of Islam had between 65,000 and 100,000 members by 1960 (Cashman 1991:171). In 1960, Elijah Muhammad made the call for a separate black nation, rejecting the goal of integration that so many American blacks believed in.

However, it was Malcolm X, a charismatic minister, who succeeded in attracting more young adherents to the Nation of Islam. Under his guidance, the Nation gave a sense of dignity and purpose to thousands of disenchanted black youths in urban areas. Malcolm X was an articulate speaker, and he did not back down or comfort those who wanted a softer approach to the problems of racism. Because of differences with Elijah Muhammad, Malcolm X left the Nation of Islam in March 1964. After traveling to Mecca and meeting Muslims of many different races, he created the Organization of African Unity. While still adhering to a philosophy of black nationalism, Malcolm X had changed his perspective from one of fighting racism to one of fighting oppression generally on a worldwide basis. Before he could implement his ideas, he was assassinated on February 21, 1965.

The Nation of Islam had been successful in getting young people off drugs, establishing a network of businesses, and generally making its members better off. After Elijah Muhammad died in 1975, his son, Wallace Deen Muhammad, sought to "seek integration into the American system" by shifting the group to Sunni Islam; establishing a new organization, World Community of Al-Islam in the West; admitting whites; and becoming known as Bilalians. In 1977, Louis Farrakhan and other members of Elijah Muhammad's organization reestablished the Nation of Islam (Cashman 1991:178; Walker 1999:119–120). Farrakhan was instrumental in bringing about the "Million Man March" on

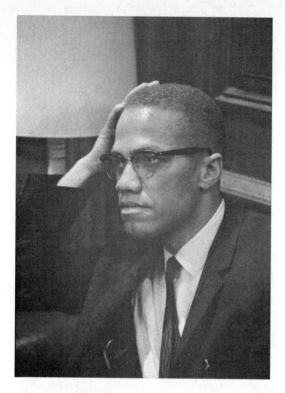

Malcolm X (1925–1965).

Washington in 1995, but his racism and anti-Semitism, as well as the initial exclusion of women, brought him a good deal of criticism.

THE RISE OF BLACK POWER AND THE END OF THE CIVIL RIGHTS MOVEMENT

As the 1960s wore on and more and more strides toward ending legal segregation were made, the nature of the civil rights movement began to change. In many ways, the rise of the black power movement was the product of generational differences as well as ideological shifts. Not content to practice the nonviolence that had become part and parcel of black protest, younger members of the civil rights movement promoted militancy and even violence in the pursuit of black goals. And because of the increasing violence against blacks in general, black political figures, and the growing threat to young black

men of the military draft, it was harder and harder to justify nonviolence as a strategy. Riots across the United States broke the decorum established by the nonviolent protests in the South. Young people in Los Angeles, Detroit, Philadelphia, and New York did not have the patience of their elders who had dismantled legal segregation in the South.

Led by Stokely Carmichael, chairman of SNCC, the Student Nonviolent Coordinating Committee shifted from its nonviolent, integrationist stance to one of black separatism, effectively destroying the organization by splitting its membership. According to Carmichael, black power was "a call for black people in this country to unite, to recognize their heritage, to build a sense of community" (cited in Cashman 1991:199). Black power protests drew upon different kinds of people than those who had started the movement; they were from the North and West, concerned with the plight of blacks in cities, and were not religious leaders. For example, in 1966, Huey P. Newton and Bobby Seale founded the Black Panther Party in Oakland, California, and openly challenged the authority of the state and police, adopting a radical agenda and openly carrying firearms.

The decade of the 1960s ended with the assassinations of Martin Luther King, Jr. (April 4, 1968), in Memphis, Tennessee, and Robert Kennedy (June 5, 1968) in Los Angeles, California. Although blacks would continue to take advantage of affirmative action and civil rights legislation enacted during the Johnson administration, the formal civil rights movement had clearly come to an end, partially eclipsed by the conflict in Vietnam. War protests began to replace civil rights protests, especially when young men were drafted in great numbers. Black men served disproportionately in this conflict and died disproportionately as well. The 1970s brought the end of the war in Vietnam and the beginning of economic recession in the United States. In the decades approaching the end of the twentieth century the problems confronting African Americans were largely social and economic, but as a group they had made more progress than ever before.

ECONOMIC DOWNTURNS AND THE RISE OF THE UNDERCLASS

Throughout the decades following the civil rights movement, a growing number of African Americans began to make impressive intellectual and cultural contributions. Spurred on by their success in dismantling segregation and identifying problems in the urban North, they continued to identify problems and work toward solutions. However, a new set of problems began to emerge, tied particularly to the economic shifts within the nation and the world.

African Americans as a group had always achieved economic success at a lesser rate than Americans as a whole. However, in the 1970s, social scientists began to realize that a great disparity had emerged between middle-class blacks and those at the very bottom of the economic ladder, the underclass. In a series of studies published as three books, William Junius Wilson, a Chicago sociologist, described dramatic changes that had taken place within the African American population. In *The Declining Significance of Race* (1980), Wilson pointed out that middle-class blacks had been able to take advantage of new opportunities arising out of the increased prosperity following World War II and the elimination of many of the racial obstacles that had previously stymied their progress. However, those without the necessary education and skills actually became worse off. At the very bottom of the lower class was an underclass, the subject of Wilson's second book, *The Truly Disadvantaged* (1987).

According to Wilson, the underclass reached a state of crisis in the 1970s that had not before been known among ghetto-bound poor people. This crisis took the form of what he called "social dislocation"—that is, the increase in "inner-city joblessness, teenage pregnancies, out-of-wedlock births, female-headed families, welfare dependency and serious crime" had reached "catastrophic proportions" (1987:3). The loss of middle-class and working-class families from the neighborhoods resulted in a destabilizing of ghetto communities and the erosion of patterns of mainstream behavior. Wilson also argued that racism in the standard sense couldn't explain the situation. Rather, the historical effects of racism and their institutionalized expression in labor markets were to blame and perhaps constituted an ongoing problem (1987:7–12).

Wilson tied the plight of the underclass to the continuous migration of blacks to cities just as the labor market was changing, so that relocation of many industries outside city centers, along with a general shift to service industries, constituted a major economic disadvantage to those blacks with the fewest skills and mobility. Because more blacks were always arriving, there was always a critical level of poor blacks (1987:142). The ensuing joblessness had a profound effect on family structure that Wilson says led to the particular inner-city pathologies he identified.

In his third book on the topic, *When Work Disappears*, Wilson reinforced the idea that it is the severity of unemployment that leads to the problems of the inner-city underclass: "As the population drops and the proportion of non-working adults rises, basic neighborhood institutions are more difficult to maintain: stores, banks, credit institutions, restaurants, dry cleaners, gas stations, medical doctors, and so on lose regular and potential patrons" (1997:44). Thus, neighborhoods deteriorated more and more, and blacks who might have shared the same values as other Americans found it impossible to implement them in such dire circumstances.

FAMILY, RELIGION, AND THE AFRICAN AMERICAN EXPERIENCE IN THE TWENTY-FIRST CENTURY

The identification of a black underclass fed into an ongoing American myth about the pathology of the black family—myths reinforced by social scientific studies such as Gunnar Myrdal's *An American Dilemma* (1944), which concluded that African American culture was "*a distorted development, or a pathological condition, of the general American culture*" (p. 928, emphasis in original) or that "peculiarities in the Negro community may be characterized as social pathology," or that "the average Negro family is more disorganized than the white family" (pp. 929, 931); or such as *The Negro Family*, by Daniel Patrick Moynihan, which states that "at the heart of the deterioration of the fabric of Negro society is the deterioration of the Negro family" (1965:5). Although both reports, among others, were meant to spur action on behalf of African Americans, the assimilationist assumptions, also inherent in the earlier work of E. Franklin Frazier (1966), came close to declaring that any forms of family not exactly like the "typical" American family were inherently pathological and that female-headed households so prevalent in the black community were inherently pathological. And while truly disintegrating families characterized only a small percentage of all African American families, this image came to stand for the whole, once again invalidating the lives and culture of the group.

However, as Robert Staples has pointed out, changes in the American family generally have followed the same pattern as African American families in terms of single-parent households and out-of-wedlock pregnancies. For example, in 1992, 25 percent of all white mothers were not married, 30 percent of all families were presided over by single parents in 1991, and 30 percent of all households were made up of single people (1999:286). In other words, the constitution of the American family generally has undergone changes that were once considered pathological among African Americans but that seem to reflect lifestyle shifts and structural changes in the dominant society.

Although family has always been a central value of African Americans, the form of the family in the black community did not always conform to the larger society's idea of the isolated nuclear family headed by a male with a stay-at-home mother. Rather, African Americans tended to place emphasis on extended family relationships, parent–child bonds, sibling bonds, and kin networks—facts substantiated by a number of studies (see Cheatham and Stewart 1990; Collins 1991; Martin and Martin 1978; Shimkin et al. 1978; Stack 1974; Staples 1999)—and African American women tend to be employed outside the home. The fate of the black family in the twenty-first century will most likely depend on the social and economic climate of the country as a whole. As of 2008, 64 percent of all black households consisted of families and 45 percent of black families consisted of married couples.

However, an enduring characteristic of African Americans has been their deep religious conviction. In the last decade of the twentieth century, pollsters George Gallup and Jim Castelli not only declared the United States the most religious of developed countries, but also African Americans as the most religious Americans and some of "the most religious people in the world" (1989:122). Gallup and Castelli also report that 77 percent of all African Americans are Protestants, 11 percent are Catholic, and 10 percent have no affiliation. More than half of all African Americans are Baptists. "They account for 29 percent of all Baptists" (1989:124). Thus, a deep spirituality, taking many forms, constitutes an abiding continuity with the past.

The rise of black feminism, the rise of Afrocentrism, and the coming into prominence of black intellectuals as end-of-the-century developments indicated that African Americans continued to act as agents of change and contributors to culture within the United States as the twenty-first century began. But the biggest change to occur in the twenty-first century was the election on November 4, 2008, of Barack Hussein Obama, an African American, as the forty-fourth president of the United States. This election was heralded by many as a turning point in history, both for African Americans and for the United States as a whole.

Notes

1. African Americans have been called many
   things over the years. First, they were referred
   to as Africans, then Blacks, Negroes, colored,
   blacks, Afro-Americans, and finally African
   Americans. Although African American is my
   term of choice and the appropriate contemporary usage, I will occasionally quote from
   works of an earlier era in which other names
   are used. I will also use black interchangeably
   with African American for the sake of brevity
   and variety.

2. The name *Seminole* means "seceders," those Native
   Americans originally known as the Lower Creeks,
   who separated from other Lower Creeks by moving
   into Florida in the 1700s (Porter 1996:5).

3. Reconstruction is a complex and controversial
   subject among historians, and I cannot do justice
   to it here. For more elaborate treatment of this
   period and of the role of African Americans, see
   Anderson (1988), Foner (1988), Gutman (1976),
   Holt (1977), Schweninger (1990), and Shenton
   (1963)—to name only a few.

References Cited

ABERNATHY, RALPH DAVID. 1989. *And the Walls Came Tumbling Down: An Autobiography.* New York: Harper & Row.

ANDERSON, JAMES D. 1988. *The Education of Blacks in the South, 1860–1935.* Chapel Hill, NC: University of North Carolina Press.

ASANTE, MOLEFI KETE. 1990. African elements in African-American English. In *Africanisms in American Culture.* Joseph E. Holloway, ed. Pp. 19–33. Bloomington, IN: Indiana University Press.

BERNSTEIN, DAVID E. 1998. The law and economics of post–Civil War restriction on interstate migration by African Americans. *Texas Law Review* 76(4):781–847.

CASHMAN, SEAN DENNIS. 1991. *African-Americans and the Quest for Civil Rights, 1900–1990.* New York: New York University Press.

CHEATHAM, HAROLD E., and JAMES B. STEWART, eds. 1990. *Black Families: Interdisciplinary Perspectives.* New Brunswick, NJ: Transaction.

COLLINS, PATRICIA HILL. 1991. *Black Feminist Thought: Knowledge, Consciousness, and the Politics of Empowerment.* New York: Routledge.

CREEL, MARGARET WASHINGTON. 1990. Gullah attitudes toward life and death. In *Africanisms in American Culture.* Joseph E. Holloway, ed. Pp. 69–97. Bloomington, IN: Indiana University Press.

CURTIN, PHILIP D. 1969. *The Atlantic Slave Trade: A Census.* Madison, WI: University of Wisconsin Press.

———. 1990. *The Rise and Fall of the Plantation Complex: Essays in Atlantic History.* Cambridge: Cambridge University Press.

DEAGAN, KATHLEEN, and DARCIE MACMAHON. 1995. *Fort Mose: Colonial America's Black Fortress of Freedom.* Gainesville, FL: University Press of Florida/Florida Museum of Natural History.

DEETZ, JAMES. 1996. *In Small Things Forgotten: An Archaeology of Early American Life.* Expanded and Revised. New York: Anchor/Doubleday.

DRAKE, ST. CLAIR, and HORACE R. CAYTON. 1945. *Black Metropolis: A Study of Negro Life in a Northern City.* New York: Harcourt, Brace and Company.

DU BOIS, W. E. BURGHARDT. 1970. *Black Folk Then and Now: An Essay in the History and Sociology of the Negro Race.* New York: Octagon Books.

FONER, ERIC. 1988. *Reconstruction: America's Unfinished Revolution 1863–1877.* New York: Harper & Row.

FRANKLIN, JOHN HOPE, and LOREN SCHWENINGER. 1999. *Runaway Slaves: Rebels on the Plantation.* New York: Oxford University Press.

FRAZIER, E. FRANKLIN. 1966. *The Negro Family in the United States.* Revised and Abridged. Chicago, IL: University of Chicago Press.

GALLUP, GEORGE, and JIM CASTELLI. 1989. *The People's Religion: American Faith in the 90's.* New York: Macmillan.

GENOVESE, EUGENE D. 1974. *Roll, Jordan, Roll: The World the Slaves Made.* New York: Pantheon.

GUTMAN, HERBERT G. 1976. *The Black Family in Slavery and Freedom, 1750–1925.* New York: Vintage.

HENRI, FLORETTE, 1976. *Black Migration: Movement North 1900–1920.* Garden City, NY: Anchor Books.

HERSKOVITS, MELVILLE J. 1990 [1941]. *The Myth of the Negro Past.* Boston, MA: Beacon Press.

HOLLOWAY, JOSEPH E. 1990. The origins of African American culture. In *Africanisms in American Culture.* Joseph E. Holloway, ed. Pp. 1–18. Bloomington, IN: Indiana University Press.

HOLT, THOMAS. 1977. *Black Over White: Negro Political Leadership in South Carolina during Reconstruction.* Urbana, IL: University of Illinois Press.

JONES, STEVEN L. 1985. The African-American tradition in architecture. In *The Archaeology of Slavery and Plantation Life.* Theresa A. Singleton, ed. Pp. 195–213. San Diego, CA: Academic Press.

LEMANN, NICHOLAS. 1991. *The Promised Land: The Great Black Migration and How It Changed America.* New York: Vintage.

LIGGIO, LEONARD P. 1976. English origins of early American racism. *Radical History Review* 3(1):1–36.

MABUNDA, L. MPHO. 1997. *The African American Almanac.* 7th edition. Detroit, MI: Gale.

MARKS, CAROLE. 1989. *Farewell—We're Good and Gone: The Great Black Migration.* Bloomington, IN: Indiana University Press.

MARTIN, ELMER P., and JOANNE MITCHELL MARTIN. 1978. *The Black Extended Family.* Chicago, IL: University of Chicago Press.

MAULTSBY, PORTIA K. 1990. Africanisms in African-American music. In *Africanisms in American Culture.* Joseph E. Holloway, ed. Pp. 185–210. Bloomington, IN: Indiana University Press.

MINTZ, SIDNEY W., and RICHARD PRICE. 1976. *The Birth of African-American Culture: An Anthropological Perspective.* Boston, MA: Beacon Press.

MORGAN, PHILIP D. 1998. *Slave Counterpoint: Black Culture in the Eighteenth-Century Chesapeake and Lowcountry.* Chapel Hill, NC: University of North Carolina Press.

MOSES, WILSON JEREMIAH. 1996. *Classical Black Nationalism: From the American Revolution to Marcus Garvey.* New York: New York University Press.

MOYNIHAN, DANIEL PATRICK. 1965. *The Negro Family: The Case for National Action.* Washington, DC: Office of Policy Planning and Research, U.S. Department of Labor.

MYRDAL, GUNNAR. 1944. *An American Dilemma: The Negro Problem and Modern Democracy.* New York: Harper & Bros.

NASH, GARY B. 1983. Forging freedom: The emancipation experience in the northern seaport cities, 1775–1820. In *Slavery and Freedom in the Age of the American Revolution.* Ira Berlin and Ronald Hoffman, eds. Pp. 3–48. Charlottesville, VA: University Press of Virginia/United States Capitol Historical Society.

NORTON, MARY BETH, HERBERT G. GUTMAN, and IRA BERLIN. 1983. The Afro-American family in the age of revolution. In *Slavery and Freedom in the Age of the American Revolution.* Ira Berlin and Ronald Hoffman, eds. Pp. 175–191. Charlottesville, VA: University Press of Virginia/United States Capitol Historical Society.

OTTENHEIMER, HARRIET. 1992. Comoro crossroads: African bardic traditions and the origins of the blues. *Human Mosaic* 26(2):32–38.

PHILIPS, JOHN EDWARD. 1990. The African heritage of white America. In *Africanisms in American Culture.* Joseph E. Holloway, ed. Pp. 225–239. Bloomington, IN: Indiana University Press.

PORTER, KENNETH W. 1996. *The Black Seminoles: History of a Freedom-Loving People.* Revised and edited by Alcione M. Amos and Thomas P. Senter. Gainesville, FL: University Press of Florida.

POWDERMAKER, HORTENSE. 1993. *After Freedom: A Cultural Study in the Deep South.* Madison, WI: University of Wisconsin.

QUARLES, BENJAMIN. 1964. *The Negro in the Making of America.* New York: Collier.

ROBINSON, JO ANN GIBSON. 1987. *The Montgomery Bus Boycott and the Women Who Started It.* Knoxville, TN: University of Tennessee Press.

SCHWENINGER, LOREN. 1990. *Black Property Owners in the South 1790–1915.* Urbana, IL: University of Illinois Press.

SHENTON, JAMES PATRICK, ed. 1963. *The Reconstruction: A Documentary History of the South after the War: 1865–1877.* New York: Capricorn Books.

SHIMKIN, DEMITRI B., EDITH M. SHIMKIN, and DENNIS A. FRATE. 1978. *The Extended Family in Black Societies.* The Hague: Mouton.

SINGLETON, THERESA A., ed. 1985. *The Archaeology of Slavery and Plantation Life.* San Diego, CA: Academic Press.

SINGLETON, THERESA A., and MARK D. BOGRAD. 1995. *Archaeology of the African Diaspora in the Americas.* Guides to the Archaeological Literature of Immigrant Experience in America, No. 2. Tucson, AZ: Society for Historical Archaeology.

SMEDLEY, AUDREY. 2007. *Race in North America: Origin and Evolution of a Worldview.* 3rd edition. Boulder, CO: Westview Press.

SOBEL, MECHAL. 1987. *The World They Made Together: Black and White Values in Eighteenth-Century Virginia.* Princeton, NJ: Princeton University Press.

STACK, CAROL B. 1974. *All Our Kin: Strategies for Survival in a Black Community.* New York: Harper Torchbooks.

STAPLES, ROBERT. 1999. *The Black Family: Essays and Studies.* Belmont, CA: Wadsworth.

STOPER, EMILY. 1989. *The Student Nonviolent Coordinating Committee: The Growth of Radicalism in a Civil Rights Organization.* Brooklyn, NY: Carlson.

STRAUSS, CLAUDIA, and NAOMI QUINN. 1997. *A Cognitive Theory of Cultural Meaning.* Cambridge: Cambridge University Press.

THOMPSON, ROBERT FARRIS. 1990. Kongo influences on African-American artistic culture. In *Africanisms in American Culture.* Joseph E. Holloway, ed. Pp. 148–184. Bloomington, IN: Indiana University Press.

TROTTER, JOE WILLIAM, ed. 1991. *The Great Migration in Historical Perspective: New Dimensions of Race, Class, and Gender.* Bloomington, IN: Indiana University Press.

U.S. CENSUS BUREAU. 2008. *Facts for* Features. CB09-FF.01 (December 2, 2008). Washington, DC: U.S. Census Bureau News, U.S. Department of Commerce.

WALKER, DENNIS. 1999. America's Western system and Black Muslim protest. *Eastern Anthropologist* 52(2):119–143.

WILSON, WILLIAM JUNIUS. 1980. *The Declining Significance of Race: Blacks and Changing American Institutions.* 2nd edition. Chicago, IL: University of Chicago Press.

———. 1987. *The Truly Disadvantaged: The Inner City, the Underclass, and Public Policy.* Chicago, IL: University of Chicago Press.

———. 1997. *When Work Disappears: The World of the New Urban Poor.* New York: Knopf.

WOODSON, CARTER G. 1936. *The African Background Outlined.* No publisher listed.

10

Hispanic Americans/Latinos

Ellen Bigler, *Rhode Island College*

What's in a name anyway? Terms of identity can reflect a people's self-perception and their power to name themselves. Terms of identity can be imposed from outside. They can mask internal differences and construct new categories that may or may not be accepted by those they seek to label. Terms of identity can change meaning from one generation to another. For Americans who originate from Spanish-speaking cultures, terms of identity—both imposed and chosen—can provide clues to their perceived internal differences and commonalities, as they struggle to find their place in the racialized hierarchy of the United States.

The popular term *Hispanic* is actually an umbrella term used first by the U.S. government in the 1970s and then in the 1980 census to identify U.S. residents originating from Spanish-speaking regions of the world. As such, it is a term fraught with difficulties. It embraces Mexican Americans who trace their roots to families living on the land the United States acquired from Mexico in 1848, alongside Salvadorans who entered in the 1980s as political refugees. It includes Afro-Cubans descended from enslaved Africans and "white" Argentineans whose ancestors originated from Italy. It incorporates the rural indigenous Guatemalans speaking only Kanjobal Maya (an Indian language) and bilingual academics from Peru who immigrate for greater professional opportunities. It embraces U.S.-born Chicanos who don't use or perhaps even understand Spanish. It subsumes Puerto Ricans who enter the mainland as citizens and undocumented Dominicans who reside in the United States in constant fear of deportation. It is, without question, a term that masks important differences among the groups it embraces.

What can such disparate peoples share? How did such a term come to gain entry and legitimacy in the public discourse? Why is it contested by many Hispanics? How useful a label is it for those it encompasses? Are we perhaps witnessing the creation of a new panethnic group akin to the construction of an "African American," "Italian," or "Indian" identity in the United States? What ultimately does it mean to be Hispanic in the United States today, and what forces have helped shape their existence? These are questions this chapter seeks to address.

HISPANIC OR LATINO? RACIAL OR ETHNIC GROUP? OR NEITHER?

Most people the government classifies as Hispanic, if asked their group membership, won't actually define themselves as such. Typically, Hispanics will identify by their place of origin or by terms for ethnic groups that have become popular in U.S. ethnic communities: Mexican American or Chicano, Nuyorican, Puerto Rican, Dominican, Cuban, and so forth. A 2006 survey by the Pew Hispanic Center, for instance, found that 48 percent of Latino adults describe themselves first by their country of origin; 24 percent call themselves American first; and 26 percent used the terms Latino or Hispanic initially (Passel and Taylor 2009). Panethnic terms like *Hispanic* or *Latino* can be useful, of course, and Hispanics have long recognized the political potential of such a label to unite diverse groups and encourage them to recognize similarities they share with others (Duany 2003; Flores 2000; Padilla 1985; Sánchez Korrol 1988). Latino academics express concern, though, about the imposition from outside of such an umbrella term, and its potential to foster stereotyped public perceptions of "Hispanics" with grave consequences for Latinos (e.g., Dávila 2001; Gimenez 1997; Oboler 1995; Santiago-Irizarry 2001). At the same time, the increasing diversity of Latinos and new settlement patterns in cities such as New York, Chicago, Boston, Miami, and Los Angeles suggest that in some cases a panethnic identity may be emerging in particular contexts, not necessarily replacing, but rather adding to, identities to the home country (e.g., Duany and Matos-Rodríguez 2006; Ricourt and Danta 2003; also see Duany 2003 for an overview of such literature).

The use of Hispanic is also criticized for the term's association with Spanish hegemony and for acknowledging only the Spanish heritage of Latin Americans. This concern with the privileging of Spanish culture has long-standing roots in Latin America. The valuing of the Spanish side of Latin Americans' heritage over their hybridized cultures and their indigenous and African roots has been a topic addressed by intellectuals and political leaders throughout much of Latin America's history. Many Latino academics (e.g., Nieto 2000) argue that if an umbrella term is to be used, *Latino*[1]—a sort of shorthand for *latinoamericano*[2]—at least acknowledges their Latin American roots and therefore the presence of their African and indigenous heritage. The term *Latino* currently appears to be more widespread among politically active members of the community, and *Hispanic* has more currency in the East and *Latino* in the West. In this chapter both terms are used.

As the opening paragraph suggests, Hispanics do not constitute one "racial" group.[3] Because of more racial intermixing in Latin America than in the United States, the peoples of Latin America have evolved a broad range of physical appearances that blend to varying degrees their Indian, African, and European roots. While Latin American societies did not escape the privileging of light skin that mars U.S. ethnic group relations, racial boundaries in Latin America are more fluid (Rodríguez 2000). There is a range of intermediary terms used to refer to a person's physical appearance, depending on factors such as skin color, hair texture, and facial features. "Race" is not necessarily viewed as a fixed biological inheritance from parents, as in the United States, but rather is dependent in part on appearance or social status. Children of the same family, therefore, may be classified as members of different racial groups based on their physical appearances. An individual's racial designation can change with that person's change in social status.

The racial category a Latino is conceptualized as belonging to in the United States can be different from the categorization in his or her homeland. It can be disconcerting for dark-skinned Puerto Ricans, for instance, to become "black" on the mainland, or for Dominicans considered *blancos* (whites) in the Dominican Republic to be viewed as "nonwhite" in the United States. The Latino presence, though, is shaking up the dichotomous racial categories that have dominated in the United States for so long (see Rodríguez and Cordero-Guzman 1992). In this respect—and, as we shall see, in other respects—they are "Latinizing" aspects of U.S. culture.

THE LATINO PRESENCE IN THE UNITED STATES: A TROUBLED PAST

Settlers of Spanish and Indian descent were present early on in what is now the United States. Mestizo communities in New Mexico predate the first so-called North American settlement of Jamestown, Virginia, established in 1609, and people with Spanish roots were incorporated with the acquisition of Florida. Mexicans were incorporated into the political boundaries of the United States beginning in the mid-1800s, and since then the numbers and diversity of Hispanics have continued to grow. The rate of growth has been greatest in recent decades, with the population tripling since the 1980 census, due to their relative youthfulness, high immigration rates, and higher birth rates. Hispanics, according to the U.S. Census Bureau (Hispanic Americans: Census Facts, 2010), now number 48.4 million and make up almost 16 percent of the U.S. population. In 2008, 66 percent of the U.S. Hispanic population was of Mexican descent, followed by Puerto Ricans (9 percent), Cuban origin Hispanics (3.4 percent), Hispanics of Salvadoran origin (3.4 percent), and another 2.9 percent of Dominican-origin. Only Mexico, at 111 million, has a larger Hispanic population than the United States.

Mexican Americans, to the 1960s

Mexicans did not originally cross the border to enter the United States; rather, the border crossed over them. Mexico in 1848 lost fully half its territory to the far more economically and militarily powerful United States after Texas declared its independence and Mexico lost the Mexican War. What are now the states of California, Colorado, New Mexico, Nevada, Utah, and most of Arizona were, along with Texas, originally Mexican land. Mexicans thus became part of the U.S. population through conquest, and this means of incorporation profoundly affected Anglos' views of them and their relations with Mexican Americans in the ensuing decades.

Mexicans living on the land when the United States acquired it were promised full rights and protections by the federal government

if they chose to remain and become American citizens. That promise, however, was quickly broken. Within a year, the discovery of gold in California led to a massive in-migration of Anglos. The 13,000 original Mexicans there were quickly outnumbered, and by 1849 the Anglo population had reached 100,000. Anglos soon dominated in the state legislature, passing discriminatory laws aimed specifically at the Mexican-origin population. These included an antivagrancy "Greaser" act and a foreign miner's tax of $20 monthly, aimed at all who spoke Spanish—including American citizens. Mexican Americans were driven from their mines, and along with Chinese miners, assaulted and lynched on occasion. Ironically, it was the Mexican miners who brought with them knowledge of mining techniques that aided the Anglo miners, and who performed much of the grueling manual labor (Takaki 1990).

The extent of Anglo–Mexican American conflict varied across the Southwest. In courts throughout the region, Mexican Americans were divested of their preexisting claims to land titles guaranteed them through the 1848 Treaty of Guadalupe Hidalgo. While some Mexican American elites initially succeeded in forging alliances with Anglos, wealthy *californios* in northern California began to lose economic clout early on. Conflict and racial violence were commonplace in Texas. The Mexican Americans of New Mexico were somewhat better off, living in relative isolation for several more decades. They succeeded in retaining some numerical plurality and degree of control in political matters, and Spanish along with English became an official state language of New Mexico. There too, though, the tolerant mood between Anglos and Mexican Americans began to evaporate by the early 1900s, as resident Mexican Americans were forced into the status of a dependent minority.

Mexicans are overwhelmingly mestizos, an outcome of Spanish and Indian intermixture over the previous four centuries. After 1848, Mexicans now in the United States found themselves surrounded by Anglo-Americans who brought with them attitudes about white superiority forged in earlier contacts and interactions with Africans and Native Americans. In the eyes of many Anglos, Mexican Americans were an inferior, mongrelized people (Takaki 1993). Even their allegedly superior "Spanish blood" had long been viewed by the English as racially impure due to the *mestizaje* (mixing) between Spaniards and Moors in Spain. Cultural traits were linked to "racial" characteristics, so that Mexicans, for instance, were seen as naturally "superstitious, cowardly, treacherous, idle, avaricious, and inveterate gamblers" (De León 1998:163).

To avoid this stigmatization, wealthy Mexican Americans (*los ricos*) struggled to maintain their status of *pureza de sangre* (pure-blooded [Spanish]) and to differentiate themselves from *mexicanos pobres* in the eyes of Anglos. In New Mexico, as the power and wealth of these elites declined, they began to refer to themselves as *hispanos* and to emphasize their "pure" Spanish (read "European") ancestry.[4] It was, of course, a cultural "invention" that ignored the realities of their own indigenous roots,[5] as they struggled to insert themselves into the "imagined (white) American community" (Oboler 1995; Takaki 1993).

The end of slavery in the United States in 1865 represented an aperture, a moment of opportunity, for reenvisioning the "American" community to be a more inclusive one. It was, unfortunately, a missed opportunity. African Americans continued to be denied equality through a variety of legal and extralegal means. Native Americans were rounded up and put on reservations. Immigration of the Chinese, who had contributed so much to the economy of the West and the construction of the transcontinental railroad, ground abruptly to a halt with passage of the Chinese Exclusion Act in 1882. Mexican Americans continued to be oppressed throughout the Southwest.

Virtually reduced to a class of exploited laborers, most Mexican Americans found themselves stigmatized, socially segregated, and politically marginalized through a variety of means. The southwestern territories were given the power to determine citizenship eligibility requirements when applying for statehood, and could elect to bar Native Americans from citizenship.[6] This became a basis in parts of the Southwest for denying Mexican Americans of predominantly Indian heritage their political rights (see Menchaca 1993). Mexican Americans in Texas were denied the vote by the use of white primaries, poll taxes, and intimidation tactics. While courts sometimes ruled that Mexican Americans be considered "white"—and the Treaty of Guadalupe Hidalgo recognized them as having the right to citizenship at a time when only whites could become naturalized citizens—Anglo cultural constructions forged in European contacts with Africans and Indians oftentimes prevailed.

Mexican Americans and Mexican nationals labored in agriculture and ranching, in mines, and on the railroads. Their labor played a significant role in the expansion of American capitalism into the Southwest, and these contributions to the well-being of the nation were clearly not limited to the Southwest. As Carey McWilliams, in his classic historical analysis *North from Mexico: The Spanish-Speaking People of the United States* (1990), emphasized in a masterfully understated fashion, "One might say . . . that Mexican miners in the copper mines of Arizona, Utah, and Nevada, have played an important role in making possible the illumination of (all) America by electricity" (p. 144).

Mining companies in search of cheap labor in the Southwest developed a caste labor system that exploited these workers. As miners, they were paid an average of 37¢ per day in 1860, compared to $1.25 for Anglos; in 1880, Mexican Americans earned $1.50 and Anglos $2.75. Anglos also usually received board while Mexican Americans were given only a ration of flour. "Mexicans," one mine owner pointed out in rationalizing such practices, "have been 'peons' for generations. They will always remain so, as it is their natural condition" (Takaki 1990:163).

Both push and pull factors contributed to the growth of the Mexican American population in the early twentieth century. The Mexican Revolution in the 1910s and its aftermath dramatically increased the numbers of Mexicans entering the United States. Agriculturalists and the burgeoning industries came to depend heavily on Mexican Americans as a cheap source of labor, particularly after Southern and Eastern European immigration was severely curtailed in the 1920s. Until the early 1920s there was little policing of the U.S.–Mexican border, and Mexicans genera-lly moved freely back and forth as economic conditions demanded.

Mexican Americans did not passively accept their poor treatment, stereotypes of docility and submissiveness aside. Workers on numerous occasions went out on strike. In one such strike Mexican American farm workers joined forces with fellow Japanese American laborers and formed a successful union. Their bid for affiliation and support from national labor leaders, however, was rebuffed. When they approached Samuel Gompers of the American Federation of Labor to charter their organization, they were told that a charter would be issued under only one condition: that Chinese and Japanese workers not be accepted as members. Mexican American union leaders refused the conditions, and the union, without the support of organized labor, soon passed out of existence (Takaki 1993).

Where Mexican American labor leaders could count on support was from within their own communities. These early labor strikes drew on the ethnic solidarity of Mexican American communities. The merchants provided support, and musicians provided entertainment. Mexican American *mutualistas* (benevolent associations), common throughout the Southwest, were formed to help individual members cope with life on the margins (Acuña 1988). They made loans, raised money for emergencies, and helped cover funeral expenses. Through such organizations, Mexican Americans sought to resist labor exploitation and racism when assistance from government or national labor organizations was not forthcoming.

In segregated Mexican American communities their language and cultural traditions, abetted by the continued influx of newcomers and frequent movement across the border, flourished and provided some measure of comfort. Extended families were their primary social networks and their safety nets in times of crisis. Opportunities for their children, meanwhile, were essentially nonexistent; if they had schooling at all, it was typically in segregated schools where they were given inferior educations and discouraged from going on in school (Carter and Segura 1979; Takaki 1993).

The Great Depression dramatically worsened the situation for Mexican Americans. They lost their jobs to Euro-Americans, and were routinely denied welfare benefits. Many were rounded up and deported, others driven "voluntarily" out of the country. In all, over 400,000 Mexicans and Mexican Americans—including legal residents and citizens among them—were repatriated to Mexico, without benefit of formal deportation proceedings (Carrasco 1998).

With the onset of World War II, however, Mexican labor was again in demand. Mexican and U.S. government officials negotiated the Bracero Program to help meet the increased demands for laborers. While the program provided protections for temporary Mexican workers, these stipulations were largely ignored. With no bargaining rights, they lived and worked in deplorable conditions for substandard wages. The Bracero Program also freed Mexican American men to serve as soldiers. Despite the racism they faced at home, they distinguished themselves in the war effort and won more Medals of Honor than any other identifiable ethnic or racial group. They also died in disproportionate numbers; Mexican Americans, for instance, represented one-tenth of the Los Angelinos but comprised one-fifth of the city's casualties (Acuña 1988:253).

What these Mexican American soldiers discovered upon returning home was that their sacrifices for the nation did not end their poor treatment. Sergeant Macario Garcia, recipient of the Congressional Medal of Honor, found, for instance, that he could not purchase a cup of coffee in a Richmond, California, restaurant. Incidents such as the "Sleepy Lagoon" case (1942) and the Zoot-Suit Riots (1943) in Los Angeles dramatized the continuing racism toward Mexican Americans.

The Sleepy Lagoon case began when a group of Mexican American youth, who called themselves members of a *barrio* club, crashed a party at a ranch. A fight soon ensued. When an invited guest was found dead in the road the following morning—without any wounds and a likely victim of a hit-and-run—authorities jailed the entire gang of Mexican American youth, alleging that they had beaten the dead youth. The response of societal institutions was appalling. The press depicted the *barrio* club members as hoodlums. A report by the Sheriff's Department of Los Angeles concluded that Mexican Americans were inherently criminal and violent: they were Indians, Indians are Orientals, and Orientals have no regard for life. In addition, the report went on, Mexican Americans were descendants of the Aztecs who allegedly sacrificed 30,000 victims a day and had an innate desire to wield a knife and spill blood. The report further urged that all club members be jailed. Sleepy Lagoon Defense Committee members, including noted journalist and lawyer Carey McWilliams, were harassed and red-baited by both the press and government agencies. Only in a court of appeals were the verdicts, ranging from assault to first-degree murder despite the lack of evidence, overturned (Acuña 1988).

The Zoot-Suit Riots occurred shortly thereafter. Sailors went on a rampage in Mexican American communities in Los Angeles, and Mexican American "zoot-suited" youth were attacked while police did little to quell the unrest. Sensationalist headlines fanned the flames. In all, over 600 Mexican American youth were arrested without cause. Military shore patrols finally intervened to put down the riot (Acuña 1988). These two incidents came to symbolize the gross injustices that Mexican Americans confronted as they went to war for what was being denied them at home, democracy and equality.

World War II profoundly affected Mexican Americans, as it did African Americans. The soldiers for the first time experienced social climates where they were not treated in a discriminatory manner. The expanding war economy meanwhile drew more Mexican Americans to urban centers and industrial employment, and the rhetoric designed to win support for the war positively depicted Latin Americans in the media. Mexican Americans were proud of their sacrifices and contributions, further increasing their sense of entitlement to equality as Americans (Moore and Pachon 1985). Political activism in turn increased. The American G.I. Forum, for instance, was formed by Mexican American veterans in 1948, when private cemeteries and mortuaries in Texas refused to handle the body of a Mexican American soldier.

Progress in the postwar years, however, was distressingly slow. Like African Americans, Mexican Americans contended with segregated public facilities and schools and discriminatory jury selection procedures. "Operation Wetback," organized by the federal government in 1954 to address the issue of illegal immigration, only worsened Anglo–Mexican American relations. Looking "Mexican" was enough to get someone stopped and told to prove his citizenship. Almost 3.8 million persons were rounded up and sent back to Mexico, most without formal proceedings (Moore and Pachon 1985). Given these sorts of conditions, Chicano historian Rudolfo Acuña and others asserted that Mexican Americans represented an "internal colony" in the United States: they were a colonized people in their own home, with little or no control over their political, economic, and educational destinies (Acuña 1988).

At the same time that Mexican Americans were an oppressed population, a small middle class had established itself. Mexican Americans were also becoming an urban population, and these developments favored greater political activism in the 1950s. The lower profile this activism assumed at the time was likely a response to the McCarthyism of the era and the backlash against Mexican Americans during Operation Wetback (Moore and Pachon 1985). Oppression was challenged through labor strikes, use of the courts when feasible, and political organizations such as the assimilation-oriented LULAC (League of United Latin American Citizens). The continuing racism and marginalization they encountered in turn set the stage for the particular form of political mobilization many Mexican Americans came to adopt in the 1960s and 1970s.

Puerto Ricans, to the 1960s

While the Mexican American presence was initially established in the Southwest and increasingly in midwestern industrial cities like Chicago, the Puerto Rican presence was concentrated in the Northeast, overwhelmingly the New York City area. The Caribbean migration that Puerto Ricans are part of is driven in large measure by the area's proximity and relationship to its powerful northern neighbor.

> By the early 1900s, the Caribbean had become effectively a North American lake. Hegemony was mostly exercised through economic power but, when necessary, it took political and military form. . . . The effect of overwhelming external hegemony was the creation of insular economies molded entirely by North American interests and the emergence of local societies profoundly dependent in their political and cultural outlook. This orientation established the broad framework for subsequent U.S.-bound migration, although the actualization of each individual outflow responded to specific circumstances. [Portes and Grosfoguel 1994:52]

Small communities of Puerto Ricans and Cubans were in place on the U.S. mainland by the late 1800s in Tampa, Key West, New Orleans, and New York City. Many of the men were *tabaqueros*, skilled cigar rollers who were politically active and ardent supporters of the struggle for Cuban and Puerto Rican independence from Spain. Caribbean political activists like José Martí frequented such communities, seeking support for the independence movement.

The status of Puerto Ricans journeying to the mainland changed dramatically in 1898. Spain, in its waning days as a colonial power, had awarded Puerto Rico greater autonomy in 1897. Eight days after the first meeting of the newly elected Puerto Rican legislature, U.S.

troops at war with Spain invaded the island. The United States defeated Spain and elected to maintain control of Puerto Rico, an island that represented a desirable possession given its strategic location, potential markets, and agricultural possibilities. Puerto Rican *independentistas* now sought their freedom not from Spain, but from the United States. Puerto Ricans migrating to the mainland after 1898 now entered the United States not as immigrants from another country but, like Mexicans in the Southwest after 1848, as a colonized people. Some 100,000 Caribbean migrants arrived between 1901 and 1910, and the mainland population climbed to 135,000 in the following decade (Portes and Grosfoguel 1994).

Cultural and artistic activities flourished in these mainland Spanish-speaking communities in the Northeast. Spanish newspapers, like other immigrant presses, kept the new arrivals informed. Social organizations formed around shared interests. The Liga Antillana, for instance, was formed in New York City by working-class Cuban and Puerto Rican women related to *tabaqueros*. East Coast attitudes about "racial" mixing, however, conflicted with the interracial complexion of Caribbean communities. While racial intermixing may have been commonplace among island Puerto Ricans and Cubans, on the mainland newcomers entered into another world where "race" separated people and profoundly shaped people's life experiences. Because the Liga Antillana was an interracial group, most meeting halls closed their doors to them (Vega 1984).

When the U.S. government granted them citizenship in 1917, Puerto Ricans became eligible to migrate to the mainland without restriction. As citizens, they constituted a readily available labor pool in the Northeast, and some 12,000 migrated to fill jobs created by the war effort. Another 18,000 were inducted into the military, where they served in segregated units (DeFreitas 1999).

The racialized social order that existed in the United States shaped Americans' relations not only with Puerto Ricans on the mainland but also with Puerto Ricans on the island. In Puerto Rico, American government officials' and business men's assumptions of the "racial" inferiority of the Puerto Ricans—they were a mixture of Spanish, African, and Indian—went hand in hand with assumptions of Anglo-American cultural superiority. Puerto Ricans were deemed not ready for self-government.

The policy that government officials adopted in relation to the island was to deliberately "Americanize" Puerto Ricans. The island's name was Anglicized to "Porto Rico." A secular public school system was established, with English-only as the dominant policy until 1948. Victor Clark, architect of the new educational system, expressed the prevailing sentiments of the time.

> The great mass of Puerto Ricans are as yet passive and plastic.... Their ideals are in our hands to create and mold. If the schools are made American and the teachers and pupils are inspired with the American (spirit) . . . the island will become in its sympathies, views, and attitude . . . essentially American. [cited in Negrón de Montilla 1975:13]

To assist in the process, U.S. heroes, holidays, symbols, and textbooks and curricula were imported. Americans were recruited as teachers, and teacher certification required fluency in English (Negrón de Montilla 1975). Even Puerto Ricans' own Spanish dialect, forged over centuries of separation from Spain, was labeled inferior.

The degree and persistence of U.S. cultural and linguistic imperialism on the island have contributed to a legacy of resistance to Anglo-American dominance that is felt today (Zentella 1981). As sociologist Clara Rodríguez notes, this existence of an "articulation of resistance, defiance, and struggle against oppression" (1989:14) provides a different context from which Puerto Ricans may interpret their relationship to the dominant society on the mainland.

Under U.S. occupation, growing numbers of Puerto Ricans were also displaced from the land to work on plantations established by American entrepreneurs. By 1930, four U.S. corporations controlled a quarter of all the land in Puerto Rico devoted to sugarcane. Puerto Rico had become economically dependent on the United States, which now accounted for 96 percent of its exports and 87 percent of its imports (Centro de Estudios Puertorriqueños 1979).

The consequences of this dependent relationship were devastating. In the early years of the Great Depression, the per capita income in Puerto Rico fell 30 percent. The growth of absentee-owned sugar corporations that displaced small independent growers reduced Puerto Ricans to "virtual economic serfdom," U.S. Secretary of the Interior Harold Ickes noted in 1935. "There is today more widespread misery and destitution and far more unemployment in Puerto Rico than at any previous time in its history" (Dietz 1986:132). The despair of Puerto Ricans fanned the flames of the independence struggle on the island, and contributed to a small but steady growth in migration to the mainland. By 1940, the mainland Puerto Rican population stood at 70,000. Puerto Rican communities were also appearing in cities outside the New York City area that provided job prospects, including Chicago, Illinois (Padilla 1985), and Hartford, Connecticut (Glasser 1997).

What was to become known as the Puerto Rican "diaspora" in the post–World War II period was the product of several interrelated events. Operation Bootstrap, designed to transform Puerto Rico's plantation economy into an industrial one, was set in motion by the U.S. government beginning in 1947. The economic displacement it stimulated occurred at a time when the population was expanding rapidly. With U.S. employers eager to recruit from this ready pool of surplus labor, agreements between the Truman administration and the colonial government were concluded leading to lower airfare from the island to New York City (Grosfoguel and Georas 1996). Puerto Ricans, as citizens, were assured entry. The mainland population between 1940 and 1960 grew over twelvefold, jumping from 70,000 to nearly 900,000. Most of these economic migrants settled in the New York metropolitan area, filling lower-level jobs vacated as Euro-Americans migrated to the suburbs.

To the great misfortune of this growing mainland Puerto Rican community, however, economic changes were simultaneously underway that undermined their opportunities for wide-scale upward mobility (Torres 1995). The U.S. economy, despite the postwar economic boom, was undergoing a massive shift from manufacturing to a service-based economy. Sixty percent of Puerto Ricans were employed in manufacturing in 1960, and New York City lost almost 450,000 manufacturing jobs in the subsequent two decades. The better-paying unionized manufacturing jobs that had allowed earlier generations of European immigrants to establish a solid economic foothold were rapidly disappearing, as manufacturers in search of greater profits sought cheaper labor in the South and then overseas. The growing numbers of informal-sector manufacturing jobs paid substandard wages and relied on new Latino immigrants (Grosfoguel and Georas 1996). Discriminatory policies further reduced opportunities for stable employment. In turn, "white flight" to the suburbs contributed to the erosion of the city's tax base.

The outcome of this was Puerto Ricans' heavy concentration in the secondary labor market and declining urban areas. Yet Puerto Ricans themselves were oftentimes scapegoated for the changing urban environment and blamed for their own poverty. The New York *World Telegram* informed its readers as early as 1947 that "Puerto Ricans are destroying the economy and suffocating the culture of their adopted community. . . . (They) are the cause of the incredibly bad housing situation . . . (and upon arrival head) straight for the welfare offices in East Harlem" (cited in Vega 1984:230).

Puerto Ricans moving to the mainland also confronted a black–white racial binary. In Puerto Rico racial membership is based primarily on physical appearance rather than biological descent, and socioeconomic variables such as education or occupation can affect racial categorization. Membership is more fluid, with more intermediary categories. Intermarriage across "racial" lines is fairly frequent, and members of the same family can be classified as belonging to different racial categories. (There is racial prejudice in Puerto Rico, though generally regarded as not as virulent as that in the United States [see Duany 1998].) Ironically, as sociologist Clara Rodríguez noted,

> Puerto Ricans entered a heterogeneous society that articulated an assimilationist, melting-pot ideology, but that, in fact, had evolved a racial order of dual ethnic queues, one White and one not-White. . . . (Yet) Puerto Ricans represented the ideal of the melting-pot ideology—a culturally unified, racially integrated people. [1989:49]

In this situation of extreme residential and occupational segregation and oppression on the mainland, not surprisingly, "the elaboration of ethnic ties provides a ready system of support for groups distinguishable by race, national origin or language" (Nelson and Tienda 1988:51). In addition, the ongoing *va y ven* (back and forth) movement between the island and mainland, propelled by economics, ensured a constant infusion of Puerto Rican culture and the Spanish language. "Ethnicity theory," which assumes that all ethnic groups are in line to assimilate as they move up the social class ladder (see Omi and Winant 1994), failed to recognize how racial formations, the colonial status of Puerto Rico, and the changing economy would play out for many Puerto Ricans. Like Mexicans, they were racialized and excluded from the imagined U.S. community. They became Americans through conquest, and experienced U.S. economic and cultural imperialism on the island; they remain concentrated on the lowest economic rungs on the mainland; and they experience ongoing ethnic revitalization from their home communities. These factors positioned them quite differently from the descendants of Euro-American immigrants in the United States by the 1960s and 1970s.

Cubans, to the 1960s

The United States acquired not only Puerto Rico but also Cuba after the Spanish–American War. By 1902, though, the United States had helped set up an independent, albeit U.S.-dominated, Cuban nation. The numbers of Cubans in the United States grew slowly up through the 1950s; by 1930, an estimated 18,000–19,000 Cubans were residents; by 1960, that number climbed to approximately 79,000. But when Fidel Castro overthrew the Cuban dictator Fulgencio Batista in 1959, the numbers of migrants from this island, only 90 miles off the tip of Florida, jumped dramatically. By 1965, 210,000 Cubans had entered the United States, most of them settling in Miami. Between 1965 and 1973, their numbers increased by another 345,000 (Portes and Bach 1985).

Demographic data on these refugees point to significant differences between this early Cuban wave and other Hispanic populations. These differences also help explain their rapid economic ascendancy in the United States. The first wave of post-1959 Cubans to arrive comprised overwhelmingly professionals, government officials, and businesspeople. Under the socialist system that Castro put into place, this group's social and economic positions in Cuba were threatened. Florida was the logical place to "wait out" the Castro years. Before Castro, many of the upper class had traveled regularly for play and work between the island and southern Florida, and for many middle-class Cubans a sojourn to the United States was an annual ritual. Miami, therefore, did not produce "culture shock," nor were the arriving Cubans viewed by established residents as the quintessential "tired and poor" immigrants. Most of these Cubans came to Miami intending to reestablish themselves only

temporarily while they waited for Castro to be deposed.

This first wave was also 94 percent white, and averaged 34 years of age and 14 years of schooling (Moore and Pachon 1985). Thus, they brought considerable cultural and social capital with them as a result of their professional status and educational backgrounds. At the school level this translated into the establishment in the Dade County public schools of the first bilingual program in the United States since World War I, when German Americans facing anti-German sentiments had abandoned their successful programs (Rodríguez-Morazzani 1997). And because they were deemed political refugees fleeing a Latin American leader the United States wanted overthrown, Cubans were welcomed and given financial assistance from the government to facilitate their resettlement. "Rapid entrepreneurial advance of the Cubans," as Alejandro Portes and Alex Stepick point out, "was not due entirely to their business acumen or community solidarity. U.S. government agencies . . . favored them disproportionately" (1993:46). The Small Business Administration, for instance, granted over $47 million in loans to Cuban-owned small businesses between 1968 and 1980 and only $6.5 million to black businesses, further contributing to ethnic group tensions in the area (Portes and Stepick 1993:46).

Despite a significant federal effort to disperse Cubans across the United States, the overwhelming majority chose to settle in the Miami area. Many who agreed to be relocated in exchange for federal assistance returned to Miami after establishing themselves elsewhere; by 1978, the *Miami Herald* estimated that about 40 percent of Cuban Americans in the Miami area were returnees (Portes and Stepick 1993:104). The ethnic enclaves they established in Miami also provided jobs and assistance for later immigrating waves of Cubans. Although the 1965–1973 refugees were less well educated, they benefited from the presence of the 1959–1965 refugees and U.S. government support.

TURNING POINTS: THE CIVIL RIGHTS MOVEMENT AND LATINOS

The 1960s marked an important turning point for the nation. People of color and other Americans disturbed by the continued existence of racism gained space on the national stage to confront the nation with the continuing persistence of racism in U.S. society. Government actions in response to community activism helped move their agenda forward. The *Brown v. Board of Education* decision in 1954, the 1964 Civil Rights Act, the Voting Rights Act of 1965, and presidential responses among other initiatives affirmed the greater willingness on the part of the federal government to address racial oppression in the United States.

The black civil rights movement and black power movement of the 1950s and 1960s provided inspiration to many in Latino communities, who saw parallels between the conditions that African Americans struggled against and their own situations. These were also years in which struggles against European colonialism were articulated on the international scene. Views of Chicano and Puerto Rican communities as exploited "internal colonies" gained credence. Challenges to ethnicity theory that assumed the comparability of all groups and their eventual assimilation into the American melting pot were mounted. Community leaders pointed to their long history of "unassimilability" as evidence of the failure of the American "melting pot." Claims of universal accessibility to the American Dream, so long given lip service in the United States, were resoundingly challenged in the public sphere. Puerto Rican and Chicano activists and artists challenged the need to abandon their language and cultures, articulating a new vision of the United States as culturally pluralistic, a "salad" or a "tapestry" rather than a "blended soup."

Mexican Americans

Political and social action in Mexican American communities coalesced into *el movimiento*, the Chicano Movement, by the later 1960s. César Chávez, whose charisma and political brilliance ultimately led to the creation of the United Farm Workers (UFW), remains perhaps the most well-known Mexican American leader. With Delores Huerta, he sought to address the pervasive poverty and the caste-like status of rural Mexican Americans and Mexican immigrant labor by organizing farm workers.[7] Chávez, himself a former migrant worker, drew on their ethnic pride, religious beliefs, and sense of community and history to organize farm workers. He adapted the Mexican eagle, a key symbol in Mexico, for use on the UFW flag and borrowed tactics of nonviolence and the effective use of boycotts from Mahatma Gandhi. Chávez and his followers organized massive consumer boycotts of nonunionized grapes and lettuce to force the agricultural corporations to allow workers to unionize. Their aims were further aided by two other factors: the end of the *bracero* program, thereby reducing growers' access to easily exploitable labor, and the growing urbanization and stabilization of the Mexican American community (Acuña 1988).

Other Mexican American leaders also emerged on the regional scene. Reies López Tijerina formed the Alianza de las Mercedes, a movement that sought to reappropriate lands taken improperly from Mexicans and Mexican communities. Rodolfo Corkey Gonzáles organized the Chicano power youth movement. José Angel Gutiérrez formed a third political party, La Raza Unida, which achieved some political successes in Texas. Mexican Americans were becoming a force to be reckoned with, and the major political parties began to court their vote.

CHALLENGING ASSIMILATION. Given the negative stereotypes and anti-Mexican American sentiments that Mexican Americans routinely encountered, many downplayed their Mexican roots ("I'm Spanish") and sought to "pass" where feasible (e.g., Johnson 1999). The use of "Mexican-American," signaling as it did that they were one among many other "hyphenated" immigrant groups, was popular. This more assimilationist orientation, however, was profoundly challenged by the new postwar generation, who were no longer willing to wait for acceptance and equality.

Cultural nationalism challenged the acceptance of assimilation as a goal. It also provided the theme that succeeded in mobilizing and unifying individuals of Mexican descent, strengthening and reinforcing ethnic identity. "Two crucial decisions were made during this period by these guardians of the culture. . . . 'Somos Chicanos.' . . . By using this term the Chicano community consciously and publicly acknowledged its Native American heritage. . . . 'Aztlán is our homeland' was the second," Chicano writer and activist Rudolfo Anaya asserted a generation later (1989:232). Young and politically active Mexican Americans renamed themselves *Chicanos*, a term used earlier to refer to lower-class Mexican Americans. *La Raza*, a term that Latin Americans used to signify their identity as a new hybrid people, also gained popularity. *Spanish*, a euphemism for the more derogatory *Mexican*, meanwhile was challenged for its implicit rejection of Chicanos' Indian heritage.

The Aztec heritage of the Mexican people became a source of pride for Mexican Americans and its emphasis an affirmation of their hybrid roots. Chicano writers, artists, and activists popularized an image of the Southwest as the land of Aztlán,[8] which, according to Aztec myth, was the original homeland of the Aztec people of central Mexico. The idea of the Southwest as Aztlán was a powerful one, as it situated Chicanos not as unwelcome outsiders but as the original inhabitants fully entitled to be there; it asserted ethnic pride in their connections to the civilizations of ancient Mexico; it affirmed their separate identity, in contrast to their Mexican heritage and Anglo environment; and it effectively unified the heterogeneous Mexican American communities in the United States (Klor de Alva 1989). This new terminology, like the evolution in the African American community of "colored" to "Negro" and then to "black" or "African American," affirmed an emerging and positive vision of themselves.

The arts also flourished, used as a vehicle to reinforce a sense of community, to build Mexicans' pride in themselves and their heritage, and to inspire community action. Playwright and film and stage director Luis Valdez organized Teatro Campesino to take these works to the people. Chicano artists took inspiration from Mexican muralists and organized to paint their interpretations of the Chicano experience on walls across the Southwest. Here representations of Donald Duck shared space with traditional Mexican heroes. Singers taught a new generation the traditional Mexican *corridos* (ballads) that told their folk history. At community centers across the Southwest, Chicanos learned the steps of the various Indian and Mexican *ballet folklorico* dances. Chicanos, like African Americans and other politically active minority groups, also challenged their representation in the media (e.g., Cortés 1983) and in school curricula and textbooks (e.g., Martínez 1989; New York State Education Department 1987), a process that continues today.

Puerto Ricans

Puerto Ricans, like Chicanos, African Americans, and Native Americans, also challenged the validity of the melting pot and asserted their entitlement to a distinctive cultural identity beginning in the 1960s. The children of the massive postwar diaspora came of age during the explosive years of the anticolonial and civil rights movements of the 1960s. Puerto Ricans organized around a variety of issues relevant to their communities: decent housing, health care and community services, the elimination of racial discrimination and police brutality, drug abuse programs, and better educational services for their children. One important component of their struggle for better educational services included support for bilingual education (Del Valle 1997). This objective was furthered by the 1973 U.S. Supreme Court case *Lau v. Nichols*, in which the court ruled that non-English-dominant children were entitled to assistance in learning English.

Political activists in the mainland Puerto Rican communities of the 1960s and 1970s recognized the shared concerns of Puerto Ricans and African Americans. Puerto Ricans in New York City live in close proximity to African Americans. As a racialized group in the United States, Puerto Ricans too have experienced prejudice and discrimination. Furthermore, different shades of color within the community translate into different experiences for darker-skinned Puerto Ricans (Klor de Alva 1989; Rodríguez 1989). Piri Thomas's autobiography, *Down These Mean Streets* (1967), early on traced the significance of skin color in shaping Puerto Ricans' experiences and life opportunities on the mainland. Piri recounts his painful discovery of what it means to be a dark-skinned Puerto Rican when he applied for a sales job. He is told that he will be contacted when something opens up, but his light-skinned Puerto Rican friend who goes in after him is hired on the spot. "I didn't feel so much angry as I did sick, like throwing-up sick. Later, when I told this story to my buddy, a colored cat, he said, 'Hell, Piri, Ah know stuff like that can sure burn a cat up, but a Negro faces that all the time.' 'I know that,' I said, 'but I wasn't a Negro then. I was still only a Puerto Rican' " (p. 104).

The political activists who organized the Puerto Rican Young Lords Party in New York City sought to build connections with the African American community,[9] and to address the racism embedded in the Puerto Rican community itself (Laó 1995). Many of the programs and calls to action by the Young Lords (e.g., their breakfast program, the garbage protest to bring attention to the city's neglect of their neighborhoods) served both Puerto Rican and African American community members. Pablo Guzmán, a leader of the group, spoke for many when he wrote that for "Puerto Ricans like myself, who are darker-skinned, who look like Afro-Americans, (we) couldn't avoid do(ing) that (seeing connections between the Black and Puerto Rican experiences), 'cause to do that would be to escape into a kind of fantasy. Because before people called me a spic, they called me a nigger" (Young Lords Party 1971:74).

Another important rallying point for the mainland community was Puerto Rico's ambiguous status as neither a state nor an independent nation. On the island, the movement for independence waxed and waned over the course of the twentieth century. The granting of commonwealth status in 1952 did little to alleviate the perception that the island still retains its colonial relationship to the United States; Puerto Ricans on the island cannot vote for president, nor do they have voting representatives in Congress. While both islanders and mainlanders remain divided on what Puerto Rico's status should be—independent, continuing as is, or statehood—the struggle for independence provides a forum for asserting the cultural nationalism of Puerto Ricans (Rodríguez 1989). Puerto Ricans today continue to maintain a distinct sense of "peoplehood," both on and off the island (Morris 1995).

Over time, however, Puerto Ricans on the mainland become culturally differentiated from island Puerto Ricans. They may lose their mastery of Spanish and acquire different cultural preferences and views than their island counterparts. The women's movement on the mainland, for instance, contributed to politically active Puerto Rican women challenging men's domination of their organizations (Laó 1995). As in the Mexican American community, women demanded that they move from being subordinated to men to being treated as equals.

So, too, the differing experiences of mainland Puerto Ricans with "race" and their own racialization on the mainland affected their understanding of such matters. These different sensibilities were apparent in mainland Puerto Rican responses to Mattel's release of "Puerto Rican Barbie" in 1997. The doll was well received in Puerto Rico as a welcome acknowledgment of their presence in American society. On the mainland, however, many were offended by her depiction as light-skinned with Anglicized features and her colonial-tiered dress. The failure of the accompanying literature to acknowledge the Tainos, the original inhabitants of the island, was also criticized (Navarro 1997).

The cultural and linguistic fusion that grows out of shared spaces and lives is readily visible in literary and artistic productions of New York Puerto Ricans,[10] oftentimes called "Nuyoricans."[11] The poetry of Nuyorican Tato Laviera evokes these interconnections, seen here in his poem "melao"[12] (Laviera 1988:27):

> melao was nineteen years old
> when he arrived from santurce   (city in
> Puerto Rico)
> spanish speaking streets. . . .
> melaíto his son now answered
> in black american soul english talk
> with native plena sounds   (African-based
> Puerto Rican music)
> and primitive urban salsa beats.

Latino rap also creatively comments on these lived realities when it intermingles Spanish and Black English and addresses shared interests, as the lyrics of KT's "We're Puerto Rican and Proud!" illustrate (Flores 2000):

> I rarely talk Spanish and a little
> trigueño   (Spanglish)
> People be swearin' I'm a moreno   (black)
> Pero (but) guess what? I'm
> Puertorriqueño.
> Word 'em up.
> All jokes aside, I ain't tryin' to dis any
> race.

When Puerto Ricans do return to the island, the cultural differentiation that arises between these two communities can be brought home all too painfully. Children raised on the mainland may be rejected by their island peers for not being "real" Puerto Ricans. "If I am an American, a gringo, a Yankee down here, and up north I am a Puerto Rican, a spik; what in hell am I really? Who am I? Where do I belong?" asks the main character in Pedro Juan Soto's "Hot Land, Cold Season" (in Seda-Bonilla 1977:115). At the same time that cultural differentiation is taking place, the ongoing movement back and forth across the "air bridge" that links island and mainland also contributes to the movement of

elements of culture in both directions, producing heated debates on the island about American cultural influence.

Tato Laviera acknowledges both the cultural hybridization taking place and the psychic costs that this rejection engenders in his poem "nuyorican" (Laviera 1985, translated from Spanish in Flores 2000:54):

> I fight for you puerto rico, you know?
> I defend myself for your name, you know?
> I enter your island, i feel foreign, you
> know?
> I enter searching for more and more, you
> know?
> But you, with your insults,
> you deny me your smile,
> i feel bad, indignant.
> I am your son, of a migration,
> a sin forced on me,
> . . . .
> Now i return with a boricua[13] heart, and you,
> you scorn me, you look askance, you attack
> the way i speak,
> while you're out there eating mcdonalds in
> american discotheques.

This circular migration from island to mainland that became so pronounced by the 1960s, and that many Puerto Ricans continue to participate in, seems at first glance to be an outcome of individual decisions. When conditions improve on the mainland, migration increases; when conditions decline, migration decreases and more people return (Maldonado 1976). What often go unnoticed, though, are the macrostructural factors contributing to this movement (Bonilla and Campos 1981; Morales 1986). Puerto Rican analysts point to the economic and political dependence of Puerto Rico and its position in the global economy, and the grave consequences for Puerto Rican migrants. "Direct colonial relations," underlines ethnographer Juan Flores, "as an uninterrupted legacy and ever-present reality, govern the motives and outcomes of the whole migratory and settlement process, and fix a consistently low ceiling on the group's expectations and opportunities" (1996:67). Puerto Rican migrants, Flores points out, might be better categorized as "colonial emigrants," like the Jamaicans in England or Martinicans in Paris, because of this differing context and the consequences of discrimination and economic marginalization in the United States. Cultural nationalism, Duany asserts (2003), emerges from this differing set of relations to the mainland and Puerto Ricans' lived experiences. Among the various Latino groups, "only Puerto Ricans insist on calling themselves simply Puerto Ricans, rather than Puerto Rican-Americans, which speaks volumes about their persistent stress on national origin and their adamant rejection of a hyphenated ethnicity (437–438)." For Puerto Ricans, Pantojas-Garcia (2005) argues,

> the Island—as the Torah for the Jewish— provides the fulcrum that affirms Puerto Rican national identity. On the Island, Puerto Ricans are not a minority, and Puerto Rican culture flourishes there as an autonomous force on equal terms with other world cultures. Thus the imagined foundational myth(s) may not be fixed but constitute a point of reference which all Puerto Ricans can "evoke" in constructing their version of national identity. [p. 174]

Puerto Ricans have defied both the melting pot and the cultural diversity ideologies that would predict their unilineal assimilation or hyphenation into the ethnic American mainstream (see Pantojas-Garcia 2005 for a literature review). They have in the process challenged the binary system operating on the mainland that provides no middle ground: a person should speak either Spanish or English, identify as either white or black, be either Puerto Rican or American (Bruce-Noboa 1987; Flores 1985; Flores et al. 1981; Klor de Alva 1988). The rejection of such binary assumptions in Puerto Rican communities and their renaming themselves "Nuyoricans," or most recently "Floricans" (Duany and Matos-Rodríguez 2006), attest to similar processes occurring in both Puerto Rican

and Chicano communities. For most Puerto Ricans, their sense of "puertoricanness" and connectedness with the Island, however symbolically, endures, captured by the poet Mariposa (María Teresa Fernández) in "Ode to the DiaspoRican":[14]

> *Some people say I'm not the real thing*
> *Boricua that is*
> *cause I wasn't born on the enchanted*
> *island*
> *cause I was born on the mainland*
> *north of Spanish Harlem . . .*
> *What does it mean to live in between*
> *What does it take to realize*
> *that being Boricua*
> *is a state of mind*
> *a state of heart*
> *a state of soul . . .*
> *¡Mira!*
> *No nací en Puerto Rico. (I wasn't born in*
> *Puerto Rico.)*
> *Puerto Rico nacío en mi. (Puerto Rico was*
> *born in me.)*

Puerto Ricans remain the poorest Latino group (Baker 2002), but they have been the "front line that opened doors for every Latino that came after them" in New York City.

Puerto Ricans have collectively altered the face of New York and are now increasingly migrating to other regions of the nation beyond their initial out-migration into New Jersey. Central Florida in particular has become attractive, drawing both northeasterners and Island residents; the numbers of Puerto Ricans in Florida increased from 241,000 in 1990 to nearly 750,000 by 2009 (Allen 2009). Many of these newcomers to the mainland are middle-class professionals fleeing the Island's inflation, unemployment, and rising crime rate (Robles 2008). Puerto Ricans on the mainland now outnumber those on the Island, 4.1 million and 3.9 million, respectively (Passel and Taylor 2009); only the Irish out-migration to the United States in the face of famine and poverty comes close to Puerto Rico's precipitous population decline since the 1940s. Their influence is already being felt; in Florida they helped Barack

Obama carry the state in 2008. Florida in the next census may become the nation's third most populous state, owing much of their increase to the rapid growth of the Puerto Rican community (Allen 2009). These "FloRicans," as some people are calling them, appear to be poised to become an important swing vote in upcoming years.

THE CHANGING U.S. LATINO COMMUNITY: THE 1970S AND BEYOND

The diversity of Latinos in the United States shifted with changes in U.S. immigration law in 1965. The national origins quota system that favored Northern and Western Europeans since its inception in the 1920s was abolished in an effort to address the racism embedded in earlier laws. This effectively opened the door to massive immigration from parts of Asia and the Latin American and Caribbean countries, with undocumented immigrants representing an additional unknown number of newcomers. The Hispanic population has tripled since 1980, increasing from 14.6 million to 48 million in 2010 (Passel 2010).

The cultural revitalization and access to the home communities that characterized Puerto Ricans' and Mexican Americans' experiences are ongoing for virtually all newcomers to the United States today. Analysts of immigrant communities in the United States (e.g., Basch et al. 1994; Smith 2005) speak of the emergence of transnational communities, "characterized by a constant flow of people in both directions, a dual sense of identity, ambivalent attachments to two nations, and a far-flung network of kinship and friendship ties across state frontiers" (Duany 1994:2). The process of conceptualizing migrants as part of transnational sociocultural systems provides a new model for understanding the immigrant experience:

> Transnational identities cross over territorial boundaries and national cultures in ways that are difficult to grasp from a traditional ethnographic perspective [Appadurai 1991,

1990]. Recent approaches to transnational communities have begun by discarding the conventional image of immigration as a form of cultural stripping away and complete absorption into the host society [Rosaldo 1989]. Rather, immigrants belong to multiple communities with fluid and hybrid identities that are not necessarily grounded in geopolitical frontiers but perhaps in subjective affiliations. Border crossing becomes an apt image for not just the physical act of moving to another country but also the crossover between cultures, languages, and nation-states in which transnational migrants participate. [Duany 1994:2]

Puerto Ricans 'and, to some extent, Mexicans were in many respects the earliest such communities.

Mexico is by far the largest source of immigrants in recent decades (Pew Hispanic Center 2009b). The numbers of Mexican immigrants doubled between 1980 and 1990 and more than doubled again in the succeeding decade; since 2006 that growth has slowed considerably, standing in 2008 at 12.7 million. Mexicans now constitute 32 percent of the U.S. foreign-born population. As such, their presence roughly parallels that of the Irish and Germans in the later nineteenth century; Irish immigrants represented one-third or more of all immigrants from 1850 to 1870, and Germans constituted 26–30 percent of the foreign-born from 1850 to 1900. More than half (55 percent) of Mexican immigrants lack legal status. During the year ending in August 2008, however, a dramatic decline in the number of Mexicans going to the United States—25 percent less Mexicans emigrated from Mexico to other countries—occurred, owing most likely to the dramatic downturn in the U.S. economy and more debatably to greater enforcement of the border (Preston 2009a).

While the Latino population has become far more dispersed in recent decades, each of the three largest populations remains geographically concentrated in a particular region of the United

States. The majority of Mexican Americans according to the 2000 census lived in the West (55.3 percent) and the South (31.7 percent), with 10.7 percent in the Midwest and 2.3 percent in the Northeast. Almost 61 percent of Puerto Ricans lived in the Northeast, with 22.3 percent in the South and 9.6 percent in the Midwest. More than two-thirds of all Cubans live in Florida (Pew Hispanic Center 2006), with about half the total population living in Miami-Dade County. But looking at the distribution of Latinos nation-wide, their presence is being felt far beyond these areas; 16 states have at least a half a million Hispanic residents, and Hispanics are the largest minority group in 21 states (Hispanic Americans: Census Facts 2010).

Today's Hispanics are overwhelmingly urbanites and are a significant presence in many cities. Demographers predict that if current trends continue, non-Hispanic whites will soon be the minority in 35 of the nation's 50 largest cities, as has occurred most recently in Phoenix, Tucson, and Denver (Asthana 2006). Longtime sites are becoming more ethnically diverse as Latino newcomers from other parts of Latin America join established Latino populations. In New York City, for instance, from 2000 to 2007, the percent-age of Puerto Ricans, once the overwhelming majority of the city's Latino population, declined from 36 percent to 33.3 percent; meanwhile the Dominican share rose from 24.6 to 25.8 percent. Most dramatically, the Mexican-origin population grew from 8.5 to 12.4 percent, increasing from almost 184,000 to almost 290,000 in only seven years (Limonic 2008). How these numbers will be affected by the sharp economic downturn remains uncertain, though it appears that growth rates of Latino immigration have slowed.

Nearly 90 percent of Hispanics live in just 10 states (Jones-Correa 2007). At the same time that Latinos remain concentrated regionally, both the old and the newcomers are spreading out to other nontraditional areas of the country. (Cuban Americans remain the exception to this trend; their concentration in Florida actually increased in recent years [Portes and Grosfoguel 1994].) The percentage of Latinos grew over 60 percent between 2000 and 2007 in states that had rela-tively low numbers in 2000, including Georgia, Nevada, North Carolina, Minnesota, South Carolina, Arkansas, Nebraska, and Iowa (Pew Hispanic Center 2009a). These newcomers and their children spreading out on the mainland have oftentimes found themselves struggling again over many of the very issues that confronted earlier generations of newcomers in the more tra-ditional regions of settlement (e.g., Bigler 1999; Glasser 1997; Soto 1997; Stains 1994; Villenas 2002; Wortham et al. 2002).

Many Latino newcomers are also part of a "brain drain" from less developed nations to the developed nations, as the economic disparities between the "have" and the "have-not" nations continue unchecked. Professionals, including engineers, academics, and entrepreneurs, from Latin American countries and Puerto Rico are migrating and joining established later-generation Latinos further up on the social class ladder.

The Mariel Exodus: Expansion of the Cuban Community

Most Cuban Americans did not participate in the ethnic movements of the 1960s and 1970s. They had little identification with other oppressed groups in the United States,[15] and many viewed themselves as political exiles rather than a racial/ethnic minority. That changed, however, after 1980, with the arrival of 125,000 *marielitos* from Cuba. Cuban president Fidel Castro, embarrassed by a sudden surge of refugees seek-ing to leave the island through the Peruvian embassy, opened the port of Mariel and declared that anyone wanting to leave could do so. Cuban Americans were invited to pick up their relatives. Castro, deliberately seeking to discredit the refugees, also sent ex-convicts and mental patients among them. While they represented perhaps only 10 percent of the *marielitos*, their presence tarnished the entire group of new-comers, many of whom also wrestled with the difficulties of being poorer and darker-skinned than the initial refugee waves. The *Miami Herald*, controlled at the time by the Anglo population, sensationalized the story. A negative stereotype of *marielitos* quickly crystallized within the established Cuban American community and the larger society. Anglos organized an "antibilingual" referendum that passed overwhelmingly. Earlier Cuban exiles, long considered "model minorities," now found themselves tarnished by negative stereotypes.

This turn of events prompted the transformation of Miami Cuban Americans "from a political exile group into a self-conscious ethnic minority" (Portes and Stepick 1993:105), producing what Portes and Stepick characterize as a process of "reactive formation." Cuban Americans came together to work to redefine the situation positively and to depict themselves as the impetus for Miami's economic transformation. Ethnic organizations formed, and the Cuban American community in Miami became more politically active. A great advantage they enjoyed over other Latino groups seeking similar goals was the economic resources they controlled.

Growing Diversification of the Latino Population

Immigration from other areas of Latin America also increased from the 1980s on, with the largest growth occurring among Dominicans, Guatemalans, Salvadorans, Nicaraguans, and Colombians.

NICARAGUANS. Cubans in Miami have been joined by other immigrant groups from Central and South America. Most numerous are the Nicaraguans who, like the Cubans before them, fled a leftist government. Like the Cubans, the earliest were the wealthy, who often had already established roots in the United States; many had also transferred their assets to U.S. banks in the late 1970s. They were soon followed by the middle class, and then the working class in the mid-1980s.

The reception of Nicaraguans in the United States, however, has been quite different from that of the Cubans. While virtually all Cubans up until 1980 had their passages paid for and were automatically granted permanent residence, most Nicaraguans found themselves classified as unwanted illegal aliens. By 1985, only around 10 percent of Nicaraguan applicants had been granted political asylum. The rest remained ineligible for refugee assistance, resettlement aid, welfare, or government loans. This changed briefly as Nicaraguan elites cemented their ties with the Cuban exile community and the Reagan White House courted potential Republican votes. By 1988, however, the policy reverted to its earlier phase, and Nicaraguans were again deported and actively discouraged from migrating (Portes and Stepick 1993:159). In 1997, the U.S. government finally made application for legal residency easier (Brinkley 1999).

DOMINICANS. Large-scale migration from the Dominican Republic is a more recent phenomenon, beginning in the 1960s when emigration restrictions loosened after the dictator Rafael Trujillo was killed. Since then, emigration has been largely economically driven, responding to rising expectations and economic downturns. Sixty percent of the Dominican population of 1.2 million is foreign-born, with New York the major haven for the new arrivals. Dominicans have christened Washington Heights, where so many settled, *Quisqueya*, the indigenous term for their island. Dominicans, 26 percent of New York City Latinos, now represent the second largest Latino group, trailing Puerto Ricans, and the single largest immigrant group in New York City (Limonic 2008). These newcomers are primarily urban middle class or working class, and, like other immigrants, typically come as part of a preexisting *cadena* (chain) that links immigrants through kinship networks. They concentrated in light manufacturing and low-income service economies; with the decline in manufacturing since 1980, massive job loss has occurred. Manufacturing went from providing employment for close to half the workforce in 1980 to providing only 12.4 percent by 2000. The shifting economy and the consequences of racial discrimination, along with the lower rates of English proficiency and educational attainment among newcomers, has meant great economic marginalization for Dominicans as a whole. Dominicans have among the lowest per capita incomes in the United States, and their unemployment rate was more than double that of the general population in 2000, with 32 percent living below the poverty rate (Hernández and Rivera-Batiz 2005). Low rates of high school completion—49 percent over age 25 had not completed their secondary educations in 2000—further limit job opportunities. These data vary tremendously though when disaggregated by immigrant status; the proportion of U.S.-born Dominicans who attained some college education rose from 31.7 percent in 1980 to 55.1 percent in 2000 (Hernández and Rivera-Batiz 2005). While collectively Dominicans lag behind Puerto Ricans, it is useful to recall three major differences contributing to their lower status. The Dominican Republic is poorer; they are the most recent migrants, with less time to acculturate and acquire English; and they do not arrive as U.S. citizens entitled to economic assistance when needed (Boswell and Jones 2006).

Not surprisingly, Grasmuck and Pessar (1991) found skin color among Dominican Americans to be a very significant predictor of poverty. Dominicans, like Puerto Ricans, oftentimes find themselves taken for African Americans, whereas on the island anyone partly "white" is considered not black. Dominicans' placement in a different racial hierarchy in the United States is a challenging one to negotiate. Jorge Duany's 1998 ethnographic study highlights some of the ways in which Dominicans seek to negotiate their identities in the racially divided United States:

Racial prejudice and discrimination have forced many Dominicans in New York to settle in areas adjacent to African American concentrations. . . . Despite physical proximity, most Dominicans strive to distance themselves culturally from African Americans by speaking Spanish, dancing the merengue, rejecting black hairstyles and speech patterns, and associating primarily with other Latinos. . . . Dominican immigrants strongly resist assimilation into the dominant culture. This tendency is partly a response to racial and ethnic exclusion. [p. 11]

Second-generation Dominican Americans, however, may be more likely to acknowledge the links and experiences they share with African Americans and identify as "Afro-Caribbean" (Pessar 1995; see also Torres-Saillant 2005). Duany concurs:

(Y)ounger members of the second generation often adopt the black dialect, hip-hop fashion, and rap music popular among African American teenagers. Some dark-skinned Dominicans are following the path of a segmented assimilation in which the main frame of reference is an adversarial African American culture rather than a mainstream white identity (see Portes 1994). Slowly but surely, Dominican immigrants are developing an awareness of their black roots and reaching out to other Caribbean and Latino peoples. [p. 11]

Many Dominicans, like other immigrants and Puerto Ricans, are choosing, for a variety of reasons, to forge lives both *aqui* ("here") and *allá* ("there") (Pessar 1995). Transportation, communication, and technology enhance access to the homeland. A greater tolerance for ethnic pluralism exists than for earlier immigrants. Economic uncertainties both at home and in the United States make it wise to keep options open. Emigrants are increasingly viewed by the home communities as important resources to be courted. Finally, as people of color, they may feel more valued in their homeland than in the United States. However, when they do return, like Puerto Ricans they may find themselves ostracized for being "Americanized." At the same time, "Dominican

Yorks" are emerging as a distinctive ethnic group in New York. More politically involved, they are demanding recognition and respect and seeking alliances with other ethnics. They are also enfranchised in the Dominican Republic, further strengthening their ability to feel invested in two countries.

SALVADORANS AND GUATEMALANS.   Among the estimated 2 million refugees fleeing the conflicts in Central America by the late 1980s were the Salvadorans and Guatemalans. Large-scale immigration from El Salvador north followed the outbreak of civil war in 1979. Salvadorans initially entered the United States largely as undocumented refugees, assisted by the U.S. Sanctuary Movement. By 1990 they were present on both coasts, almost half in Los Angeles, and significant populations in greater New York, Washington, D.C., San Francisco, and Houston. As a whole they are poorer, younger, and less educated than the average American (Mahler 1995). Their status, lack of education, and lack of English limit their employment opportunities primarily to the poorly paid informal and service sectors, and they settle where they find niches for their labor. Large cities are not the only destinations for new immigrants; Sarah Mahler (1995), for instance, found an estimated 60,000–100,000 Salvadorans living on Long Island, filling spaces in the labor force created by a growing demand for service jobs and an aging and shrinking native-born population. The limited skills and oftentimes undocumented status of these newcomers, unfortunately, leave them vulnerable to mistreatment from their employers. They also live with the uncertainty of their permanent status. The president in El Salvador has pushed the United States to permit more to enter, and continued to request extensions of the temporary legal status that the United States granted in 2001. Salvadorans in the United States meanwhile provide invaluable assistance to Salvadorans back home; in 2006 Salvadorans were reported to be sending home $2.8 billion annually (Aizenman 2006). Salvadorans in the United States today number 1.37 million.

One-quarter million Guatemalans of Mayan descent also fled for their lives from government troops. Like the Nicaraguans, many of these refugees entered the United States as undocumented immigrants. Unlike the Nicaraguans, the Salvadorans and Guatemalans fled from conflicts where the U.S. government supported their military rulers, and Americans were generally uninformed about the U.S. government's role in such conflicts. These refugees thus had no allies like the vocal anti-Communist Cuban American community to advocate on their behalf. Recently, however, the U.S. government reversed long-standing policy and agreed that refugees from right-wing governments will be accorded the same treatment as the Nicaraguans fleeing a left-wing government. They can now apply for legal residency and are spared the earlier difficulties of having to appear before a judge, prove that they have been in the United States for seven years, and document that their lives are in danger if they return (Brinkley 1999). In 1999 President Bill Clinton recognized the U.S. role in this civil war when he apologized to the Guatemalan people for the U.S. support of right-wing Guatemalan governments that killed tens of thousands of Mayan Indians and rebels in recent decades (Broder 1999). Guatemalans currently in the United States number 986,000 (Pew Hispanic Center 2010).

For the Guatemalan Maya fleeing the destruction of their communities and widespread murders, life in the United States has been difficult. They came in large family groups, with many settling in southern Florida. Indiantown, Florida, became one such popular destination in the early 1980s, providing work and a safe environment for the refugees (Burns 1993). It was, however, an environment very different from what they had previously known. In the United States the Maya face prejudice and discrimination not only from Anglos but also from other Latinos. Mexican immigrants, for instance, echoing prejudices in Mexico, may disparage them as *indios*. In the United States the Maya also became one among many diverse groups. No longer identifying and identified as indigenous Maya, they have become "migrant workers" or "illegals." After several years in the United States, they also become culturally differentiated from the Maya that remained behind (Burns 1993).

INDIGENOUS MEXICANS AND TRANSMIGRATION. Indigenous communities in Mexico have been sources for American labor for almost half a century, with back and forth migration a way of life for generations. The Mixteca of Oaxaca's region is one such population; an estimated half million indigenous people from Oaxaca are estimated to live in the United States (Bacon 2008). Faced with extreme poverty (75 percent of Oaxaca's residents live under such constraints), their choices have been further circumscribed by the impact of World Bank and U.S. loan conditions that cut subsidies and raise prices for necessities. They are now organizing for the "right to stay home" (Bacon 2008). Rufino Dominguez, a farmer and one of the founders, would choose to stay in his village, but "there are no jobs here, and NAFTA made the price of corn so low that it's not economically possible to plant a crop anymore. We come to the U.S. to work because we can't get a price for our product at home. There's no alternative" (Bacon 2008). Indigenous Mexicans are even more vulnerable than other migrants when attempting to cross the border in search of work, as many do not even speak Spanish. An estimated 11.9 million unauthorized immigrants are believed to be in the United States, with 81 percent from Mexico and other Latin American countries (Terrazas and Batalova 2008). Ismael Rojas, one such Mexican who arrived without papers, articulated what drives so many: "You can either abandon your children to make money to take care of them, or you can stay with your children and watch them live in misery. Poverty makes us leave our families" (Bacon and Hing 2009). Despite what appears to be a dip in the numbers crossing, deaths are up along the U.S.–Mexican border (Government Accountability Office 2006; Marosi 2005). Most recently 128 people were found during a six-month period in 2008

as the risks with increased surveillance increased (Rotstein 2009). Further terrifying many along the border, a splinter group of the Minutemen movement, set up in 2005 by private citizens to patrol the border, entered a home in a border community and killed the father and 10-year-old daughter (McKinley and Wollan 2009).

THE IMMIGRATION DEBATE INTO THE TWENTY-FIRST CENTURY

The surge in nativism that has accompanied the growth of the Latino population in recent decades, in particular Mexican immigration, has long-standing antecedents that anyone familiar with U.S. "racialization" processes in the United States can cite (see Takaki 1993). The Irish, the Germans, Japanese and Chinese, and southern and eastern Europeans have all been perceived as threats to the American way in their time. "Each (discourse of threat) was pervasive and defined 'truths' about the threats posed by immigrants that, in hindsight, were unjustified or never materialized. . . . And each of these discourses generated actions . . . riots, restrictive immigration laws, forced internments, and acrimonious public debates over government policies" (Chavez 2008:3). While the economic boom of the 1990s helped quell the most strident voices of the late twentieth century, they returned in full force following the September 11, 2001, attack on the World Trade Center. What Chavez terms the "Latino Threat Narrative" is a discourse that holds that Latinos are unlike any earlier groups and are part of an invading force (note the military terminology) south of the border, bent on the *reconquista* of the Southwest and the destruction of the American way of life. It is the very repetitiveness of this set of claims in recent decades, repeatedly endlessly in public discourse and the media, and resting as it does on a taken-for-granted set of assumptions, that gives it such power. California governor Pete Wilson, for instance, when campaigning for re-election, spoke of "hordes of Mexican immigrants," of "invaders" pouring across the border, and of the state as "awash under a brown tide" (Santa Ana 2002:286–287). The greater social changes and economic vulnerability in the United States have left many more Americans receptive to such facile explanations for the nation's current difficulties.

An article in *Foreign Policy* in 2004 by the magazine's founder, the distinguished academic Samuel Huntington of Harvard, lent credibility to the Latino Threat Narrative. "One index foretells the future," he warns the reader ominously, "In 1998, 'Jose' replaced 'Michael' as the most popular name for newborn boys in both California and Texas" (Huntington 2004a:38). The nation, he argued, is in great danger:

As Chavez (2008) argues in *The Latino Threat: Constructing Immigrants, Citizens, and the Nation*, the Latino Threat Narrative articulated so eloquently by Huntington is also part of a larger contemporary crisis in the meaning of citizenship. Notions of citizenship and belonging, who is and who is not "American," are played out in public arenas. No longer is "citizenship" unproblematically contained within national borders or past legalistic definitions; in a time of increasingly permeable borders, both literally and figuratively, the very meaning of the term is contested in public spaces.

Other meanings of citizenship—economic, social, cultural, and even emotional—are being presented in debates, marches, and public discourse focused on immigrants, their children, and the nation [4]. . . . The images we constantly consume . . . help construct our understanding of events, people, and places in our world. . . . How we, as a nation of diverse people, derive our understanding of who to include in our imagined community of fellow citizens is a product of many things, not the least of which is what we glean from the media. [5]

(S)pectacles [that give voice to aspects of the Latino Threat Narrative] objectify Latinos. Through objectification (the process of turning a person into a thing) people are dehumanized . . . (and) it is easier to lack

empathy for those objects and to pass policies and laws. . . . Portraying Latinos as objects or things makes it easier to see immigrant marchers as a chaotic mass rather than as a people struggling to be recognized as contributing members of society. [6]

The immigration debates over the past three decades have provided ample opportunity for this Latino Threat Narrative to be reinforced, and the names of ensuing legislation evoke this Narrative. The 1986 Immigration "Reform and Control" Act put in place sanctions for employers who use undocumented immigrant workers, along with an amnesty program for over 1 million of undocumented immigrants. (In 1990 the Immigration Act increased the numbers allowed in to 700,000); the "Illegal Immigration Reform and Immigrant Responsibility" Act of 1996 made the requirements more difficult for those who sought to become legal immigrants, the same year that the "Personal Responsibility" and Work Opportunity Reconciliation Act ended cash assistance to poor families with children, restricting legal immigrants' use of those benefits in the process. In 2005 the House of Representatives passed HR 4437, entitled the "Border Protection, Antiterrorism, and Illegal Immigration Control" Act, replete with provisions for border fences, surveillance technology, more detention provisions, and increases in penalties for hiring undocumented immigrants. To be an undocumented immigrant would have been branded a felony (making later legal residence status an impossibility); and anyone assisting or shielding illegal immigrants—including doctors, teachers, social workers, nurses, priests—could be prosecuted, spend up to five years in prison, and have some of their assets seized.

The bill did not become law—immigration reform is still on the table for the new Obama administration—but the message to Latinos and other immigrants was impossible to miss. Such enforcement tactics have had profound effects. They have split families, with adult caretakers disappearing without notice for prolonged periods; traumatized Latino communities;[16] disrupted businesses, and with that the work lives of documented workers and American citizens; and contributed to a climate fostering still greater exploitation of unprotected workers.

Under the Obama administration, there has been a move away from the raids and their devastating consequences. Rather than criminal warrants and military tactics when rounding up suspected undocumented immigrants, Immigration and Customs Enforcement (ICE) agents in June 2009 notified American Apparel in Los Angeles, which hires over 5,600 employees in the city, that they were facing civil fines and would be required to fire undocumented workers, probably within two months; workers were given time to prove their status. Federal agents, the *New York Times* reports, will now focus on businesses suspected of undocumented workers and utilize tough criminal charges primarily for those who also exploit such workers, violating labor and wage laws (Preston 2009b). The issue of how to address the high numbers of undocumented immigrants, drawn by employment opportunities, remains a significant challenge to the Obama administration, albeit one that has most recently taken a back stage to the consequences of what some are now referring to as "The Great Recession" of 2008–2009.

The sensationalist media stories of immigration raids and the need for military-like tactics to control the border have contributed to greater hostility toward Latinos. The sorts of charges leveled against Latinos (and it is Mexicans—and to a degree Mexican Americans—that are typically portrayed as the invading masses in public discourse) rest on a set of unexamined assumptions. They are seen as unable or unwilling to learn English or integrate into the larger society; unchanging culturally; a reproductive threat; and conspiring to reconquer the Southwest and return it to Mexico (Chavez 2008:51). But how valid are the concerns that undergird the Latino Narrative Threat? On the right, supporters of this thesis were reaffirmed in their perceptions of the threat Mexicans represent to the United States, with Patrick Buchanan, well-known spokesperson for right-wing causes and editor of *The American Conservative*, concurring:

Will the U.S. Southwest cease to be truly American by mid-century? Is Mexifornia reality and Mexamerica[17] a certainty? (. . .) It is impossible to see who, or what, is going to stop the invasion of the United States before the nation's character is altered forever, and we become two nations with two languages and cultures—not unlike the Palestinians and Israelis on the West Bank. [2004]

Huntington's article (2004a) and subsequent book (2004b) also evoked reasoned sociological treatises and impassioned responses from many, challenging his arguments with a wealth of social science data (see, e.g., Citrin et al. 2007; Chavez 2008; Drezner 2004; Fuentes 2004; Suarez-Orozco and Orfield 2004; Suro 2004). The unquestioned assumptions undergirding this most recent iteration of the Latino Threat Narrative do not hold up when subjected to close scrutiny.[18] We may first dispense of Huntington's claim to the nation as Anglo-Protestant, as the impact of its diverse roots on American culture is readily documented (e.g., Takaki 1993). Indeed, Mexicans do represent in some ways a different immigrant wave than earlier waves of southern and eastern European immigrants a century ago and to whom they are often compared. They are from a neighboring country with a long permeable border and a troubled relationship to its neighbor; they come at a different moment in time in terms of their options in the United States and the forces driving their immigration; and their mixed "racial" heritage makes them less likely to be viewed as "white," with all its attendant difficulties. They are more likely to retain ties to their country of origin, abetted by improved transportation and communication; yet as Drezner points out (2004), 30 percent of European immigrants returned to their countries of origin between 1870 and 1930, and with Italians the rate was closer to 50 percent.

Mexicans, Mexican Americans, and other Latinos are not static and immutable, as Huntington's thesis implies. Analyses of their demographic characteristics across generations in the United States underline the changes that occur, challenging Huntington's underlying assumptions. Most Mexican immigration is relatively recent, and like past immigrants they cluster in ethnic neighborhoods, but they are becoming geographically more dispersed; they are more likely to marry across "racial" lines the longer they are in the United States (see discussion below). The children of Mexican immigrants rapidly acquire English-language skills at rates comparable to other immigrants, while their support for bilingualism suggests more of a symbolic affirmation of their roots than a reality in subsequent generations (Citrin et al. 2007). Three-quarters of English-speaking Latinos disagree with the fatalistic statement that "It doesn't do any good to plan for the future because you don't have any control over it" (Suro 2004), thus reaffirming their belief in a basic American creed. On the criticism of their rates of reproduction, Mexican American birth rates approach other Americans' in subsequent generations as they acquire more education, and indeed Mexican birth rates are dropping (Chavez 2008). They become less religious and more likely to take up Protestant religions with time (Citrin et al. 2007), and they complete more years of school than did immigrants a century ago (Suarez-Orozco and Orfield 2004). Mexican Americans serve in the military at comparable rates to other ethnic groups (Brooks 2004), and Hispanic names are well represented on the lists of Americans that have died in Iraq and Afghanistan. They increasingly identify as "Americans" with each successive generation (Citrin et al. 2007). Even the name Jose has been declining in popularity for years, Roberts (2009) notes, reflecting the growing numbers of second- and third-generation Mexican-origin Americans who are adopting more Americanized names for their children. In California, the name Jose slipped from the most popular in 1998 to thirteenth in 2007, and in Texas, while Jose is still the most popular name, the number of Joses has been on the decline every year since 2000.

"American" and "Chicano" or "Latino" identities, English and Spanish, can indeed coexist without presenting a threat to the nation. And finally, contrary to popular perceptions, the proportion of foreign-born in the United States is not unprecedented. Immigrants in 2007 made up 12.6 percent of the U.S. population; in 1890 immigrants represented 14.8 percent of the U.S. population (Terrazas and Batalova 2008). Mexicans, 30.8 percent of today's immigrants, do comprise the largest share of the immigrant population when taken by country of origin. As will become apparent below, any threat lies not in the inherent nature of the Mexican-origin population or Latinos in general, but rather in the forces that conspire to limit their upward mobility and integration into the mainstream.

CHALLENGES AND OPPORTUNITIES

Latinos are beyond dispute now a numerical force in the United States, yet their troubled past in this country and current social and economic situations combine to limit their access to equal participation in the American mainstream. Particularly problematic are the stubborn disparities in educational attainment, given the changing nature of the American economy and the severe economic downturn in the United States that came to the fore in 2008.

Economic and Educational Challenges

A growing number of Latinos have gained access to the middle class, in part due to their mobilization in the 1960s. Most Latinos, however, continue to confront significant structural barriers to upward mobility that negatively affect the quality of their life experiences and their life chances (Massey 2007). They suffer the consequences of racial and ethnic discrimination, and of the decline of the central cities. Economic restructuring, with jobs moving overseas and a shift from a manufacturing to a service economy, has meant the elimination of the unionized better-paying blue-collar jobs that provided white ethnics opportunities to establish economic stability and ultimately enter the middle class.

U.S. News & World Report in May 1997 featured a superhero flying through the air with the caption "The Amazing American Economy." What may be more amazing is how economic trends have led to greater, rather than lesser, income inequality across the U.S. population, exacerbated all the more by the economic downturn a decade later. Since the 1960s the gap between the rich and the poor has dramatically increased—the top 10 percent for instance garnered 43.9 percent of income in 2000, compared to 32.9 percent in 1980, with the share going to the top 1 percent nearly doubling between 1973 and 2000 (Massey 2007). Meanwhile real wages for those on the lower rungs of the economic ladder actually declined (Collins and Yeskel 2000; Massey 2007). The real value of the minimum wage was boosted only in 2007, after 10 years without an adjustment, to a value in 2009 dollars of $7.25; this still falls far short of its value in 1968 of $9.47 in 2009 dollars. In 1968 a worker earning minimum wage earned 93 percent of the federal poverty limit in a year; by 2005 minimum wage was such that it was worth only 53 percent of the federal poverty rate (Massey 2007).

Despite the thriving economy of the 1990s, Latinos remain concentrated in the secondary labor market, with its low-wage jobs vulnerable to market swings and with virtually nonexistent benefits (Fletcher 2000). Massey (2007) documents the decline of Latino incomes and increased poverty rates in the 1990s, which in part is also an outcome of the militarization of the Mexico–United States border after 1986. Return migration dropped significantly, leaving many north of the border without social, economic, or political rights, and the criminalization of undocumented hiring further increased discrimination and contributed to labor subcontracting. Since then the situation has become more dire, as the economy has experienced a marked downturn.

This situation of stubbornly entrenched income inequality is ominous for all Americans, and African Americans and Latinos who are disproportionately worse off will feel the impact most. A brief overview of unemployment, income, and education statistics (Table 10-1) suggests the extent of these different locations in the socioeconomic structure and the challenges confronting us. Latinos, both native-born and foreign-born, like blacks, suffered more from the economic downturn than whites. Taken

TABLE 10-1 Social and economic characteristics of whites, Hispanics, and blacks, 2008, 2010

	Total White[a]	Total Black	Total Hispanic
Poverty rate (2008)	8.2%	21.9%	19.5%
Unemployment rate (2008)	5.5%	11.5%	8/9.5%
Unemployment rate (2010)	8.0%	15.6%	11.9%
High school graduate (25+)[b]	90.0%	80.9%	60.8%
College completion (25+)[b]	30.7%	17.5%	12.9%
Median household income[b]	$56,826	$35,644	$41,041

Source: 2008 data from Pew Hispanic Center 2010; unemployment rates second quarter 2010, from Kochhar 2010.

[a]Non-Hispanic white.

[b]2008 data.

collectively, one-fifth of all Hispanics live below the poverty level. The median household income of Hispanics, who typically have larger families, is only 72 percent that of Euro-Americans. (Cubans, for reasons discussed earlier, fare best of the Latino groups.) Differences in education, so critical in today's new economy, translate into differences in access to better-paying employment opportunities.

Recent statistics underline the costs of less education for younger generations. High school graduates on the average will earn 1.2 million dollars during their working life, while college graduates with a bachelor's degree will earn almost double that, 2.1 million dollars (Longley 2010).

BEYOND THE IMMIGRANT ANALOGY. In many respects, Latinos as a whole are better conceptualized as "racial," rather than "ethnic" minorities. Their limited opportunities as racial minorities in turn differentiate them from their Euro-American counterparts.

Why Latinos were not culturally and structurally assimilating into the dominant population and ascending the social class ladder like their Euro-American counterparts became a contentious subject of debate by the 1960s. "Cultural deficit" explanations that attributed their low socioeconomic status to "culturally determined" behaviors were prevalent.[19] Hispanic culture (with most early studies based on Mexican Americans) was alleged to be deficient because of its supposed anti-intellectualism, parental indifference, doting child-rearing style, and absence of future orientation, as well as a lack of commitment to the English language.[20] A "noncompetitive, nonprogressive, easily satisfied psychological makeup that caters to a family-oriented fatalistic world view" was defined as the barrier to rapidly ascending the social class ladder (Klor de Alva 1988:116). Fatalism and familism (family needs taking priority over emphasis on the individual's fulfillment) were widely accepted as explanations for Mexican Americans' poverty, without investigating whether these traits existed in urban

barrios or, for that matter, led to poverty (Moore and Pinderhughes 1993). These images of Latinos and explanations for their economic situations arose from a variety of sources: popular culture, ethnocentric scholarly analyses (e.g., Heller 1966), and overgeneralization of findings from anthropological studies of isolated rural Mexican American communities (e.g., Madsen 1964; Rubel 1966) to urban settings.

While the idea that cultural and linguistic "deficits" held back Latinos may have been a popular assumption among many educators, social service providers, and policy makers in the 1960s, a growing number of anthropologists and other qualitative researchers—including among them a new generation of Chicano and Puerto Rican academics—took issue with then-popular social science assumptions. Chicano academics attacked depictions of Mexican American culture that portrayed it as static, oppressive, and backwards[21] (Griswold del Castillo 1984). Mexican American anthropologist Octavio Romano's work, published in the Chicano journal *El Grito* from 1967 to 1970, was central. Romano, noted one Chicano anthropologist, "taught his many readers to argue against cultural determinism, the idea that Chicanos (or any other group) are victims of their own values, such as passivity, fatalism and envy. . . . (These are) new ways to blame the victim" (Rosaldo 1986:8). Chicano folklorist Américo Paredes, in his critiques of portrayals of Mexican Americans (1978), aptly demonstrated how Euro-American anthropologists, as cultural outsiders, easily missed the subtle double meanings in many Mexican oral traditions when arriving at their conclusions.

Puerto Ricans' continuing poverty was also a focus in the social science literature. Anthropologist Oscar Lewis popularized the notion of a "culture of poverty" that reproduced itself in his ethnography *La Vida, A Puerto Rican Family in the Culture of Poverty* (1966). Though Lewis did not intend to equate a culture of poverty with race or ethnicity, many felt that it read as characteristic of Puerto Ricans rather than as an outcome of dislocation in a capitalist economy. Critics attacked it as a "blame the victim" approach to understanding the root causes of poverty, and instead argued for attention to the system that produces such profound poverty. Cultural practices, they argued, needed to be understood as adaptive responses to life difficulties rather than causes of poverty. This sort of understanding would, for instance, see familism as a "smart" choice when resources and opportunities are limited, rather than a barrier to upward mobility. Anthropologists' own tendencies to depict culture as bounded, unchanging, and homogeneous, and to ignore oppression and inequality (Rosaldo 1989), came under attack within anthropology at home as a new generation of scholars, many of them "natives" themselves, came of age and entered the discipline.

Culture, Language, Identity . . . and Education

If greater educational success is increasingly a prerequisite for achieving economic stability in the United States, it is instructive to examine what educational anthropologists have found in exploring disparities in educational performance across groups. The criticism in the 1960s and 1970s of mainstream social science explanations for minority groups' lack of achievement had its counterpart in new theorizing on education and minority student performance coming out of educational anthropology, a field then in its infancy.

Anthropologists working in schools brought a number of strengths to their study of educational institutions. For one, schools and students are contextualized as existing within a larger framework, both historically and societally. For another, anthropologists are interested in how various groups experience and view their worlds, ensuring a broader range of perspectives and understandings. They also seek to distance themselves from their own cultural biases and assumptions and frequently challenge common,

taken-for-granted understandings. Both the macro perspective, looking at things from outside the schools, and the micro perspective, close-up ethnographic projects within schools themselves that examine the complex ways in which culture and language differences can enter into educational performance, were utilized. These orientations provided new understandings of how culturally and linguistically diverse students and their communities participate in the school experience.

REFUTING CULTURAL DEFICIT NOTIONS.   Early analyses of Latinos' school performance often took for granted that the practices of the schools themselves were neutral, and that the "problems" lie in the cultural and linguistic practices of non-mainstream families. It was taken as a given that all students had equal educational opportunities. Yet we know that was not (e.g., Carter and Segura 1979; Pedraza 1997), and still is not the case, when de facto segregation and gross economic disparities across suburban and urban schools make quality education far less likely for Latinos and other urban minorities (Kozol 1991).

The early explanations (e.g., Bereiter and Engelmann 1966; Hess and Shipman 1965) alleged that cultural and linguistic deficits in lower-class homes were the causes of their lower educational performance.[22] This "culture of poverty" explanation, as critics termed it (e.g., Leacock 1971), was flawed for its assessment of these groups from an ethnocentric, middle-class point of view rather than a culturally relativistic point of view that seeks to understand people's behavior from their own perspectives and experiences. Working and living in minority communities, they documented the strengths of culturally different students' home environments (e.g., Au 1980; Labov 1972; Philips 1972) and argued that the issue was not one of cultural deficiencies in their homes, but rather cultural mismatches in interaction and learning styles within the schools. Cultural differences in school settings when teachers are unaware of them can lead to systematic miscommunication and contribute to academic difficulties.

BEYOND "CULTURAL DIFFERENCE." But cultural difference alone doesn't always lead to problems, and John Ogbu (1978) took the lead in theorizing the significance of factors beyond the school doors. Put briefly, Ogbu argues that the way that racialized groups have been treated in the United States affects their attitudes toward mainstream institutions. "Involuntary" minorities such as African Americans, Chicanos, or Native Americans, all longtime U.S. citizens, have suffered the consequences of an enduring, ongoing history of discrimination that affects their sense of whether education can improve their lives. They may manifest oppositional behavior in schools. Secondary cultural practices forged in segregated social environments (e.g., dress, ways of speaking) for instance become important markers of identity, and conformity to school rules may be read as "acting white," an important contribution by Signithia Fordham to Ogbu's work (Fordham and Ogbu 1986).[23]

"Voluntary" minorities, on the other hand, the new immigrants, have a different history and thus a different perspective. They look back to their homelands as the basis of comparison. They see opportunities denied to them there, but if all else fails in their new homeland, they can return. Therefore they are more willing to comply with school expectations, firm in the belief (for the first generation, anyway) that they have opportunities to succeed.

Ethnographic research has found support for Ogbu's theory. Maria Matute-Bianchi, for instance, found an oppositional identity among second- and third-generation Chicano students (1986). Marcelo Suarez-Orozco (1987) found that Central American newcomers—immigrant minorities—had a better track record in schools than their Chicano and Puerto Rican peers. While these students faced significant institutional barriers—a drug-infested environment, low expectations, and placement into non-academic tracks, among them—they saw schooling as their window of opportunity and felt duty-bound to succeed for their suffering parents.

John Ogbu's work is valuable for fostering awareness of how the larger sociohistoric context can affect people's relations to educational institutions, but a number of anthropologists have also pointed out some of the limitations of his theory (e.g., Davidson 1996; Erickson 1987; Foley 1991; Gibson 1997; MacLeod 1995; Tapia 1998).[24] Among them: it assumes the neutrality of schools and can easily be read as deterministic, with nothing to be done about it; it doesn't explain why *some* involuntary minorities succeed, and why *some* immigrant minority youth come to display oppositional identities; it doesn't consider class differences adequately; it doesn't allow for the possibility that students may manifest an oppositional identity and still succeed academically.

The ethnographic findings these anthropologists draw on have a great deal to tell us about Latinos: the variability within any given ethnic group in the United States; the difficulties with assuming a linear progression from "immigrant" to "ethnic" to "assimilated"; and the significance of the ways in which individual actors negotiate and construct new, and oftentimes multiple, identities. Douglas Foley (1990), studying working-class and middle-class Mexicanos (the regional term for Mexican Americans) in a south Texas town, found significant intragroup differences among the Mexicanos. Both groups expressed "chicanismos," or "pochismos," expressive cultural practices (dress, greetings, etc.) associated with Mexican Americans. Middle-class youth, though, when the situation demanded, put into action mainstream communicative competencies in impression management such as feigning interest in teacher talk or asking questions designed to get teachers "going" on a topic. These practices fostered positive relations with Anglos and authority figures, unlike those of their working-class peers. Cynthia Bejarano (2005) found competing identities among Mexican-descent youth along the border, articulated through markers such as dress and use of language, and reflecting their differing locations along the "Mexican cultural continuum." Her work serves as a cautionary tale for those who would assume a singular cultural identity among Mexican-descent students.

Maria Matute-Bianchi (1991) and Katherine Hayes (1992) found immigrant minority youth who acted like involuntary minority youth. Matute-Bianchi documented immigrant Mexican students seeking acceptance by their Chicano peers through adoption of a *cholo* identity (including expressive aspects such as their dress, walk, and speech) and the antischool attitudes that are common among many *cholo* youth. Similarly, Hayes found that the children of Mexican immigrants felt that school offered nothing to them; their classroom behaviors echoed those of involuntary minority students who rejected the symbols, behaviors, and ideals of Anglo-American society. The time of arrival of immigrant youth may be significant, she suggests. Those who come later in elementary school may have positive identities already in place, whereas those who have all their schooling in the United States may have experiences that lead them to see the world in ways more similar to those of involuntary minorities.

Javier Tapia (1998) found considerable variability in academic performance among the children of poor Puerto Rican families in Philadelphia. His ethnographic study documents the critical nature of family stability, in turn influenced by economic stability, for stronger academic performance. This family stability appeared to matter more than the language of instruction and method of teaching. Nilda Flores-González (1999) found Puerto Rican students in an urban Chicago school who displayed an ethnic identity and were also high achievers, without being accused of "acting white" by their lower-achieving peers.

If raising students' academic success rates is an educational goal, there is also much that educational anthropologists can tell us about what sorts of conditions affect culturally diverse students' educational engagement. School practices, as we now know from ethnographic research, can negatively affect culturally diverse students' orientations to schooling. Marginalization and alienation can be the unanticipated outcomes of unquestioned school practices, including the choice of instructional language, tracking, differential treatment, speech acts that stigmatize cultural expressive practices, and writing off parents who fail to conform to middle-class ways of showing interest in their children's education (Davidson 1996).

On the other hand, certain conditions appear to foster the educational engagement of minority youth. One major finding, drawing on both international and U.S. cases, is that "minority students do better in school when they feel strongly anchored in the identities of their families, communities, and peers and when they feel supported in pursuing a strategy of selective or additive acculturation" (Gibson 1997:445–446). Students can be academically successful without losing their ethnic identity if the schools are structured in ways that affirm students' identities and sense of empowerment (Mehan et al. 1994). Mexican-origin adolescents whose parents lack the cultural, social, and economic capital to help their children navigate their schooling can benefit from the construction of what Gibson et al. (2004) term "peer social capital," in which peer social relations provide access to tangible forms of support and a sense of belonging. A culturally sensitive pedagogy, a multicultural curriculum, and recognition and utilization of the "funds of knowledge" that all students bring to school can create a more inclusive and empowering environment while educating all students to the diversity of the world around them (e.g., Bigler 1999; Mercado and Moll 1997; Osborne 1996). Schools can adopt multiculturalism as a *process*, whereby all school practices and outcomes are constantly required to foster more equitable outcomes (Nieto 2000).

LANGUAGE AND IDENTITY. Sociolinguists—anthropologists who study language in its social context—also have a great deal to say about the relationships among culture, identity, language, historical processes, and educational well-being.

We take our cues for language usage from those around us, so that our class locations and ethnic roots, particularly in a society like our own that remains very segregated, provide us with diverse understandings of appropriate "ways of speaking." Latinos are linguistically diverse. Some speak only English, some only Spanish, some are bilinguals; various dialects of English and Spanish coexist, and many Latinos use "Spanglish." Code-switching, or moving back and forth between languages or styles of speaking, is common in regions of the world where different speech communities live in close contact. Linguistic borrowing from one language to another is also common, so that Spanish-speaking Puerto Ricans in New York speak of *el bloque* ("the block") and *lonchar* ("to lunch"). English, in fact, is peppered with words that were originally Spanish: *adobe*, *bronco*, *canyon*, *corral*, *lasso*, *lariat*, *mosquito*. Mexican Spanish contains words from Nahuatl, the language of the Aztecs. Some of these "nahuatlismos," in turn, entered English through the Spanish: *cocoa*, *tomato*, *coyote*, *chocolate*, *chile*. In Puerto Rico, remnants of the Arawak language, spoken by the original inhabitants, are woven into their Spanish and made their way into English: *papaya*, *yuca*, *maíz*, *iguana*, *barbacoa* (*barbecue*), *huracán*. Today English Internet terms make headway in Spanish-speaking countries, as speakers adapt them to their own linguistic rules: *el backup*, *fordwardear*, *chatear*, *la windo* (Dillon 2000). These sorts of processes of linguistic change are normal anticipated responses to contacts with other speakers, not signs of linguistic "deficiencies."

Yet Puerto Ricans and Spanish-speaking Mexican Americans have a long history of being stigmatized for their speech patterns, as well as being pressured to abandon Spanish. There is a hierarchy of Spanish dialects among Latinos, and Puerto Ricans may be told by other Spanish speakers—or even Spanish-language teachers—that their Spanish is ungrammatical. Mexican American children in the Southwest up to the 1960s were required to use only English in school, even when playing with their classmates on the playground. Stories abound among Chicanos of physical punishment or loss of privileges like recess for using Spanish on school grounds (Montoya 1998).

Thus, many Latinos come to believe their own language patterns are inferior (e.g., Urciuoli 1996; Zentella 1997, 2005). To be pressured to reject the language of the home and community, with all that implies, is a traumatic experience (Rodríguez 1982), and such acts also have unanticipated consequences. They increase the possible alienation of children from school, particularly when accompanied by other practices such as cultural exclusion, inappropriate evaluation of cultural differences, and the like, so that they may come to view school as a "white" institution. If these practices result in language loss, children may be denied important links to their families and communities. And for those caught up in the migrant stream and transnational communities, language loss complicates their return.

The negative evaluation of Spanish in public places has grown as anti-immigrant, anti-bilingual education, and English-only movements have flourished since the 1980s.[25] Not unexpectedly, Latinos asked by Pew Hispanic Center researchers in three different surveys to identify sources of discrimination against them chose insufficient English-language skills more often than other possible causes of discrimination (Hakimzadeh and Cohn 2007). Speaking Spanish in public is viewed by segments of the Euro-American population as "unAmerican" and evidence of speakers' laziness and/or unwillingness to assimilate (Bigler 1997; Crawford 1992; Woolard 1989; Zentella 1988). Bilingual education has increasingly come under attack, despite significant evidence of its benefits when done well.[26] Puerto Rican academic Ana Zentella takes a different view of the real issues:

Blaming linguistic and cultural diversity (for the political, social and economic problems facing the US today) is a smoke-screen for the fact that the US has not resolved fundamental inequalities. The root of the problem lies in an inability to accept an expanded definition of what it is to be a US American today. . . . The nation's problems would not disappear if we all spoke the same language, unless by speaking the same language we mean that we have the same rights and obligations toward each other. [1997:286–87]

Ironically, arguments that Spanish maintenance threatens the status of English and leads to ethnic fragmentation ignore the linguistic research that indicates that second- and third-generation Americans are losing their native languages at rates roughly comparable to those of earlier immigrants. Summarizing various data sets, Citrin et al. (2007) found traditional patterns of linguistic assimilation among immigrants, with the vast majority monolingual English by the third generation. They conclude that "Mexican immigrants may know less English than newcomers from other countries . . . but the trajectory of their progeny's assimilation resembles that of their European predecessors of a century ago, and their rate of linguistic assimilation is on par with or greater than those of other contemporary immigrant groups" (p. 35).

Rather than to assume that there is room for only one language, a common American assumption, linguistically diverse children can be more productively taught to value both languages and to code-switch when their community dialect differs from the standard. While the Latino Threat Narrative (Chavez 2008) casts Latinos' use and valuing of Spanish as evidence of their failure to assimilate, we might better conceptualize their attachment to Spanish as an asset to our collective well-being to have multilingual citizens in today's globalized world, and a productive move toward displacing the long-standing discourse of English-Only as evidence of "Americanness."

Past Imperfect, Present Tense, Future Conditional?[27]

As Latinos are changed by their experiences in the United States, so too is the United States changed by the growing presence of Latinos and their increased access to mainstream institutions. Latinos have historically gone unrecognized for their contributions to the national economic well-being, and today's situation remains little changed. The continued economic strength of the United States is in part made possible by the labor and tax revenue contributions that Latinos and the newest immigrants, both documented and undocumented, contribute. Popular impressions notwithstanding, Latinos' contributions exceed their costs to the government (Brand 2000).

Latino immigrants have helped revitalize declining cities and suburbs where they have settled. Many cities, including Boston, Dallas, and Los Angeles, would have declined in population over the 1990s were it not for Hispanics (Schmitt 2001). Current Hispanic spending power is estimated at $869 billion, with California accounting for more than a quarter of it (Nelson 2008). Many Hispanics, like earlier generations of Americans, also see owning their own businesses as a stepping-stone on the way to the American Dream (Fletcher 2000; Kotkin 2000). There were 1.6 million Hispanic-owned businesses in 2002, and Hispanic-owned businesses grew at a rate of 31 percent between 1997 and 2002, compared to a national average of 10 percent. Forty-five percent of those businesses, which generated $222 billion, were owned by Mexicans and Mexican Americans. The number of Hispanic-owned firms that had receipts of $1 million or more increased 52 percent between 2002 and 2007 to 44,206 (U.S. Department of Commerce 2010). " 'Without the Latino entrepreneur, New Jersey's cities would be falling into urban decay,' says Guillermo Beytagh-Maldonado, executive director of New Brunswick's Puerto Rican Action Board. . . . 'Latino entrepreneurs are the (New Brunswick) owners of the mom-and-pop shops' " (Brand 2000). Meanwhile, Latinos are rapidly emerging as a significant market. From 1990 to 2006 the disposable

Hispanic American family.

income of Hispanics rose by $832 billion, and is projected to grow to almost $1.2 trillion by 2011.[28] Marketers are quick to seize the opportunity to win their allegiance, and to reach this market they have begun to attend to Hispanic cultural tastes, the images they project in their ads, and even the models they select to sell their products (Cortese 2007).

Latinos holding public office are on the increase. The election in 2004 of Antonio Villaraigosa as mayor of Los Angeles, the nation's second largest city, was a continuation of an upward trend in the numbers of elected Hispanics, from 3,743 in 1996 to 4,853 by 2004, a growth rate of 30 percent (Wood 2005). The increased turnout (Lopez and Taylor 2009) of Hispanic voters—voter turnout in the 2008 election rose from 47.2 to 49.9 percent—further challenges the Latino Threat Narrative's claim of Latinos' noninvolvement in the American political sphere. The growing Latino population is now actively courted by political candidates.

The number of Latino eligible voters grew from 16.1 million to 19.5 million between 2004 and 2008; if the major political parties are going to successfully court Latino voters, they will want to address not only the concerns they share with many other Americans but also their shared interests, including government policies toward Latin American nations and immigration and language policies.

The cultural influence of Latinos is, meanwhile, undeniable. By 1988 *Time* magazine was calling attention to the presence of Latinos on the cultural scene. "A Surging New Spirit: In film, music, theater, art, design—the Hispanic influence is exploding into the American cultural mainstream," the feature article proclaimed.

True, these influences are not felt uniformly around the nation, but they are there nonetheless. New crossover artists join other Latinos with national name recognition: Gloria Estafan, Jennifer Lopez, Ricky Martin, and Andy García;

Jennifer Lopez (Puerto Rican American).

Edward James Olmos, Jimmy Smits, Linda Ronstadt, and Rosie Perez. Americans of all backgrounds dance increasingly to a Latin beat: Latin hip-hop, reggaeton, bachata, and salsa, among others. Meanwhile Latin American musicians filter American rock through their own sensibilities, producing the new phenomenon "rock *en español*" that wound its way back into the U.S. music scene (Rohter 2000).

A new generation of Latinos, like earlier generations of ethnic writers, pen bittersweet memoirs about their coming of age in the United States: *How the Garcia Girls Lost Their Accents*, by Julia Alvarez (1992); *When I Was Puerto Rican*, by Esmeralda Santiago (1993); *The House on Mango Street*, by Sandra Cisneros (1989); *Always Running: La Vida Loca*, by Luis Rodríguez (1993). Quality movies with Latinos as stars are hailed as box-office successes: *Mi Familia, Stand and Deliver, American Me, The Mambo Kings Play Songs of Love*. Salsa and flour

tortillas are ubiquitous, having even gone trendy for "roll-ups" in chic eateries; design and architecture magazines borrow heavily from Hispanic decorating styles in the South and West; Spanish has become the preferred second language in schools across the nation.

A sense of affinity is palpable at times among Latinos when they come together to share their common concerns.[29] But there is no one "Latino" experience, any more than there is one "Chicano" or one "Puerto Rican" experience—or for that matter, one "American" experience. Latinos are taking a variety of paths in the United States. Many, particularly the lighter-skinned, may assimilate into the Euro-American mainstream, as intermarriage, largely across Latino-Anglo lines, increases. The possibility of Latinos intermarrying across "racial" lines—most typically to whites—increases across time in the United States, rising from 10 percent for Hispanic foreign-born noncitizens to 30 percent of U.S.-born Latinos (Lee and Edmonston 2005), yet one more challenge to the Latino Threat Narrative. Not that they will necessarily be absorbed into the dominant society; the assimilation may also be in the opposite direction (Rosaldo 1985). Others may assimilate into the African American urban culture, or children of mixed Latino–African American marriages may choose to identify as Latino.

Undoubtedly, the homelands will continue to be not only spiritual but also material realities for many Latinos. And many Latinos, if current trends hold, may be "not neither," as Sandra Maria Esteves (1984:26) puts it, continuing to maintain their claims to the right to distinctive identities, to exist in the "borderlands" (e.g., Anzaldua 1987) and carve out new ways of being "American." Some will have more choice than others.

The very nature of Latinos' experiences has required them to be adept "border crossers," crossing racial, ethnic, national, and language borders. But there is one border that will remain particularly problematic: Without the public will to address the continuing and growing inequalities among us that rob so many of a decent quality of life, many will remain on the wrong side of an economic divide that continues to threaten American society well into the twenty-first century.

Notes

1. In Spanish, the ending *-o* is used for the masculine form of a word, and *-a* for the feminine. Much like in the arguments for replacing "mankind" with "humankind," the term *Latino* is also sometimes written as *Latina/o* to signal more inclusiveness.

2. The word *Latino* would technically incorporate speakers of other Latin-derived languages. Indeed, Portuguese-speaking Brazilians in the United States in many respects could be logically grouped with other Hispanic groups, but instead fall between the cracks of U.S. racial/ethnic categories. For a research-based analysis of the Brazilian population's positionality, see selections in "Brazilian Immigration," in the collection *The Other Latinos* (Falconi and Mazzotti 2007).

3. By "racial" group, here I mean it in the sense of those who see distinctive biological races existing. Latinos to varying degrees have white, Indian (Asian), and black ancestry when seen from this perspective.

4. While this reflects to some extent the valuing of "European" ancestry in Latin American countries, it can also be understood in part as a politically expedient choice given the racism toward American Indians in the United States (see Menchaca 1993).

5. Even the federal government could not agree on how to classify Mexicans. When the 1930 census sought for the first time to capture the number of Hispanics in the United States, "Mexican" (meant as a label for Mexican Americans) was placed under the rubric of "other races"; in the 1950 census, Mexican Americans were considered to be whites.

6. Ironically, Indians in Mexico had been eligible for citizenship since 1812 under Mexican law (see Menchaca 1993).

7. The National Labor Relations Act, passed during the Great Depression, had given American workers the right to join labor unions but excluded farm workers.

8. The term is found throughout the political and artistic productions of the day: in the name of a scholarly Chicano journal, in political tracts like the *Plan Espiritual de Aztlán*, and in titles of literary works and organizations.

9. Their interests extended beyond North America to embrace independence and rebel movements across Latin America, symbolically "linking arms" with others in their struggles for equality (Arguello 2009).

10. There are many excellent anthologies; for an overview, the reader may want to begin with *Hispanic-American Literature: A Brief Introduction and Anthology*, edited by Nicolás Kanellos (1995).

11. "Nuyorican" refers to Puerto Ricans who grew up in New York City. Alternatively, they sometimes label themselves "neoricans." The term is not universally accepted.

12. The many nuances of this poem are developed in depth in Juan Flores' essay "Broken English Memories" (2000).

13. *Boriquen* was the name the indigenous people called Puerto Rico, and Puerto Ricans oftentimes refer to themselves as *boricuas*.

14. Poem available at http://www.virtualboricua.org/Docs/poem_mtf.htm; video clip available on YouTube or at http://sarahrettger.blogspot.com/2008/05/poetry-friday-ode-to-diasporican.html.

15. Some Afro-Cubans did see themselves as a racial minority, however.

16. The impact of recent immigration enforcement policies has reverberated throughout all Latino communities, regardless of residents' legal status or citizenship. A 2008 National Survey of Latinos found that 1 in 10 Hispanics had been stopped in the past year by authorities and asked about their immigration status. Approximately 3 of every 4 disapproved of recent enforcement measures: workplace raids, the use of local police, and criminal prosecution of undocumented immigrants and employers hiring them (Lopez and Minushkin 2008). American citizens have been swept up in such raids (Preston 2009b).

17. The terms *Mexifornia* and *Mexamerica* combine the word *Mexico* with the words *California* and *America*, signifying the "takeover" by Mexicans.

18. See Chavez (2008) for an excellent overview of evidence undermining Huntington's thesis.

19. As late as the 1950s, and even into the 1960s, social science researchers were asking similar questions about why Italian Americans were not climbing the social class ladder at the rates of other "model minorities," like the Jews (di Leonardo 1992).

20. A small number of early studies (e.g., McWilliams 1990) did argue that poverty was the result of structural factors rather than the product of "deficient" cultural behaviors, anticipating current understandings.

21. Several people attacked by Romano and other Chicanos subsequently left the field of Chicano studies.

22. See Jacob and Jordan (1993) for a summary of these works and anthropologists' refutations.

23. This sort of oppositional identity is not inherently linked with racial minorities. Paul Willis (1977), for instance, found a similar oppositional identity among disaffected white working-class males in Britain, who believed they had little chance to succeed. See also Noguera (2003) for an instructive look at how educators are challenging deterministic interpretations of "oppositional identity" formation.

24. Ogbu has begun to address some of these concerns in recent work; see, for instance, Ogbu and Simmons (1998).

25. Some Latinos are refusing to surrender to this hegemonic evaluation of their languages and dialects, and now proclaim their use of Spanish and Spanglish as positive and as an affirmation of ethnic pride (Anzaldua 1987; Zentella 1997).

26. The merits of bilingual education are well documented in a number of works. See Nieto (2000) for a rationale and an excellent summary of findings on the merits of strong late-exit bilingual programs for students' academic development.

27. This, of course, is a play on words, using real and "imagined" verb conjugations.

28. This estimate however predates the dramatic economic downturn of 2008–2009.

29. Numerous academic works address these commonalities, including Bonilla et al. (1998), Flores and Benmayor (1997), and Flores (2000).

References Cited

ACUÑA, RUDOLFO. 1988. *Occupied America: A History of Chicanos*. 3rd edition. New York: Harper & Row.

AIZENMAN, N. C. 2006. Salvadorans ambushed by memories in Iraq. *Washington Post*, March 25, p. A1. http://www.washingtonpost.com/wp-dyn/content/article/2006/03/24/AR2006032402126_pf.html (accessed July 1, 2009).

ALLEN, GREG. 2009. Puerto Ricans gain political clout in Florida. *National Public Radio*, June 28. http://www.npr.org/templates/story/story.php?storyId=105691084&ft=1&f=1001 (accessed June 28, 2009).

ALVAREZ, JULIA. 1992. *How the Garcia Girls Lost Their Accents*. New York: Penguin.

ANAYA, RUDOLFO. 1989. Aztlán: A homeland without boundaries. In *Aztlán: Essays on the* Chicano *Homeland.* R. Anaya and F. Lomelí, eds. Pp. 230–241. Albuquerque, NM: Academia/El Norte.

ANZALDUA, GLORIA. 1987. *Borderlands/La Frontera: The New Mestiza.* San Francisco, CA: Spinsters/Aunt Lute.

APPADURAI, ARJUN. 1990. Disjuncture and difference in the global cultural economy. *Public Culture* 2(2):1–24.

———. 1991. Global ethnoscapes: Notes and queries for a transnational anthropology. In *Recapturing Anthropology: Working in the Present.* R. Fox, ed. Pp. 191–210. Santa Fe, NM: School of American Research Press.

ARGUELLO, MARTHA. 2009. Sisters, brothers, Young Lords. *ReVista, The Harvard Review of Latin America* VIII(18):43–45.

ASTHANA, ANUSHKA. 2006. Hispanic influx reshaping big cities. *Seattle Times* (*Washington Post* article), August 24. http://seattletimes.nwsource.com/html/nationworld/2003216185_whites22.html (accessed June 30, 2009).

AU, KATHRYN. 1980. Participant structure in a reading lesson with Hawaiian children: Analysis of a culturally appropriate instructional event. *Anthropology & Education Quarterly* 11(2):91–115.

BACON, DAVID. 2008. The right to stay home. *TruthOut.* http://dbacon.igc.org/Mexico/2008stayhome.html#top (accessed June 25, 2009).

BACON, DAVID, and BILL ONG HING. 2009. Rights, not raids. *The Nation,* May 18. http://www.thenation.com/doc/20090518/hing_bacon (accessed June 23, 2009).

BAKER, SUSAN. 2002. *Understanding Mainland Puerto Rican Poverty.* Philadelphia, PA: Temple University Press.

BASCH, LINDA, NINA GLICK SCHILLER, and CRISTINA SZANTON BLANC. 1994. *Nations Unbound: Transnational Projects, Postcolonial Predicaments, and Deterritorialized States.* Basel: Gordon & Breach.

BEJARANO, CYNTHIA. 2005. *¿QUÉ ONDA? Urban Youth Cultures and Border Identity.* Tucson, AZ: University of Arizona Press.

BEREITER, CARL, and SIEGFRIED ENGELMANN. 1966. *Teaching Disadvantaged Children in the Preschool.* Englewood Cliffs, NJ: Prentice Hall.

BIGLER, ELLEN. 1997. Dangerous discourses: Language politics and classroom practices in upstate New York. *Centro* 9(1):8–25. New York: Centro de Estudios Puertorriqueños, Hunter College, CUNY.

———. 1999. *American Conversations: Puerto Ricans, White Ethnics, and Multicultural Education.* Philadelphia, PA: Temple University Press.

BONILLA, FRANK, and RICARDO CAMPOS. 1981. A wealth of poor: Puerto Ricans in the new economic order. *Daedalus* 110(Spring):133–176.

BONILLA, FRANK, EDWIN MELÉNDEZ, REBECCA MORALES, and MARÍA DE LOS ANGELES TORRES, eds. 1998. *Borderless Borders: U.S. Latinos, Latin Americans, and the Paradox of Interdependence.* Philadelphia, PA: Temple University Press.

BOSWELL, THOMAS, and TERRY-ANN JONES. 2006. Puerto Ricans, Cubans and Dominicans. In *Contemporary Ethnic Geographies in Americ*a. Ines M. Miyares and Christoper Airriess, eds. Pp. 123–150. Lanham, MD: Rowman & Littlefield Publishers, Inc.

BRAND, RICHARD. 2000. The second great wave; Hispanic immigrants are changing the face of central Jersey. *New York Times,* May 28.

BRINKLEY, JOEL. 1999. U.S. acts in behalf of immigrants who fled right-wing governments. *New York Times,* May 21.

BRODER, JOHN. 1999. Clinton offers his apologies to Guatemalans. *New York Times,* March 11.

BROOKS, DAVID. 2004. The Americano dream. *New York Times,* February 24.

BRUCE-NOBOA, JAMES. 1987. A question of identity: What's in a name? Chicanos and Riqueños. In *Images and Identities: The Puerto Rican in Two World Contexts.* Asela Rodrígues, ed. Pp. 229–235. New Brunswick, NJ: Transaction.

BUCHANAN, PATRICK. 2004. Huntington and Hispanics (Letters to the Editor). *Foreign Policy* 142(May–June): 12–13.

BURNS, ALLAN. 1993. *Maya in Exile: Guatemalans in Florida.* Philadelphia, PA: Temple University Press.

CARRASCO, GILBERT PAUL. 1998. Latinos in the United States: Invitation and exile. In *The Latino/a Condition: A Critical Reader.* R. Delgado and J. Stefancic, eds. Pp. 77–85. New York: New York University Press.

CARTER, THOMAS, and ROBERT SEGURA. 1979. *Mexican-Americans in School: A Decade of Change.* New York: CEEB.

CENTER FOR LATIN AMERICAN, CARIBBEAN & LATINO STUDIES. 2008a. The Latino population of New York City, 2007. Latino Data Project, Report 20. http://web.gc.cuny.edu/lastudies/latinodataprojectre ports/The%20Latino%20Population%20of%20New%20 York%20City%202007.pdf (accessed June 30, 2009).

————. 2008b. Latinos and the 2008 presidential elections: A summary data base. Latino Data Project Report 25. http://web.gc.cuny.edu/lastudies/latino-dataprojectreports/Latinos%20and%20the%202008%20Presidential%20Elections%20A%20Visual%20Data%20Base.pdf (accessed June 30, 2009).

CENTRO DE ESTUDIOS PUERTORRIQUEÑOS (CENEP), CITY UNIVERSITY OF NEW YORK. 1979. *Labor Migration under Capitalism: The Puerto Rican Experience.* New York: Monthly Review Press.

CHAVEZ, LEO R. 2008. *The Latino Threat: Constructing Immigrants, Citizens, and the Nation.* Stanford, CA: Stanford University Press.

CISNEROS, SANDRA. 1989. *The House on Mango Street.* New York: Vintage.

CITRIN, JACK, AMY LERMAN, MICHAEL MURAKAMI, and KATHRYN PEARSON. 2007. Testing Huntington: Is Hispanic immigration a threat to American identity? *Perspectives on Politics* 5(1):31–48. http://www.apsanet.org/imgtest/PerspectivesMar07Citrin_etal.pdf (accessed June 23, 2009).

COLLINS, CHUCK, and FELICE YESKEL (with United for a Fair Economy). 2000. *Economic Apartheid in America: A Primer on Economic Inequality and Insecurity.* New York: New Press. [excerpted in journal online]; http://www.tompaine.com/print.php3?id+1245 (accessed August 8, 2000).

CORTÉS, CARLOS. 1983. The greaser's revenge to boulevard nights: The mass media curriculum on Chicanos. In *History, Culture, and Society: Chicano Studies in the 1980s.* National Association for Chicano Studies. Pp. 128–131. Ypsilanti, MI: Bilingual Press.

CORTESE, AMY. 2007. At the mall, mariachi instead of muzak. *New York Times*, May 20.

CRAWFORD, JAMES. 1992. *Hold Your Tongue: Bilingualism and the Politics of "English Only."* Reading, MA: Addison-Wesley.

DAVIDSON, ANNE LOCKE. 1996. *Making and Molding Identity in Schools: Student Narratives on Race, Gender, and Academic Engagement.* Albany, NM: State University of New York Press.

DÁVILA, ARLENE. 2001. *Latinos Inc: The Marketing and Making of a People.* Berkeley, CA: University of California Press.

DE LEÓN, ARNOLDO. 1998. Initial contacts: Niggers, redskins and greasers. In *The Latino(a) Condition: A Critical Reader.* Richard Delgado and Jean Stefancic, eds. Pp. 158–164. New York: New York University Press.

DEFREITAS, GREGORY. 1999. The emergence of the Hispanic American labor force. In *Rethinking the Color Line: Readings in Race and Ethnicity.* Charles Gallagher, ed. Pp. 237–275. Mountain View, CA: Mayfield.

DEL VALLE, SANDRA. 1997. BPO v. Mills and the struggle for bilingual education. *Centro* 9(9):74–85. New York: Centro de Estudios Puertorriqueños, Hunter College, CUNY.

DI LEONARDO, MICAELA. 1992. White lies, black myths. *Village Voice* 22(September):29–36.

DIETZ, JAMES. 1986. *Economic History of Puerto Rico.* Princeton, NJ: Princeton University Press.

DILLON, SAM. 2000. Click to be subsumed: On the language of Cervantes, the imprint of the Internet. *New York Times*, August 6.

DREZNER, DANIEL. 2004. Hash of Civilizations. *The New Republic Online*, March 3. http://www.daniel-drezner.com/policy/hash.htm (accessed June 22, 2009).

DUANY, JORGE. 1994. *Quisqueya on the Hudson: The Transnational Identity of Dominicans in Washington Heights.* New York: Dominican Studies Institute, City University of New York.

————. 1998. Reconstructing racial identity: Ethnicity, color, and class among Dominicans in the United States and Puerto Rico. *Latin American Perspectives* 25(3):147–172.

————. 2003. Puerto Rican, Hispanic, or Latino? Recent debates on national and pan-ethnic identities. *Centro* XV(2). New York: Centro de Estudios Puertorriqueños, Hunter College, CUNY.

DUANY, JORGE, and FÉLIX V. MATOS-RODRÍGUEZ. 2006. Puerto Ricans in Orlando and central Florida. Policy Report. *Centro* 1(1). New York: Centro de Estudios Puertorriqueños, Hunter College, CUNY. http://www.centropr.org/documents/working_papers/FloridaBrief(F).pdf (accessed June 28, 2009).

ERICKSON, FREDERICK. 1987. Transformation and school success: The politics and culture of educational achievement. *Anthropology & Education Quarterly* 18(4):335–356.

ESTEVES, SANDRA MARÍA. 1984. *Tropical Rains: A Bilingual Downpour.* New York: African Caribbean Poetry Theater.

FALCONI, JOSÉ LUIS, and JOSÉ ANTONIO MAZZOTTI, eds. 2007. *The Other Latinos: Central and South Americans in the United States.* Cambridge, MA: Harvard University David Rockefeller Center for Latin American Studies.

FERNÁNDEZ, MARÍA TERESA. 2009. Boricua Poetry (Ode to the Diasporican). http://www.virtualboricua.org/Docs/poem_mtf.htm (accessed June 25, 2009).

FLETCHER, MICHAEL. 2000. Latinos missing American dream: Report finds many stuck in low-wage jobs. *San Jose Mercury News*, July 5.

FLORES, JUAN. 1985. "Que assimilated, brother, yo soy asimilao": The structuring of Puerto Rican identity in the U.S. *Journal of Ethnic Studies* 13(Fall):1–16.

———. 1996. Pan-Latino/trans-Latino: Puerto Ricans in the "New Nueva York." *Centro* 8(1–2):170–186. New York: Centro de Estudios Puertorriqueños, Hunter College, CUNY.

———. 2000. *From Bomba to Hip-Hop: Puerto Rican Culture and Latino Identity*. New York: Columbia University Press.

FLORES, JUAN, JOHN ATTINASI, and PEDRO PEDRAZA. 1981. La carreta made a U-turn: Puerto Rican language and culture in the United States. *Daedalus* 110(Spring):193–217.

FLORES, WILLIAM, and RINA BENMAYOR, eds. 1997. *Latino Cultural Citizenship: Claiming Identity, Space, and Rights*. Boston, MA: Beacon Press.

FLORES-GONZÁLEZ, NILDA. 1999. Puerto Rican high achievers: An example of ethnic and academic identity compatibility. *Anthropology & Education Quarterly* 30(3):343–362.

FOLEY, DOUGLAS. 1990. *Learning Capitalist Culture: Deep in the Heart of Tejas*. Philadelphia, PA: University of Pennsylvania Press.

———. 1991. Reconsidering anthropological explanations of ethnic school failure. *Anthropology & Education Quarterly* 22(1):60–86.

FORDHAM, SIGNITHIA, and JOHN OGBU. 1986. Coping with the burden of "acting white." *Urban Review* 18(3):176–206.

FUENTES, CARLOS. 2004. Huntington and the mask of racism. *New Perspectives Quarterly* 21(2, Spring). http://www.digitalnpq.org/archive/2004_spring/fuentes.html (accessed December 1, 2008).

GIBSON, MARGARET. 1997. Complicating the immigrant/involuntary minority typology. *Anthropology & Education Quarterly* 28(3):431–454.

GIBSON, MARGARET, PATRICIA GANDARA, and JILL PETERSON KOYAMA. 2004. *School Connections: U.S. Mexican Youth, Peers, and School Achievement*. New York: Teachers College Press.

GIMENEZ, MARTHA. 1997. Latino/"Hispanic"—who needs a name? The case against a standardized terminology. In *Latinos and Education*. Antonia Darder, Rodolfo Torres, and Henry Gutíerrez, eds. Pp. 225–238. New York: Routledge.

GLASSER, RUTH. 1997. Aquí Me Quedo: *Puerto Ricans in Connecticut*. Middletown, CT: Connecticut Humanities Council.

GOVERNMENT ACCOUNTABILITY OFFICE. 2006. Illegal Immigration: Border-Crossing Deaths Have Doubled Since 1995; Border Patrol's Efforts to Prevent Deaths Have Not Been Fully Evaluated. United States Government Accountability Office (August). http://www.gao.gov/new.items/d06770.pdf (accessed July 1, 2009).

GRASMUCK, SHERRI, and PATRICIA PESSAR. 1991. *Between Two Islands: Dominican International Migration*. Berkeley, CA: University of California Press.

GRISWOLD DEL CASTILLO, RICHARD. 1984. *La Familia: Chicano Families in the Urban Southwest, 1848 to the Present*. Notre Dame, IN: University of Notre Dame Press.

GROSFOGUEL, RAMÓN, and CHLOÉ GEORAS. 1996. The racialization of Latino Caribbean migrants in the New York metropolitan area. *Centro* 8(1–2):190–201. New York: Centro de Estudios Puertorriqueños, Hunter College, CUNY.

HAKIMZADEH, SHIRIN, and D'VERA COHN. 2007. English usage among Hispanics in the United States. November 29. http://pewhispanic.org/files/reports/82.pdf (accessed November 7, 2010).

HAYES, KATHERINE. 1992. Attitudes toward education: Voluntary and involuntary immigrants from the same families. *Anthropology & Education Quarterly* 23(3):250–267.

HELLER, CELIA. 1966. *Mexican-American Youth: Forgotten Youth at the Crossroads*. New York: Random House.

HERNÁNDEZ, RAMONA, and FRANCISCO RIVERA-BATIZ. 2005. *Dominicans in the United States: A Socioeconomic Profile, 2000*. Dominican Research Monograph. New York: CUNY Dominican Studies Institute.

HESS, ROBERT, and VIRGINIA SHIPMAN. 1965. Early experience and the socialization of cognitive modes in children. *Child Development* 36:869–886.

HISPANIC AMERICANS: CENSUS FACTS. 2010. Infoplease. http://www.infoplease.com/spot/hhmcensus1.html (accessed November 8, 2010).

HUNTINGTON, SAMUEL. 2004a. The Hispanic challenge. *Foreign Policy* 141(March–April): 30–45.

———. 2004b. *Who Are We*. New York: Simon & Schuster.

JACOB, EVELYN, and CATHIE JORDAN, eds. 1993. Introduction. In *Minority Education: Anthropological Perspectives*. Norwood, NJ: Ablex.

JOHNSON, KEVIN. 1999. *How Did You Get to Be Mexican? A White/Brown Man's Search for Identity.* Philadelphia, PA: Temple University Press.

JONES-CORREA, MICHAEL. 2007. Swimming in the Latino sea: The other Latinos and politics. In *The Other Latinos: Central and South Americans in the United States.* Jose Luis Falconi and Jose Antonio Mazzotti, eds. Pp. 21–38. Cambridge, MA: Harvard University Press.

KANELLOS, NICOLÁS, ed. 1995. *Hispanic-American Literature: A Brief Introduction and Anthology.* New York: Addison-Wesley.

KLOR DE ALVA, JORGE. 1988. Telling Hispanics apart: Latino sociocultural diversity. In *The Hispanic Experience in the United States: Contemporary Issues and Perspectives.* Edna Acosta-Bélen and Barbara Sjostrom, eds. Pp. 107–136. New York: Praeger.

———. 1989. Aztlán, Borinquen and Hispanic nationalism in the United States. In *Aztlán: Essays on the Chicano Homeland.* Rudolfo Anaya and Francisco Lomelí, eds. Pp. 135–171. Albuquerque, NM: El Norte Publications/Academia.

KOCHHAR, RAKESH. 2010. After the Great Recession: Foreign Born Gain Jobs, Native Born Lose Jobs. October 29. http://pewhispanic.org/files/reports/129.pdf (accessed November 7, 2010).

KOTKIN, JOEL. 2000. A revival of older suburbs as ethnic businesses take hold. *New York Times*, February 27.

KOZOL, JONATHAN. 1991. *Savage Inequalities: Children in America's Schools.* New York: Crown.

LABOV, WILLIAM. 1972. The logic of Nonstandard English. In *Language and Social Context.* Pier Paolo Giglioli, ed. Pp. 179–215. London: Penguin.

LACAYO, RICHARD. 1988. A surging new spirit. *Time*, July 11, pp. 46–49.

LAÓ, AUGUSTÍN. 1995. Resources of hope: Imagining the young Lords and the politics of memory. *Centro* 7(1):34–49. New York: Centro de Estudios Puertorriqueños, Hunter College, CUNY.

LAVIERA, TATO. 1985. *AmeRícan.* Houston, TX: Arte Publico.

———. 1988. *Mainstream Ethics (Ética Corriente).* Houston, TX: Arte Publico.

LEACOCK, ELEANOR, ed. 1971. *The Culture of Poverty: A Critique.* New York: Simon & Schuster.

LEE, SHARON M., and BARRY EDMONSTON. 2005. New marriages, new families: U.S. racial and Hispanic inter-marriage. *Population Bulletin* 60(2). Washington, DC: Population Reference Bureau. http://www.prb.org/pdf05/60.2NewMarriages.pdf (accessed July 1, 2009).

LEWIS, OSCAR. 1966. *La Vida: A Puerto Rican Family in the Culture of Poverty.* New York: Random House.

LIMONIC, LAURA. 2008. The Latino population of New York City, 2007. Latino Data Project, Report 20. *Center for Latin American, Caribbean & Latino Studies.* http://web.gc.cuny.edu/lastudies/latino-dataprojectreports/The%20Latino%20Population%20of%20New%20York%20City%202007.pdf (accessed June 30, 2009).

LONGLEY, ROBERT. 2010. Lifetime earnings soar with education. About.com, February 13. http://usgovinfo.about.com/od/moneymatters/a/edandearnings.htm (accessed November 7, 2010).

LOPEZ, MARK HUGO, and SUSAN MINUSHKIN. 2008. Hispanics see their situation in U.S. deteriorating; Oppose key immigration enforcement measures. Pew Hispanic Center, September 18. http://pewhispanic.org/files/reports/93.pdf (accessed June 10, 2009).

LOPEZ, MARK HUGO, and PAUL TAYLOR. 2009. Dissecting the 2008 electorate: Most diverse in U.S. History. Pew Hispanic Center, April 3. http://pewhispanic.org/reports/report.php?ReportID=108 (accessed June 20, 2009).

MACLEOD, JAY. 1995. *Ain't No Makin' It: Aspirations and Attainment in a Low-Income Neighborhood.* 2nd edition. Boulder, CO: Westview Press.

MADSEN, WILLIAM. 1964. *Mexican-Americans of South Texas.* San Francisco, CA: Holt, Rinehart and Winston.

MAHLER, SARAH. 1995. *Salvadorans in Suburbia: Symbiosis and Conflict.* Boston, MA: Allyn & Bacon.

MALDONADO, RITA. 1976. Why Puerto Ricans migrated to the United States in 1947–73. *Monthly Labor Review* 99(Summer):7–18.

MAROSI, RICHARD. 2005. Border crossing deaths set a 12-month record. *Los Angeles Times*, October 1. http://www.ccis-ucsd.org/news/latimes10-1-05.pdf (accessed July 2, 2009).

MARTÍNEZ, ELIZABETH. 1989. Histories of the "sixties": A certain absence of color. *Social Justice* 16(4): 175–185.

MASSEY, DOUGLAS. 2007. *Categorically Unequal: the American Stratification System.* New York: Russell Sage Foundation.

MATUTE-BIANCHI, MARIA. 1986. Ethnic identities and patterns of school success and failure among Mexican-descent and Japanese-American students in a California high school: An ethnographic analysis. *American Journal of Education* 95(1):233–255.

———. 1991. Situational ethnicity and patterns of school performance among immigrant and nonimmigrant Mexican-descent students. In *Minority Status and Schooling: A Comparative Study of Immigrant and Involuntary Minorities*. Margaret Gibson and John Ogbu, eds. Pp. 205–247. New York: Garland.

MCKINLEY, JESSE, and MALIA WOLLAN. 2009. New border fear: Violence by a rogue militia. *New York Times*, June 27, p. 1.

MCWILLIAMS, CAREY. 1990 [1948]. *North from Mexico: The Spanish-Speaking People of the United States*. New edition updated by Matt Meier. New York: Greenwood Press.

MEHAN, HUGH, LEA HUBBARD, and IRENE VILLANUEVA. 1994. Forming academic identities: Accommodation without assimilation among involuntary minorities. *Anthropology & Education Quarterly* 25(2):91–117.

MENCHACA, MARTHA. 1993. Chicano Indianism: A historical account of racial repression in the United States. *American Ethnologist* 20(August):3.

MERCADO, CARMEN, and LUIS MOLL. 1997. The study of funds of knowledge: Collaborative research in Latino homes. *Centro* 9(9):27–42. New York: Centro de Estudios Puertorriqueños, Hunter College, CUNY.

MONTOYA, MARGARET. 1998. Law and language(s). In *The Latino(a) Condition: A Critical Reader*. Richard Delgado and Jean Stefancic, eds. Pp. 574–578. New York: New York University Press.

MOORE, JOAN, and HARRY PACHON. 1985. *Hispanics in the United States*. Englewood Cliffs, NJ: Prentice Hall.

MOORE, JOAN, and RAQUEL PINDERHUGHES. 1993. Introduction. In *In the Barrios: Latinos and the Underclass Debate*. Joan Moore and Raquel Pinderhughes, eds. Pp. xi–xxxix. New York: Russell Sage.

MORALES, JULIO. 1986. *Puerto Rican Poverty and Migration: We Just Had to Try Elsewhere*. New York: Praeger.

MORRIS, NANCY. 1995. *Puerto Rico: Culture, Politics, and Identity*. Westport, CT: Praeger.

NAVARRO, MIREYA. 1997. A new Barbie in Puerto Rico divides island and mainland. *New York Times*, December 27.

———. 2000. Falling back: A special report. Puerto Rican presence wanes in New York. *New York Times*, February 28.

NEGRÓN DE MONTILLA, AIDA. 1975. *Americanization in Puerto Rico and the Public School System, 1900–1930*. 2nd edition. Rio Piedras, PR: Editorial Edil.

NELSON, FRANK. 2008. The 100 most influential U.S. Hispanics, 2008. *Hispanic Business Magazine*, September 30. http://www.hispanicbusiness.com/news/news_print.asp?id=129770 (accessed June 27, 2009).

NELSON, CANDACE, and MARTA TIENDA. 1988. The structuring of Hispanic ethnicity: Historical and contemporary perspectives. In *Ethnicity and Race in the U.S.A.* Richard Alba, ed. Pp. 49–74. London: Routledge.

NEW YORK STATE EDUCATION DEPARTMENT. 1987. *The Ibero-American Heritage Curriculum Project: Latinos in the Making of the United States of America: Yesterday, Today, and Tomorrow*. First Annual Meeting Conference Proceedings, Albany.

NIETO, SONIA. 2000. *Affirming Diversity: The Sociopolitical Context of Multicultural Education*. 3rd edition. New York: Addison Wesley Longman.

NOGUERA, PEDRO. 2003. How racial identity affects school performance. *Harvard Education Newsletter*, March/April. http://www.edletter.org/past/issues/2003-ma/noguera.shtml (accessed July 1, 2009).

OBOLER, SUZANNE. 1995. *Ethnic Labels, Latino Lives: Identity and Politics of (Re)presentation in the United States*. Minneapolis, MN: University of Minnesota Press.

OGBU, JOHN. 1978. *Minority Education and Caste: The American System in Cross-Cultural Perspective*. New York: Academic Press.

OGBU, JOHN, and HERBERT SIMONS. 1998. Voluntary and involuntary minorities: A cultural-ecological theory of school performance with some implications for education. *Anthropology & Education Quarterly* 29(2):155–188.

OMI, MICHAEL, and HOWARD WINANT. 1994. *Racial Formation in the United States from the Late 1960s to the 1990s*. 2nd edition. New York: Routledge.

OSBORNE, A. BARRY. 1996. Practice into theory into practice: Culturally relevant pedagogy for students we have marginalized and normalized. *Anthropology & Education Quarterly* 27(3):285–314.

PADILLA, FELIX. 1985. *Latino Ethnic Consciousness: The Case of Mexican Americans and Puerto Ricans in Chicago*. Notre Dame, IN: University of Notre Dame Press.

PANTOJAS, GARCÍA. 2005. The Puerto Rican paradox: Colonialism revisited. *Latin American Research Review* 40(3):163–176. http://0-muse.jhu.edu.helin.uri.edu/journals/latin_american_research_review/v040/40.3garcia.html (accessed June 22, 2009 from Project MUSE database).

PAREDES, AMÉRICO. 1978. On ethnographic work among minority groups: A folklorist's perspective. In *New Directions in* Chicano *Scholarship.* R. Romo and R. Paredes, eds. Pp. 1–32. Chicano Studies Monograph Series. La Jolla: Chicano Studies Program, University of California at San Diego.

PASSEL, JEFFREY. 2010. Census history: Counting Hispanics. March 3. http://census.pewsocialtrends.org/2010/census-history-counting-hispanics-2 (accessed November 7, 2010).

PASSEL, JEFFREY, and PAUL TAYLOR. 2009. Who's Hispanic? Pew Hispanic Center. http://pewhispanic.org/reports/report.php?ReportID=111 (accessed June 26, 2009).

PEDRAZA, PEDRO. 1997. Puerto Ricans and the politics of school reform. *Centro* 9(9):74–85. New York: Centro de Estudios Puertorriqueños, Hunter College, CUNY.

PESSAR, PATRICIA. 1995. *A Visa for a Dream.* Needham Heights, MA: Allyn & Bacon.

PEW HISPANIC CENTER. 2006. Cubans in the United States. August 25. http://pewhispanic.org/files/factsheets/23.pdf (accessed June 29, 2009).

———. 2009a. Statistical Portrait of Hispanics in the United States, 2007. Based on U.S. Census Bureau's 2007 American Community Survey. http://pewhispanic.org/factsheets/factsheet.php?FactsheetID=46 (accessed June 24, 2009).

———. 2009b. Mexican Immigrants in the United States, 2008 (Fact Sheet). http://pewhispanic.org/factsheets/factsheet.php?FactsheetID=47 (accessed June 28, 2009).

——— 2010. Statistical Portrait of Hispanics in the United States, 2008. http://pewhispanic.org/factsheets/factsheet.php?FactsheetID=58 (accessed November 7, 2010).

PHILIPS, SUSAN. 1972. Participant structure and communicative competence: Warm Springs children in community and classroom. In *Functions of Language in the Classroom.* Courtney Cazden, Dell Hymes, and Vera John, eds. Pp. 370–394. New York: Teachers College Press.

PORTES, ALEJANDRO, ed. 1994. The new second generation. *International Migration Review* 28(4), Ithaca, NY: CUP Services.

PORTES, ALEJANDRO, and ROBERT BACH. 1985. *Latin Journey: Cuban and Mexican Immigrants in the United States.* Berkeley, CA: University of California Press.

PORTES, ALEJANDRO, and ALEX STEPICK. 1993. *City on the Edge: The Transformation of Miami.* Berkeley, CA: University of California Press.

PORTES, ALEJANDRO, and RAMÓN GROSFOGUEL. 1994. Caribbean diasporas: Migration and ethnic communities. *Annals of the American Academy of Political and Social Science* 533(May):48–69.

PRESTON, JULIA. 2009a. Mexican data show migration to U.S. in decline. *New York Times,* May 15.

———. 2009b. A new strategy on illicit work by immigrants. *New York Times,* July 3, p. 1.

RICOURT, MILAGROS, and RUBY DANTA. 2003. *Hispanas de Queeens: Latino Panethnicity in a New York City Neighborhood.* Ithaca, NY: Cornell University Press.

ROBERTS, SAM. 2009. Study reveals changes among second-generation Hispanics. *New York Times,* May 29.

ROBLES, FRANCES. 2008. Recession drives educated Puerto Ricans to South Florida. *Miami Herald,* August 13. http://juantornoe.blogs.com/hispanic-trending/2008/08/recession-drive.html (accessed June 25, 2009).

RODRÍGUEZ, CLARA. 1989. *Puerto Ricans: Born in the USA.* Boston, MA: Unwin Hyman.

———. 2000. *Changing Race: Latinos, the Census, and the History of Ethnicity in the United States.* New York: New York University Press.

RODRÍGUEZ, CLARA, and HECTOR CORDERO-GUZMAN. 1992. Placing race in context. *Ethnic and Racial Studies* 15(4):523–529.

RODRÍGUEZ, LUIS. 1993. *Always Running: La Vida Loca: Gang Days in L.A.* Willimantic, CT: Curbstone Press.

RODRÍGUEZ, RICHARD. 1982. *Hunger of Memory: The Education of Richard Rodríguez.* Boston, MA: Godine.

RODRÍGUEZ-MORAZZANI, ROBERTO. 1997. Puerto Ricans and educational reform in the U.S.: A preliminary exploration. *Centro* 9(9):59–73. New York: Centro de Estudios Puertorriqueños, Hunter College, CUNY.

ROHTER, LARRY. 2000. Rock en español approaching its final border. *New York Times,* August 6.

ROMANO, OCTAVIO. 1967. Minorities, history and the cultural mystique. *El Grito* 1(1):5–11.

ROSALDO, RENATO. 1985. *Assimilation Revisited.* Stanford Center for Chicano Research. Working Paper Series No. 9 (July). Stanford, CA.

———. 1986. *When Natives Talk Back:* Chicano *Anthropology since the Late Sixties.* Renato Rosaldo Lecture Series Monograph. Vol. 2, pp. 3–21. University of Arizona, Tucson.

———. 1989. *Culture and Truth: The Remaking of Social Analysis.* Boston, MA: Beacon Press.

ROTSTEIN, ARTHUR. 2009. Border deaths up despite apparent dip in crossings. *Cleveland Plain Dealer,*

April 8. http://www.cleveland.com/nation/index. ssf/2009/04/border_deaths_up_despite_appar.html (accessed July 2, 2009).

RUBEL, ARTHUR. 1966. *Across the Tracks*. Austin, TX: University of Texas Press.

SÁNCHEZ KORROL, VIRGINIA. 1988. Latinismo among early Puerto Rican migrants in New York City: A sociohistoric interpretation. In *The Hispanic Experience in the United States: Contemporary Issues and Perspectives*. Edna Acosta-Bélen and Barbara Sjostrom, eds. Pp. 151–162. New York: Praeger.

SANTA ANA, OTTO. 2002. *Brown Tide Rising: Metaphors of Latinos in Contemporary American Public Discourse*. Austin, TX: University of Texas Press.

SANTIAGO-IRIZARRY, Vilma. 2001. *Medicalizing Ethnicity: The Construction of Latino Identity in a Psychiatric Setting*. Ithaca, NY: Cornell University Press.

SANTIAGO, ESMERALDA. 1993. *When I Was Puerto Rican*. New York: Addison-Wesley.

SCHMITT, ERIC. 2001. Census shows big gain for Mexican-Americans. *New York Times*, May 10.

SEDA-BONILLA, EDUARDO. 1977. Who is a Puerto Rican? Problems of sociocultural identity in Puerto Rico. *Caribbean Studies* 17(April–July):105–121.

SMITH, ROBERT. 2005. *Mexican New York: Transnational Lives of New Immigrants*. Berkeley, CA: University of California Press.

SOTO, LOURDES DIAZ. 1997. *Language, Culture, and Power: Bilingual Families and the Struggle for Quality Education*. Albany, NY: State University of New York Press.

STAINS, LAURENCE. 1994. The Latinization of Allentown, Pa. *New York Times Magazine*, May 15.

SUAREZ-OROZCO, MARCELO. 1987. Becoming somebody: Central American immigrants in U.S. inner-city schools. *Anthropology & Education Quarterly* 18(4):287–299.

SUAREZ-OROZCO, MARCELO, and GARY ORFIELD. 2004. Huntington and Hispanics (Letters to the Editor). *Foreign Policy* 142(May–June):88–89.

SURO, ROBERTO. 2004. Huntington and Hispanics (Letters to the Editor). *Foreign Policy* 142(May–June):4–6.

TAKAKI, RONALD. 1990. *Iron Cages: Race and Culture in 19th-Century America*. New York: Oxford University Press.

———. 1993. *A Different Mirror: A History of Multicultural America*. Boston, MA: Little, Brown.

TAPIA, JAVIER. 1998. The schooling of Puerto Ricans: Philadelphia's most impoverished community. *Anthropology & Education Quarterly* 29(3):297–323.

TERRAZAS, AARON, and JEANNE BATALOVA. 2008. The most up-to-date frequently requested statistics on immigrants in the United States. Migration Policy Institute, December 12. http://www.migrationinformation.org/USfocus/print.cfm?ID=714 (accessed June 30, 2009).

THOMAS, PIRI. 1967. *Down These Mean Streets*. New York: Knopf.

TORRES, ANDRES. 1995. *Between Melting Pot and Mosaic: African Americans and Puerto Ricans in the New York Political Economy*. Philadelphia, PA: Temple University Press.

TORRES-SAILLANT, SILVIO. 2005. Dominican Americans. In *Multiculturalism in the United States: A Comparative Guide to Acculturation and Ethnicity* (revised and expanded). John Buenker and Lorman Ratner, eds. Pp. 99–117. New York: Greenwood Press.

U.S. DEPARTMENT OF COMMERCE. 2010. Hispanic-Owned Businesses Grow by more than Double the National Rate. http://www.commerce.gov/print/blog/2010/09/21/hispanic-owned-businesses-grow-more-double-national-rate September 21 (accessed November 7, 2010).

URCIUOLI, BONNIE. 1996. *Exposing Prejudice: Puerto Rican Experiences of Language, Race, and Class*. Boulder, CO: Westview Press.

VEGA, BERNARDO. 1984. *Memoirs of Bernardo Vega*. César Andreu Iglesias, ed. New York: Monthly Review Press.

VILLENAS, SOFIA. 2002. Reinventing *educación* in new Latino communities: Pedagogies of change and continuity in North Carolina. In *Education in the New Latino Diaspora: Policy and the Politics of Identity*. Stanton Wortham, Enrique Murillo Jr., and Edmund T. Hamann, eds. Pp. 17–35. Westport, CT: Ablex Publishing.

WILLIS, PAUL. 1977. *Learning to Labor*. Westmead, England: Saxon House.

WOOD, DANIEL B. 2005. Latino politicians gain clout in US. Christian Science Monitor, May 19. http://www.csmonitor.com/2005/0519/p01s01-uspo.html# (accessed June 15, 2009).

WOOLARD, KATHRYN. 1989. Sentences in the language prison: The rhetorical structuring of an American language policy debate. *American Ethnologist* May(16):268–278.

WORTHAM, STANTON, ENRIQUE MURILLO Jr., and EDMUND T. HAMANN. 2002. Education and policy in the new Latino diaspora. In *Education in the New Latino Diaspora: Policy and the Politics of Identity*. Stanton

Wortham, Enrique Murillo Jr., and Edmund T. Hamann, eds. Pp. 17–35. Westport, CT: Ablex Publishing.

YOUNG LORDS PARTY. 1971. *Palante: Young Lords Party.* New York: McGraw-Hill.

ZENTELLA, ANA CELIA. 1981. Language variety among Puerto Ricans. In *Language in the USA.* Charles Ferguson and Shirley Brice Heath, eds. Pp. 218–238. Cambridge: Cambridge University Press.

———. 1988. Language politics in the U.S.A.: The English-only movement. In *Literature, Language and Politics.* B. J. Craige, ed. Pp. 39–51. Athens, GA: University of Georgia Press.

———. 1997. *Growing Up Bilingual: Puerto Rican Children in New York.* Malden, MA: Blackwell.

———. 2005. Perspectives on language and literacy in Latino families and communities. In *Building on Strength: Language and Literacy in Latino Families and Communities.* Ana Celia Zentella, ed. Pp. 1–12. New York: Teachers College Press.

11

■ ■ ■

Asian Americans

Janet E. Benson, *Kansas State University*

While significant numbers of Asians have migrated to the United States since the nineteenth century, by far the most dramatic population growth has taken place since the passing of the 1965 Immigration Act. Chinese and Japanese came first during the nineteenth century, followed by Filipinos and Koreans; since the 1960s, however, the numbers of Asian Indians, Vietnamese, and other Southeast Asians have rapidly grown, as well as those of Chinese newcomers from the mainland and Taiwan. The term *Asian American*, created during the 1960s for political purposes by second- and third-generation Americans of Asian descent, implies a homogeneity of culture that does not exist (Cheng and Yang 1996:341). Not only does Asia include more than half the world's population, but people of Asian descent live in the Western Hemisphere (in Latin America or the West Indies, for example) and have emigrated from these regions to the United States. They differ culturally from ancestral groups in the country of origin. An "East Indian" (Asian Indian) person from Trinidad, for example, comes from a very different cultural background than that of his or her contemporaries in India.

Many recent immigrants identify themselves first by nationality of birth or ethnic group and only second, if at all, as "American" (often used as a synonym for "white" in everyday language). However, non-Asian Americans frequently cannot distinguish among different Asian groups, or even between Asians and Latinos, and hostility toward one ethnic group is often mistakenly directed at another. Generation is another complicating factor. Even the post-1965 newcomers have produced second and third generations whose members are, to a large degree, culturally American. By 2000, there were more third-generation than second-generation people among Asian Indians, Chinese, and Koreans (Yang 2006:295). Today no one should assume that a person with an "Asian" appearance is foreign-born or non-English-speaking. The individual may very well have been born and raised in the United States with little knowledge of any language other than English.

The first part of this chapter will focus on Asian immigration from the nineteenth century to 1965; the remainder will emphasize post-1965 immigration. Only the largest groups can be covered here. For our purposes these will include the Chinese, Japanese, Korean, Filipino, South Asian (particularly Asian Indian), and main Southeast Asian groups (particularly Vietnamese). Rates of citizenship vary among the groups, depending on recency of arrival and other factors, but the majority are American citizens today.

EARLY ASIAN IMMIGRATION

The Chinese, who were the first Asian immigrants to enter the United States in significant numbers, arrived in Hawaii in the 1830s to cultivate sugarcane and in California during the 1840s to work as miners following the discovery of gold. Chinese laborers built the Central Pacific Railroad (1865–1869) (Takaki 1990:21, 84–86). Japanese immigrants followed in the 1880s, and other Asians arrived after the turn of the century. The Japanese found employment as agricultural laborers, first in Hawaii and then California (Takaki 1990:42–45). Between 1820 and 1930, newcomers from China numbered 377,245, and from Japan, 275,643; not all of these remained in the United States, however. Other Asian groups were much smaller in total numbers due to racist opposition following the Chinese arrival. Before World War II, the total immigrant flow from Korea, India, and the Philippines numbered less than 150,000 (Reimers 1992:3).

Chinese Americans

Old-stock Americans were historically ambivalent about immigration. They supported the ideology of religious and political freedom and wanted cheap labor, but they also wanted to avoid social contact with newcomers. Immigration peaked during the period 1890–1920, with opposition to Southern European immigrants as well as Asians resulting in restrictions being implemented at the end of that period. As the first Asians to arrive, the Chinese were the first to encounter severe discrimination. The Foreign Miners' Tax (originally created to discourage Mexican and Latin American miners) was imposed on the Chinese in the 1850s; by the 1880s, nativist feelings on the West Coast led to mob violence against them (Reimers 1992:1–2). In 1882, Congress passed the Chinese Exclusion Act, "the first federal law ever passed banning a group of immigrants solely on the basis of race or nationality" (Gyory 1998:1). The act suspended immigration for 10 years and was later renewed, with devastating social consequences for Chinese people in the United States. After the Scott Act of 1888, which imposed

further restrictions, even the reentry of Chinese with return certificates was prohibited. Men other than merchants were not allowed to bring their wives from China, nor were Chinese allowed to marry "white" women in California until 1948 (Ling 1998:2; Nee and Nee 1972:18–19). As a result, communities of permanent bachelors developed in the western United States. The situation was somewhat different in Hawaii, where planters encouraged families to settle, and intermarriage between Chinese and Hawaiians took place (Takaki 1990:159, 169). After 1943, when Congress repealed the Chinese Exclusion Act and granted the right of naturalization, Chinese men were allowed to bring their wives to the mainland again. Ninety percent of Chinese immigrants between 1948 and 1952 were women (Reimers 1992:27).

Among the causes suggested for discrimination against the Chinese, and Asian Americans in general, are economics and racism. The Chinese worked for lower wages than those of white miners and laborers, who saw them as competing unfairly. Nativists also accused them of having lower moral standards and being unassimilable due to their race (Reimers 1992:4). Andrew Gyory argues, however, that "the motive force behind the Chinese Exclusion Act was national politicians who seized and manipulated the issue in an effort to gain votes" (1998:1). On the West Coast, the Chinese were systematically excluded from economic sectors where they competed with native-born Americans, for example in gold mining, but they were allowed to fill niches such as the laundry business where their services were needed and they did not compete with established Americans. "Chinatowns," today a magnet for tourists in American cities from San Francisco to New York, are relics of nineteenth-century segregation (see Nee and Nee 1972).

During and after World War II, public attitudes toward Chinese Americans improved somewhat. The United States was an ally of China against Japan, which led to the repeal of the Chinese Exclusion Act. Labor shortages during the war created opportunities for Chinese Americans in defense industries; and ethnic and religious groups and voluntary organizations involved in refugee resettlement lobbied against laws restricting Chinese immigration and naturalization. The United States also experienced relative prosperity after the 1940s, which eased racial tensions (Ling 1998:2; Nee and Nee 1972:154; Reimers 1992:11–12).

Japanese Americans

The Japanese initially worked on Hawaii's sugar plantations but migrated to California by the 1880s, where anti-Japanese feelings quickly developed. The San Francisco school board nearly created an international incident by segregating Japanese students in 1905; it rescinded the order in return for the Gentlemen's Agreement of 1908, which was an understanding between the United States and the Japanese government that the latter would withhold visas from laborers headed to the United States (Reimers 1992:5).

Japanese newcomers wanted to move from being agricultural laborers to farmers, but were resisted by white Californians, who passed restrictive land laws. The Alien Land Law of 1913 (amended in 1920–1921) barred aliens ineligible for citizenship from owning or leasing agricultural land. In practice, this meant "Orientals," all those not classified as "white" or African American. The laws affected Chinese, Koreans, and Asian Indians as well (Leonard 1997:41). The Japanese were declared ineligible for citizenship by the U.S. Supreme Court in 1922, which cited naturalization statutes dating back to 1790. Congress then banned virtually all immigration from Asia in 1924, when it passed the Oriental Exclusion Act, declaring all Asians "ineligible for citizenship" (Reimers 1992:5–6).

The worst case of civil rights violation during World War II took place shortly after Pearl Harbor when President Roosevelt interned 110,000 Japanese Americans, many of whom were American-born citizens, in internment camps far from their homes. The action placated racist fears, despite the fact that no sabotage had been committed by this population. The Japanese Americans were not only deeply shamed and

disillusioned but also lost most of their property, for which they were never adequately compensated (Reimers 1992:9). After World War II, intermarriage between American soldiers and Japanese women became the main reason for immigration from Japan. Between 1947 and 1975, 66,681 women from Japan joined their husbands in the United States (Reimers 1992:23, 26). In recent years Japanese Americans have been characterized by a high rate of intermarriage with established Americans; they are the only Asian American group in which a minority are foreign-born (Okamura 1998:22).

As with other Asian Americans, important generational differences exist. Most Japanese Americans distinguish several generations including *Issei*, the first generation, born in Japan; *Nisei*, the second generation, born in the United States to Issei parents between 1910 and 1940; and *Sansei*, or the third generation, born in the United States to Nisei parents since World War II (Kitano 1976:5–9). Antimiscegenation laws in California between 1905 and 1948 made legal marriage with whites impossible, so there are very low rates of intermarriage with whites among members of the first two generations. However, such marriages were very common among Sansei (O'Brien and Fugita 1991:98).

Japanese Americans had different postwar experiences in Hawaii and on the mainland. Hawaii, with its tourist industry, military bases, and plantations, offered more limited economic opportunities than the West Coast. On the other hand, Japanese Americans there had not suffered the massive property losses that those on the mainland had because of their internment. The return of the famous 442nd soldiers, an all-Japanese American combat unit that distinguished itself during the war, also resulted in political changes. Returning veterans were unwilling to be treated as second-class citizens, and a number of them went to law school on the GI Bill and became active in politics. By 1950, 40 percent of Hawaii's voters were of Japanese ancestry. The Nisei veterans used the Democratic Party as a vehicle for change (Republicans had been dominated by the sugar plantations), campaigning for Hawaii's statehood[1] and entering the state house and senate. Half of the legislators were Nisei, mostly war veterans and law school graduates (O'Brien and Fugita 1991:87–88).

On the mainland, discrimination had been more severe, culminating in internment and massive property loss. However, Japanese Americans were able to make a remarkable comeback after 1945. First, American attitudes toward Japan changed. Once defeated, it was no longer a threat but remained strategically important to the United States as an outpost in the Far East during the cold war. The War Relocation Authority, which had been responsible for interning Japanese Americans, encouraged them to disperse upon their release. Many moved to the Midwest or East, where discrimination was less and smaller numbers encouraged greater acculturation. Japanese Americans also had more resources than many other ethnic groups, particularly a high level of education which exceeded that of whites from 1940 on (O'Brien and Fugita 1991:90–94).

Korean Americans

The earliest-arriving Koreans were a much smaller group than the Chinese or Japanese. A few students came around the turn of the century, but the main flow began when several thousand laborers were recruited to work on plantations in Hawaii. Some former plantation workers later traveled from Hawaii to the West Coast. Nativists complained to the U.S. government, and Japan, in control of Korea at the time, halted emigration (Reimers 1992:5). After World War II, the American military presence in Asia led to marriages between Korean women and American servicemen: 28,205 Korean women emigrated to join their husbands between 1950 and 1975 (Reimers 1992:23).

Filipino Americans

Filipino Americans share a common historical background with Chinese, Japanese, and Korean Americans as labor migrants, particularly in Hawaii, and as groups experiencing exclusion and discrimination before World War II. Some authors

feel that of all the Asian American groups, Filipinos occupy the most marginalized and subordinate status (Okamura 1998:3).

Yen Le Espiritu argues persuasively that Filipino American history must be understood in the context of the colonial and postcolonial relationship between the Philippines and the United States. Following the Spanish–American War in 1898, the United States assumed colonial rule. The U.S. annexation affected all aspects of Philippine life, from the economy to the educational and political systems, and encouraged emigration (Espiritu 1995:2–3, 1996:30). Filipinos were exempted from the Oriental Exclusion Act of 1924 and allowed to immigrate as American nationals, though they lacked full citizenship. The first Filipino newcomers were college students arriving between 1903 and 1910; however, most Filipinos came to Hawaii as plantation workers. The Hawaiian Sugar Planters' Association recruited heavily in the Philippines, bringing 126,000 Filipinos between 1909 (when Japanese workers organized a major strike) and 1946. Although almost half of them eventually returned home, Filipinos numbered 70 percent of plantation workers by the 1930s. They were hit hard by the depression, particularly because, as a recent immigrant group with little education, they had no means of employment other than agricultural or service work. Chinese and Japanese American residents of Hawaii were already employed in the business and skilled or semiskilled sectors by this time. Since most of the Filipino workers recruited were young single men from rural areas, an imbalanced sex ratio existed (five men to one woman in 1930); this in turn contributed to racial stereotyping of Filipinos as violent and immoral (Okamura 1998:37–39).

Most Filipino immigrants who reached the U.S. mainland were former plantation employees who continued to work in agriculture, following crops up and down the West Coast. There were only 6,000 on the mainland in 1924, but they grew to 30,000 by 1930. Discrimination was much worse than in Hawaii. During 1928–1930, race riots directed at Filipinos broke out in farming towns in Washington, California, and Oregon.

In 1930, in Watsonville, California, a mob of whites attacked agricultural workers and killed one person (Okamura 1998:39–40). Whites viewed Filipinos as "unfair competition" because they worked for lower wages and courted white women.[2] Organized labor and other conservative groups lobbied for laws (declared unconstitutional in 1948), which were passed in several states in the 1930s, to keep Filipinos from marrying whites (Okamura 1998:40). Although the War Department and Hawaiian sugar planters wanted Filipino labor, opposition grew during the 1920s and 1930s from nativist groups and trade unions. As part of the Philippine independence bill, the country was given an annual quota of only 50 (Reimers 1992:6–7). Between 1946 and 1965, only 34,000 Filipinos came to the United States, 16,000 of them wives of American servicemen.

Asian Indians

Early South Asian, or Asian Indian, immigrants consisted mainly of a few thousand Sikhs (a minority religious group) from the Punjab in north India, farmers who came to California to work as agricultural laborers around 1900. Capital-intensive agriculture and large-scale irrigation led to strong labor demands by the 1870s, with Asian immigrant groups contributing in different ways to agricultural development. The Japanese, for example, came as contract laborers, but many became tenants and specialized in labor-intensive crops like strawberries (Leonard 1997:40–41). The Punjabis cultivated rice in northern California and grapes in central California and established cotton growing in the southern Imperial Valley. Although they initially worked as laborers, many were soon farming in their own right until the U.S. Supreme Court's Thind decision of 1923. In this ruling, people from India were considered Caucasian but not "white persons" as popularly defined. This made Asian Indians "aliens ineligible to citizenship" (like other Asian groups) and subject to California's Alien Land Laws, discussed earlier. Citizenship was not granted until 1946.

By 1917, Congress had created the Asiatic Barred Zone, an area including India, from which immigration was banned (Reimers 1992:5–6). The farm workers from India were placed in the same situation that the Chinese had faced earlier: they were not allowed to bring wives from India (since immigration was banned and Asians in any case were "aliens ineligible for naturalization"), nor were they allowed to marry "white" women due to miscegenation laws.

Karen Leonard has written a fascinating account of how a new ethnic group, the so-called "Mexican Hindus" (the misnamed "Hindus" were actually Sikhs), developed due to discriminatory laws and practices. Many Punjabi Sikhs already had wives and families in India but were not allowed to bring them to the United States. Because most of the immigrants were male, those who wanted a stable family life had to marry women of an ethnic group other than their own. White justices of the peace would not conduct marriages between Sikh men and white women but would for Sikhs and the darker-skinned Mexican women, with whom Sikhs often worked. Husband and wife could communicate verbally but only in limited ways, neither fully mastering the other's language. Children generally learned Spanish and grew up culturally more similar to mothers than fathers. The current generation tends to identify more with their Indian ("Hindu") heritage, but has minimal knowledge of it and little in common with recent immigrants from South Asia (Leonard 1997:47–57).

The War Brides Act and Asian Immigration

The passage of the War Brides Act in December 1945 allowed spouses and minor children of American servicemen to join the men and become citizens more easily. In spite of this, Korean and Japanese wives were barred from entering the United States prior to 1952 because they were members of races "ineligible for immigration or naturalization." After Congress changed the law, several thousand Asians (from a total of 117,000 women) entered under the act.

The end of racial barriers to immigration and naturalization allowed other wives to join husbands after the end of the War Brides Act in 1952. A total of 165,839 wives came between 1947 and 1975, with by far the largest numbers from Japan, the Philippines, and Korea (Reimers 1992:21–23).

Discrimination and Prejudice

As seen in this account, the early Asian immigrants encountered nativist reactions ranging from negative newspaper editorials to mob violence, restrictive land laws, confinement to internment camps, and denial of citizenship rights. Like other minority groups, Asian Americans experienced segregation in the wider society well into the 1940s and 1950s with regard to public facilities like schools, restaurants, and swimming pools (see Leonard 1997:61). Because of their small numbers and vulnerable position, individual groups (the Japanese internees, for example) were seldom willing or able to protest effectively against discrimination. This situation changed after World War II, when veterans returned no longer willing to accept second-class citizenship, and especially after the civil rights movement of the 1960s.

POST-1965 IMMIGRATION

The New Asian Americans

By the 1950s, Asian immigration to the United States had slowed to a trickle (about 15,000 per year) due to restrictive immigration laws. However, it dramatically increased after 1965 because of two factors, the 1965 Immigration Act and the end of the war in Vietnam (Lee 1998:10). The 1965 act reflected new relationships between the United States and Asian countries, less discriminatory attitudes in general, and the effects of the civil rights movement. It abolished the old national origins quota system, which privileged Northern European immigrants and severely restricted flows from other countries, and it emphasized family reunification (Takaki 1990:419).

Because Asian Americans were a small minority in 1965, few supporters of the act expected the dramatic increase in Asian immigration that took place. However, Asians tend to have larger families than the American norm, and once established, newcomers often sponsor relatives. As a result, although total numbers are small (an estimated 14.9 million in 2006, including those of mixed ancestry) (U.S. Bureau of the Census 2007a), Asian Americans are increasing exponentially—at a much faster rate than Latinos or African Americans. Although only about 5 percent of the U.S. population (U.S. Bureau of the Census 2008) at the present rate of growth they will equal African Americans in number (75 million) and proportion (13 percent) by the end of the twenty-first century (Yang 2006:310).

Some older, established Asian American groups, such as Chinese, Korean, and Filipino, have received an influx of recent immigrants. Chinese from the mainland, Taiwan, and Hong Kong have arrived in the United States, particularly on the East and West coasts, and Korean and Filipino populations have mushroomed. One group, the Japanese Americans, has declined due to current low immigration. Asian American diversity has also increased, as more groups are named in every census. The South Asian immigrant population, for example (which consists largely of Asian Indians but also includes newcomers from Pakistan, Bangladesh, Sri Lanka, Nepal, and Bhutan), is almost entirely a product of the post-1965 period. The ability to sponsor family members has made a dramatic difference to Asian American populations in the United States. With some exceptions, recent immigration involves more families and more women in relation to men than in earlier periods (Chen 1992:6; Lee 1998:1; Ling 1998:2, 113).

The 1990 Immigration Act increased the numbers of legal immigrants[3] but also created an annual quota for family members brought in by sponsoring relatives. The preference quotas have also been changed to reflect the old national origins quota system of 1925, so that the pool of legal entrants is now dominated by Latin Americans and Asians from only a few countries, particularly China, Korea, the Philippines, and India (see Salins, as cited in Williams 1996:24).

The estimated total in Table 11-1 does not include children of mixed Asian and White marriages (about 1 million people). "Other Asian" refers to people reporting ancestry from a group not detailed in the survey or two or more Asian groups. "Other Asian not specified" refers to people who checked the "other Asian" response category or gave generic terms (U.S. Bureau of the Census 2007b).

According to recent estimates, Chinese (mainland and Taiwanese) and Asian Indians are the two largest Asian American groups, followed by Filipinos, Vietnamese, and Koreans. Approximately 1.7 million residents belong to other Asian groups including those combining two or more Asian categories (U.S. Bureau of the Census 2007b). Asian Indians, Koreans, and Vietnamese have outnumbered Japanese Americans since 1990 (Lee 1998:15–16). Civil war in Vietnam and the neighboring countries of Laos and Cambodia began a massive refugee flow in 1975, which continued into the 1990s and fundamentally altered American demographics. There were only about 20,000 Southeast Asians in the United States in 1975, but by September 1987, they totaled well over 1 million people (Haines 1989:2).

The Vietnam War and the Southeast Asian Refugees

To understand the how and why of the sudden increase of Southeast Asians in the United States, as well as American reactions to the refugees, some knowledge of the Vietnam War is essential. Most of these events seem remote and irrelevant to young people today. However, 15 years of military involvement in Vietnam, Laos, and Cambodia had a profound and lasting effect on both America and the war-torn Southeast Asian countries. By 1975, 60,000 Americans were dead and 300,000 wounded, and the country was deeply divided over the war's morality (Robinson 1998:7). American political involvement in Southeast Asia created military, economic, and personal ties as well as (in the minds of at least some Americans) moral responsibility for the fate of those who had worked for or had been associated with Americans.

Following the withdrawal of the French colonialists in 1954, the partition of Vietnam into North and South, and the creation of Cambodia, Laos, and Vietnam as independent states, the United States became increasingly embroiled in the wars and internal conflicts of these countries (Robinson 1998:12). It was the cold war era, and American foreign policy emphasized opposition to Communist influence. In Vietnam's case, this meant supporting the South Vietnamese government against the North Vietnamese Communists led by Ho Chi Minh.

TABLE 11-1 U.S. Asian alone population (selected groups)

	Estimate
Total	13,233,287
Asian Indian	2,570,166
Bangladeshi	72,237
Cambodian	218,624
Chinese (except Taiwanese)	2,953,091
Filipino	2,412,446
Hmong	201,701
Indonesian	61,384
Japanese	803,092
Korean	1,344,171
Laotian	195,201
Malaysian	17,077
Pakistani	195,037
Sri Lankan	27,965
Taiwanese	92,501
Thai	154,235
Vietnamese	1,508,489
Other Asian	292,107
Other Asian, not specified	113,763

Source: U.S. Census Bureau, 2007 American Community Survey, B02006, Asian alone by selected groups.

Meanwhile, in neighboring Laos, leftist fighters known as the Pathet Lao opposed the government of Prince Souvanna Phouma, and North Vietnamese troops moved soldiers and supplies down the Ho Chi Minh Trail into South Vietnam. To interfere with this supply line, in 1961 the American Central Intelligence Agency began to train a highland ethnic minority, the Hmong, as guerrilla fighters. By 1967, when the Americans had turned to conventional warfare and guerrilla tactics were becoming increasingly irrelevant, the Hmong guerrillas numbered nearly 40,000. They suffered terrible losses, with 18,000–20,000 killed in combat and 120,000, nearly half the population, becoming internal refugees by 1973. Following a cease-fire agreement that year, U.S. forces withdrew and the situation became increasingly desperate for the Hmong. In the spring of 1975, as a Communist victory was about to take place in Laos, the Americans finally agreed to rescue Hmong leader Vang Pao, his most important officers, and their families. About 2,500 Hmong were airlifted into Thailand. Abandoned by their former American allies and fearful of retribution, thousands of other Hmong, as well as lowland Lao who were associated with the previous government, sought refuge in Thailand (Robinson 1998:12–14). Attacked by the Pathet Lao and Vietnamese troops in 1977 and 1978, 100,000 Hmong and other highland groups fled to Thailand by 1980 (Robinson 1998:107).

When Saigon fell to the Vietnamese Communists on April 30, 1975, an unprecedented refugee flight out of Southeast Asia began. The U.S. State Department was unprepared for the rapidity of South Vietnam's collapse, and departure conditions were chaotic. Approximately 130,000 Vietnamese refugees managed to escape within the first few weeks of Saigon's fall, including a segment of elite with close ties to the U.S. government. They were quickly settled in America with the help of voluntary organizations, particularly the Catholic Church. A second wave peaked in 1980–1981 when the new Vietnamese government expelled Chinese from Vietnam; large numbers of

Vietnamese fled by sea in small, crowded boats; and lowland Lao and Hmong escaped from Laos (Haines 1989:2; Rutledge 1992:5–6). Accounts of the "boat people" being repeatedly attacked by Thai pirates, or being pushed back into the ocean by hostile residents of neighboring countries, alarmed the international community and led to increased humanitarian efforts.

Cambodia's government also experienced rapid collapse in April 1975. The Communist Party of Kampuchea (the Khmer Rouge, or "Red" Khmer, supported by the North Vietnamese) took Phnom Penh, the country's capital, on April 17 and immediately began a campaign to empty the cities and move all the people to the countryside. Markets and currency were to be abolished and cooperatives established with communal eating arrangements. Buddhist monks were set to work in the fields, and leaders of the U.S.-backed Lon Nol regime were targeted for execution. The entire Vietnamese minority population (between 170,000 and 270,000 people) was expelled in 1975, many Cambodians and Chinese fleeing with them into Vietnam. Up to 2 million people died in this brutally enforced social revolution (death was the punishment for any fault); many Cambodians witnessed the murder of close relatives (Robinson 1998:10–12).

The U.S. government did not initially plan to admit large numbers of refugees. High-ranking Vietnamese officials and military personnel and their families were to be evacuated, as well as a token number of Cambodians and Laotians. However, conflict in all three states created so many refugees that "first asylum" countries (neighboring states like Thailand, Malaysia, and Indonesia) and the then-British colony of Hong Kong were soon overwhelmed. Because of U.S. involvement in Vietnam, support for the refugees was seen as an American responsibility. While "first asylum" countries felt that the "displaced persons" should be sent home, the countries of origin did not want them. The use of the term *refugee* for this population allowed the United States to blame Communism for the exodus and to draw on international aid (Robinson 1998:7–8). Refugee camps were created and funded, processing centers were set up in the Philippines and Indonesia to resettle refugees more rapidly, and a number of countries, including the United States, agreed to admit more refugees.

The presence of Vietnamese, Lao, Cambodians, Hmong, and other Southeast Asians in the United States cannot be understood without reference to this brief history. At least in the case of the early arrivals, most refugees did not want to leave their homes and relatives, but were forced out by political circumstances. Faced with reprisals in their own countries, or living in spartan refugee camps with no chance of returning home, they chose to start over in a new and unfamiliar third country. For most, this meant separation from family for years if not forever.

In addition to these Southeast Asian ethnic groups, another subset of the refugee population are the *Amerasians*—children of American servicemen and Vietnamese women. As children of the enemy, they were denied education and economic opportunities in Vietnam and relegated to the lowest social status. Special efforts were made to bring them to the United States. By the 1990s, the last Southeast Asians to enter as refugees (rather than as immigrants sponsored by families) included Amerasians and people who had been confined to Vietnamese Communist "reeducation camps" because of their close contact with Americans. The Amerasians and other groups from Southeast Asia have greatly increased the diversity of America's Asian heritage population.

The 1980 Refugee Act

After 1980, a major shift in American policy permitted large numbers of refugees, including Vietnamese and other Asians, to enter the United States for the first time. Prior to 1980, refugee acts or the use of presidential "parole power"[4]— an executive decision made by the president through his attorney general to admit whole groups of people—mainly focused on European refugees fleeing Communist countries. (Hong Kong Chinese were, however, admitted in 1962.) Large numbers of Vietnamese were initially paroled, as well as Cubans who fled after Castro

came to power in 1959 (Reimers 1992:157–159). Problems with the ad hoc, inconsistent nature of refugee policy and the basically anti-Communist definition of "refugee" led to major reforms of the 1980 Refugee Act. The United States formally accepted the United Nations definition of "refugee," namely, any person outside his or her country who is unable or unwilling to return "because of persecution, or a well-founded fear of persecution, on account of race, religion, nationality, membership of a particular social group, or political opinion" (Reimers 1992:194).[5] The act also created refugee programs in the U.S. Department of Health, Education, and Welfare, and allocated funding for refugees (Reimers 1992:195–197). Since then, the Office of Refugee Resettlement has been responsible for allocating federal money to state-level agencies to pay for resettlement costs.

The Significance of Refugee Status

In discussing displaced populations, a distinction is generally made between refugees and immigrants. The United Nations definition applies to individuals unable to return home because of the possibility of persecution or death; they are exempt from immigrant quotas (Rutledge 1992:10). Unlike immigrants, who may have years to plan a move from one country to another, refugees are often forced to risk their lives in a hasty departure. In actuality, it is not always easy to distinguish between political and economic motives for flight. "Refugee" is a temporary legal status that entitles people to enter the United States and to receive medical aid, cash assistance, and other benefits for a limited period of time. From the beginning, the refugee resettlement program has emphasized self-sufficiency, due to taxpayer concerns about costs. The government also expects that refugees will soon become U.S. citizens. In fact many of the escapees from Vietnam, Laos, and Cambodia are now naturalized Americans, while their children have been born or largely raised in the United States.

The fact that refugees receive government assistance has been misunderstood and often resented by established Americans. It is important to understand that once awarded refugee status by the government, an individual has the legal right to be in the United States and to receive certain types of aid. The government's assumption is that people who have recently fled for their lives will need medical and mental health services, initial financial support, and perhaps language instruction in order to adapt and become self-supporting.

Most recent arrivals from Southeast Asia today are not refugees, but legal immigrants sponsored by relatives. The relatives undertake full legal responsibility for their support, as individuals with immigrant status receive no government assistance. With this background, we turn to a more detailed discussion of contemporary Asian American groups.

ASIAN AMERICANS TODAY

Chinese Americans

Nineteenth-century Chinese immigrants were relatively homogenous culturally, since most came from Kwangtung Province in southeast China, and they lived in Hawaii or the West Coast. As anti-Chinese sentiment peaked, many returned to China. Others moved to the central and eastern United States, which were relatively safer regions and offered more job opportunities. Until the 1960s, highly educated Chinese immigrants were often barred from professional occupations and restricted to menial work (Chen 1992:5).

In his book *Chinatown No More* (1992), the anthropologist Hsing-shui Chen describes a considerably more diverse post-1965 flow of newcomers from China and argues that contrary to popular stereotypes, most Chinese immigrants do not live in isolated Chinese communities ("Chinatowns"). Some of the first post-1965 immigrants were college students from Hong Kong and Taiwan who were studying in the United States when immigration laws changed and who decided to stay on[6] (1992:6). Many others came through family sponsorship. By the early 1980s, Chinese from Taiwan, Hong Kong, mainland China, Southeast Asia, the Caribbean,

and South America were present in New York City, where Mandarin, Taiwanese, and other languages besides Cantonese could be heard (1992:vii–ix). As early as the late 1960s, however, the Chinese American population was divided into "Chinatown Chinese," older immigrants involved in the ethnic economy, and "non-Chinatown Chinese," professionals and university faculty living in white neighborhoods. Examples of outer-city or suburban settlements of Chinese Americans include Flushing and Elmhurst in New York City (the site of Chen's study) and Monterey Park in California (Chen 1992:6–7; Fong 1994).

While the pre-1965 Chinese immigrants had been manual workers, professional and technical workers form the largest group of Chinese immigrants today due to immigration law preferences. In addition, many are entrepreneurs or factory workers. Decreased job discrimination has also meant more opportunities for the second generation of these new Chinese Americans, born and raised in the United States. Favored locations for new immigrants, because of expanding job markets and good public transportation, have been San Francisco, New York City, and Los Angeles (Chen 1992:8–9). While the Los Angeles region exceeds all other centers in terms of total Asian population[7] (Cheng and Yang 1996:308), by some estimates as many as one-fourth of all new Chinese immigrants are now in the New York City metropolitan area. Immigrants provide a cheap labor force that has helped revive declining industries like garment manufacturing.[8] Immigrants also invest capital in stores and small retail shops, which produce taxes for the city and provide jobs for native-born Americans as well as other immigrants (Chen 1992:28–32). Though commonly scapegoated as "taking jobs away from Americans," the reverse—job creation—is more likely to be true.

Chen argues that Chinatowns have changed since the 1940s. The repeal of the Chinese Exclusion Act, access to citizenship, voting rights laws, war bride legislation, and the family reunification policy have all weakened the traditional bachelor organizations of urban

Chinatowns. Second-generation Chinese are more assimilated into the majority population and not reliant on ethnic businesses (1992:11). Although New York City's Chinatown has mushroomed in recent years, many new immigrant Chinese live elsewhere.

Chen points out that Chinese Americans are not homogenous (see also Lien 2008; Ong 2003). Those born and raised in the United States since the 1950s tend to be highly educated and middle class, are unlikely to know any language other than English well, and may feel they have little in common with new arrivals. Post-1965 immigrants are very diverse in terms of education attained, level of English spoken, and other characteristics. Chen observes that Chinese of different classes do not interact with each other. Although a "Chinese" ethnic consciousness does emerge in some situations, such as political campaigns, Chen found that the ethnic group concept was not suitable for his purposes. He focused instead on differences within the Queens (Taiwanese) Chinese, who, occupationally speaking, fall into four classes: working class (workers in factories, restaurants, and stores); small business owners; the new middle class (professionals, medical doctors, civil servants, university faculty); and capitalists (owners of businesses with more than 30 employees). Considerable mobility takes place among these classes, with the middle class moving in and out of small business, for example, and workers becoming capitalists (1992:42–44).

Like many other researchers, Chen found that the revolution in international communications has removed barriers between countries. What is true for Taiwan is no less true for most of the other Asian countries discussed in this chapter: jet travel, the telephone, television, video recorders, cell phones, and the Internet make possible the rapid exchange of information and the maintenance of family relationships across continents (see Cheng and Yang 1996). Travel to the United States is seen as desirable, and friends and relatives who have made the journey can easily give up-to-date information and advice. Modern communications also influence ethnic identity, since people who can travel frequently from one continent to another may

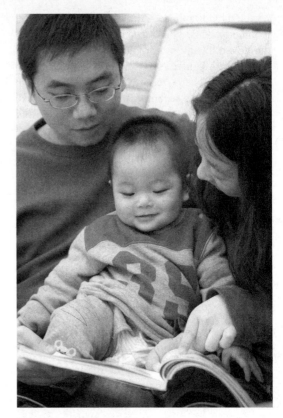

Chinese American family.

be less willing to settle permanently in, and identify with, a new homeland. Especially when first trying to establish themselves, immigrants may maintain family units spread between continents. Among his sample of 100 households, Chen found 19 cases of what he calls "divided family ties" (all among working-class or business-class people)—cases in which a husband or wife cared for children alone while the spouse was back in Taiwan. Taiwan residents refer to these absent spouses as "wife in America" or "astronaut" (in the case of a husband who has to fly frequently back and forth). Some couples come as tourists, leaving children temporarily in Taiwan with grandparents. Child care is extremely expensive in New York City, and both parents must work to support themselves; also, boys older than 16 are of military-service age and are not permitted to travel until the service has been completed (Chen 1992:54–56).

Not only do patterns of migration differ today from those of the early Chinese, with families arriving rather than single males, but motives also differ. Economic gain is not the only consideration. Parents value education highly and want their children to learn English, and some wish to remove their children from Taiwan's high-pressure educational system. Sponsorship is another important factor; 80 percent of immigrant Chinese are said to have come to the United States through kin sponsorship (Chen 1992:59, 65–66). Once in the United States, both men and women work (in 68 of 100 households in Chen's sample), resulting in a median family income that is higher than the national average (1992:76).

Chen found that working-class immigrants, who do not know English, find language so great a barrier that they prefer to work in businesses run by other Chinese: garment and knitting factories, for example, and Chinese restaurants. Immigrants often suffer downward social mobility; women teachers from Taiwan, for example, find it difficult or impossible to work as teachers in the United States. Their children have adjustment problems because parents do not know enough English, or have enough time, to adequately supervise them. For small business owners, earning money is the most important value; they often bring capital from Taiwan, though owners may also start out as workers, accumulate capital, and borrow from banks. Not all of these businesses are successful, and busy entrepreneurs often have problems with their children as well. Professionals, by contrast, have more stable family lives, encounter fewer language problems, usually own their own homes, and frequently start businesses. Female community leaders come from this class (Chen 1992:248–254).

Japanese Americans

Japanese Americans are the only Asian American group that has not experienced rapid growth during the post-1965 era. They are distinguished by relatively high levels of income and education and high levels of intermarriage with white Americans among the third and later generations. The degree of intermarriage is especially remarkable given the rampant discrimination they faced before and during World War II. Less than 40 years after internment, half of all new Japanese American marriages took place with whites. David O'Brien and Stephen Fugita attribute this assimilation to a number of factors: the postwar economic boom, various government actions, and such cultural factors as high education levels, a strong work ethic, and emphasis on group survival (1991:84–85).

After release from the internment camps, mainland Japanese Americans experienced dramatic changes in employment opportunities. Formerly they had been excluded from professional services and public administration, but new openings were available to them in a booming postwar economy. By 1980, 21.8 percent were in professional services (although 35.9 percent were in trade, a common prewar occupation given other constraints on employment), and 4.8 percent were still employed in agriculture versus 3 percent for the general population (O'Brien and Fugita 1991:95).

One issue that eventually united Japanese Americans of different generations and social classes was the redress movement (also known as the reparations movement), which called for an apology from the U.S. government and financial restitution for the internment of Japanese Americans during the war. It began in the late 1960s on the West Coast and had become a priority issue by 1974. The Japanese American community was not always united in support of it; some feared a backlash by white Americans or felt that payment would trivialize their experiences. After concerted efforts by Japanese Americans, with help from the Jewish lobby, the Civil Liberties Act of 1988 was finally signed into law by President Reagan. It mandated a payment of $20,000 to all living internees and a formal apology by the government. O'Brien and Fugita note that "only in the 1980s with the discussion and soul searching associated with the successful redress movement has the community as a whole cleansed itself of many of the repressed and unresolved feelings toward the incarceration"

(O'Brien and Fugita 1991:81). Before this, many Japanese Americans were afraid to show reactions that might lead to reprisals from white Americans, but they are not likely to feel this hesitancy in contemporary America's more open social climate.

Filipino Americans

Like the nineteenth-century Chinese immigrants, early Filipino migrants came to Hawaii and California to work primarily as manual laborers. Also, as in the case of Chinese Americans, ongoing immigration since 1965 has resulted in a much more diverse Filipino American population today (Espiritu 1996). Third- and fourth-generation Filipino Americans do not speak any of the Philippine languages, and they tend to have a higher socioeconomic status than the first generation. Like the children of the post-1965 immigrants, they are more integrated into U.S. society than newcomers. On the other hand, almost two-thirds of Filipino Americans are foreign-born and speak a Philippine language at home. The majority (71 percent) live in the western United States, particularly California and Hawaii (Okamura 1998:34–35).

Because of *chain migration*, in which earlier immigrants sponsor other family members, Filipino American numbers have doubled with every census. Since 90 percent prefer to live near relatives, the number of Filipino Americans in specific states and cities increased over time (Okamura 1998:42–43).

Agriculture employed most Filipino Americans until recently; even as late as the 1960s, they made up 47 percent of plantation employees in Hawaii and 31 percent of agricultural laborers in California. Many are also service workers in factories and restaurants. Shortly after the 1965 act was passed, several thousand Filipino doctors, engineers, and scientists arrived to work in the United States, and during the 1980s thousands of Filipino nurses obtained H1-B visas[9] during a nursing shortage in the United States (Okamura 1998:45; Williams 1996:16).

The anthropologist Jonathan Okamura argues that Filipinos have experienced little occupational mobility since 1980, in spite of a relatively high educational status among post-1965 immigrants. In California, Filipinos have the highest high school dropout rate and, in the case of the third and fourth generations, are underrepresented in higher education. Service work is still the most important occupational category for men and the second largest for women, especially in Hawaii, where the tourist industry is a big employer. Filipino Americans have very high work force participation rates (75 percent among persons aged 16 or older). Median household incomes ($42,600 in 1989) were higher than those of both Asian Americans and whites in the late 1980s, simply because the average Filipino American household had more working adults (Okamura 1998:44–47).

Okamura argues that Filipino Americans have been particularly disadvantaged by the "model minority" stereotype of Asian Americans, the popular assumption that all are highly educated and well-to-do. Beginning in 1986, Filipino Americans were no longer considered a special target group for recruitment and admission in the University of California's affirmative action program. According to Okamura, not only did their acceptance rate decline at UCLA in the 1990s, but Filipino American enrollment at UCLA and Berkeley also decreased. In July 1995, the University of California Board of Regents voted to eliminate affirmative action programs based on racial and other preferences starting in the fall of 1997. Okamura argues that Filipino Americans also face employment discrimination due to their accented English and stereotyping, perpetuated by ethnic jokes in the mass media (Okamura 1998:51–52).

South Asians

South Asia includes India, Pakistan, Bangladesh, Sri Lanka, Nepal, and Bhutan. Asian Indians are by far the largest South Asian group represented in the United States today (according to current estimates, the second largest Asian group after Chinese) and will be discussed here more.

Culturally and linguistically, South Asia is one of the world's most complex regions. Although its roots extend back more than 5,000 years to the Indus Valley civilization, it has been periodically invaded by newcomers entering through the northwest passes or by sea: Greeks, Mughals, Pathans, Portuguese, Dutch, French, English—all have left their mark. Within India, there are two major language families, Indo-Aryan (a branch of Indo-European) in the north and Dravidian (consisting of indigenous languages) in the south. Modern states in India and Pakistan have been formed along linguistic lines (e.g., Andhra Pradesh in the south is dominated by speakers of Telugu, a Dravidian language), although many people speak more than one language, including English. At least within India and Pakistan, individuals tend to identify strongly with regional cultures of the different states.

Modern South Asia is very much a product of British colonial history. The British came first as traders during the period of Mughal rule and stayed to gradually take control of the Indian subcontinent. By the time India gained independence in 1947, the British had created a system of government and law and a modern infrastructure in the region. It also created a mostly Hindu, English-speaking elite oriented toward the West. At Independence, India was divided; Partition led to the creation of Pakistan with its two wings, East and West, separated by 1,500 miles of territory. Millions of people became internal refugees, and the older generation has never forgotten the violence of that period. Following civil war in 1971, West Pakistan became simply Pakistan and East Pakistan, Bangladesh.

By the time of Sri Lanka's independence in 1948, a Western-educated Tamil elite coexisted uneasily with a Buddhist majority largely educated in the indigenous Sinhalese language. Colonialism created conditions favorable to emigration, including political and economic ties between India and the West and a highly educated, English-speaking professional elite who could adapt quickly to U.S. culture and society. Almost all of the early post-1965 immigrants studied in English-language schools in India

(Williams 1996:12). Conflict in the region over the past two decades (civil war in Sri Lanka between Buddhists and Tamils, Sikh separatism in the Punjab) has also spurred minorities to leave South Asia. One important feature of the South Asian diaspora has been the establishment of Hindu temples, Muslim mosques, and Sikh gurudwaras in many American cities, sometimes against the opposition of local established Americans. Indian Christians, some recent converts and others with a 2,000-year-old religious tradition, have also added new elements to Christianity in the United States (Williams 1996:5).

Some of the Asian Indian Christians were among the first of the "pioneers" to enter the United States after 1965. Numerous Indians were students in American universities at the time and decided to stay on to work in the United States. They were engineers, physicians, scientists, and university faculty; many hold prominent positions in their fields today. This pattern continues as every fall, bright young graduate students arrive from India to be welcomed by their American university's India Student Association. Many of them will later work for an American employer and obtain H1-B status. This "brain drain" is the result of India's Western-oriented educational system and (until recently) stagnant economy. Indians and other South Asians seek better employment, the opportunity to conduct cutting-edge research, and the best education for their children (Williams 1996:12–13).

In the 1960s and 1970s, and again in the 1990s, employer demands for scientifically trained specialists from foreign countries led to the growth of Indian populations in major cities like New York and Dallas (see Brettell 2005). Earlier in this period, the beginning of Medicare and Medicaid, coupled with the drafting of physicians and nurses for the Vietnam War, resulted in a shortage of health personnel. Because of India's colonial background, Indians were able to establish professional credentials in the United States and adapt quickly (Williams 1996:13). Today, Indian physicians and nurses can be found working in isolated rural settings and big-city hospitals where most established

American physicians prefer not to practice. They provide services to populations who would otherwise go without care.

Indian Christian nurses had a particularly interesting role to play in immigration. A nursing shortage in the 1970s led to the recruitment of nurses in India by agents of American hospitals. Almost all of these nurses were Christian because, until recently, nursing occupied a very low social status in India due to its polluting aspects. The nurses in turn brought their husbands and other family members. In the case of other Asian Indian groups, a man with high professional qualifications usually was offered a job or a position and then returned home to India to marry, or brought his wife and children to join him (Williams 1996:16–18). The sponsorship of relatives in recent decades has brought less highly educated and less English-proficient Indians to the United States, creating a more socioeconomically diverse population, as in the cases of other Asian American immigrant groups. It is more difficult for elderly relatives and non-English-speaking spouses to adjust (although highly educated men often have highly educated wives who are also technicians, teachers, or professionals). In the 1990s, with the growth of the computer industry and a shortage of technically trained American personnel, U.S. computer companies demanded an increase in H1-B visas in order to bring more computer specialists from India to the United States. Development of an Indian computer industry and a growing economy at home have led to increased transnationalism today, as elite migrants maintain (often work-related) social relationships between the homeland and the host country. Asian Indians have the highest population growth rate of all Asian groups (133 percent in the 1990s) and census estimates suggest that they are currently moving into second place among Asian American ethnic groups relative to group size (Yang 2006:294).

Korean Americans

Pre-1965 Korean immigrants shared a number of characteristics with Chinese, Japanese, and Filipino immigrants and endured similar experiences of racial exclusion. Because of U.S. military involvement in Asia, Korean women married to American servicemen have been one subgroup in the immigration flow since World War II to the present. However, as did other Asian Americans, many came to join close relatives through the family reunification provisions of the 1965 Immigration Act. There are also reports of middle-class people being recruited by Korean brokers to work in low-level occupations like poultry processing. The immigrants pay high fees to the brokers, who require that they stay in the job for a certain period of time.[10] One of the major motivations for emigration is a better future for their children.

Korean Americans are probably best known for running small businesses, such as greengrocer shops and liquor stores, in large urban centers like New York City and Los Angeles. However, they also operate restaurants and stores in many small towns throughout the United States, especially near army bases. The entrepreneurs are often relatively well-educated, middle-class people who lack the English-language skills and credentials to move into professional occupations (though their children may do so); self-employment, which represents downward social mobility for many, is the best option given their constraints. Other Korean Americans, particularly those who came originally as graduate students, do have the English proficiency and skills to enter mainstream occupations.

A great deal has been written about one current issue related to Korean Americans, namely, conflict between Korean shopkeepers and African Americans in urban settings (Abelmann and Lie 1995; Kim 1999; Lie and Abelman 1999; Min 1996; K. Park 1999). On April 29, 1992, South Central Los Angeles flared into flames and violence that continued for three days and attracted national attention. Sparked by the Rodney King verdict, in which white police officers were acquitted in the beating of an African American suspect, the riots destroyed many businesses in South Central Los Angeles and Koreatown. While the violence began as a protest against white society, the media recast it as group conflict between two minorities; in fact, all ethnic groups were

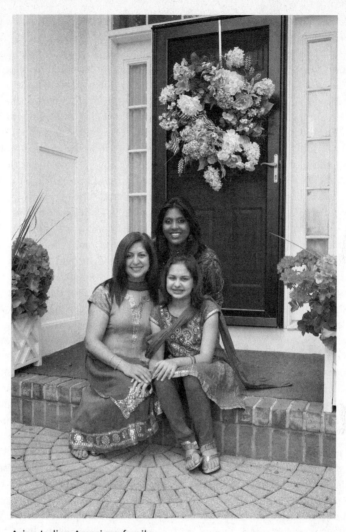

Asian Indian American family.

involved, both as victims and looters. Pictures of armed Korean store owners reproduced a negative stereotype of Korean businesspeople as ruthless exploiters and vigilantes (Kim 1999:1). Korean merchants suffered catastrophic economic losses, $350 million to $400 million and approximately 2,300 Korean American businesses out of a total of 4,500 damaged or destroyed. Half could not rebuild at all, and many lost their homes (Kim and Kim 1999:26).

Kwang Chung Kim and others have argued that Korean merchants in Los Angeles were victimized twice, first by economic loss and psychological trauma and again when they were blamed for the destruction of their own property: "Thus, along with African Americans' racism, jealousy, and scapegoating, Korean merchants' rude treatment of customers, prejudice, economic exploitation, cultural misunderstandings, limited assimilation, and foreignness were all identified as sources of the conflict" (Kim 1999:2).

Kim points out that the Los Angeles racial disturbance does not represent the whole

Korean American experience; racial relations in other cities, like Chicago and New York, are similar in some ways to those in Los Angeles and different in others (1999:2). One constant is the structural position of Korean merchants, literally "caught in the middle" (Min 1996) between poor urban minorities and dominant white society. White-owned corporations—industries providing "good" jobs as well as large retail stores—had abandoned poor minority urban neighborhoods by the 1970s, just as Korean immigrants were beginning to arrive in the United States. Unable to compete with white-owned chains in middle-class locales, Korean entrepreneurs purchased inexpensive property in inner-city neighborhoods and started small stores. Some African Americans see this situation as exploitative and feel that banks or the government discriminate against African Americans in favor of Korean Americans. In fact, Korean American researchers argue that merchants compete fiercely with other Korean American entrepreneurs, keeping overall prices down. They find no evidence of bank or government help (Kim and Kim 1999:30; Lee 1999b:123). They argue that native-born residents are often too poor to start their own businesses or lack the necessary skills.

Given their different experiences in U.S. society, African Americans and Korean Americans take opposing perspectives on the presence of Korean merchants in poor urban neighborhoods and negative responses by African American residents (Kim 1999:4). Both African Americans and Korean Americans explain intergroup conflict in terms of culture, while the media focus on race and ignore the role of whites in creating the situation (K. Park 1999). Because of their own desperate circumstances, any outside businesses are viewed with suspicion by African Americans living in poverty. Korean American merchants are culturally and racially distinctive, easily labeled as "foreigners."

Intergroup conflict includes interpersonal disputes, boycotts, and (rarely) mass violence. Studies of boycotts of Korean American businesses in New York City (Lee 1999a) and Chicago (Choi 1999) indicate that such boycotts are organized by African American leaders involved in intense political competition. Actual relations between Korean merchants and African American customers are not as bad as suggested by the media and popular stereotypes, although communication difficulties do exist. For example, shopkeepers have been accused of rudeness for not smiling at customers, not looking them in the eyes, and following them around the store. These behaviors are related not only to cultural differences (looking someone in the eyes is regarded as rude behavior in a number of Asian societies) but also to merchants' negative experiences (shoplifting, armed robberies) with customers in high-crime locations.

In Chicago, there have been outbreaks of rioting, endangering store owners of all ethnic groups, whenever the Chicago Bulls basketball team has won NBA championships. Mediation efforts on the part of Korean American and African American representatives, coupled with prompt police action, have helped forestall violence (Choi 1999). The anthropologist Jung Sun Park (1999:216–222) points out that Korean Americans in Chicago were shocked by media coverage of the Los Angeles riots that portrayed Korean Americans as powerless and marginalized "foreigners" (although two-thirds in fact are American citizens). First-generation immigrants in Chicago turned to the second generation for leadership; as a result, the Chicago ethnic community began to identify with the term *Korean American* in order to claim full membership in American society.

Korean immigration has been declining since the early 1990s, and recent immigrants are not entering business. As the present Korean merchants age, many are selling out; their children, often highly educated professionals, are not interested in maintaining retail businesses in high-risk urban areas. Less antagonism will probably be directed against Korean Americans in the future, though it may well affect the Arab and Pakistani American merchants now moving into inner-city locations (Choi 1999:175; Kim 1999:240–241).

Vietnamese and Other Southeast Asians

Southeast Asians are unique among post-1965 Asian groups due to their origin as refugees, the recentness of their arrival, and the problematic fact of their association with the war in Vietnam. The main ethnic groups from Southeast Asia in the United States today come from Vietnam, Cambodia, and Laos. The largest groups resettling in America are the Vietnamese, Sino-Vietnamese (Vietnamese of Chinese descent, including merchants from Vietnam), Lao and Hmong from Laos, and Khmer (Cambodian). The Vietnamese are by far the largest group. (The many smaller ethnic groups will not be discussed here.) "Southeast Asian," a broad category used by the government and recent scholars, is not a term applied by most former refugees to themselves. As the anthropologist David Haines points out (1989:8), each of these groups has its distinct culture, language, and prearrival history; each has also had different experiences resettling in the United States.

Of all the Southeast Asian groups, the Vietnamese were the best educated, the most familiar with English, and the most apt to have technical or professional backgrounds before leaving Vietnam. The Sino-Vietnamese are similar in characteristics but were even more urban as a group. Together with the Vietnamese, with whom they sometimes intermarried, they had relatively small households and fewer children. The Hmong, a hill people who were enlisted by the U.S. military to fight against Communist forces in Laos, are just the opposite; the most rural and least educated and with the largest families, they have had the most difficult adjustment problems in the United States. The Lao and Khmer are in between, both having urban and rural people, a moderate education level, and a wide range of occupations. The Khmer, however, suffered the genocidal activities of the Pol Pot regime (1975–1978) and have endured the most psychological trauma of all the Southeast Asian refugees (Haines 1989:8; see also Ong 2003).

Considerable diversity exists within, as well as between, the different ethnic groups. The Vietnamese, for example, include Catholics, Buddhists, and members of other religions. Some were white-collar workers in Saigon, and others were farmers or fishermen. Some came from highly educated, well-to-do families; others had an impoverished background. Laotians include former military officials and educated professionals, as well as older people, men and especially women, who may be completely illiterate. Education and previous occupation in turn affect individual adjustment in the United States.

The pattern of settlement of the Southeast Asian refugee population in the United States is similar to that of other Asian groups. At the time of the 1980 census, there were relatively few Southeast Asians in New England, for example, and more on the West Coast, as is the case with other Asian Americans. However, a large proportion were living in the west central states, such as Texas, Louisiana, Minnesota, and Iowa (Haines 1989:5–6). This is partly due to the refugee resettlement process, which emphasized dispersal of the refugee population in order to avoid overburdening communities with large numbers of newcomers.

At first, the Southeast Asians had no choice about where to move; they were placed where sponsors and services were available. However, the refugees quickly relocated, often several times, to reunite with kin, seek better employment, and find more congenial locales. While refugees commonly refer to the climate as a reason for moving (not surprisingly, people from tropical countries prefer warmer climates), the presence of relatives and/or a sizable ethnic community are probably more important concerns. The concentration of Southeast Asians, for example, has steadily increased in California (over 40 percent of the refugee population had settled there by 1984), a state with a long history of Asian immigration. Texas has consistently been the second most populous state for 1975 arrivals (Haines 1989:3–5). Former refugees from fishing communities in Vietnam prefer to live on the Gulf Coast, in Texas or Louisiana, where they can be near the water, enjoy a seafood diet as they did in Vietnam, and work in shrimping or seafood processing (Durrenberger 1996).

The Context of Reception

Because the war in Vietnam was such a divisive experience for Americans, and because this refugee flow has been unusually large and long term, the reception of Southeast Asians by established Americans has not been uniform. Some refugees arrived as late as the 1990s when many earlier refugees were well-established citizens of American communities. A whole generation of Vietnamese American children has grown up in the United States. Though native-born citizens and often more American than Vietnamese in culture, they are likely to be categorized as "foreign" by established Americans of other ethnic groups. "First-wave" arrivals, those who came in 1975, were generally warmly received. Catholic church congregations often sponsored fellow Catholics and developed enduring relationships with refugee families. However, cross-cultural misunderstandings occurred as well. The refugee flow began so suddenly that there was no time to properly train or orient either the refugees or their sponsors, who might be individual families, churches, voluntary organizations, or even companies. Eventually, "donor fatigue" set in as numbers increased in the late 1970s and 1980s (Rutledge 1992:41–42).

Other misunderstandings occurred with regard to church attendance. For many established Americans, being Christian is synonymous with being American; but the majority of Vietnamese, as well as Lao and Khmer, are Buddhist. While they might feel obligated to attend a sponsor's church at first out of politeness, in most cases they had no desire to change religion. This was sometimes a source of disillusionment for sponsors. Some ministers and church groups focused on the attempted conversion of Vietnamese and Lao refugees as a mission, even to the extent of learning the language and preaching in it. Because they did not see Buddhists attending temples regularly (often none were

available, especially in small towns), Christians tended to assume that the newcomers "had no religion." In fact, just the opposite was true; religion was a great source of comfort and identity as people struggled to re-create their lives in a new land. A small shelf in the living room often served as an altar on which photographs of deceased relatives were displayed, and offerings of food and drink were made weekly and annually to commemorate deceased individuals (called ancestor worship in the literature, this custom is similar to Memorial Day observations in America). Southeast Asians did travel to temples in other communities on special occasions. But, as one Vietnamese refugee told the author, "I don't need to go to a temple; the Buddha is in my heart."

A persistent response of some established Americans—particularly some Vietnam veterans, though not confined to them and certainly not true of all—is a negative reaction to the Vietnamese (or even Asian Americans in general) because of an association with bad memories of the war in Vietnam. Some veterans suffer from posttraumatic stress syndrome—nightmares, depression, anxiety, and other symptoms resulting from wartime experiences—which can be triggered by seeing an Asian face. Others felt they had been rejected by fellow Americans after their return home because of the war's unpopularity, and they resented the "special treatment" supposedly given to refugees.

The effects of these feelings can range from discrimination in hiring practices to casual insults and harassment in daily life. For example, young Lao men in southwest Kansas in the late 1980s told the author that they were sometimes targets for hostility when driving to work; cars would cut them off and the occupants would spit at them. When asked why this happened, they said, "They think we're Vietnamese and they don't like the Vietnam War." Former South Vietnamese army officers were confused by the behavior of some individuals who apparently thought that they were Communists. The established Americans did not distinguish between North and South Vietnamese (enemies during the conflict): "Don't they know we fought on the American side?"

asked the Vietnamese newcomers. However, some white American veterans have formed close relationships with Vietnamese Americans and have reconciled feelings of hostility or guilt over Vietnam by making return visits with them in recent years as the country has opened up to the outside world. Over time, particularly in smaller communities, the Vietnamese and other former refugees have gradually been accepted.

Economic conditions also greatly influenced the reception of Southeast Asians, both generally and in the specific communities where they settled. Increasing numbers of refugees in the early 1980s coincided with an economic recession in the United States (Haines 1989:11). By 1981, more than 500,000 Southeast Asians had been resettled in hundreds of American communities, and domestic pressure to scale back the U.S. refugee program was growing. Local governments and service providers felt overwhelmed and underfunded (Robinson 1998:113). Competition grew between refugee groups, and between newcomers and established American minorities, for scarce resources in poor local employment markets. For example, anthropologists Paul Durrenberger (1996) and Paul Starr (1981) have discussed competition and conflict between Vietnamese fisherfolk and established white Americans on the Gulf Coast. Refugees from Vietnam were placed with seafood company sponsors in Florida, Louisiana, and Texas who needed workers for fishing and packing. The Vietnamese soon bought boats, however, and went into business for themselves. The Vietnamese initially broke many boating and fishing regulations, angering local fishermen. Starr suggests that some of the complaints, however, can be understood as jealousy expressed "toward those who work harder, longer, and more efficiently than is regarded as 'normal'" (Starr 1981:233). The Vietnamese came at a time when shrimp supplies were declining and government regulations made it increasingly hard for fishermen to survive. Racial violence broke out along the Gulf Coast in the early 1980s—boat burnings in Seadrift, Texas; a Ku Klux Klan rally in Galveston, Texas; and a brawl among

shrimpers in Gulfport, Louisiana (Durrenberger 1996:37–39). Durrenberger points out that Vietnamese shrimpers were deliberately recruited by Mississippi processors who wanted workers and a reliable shrimp supply (1996:68). By the late 1980s, although competition still persisted, the violence had lessened. Local and immigrant shrimpers adjusted to each other, even uniting in a spontaneous Gulf port blockade in 1989 to protest government regulations (1996:69–70).

Where jobs were readily available and newcomers were not seen as competing with the established population for employment or resources, as in the meatpacking town of Garden City, Kansas, during the 1980s and 1990s, minimal conflict took place. The newspaper and the local ministerial alliance played a vital role informing the public about reasons for the presence of Southeast Asians, almost all of whom had come to work in local meatpacking plants. Most employers came to appreciate the strong work ethic of the Vietnamese and Lao newcomers. Although discrimination and stereotypes persist, mutual adjustment and accommodation between Vietnamese and other, established groups has been the norm (see Benson 1990, 2001; Stull et al. 1990).

The previous discussion leads us to larger questions about perceptions of Asian Americans—and nonwhite groups in general—by native-born Americans.

PREJUDICE AND ASIAN AMERICAN IDENTITY

In general, American attitudes toward Asian groups mirror America's relationship to the countries of origin at any given time. World War II led to marked antagonism toward Japanese Americans; the Vietnam War created considerable hostility toward Vietnamese refugees. Most established Americans know little about the post-1965 immigrants, and misinformation and rumors easily spread.

A persistent problem for Asian Americans, and for nonwhite individuals in general, is that regardless of their own perceptions of ethnic identity, they are often inappropriately categorized by established Americans. Prejudices directed against a particular population or ethnic group are generalized and applied to others. Native-born Asian Americans, for example, are confused with recent immigrants from China, India, or other countries. As we have seen, media treatment of Korean American merchants in Los Angeles as "foreigners" led to greater self-consciousness among Chicago's Korean Americans. The September 11, 2001 terrorist attack on the World Trade Center led to hundreds of cases of persecution of Muslims and Asian Americans, particularly South Asians. A Sikh gas station owner was murdered, possibly because he wore a turban vaguely similar to that of the Saudi Arabian terrorist Osama bin Laden, as pictured on television. As long as Asian Americans are considered "others," they are likely to face a certain amount of prejudice and discrimination from established residents. At the same time, it must be recognized that first-generation Asian Americans, many of whom have already absorbed American racial stereotypes from the mass media before emigrating, are also capable of prejudice against outsiders and those they perceive to be of low status in U.S. society.

The longer a group has been in the country, the more politicized it is apt to become in its awareness of the need to protect civil rights. At the same time, the more established the group, the more likely that it has become incorporated into U.S. society, at least economically if not culturally. Here we turn to the issue of achievement among Asian Americans and whether they should be considered a "model minority."

ACHIEVEMENT AND DIVERSITY AMONG ASIAN AMERICANS

As we have discussed, great diversity—economic, cultural, linguistic, generational—exists within the population referred to here as "Asian American." Some are fourth-generation Americans, and others are recent immigrants or refugees not yet eligible for citizenship. Some can speak, read, and write one or more Asian languages, and others are fluent only in English. Some are well-to-do, successful entrepreneurs or professionals; others have difficulty finding employment. Given this diversity, we would expect considerable variation in the degree to which Asian American individuals and groups have been integrated into U.S. society, economically and otherwise.

Income and Occupation

Newcomers enter U.S. society in several ways, most commonly as labor migrants, professionals, entrepreneurs, refugees, or capitalists (Cheng and Yang 1996:325; Portes and Rumbaut 2006). As we have seen, the first Asian immigrants were primarily labor migrants, while post-1965 newcomers came initially as professionals or refugees. Many others, sponsored by family members, have turned to food processing, garment and electronic manufacturing, or self-employment in the form of entrepreneurship. For refugees, especially minority groups from rural Southeast Asia, employment has been far more challenging than for professional migrants. The Immigration Act of 1990 also granted permanent residence to wealthy investors, a number of whom have settled in the Los Angeles and San Francisco areas (Cheng and Yang 1996:331; Ong 2003:270; Wong 1998:35).

Although the influx of refugees has resulted in more varied public reactions, to a large extent Asian Americans still retain a *model minority* image in the wider society. This term was first used by the press in the mid-1960s to praise Japanese and Chinese Americans for their achievements (Cheng and Yang 1996:312; Ong 2003:77), and has been a source of controversy ever since. It has been criticized as a racial stereotype which implies that there is no problem with racism in U.S. society because Asian Americans have "made it," creating a standard of behavior that is difficult for other, more stigmatized minorities to match. The concept conceals great differences in economic outcomes. Many Asian Americans resent the common assumption that all those of Asian heritage are privileged or not "real" minorities in the same sense as African Americans, Latinos, and Native Americans. Asian Americans are quick to point out that whatever success they have achieved has been the result of extremely hard work and sacrifice, often in the face of discrimination. This is a particularly sensitive point for professionals who compete with other minorities under affirmative action guidelines.

Census materials summarizing Asian American income and education may give the misleading impression that all individuals in this externally imposed category are well-off compared to other minorities. According to the U.S. Census Bureau estimates, the median income ($64,238) of Asian and Pacific Islander families in 2006 was the highest among all race groups.[11] But researchers (cf. Sakamoto and Xie 2006) note that income figures mask great variation among Asian populations. For example, Asian Indians, many of whom arrived as highly educated professionals under 1965 Immigration Act provisions, averaged a household income of $78,315 in 2006; the corresponding figure for Vietnamese Americans, many of whom are former refugees, was $52,299.[12] Relatively high household incomes for the latter group are partly explained by the fact that Asian American families tend to have more wage earners than white families. Wives make a major economic contribution in almost all of the Asian groups, while additional workers (adult children or other relatives) may be present in the household as well (Benson 1994; Ling 1998:168; Sakamoto and Xie 2006). In the past, Asian American professionals have sometimes felt that underrepresentation in managerial jobs—the so-called "glass ceiling"—limited their earnings potential (Cheng and Yang 1996). However, based on their analysis of the 2000 census, Sakamoto and Xie (2006:70) do not find that Asian Americans are less likely to be employed as managers, except possibly at the highest levels. Evidence of disadvantage is clearest before the Civil Rights Act of 1964, with less systematic racial discrimination since the 1990s (Sakamoto and Xie 2006:65, 67). The authors conclude that "native-born Asian Americans appear to have achieved at least approximate equality with white workers in the post-civil rights period" (Sakamoto and Xie 2006:67). However, *foreign-born* Asian Americans and their children, particularly those who have come as refugees rather than highly educated professionals, have not done as well. And poverty rates for Asian Americans in the 2000 census (11 percent for native-born, 13 percent for foreign-born) exceed those for whites (9 percent) though not African Americans (24 percent) (Sakamoto and Xie 2006:73).

The general Asian American population is split between those at the top of the socioeconomic ladder (professionals and capitalists) and those at the bottom (workers in service and manufacturing). The overall poverty rate for Asian and Pacific Islander families was about 10 percent in 2006 (U.S. Bureau of the Census 2008) and would be higher except for the income-pooling strategy of multiple-earner households mentioned above. Sakamoto and Xie (2006:74–75) discuss the economic polarization among Asian Americans—those who can achieve middle-class status versus those who remain economically deprived—and observe that Vietnamese and the census category of "other Asians" (including former refugee groups like Lao and Cambodian), together with their children, are significantly disadvantaged.

Aihwa Ong (2003) is one of the few authors who discusses both the crucial role of Asian entrepreneurs in the emergence of Silicon Valley as a center for the global information (IT) industry and the exploitation of low-wage workers by fellow Asians or Asian Americans (2003:260–265). Since the 1980s, local production networks have heavily utilized immigrant and ethnic workers, often Southeast Asian women who earn below-minimum wages under poor labor conditions (2003:263). It is questionable whether these workers can escape from poverty within one generation or even two, since their children may not have the resources for a college education. Ong notes that "there has been very little interest in the indentured servitude of Southeast Asian migrants and smuggled Chinese workers, whose sufferings recall the earlier decades of Asian labor exploitation in the United States" (Ong 2003:273).

Education

Education is another area in which many Asian Americans excel, although the model minority image is problematic here as well. While educational levels are high, school completion rates vary greatly among Asian American groups. Sakamoto and Xie (2006) find that native-born Chinese, Korean, and Asian Indians have the highest levels of college graduation, which is not surprising since most are the children of professionals or entrepreneurs who possess considerable resources and high expectations for the next generation. The academic success of other refugee and immigrant children is more problematic as discussed below.

A number of studies have attempted to explain Asian American academic achievement (e.g., Caplan et al. 1991; Gibson 1988; Zhou and Bankston 1998). One study, by Nathan Caplan, Marcella Choy, and John Whitmore in the early 1980s, was a national survey of educational outcomes among Vietnamese, Lao, and Sino-Vietnamese refugee children. These were children of farmers and fishermen, not highly educated people. Most lost between one and three years of formal schooling in the resettlement process, and they lacked English skills and a basic knowledge of American culture. However, at the time of the study, 8 out of 10 students had a B average or better in terms of GPA, with almost half receiving A's in mathematics. They did not do as well in writing and English, since they had had only about three and a half years of experience with the new language. Families with four or more children did just as well or better than smaller families, and

girls did just as well as boys. The authors attribute this success to cultural values (particularly a high value placed on education), family lifestyle (a low divorce rate, parental involvement, and cooperative learning), and a willingness to seize opportunities. Min Zhou and Carl Bankston (1998) also studied the adaptation of Vietnamese American children and found that the ethnic group is an important source of identity and support. Those children who do best academically are least acculturated and have the strongest ties to their ethnic community (1998:235). In spite of the admirable struggle for academic achievement described in these studies, parents do not always succeed in controlling their childrens' socialization, nor is it easy to finance college. According to Sakamoto and Xie, Vietnamese are less likely than African Americans to finish high school and, together with smaller Asian groups, experience higher poverty rates than other Asian Americans (2006:58, 74). The "model minority" stereotype is most likely to disadvantage children from this socioeconomic background.

The Future of Asian American Ethnicity

Asian American authors are somewhat ambivalent about the future of their ethnicity. "Asian American" is, after all, a government-constructed racial category, not a biological or cultural reality. On the one hand, they recognize the need for political unity with regard to civil rights issues; on the other, they acknowledge that the idea of Pan-Asian unity embodies hope rather than reality. Members of different Asian

---

TABLE 11-2   Educational achievement: Asian Americans compared with all Americans

Race	High School Diploma (%)	Bachelor's Degree (%)	Graduate/Professional Degree (%)
Asian Americans	86	49	20
All Americans	84	27	10

Source: U.S. Bureau of the Census 2008. Figures refer to single-race Asians only and individuals aged 25 and older.

groups do not necessarily live in the same neighborhoods, interact with each other more than other Americans, or see themselves as having interests in common. They may or may not identify strongly with an ethnic group from a particular country of origin. Class and generation also divide co-ethnics: on certain issues, university professors will have different concerns from those of shopkeepers, recent arrivals from third- or fourth-generation Asian Americans (see Espiritu 1996). This is not to say that national origin groups cannot become politicized and recognize a common identity in certain situations, such as Japanese Americans with reference to the redress movement or Korean Americans in reaction to negative media portrayals. However, a Pan-Asian identity is still in its beginning stages. As long as immigration continues at high levels, and easy travel and communication are possible, broad solidarity among Asian-origin groups will not come easily (Cheng and Yang 1996:342–343; see also Espiritu 1992; Ong 2003; Yang 2006). Ong argues persuasively that the basic black–white

racialization of the United States affects Asian Americans as well, stratifying this population into those who "become white"—that is, are seen as "deserving" citizens, like professionals and elite entrepreneurs—and those who are considered "undeserving" because of their poverty and cultural differences from the mainstream. According to Yang (2006), the most likely scenario for the twenty-first century is that Asian Americans will neither be fully accepted nor completely assimilated into mainstream society and that multiple identities (American, Asian American, ethnic or subethnic, specific Asian groups) will continue to coexist simultaneously. Generational differences will continue to be very important, with second and subsequent generations more likely than the first to adopt a hyphenated American identity in their quest for social acceptance (Yang 2006:306–307). It may be that while ethnicity does not disappear, it will become increasingly symbolic as kinship integrates Asian groups into U.S. society (Yang 2006:307; Zhou and Bankston 1998:240).

Notes

1. Hawaii became the fiftieth state on March 12, 1959.
2. California suffered a very unbalanced sex ratio in the 1930s, with 14 men to every woman (Okamura 1998:40).
3. The country quota does not include close relatives, refugees, and special immigrants, so actual numbers coming from a particular country per year may greatly exceed the total.
4. Through the attorney general, the president could grant admission to whole groups of people.
5. In actual practice, previous policies continued; most refugee admissions after 1980 were of persons supposedly fleeing communism, including those from Vietnam, Laos, and Cambodia.
6. The People's Republic of China did not permit emigration until recently (Chen 1992:ix).
7. In 1990, it had more than 1.3 million Asians, or 9 percent of the total population.

8. Many American companies moved their factories to other countries or Sunbelt states in the 1970s to take advantage of cheaper labor and overhead (Chen 1992:31).
9. H1-B visas allow foreigners temporary residence for employment purposes, and can be converted into the coveted "green card" (no longer actually green) of permanent residence.
10. These newcomers enter with H1-B status as workers fulfilling employer needs.
11. "Asian and Pacific Islander" is the government category used in the 1990 census, with Pacific Islanders representing only a small portion of the total. The 2000 census separated the two categories and allowed people to report mixed racial backgrounds for the first time (Yang 2006:292).
12. U.S. Bureau of the Census, Asian/Pacific American Heritage Month: May 2008, http://www.census.gov/newsroom/releases/pdf/cb08-ff05.pdf

References Cited

ABELMANN, NANCY, and JOHN LIE. 1995. *Blue Dreams: Korean Americans and the Los Angeles Riots.* Cambridge, MA: Harvard University Press.

BENSON, JANET E. 1990. Good neighbors: Ethnic relations in Garden City trailer courts. *Urban Anthropology* 19:361–386.

———. 1994. The effects of packinghouse work on Southeast Asian refugee families. In *Newcomers in the Workplace.* Louise Lamphere, Alex Stepick, and Guillermo Grenier, eds. Pp. 99–126. Philadelphia, PA: Temple University Press.

———. 2001. Vietnamese refugees, Mexican immigrants, and the changing character of a community. In *Manifest Destinies: Americanizing Immigrants and Internationalizing Americans.* David W. Haines and Carol A. Mortland, eds. Westport, CT: Praeger.

BRETTELL, CAROLINE B. 2005. The spatial, social, and political incorporation of Asian Indian immigrants in Dallas, Texas. *Urban Anthropology* 34(2–3):247–280.

CAPLAN, NATHAN, MARCELLA H. CHOY, and JOHN K. WHITMORE. 1991. *Children of the Boat People: A Study of Educational Success.* Ann Arbor, MI: University of Michigan Press.

CHEN, HSIANG-SHUI. 1992. *Chinatown No More.* Ithaca, NY: Cornell University Press.

CHENG, LUCIE, and PHILIP Q. YANG. 1996. Asians: The "model minority" deconstructed. In *Ethnic Los Angeles.* Roger Waldinger and Mehdi Bozorgmehr, eds. Pp. 305–344. New York: Russell Sage Foundation.

CHOI, INCHUL. 1999. Contemplating Black-Korean conflict in Chicago. In *Koreans in the Hood: Conflict with African Americans.* Kwang Chung Kim, ed. Baltimore, MD: Johns Hopkins University Press.

DURRENBERGER, PAUL E. 1996. *Gulf Coast Soundings: People and Policy in the Mississippi Shrimp Industry.* Lawrence, KS: University Press of Kansas.

ESPIRITU, YEN LE. 1992. *Asian American Panethnicity.* Philadelphia, PA: Temple University Press.

———. 1995. *Filipino American Lives.* Philadelphia, PA: Temple University Press.

———. 1996. Colonial oppression, labor importation and group formation: Filipinos in the United States. *Ethnic and Racial Studies* 19:29–48.

FONG, TIMOTHY P. 1994. *The First Suburban Chinatown: The Remaking of Monterey Park, California.* Philadelphia, PA: Temple University Press.

GIBSON, MARGARET A. 1988. *Accommodation without Assimilation: Sikh Immigrants in an American High School.* Ithaca, NY: Cornell University Press.

GYORY, ANDREW. 1998. *Closing the Gate: Race, Politics, and the Chinese Exclusion Act.* Chapel Hill, NC: University of North Carolina Press.

HAINES, DAVID W., ed. 1989. Introduction. In *Refugees as Immigrants.* Pp. 1–23. Totowa, NJ: Rowman and Littlefield.

KIM, KWANG CHUNG. 1999. Introduction. In *Koreans in the Hood: Conflict with African Americans.* Kwang Chung Kim, ed. Pp. 1–13. Baltimore, MA: Johns Hopkins University Press.

KIM, KWANG CHUNG, and SHIN KIM. 1999. The multiracial nature of Los Angeles unrest in 1992. In *Koreans in the Hood: Conflict with African Americans.* Kwang Chung Kim, ed. Pp. 17–38. Baltimore, MA: Johns Hopkins University Press.

KITANO, HARRY L. 1976. *Japanese Americans: The Evolution of a Subculture.* Englewood Cliffs, NJ: Prentice Hall.

LEE, HEON CHEOL. 1999a. The dynamics of Black-Korean conflict: A Korean American perspective. In *Koreans in the Hood: Conflict with African Americans.* Kwang Chung Kim, ed. Pp. 91–112. Baltimore, MA: Johns Hopkins University Press.

———. 1999b. Conflict between Korean merchants and black customers: A structural analysis. In *Koreans in the Hood: Conflict with African Americans.* Kwang Chung Kim, ed. Pp. 113–130. Baltimore, MA: Johns Hopkins University Press.

LEE, SHARON M. 1998. Asian Americans: Diverse and growing. *Population Bulletin* 53(2):1–40. Washington, DC: Population Reference Bureau.

LEONARD, KAREN ISAKSEN. 1997. *The South Asian Americans.* Westport, CT: Greenwood Press.

LIE, JOHN, and NANCY ABELMAN. 1999. The 1992 Los Angeles riots and the "Black-Korean conflict." In *Koreans in the Hood: Conflict with African Americans.* Kwang Chung Kim, ed. Pp. 75–87. Baltimore, MD: Johns Hopkins University Press.

LIEN, PEI-TE. 2008. Homeland origins and political identities among Chinese in southern California. *Ethnic and Racial Studies* 31(8):1381–1403.

LING, HUPING. 1998. *Surviving on the Gold Mountain: A History of Chinese American Women and Their Lives.* Albany, NY: State University of New York Press.

MIN, PYONG GAP. 1996. *Caught in the Middle: Korean Communities in New York and Los Angeles.* Berkeley, CA: University of California Press.

NEE, VICTOR G., and BRETT DE BARY NEE. 1972. *Longtime Californ': A Documentary Study of an American Chinatown.* New York: Pantheon.

O'BRIEN, DAVID J., and STEPHEN S. FUGITA. 1991. *The Japanese American Experience.* Bloomington, IN: Indiana University Press.

OKAMURA, JONATHAN. 1998. *Imagining the Filipino American Diaspora.* New York: Garland.

ONG, AIWA 2003. *Buddha is Hiding: Refugees, Citizenship, the New America.* Berkeley, CA: University of California Press.

PARK, JUNG SUN. 1999. Identity politics: Chicago Korean-Americans and the Los Angeles "riots." In *Koreans in the Hood: Conflict with African Americans.* Kwang Chung Kim, ed. Pp. 202–231. Baltimore, MD: Johns Hopkins University Press.

PARK, KYEYOUNG. 1999. Use and abuse of race and culture: Black-Korean tension in America. In *Koreans in the Hood: Conflict with African Americans.* Kwang Chung Kim, ed. Pp. 60–74. Baltimore, MD: Johns Hopkins University Press.

PORTES, ALEJANDRO, and RUBEN G. RUMBAUT. 2006. *Immigrant America: A Portrait.* 3rd edition. Berkeley, CA: University of California Press.

REIMERS, DAVID M. 1992. *Still the Golden Door.* 2nd edition. New York: Columbia University Press.

ROBINSON, W. COURTLAND. 1998. *Terms of Refuge: The Indochinese Exodus and the International Response.* London: Zed Books.

RUTLEDGE, PAUL JAMES. 1992. *The Vietnamese Experience in America.* Bloomington, IN: Indiana University Press.

SAKAMOTO, ARTHUR, and YU XIE. 2006. The socioeconomic attainments of Asian Americans. In *Asian Americans: Contemporary Trends and Issues.* 2nd edition. Thousand Oaks, CA: Pine Forge Press.

STARR, PAUL D. 1981. Troubled waters: Vietnamese fisherfolk on America's Gulf Coast. *International Migration Review* 15:226–238.

STULL, DONALD D., JANET E. BENSON, MICHAEL J. BROADWAY, ARTHUR L. CAMPA, KEN C. ERICKSON, and MARK A. GREY. 1990. *Changing Relations: Newcomers and Established Residents in Garden City, Kansas.* Institute for Public Policy and Business Research. Report No. 172. Lawrence, KS: University of Kansas.

TAKAKI, RONALD. 1990. *Strangers from a Different Shore: A History of Asian Americans.* New York: Penguin.

U.S. BUREAU OF THE CENSUS. 2007a. American Community Survey 1-Year Estimates. B02011. Asian alone or in Combination with One or More other Races. http://factfinder.census.gov.

U.S. BUREAU OF THE CENSUS. 2007b. American Community Survey 1-Year Estimates. B02006. Asian Alone by Selected Groups. http://factfinder.census.gov.

U.S. BUREAU OF THE CENSUS. 2008. Asian/Pacific American Heritage Month: May 2008. http://www.census.gov/newsroom/releases/pdf/cb08-ff05.pdf

WILLIAMS, RAYMOND BRADY. 1996. *Christian Pluralism in the United States.* Cambridge: Cambridge University Press.

WONG, BERNARD. 1998. *Ethnicity and Entrepreneurship: The New Chinese Immigrants in the San Francisco Bay Area.* Needham Heights, MA: Allyn and Bacon.

YANG, PHILIP Q. 2006. Future prospects of Asian Americans. In *Asian Americans: Contemporary Trends and Issues.* Pyong Gap Min, ed. 2nd edition. Pp. 292–316. Thousand Oaks, CA: Pine Forge Press.

ZHOU, MIN, and CARL L. BANKSTON III. 1998. *Growing Up American: How Vietnamese Children Adapt to Life in the United States.* New York: Russell Sage Foundation.

12

■ ■ ■

Arab Americans

Barbara C. Aswad, *Wayne State University*
Thomas Abowd, *University of Massachusetts, Amherst*

The Arab world is a large area composed of 21 major countries, extending from Morocco on the Atlantic Ocean to Iraq and the Persian Gulf. It includes over 250 million people and exhibits great diversity, which is also reflected in the many religious traditions and national groups that comprise the Arab American community. In reference to Americans of Arab background, the term *Arab* connotes a linguistic, cultural, and sometimes political term used to identify those who have migrated primarily from Lebanon, Syria, Palestine, Iraq, Egypt, Yemen, and Jordan. For historical and cultural reasons, some persons from these areas may not identify with the designation. Also, Americans often confuse "Arab" with "Middle Eastern," a term that refers to an area that includes not only the Arab countries but also Turkey, Iran, and Israel, where languages other than Arabic are spoken by the majority and are official languages. Arabic is a Semitic language, related historically to Hebrew, Aramaic, and Chaldean.

WHERE AND HOW DO ARAB AMERICANS FIT IN?[1]

There are an estimated 3.5 million Arabic-speaking people and their descendents living in the United States, constituting about 1 percent of the population. The majority have arrived during the last third of the twentieth century (Haddad 2004:2). The 2000 census cites a figure much lower, estimating Arab Americans at 1,250,000. However, the Arab American Institute census estimates, based on research done by the Zogby International polling and marketing firm, place the population at more than 3,500,000.[2] Policies of the American government have been important in the regulation of Arab immigrants to the United States. Limits and conditions are not uncommonly placed on these new arrivals to the country. In addition, foreign policies and wars have often propelled residents of the Arab world to seek refuge in the United States, frequently with relatives or with existing communities of Arabs.

The positive impact of joining people with a similar culture, history, and language; greater employment possibilities; and the apprehension of prejudice toward Arabs and Muslims by the host society also affect the character of settlement patterns. About 94 percent of Arab Americans live in major metropolitan areas. More reside in the greater Los Angeles than in any other city, followed by Detroit, New York City, Chicago, and Washington, DC. Lebanese Americans constitute the single largest group nationally. But in particular areas, other communities are as big or bigger. For example, in the Detroit area immigrants from Iraq (Muslim and Christians) are as great or greater in number than the Lebanese population. In New Jersey, Egyptian Americans constitute the single largest Arab group (Arab American Institute Web site: http://www.aaiusa.org/arab-americans/22/demographics).

Arab Americans are diverse, representing different religions, denominations, regions, classes, generations, income levels, and degrees of social and political acculturation to America. Approximately 25 percent are Muslims representing Sunnis, Shiites, and Druze, while the majority are Christian, representing Catholics (42 percent), Orthodox (23 percent), and Protestants (12 percent).[3] Some Americans believe that the percentage of Muslims is higher, as much as a third. However, this is a stereotype and what is found is a reverse pyramid of the Middle East, where at least 90 percent are Muslims. This is due to the fact that most of the early immigrants were Christian Lebanese and Syrians, and there are now up to six generations in the country. The more recent migration patterns, however, are mostly Muslim, coming from a variety of countries including Lebanon, Yemen, Syria, Palestine, Iraq, and North Africa. The specifics of these waves of migration will be discussed latter.

Despite their differences, immigrants from the Arab world share a range of cultural characteristics: the Arabic language, art and music, culinary traditions, myths, and social customs such as patrilineal descent, extensive and intensive kinship obligations, values of hospitality, and a stress on educating their children. They are well aware of the many contributions in science, mathematics, medicine, literature, and architecture made by Arab and Islamic Empires from the eighth through the twelfth centuries A.D., when Europe experienced what has been referred to as the "Dark Ages." Most Arab Americans also share a common history, in which their ancestors lived for 400 years under Ottoman Turkish control. This was followed by several decades of European colonial control, influence, and suppression, against which people of the region fought wars of liberation in the twentieth century.

Algeria was the first Arab country colonized by a European power. France conquered this North African people in 1830 and controlled it until the Algerians gained their independence in 1962. Most of the other peoples of the Arab world won their freedom from British and French colonial governments in the 1950s and 1960s. The Palestinian people, having lived in historic Palestine under both Ottoman rule and then British colonialism, have still not rid themselves of Israeli occupation. Today, over one-half of all Palestinians reside as refugees or exiles outside of their former villages and towns. The majority of the remainder has lived under Israeli occupation and control since 1948.

Until recently, Arab Americans represented a small ethnic group and were often marginalized in discussions of ethnicity and racism. Some names are familiar to the public, such as consumer advocate and politician Ralph Nader; Senator George Mitchell; journalist and White House dean of the press corps Helen Thomas; football player and Heisman Trophy winner Doug Flutie; merchants Haggar and Farah Brothers; former CEO of Ford Motor Company Jacques Nasser; former UAW president Stephen Yokich; actors Salma Hayak, Kathy Najimy, Marlo Thomas, F. Murray Abraham, Tony Shalhoub, and Jamie Farr from *M*A*S*H*; singers Paula Abdul and Paul Anka; and radio host Casey Kassem.[4]

However, with increased American involvement in the Arab world, its increased dependence on oil particularly after the al-Qaeda attacks of September 11, 2001 on the World Trade Center and the Pentagon, the American war, and occupation of Iraq, Arab Americans became targets of U.S. government surveillance, especially in the George Bush administration (2000–2008). Their lives have been altered in many ways as they find themselves in the spotlight, the focus of greater levels of suspicion and surveillance.

Thus, Arab Americans, proud to be citizens of the United States and having made many contributions in their new country, find themselves with an uncomfortable struggle as they try

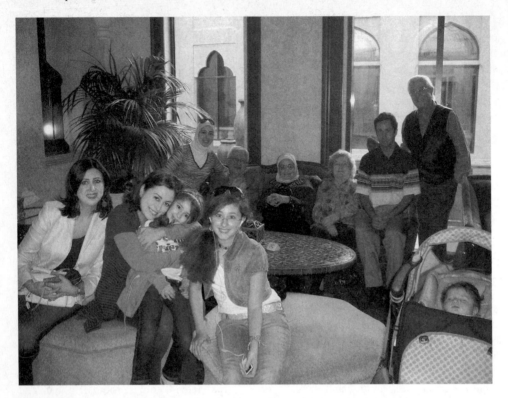

Arab American extended family.

to explain themselves, exhibit their patriotism, and yet show ethnic pride and examine their identity. Nadine Naber insightfully describes four paradoxes of "Arab American invisibility" as an ethnic group: (1) Arab diversity while represented as a monolith, (2) simultaneous racialization as whites and nonwhites, (3) racialization by religion (Islam), and (4) the intersection between the religious forms of identity that Arab immigrants bring to the United States and the racial forms that characterize U.S. society (2000:37–81). Aswad would add to these a misunderstanding of Middle East history and a misunderstanding of Arab kinship, gender, and family roles in society.

Howell states that these identity formations take place outside the American mainstream. "In these marginal locations, Arab immigrants from various national and village 'homes' construct identities that flow constantly across the globe. They maintain transnational marriages, religious institutions, commercial networks, and village

clubs" (Howell 2001:61). Suleiman's collection of essays clearly shows these connections (1999). A good example is Seikaly's study of 50 Palestinians in the Detroit area, demonstrating "through their memories, they reweave the experience of Palestinian hope and despair and have shown its impact on their thoughts, actions and identifications today" (1999:36). "The community, which has bound its identity with the fate of its homeland, has been on a roller coaster of euphoria, expectations, and disappointments leading to the current state of uncertainty and anguish" (ibid.). She discusses conditions of resignation, hope of return, and activism in their thoughts, actions, and identity. The difference of experiences and the importance of background factors such as education and number of relatives to assist in adjusting to this country, yet who live in the same Dearborn ethnic neighborhood, are seen in Aswad's comparison of Yemeni and Lebanese women in Dearborn in the 1980s

(1991b). Earlier studies showing the background diversity and adaptations of different Arabic-speaking communities in the Detroit area including Christian Lebanese and Iraqis, Christian Palestinians from Ramallah, and Muslim communities (Aswad 1974).

The early imagery of exotic Arabs, or the Holy Land imagery, and what Naber refers to as "racialization of ambiguity" (Naber 2008:23) refer to early Arab immigrants when the U.S. Census Bureau took the position that "Arab-Americans were to be treated like Italian-Americans, Greek Americans and some other European immigrant communities" (Hassan 2002:4). However, much of the current identification of "Arab" has been created within the United States in the last 50 years. During this period, the words *Arab* and *Islam* have received numerous negative stereotypes that have affected Arab American communities. As with other minority groups, members of the Arab community have experienced the sting of prejudice, stereotypical representations in popular culture, institutional racism, and fears of harassment. Arabs have witnessed their religions and traditions misrepresented as primarily violent and their communities as inferior. Arab women have been stereotyped and represented in a range of simplistic and crude ways. These attitudes were present before the violent attacks organized by al-Qaeda on September 11, 2001 and the rise of the Taliban in Afghanistan. The attacks increased the fervor of stereotypical views and violent assaults directed against the Arab American population more generally. Further, they also raised questions about the origins of these terrorist acts and the relation of religious and cultural customs to them. The American government initially tried, with some success, to separate this horrific deed from the beliefs of most Muslims. President Bush and others spoke against attacking people because they looked Arab, Muslim, or Eastern.[5] However, the governmental policies that followed had the effect of profiling and detaining these very same communities.

Initially after the 9/11 attack, more than 1,100 Arab, South Asian, and Muslim men were rounded up and detained without charge by the FBI, the Immigration and Naturalization Service (INS), and local law enforcement agencies (Howell and Jamal 2009:88). Nearly every last detainee was eventually cleared completely of any link with any violent organization or individual. As a result of these government policies, many Arabs in the Detroit area stayed inside their homes and communities for weeks and reported that they felt extremely anxious and scared in their own country. Many women did not shop; several had their Islamic head scarves *(hijabs)* pulled off. A suburban Arab commented that he now knew how African Americans felt walking in primarily white neighborhoods. Some Christian Arabs distanced themselves from Muslim Arabs, and some wore large crosses. Muslims in Detroit (71 percent) and elsewhere (82 percent) report greater worries about their future in the United States than do Christian Arabs (39 percent in Detroit and 57 percent nationally) (Howell and Jamal 2009:85). Zogby found in 2002 that nationally 25 percent had experienced attacks (Arab American Institute 2002). These concerns were not unfounded. A 2006 Gallup Poll found that 39 percent of Americans favored the requirement that Muslims carry special identity cards, 51 percent believed that Muslims were not loyal to the United States, and 25 percent said they would not want a Muslim neighbor. Few had a positive view of Islam, while 65 percent knew little or nothing about it (Cainkar 2009:407).

Shryock, on the other hand, found that in the Detroit area in 2003, only 15 percent felt that they had had a "bad" experience, while 33 percent said that someone "not of Middle Eastern background" had shown them solidarity or support after 9/11 (2008:109). For example, in the Claremont and Pomona areas of California, 30 religious and community groups accepted the local mosque's invitation to enter and learn about Islam in the Claremont and Pomona areas of California. Because of the attack, many thoughtful Americans also acquainted themselves with the history, religion, literature, and politics of the Middle East, Afghanistan, Pakistan, and Central Asia. As in the Vietnam War, they also examined America's role in global affairs.

More recently, many hundreds of thousands of Iraqi Americans, whose families experienced the American attack on Iraq in 1991 and 2003, have been deeply affected by the policies of their new country. These two U.S. interventions have resulted in the destruction of substantial portions of Iraq, large-scale sectarian violence, and the death of an estimated 1 million people through sanctions and war. A series of Israeli invasions of Lebanon (1978, 1982, 1993, and 2006) and its occupation of southern Lebanon from 1978–2000 have impacted both Lebanese in their native country and Lebanese Americans. The massacre of over 1,400 Palestinians of Gaza by Israel in December 2008 and January 2009 was felt by Arab Americans, many of whom have relatives in these areas. Their worldview includes information from media in the Arab world that the majority of Americans do not receive. For example during the massacre in Gaza, al-Jezeera and other Arab TV stations vividly and constantly showed the events while the al-Jezeera in English is banned by many U.S. cable stations and TV coverage was limited.

Stereotypes and institutional policies of discrimination and profiling have emerged not simply because of the 9/11 attack. In the last 60 years the United States has been engaged in a political-economic struggle in the Arab world because of the importance of oil to industrialized economies. However, contrary to much of public discourse on oil and the Arab world, the United States has consumed only a small percentage of its oil from this region. Its interest in the petroleum of the Arab world and Middle East has largely to do with the control of resources that competitors like China and Japan rely on much more heavily.

The U.S. government's war in Iraq was partially motivated as a means to control the flow of oil in the Middle East. Government officials know that increased stereotypes of Islam could injure relations with highly religious Saudi Arabia and other countries where U.S. military bases exist. Attitudes are also influenced by the Palestinian–Israeli conflict in which elements of the U.S. elite have allied themselves with Israel and its occupation of Palestinian, Lebanese, and Syrian lands.

A general lack of knowledge exists in the United States about the history of the Arab world and the tenets of Islam, Arab families, and the complexities of foreign conflicts. However, in the last two decades, there has also been a major increase in scholarship relating to Arab Americans after the events of 9/11 and an increased interest in the Arabic language.[6] The mainstream media, nonetheless, still lag behind in presenting positive views of Arab culture. Shaheen has long studied media portrayals scrutinizing the cascade of stereotypes that demonize whole groups and create fear and hatred (1984, 2008). Al Sultany states, "The rhetoric of the nation in danger, through the news media and TV dramas, has become accepted as truth and common sense. Discourses on safety and risk are a form of governmentality. In this case, 'crises' is used to justify racist views and practices: to racialize Arabs, Arab Americans, Muslims, and Muslim Americans as threats to the nation: and hence to use them as the contemporary racialized enemy through which the nation defines its identity and legitimizes it abuse of power" (Shaheen 2008:228).[7] Others have analyzed newspapers before and following 9/11 and report, "Major US newsprint media have contributed to the uninhibited bullying of Arab and Muslim Americans through misrepresentations . . . " (Naber, D'Harlingue with Wong 2008:274). In addition to their struggle with governmental pressures and social pressures, Arab Americans have found themselves in competition with far more powerful pro-Israeli lobbies, such as the American Israeli Political Action Committee (AIPAC). The power of this lobby was exhibited in the 2008 presidential election, in which Clinton and Obama sought these groups' support. The lack of substantial criticism of Israeli human rights abuses by U.S. administrations, including the Obama administration, and the sanctioning of the one-sided war against Gaza by the U.S. Congress are lucid examples of AIPAC's power. Recent American Jewish organizations such as J street, Jewish Voices for Peace, Jews for Peace, the Union of Progressive Zionists, and the Jewish Alliance for Justice and Peace have begun to offer pressures against AIPAC and for peace with the Palestinians.

Shryock (2008:111) argues that there are intellectual, moral, and political benefits to the "taxonomic uncertainty that suspends Arab Americans between zones of whiteness, Otherness, and color." He found in a major study in the Detroit area that 64 percent identify as "white" and that 32 percent of Arab and Chaldean respondents chose "other." Cainkar on the other hand in her study of Muslims in Chicago finds little identification as "white" and found that 53 percent said they had experienced discrimination after 9/11, with 47 percent saying they had not (2008:79).

Shryock also argues that a major organization ACCESS, located in the heart of Dearborn, a suburb of Detroit, has evolved from a grassroots organization begun by political radicals into a mainstream organization with a large budget. This is accurate and the alliances mainstream and otherwise have allowed major extension of services to the local community (Aswad and Gray 1996; Rignall 2000). However, it seems to Aswad, who has worked with ACCESS for many years, that Shryock and others dismiss too easily the historical economic class variable when discussing relative poor communities and their struggles such as Dearborn and Chicago. In the 1970s, the smaller and weaker Arab community was under the threat of removal by the city of Dearborn, and Ford Motor Company, when ACCESS was organized (Aswad 1974). The good reputation of the organization, locally, nationally, and abroad, served to buffer attacks on the community. A primary ethnic community also has the advantage of revivalism after attacks, while those which are spread out do not have. The localized African American community in Detroit is another good example of that kind of power.

In any discussion of race and its relation to Arabs Americans, it is vital to understand the particular dimensions of racial politics in the United States. Much analysis of the subject is hampered by a binary notion of race which so often places people in either a "black" or a "white" category. These assumptions about race simplify the multiple and shifting experiences of the diverse groups that comprise Arab Americans and other communities. Abowd argues that any discussion concerning race and Arabs in the United States must examine this group in relation to others. For example, David and Abowd have examined Arab relations in the Detroit area with African Americans, around the sites of Arab-owned small businesses in poor and majority black areas of the city. Detroit, like many U.S. urban centers, has witnessed in recent decades the rise of substantial encounters between an increasingly destitute and marginalized African American community and Arab small business owners. Abowd writes about some of the gendered implications of these interactions as well as the way gender intersects with race and class in the construction of intercommunal politics (2009).

The tendency to eliminate race when talking about Arabs has much to do with, as Abowd and Gualtieri argue, the general confusion about where Arab Americans lie in relation to white populations and people of color communities. It should be noted that Arab Americans themselves are in disagreement about what their racial assignment is. Older, more established and wealthier Christian families overwhelmingly regard themselves as "white." Arab Muslims who have arrived in recent decades and who face greater degrees of profiling and discrimination are much more likely to define themselves as something other than "white"—but, consistent with the complexity of racial politics in the United States, usually not "black."

In the United States, diverse cultural groups are often lumped together by language. Thus, Spanish speakers include such diverse groups as Cubans, Puerto Ricans, and Mexicans. Similar differences occur with communities from Arabic-speaking areas. The U.S. census has categorized immigrants by language, skin color, and country of origin, which often confounds the process of identification for Arabic speakers. In the census, they were considered "Caucasian" and, with other Middle Eastern groups, are the only Third World peoples not afforded "minority" status. Many could be considered Asian or African since they were born in those geographic areas, but they are not for the purposes of the census or policies of affirmative action.

The privilege of "whiteness" in the social stratification of the United States and the discrimination against those of darker pigmentation affect some members of the Arab communities. Although legally classified as Caucasian, a dark-skinned person from Yemen or Lower Egypt is not granted that privilege by white Americans, who are also ambivalent toward other olive-skinned Arabs. African Americans, on the other hand, generally view Arab Americans as white. Because skin color is not a major social category in the Middle East, being part of the U.S. system of racial stratification has raised debates within the communities as to how they should be classified. Official minority status obviously brings some benefits, especially for those of low income.[8] Still, other members wanting to assimilate speedily, and fearful of many of the negative terms often associated with "Arab," would disassociate themselves and be glad to be considered members of the dominant society. Others decline to identify themselves, fearful of documentation or discrimination. Educated Arab Americans and those who have language fluency have been more accepted.

Naber points out that "Arab-Americans do not always possess the power to choose 'to pass' or 'not to pass' as white" (2000:49). This is especially true during a political crisis. She cites documentation by the American Arab Anti-Discrimination Committee (ADC) of harassment that began in the Nixon era by the FBI, such as visiting homes and making phone calls to individuals as well as to relatives, neighbors, friends, and employers (ADC 1986:2). According to the ADC, "Invariably, no criminal charge is involved and the individuals are being investigated because of their origin and/or political beliefs" (ibid.). Detention camps for Arab Americans were planned by the FBI and the Immigration and Naturalization Service in 1987 in Oakdale, Louisiana (Naber 2000:49). These pressures intensified after the 1991 Gulf War, and most recently there have been trials and deportations based on secret evidence in which the attorney for the accused does not have access to evidence brought against the client.

As a reaction to the increased tension in the communities, increased political mobilization by Arab Americans began in 1996, when the Anti-Terrorism Act of 1996 allowed the then Immigration and Naturalization Service to arrest, detain, and deport noncitizens on secret evidence if they were deemed to be national security threats, at the same time denying the accused and their lawyers to documents revealing their charges (Bakalian and Bozermeir 2009:6). This was followed after 9/11 by the Homeland Security Act in 2002, when the INS was transferred to the Department of Homeland Security. The first office was established in Dearborn, Michigan, the heartland of Arab Americans. Howell and Jamal report that the FBI announced a doubling of agents—the third since 9/11—and in 2007 broke ground for a new facility that triples the size of its current office space (2009:92). Another system, called NSAAEERS, also known as entry–exit system, required males to be fingerprinted, interviewed, and registered within 30 days of entering the United States and report annually. Arabs and Muslims were represented in all these systems in a disproportionate manner (Kayyali 2006:26). There has also been a mobilization of Muslims in the United States recently, which will be discussed below in the section on religion.

As with other immigrants, working out their positions in the U.S. system of stratification includes both acceptance and resistance to Americanization. Sensitive life stories illustrate the variety of identifications and swings back and forth, helping Arab Americans to get around labels of "us," "them," and "others." For example, Nabeel Abraham (2000) recounts the upheavals in his family and homeland from which his parents had to flee after the creation of the Israeli state in 1948. He discusses his initial marginality with his schoolmates, then acceptance, then increased identification with Arabs and Palestine, which he later visits, and his final career choice of studying Arab culture as an anthropologist.

Linda Walbridge and T. M. Aziz (2000) explain, writing about the Southern Iraqi Muslim population, that building a community is a strategy of survival for these poor refugees who were victims of the Gulf War in 1991. They contrast these immigrants with the well-established Lebanese community in the same area, who distance themselves from these "boaters" from another region of the Middle East. Few Iraqi refugees have been allowed into the United States since the Iraq war begun by the United States in 2003, but again even though they will be scattered to live in many regions of the United States, many Muslims and Chaldeans will find their way to their established communities in the areas such as Detroit. Many of these Iraqis will be those who participated as translators and in other services for the American occupation and will be seen as different from the earlier Iraqi refugees.

Labels found within the community, such as "old world" and "boaters" (those just off the boat) versus "American born" or "integrationist" or "isolationist," or those used by academics (Abraham 1989), show these processes and a certain consciousness. Outsiders use such derogatory terms as "camel jockey" and "sand nigger" (Charara 2000:405). "Rag head" is often directed at Muslim girls in Dearborn high schools. Associations between Arabs and terrorism are also made in facile ways that have stark, racist dimensions.

Thus, identity might be thought of as a mixture of the changing identities found in the Middle East, the existing and changing perceptions, stereotypes, and stratification in the United States, and the variables found among the different communities and individuals, such as generation, region of origin, circumstances of migration, international political conditions, religion, urban or rural background, education level, occupation, and economic status. Current tensions have been created because of the violent response by some members of the Islam and Arab world to U.S. dominance in the twenty-first century, the U.S. government's harsh treatment of Arab Americans and Muslims, and some negative reactions by the general society and media. All individuals have multiple identities and will change them when necessary, beneficial or possible.

Now we will examine historical and cultural background factors important to identity and community organization, in two sections: first the major immigration periods, and second, specific social factors, such as religion, family, and political organization.

THE IMMIGRATION EXPERIENCES

The Early Settlers

Many empires affected the roots and identities of today's Arab peoples. Arabs lived in the Arabian Peninsula for many years before the rise of the Islamic state in the seventh century under the Prophet Muhammad. At that time, religion, politics, and society were strongly linked, and the Islamic empire spread the Arabic language and Islam religion across North Africa into Europe and into other areas of Asia, where they were incorporated to different degrees into the local customs of many diverse groups.

FORMATION OF SUBCOMMUNITIES AND IDENTITIES.   It is important to realize, as they do, that Arab Americans form many distinct subcommunities, both abroad and in the United States. The relationships among the groups and their identity depend, as we mentioned, on their historical, social, and geographic relationships and on current events in the Middle East. The usual basis for group identity is, first, the family, then religion, region, economic class, and generation. The importance of religion in identity, custom, history, and politics is seen for example in the fact that immigrants from the same village in Lebanon nonetheless live in separate areas of Detroit, divided by their religious identities (Aswad 1974). Other examples are seen in the situation in Dearborn between the established Muslim Shiite Lebanese community and the recently arrived Iraqi Muslim Shiite community. The Iraqis settled in Dearborn because the Lebanese Muslim Shiite community was there; however, social, educational, and generational differences between the two communities produce tensions. Many Iraqis, moreover, reported more affinity with the Yemeni, who also came from rural, quasi-tribal backgrounds (Walbridge and Aziz 2000).

WHEN AND WHY DID THEY COME? According to some authors, among the belongings of Columbus was a book by the Arab geographer al-Idrisi, which mentions that eight Arabs sailed from Lisbon and landed in South America, long before 1492. We are also told that Istephan, a Moroccan Arab, served as a guide to the Spanish explorers and conquerors in what is now Arizona and New Mexico in the 1500s (Mehdi 1978). Arabs had been the major navigators and geographers for centuries before Portuguese and Spanish explorers. Andalusia, in southern Spain, was part of the Arab and Islamic empires for 800 years until the Inquisition in 1492, in which Spain expelled the majority Muslim and minority Jewish populations. The exchange of knowledge, technical and navigational skills, and personnel among these Mediterranean cultures, which settled the Americas, is well documented.

Although a few Arabs settled in the United States during the nineteenth century, the first sizable wave arrived between 1900 and 1914. The overwhelming majority were Christians from the Syrian Lebanese region. It was a region that had been the Syrian Province of the Turkish Ottoman Empire for 400 years, until it was divided by the imperial British and French powers into the four states of Lebanon, Palestine, Syria, and Transjordan. The immigrants thus identified themselves as Syrians. The famous secret Sykes–Picot Treaty of 1915 had divided Syria, and it was soon followed by the Balfour treaty of 1916, which granted a homeland to Jews in Palestine, was in contravention of the Covenant of the League of Nations and its World War I pledge of independence for the Arabs (Khalidi 2006:32–33). This set the framework for future political organizations among Arab Americans.

Because the Lebanese region of Syria was the home of the early group, as well as providing a continuous stream of immigrants, we will discuss it in some detail. It is a mountainous region, with villages and regions that have a high degree of autonomy and well-developed networks of rural markets. The entrepreneurial skills of the Lebanese, both in the mountains and especially in the coastal communities, are well known. There are 17 religious communities, primarily Christian and Muslim, which are like ethnic groups due to their high degree of endogamy, or marriage within the group, as well as social and economic networking within these communities (see Chapter 15). Quotas in the Lebanese parliament represent these religioethnic communities. They are not as economically stratified as the ethnic or racial groups in the United States; however, in the nineteenth century, when Lebanon was part of Syria, the French colonists, who ruled Syria–Lebanon for a century, used a divide-and-rule strategy by patronizing a minority, the Maronite Roman Catholics, to control a majority of Muslims. France gave the Catholics privileges, introduced the cash crop and silk into their regions, placed them in government positions, and greatly influenced their culture to a higher extent than that of other Lebanese. The politicization and racialization of religious and ethnic groups in the Middle East by Europeans still affect members of the Arab American communities. These same complicated rules of divide and rule were part of the ruling strategy used by the British and later the Americans in Palestine and Israel.

The mainly Christian immigrants left Lebanon for several reasons. The cash crop gave them the financial means to emigrate (Owen 1992). On the other hand, competition from the Japanese and Chinese silk trade, which had increased after the opening of the Suez Canal in 1856, and a deadly mulberry tree disease, forced many who had specialized in silk, which decreased subsistence products, to find other sources of income and migrate. In addition, the population had increased due to cash cropping, where young hands formed a cheap labor pool. These processes occurred throughout the world with other crops such as cotton in Egypt, rubber in Java, and many crops in Africa. Thus, the result is a larger population, fewer subsistence crops, and less trade. Some populations reacting to these stresses, such as those in Egypt, just became poorer; some, such as the Lebanese, were able to migrate.

Increased military conscription and taxation by the deteriorating Ottoman Turkish administration added to the economic pressure to leave (Khalif 1987). Some Christians reported that the violence of the earlier Christian–Muslim conflicts of the mid-nineteenth century also affected their decisions (Suleiman 1999). The stories of wealth in America, and in many cases the enticements of steamboat agents and the influence of Western missionary educators, were part of the many push–pull factors of early migration (Naff 1985).

Although some were urbanites and well educated, many more were middle peasants from rural villages or towns. A "middle peasant" is one who is neither a large landlord nor a sharecropper but who owns a medium amount of land and works it with his family. This emphasis on family work assisted them in opening up family-run businesses in the United States. Many members of the early communities were single men who wanted to earn money and return to Lebanon; others feared persecution if they returned. Eventually, they brought their wives and started families. Rouf Halaby (1985) reported that by 1919, 70,000 immigrants supported nine Arabic-language newspapers. Journals such as *The Syrian World*, published in English in the late 1920s, featured poetry, fiction, essays, and prose. In 1923, the well-known Lebanese immigrant Khalil Gibran published *The Prophet*, which became one of the all-time best-selling books in the United States.

Bawardi (2009) has recently analyzed archival documents regarding several political organizations that reflected transnational political consciousness and development of an Arab American identity among the early immigrants who have often been described in scholarly works as apolitical and assimilationists or keeping their politics to themselves (Suleiman 1999). Bawardi found strong sentiments of Arab nationalism against the Ottoman Empire, the dismembering of Syria, and the encroachment of European Zionism as bases for the secret Free Syrian Society (FSP) in 1915. Later, in 1925, when France was ruling Syria as a mandate power, the New Syria Party (NSP) was formed after the brutal French repression of a Syrian revolt in 1925–1926, in which France killed 1,200 Syrian prisoners. Membership of the FSP and NSP included persons of various religious groups.

The Arab National Institute became the preeminent American Arab political organization following the Palestinian uprising and general strike in 1935–1936 until World War II disrupted that effort in 1939. Meanwhile numerous Arab Americans served the United States in the War, and demonstrated their loyalty to the United States. The last organization discussed by Bawardi in the period during the first half of the twentieth century was the Institute of Arab American Affairs from 1945–1951 formed by the surviving members of the League. The Institute responded to the Anglo-American Commission when partition of Palestine loomed as the preferred option in the United Nations. This partition allocated a disproportionate amount of fertile lands to the Zionists and crippled Palestinian society. Feeling their impotence beside the heavily funded Zionist interest groups in the United States, the Institute instead focused on the importance of Arab interests to the United States (Bawardi 2009). These four organizations combined aid activities for victims of the atrocities brought on their relatives abroad, exchanged visits by dignitaries, and distributed thousands of bulletins and newsletters.

What were the occupations of the early immigrants? Many started as peddlers and became small shop owners, industrial workers, and farmers.[9] Women worked in textile factories on the East Coast and in family-run stores. Later, some enterprises grew into large businesses such as the Haggar and Farah companies. The large and cohesive nature of the Arab family, which is discussed below, allowed family business to become important agents of integration in the United States. The auto industries attracted many Arab Americans from other parts of the country, and continue to do so today. Due to the nature of the industry, fewer women participated in the labor force of the auto companies. Also, although contacts for auto jobs were common, and labor bosses brought workers from the Middle East, village and kinship could not enter in such an important fashion as evidenced in small and larger food and textile enterprises.

The American government emphasized a nationalistic policy during and after World War I that encouraged assimilation. Restrictive immigration quota laws such as that of 1924 favored European migration and curtailed immigration from Third World countries. Those who spoke a different language were made to feel ashamed, and the melting pot ethos affected the second generation. Consequently, much of the native literature and history was systematically ignored. Islam was seen as very foreign to Americans.

Communities adapted differently according to the ethnic/racial character of the region in which they settled. The Lebanese Catholics who settled in the southern United States, where Baptists were dominant and plantations and lumber provided the economic base, entered the small-shop niche, a niche not available to poor blacks and stigmatized by upper-class whites. This niche was also entered by Italians, Chinese, and European Jews. All were marginalized from the major economic and political arena. However, in southern Texas, the Catholic Lebanese who had arrived by way of Mexico spoke Spanish and became a more accepted integrating link between upper-class Anglos and lower-class Mexican Catholics (John 1987). In the northeastern United States bordering Canada, where their French might have been useful, they worked as unskilled laborers in textile mills, because the Quebecois scorned the Lebanese usage of French (Hooglund 1987). Thus, each area affected adjustment differently. Gualtieri found there had been early violence against some Arab Americas despite their classification as "white." She discusses the case of a Syrian grocer Romey, who was lynched in Florida in 1929 (2008:157).

The immigrants and their descendants describe these early migrants as hardworking, and they certainly were. However, it is important to be aware that Europeans and other nonblack immigrants were able to "make it" to the middle class, but American blacks did not because of the politics of racial inequality in the United States. In this period, the "not quite white" Lebanese Catholic Christians identified with the dominant European Christians if possible. Muslims identified as being Lebanese or Syrians, or Muslims, but had the disadvantage of there being few Muslims in America, a reason given for the limited numbers of Muslims in the early immigrant groups. They feared a loss of religious faith among their children. Catholic Christians, meanwhile, often sent their children to Catholic schools, another institution of assimilation. Muslims usually sent their children to the public schools. Names were often anglicized by both Christian and Muslim immigrant groups. Muhammad became Mike, Adnan became Ed, and Salwa became Sally. During the depression years, there was little immigration, and often the Lebanese returned to Lebanon because of unemployment. The identification as Arab was also present, as we have seen in the above discussion of political organizations, but became more common after World War II. Arabic as a language of communication was still basic in most homes and magazines.

Changes in Immigration after World War II

Following World War II, the demographics of Arab immigration changed. Although the Lebanese continued to come, other Arab countries were represented, and there were other reasons for coming. The new geographic areas for Arab emigrants included Palestine, Yemen, Egypt, Iraq, Syria, and Jordan.

A new and influential group of professional members began to arrive in the 1960s. They were part of the "brain drain," a term referring to the expertise lost to the country that provided the professionals' initial education. Changes in the U.S. immigration laws in the 1960s allowed increased immigration from Third World countries, favoring professionals and family members. Many professionals married Americans and became more secular; their children usually had dual cultures. Yvonne Haddad and Adair Lummis (1987) mention that many of the professionals were influenced by Western ideas before they came. Since the 1980s, members of the professional cadre married primarily from their home countries. This began a major trend of upper-class more educated Arab Americans who differed in their settlement patterns from the earlier communities, as they spread into the suburbs in secondary ethnic communities where they formed national and religious ethnic organizations. This is discussed later below.

During the post–World War II period, there was an increase in the numbers of people who were pushed or fled political unrest, oppression, and wars. Palestinians began their diaspora, due to the occupation of their lands by Israel in the wars of 1948, 1957, and 1967, and emigration continues today. The 1980s witnessed major immigration because of warfare in Lebanon and Iraq. A civil war in Lebanon occurred in the 1970s and 1980s. In particular, the Israeli invasion of Lebanon in 1982, which included the bombing of Beirut and occupation of south Lebanon, resulted in massive immigration to the United States. Many came to the Detroit area and other regions where they had relatives. Iraqis fled the Iraq–Iran War in the 1980s and the Gulf War in the 1990s. A sizable number continues to wait in Jordan hoping to immigrate. Struggles between South and North Yemen increased their numbers in the United States. The often-violent treatment of Christian Copts in Egypt in the last 20 years has forced many, primarily of the professional class, to immigrate to the United States. Most recent have been the Lebanese from the Israeli War on Lebanon of 2006 and the war victims from Iraq since the 2003 American war on Iraq.

The availability of professionals who came to study and stayed or who were forced from their countries due to violence and political unrest has been useful to the immigrant communities and to social service organizations such as ACCESS in Dearborn, which has numerous doctors, psychiatrists, psychologists, and social workers from the Middle East who are bilingual. This was not the case even 30 years ago.

We mentioned earlier that Arab Americans have experienced a sense of hostility in the United States during the last 40–50 years—primarily because of the struggle over oil and the political power of Israel and its supporters in the U.S. Congress. Movies and TV in particular portrayed Arabs as villains and terrorists. One could not find an Arab "good guy" in the movies. As negative stereotypes of Arabs, Islam, and Arab culture increased, Arab Americans were forced to reconsider their identity, to defend it and reconnect with it, or shun it. New organizations were created to help Arab Americans cope. In the 1960s, America was also changing. The Civil Rights Movement and cultural protests of the African American

communities increased ethnic revival among other communities. In the Arab American community, one could hear, "We want to be called Muhammad instead of Mike in public." It had always been Muhammad in the home.

Definitions of ethnicity often use art, dance, drama, literature, poetry, and food in their celebrations and ethnic fairs. The Arab American National Museum in Dearborn, Michigan, built in 2005, has been a major location for many Arab American and foreign Arab artists to exhibit their talents. Sawalha (2008, 2009) points to the increase in artistic activism and challenges of such groups as the al-Jisser Group in bringing the exhibit Made in Palestine. Emily Jacir, a Palestinian American, won the prestigious Hugo Boss award in 2008 and had her photographic exhibit "Where we Come From, a history of the Palestinian experience" exhibited in the Guggenheim Museum. Annnemarie Jacir, a filmmaker, produced *Salt of the Sea* and other award-winning films. The increase in Arab comedians has also been political as well as ethnic, and Arab comedians have increasingly made appearances outside the ethnic community. Freij concludes, however, that while Arab American artists infuse the "largely commercial aesthetic economy with political and ethnic sentiments," they should be understood to be outside formal networks of influence on politics itself (2008:10).

Ethnic identity may also change in relation to foreign relations between the communities abroad, the size of the local community here, relations with other American ethnic groups, and how other Americans identify them. For example, if there are few in an area, they may seek out others from their general area or state of origin such as Lebanon. If they are a large community, they may separate into ethno-religious groups on their own and have their own newspapers, clubs, or organizations. Thus, ethnicity is a fluid variable and, of course, we need to remember that people have multiple identities, changing them according to the circumstances. Christian Arabs may emphasize their religion, light-skinned Arabs may stress phenotypic characteristics, and those who know English or are educated may identify with other Americans in their economic class.

Factors of religion, such as Islam, or phenotypic characteristics, such as dark skin, as well as economic class, rank some Arabs low in the American stratification scheme. Thus, a dark-skinned Muslim from a village who has low educational or occupational skills may experience more discrimination than, for example, an educated light-skinned Christian doctor. However, if the former remains in his or her community or with other minorities, which share class or education similarities, and does not interact with the dominant Anglo-Americans, one may feel less everyday discrimination than someone in a more affluent predominantly Anglo suburb who is separated from others like him or her. A person living in a "Little Arabia" also has the psychological satisfaction of speaking his or her own language and living with those who share his or her values.

In the world of higher education during the early post–World War II period, many Arab scholars writing on Arab topics were marginalized and relegated to small colleges. Due to organizing abilities through such organizations as the Middle East Studies Association, the Arab American University Graduates, increased publications, as well as their knowledge of Middle East sources and languages, they became hired by major universities. It was always difficult for them, as well as others who taught on Arab topics, due to the question of Palestine and racism in academia.

SOCIAL DIMENSIONS OF ORGANIZATION AND IDENTITY

Religion

Religion is a major social and cultural boundary among Arabic speakers in the Middle East, and it has been important in the location of today's Arab American communities. It is the most difficult boundary to marry across, unlike skin color or language or geographic area. Thus, even though there is a considerable amount of identification, organization, and marriage within state, city, and village communities, there is little marriage between Muslims and Christians from the same region. For example, there are fewer stigmas for a Lebanese Muslim to marry a Pakistani or Yemeni Muslim than to marry a Lebanese Christian from his or her village, and vice versa. A Christian Arab could marry an Italian Christian with less negative social pressure from his or her family than a Muslim Arab from his or her village. Due to the rules of patrilineality, in which the children, both male and female, assume their father's lineage, there are more restrictions on Arab women's marriages than those of Arab males. It is assumed that children will take the father's religion and identity. Consequently, if a Muslim Arab woman wishes to marry "out," strong pressure is placed on the future husband by her family to convert to Islam. It is also easier for a Muslim male to marry a non-Arab Christian than an Arab Christian. In the same fashion, many more Arab Catholics marry Catholics than Protestants, and again it is easier for males to cross these lines than for females.

Immigrants, especially nonprofessionals, will typically settle with village and family members, who are of their same religion. For example in the Detroit area, Lebanese Catholics settled on the east side with other Catholic minorities, and working initially at the Chrysler Plant. Muslims and Lebanese Orthodox Christians settled near the Ford Plant in Highland Park (a small city within Detroit boundaries), and the Muslims moved to Dearborn when Ford Motor Company did. Later Iraqi Chaldeans moved into Highland Park (Aswad 1974). There are secondary ethnic communities that expand from the primary enclaves and maintain their distinctive background; however, many professionals and more members often reflect settlement in the area of their jobs.

Many religious groups are represented among American Arabs. Lebanon itself has 17 religious groups, which are all represented. The major Christian Catholic groups include the Maronite (Lebanese), Chaldean (Iraqi), Assyrian (Syrian), Melkite (Lebanese), and Coptic Catholics (Egyptian). Christian Orthodox sects include Byzantine, Antiochian and Syrian Orthodox (from Lebanon, Syria, and Palestine), and Coptic Orthodox (Egyptian). Since the Europeans drew the boundaries of current states in 1922, religious communities and country boundaries do not coincide.

Among the Muslim sects, the largest are the Shi'a from Lebanon and, most recently, southern Iraq as well as Yemen. It should be noted that the Shi'a are a numerical minority in the Middle East but are a numerical majority, for example, in Detroit, where there are five or six Shi'a mosques. Linda Walbridge (1996), in a sensitive study of the differences among these mosques, comments that at times it is a "battle of the headscarves," referring to how much hair should be covered by women's apparel. The Sunni, the vast majority of Muslims in the Arab world, are also building mosques in the United States, and it should be noted that their number rose after the 1960s, when many professionals and upper-class Muslims came to the United States. Some of this group were secular and often married Americans, and thus their children are often not associated with the mosque as much as the earlier or later arrivals. The Druze, an offshoot of Shi'a Islam, also have active societies in the United States.

Those who came before 1950, during the period of strong assimilation pressures in the United States, had outwardly accepted many American customs, including Anglo names, marriages to non-Muslims, and often the loss of Arabic. When communities were influenced by immigrants from countries experiencing a reemergence of Islamic laws and Islamic dress codes during the past 30 years, and when the communities experienced growth so that there were many mates to choose from, the push toward assimilation was weakened. The emergence of African American ethnicity since the 1960s raised ethnic pride among other groups as well, Arabs and Muslims among them (Aswad and Bilge 1996:1–14). In fact, the two tendencies of assimilation and revitalization produce conflicts in some areas, especially over female behavior. Still, one sees family and friendship groups where women wear a variety of dress, from Islamic scarves and dresses to typical American, and no one seems to notice. Early Christian groups sponsored newspapers, some of which continue today, and an increasing number of Islamic newspapers in both Arabic and English are currently published. More recently, there are cable TV and video programs in Arabic, as well as Internet Web pages, which access religious and other programs in the United States and in the Middle East.

The church and mosque are major institutions for socialization of young people, and a place to select marriage partners, as well as for religious education. In addition, Christian Arabs, especially Catholics, often attend religious schools. Recently, there has been a major push by Muslims across the United States to open Islamic schools. With the rise of Islamic movements in the Middle East, many Muslim communities in the United States have been faced with stricter adherence to Islamic customs and laws. Yvonne Haddad and John Esposito state that a primary question facing Muslims in America is whether or not to live Muslim lives in a non-Muslim territory. "Islamic law provides the ideal blueprint for society delineating what can and cannot be done" (1998:5). Islamic law was formed in the early centuries of Islamic history and was affected by nineteenth-century reformers who called for reinterpretations. Much of this law pertains to family law, and thus informs everyday decisions. The role of the clergy is important, due to the significance of religion as an ethnic boundary. They assist members in adjusting to the United States and its laws. They become enforcers of Islamic laws at times and can be crucial in cases of, for example, domestic violence. Aswad has heard women complain that some imams side with men. Men have been heard to explain that America is a country that favors women: "they get the custody and welfare." As we discuss the family and women's roles, we will find that members of the family may often be a woman's best protector as well as disciplinary figure, and thus complicated dramas between the clergy and the family may be played out. Women have become very active in discussions of Islam and in Islamic organizations and mosques in the United States. The president of the Islamic Society of North America, Ingrid Mattson, is a convert, scholar, and activist.[10]

Recent and historical conflicts in the Middle East may cause some Arab Americans to minimize socialization with members of another religion. The civil war in Lebanon during the 1970s and 1980s had many dimensions, especially economic, but it also involved military conflicts between religious communities in the Middle East. This caused tensions among Arab communities in the United States. However, because these religious communities usually settle in different areas, the opportunity for interaction was minimized. Although separateness has existed between the Muslims of the African American and Arab American communities, relationships between some groups, both nationally and within communities, has been increasing.[11] Read has explored differences in racial discrimination between Christian and Muslim Arab Americans, and found that Muslims, across the board, experience higher levels of discrimination than do their Christian counterparts and are " . . . uniformly disadvantaged in American society today, irrespective of their racial and ethnic identifications" (2006:315).

Islam is the fastest growing religion in America. Mohammed Khan (1998) found that immigrants may adhere more strictly, while those born and raised in the United States are more open, inclusive, and less sectarian. Arab Americans have been affected by the Middle East calamities. For example, the 34-day Israeli War on Lebanon in 2006 destroyed much of the infrastructure and claimed 1,191 lives. In the reader *The War on Lebanon* (Hovsepian 2008), numerous writers recount the destruction of entire villages, the destruction of the infrastructure in Lebanon, and the anger toward the United States which supplied and resupplied the Israeli weaponry. In the village of Bint Jbeil (Southern Lebanon), which has 3,000 members in Dearborn, Michigan, family members, particularly women and children on vacation visiting their families, were visiting the village when Israel destroyed it. Immediately fund-raising dinners were held to assist relatives and to assist in rebuilding the town. Turfe, along with 15 members of her immediate family, was visiting Lebanon that summer and was in the town at the time of the seven-day attack. She describes

it "The thunder of outgoing and incoming fire was unbearable. We knew a missile hit nearby when the house rumbled and the earth shook. Sleep was not possible as the bombing continued throughout the night. We estimated that 70 missiles pounded Bint Jbeil in the first three hours. We all prayed as children asked what would happen to them if they died" (2008:201). Turfe finally escaped but lost her grandmother and aunt.

Bakalian and Bozorgmehr discuss the political mobilization of Muslims as a reaction to the prejudices and governmental targeting after 9/11 against Muslims in the United States (2009). Although most Muslims in the world are not Arabs, the 9/11 incident stereotyped the religion. Also like other religions, a sizable proportion of Muslims are secular, and many identify primarily with their heritage (Arab, Turkish, Iranian, Indonesian); there has been a definite increase in religiosity among many. "Islam has gained political currency and come to incorporate ethnicity, nationality, religiosity and community as one construct in American society" (Bakalian and Bozorgmehr 2008:2). The increase in Islamic head coverings in the Middle East created a definite increase in the United States. However, in the same family some women choose to and others don't. Haddad discusses how Muslims came out of the shadows by building mosques and Islamic centers whose number grew from 598 in 1986 to over 1,000 by 2000. Over 200 Islamic schools were established (2004:27). This created some divisions within the local communities. Some Islamists felt that Arab identity had been divisive and had led to the disempowerment of the Arabs, feeling they place national over religious identity (ibid.).

The *Los Angeles Times* reported in 2009 that "The US government had met privately with Muslim leaders, assuring them that a spate of hate crimes would be vigorously investigated and at the same time asking for help in the campaign against terrorism" (Watanabe and Palonea March 01, 2009:A5). However, it also reported that "The agency's infiltration of mosques and schools has influential groups reconsidering their post 9/11 cooperation" (ibid.). One agent told his story about his infiltration activities (ibid.).

In sum, religion is one of the most important organizing factors of identity among Arabs in America; the other is kinship and the family. Sometimes the two are blurred. Of course, Islam was founded in an area of the world where patrilineal rules were customary and it reinforced them. However, among the Arab Christians, family organization is also patrilineal and in most customs parallels that of Muslims. Let us now discover how patrilineality and extended connectivity characterize the Arab family, resembling more the structure of families of Indians and other Asians than that of Euro-Americans.

Family, Kinship, and Gender

The family is the major social institution in the Middle East, as well as among Arab Americans. Arab families are very gregarious, and visiting among members is expected and frequent (Aswad 1974). In all societies, there are many family types, which may vary among lines of socioeconomic background and individual histories and experiences. However, the ideology and practice of family rules, in Arab culture, include being large and extended, based on intimate social reciprocal relations, and patrilineally organized.

Arabs share with other cultures, such as Indian, Chinese, and Mediterranean, the institution of large families. Socialized as a member of a group rather than as an individual within a nuclear family is a basic difference from that of many American families. The importance of the honor of the family and the rules and obligations of etiquette are opposed to the bilateral, nucleated form of traditional American families, and even more so from the increasingly one-parent households in the United States. An emphasis on individualism and individual space in many American families is also at variance with the idea of shared obligations, hierarchies of power, and living styles of Arab Americans.

Pressures are often put on young people to socialize with their relatives, not to live alone, and not to travel far away to college. A youth may ask, "You went to the movies or shopping with your cousins, not your friends?" The Arab youth will respond, "They are my friends." Arab youth may

criticize the restrictions but usually come to terms and carry on the teachings of their parents. Life stories bring out the importance of these connections. Lara Hamza writes, "My emerging divided identity troubled and confused me. My family life increasingly appeared 'foreign' to me, and I longed to fit in with the majority, to fully assimilate into the American lifestyle. This displaced loyalty made me resent not only my Arab heritage but, much to my later misfortune, my family life as well" (2000:392). In her essay, she also discusses confusing perceptions of gender roles and arranged marriages in a culture of individual choice. Only later did she come to appreciate some of the values of a philosophy that emphasized the unit rather than strictly individual choices. In cases of mixed marriages, however, this struggle of dependence and connectivity versus independence and space often presents a problem for the parents and mixed messages for the children. The degree of patriarchy, discussed below, may also present problems.

For most immigrants, the family has been influential in migration. Kinship and marriage are of primary importance in the system of chain migration, whereby one member in a family immigrates to the United States and establishes oneself, then brings other members of the family, and so on, until many relatives have settled together. Relatives often provide the economic basis for an enterprise such as operating or owning a store. In ethnic villages, members can name 200 or more relatives who live around them. These family networks often span many continents, providing links to Africa, Latin America, the Caribbean, and the United States (Aswad and Bilge 1996). For example Aswad found that 65 percent of the Arab population she studied in the Dearborn working-class community came to the area because of relatives, and 41 percent said relatives helped them with employment. A strong 85 percent said they ate at least once a week with relatives other than their immediate family and 34 percent said they ate daily with such relatives. Fifty percent were married to their relatives. Marriage patterns often reinforced chain migration. Compared to other ethnic groups in this same community, when asked what they liked best about the community, Arabs said because their relatives lived here while non-Arabs indicated their neighbors (1974:66–68). Members of the professional or upper classes who may not have these large kin groups establish for themselves a circle of friends who operate in a similar fashion regarding visiting and hospitality.

What are patrilineality and patriarchy? *Patrilineality* is being a member of one's father's descent group at birth, sharing many special rights and obligations with this group. This is true for daughters as well as sons. This is not to say that one's mother's descent group is not important; in fact, migration may increase dependence on the mother's kin. However, one traces his or her descent through the father and is known to the community as a member of that line of descent; one's behavior reflects favorably or unfavorably on that name and group, not just upon oneself or merely on one's parents. Marriages can be used in a manipulative fashion which serves to preserve family and individual rights, to extend relations with a new family and especially in villages and tribes, to build large kin-lineage units. In tribal cultures of the Middle East, this group will defend one's life. The honor or reputation of the family acts very much as a mechanism of social control.

In the United States, where the dominant pattern of descent brought from Europe is bilateral descent, kinship is constructed through both mother's and father's lines, and is more flexible, and identity is often characterized by whom you live close to, whom you see, or other circumstantial variables. Under situations of industrial capitalism, individual achievement is stressed more than family or group achievement. In meeting someone in the United States, people often ask, "What do you do (referring to an occupation)?" Arabs usually want to know what family and region you are from.

Males have more privileges in patrilineal systems—plural wives, more inheritance, fewer restrictions on sexuality, and the like—and more power is given to males, especially elders, in the patriline. This is called *patriarchy*. Fathers are usually treated with respect in public and often get preferential treatment at home. What is often seen by the outsider is the modesty or public restriction placed on some females. The patriline also pressures the behavior of men, often influencing their occupations and marriages.

Patrilocality, in which men live near their fathers and brothers after marriage, reinforces male power, since women then are separated from their own patriline. Cousin marriage within the patriline, a tradition in the Middle East, mitigates against this separation. It is important to distinguish patrilineality (male descent) from patriarchy (male power). Most Americans see only the latter. In the United States there is also patriarchy despite the ideology of equal partnership and it certainly exists in the corporate and governmental structures. In cases of migration, it has been found difficult to follow these patterns, and in many cases, the immigrants settle near the mother's family (Aswad 1999). Also Arab women in the Middle East and in the United States are challenging many of these rules, forming groups to seek protection from abuse and entering public roles more often.

Patrilineality explains restrictions placed on female sexuality, in order to preserve the legitimacy of the male line. This is especially true where lineages are a major form of organization, such as India and the Middle East. One does not find such restrictions on females in matrilineal systems, where the identity of the child is obvious, and most property passes through women such as the Hopi Native Americans. It is also less in countries where other institutions such as age grade or associations offer alternative forms of organization, such as in sub-Saharan Africa. The emphasis on female virginity before marriage helps to explain the double standard where dating is tolerated for males but not for females. When placed in the American situation where dating is common for mate selection, this area of inequality between brother and sister becomes obvious. Immigrant parents, fearful of American styles of behavior, especially dating, alcohol, and drugs, usually feel the need to protect their daughters even more than in their countries of origin.

Women have gained in numerous areas of freedom in the United States, especially due to high levels of education, the opportunity for employment, and the successes of the last 40 years by women in America to attain their rights alongside men. Arab American women have attained prominent positions as judges, politicians, medical doctors, and professors. Their obvious inclusion and leadership are seen in organizations such as Arab American women's professional societies, the preponderance of employees in social service agencies such as ACCESS, increased roles in mosques, churches, ethnic and national groups such as the Syrian Club, or town organizations such as the Ramallah Federation. Helen Thomas, Donna Shalala, and others were mentioned earlier. The extreme importance of family and women in time of war for Arab Americans is sensitively analyzed through interviews by Naber in her study of Lebanese Shia in Dearborn after the 2006 invasion and siege of Lebanon and their natal towns by Israel (2009). Joseph addresses the role of women as transnationals and men as nationals in times of political conflict (2009).

Several interesting books and studies have been written on Arab American women caught in the tug of war between American "freedoms" for women and the sometimes restrictive nature of their homes.[12] The concept of male honor and the expectation to provide for his family, especially among immigrants from rich peasant backgrounds, meant that men sometimes were proud their wives didn't "have to work," and some restricted them (Aswad 1991b). This was undoubtedly true for other classes as well; however, the economic challenges, women's increased education, and their insistence have changed some male attitudes especially as two jobs became important to sustain a family. Among lower income families on welfare, money going to women meant a raise in their status, as it had among other minorities, although this differed according to their migration background (Aswad 1999).

In Western societies, there is a stereotype that women in the Arab family have very little power. However, women get their status and reputation in the same way as men, through their patriline. For example, Pakistan's former prime minister Benazir Bhutto followed her father to power, as did Indira Gandhi, both from patrilineal systems. (So far there has been no woman president of the United States.)

In Arab society, women continue to belong to their patriline after they marry, thus preserving protection from their brothers and fathers. It is important to distinguish patrilineality (male descent) from patriarchy (male power).

Fadwa el-Guindi (2000), in a comprehensive analysis of the head scarf (*hijab*) and veil, challenges Western and feminist ideas and indicates how dress serves to establish a woman's identity and status, as well as its use in the contemporary political context.

Due to the extended nature of family relations, women are a major part of social configurations and have most of the power in running the household and raising children. They negotiate their positions through sons, brothers, fathers, education, alliances with other women, gossip, and other mechanisms of power. Families try to influence marriages to a great extent, especially in the case of girls. In extreme cases, where it is felt that a youth is violating family rules, he or she may be sent "back home" for a mate (Aswad 1991b). Marriage can be used in a manipulative fashion which then serves to promote family and individual property rights, to build up relations with another family, and to build large kin-lineage units. This allows cohesion with kinsmen, relations economically, and political alliances. Although sometimes these can be competing motivations, marriages usually involve major planning. The difference between Christian and Muslim rules is notable in the lack of polygyny among Christians, but most other rules are the same. Divorce is viewed as unfavorable among many Arabs, and the rate found by John Zogby (1990) was 4.5 percent in the 1980 census, although recently it is said to be increasing.

Norms with regard to homosexuality and divorce are also shifting, particularly among Arab American young adults. Mirroring changes more broadly in the United States in the last two decades, Arab American women have increasingly joined the workforce and, with what is often a newfound economic independence, have forged greater social autonomy. Further, Arab American activists, particularly in the last two decades, have organized many gay and lesbian organizations that bring "queer" Arabs together in solidarity as well as with these communities more generally. This has been most pronounced in the large urban centers where a majority of Arab Americans reside.

Still, because of the importance of the family, children, and patrilineality, homosexuality is often viewed with disfavor and stigmatized. Little has been written about this subject, but Naber (2006) has a very insightful discussion regarding a group of Arab American girls she interviewed in San Francisco. Noting that the culture of San Francisco is more liberal than many parts of the United States, she states that in her own bicultural experience growing up in a bicultural Arab American familial and communal context, "Al American (Americans) were often referred to in derogatory sexualized terms. It was the trash culture-degenerate, morally bankrupt and not worth investing in. Al Arab (Arabs) on the other hand were referred to positively and associated with Arab family values and hospitality" (ibid.:87). Naber interviewed 30 second-generation girls and writes about the struggles of several young activist women and their parents as they decide between following traditional marriage patterns, dating in the American fashion, and even choosing to be openly lesbian. She brings the intersections of class, race, gender, religion, and politics in different locations, noting that due to these differences we cannot generalize about Arab American women (2006:91). The subject of virginity is crucial, but issues of class, religion, village, and national origin also are brought to control marriage and sexual orientation. She ranks them as the ideals regarding marrying one's kin, within religious group (Muslim or Christian), village of origin, economic class, national, and racialized/ethnic (Arab) group (ibid.:93).

During her research she saw a graffiti reading QUEER ARABS EXIST, and interviewed lesbian activists, and writes of their struggles. An idealized "Arab culture" was invoked as a strategy for harnessing markers of middle-class whiteness, in many cases, while in other cases controls on their daughters' sexuality to protect the family and an imagined Arab people from degeneracy in white middle-class terms. In this struggle, extended family members, local religious figures, and others are brought in to support the ideology, as well as some U.S. racial ideas about intermarriages and gayness.

Caring for the elderly is a requirement in the ideology of the extended family. When Aswad inquired regarding a retirement home for their parents, Arab Americans in Dearborn reacted with negative surprise, saying it brought "shame." Later, some added, "Well, if it was right in the middle of the community, maybe." It is the exceptional family that does not care for their elderly in the home. In describing the needs of elderly Muslims, Mary Sengstock (1996) found a discrepancy between the subjects' perceptions of their own needs and the perceptions of the (generally non-Arab) interviewers. The interviewers' vision of the elderly was that of being surrounded by family members and community, yet the elderly reported being "lonely." They missed the members of the extended family who were abroad.

Mental illness is stigmatized in many cultures, and so is it in Arab culture. Organizations like ACCESS provide assistance to families and consumers, and some communities are slowly beginning to discuss it publicly. As with other family-oriented cultures, mental illness is often accommodated or hidden but not discussed in public. Organizations like ACCESS have been important in addressing these problems. The method of treatment focuses on a family approach, rather than therapist to individual.

There are some problems when Arab family customs meet with the American legal system. They will be discussed below.

Language

Language, folktales, literature, and expressions are primary ethnic identifiers. There are numerous dialects in the Arab world, and likewise among the immigrants. There is also a standard Arabic used in the media, so people from different parts of the vast region can understand each other, except for certain vocabulary. In the Detroit area, language distinguishes the Arab communities from the Chaldean community. Chaldean is a dialect of Aramaic, which, like Arabic, is a Semitic language. Many Chaldeans also know Arabic because they grew up in Iraq, but the language, as well as the origin of their homeland in northern Iraq, creates a major social boundary for the community. Many non-Arab or non-Chaldeans confuse between the two communities, usually calling them both Arab. And, indeed, some bilingual Chaldeans regard themselves as Arabs, which definitely confuses those outside the communities.

There are also certain languages that are liturgical, spoken by priests in churches but not by the communities outside the church. These include the Coptic language in the Egyptian Coptic Church and Assyrian in the Lebanese Maronite Roman Catholic Church. In places such as Michigan, which has a large Arab community, Arabic had a first-language status early on and changed to become an ethnic language, understandable primarily to that community (Rouchdy 1992). With recent increases in immigration, the first-language status has returned for many, and many are learning standard Arabic in school.

Arabic is not a language easily learned by Americans, and although it has become a major language in the international realm, few Americans know it compared, for example, with Spanish or French. Preserving the language is seen as important to most immigrants, since many members see its loss as a major loss of the culture. Aleya Rouchdy (2004) reports that when many young people study classical (or standard) Arabic in schools it revives their sense of pride in the language and increases their desire to learn the colloquial. But they also know the importance for their future of learning the dominant language of the host country. For students who immigrate not knowing English, it can be very problematic and bilingual programs in areas of Arabic speakers have had some successes. The negative perceptions and racism of non-Arabs in the local communities have often made it difficult to fund such programs.

Literature has been an equally vital part of the Arab communities. The immigrants brought books and stories from the Arab world, but until recently, there has been little translation into English. Newspapers, magazines, and books are now being translated. American Arab writers in the diaspora such as Naomi Shihab Nye, Larry Joseph, Antoun Shammas, Gregory Orfalea, and others have become popular. The worldwide proliferation of cable TV has infused local communities with new and old movies, cultural events, and news analysis from the Arab world. New immigrants and increased technology have revived an interest in Arabic so that the older generations are pushing the younger to learn Arabic. Mosques have been active in offering Arabic courses and Koranic studies. At the university level, classes at Wayne State University, for example, have risen from 20 students in the 1980s to 200 today (Rouchdy, personal communication).

Overall, the challenge of maintaining the Arabic language increases as generations pass. Generational problems, caused by lack of knowledge of the parental language, are well known in all immigrant cultures. Parents and children alike often feel the culture is diminished if the language is not known. Young people have been heard to comment, "My parents say I am not an Arab because I don't know the language well." Children may understand but not speak or read. Parents may be disappointed and children may feel inadequate in meeting their parents' expectations, or embarrassed in front of their friends. Feelings of alienation can arise on many levels. This is especially true in mixed marriages, where children often don't know the language. On the other hand, if parents don't know English well, and children do, there can be cases of "role reversal," where children gain power over parents in some situations, or are called on to translate.

The predominance of Arabic as a language in a working-class community where Arabic is a primary language may present a problem in school success for some children. Some of their parents may not have had much schooling in Arabic as well. Organizations such as ACCESS have instituted tutorial programs to assist the children and offer classes for adults (Aswad and Gray 1996). Rouchdy (2004) comments that because of classical (or standard) Arabic, Arabs have a great respect for the language and they do not feel it is subordinate, rather they feel it is fundamental to the revival and maintenance of the community.

The increased importance of Islam and the Qur'an would assist this in Muslim communities.

Economic Class and Occupations

We mentioned earlier that many Arabs began by peddling and running grocery stores and dry goods stores, and then changed to other occupations (Sengstock 1974, 1996). The entrepreneurial spirit is still strong. Zogby indicates that 25 percent are involved in retail trade, substantially higher than the 16 percent of the U.S. population (1990:15). In small shops, one doesn't need much English to get by, and, more importantly, family networks, family labor, and community networks make it possible to start a business with few financial resources. The patrilineal and extended nature of the family, plus long hours of work, has assisted many in becoming successful. Those without the networks might suffer a handicap unless they have professional training. Gary David (2000) notes that the Chaldeans in Detroit trace their history of small store ownership back to Iraq, where Muslims couldn't have liquor licenses and Christians could and did. In Toledo and Detroit, however, Muslims do own liquor shops. The nature of kin corporations is understood by some ethnic groups such as the Chinese and Koreans, but seldom by those in whose neighborhoods they operate. Stores become an area of interracial and cross-cultural interaction, and there may be conflicts, some of them violent. The community becomes suspicious and resentful as the foreign culture profits from the community and then leaves without doing anything to economically help the neighborhood residents (Shadroui and Bahhur 1995).

In the upheavals in Detroit in 1967 and in Los Angeles in 1988, stores were burned. In Detroit, Chaldean merchants work behind bullet-proof glass cages and often complain of the feeling of separation from their customers (David 2000). While teaching in Detroit, the author has heard complaints by local non–Middle Eastern people of feeling exploited by Arab American merchants, their lack of cleanliness, food that wasn't fresh, rude behavior by clerks, talking in Arabic or Chaldean, and their encouraging liquor consumption. Also, they feel that the merchants should hire them. Of course hiring local persons undermines the cheap labor of family members. Merchants who have stayed in areas without hostile feelings do, in fact, find ways of serving their communities by having clean stores, extending credit, having good merchandise, offering food to the poor, hiring local people, and contributing to scholarship funds. Comments by the local community are very positive for these merchants.

When large sums of money are necessary for start-ups, trust and reciprocity are primary, and those are found in the family and community, seldom outside it. Store owners working in another culture work many hours, only trust each other for sums of money to start up businesses, and owe each other. They also run the risk of murder. More than 80 shopkeepers have been shot over the years in Detroit. Store owners prefer to operate within their cultural enclaves, such as Atlantic Avenue in Brooklyn or Warren Avenue in Dearborn, where there are 125 shops of every nature (Abraham 2000). Sometimes saturation occurs, and stores and restaurants go out of business. Even within a large city such as Detroit, a saturation point emerges, and store owners encourage their children to go into other professions (David 2000; Sengstock 1999). Gas stations are another niche for Lebanese and Yemeni. Factory work was a major tradition in Detroit. With mechanization, such work has become less available; however, the high wages still attract immigrant workers if they are able to find networks offering them jobs.

There are also an increasing number of large and wealthy Arab American entrepreneurs who trade with the Middle East. This class lives in spacious homes in the suburbs and, in most cases, supports Republican politics in their communities. As a group, they have not been studied as much as smaller entrepreneurs have. Likewise, the richer members of the kin corporations, who have gone into wholesale and ownership of large food businesses, and have benefited from the small shopkeepers, have received less attention. The brain drain, begun in the 1960s, still continues, along with the increased education of generations raised in the

United States, so that today many Arab Americans are in the professional class. Significant groups include doctors, lawyers, engineers, and professors. Among women in the Detroit area, a major profession of choice is pharmacy. Zogby (1990:18) found that Arab Americans are twice as likely as the national population to be health professionals and more likely than most other ethnic groups. They are less likely to be in agriculture, forestry and fishing, construction, and manufacturing.

Thus, there is an increasing wealth differential within the Arab American communities, with a growing class of wealthy professionals and large entrepreneurs, a growing middle class, and a growing poorer, less skilled class of rural immigrants. These last may, in fact, be quite poor. Zogby's 1990 study found a higher disparity among household and economic status for Arabs than for other ethnic groups. For example, they have a high mean income, yet have a larger percentage below the poverty level than the U.S. population as a whole and than those of European background. On the other hand, he found that Arab Americans as a whole, both native-born and immigrant, had a higher educational achievement level than the U.S. population as a whole and many European groups. His figures represent populations before immigrants reacting to the recent Iraqi war migrated to the United States. This corresponds to a greater poverty level among those most recently arrived and those who are American-born (Zogby 2000:10).

There has been an increase in education. Zogby's analyses of the 2000 census found that 85 percent have a high school diploma, and 40 percent have a BA or higher compared to 24 percent of Americans at large, and 17 percent having post-graduate degrees, nearly twice the American average (9 percent). Seventy-three percent were employed in managerial, professional, technical, sales, or administrative fields. Nearly half as many are employed in service jobs (12 percent) in relation to Americans overall (27 percent). Most work in the private sector (88 percent) while 12 percent are government employees (Zogby 2000). Their median income in 1999 was $47,000 compared with $42,000 for all households in the United States. Close to 30 percent have an income of more than $75,000 (Zogby 2000).

Read explores theories of U.S. gender inequality and their relation to Arab American women and work. Citing the 1990 census she found that Arab American women's labor participation (59.9 percent) is lower than other U.S. ethnic groups of women. A low rate among Arab immigrant women (49 percent) contrasts with U.S.-born Arab Americans, which resembles U.S. white women in the low 70 percent, and is thus responsible for an overall rate lower for Arab American women (Read 2006:4). Read mailed surveys in English to 1,500 women with Arab surnames, which restricted some lower income recent immigrant participation; however, she found a positive correlation between the degree of religiosity and marriage to another Arab, which both strengthened family values. She agrees with Haddad and Smith (1996) that adherence to domestic duties reflects a feeling of pressure to maintain ethnicity against certain Western cultural influences and consequently reduced employment. Obviously women from rural and poor backgrounds, with few industrial skills, inadequate English language, and education, are at a disadvantage, regardless of their religious involvement (Aswad 1991a). However, Read found that although many foreign-born women have high education and high incomes, if they do not work before 15 years in this country their rate of employment is low. She found the role of an Arab spouse in influencing and sometimes restricting employment to be siginificant.

Arabs and the American Legal System

Fatima al-Hayani found that many Arabs and lawyers feel the law can be and is sometimes negatively biased against Arab Americans, and she reports that many lawyers avoid jury trials because they feel "juries are affected by the negative depiction of Arabs" (1999:80). Particular areas that present a lack of understanding of social customs involve custody cases and Arab parenting practices and domestic violence. Racial profiling and targeting by police are also felt by the community and lawyers. Cases of child abuse obviously do occur in the community; however, sometimes misunderstandings of language and custom have resulted in children being taken from their homes, so that people fear involvement with the law. Adoption is not a policy of patrilineal families because it is the close patrilineal relatives who care for children in cases of abuse or death of parents, with the result that few Arabs become foster parents. Some Muslim children were put in Christian foster homes where Muslim dietary laws and religious beliefs were not observed.

In the area of domestic violence cases, al-Hayani (1999) found that cultural problems result in the police either ignoring the wife's complaints or overreacting. Al-Hayani contends that this is due to the erroneous view that wife-beating is acceptable Arab behavior and custom, a reason found in police statements for noninvolvement (ibid.:74). Kulwicki found (25 percent) of the 277 women she interviewed reported domestic violence through beating, 18 percent said they were kicked (1996). In some cases women are afraid that their husbands will be deported and thus do not report mistreatment. Aswad is often asked about how domestic violence in the Arab community is compared to that in other groups in the United States. Without comparable statistics, we would venture that the stress of adaptation to another culture will certainly present increased chances for violence among immigrant families. On the other hand, it seems through observations that the nature of the extended family attempts to limit the degrees of violence. There are usually relatives or others who will try to intervene in cases of violence. They feel this is their obligation. This intervention scheme is not part of many American two-parent families or neighbors, who feel they "should mind their own business." Yet concepts of honor and shame prevent many from admitting to this abuse, and seeking outside help. Community organizations such as ACCESS and ACCSSA in the Detroit area have been important as culture brokers and in assisting members of the Arab community (Aswad and Gray 1996). A recent study conducted by Kulwicki of victims and those involved in response such as religious leaders, police, shelters, social service agencies,

doctors, lawyers, community leaders, and others. She found that special programs have helped women, but there was inadequate understanding in emergency rooms, a lack of education and economic resources, fear of losing child custody, perception of lack of confidentiality on the part of the victims regarding services offered by Arab American providers, lack of services for the batterers, little confidence in religious leaders, and a lack of continuation of services. Certainly shame was a major barrier (Kulwicki and Aswad 2008).

Welfare is another area in which American laws may affect family relations. The author found that it provides an alternative means of support for some women who are mistreated. However, the majority use it to improve their power in the home by gaining access to revenue. The additional money is useful to men also and although it may give women more decision-making power, it does not always cause conflicts. Changes in the laws, which require recipients to find jobs or take classes after two years, affect

Ralph Nader (Arab American).

those families in which husbands do not want their wives to work outside the home. In some poor communities, women also do not have the educational level or linguistic ability to hold jobs or even to apply for job training (Aswad 1999).

Several recent pieces of legislation have particularly affected Arab immigrants. The Anti-Terrorism and Effective Death Penalty Act was signed into law in 1996. Under the terms of this law, "the government may deport an immigrant even if she or he has not committed any crime" (Moore 1999). A new court, called the removal court, hears the government's deportation cases behind a cloak of secrecy. Kathleen Moore, a legal scholar, states that "while the court accepts the government's case against a suspected alien terrorist, the defendant receives an unclassified summary of the evidence against her or him, without showing the identity of informants, which could be used in preparing a defense" (p. 85). This ruling affects other immigrants as well, but targets Arabs in particular (Hajjar 2001:8).

After the World Trade Center and Pentagon attacks, the USA Patriot Act of 2001 [H.R. 3162] was passed by Congress and signed by President Bush with limited opportunity for debate or committee hearings. Many civil rights groups have been concerned that civil rights could be compromised in the rush to put in place new laws to fight terrorism. The issues regard longer detention, increased use of secret evidence, expanded federal electronic surveillance authority, and deportation for acts vaguely defined as "terrorist." In a summary of issues affecting Arab Americans, Anton Hajjar (2001:10) quotes U.S. Senator Russ Feingold (D-WI) on October 25, 2001,

Although the Administration requested the power "to detain immigrants indefinitely," including legal permanent residents, "the Senate bill required the detainee to be charged with a criminal or immigration violation within seven days or release the detainee." Under the Act, however, "immigrants who win their deportation cases could continue to be held if the Attorney General continues to have suspicions." The bill also

continues to deny detained persons a trial or hearing where the government would be required to prove that the person is, in fact, engaged in terrorist activity. [H.R. 3162, Sec. 411–412]. "To avoid deportation, the immigrant is required to prove a negative; that he or she did not know, or should not have known, that the assistance would further terrorist activity . . . Groups that might fit this definition could include Operation Rescue, Greenpeace and even the (Afghan) Northern Alliance . . . " [H.R. 3162, Sec. 411–412]. Feingold concludes "In the wake of these terrible events, our government has been given vast new powers and they may fall most heavily on a minority of our population who already feel particularly acutely the pain of this disaster." [p. 11]

There has also been extensive discussion on political processes in the Arab world. In a 1999 article examining inaccuracies and myths in the media and in some academic circles, Joseph finds that political processes in the Arab world are described as undemocratic and as part of Islam. They are frequently represented as resistant to modernity, blindly traditional, hierarchical, and oppressive to women. Little is shown of the relationships that occur, especially kinship and family systems, even under conditions of authoritarian regimes. Both Arabs and Arab Americans are in fact becoming more critical of these regimes.

Ethnic and Political Organizations

We have discussed origins and activities of early organizations and the political, social, and economic roots of later groups. Arab identity was revitalized in the United States after the 1967 Arab–Israeli War, in which Israel occupied the territories of Lebanon, Syria, Egypt, Jordan, and Palestine. These events motivated the establishment of organizations that cut across religious and regional groups, such as the Association of Arab-American University Graduates (AAUG) in 1967. The National Association of Arab Americans (NAAA) was founded in 1972, and the Arab-American Anti-Discrimination Association

(ADC) was formed in 1980 to combat discrimination. Later, the Arab American Institute (AAI) was founded in 1985 to increase Arab American participation in the U.S. political system. At a national level these organizations have attracted notable speakers at their conferences. These organizations were very active after the September 11, 2001 attacks. The Arab-American Press Guild was founded in 1985 in Los Angeles by Joseph Al-Haiek, Samir Twair, and Ghazarian to coordinate Arab American journalist, and educate the American public by holding public forums, radio and TV broadcasts, and by their newspapers. Other locals have their newspapers such as Sada al Watan in Dearborn.

Political organizations and events respond to events in the Middle East. There are many active state and city or village organizations. Perhaps the largest in the United States is the Federation of Ramallah Palestine, which had its fifty-first annual banquet in 2009. Ramallah is one of the prominent capitals of occupied Palestine. In 2000, thousands of Lebanese (most from south Lebanon) held a two-week celebration in the streets of Dearborn after Israel quit its occupation of south Lebanon. One of the largest villages, Bint Jbail has perhaps 3,000 members living near Dearborn, Michigan. It was mentioned earlier how this village was destroyed by Israel in 2006 and the effect it had on the American community.

Sally Howell (2000a) documents how traditional art, dancing, and food are revitalizing the communities. She also notes that the vast number of artists using Middle East themes is made up of recent immigrants from the Arab world. The annual three-day Arab Festival, also in Dearborn, attracted a quarter of a million persons in 2009. Events such as the annual dinner for ACCESS also drew over 2,000. In recent years, it has become the second largest ethnic dinner after the NAACP in Detroit. Music is another venue that has energized and expanded in the Arab American community, and Anne Rasmussen discusses how "memory and imagination are fueled by musical style, textual references, and regional repertoires" (2000:568). And it has become an ethnic occupation. In an attempt to be more inclusive and less insular, some organizers are including performances of other ethnic groups,

such as Hispanic and African American. The Arab American National Museum in Dearborn hosts a variety of Arab and other artists and musicians weekly and has a multiethnic attendance.

In sum, there are strengths and challenges for Arab Americans, in their varieties of adaptations and identities. Their identity has been acutely challenged, especially Muslim Arab Americans, since the terrorist attack on September 11, 2001. The event has also caused Christian communities to further distance themselves from Muslim communities. One particular strength that Arab Americans have is the sense of family and kinship with reciprocal relationships, connectivity, and generosity. Those visiting the communities feel a vibrancy and enthusiasm. However, strains are also apparent because of its misfit with much in the United States, especially the legal and religious systems, where Arabs feel discrimination and misunderstanding. Yet kin relations form their own adaptations, thereby contributing to American values, as do other minority ethnic groups. Kin corporations have been beneficial in some economic niches, yet may be restraining in other areas since time and finances must be shared. Arab Americans are considered both white and nonwhite by U.S. culture and are thus often marginalized. They feel they are a Third World minority, yet do not receive the benefits of special programs. This is especially true for the poor. Muslims feel that their religion is attacked in the United States.

A special area of discomfort for Arab Americans has been the political realm due to tensions between the United States and the Middle East, the U.S. support of Israel, the Gulf War, the Iraq war, the Bush administration's targeting of Muslim and Arab Americans, and tensions between groups within the Middle East. They feel their contributions throughout history have not been given exposure in textbooks. But as they increase in numbers, Arab Americans and Muslims will undoubtedly become more evident in the U.S. ethnic, social, and political arenas. Their culture, religion, and literature will continue to add to the culture as much as their food has.

Notes

1. For an extensive annotated classified bibliography on Arab Americans, consult Michael Suleiman (2006). Another bibliography, by Gen'nan Ghazal Read, was produced for the American Arab Institute in 2006.
2. They feel that the differing results are due to sampling, combined with nonresponse by some, under-response (only two ethnic backgrounds are tabulated and reported), and reporting ancestry as race, which results in relatively higher under-reporting among Arab Americans. They also believe that many Arab Americans simply "do not understand the relevance of the census, its confidentiality or did not respond to the question on the sample 'long form' that measures ethnic ancestry" (Arab American Institute. Wikipedia:2). In 2001 the Coalition of American Assyrians and Maronites rebuked the Arab American Institute for categorizing them as Arabs (ibid.:3). Approximately one-quarter are noncitizens, that is, had temporary and permanent green cards or are students, whereas the national figure is 6.65 percent (Kayyali 2006:25).
3. Kayyali 2008: http://www.aaiusa.org/demographics.htm#religion3
4. For more noted Arab Americans, see Arab American Institute, Arab Americans. 2009. http://www.aaiusa.org/arab-americans
5. Shortly after the attack, a Detroit newspaper headline from a survey of 306 persons stated, "Few blame local Arab Americans for attacks: More than 63 percent say they don't feel hostile; 59 percent support profiling"; 14.7 percent reported feeling "somewhat hostile"; and 4.6 percent "very hostile" (*Detroit News*, September 16, 2001). Ethnic profiling became a major problem for Arab Americans. A local poll of 527 Detroit area Arab Americans, half of whom were Christians, half Muslims, stated, "Arab Americans expect scrutiny, feel sting of bias: 61 percent in poll say profiling is justified" (*Detroit Free Press*, October 1, 2001). This reaction appears to reflect fear in the communities. The poll reported only 22 percent of the Arab Americans said they had felt acts of bias. Of this figure, 22 percent had experienced strange looks, 19 percent nasty comments, 15 percent racial slurs, and 10 percent threats. Few had met with physical assault (2 percent) or objects thrown (2 percent). Imad Hamad, Regional Midwest director of the American-Arab Anti-Discrimination Committee, reported that there were 500 incidents nationally, including 5 deaths (personal communication, November 6, 2001). Windows had been broken and threats made in local community centers and mosques, but there were also many messages of support. In Chicago an angry crowd marching on a mosque was stopped by police. A mosque was fire bombed in Texas. The incidents initially, however, seemed somewhat less violent than during the Gulf War. Locally Arab Americans felt the need to proclaim their loyalty and love of the United States (*Detroit Free Press*, October 2001). Imams spoke out explaining their faith and disassociating themselves from the attack and from the al-Qaeda organization (*Detroit Free Press*, October 27, 2001).
6. Particularly useful recent books include Jamal and Naber (eds.). 2008. *Race and Arab Americans Before and After 9/11*; Bakalian and Bozermehr. 2009. *Backlash*; Cainkar, 2009 *Homeland Insecurity*; Salaita, 2006 *Anti-American Racism in the USA*; Haddad, 2004. *Not Quite American?*; Orfalea, Gregory. 2006 *The Arab Americans*; Ewing. 2008. *Being and Belonging: Muslims in the United States since 9/11*; Gualtieri, 2009, Baker, Howell, Jamal, Lin, Shryock, Stockton, Tessler. 2009 *Citizenship and Crisis: Arab Detroit after 9/11*. The article by Howell and Shryock (2003) is also very useful.
7. A recent study by Tom Jon Semmerling (2006) gives detailed analyses of films, using history, social systems, and myth to explore how the United States sees Arabs as "evil," and allows it to control the minority at home and continue its occupation abroad.
8. Some social service organizations for Arabs, such as ACCESS in Dearborn, Michigan, receive funds under the title of "special populations."
9. Read the stories by Alixa Naff (1985) and Nabeel Abraham (2000) to see how they went back and forth between peddling and shopkeeping.
10. For an engaging discussion of the diversity of Muslims and Muslim organization in America,

see Geneive Abdo, *Mecca and Main Street: Muslim Life in America after 9/11* (2006). Also the diversity of contemporary Muslim life experiences in the world is portrayed in *Muslim Voices: Muslim Lives*. Ed. Francis Trix, John Walbridge, Linda Walbridge (2009).

11. See Yvonne Haddad (1991) and Yvonne Haddad and John Esposito (1998).
12. See examples of these life stories in Barbara Aswad and Barbara Bilge (1996), Evelyn Shakir (1997), Joanna Kadi (1994), and Nabeel Abraham and Andrew Shryock (2000).

References Cited

ABDO, GENEIVE. 2006. *Mecca and Mainstreet: Muslim Life in America after 9/11*. New York: Oxford University Press.

ABOWD, THOMAS. 2009. The gendered racialization of Arab and African American women in an age of deindustrialization in Detroit. Work in progress.

ABRAHAM, NABEEL. 1989. Arab-American marginality: Mythos and praxis. In *Arab Americans: Continuity and Change*. Baha Abu-Luban and Michael Suleiman, eds. Pp. 17–43. Belmont, MA: Association of Arab-American University Graduates.

———. 2000. To Palestine and back. In *Arab Detroit*. Nabeel Abraham and Andrew Shryock, eds. Pp. 425–462. Detroit, MI: Wayne State University Press.

ABRAHAM, NABEEL, and ANDREW SHYOCK. 2000. *Arab Detroit*. Detroit, MI. Wayne State University Press.

AL-HAYANI, FATIMA AGHA. 1999. Arabs and the American legal system: Cultural and political ramifications. In *Arabs in America*. Michael Suleiman, ed. Pp. 69–73. Philadelphia, PA: Temple University Press.

AMERICAN ARAB ANTI-DISCRIMINATION COMMITTEE (ADC). 1986. *Report on the FBI and Civil Rights of Arab Americans*. 1732 Wisconsin Ave. Washington, DC, 2007.

ALSULTANY, EVELYN. 2008. The prime-time plight of the Arab Muslim American after 9/11: Configuration of race and nation in TV dramas. In *Race and Arab Americans before and after 9/11: From Invisible Citizens to Visible Subjects*. Amaney Jamal and Nadine Naber, eds. Syracuse, NY: Syracuse University Press.

ASWAD, BARBARA C. 1974. The Southeast Dearborn Arab community struggles for survival against urban "Renewal." In *Arabic-Speaking Communities in American Cities*. Barbara C. Aswad, ed. Staten Island, NY: Center for Migration Studies Press.

———. 1991a. *The Effect of the Rich Peasant Mentality and Welfare on Arab American Women and Employment in Dearborn Michigan*. Working Paper #1. Los Angeles, CA: Center for Middle East Studies, UCLA.

———. 1991b. Yemeni and Lebanese Muslim immigrant women in southeast Dearborn, Michigan. In *Muslim Families in North America*. Earle Waugh, Sharon McIrvin Abu-Laban, and Regula Burchkardt Quershi, eds. Pp. 256–281. Edmonton: University of Alberta.

———. 1992. The Lebanese Muslim community in Dearborn, Michigan. In *The Lebanese in the World*. Albert Hourani and Nadim Shehadi, eds. Pp. 167–188. London: I. B. Tauris.

———. 1998. Arab American families. In *Families in Cultural Context*. Mary Kay DeGenova, ed. Pp. 213–238. Mountain View, CA: Mayfield.

———. 1999. Attitudes of Arab immigrants toward welfare. In *Arabs in America*. Michael W. Suleiman, ed. Pp. 177–191. Philadelphia, PA: Temple University Press.

———. 2005. Women, gender and family relations: United States. In *Encyclopedia of Women and Islamic Cultures*. Suad Joseph, ed. Leiden: Brill.

ASWAD, BARBARA C., and BARBARA BILGE, eds. 1996. *Family and Gender among American Muslims*. Philadelphia, PA: Temple University Press.

ASWAD, BARBARA, and NANCY GRAY. 1996. Challenges to the Arab-American family and ACCESS (Arab Community Center for Economic and Social Services). In *Family and Gender among American Muslims*. Barbara C. Aswad and Barbara Bilge, eds. Pp. 223–241. Philadelphia, PA: Temple University Press.

ARAB AMERICAN INSTITUTE. Wikipedia 2009.

BAKALIAN, ANNY, and MEHDI BOZORMEHR. 2009. *Backlash 9/11: Middle Eastern and Muslim Americans Respond*. Los Angeles, CA: University of California Press.

BAKER, WAYNE, SALLY HOWELL, AMANEY JAMAL, CHIH LIN, ANDREW SHRYOCK, RON STOCKTON, and MARK TESSLER. 2009. *Citizenship and Crisis: Arab Detroit after 9/11*. New York: Russell Sage Foundation.

BAWARDI, HANI. 2009. *Arab American Political Organizations from 1915 to 1951: Assessing*

Transnational Political Consciousness and the Development of Arab American Identity. Ph.D. diss. Detroit. Wayne State University.

CAINKAR, LOUISE. 1991. Immigrant Palestinian women evaluate their lives. In *Family and Gender among American Muslims.* Barbara Aswad and Barbara Bilge, eds. Pp. 41–58. Philadelphia, PA: Temple University Press.

———. 2008. Thinking outside the box: Arabs and race in the United States. In, *Race and Arab Americans before and after 9/11.* Amaney Jamal and Nadine Naber, eds. Pp. 46–80. Sryacuse: Syrause University Press.

———. 2009. *Homeland Insecurity: The Arab American and Muslim American Experience after 9/11.* New York. Russell Sage foundation.

CHARARA, HAYAN. 2000. Becoming the center of mystery. In *Arab Detroit.* Nabeel Abraham and Andrew Shryock, eds. Pp. 401–424. Detroit: Wayne State University Press.

DAVID, GARY. 1999. *The Mosaic of Middle Eastern Communities in Metropolitan Detroit.* Detroit: United Way Community Services.

———. 2000. Behind the bulletproof glass: Iraqi Chaldean store ownership in Metropolitan Detroit. In *Arab Detroit.* Nabeel Abraham and Andrew Shryock, eds. Pp. 151–178. Detroit: Wayne State University Press.

EISENSENLOHR, CHARLENE. 1996. Adolescent Arab girls in an American high school. In *Family and Gender among American Muslims.* Barbara C. Aswad and Barbara Bilge, eds. Pp. 250–270. Philadelphia, PA: Temple University Press.

EL-GUINDI, FADWA. 2000. *Veil: Modesty, Privacy and Resistance.* New York: Berg Press.

ELKHOLY, ABDO. 1966. *The Arab Moslems in the United States: Religion and Assimilation.* New Haven, CT: College and University Press.

EWING, KATHERINE. 2008. *Being and Belonging: Muslims in the United States since 9/11.* New York: Russell Sage Foundation.

FREIJ, MAYSOUN. 2008. Art as a proxy for politics among Arab American artists in New York. Paper presented at the Middle East Studies Association Annual meeting. Washington, DC.

GUALTIERI, SARAH. 2008. Strange fruit? Syrian immigrants, extralegal violence and racial formation in the United States. In *Race and Arab Americans before and after 9/11.* Amney Jamal and Nadine Naber, eds. Pp. 147–169. Syracuse, NY: Syracuse University Press.

GUALTIERI, S. M. 2009. *Between Arab and White: Race and Ethnicity in the Early Syrian American Diaspora.* Berkeley, CA: University of California Press.

HADDAD, YVONNE Y., ed. 1991. *The Muslims of America.* New York: Oxford University Press.

———. 2004. *Not Quite American? The Shaping of Arab and Muslim Identity in the United States.* Waco, TX: Baylor University Press

HADDAD, YVONNE Y., and JANE I. SMITH. 1996. Islamic values among American Muslims. In *Family and Gender among American Muslims; Issues Facing Immigrants and Their Descendants.* Barbara C. Aswad and Barbara Bilge, eds. Philadelphia, PA: Temple University Press.

HADDAD, YVONNE Y., and JOHN L. ESPOSITO, eds. 1998. *Muslims on the Americanization Path?* New York: Oxford University Press.

HADDAD, YVONNE, and ADAIR LUMMIS. 1987. *Islamic Values in the United States.* New York: Oxford University Press.

HAJJAR, ANTON GEORGE. 2001. *Selected Legal Issues Affecting Arab Americans* (Manuscript). Washington, DC. The Division of United States Studies of the Woodrow Wilson Center.

HALABY, ROUF. 1985. Introduction. In *Arabic Speaking Immigrants in the United States and Canada.* Muhammed Sawaie, ed. Lexington, NY: Mazda.

HASSAN, SALAH. 2002. Arabs, Muslims, and race in America: Arabs, race, and the post September 11th National Security State. *Middle East Report* 32(3):16–21.

HAMZA, LARA. 2000. Coming home. In *Arab Detroit.* Nabeel Abraham and Andrew Shryock, eds. Pp. 391–400. Detroit, MI: Wayne State University Press.

HOOGLUND, ERIC, ed. 1987. *Crossing the Waters.* Washington, DC: Smithsonian Institute Press.

HOVSEPIAN, NUBAR, ed. 2008. *The War on Lebanon: A Reader.* Northampton, MA: Olive Branch Press.

HOWELL, SALLY. 2000a. The art and artistry of Arab Detroit. In *Arab Detroit: Detroit.* Nabeel Abraham and Andrew Shryock, eds. Pp. 487–514. Detroit, MI: Wayne State University Press.

———. 2000b. Finding the strait path. In *Arab Detroit.* Nabeel Abraham and Andrew Shryock, eds. Pp. 241–278, Detroit, MI: Wayne State University Press.

———. 2001. Cultural Interventions: The Arab American aesthetics between the transnational and the ethnic. *Diaspora* 9(1):52–82.

HOWELL, SALLY, and ANDREW SHYOCK. 2003. Cracking down on Diaspora: Arab Detroit and America's "War on Terror." *Anthropological Quarterly* 76(3):443–462.

HOWELL, SALLY, and AMANEY JAMAL. 2009. The aftermath of the 9/11 attacks. In *Citizenship and Crisis:*

Arab Detroit after 9/11. W. Baker, A. Jamal, A. Lin, A.Shyrock, R. Stockton, and M. Tessler, eds. New York: Russell Sage Foundation Press.

JAMAL, AMANEY, and NADINE NABER. 2008. *Race and Arab Americans before and after 9/11. From Invisible Citizens to Visible Subject.* Syracuse, NY: Syracuse University Press.

JOHN, SARAH. 1987. Arabic speaking immigration to the El Paso area, 1900–1935. In *Crossing the Waters.* Eric Hooglund, ed. Washington, DC: Smithsonian Institution.

JOSEPH, SUAD. 1999. Against the grain of the nation–the Arab. In *Arabs in America.* Michael Suleiman, ed. Pp. 256–271. Philadelphia, PA: Temple University Press.

———. 2009. Geographies of Lebanese families: Women as transnationals, men as nationals and other problems with transnationalism. *War and Transnational Arab Families, Journal of Middle Eastern Women's Studies* 5(3):120–144.

KADI, JOANNA, ed. 1994. *Food for Our Grandmothers. Writings by Arab-American and Arab Canadian Feminists.* Boston, MA: South End Press.

KHALIDI, RASHID. 2006. *The Iron Cage: the Study of the Palestinian Struggle for Statehood.* Boston, MA: Beacon Press.

KAYYALI, RANDA. 2006. *The Arab-Americans.* Westport, CT: Greenwood Press.

KHALIF, SAMIR. 1987. The background and causes of Lebanese/Syrian immigration to the United States before World War I. In *Crossing the Waters.* Eric Hooglund, ed. Pp. 17–36. Washington, DC: Smithsonian Institute Press.

KHAN, MOHAMMED A. MUQTEDAR. 1998. Muslims and identity politics in America. In *Muslims on the Modernization Path?* Yvonne Y. Haddad and John L. Esposito, eds. Pp. 87–104. New York: Oxford University Press.

KULWICKI, A. 1996. Arab Domestic Violence Education Project: Executive Report. Unpublished Report. Arab Community Center for Economic and Social Services. (ACCESS) Dearborn Michigan.

KULWICKI, A., and B. ASWAD. 2008. *Barriers in the Utilization of Domestic Violence Services among Arab Immigrant Women* (Manuscript). Rochester, MI: Oakland University School of Nursing.

KULWICKI, A., and J. MILLER. 1999. Domestic violence in the Arab-American population. *Mental Health Nursing* 20(3):199–216.

MEHDI, BEVERLEE TURNER. 1978. *The Arabs in America, 1942–1991.* Dobbs Ferry, NY: Oceana.

MOORE, KATHLEEN M. 1999. A closer look at anti-terrorism law: *American-Arab Anti-Discrimination Committee* vs. *Reno and the Construction of Aliens' Rights.* In *Arabs in America.* Michael Suleiman, ed. Pp. 84–99. Philadelphia, PA: Temple University Press.

NABER, NADINE. 2000. Ambiguous insiders: An investigation of Arab American invisibility. *Ethnic and Racial Studies* 23(1):37–61.

———. 2006. Arab American feminities: Beyond Arab Virgin/American(ized) whore. *Feminist Studies* 32(1, Spring):87–111.

———. 2008. Introduction. Arab Americans and US racial formations. In *Race and Arab Americans before and after 9/11. From Invisible Citizens to Visible Subjec*t. Pp. 1–45. Syracuse, NY: Syracuse University Press.

———. 2009. Trans-national families under Siege: Lebanese Shi'a in Dearborn Michigan and the 2006 War on Lebanon. *War and Transnational Arab Families, Journal of Middle Eastern Women Studies* 5(3):145–174.

NAFF, ALIXA. 1985. *Becoming American: The Early Arab Immigrants' Experience.* Carbondale, IL: Southern Illinois University Press.

OWEN, ROGER. 1992. Lebanese migration in the context of world population movements. In *The Lebanese in the World.* Albert Hourani and Nadim Shehadi, eds. Pp. 32–40. London: I. B. Tauris.

ORFALEA, GREGORY. 2006. *The Arab Americans: A History.* Northampton, MA: Olive Branch Press.

RASMUSSEN, ANNE. 2000. The sound of culture, the structure of tradition. In *Arab Detroit.* Nabeel Abraham and Andrew Shryock, eds. Detroit, MI: Wayne State University Press.

READ, JEN'AN GHAZAL. 2006. A Complete Bibliography of Selected Reference on Arab Americans. Arab American Institute Foundation. www.aaiusa.org

RIGNALL, KAREN. 2000. Building the infrastructure of Arab American identity in Detroit: A short history of ACCESS and the community it serves. In, *Arab Detroit: From Margin to Mainstream.* N. Abraham and A. Shrock, eds. Detroit, MI: Wayne State University Press.

ROUCHDY, ALEYA, ed. 1992. *The Arabic Language in America.* Detroit, MI: Wayne State University Press.

———. 2004. *Language Contact Phenomena in Arabic: Variations on a Sociolinguistic Theme.* Richmond, UK: Cuzon.

SAWALHA, ASEEL. 2008. Palestinian Art Exhibit in Diaspora and the International Social Justice Movement. Paper presented Middle East Studies Association Annual meeting. Washington, DC.

————. 2009. Being an Arab, a Woman and an Artist in New York: Then and Now. Paper presented at the 2009 Diwan Forum for the Arts, Arab American National Museum, March 29, 2009.

SALITA, STEVEN. 2006. *Anti-Arab Racism in the USA. Where It Comes from and What It Means for Politics Today.* Ann Arbor, MI: Pluto Press.

SEIKALY, MAY. 1999. Attachment and identity: The Palestinian community of Detroit. In *Arabs in America.* Michael W. Suleiman, ed. Pp. 25–38. Philadelphia, PA: Temple University Press.

SEMMERLING, TIM JON. 2006. *"Evil" Arabs in American Popular Film.* Austin, TX: University of Texas Press.

SENGSTOCK, MARY. 1974. Iraqi Christians in Detroit: An analysis of an ethnic occupation. In *Arabic Speaking Communities in American Cities.* Barbara C. Aswad, ed. Pp. 21–38. New York: Center for Migration Studies.

————. 1996. Care of the elderly within Muslim families. In *Family and Gender among American Muslims.* Barbara C. Aswad and Barbara Bilge, eds. Pp. 271–297. Philadelphia, PA: Temple University Press.

————. 1999. *Chaldean Americans.* New York: Center for Migration Studies.

SHAHEEN, JACK. 1984. *The TV Arab.* Bowling Green, OH: Bowling Green State University Popular Press.

————. 2008. *Guilty. Hollywood's Verdict on Arabs after 9/11.* Northampton, MA: Olive Branch Press.

SHADROUI, GEORGE, and RIAD BAHHUR. 1995. *Arab American Merchants and the Crisis of the Inner City: Cleveland—a Case Study.* Washington, DC: Arab American Institute.

SHAKIR, EVELYN. 1997. *Bint Arab: Arab and Arab American Women in the United States.* Westport, CT: Praeger.

SHRYOCK, ANDREW. 2008. The moral analogies of race. In *Race and Arab Americans after 9/11.* Amaney Jamal and Nadine Naber, eds. Pp. 81–113. Syracuse, NY: Syracuse University Press.

SULEIMAN, MICHAEL W. 1999. Introduction. In *Arabs in America.* Michael W. Suleiman, ed. Pp. 1–24. Philadelphia, PA: Temple University Press.

————. 2006 *The Arab-American Experience in the United States and Canada: A Classified Annotated Bibliography.* Ann Arbor, MI: Pierian Press.

TRIX, FRANCES, JOHN WALBRIDGE, and Linda Walbridge, eds. 2009. *Muslim Voices and Lives in the Contemporary World.* New York: Palgrave Macmillan.

TURFE-BRINJIKI, HAIM. 2008. A fateful visit to Lebanon: A diary. In *The War on Lebanon: A Reader.* Nubar Hovsepian, ed. Pp. 200–207. Northampton, MA: Interlink Publishers.

WALBRIDGE, LINDA. 1996. Sex and the single Shi'ite: Mut'a marriage in an American Lebanese Shi'ite community. In *Family and Gender among American Muslims.* Barbara C. Aswad and Barbara Bilge, eds. Pp. 143–154. Philadelphia, PA: Temple University Press.

WALBRIDGE, LINDA, and T. M. AZIZ. 2000. After Karbala. In *Arab Detroit.* Nabeel Abraham and Andrew Shryock, eds. Pp. 321–342. Detroit, MI: Wayne State University Press.

WATANABE, TERESA, and PALONEA ESQUIVEL. 2009. L.A. area Muslims say FBI surveillance has a chilling effect on their free speech and religious practices. *Los Angeles Times,* March 1, 2009:A5.

ZOGBY, JOHN A. 1990. *Arab America Today: A Demographic Profile of Arab Americans.* Washington, DC: Arab American Institute.

————. 2000. *Zogby Culture Polls.* New York: Zogby International.

13

■ ■ ■

Latin America and the Caribbean

Ronald Kephart, *University of North Florida*

Latin America and the Caribbean provide one of the richest tapestries of human biological, linguistic, and cultural diversity on earth. Anyone who travels to any part of this vast region witnesses an astonishing variety of skin colors, hair forms, facial features, and overall body types. They see dark-skinned, very curly-haired "African"-looking people in Port-au-Prince and Bridgetown; brown-skinned East Indians with straight black hair in Port-of-Spain and Georgetown; Europeans with light skin and thin straight or wavy hair in Buenos Aires and Bogotá; and Native American peoples with eyes and hair similar to those of many Chinese in La Paz and Cuzco.

At the same time, travelers may suspect that many of the people they encounter appear to be a "mixture" of some or all of these groups, and they are correct. In Latin America and the Caribbean, people from all major parts of the world—the only exception being indigenous Australians—came together and mixed to form what is essentially a new, modern human gene pool. Those who pay close attention in their journey are also impressed by the variety of languages and cultural practices they encounter. Of course, they may hear any number of standard European languages, such as Spanish, English, Portuguese, French, and Dutch. But they may also hear languages as diverse as Jamaican English Creole, which has been spread worldwide by Bob Marley and other performers of reggae music; Garifuna, spoken in Central America by descendants of "black Caribs"; and Quechua, the imperial language of the Incas at the time of the Spanish Conquest. And this is only the tip of the iceberg, because hundreds of languages are spoken all over Mexico and Central and South America. People are often surprised to learn that only about one-third of the population of Bolivia speak Spanish as their first language: the other two-thirds are native speakers of Aymara, Quechua, or other Native American languages, as well as Japanese, German, and the like.

Similarly, observers may see diverse cultural practices, such as Mayans blessing the corn seed; or Carriacouans honoring their African ancestors by setting out a special table of food called the *saraka*; or perhaps a group of Aymara offering a llama fetus to the *awki* spirits. And, if the travelers are North Americans, they may be puzzled by the fact that people who they would call

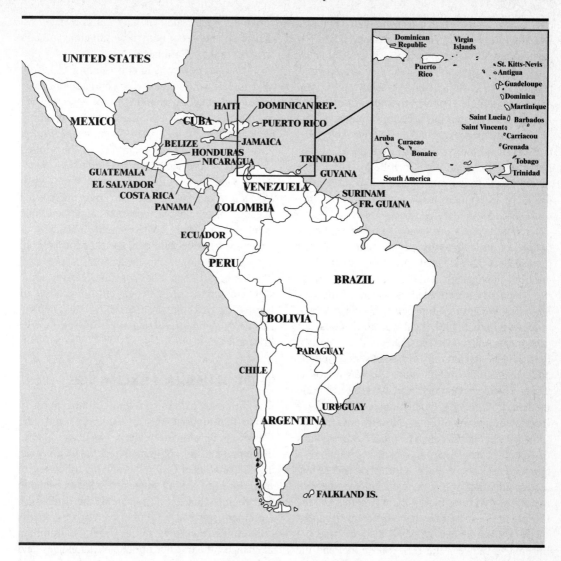

"black" in the United States are not always called "black" in the Caribbean and in Latin America. We shall return to this important observation later.

Obviously, this is a vast topic, and organizing it into a coherent and meaningful presentation is not easy. I have chosen to follow anthropologist Charles Wagley, who, for broad purposes of discussion, suggested that we think of the New World in terms of three basic "culture spheres": Euro-America, Indo-America, and Plantation America (Wagley 1957). Euro-America consists of those regions whose present-day populations

consist primarily of people of European descent: Argentina and Uruguay, for example. The population of Indo-America is primarily of Amerindian or mixed Amerindian-European origin. Plantation America consists of the regions to which the majority of African slaves were imported, and is distinguished by populations that are largely of African and African European descent. It is important to note that the borders between these "culture spheres" do not always correspond to national borders. For example, southern Brazil, like neighboring Argentina and Uruguay, is essentially Euro-America, whereas northern Brazil with its strong African presence is clearly part of Plantation America.

In this chapter I shall be concerned primarily with Plantation America and Indo-America, which I prefer to call Amerindian America. After making a few comments about the Amerindian background and Native American notions of ethnicity, I shall move on to survey Latin America and the Caribbean. Here and there, I will focus more sharply on particular problems in ethnicity or "race," as illustrations of the broader generalizations.

Before going on, I want to make explicit a couple of crucial assumptions underlying my presentation. As indicated within this textbook, it has been convincingly demonstrated that "race," as it is popularly constructed, is a part of the *folk model* of Western culture, and that an *analytic model* of human biological variation does not support this folk model (see Chapters 1, 2, 3, and 4). Folk models are culturally constructed descriptions and explanations of the natural and social worlds that do not depend for their validity on the scientific method. Folk models typically take their validity from an authority, often a religious authority of some sort. In contrast, analytic models are products of scientific investigation, which is grounded in empirical evidence, hypothesis formation and testing, replicability, and so on. As we shall see, the folk models of "race" we find in Latin America and the Caribbean are sometimes quite different from that of the United States. We shall also see that the differences between the U.S. folk model and the Caribbean and Latin American folk models sometimes cause conflicts, especially in the areas of culture contact.

As indicated in this textbook (see Chapter 4), the standard anthropological notion of *ethnicity* is self-identification centered on belonging to a group whose members believe that they share a history, culture, and language. People who differ biologically may belong to the same ethnic group, and people who are biologically very similar may belong to different ethnic groups. In other words, within their analytic models, anthropologists recognize ethnicity and biology as independent

variables, which may or may not correlate. We shall see examples of both these situations in Latin America and the Caribbean.

People, however, in constructing their folk models, frequently confuse or conflate notions of "race" and ethnicity, resulting in the *essentializing* of ethnicity. Ethnicity is then viewed as resulting from *descent*, rather than from *enculturation* (Gil-White 2001). For example, in the United States *Hispanic* is sometimes referred to as a "race" rather than an ethnic group. And then, when *Hispanic* is taken to be an ethnic group, there is the question of whether it represents a single ethnic group or many: Are Cubans the same, ethnically, as Argentines, just because both speak Spanish? From our perspective, of course, the answer must be "no."

When it seems appropriate, I offer some statistical data on various ethnic groups of Latin America and the Caribbean, taken from the *Encyclopaedia Britannica* online (www.britannica.com).

THE COLUMBIAN EXCHANGE

The biological, linguistic, and cultural diversity found throughout Latin America and the Caribbean is, ultimately, the result of one fateful event in the history of humankind. On October 12, 1492, Christopher Columbus and his followers, in their three tiny sailing ships, arrived at an island in the region that is now called the Bahamas. Columbus's arrival set in motion a process that is sometimes referred to as the "Columbian exchange," the transfer of peoples, languages, and cultures (both ideal and material) between the Old World and the New (Crosby 1972).

Most evidence suggests that the New World was peopled initially by migrants from northeastern Asia who traveled across the Bering Strait during periods of intense glaciation, between about 20,000 and 10,000 years ago. The date for the earliest of these migrations is in dispute, but about 10,000 years ago the melting Ice Age glaciers ended the possibility of walking from Asia to North America. And, by around 8,000 years ago, and probably earlier, the descendants of these early migrants had reached the far corners of the vast territory at their disposal. Physically, the indigenous peoples of the Americas were relatively homogeneous, suggesting that the number of original migrants was small. Similar outward physical appearance, and the very high frequency (100 percent in many populations) of type O blood throughout the Americas, attests to the probability of a genetic "founder's effect" at some point in the past.

The relative lack of physical differences among Native American peoples is dramatically counterbalanced by the cultural and linguistic differences we find among them. In Latin America and the Caribbean, people are organized into bands subsisting on foraging like the Ciboney, Siriono, and Ache. We also find societies subsisting on a mix of foraging and horticulture, such as the Yanomama of Venezuela and Brazil and the Shuar (Jívaro) of Ecuador. Historically, there were chiefdoms based on more intensive horticulture, such as the Taíno of the Greater Antilles. And finally, before and at the outset of the Columbian exchange, complex, stratified, state societies based on intensive agriculture had developed, the most well known of which are the Maya of Central America, the Inca of the central Andes, and the Aztec of Mexico.

Presently, there are no Native American states; most indigenous peoples now find themselves, for better or worse, integrated into European-dominated state societies as peasant farmers, like the Maya or the Aymara of Perú and Bolivia. Many have also come to be part of an ever-growing rural and urban proletariat. Relatively few have managed, like some Yanomama communities, to maintain their traditional lifeways.[1]

Linguistically, we find literally hundreds of indigenous languages across the Caribbean and Central and South America. The relationships between and among these languages are often difficult to determine, but linguists generally agree that most belong to one of the following groups (O'Grady et al. 2001):

- *Uto-Aztecan* (Mexico, northern Central America, southwestern United States). Many speakers of these languages, especially Nahuatl and related languages, are descendants of peoples who were organized into states at the time of the arrival of Europeans. Other related languages include Hopi and Papago (Tohono O'odham) of the southwestern United States.
- *Mayan* (southern Mexico, Guatemala, Belize). Varieties of Mayan include Yucatec, Kekchi, Tzeltal, and Tojolabal. Most present-day Maya are peasant farmers.
- *Andean-Equatorial* (the Andes, other parts of South America). Many scholars place Aymara and Quechua into this group; however, the two languages are not historically related, and their exact relationship is contested. The Inca used both as imperial languages: languages related to Aymara had been replaced by Quechua just before the Spanish arrived. Arawak is still spoken in northern South America; and Guaraní, along with Spanish, is an official language of Paraguay.
- *Ge-Pano-Carib* (South America). Languages in this group include Carib (Guyana, Surinam, French Guiana, and also formerly the Lesser Antilles) and several minority languages of Perú, Brazil, and Argentina.
- *Macro-Chibchan* (northwestern South America, southern Central America). Languages include Cuna (Panama and Colombia), Warao (Venezuela), and some others.

It seems that among most of these Native American groups, classification of people is based on linguistic and cultural factors rather than on any visible biological traits that might qualify as "racial." For example, the Yanomama, who are forager-horticulturalists of the upper Orinoco (northwestern Brazil and southern Venezuela), classify people into *Yanomama*, those who speak the Yanomama language and who also know how to operate within Yanomama culture; and *nabuh*, those who don't. Kenneth Good (1991), who studied the Yanomama for 15 years, reports that at first his hosts called him "Ghost Tongue," meaning that he was like a child who had not yet learned to talk, until he was able to speak Yanomama fluently. In the Andes, similar concepts exist. For example, the native people living around Tupi, Perú, speak a language they call *Jaqaru*, from the words *jaqi* "human being" and *aru* "speech"; they also refer to themselves as *Jaqaru* people. Thus, their concept of self-identity is tightly bound up with their language and culture (more about this later). Similarly, Ecuadoran Quechua speakers call their language *runa shimi*, "human language" (Carpenter 1983).

In the Columbian exchange, the Old World received from the New World many new foods, including corn, potatoes, tomatoes, peanuts, squash, beans, chili peppers, manioc (yuca, or casava), and turkeys. Some of these have become supremely important in the Old World. (Who can imagine Italian cooking without tomatoes, the Swiss without chocolate, or the Irish without potatoes?) Indeed, there are now parts of the Old World, especially in Africa, that could not feed their people without the New World crops they gained from the Columbian exchange. And finally, we might mention the millions of people around the world addicted to the nicotine in tobacco, a New World product.

In the reverse direction, the Old World contributed important food and work animals (cattle, horses, pigs, sheep, goats, donkeys), although these were frequently more destructive than beneficial. But perhaps the most consequential Old World product introduced to the New World was sugarcane. Its arrival and subsequent development into one of the New World's most important tropical exports had enormous consequences for the human component of the Columbian exchange and for European constructions of "race."

The consequences of the Columbian exchange included the decimation and outright disappearance of many Native American groups, the oppression and exploitation of others, and their reduction to marginalized existences within newly formed state societies dominated by Europeans. In addition, over 10 million Africans were enslaved and transported to the New World to provide labor for the growth and expansion of European capitalism. Later, when these African slaves were freed, people of other diverse origins—India, Indonesia, the Middle East, and even Africa—

were brought, sometimes by enticement, sometimes by trickery, sometimes by force, to take their place. All the while, Europeans themselves came to labor, not always willingly and not always as members of an elite ruling class. The Caribbean, along with some parts of the South American mainland (especially northeastern Brazil and the Guianas), provided the settings for the first large-scale experiments in tropical plantation agriculture. These in turn provided the model, and also much of the investment capital, for the development of the Industrial Revolution in Europe and the United States (Williams 1994).

Meanwhile, the Columbian exchange also gave the peoples of the New World something they had never had before: an all-inclusive name for themselves. Columbus, mistakenly thinking that he had sailed all the way to the Indies, called the people he encountered *indios*, or "Indians." Before this, they had defined themselves according to their languages and cultures; after Columbus, they were defined by the Europeans as people from a place they had never heard of, much less visited. Over time the word became, like *nigger* in the United States, a term of deprecation, and most Native American peoples today prefer to be called by their ethnolinguistic name (Aymara, Maya, etc.), or even *indígena*, meaning "indigenous." Further confusion arises when we realize that in a number of places, such as Guyana and Trinidad, there are people who really qualify as "Indians," that is, people from India. They are often referred to as "East Indians" to distinguish them from Native Americans.

As we continue our survey, we shall see that the fates of Native American peoples were different in different areas of Latin America and the Caribbean. They all but disappeared from the Caribbean islands, but in other areas, such as Mexico, Guatemala, Paraguay, and the Andean countries, they remain significant, although often abused and exploited, segments of society. And in some regions, notably the drainage basins of the Amazon and Orinoco rivers, small populations attempt to hang on to their traditional ways of life in the face of the ever-increasing challenges of "development" and their ever-intensifying integration, willing or not, into the economies of state societies.

AMERINDIAN AMERICA

Amerindian America consists primarily of those regions that had relatively large and dense populations of indigenous peoples at the time of Columbus's arrival. These regions include Mexico, the interior of Central America, and the cordillera of the Andes. Indigenous peoples in these regions had created complex societies with all the characteristics of states: a ruling elite; a full-time priesthood that managed the state religion; a bureaucracy; a middle class of tradespeople and artisans; and an army to defend and, if possible, extend the dominion of the state. At the time of the Spanish Conquest, the Aztecs of Mexico and the Inca of the central Andes had created empires, in the latter case an empire of greater extent than the Roman Empire. A smaller but equally complex state society, that of the Maya, had existed previously in Central America and Mexico, but this society had collapsed and the Mayans whom the Spanish encountered were living in essentially village-scale communities.

The dense populations of these Amerindian states ensured that relatively high indigenous populations would survive to be incorporated into the new Spanish domains, and it is indeed in these areas that we find the highest percentages of people claiming Amerindian status, as shown in Table 13-1. In contrast, we will see later that the percentages of Amerindians in the countries making up Plantation America approach or equal zero.

The incorporation of Amerindians into the newly created Spanish domains typically entailed becoming a *peón*, or serf, on a plot of land granted to the conquerors and their allies by the Spanish rulers as part of the *encomienda* system. Under this system, the Spanish *encomenderos* had rights to the land and its produce, as well as to the labor of the Amerindians, who came attached to the land

as a result of their *reducción* (reduction) to territories determined by the colonizers. The labor extracted was typically in the form of mining, as well as public works such as road building and the like, in addition to their obligation to grow crops portions of which were owed to the landowners. Hence, in many places the system closely resembled the feudalism that was disappearing in other parts of Europe at the time but that was still a vital part of the Spaniards' worldview.

As we have seen, Columbus called the people he encountered *indios* (Indians) because he thought that he had reached the Indies. From the beginning, most of the Spanish who came to the New World were males, looking for adventure and wealth; they were not averse to finding mates also. The term *blanco* refers to people of European descent, who are generally rare in the highlands, except in the larger towns and cities, where they are concentrated. In Spanish, the word *mestizo* was applied to the offspring of matings, and it is still used to refer to someone who is a mixture of European and Amerindian descent. *Mestizaje*, the mixing of Amerindians and Europeans, has been the subject of differing ideologies over the centuries. As Martínez-Echazabal (1998) reports, the Amerindians were at first viewed as even more savage and less human than Africans, and it was thought by some that mestizaje would result in the disappearance of "civilized" European society in the Americas. As time went on, however, mestizaje became part of an ideology centered on creating new societies distinct from the European colonizers, as in the ideology of *la raza* (the race) in Mexico.

The result of mestizaje is that in those areas that had the largest indigenous populations, populations that were not obliterated early on, mestizos form a very significant portion of the population, as illustrated in Table 13-2.

TABLE 13-1 Amerindian populations, as percentage of total population, for selected countries of Amerindian America

Country	Bolivia	Perú	Guatemala	Ecuador	Mexico
Percent	55	54	43	40	30

TABLE 13-2	Mestizos as percentage of total population, for selected countries of Amerindian America			
Country	Honduras/El Salvador	Nicaragua	Venezuela	Mexico
Percent	90	69	67	60

The Andes

In the Andes, the distinct, yet interdependent, nature of these three groups is especially well illustrated by the relationships among the indigenous Aymara and their mestizo and blanco neighbors. The Aymara were, before the Spanish arrived, one of the principal groups in the Inca Empire. There is evidence that a language related to Aymara was used by the Incas in their first territorial expansion along the Andean chain; just prior to the conquest, however, Quechua had replaced Aymara as the imperial language.

Today, the Aymara live in scattered communities throughout a large region surrounding Lake Titicaca, where Perú, Bolivia, and Chile come together, a region known as the *Altiplano* ("high plain"). They occupy an ecological niche similar to that of the Sherpas of Tibet, with crops and animals adapted to high altitudes and extreme daily fluctuations in temperature. Frequently, in the preconquest Andes, indigenous peoples used a "vertical archipelago" system of farming, under which each family had plots at different altitudes from near sea level to around 12,000 feet (Murra 1972). This allowed families access to foods and products from tropical, temperate, and alpine environmental niches. After the Spanish imposed their limited European view of landholding, sometimes in rather arbitrary and capricious ways, this spectrum of resources was closed off to most native groups, with far-reaching consequences for their subsistence strategies.

Before the Bolivian revolution of the 1950s, many Aymara were essentially serfs in a feudal system that tied them economically as well as physically to large haciendas owned by the Spanish-speaking elite. Presently, they typically work their own small plots, planting especially potatoes (some 2,000 varieties) and quinoa using traditional technology such as the foot plow. They also herd sheep and camelids, and they keep guinea pigs for food as well. Many Aymara have gone beyond this, however, by integrating themselves into the national marketing system connecting rural producing areas to consumers in the cities.

To supplement their income, they may also hire themselves out to work on the mestizos' land, which is usually better than their own, more marginal land. The *misti*, as the Aymara call them, need the Aymara's labor; the Aymara need the misti's cash. There is a certain element of mutual distrust and deprecation: the Aymara may feel that the misti are too lazy to work their own land; the misti complain about the Aymara's addiction to cycles of fiestas. For the Aymara, the sponsorship of a fiesta, which impoverishes the sponsors but at the same time binds them to their community, is an essential part of adult life; for the misti and the blancos, the fiestas are distractions from work.

The Aymara have maintained many elements of their traditional religion, and these are practiced alongside Roman Catholic rites and ceremonies: the Catholic god and saints must be invoked, as well as the *awki*, the spirits of high places, and also the ancestors. Crucially, both the Aymara and the misti need the "white" priest for the blessing of the Virgin. The Aymara sometimes use the term *viracocha* to refer to the white elites, a reference to the light-skinned, bearded god who in Andean myth was supposed to have gone away and then returned in the form of the Spaniards.

Because many people in the highlands are mestizos who may be physically indistinguishable from the indios, the principal markers of "Indian-ness" are language and clothing. The colorful and "exotic" clothing worn by "traditional" Native Americans in the Andes frequently

Evo Morales, Aymara Indian President of Bolivia.

represents costumes originating in medieval Spain that were imposed by the Spanish in the years of the conquest. In any case, to "pass" into mestizo society Native Americans may need only to put on European-style clothes and speak Spanish instead of Quechua or Aymara (Buechler and Buechler 1971; Hardman 1981).

The Aymara language is co-official with Quechua and Spanish in Bolivia; Quechua is co-official with Spanish in Perú. These languages, plus Guaraní, which is co-official with Spanish in Paraguay, are the only Amerindian languages that enjoy official status in Latin America and the Caribbean.

PLANTATION AMERICA

Plantation America encompasses primarily the tropical and subtropical lowland areas that were best suited for the development of export agriculture based on tropical cultigens. This includes most of the Caribbean islands, as well as the low-lying Caribbean coastal regions of Central and South America: the Guianas (Guyana, French Guiana, and Surinam) and northern Brazil. The distinguishing demographic feature of these areas is the large presence of the descendants of African slaves, people who in censuses are referred to as "black" or "African." Figures for some selected countries of Plantation America are given in Table 13-3.

These regions, especially the French and British territories in the Caribbean, are special in any discussion of "race" and ethnicity. It was here that Europeans put into place the system of using enslaved West Africans as labor for the production of sugar and other tropical staples. However, this in itself might not have produced the virulent racist ideology that developed, had not the particular social, political, and economic context for this contact been as it was. Within this context, a tiny European "white" elite dominated a much larger African "black" population that was enslaved and that existed as chattel property of the white elite. The labor of this enslaved work force was directed toward the planting, cultivation, and processing for export of tropical staples, with sugarcane being especially important.

The virtual elimination of native peoples in these areas, itself a principal reason for the importation of African slaves, had another consequence: the early and continued reproductive mixing of Europeans and Africans, usually the outcome of mating between African females and European males. The result was an ever-growing population of people of mixed descent, whose status was,

TABLE 13–3	People reported as "black," as percentage of total population, for selected countries of Plantation America		
Country	Haiti	Barbados	Antigua	Grenada
Percent	95	93	91	85

TABLE 13-4 Percentages of mulatto or "mixed" for selected countries of Plantation America

Country	Martinique	Dominican Republic	Cuba	Brazil
Percent	94	73	51	40

historically, often ambiguous. At first, it was thought that the offspring of such matings would be infertile, like mules, the product of mating between horses and donkeys. Hence, they acquired the labels *mulato* (Spanish and Portuguese) and *mulatre* (French), words that found their way into English as *mulatto*; the corresponding process is sometimes referred to as *mulataje*, on a parallel with *mestizaje*. Of course, any photograph of a crowd of people in Cuba or Brazil refutes the notion of their infertility! Table 13-4 lists the percentages of people classed as mulatto or "mixed" for selected countries of Plantation America.

An additional aspect in this context was the rise of empiricist science in the West, and with it the quest to classify things, living and nonliving, into orderly categories. In the eighteenth century, Linnaeus' classification of humans into four types (white, black, red, and yellow) was soon followed by Blumenbach's revision, which included a fifth category (Ethiopian, Caucasian, Mongoloid, American, and Malay; see Chapter 2). Soon, schemes with many more categories were proposed. But, most importantly for our topic, in addition to the supposed physical traits that separated these alleged "races," mental and behavioral traits were also concocted, mostly out of the clouded pseudoscientific world of European

ethnocentrism. In this way, an ideology of racial inferiority, inferiority represented not just in physical features but also in linguistic and cultural forms, developed as a means of justifying slavery, or at least making it easier for the slave owners and traders to live with the system they had created. As the historian and former prime minister of Trinidad and Tobago Eric Williams (1994), argued, in this view African slavery was the cause of the racist ideology that developed in its support, not the other way around.

One outstanding feature of Plantation America is the predominance in nearly every country of a *creole* language. Creole languages take the majority of their vocabularies from one of the European languages (Spanish, Portuguese, French, English); they take their syntax, to at least some degree, from the West African languages spoken by the slaves who were brought to the New World. Linguists disagree about the details of their genesis, but it is clear that they are the product of the linguistic creativity of West Africans. Table 13-5 provides a sample sentence in the Jamaican (English) Creole, Haitian (French) Creole, and Papiamentu, a Spanish / Portuguese Creole spoken in parts of the Netherland Antilles. All the words are from European languages except the Jamaican *nyam*, which is from a West African language.

TABLE 13-5 The sentence "I am eating" as translated into three creole languages of Plantation America

Language	Subject I	Progressive (am) . . . -ing	Verb eat
Jamaican Creole	Mi	a	nyam
Haitian Creole	M	ap	manje
Papiamentu	Mi	ta	kome

The structure, which in all cases places the progressive marker corresponding to the English *-ing* suffix before the verb, is typical of a number of West African languages spoken by the slaves.

Creole languages are the majority languages throughout Plantation America, with the exception of the Spanish countries and Brazil (although some linguists claim semicreole status for Brazilian Portuguese). The lack of creole languages in Cuba, the Dominican Republic, and other Spanish-speaking areas is generally thought to be due to the fact that in the early years of settlement only small numbers of African slaves were brought to these places. Furthermore, these slaves mostly worked on small farms alongside their Spanish-speaking owners, and thus had access to more or less normal acquisition of Spanish as a second language. Their descendants were able to pass on Spanish to the slaves who arrived later and in larger numbers. In contrast, in the French- and English-speaking territories, the European population was typically very small and the slaves interacted mostly with each other, rather than directly with Europeans, reinforcing the separateness of the creole languages from the European ones.

Despite their ubiquity, creole languages enjoy official recognition only in Haiti, where Haitian *Kreyòl* is co-official with French, and in the Netherlands Antilles, where Papiamentu shares official status with Dutch and English. A standardized writing system and materials for literacy education have been developed for Kreyòl, and books, both fiction and nonfiction, have been written in Kreyòl. In other areas, and, for that matter, even in Haiti among some elite circles, the debate about the appropriate use of creole languages continues, and children are expected to deal with the official European language from the time they enter school, often in a sort of sink-or-swim way (Holm 1989).

Brazil

It was in northeastern Brazil that the Portuguese, in the sixteenth century, established the first sugar plantations in the New World. These plantations were modeled on those they had already been operating, with African slaves, on the Azores and other islands near the coast of Africa. The Native Americans who inhabited Brazil, especially the part of Brazil that forms the Amazon drainage basin, were (and are) generally foragers and small-scale slash-and-burn farmers living in villages scattered through the rain forest. Hence, they were not available for plantation labor. To provide labor for the plantations, then, more than 3.6 million African slaves were taken to Brazil between the sixteenth and nineteenth centuries (Richardson 1992). Hence, the area making up primarily the state of Bahia is the region of Brazil with the strongest African presence. Population figures for Brazil are given in Table 13-6.

Afro-Brazilians, like people of African descent in Haiti, Cuba, and elsewhere, have conserved and also embellished important aspects of their African culture. This is especially true in the domain of religion. Many Brazilians participate in religious activities and rituals associated with *Candomblé*, a syncretism of West African and European Catholic religions similar to the Haitian *Vodoun* and the Cuban *Santería*. In these religions West African spirits are identified with Catholic saints; important components include the veneration of ancestors and possession by spirits during intense ceremonies.

As slaves, of course, Afro-Brazilians were subject to the same aspects of "race" ideology as were Africans in other parts of Latin America and the Caribbean. This ideology includes the devaluing of Africans' physical features and also their mental abilities, and these attitudes are present today. Nevertheless, Brazil promotes itself as a sort of racial democracy, a "mixed-race nation," an idea that was expressed widely in 1988, the centennial of the abolition of slavery in Brazil. But the popular saying, "Every Brazilian male

TABLE 13-6 Brazilian ethnic groups as percentages of total population

Category	White	Mulatto	Black	Other
Percent	54	40	5	1

needs three women in his life: a white woman to bear his heirs, a black woman to cook for him, and a *mulata* to make love to" suggests that Brazilians are not as color-blind as they might like to think (Winn 1999). It may be true that Brazilian culture is different in terms of the way it models and interprets "racial" differences, but these differences still play an important role in Brazilian culture.

While doing research in Brazil in the 1950s, the anthropologist Marvin Harris (1964) noticed that Brazilians used a much greater variety of terms to refer to people of different physical types. To explore this phenomenon, Harris showed Brazilians photographs of people and asked them to tell what "race" the person in the photo belonged to. Surprisingly, he found that the same person could be categorized differently depending on the context in which they were observed. For example, a person called *preto* (black) when wearing old clothes and standing in front of a poor-looking house might be called *moreno* (brown) or even *branco* (white) when seen dressed up in front of a wealthy-looking house.

In an attempt to attack this problem systematically, Harris designed a set of cards, each of which contained a simple drawing of a person. There were 36 male and 36 female portraits. The portraits differed by three skin tones (light, medium, dark), three hair types (straight, wavy, curly), two nose widths (narrow, wide), and two lip types (thin, full). All 36 combinations were represented for each sex. Harris showed people the cards and asked them to characterize each drawing, with the hope of uncovering the rules Brazilians use to place people into "racial" categories. Harris found a wide variety of terms available to Brazilians which allows them to call attention to different combinations of physical traits (skin color, hair form, etc.). In addition, as shown by the earlier experiments with photographs, Brazilians can also take into account social and economic circumstances in calculating their "race." The result is that the Brazilian system is a continuum, from *preto* at one end to *branco* at the other and a number of categories in between.

In contrast, North Americans, at least as far as "black" and "white" are concerned, produce a simple dichotomy. The North American rule is a *hypodescent* rule because it places people into the category that has the *lower* prestige in the society. Under the hypodescent rule, people with *any* known African ancestry can be considered "black."

Harris's explanation for the difference between U.S. and Brazilian folk models involves taking into account the different socioeconomic conditions that prevailed in these places during colonial times. In the United States, during the period of slavery, the ratio of slaves to Europeans was relatively small; only in places like coastal South Carolina, where rice (to help feed Caribbean slaves) was grown on large plantations, were the ratios anything like those of Brazil or the Caribbean. There were plenty of European immigrants available to fill the middle-level jobs, such as blacksmith, carpenter, and wheelwright, as well as to work on small farms providing food for the plantations, and even to serve as militia. The strict categorization of both slaves and former slaves, as well as people of "mixed" descent, into a "black" (Negro, Colored) category, helped keep them from competing for these jobs. At the same time it helped keep the power of the planter class secure, by ensuring that poor whites saw themselves as belonging to a category distinct and separate from both slaves and ex-slaves, and thus preventing the two groups of exploited people from joining together against the planters.

In Brazil, In contrast, there were relatively fewer Europeans available to do these sorts of jobs, which still needed to be done. Harris concluded that this led to a more open system that allowed people to move around and occupy a greater variety of roles in the society. In Brazil, and in other parts of Plantation America, there was less need to maintain a strictly defined boundary between the Europeans and everyone else.

This is not to suggest that Brazilians are "color-blind" or that skin color and other physical features do not make any difference to Brazilians. In Brazil, light skin and European features are valued over darker skin and non-European features. In fact, Brazilians are probably more consciously aware of these differences than North Americans typically are. The saying quoted earlier, about men needing white women to give them heirs (i.e., as legal wives) and black and brown women to cook for them and to give them (extramarital) sex, has no analog in U.S. culture. What it does suggest is that in Brazil people are spread out along a continuum with many more points on it, rather than being squeezed into two mutually exclusive categories.

More recently, Francisco Gil-White (2001) has called Harris's conclusions into question by pointing out that Harris did not follow up to discover whether the terms he elicited actually represented "racial" or ethnic groups, that is, groupings based on descent or enculturation. Instead, they may have simply represented sorting by physical features. This is an important criticism, and more work needs to be done in this area. We will revisit this issue when we discuss concepts of "race" in the Caribbean. Meanwhile, it is worth noting that in recent years officials in Brazil appear to be adopting a form of the U.S. hypodescent rule for legalistic purposes, so that people are not being asked to decide whether they are "black" or "white" for purposes such as fulfilling quotas in university admissions (Bailey 2008).

The Caribbean

THE AMERINDIANS. When Columbus arrived in the Caribbean in 1492, several ethnolinguistic groups inhabited the region. Small numbers of a foraging people known as the Ciboney could be found on Cuba. However, by about 700 A.D. most of the Greater Antilles and the Bahamas were occupied by Arawakan-speaking peoples who had migrated northward from South America along the chain of islands. They called themselves by various names such as *Taíno* (Hispaniola), *Lucaya* (Bahamas), and *Iñeri* in the Lesser Antilles. These Arawakan-speaking groups were organized into villages that subsisted on horticulture supplemented by fishing and hunting. They had a ranked system of social hierarchy, and their word for their leaders gave us the Spanish word *cacique*. Some other words that

entered European languages from Arawak are *hammock* and *hurricane*. The Dominican Spanish word *bohío*, meaning a rural shack, was the Arawaks' name for the island that the Spanish called *Hispaniola*.

The Arawaks essentially disappeared from the Greater Antilles within half a century or so of Columbus's first visit. Their disappearance was due in part to their lack of immunity to certain diseases, especially smallpox and influenza, to which both Europeans and Africans carried some immunity due to their long association with domesticated animals, like cattle, sheep, poultry, and so on, from which these diseases migrated to humans in the Old World (Diamond 1998). However, abusive and even genocidal behavior on the part of the colonists also factored in their disappearance, as it did in parts of North America.

In the Dominican Republic, the Taíno are gone but by no means forgotten. In Santo Domingo, the capital, there is a statue of a woman named *Anacaona*, who is revered as a symbol of the Arawak people. She was hanged in 1503, after participating in an unsuccessful uprising against the Spanish. The Arawaks on Puerto Rico called their island *Borikén*, and this is the name used by the Puerto Rican independence movement as a symbol of their desire to break from past colonial relationships. The group works to preserve and increase awareness of Taíno language and culture (Rouse 1992). Arawak-speaking people today live along the northern fringe of South America. They include the Guajiros of the Guajira Peninsula between Colombia and Venezuela and the Locono of Venezuela.

Just prior to the European encounter, another group, the Caribs, had invaded the Windward and Leeward Islands from the region of South America near the mouth of the Orinoco River. In the Lesser Antilles, the indigenous peoples survived, marginally, on some of the Leeward and Windward Islands. These small islands, while claimed initially by Spain, did not offer the gold and other riches that the Spanish adventurers sought and thus were mostly ignored by the Spanish. After 1600, the French and English began to settle them and set up sugar and other plantations. By this time a culture had developed that consisted of a mixture of the Arawaks, who had arrived earlier, and the more recent Caribs; this culture came to be known as Island Carib and extended from Grenada in the south to Dominica in the north.

At first, the Island Carib society was probably bilingual, with both women and men speaking Arawak while Carib was maintained as a men's prestige language. Eventually, though, a "new" language developed that was essentially Arawakan in structure but that contained some dual vocabulary: Arawakan for women, Carib for men. For example, to this day women and men use different pronouns meaning "I": *nuguya* for women and *aw* for men. Historically, there were other differences. The new language came to be known as *Garifuna*.

On Grenada, French forces eventually drove the Island Caribs to the very northern tip of the island, where they jumped off a cliff into the sea rather than face defeat. The place where this happened is called Morne des Sauteurs, "hill of the jumpers"; the nearby town is called Sauteurs. In contrast, on Dominica, which is a larger and more rugged island, a community of Island Caribs has survived on the windward (east) coast. These are "true" Caribs, and their reserve was set aside for them by the government of Dominica in 1903. The reserve serves as the focal point for their ethnic revitalization (Hulme and Whitehead 1992).

As a further complication, the Island Caribs on St. Vincent were joined at some point by African slaves who had escaped from a shipwreck and managed to reach shore. The resulting group came to be known as the Black Caribs. As on Grenada, there was a lengthy conflict between these people and the British, who wanted to make the island safe for settlement. In 1797, in one of the more bizarre stories from the Caribbean past, most of the remaining Black Caribs were rounded up and put on vessels that carried them to the Bay Islands lying between Belize and Honduras. The British left them there, charitably, with some supplies.

These forced migrants and their descendants prospered, spreading to the neighboring mainland territories of Belize, Guatemala, Honduras, and Nicaragua. They have maintained the Garifuna language and many elements of their culture, and see themselves as distinct from the "Creole" population, which consists of Anglophone West Indians. In Nicaragua, they mixed to some extent with the Miskitu, who occupy the region known as the Mosquito Coast (Gonzalez 1988). The Garifuna are renowned as "linguists," that is, people who have a facility for languages; they are prominent in the teaching profession in Belize. They maintain important aspects of their culture, which include the *punta* drumming and singing in honor of their ancestors. They also retain in their ethnohistory knowledge of their homeland, St. Vincent.

Although it is sometimes claimed that there are no longer any Caribbean Amerindian people, on Puerto Rico there exists a group who call themselves the *Jatibonicu Taíno*. Furthermore, the Caribbean Amerindian Centrelink is an Internet site maintained to "focus upon or shed light upon the Native peoples of the Caribbean and circum-Caribbean."[2]

"WHITES," "BLACKS," AND OTHERS IN THE CARIBBEAN.

As a result of the African slave trade, and the subsequent mating of Europeans and others with Africans, approximately two-thirds of the people of the Caribbean can claim at least some African ancestry, making them, for census purposes, either black or mulatto/mixed. Because the Spanish territories didn't import large numbers of African slaves until the second half of the nineteenth century, the numbers there are fairly low, but note the high percentage of the populations that is mixed, as shown in Table 13-7.

In contrast, on Haiti the black population is about 95 percent, with whites and mulattos making up the other 5 percent. This is a direct result of the fact that Haiti was a French sugar colony almost from the start. Then, during the Haitian revolution (1790–1894), many of the already small white elite were either killed or forced to flee the country.

Other Caribbean countries fall somewhere in between the extremes of Haiti, on the one hand, and Cuba and the Dominican Republic on the

TABLE 13–7 Ethnic groups as percentage of population for two countries of the Hispanic Caribbean

	White	Black	Mulatto	Other
Cuba	37	11	51	1
Dominican Republic	16	11	73	—

other. For example, Table 13-8 provides figures for blacks, whites, and mulattos for a selected sample of Lesser Antillean states.

But how do people in the Caribbean place people into "racial" categories? Since the Caribbean belongs mostly to Plantation America, it seems reasonable to presume that most places in the Caribbean should follow a pattern more like the Brazilian one than the North American pattern. Nevertheless, the Caribbean subsumes a number of differently structured societies. As described by Lowenthal (1972), social stratification in Caribbean societies may take place along lines of "color" (i.e., "race") or "class" (social and/or economic status). Some societies are stratified along one or the other dimension; some are stratified along both; a few are relatively unstratified, or homogeneous.

Following Lowenthal, I formulated the following hypotheses regarding the way in which people from the Caribbean would deal with Harris's drawings:

- Societies that are stratified by both by color and social class, like Trinidad and Barbados, should show the most "racial" terms. In these societies, people in the upper classes tend to be "white" or light-skinned, while people in the working classes tend to be "black" or dark-skinned. However, there are wealthy upper-class "blacks" as well as poor lower-class "whites."
- Homogeneous societies, like Carriacou, should show the fewest "racial" terms. In these societies there is little or no stratification along lines of color or class.
- Societies stratified by class or color but not both should fall somewhere between the two extremes. Examples of these societies are Grenada and Dominica, which have no "white" elite and in which there is little or no correlation between skin color and social class.

I tested these hypotheses using the drawings from Harris's Brazil study.[3] Both "black" and "white" North Americans placed most of the portraits into discrete categories labeled white, black, and Indian or Asian. What happened after that varied; usually there were one or two extra categories like Hispanic, American Indian, or Australian Aborigine, into which they put the portraits that didn't seem to fit the three basic categories.

I then used the portraits on informants from Barbados, Trinidad, Jamaica, Bahamas, Dominica, and Grenada; I also tried them out on people in

TABLE 13–8 Ethnic groups as percentage of population in selected countries of the Lesser Antilles

	Barbados	Grenada	St. Lucia	Trinidad
Black	92	85	90	40
White	3	1	1	1
Mulatto/mixed	3	11	6	18
Other	2	3	3	41

Carriacou. In general, I found an overall pattern that more closely resembled Harris's Brazilian pattern than the North American pattern. I also found that the hypothesis about the correlation between social stratification and complexity of categorization was confirmed: Trinidad and Barbados had the most categories, Grenada and Dominica had fewer, and Carriacou had the fewest of all.

TRINIDAD. Trinidad (the larger part of the state of Trinidad and Tobago) is a complex society stratified along the lines of both class and color. It was Spanish for a while, then French, and then British. It became an independent state in 1962. Because of its historical background, the ethnic makeup of Trinidad is especially complex. The Spanish, French, and British all brought African slaves to work in the sugarcane fields. After emancipation (1835), when many ex-slaves preferred working their own small farms rather than continuing to work on the sugar plantations, tens of thousands of East Indians, as well as a number of Chinese, were brought in as indentured laborers. Consultants from Trinidad offered the following seven basic terms in response to the portraits: *negro, indian, dogla* (a mixture of East Indian and African), *mestizo, panyol* (i.e., Venezuelan), *Spanish* (i.e., European), and *white*. In addition, nine compound terms occurred: *madrasi-Indian, kuli-indian, Tobago-negro, chinee-negro, French-creole* (= *local-white*), *clearskin-dogla, koko-panyol, half-white* (= mulatto), and *local-white*.

DOMINICA. Dominica, in the Windward Islands, is a society stratified by economic class rather than by color. This means that there are social classes, but the classes are based on wealth rather than "racial" affinity, and there is no substantial "white" elite as there is in places like Jamaica, Barbados, and Trinidad. The Dominican consultant offered the following five terms in response to the portraits: *nèg* (= black), *blan* or *beke* (= white), *kuli* (= East Indian), *black-and-kuli*, and *chaben*. Besides these five terms, the consultant offered the descriptive modifier *fairskin-*, which can be used to modify the first three terms. None of Harris's faces

elicited the term *Carib*, which is an important ethnic group within Dominica.

CARRIACOU. Carriacou is a relatively homogeneous society with a strong cultural ideal of egalitarianism that is reinforced in a number of ways, including informal food sharing and more formal redistributive feasts at special occasions such as boat launchings, weddings, and the like. Harris's faces elicited no single-word terms such as *white* or *black* to identify the portraits. Instead, the Carriacouans used color terms as descriptive adjectives: they were always accompanied by a noun such as *people, woman, man, girl,* or *boy*. The terms included *dark-/black-, brown-/brownskin-, red-/redskin-, pink-* (i.e., albino), and *white-*.

On Carriacou, the term *white people* is sometimes used to describe the people of Windward, a village that was traditionally inhabited by descendants of British and French indentured workers. Until well into the twentieth century this group was a "closed community"; however, for some time now there has been intermarriage between the "white people" and the much more numerous people of African descent. Still, for most Carriacouans, "white" implies someone not born on Carriacou; no one born and raised in Carriacou is normally thought of as "white."

My research reported here, which used Harris's drawings of faces, is equally open to Gil-White's (2001) criticism of Harris: Were my informants simply sorting by physical features visible on the cards, but not really telling me anything about any "racial" or ethnic categories they might have had? This is really a question for further research. However, it seems clear that the way in which the faces are approached varies significantly, both between the United States and the Caribbean and also within the Caribbean itself. In the United States and Trinidad, people used terms that could be plugged into a sentence, like "The *x* live on that side of town," where *x* might be *whites* or *blacks*, and so on. The principal difference between the United States and Trinidad (and other societies stratified by both class and "race") seems to be the number of terms given. In the United States, the faces can be fitted pretty easily into four or five categories; in Trinidad, more categories are available.

On the other hand, I do think that my Carriacouan informants were simply sorting or, rather, describing in the way that they might use to call attention to someone. They provided not terms, but adjectives: "You know Mary; she is the *brown-skin* one." This was their response to the physical features presented in the faces. And yet, they clearly also have ways of constructing for themselves identities that set them apart from other people in the world, and that also divide them into groups internal to Carriacou.

First, Carriacou people see themselves as distinctive, by virtue of having been born and raised on Carriacou of parents who were also born and raised on Carriacou, and so on. This sets them apart from everyone else in the world, even nearby Grenadians. They are *Carriacou people*: more honest, thrifty, and hardworking than people from other places.

Carriacou people are also very aware of their African ancestry. They conceptualize at least some of their behaviors and beliefs as "African," and they contrast these with "white" behaviors and beliefs. One such behavior is the food sharing mentioned earlier. One evening when I had prepared a little fish broth, an elderly friend dropped by just as I was about to eat. So I shared out all the broth between the two of us. As we were about to eat, a young man happened by; I asked if he had eaten, and he said no. So, after asking permission, I took enough broth from each of us to make a plate for him. The elderly Carriacouan commented that I was behaving "like *negro people*," since everyone knew that *white people* would not share their food in this way.

Finally, Carriacou people traditionally categorized themselves as belonging to different African *nations* or *bloods*. This is described in the next section.

Whatever is going on, description or categorization, the situation is not significantly different for the Hispanic and Francophone Caribbean. For example, in Spanish America, the term *negro* tends to be reserved for people with very dark skin; it is not a hypodescent term. The classificatory term

mulato, which was formerly used as a term for someone of mixed African and European descent, has been mostly replaced by descriptive terms such as *trigueño* (wheat colored), *acanelado* (cinnamon colored), and *cobrizo* (copper colored). In addition, the term *moreno* can be used for anyone, from European brunettes to people with dark skin. All these terms can be modified in various ways. For example, a person might be *moreno claro* (light brown), or *blanco quemado* (sunburned white), or *negro fileno* (dark-skinned with a straight nose) (Solaún et al. 1987).

It is worth mentioning that in some Hispanic areas, *negrito* and *negrita* (literally "little black") are used as terms of affection. Similarly, on Haiti the Creole term *nèg* (from French *negre*) means something like "guy" or "buddy" and can be used with people of any skin color.

African Ethnicities: Carriacouan "Nations"

One frequently ignored aspect of Caribbean ethnic identity is that different African ethnolinguistic groups were represented among the early slave populations. In early censuses, slaves born in Africa were designated by a given name (George, Mary), as well as by the name of the ethnic group they belonged to (e.g., "Georges Bambara"). Slaves born in the New World were designated as "creole." The 1750 census of Carriacou identify several African ethnolinguistic groups (Brinkley 1978): Bambara, Congo, Ibo, Arada, Anan. A number of others were added to the culture later.

On Carriacou, people self-classified themselves traditionally by the African "nation" (ethnic group) into which they were born, as determined by the nation of their mother (a matrilineal descent rule). There was a hierarchy of nations, with the *Kromanti* and *Mandingo* at the top. The term *Kromanti*, sometimes spelled *Cromanti*, refers to the port city of Cormantyn, in what is now Ghana, which served as a holding area for many Africans on their way to enslavement in the New World. At a *Big Drum* ceremony, which is performed on special occasions and involves summoning the ancestors back from Africa, the *Mandingo* and

Kromanti songs are the first of the actual nation songs to be played. Each nation has its own drumming pattern and associated songs. There were also stereotypical beliefs about physical and mental attributes of particular nations, for example: *Kongo* people are very dark; *Kromanti* women are independent and prefer to remain single (Hill 1977). This knowledge of one's African ethnic roots is less important today than it was in the past; traditionally, it set limits on possible marriage partners, because a person was not supposed to marry someone from the same nation (Hill 1977; Kephart 2000; McDaniel 1998; Smith 1962).

The "Redlegs" of Barbados

In the earliest years of the developing Barbadian sugar industry, planters tried to satisfy their need for labor by recruiting workers from the British Isles. Sometimes, workers were enticed by promises of a plot of land after serving their period of contract; sometimes, they were shipped out involuntarily for a variety of reasons. On Barbados, once their contract was completed, they found that virtually all the decent land was already in sugar production; they were thus forced to accept marginal lands on the windward side of the island. Those who did developed a closed community of small farmers similar to, but if anything more closed than, the one at Windward, Carriacou.

For many years, these "redlegs," as they came to be called, were the poorest group on Barbados; they nevertheless took pride in the fact that they were "white," and therefore united by color, if not by class, with the planters. By the middle of the twentieth century, some of them had begun to mix with the "African" population; and some became successful as merchants. Still, some redlegs retained their prejudicial attitudes toward the African population (for an in-depth history of the redlegs, see Sheppard 1977).

Some European indentured laborers who were unable to obtain land on Barbados migrated westward to the Windward and Leeward Islands, where they founded communities similar to that on Barbados. Two such communities are the one at Windward, Carriacou, and another at Mount Moritz, Grenada. These white nonelites are known as *mongmong* (from French Creole *moun-mòn*, "mountain people") on Grenada. As on Barbados, historically, they have been looked down upon by other segments of the population. Interestingly, on Carriacou, until they began intermarrying with the "African" population, they belonged to no nation; this limited the extent of the social networks available to them. (See Howard Johnson and Karl Watson [1998] for essays on these and other white minorities in the Caribbean.)

The East Indians

After emancipation, many ex-slaves refused to work for their former masters on the sugar plantations. To supply the need for labor, the industry turned again to indentured laborers, imported this time from India and other parts of Asia. The majority went to Trinidad and the Guianas. In Trinidad they are about 40 percent of the population; in Guyana, 50 percent; in Suriname, they are about 33 percent, but the number rises to 49 percent if the Javanese, also East Asians, are included. The anthropologist Morton Klass (1988) has written about the East Indians of Trinidad.

The indentured laborers were frequently able to complete their period of indenture and acquire a farm or shop or, eventually, a business. Their descendants have been relatively successful in the societies in which they are a substantial part of the population and have integrated themselves into the social, political, and economic spheres of the countries where they live. In the process, they have maintained much of their culture. This success has come at a price, however. The price is a long-standing, and sometimes violent, relationship with the descendants of African slaves. Afro-West Indians at times felt that the East Indians had kept them from making a living by selling their own labor at a price lower than the former slaves were willing to do. In turn, East Indians have often seen Africans as lazy, unwilling to work hard in order to get ahead. In both Guyana and Trinidad, especially, East Indians and Africans have vied with each other for political power (Eriksen 1992).

The Maroons

Whenever and wherever possible, the African slaves ran away from their plantations and founded *maroon* communities (from Spanish *cimarrón* "wild"), documented extensively by anthropologist Richard Price (1979). This *maroonage* was feasible on the larger islands, like Jamaica, and the South American mainland, where ample unsettled land was available outside the reach of the authorities. One area where this occurred, and where the descendants of the original maroons continue to maintain an existence separate from the larger society, is the so-called "Cockpit Country" of Jamaica, settled in the eighteenth century and described by anthropologist Zora Neal Hurston (1990). Another is San Basilio de Palenque, near Cartagena, Colombia. A third, and perhaps the most famous, consists of various groups, including the Saramaka, Ndjuka, and others, inhabiting the interior of Suriname (see also Herskovits 1966).

Perhaps more than any other Africans in the New World, these maroon groups, by separating themselves early on from the plantation culture, were able to maintain aspects of the African cultures from which they had come. These include religious practices, various arts and crafts, verbal performance, horticultural methods, and so on. In all cases, they speak creole languages, languages that contain European vocabulary grafted onto West African sentence structures.

ETHNIC REVITALIZATION

As is evident throughout much of the world, in the Caribbean and Latin America contemporary humans have adjusted to living in large-scale societies influenced by globalization and nationalization trends. Within these once traditional societies, many of the human interactions that occur are anonymous. There is, too, often a culturally homogenizing trend reinforced by the declaration of particular languages (usually the languages of the former European colonists) as "official." National systems of education attempt to reinforce this by teaching in the "national" language and emphasizing a "national" ideology. People are encouraged through a long process of enculturation to speak Spanish, English, or whatever the national language happens to be; to identify with the flag; and to behave in ways that are indicative of nationhood, be it Cuban, Jamaican, or Haitian.

At the same time, from the perspective of anthropology, nation-states like these are relatively new in the history of humankind. Before this, people had lived for tens, perhaps hundreds, of thousands of years in small-scale societies in which nearly all interactions were face-to-face and usually with someone known or even related. Given these facts of history, and especially given the relatively short time (about 5,000 years) that humans have lived in large-scale societies, it seems reasonable to assume that we have not had time to adjust biologically to our new living arrangements. In particular, we almost certainly retain from our not-that-distant past a proclivity for life in small, face-to-face societies. Within such societies, it is easy to construct ethnic markers that help let us create an identity for ourselves as a group, in contrast to others who don't share those ethnic markers and therefore are outside the group. The ethnic markers may be linguistic (as in some of the cases we noted earlier among Native Americans); they may be cultural (beliefs, behaviors, dress, tattooing, or other body decorations); they may include aspects of physical appearance, such as skin color or hair form. One anthropologist has referred to this predisposition among humans toward the formation of relatively small in-groups as the *social imperative* (Cring 1992).

The social imperative provides us with an explanation for why, all across Latin America and the Caribbean, people have sought, and continue to seek, ways of forming themselves into more manageable groups than the large-scale states they find themselves in tend to provide. When we couple this with the fact that most Caribbean and Latin American societies contain within themselves minority groups that are in structurally subordinate positions (economically, socially, politically), we have a situation ripe for the development of *ethnic revitalization movements* or *ethnonationalist movements*.

Often, ethnic revitalization movements are centered on religion, and while this is true for the Caribbean and Latin America, it is also possible to identify a component of ethnicity in some cases. Let us look briefly at a case that illustrates these ethnic (rather than strictly religious) revitalizations.

The Rastafarians

As we have seen, Africans in Jamaica are descended from slaves who were brought there by the Spanish and then the English to work on plantations. After emancipation, the ideology of African as inferior, and European as superior, was maintained, and, as often happens, found its way into the worldview of even the slaves' descendants. All things European were prized: hair, dress, language, religion. All things African were devalued.

In the 1930s, a movement to revalue all things African began, largely under the impetus of Marcus Garvey. Garvey found passages in the Christian Bible that allowed him to declare that Haile Selassie, the newly crowned emperor of Ethiopia, was a living god. Black people should worship him and turn away from the Christian god. Haile Selassie's title was *Ras* ("king") *Tafari*, so the movement's followers came to be known as *Rastafarians*.

One of the ethnic markers Rastafarians (or Rastas, for short) used to set themselves apart not only from the European elite but also from the masses of African descent was by their hairstyle. Rastafarians refused to cut their hair, allowing it to grow into long "dreadlocks." They also refused to comb their hair in the conventional European way. It must be understood that this was not the copying of an African custom; no Africans wore their hair this way traditionally (those that wear "dreads" now are copying the Rastafarians!). The growing of dreadlocks, then, began as an explicit rejection of European cultural norms—a defiant symbol of resistance to the cultural values and norms imposed by the white Europeans (Barrett 1977).

Another ethnic marker setting Rastas apart is language. Although Rastas essentially speak Jamaican, English Creole, locally called *Patwa*, they consciously made some changes to it, especially in vocabulary. One noticeable shift is the Rastas' use of the first person pronoun *I*, pronounced [ay], for all functions of the pronouns (Patwa speakers use *mi* for all functions). So, a Rasta might say, "Give I a book," where speakers of both English and Patwa would say, "Give me a book." Rastafarians also creatively alter the forms of words to make a political point, such as using *overstand* for *understand* and *downpress* for *oppress*. The use of *I* also makes a point, since it is homophonous with *eye*, the organ of sight.[4]

A third ethnic marker is *reggae* music, which developed from urban *ska*, played in the poor sections of Kingston, the Jamaican capital. The music was first carried out of Jamaica by artists like Jimmy Cliff, Peter Tosh, and especially Bob Marley. It is heard and copied all over the world.

Bob Marley (1945–1981).

The Illogic of "Black Power" and the Maintenance of Inequality

The Rastafarians were successful in rekindling a consciousness of Africa and Africa-ness among many Caribbean people. However, the *black power movement*, which attempted to do the same thing in the United States beginning in the 1960s, found little sympathy in the Caribbean. Our earlier discussion of the meanings and use of *black* and "white" among West Indians should make the reason obvious. For Caribbean people, *black* is a descriptive term used for people with very dark skin color, not a term for a descent group, as it is in the United States. At the same time, though, the lack of a strict hypodescent rule and the resultant merging of Afro-Caribbean people into a "creole" (in contrast to a non-creole or metropolitan) identity has served to obfuscate internal structures of stratification and inequality (Hintzen 2002).

SUMMARY

In this chapter, we have provided an overview of the physical, cultural, and linguistic diversity displayed by the peoples of Latin America and the Caribbean. We have noted that in some areas (the Caribbean, for example) the Native American populations were almost totally obliterated. In others (Perú, Bolivia) they remain an important, even dominant, segment of the population, although they are integrated, principally as peasant farmers and urban and rural proletariat, into national (and even global) economies. In some scattered regions, especially the Amazon and Orinoco river basins of Brazil and Venezuela, indigenous groups like the Yanomama attempt to carry on their traditional life ways largely separated from their respective national cultures. And yet, even these groups have become integrated, if only at arm's length, into larger economies by their acceptance of and increased dependence on products of Western technology, such as machetes and firearms.

The descendants of people who came from Europe, Africa, and Asia as part of the Columbian exchange dominate large portions of Latin America and the Caribbean. Some regions display their history of plantation slavery in the large numbers of people who claim African descent. As with the majority of surviving Amerindians, these peoples have mostly been integrated into national cultures, but some groups of descendants of African slaves, like the Saramaka of Suriname, have managed to carry on cultural and linguistic traditions that tie them directly to Africa. People of European descent are the majority in some regions, such as southern Brazil, Argentina, Uruguay, and Chile. In other places, like Barbados, Europeans form minorities that, perhaps paradoxically, are divided into elite and nonelite classes.

However, the overall theme uniting the peoples and cultures of Latin America and the Caribbean is *mestizaje*, or "mixture." First, there is mixture of gene pools: Amerindian, European, African, and Asian. Second, the languages and cultures found throughout the region reflect the creation of new from old, so that "Cuban," "Barbadian," and "Haitian," to mention three examples, are all distinct, in their own ways, from the cultures of their founding populations (see Yelvington 2001).

Notes

1. However, as of this writing (2009) Bolivia is the first Latin American nation to have an elected president who is a Native American: Evo Morales, an ethnic Aymara.
2. The Web address for the Jatibonicu Taino is http://members.dandy.net/∼orocobix/index.html. The Web address for the Caribbean Amerindian Centrelink is http://www.centrelink.org.
3. The research reported here is not published. However, it is described in more detail and in the context of a longer discussion of "race" at http://www.unf.edu/∼rkephart/Writings/Race_Essay.html.
4. The observations on Rastafarian language are from a presentation by Mervyn Alleyne during a conference on San Andrés, Colombia, in May 1999.

References Cited

BAILEY, STANLEY R. 2008. Unmixing for race making in Brazil. *American Journal of Sociology* 114(3): 577–614.

BARRETT, LEONARD E. 1977. *Rastafarians: Sounds of Cultural Dissonance.* Boston, MA: Beacon Press.

BRINKLEY, FRANCES. 1978. An analysis of the 1750 Carriacou census. *Caribbean Quarterly* 24(1–2): 44–60.

BUECHLER, HANS, and JUDITH-MARIA BUECHLER. 1971. *The Bolivian Aymara.* New York: Holt, Rinehart & Winston.

CARPENTER, LAWRENCE. 1983. Social stratification and implications for bilingual education: An Ecuadorian example. In *Bilingualism: Social Issues and Policy Implications.* Andrew W. Miracle, ed. Pp. 96–106. Athens, GA: University of Georgia Press.

CRING, DAN. 1992. The ontogeny and phylogeny of discrimination. Paper presented at the Annual Meeting of the Louisiana Academy of Science.

CROSBY, ALFRED. 1972. *The Columbian Exchange: Biological and Cultural Consequences of 1492.* Westport, CT: Greenwood Press.

DIAMOND, JARED. 1998. *Guns, Germs, and Steel: The Fates of Human Societies.* New York: Norton.

ENCYCLOPAEDIA BRITANNICA. Electronic document, http://www.britannica.com.

ERIKSEN, THOMAS H. 1992. *Us and Them in Modern Societies: Ethnicity and Nationalism in Trinidad, Mauritius and Beyond.* Oslo: Scandinavian University Press.

GIL-WHITE, FRANCISCO. 2001. Sorting is not categorization: A critique of the claim that Brazilians have fuzzy racial categories. Unpublished manuscript.

GONZALEZ, NANCY. 1988. *Sojourners of the Caribbean: Ethnogenesis and Ethnohistory of the Garifuna.* Urbana, IL: University of Illinois Press.

GOOD, KENNETH. 1991. *Into the Heart: One Man's Pursuit of Love and Knowledge among the Yanomama.* New York: Simon & Schuster.

HARDMAN, M. J., ed. 1981. *The Aymara Language in Its Social and Cultural Context.* Gainesville, FL: University Press of Florida.

HARRIS, MARVIN. 1964. *Patterns of Race in the Americas.* New York: Norton Library.

HERSKOVITS, MELVILLE. 1966. *The New World Negro: Selected Papers in Afroamerican Studies.* Frances S. Herskovits, ed. Bloomington, IN: Indiana University Press.

HILL, DONALD. 1977. *The Impact of Migration on the Folk and Metropolitan Society of Carriacou, Grenada.* New York: American Museum of Natural History.

HINTZEN, PERCY C. 2002. The Caribbean: Race and Creole ethnicity. In *A Companion to Racial and Ethnic Studies.* David Theo Goldberg and John Solomos, eds. Pp. 475–494. Malden, MA: Blackwell Publishers.

HOLM, JOHN. 1989. *Pidgins and Creoles*, vol. II. *Reference Survey.* Cambridge: Cambridge University Press.

HULME, PETER, and NEIL WHITEHEAD, eds. 1992. *Wild Majesty: Encounters with Caribs from Columbus to the Present Day.* Oxford: Clarendon Press.

HURSTON, ZORA. 1990. *Tell My Horse: Voodoo and Life in Haiti and Jamaica.* New York: Perennial Library.

JOHNSON, HOWARD, and KARL WATSON, eds. 1998. *The White Minority in the Caribbean.* Kingston: Ian Randle.

KEPHART, RONALD. 2000. *"Broken English": The Creole Language of Carriacou.* New York: Peter Lang.

KLASS, MORTON. 1988 [1961]. *East Indians in Trinidad: A Study in Cultural Persistence.* Prospect Heights, IL: Waveland Press.

LOWENTHAL, DAVID. 1972. *West Indian Societies.* London: Oxford University Press.

MARTÍNEZ-ECHAZABAL, LOURDES. 1998. Mestizaje and the discourse of national/cultural identity in Latin America, 1845–1959. *Latin American Perspectives* 25(3):21–43.

McDANIEL, LORNA. 1998. *The Big Drum Ritual of Carriacou: Praisesongs in Rememory of Flight.* Gainesville, FL: University Press of Florida.

MURRA, JOHN V. 1972. Control Vertical de un Máximo de Pisos Ecológicos en la Economía de las Sociedades Andinas. In *Visita de la Provincia de León de Huánuco en 1562,* vol 2. John V Murra, ed. Pp. 427–468. Huánuco, Perú: Universidad Nacional Hermilio Valdizán. Facultad de Letras y Educación.

O'GRADY, WILLIAM, J. ARCHIBALD, M. ARONOFF, and J. REES-MILLER. 2001. *Contemporary Linguistics: An Introduction.* 4th edition. Boston, MA: Bedford/St. Martin's Press.

PRICE, RICHARD, ed. 1979. *Maroon Societies: Rebel Slave Communities in the Americas.* Baltimore, MD: Johns Hopkins University Press.

RICHARDSON, BONHAM. 1992. *The Caribbean in the Wider World: A Regional Geography.* Cambridge: Cambridge University Press.

ROUSE, IRVING. 1992. *The Tainos: Rise & Decline of the People Who Greeted Columbus.* New Haven, CT: Yale University Press.

SHEPPARD, JILL. 1977. *The "Redlegs" of Barbados.* Millwood, NY: KTO Press.

SMITH, M. G. 1962. *Kinship and Community in Carriacou.* New Haven, CT: Yale University Press.

SOLAÚN, M., E. VÉLEZ, and C. SMITH. 1987. Claro, Trigueño, Moreno: Testing for race in Cartagena. *Caribbean Review* 15(3):18–19.

WAGLEY, CHARLES. 1957. Plantation-America: A culture sphere. In *Caribbean Studies: A Symposium.* Vera Rubin, ed. Pp. 3–13. Seattle, WA: University of Washington Press.

WILLIAMS, ERIC. 1994. *Capitalism and Slavery.* Chapel Hill, NC: University of North Carolina Press.

WINN, PETER. 1999. *Americas: The Changing Face of Latin America and the Caribbean.* Berkeley, CA: University of California Press.

YELVINGTON, KEVIN. 2001. The anthropology of Afro-Latin America: Diasporic dimensions. *Annual Review of Anthropology* 30:227–260.

14

Africa

Sheilah Clarke-Ekong, *University of Missouri, St. Louis*

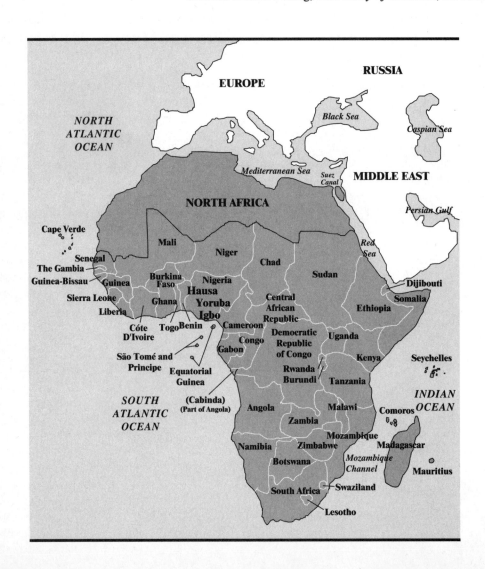

In just the last generation, many North American students and their teachers have become significantly more informed about Africa and increasingly more aware of how Africans construct their own worldviews. This enhanced knowledge base is a very good thing within our academic communities. Unfortunately, for many outside the venues of formal education, some of the most fundamental facts about Africa are still clouded in myth and misinformation. It is the misinformation, often sustained by Western media exposés and biased historical accounts, that is most challenging. For starters, there is no distinguishable African race or tribe, no mono-African language (written or spoken), and the African continent comprises 61 territories of which 56 are independent countries. Fifty-two of these nation-states make up sub-Saharan Africa, the most likely area of focus when the topic of Africa comes up for discussion. Within these independent countries are approximately 922 million people. Sub-Saharan Africa is home to the largest populated country, Nigeria, with an estimated population of 140 million, and Seychelles, the smallest country, with only 80,000 people, as well as Zambia, with an urban population of nearly 50 percent, and Burundi, with only 6 percent city dwellers (Middleton 2000). Africa gave us the world's earliest civilizations, and hominid fossils found in Africa date the origins of humankind. This is a continent that still houses some of the few remaining hunting-and-gathering societies, the longest sustaining human subsistence pattern recorded. We also know now that these societies might well have been referred to as "gathering and hunting" societies, as the women's gathering activity supplied at least 80 percent of the caloric intake. With over 11 million square miles of landmass, Africa is more than three times larger than the continental United States. Given the facts stated above, it remains unfortunate that the mention of Africa still too often conjures up the image of tribal peoples, less civilized than the rest of us, who live in tropical jungles, barren deserts, and undeveloped countries. Our interest in the developing world is very often driven by our own local ethnocentric agenda of the processes of globalization as it impacts Western economic and political well-being. When thinking of Africa, in particular, we may likely have images of famine, poverty, and violence, reinforced by portrayals of starving women and children and "tribal-ethnic" violence that come across the airwaves of Western media. Although there are a number of politically charged hot spots in Africa at any given time, none of these can be totally reduced to tribal or ethnic conflicts in an informed analysis. Where ethnic hostilities exist, we need to use historical and contemporary assessments to holistically assess the situation.

Many more of the conflicts taking place since the new millennium are struggles for power among rival factions. In several African countries (e.g., Liberia, Sierra Leone, Somalia, and Sudan), rival forces often recruit heavily from one region (giving rise to the ill-conceived notion that these are ethnic conflicts) in order to make use of local leaders and loyalties to control their followers. In fact, if we examine just three specific cases, a clearer picture presents itself. In Somalia's capital, Mogadishu, heavy fighting between the transitional government soldiers and Islamist forces keeps the battle-torn region destabilized. An estimated 300,000 people have been killed in Darfur and another 2.7 million forced from their homes since violence erupted in 2003, pitting various rebel groups against government forces and their allied Janjaweed militiamen. The multinational invasion of the Democratic Republic of Congo (DRC) was in full swing, while brutal rebellions were wreaking havoc in Angola and Sierra Leone, and Ethiopia and Eritrea were engaged in heavy fighting over their border. These ongoing conflicts cannot be described nor explained in ethnic terms.

Many sources of African conflict may have cultural components, but these are often manifested through political and economic arenas. Villages, regions, ethnic groups, nationalities, and religious groups—all have distinct cultures at different levels of cultural and social heterogeneity. It is the number of ethnic groups and their relationships to power, not diversity, per se, that strongly affect political stability. Interactions among peoples of different societies and backgrounds may very well enhance their "ethnic" consciousness and reignite differences and animosities stretching back deep into their history. Another way of thinking about the dynamic nature of ethnicity, according to anthropologist Jack David Eller, "is that ethnic groups do not fight about culture but with culture—with culture as a weapon in a struggle of a different kind, whether it is political, economic, religious, or irredentism" (1999:3).

As indicated throughout this textbook, the idea that the world's current conflicts are fueled by age-old ethnic loyalties and cultural differences without due consideration for other social, economic, and political dynamics is an oversimplification. If ethnicity does not necessarily mean conflict, neither is conflict everywhere traceable to politicized ethnicity. Somalia, one of the most conflict-ridden states anywhere in the continent, is a case in point. Ethnically and culturally, Somalia is one of the most homogeneous countries in Africa. The real diversity for Somalia, a country slightly smaller than Texas, might have been during the colonial period when the French, the Ethiopians, the British, and the Italians all took a part for themselves.

In Somalia, family loyalty is the premier value. Clans, a systematic genealogical structure, with numerous branches called lineages, constitute the heart of Somali society. By the twelfth century, the ancestors of some clan families were already established in their present locations. The major challenge facing modern Somalia is how to unify a country whose people often give greater allegiance to their lineage and clan than to the nation-state. The contemporary situation continues to show the importance of clans in that by the mid-1980s, government and opposition movements were still clan-based, as they were prior to colonization in the nineteenth century. The primary divisions in the Somali nation are based on kinship, culture, economy (occupation), history, and geographic location. The northern Somali are those clans and lineages primarily engaged in nomadic subsistence strategies. The southern Somali are settled in the arable regions and practice either agriculture or agro-pastoralism (Putman and Noor 1993).

Conflict, like any other social dynamic, must be looked at holistically. Unfortunately, the phrase *ethnic conflict* has become a shorthand way to speak about any and all violent confrontations between groups of people living in the same country. Indeed, some of these conflicts may involve ethnic and cultural identity, but many are about equitable resource distribution and allocation (Bowen 2001:356).

Before we can fully engage a conversation about African ethnicity, we must lessen the shadow of tribalism and the notion that African peoples are behaving in tribal ways. According to Africa Policy Information Center (2005), "Not only does using the term 'tribe' promote a racist conception of African ethnicities as primitive and savage, it prevents observers from coming to an accurate understanding of the causes of certain regional and country conflicts." As the term *tribe* is currently used, it can mean any number of group associations based on language competency, ancient kingdoms, shared history, shared geographical location, shared kinship, similar lifestyles and livelihoods, shared religious belief systems, common cultural practices, and more. In conclusion, the word *tribe* as often used in everyday context has no coherent meaning.

Ethnicity is both a personal and group identity marker which is self-imposed and externally assigned. As such, it relies on the ways in which people consider themselves as sharing common characteristics that are different from other people. Attachment to ethnicity, as distinct from attachment to race, may arise in several different ways. First, culturally patterned forms of behavior by which individuals satisfy their needs may bring them closer to some people rather than others. Second, the similarities between members of an ethnic group may be based on physical characteristics as much as cultural characteristics, to create a "consciousness of kind." Third, similarity of cultural behavior may be seen as a sign of cultural relatedness (Loukas 1929).

Africa, the second-largest continent of the world's seven, presents both similarities and certain uniqueness when one examines topics of identity. Legacies of colonialism, military coup d'états and destabilized governments, the HIV/AIDS epidemic, mineral reserves, ethnic and civil strife, genocide, and Apartheid and post-Apartheid are just some of the issues shaping both the insider's and outsider's perceptions of Africa. In reality, Africa's history, as well as its contemporary evolution, reflects the complexity of the entire world, from the most technologically advanced to the most marginal. Globalization par excellence is being played out in Africa, with its emerging markets and unrelenting need from the Western powers for access to her wealth of natural and mineral resources.

In this chapter we will examine some of the more significant expressions of ethnicity in Africa as a social construction of identity that serves many people around the world. We will also give consideration to some of the historical legacies that help sustain this form of identity in contemporary Africa. Africans, like all people, have multiple levels of identity and symbols of representation. Examples that readily express this "situational selectivity" are many. An Ibibio may be a mainland Ibibio or an Ibibio from the Ibesikpo clan, when the reference point is the southeastern region of Nigeria. In Lagos, the commercial capital, and Abuja, the government capital, he/she is simply an Easterner. In London, he is a Nigerian. In Missouri, she is an African. Having several "ethnic" identities also holds true for some Tanzanians within their own country. Postcolonial policy encouraged the use of Kiswahili as the national lingua franca and socialism (*ujaamaa*) as a means of uniting the citizens. "Thus, a man in Tabora, a center of the nineteenth century Arab slave trade, may point to distant Arab origins of his father and Sukuma or other Bantu origins of his mother, and may speak both Swahili and the Sujuma language, according to the situation" (Middleton 2000:90).

In anthropological terms, the use of the comparative method makes multiethnicity and statehood part of the same process. Multiethnicity becomes a way of adding power through numbers of supporters, which overrides chance demographic factors. In such instances, claims of common ethnicity can be used to mobilize

previously autonomous groups under a unified leadership. According to Paul Bohannan, "When states developed to become nation-states, a new dimension of difficulty was added with the idea that the state should now be associated with both a specific ethnic group and with a specific territory" (1995:180). The fact that almost no states were actually of this sort made little difference to those responsible for creating this imaginary model and subsequent policy implementations (Lemarchand 1999). The idea appeared early among the Portuguese in the fourteenth century. It logically led to the proposition that the state should be the representative of what we today would call a dominant ethnic group, which should occupy and control its own property. Its members become the only people with full rights within the territory (Cohen 1993).

Ethnicity is just one way of categorizing a group of people. It is not an immutable phenomenon but a changing feature of society. Just as people are able to self-define, they are able to redefine themselves, and as a result ethnic compositions and boundaries do change. Knowing that culture is primarily adaptive, it is reasonable to conclude that identity can be and is often situational, and may change in response to any number of extenuating historical, territorial, economic, or political factors. An individual or group attachment to shared ethnicity can also set moral boundaries and values determined by rules of tradition (Maybury-Lewis 1997).

ETHNICITY OR TRIBALISM?

The conventional use of the word *tribe* stems in part from a view that African cultures have remained largely static and fixed at some pre-twentieth-century stage of development. "Tribe" comes from the Latin *tribus*. Throughout time, this term has been tied to classical Judeo-Christian biblical images. Many nineteenth- and early twentieth-century Europeans and Americans who used Latin and English Bibles adopted the term for the 12 lineages of Hebrews who settled the Promised Land. This link of tribes to the glorified periods of early Western culture supported the notion that "the tribe" had some universal validity in social evolution. According to David Wiley, "It is no accident that the contemporary uses of the term 'tribe' were developed during the nineteenth century rise of linear evolutionary and racist theories to designate alien non-white peoples as inferior or less civilized" (1999:56). From 1885 on, the colonial partition and conquest of Africa divided communities, created new ones, and fostered new identities.[1]

There is sufficient evidence that in the precolonial era, Africans thought of themselves primarily as members of descent-based lineage groups. Personal identification arose first out of familial sentiment and socialization, reinforced by community membership and respect for recognized authority figures (Falola 2000; Williams 2001). The renowned Igbo novelist and social critic Chinua Achebe says that the proverb, "*Nku di na mba na-eghelu mba nni*,"—Every community has enough firewood in its own forests for all the cooking it needs to do—underscores the importance of community (2000:7). At yet another level, the occupational or subsistence niche associated with many groups is basic to distinguishing them from neighboring groups. Ethnic groups occupying the Horn of Africa are classically distinguished by their subsistence patterns. Among peoples with established chieftaincy institutions, such as the Yoruba of Nigeria, loyalty to the chiefdom provides an active identity marker. While modernity tends to play down the influence of customary law, chieftaincy is an identity above and beyond any secular constitutional arrangements and/or mandates. The chieftaincy institution as a repository of tradition and customary law was incorporated into the colonial administration, making traditional rulers the middlemen. Colonial rule very often subordinated indigenous African authority.

Among the Asante of Ghana, distance to or from the royal lineage sustains group identification. The coastal Fante are very keen to impress other Ghanaian groups with their level of Western education and long-term European exposure. We might also see groups sharing so much in common, like the Lele and Bushong of the former Belgian Congo, that outsiders would hardly notice any difference. Both peoples recognize a common ancestry, share similar customs, live in the same geographic zone, and speak languages very closely related. The major distinguishing feature, the Kasai River, provides for rich and poor soils. The Lele are poor subsistence farmers; their soils support only steppe-like vegetation. The Bushong, even before colonialism, produced for exchange, and their native economy was noted for its use of money and its specialized traders and markets (Douglas 1997:101–102).

In the mergers of colonial and indigenous political systems, we begin to see the linkage between politics and kinship. The Nuer of southern Sudan were scattered over an immense area of land and seemed to have no discernible system of relationships linking them together. With more than 200,000 persons over an area of more than 30,000 miles there were fewer than seven people per square mile. E. E. Evans-Pritchard (1940) concluded that one could make sense of the Nuer world—that they had a well-organized political system uniquely suited to their ecological and social needs and one that operated according to genealogy and kinship relations (Grinker and Steiner 1997:5).

The examples cited here show that in all the different articulations and manifestations of group identity and affiliation, relationships are sustained and/or diminished and subsequently reinforced and understood in relation to other similar and dissimilar groups, situations, and events.

For Africa, much of the early history was passed down orally and there is still considerable uncertainty and variability about the essential nature of social interactions before the colonial era. The topics most often discussed are what indigenous peoples called themselves and the existing relationships between different groups. Social anthropologist S. Nadel (1942) presents evidence that affirms the existence of specific forms of self-group identification in the precolonial era. "The Nupe ethnic group was not different from the Nupe State. A Nupe was anyone—whether warrior, peasant, pastoralist, or craftsman—who was defined as a subject of the Nupe sovereign" (Middleton 2000:84).

From a different point of view, and drawing insight from official colonial documents and missionary records from the early 1900s, David Simmons (2000) asserts that there was a colonialist need to ascribe identities to native peoples as a means of reordering the native perception of reality. This also provided a justification for allocating resources to some and excluding others. An example includes the following account by a British War Office official in 1917 as he reportedly assessed the situation as such:

[The] spirit of nationality, or perhaps it would be more correct to say, of tribe, should be cultivated and nowhere can this be done with better chance of success than in British East Africa and Uganda, where there are numerous tribes ethnographically quite distinct from one another. It is suggested that in each ethnographically distinct district the schools should, as far as possible, form integral parts of the tribe and centers of folklore and tradition.

A method may also be found whereby the efforts of missionaries may also assist in the cultivation of national spirit. This it seems might be done by allowing only one denomination to work in each demographic area and by not allowing the same denomination to work in two adjacent areas. [Malawi National Archives, GOA 2/4/12, "Mohammadanism and Ethiopianism" (circular letter, Lt. Col. French to Governor Smith, 7 Aug. 1917)]

The colonial powers—Belgians, Spanish, Germans, French, British, and Dutch—also realized that, given their small numbers in their colonies, they could only effectively govern and exploit by making "partners" from among local people, sometimes from minority, marginalized, or Christianized groups. After affirming this relationship, the state then had to separate its partners from all others, thereby creating firmly bounded "ethnic groups" (Bowen 2001:358; Middleton 2000).

When introduced by European missionaries and anthropologists, and used strategically by colonial officials, the concept of "tribe" in Africa became an effective mechanism for implementing colonial policies. These policies determined the relationship between ruler and subject, exploiter and exploited. Commonly referred to as "indirect rule or divide and rule," the British policy was designed to leave traditional leaders and local institutional structures essentially intact. Indirect rule in northern Nigeria aimed to maintain British economic interests in a caste-like structure in which the Fulani were to serve as allies. The British official Frederick Lugard endeavored to enlist the conquered Fulani as captains, ensure their loyalty through the establishment of a taxation system that would give them appropriate compensation, control the collection of taxes through partnership, and guide the people on the road to "civilization." Inherent in the process was the need for centralization requiring all sources of separate identity being either destroyed or subdued. It was then directed that European officers or their Fulani delegates would work within this framework to extract resources for the British Empire. There was little interest on the side of the British to have Africans take on their masters' cultural attributes or values.[2] However, with the change in institutional structures and the imposition of new authority figures, new cultural values did come into existence.

The French had a different approach for administering their African colonies. Their policy of assimilation was much more obtrusive to local leadership and critical of local institutional structures. Africans under French colonial rule were encouraged to "become French" by relinquishing indigenous cultural beliefs and values. Taking on French cultural attributes and achieving competency in spoken French became the markers of "civilization" and elite status (Grinker and Steiner 1997; Simmons 2000; Southall 1997:41–43). The Portuguese and Belgians were notably the most authoritarian and rigid in their native-rule policies (Scupin 2008). Whether for administrative convenience or as part of the civilizing mission, colonialism had a systemic and fundamental impact on Africa's indigenous social order. Over time, and often unwittingly, Africans also began to think of themselves in terms designated by their colonial masters.

Compounding our lack of understanding is confusion about the term *tribalism*, often used, even by academics, interchangeably with ethnicity, as if they were one and the same. Try to imagine, if you will, a news release announcing tribal violence breakouts between the Israelis and the Palestinians, or ethnic clashes between the Irish Catholics and Protestants. This with a full description of white-on-white violence!

Although ethnic violence is commonplace in many parts of the world today, ethnicity in Africa is often treated differently and frequently dismissed as tribalism among native peoples. Increasingly, scholars of African area studies are promoting the view that the conflicts commonly attributed to tribalism are as much an outgrowth of such modern phenomena as political instability, urbanization, and economic hardship as they are a continuation of age-old traditional alliances (Bowen 2001).

So the question remains: Are there tribes in Africa, and if so, what function do they fulfill? Yes, there are tribes in Africa. Many terms change meaning over time in social science discourse, and anthropologists are particularly sensitive to this phenomenon as we attempt to explain the reality of our informants. Tribe can refer to groups with a range of social realities such as a common language, a common culture, common ancestral lineages, or recognition of the same authority figure. Tribe may also appropriately refer to types of subsistence, such as horticulture and pastoralism (Scupin 2008).

It was only in the 1960s that the concept of tribe came under criticism from the academic community as part of a critique of Eurocentric perspectives and analyses. Because the word was also normally used in conjunction with describing rural peoples, there was the unfortunate implication that it explained some largely unchanged and or stagnant stage of development. Many scholars now agree that the word *tribe*, in sociological and anthropological literature, as well as in the popular press, is essentially derogatory, ambiguous, and imprecise.

ETHNICITY: THE AFRICAN PARTICULAR

In Africa, one finds, in addition to cultural pluralism, *syncretism*, that is, the coexistence of different beliefs and practices without necessarily being merged into new entities. Among Africans, an ethnic group is defined both by common objective elements, such as ancestry, kinship and descent, language, history, religion, customs (i.e., even food and initiation rights), institutions, and physical type, and by subjective self-identification. Increasingly, the inherent struggle for political power as it revolves around the state allocation of resources is also equally important in modern times. According to Rene Lemarchand, in an article titled, "Ethnicity as Myth: The View from the Central Africa," "Ethnicity is never what it seems. What looks to the profane like ancestral atavism others identify as a typically modern phenomenon, anchored in the impact of colonial rule. Where neo-Marxists detect class interests parading in traditional garb, mainstream scholars unveil imagined communities. And what many see as the bane of the continent others view as the basis of a moral social contract that carries the seeds of accountability and transparency" (1999:1). Myth or not, "Ethnicities arose from the people's varied experience of migration and urbanization, subordination and competition, religious belief and conversion. These brought people into new relations and differentiated them in new ways. What multiple forms have in common is access to public resources" (Williams 2001:3).

Ethnic groups are meaningful entities, and while the lines between them are seldom sharp, they are, nonetheless, real (Harf and Lombardi 2001:341). According to Susan Greenbaum, ethnicity is a process rather than a finite set of categories. "What endures, however, is kinship. Ethnic groups are basically ancestral groups; in which shared origins provide the basis of a common identity. Ethnicity is both voluntary and imposed. Both elements reflect a continuum, and divided ancestry represents choice as well as ambiguity" (1992:8). The Yoruba of southwestern Nigeria say, "*Ajobi a gbe wa o*"—May the bond of our common ancestry bless, protect, and nurture us all!

Most Africans identify themselves in terms of their local societies, not as members of any monolithic ethnic groups. Within Africa and among its many diverse communities, a critical part of the contemporary articulation of ethnicity includes a "we-group feeling," sustained by land tenure/ownership, subsistence patterns, language proficiency, and chieftaincy. Whether self-defined, attributed by others, or both, these usually descent-based associations constitute a process of ethnic identification dependent upon real-world causes. The most widespread and apparent expression of this "we/them" worldview comes into play and is defined by the presence of an outsider, "the other(s)." Other indicators of group affiliation include a real or putative common historical experience (i.e., colonialism, migration, etc.) that provides a sense of shared fate. African leaders may also facilitate notions of group membership in an effort to build constituencies by using ethnic loyalties and fears to mobilize supporters. And as Ronald Cohen emphasizes, "The competition for scarce resources intensifies allegiance to racial or ethnic groups" (1978:402).

Anthropologists, responsible for many of the early African ethnographies, have been key participants in the effort to understand the concept of ethnicity in Africa. The focus on ethnicity took hold with the study of rapidly changing communities, many of them African cities. Urban anthropologists, such as Clyde Mitchell, Max Gluckman, A. L. Epstein, and Abner Cohen, set the stage and made some of the most important strides in the transition from tribal to ethnic studies (Grinker and Steiner 1997:6; Toland 1993:233). Additionally, a number of different explanations were given for the sustainability of ethnic groups, such as socially constructed groups' efforts at boundary maintenance (Barth 1969), primordial ties of language and culture (Geertz 1973), and a group's instrumental strategies (Cohen 1969).

Frederik Barth (1969) wrote a treatise entitled *Ethnic Groups and Boundaries*, in which he challenged prevailing views of how ethnicity operates in the modern world. Barth argued that ethnic identification reflects neither cultural inertia nor the incomplete process of integration in modern nation-states but, rather, that those persistent ethnic distinctions are an essential feature of such political systems. He observed that boundaries remain between groups in spite of groups' frequent interactions, including intermarriage. In his terms, ethnicity serves as a "vessel" for the mobilization of group interests. The articulation of such interests is a dynamic, ongoing process, not a historical artifact. Barth's ideas strongly influenced a generation of anthropologists and other social scientists interested in the subject of ethnicity (Greenbaum 1992; see also Chapter 4).

Two distinct strands of thought on the nature of ethnicity have emerged. On the one hand, ethnicity is presented as a "primordial" sentiment embedded in human nature (Stack 1974; see also Chapter 4). And given this inherent nature of ethnicity it actually thrives in societies that extol group values over individual rights. Here we consider ethnicity as to how it relates mainly to the abstract symbol system of a group, functioning largely as a repository of social categories that play an important role in group boundary maintenance and identification. On the other hand, ethnic identification represents a strategic axis around which groups and individuals organize to compete for resources and power. Here we acknowledge that ethnicity is about group consciousness and exclusivity and manifests itself in interethnic discrimination. But ethnic identification and solidarity need to be activated before they can assume relevance as a vehicle for social action. Ethnic diversity need not mean ethnic conflict, but in the modern African state, ethnicity has been commonly mobilized and exploited by elite groups to advance or defend their positions within the political economy. Although somewhat contradictory in their implications, both perspectives emphasize the fact that ethnic divisions are permanent forces in modern society. These newer conceptions also make it more difficult to define ethnicity and what makes for an ethnic group.

In the African context this meant that the national integration thesis that became so prominent was hinged on the wrong assumption that ethnic loyalties are temporal survivals from the past that will wither away in the course of urban and industrial development and modernization. With this development, attention shifted from the "detribalization" thesis, which assumes that ethnic ties would be eliminated by modernization, to the "retribalization" or "supertribalization" thesis, in which ethnicity is seen as a consequence of modernization and is heightened by it. According to John Middleton, "Ethnicity is rarely a mere classification system of parallel groups operating at the same level of power, esteem, and privilege. It usually implies an element of vertical subordination: ethnic group membership is a status position in a hierarchy of political-economic power and prestige, and ethnicization aims at improving the position of the entire ethnic group" (2000:93).

We anthropologists were much more comfortable with issues of ethnicity that stressed group solidarity and explaining cultural phenomena in terms of the "ethnographic presence," even if perpetuating, at times, a historical perception. We now know that ethnicity is realistically a process, both voluntary and imposed. Elements reflecting a continuum and divided ancestry represent choice as well as ambiguity. Fragmentation and intensification can, in fact, be part of the same process.

The fluid nature of ethnicity in Africa is particularly interesting from an anthropological perspective. Changes in political, economic, and occupational positions have led to changes in identities leading to stability in interethnic relationships. From ancient times trade encouraged a symbolic interethnicity among people who regularly came into contact with one another (Falola 2000). African ethnicity is syncretic, multilayered, and transitional. It may be the most adaptable component of anything close to a pan-African phenomenon.

In Africa, indigenous group identities are, more often than not, negotiable. Interesting examples of the fluidity and the negotiable nature of ethnicity include the Diakhanke, inhabitants of the Senegambia hinterland, who specialized in trade, carrying goods from the Upper Niger to the Senegal and Gambia Rivers and establishing trading colonies throughout West Africa (Falola 2000:29–30). And a more systematic ethnic manipulation was evident in apartheid South Africa, where eugenicists, with the assistance of the academic community, codified ethnic boundaries for political and economic advantage (Gates 2000).

Ethnicity and Ritual

Reinvention, resynthesis, and appropriation of cultural forms all influence the expression of ethnicity. Culture helps us organize a worldview. Many of the customs and associated rituals in Africa reinforce a sense of belonging to communal living and the importance of group membership. There are many examples throughout Africa. We now find "ethnic" associations that enable urban dwellers to organize themselves for mutual aid and benefit. These associations are an important source of security for those finding themselves away from the comforts of lineage and community. In Migwani, in central Kenya, local identity is expressed outwardly in distinctive traits such as styles of dress and body decorations, hairstyles, popular songs and dances, and nuances of language. For the Kaguru of Tanzania, East Africa, the initiation of adolescent boys and girls defines them as a culturally unique people. The rituals and symbolism associated with this transformation of children into adult members of society mark them as a distinct ethnic group (Beidelman 1997).

Ritually important festivals in contemporary Ghana keep alive much that people have lost; it supplies what modernization and Westernization have eroded and allows participants to look into their past with joy and pride. In addition, there exists a link to tradition where the rites somehow embody what only a few select individuals are privileged to know, thus marking it with prestige. Being scarce, this selective knowledge is cherished. The tenacity of age-old tradition has preserved some archaic language forms, used by select individuals, that few others are able to understand or appreciate. This has effectively become a ritual and performance language that provides an added sense of authenticity to cultural events and displays. Among African governments that now encourage the revitalization and reinvention of tradition, those proficient in select areas gain renewed status. The ability to improvise becomes key to the continuity and genius of it all. Interesting are the analogies that are made to Christendom, as Ghanaians convert to this tradition, to ensure that the net of inclusive grows larger as time goes on. The main concern is to attract the largest possible following and support by winning over the community.

In contemporary Ghanaian society, some festivals take the place of traditional rites of passage, dictating rights and obligations of a new generation to the past and as enforcers of values for the future. Many of the more extensive traditional ceremonies that once marked major transitions in the lives of young men and women have, for the most part, been replaced by Western schooling and other local institutional arrangements for passing on knowledge.

Historical events also represent oneness of society, ethnic unity, and togetherness. For example, the Hogbetsotso festival is a celebration to commemorate the migration of the Ewes from Notsie and to rekindle a keener appreciation of the cultural heritage and traditional values of Anlo. It is also meant to foster a sense of belonging and ethnic unity (Kodzo-Vordoagu 1994). From traditional times, Anlo, like other Ewe states, has been a monarchy, the chief being the constitutional head (i.e., he reigns rather than rules). In traditional times, a hierarchy of officials ranging from the lineage—head through the ward chiefs, subchiefs, and chiefs (*dufia*) to the paramount chief—conducted the administration of the state.

IMPORTANCE OF POLITICAL CHOICES

Clifford Geertz, best known for *The Interpretation of Cultures* (1973), wrote in an essay:

At the political center of any complexly organized society (to narrow our focus now to that) there exist a governing elite and a set of symbolic forms expressing the fact that it is governing. No matter how democratically the members of the elite are chosen (usually not very) or how deeply divided among themselves they may be (usually more than outsiders imagine), they justify their existence and order their actions in terms of a collection of stories, ceremonies, insignia, formalities, which they have inherited or, in more revolutionary situations, invented. [1985:15]

The state, through its nature of incorporation of the many into a united one, articulated with an official origin myth, charter, and dominant system of values and beliefs, has always constituted a more or less believable, stable-unstable entity at the ethnic level. Precolonial Africans may have formed something analogous to ethnic units within a compact territory but not as a political unit. Leadership and political authority in African societies within state development, at least comparable to Europe, was never defined exclusively by ethnic terms. It has been argued that colonialism-interrupted political autonomy left the continent with bitter ethnic, class, and intercountry hostilities, which have been at the root of many contemporary problems (Evans-Pritchard 1951).

Other forms of changing inter-ethnic contact, especially in the context of the social-political changes associated with colonial rule include: (1). Peripheral Contact, people exchanging goods without much interaction, (2). Institutional Contact, a mostly peripheral contact based upon some institutionalized meeting point such as trade or conflict, (3). Acculturation, a partial merging, where the weaker society makes more adjustments than the stronger and accepts some of the outward manifestations of identity of the dominant group, (4). Dominance, a single society with two categories distinguished primarily by non-ethnic characteristics such as income, education and religion, (5). Paternalism, a specialized form of institutional contact that, unlike domination involves the retention of distinctiveness among the interactive societies; (6). Integration, a reduction of identifying with ethnic group and instead the establishment of a larger unity based upon association ties, and (7). Pluralism that is similar to an integrated situation, but the distinction being the existence of a larger order without the clear dominant-subordinate relation. [Paden and Soja 1970:26]

Contemporary sub-Saharan Africa presents some interesting case studies. Nigeria is a good example of the inherent intricacies of ethnicity in public and private life. In early contact with the British, an ideology developed in which the Hamitic Hausa-Fulani became models for "civilization" and partners in its spread. An example is the Yauri emirate, located in the northwest part of Sokoto State, Nigeria. By the time of the British conquest, it was the smallest of the Hausa emirates, and the westernmost station along the Niger River. Yauri never was a Fulani state, although it had paid tribute to the Fulani Sultan Sokoto. Its rulers have generally been careful to stress their separate Hausa identity and, therefore, their distinction from the Fulani. Yauri's rulers form a Hausaized minority among an ethnically heterogeneous population. Changes in political, economic, and occupational position have led to changes in such identities. The stability resulting from the imposition of British rule frustrated resistance to the emir's power. The traditional patterns of migration into Yauri were changed and the Hausa population grew significantly. In addition, there was an increase in the number of people changing ethnic identities from Reshe to Yaurawa and then to Hausa (Salamone 1974, 1985).

People are strength. Ethnic group enclaves reproduce their heritable cultures (and traditions) with the polity while more slowly assembling alliances. In comparative and historical perspective, uni-ethnic states are the exception, not the rule. It was the colonial powers, and the independent states succeeding them, that reinforced the concept that each and every person had an "ethnic identity" that determined his or her place within the colony or the postcolonial system. Even such seemingly innocent events as the taking of a census created the idea of a colony-wide ethnic category to which one belonged and had loyalties.

In the postcolonial period, most African countries have, like other world areas, tried to integrate their diverse peoples. It is a policy that has risks and sometimes runs into difficulties. At the beginning of the colonial period, Frederick Lugard, a British military-trained administrator, realized the value of governing this protectorate through local rulers, if possible. Nigeria was initially divided into north and south, for administrative purposes. In the north, the emirs, who held religious and political influence, were recruited, especially those who had been defeated, to cooperate with and work for the British government. In return, the British government would confirm them in office. In the southwestern region, largely occupied by another major ethnic group, the Yoruba, officeholders were identified among traditional kingdoms and chieftaincies. The problem came when assessing centralized leadership and/or authority holders in the eastern region. Many of the groups in the southeastern part of the country had decentralized authority frameworks. Important leadership positions were held at very local levels, such as clan and village heads. A new and foreign officeholder, the district officer, was created by the British to administer colonial rule in these areas.

At the dawn of independence Nigeria was divided into three regions: north, south, and east—each with its own party supported by ethnic allegiances. In 1963, the Midwestern region was created in response to minority interests within the former western region. The intensity and discord of this three-way division, a pogrom against the Igbo in the north, and a feeling of disenfranchisement drove the Igbo in the southeast region of Biafra to attempt to break away from Nigeria in 1967. The traumas of the civil war and those that followed led politicians to try a new system in the politically and ethnically divided country. They carved the country into 12 states, the boundaries of which cut through the territories of the three largest ethnic groups (Hausa, Yoruba, and Igbo), encouraging a new federalist politics based on multiethnic coalitions.

Nigeria's 1979 government put in place the *Federal Character Principle.* The principle was grounded in sensitivity to ethno-regional representation in the federal government and its agencies. The policy of federal character representation was nurtured by the Mohammed/Obasanjo regime, which introduced the concept as a panacea to the problem of ethnic balancing in federal government appointments. The basis of representation now, however, was states rather than geographic regions, which nevertheless continued to be important. In 1976, the Nigerian government, under military rule, further divided the country by creating seven more states. By creating 19 states, it was hoped that ethnic coalitions would be weakened, and even disappear. Once again, the ruling government decided to renegotiate the sharing of national resources (Diamond 1988; Joseph 1987). In 1991, 11 more states were created, and in 1996 the number rose to, and is currently holding at, 36. The Federal Territory was situated strategically to avoid ethnic domination by any one group and is located centrally within the country's middle belt.

The facts of ethnic differentiation in terms of language, culture, territory, and even loyalty as an "objective" reality remain problematic from the point of view of governance. The problem is only made worse by the competition for scarce resources between the groups. Increasing the number of states was a direct response to the demands and agitation of groups that were not satisfied with their positions in the federation.

Initially, it was the minorities who agitated for more states, but in 1990 the need for states had changed. They were no longer needed to protect group identity and autonomy. Any group that sought a share of the "national cake" or that wanted to maximize its share of the cake demanded more states, although states were not designed to have an ethnic basis. An example of the latter was the Igbo, who constituted the majority in only two states, Anambra and Imo; the other major groups, the Hausa/Fulani and the Yoruba, represented majorities in about five states each. The Igbo had persistently pressed for equality with other major groups by demanding new states. Realizing that the creation of states could go on endlessly, the federal government tried to bolster local governments as another way of meeting the demands. The subordinate status of local governments, however, coupled with the continued use of the states as units for distributing national resources, made demands for more states a recurrent theme in Nigerian federalism (Udogu 1999).

Elections can and will stir up intergroup tensions. African governments have taken different approaches to the problem. In the 2000 presidential election in Ghana, each candidate had to secure a percentage of votes from each of the country's 11 regions. At the other extreme, Kenya's Daniel Moi has created an ethnic electoral base that excludes most Kikuyus, thus increasing the relevance of ethnicity in politics and therefore the level of intergroup tensions.

RELIGION

A person can be half-African and half-Arab and simultaneously a citizen of two countries, but it is more difficult to be half-Catholic and half-Muslim. As people define their identity in ethnic and religious terms, they are likely to view their world in an "us versus them" basis (Huntington 2001). Mobilizing support and forming coalitions on the basis of ethnic and religious ideology has become a powerful tool among some African governments.

Islam was introduced into West Africa during the fifteenth century. The people in northern

Nigeria who accepted Islam took on the name "Hausa," and those who did not remained "Maguzawa." This process of fission essentially divided the community into two distinct ethnic societies. On the other hand, in the nineteenth century, after the Fulani conquered the area, there was a merger of the urban Hausa and Fulani into a new group called "Hausa-Fulani." Southerners now routinely refer to all these people as Hausa.

In contemporary times, the link between religion and politics has become very complex. Muslims in Nigeria are about 47 percent and Christians make up 35 percent of the population. Since 1999, Nigeria has 12 states with Shari'ah law in place. Muslims are also members of every dominant political and ethnic group in the country. Islam is generally associated with the Hausa-Fulani segment of the population, though an increasing number of Yoruba are now practicing Muslims. With the political amalgamation of the various ethnic groups in Nigeria into one political entity, and since Hausa-Fulani ethnicity and the Islamic religion pioneered a political party for central political power, no major decisions are ever taken without prior consultations and approbation of certain powerful emirs. Currently, there is a Taliban-like Islamic movement known as the al-Sunna wal Jamma (Followers of Muhammad's Teachings) based in the 12 states with Shari'ah law (Abubaker 2009). The young Nigerian leaders of this movement want to impose a very strict version of the Shari'ah. Although this sectarian movement does not appear to have connections with the Taliban or al-Qaida, they have been launching attacks on local populations in the northern states. These Islamists are also referred to as "Boko Haram," which translates as "Western education is prohibited" in the local Hausa dialect. The leaders of this sect are saying that their followers are ready to die to ensure the institution of the Taliban-like form of Shari'ah (Abubaker 2009).

People "became" Hausa in order to reap the benefits of affiliating with the Islamic religion: political centralization, administrative organization, trade, and connections with a far-reaching network of states sharing a common civilization and religion. In attempting to overcome the various hazards of trade, traders had to build relations of trust and confidence with those whom they encountered during their journeys. Learning languages was common. Next, intermarriage was a social bond and alliance-building mechanism for promoting shared interests (Falola 2000:29; Salamone 1974). Ethnic bonds were also created through "blood brotherhoods." In northwestern Uganda during the nineteenth century, the salt trade became a very contentious one, with struggle over control of the trade. Religion was used to facilitate trade. Likewise, the Hausa, also long-distance traders, used Islam to create an effective bond of unity among themselves in order to control trade (Cohen 1969).

RELIGION AND ETHNICITY IN SUDAN

Sudan is the largest nation in Africa, covering nearly a million square miles. The population is estimated at 34 million, and 70 percent are Muslim, 5 percent Christian, and 25 percent animist. Many different ethnic groups occupy the country, and over 400 languages are spoken. Northern Sudan represents Arabic Islamic culture, with both pastoralists and agriculturists. Southern Sudan is composed primarily of more "African" people who follow indigenous animist beliefs and/or Christianity. The country is effectively divided between the north and the south, with all real power, economic and political, residing in the north. Sudanese have engaged in destructive civil wars for years (Middleton 2000).

The British colonized the Sudan in 1896–1898. They allowed for Anglo-Egyptian administration until 1924, when they introduced "indirect rule" through local chiefs. The tensions and disparities between the north and south in large part emerged as a result of British colonial policy, which sought favor with the northerners, bringing Western education and infrastructure developments, with benign neglect and control as the overall approach toward southerners. The British southern policy led to a depopulated no-man's land between the two regions, which kept peace during the colonial era. When Sudan gained independence in 1956, the better-educated and Western-trained northerners were the beneficiaries of almost all of the government and administrative positions; only 4 such positions out of 800 went to southerners (O'Ballance 1977:70). The frustrations and insults felt among southerners led to the first Sudanese separatist movement. A 16-year civil war ensued, ending with autonomy for the south, which devolved into chaos.

Military and civil governments seized power alternately, until in 1969 a coup d'état brought in a military government headed by Colonel Jaafar Nimeiri. In 1972, his government sanctioned a constitution that mandated a single political party, the Sudan Socialist Union. A second southern revolution broke out in 1983, when the military government introduced Shari'ah law for the entire country, which is still in progress, the impasse halted only by an uneasy cease-fire. As a result, the Sudan People's Liberation Army (SPLA) was formed in the south, with its goal of a "unified, secular, democratic Sudan." Martial law was enacted in 1984 as southern Sudan sank into full-scale famine, partially caused by drought but primarily by political troubles. The religious-based ethnic struggle between the north and south continues today.

In response to growing global attention to the ongoing crisis in Sudan, often referred to only as the "humanitarian crisis in Darfur," the U.S. special envoy to Sudan on June 23, 2009, gave the following remarks in support of the Comprehensive Peace Agreement (CPA):

But I'd really like to welcome all of you here today. This really is a very special event, the first high-level conference of its type since the signing of the CPA back in 2005, and we thank you for coming from near and from far. And we have people that have arranged their schedule significantly to be part of this event, and we're deeply grateful because this is a critical effort that's occurring at a crucial time as we approach the final push to fully implement the CPA.

As all of you know well, the Governments of Southern Sudan and the Sudanese People Liberation Movement signed the CPA back in January of 2005 ending a 22-year civil war between the north and the south, and this CPA has resulted in a peace for over four years. But none of this would have been possible without the support of the international community. Without your tireless efforts and those representatives of your country. Some of the people sitting here today were out in Naivasha, were part of those negotiations, and witnessed, and some even signed that special document. Now, I want to thank you personally for your continued commitment to peace in Sudan.

GENOCIDE IN RWANDA

Rwanda has experienced Africa's worst-attempted genocide in modern times and is still recovering from the shock. Even where mass murder appears aimed at a specific ethnic community, questions still arise as to the meaning of ethnicity where the groups in conflict share the same language, the same national territory, the same customs, and for centuries have lived more or less peacefully side by side. The country has been beset by ethnic tension associated with the traditionally unequal relationship between the dominant Tutsi minority and the majority Hutus. Mass conflict began when Belgian colonial rulers gave the Tutsi a monopoly of state power (Middleton 2000). Using "ethnicity" as a political weapon is a product of modern politics that often reflects a real or imagined inequity of resource distribution and allocation (Bowen 2001; Falola 2000; Middleton 2000). (See: http://www.youtube.com/watch?v=Pw12KGSj53k&NR=1.)

Before the modern era some Africans did consider themselves Hutu or Tutsi, Nuer or Zande, but these labels were not the characteristic of everyday identity. A woman living in Central Africa drew her identity from where she was born, from her lineage and in-laws, and from her wealth. Tribal or ethnic identity was rarely important in everyday life and could change as people moved over vast areas in pursuit of trade or new lands. Conflicts were more often within tribal categories than between them, as people fought over sources of water, farmland, or grazing rights.

In Rwanda and Burundi, German and Belgian colonizers admired the taller people called Tutsis, who formed a small minority in both colonies. The Belgians gave the Tutsis, the minority group, privileged access to education and jobs, and even instituted a minimum height requirement for entrance to college. To enable colonial officials to distinguish Tutsi from non-Tutsi, everyone was required to carry identity cards with tribal labels. Fortunately, people cannot be forced into the neat compartments that this requirement suggests. Many Hutus are tall and many Tutsis short; furthermore, many Hutus and Tutsis had intermarried to such an extent that they were not easily distinguished physically (nor are they today). They spoke the same language and carried out the same religious practices. In most regions of the colonies the categories became economic labels: poor Tutsis became Hutus, and economically successful Hutus became Tutsis. Where the labels Hutu and Tutsi had not been much used, lineages with lots of cattle were simply labeled Tutsi; poorer lineages, Hutu. Colonial discrimination against Hutus created what had never existed before: a sense of collective Hutu identity, a Hutu cause. In the late 1950s, Hutus began to rebel against Tutsi rule (encouraged by Europeans on their way out) and then created an independent, Hutu-dominated state in Rwanda; this state then gave rise to Tutsi resentments and to the creation of a Tutsi rebel army, the Rwandan Patriotic Front.

In Rwanda, the continuing slaughter of the past few years stemmed from efforts by the dictator-president Juvenal Habyarimana to wipe out his political opposition, Hutu as well as Tutsi. In 1990–1991, Habyarimana began to assemble armed gangs into a militia called Interahamwe. The militia carried out its first massacre of a village in March 1992, and in 1993 began systematically to kill Hutu moderates and Tutsis (Bowen 2001:356–366; Lemarchand 1999).

Paul Kagame, the current president of Rwanda, grew up in Uganda where his parents fled to escape Hutu violence. He has attempted to play down any ethnic agenda in Rwanda, presenting himself as a Rwandan and not a Tutsi. Like other African countries, Rwanda is attempting to forge a national identity that will supersede any ethnic identity (Scupin 2008).

SOUTH AFRICA IN TRANSITION

In some ways South Africa is a mirror reflection of all other countries in the sub-Saharan region, and at the same time, it is very different. In many countries, colonial authorities exploited and exacerbated ethnic differences for their own ends, and the white regimes of southern Africa pursued an aggressive policy of retribalization (Bowen 2001; Wiley 1999). Prior to 1994 and the "official" end of Apartheid, South African identity was scripted by ethnicity and language competency. Most notably, the majority groups were, in alphabetical order, Afrikaner, Colored, English, Indian, Ndebele, Pedi, Sotho, Tswana, Tsonga, Venda, Xhosa, and Zulu (Goldschmidt 2003:204).

The Republic of South Africa, also referred to simply as South Africa, came into being in 1961. It is the most populous country in southern Africa. It is also the most industrialized and has the largest white population in sub-Saharan Africa. Population estimates show that South Africa has 34.5 million blacks, 5 million whites, 3.5 million coloreds, and 1 million Asians. Eight million people, mostly blacks, live in the squalor of squatter settlements. Many blacks were resettled into reservation areas called "homelands." About 18 million black families earn less than $220 a month. Half the black population is illiterate and half of its workforce is unemployed. The urban population continues to grow, while the infrastructure of social services and amenities fails to meet urgent needs. Currently, only 15 percent of the urban population has access to potable water; about 8 million have access to only minimal sanitation; about 17 million do not have electricity; and about 8 million do not have formal road access to their homes. Of the white population, 60 percent are Afrikaans-speaking. These are descendants of Dutch, Huguenot, and German ancestry. Forty percent are English-speakers, descendants of British rule in the Cape Province (Middleton 2000).

For most of South Africa's contemporary history, social identity has been tied to a political agenda of legitimized racial separation and discrimination. In apartheid South Africa, race or skin color was enclosed within the net of ethnicity, thus clouding the issues particular to each.[3] This is even more problematic because the social categories of apartheid were defined by crude racial measures (see Chapter 4). Phenotype, as perceived by those in power, was the most salient component of apartheid social categories.

The white minority population was privileged by the state. Blacks, members of the native populations of South Africa, were largely disenfranchised, while those designated as colored fell somewhere in between. Some coloreds were able to pass for white; some were accused of being black. Whites took all that was good; blacks were denied all that was good. The colored population was systematically relocated over a period of 40 years, at the whim of how much privilege they were deemed deserving of to serve the needs of the apartheid system. Residential patterns, school attendance, job niches, and entertainment venues still, for the most part, represent the social structure of apartheid, lagging behind the rapid ideological changes mandated by the "Post-Apartheid era." Those designated as "colored" are, perhaps, the most interesting of apartheid's creations: white is privilege, black is disenfranchised, and colored is neither.

According to Jamie Gates (2000:58), Birgit Pickel (1997) argues from the literature that the colored category was constructed as a buffer between privileged white and subjugated black South Africans. The colored category, as with the white, black, and Indian categories, was reified and given the meaning most conducive to the goals of apartheid. A colored identity remains, in some ways, a disclaimer. It is the perception that one is not black, white, Indian, Chinese, or a member of any other socially meaningful category—in other words, it is more a perception of what coloreds are not than what they are.

About 1995, 9 new provincial capitals, the dissolution of the 10 black homelands, successful national/local government elections, the inauguration of the human rights commission, and other transformations of the social order set the stage for new dispensations. The new flag of six colors symbolizes the people, their blood, their land, the gold under the ground, the sky, and peace. The importance of language is expressed in the interim constitution, which accords official status to 9 of South Africa's 11 indigenous languages (isiZulu, Setswana, North Sotho, South Sotho, Xhosa, Swazi, Ndebele, Venda, and Shangan), putting them on a par with English and Afrikaans in all spheres of life. This document, referred to as a "model" by many a news correspondent, has left out in the cold the "language of apartheid"—the words, phrases, and idiomatic expressions that continue to color daily interactions among South Africans.

The language of the "new" South Africa stresses the need for a nonracial, nonsexist society and provides hope for a positive transformation. The African National Congress's Reconstruction and Development Program (RDP) promises transparency, socioeconomic restructuring, growth, and equity for all. The National Government of Unity has put in place the Truth and Reconciliation Commission, the Human Rights Commission, and the Anti-Corruption Commission. National and local decisions are being taken on affirmative action, gender equity, house subsidy grants, industrial development, and the integration of universal primary education. Workers now have the Labor Relations Act and a Commission of Conciliation, Mediation and Arbitration (CCMA), which are independent of the state, trade unions, and employers, to resolve disputes through conciliation.

Even with all the positive social and political policy transformations, the built-up shanties of the blacks that have been marginalized by the system of institutionalized racism of apartheid, remain appalling. In these slum conditions there is no plumbing, no electricity, and no waste collection. Homes are made of battered aluminum, cardboard, and wood strips salvaged from demolished construction sites. In contrast, the designated areas for resident Indians are crowded with some massively impressive buildings, showing the entrepreneurial successes of the owners. Locked into small plots with nowhere else to go, they overbuilt. Mitchell Plain is one model community for Indians. Bishops Court, the exclusive reserve for whites, is all that wealth can afford. High walls shield occupants from the eyes of those who pass on the surrounding roadways, as each house is self-contained with a state-of-the-art security system.

The real problem for contemporary South Africa is the urgency to meet the needs of its many ethnic and communal groups, especially those facing dramatic social, political, and economic changes for which their history has not prepared them. People will be drawn into groups with which they feel an affinity, for mutual assistance, and in reaction toward hostility against them. South Africans who are making a public claim for a nonracial, nonsexist society that forbids discrimination will have to find a way to bargain for an equitable division of the state's resources if they hope to avoid the ethnic clashes being played out in many other parts of the African continent.

CONCLUSION

All cultural concepts are inherently interconnected in complex and often complicated ways. Ethnicity is just one cultural construct for self- and group identity with both historical and contemporary references. In Africa, traditional ethnic categories were influenced by changes in the social-economic structure attendant to the colonial and postcolonial eras, leading to a complex identity paradigm. Communal self-perception and identification by others are equally powerful issues to contend with in Africa. An assessment of "ethnicity" in the present day requires an evaluation of (1) ethnic minorities who are nationals, (2) ethnic minorities who are migrants and/or refugees, (3) ethnic majority populations who are politically dominant, (4) ethnic majority populations who are politically subordinate, and (5) ethnic minority populations who are politically dominant.

Most African instrumental and symbolic features sustain the continuing value for ethnic association and affiliation. Ethnicity in Africa is now being used to integrate the trajectories of political power, prestige, and privilege through access to economic resources. Attendant issues include spatial integration and social boundaries, physical expressions, and symbolic representations.

Group and individual identity based along ethnic lines serves to secure a community's place in the nation-state, as well as the nation-state's preeminence in the lives of communities. Among Africa's multiethnic societies this means bargaining for the group's share of the resources available in the state against other groups, defending the group against discrimination, and, in general, maximizing its members' chances and minimizing their disadvantages (Hobsbawn 1991).

Notes

1. At the Berlin Conference of 1884–1885, European countries with interests in expanding into the African continent met to determine the rules that would guide them. This is sometimes referred to as "the scramble for Africa."
2. Flora Shaw (Lady Lugard) (1964) developed an elaborate scheme for racial ranking.
3. Apartheid, "apartness," was maintained by a massive legal and institutional structure to ensure the perpetuation of white rule. Some of the laws:

1893	Indians disenfranchised
1902–1909	Location laws (Jim Crow in the United States)
1905	Schools Board Act in the Cape
1902	Native Reserve Location Act
1904	Locations Act
1909	South Africa Act, basis for Constitution Act of 1961; established places for prime minister and parliament government; coloreds and blacks could elect whites to represent them in parliament until this "privilege" was abolished for Africans in 1959 and for coloreds in 1968.
1913	Native Land Act (scheduled areas)
1923	Natives (urban areas) Act

1910–1924	Definitive legislative acts to institution-alize segregation politically, territorially, and residentially. First restriction of black and colored voters to the Cape alone, and the exclusion of blacks everywhere from parliament.	1984	New Constitution Act, creating a three-chamber parliament dominated by the white chamber with subordinate chambers for coloreds and Asians.Africans, making up 73 percent of the population, were still excluded. Prime minister position abolished and a "president" position, which is now head of state and head of government, is new government profile.
1969	Terrorism Act; backdated to 1962. Terrorism now receives death penalty; no appeal.		

References Cited

ABUBAKER, AMINU. 2009. Nigerian army attack rebels in North. *Los Angeles Times*, July 29, 2009. http://www.latimes.com/news/nationworld/world/la-fg-nigeria29-2009jul29,0,7741454.story.

ACHEBE, CHINUA. 2000. *Home and Exile.* Oxford: University Press.

AFRICA POLICY INFORMATION CENTER. 2005. "Talking about 'Tribe': Moving from Stereotypes to Analysis." Africa Policy Information Center (APIC). Background Paper (Originally published 1997). http://www.africafiles.org/article.asp?ID=9130&ThisURL=&URLName=

BARTH, F., ed. 1969. *Ethnic Groups and Boundaries: The Social Organization of Cultural Differences.* Boston, MA: Little, Brown.

BEIDELMAN, T. O. 1997. *The Cool Knife: Imagery of Gender, Sexuality, and Moral Education in Kaguru Initiation Ritual.* Washington, DC: Smithsonian Institution Press.

BOHANNAN, PAUL. 1995. *How Culture Works.* New York: Free Press.

BOWEN, JOHN R. 2001. The myth of global ethnic conflict. *Journal of Democracy* (October 1996). *Taking Sides: Clashing Views on Controversial Global Issues.* James E. Harf and Mark Owen Lombardi, eds. Guilford, CT: McGraw-Hill/Dushkin.

COHEN, ABNER. 1969. *Custom and Politics in Urban Africa: A Study of Hausa Migrants in Yoruba Towns.* Berkeley, CA: University of California Press.

COHEN, RONALD. 1978. Ethnicity: Problem and Focus. *Annual Review of Anthropology* 7:379–403.

———. 1993. Ethnicity, the state, and moral order. In *Ethnicity and the State. Political and Legal Anthropology Series*, vol. 9. Judith D. Toland, ed. New Brunswick, NJ: Transaction.

DIAMOND, LARRY. 1988. Nigeria: Pluralism, statism, and the struggle for democracy. In *Democracy in Developing Countries: Africa.* Larry Diamond, Juan J. Linz, and Seymour Martin Lipset, eds. Boulder, CO: Lynne Rienner.

DOUGLAS, MARY. 1997. Lele economy compared with the Bushong. In *Perspectives on Africa: A Reader in Culture, History, and Representation.* Roy R. Grinker and Christopher B. Steiner, eds. Cambridge, MA: Blackwell.

ELLER, JACK D. 1999. *From Culture to Ethnicity to Conflict: An Anthropological Perspective on International Ethnic Conflict.* Ann Arbor, MI: University of Michigan Press.

EVANS-PRITCHARD, E. E. 1940. *The Nuer: A Description of the Modes of Livelihood and political institutions of a Nilotic Peoples.* Oxford: Clarendon Press.

———. 1951. *Kinship and Marriage among the Nuer.* Oxford: Clarendon Press.

FALOLA, TOYIN, ed. 2000. *Africa: African Cultures and Societies before 1885*, vol. 2. Durham, NC: Carolina Academic Press.

GATES, JAMIE. 2000. Review of coloured ethnicity and identity: A Case study in the former coloured areas in the Western Cape, South Africa. *Transforming Anthropology* 9(1):58–60.

GEERTZ, CLIFFORD. 1973. *The Interpretation of Cultures.* New York: Basic Books.

———. 1985. Centers, kings, and charisma: Reflections on the symbolics of power. In *Rites of Power, Symbolism, Ritual and Politics since the Middle Ages.* Sean Wilentz, ed. Philadelphia, PA: University of Pennsylvania Press.

GOLDSCHMIDT, MYRA M. 2003. Identifying labels among university students in the new South Africa: A retrospective study. *Journal of Black Studies* 34(2):204–221.

GREENBAUM, SUSAN. 1992. *Race/Ethnicity/Culture.* Essay produced under sponsorship for USF Center for Teaching Enhancement, Resource Guide for the General Education Curriculum, Department of Anthropology, University of South Florida.

GRINKER, ROY RICHARD, and CHRISTOPHER B. STEINER, eds. 1997. Introduction: Africa in perspective. In *Perspectives on Africa: A Reader in Culture, History, and Representation.* Cambridge, MA: Blackwell.

HARF, JAMES E., and MARK OWEN LOMBARDI, eds. 2001. *Taking Sides: Clashing Views on Controversial Global Issues.* Guilford, CT: McGraw-Hill/Dushkin.

HOBSBAWN, E. J. 1991. *Nations and Nationalism since 1780: Program, Myth, Reality.* Cambridge: University of Cambridge Press.

HUNTINGTON, SAMUEL P. 2001. The clash of civilizations? In *Taking Sides: Clashing Views on Controversial Global Issues.* James E. Harf and Mark Owen Lombardi, eds. Guilford, CT: McGraw-Hill/Dushkin.

JOSEPH, RICHARD A. 1987. *Democracy and Prebendal Politics in Nigeria: The Rise and Fall of the Second Republic.* New York: Cambridge University Press.

KODZO-VORDOAGU, J. G. 1994. *Anlo Hogbetsotso Festival.* Accra, Ghana: Domak Press.

LEMARCHAND, RENE. 1999. Ethnicity as myth: The view from the Central Africa. Occasional paper. Centre of African Studies, University of Copenhagen.

LOUKAS, CHRIST. 1929. Consciousness of Kind Among University Students. *Social Forces* 7(3):385–388.

MAYBURY-LEWIS, DAVID. 1997. *Indigenous Peoples, Ethnic Groups, and the State.* Boston, MA: Allyn & Bacon.

MIDDLETON, JOHN, ed. 2000. *Encyclopedia of Africa: South of the Sahara,* vol. 2. New York: Simon & Schuster/Macmillan.

NADEL, S. F. 1942. *A Black Byzantium: The Kingdom of Nupe in Nigeria.* Cambridge, MA: Blackwell.

O'BALLANCE, E. 1977. *The Secret War in the Sudan, 1955–1972.* London: Faber & Faber.

PADEN, JOHN, and EDWARD SOJA, eds. 1970. *The African Experience,* vol. 2. Evanston, IL: Northwestern University Press.

PICKEL, BIRGIT. 1997. *Coloured Ethnicity and Identity: A Case Study in the Former Coloured Areas in the Western Cape/South Africa.* Hamburg, Germany: Lit Verlag.

PUTMAN, DIANA, and MOHAMOOD C. NOOR. 1993. *The Somalis: Their History and Culture. CAL Refugee Fact Sheet No. 9.* Washington, DC: Refugee Service Center.

SALAMONE, FRANK A. 1974. *Gods and Goods in Africa. Persistence and Change in Ethnic and Religious Identity in Yauri Emirate, Northwestern State, Nigeria.* HRA Flex Books, Ethnography Series FF 36-001. New Haven, CT: Human Relations Area Files.

———. 1985. The social construction of colonial reality: Yauri emirate. *Cahiers d'Etudes Africaines* 98(XXV-2):139–159.

SCUPIN, RAYMOND. 2008. *Cultural Anthropology: A Global Perspective.* 7th edition. Upper Saddle River, NJ: Prentice Hall.

SIMMONS, DAVID. 2000. Signs of the times: Missionaries and tribal genesis in southern Rhodesia. *Transforming Anthropology* 9(2):3–18.

SOUTHALL, AIDAN W. 1997. The illusion of tribe. In *Perspectives on Africa: A Reader in Culture, History, and Representation.* Roy R. Grinker and Christopher B. Steiner, eds. Cambridge, MA: Blackwell.

STACK, CAROL B. 1974. *All Our Kin: Strategies for Survival in a Black Community.* New York: Harper & Row.

TOLAND, JUDITH D. 1993. *Ethnicity and the State: Political and Legal Anthropology Series,* vol. 9. New Brunswick, NJ: Transaction.

UDOGU, IKE E. 1999. Ethnicity, the state and the issue of nation-building in Nigeria's fourth republic. *Scandinavian Journal of Development Alternatives and Area Studies* 18(4):5–22.

WILEY, DAVID. 1999. If it's Africa, this must be a tribe. In *Capturing the Continent: U.S. Media Coverage of Africa.* Special 1990 edition of *Africa News.*

WILLIAMS, GAVIN. 2001. *Reforming Africa: Continuities and change.* In *Africa South of the Sahara.* John Middleton, ed. 30th edition. London: Europa.

15

●●●

The Middle East

Laurie King-Irani, *Georgetown University*

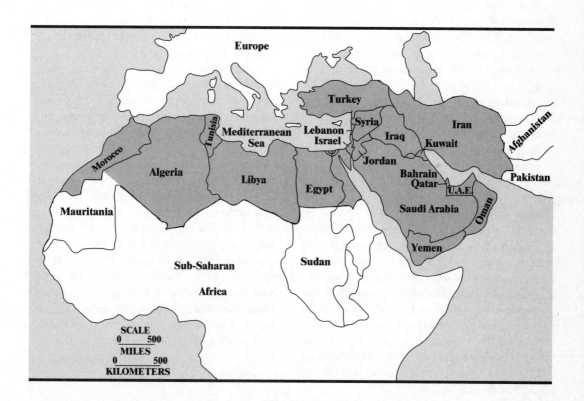

Scarcely a day passes without a dramatic news report about ethnic conflict and violence in the Middle East. Whether clashes between Israeli soldiers and Palestinian youths; civil war, famine, and population displacements in the Sudan; or Iraqi Sunnis and Shi'i carrying out suicide bombings against one another, the region seems to endure more than its fair share of political strife and ethnic conflict.

The unique historical, strategic, and geographic aspects of this region, as well as the interplay of these aspects with a multiplicity of local political interests and goals, may well predispose the societies and states of the Middle East to a greater degree and variety of political and ethnic conflicts than many other regions of the contemporary world.

Along with Central Africa and the Balkans, the Middle East registers in the consciousness of most Westerners as an area of chronic conflict, political volatility, and dangerous divisiveness, all of which, it is assumed, arises from age-old ethnic disagreements or religious antagonisms between the human components of the supposedly static and eternal Middle Eastern mosaic of communities (Coon 1961). The mainstream media's depictions of such conflicts as being rooted in ancient tribal animosities might lead casual observers to conclude that ethnic tensions in this large and diverse region are simply inevitable—encoded in the very genetic makeup or cultural "programming" of Middle Eastern populations. It is easy to assume that the sharp edges of the individual pieces of the Middle East mosaic are immutable, inherently antagonistic, and fated to "rub each other the wrong way" forever. Yet nothing could be farther from the truth.

In contrast to these popular—and mistaken—notions about ethnicity and ethnic conflict in the contemporary Middle East, this chapter will examine the emergence, mobilization, consolidation, and institutionalization of the region's ethnic identities not as examples of unchanging biological predispositions or cultural "essences" but, rather, as humanly shaped and strategic responses to specific environmental, geographic, historical, political, and economic realities. Changing configurations of ethnic identity and the dynamics of majority–minority relations in the various states in this region offer valuable lessons in the contingent and political—and therefore constructed and strategic—nature of ethnicity in the Middle East.

To understand the genesis, nature, and trajectory of Middle Eastern ethnic phenomena, we must first survey the region's ecological, historical, geographic, and administrative contexts. In other words, we must investigate the politics of identity. The formation of ethnic groups in the Middle East, as well as the dynamics of collaboration and competition among and

between such groups and the states in which they are located, arise from ever-changing balances of power and shifting frameworks of decision making and resource distribution at the local, national, regional, and international levels. Such political processes are present in every region of the world, but in the Middle East, long a "crossroads" of diverse cultures, languages, economies, and environments, political phenomena arising from the cross-fertilization of diverse peoples have taken distinct forms. Since ancient times, and indeed, up until the present, the region has been a key prize for various world powers, from the ancient Roman and Persian empires, to the European colonial powers of the nineteenth and early twentieth centuries, and ultimately to the multinational corporations and high-tech Western armies of the present era.

Thanks to its marked strategic importance, the Middle East and its peoples are no strangers to the intrigues and interventions of local, regional, and global politics. As we shall see in some of the case studies presented here, the most harrowing episodes of interethnic conflict in the Middle East have occurred when all three dimensions of competition for political power and economic resources—global, regional, and local—have coincided, as they did in Lebanon during its long and bloody civil war, which was also a regional war fought out on Lebanese soil (Hanf 1992; Harf 1993; al-Khazen 2000; King-Irani 2000), or in Iraq, where the nation's marginalized Shi'i and Kurdish communities rose up in a bloody, but ultimately futile, challenge to the ruling Sunni Ba'athist regime of Saddam Hussein in 1991 (Abd al-Jabber 1992; Graham-Brown 1999; Hiltermann 1999).

DEFINING THE TERMS

Before embarking on a journey through the ethnopolitical map of the Middle East, we shall first clarify what is meant by such easily taken-for-granted terms as the "Middle East" and "ethnicity."

The *Middle East* or *Near East* has been characterized as such in relation to the "Far East" (China, Southeast Asia, and Japan), indicating that the vantage point for determining these locations was not indigenous but Eurocentric. The perspective from which this label was coined was that of Britain and France, former colonial powers. Here, we find an initial, and telling, indication of the historical tensions and conflicts surrounding issues of identity and power in the Middle East: the region has been defined and represented from the outside, not from within (Said 1978). This discomfiting reality has sparked various nationalist and religious movements over the years to assert regional or national autonomy from Western political and cultural domination.

Even many decades after the end of colonial rule, Western interests and interventions can still evoke deep emotions and great controversies. The West's direct or implicit role in some of the continuing tensions and injustices in the region, particularly those associated with Israel's occupation of Palestinian territory and Israeli military attacks on Lebanon, or the U.S. role in the current militarization of the Arab Gulf region, are interpreted through a lens of suspicion, outrage, and anger. Ironically, although direct colonial rule has long since ended, the dynamics of the current global capitalist economy and the Middle East's weak role therein replicate relationships of dependency between the region and the leading industrialized nations of the West (Barakat 1993; Halliday 1999; S. Makdisi 1990; Pfeifer 1998).

The imperialist roots of the region's geographic labeling notwithstanding, the Middle East is conventionally described as stretching from Morocco and Mauritania in the west to Iran in the east, and from Turkey in the north to Sudan in the south. The area of this large and culturally diverse region, which is double the size of the continental United States, encompasses territory on three continents (Africa, Europe, and Asia) and is home to over 370 million people, among whom Muslims constitute 82 percent of the population, Christians 9 percent, and Jews 7 percent[1] (Eickelman 1999). The region also includes other religious groups that do not fit neatly into the categories of the three monotheistic faiths, such as followers of the Druze faith,[2] adepts of the ancient Zoroastrian faith (found in Iran and India), and followers of the relatively new Baha'i faith that originated in Iran, where it is now subject to repression (Sanasarian 2000).

Despite Islam's crucial historical and cultural roles in unifying most of the region between the seventh and the ninth centuries (Esposito 1998), no less than its contemporary galvanizing role as a basis of political mobilization and ideological guidance in a rapidly changing world, the Islamic world is far from unified and harmonious: Sunni and Shi'i Muslims have been known to fight each other more ferociously than either has fought against Christians and Jews.[3] Furthermore, with the rise of politicized Islam throughout the region during the last quarter of the twentieth century, there have been ideological divisions and disagreements between members of the same Islamic sects over the proper role of religion and religious organizations in contemporary Arab society (Silverstein 1996) as well as within the Iranian government.

In addition to the region's multiplicity of religions, the diversity of languages is also pronounced and frequently corresponds to religious distinctions: Arabic, Persian, Turkish, Hebrew, Kurdish, Berber, and Armenian are spoken in the region, in addition to lingering colonial languages: French in North Africa, Syria, and Lebanon; English in Egypt, Jordan, Palestine, and Iraq; and Italian in Libya. Some languages, such as Berber (Tamazight) and Kurdish, are subdivided into a variety of dialects, some of which have yet to be standardized.

Because the newly formed states of the region did not emerge as a result of long-term, organic economic and political processes but from the quick sketching of colonial powers' pens (Fromkin 1988; Manners and Parmenter 2004; Tibi 1989), few Middle Eastern states' boundaries coincide with preexisting geographic, linguistic, or cultural borders. (Egypt is the only exception.) Consequently, a variety of identity crises and ethnic conflicts were built into the new states—and thus into the new regional state system—of the postcolonial Middle East from the outset.

The crisis of national integration has been a continuing theme (Drysdale and Blake 1985), expressed through a variety of permutations:

military coups, politicized religious movements, strict language policies, and the sedentarization or transfer of population groups that posed direct or indirect challenges to the legitimacy of state borders or the control of state resources. Although few states in the Middle East can boast ethnic, linguistic, or cultural homogeneity, nearly all have tried to achieve it (Bengio and Ben-Dor 1999; Drysdale and Blake 1985; Eickelman 1999; Tétreault 2001), some by force, particularly in the Sudan (Lesch 1997; Ronen 1999), and usually at the expense of weaker ethnic groups.

Although fabulous oil wealth can easily be found in the Middle East, particularly in the countries of the Arab Gulf (Saudi Arabia, Kuwait, Qatar, Bahrain, the United Arab Emirates, and Oman), the vast majority of Middle Eastern peoples are more familiar with poverty or the fear of its imminent arrival (World Bank 2008). The gap between the region's haves and have-nots is profound, dramatic, and deepening. Perceived and actual economic inequalities influence the formation and mobilization of ethnic groupings, particularly in those countries in which the rich and poor live in close proximity, such as Lebanon, Egypt, and Turkey.

In assessing *ethnicity* in any region, including the Middle East, we must avoid the easy assumption that ethnic differences are essentially physiological differences. The conclusion that ensues from this view—that is, that ethnic groups are determined primarily by objective biological criteria such as hair, skin, and eye color, or height and physique, and only further distinguished by such characteristics as language, cultural patterns, and religious faith—has facilitated racial stereotyping and racism in many societies. Social scientists examining the phenomenon of ethnicity stress that it is a strategic more than a genetic phenomenon (Anderson 1983; Cohen 1978; Eller 1999; Royce 1982).

Identity is neither programmed nor preexisting; it is constantly being shaped by the interplay of contexts and the dynamics of power inherent in such contexts. If identities were determined by virtually immutable genetic realities alone, then we would expect to see the same categorizations, symbols, and expressions of identity enduring over time in the same place, regardless of economic, cultural, or political developments. This is clearly not the case in the Middle East, a region that has experienced rapid metamorphoses from empire to colonial regimes to modern nation-states in less than a century, and in which organized ethnic and religious groupings have emerged in different periods to compete for power, resources, and privileges, thus highlighting the contingency and relativity of identity.

Under conditions of empire, familial and religious (sectarian) identities were most significant in the region. Under conditions of centralized state administrations, new regional, class, cultural, and ethnic identities—and, consequently, new conflicts—have come to the fore as laws and policies imposed identities on people that were new, uncomfortable, and even, in some cases, objectionable.

A dual dynamic of identity is evident in the context of the modern nation-state in the region. One aspect of this dynamic is that identities can be claimed actively by people affiliating as members of a particular group in order to secure access to scarce resources or threatened rights, or in competition with other groups for control of the state's resource-distribution mechanisms. The opposite aspect of this dynamic is identification as an involuntary process, as in those situations in which the state, desiring to safeguard or project a vision of its own ethnic purity or religious unity, imposes limited and limiting identities from above while forbidding the expression of contradictory identities from below.

The phenomenon of Middle Eastern ethnicity presents a number of definitional and methodological challenges for researchers because ethnic groups often behave like kin-based groupings, such as lineages and tribes, especially in the way they mobilize their members by invoking a common historical identity and ties of mutual obligation (Tibi 1989). At the same time, ethnic differences frequently correspond closely to socioeconomic distinctions. For example, in Israeli society,

Western-oriented Ashkenazi Jews (who emigrated from Central and Eastern Europe), though numerically the minority community, are the dominant group with respect to wealth and control of the state's decision-making bodies—this in comparison with the more numerous Sephardic Jews (Arab, Iranian, and Turkish), whose cultural attitudes and practices have long been denigrated as "backwards" by Ashkenazi Jews (Avruch 1987).

Prior to the convulsions of the Lebanese civil war (1975–1990), wealthy power brokers and owners of factories, banks, and businesses in Lebanon tended to be Maronite Christians, while the poorer, less powerful agricultural communities in Lebanon were invariably populated by Shi'i Muslims in the south and Sunni Muslims in the north (Salibi 1988). In Iraq, a country cobbled together from three distinct ethnoreligious groups—Sunni Kurds, Shi'i Arabs, and Sunni Arabs—divisions of wealth and poverty have historically mirrored the divisions between Sunni and Shi'i communities, with Sunni Arabs enjoying a far greater share of power and wealth than either the Sunni Kurds or the more numerous Shi'i community. This political and economic configuration predates the Iraqi nation-state, as Sunnis have enjoyed a greater scope of economic and political power than Shi'i Muslims since Ottoman times and were the "favored community" during the period of British colonization.

To understand how ethnic groupings became key players in the contemporary Middle Eastern political scene, we now turn to an examination of the ecological, historical, and political processes that have shaped individual and collective political perceptions, organizations, and actions in the region. Important factors have been the dismantling of the Ottoman Empire (1359–1918), European colonization and its repercussions, the regional economy's incorporation into a world capitalist system, and last but not least, the formation of nation-states. All of these developments have exacerbated inequalities, mobilized groups, catalyzed competition, and thus occasionally engendered conflicts in the region.

CONTEXTS AND CATALYSTS OF ETHNICITY IN THE MIDDLE EAST

The peoples of the Middle East are no strangers to harsh and uncertain environments, whether natural, economic, or political. Inhabiting an ecological zone characterized by aridity, steep valleys, rugged mountains, few rivers, scant rainfall, and poor soils, Middle Eastern communities were traditionally compelled to combine a variety of modes of subsistence, such as pastoral nomadism, small-scale agriculture, commerce, and fishing, in order to make a living. Groups dwelling in this arid and semiarid region also developed distinctive cultural patterns and sociopolitical institutions that served to minimize the hardships and uncertainties of their natural environment. Up until the present era, the peoples of the Middle East have remained justly famous for loyal attachment to their families and religious communities, and distinctive rituals of hospitality and conflict mediation. They have a preference for shifting and fluid coalitions rather than enduring, corporate sociopolitical organizations and for flexible kin-based collectivities, such as the lineage and the tribe, which until quite recently performed most of the social, economic, and political functions of communities in the absence of centralized state governments (Khoury and Kostiner 1989; King-Irani 2004).

Before the nation-state system, and even before the colonial era, most of the peoples of the region (with the exception of those living in Morocco, Mauritania, and Iran) lived under Ottoman rule in the sociopolitical framework of a vast and multiethnic Islamic empire. Day-to-day matters of administration and basic governance were overseen and discharged by local political elites chosen by the Ottoman rulers, as well as the local clergy.

The Ottoman Empire was organized not according to ethnic or national principles and categories but according to religious distinctions (Bosworth 1982). Subjects of the Ottoman sultan did not identify themselves as Ottomans, Turks, Arabs, Azeris, Berbers, or Kurds but as Muslims, Christians, Jews, or Druze. The crucially distinguishing social categories were religion, class, and gender. Accordingly, Muslims, men, and the well-to-do enjoyed power and privileges that women, the poor, and non-Muslim communities could never hope to attain.

Within this sociopolitical setting, Muslims constituted the majority, both in terms of absolute numbers and in terms of power, rank, status, and opportunities. Christians and Jews were formally recognized as respected religious minorities— "Peoples of the Book"—and categorized as *dhimmi* communities (literally, "on the conscience" of the larger and more powerful Muslim community). Christians and Jews were to be protected from harm or persecution by the majority Muslim community in return for their acceptance of a subordinate social and political status, payment of a special head tax (*jizya*) in exchange for their exemption from military service, and refraining from any public display of their religions, such as processions and liturgical ceremonies.

Dhimmi communities were under the jurisdiction of Islamic courts in the event of criminal cases and some property disputes, but otherwise obeyed the jurisdiction of their own communities' religious laws and precepts concerning any issues touching upon religious and family matters. As non-Muslims, Christians, Druze, and Jews were not subject to the rulings of *Shari'ah* (Islamic law) in matters of personal status, such as marriage, divorce, inheritance, adoption, and other family issues. Instead, Christian sects and Druze and Jewish communities sought guidance, mediation, and rulings from their own religious leaders, who had the power to make binding judicial decisions in the domain of family law and to represent their religious communities in official dealings with the Ottoman authorities. This system of legally recognized, non-Muslim communal autonomy was known as the *millet* system (meaning "people" or "community" in Turkish).

The Middle East's cultural heterogeneity stemmed from geography as much as from Ottoman social categorizations, however. The ecological characteristics of the region, combined with the prevalence of rugged mountains, deep valleys, and virtually impassable desert expanses,

compelled different communities to live in small, close-knit family groupings widely separated from each other with no overarching political or economic organization (Meeker 1979). This facilitated pronounced diversity in the region. For example, the three key cities of present-day Iraq all of which are linked by rivers (Mosul, Baghdad, and Basra), had completely different systems of weights and measures and currencies until the late nineteenth century (Batatu 1978). Until the advent of advanced communications technology and the construction of paved roads and railways in the late nineteenth and early twentieth centuries, some areas of the Middle East were virtually inaccessible. Existing independently of each other for so many centuries, it was only natural that marked linguistic, cultural, and religious differences would develop among the dispersed populations of the Middle East.

During the Ottoman era, the rugged mountainous areas of the eastern Mediterranean became a refuge for various Christian sects and Islamic splinter groups seeking to escape persecution by orthodox religious authorities. Dwelling high atop these mountains, minority groups such as the Maronites, Druze, Shi'a, and Alawites could pursue their religious traditions free of interference from either Christian or Muslim authorities. Religious refugees thus rendered the mountainous zones of the region culturally and religiously diverse: not only the mountains of Lebanon and Syria but also the mountainous regions of northern Iraq and eastern Turkey, as well as those of North Africa, have traditionally been home to minority groups such as the Kurds, Assyrians, and Berber tribes.

Middle Eastern cities have always evidenced cultural and religious heterogeneity. The plural nature of Middle Eastern urban space is inscribed in the very towers, walls, and gates that marked off the various named sections of traditional urban settlements (the "Muslim Quarter," the "Armenian Quarter," the "Jewish Quarter," and the "Orthodox Quarter"), as we find in such ancient cities as Jerusalem, Cairo, Damascus, and Baghdad. The spatial separation of different religious and ethnic groups in the traditional Middle Eastern city was paralleled by a division of labor among these distinct communities. Muslims, Christians, and Jews occupied different professional categories in the Ottoman social and economic structure.

The city's traditional division of labor was usually characterized by accommodation, complementarity, and integration rather than by competition and conflict. Muslims held influential positions in religious courts and schools as well as in the military and in local government administration. Non-Muslims were primarily doctors, merchants, advisers, artisans, and religious and legal specialists for their own sectarian communities. The Ottoman era division of labor is recorded to this day in the names of many Christian families from Lebanon, Palestine, and Syria designating the professional and artisan roles that their ancestors played in Ottoman society: *sabbagh* (dyer), *hakim* (doctor), *khabbaz* (baker), *sayigh* (goldsmith), *hayek* (weaver), *najjar* (carpenter), *khoury* (priest), and *shammas* (sexton).

Thus, the cultural and religious heterogeneity of the Middle East is neither a new phenomenon associated with rapid urbanization nor a function of the creation of modern nation-states. Nor is cultural diversity a by-product of colonialism (although colonial powers certainly employed "divide and rule" tactics to consolidate their control of local societies and political systems under their rule). Different ethnic and religious groups have been living side by side in the Middle East for centuries, occasionally in conflict, but more often than not in harmony.

What *is* new is a transformed structure of relationships among the different ethnic and religious groups within the contemporary Middle Eastern nation-state. Here we see the aforementioned interplay of context and ethnic identity: in the administrative context of the nation-state, the social, political, and economic frameworks in which different groups interact, work, and struggle are no longer characterized by traditional guidelines of complementarity but by the uncertainties of competition. Although the Ottoman Empire was hardly a model of economic efficiency or social justice, it nevertheless encouraged intercommunal accommodation and cooperation to a greater degree than did subsequent colonial regimes or the imposed nation-state.

The relative balance and insularity of the Ottoman social universe was increasingly disturbed in the eighteenth and nineteenth centuries by European peoples, processes, and events. By the late eighteenth century, Ottoman authorities had grown alarmed by Europe's increasing military prowess and administrative efficacy, and accordingly attempted to copy European developments and practices so as to enhance their own control over the empire's far-flung territory and resources (Drysdale and Blake 1985; Goldschmidt 2000).

By the middle of the nineteenth century, European powers were lobbying the Ottoman sultan for better treatment and even protection of particular *dhimmi* communities, as well as special protections for European commercial agents and representatives in the region and for their local employees and contacts among the Ottoman Christian and Jewish population. Under European pressure, the Ottoman sultan issued a decree giving Christians and Jews legal equality with Muslims in the empire (Goldschmidt 2000), just at a time when the region's incorporation into a European-dominated market economy and the resulting transformation of the local economic system (particularly the shift from subsistence to cash crops) were having a noticeable impact on social and economic relations in the Ottoman world.

European powers' concerns about the local non-Muslim population stemmed not from charitable impulses alone. Aiding and allying with local Christian and Jewish interests enabled European states to get their "foot into the door" of the declining Ottoman Empire. European actions in the empire were part and parcel of the "Great Game"—the race among various European powers to control the routes to and the extraction of resources from the East, particularly India, where the British enjoyed—and naturally endeavored to maintain—a decided strategic advantage (Fromkin 1988).

In their pursuit of the "Great Game," the European powers backed different communities' interests, thereby establishing, whether by design or happenstance, the groundwork for the "divide and rule" policies so effectively implemented during the colonial period following the Ottoman Empire's collapse at the end of World War I. The British supported the Druze and the desert tribes of the Hejaz region of what is now Saudi Arabia (dramatized in David Lean's epic film, *Lawrence of Arabia*), the French backed the Maronites in the Levant and the Berbers in North Africa, and the Russians backed the Greek Orthodox in what are now Lebanon, Palestine, and Syria. During the colonial era, different groups received differential treatment from the British and French authorities. The colonial policy of playing various groups off against one another was later echoed in the practices and policies of the new nation-states that the colonial powers carved out of the region—heedless of any coincidence of ethnic, natural, or linguistic borders. Those who had been favorites during the colonial era frequently became scapegoats after independence.

CRUCIBLE OF COMMUNITY OR CAULDRON OF CONFLICT? THE NATION-STATE IN THE MIDDLE EAST

Although the bureaucracies of most Middle Eastern states are well entrenched and heavily subsidized, few have succeeded in distributing resources equitably, administering justice fairly, protecting and advancing the interests of the majority of their people, establishing a strong sense of common identity and mission, and thereby winning public support and popular participation through legitimate means (Ayoubi 1995; al-Khafaji 1995). Most states in the Middle East serve narrow elite interests rather than the broad common good (Barakat 1993; Tibi 1989). The overwhelming majority of the region's population does not participate in the economic and political decision-making processes that greatly influence their and their children's lives. Middle Eastern states usually rule rather than govern their populaces, employing coercion, manipulation, and co-optation of various ethnic groups to achieve control and compliance (Bengio and Ben-Dor 1999).

As an externally imposed, internally weak, and relatively new form of sociopolitical organization lacking roots, precedents, and traditions, the Middle Eastern nation-state still cannot claim the same kind or degree of support, loyalty, and legitimacy that Middle Eastern kin, ethnoreligious, and patron-client networks have always claimed. Even half a century after the nation-state's appearance in the region, kinship relations (including ethnic relations modeled on a kinship pattern) mediate individuals' personal, economic, and political lives to an extent almost unimaginable to anyone who has grown up in Western Europe or North America.

For example, individuals' interactions with state bodies and government bureaucracies take place primarily through patron–client relationships mediated by ties of kinship (actual or fictive lineages, or, as in Palestine, the *hamoula*, a patronymic association; see Eickelman 1999) or ethnic and sectarian affiliation (Cunningham and Sarayrah 1993). In most Middle Eastern societies, full government services are available only to those who have connections (*wasta* in Arabic; *protektzia* in Hebrew), and such links are usually contingent on one's family or ethnic networks. Citizenship, an identity category deriving its significance from the jural relationship of each individual to the nation-state, carries much less emotional, moral, legal, and political weight in the Middle East than do the identity categories of kinship, ethnicity, and religion.

Understanding the reasons why peoples throughout the Middle East preserve and value pre-state social and political institutions based on primordial affiliations such as kinship, ethnicity, and religion can help us appreciate the genesis of intrastate turmoil and interstate hostilities. Discovering how Middle Eastern peoples strategically invoke and manipulate ethnic affiliations will give us a new awareness of the creative and effective means individuals and groups have developed in order to survive and thrive in a challenging socioeconomic environment while preparing for future contingencies.

PUTTING IT ALL TOGETHER: SOME CONTEMPORARY CASE STUDIES

We will now examine the emergence, mobilization, and institutionalization of ethnic identity in relation to the historical, geographic, economic, and political contexts described above by examining the following case studies: Copts in Egypt, Berbers in Algeria, the multiconfessional Republic of Lebanon, and the Kurdish tragedy in Iraq. These examples are presented in order of increasing complexity as well as according to the degree of conflict and violence associated with each, from least to most conflictual given present realities.

Copts: Original Egyptians and a Non-Muslim Minority

The Copts (whose name is etymologically related to the ancient name "Egypt") are indisputably Egyptians and Arabs; indeed, they are the original Egyptians. Yet their non-Muslim status is a sensitive issue that is seldom discussed openly and frankly in Egyptian society. Egypt experienced less virulent ethnic and religious unrest than virtually any other Arab state in the immediate postindependence period. Indeed, Copts, 5 percent of the country's population, played an important role in the Egyptian struggle for independence from British colonial rule, achieved in 1922. For the next 30 years, Coptic–Muslim relations in Egypt were fairly unproblematic, but the nationalization of Egypt's private industries and businesses after the 1952 revolution affected Coptic interests disproportionately. Many wealthy Coptic families left the country during this period.

A key complaint of Egypt's Coptic community over the last several decades has been the difficulty—in some cases, the impossibility—of obtaining the requisite official permits to undertake the construction of new churches or the repair of old ones. In 1972, a Coptic church that had been built without government authorization was mysteriously burned to the ground, sparking violent riots.

The government's policy was to move carefully, quietly, and judiciously in protecting the rights and answering the demands of the Copts. To focus too much attention on the nature of the Copts' minority status would have the effect of activating Islamists' concerns and emotions. In other words, defining and treating the Copts publicly as a religious minority would implicitly define Egypt as a religiously based—that is, an Islamic—state, and the government did not wish to give this impression, internally or externally. Coptic expatriate communities in Europe and North America did not take so circumspect an approach to the debate, however, and many pressured their adopted Western governments to look into the issue of Coptic rights in Egypt. In 1997, when radical Islamist groups massacred several Copts in villages in Upper Egypt, some felt that the heightened attention to the Copts, although intended as a positive measure, had in fact led to a very negative conclusion.

The situation of Egypt's Copts says as much about regional and international politics and ideological developments as it does about internal Egyptian issues and problems. Strong anti-Western sentiments and associated tensions throughout the region as a whole, largely in response to U.S. policies universally perceived as unfair in the Islamic world, can and have had tragic repercussions for Coptic Christians in remote Egyptian villages (Graham-Brown 1999).

Here we have an illustration of the *transnational* character of ethnic sentiments and political movements in the region. Islamist movements are not geographically constricted or delimited. Events in one country can and frequently do have immediate and unpredictable echoes in other countries, despite national borders that have been in existence for over half a century. The dilemmas of the Egyptian Copts are but one example of the challenges of national integration and the crisis of citizenship in the states of the region. This case study also shows that many states in the region are fearful of actual or potential Islamist mobilization within or outside their borders.

Berbers in Algeria: Creatively Reclaiming Colonial Stereotypes

The shocking episodes of violence in Algeria over the last decade, most notably a series of heinous massacres in several cities and remote villages, is only tangentially related to Algeria's mixed ethnic composition, in which Arabs are 75 percent of the population and Berbers[4] (representing four different tribal groups, the largest and most influential of which are the tribal groups from the mountainous region of Kabylia) constitute 25 percent.

Algeria's 10 years of torment stem from sharp ideological and political differences over the benefits and drawbacks of an Islamic form of government. In 1991, Algerians went to the polls to elect a new government. It soon became clear that Islamist parties were poised to win the elections in a landslide. Fearing their ascension to power, the incumbent Algerian government and its military apparatus cancelled the election results and ultimately seized control of the country, ironically in the name of protecting democracy. Thus was set in motion a vicious cycle of attacks and counterattacks whose protagonists are often ambiguous. Rumors abound that some Islamist-orchestrated massacres may in fact have been carried out by army units disguised as Muslim radicals. In the current atmosphere of violence, fear, and chaos, public trust and common points of reference have been badly eroded (Silverstein 1997).

In this troubled setting, the country's Berber minority has creatively reworked an identification imposed upon it by the French colonial authorities in the nineteenth century. In an effort to divide and rule the Algerian population, France, like all colonial powers everywhere, had selected some groups for favored treatment, particularly in the areas of legal rights, educational opportunities, and employment in the colonial administration. In Algeria, Berbers and Jews represented the chosen, colonial favorites (Maddy-Weitzman 1998). French officials considered Berbers to be more refined, educable, and civilized than their Arab counterparts, and therefore more promising candidates for France's

"civilizing mission." As such, Berbers were afforded special educational opportunities, were not supposed to learn Arabic, and in 1874 were exempted from the rulings of Islamic law and encouraged to use customary law instead. All of these moves were meant to wean Berbers away from "primitive" cultural, social, and political behaviors in preparation for being "civilized" according to French tastes and specifications.[5] Berbers ultimately became overrepresented in the ranks of the colonial era elite—bureaucrats, teachers, lawyers, and so on.

Because France treated Algeria differently than its other colonies—considering it an integral part of France and turning over most of the country's cultivable land to French settlers—human traffic between France and Algeria was constant and significant in both directions. Berbers and Jews, more than their fellow Arab Muslim Algerians, went to study, work, and live in France, many of them remaining for their entire lives. To this day, Algerian political movements, organizations, and events frequently originate from—and impact upon—Algerian communities in France as much as the Algerian homeland.

Upon independence, the Algerian government wanted to stress the country's Arab and Muslim heritage first and foremost. This desire was a natural psychological reaction to France's inherently racist "civilizing mission," which had denigrated, marginalized, and denied Arab culture, language, and history. Yet this emphasis also sidelined and marginalized the Berbers, who began organizing, first among their expatriate community in France, to protect and advance their own cultural interests and the teaching of their language, Tamazight (Goodman 1996; Maddy-Weitzman 1998; Silverstein 1996, 1997). The initial crux of Algeria's Berber issue was the language issue. The Berbers were fighting to preserve a respected place in the new Algerian nation-state for their own unique cultural heritage. In the 1960s, this was particularly urgent, as the state forbade parents to give their children Berber names and repressed the public use of Berber dialects.

The Berbers have never demanded political autonomy, secession, or self-rule, only the right to be considered a legitimate and integral component of the Algerian nation-state. In advancing this goal, Berber activists and cultural groups promoted a view of Algeria as Arabic *and* Berber. The key vehicles for communicating this vision in the 1970s were the new Kabylian Berber popular songs (Goodman 1996; Silverstein 1996) and the Berber cultural movement, composed primarily of Kabylian students and expatriate Berber intellectuals in France (Maddy-Weitzman 1998). In addition to advancing Berber linguistic and cultural expressiveness and heritage, this movement also called for Western-style political liberalization and democratization because, "at bottom, the Berberists saw democratization as the only way to guarantee their cultural and ethnic rights within the Algerian state" (p. 39).

With the rise of the Islamist movement, the Berbers' identity in the Algerian context took on new dimensions, as some Berber groups and spokesmen invoked their unique cultural and historical role as a countervailing force to the drive for Islamization. Artists and singers were particularly prominent in this effort, particularly members of the Rassemblement de la Culture et la Démocratie (RCD), a movement that espoused an explicitly modernist/secularist Berber stand in the face of the violence tearing the country apart.

The RCD's guiding agenda was a new vision of modern Algerian culture that would include "the Kabylian synthesis of village customs and rituals, many undoubtedly pre-Islamic in origin, an attenuated Islam, Tamazight, and French-centered modernity, epitomized by the French language spoken by much of the intelligentsia and the middle and upper classes" (Maddy-Weitzman 1998:43). This agenda represented an intriguing reworking of the French colonial image of the wise and noble Berbers in comparison to the less cultured Arab Muslims of Algeria. Paul Silverstein (1996) argues that the Berber movement "consciously selected and reworked elements of this colonial era myth, or stereotype, of the essential Berber character to

stake out a position between the Algerian military regime and the Islamists" (p. 11).

This strategic choice of identification seems to have been fruitful initially. In 1994, a well-organized, extended school strike on behalf of the Tamazight language as a vehicle of educational instruction took place throughout Kabylia. By the spring of 1995, Tamazight's role and legitimacy in the Algerian social, cultural, and political contexts received official recognition after a series of negotiations to end the strike. The Algerian government announced that it would create a "body with executive powers, attached to the presidency, [and] charged with the rehabilitation of Tamazight culture, one of the foundations of Algerian culture" (Embassy of Algeria 1995).

Perhaps the Algerian government perceived a strategic value in aligning with Berber demands for inclusiveness and cultural plurality at a time when militant Islamic factions were attempting to impose a strict form of religious and cultural homogeneity and purity on the Algerian populace by force of arms. Nonetheless, as dramatic as these developments were in the history of Berber struggles in Algeria, the regime's new open-mindedness regarding Berber demands did not endure: "Although the new draft constitution [of 1995] recognized that Amazighité (Berber identity) was part of Algeria's common heritage, along with Islam and Arabism, it failed to recognize Tamazight as Algeria's official second language" (Embassy of Algeria 1995:47). As long as significant segments of Algerian society remain committed to emphasizing a strictly Muslim or Arab identity, Berber cultural aspirations are not likely to be fully realized.

Lebanon: A Living Remnant of the Ottoman *Millet* System

Moving east to the Levant, we find another nation-state in which French colonial policies of preferential treatment influenced interethnic relations in the postcolonial period. Lebanon, a country marked by profound ethnic diversity, first, because its mountainous terrain was historically so attractive to religious and ethnic minorities fleeing persecution, and second, because of the manner in which it was patched together as an administrative territory following the collapse of the Ottoman Empire, represents a living remnant of the Ottoman *millet* system disguised as a centralized nation-state. Lebanon began as the autonomous region of Mount Lebanon that the French exacted from the Ottoman authorities in the 1860s to protect the Christian *dhimmis* (primarily the Maronites, an Eastern Rite church that was always in communion with Rome and thus had more of a Western orientation than the other Christian sects).

Before Lebanon's independence in 1943, the French colonial powers had attached to Mount Lebanon the northern regions of Akkar Province, the city of Tripoli and its surroundings, the capital city of Beirut, and the southern cities of Sidon and Tyre. This deft carving of territories added Sunni, Greek Orthodox, Armenian Orthodox, Jacobite, Assyrian, and Shi'a communities to the largely Maronite and Druze communities of Mount Lebanon. France's creation of the Republic of Lebanon did not sit well with Syrian leaders or the Syrian populace, who had always considered some of the new territories of Lebanon, particularly the northern provinces and the Beqa'a Valley, its territory. To this day, Syria, which plays an active role in Lebanese affairs behind the scenes, does not have an embassy in Beirut.

Adding to the inherently unstable mix of religious groups in the newly forged Lebanese Republic (which, at independence, was said to be 51 percent Christian and 49 percent Muslim by some manipulations of statistical data) was the arrival in 1948 of tens of thousands of Palestinian refugees fleeing war and violence between Palestinian Arabs and European Jews who had been living and settling in Palestine since the last decades of the nineteenth century. The Jews obviously won that battle, founding the State of Israel in 1948 and forbidding the return of the majority of the refugees who had fled or who had been driven out.

The presence of the Palestinian refugees in Beirut presented not only a logistical and economic problem of immense proportions for a new state lacking in resources. The biggest threat posed by the refugees' presence was the potential demographic and political significance of a large Sunni Muslim group in a state dominated by Christians. Many Christian—and even a few Muslim—leaders of the new republic feared that the refugees might one day tip the delicate religious balance and the verbal national pact that enabled Western-oriented Christians to coexist and collaborate with Muslims who looked to the Arab and Islamic world for their identity and ideological influences.

The Lebanese political system is based on religious (sectarian) power-sharing (called *taa'ifiyya* in Arabic, from the word *ta'ifa*, meaning "sect"). As Barbara Harf (1993) has noted, no single Lebanese group constitutes a majority; Lebanon is unique in being a country composed solely of minorities—18 officially recognized ethnoreligious groups, to be precise. Each group has its guaranteed number of seats in the parliament, and each expects to receive its fair share of ministerial posts. The three largest groups—the Maronites, the Sunnis, and the Shi'i—get the presidency, the prime ministerial, and the speaker of the parliament positions, respectively.[6] Theory and practice rarely coincide in politics, however, and the Christian Maronite community's historic domination of Lebanon's political and economic power structures since before the state's establishment, no less than the context of relative and absolute deprivation and economic inequalities, rising regional Arab nationalist sentiments (particularly pro-Palestinian feelings), and the polarizing influences of the cold war between the United States and the USSR in the region—all led to the eventual conflagration of the war.

In Lebanon, the entire population, being a mosaic of contending minorities, was thinking and feeling like potential victims even before war broke out on April 13, 1975. It is no wonder, then, that the war was so violent, so bitter, and so protracted. As Theodore Hanf describes the nature of the conflict in his Lebanon, "It was a macabre game of musical chairs in which no one wanted to be the only one left standing. . . . The fear of being the ultimate loser is the motivating force in [Lebanese] politics" (1992:1–2). Long before the war began, the Lebanese were enmeshed in a political and psychological "economy of scarcity" that left everyone feeling both vulnerable and opportunistic, and thus prone to aggressiveness.[7]

Clearly, many of Lebanon's 18 sects had valid reasons to worry about scarcities of power, security, and resources. *Taaʿifiyya*, however, actually obstructs power-sharing at the grassroots level and gives rise not to a nation of fellow citizens but to an arena of pronounced conflict and competition among many anxious and agonistic minority groups. Because of Lebanon's religiously based system, every individual is encouraged to think of himself or herself as a Maronite, a Shiʿi or a Sunni first, and only secondarily as a Lebanese citizen. By emphasizing the group over the individual (and thereby minimizing the individual's choice, power, and sense of responsibility), and by privileging the sect over the state (thus contributing to the fragmentation of the polity), *taaʿifiyya* cannot but set the stage for future violent conflicts.[8]

In the Middle Eastern context, Lebanon represents an extreme example of the triumph of the ethnic group over both the individual citizen and the overarching state. Lebanese sociologist Samir Khalaf notes that the tragedy of Lebanon lies in the fact that "the very factors that account for much of the viability, resourcefulness, and integration of the Lebanese are also the factors that are responsible for the erosion of civic ties and national loyalties. . . . In short, the factors that enable at the micro and communal level disable at the macro and national level. This is indeed Lebanon's predicament" (1985:14).

Not only has Lebanon's system of religious power-sharing had detrimental effects on national identity and the consolidation of the institution of citizenship, it also has complicated Lebanese conceptions, attitudes, and behaviors associated with power. In Lebanon, power is not vested in the individual; rather, individuals can only attain power through their community, or, more specifically, through the leader (*zaʿeem*) of their community. The *zaʿeem* usually wields absolute power (backed up by credible threats of force) in the context of his ethnoreligious group, which is also a kinship group, so family obligations and duties also influence individual and communal political behavior and choices.

It is often observed that "absolute power corrupts absolutely," and in most cases in Lebanese history this has, unfortunately, been true. The concentration of power in the hands of a few individuals (and families) in Lebanon's political system has increased the sense of powerlessness and dependency that is already so prevalent among the members of the contending minority communities. If two communal leaders become embroiled in a personal conflict, the strife can quickly spread to their supporters in each respective community. The good of the community is thus sacrificed for the political or economic interests of corrupt and grasping leaders, who often have more in common with each other than they do with the wider communities they supposedly represent.

The complexities and tragedies of the long and destructive Lebanese civil war, which took 150,000 lives, were profound and mind-boggling and seemed to necessitate a complex, elaborate, and carefully calibrated solution to effectively end the fighting. This was a mistaken notion. What finally ended the war was a blunt, unambiguous, and decisive show of force by the Syrian military in 1990. In a land beset by a plethora of armed bullies (a wide variety of warlords representing different confessional communities), the Syrians stopped the war in its tracks simply by acting as the biggest bully of all.

In 2006, another tragedy struck with an Israeli military invasion targeted at the Shiʿi group known as Hezbollah (party of God) that has had political links with the regime in Iran. Hezbollah had been firing rockets directed at border towns in Israel. The Israeli military bombed numerous areas throughout Lebanon while Hezbollah continued to launch rockets into northern Israel. The month-long conflict left considerable damage throughout Lebanon. Hezbollah has continued to become an important ethnic-religious-political player in Lebanese politics.

Iraq's Ethnic Trio: Kurd, Sunni, and Shi'a in a Weak State System

In 1991, at the end of the United States–led Gulf War against Iraq to free Kuwait from Iraqi occupation, few could have predicted that the Ba'thist regime of Saddam Hussein, a Sunni who seized power in 1978, would still be firmly ensconced in Baghdad a decade later. Although Saddam and his regime and inner circle have survived—and according to some, have even thrived—since the Gulf War (Graham-Brown 1999), the Iraqi people, be they Kurds in the north, Shi'a in the south, or Sunnis and Christians in the central area, have suffered from both externally imposed sanctions and internally imposed oppression.

Iraq under Saddam Hussein constituted the extreme example of the crises of national integration and representative governments in the Middle Eastern context. Iraq remained an integrated nation-state only by the narrowest of definitions: both the Kurdish-dominated north and the Shi'i-dominated south were under constant Western (United States and British) aerial surveillance and were transformed into "no-fly" zones in which Iraqi air force planes and helicopters ventured only at their own risk. The Kurds, who are part of a larger, stateless ethnicity spread out over five nation-states (Iraq, Iran, Turkey, Russia, and Syria), looked to foreign assistance programs, primarily that of the United Nations, rather than to the central Iraqi bureaucracy in Baghdad for their basic social needs. The Shi'a suffered from imposed sanctions as well as from the regime's brutal repression and their historically marginal status in Iraq. With the 2003 U.S.–British invasion of Iraq and the collapse of the Saddam Hussein regime, new configurations of ethnic and political developments have emerged.

The British cobbled Iraq together as a nation-state following World War I by joining the provinces of three distinct cities into one territorial unit: Mosul in the north, Baghdad in the center, and Basra in the south. In patching together this new state, the British colonial powers were far more interested in their own needs and aims than those of the Arab and Kurdish, Shi'i and Sunni, peoples of the new, hybrid nation-state. The Kurds had wanted to have their own state, one that would have joined various, dispersed Kurdish tribal groups, speakers of various languages and subdialects, and communicants of several different religions[9] into one territorially delimited state (Eller 1999). Britain's strategic interest in oil, which is particularly prevalent in the region around Mosul, meant that this Kurdish-dominated region, which had been linked with Turkey through trade, language, culture, and administrative structures and networks during the Ottoman era, would be given to the new state of Iraq, against the wishes of the Kurdish population (Batatu 1978).

The British placed a compliant ruler (King Faisal, a Sunni who was not even an Iraqi but a member of the Jordanian Hashemite family) on a newly created Iraqi throne in 1921. Nine years later, the nation-state of Iraq—a newly minted monarchy—gained its independence from the British. For the next 20 years, Iraq was run by a British-backed monarchy and an elite class of tribal landlords. This system, in which the gap between rich and poor grew ever more pronounced, did not encourage national integration.

King Faisal's solution to this problem, for which he received help from the British, was to build up a strong army capable of maintaining internal order, representative of all Iraqi ethnic and regional groups but commanded by Sunnis. The strength and consolidation of the Iraqi armed forces were to prove decisive to state unity in the coming years. Indeed, by the time Saddam Hussein came to power, the army, particularly key units known as the special protection forces, already had a well-entrenched role as the keystone of Ba'thist state power.

The Ba'thist regime that took power in 1968, the forerunner of the Saddam Hussein regime, survived longer not because it had achieved national integration but because it relied upon tribal and ethnic integration to consolidate the ruling inner circle of the regime in a matrix of overlapping, mutually supportive ties at the expense of the nation as a whole. Kurds and Shi'a were largely excluded from these networks, which meant that they had little power, little say over resource allocation, and little control over the coercive mechanisms of state power and surveillance, all of which remained in the hands of the Sunnis.

The leaders and the rank and file of the post-1968 regime were composed of interlocking networks of tribal members from a limited number of Sunni towns and villages in the central part of the country (Abd al-Jabbar 2000; Bengio 1999; Graham-Brown 1999). Relying on and invoking their own tribal and family ties, they shored up the regime while playing different tribal and ethnic factions off against one another to the regime's advantage, particularly in the very fragmented social milieu of Kurdistan, where tribal, linguistic, regional, and political divisions fragmented Kurdish political demands and rendered coordinated action impossible.

While manipulating tribal and ethnic ties to consolidate power, Saddam Hussein also attempted to manipulate regional politics to his regime's advantage by using warfare to build up the state and focus national attention on expansionary and adventurist projects, such as Iraq's war with Iran (1980–1988) and the ill-fated Iraqi invasion of Kuwait in 1990. In addition to squandering Iraq's considerable oil wealth and political capital on such disastrous campaigns, Hussein also used the army against recalcitrant or unruly ethnic groups in Iraq, most notoriously during the Iraqi government's *anfal* campaign in the late 1980s, the goal of which was to control Kurdish elements through ethnic cleansing, population transfers, village demolitions, mass murder, and torture in the Kurdish north.

Similarly, following the failed uprisings against the regime after Iraq's rout from Kuwait in the spring of 1991, Saddam Hussein used the army to drain the swamps of southern Iraq (causing dramatic ecological damage) in order to flush Shi'i rebels out of hiding. Many participants in the Iraqi *intifada* ("uprising") of 1991 were summarily executed. Although Western powers and neighboring Arab states were well aware of the Iraqi regime's massive human rights abuses against its own people, they never interfered, despite the fact that the United States had urged Kurds and Shi'ites to rise up against the Iraqi regime in early 1991.

The failure of the Kurdish and Shi'i uprisings attested to the deeply fragmented nature of Iraqi society and the relative advantage this fragmentation gave to a highly centralized, powerful army composed mostly of Sunnis. Since 1991, the fragmentation of the Iraqi population along ethnic, and even subethnic, tribal lines had rendered all potential and actual opposition to the regime unlikely. The Ba'thist army, though feared and hated, was still well entrenched enough to crush future uprisings. Furthermore, the impact of the United States–led economic sanctions against Iraq had served to enrich the regime (through black market economies dominated by Hussein's family) while weakening the Iraqi population physically, economically, psychologically, and politically (Graham-Brown 1999).

The 2003 U.S.–British invasion of Iraq and collapse of the Ba'thist regime set in motion numerous ethnic–political conflicts and violence between the Shi'i majority and Sunni minority ethnic groups that have become all too familiar in the world media. The Shi'i were able to mobilize their formerly persecuted status to become the dominant ethnic-political group in Iraq. The Kurds in the north have been struggling to develop their autonomy from the Shi'i-dominated regime in Baghdad. Whether the new democratically based government that emerged after the downfall of the Ba'thist regime can achieve a modicum amount of ethnic–political harmony in Iraq will remain a formidable challenge for the future.

MIDDLE EASTERN ETHNICITY ASSESSED: STRATEGY OR STRAITJACKET?

Perhaps it is not too far-fetched to argue that extensive, overlapping kin and ethnic-based networks and patron–client relationships constitute the actual "glue" that holds the Middle Eastern nation-state together. Rather than being sustained by a sense of shared identity, the formal institution of citizenship, and broadly shared interests and goals, the nation-state in the Middle East survives because of the public's considerable investments of time, energy, resources, and money in the cultivation and maintenance of innumerable dyadic relationships (often utilizing the idiom of ethnicity or kinship) with influential incumbents of the government bureaucracy.

Although resorting to primary identities and traditional relationships in order to survive in a challenging world is instrumental, logical, and strategic, it also entails costs and consequences that can have negative repercussions on individuals and collectivities in the region. Relying on kin, rather than the state; affiliating with narrowly defined ethnoreligious groups, rather than forming broad-based coalitions and solidarities; and participating in patron–client exchanges of goods and services that perpetuate socioeconomic inequalities while consolidating age-old forms of political domination—all serve to impede economic, cultural, and political integration on the regional and national levels while also discouraging processes of empowerment, the attainment of social justice, and the implementation of democratic reforms on the local level. Also, a public that has fragmented into separate, competing blocs of kin ethnoreligious communities is facilitating its own control, exploitation, co-optation, and manipulation by repressive state governments. A divided population is much easier to rule, as the colonial powers so deftly proved.

The institutionalization of ethnic and religious identities for legal and administrative purposes, seen most clearly in states such as Lebanon and Israel, can be a double-edged sword. Official recognition of cultural heritage and religious laws may provide answers to individuals' psychological needs and communal organizational problems. However, it can also trap individuals (particularly women[10]) in the vise of inflexible identity categories not of their own choice or making, thus limiting their personal options and opportunities while preventing the development of a more inclusive sense of overarching national loyalty and identity.

CONCLUSION

This chapter has analyzed and interpreted ethnicity as a dynamic process in the contemporary Middle East by showing how identities and the political agenda associated with them are influenced by ecological, economic, historical, administrative, and political realities. We have learned that sociopolitical categorizations and behaviors in the Middle East have historically been affected by the limitations of a harsh natural environment in which economic scarcity and pronounced political competition were constants, and sustained and enduring relationships of mutual trust and permanent, broad-based, sociopolitical formations were rare. Furthermore, we noted that the region underwent rapid economic and political changes in the nineteenth century, which permanently altered the traditional class structure and gave rise to sharp socioeconomic inequalities that were exacerbated by colonialism and the incorporation of the region into a competitive world capitalist economy. These inequalities and sociopolitical disparities remain unresolved to this day.

Lacking satisfying representation or assistance from the nation-states of the region, Middle Eastern peoples have resorted to primary identity categories and traditional organizational structures in an effort to make a living—and to discern meaning—in the challenging world that confronts them. Although they have succeeded in this effort, it has not been without costs and consequences. In the long run, resorting to kinship, ethnicity, and ties of patronage based on subnational identifications may have a negative effect on societies that are increasingly pressured to reconcile their segmented and fragmentary nature with increasing demands for political and economic integration, coordination, and cooperation in the global economy. In the current era of dramatic cultural and technical innovations and global economic fluctuations, we should not be surprised to see new political configurations and identities emerging in the Middle East.

Notes

1. Although most Jews in the region now live in Israel, it is an oft-neglected fact that small but vibrant Jewish communities continue to live in Morocco, Tunisia, Lebanon, Iran, Syria, and Yemen.

2. The Druze faith is sometimes categorized as an Islamic sect, but Sunni Muslims do not consider it as such. It is an offshoot of Ismaili Shi'i Islam that incorporates Neoplatonic doctrines as well as a belief in reincarnation. Druze communities are found in mountainous regions of Syria, Lebanon, and northern Israel. Although all Druze are ethnically and linguistically Arabs, in Israel they are categorized as a separate ethnic group from Muslim and Christian Arab citizens of the state and are required to serve in the Israeli defense forces. Just 80 miles north, in the Shouf region of Lebanon, the Lebanese Druze community was aligned with Arab nationalist, socialist, and pro-Palestinian factions during the Lebanese civil war, thus illustrating the flexibility and fluidity of ethnic politics in this region (Firro 1999; Hajjar 2000).

3. The Shi'i branch of Islam traces its leadership to the cousin of the Prophet Muhammad, 'Ali ibn Abi Talib. Shi'ites are the largest Islamic community after that of Sunni Muslims. Shi'ism originated from a split in the early Muslim community over the issue of succession in the leadership of the Islamic community (the *ummah*). After the assassination of the Caliph Uthman, 'Ali, a blood relative of the Prophet, who was married to the Prophet's daughter Fatima, acceded to the caliphate. 'Ali was opposed by some of the surviving companions of the Prophet, and this disagreement began a conflict between those who opposed his role as leader of the faithful and those who supported him, known as the partisans of 'Ali (*shi'at 'Ali*, in Arabic). Since many tribal groups in Syria and Mesopotamia opposed 'Ali, he moved the caliphate from Damascus to Kufa, a city in what is now southern Iraq. 'Ali was assassinated in 661, and his martyrdom continues to be a powerful organizing theme in Shi'i faith and tradition. Shi'i communities are found today in Lebanon, where they are numerically the largest of all of Lebanon's confessional sects, as well as in Iraq, where they are a majority of the population, concentrated in southern Iraq, though they are marginalized from centers of political power; and last but not least in Iran, where virtually the entire Muslim population is Shi'i.

4. The name "Berber" is not used by this community. "Berber" derives from the Greek word for "barbarian," or perhaps from a colloquial Arabic expression, "*ber-ber*," which indicates that a person does not speak properly (i.e., does not speak Arabic correctly). The name used by Berbers among themselves is *Amazigh* (plural, *Imazighen*), meaning "free man" in the Tamazight language. Before the advent of Islam in North Africa, the entire population was Imazighen, speaking several different dialects of Tamazigh. Today the largest and most influential Amazigh tribal group is that of the Kabylian Berber community. All Amazigh are Sunni Muslims, with few exceptions, and are distinguished from non-Amazigh primarily by their spoken language, which was standardized only in the twentieth century.

5. Although Berbers played a key role in Algeria's independence struggle, many Arab nationalists and Islamists cited the Berbers' special treatment under the French, particularly their exemption from Islamic law, as marks against this community's loyalty, patriotism, and steadfastness. Despite the special treatment accorded them by the French colonial regime, the Berbers did not profit economically or politically in the long run. As revealed in a series of 11 essays by Albert Camus that appeared in the *Alger-Republicain* newspaper in 1939 under the title "Poverty in Kabylia," the Berbers were as impoverished as ever in the years leading up to World War II (Maddy-Weitzman 1998:50).

6. Religious affiliation in Lebanon is not a matter of individual choice but something one is born into. In Lebanon, individuals are considered to belong to the religious sect of their father. This conflates a patrilineal (and patriarchal) kinship system with the state's confessional system of government and resource allocation. In Lebanon, religion determines one's relationship to the state, and since religious affiliation determines how one will be married, buried, divorced, and inherited, family membership is intimately tied to political

membership. At the national level, this is evident in the "dynasties" of various sectarian leaders and their sons, who have assumed the mantle of power for their respective religious communities generation after generation—for example, the Cham'oun and Frangieh families among the Maronites, the Jumblatt and Arslan families among the Druzes, and the Husseinis and Asads among the Shi'ites. Conflicts frequently erupt *within* religious communities when members of these families compete for the role of the lead family within their respective sects. During the civil war, the rise of militias and the breakdown of the state's role as guardian of civil order exacerbated these interfamily, intrasectarian conflicts, particularly among the Maronites.

7. The author, who lived and worked in Lebanon for five years in the postwar period, often heard colleagues and friends refer to Lebanon's tragedy as being analogous to "one hundred dogs trying to chew on the same bone," the bone here being the state and its various material and nonmaterial resources.

8. The Ta'ef Accord, an agreement that set the terms for the end of the Lebanese conflict in 1989 (and which takes its name from the Saudi Arabian city where the negotiations were held), clearly stipulated that the Lebanese system would be deconfessionalized in an orderly progression of steps, culminating in complete deconfessionalization by the mid-1990s. To date, this process has scarcely been initiated or attempted (U. Makdisi 1997).

9. Kurds in Iraq are primarily Sunni Muslims, but there are also Shi'i, Christian, and Jewish Kurdish tribes in neighboring countries.

10. Because both Israel and Lebanon have retained elements of the *millet* system and Ottoman legal specifications concerning ethnoreligious groups, most notably the retention of "personal status laws," which give different religious communities' leadership effective legal and moral control over issues such as marriage, divorce, inheritance, and adoption, women are particularly disadvantaged by the lack of modern, liberal laws concerning alimony, child-support payments, and fair inheritance practices. Neither Israel nor Lebanon recognizes civil marriage. All couples must marry in a religious ceremony, and if they are from different religious backgrounds, this implies that one must convert to the faith of the other. Usually, it is the woman who converts. In such cases, however, it is far more common that the couple will go to Cyprus, marry there in a legally binding civil ceremony, and return to either Lebanon or Israel, where the state does recognize civil marriage certificates originating in other states.

References Cited

ABD AL-JABBAR, FALAH. 1992. Why the uprisings failed. *Middle East Report* 176:2–14.

———. 2000. Shaykhs and ideologues: Detribalization and retribalization in Iraq, 1968–1998. *Middle East Report* 215:28–31.

ANDERSON, BENEDICT. 1983. *Imagined Communities: Reflections on the Origins and Spread of Nationalism.* London: Verso.

AVRUCH, KEVIN. 1987. The emergence of ethnicity in Israel. *American Ethnologist* 14(2):327–339.

AYOUBI, NAZIH. 1995. *Overstating the Arab State.* London: I. B. Tauris.

BARAKAT, HALIM. 1993. *The Arab World: Society, Culture, and State.* Berkeley, CA: University of California Press.

BATATU, HANNA. 1978. *The Old Social Classes and the Revolutionary Movements of Iraq.* Princeton, NJ: Princeton University Press.

BENGIO, OFRA. 1999. Nation building in multi-ethnic societies: The case of Iraq. In *Minorities and the State in the Arab World.* Ofra Bengio and Gabriel Ben-Dor, eds. Pp. 149–170. Boulder, CO: Lynne Rienner.

BENGIO, OFRA, and GABRIEL BEN-DOR, eds. 1999. *Minorities and the State in the Arab World.* Boulder, CO: Lynne Rienner.

BOSWORTH, C. E. 1982. The concept of dhimma in early Islam. In *Christians and Jews in the Ottoman Empire,* vol. 2. Benjamin Braude and Bernard Lewis, eds. Pp. 37–54. *The Arabic Speaking Lands.* New York: Holmes & Meier.

COHEN, RONALD. 1978. Ethnicity: Problem and focus in anthropology. *Annual Review of Anthropology* 7:379–403.

COON, CARLETON. 1961. *Caravan: The Story of the Middle East.* New York: Holt, Rinehart & Winston.

CUNNINGHAM, ROBERT, and YASIN K. SARAYRAH. 1993. *Wasta: The Hidden Force in Middle Eastern Culture.* Westport, CT: Praeger.

DRYSDALE, ALASDAIR, and GERALD H. BLAKE. 1985. *The Middle East and North Africa: A Political Geography.* Oxford: Oxford University Press.

EICKELMAN, DALE. 1999. *The Middle East and Central Asia: An Anthropological Approach.* 3rd edition. Upper Saddle River, NJ: Prentice Hall.

ELLER, JACK DAVID. 1999. *From Culture to Ethnicity to Conflict: An Anthropological Perspective on International Ethnic Conflict.* Ann Arbor, MI: University of Michigan Press.

EMBASSY of ALGERIA. 1995. Amazighté—communiqué de la présidence. Washington, DC, April 3.

ESPOSITO, JOHN. 1998. *Islam: The Straight Path.* 3rd edition. New York: Oxford University Press.

FIRRO, KAIS M. 1999. *The Druzes in the Jewish State: A Brief History.* Leiden: Brill.

FROMKIN, DAVID. 1988. *A Peace to End All Peace: The Fall of the Ottoman Empire and the Creation of the Modern Middle East.* New York: Avon.

GOLDSCHMIDT, ARTHUR JR. 2000. The historical context. In *Understanding the Contemporary Middle East.* Deborah J. Gerner, ed. Pp. 33–80. Boulder, CO: Lynne Rienner.

GOODMAN, JANE. 1996. Berber associations and cultural change in Algeria. *Middle East Report* 200:16–20.

GRAHAM-BROWN, SARAH. 1999. *Sanctioning Saddam: The Politics of Intervention in Iraq.* London and New York: I. B. Tauris, in association with MERIP.

HAJJAR, LISA. 2000. Speaking the conflict, or how the Druze became bilingual: A study of Druze translators in the Israeli military courts in the West Bank and Gaza. *Ethnic and Racial Studies* 23(2):299–328.

HALLIDAY, FRED. 1999. The Middle East at the millennial turn. *Middle East Report* 213:4–7.

HANF, THEODORE. 1992. *Coexistence in Wartime Lebanon: The Decline of a State and the Rise of a Nation.* London: Center for Lebanese Studies, in association with I. B. Tauris.

HARF, BARBARA. 1993. Minorities, rebellion, and repression in North Africa and the Middle East. In *Minorities at Risk: A Global View of Ethnopolitical Conflicts.* Ted Gurr, ed. Washington, DC: United States Institute of Peace.

HILTERMANN, JOOST. 1999. Clipped wings and sharp claws: Iraq in the 1990s. *Middle East Report* 212:58–60.

KHALAF, SAMIR. 1985. *Lebanon's Predicament.* New York: Columbia University Press.

AL-KHAZEN, FARID. 2000. *The Breakdown of the State in Lebanon: 1967–1976.* Cambridge, MA: Harvard University Press.

KHOURY, PHILIP, and JOSEPH KOSTINER, eds. 1989. *Tribes and State Formation in the Middle East.* Berkeley, CA: University of California Press.

KING-IRANI, LAURIE. 2000. Rituals of forgiveness and processes of empowerment in Lebanon. In *Traditional Cures for Modern Conflicts: African Conflict "Medicine."* I. William Zartman, ed. Pp. 129–140. Boulder, CO: Lynne Rienner.

———. 2004. Kinship, ethnicity and social class: Strategies of diversity in the Middle East. In *Understanding the Contemporary Middle East.* 2nd edition. Deborah J. Gerner, ed. Boulder, CO: Lynne Rienner.

LESCH, ANN. 1997. *The Sudan: Contested National Identities.* Bloomington, IN: Indiana University Press.

MADDY-WEITZMAN, BRUCE. 1998. The Berber question in Algeria: Nationalism in the making? In *Minorities and the State in the Arab World.* Ofra Bengio and Gabriel Ben-Dor, eds. Pp. 31–52. Boulder, CO: Lynne Rienner.

MAKDISI, SAMIR. 1990. The Arab world and the world economy: An overview. In *The Economic Dimensions of Middle East History: Essays in Honor of Charles Issawi.* Hala Esfandiari and A. L. Udovich eds. Pp. 123–146. Princeton, NJ: Darwin Press.

MAKDISI, USAMA. 1997. The modernity of sectarianism in Lebanon. *Middle East Report* 200:23–26.

MANNERS, IAN, and BARBARA MCKEAN PARMENTER. 2004. The Middle East: A geographic preface. In *Understanding the Contemporary Middle East.* 2nd edition. Deborah G. Gerner, ed. Boulder, CO: Lynne Rienner.

MEEKER, MICHAEL. 1979. *Literature and Violence in Early Arabia.* London: Cambridge University Press.

PFEIFER, KAREN. 1998. How Tunisia, Morocco, Jordan, and even Egypt became IMF "success stories" in the 1990s. *Middle East Report* 210:23–27.

RONEN, YEHUDIT. 1999. Religion and conflict in the Sudan: A non-Muslim minority in a Muslim state. In *Minorities and the State in the Arab World.* Ofra Bengio and Gabriel Ben-Dor, eds. Pp. 73–90. Boulder, CO: Lynne Rienner.

ROYCE, ANYA PETERSON. 1982. *Ethnicity: Strategies of Diversity.* Bloomington, IN: Indiana University Press.

SAID, EDWARD. 1978. *Orientalism.* Harmondsworth, UK: Penguin.

SALIBI, KAMAL. 1988. *A House of Many Mansions: The History of Lebanon Reconsidered.* London: I. B. Tauris.

SANASARIAN, ELISE. 2000. *Religious Minorities in Iran.* Cambridge: Cambridge University Press.

SILVERSTEIN, PAUL. 1996. Realizing myths: Berbers in France and Algeria. *Middle East Report* 200:16–20.

———. 1997. "The rebel is dead! Long live the martyr!" Kabyle mobilization and the assassination of Lounes Matoub. *Middle East Report* 208:3–4.

TÉTREAULT, MARY ANN. 2001. International relations. In *Understanding the Contemporary Middle East.* Deborah J. Gerner, ed. Pp. 129–160. Boulder, CO: Lynne Rienner.

TIBI, BASSAM. 1989. The simultaneity of the unsimultaneous: Old tribes and imposed nation states in the modern Middle East. In *Tribes and State Formation in the Middle East.* Philip S. Khoury and Joseph Kostiner, eds. Pp. 127–152. Berkeley, CA: University of California Press.

WORLD BANK. 2008. *Shaping the Future: A Long-Term Perspective of People and Job Mobility for the Middle East and North Africa.* Washington, DC: The World Bank.

16

...

Asia

Raymond Scupin, *Lindenwood University*

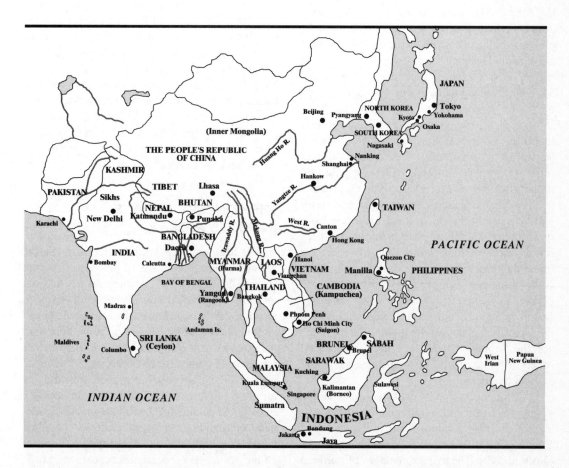

Asia is a culturally diverse region with a wide variety of languages, ethnic groups, and religions. This chapter focuses on race and ethnic relations in three general regions: South Asia, East Asia (China and Japan), and Southeast Asia. These regions contain most of the world's population—over 3 billion people. Different forms of societies have developed in these regions, ranging from hunter-gatherer and horticultural societies of the tropical rain forests, to the pastoral nomads of northern China, to vast, complex, intensive agricultural societies, to the advanced industrial societies such as those in Japan. As we will see, race and ethnic relations have been shaped by the traditional cultural beliefs, worldviews, and ideologies, as well as Western concepts and the rapid globalization processes affecting these different regions.

SOUTH ASIA

South Asia is a distinct geographic region extending from the Himalaya Mountains in the north, through the tropical forests and vast agricultural plains of India, and south to the island nation of Sri Lanka. The major countries of South Asia include Pakistan, India, Bangladesh, Nepal, and Sri Lanka. To some extent, the geographic locations of the populations of South Asia have influenced the development of diverse ethnic identities. Historically, as various groups were separated by mountains, tropical forests, and other geographic barriers, regional ethnic and linguistic differences emerged within these countries. Additionally, these peoples began to classify and distinguish their own local identities from one another. Therefore, each of these countries has distinctive ethnic groups that differ in their linguistic, historical, and cultural experience. And, for the most part, the ethnic identities of the peoples of South Asia do not correspond to the nation-states or countries. For example, within the country of Pakistan the major ethnic groups are the Punjabi, Sindhi, Pathan, Baluch, and others who maintain distinct languages and cultural traditions.

India, a country that contains over a billion people, has tremendous ethnic, linguistic, and cultural diversity. A recent ethnographic survey of India has identified over 324 distinct languages (Norton 1999). The major languages of northern India include Hindi, Bengali, Punjabi, Gujarati, and Bihari, all part of the Indo-European language family. Southern India has languages such as Tamil, Telugu, and Malayalam that belong to a completely different language family, the Dravidian. Officially, the government of India recognizes 18 different languages; however, no single language is spoken by more than 40 percent of the population. Thus, India does not have a uniform language that serves to unite all of its various ethnic groups.

South Asia also includes various religious traditions that result in ethnic complexity. For example, although Hinduism is the religion of 80 percent of the population in India, over 100 million Muslims reside in the country. In addition, religious minorities include Sikhs, Jains, Christians, and a wide variety of Buddhist traditions. Pakistan and Bangladesh are Islamic countries, whereas Nepal and Sri Lanka have both Hindu and Buddhist traditions that are widely divergent. All of these religious faiths have been a source of boundary markers of ethnic identity in different regions of South Asia. Combined with linguistic differences, this religious diversity has produced an immense variety of cultural traditions and ethnic complexities throughout South Asia.

THE CONCEPT OF RACE IN SOUTH ASIA

As has been emphasized in earlier chapters, the scientific concept of "race" is problematic within anthropological research. Anthropologists find that there is too physical and genetic complexity to identify clearly bounded, easily separated "races" throughout the world. However, as we have seen (Chapter 2), as the concept of "race" began to be formulated by scientists in European society in the eighteenth and nineteenth centuries, it held many misconceptions about the relationship between biology and culture. It led to stereotypes and essentialist constructions of "racial identities" based on blood or inheritance combined with cultural or ethnic traits. These early European scientists, including anthropologists, were conflating physical characteristics with cultural attributes. Today, we would consider these notions as "folk" or "pseudo-scientific" constructions of race.

As we have seen, many people throughout the world have maintained nonscientific folk concepts of race and ethnicity within their cultural traditions (Chapter 4). Thus, some people classify groups into separate categories based on skin color or other traits, including cultural attributes. These folk concepts of race have been identified within the various cultures of South Asia. Though the English term *race* or the German word *Rasse* does not appear in South Asia until after European colonialism, there are close equivalents of this notion of race found in earlier popular or indigenous traditions in the area. These folk categories of race were based not only on purely biological characteristics but on indigenous notions of cultural "essences" as well. Subsequently, in many cases, following European colonialism and the introduction of Western concepts of "race," indigenous folk categories were often combined and synthesized into new forms of "race" categories in South Asia.

Some of the indigenous concepts that are close equivalents to the concept of race are intimately connected with the caste system of India. Most scholars associate the origins of the caste system with the Indo-Aryan peoples who settled in northern India after about 2000 B.C.E. The Indo-Aryan peoples were a pastoralist society that gradually gained control of the Punjab region and most of northern India by 600 B.C.E. Prior to the settlement of the Indo-Aryans, agricultural civilizations developed by peoples speaking Dravidian languages existed throughout northern India. Gradually, these peoples were absorbed into the political and cultural system of the Indo-Aryans.

Between 1800 and 600 B.C.E, the Indo-Aryans had produced a massive collection of sacred texts known as the Vedas, the earliest texts of the Hindu religious tradition. In the oldest text of the Vedas, the *Rig Veda*, the term *varna* is introduced to distinguish the Indo-Aryan people from others who were designated as slaves. *Varna* is translated as "color" or "complexion," but it refers primarily to linguistic and cultural differences between the populations (Klass 1997; Trautmann 1997).[1] Within a sacred hymn, the *Purusha-Skuta*

("Hymn of Man") in the *Rig Veda*, the creation of the universe and of humans is described. According to the myth, four social orders, or *varnas*, are associated with different types of humans who are born from the cosmic giant *Purusha*, the primeval man. The *Brahman*, priests or ritual specialists, emerge from the head or mouth of *Purusha*; the *Kshatriya*, warrior princes and chieftains, from the arms; the *Vaisya*, a group of agriculturalists, merchants, and traders, from his thighs; and the *Sudras*, laborers and servants, come from his feet. The levels of origins implied that these various groups had different natures, temperaments, behaviors, and personalities.

This fourfold *varna* scheme provided the ideological framework for organizing thousands of diverse groups within Indian society. Eventually, the functional groupings in the *varna* ideological scheme imposed categories that became the castes and subcastes, or, more precisely, what Indians refer in Hindi as *jatis*, of which there are several thousand. The *jatis* are hierarchically ranked in accordance with descent, occupational, marital, and ritual-religious factors. One is born within a specific family determining one's caste. Ideally, one is supposed to practice the same occupation associated with one's caste, marry within one's caste, and practice Hinduism as a member of a particular caste. As the religious tradition of Hinduism evolved in India, *varnas* were associated with the doctrinal concepts of reincarnation and *karma*. The doctrine of reincarnation refers to how after death one's soul transmigrates to another being to be reborn. Popularly, the doctrine of *karma* suggests that one inherits a particular type of soul that will influence one's temperament and lifelong destiny (Daniel 1983). In other words, an individual will be born within a high-ranking or low-ranking *varna* based on one's *karma*; and, one will inherit a particular "essence" that will shape one's personality and behavior. To some extent, the term *jati* is equivalent to "species," which would imply a concept of a "race" (Dumont 1970).

As is obvious, this indigenous concept of inherited temperament and behavior associated with a particular rank based on one's family and birth is somewhat equivalent to a folk concept of race. In this folk concept, an individual inherits a particular status and "essence" that are connected with specific behaviors and culture. Although the caste system is extremely varied, differing from one region to another and from one village to another, and is constantly being transformed, the basic ideals tend to associate biological inheritance and the determination of one's status, temperament, and behavior.[2]

With Western colonialism, the early European concepts of race were imported into South Asia. During the eighteenth and nineteenth centuries, as the British were colonizing India, colonial officials along with ethnographers and scholars were ordering, counting, and classifying various populations according to "racial," tribal, and caste identities (Bayly 1995; Trautmann 1997). These processes were part and parcel of the colonial project in order to exert political and economic control of the different regions of India. This colonial project also led to the circulation of ideas of "race" that became the predominant myths of European society. For example, the British linguistic scholar William Jones discovered that the Indo-Aryan language of Sanskrit was historically related to other European languages such as Greek and Latin. Jones deduced from this that the "Aryan" peoples represented a conquering "race" that built the civilizations of Greece, Rome, and later European countries (Bayly 1995; Trautmann 1997). This Aryan conquest myth provided the fodder for the theories of the scientific racists such as the French thinker Joseph Gobineau, whose thesis later influenced the Nazi beliefs about the superiority of the so-called Aryan race (see Chapter 2). Other early British scholars, relying on the Hindu texts, distinguished the Aryans from other peoples in India by skin color. In addition, the upper castes were distinguished from the lower castes based on skin color. Thus, the Brahmans, the upper caste associated with the Aryans, were lighter in skin color than the lower castes. The British colonial project resulted in essentialist stereotypes about the hierarchy of various "racial" and caste groups in India, which influenced European conceptions of India for generations (Bayly 1995; Inden 1990).

The European concepts of race were imported by a number of Indian thinkers and were synthesized with indigenous conceptions of "race" and "caste." As more native people became literate in English, and Indian nationalism developed in the nineteenth and twentieth centuries, various essentialist ideas of race and caste began to percolate into Indian thought. Racist beliefs about the superiority of the Aryan race were incorporated into a Hindu revivalist and nationalist movement known as *Hindutva*. One of the important leaders of the Hindutva revivalist movement, V. D. Savarkar, wrote about how Hindus "share a common blood of the mighty race of Aryans," and that this "blood" should be the basis of a nationalist consciousness (Jaffrelot 1995). Later Hindu nationalist ideologues adopted modified myths of Aryan racial superiority to help provide the foundation of a postcolonial independent nation in India. Though, eventually, the Hindutva nationalist ideologies minimized the "racial" aspects of Hinduism and emphasized the cultural and religious traditions, they promoted the dominance of the Hindu majority over other ethnic groups in the building of the Indian nation.

Recently, in the 1980s and 1990s, the Hindutva movement resurfaced as an integral aspect of contemporary Indian politics. A political party, the Bharatiya Janata Party (BJP), which is linked with the Hindutva movement, managed to gain control of the political system. The Hindutva movement emphasizes a resurgence of Hindu religiosity and ethnic purity against other ethnic and religious groups in India. Hinduism is interpreted as a unified ethnic and religious tradition as distinct from other minority religions such as Islam. The BJP and the Hindutva movement were associated with the destruction of a Muslim mosque in Ayodhaya, India, in 1992. Hindus claim that the mosque was actually the temple and birthplace of the Hindu god Rama, prior to the settlement of the Muslims in India. Hindu mobs violently attacked and burned the mosque. The Muslim minority community in India, a population of 140 million people, is fearful of the status of their mosques and their ethnic and religious identity in India.

The Hindu ethnic and religious resurgence is partly a response to the globalization process that has fragmented and divided the traditional regional, village, religious, and ethnic communities in India. The basic aim of the Hindutva religious and ethnic resurgence is to restore an "original" ethnic and organic community that represents a harmonious India. This ethnic and religious Hindu movement has created conflict among different ethnic communities in India. The BJP took pride in the explosion of a nuclear device in 1998, which they perceived as a symbol of the political power of the Hindutva agenda. This has exacerbated geopolitical relationships with India's Islamic neighbor Pakistan, which then detonated its own nuclear devices. Ethnic and religious resurgence within this South Asian region may have consequences for the entire global community.

The Sikhs

Another ethnic problem that has confronted India involves the Sikh community. The Sikhs are a population of about 18 million who live in the Punjab region bordering India and Pakistan. The Sikh religion developed in the fifteenth century as a blend of Hindu and Islamic beliefs. Sikhism is a mystical religious tradition centered on venerated leaders who founded a military fraternity that offered protection from both Muslims and Hindus. The Sikhs pride themselves on their warrior spirit. Every male carries the name Singh, which translates as "lion." The Sikhs have built a major house of worship—the Golden Temple of Amritsar—in the Punjab.

Anthropologist Richard Fox (1985) conducted ethnographic research among the Sikhs in 1980–1981. Using historical material and ethnographic data, he focused on the development of Sikh ethnic and religious identity as a response to external pressures. The Sikhs, who had freed themselves from Muslim and Hindu domination, were confronted with colonialism and the capitalist world system that penetrated the Punjab. The British viewed the Sikhs as an important military shield that could be used for extending their control over India. Colonial and military officials,

therefore, treated and classified the Sikhs as a separate "race" of warriors.[3] These British conceptions tended to reinforce Sikh ethnic separateness from Muslims, Hindus, and other groups.

Eventually the Sikhs recognized that the incorporation of their territory into the British empire would reduce their political and economic autonomy. Therefore, they initiated reform movements that sought to unify urban workers and rural peasants. These movements led to violent resistance against the British and, following national independence in 1947, to secessionist movements against the Indian government. The Sikhs wanted their own nation-state called Kalistan based on their ethnicity in the Punjab region. This ethnonationalist movement accelerated during the 1970s and 1980s, and was met with increased police and military repression by the Indian government.

In 1984, a group of militant, armed Sikhs took refuge in the Golden Temple of Amritsar, demanding political autonomy from India. The Indian government responded by sending military troops into the Punjab, some of whom entered the temple. The temple complex was destroyed and hundreds of Sikhs were killed. This violation of their sacred temple outraged many Sikhs, many of whom were not militant. Later in 1984, as resistance to Hindu domination grew, a Sikh militant assassinated Prime Minister Indira Gandhi. This event was marked by wide-scale violence, and Hindus killed over 3,000 Sikhs in the capital city of Delhi. Although this conflict between Sikhs and Hindus was a problem in the recent past, ethnic and religious tension has declined since the election in 2004 of a Prime Minister in India, Manmoham Singh, who is a Sikh.

Ethnic Problems in Sri Lanka

Another South Asian country facing severe and troubling ethnic problems is Sri Lanka. For many years, this island country south of India was called Ceylon. It became known as Sri Lanka in 1972. The indigenous majority population of Sri Lanka is the 12 million or so Sinhalese-speaking Buddhists. Sinhalese is a Sanskrit-derived Aryan language. The Sinhalese Buddhists are concentrated in the central, southern, and western portions of the island. Under British colonialism, Tamil-speaking Hindus were imported as indentured workers from southern India to work on rubber plantations. Tamil is one of the languages of the Dravidian family in India. Although the majority of Tamil-speaking Hindus were already in residence in Sri Lanka, British policies increased their population. There are some internal ethnic divisions between the original Tamil settlers and the later immigrants (Daniel 1997). Today, the Tamil Hindus make up 18 percent of the population, about 3 million people, and constitute a majority in northern Sri Lanka. Both the Tamil Hindus and Sinhalese Buddhists are internally differentiated by caste differences that have played a role in the development of their ethnic identities.

The history of the ethnic conflict between the Tamil Hindus and the Sinhalese Buddhists is extremely complex.[4] Anthropologists have been studying how the myths of nationalism and religion have been used to accentuate ethnic differences in Sri Lanka (Kapferer 1988; Spencer 1990; Tambiah 1992). They indicate how the Sinhalese have employed an ancient Buddhist cosmological tradition known as the *Mahavamsa*, which is interpreted to demonstrate that they are clearly the dominant group. This Buddhist tradition suggests that the original inhabitants of the island were demons ruled by the demon-king Ravana. According to this tradition, the first human settlers were the Sinhala (Sinhalese), "people of the lion." Thus, this cosmological tradition is used as a charter myth to justify claims of ownership of the entire island by the Sinhalese. The myth also emphasizes how after Buddhism was established in Sri Lanka, under a Sinhalese Buddhist king, a Dravidian-speaking Tamil Hindu usurped the throne. Therefore, the Tamils are introduced in the chronicle as an enemy of the Sinhalese people. The Tamils are also associated with the decline of the original Sri Lankan Buddhist civilization. This sets up a cosmic struggle between the Tamil Hindus and Sinhalese Buddhists within the myth.

During the period of British colonialism in Sri Lanka (Ceylon), a number of factors developed that resulted in intense ethnic tensions between the Sinhalese and Tamils. As part of the resistance to British colonial domination, both the Sinhalese and Tamils began to publish newspapers, books, and pamphlets in their respective languages to reform and revitalize their own ethnic and religious traditions. As we have seen elsewhere (Chapter 4), print media is an important stimulant to the development of ethnonationalism. The Sinhalese emphasized the Buddhist traditions such as the *Mahavamsa* to claim their ethnic domination and rights over the entire island. In addition, they also drew on the British colonial scholarship and notions of the "Aryan race superiority" that were circulating among Europeans, suggesting that the Sinhala were the superior race of Sri Lanka. The Tamil ethnonationalism movement produced its own interpretations of the Hindu chronicles to suggest that the Sinhalese identity is not really "Aryan" but rather a mixture of various cultures, and that their own Tamil language and religion are superior to those of the Sinhalese. In addition, an economic factor influenced the ethnic relationship between the Tamils and Sinhalese. Generally, the Tamil adopted the English language rapidly and tended to be favored by the British for high-status positions within the colonial regime. The Sinhalese perceived this tendency, and were fearful of losing their majority control of the island following independence. All these factors crystallized the ethnic division between the majority "Sinhala/Buddhist/Aryan" and minority "Tamil/Hindu/Dravidian" populations.

In 1948, after independence from the British, the Sinhalese were able to dominate politically and elect people to office from their own community. During the 1950s, to extend their ethnic hegemony they began to promote a Sinhalese-only language policy. In addition they emphasized that Buddhism was the official religion of the country. Tamils demonstrated against these policies, and interethnic violence erupted. Eventually, in the 1970s Tamil militants formed an organized paramilitary group, the Liberation Tigers of Tamil Eelam (LTTE) or Tamil Tigers, who called for the liberation of northern Sri Lanka as an independent Tamil nation-state. By 1983 extensive violence broke out between Tamils and Sinhalese in the north. The Sinhalese army responded with an invasion and indiscriminate killings in the Tamil communities. The Tamils responded in kind with terrorist activities including suicide bombing against the Sri Lankan military. Some ethnic Tamils based in Tamil Nadu in India supported the Tamil Tigers and sent funds for military equipment to them. In 1987, India sent soldiers to quell the violence. Pressured by the Sri Lankan government, India withdrew in 1989. As anthropologist Stanley Tambiah noted (1986), the ethnic fratricide that was ongoing in Sri Lanka is exacerbated by the continuing delivery of strategic arms from the industrialized world into the hands of these ethnic groups. During 2008 and 2009 the Sri Lankan military carried out a frontal assault on the LTTE located in northern Sri Lanka. In May of 2009, the Sri Lankan government declared victory over the LTTE, some of whom committed suicide rather than surrender. This ethnic war was very costly for Sri Lanka resulting in more than 80,000 deaths. Currently, the Sri Lankan government has some 300,000 Tamils imprisoned in camps surrounded by barbed wire. The country of Sri Lanka will need to develop policies of reconciliation in order to restore political and economic stability that was disrupted by three decades of ethnic conflict.

RACE AND ETHNICITY IN EAST ASIA: CHINA AND JAPAN

At first sight, unlike South Asia, the East Asian countries of China and Japan appear not to have great ethnic diversity. Many people assume that these countries have been dominated by one ethnic group for centuries, and the percentage of people who are not part of the dominant ethnic group is fairly small. For example, China (mainland China, not including the island of Taiwan), with 1.3 billion people, includes 104 million people (9.1 percent of the population) who are referred to as "national minorities." These minorities are ethnically distinct from the Han majority population, which make up 92 percent of the population. These official national minorities

consist of 55 groups, 18 of which have more than 1 million members. Japan appears to have even more ethnic homogeneity. The Japanese make up 99.4 percent of the population of 126 million people, with only 0.6 percent of the population being ethnic minorities (mostly Korean).

Thus, both of these countries appear to have more cultural and ethnic homogeneity than many other areas within Asia. Nevertheless, as we will see, they do have interethnic tensions, and the appearance of cultural homogeneity is rather superficial. And, most recently, global factors have begun to stimulate more ethnic diversity in these areas. Anthropologists have been doing research on the ethnic relations in China and Japan to investigate how these countries deal with their interethnic tensions, and how the dominant majority has to maintain its ethnic and cultural dominance.

The Concept of Race in China and Japan

As in South Asia and many other areas of the non-Western world, within China and Japan "folk" concepts of group membership were equivalent to the pseudoscientific concept of "race" that was developed in European society in the eighteenth and nineteenth centuries. In both China and Japan these folk notions of race were related to family, blood relationships, and descent. From the earliest centuries of Chinese civilization one's social identity revolved around membership within a particular family, a family that had deep historical roots. In traditional China a family was part of a patrilineage, or *zu*, a group of people who could demonstrate through written records or oral history that they were descended from particular ancestors. A group of patrilineages was referred to as a *clan*. Clans shared the same surname, such as Li, Mao, or Chang, and often shared property, such as an ancestral temple, cemetery, or common land. In some regions of China this emphasis on patrilineal clans led to villages where almost all the inhabitants shared the same surname.

Throughout much of traditional Chinese history these patrilineal clans were involved in competition and conflict over land, power, and status. They became militarized, and struggled with each other for leadership. Those patrilineal clans that attained leadership success and were able to rule over various regions gained higher status. To justify their claims to high status, various concepts of descent, blood ties, and kinship solidarity were developed. Cults and folk notions of patrilineal descent emphasizing specific families as superior "peoples" and "culture" were acknowledged. As expected, the Chinese emperor's patrilineal clan was superior to all.

Various peoples outside the confines of traditional Chinese civilization were classified as "barbarians," *yongxiabianyi*, and the physical characteristics of these people were conflated with cultural attributes (Dikötter 1992). The barbarians living beyond the realm of Chinese civilization were classified as nonhuman animals. The only people who were *ren*, "human beings," were the Chinese. Skin color was often used as a marker of animality and bestiality for the barbarians. In both the mythological and elite literate traditions of China, color consciousness was used to classify different peoples outside the empire. When trading activities took the Chinese to areas such as Southeast Asia, Africa, and Central Asia, they encountered people of different skin colorations. This resulted in linking skin coloration with cultural characteristics, and defining these peoples as nonhuman and uncivilized. Thus ideologies that emphasized the "purity" of the Chinese versus the "impurity" of barbarians based on natural "essences" emerged. One of the principal duties of the Chinese emperor was to keep the boundaries between these groups distinct. Thus, folk-based ideologies of "racial" taxonomies were being formed well before European intrusions into China (Dikötter 1992, 2008).

Likewise, the Japanese had similar folk and ideological notions that were parallel to the early European pseudoscientific concepts of race. Purported links between blood, descent, and status were inextricably tied together in Japanese myth and cultural traditions. During the Classical period in Japanese history (400–1200 C.E.) cultural traditions, including writing, literature,

religion, and political forms, were borrowed from China and grafted onto the indigenous traditions within Japan. Political institutions, including the institution of the emperor, were adopted from China into Japan. The notion that the bloodline of the imperial family was superior became even more important in Japan than in China. The Japanese emperor and his family were associated with cosmological traditions that designated them as divine beings. The emperor's family and clan were at the top of a traditional hierarchy of families, resembling the caste system of India, which distinguished between pure and impure individuals. Therefore, rank, status, and hierarchy were believed to be determined by birth, blood, kinship, and descent in traditional Japanese society. This was similar to the folk concepts of race found in other areas of the world.

Western Influence and Race

With the exception of the colonization of Hong Kong and nearby regions by the British, neither China nor Japan were taken over as colonies by European powers. However, with Western penetration into Asia, European pseudoscientific beliefs about race were diffused and integrated with indigenous concepts into China and Japan. In China, the Western pseudoscientific category of "race" and the purported evolutionary superiority of specific "races" were fused with folk models of patrilineal descent and the pure origins of the emperor (Dikötter 1992, 1997, 2008). After resistance to the British during the Opium War (1839–1842) and then with Japan's defeat of China in 1894–1895, Chinese intellectual reformers began to draw on evolutionary theories from the West to construct a new group identity. They postulated a world in which different "races" struggled for survival. They argued that all inhabitants of China were descended from the patrilineal line of the Yellow Emperor. As Frank Dikötter states, "Extrapolating from an indigenous vision of lineage feuds, which permeated the social landscape of late imperial China, reformers constructed a racialized worldview in which 'yellows' competed with 'whites' over degenerate breeds of 'browns', 'blacks' and 'reds' " (2008:11). This notion of race provided a common descent linked by blood to unite the Chinese. The term *zu* for patrilineage was eventually redefined as *minzu*, which integrated people (*min*) and descent (*zu*) to refer to the people, "race," or nation of China.

The term *minzu* was introduced into China from Japan in the late nineteenth century when other Western concepts were translated into Japanese and transmitted to China. In particular, the "Han race" was identified with the most pure "race" descended from the emperor. The leader and first president of the Republic in China, Sun Yat-sen, promoted a racial nationalism as a basis for the nation-state in the early twentieth century. He wrote about how the Han had common blood, common language, common religion, and common customs, and was a single, pure race. Sun believed that groups such as the Mongols, Manchus, Tibetans, and Mohammedan Turks were different *minzu*, or peoples or nationalities. Textbooks were used to educate the children of China about these "races." For example, one elementary textbook of 1921 asserts: "Mankind is divided into five races. The yellow and white races are relatively strong and intelligent. Because the other races are feeble and stupid, they are being exterminated by the white race. Only the yellow race competes with the white race" (cited in Dikötter 1992:163, 2008). Following the Communist revolution in China led by Mao Zedong in the 1950s, racialized notions were still perpetuated. Mao perceived the Chinese nation (*minzu*) as a biologically distinct group, a matter of "culture" as well as "race."

Japanese nationalists also adopted the European pseudoscientific concepts of race to reinforce indigenous concepts of blood and descent. A conjunction of blood, culture, history, and political form became the dominant discourse of Japanese intellectuals during the Meiji period (1868–1912). During the Meiji period many Japanese studied Western traditions as a means of inducing rapid modernization. As the Japanese investigated Western writings on "race," these ideas were incorporated and synthesized with indigenous conceptions. "Japaneseness" became

Mao Zedong (1983-1976).

associated with a particular "race" of people who were part of one family nation (*kazoku kokka*), with the emperor as a semidivine father. Various Japanese intellectuals identified the nation, or *minzoku*, as a manifestation of common blood and ancestry as well as culture (Weiner 1997; Yoshino 1998). Ultimately, this racialistic thinking was extended in the Japanese notion that they were the superior "race" of Asia, and this became the basis for an ethnonationalistic movement and imperialistic expansion in the twentieth century resulting in World War II. Many Japanese began to believe that they were a superior "race" compared to the inferior races of China, Korea, or their own indigenous native population of Ainu in northern Japan (Ohnuki-Tierney 1998; Weiner 1997). Family, kinship, blood, and culture became inextricably bound to produce a sense of superior Japaneseness. Following World War II, with the U.S. occupation and the ideological attack on these notions of the superior Japanese race and blood, these beliefs became muted.

Yet, as sociologist Kosaku Yoshino says, in the Japanese subconsciousness the nation as "imagined kinship" and metaphors of blood remain alive and well (1998:201).

The Muslim Minority in China

Anthropologist Dru Gladney has been conducting ethnographic research on the Muslim minority in China illustrating how ethnic relations between the national minorities and Han majority have evolved and persist (1991, 1998). Sun Yat-sen, the nationalist leader, had divided China into five different peoples: the Han, Man (Manchu), Meng (Mongolian), Zang (Tibetan), and Hui (all Muslims in China). He used the term *Han minzu* to refer to the majority group, in contrast and opposition to these other "internal foreigners." After the Communist revolution in China, the 56 different nationalities, including the Han majority, were recognized by government authorities in order to control and consolidate the nation-state. Included within these 56 nationalities are 10 Muslim nationalities: Hui, Uygur, Kazak, Dongxiang, Kirghiz, Salar, Tadjik, Uzbek, Baonan, and Tatar—consisting of over 17 million people.

The earliest Muslim groups in China were descended from Arab, Persian, Central Asian, and Turkish peoples who migrated into China and settled in the northwest and southeast coastal regions. As noted, prior to 1949 the term *Hui* was a general term for "Muslims." However, following the Communist revolution, the Muslims were separated into the 10 separate groups, based on language. The Hui, who are the largest Muslim group, have a population of over 8 million people and are widely distributed throughout China. They did not have a separate language of their own, and spoke the language (mostly Chinese Mandarin) where they lived. The Hui reside in most of the counties and cities throughout China, including the large cities of Beijing and Shanghai. Unlike the other Muslim nationalities in China, the Hui speak the dialects of the other ethnic groups among whom they live, primarily the Han. Some of the Hui, however, reside in areas such as Tibet or Mongolia, where they speak the Tibetan or Mongolian language. Since the Hui did not reside in one locale in China, Gladney had to do multisited ethnographic work. This enabled him to investigate how the Hui have managed to maintain and emphasize their ethnic identity in different cultural contexts throughout China.

The focus of Gladney's research was on the ethnogenesis of the Hui. How have these widely dispersed people been able to develop and sustain an ethnic identity that differentiates them from other people in China? Before the 1950s, the Hui were not recognized by the state as a distinctive nationality. Instead, they were referred to in general terms as "Muslims," along with other groups of Muslims. In order to examine the question of how they became "Hui," Gladney concentrated his ethnographic research on several different regional locations where the Hui resided. He studied the Hui in the city of Beijing, in Ningxia, a rural area in the northwest, in a rural community on the outskirts of Beijing, and in the southern city of Chendai in Fujian Province. Gladney discovered that it was only after the Chinese state began to categorize and designate these people as "Hui" for political purposes that these people began to objectify their own ethnicity. Though they previously related to one another on a local level as fellow Muslims, after government classification and designation, the Hui began to think of themselves as "*Hui minzu.*" However, as Gladney discovered from his research in these four areas, the expression of ethnicity was dramatically different in these various locales.

One important expression of ethnic and religious identity does appear to cut across the dispersed Muslim population in China. The notion of belonging to the Islamic faith, which is the "pure and true" (*qing zhen*) religion, is emphasized by all Hui Muslims. This phrase *qing zhen* is found wherever Hui Muslims reside, and it refers to such Islamic dietary rules as the avoidance of pork consumption. To some extent, it is similar to Jewish notions of "kosher" and approximates the Arabic concept of "halal." Among the approximately 200,000 Hui Muslims in the capital city of Beijing, the most important expression of ethnic identity is based on their dietary restrictions, especially the absence of pork, which is maintained through their own ethnic restaurants. Pork is the staple meat of the Han majority in Beijing and throughout China, and many of the Han cannot fathom why the Hui do not eat pork. Thus, the pork taboo has become the most significant aspect of Hui identity within Beijing. Muslim restaurants where the phrase *qing zhen* is displayed openly are the foremost centers of cultural and religious identity for the Beijing Hui. The Hui meet in the restaurants to discuss religious and other community issues while maintaining their *qing zhen* lifestyle. Young Hui go to restaurants to socialize and meet prospective spouses. Though the Hui of Beijing do not wear traditional Muslim clothing, and are more secular than Muslims in rural areas, Gladney found vibrant signs of ethnic identity within this community.

Gladney resided in the Hui rural community in Ningxia, which is representative of many of the Muslim communities of northwest China. Ningxia is the Ningxia Hui Autonomous Region, one of the five minority autonomous regions in China (including Tibet, Uygur, Inner Mongolia, and Zhuang in Guangxi). The Ningxia Hui community has a completely different form of ethnic expression than that of the Beijing Hui. Within this community, the emphasis on *qing zhen* is sought through a close identity with the Islamic religious tradition. They maintain a rigid notion of *qing zhen*, which results in strict rules of pure and impure behaviors. These pure and impure regulations divide the Hui from the Han in the northwest area. For example, Hui Muslims cannot accept food from their Han neighbors because of pure/impure cultural norms. In addition, an Islamic resurgence movement has developed among these Hui Muslims. Increases in religious education, mosque attendance, traditional restrictions on male–female interaction, decreases in Hui–Han intermarriages, and extensive contact with other areas of the Islamic world are recognizable signs of an enhanced ethnic and religious identity among these Hui Muslims in Nangxia.

In the two other Hui communities Gladney discovered other indications of ethnic identity.

In Chang Ying village, on the outskirts of Beijing, Hui Muslims maintain their identity primarily through marriage arrangements. They practice a strict form of ethnic endogamy (marriage within their own ethnic group) as a means of preserving their identity. To live the *qing zhen* "pure and true" Islamic life among the Hui in Chang Ying is to marry only within one's own ethnic group. In order to maintain this ethnic endogamy, the Chang Ying Hui have had to develop extensive marriage networks throughout China. Though this ethnic endogamy has sometimes resulted in birth defects, it reinforces their identity with their original purported Muslim ancestors.

In contrast to this mode of ethnic expression, Hui Muslims of the town of Chendai, in southern Fujian Province, have another understanding of *qing zhen*. The Chendai Hui consist of one patrilineal group with the surname Ding. The Ding do not practice Islam, they consume pork, and they are the most highly assimilated Hui within China. However, the Chendai Hui do assert their ethnic affiliation with Arab and Persian ancestors through various tombs of Muslim saints in their city, and ancient texts that refer to their Ding patrilineal group. Various rituals surrounding the use of these texts and graves are maintained to reinforce their own unique interpretation of *qing zhen*, an identification with their ancient Arab and Persian ancestry.

Through his ethnographic research Gladney demonstrates how ethnic expression varies within the group classified as "*Hui minzui*" in China. However, he also illustrates how Chinese nationality and Han nationality are "imagined" by both the Chinese state and scholars of China. He shows how the assumptions of cultural and ethnic homogeneity regarding China are misconceived, in that they underestimate the degree of ethnic and cultural diversity within China. Aside from his own case studies of the Hui, Gladney notes that with the new forms of globalism and economic expansion in southern China, different groups from within the Han majority have begun to reassert, reinvent, and rediscover their own ethnic and cultural differences. The Cantonese (in southern China and Hong Kong), the Hakka (*Kejia*), and the Hokkien-speaking people are beginning to distinguish themselves from other Han. As these groups benefit from the opening of China to the global economy, and freedom from the severe political restraints of Maoism, they are beginning to emphasize their own local histories, genealogies, and cultural traditions. These new ethnic movements belie the traditional assumptions about China being a monocultural and culturally homogeneous society.

Japan as a Multiethnic Society

The perception of Japan as one of the most ethnically homogeneous societies in the world is not just an outsider's stereotypical understanding of Japan but is also the dominant Japanese perception of their own society. The Japanese tend to believe that they are a distinctive "race" and that they differ from the other "races" of Asia. They imagine themselves as all related with one another "by blood," and this metaphor of "Japanese blood" (*Nihonjin no chi*) is used to strengthen their ethnic identity. Although the Japanese, like all other peoples, are the result of a long evolutionary history of mixture of different groups, this racialized notion of ethnic identity remains a myth of cultural identity for the Japanese (Diamond 1998; Yoshino 1992, 1998). These social constructions of "race" are similar to other peoples' "folk" notions of "race" that we have encountered (see Chapter 4). This social construction of "race" is also the basis of the *Nihonjinron* (works on Japanese distinctiveness) that have been promoted within the media and intellectual circles in Japanese society. In the media and in the *Nihonjinron* literature, the Japanese economic miracle and absence of social problems were attributed to this "racial" and ethnic uniqueness. These folk notions of "race" maintained within Japanese society also resulted in various ethnic problems.

In a provocative essay, anthropologist Emiko Ohnuki-Tierney (1998) suggests that the construction of Japaneseness is related to the dominant symbols and metaphors of nature, which include rice and animals. She argues that Japanese ethnic identity is tied to the traditions of agrarian Japan, where peasants produced rice on the land. This form of agricultural production lasted for some 2,000 years and provided the foundations for the nation-state in Japan. Additionally, the Buddhist tradition, with its strong prohibition on the killing of animals, became integral to Japanese culture. In fact, until after World War II, most Japanese did not consume meat. As Ohnuki-Tierney emphasizes, the Japanese vision of nature does not have much room for "wild nature," in contrast to European cultures in which hunting and pastoralism have been important (1998:35). These two traditions of agricultural rice production and taboos against the killing of animals have had negative consequences for two different ethnic minorities in Japan: the people known as the *hisabetsu burakumin* and the indigenous Ainu.

Ohnuki-Tierney underscores the fact that during the medieval period in agrarian Japan there were categories of people associated with different occupations, ranks, and statuses that were classified as "pure" or "impure." This stratified society was composed of low-status peoples: cleaners of temples, entertainers, prostitutes, undertakers, plasterers, carpenters, arms manufacturers, butchers, tanners, and leather workers. All of these low-status occupations and peoples were considered impure, and all were nonagrarian (Ohnuki-Tierney 1987, 1998). Later, during the Tokugawa period (1603–1868), this stratification system evolved into a rigid caste system of warriors, farmers, manufacturers, and merchants, with an "outcaste" group at the bottom. This lowest outcaste group has become known as the "*etta*," or *hisabetsu burakumin*, who were employed as leather workers, fur processors, or butchers. This nonagricultural occupation was associated with "death and violence" against animals, and the people were considered as the most "defiled" and "impure" group in Japan.

Presently, the *burakumin* consist of about 3 million people, and remain a discriminated ethnic minority in Japanese society. They are sometimes referred to as "Japan's invisible race," because no physical characteristics distinguish this population from other Japanese.

Nonetheless, they reside in separate ghetto areas in Japan and most still work primarily in shoe shops and other leather-related industries. Marriage between *burakumin* and other Japanese is still restricted, and other patterns of ethnic discrimination against this group continue (DeVos and Wetherhall 1983). This ethnic discrimination has resulted in poverty, lower education attainment, delinquency, and other social problems for the *burakumin*, just as it has for some ethnic minorities within the United States. The *burakumin* also score lower on IQ tests. Since these people are not biologically or racially different from other Japanese people, this finding indicates, as was emphasized in the discussion in Chapter 2, that ethnic discrimination, poverty, and related environmental conditions are more responsible for differences in intelligence than any purported biological differences.

The indigenous Ainu people of the northern island of Hokkaido in Japan are also considered another "race" distinctive from the Japanese. They are referred to as *Kyuudojin* ("aborigines") or *Dojin* ("natives") in colloquial Japanese. The Ainu have some physical traits that distinguish them from the Japanese population, but there has been extensive intermarriage between these people and other Japanese. Because of the intermarriage, it is difficult to estimate the population of the Ainu, which ranges from 20,000 to 300,000 (Sjoberg 1993; Dubreil 2007). However, the offspring of marriages between other Japanese and Ainu are classified as "Ainu" by the majority population. The fraction of "foreign" blood in a child's veins is sufficient to deny it "pure" Japaneseness (DeVos and Wetherhall 1983). Traditionally these people were hunters and gatherers, and, like many indigenous peoples elsewhere in the world, were conquered and eventually incorporated into the expanding imperial agrarian state of Japan. According to Ohnuki-Tierney (1998), the fact that these people were engaged in hunting animals and were nonagriculturalists reinforced their low status and resulted in negative stereotypes against them. The Ainu are sometimes referred to as *gaijin*

("outside person," "non-Japanese," "foreigner") by other Japanese. Until the 1930s the Japanese government maintained separate schools for the Ainu, which reinforced their minority status. Presently, they remain in the lowest income bracket in Japan, and only 8.1 percent graduate from high school (Sjoberg 1993). Although the Japanese government has been reluctant to recognize the social and cultural problems that have faced the Ainu, the local government in Hokkaido has opened an Ainu research center in 1994 to gain an understanding of these people. Currently, there is an ethnic awareness campaign associated with a unique Ainu flag and other cultural symbols including Ainu indigenous art work that has emerged within Japan (Dubreil 2007).

Other ethnic minorities, such as the Koreans, Chinese, and Okinawans, have had their share of difficulties in Japanese society. These groups have experienced widespread discrimination, even though they have adopted the Japanese language, norms, and values. A common attitude found in Japan is that because these people do not share "Japanese blood" they do not think like "us" (Yoshino 1992, 1998). The fact that some Korean well-known entertainers and sports figures are accepted as "ethnically Japanese" has not dislodged this racialistic thinking. The metaphor of "Japanese blood" is embedded strongly within Japanese culture. The blurring of race and culture, and the beliefs regarding the genetic transmission of Japanese uniqueness, has been perpetuated for centuries. These folk beliefs have a tenacious hold on the minds of both Japanese lay people and intellectuals (Yoshino 1992, 1998).

Globalization trends, however, are beginning to have an effect on the indigenous folk notions of Japanese blood, descent, and race. Despite official policies that restrict immigration of foreigners into Japan, the country has witnessed a growing number of immigrants in recent years. Since the mid-1980s Japan has faced a labor shortage, and many immigrants are coming to seek work. Many of these jobs are unskilled or low-skilled, and the Japanese government is willing to open its doors to immigrants to work in jobs that most Japanese will not accept. These newcomers work in so-called 3-K jobs: work that is *kitsui* ("hard"), *kitanai* ("dirty"), or *kiken* ("dangerous") (Wehrfritz and Takayama 2000). Koreans, Chinese, Indians, and smaller numbers of people from Africa and the Middle East are now immigrating to Japan for these jobs, as well as many illegal and undocumented immigrants.

Faced with new ethnic minority problems, in 1989 the Japanese government gave special residency status to *Nikkeijin*, descendants of Japanese emigrants, mostly from Brazil and Peru. By the end of 1998, some 222,000 Brazilians and 41,000 Peruvians of Japanese ancestry had established residency in Japan. The assumption of the government is that these people will be able to assimilate into Japanese society more easily than other foreigners (Potter and Knepper 1998). However, the folk notion that Japanese culture is the exclusive property of the Japanese race is being challenged by new immigrants, who, though different in physical appearance, can speak Japanese as well as native Japanese. The concept of Japan as a culturally and ethnically homogeneous society is less likely to be maintained in the face of these new globalization tendencies.

ETHNICITY AND RACE IN SOUTHEAST ASIA

Southeast Asia is divided into two geographic zones: mainland and island Southeast Asia, which include countries with different environments and histories that have contributed to cultural and ethnic complexity. The countries of mainland Southeast Asia include Myanmar (Burma), Thailand, Kampuchea (Cambodia), Laos, and Vietnam. The countries of island Southeast Asia are Malaysia, Singapore, Brunei, Indonesia, and the Philippines. All of the mainland Southeast Asian countries have a dominant ethnic majority with various ethnic minorities. For example, Myanmar consists of ethnic Burmese, who make up 65 percent of the population of 47 million, and a variety of other ethnic groups, including Shans, Karens, Mons, Indians, and Chinese. Ethnic Thais make up 75 percent of the population of Thailand of 62 million, with a number of other

ethnic minorities such as Chinese, Malay, Indian, and smaller numbers of "Hill tribes" residing in the mountain areas bordering southern China. The countries of Vietnam, Kampuchea, and Laos have ethnic majorities with smaller populations of ethnic minorities residing in different regions.

Island Southeast Asia has countries that range from extreme ethnic diversity to those that have ethnically homogeneous populations. The most ethnically diverse country is Indonesia, which encompasses over 13,000 islands extending over 3,000 miles from west to east. Indonesia has a total population of about 210 million people. The largest ethnic group, the Javanese, on the major island of Java, makes up 45 percent of the population. Other ethnic minorities on different islands of Indonesia include the Sundanese, Achenese, Madurese, Alorese, Timorese, Sumatrans, Balinese, Moluccans, Iban, Dani, and many others. Altogether there are over 100 different ethnic groups speaking some 300 different languages extending throughout the Indonesian archipelago. The country of Malaysia consists of the ethnically Malay population, 58 percent of the population of 21 million people, and other ethnic minorities, such as the Chinese, Indian, and other smaller groups. In contrast, the country of Singapore has a Chinese majority of 77 percent of its 3 million plus population, along with Malay and Indian minorities. The small country of Brunei, with approximately 300,000 people, also has an ethnic Malay majority, a Chinese minority, and smaller numbers of other ethnic groups. The ethnic majority, the lowland Filipinos, are 90 percent of the 77 million people in the Philippines, where nine different languages are spoken, including Tagalog, Cebuana, and Ilocano. Minorities such as the Chinese and Muslims and smaller upland ethnic groups also reside in the Philippines.

Other factors that have complicated ethnic relations throughout most of Southeast Asia are the historical experience of European colonialism and the Japanese occupation during World War II. During the nineteenth century, to extend its Asian empire from India the British colonized the countries of Burma and Malaysia. At about the same time, to compete with the British the French colonized Indo-China (Cambodia, Laos, and Vietnam). Earlier, the Dutch colonized the various islands of Indonesia. Spaniards were the colonizers of the Philippines in the 1500s, but following the Spanish-American war in 1898, the United States took control over the Philippines. In World War II Japan controlled most of the countries of Southeast Asia. Following World War II most of these countries developed independence and nationalist movements, gradually resulting in their liberation from their colonial masters. However, colonialism in Southeast Asia had major consequences for the content and form of ethnic relations in these societies. For examples of the dynamics of ethnic relations in Southeast Asia, we will concentrate on the countries of Thailand and Malaysia.

Thailand

Thailand is an atypical country in Southeast Asia because it was not directly colonized by European powers. The Thai monarchy, which had some experience with Western interests, developed economic and political strategies to play European rivals against one another while adopting Western innovations. European business interests were allowed to aid in the development of some goods, but not to exercise direct political control. To some extent, this suited the geopolitical strategies of both the British and the French, who preferred Thailand as a buffer state between their colonial domains of Burma and Indo-China.

To some degree, Thailand, like China and Japan, is perceived as an ethnically and culturally homogeneous society (Winichakul 1994). Siam, Thailand's original name, was established through the expansion of monarchical rule beginning in the sixteenth century. Gradually, as the Siamese state developed from its centers in Sukothai, Ayudhaya, and finally Bangkok, it incorporated bordering regions in the north, northeast, and south. Within these geographic regions were people who were different ethnically, linguistically, and culturally from the ethnic Tai. For example, in the north were many tribal minorities speaking different languages, in the central region there

were Mon- and Khmer-speakers, and in the south was a large number of Malay-speaking people. Even within the capital city of Bangkok, ethnic minorities resided among the majority Tai.

Despite the ethnic diversity within the country, Siamese nationalist leaders and state officials promoted a uniform ethnic collective identity based on notions of race, culture, and what has been referred to as the "Three Pillars." Various Siamese monarchs promoted the Three Pillars of national and ethnic identity for the country. The Three Pillars of this Thai collective identity were the "Nation" (*chat*), "Religion" (*sasana*), and "Monarchy" (*phramahaksat*). This Siamese political and cultural code represented a symbol of a unified ethnic identity that was formulated to mediate the actual ethnic ambiguities and contradictions within the country.

The first pillar, *chat* (derived from the Sanskrit-Hindi *jati*, which translates roughly as "caste"), is used by the Siamese majority to refer to birth, race, lineage, and origin. Historically, the second pillar, *sasana*, religion, was synonymous with Theravada Buddhism, which is practiced by the majority of people in Thailand. The third pillar, *phramahakasat,* is an honorific term for "king" or "monarch" and embodies the vertical or hierarchical symbolic relationship between the ruler and the people in Siamese society.

These Three Pillars were cultivated as the basis of ethnic and national identity within Siamese society. In particular, *chat* (nation) also has the connotations of biology, birth, lineage, and descent, which makes it somewhat equivalent to the European concept of race. In linguistic usage *Chon Chat Thai* was used to refer to the Thai race/nation/culture. This racialistic term of identity became the basis of ethnonationalism in Thailand (Barmè 1993; Vella 1978). It was also used to promote government policies that affected ethnic relations. For example, by the twentieth century, approximately 10 percent of the population in Thailand was Chinese who had immigrated for economic and political purposes. Many of the Chinese had become successful in the Siamese economy. For many years, unlike other citizens, the Chinese were not subject to head taxes because the Siamese economy was dependent on their labor. When, in 1910, the Chinese were required to pay the head tax, they organized a general strike and closed all their businesses and shops. Also, some of the Chinese community had been involved in a political plot against the royalty.

In response to these perceived economic and political threats, the king, Rama IV, wrote two books outlining his fears of the Chinese: *The Jews of the Orient* and *Wake Up Siam: A Reminder to the Thais*. Obviously, his perceptions were based on Western racial stereotypes perpetuated in the early twentieth century. However, understanding the important role that the Chinese had played in developing the Siamese economy, the king did not implement restrictive immigration policies. Additionally, he initiated a Thai nationality law in 1913 which stated that everyone born in Siam, regardless of parentage, was Thai. This official policy tended to encourage the assimilation of the Chinese and other ethnic minorities.

Later developments in Thai history provoked extreme nationalistic policies that were based on notions of "race" drawn from European and Japanese sources. In particular, Luang Wichit Wathakan, who was director general of the department of fine arts during the years 1932–1941, drew on racist and fascist ideas from Europe and Japan to promote nationalism in Thailand. During World War II he became minister of foreign affairs. Wichit, like Hermann Goebbels of Germany, with whom he is compared, became the major propaganda minister in Thailand. He provided a conceptual framework that was sanctioned by the state to create a racial and nationalistic identity for the Thai people (Barmè 1993). Wichit propagated the idea that the Thai were a heroic and martial "race." The Thai "race" was conceptualized to be different from that of the Chinese, Indian, European, or American. There were specific behaviors and cultural conventions that were assumed to be associated with the Thai "race." Thai culture and race (*Thai Rathaniyom*) and a cultural policy based on "Cultural Rules" (*Kot Wattanatham*) were publicized and propagated through the educational system and media.

At this same time, the name of the country was changed from Siam to Thailand. Part of the reason for this name change was to distinguish the Thai "race" from the Chinese and other ethnic minorities and to encourage a more unified basis for this ethnonationalist movement. The promotion of "Thainess," emphasizing various behaviors and etiquette, was used along with other national symbols such as the Three Pillars to emphasize an ethnically homogeneous society. Official legislation was passed to expand the use of the Thai language and reduce the use of other languages such as Chinese, Lao, Shan, and Malay within Thailand. All of these policies have had consequences for ethnic minorities in Thailand up to the present.

The Muslim Minority in Thailand

In Thailand, one of the largest ethnic minorities is the Muslim population. Muslims are approximately four percent of the population. About 4 million Thai citizens profess the Islamic faith and maintain over 2,700 mosques. Muslims in Thailand include the Malay Muslims, who speak the Malay language and reside primarily in south Thailand in a number of provinces bordering on Malaysia. The Malay Muslims of south Thailand make up over 70 percent of the population in that region. A second category of Muslims sometimes refer to themselves as Thai Muslims, or, *Thai Isalam*, and reside in central and north Thailand. The Thai Muslims are smaller heterogeneous ethnic and religious minorities in these regions and speak Thai. Historically, the Muslims of south Thailand lived in a region imbued with a Malay-Indonesian Islamic political and religious cultural ethos, whereas the Muslims of central and north Thailand have been influenced by the political-religious culture of the Theravada Buddhist traditions. However, because of the administrative practices and policies of the Thai state during the course of the twentieth century, all Muslims in Thailand have been largely affected by the dominant Buddhist political and religious culture (Scupin 1998).

The Malay-speaking Muslims are in south Thailand as a result of the expansion of the Thai state into that region. The four southern provinces of Patani, Narathiwat, Satul, and Yala bordering on Malaysia have been gradually integrated into Thailand since at least the sixteenth century. These Malay Muslims identify themselves as *ore nayu* (the Malay people), and they refer to the Thai Buddhists as *ore siye* (the Siamese people). The Thai Buddhists, or *chat Thai*, use the ethnic category *khaek Musalayam* to refer to the Malay Muslims, which was perceived as a pejorative term by the native Muslims in the south. In the early twentieth century, the Thai government aggressively began to incorporate this Malay Muslim population through the appointment of Thai Buddhist bureaucrats throughout southern Malay regions (Pitsuwan 1985; Thomas 1975). In addition, Thai authorities began to interfere directly with the religious practices of the Muslims in the South. Bangkok authorities attempted to assume all legal matters under Thai law. In effect, this meant that the Muslim legal code, structured by the *Shari'ah* and *adat* (Malay custom) and administered by the local *qadi* (Muslim judge), was to be controlled by Thai Buddhist officials.

During the 1930s, the Thai government promoted education as the means of integrating this region into the Thai nation. This created a dilemma for the Malay Muslims in the south, because the Thai educational system was based on Buddhist values, and the language of education was Thai. Therefore, to become involved in the Thai educational process necessitated a rejection of one's language and religion, the primordial basis of ethnic identity for these Malay Muslims. To resolve this dilemma, the *ulama*, the local Muslim religious leaders and the source of political legitimacy, played a prominent role in mobilizing political support around Islamic religious and cultural symbols. However, the Thai government, based on the racist notion of *chon chat Thai*, attempted to enforce central Thai "race" and culture at the expense of other minority groups in Thailand. As part of these policies, the Malay Muslims were not allowed to wear their traditional clothing, elements of Islamic religion that applied to marriage and inheritance were banned, non-Buddhists were deliberately discriminated against in government, and conscious attempts at proselytization of the Buddhist faith in the south were to be carried out within the government-sponsored educational system—all in all an aggressive attempt at forced assimilation.

Eventually, in the 1950s and 1960s the Thai government began to develop socioeconomic programs as an instrument of assimilation. Nonetheless, these national integrationist policies continued to include the imposition of Thai Buddhist cultural ideals in the southern Malay areas. The result was resentment among the Malay Muslim minority.

A number of Islamic-based factions emerged during the 1960s and 1970s in south Thailand, reflecting a diversity of political views and engaging in secessionist activities. One of the most influential secessionist groups, PULO, the Patani United Liberation Organization, emerged in the late 1960s and became the most well-known and most effective guerrilla and separatist movement in the region. PULO was devoted to preserving "Malayness" and the Islamic way of life in south Thailand. Their militant activities created deeper divisions between the Malay Muslims and the Thai Buddhists associated with central Thai authorities. The overall goal of PULO was to create an autonomous Islamic state. Although there were sporadic skirmishes, since the 1990s PULO began to decrease in membership and Malay Muslim communities of Patani changed their political strategies by actively mobilizing their communities and seeking a voice in the Thai political system.

Ethnic and religious-based violence erupted dramatically in southern Thailand on January 4, 2004, when over a hundred Muslim insurgents raided an arms depot of the 4th Army Engineers in Narathiwat province. As diversionary moves, they also torched 20 public schools, burnt rubber tires, and planted fake explosives in a neighboring Yala province. Shortly thereafter a number of Buddhist monks were attacked and killed. Sporadic violence has continued for the past five years in southern Thailand. Since 2004 there have been over 3,200 deaths of both Buddhist and Muslims in this southern insurgency in Thailand (Askew 2007, 2009; Liow 2007; McCargo 2007, 2008, 2009). The Thai government has militarized various Buddhist temples in the southern provinces in order to quell the ethnic and religious violence (Jerryson 2009). This has led to ethnic polarization, mistrust, and continuing tensions between the Muslim and Buddhist populations in the south. Resolving this Muslim–Buddhist ethnic-religious tension and insurgency is a major concern and challenge for the Thai government.

Malaysia

Malaysia is an ethnically plural society. Before the fourteenth century the Malay archipelago consisted of a number of small states each of which had its own ruling monarch. These states were influenced strongly by the religious traditions of Hinduism and Buddhism, which, since the first century C.E., had diffused to this region through trading and political contacts with India. The rulers of these small kingdoms were believed to be semidivine. The peoples residing in the interior regions of what was then known as Malaya were mostly peasants who cultivated rice; most of the coastal peoples were involved in fishing, trading, and piracy. During this period, there were active trading contacts among different Asian countries and the Malaya region. Following the fourteenth century, Islamic traders from the Middle East and South Asia entered the region of Malaya. Gradually, some of the rulers of Malaya began to convert to the Islamic tradition, and in most cases the people converted to the religion of their rulers. Though Islam coexisted with the traditions of Hinduism and Buddhism for many years in Malaya, eventually the Islamic religion began to predominate. During the sixteenth century Western expansion into Malaya began with the Portuguese. The religious tradition of Islam became a means of mobilizing and unifying different Malay principalities as the Western colonial powers arrived on the scene. Eventually,

during the nineteenth century, the British took control of the region of Malaya as one of its primary colonies in Southeast Asia, and British colonialism persisted there until the 1950s.

Under the British, new patterns of ethnic relations in Malaya developed. As a means of developing the colonial economy in Malaya, the British actively recruited and imported cheap labor from China and India. The native population of Malaya was reluctant to work in the tin mines and on the rubber plantations developed by the British. Thus, thousands of Chinese, mainly from the southeast area of China, came to work in mines, commercial businesses, and other occupations. Indians were imported from colonized India to work on the rubber plantations. These groups from China and India were themselves linguistically and ethnically diverse. The Chinese included Cantonese, Hakka, Hainanese, Kwongsai, Hokkien, and other different linguistic groups. The Indians comprised Tamil, Telegu, Punjabi, Bengalis, Sikhs, and others. There were also migrant workers from many different ethnic backgrounds in Indonesia. The effects of these developments in British Malaya were to create a plural society that would result in ethnic divisions and tensions in postcolonial Malaysia.

Prior to Western colonialism in Malaya, as in the other areas of Asia we have examined, an indigenous concept was used to categorize people that closely resembled a notion of "race." The Malay term *bangsa* was used to refer to the common culture, descent, and origin of a particular group of people. *Bangsa* is derived from the Sanskrit word *vamsa*, which is translated as "line of descent" or "blood" (Hirschman 1987; Nagata 1981). Originally, the term *bangsa* was used to differentiate different families, and in particular to distinguish the royal family from other patrilineages. Thus, the term had similar connotations of a folk concept of "race," referring to blood, birth, biological inheritance, and origins. When the British colonized the region of Malaya, colonial officials, census takers, and scholars imposed their nineteenth-century pseudoscientific conception of race onto the various populations. Thus, the racially conscious British divided the major populations into the Malay, Chinese, and Indian races, with other subdivisions based on language, religion, and culture. These racial categories hopelessly confused "race" with "culture." Eventually, these British notions were combined with indigenous beliefs of *bangsa* to crystallize into racial ideologies that were to become the foundation of the nationalist and independence movements in Malaysia (Hirschman 1987; Milner 1998). They continue to influence ethnic relations today.

The Ethnic Struggle in Malaysia

Following independence and the withdrawal of the British in 1957, a major challenge confronted the Malay majority. Despite the fact of the Malay's slight majority in population, the Chinese had become the dominant ethnic group in the private sector of the economy. Thus, as in most of the other areas of Southeast Asia, the Chinese population became extremely successful in businesses and entrepreneurial activities. Though the Malay majority gained control of the political institutions, the Chinese tended to control the economy. The various reasons for the economic success of the Chinese in Southeast Asia have been studied by many scholars over the years. In Malaysia during the colonial period various stereotypes were perpetuated by the British regarding the Malay and Chinese "races." The Malay were considered "lazy and indolent," whereas the Chinese were assumed to be "industrious and hardworking."

Modern researchers have examined the various factors that resulted in Chinese economic success in Southeast Asia and have debunked these racist stereotypes. Historians emphasize the business experience that the Chinese had at home, which preadapted them for success in Southeast Asia. The fact that the Chinese had some prior experience in small- and medium-scale businesses and in handling money and loans gave their group advantages in comparison with native populations in Southeast Asia (Mackie 1998). However, this explanation tends to underestimate the traditional economic activities that native populations of

Southeast Asia had been engaged in prior to the arrival of the Chinese (Hefner 1998; Mackie 1998). Later research compared the "overseas Chinese" in Southeast Asia to other ethnic groups such as the Jews of Europe as "middleman minorities." Because of their business skills, the various governments drew on these "middleman minorities" to act as intermediaries between them and the native peoples. For example, the Chinese were recruited to collect taxes and work in a variety of state-owned businesses. Other scholars note how the patrilineal kinship system of the Chinese, which involves the commitment of all members of the family in family businesses, was significant in stimulating economic development. In addition, traditional practices of personal patron–client networks, or *guanxi* relationships, for building trust and community ties within the Chinese business community played a significant role in success in Southeast Asia (Hefner 1998; Mackie 1998).

After independence, the economic success of the Chinese (and, to some extent, the Indian population) compared with that of the Malaysian majority resulted in ethnic tensions. As the majority of the Malays was rural farmers and was not benefiting from the modern industrializing economy, they felt deprived compared to the Chinese and Indian segments of the country. During the late 1960s, riots ensued directed against the perceived ethnic inequalities and lack of opportunities within the newly developing economy. Two thousand lives were lost, mostly Chinese. As a result of these demonstrations, in the 1970s the Malaysian government designed an affirmative action plan that gave preference to ethnic Malays in education and employment in the private sector of the economy. The aim of the government was to reduce the "structural barriers" that prevented the Malays from enjoying the benefits of the economic boom taking place in Malaysia. The government set a target of Malay participation in 30 percent of Malaysian businesses. In addition, to reinforce these ethnically based policies the government introduced a new Malay term, *Bumiputras* ("sons of the soil"), to distinguish the Malay from the immigrant communities of Chinese and Indians. Although this system of preferential treatment has resulted in some success for Malay involvement in the economy, the Chinese and Indian communities are concerned that the privileges given to the *Bumiputras* are being abused by the government to discriminate against them. These ethnic tensions are reflected within the political party system in Malaysia presently. Each of the major ethnic groups has its own political party that competes with the others in elections. Some analysts have referred to Malaysia as an "ethnocracy," as the Malays, through the *Bumiputra* policies, have created a political and economic framework that excludes and deprives non-Malay peoples of educational, economic, and political opportunities (Wade 2009).

Ethnicity and Religion in Malaysia

Anthropologist Judith Nagata has been engaged in a long research project on ethnicity and religion in Malaysia. In one of her ethnographic studies in the 1970s she observed ethnic interaction in the Malaysian city of George Town, Penang (1974, 1981). George Town, a port city, is ethnically diverse, with the Chinese population making up 71 percent and smaller communities of Indians, Malays, Indonesians, Arabs, and Europeans. The Chinese population was mostly Buddhist, the Indians mostly Hindu, and Malays, Indonesians, and Arabs were Muslims. Traditionally, in rural areas to become "Malay" meant converting to Islam and becoming a practicing Muslim and speaking Malay. In fact, the constitution of Malaysia is based on a salient definition of "Malay": It is a person who is a Muslim and speaks the Malay language and follows the traditional customs *adat* of Malay culture (Nagata 1974:335). Nagata, however, found that the ethnic interaction among these different communities was marked by tremendous fluidity and modifiability in various social contexts. In some situations, people descended from the Arab or Indian Muslims considered themselves Malay and at other times classified themselves as Arabs or Indians. Thus, the Islamic religious tradition was used to unify their ethnic identity in some circumstances, while other traits were utilized to distinguish themselves from others. Nagata found that the variances in self-categorization were dependent on whether individuals wanted to express social solidarity or distance from one another, or to expedite social or political benefits, or a consideration of social status. For example, in some contexts, Arabs would claim higher ritual purity by referring to their ancestors associated with the "Holy Land" versus the lower impure status of "Malays."

At the same time, some "primordial" features of ethnicity were used to demarcate boundaries among various groups. Nagata found that people distinguish between different types of Muslims: Arabs, Indian, and a variety of groups from Indonesia. In addition, some Chinese Muslims who lived in George Town had intermarried with Malay and had adopted Malay culture, including dress, diet, and other norms. These Chinese Muslims were not considered Malay. Usually Malays revert to the racialistic term *bangsa* to refer to these Chinese Muslims. In this case a commonality of religion and culture does not become a primordial charter for ethnicity. Thus, Nagata found that some ethnic traits have become primordialized for identity purposes, but others do not. Regardless of religious and cultural practices, the notions of race (*bangsa*) would enter into Malay discourse when discussing Chinese Muslims. Thus, in some contexts, the building blocks of ethnicity appear to be based on irreducible givens, whereas in other situations group economic, social, and political interests result in permutations of ethnic identity.

Another dimension of ethnicity and religion that Nagata (1984) emphasizes has to do with the emergence of Islamic revitalization in Malaysia. During the 1970s, an Islamic movement known as *dakwah* (Islamic revival) developed in Malaysia, primarily among young Malays who had moved from rural areas into the cities and were adapting to the new demands of education and modernist developments. The *dakwah* movement led to an increasing emphasis on religious ritual, mosque and religious school attendance, the introduction of Arabic dress and language, and political Islamic themes.

Despite the fact that Islam is perceived as a universal religion that is antithetical to racism, nationalism, and parochial identities, the *dakwah* movement has tended to be bound with the ethnic identity of "Malayness." Though the religious leaders espouse the universality of Islam in their discourse, the reality of ethnic politics and ethnic categorization constrains this universalism in Malaysia.

The *dakwah* movement tends to concentrate on the Malay community, and tends to be associated with the politics of that ethnic bloc. Even though some Chinese convert to Islam, as a means of assimilating to Malay culture, they are not integrated within the Malay ethnic community. Islamic religious revitalization has exacerbated the ethnic divisions among the Malay, Indian, and Chinese populations in Malaysia. Additionally, religious revitalization has been developing among the Chinese (Buddhist and Christian) and Indian (Hindu), which tends to reinforce ethnic segmentation and polarization. The overtly pro-Malay and pro-Islamic programs of the Malaysian government have revived apprehensions among the non-Malay communities. Whether Malaysia can adopt a more tolerant civic form of nationhood that will provide the basis for a multiethnic society is a challenge for the future.

CONCLUSION

Throughout the region of South, East, and Southeast Asia are found indigenous concepts similar to notions of race emphasizing the intimate connections between biology and culture. Following contact with Western countries, the pseudoscientific concept of race was incorporated and synthesized with earlier native conceptions. These concepts of race were promoted by the different governments, both colonial and postcolonial, to distinguish among various ethnic majorities and minorities. These concepts of race persist, perpetuating specific patterns of ethnic interaction and dynamics throughout Asia. Presently in Asia many different ethnic and cultural traditions are colliding with the rapid process of globalization. Globalization is disrupting the traditional values and practices within the region. In some cases, the overall reaction is to revert to a nostalgic past in which the traditional ethnic or "racial" community, the extended family, and other communal practices provide sustenance. This reaction has at times led to tensions among ethnic groups. Continuing ethnographic research is needed to help people understand each other's traditions as one major step in helping to reduce these tensions.

Notes

1. The indigenous Indian tradition was not immune to considerations of skin color and the classification of different peoples. In one classic work, the *Mahabhasya*, the people of northern India are "fair," those of eastern India are "dusky," those of the south are "dark," and those of the west are "pale, yellowish-white." The people of the central areas are mixed. But these "folk" constructions of peoples by skin color were not the basis of any type of scientific objective notion of race (Trautmann 1997).

2. The Indian caste system is not the only social structure that connects birth with status and rank. As we saw in Chapter 2, the Greek philosophers maintained similar ideas regarding the relationship between inheritance of different types of souls and "essences." This type of classification, based on the idea of inherited blood, essences, and humors, continued to influence many people during the medieval period in Western society, and resulted in simplified stereotypes of behavior and temperaments of people around the world. In the medieval period it was accepted that there was a "Great Chain of Being," which posited natural essential categories based on a hierarchy established by God and nature. Thus, the social differences among aristocrats and serfs were purportedly based on innate biological characteristics and birth.

3. The Sikhs were not the only people used for military and strategic purposes by the British. Lionel Caplan (1995) discusses how the British classified the Gurkhas of Nepal as a "martial," "warlike," "masculine" "race," and recruited

them into the Indian army. This nineteenth-century racial essentialistic discourse about the Gurkhas has had very real economic and political effects for these people.

4. For a thorough summary of the literature and history of the Sri Lankan ethnic conflicts, see Chapter 3 in Jack Eller's *From Culture to Ethnicity to Conflict: An Anthropological Perspective on International Ethnic Conflict* (Ann Arbor, MI: University of Michigan Press, 1999).

References Cited

ASKEW, MARC. 2007. *Conspiracy, Politics, and a Disorderly Border: The Struggle to Comprehend Insurgency in Thailand's Deep South.* Policy Studies 29. Washington, DC: East-West Center Washington.

———. 2009. "Landscapes of fear, horizons of trust: Villagers dealing with danger in Thailand's insurgent south." *Journal of Southeast Asian Studies* 40(1):59–86.

BARMÈ, SCOTT. 1993. *Luang Wichit Wathakan and the Creation of a Thai Identity.* Singapore: Institute of Southeast Asian Studies.

BAYLY, SUSAN. 1995. Caste and "race" in the colonial ethnography of India. In *The Concept of Race in South Asia.* Peter Robb, ed. Pp. 165–218. Delhi: Oxford University Press.

CAPLAN, LIONEL. 1995. Martial Gurkhas: The persistence of a British military discourse on "race." In *The Concept of Race in South Asia.* Peter Robb, ed. Delhi: Oxford University Press.

DANIEL, VALENTINE E. 1983. Conclusion: Karma, the uses of an idea. In *Karma: An Anthropological Inquiry.* Charles F. Keyes and Valentine Daniel, eds. Pp. 287–300. Berkeley, CA: University of California Press.

———. 1997. *Charred Lullabies: Chapters in an Anthropography of Violence.* Princeton, NJ: Princeton University Press.

DEVOS, GEORGE, and WILLIAM WETHERHALL. 1983. *Japan's Minorities: Burakumin, Koreans, and Ainu.* New York: Minority Rights Group.

DIAMOND, JARED. 1998. Japanese roots. *Discover*, June, pp. 86–94.

DIKÖTTER, FRANK. 1992. *The Discourse of Race in Modern China.* Stanford, CA: Stanford University Press.

———, ed. 1997. *The Construction of Racial Identities in China and Japan: Historical and Contemporary Perspectives.* Honolulu, HI: University of Hawaii Press.

———. 2008. The racialization of the globe: An interactive interpretation. *Ethnic and Racial Studies* 28(4):1–19.

DUBREIL, CHISATO. 2007. The Ainu and their culture: A twenty-first century assessment. *Japan Focus*, November 26.

DUMONT, LOUIS. 1970. *Homo Hierarchicus: An Essay on the Caste System.* Mark Sainsburg, trans. Chicago, IL: University of Chicago Press.

FOX, RICHARD G. 1985. *Lions of the Punjab: Culture in the Making.* Berkeley, CA: University of California Press.

GLADNEY, DRU C. 1991. *Muslim Chinese: Ethnic Nationalism in the People's Republic.* Cambridge, MA: Harvard University Press.

———. 1998. *Ethnic Identity in China: The Making of a Muslim Minority Nationality.* Orlando, FL: Harcourt Brace.

HEFNER, ROBERT W., ed. 1998. *Market Cultures: Society and Morality in the New Asian Capitalisms.* Boulder, CO: Westview Press.

HIRSCHMAN, CHARLES. 1987. The meaning and measurement of ethnicity in Malaysia: An analysis of census classifications. *Journal of Asian Studies* 46(3):555–582.

INDEN, RONALD. 1990. *Imagining India.* Oxford: Oxford University Press.

JAFFRELOT, CHRISTOPHE. 1995. The ideas of the Hindu race in the writings of Hindu nationalist ideologues in the 1920s and 1930s: A concept between two cultures. In *The Concept of Race in South Asia.* Peter Robb, ed. Pp. 327–352. Delhi: Oxford University Press.

JERRYSON, MICHAEL. 2009. Appropriating a space for violence: State Buddhism in southern Thailand. *Journal of Southeast Asian Studies* 40(1):33–57.

KAPFERER, BRUCE. 1988. *Legends of People, Myths of State: Violence, Intolerance, and Political Culture in Sri Lanka and Australia.* Washington, DC: Smithsonian Institution Press.

KLASS, MORTON. 1997. *Caste: The Emergence of the South Asian Social System.* Prospect Heights, IL: Waveland Press.

LIOW, JOSEPH CHINYONG. 2007. *Muslim Resistance in Southern Thailand and Southern Phillipines: Religion, Ideology, and Politics.* Policy Studies

24. Washington, DC: East-West Center Washington.

MACKIE, JAMIE. 1998. Business success among Southeast Asian Chinese: The role of culture, values, and social structures. In *Market Cultures: Society and Morality in the New Asian Capitalisms.* Robert Hefner, ed. Pp. 129–146. Boulder, CO: Westview Press.

McCARGO, DUNCAN, ed. 2007. *Rethinking Thailand's Southern Violence.* Singapore: NUS Press.

———. 2008. *Tearing Apart the Land: Islam and Legitimacy in Southern Thailand.* Ithaca, NY: Cornell University Press.

———. 2009. Thai Buddhism, Thai Buddhists and the southern conflict. *Journal of Southeast Asian Studies* 40(1):1–10.

MILNER, ANTHONY. 1998. Ideological work in constructing the Malay majority. In *Making Majorities: Constituting the Nation in Japan, Korea, China, Malaysia, Fiji, Turkey, and the United States.* Dru C. Gladney, ed. Pp. 151–172. Stanford, CA: Stanford University Press.

NAGATA, JUDITH A. 1974. What is a Malay? Situational selections of ethnic identity in a plural society. *American Ethnologist* 1(2):331–350.

———. 1981. In defense of ethnic boundaries: The changing myths and charters of Malay identity. In *Ethnic Change.* Charles F. Keyes, ed. Pp. 88–116. Seattle, WA: University of Washington Press.

———. 1984. *The Reflowering of Malaysian Islam: Modern Religious Radicals and Their Roots.* Vancouver: University of British Columbia Press.

NORTON, JAMES H. K. 1999. *India and South Asia.* 4th edition. Guilford, CT: Dushkin/McGraw Hill.

OHNUKI-TIERNEY, EMIKO. 1987. *The Monkey as Mirror: Symbolic Transformations in Japanese History and Ritual.* Princeton, NJ: Princeton University Press.

———. 1998. A conceptual model for the historical relationship between the self and the internal and external others: The agrarian Japanese, the Ainu, and the special-status people. In *Making Majorities: Constituting the Nation in Japan, Korea, China, Malaysia, Fiji, Turkey, and the United States.* Dru C. Gladney, ed. Pp. 31–54. Stanford, CA: Stanford University Press.

PITSUWAN, SURIN. 1985. *Islam and Malay Nationalism: A Case Study of the Malay-Muslims of Southern Thailand.* Bangkok: Thai Kadai Research Institute.

POTTER, DAVID, and PAUL KNEPPER. 1998. Comparing official definitions of race in Japan and the United States. In *The Social Construction of Race and Ethnicity in the United States.* Joan Ferrante and Prince Brown, Jr., eds. Pp. 139–156. New York: Longman Press.

SCUPIN, RAYMOND. 1998. Muslim accommodation in Thailand. *Journal of Islamic Studies* 9(2):229–258.

SJOBERG, KATARINA. 1993. *The Return of the Ainu.* Switzerland: Harwood Academic Publishing.

SPENCER, JONATHAN, ed. 1990. *Sri Lanka: History and Roots of Conflict.* London: Routledge.

TAMBIAH, STANLEY. 1986. *Sri Lanka: Ethnic Fratricide and the Dismantling of Democracy.* Chicago, IL: University of Chicago Press.

———. 1992. *Buddhism Betrayed: Religion, Politics, and Violence in Sri Lanka.* Chicago, IL: University of Chicago Press.

THOMAS, LADD. 1975. *Political Violence in the Muslim Provinces of Southern Thailand.* Singapore: Institute of Southeast Asian Studies.

TRAUTMANN, THOMAS R. 1997. *Aryans and British India.* Berkeley, CA: University of California Press.

VELLA, WALTER F. 1978. *Chaiyo! King Vajiravudh and the Development of Thai Nationalism.* Honolulu, HI: University Press of Hawaii.

WADE, GEOFF. 2009. The origins and evolution of Ethnocracy in Malaysia. *The Asia-Pacific Journal* 47(4), November 23.

WEHRFRITZ, GEORGE, and HIDEKO TAKAYAMA. June 5, 2000. The Japan that can say yes. *Newsweek*, pp. 34–35.

WEINER, MICHAEL. 1997. The invention of identity: Race and nation in pre-war Japan. In *The Construction of Racial Identities in China and Japan: Historical and Contemporary Perspectives.* Frank Dikötter, ed. Pp. 96–117. Honolulu, HI: University of Hawaii Press.

WINICHAKUL, THONGCHAI. 1994. *Siam Mapped: A History of the Geo-Body of a Nation.* Honolulu, HI: University of Hawaii Press.

YOSHINO, KOSAKU. 1992. *Cultural Nationalism in Contemporary Japan: A Sociological Inquiry.* London: Routledge.

———. 1998. Culturalism, racialism, and internationalism in the discourse on Japanese identity. In *Making Majorities: Constituting the Nation in Japan, Korea, China, Malaysia, Fiji, Turkey, and the United States.* Dru C. Gladney, ed. Pp. 13–30. Stanford, CA: Stanford University Press.

17

■■■

Europe

Pamela Ballinger, *Bowdoin College*

This chapter examines race and ethnicity in Europe, situating contemporary understandings in broad historical processes of state building, ethnic and nationalist movements, and colonialism. We first look at the historical diversity of nationalist movements in Europe and their associated ideas of ethnic and racial identity; the types of nationalism explored range from romantic, national liberation movements in the nineteenth century to the Nazi race regime and state socialist experiments in multiethnic federalism in the twentieth century. We then consider two cases that demonstrate the close and sometimes explosive relationship between religious and ethnic identities, those of Northern Ireland and the former Yugoslavia (with a focus on Bosnia-Herzegovina). In both examples, violent conflict reflects the interplay between long-standing tensions and new challenges confronting Europe after the cold war and the integration of the European Union (EU).

Whereas the EU implies a model of inclusion designed to overcome the ethnic and nationalist hatreds that ravaged Europe with two bloody world wars in the last century, a European identity also appears to exclude many "nonwhite" immigrants, as well as those peoples from Eastern Europe whose states remain outside of the EU. How are notions of "European" identity changing, and how can we understand a pan-European identity in terms of ethnicity, and race? What is the relationship among "culture," ethnicity, and race in the "old" and "new" Europes? Answering such questions illuminates the differences, as well as the similarities, between European societies and the United States as they struggle to build multicultural polities in a globalized world.

THE IDEA OF EUROPE AND THE IDEA OF NATION

Notions of race and ethnicity in contemporary Europe cannot be understood without reference to ideologies of nationhood, commonly said to have originated in Europe in the eighteenth and nineteenth centuries (see Chapter 4). The broad historical circumstances in which nationalism came to the fore as a political ideology included the European conquest of much of the world and the Industrial Revolution, both of which reflected and facilitated the creation of centralized states and bureaucracies. As a result, peoples living within what we today call Europe began to view themselves as "Europeans," as well as members of a specific nation or state.

From Christians to Europeans

The very notion of "Europe" was made possible by radical transformations from the fifteenth century onward. Inhabitants of medieval Europe typically identified either at a narrow, local level, on kinship lines (genealogies, dynasties) or as part of a religious community. Prior to the Protestant schism, to be a Christian in Europe generally meant to view oneself as part of a universal, religious kingdom. (This held true despite the split between Catholicism and Orthodox Christianity in 1054, which followed the division between the Western and Eastern halves of the old Roman Empire.) In the Christian mind, the world was made up of Christians and infidels; in theory, then, any pagan could join the Christian community through a process of religious conversion. This understanding built upon an older worldview that distinguished citizens of the Roman Empire (as well as the earlier Greek polities; see Chapter 4) from so-called "barbarians," who nonetheless might potentially become Romans. Such perspectives contrast sharply with modern understandings of ethnicity and, above all, "race," in which one is said to be literally born into a community and where identity does not prove a matter of choice.

The medieval division of the world into Christians/pagans had already begun to change even before "Europeans" ventured out in transoceanic sailing ships to encounter other peoples. The geographic expansion of Christian states followed upon the humanistic rediscovery of the ancient Greek and Roman past, which had been largely forgotten, condemned, or misunderstood during the medieval period. Just as the explorers encountered strange peoples separated from Europeans in space, the humanists discovered exotic peoples (the ancient Greeks and Romans) separated from Europeans in time. Eventually, the Greeks and Romans were embraced as "ancestors" who laid the foundations of Europe. From this dual encounter in time and space, there emerged a notion of being "European" that built upon and yet reconfigured the older Christian–pagan distinction. The label "Europe" stood for a geographic space, as well as a moral entity, distinguished from a host of other peoples and ways of life (Chabod 1991). These other peoples eventually came to be understood as belonging to diverse nations (*nationes*, from the Latin *natio*) and races.

The purity of this emerging European identity had to be policed from within, as well as from without. Internal "others," like the Jews and Moors (Muslims), were increasingly recognized as alien and expelled from various parts of the European continent, most notably from the Iberian Peninsula with the *Reconquista* of 1492. The timing of this violence coincides with Columbus's first voyage to the New World, further underlining the ways in which the consolidation of forms of European and national identity went hand in hand with the identification, labeling, and frequent persecution of "racial" and religious "others." The brutality of the Iberian reconquest prefigured the tragic genocide carried out in the New World, whereby Spanish violence, enslavement, and other harsh labor policies and diseases decimated native populations.

As Spain and other European powers carved out empires in the New World in the sixteenth and seventeenth centuries, fierce debates ensued over the policies to be adopted toward native populations and over how to classify such peoples (and, by extension, oneself). When Europeans first encountered different plants, animals, and peoples, they sought to incorporate them into their traditional classification systems (Todorov 1987). No matter how exotic or odd other peoples appeared to such Europeans, for Christians all men were thought to be descendants of a common ancestor (Adam) and thus fundamentally the same (Hodgen 1963:386–426). Yet not all Europeans were heterodox Christians, or even believers at all; indeed, the secularizing impulse of Renaissance humanism created a space for questioning an older view of the universe centered on the notion of a "Great Chain of Being" linking the divine to the most minute forms of life. Thus, when European conquistadors, missionaries, traders, and scholars encountered other peoples in the New World, Africa, and Asia, their responses were not uniform.

One reaction was to view other peoples in terms of devolution. This understanding followed out of a traditional Christian belief that Man, perfect at his creation, had subsequently been exposed to different environments after his expulsion from the perfect and balanced climate of the Garden of Eden. These different climates not only modified Man's temperament (thereby explaining cultural diversity) but also led to his degeneration or devolution (Hodgen 1963). According to this theory, peoples like the American Indians could be seen as the most degraded and hence in need of European administration. An opposing but related view held that these natives were the least degenerated of peoples and thus in their childlike and pure state required protection from the corrupting influences of the European colonizers. The French philosopher Jean Jacques Rousseau would later reformulate and secularize this idea as that of the "noble savage."

Others, however, began to question that all these peoples had a common ancestor or even their basic humanity. Some thinkers suggested that these populations represented either a transitional form between Man and other animals or a type of human very far removed from modern European Man. This shift was accompanied by a new interest in taxonomy and "scientific" classification, what became known as natural history. Though Carolus Linnaeus, the founder of modern taxonomic systems, continued to believe that species were immutable or fixed (as given by God), contemporaries like Comte de Buffon suggested that change could occur between forms. In the nineteenth century, the seeds of such thought would blossom into a fully developed theory of biological evolution that profoundly challenged traditional religious worldviews.

The traditional Christian perspective viewed not only species but also history as fixed, with time unfolding toward a preordained end point (the Last Judgment). From the eighteenth century onward, however, this view of sacred history increasingly gave way to a secular understanding of history and a search for general laws governing the development of society and culture. New forms of classification—given tangible form in encyclopedias and museums—broke with medieval and Renaissance systems of arrangement according to outward resemblance or "similitude" and instead sought to organize things from simple to complex. This entailed a shift from seeing Man's development in terms of devolution to viewing it as a process of (social) evolution.

With the secularization of older, Christian views of sacred history, time now became something standardized, marked out on a clock. This reflected not just Enlightenment philosophizing but the beginnings of industrialization in Europe, which profoundly altered individuals' rhythms and sense of identity and belonging. The peasant-turned-factory-worker now measured time by the clock (punching in and out) rather than by the position of the sun in his field (Thompson 1967). Changing understandings of time, together with what Benedict Anderson (1987) calls "print capitalism"—the development of the printing press and the subsequent spread of the printed word—helped create new senses of community and belonging (see also the discussion in Chapter 4).

Our having just seen how "(white) Europeans" began to identify themselves as such in relation to other populations of the globe, Anderson's discussion helps us to understand how Europeans simultaneously came to differentiate themselves in ethnic and national terms from their more immediate neighbors. The advent of print capitalism made possible the proliferation of books and newspapers in vernacular, or local, languages. Now that writings were widely available in, say, French or Spanish rather than Latin, the reading public greatly increased. This helped create a sense of identification, for example, between French-speakers as a group as opposed to Spanish-speakers and also served as a vehicle for elites interested in welding diverse local dialects into one "national" language, like French.

Anderson cites the newspaper as a primary means by which such "national" identities were created. He suggests that the newspaper also fostered a new sense of time: that of simultaneity.

Each reader of the paper knows that many others are reading the same news at the same moment. Even if the reader will never meet most of these fellow newspaper consumers, he or she has a sense of what Anderson deems an "imagined community" of readers. Since the nineteenth century, this community has been imagined primarily in terms of the nation. According to Anderson, the idea of the sovereign nation that embodies the will of the people ultimately supplanted the older understanding of a "universal" kingdom of God. As we shall see in subsequent sections, this did not mean that religious identities lost all salience in Europe. Religion, ethnicity, race, and nationhood continue to intersect in dramatic and sometimes tragic ways. Let us now untangle the complicated intersections in Europe of the ideas of nation, ethnicity, and race.

The Idea of Nation

Although the idea of the nation is thoroughly modern, it drew upon older understandings about people and place (Kedourie 1993; Kohn 1965, 1967). The word *nation* derives from the Latin *natio* ("to be born"), suggesting a sense of naturalness rooted in time immemorial (Verdery 1993). Not surprisingly, the nationalist movements that arose in early modern Europe often drew upon traditional symbols, at times using them to confer authenticity on "invented" national histories, heroes, and rituals. One famous example is that of the coronation ceremonies associated with the British monarchs. Though seemingly age-old, ceremonies like that for the coronation of England's Queen Victoria were newly minted but nonetheless suffused with an antique air (Cannadine 1983).

Other traditions that became part of a "national heritage" included folk poetry and songs. In some instances, these poems were fabricated by scholars and presented as newly discovered ancient traditions, as in the case of the Ossian poems "recovered" by the Scottish scholar James Macpherson. In many cases, traditional folk forms were edited and selected by scholars (most famously, the Grimm brothers) in a creative process of reworking (Cocchiara 1952; Ellis

1963). The intense interest in these popular traditions proved one of the enduring legacies of the Romantic movement in philosophy and art. Broadly speaking, Romanticism proved a response to the Enlightenment faith in reason and progress. Belief in the perfectibility of Man and society had been profoundly shaken by the events of the French Revolution in which the cult of reason and liberty ultimately descended into tyranny. The dehumanization and degradation of Man wrought by the Industrial Revolution further disillusioned a generation of intellectuals. Romanticism exalted emotion, irrationality, and the sublime together with those things rejected by Enlightenment thinkers: the "primitive," the folk, and the past.

For the development of romantic nationalism in Europe, among the most outstanding intellectual figures are Jean Jacques Rousseau (1712–1778) and Johann Gottfried Herder (1744–1803). Skeptical of the Enlightenment's universal histories, search for laws, and belief in an ever better society, the French philosopher Rousseau instead valorized the simple and the "primitive" (i.e., the noble savage). He also addressed himself to broad questions of sovereignty (expressed in the "general will" of the people) and the specific issue of the Polish nation. Like those philosophers he criticized, however, Rousseau proved less interested in the way of life of actual "savages" than in the figure or metaphor of the savage. Rousseau used this image of the pure native uncorrupted by the conceits of society in order to critique the contemporary European societies around him.

In contrast to Rousseau, Herder's interest in the primitive extended to studying the actual examples he found at hand in contemporary Europe. Primarily a philologist (scholar of language), in later life Herder stressed the diversity of culture (*kultur*). He argued that each people, or *volk*, had a unique history and cultural development, which resulted from the interaction of the environment and the innate creative spirit or genius of a people. According to Herder, this genius was expressed in folk arts, in particular folk poetry and songs. Herder dedicated himself to collecting such folk traditions, especially among the Slavic peoples of southeastern Europe,

and encouraged other scholars to engage in hands-on fieldwork (Barnard 1965, 1969; Herder 1966, 1968).

Herder's insistence that culture could best be understood through ethnological work, rather than from the comfortable armchair of the philosopher in his salon, constitutes an important precedent for later anthropological practice. Herder also contributed to anthropology the idea that cultures were plural and that each culture must be studied with respect and in relation to its own unique development. These ideas come into American cultural anthropology in a fairly direct fashion (though a century after Herder) through the work of German-born Franz Boas, the "father of American anthropology" (Duden 1989).

Scholars like E. B. Tylor incorporated Herder's focus on popular traditions into the British tradition of social anthropology (Cocchiara 1952:392). Tylor not only contributed to the nascent discipline of anthropology an influential definition of culture but also founded the field of folklore studies in Britain. Although the role played by anthropologists in studying colonial populations and creating racial and ethnic hierarchies has received considerable attention in the last 30 years, the similar involvement of anthropologists in nation-building projects within Europe has been underexplored (Herzfeld 1987). Anthropology proved just as significant to the articulation of ethnic and national differences within Europe as to those distinctions between Europeans and other peoples. Though folklore studies only developed in the late nineteenth century in Great Britain, for example, they blossomed in continental Europe in the second half of the eighteenth century as a result of the researches of Herder and his disciples.

Folklore quickly became wedded to nation- and state-building projects, particularly in the multiethnic Hapsburg Empire. This occurred despite Herder's own rejection of the idea that a people (*volk*) proved synonymous with a state (*staat*) or territory. Herder also denounced *ethnocentrism*, the idea that one people proved superior to another. He did, however, believe in the Slavs' particular mission to regenerate Europe, a theme picked up by intellectuals who identified with their respective Slavic ethnic groups.

Slavic-speaking groups (including Czechs, Slovaks, Poles, Slovenes, Serbs, and Croats) constituted the majority of the peoples dominated by the German-speaking Austrian Hapsburgs. Other sizable populations included Hungarian Magyars, as well as Italians and Romanians speaking Romance languages derived from Latin. Vienna, the cosmopolitan capital of this multiethnic empire, became the center for both Slavicist and folklore studies under the Czech scholar Abbé Josif Dobrovski and his student, the Slovene Jernej Kopitar. As subject peoples within the empire began to demand autonomy or independence, the revival of folk traditions underwrote emerging senses of belonging to a nation or people. In most Slavic languages, the word *narod* stands for both "nation" and "people," blurring the distinctions between the two that exist in English and Romance languages. The view that the boundaries of a territorial state must coincide with the *narod* or *volk* (the people or ethnic group)—that is, nation = ethnic group—may have as its extreme consequences the removal of those populations who do not belong to the "national"/ethnic group.

The ambiguities created by this understanding of nation as ethnic group are illustrated by the view of Serbian identity put forward by the folklorist and philologist Vuk Karadžić. Encouraged by Kopitar, Karadžić began in 1814 and 1815 to record the epic folk songs of Serbian peasants, such as those of the Kosovo cycle, detailing the Serbs' legendary defeat by the Ottoman Turks in 1389 on the Field of Blackbirds in Kosovo (Wachtel 1998:32). These traditions had been preserved both by the (Serbian) Orthodox church and the folk singers who recounted the ballads to the accompaniment of the one-stringed instrument known as the *gusle*. In collecting these folk traditions, Karadžić helped codify the Serbian language, publishing a Serbian grammar and dictionary in 1814 and 1818, respectively (p. 26). The Serbian tongue, however, proved similar to other Slavic variants, such as Bulgarian and Croatian. Thus, when Karadžić declared that "Serbia is wherever Serbian is spoken," he included as Serbs those individuals whom others might identify as Bulgarians or Croats. Karadžić's work helped foster a sense of Serbian identity, which both reflected and contributed to the struggle for an independent Serbian state. The Serbs attained complete autonomy within the Ottoman Empire by 1830 and formal independence in 1878.

In roughly the same period, there arose in the Hapsburg lands the South Slav, or Yugoslav (Jugo or Yugo means "south"), movement whose intellectual proponents understood Karadžić's researches in a more inclusive manner. The Yugoslav idea had its origins in the 1830s with the cultural movement known as Illyrianism. Although various understandings of Yugoslavism competed, and some peoples (like the Bulgarians) were at times included or excluded as Yugoslavs, its advocates agreed that a South Slav cultural and linguistic unity existed and should be recognized by a corresponding Yugoslav political unit. Scholars worked to codify a standard language of this cultural expression, Serbo-Croatian (which took the Štokavian dialect as its base). For proponents of Yugoslavism, then, those traditions of epic poetry that Karadžić saw as mapping out a distinctly Serbian nation instead characterized a broader South Slav unity (pp. 38–45). Yugoslavists similarly interpreted lyric poetic forms common to Catholic "Slovenes" and "Croats" as South Slav cultural expressions, whereas for anti-Serbian nationalists like Ante Starčević and Josip Frank all South Slavic culture (and peoples) were instead "really" Croatian. Politically, these various forms of identity (i.e., Serbian, Croatian, and Yugoslav) have coexisted for more than a century, at times proving compatible and at other times mutually exclusive, depending on the form of statehood envisioned and the imagined relationship between ethnic identity and nationhood. This example reveals how the same ostensible past and folk tradition can be understood in very different ways. In the course of the Yugoslav wars in the 1990s, the insistence that territory and ethnic group coincide culminated in the policy known as "ethnic cleansing," whose tragic results we will examine later.

"Old" and "New" Nations: States before Nations, Nations before States

In considering the historical development of nationalism in what we today call "Eastern" and "Western" Europe, scholars often distinguish between the romantic, *Volkish* nationalism common to the area of the Hapsburg and Ottoman empires (as in the Serbian case) and the liberal, civic nationalism of the type associated with the French Revolution or the Italian Risorgimento (Gellner 1987; Hobsbawm 1990). Sometimes this distinction is rephrased as that of nation understood as ethnicity versus nation as citizenship (Verdery 1993); on this, see also Chapter 4. Other scholars map onto these types of nationalism different understandings of citizenship such as *jus sanguinis*, with belonging based on blood and ethnic group (as in Germany), and *jus soli*, based on common political participation (as in France) (Brubaker 1992). However scholars label the distinction, basically they contrast a "bad" nationalism, which confuses nation and ethnic group, to a "good" (or better) nationalism, which envisions the nation as a political community and hence as something more than an ethnic group.

At the most general level, these distinctions help us delineate the different experiences of nation-state building in Europe. These categories highlight, for example, the challenges faced by national independence movements in the nineteenth century where a sense of belonging to an ethnic or national group often underwrote demands for a state. This contrasts with the experience of the so-called old states and nations, like France and England. Here, political dynasties consolidated and centralized power relatively early. Inhabitants of these polities initially identified themselves as subjects of the Crown more than as French or English (Breuilly 1985:44–82). Over several centuries, centralized institutions like the bureaucracy, educational system, and army served to make "peasants into Frenchmen" (for France, see Weber 1976; on Britain, Corrigan and Sayer 1985).

Certainly, the long-term process of building national identities in centralized states/monarchies, like those of Britain and France, contrasts with those national liberation movements, often inspired by the French Revolution, which quite literally had to build states (together with educational systems and militaries) overnight. Yet scholars now recognize that the process of state building in supposedly "old" nations took much longer than previously believed, was always incomplete, and was accompanied by considerable violence (much of it now conveniently forgotten). Furthermore, the assumption that in many parts of Eastern Europe "nation" came before "state" needs to be tempered. Certainly, for *volk*-minded intellectuals like Vuk Karadžić, "nation" did exist before state. There usually exists a significant difference, however, between the sentiments of the well educated and the peasants whose culture the intellectuals codified and then exalted.

Recent historical work also reveals that in cases like those of the Serbian and Greek revolutions, where a sense of nationhood inspired intellectuals in their fight against the Ottoman Empire, considerable time and effort were nonetheless required to build a sense of national identity *after* the achievement of independent states (Herzfeld 1982; Kitromilides 1989). "Serbs" or "Greeks" thus had to be made in a similar manner to "French" or "English," although in considerably less time. This suggests that, while useful in some ways, the distinction between states before nations and nations before states should not be exaggerated. To do so takes the rhetoric of romantic nationalists—that the nation has awoken and must find its expression in a political state—at face value.

Overstating such differences may also lead us to neglect the many similarities between processes of identity formation in both "Eastern" and "Western" Europe, wrongly seeing nationalism in the East as something destructive or violent (at least potentially) in contrast to nationalism in the West. The complicated process of Italian unification illustrates some of the dangers in overdrawing these distinctions. Scholars often describe the Risorgimento, the movement that led to the creation of an Italian state in 1861, as an example of a civic or liberal (i.e., Western-style) nationalism. Unification movements such as that in Italy are typically thought to have put a "political roof over a culture (and over an economy)" (Gellner 1987:99) in a benign manner far removed from the messiness of Central and Eastern Europe, where extreme ethnic diversity and the lack of a crystallized national culture necessitated brutality in the attempt to render state and nation congruent.

Undeniably, a sense of Italianness did exist among intellectuals, despite the Italian peninsula's political division. The metaphor of a resurgence or reawakening implied by the term *Risorgimento* and the battle cry "Italy, awake!" reflected the deeply romantic impulse of much Italian nationalism (particularly in the thoughts of Giuseppe Mazzini and Giuseppe Garibaldi). This contrasted, however, with the reality of widespread linguistic diversity and extremely localized identities. Indeed, after the Italian state's establishment as a constitutional monarchy, its leaders recognized the necessity to "make Italians."

Although Italy has often been deemed an ethnically homogeneous state (at least until recent immigration), in fact there were ethnically different "others" (in addition to the division between northern and southern Italians, which in everyday life is often posited as a racial difference) who posed a problem to the project of "making Italians." The 1866 war between Austria and Italy, which brought the provinces of Veneto and Friuli into the new Italian state, for example, also incorporated a sizable population of Slovenes located in the Valli di Natisone. Many of these Slovenes assumed that the new Italian state would extend to them the same administrative, judicial, and linguistic "autonomy" they had once enjoyed under the Venetian Republic (Clavora and Ruttar 1990:13). This expectation soon proved mistaken, however, as the Italian state undertook a deliberate policy of Italianization.

An 1866 newspaper article outlined this policy: "These Slavs need to be eliminated, by means of benefits, progress and civility. We will adopt the language and culture of a dominant civilization, that of Italian civilization, in order to Italianize the Slavs in Italy" (cf. Clavora 1988:7). In the twentieth century, the Fascist regime continued and intensified such policies, which were bound up with Italian desires for coastal territories inhabited by Slovenes and Croats. In Italian frontier areas, anti-Slav chauvinism proved strong, and still does today, in border cities like Trieste. Such chauvinism speaks a language of both ethnicity and race, as suggested by an 1884 article in a Triestine newspaper. Entitled "A Microbe," the article compared the Slovenes to a "barbaric" African people, the Hottentots.

Such comments, together with the experience of minorities like the Slovenes, point up what might be called the myth of Italy's lack of racism (examined in the next section), as well as the often idealized image of Italy's benign process of state formation. Though we should not go too far in the other direction in viewing Italian unification as particularly brutal, we should be aware that the processes of nation and state building in "Western" and "Eastern" Europe are not as different or unrelated as scholars have sometimes made them out to be. Indeed, contrasting Western nationalisms to Eastern nationalisms represents one means by which negative images of Eastern Europe (and Eastern European ethnic groups) are perpetuated. As we shall see in the final section, currently such images work to exclude some East European peoples from the very definition of "European."

In understanding ethnic and racial identities in Europe, the distinction between old and new nationalisms proves somewhat more helpful than does that between Western and Eastern nationalisms. Not only did states like France and England have more time in which to build national identities out of diverse ethnic and regional identifications than did those like Italy or Serbia, these long-standing states also developed a sense of nationhood in tandem with colonial empires. In contrast, newer nation-states like Italy and Serbia were formed *out of* imperial structures. Yet, as nineteenth-century European national-imperial discourses developed in tandem with bourgeois notions of respectability and normality, the imperial experience shaped interrelated identities—those of ethnicity, race, nationality, and gender—within *and between* the European metropole and colony, as well as between the European core and its internal peripheries. Racial classifications based on supposed signs of deviance (such as certain skull shapes or noses) reveal a direct link between how internal European "others"—including Jews, Gypsies, prostitutes, and homosexuals—and colonial subjects were differentiated by means of a shared vocabulary of criminality and medical hygiene (Gilman 1985; Mosse 1985). This racialized language of "otherness," derived in part from the colonial experience, proves central to the discourses and practices of nationalism, even in those European countries like Italy and Germany that achieved statehood late and lacked significant empires. The next section explores the interpenetration of racial, national, and militaristic ideologies for German Nazism and Italian Fascism.

reminds us that the potential for genocide cannot be neatly circumscribed to a particular time, place, or culture (like Hitler's Germany).

In questioning pervasive claims that Germans were culturally predispositioned (by anti-Semitism, authoritarian cultures/personalities, and so on) toward genocide, other historians have countered that anti-Semitism proved pervasive in much of Europe and perhaps was strongest in France rather than Germany. Certainly, the negative associations of Jews with rootless cosmopolitanism, capitalism, and effete decadence had currency throughout much of Europe. The nineteenth-century Italian criminologist Cesare Lombroso even claimed to see in Jewish physiognomies signs of an innate criminality or illness (Gilman 1985:154–157; Mosse 1985:133–147).

Although we cannot hope to definitively answer here the question of the origins of the "final solution" or the degree of complicity of

NATIONALISM AND AUTHORITARIAN REGIMES IN TWENTIETH-CENTURY EUROPE: THE CULMINATION OF NATIONALISM AND RACE?

Nazism and Fascism

Scholars continue to debate the origins of National Socialism and Italian Fascism, the differences between the regimes's racial policies, and the degree of consensus obtained by the regimes among "everyday" Germans and Italians. The "final solution," Hitler's systematic campaign to exterminate the Jews, understandably provokes the most heated discussion. In a controversial book, Daniel Goldhagen argued that the Germans' deep tradition of anti-Semitism made them "Hitler's willing executioners" (1996). Picking up on Hannah Arendt's well-known thesis regarding the "banality of evil," Christopher Browning has instead suggested that the supposedly deeply anti-Semitic, willing executioners who actually carried out massacres of Jews were merely "ordinary men" (1992). Such a view

Adolf Hitler.

ordinary Germans in the Holocaust of the Jews, we can pin down the official ideology of Nazism within which this particular genocide unfolded. Hitler conceived of National Socialism as an anti-Bolshevik revolution. He created a ritual state based on spectacles that invoked Teutonic pagan glories, as with the famous rally at Nürnberg, and ceremonies like the German Harvest Festival and German Summer Solstice. Despite the Nazis' hatred of Jews, the regime proved ambivalent (and at times even hostile) to Christian traditions and sought to reinterpret the meanings attached to Christian holidays like Christmas. Regime folklorists argued that, historically, ethnically German festivals had been Christianized; accordingly, "German" folktales and songs were trotted out to replace Christian ones (Gajek 1990). The regime thus represented this pagan past as a thoroughly German one, a German ethnic or national identity here understood in racial terms as synonymous with "Aryan." Other citizens of the German state, like those who self-identified (or were identified by others) in cultural or religious terms as "Jews," were excluded from this ethnic/racial understanding of German identity.

As part of their program to instill "German pride" after the nation's humiliating defeat in World War I and the economic chaos of the postwar Weimar Republic, Adolf Hitler and other Nazi leaders codified an elaborate racial hierarchy. At its apex were Aryans, at its bottom Jews. Other "deviant" groups included Gypsies (Roma), homosexuals, and Slavic peoples (the so-called "slave races"). The Nazis thus read various ethnic, cultural, religious, and sexual differences as "racial," that is, inherently rooted in biology. The obsessive fear of homosexuality's contamination of the German "race" led to a purge of the SA (storm) troops in 1934 and the murder of its chief, Ernst Röhm; to prevent the military cult of masculinity from degenerating into male–male sex, soldiers were encouraged to seek out female prostitutes (Mosse 1985:157). Aryan women were, in turn, enjoined to produce children and thereby contribute to a healthy (and superior) *volk*, or people, what one scholar has deemed a "racist sexism" (Bock 1984:288).

This racial and sexual hierarchy informed the Nazi policy of negative eugenics, begun as a program of forced sterilization of those individuals with "undesirable" genes: the physically and mentally disabled.[1] Preventing "asocial" and undesirable elements from reproducing constituted the flip side of "racist sexism," that is, "sexist racism" or the prohibition of procreation by racially inferior women (Bock 1984.) The Nazis soon extended their eugenic policies to the Jews. By the time of World War II, Jewish and Gypsy women in Nazi concentration camps were subject to mass sterilizations. The Nazis also forced many women in the conquered eastern territories to submit to sterilization and/or abortions (Bock 1984).

As the preeminent "other," the Jews became subject to discrimination and violence from almost the moment Hitler assumed power as German chancellor in 1933. Pogroms, expropriations, and laws stripped German Jews of their property and rights. The 1935 Nürnberg laws denied German Jews citizenship and forbid intermarriage with "Germans." Any possible contamination by Jews had to be cleansed; the Nazis went so far as to condemn avant-garde art as degenerate due to its association with cosmopolitanism and the "mad" genius of the artist and hence with Jewishness (Gilman 1985:233–237). The infamous "Night of the Broken Glass," or *Kristallnacht*, in 1938 made clear the Nazis' determination to destroy all remnants of Jewish life in Germany; on this one night, Nazi supporters vandalized or destroyed Jewish synagogues, homes, and shops. In the years following *Kristallnacht*, Jews were forced to wear the Star of David as an identifying mark. Hitler announced as his goal the physical removal of Germany's Jewish population and, through psychological and physical intimidation, "encouraged" Jews to emigrate.

From 1936 on, a four-year plan detailed a plan of increasing "living space" (*Lebensraum*) through conquest of territories to the east. Initially, the lands targeted were those with a sizable German-speaking population, which provided the pretext for "unification" with the

German motherland. After 1939, the German master race (*Herrenvolk*) turned its attention to neighboring Slavic lands. This program of war and territorial expansion facilitated the Nazi plan of ridding Germany and, later, the occupied territories of their Jewish populations. Jews were confined to restricted areas (ghettos) or concentration camps where they often died of exhaustion, hunger, or disease. In the territories conquered by the Nazis, SS death squads massacred entire villages of Jews.

At the Wannsee Conference of 1942, Nazi leaders, including SS (black shirts) head Reinhard Heydrich, drew up plans for the "final solution" of the "Jewish question." Jewish populations from Nazi-occupied areas throughout Europe were transported to concentration camps in the eastern lands of the Reich. In death camps like Auschwitz and Treblinka, specifically designed to exterminate Jews, Nazis carried out their policies with bureaucratic efficiency. Methods of murder included mass shootings and gassings in chambers disguised as showers. Some scholars have seen in the gas chambers the literal culmination of the Nazi obsession with (racial) hygiene. After the Allies liberated survivors of the concentration camps, the horrors of the Holocaust were condemned, and a number of Nazi war criminals put on trial at Nürnberg.

How have German and Jewish identities been understood in the post-Nazi era? The Nazis' crimes largely discredited expressions of nationalism and racism in Germany, although the country's cold war division into two states (West Germany and the socialist German Democratic Republic) prompted different responses to the Nazi past (Herf 1997). After an initial silence and a desire to return to "normality," a younger generation of West Germans began to critically explore the Nazi past. In particular, this examination focused on the genocide of the Jews, German responsibility, and the admonition to "never forget." The dominance of the Holocaust narrative in West Germany to some extent mirrors forms of identity expressed by many Jews of European origin (including those who resettled in Israel or the United States). Increasingly, many Jews understand the Holocaust as the central Jewish experience, sometimes to the neglect of other aspects of Jewish history (Young 1988:187).

In socialist East Germany, by contrast, the historiography of the war interpreted Nazism as a form of monopolistic capitalism (the merging of big business with the military industrial complex) whose victims included working-class organizations, Slavic peoples, and Jews. In this reading, the Holocaust of approximately 6 million Jews represented one piece of the larger picture of Nazi crimes but not necessarily the dominant or defining aspect of Nazism. The issue of the Holocaust's centrality to the German experience and to what degree and in what ways it should define contemporary German identity remains a source of debate among Germans, particularly after West and East Germans were reunited in a single state in 1990. The appearance of neo-Nazi groups and violence against "immigrants," particularly in the eastern parts of Germany, suggest that the process of (re)defining German national identity proves fraught with difficulties. Despite recent changes in laws that permit some nonethnic Germans to acquire citizenship, German identity remains understood primarily in terms of blood and ethnicity.

Whereas the Nazi obsession with race (and the blurring of categories of religious and ethnic identity with those of race) proves well known, the story of the contemporary Italian Fascist regime and its understandings of nation and race have received less attention. All too often, scholars use the label *Fascism* or *totalitarianism* but then look only at the experience of German National Socialism. Rightly criticizing this tendency, in the 1970s one of the premier historians of Fascism argued for a sharp differentiation between Italian Fascism and German Nazism (De Felice 1976). According to this influential interpretation, Italian Fascism differed from Nazism in a key way: Italy lacked a racist tradition. Anti-Semitic policies were said to have come about only as a late result of the unequal partnership between Mussolini and Hitler, with the Germans imposing racial laws on the Italians.

That significant numbers of Italians defied the 1938 racial laws by sheltering and helping Jews is well documented and confirms the thesis of the different receptions in Germany and Italy of anti-Semitic measures. An estimated 85 percent of Italy's Jewish population survived the Holocaust, making Italy one of the occupied countries with the highest survival rates of Jews (Zuccotti 1987:272). Italian efforts to rescue Jews within Italy and beyond have rightly been lauded as "something unique in the annals of the Holocaust" (Shelah 1989:205; see also Steinberg 1990).

The insistence on Italians' lack of anti-Semitism, however, glosses over the Italian interest in race well before alliance with Germany. Not only did some Italians wholeheartedly embrace anti-Semitism (Stille 1991), but other forms of racism existed as well, as evidenced by pro-natalist (literally, pro-birth) concerns with reproducing the nation and expressions of racial superiority over and violence toward Italy's colonial populations in Africa and the Balkans.

As occurred in Nazi Germany, the Italian Fascist regime took an obsessive interest in the health and reproduction of the Italian people (particularly in light of declining birth rates in northern Italy). Fascist leader Benito Mussolini's 1927 Ascension Day speech launched a series of demographic campaigns to increase the Italian population (what Mussolini phrased in militaristic terms as the "battle for the births"). A language of hygiene linked what Ferdinando Loffredo, a Catholic fundamentalist and prominent proponent of a racist totalitarianism, deemed "a politics of family and a politics of race" (in *Difesa della Razza*, November 20, 1939). Far from merely imitating German ideas and policies, this demographic policy possessed deep roots in Roman Catholicism and the Italian social sciences. These policies also proved part and parcel of the regime's expansionist aims in Africa and the Balkans prior to World War II. The 1935 Italian conquest of Ethiopia (together with the colonization of Somaliland, Libya, and Albania), for example, raised concerns over miscegenation (racial mixing) and prompted laws forbidding

intercourse (social and otherwise) between Italians and Africans.

Italian colonialism was also driven by the desire to stem massive Italian emigration to the Americas by providing land to "settler colonists." Unlike Nazism, where negative eugenics culminated in the medical experiments and scientized mass death of the concentration camps, the Italian regime made sheer numbers the measure of demographic strength (sometimes deemed "euthenics"). This reflected the fact that sterilization, birth control, and other techniques for preventing undesirables from reproducing could not be reconciled with Catholic tenets. In keeping with Catholic beliefs, the regime outlawed abortion and birth control while simultaneously increasing social welfare legislation. In contrast to the almost total control enjoyed in Germany by Hitler after 1938, the Italian Fascist regime needed the support of the Church, although the

Benito Mussolini.

relationship between the two often proved ambivalent. Despite the regime's sometimes conciliatory stance toward the Church, the two came into conflict over specific issues like education (Koon 1981) and more generally over the regime's attempts to collapse the public and private spheres.

Pointing up the understandings of race and nation that came to the fore during the Fascist regime does not imply that we should now view Italian Fascism just like Nazism where it was once seen as relatively benign in comparison to its German counterpart. The differences between German Nazism and Italian Fascism are significant and should not be overlooked, especially since the prevailing understandings of race, ethnicity, and nation did not prove identical in each case. Furthermore, the response by everyday people to the respective regimes' categories of identity and policies proved distinct; Germany lacked the kind of large-scale resistance movement, for example, found in northern Italy from 1943 on. Having said this, however, it proves important to go beyond clichés about the insignificance of race to Italian Fascism and instead to see exactly what types of understandings—of gender, family, race, and national identity—operated during the 20 years (1922–1943) in which the Fascists held power.

Doing this proves particularly important for examining identity in contemporary Italy. The pervasive self-image of Italians as "good people" (*brava gente*)—which rests on an interpretation of Fascism as relatively benign—shapes current Italian responses to immigration. In the final section of this chapter, we examine the issue of "new racisms" in a Europe coping with large-scale immigration.

Socialist Multiethnic Experiments

In contrast to German National Socialism and Italian Fascism, where returning the nation or the people to greatness proved an explicit and fundamental goal, communist states in Europe organized themselves according to the principle of international working-class solidarity. Marxist theory predicted that the realization of a socialist state would overcome the pernicious ideologies of race, ethnicity, and nation that had in the past served the bourgeoisie in manipulating the working classes. According to this line of thinking, members of the working class had been duped into identifying on narrow ethnic or national lines (a "false consciousness"); this prevented workers from seeing their "true" solidarity with other members of the proletariat in other countries. Although various Marxist positions on nationalism existed,[2] in the period before World War I many communist intellectuals did not take seriously enough the enduring strength of nationalist feeling.

In laying the groundwork for the first communist state, achieved in Russia in 1917 with the Bolshevik Revolution, Vladimir Ilich Lenin did address himself to the troubling nationalities question. Lenin's theoretical writings reflected pragmatic concerns: Not only had nationalism hampered previous attempts at working-class revolution, but the Bolsheviks had assumed control of a multiethnic Russian Empire. As Lenin put it, "Russia is a state with a single national center—Great Russia. . . . The specific features of this national state are, firstly, that 'alien races' (which, on the whole, comprise the majority of the population—57 per-cent) inhabit the border regions" (1951:29).

Lenin treated the problem of nationalism together with colonialism, discussing both in terms of self-determination. U.S. President Woodrow Wilson had enshrined the principle of self-determination, the idea that each national group had the right to its own state, in his Fourteen Points at the Versailles Conference at the end of World War I. As a socialist solution to the issue of self-determination, Lenin promised, "Complete equality for all nations; the right of nations to self-determination; the amalgamation of the workers of all nations—this is the national program that Marxism, the experience of the whole world and the experience of Russia, teaches the workers" (p. 110).

At the same time, Lenin laid out a pragmatic three-pronged political strategy. He argued that prior to assuming power in a particular state, communist parties needed to promise all national groups the right to self-determination (i.e., to secede) and guarantee rights of national equality to those who chose to remain within the state. After obtaining power, the communists would then terminate the right to national secession. In its place, the party would either offer territorial autonomy to compact national groups or assimilate other ethnic and national groups. Finally, Lenin sustained that the party itself should be kept above any national interests (Connor 1984:36). Lenin's different statements point to the fact that under state socialism, the relationship between nationalism/national minorities and communism was one thing in theory but another in practice (refer also to Chapter 4).

If anything, the Marxist-Leninist regime in the USSR institutionalized, rather than abolished, the national question. At the official level, for example, Soviet passports listed the holder's ethnic/national identity, and average Soviet citizens were acutely aware of their neighbors' ethnic affiliation. At a more popular level, ethnic jokes were one means by which group distinctions became known. Such cultural markers included way of dress, codes of morality, physical appearance, and language. Initially, the Soviet regime had promoted plurilingualism; the reality of a central "Russian" state, however, facilitated linguistic assimilation by non–Russian-speaking peoples. After 1938, Stalin reversed these more open linguistic policies and required Russian in schools throughout the Soviet Union. Only in 1959 did schooling in native languages again become possible (Connor 1984:256), although Russian remained the lingua franca until the demise of the USSR. As we have seen, a vocabulary of ethnicity and nation also remained a common language, together with that of communism. This helps explain why between 1989 and 1991 nationalist movements emerged so quickly after the fall of state socialism in both the USSR and in the Soviet-dominated states in the East European bloc.

Those European states that adopted socialist governments after World War II under the "tutelage" of the Soviet Union often followed the Soviet model in addressing the national question. As the Yugoslav and Romanian examples demonstrate, national sentiment by no means disappeared under socialism but rather was harnessed to Marxist-Leninist ideology. In both these cases as well, initial support for the Soviet Union gave way to resistance and explicitly national-based forms of socialism.

The Yugoslav state formed after World War II by Marshal Josip Broz ("Tito") was initially modeled on the Soviet federation. By the eve of the 1941 Axis invasion, the first Yugoslav state—a Serb-dominated monarchy formed in 1918—had virtually collapsed due to Serb–Croat disagreements. When Tito and his communist partisans emerged as the victors from the bloody civil war carried out within occupied Yugoslavia, they built a socialist federation composed of constituent republics with the legal (albeit fictive) right to secede. In reality, the central party exercised tight control. Following the Stalinist model, Tito also sought to collectivize agriculture and institute a five-year economic plan.

Within three years after the war's end, however, Stalin and Tito had fallen out over a number of issues, notably Tito's pursuit of an independent ("nationally" minded) foreign policy. Against Stalin's wishes, Tito pressed Yugoslav territorial claims to Trieste and Istria (formerly Italian), sought a Yugoslav–Albanian federation, and gave support to the communist side in the Greek civil war. When in 1948 Stalin expelled Tito and the Yugoslav communist party from the international association of socialist states (the Cominform), he expected Tito's base of support to collapse immediately. Although the reasons for Tito's political survival are multiple, one primary factor lay in Tito's ability to appeal to a supranational Yugoslav sentiment in opposition to the Soviet Union. With the help of party leaders like Edvard Kardelj, Tito made a virtue out of necessity and articulated a "Third Way" of socialism, that of the Yugoslavs. The threat (real or imagined) of invasion by the Soviet Union helped foster a sense of defending socialist Yugoslavia, which in contrast to Soviet-imposed regimes had been built with genuine popular support.

As Yugoslavia pursued its own "non-aligned" path independent of both the Soviet Union and the United States, the sense of being a "Yugoslav" with respect to an external threat coexisted with ethnic and national distinctions such as Serb, Croat, Slovene, Macedonian, and (Bosnian) Muslim. Over time, Tito developed an elaborate system, known as the "ethnic key," for apportioning positions to members of various ethnic groups. In doing this, Tito sought to avoid any one ethnic group from dominating the federation, as had occurred in the first Yugoslavia. Identities such as "Macedonian" and "Muslim" were officially recognized as national ones for the first time (in 1945 and 1971, respectively) in order to further balance long-standing Serb–Croat tensions.

This ethnic key in no way abolished ethnic or national sentiments but rather kept them firmly in place. The new constitutions introduced in 1963 and 1974, respectively, moved Yugoslavia toward a decentralized model, giving greater power to the "national" republics (Slovenia, Croatia, Bosnia-Herzegovina, Serbia, Montenegro, and Macedonia). As we shall see in the section devoted to Bosnia, when political and economic conditions changed in the 1980s, nationalist leaders would skillfully manipulate these preexisting forms of identity. In doing so, they helped to destroy Tito's multiethnic, socialist state.

The Romanian mix of socialist and nationalist ideologies shares certain parallels with the Yugoslav case, even though the map of ethnic relations in Romania differed dramatically. In contrast to Yugoslavia, where no one ethnic group made up an absolute majority, Latin-speaking Romanians constituted the ethnic majority in Romania. (Romanian scholars have long argued, however, as to whether contemporary Romanians descend from the original inhabitants, known as Dacians, the subsequent Roman conquerors, or some combination of the two groups.) In the border region of Transylvania, there also exists a sizable population identifying as ethnically Hungarian (and, until the end of World War II, many ethnic Germans). In the postsocialist era, tensions have periodically flared between Romania and Hungary over Transylvania.

Though Romania lacks the extreme ethnic complexity that characterized socialist Yugoslavia, in both places a language of nation informed that of socialism. Anthropologist Katherine Verdery (1991) has illuminated the important role played by "national ideology under socialism" in Romania. Romania's strongman communist leader, Nikolae Ceaucescu, embraced this national vocabulary in the 1960s and 1970s in the process of distancing Romania from its Soviet master.

At the end of World War II, Romania possessed only a small communist party organization; the eventual triumph of communism in Romania depended directly on Soviet support. As a consequence, Soviet leaders expected Romanians to specialize in those items (agricultural and consumer goods) that suited Soviet needs. In 1964, General Secretary Ceausescu made what amounted to a "declaration of independence," demanding that the Soviet Union respect the state sovereignty of the bloc members. Ceausescu thus took up a language of nation that appeared to resonate with average Romanians more than the "foreign" Marxist-Leninism imported from the Soviet Union (Verdery 1991:103–105).

Intellectuals and artists elaborated this "national" language. Although competing schools and interpretations arose in fields like history, they all shared a common conceptual vocabulary centered around nationhood. This vocabulary focused on traditions and ancestors, thereby emphasizing relations of kinship into which the socialist state increasingly intervened. Verdery has called the quasi-familial forms of dependency created between the socialist state and its subjects *socialist paternalism* (1993:39, 1996:61–82). Unlike with other forms of nationalism where a sense of kinship and community generates solidarity, socialist paternalism explicitly operated to create dependency and hierarchy.

Key to this relationship, which made citizens like needy children, were gendered images that represented the state and party like patriarchal family heads (i.e., as fathers). In a manner similar to that of Nazi Germany and Fascist Italy, the Romanian state glorified the role of women as "mothers of the nation," outlawing abortion as an attack on the nation itself (Kligman 1998b; Verdery 1996:61–82). The nation's heroes consisted of those virile workers and soldiers ready to sacrifice themselves for the (female) nation. This rhetoric became widespread, despite the increased presence of women in the workplace and the feminization of certain fields, like agriculture. The prominent role of women in "traditional" ways of life like peasant agriculture only furthered the image of women as the bearers (literal and figurative) of national tradition—that is, that of the folk (Kligman 1988b).

The work of Verdery and other anthropologists helps us make sense of the ongoing transformations of ethnic and national identities in European postsocialist societies like Romania and the former Soviet Union. Their research demonstrates that, contrary to one popular belief, communism did not put a lid on ethnic and national sentiments which then "boiled over" or erupted after the fall of socialism. Rather, understandings of ethnicity and nation coexisted with these socialist regimes. Ironically, the socialist regimes that sought to use these languages ultimately failed to control them. Verdery suggests that in Romania, the socialist state's opponents ultimately turned the language of nation against it. In places like Poland, a sense of religion (Catholicism) strongly tied to a sense of national identity fueled opposition to the Soviet-backed regime. With the demise of that Soviet regime and the socialist bloc, we witnessed the sometimes violent transformations of such ethnic and national sentiments.

THE RESURGENCE OF ETHNICITY

After the horrors of World War II, both nationalism and "scientific racism" were roundly condemned in Europe. With the cold war division of Europe (and the world) into ideologically opposed capitalist and communist blocs, many scholars predicted the declining importance of ethnic and national sentiment in Europe. The creation of a West European common economic structure or market with the explicit aim of preventing future conflicts among European nation-states buoyed such optimism. In addition to those Marxist thinkers who predicted the triumph of class identifications over ethnonational ones, many other observers thought that only in the developing world did narrow ethnic or "tribal" divisions still hold sway.

In the 1960s, however, it was precisely in those "old" European states with supposedly well-consolidated national identities where regionally and linguistically based ethnic identifications emerged as political movements. In France, a movement of Breton-speakers from the northern region of Brittany put into question the success with which Frenchmen had been "made." Similarly, in the United Kingdom there emerged Scottish and Welsh ethnonational movements that criticized England's "suppression" of minority cultures.

The political language used by these minority or regional movements directly drew upon the independence struggles waged by the peoples in Europe's overseas colonies. The Bretons, for example, contended that they had been underdeveloped and exploited in a manner similar to that of the Algerians, who in 1963 had waged a hard-fought war for independence from the French. In line with this, scholars began to talk about processes of "internal colonialism" and underdevelopment (Hechter 1975; Nairn 1977). Many of these scholars worked from a political economy framework, seeking to address Marxist theory's former blind spot for nationalism.

According to the "internal colonialism" interpretation, European nation-states came into being in part as a result of the periphery's exploitation by the center. This exploitation occurred overseas (the European center extracting resources from the colonies) and at "home" in parallel and interrelated processes with similar results: cultural and economic impoverishment of the periphery. Admittedly, some scholars questioned the appropriateness of this analogy for understanding the regional ethnicities emerging in places like France (McDonald 1986) or the United Kingdom; Scotland, for example, did not represent a classic case of economic underdevelopment but rather a well-developed region within a less developed hinterland (Nairn 1977:203). Nonetheless, the idea of internal colonization proved politically useful in fostering a sense of identity within these "new" ethnic movements.

Breton activists, for instance, identified the educational system as a key means by which linguistic "colonization" and "cultural genocide" had been accomplished at home (McDonald 1989:86, 190). Although language represented the key marker of Breton identity, aspects like kinship and ancestry also lent this form of ethnicity a quasi-biological sense (p. 120; see also McDonald 1986). Bretons defined themselves ethnically as Celts, in contrast to the Latin French, and made common cause with other oppressed Celtic minorities, like the Welsh. Folkloric traditions such as dances and festivals became key to expressions of this pan-Celtic identity, as well as a more specific Breton one.

As the Breton example suggests, the ethnic identifications that (re)emerged in Europe in the 1960s and 1970s often drew upon nineteenth-century understandings of a *volk*, or people, as nation. Although Herder focused on shared culture rather than shared biology when he used the term *volk*, others who took up the idea often blurred the lines between race, ethnicity, and nation. In the 1960s and 1970s, the term *ethnic group* assumed many of the quasi-biological meanings associated with the now unpopular terms *race* and *tribe*. Although scholars recognized that ethnicity followed out of shared culture and a shared sense of descent rather than actual biological continuity, in practice "ethnic group" often came to imply a population linked together in some biological fashion (Just 1989). Increasingly, the concept of culture itself has taken over some of these old associations, at times appearing as inescapable as one's genetic makeup.

RELIGION, ETHNICITY, AND NATIONAL IDENTITY

Just as many social scientists expected ethnic distinctions to weaken or even disappear in Europe, they also predicted the decline of religious identifications. Almost every one of the classical social theorists—from Karl Marx to Max Weber to Émile Durkheim—expected religion to give way to a secular (communist, "disenchanted," scientific) worldview. At the same time when "new ethnicities" emerged in Europe in the 1960s and 1970s, however, there arose what scholars labeled "new religions," reflecting interest in alternative forms of spirituality. These beliefs often intersect with new kinds of identities, such as feminism and environmentalism, that complicate older distinctions based on class, ethnicity, and national identity.

Although individuals attracted to these "new" faiths expressed dissatisfaction with traditional churches, religious identifications with Catholicism, Orthodox Christianity, Judaism, various Protestant sects, and Islam nonetheless continue to have significance for many contemporary Europeans. In some instances, ethnic and national identities largely coincide with religious identities. In places like Yugoslavia and Northern Ireland, long-standing ethnic-religious identities acquired new salience in the 1960s, the same period that political movements centered around the new ethnicities made their presence felt in Europe. In Bosnia, for example, the ethnic and national identifications of Serb and Croat have long been associated with Orthodox and Catholic religious identities, respectively. Beginning in the 1960s, the Yugoslav state also recognized "Muslim" as an official ethnic grouping, regardless of individuals' actual religious observances. In Northern Ireland, the late 1960s and the organization of a Catholic civil rights movement signaled the beginning of the period known as "the Troubles."

The Bosnian and Irish cases reflect the enduring legacies of empire within Europe, as well as the dilemmas inherent in the building of "modern" nation-states. In both instances, religious identities have intersected social, economic, and political ones, in sometimes violent ways. To some degree, these contemporary "religious wars" have roots in the religious conflicts (Christianity versus Islam, Catholic versus Protestant) that divided early modern Europe at the same time that this violence proves thoroughly modern in its form and content.

Northern Ireland

In explaining violent conflict in Northern Ireland, a body of recent scholarship de-emphasizes its religious dimensions in favor of economic and political explanations that stress Ireland's role as Britain's "first" and oldest colony (see the discussions in Feldman 1991:19; Galliher and DeGregory 1985:53; Miller 1998). The popularity of the socioeconomic interpretation may reflect the declining significance accorded to religion in much classic social theory and hence that theory's difficulty in explaining the Northern Irish paradox: the coexistence of industrialization, advanced capitalist development, and high levels of participation in traditional religious practices (Fulton 1991:5). This paradox reflects the peculiarities of Anglo-Protestant colonization of Ireland, which ultimately created a series of nested cores and peripheries.

For much of the modern period, the northern part of the island generally possessed a more industrialized economy than the agrarian south; furthermore, within Northern Ireland, an agrarian area surrounded an industrialized core centered on the city of Belfast. The politically and economically dominant Protestants reinforced their status by restricting access to jobs in industry. Material deprivations, together with political disenfranchisement, facilitated the eventual alignment of Catholicism with Irish nationalism. Conflicts over identity in contemporary Northern Ireland thus reflect the ways in which the politics of religion historically unfolded within the context of industrialization and national "revival." Ireland's uneven economic development, which became mapped onto ethnic and religious distinctions, followed out of the island's colonization. This colonial past, and the settlers it left behind, continue to shape contemporary structures of power and group relations, as well as collective memories and myths.

The colonization of Ireland has its distant roots in the twelfth century, at which time Normans from England and France invaded the island, whose population had been overwhelmingly Gaelic (Celtic). Ireland's formal colonization occurred in the late sixteenth and seventeenth centuries, with the emigration of significant numbers of Scot and English settlers to the six counties of Ulster (in the northern part of Ireland), a policy encouraged by the English monarchs Elizabeth I and James I. These policies failed, however, in their aim of creating "Irish" loyalty to an English Crown, which now differed from its Irish subjects not just in ethnic or national terms but also in religious ones, following Henry VIII's break with the Catholic church and the establishment of the Protestant Anglican church. Abandoning efforts to create loyalty, English monarchs subsequently oversaw a campaign (the "plantation policy") in which Protestant settlers received land confiscated from Catholic landholders. By the second half of the seventeenth century, Catholic-owned lands had declined from three-fifths to one-fifth of all land in Ireland (Fulton 1991:27). The defeat of the Catholic King James II, who sought to reverse these policies, by the Protestant William of Orange (husband of James II's daughter, Mary) further reduced Catholic landownership in Ireland to a mere one-seventh of all landholding by 1707 (p. 33).

During the final decades of the eighteenth century, the battle lines between "Catholic" and "Protestant" identities in Ireland hardened. This followed out of both economic and political developments. In the northern part of the island, there emerged a prosperous commercial class made up of drapers, bleachers, and bankers. This class laid the foundations for industrialization in the nineteenth century, which would widen the economic gap between the more prosperous north and the impoverished agrarian south. Ethnic Scottish and English settlers, many of them subscribing to Calvinism (a Protestant sect), largely composed this commercial elite. The traditional landholding elite instead generally self-identified as English and belonged to the Protestant Church of Ireland.

Political events at the end of the 1700s muted any potential solidarities between the ethnically and religiously diverse components of the lower classes. By the end of the 1770s, a Protestant militia unit known as "the Volunteers" formed to resist the "Catholic threat." The Protestant-controlled parliament (relatively independent from England since 1782) sanctioned these Protestant volunteers, as well as stridently Protestant associations like the "Orange Boys," formed by James Wilson in 1793 (pp. 41–49). In response, some Catholics became militiamen known as "the Defenders." Together with the political movement the United Irishmen, the Defenders led a failed insurrection in 1798. As a result, the 1800 Act of Union restored direct English control over Irish affairs.

The nineteenth century witnessed the growing development of an Irish nationalist movement that variously demanded "home rule," or independence from Britain, and a Protestant religious revival. The growth of Irish nationalism reflected a cultural "renaissance," sometimes referred to as the "Celtic twilight." This entailed the intellectual "discovery" of the folk common to romantic movements, with particular emphasis on the linguistic revival of Gaelic and the search for cultural expressions (old and new) such as Gaelic songs and poetry. The Protestant revival embraced diverse Protestant sects and stressed enthusiastic practices such as "spirit possession" (p. 60); these understandings reflected Protestant beliefs in a direct, unmediated relationship with God and thus highlighted fundamental doctrinal differences between Catholics and Protestants. Some Irish Protestants not only saw Catholics as belonging to a different religious or cultural tradition, however, but even a different race. As Charles Darwin's ideas about biological evolution gained popularity, images of the "wild" or savage Irish often depicted them as apelike; as members of a supposedly lesser breed, the Irish were associated with criminality, sloth, and drunkenness (Curtis 1971). These racist views of the Irish were not restricted to Northern Ireland or Great Britain; they circulated widely in North America, where many Protestant-Anglos looked with disdain upon Irish Catholic immigrants (see Chapter 6).

Racialized depictions of the Irish "Paddy" became prominent in newspaper cartoons as debates over home rule unfolded in the last two decades of the nineteenth century. As pressure for some form of home rule grew, particularly under the Liberal English Prime Minister W. E. Gladstone (who in 1886 introduced the first home rule bill in Parliament), Irish Protestants prepared to resist any change that would make them a minority in an Irish Catholic state. Orangeism, dedicated to preserving Protestant ascendancy and the Irish–British Union, became a mass movement. In 1914, the home rule bill finally passed. Although a special act excepted the six counties of Ulster from home rule for a period of six years, Ireland appeared to be on the brink of a civil war.

Only the beginning of the Great War and the postponement of home rule delayed the civil conflict for which Protestant paramilitary groups—many of whose members had sworn the Solemn League and Covenant to defend the Union—had been preparing. In 1913, a group of Catholics formed the Irish Volunteers in order to forcibly prevent a possible secession by Ulster unionists. During the World War I, Protestants and Catholics alike loyally defended Britain. A faction of the Irish Volunteers, however, refused to serve what they saw as the interests of an oppressive empire. Led by the poet Padraic Pearse and Tom Clarke, a small group of the Volunteers (forming the Irish Republican Brotherhood) participated in the Easter Rebellion of 1916.

Pearse and his nationalist supporters seized the Dublin post office in what was supposed to be the beginning of a countrywide revolt. Many Irish families had a son or loved one serving in the British imperial forces, however, and Pearse's call for revolution against the colonial oppressor found little support. British forces quickly crushed the uprising, court-martialing and executing 14 of its leaders. The brutal British response ultimately galvanized Irish nationalist sentiment, and Pearse and his fellow conspirators became widely recognized as martyrs to the Irish cause. This may have been Pearse's intent; realizing the lack of widespread support for such a rebellion, he might have desired to make a "blood sacrifice" that would ultimately regenerate and liberate the nation. Pearse drew heavily on Catholic imagery, envisioning himself as a crucified Christ whose sacrifice would redeem the Irish nation (Hughes 1994:39–41).

At the conclusion of World War I, the Irish state Pearse had died for came into being by means of the Government of Ireland Act of 1920 and the subsequent Anglo-Irish Treaty of 1921–1922. Though Pearse dreamed of a unitary Irish state, the civil war that followed led to the creation of two separate units: the Republic of Ireland in the south and a Protestant-dominated Northern Ireland (made up of six of Ulster's nine counties). These agreements did not entail meaningful guarantees for the protection of the Protestant minority in the south (many of whose members emigrated) or the Catholic minority in the north.

From its creation in 1921, the state of Northern Ireland pursued undeniably discriminatory policies against its Catholic citizens. The institution of a Special Powers Act in 1922—an "emergency" measure that remained in place for almost half a century—facilitated Protestant dominance. The police force, known as the Royal Ulster Constabulary (RUC), together with the Ulster Special Constabulary (the B Specials), operated in paramilitary fashion. They enforced the religious discrimination that existed in the realms of voting, the legal and justice system, public housing allocations, and the private and public sectors of employment (Rowthorn and Wayne 1988:28–37).

In the late 1960s, Catholics (often referred to as "Nationalists") began to challenge this institutionalized discrimination. Inspired by the African American civil rights movement, in 1968 the Northern Ireland Civil Rights Association (NICRA) led a campaign of civil disobedience. By the summer of 1969, tactics of peaceful protest had given way to violent clashes. This led some Catholics to abandon the politics of nonviolence, forming paramilitary groups known as the Provisionals. The Irish Republican Army (IRA), a guerrilla group that had advocated violence in order to attain Irish independence, also re-emerged. Protestant paramilitary groups replied with equal violence. The use of terror by both sides in the conflict prompted intervention by the British army in 1971.

Although initially welcomed by some Catholics as protectors from the Ulster Protestants, the British soldiers soon became the agents of repression and martial law in Northern Ireland (Rowthorn and Wayne 1988:41). The army oversaw the internment without trial of individuals "suspected of terrorism"—not only republicans supporting the IRA and other proindependence paramilitary groups but also "loyalists" employing extreme violence. In what became known as the "Bloody Sunday" massacre (1972), the British army killed 13 protesters marching at Derry. Later that year, Britain suspended Northern Ireland's constitution and parliament and instituted direct rule. Direct rule ended only in 1999, leaving bitter memories among Catholics of human rights abuses like unconstitutional house and strip searches. The fate of Catholics imprisoned by the British provided a powerful focus for Nationalist resistance. As anthropologist Allen Feldman has argued, "The experience of arrest and interrogation is central to the political culture of violence in Northern Ireland" (1991:85).

Initially, the government accorded both imprisoned Nationalists and Unionists/Loyalists a "special category status" as political prisoners. Grouped together in a manner that facilitated organizing, "politicals" were not required to wear prison uniforms. In 1975, the policy of internment came to a halt. In 1976, various privileges and political prisoner status altogether were revoked. This reflected an attempt to criminalize the paramilitaries and to render the national and religious question in Northern Ireland merely one of "law and order" restricted to unruly ghettos (Aretxaga 1997:84). British media often described Catholic paramilitary volunteers as "hardmen," an image invoking fanatical "gunmen" dedicated to radical violence (Feldman 1991:47). Negative media images accompanied ever more intrusive forms of surveillance, including strip searches. Anthropologists like Feldman and Aretxaga have demonstrated how the bodies of individuals (symbolic of the body politic) became the sites of both repression and resistance.

Jailed Nationalists, for example, wielded their bodies as "protest weapons." Together with well-publicized hunger strikes, one of the most powerful uses of the body for resistance consisted in the so-called "blanket protest." When denied their political status and ordered to wear prison uniforms, Catholic political prisoners responded by wearing only blankets in their cells. Forbidden to wear blankets outside of their cells, and with their naked bodies exposed to physical and verbal abuse, the prisoners undertook a new, "dirty protest." This entailed a refusal to wash or leave their cells, even to use the toilets. When authorities prevented prisoners from discarding their bodily waste through the windows, the prisoners took to smearing feces on the cell walls.

Aretxaga has told the parallel but lesser known story of Catholic women's resistance. Although female activism began during the civil rights and march phase of the Nationalist movement, it crystallized in response to the disruption of family and civil life wrought by British army rule. Members of the security forces often targeted women for sexual harassment (1997:131). When house searches became daily occurrences, women organized a system of whistles and banging garbage-can lids to alert other families. In a more dramatic example, female members of the IRA in Armagh jail organized a "protest of dirt" to demonstrate their solidarity with incarcerated male members of the IRA. This women's protest, all too often treated as a mere footnote to that of the men, proved particularly disturbing for Protestant and Catholic men alike.

The sight of women in their own excrement and menstrual waste violated cultural taboos of various sorts. It also challenged the more traditional role set aside for women in Nationalist discourse: that of mothers supporting (or grieving for) their heroic sons. The IRA relied on a conservative ideal of the activist, republican male and the passive, devoted wife and mother (p. 151). The pervasive image of Mother Ireland drew upon not only a common nationalist language but also the prominence accorded to Mother Mary in popular Catholicism (p. 112). The leader of the Easter Rebellion, Padraic Pearse, had powerfully

combined these two languages, reconfiguring an older poetic image of Mother Ireland as a worn-out hag into that of a proud mother sacrificing her sons (like Mary) to the national cause. Aretxaga notes that the Armagh women's protest not only questioned the prevailing ethnic and religious hierarchy in Northern Ireland but also the gender regime. She suggests that the fragility of this feminist project parallels that of the prospects for peace in Northern Ireland at the same time that it represents the possibilities for change (p. 175).

The Anglo-Irish Agreement of 1985, which gave the Republic of Ireland a voice in Northern Ireland politics, marked the beginnings of a drawn-out peace process. Despite sporadic violence, the IRA and the Unionist paramilitaries generally agreed to end the use of violent tactics in 1994. Soon after, Sinn Féin, the political branch of the IRA, began to participate directly in the peace process. The Belfast Agreement of 1998 (otherwise known as the Good Friday Peace Accord) provided for devolution of government responsibilities to an elected assembly of Northern Ireland; devolution became a reality in December 1999. Ireland and Northern Ireland's membership in the European Union has facilitated the peace process and its practical implementation (Hume 1993), which led to the creation of a power-sharing agreement and the reform of the police (the former Royal Ulster Constabulary). Sporadic acts of violence—such as that occurring in March 2009 when extremist factions of the IRA killed two British soldiers and a policeman—are reminders of the fragility of the peace achieved in Northern Ireland. At the time, many feared that these killings might spark a cycle of retribution that would prompt a return of the polarization and quotidian violence that marked the Troubles. For the most part, however, the response of politicians (including those within Sinn Féin) and everyday citizens alike in Northern Ireland has been to condemn the work of extremists and demonstrate solidarity for the peace process. Citizens in cities around Northern Ireland, for example, gathered to protest the killings and held silent vigils in support of continued peace. In June of 2009, several of Northern

Ireland's existing paramilitary groups announced that they had destroyed their weapons and pledged to work within the legal framework of the state.

Although the recourse to violence by extremist groups remains a potential threat, (particularly splinter groups like Real IRA) perhaps the greater challenge to constituting a durable peace in Northern Ireland lies in the difficulty of reconciling divergent understandings of that country's recent violent past. Since the Good Friday Accord, for example, the city of Belfast has been the object of large-scale processes of revitalization and gentrification with the explicit aim of using public architecture and leisure activities such as sport to "normalize" the post-conflict city; these initiatives also seek to create new service-sector jobs in a postindustrial city that has lost its primacy as a center for shipbuilding (Barnier 2006:168). The city, however, remains divided by memorializations and ethnoreligious indices of various sorts (such as murals and graffiti) that mark out areas as republican or loyalist, Catholic or Protestant. An ambitious effort to create a new, neutral public space culminated in the massive sports and entertainment complex known as the Odyssey Arena, which opened in 2000. The featured sport played at the Odyssey is ice hockey, an activity with little history in the city and which many residents view as an artificial imposition. In addition, sports shirts and other symbols seen to potentially promote sectarianism are banned from the stadium, raising questions about whether the most effective way to overcome a divided past lies in erasing it or rather creating a space that can accommodate divergent identities (pp. 170–172).

Given the failure of the Odyssey to serve as an inclusive and "authentic" sports center with which the city's various populations (including the increasing number of non-Irish immigrants) can identify, the British government has promoted a plan to build a large stadium on the site of the Maze, the former prison that housed many republicans and loyalists during the 1970s and 1980s. Referred to by former prisoners as Long Kesh, the center closed in 2000. The plan to transform the

abandoned prison into a prominent public space highlights the competing understandings of the recent past. Some members of the Sinn Féin party, for example, have advocated building a museum there to memorialize republican "martyrs," comparing the Maze to Robben Island (the infamous political prison in South Africa where anti-apartheid dissidents like Nelson Mandela were sent) and even to the Nazi concentration camp at Auschwitz (Graham and McDowell 2007:357). Unionists/Loyalists reject such analogies, as well as any proposal to create a memorial site at the former prison. Transforming the Maze into a historical monument may thus potentially reinforce, rather than mitigate, divisions within Northern Ireland. As Brian Graham and Sara McDowell put it, "the Maze is essentially a zero-sum heritage site . . . [and] appears to have little potential as a site of atonement or reconciliation" (2007:363). Whether a sports complex built on adjacent land can escape associations with this divided history also proves questionable. Although Northern Ireland has enjoyed (relative) peace for over a decade since the historic peace agreement, debates about how to interpret and remember the Troubles may continue to divide, rather than unite, the citizens of that state.

Bosnia-Herzegovina

The conflict in Northern Ireland reflects the dilemmas inherent to state building in Europe's supposedly "old" nations, offering an example in which the framework of an integrated Europe may facilitate resolution of (post)colonial conflicts. Yugoslavia's violent dissolution, by contrast, unfolded within the context of an integrating Europe and raises questions about how ethnic and religious conflicts may develop in those states bordering on, but denied the privileges of membership in, the "new" Europe. Furthermore, in many contemporary societies within the European Union, the relatively recent arrival of immigrants who are not just ethnically but also religiously distinct raises new questions about the future of "national" ways of life; often these "others" come from former colonies or the postsocialist European states, sometimes as refugees. Increasingly, however, they also come from the newest member states that joined the European Union as the result of enlargement in 2004 (Cyprus, Czech Republic, Estonia, Hungary, Latvia, Lithuania, Malta, Poland, Slovakia, and Slovenia) and 2007 (Bulgaria and Romania). These dual processes of enlargement and immigration (from both within and outside the EU) have given particular urgency to the long-standing issue of what a "European" identity consists in.

In particular, Muslims appear to put into question the values associated with both the "West" and "Christianity." Regardless of their actual beliefs and practices, many individuals from Muslim societies are assumed to be proponents of "Muslim fundamentalism"; this label implies a whole host of negative images, such as the principle of theocracy (merging of religious and political rule), subordination of women, and rigid religious strictures. In countries like France, Germany, and Britain, attention has focused on whether religiously prescribed headscarves and veils should be permitted or outlawed in public institutions (such as schools); those who argue for allowing headscarves do so on the grounds of freedom of religious expression and tolerance of cultural difference whereas those who advocate prohibiting headscarves in certain public settings claim that they serve to oppress women. Contemporary stereotypes about Islam as oppressive and fanatical draw upon long-standing European fears of the Muslim "other," which date back to the medieval confrontation between Christianity and Islam in Europe and the Near East. Like the Jew, the "Moor" or the "Turk" represents the "other" whose specter has haunted Europe (Bunzl 2005; Ozyürek 2005).

After the completion in 1492 of the brutal Christian Reconquest of the Iberian Peninsula, which entailed the expulsion of both Moors and Jews, the Balkan Peninsula remained the last terrestrial frontier within Europe between Christianity and Islam. In the Balkans generally and on the territory of the South, or Yugo, Slavs especially, met competing religions (Islam and Christianity, as well as Catholicism and Orthodoxy) and empires (those of the Austrian Hapsburgs, the Venetians, and the Ottoman Turks). In the European territories controlled by the Ottomans for several centuries there lived not only large populations of Muslims who had emigrated from the imperial center (Constantinople) but also ethnic Slavs who converted to Islam. When the Ottomans withdrew and "European" nation-states came into being in the nineteenth and twentieth centuries, these Muslim populations remained. One of the largest populations of such "Islamicized Slavs" lives in the territory of Bosnia-Herzegovina; non-Slavic Albanians, thought to be descendants of the peninsula's original Illyrian inhabitants, also converted in large numbers to Islam. Among the member states of the European Union, Bulgaria claims the largest Muslim minority (in terms of percentage of overall population); as in the former Yugoslavia, these Bulgarian Muslims are autochthonous or "native" Muslims, rather than recent migrants, reminding us of the diversity of Muslim populations within Europe.

Despite the extensive religious and ethnic mixture that characterized the Yugoslav territory, when the multiethnic federation dissolved in 1991 it broke into states defined on narrow ethnonational lines. In the course of the wars of the 1990s by which these new states came into being, many populations (such as Croatia's Serbs, Bosnia's Muslims, and Kosovo's Albanians) have been "ethnically cleansed" through expulsion and/or massacres in an attempt to make the boundaries of ethnic group and territory contiguous.

Perhaps more than any of socialist Yugoslavia's other republics (Slovenia, Croatia, Serbia, Montenegro, and Macedonia), Bosnia-Herzegovina embodied the multiethnic Yugoslav mix. In Bosnia lived ethnic Serbs (generally Orthodox), Croats (mainly Catholic), Jews, Vlachs, Gypsies, and Muslims (usually referred to today as Bosniaks). The fate of Bosnia-Herzegovina illustrates the tragic failure of the Yugoslav experiment, as well as the ways in which religious affiliation may overlap with ethnic and national identity.

Nationally minded historians in the Balkans often claim that during the centuries of Ottoman domination, the Christian churches kept national sentiment and heritage alive. Serbian monasteries, for example, are said to have nurtured the memory of the medieval Serbian state, and in particular its defeat by the Ottomans in the 1389 battle of Kosovo. In reality, the historic relationship between religious and ethnonational affiliation in the former Yugoslavia proves more complex. In overseeing a vast empire of persons belonging to different ethnic and religious groups, the Ottomans did not generally attempt to assimilate or convert whole populations. Rather, they created a system for administering the different religious communities, known as the *millet*. This system gave a degree of autonomy to the various religious faiths, permitting members to practice their own religious laws and follow their own leaders (although the Ottoman sultan had ultimate authority).

As a consequence, individuals within the European territories of the Ottoman Empire defined their identity primarily in religious terms, at least until the eighteenth and nineteenth centuries. At this time, European ideologies of nationalism came into the Balkan Peninsula via Jewish and Greek traders who traveled in the West, intellectuals schooled in Europe, and various contacts with the world of Russian Orthodoxy. The Orthodox *millet*, headed by the patriarchate in Constantinople, looked with disfavor upon nationalism, given its negative associations with Western secularism. Furthermore, the patriarchate feared losing its control over the empire's Orthodox faithful as various "acephalous" churches—such as the Serbian Orthodox church and the Bulgarian Orthodox church—were restored or created.

Contrary to one commonplace assumption, then, the Orthodox church was not the unproblematic "cradle" of Serbian (or Bulgarian or Macedonian, etc.) nationalism. That said, however, these Christian identities undoubtedly informed resistance to the Ottoman Empire, specifically demands to create European nation-states. The Serbs and Greeks carved out the first independent states within Ottoman Europe. Many other peoples in the South Slav area, including some Catholic Slovenes and Croats in the Hapsburg Empire, looked to the Serbs as possible leaders for some kind of pan-Slav or Yugoslav unification (see the section on "old" and "new" nations). What place would "Muslim Slavs" occupy within such a future state? The first Yugoslav state, formed at the end of World War I with the collapse of both the Hapsburg and Ottoman empires, recognized as its three founding "peoples" the Serbs, Croats, and Slovenes. At this time, neither Muslims nor Bosnians were recognized as separate ethnic groups. Serb and Croat nationalists alike claimed the Bosnian Muslims as Islamicized Serbs or Croats, respectively. In practice, however, there existed a defined Muslim political/cultural community in Bosnia, one that resented the new Yugoslav state's centralizing tendencies (Malcolm 1994:163–173).

In the first Yugoslavia, the major source of ethnic tension derived from the differing visions of the Croats and Slovenes, on the one hand, and of the Serbs, on the other. The role of Bosnia's Muslims did not occupy center stage, although Serbian leaders devoted considerable attention to the majority population of Albanian Muslims in Kosovo; a plan for the forced transfer of the Kosovars to Turkey was halted only by the outbreak of World War II (Malcolm 1998:283–286). When a coalition of the Axis powers, led by Nazi Germany and Fascist Italy, invaded Yugoslavia in April 1941, the state rapidly collapsed, in part because Serb–Croat quarreling had weakened any sense of solidarity. The Axis powers partitioned Yugoslavia into occupied zones; in addition, Italy and Germany backed an "independent" Croatian state headed by Ante Pavelić. Founder of the extremist movement known as the Ustaša, Pavelić advocated the national "purification" of Croatia. The Ustaša carried out a campaign to exterminate Serbs, Jews, and Gypsies so brutal that it shocked even some Nazi observers. In some cases, Bosnian Muslims also participated in the persecution of ethnic Serbs, though many Muslims also fought with the communist partisans (Malcolm 1994:89–191). During World War II, then, Yugoslavia not only suffered from foreign occupation but also civil war and genocide from within.

Building a socialist Yugoslavia at war's end demanded reconciliation of Yugoslavia's diverse peoples. Tito actively suppressed the memory of some of the worst interethnic fighting during the war (as well as the violence committed by the communists in consolidating their power). In the 1980s and 1990s, interethnic conflict would again tear apart Yugoslavia, fueled by nationalist leaders who invoked past ethnic and religious violence, including that of World War II (Denich 1994; Hayden 1994).

Ironically, many observers expected that Yugoslavia—long independent of the Soviet bloc and more open and prosperous than the bloc states—would make the smoothest transition to a market democracy. Instead, the reverse occurred. Why did Yugoslavia's breakup occur with such violence? In particular, why did Bosnia become the site of expulsions and massacres that many persons believed could never happen again in Europe? The reasons for Yugoslavia's destruction lie in the economic and political character of socialist Yugoslavia, as well as changes in the broader political economy.

In the 1960s and 1970s, Tito transformed the centralized Yugoslav state into a much more loosely organized federation. Despite the growing weakness of the federal center vis-à-vis these republics (with considerable economic and political decision making at the republican, rather than federal, level), Tito and the communist party managed to hold the fragile federation together. Tito's death in 1980 not only left a power vacuum but also coincided with an economic crisis, the result of Yugoslavia's reliance on credits and loans from international banking institutions like the International Monetary Fund and the World Bank (Woodward 1995:47–81). In the 1980s, once prosperous Yugoslavs had to cope with skyrocketing inflation, unemployment, and shortages. In this context, nationalist demands—which in Tito's time had been suppressed, as occurred in 1971 after the "Croatian Spring"—became a common way to express dissatisfaction.

Usually this nationalism was couched in terms of victimization, the specific ethnic-national group claiming that its interests had been sacrificed to those of Yugoslavia and/or some other national group. Whereas Serb–Croat conflict had dominated much of Yugoslavia's history, in the 1980s the competing and intertwined nationalisms of Serbia and Slovenia first came to the fore. In Slovenia, articulations of national identity and demands for independence rooted in a sense of victimization as a small nation coincided with the flourishing of an underground, avant-garde youth scene; to many Western observers, Slovenia appeared to be enjoying an opening up of "civil society."

Many Slovenes and members of Yugoslavia's other ethnic groups complained that Serbs had disproportionate power in the socialist Yugoslavia (just as they had dominated the first Yugoslavia). Serbs, however, countered that Tito's state had victimized the Serbs, denying them rights and privileges in pursuit of an ethnic quota system. In a 1986 memorandum, intellectuals associated with the Serbian Academy of Arts and Sciences gave expression to a pervasive view of Serb "martyrdom," one that drew upon deeply rooted images from Serbian history and also contemporary events in the province of Kosovo. In the 1980s, Albanian Yugoslavs began to protest discriminatory treatment at the hands of the Serbs and demand that Kosovo, an autonomous province since 1963 but largely under the control of Serbia, become a full-fledged republic within the federation.

Serbian nationalism found its focal point in the question of Kosovo. The poorest region of Yugoslavia and one inhabited primarily by Muslim Albanians, Kosovo held a special place in narratives of Serb identity. The presence of important Serbian Orthodox monasteries in the region and the memory of the Serbs' 1389 defeat to the Ottomans on Kosovo's Field of Blackbirds, popularly viewed as signaling the end of the medieval Serbian kingdom, underwrote the belief that Kosovo represented Serbia's "Jerusalem" and, by extension, that Serbs shared with the Jews the status of a chosen, yet persecuted, people (Živković 2000). In this line of thinking, the Serbian people had been martyred again and again throughout their history. Serbian nationalists like Slobodan Milošević (taking up well-rehearsed arguments) argued that the growth of the Albanian population in Kosovo and the proportionate decline of the Serbian population there represented the latest act of martyrdom. Albanians were said to be engaging in a plan of ethnic or demographic cleansing that would drive out remaining Serbs from Kosovo; nationalists often represented these Muslim Albanians as akin to the Ottoman Turks who had forced Serbs to submit to the "Ottoman yoke" for centuries. Reports and rumors, never substantiated, charged Albanians with undertaking a systematic campaign of "nationalist rape" of Serbs (young and old, male and female). In actuality, it would be Serbs in Bosnia who would actually first use mass rape as a systematic weapon in the Yugoslav wars (Bracewell 2000).

Although Kosovo appeared the likely place in which these wars would begin, large-scale violence first occurred when Slovenia and Croatia declared independence from Yugoslavia in 1991. The Yugoslav national army, increasingly identified as the instrument of Serbian rather than Yugoslav interests, moved to prevent secession. After a 10-day war in Slovenia, Serbian leader Milošević agreed to let Slovenia leave the federation. He then turned his full attention to Croatia, home to a sizable minority population of ethnic Serbs; some of these Serbs had already declared an independent republic in the Krajina region (the mountainous zone adjacent to the Dalmatian coast). These Serbs refused to become a minority within the new Croatian state. They feared that Croatian nationalists and their leader, Franjo Tuđman (elected president of Croatia in 1990), would undertake a genocide of Serbs like that which had occurred during World War II. The revival of symbols (such as the flag, the currency) associated with Pavelić's Ustaša state and the mass firing of Serbs from the civil service and police fed such fears.

Groups of paramilitary volunteers (many of them from Serbia itself) formed in support of these Croatian Serbs. These volunteers often committed the worst violence of the wars. Although they were likely motivated by ethnonational hatred, other factors such as class antagonism and an aggressive masculinity also came into play (Ignatieff 1993; Woodward 1995). Such militias played a major role in the siege and destruction of the city of Vukovar. Here, ethnic Croatians were driven out or killed in the process that became known as "ethnic cleansing." The violence of Vukovar offered a blueprint for the war in Bosnia, which began in 1992 after that state's declaration of independence.

In the period leading up to Bosnia's first free elections, parties formed largely (though not exclusively) on ethnic lines. The major parties represented the Bosnian Serbs (SDS), the Bosnian Croats (HDZ), and the Bosnian Muslims (SDA). Under the leadership of Aliya Izetbegović, the SDA continued to express support for a multiethnic Bosnia. Without a doubt, however, the SDA was associated with the Muslims; not only had Izetbegović been imprisoned under Yugoslavia for writing a pan-Islamic tract but the SDA adopted the Islamic symbol of the crescent moon. This reflected the way in which, under Tito, "Muslim" had become a recognized cultural or ethnic identity. Whereas Bosnian Muslims had previously been counted in censuses as either ethnically Serb or Croat, the 1961 census defined Muslim as an ethnic identity, and the 1971 census recognized Muslim as a national identity on a par with those of the Serbs and Croats (Malcolm 1994:198–199). This change followed out of a desire to balance Serb and Croat rivalry in Bosnia. In addition, it helped divest a Muslim identity of those religious meanings that might make it a counterpoint for opposition to the communist state (p. 200).

In general, Bosnia's Muslims were among the most secularized in the world. Differences in the practice of being Muslim did, however, mark Bosnia's urban and rural areas. The Muslims of Bosnia's capital city, Sarajevo, possessed a reputation for their cosmopolitan ways. Little, if anything, outwardly distinguished these urban Muslims from their Serb or Croat neighbors. In some rural villages, like that studied by anthropologist Tone Bringa (1995), Muslim women wore traditional headscarves and *dimije* (baggy pants). Here Muslims lived alongside their Croat neighbors and shared bonds of friendship (symbolized by the women's coffee-drinking groups). The two groups nonetheless remained distinct, and intermarriage was infrequent. Even in this case, though, Muslim identity had a situational aspect, as village women wore Western-style clothes when going to the nearby market town; in addition, younger women sometimes adhered to Muslim ways less strictly. It is only as a result of the war and the persecution of Muslims in Bosnia that some Muslims there have begun to embrace more "orthodox" forms of religious identity.

In spite of this, some Serbs in Bosnia argued that the SDA of Izetbegović represented a party of Islamic fundamentalists. Bosnian independence was declared in 1992 after a referendum that the Serbs of Bosnia boycotted on the grounds that it violated the still-valid constitution of the Socialist Republic of Bosnia and Herzegovina (Hayden 2000:92–93). The Bosnian Serbs instead proclaimed their own independent republic, Republika Srpska. Under the political leadership of Radovan Karadžić and the military leadership of General Ratko Mladić, who had made a name for himself (and his ethnic cleansing tactics) in the Serb–Croat war, the Bosnian Serbs began to drive non-Serbs out of those areas they claimed as Serbian. Together with the expulsions, the Serbian military and paramilitary volunteers also massacred Muslims, often burying them in secret grave sites that international observers later discovered.

Many more Muslims were interned in centers where they suffered from torture, malnourishment, and disease. Paramilitary squads targeted Muslim women as the objects of a systematic campaign of mass rape, designed to physically and psychologically degrade the enemy. All these tactics had a common aim: to make it impossible for Serbs, Croats, and Muslims to live together again after the war and hence to render ethnic cleansing a permanent reality.

Initially, the Croats and Muslims of Bosnia formed a military alliance against the Serbs. By 1993, however, the Muslims' former allies had become their enemies. Bosnia's Croats, concentrated in the region of Herzegovina, increasingly sought incorporation into the neighboring state of Croatia. As chronicled in Tone Bringa's moving film, *We Are All Neighbors*, Croats and Muslims who yesterday had lived together as neighbors now regarded one another suspiciously as Croat and Muslim militaries advanced toward their villages. In the village depicted in the film and in many other parts of Bosnia-Herzegovina, Croats ethnically cleansed Muslims. Muslims thus found themselves pressed on both sides by the Serbs and Croats.

Media images of Muslim victims created growing outrage in the United States and Europe, prompting demands for both humanitarian and military intervention. Although Serbs and Croats also suffered ethnic cleansing, Bosnian Muslims were perceived by many in the West as Yugoslavia's greatest victims. The persecution of Jews during the Holocaust offered a key analogy for such media coverage and for arguments that this time the West could not stand idly by. As already seen in the case of the Long Kesh prison in Northern Ireland, the Yugoslav case likewise revealed not only the powerful moral capital attached to the Holocaust narrative—a narrative referenced by various parties (Serbs, Muslims, Albanians, members of the international community, and media) during the conflict—but also the danger that use of the Holocaust metaphor might obscure understanding of what actually happened in former Yugoslavia (Hayden 1996:731; Živković 2000:83). Furthermore, the view that events in Yugoslavia were anomalous in "civilized," late twentieth-century Europe also obscured the extensive violence that historically accompanied state and nation building in Europe, as we have seen.

Anthropologist Robert Hayden has argued that "'ethnic cleansing' is a logical corollary of self-determination in situations in which the existence of a minority can be presented as potentially threatening to the national state of the majority" (1996:735–736). If so, an understanding of events in Yugoslavia requires attention not only to nationalist ideologies espousing purity but also an international system that embraces contradictory principles like those of self-determination and inviolability of borders. The insistence on both principles may lead, as it did in the former Yugoslavia, to violent expulsions designed to render territorial and ethnic borders congruent (Woodward 1995). The extensive role played in the Yugoslav conflict by the international community—from the United Nations peacekeepers to the debates over the arms embargo on Bosnia to the series of limited air strikes conducted by the United States on Serb targets to the NATO campaign in Kosovo—proves too complicated to detail here. What should be stressed, however, is that the Dayton Accords, which ended the Bosnian fighting in 1995, largely resulted from outside pressure being brought to bear on the warring sides within Bosnia.

The Dayton Accords created a unitary Bosnian state in name only, made up of a Croat–Muslim federation and the Serbian entity (Republika Srpska). In reality, these units tend to function like autonomous states that often have little interest in fulfilling all the clauses of the treaty such as that providing for the return of refugees to their homes. Although some refugees have returned, the end result of the ethnic cleansing carried out during the war appears to be the permanent "unmixing" of the peoples of Bosnia. Currently, the existence of the fragile Bosnian state that emerged from the conflict depends on the presence of an international peacekeeping force. In 2004, NATO peacekeeping troops (known as SFOR) turned over responsibilities to EUFOR (Althea), a European Union–led mission. The EU has announced its intention to phase out EUFOR over time, though no firm deadline has been established.

The international community has played a multifaceted role in Bosnia during and after the conflict, leaving a record of mixed results, at best. A number of anthropologists have studied the ways in which international bodies and non-governmental organizations (NGOs) have become critical to the (political) economy of Bosnia, prompting criticisms that this has fostered a culture of dependency and corruption. Anthropologist Andrew Dawson, for example, has documented the growth of the sex trade in

Bosnia, noting that the country has served as both "a transit destination and an end point in itself" for prostitution (2008:126). In her research on both women's NGOs and the police in Bosnia, anthropologist Elissa Helms demonstrates the ways in which foreign-funded bodies have taken over key capacities of the state (2006:345). The prosecution of "war criminals" represents one such critical capacity, a capacity largely assumed by the International Criminal Tribunal for Yugoslavia (ICTY) established in 1993. At the same time that non-Bosnian actors have played a crucial role in shaping the Bosnian future, they have nonetheless not participated to any significant extent in Bosnian society nor have they been subject to its regulations (Coles 2002:8). Not surprisingly, international institutions and their representatives—particularly the ICTY—have often proven unpopular in Bosnia.

While what will happen when the peacekeepers leave Bosnia remains to be seen, the prospects for a unified Bosnian identity and state appear less hopeful than in Northern Ireland. As in Northern Ireland, the Bosnian conflict has bequeathed a legacy of a culture marked by specifically *masculine* violence. Increasingly, complaints within Bosnia about the international community are represented in gendered terms, as the actual members of international organizations (many of whom are women) come to be seen as figuratively emasculating Balkan males and subverting patriarchal codes (Helms 2006; Živković 2006). In addition, as in Northern Ireland, there remains in Bosnia a legacy of bitter memories of ethnic and religious hatred with no consensus about how to interpret or memorialize the civil war that tore apart Bosnia.

Debates over how to memorialize Srebrenica, the site of a 1995 massacre of an estimated 8,000 Bosnian Muslim men by Bosnian Serb forces led by Ratko Mladić, exemplify how acknowledging atrocities does not necessarily promote reconciliation—that is, how the goals of justice and reconciliation may at times prove incompatible. The events at Srebrenica have been widely condemned as an act of genocide against Bosnian Muslims, even if some Bosnian Serbs have refused

414 Chapter 17 • Europe

to acknowledge it as such or have insisted on con-textualizing the violence within a broader frame that takes account of the destruction by Bosnian Muslim forces of some Bosnian Serb villages in the area around Srebrenica in 1992 and 1993. Questions of priority—that is, who did what first and why—together with the politics of recognition and non-recognition (as Serbs often complain about their forgotten victims)—thus may lead to sharply opposed narratives and understandings of what happened.

Outright denials of the number and identities of victims have become more difficult, however, thanks to the use of new technologies like DNA identification. DNA technology has provided a more reliable form of identification of remains than traditional sources of identification, which proved particularly inadequate at Srebrenica as the result of *secondary burials* (in which perpetrators first buried victims in one grave and then exhumed and reburied them elsewhere, often purposefully jumbling bodies). Anthropologist Sarah Wagner (2008) has evidenced how implementation of a large-scale and organized effort to use DNA to *identify* victims (rather than *confirm* identities, the usual task of such DNA identification) represents an innovation in forensic work with massacre vic-tims. This process requires the cooperation of family members of the victims willing to give DNA samples at the same time that it rests upon understanding of specific socio-cultural notions of kinship. Given this, anthropologists have had an important role to play here, both in the forensic and cultural side of the identification process. Anthropologists like Wagner have also studied the efforts to memorialize these victims once their remains have been identified.

Wagner details how the Srebrenica Memorial, dedicated in 2001, plays many roles: it provides a form of recognition in tangible form, a place for survivors to mourn, and a means to educate future generations. At the same time, however, the memorial also serves as a site at which divergent narratives and voices may clash. The cemetery attached to the memorial, for example, features a prayer in three languages:

Bosnian, Arabic, and English. The choice of lan-guages there underlines the ethnic and religious identities of the victims (Muslims) but also reaches out to a more international audience, symbolizing the international community's recognition that a genocide occurred. In con-structing a varied audience of Bosnian Muslims, other adherents of Islam, and people from outside of Bosnia, the memorial does not neces-sarily serve as an instrument of reconciliation, despite the stated hopes of many members of the international community. Serbs instead gravitate to the smaller commemorative center at Kravica, built to remember their victims.

Robert Hayden (2007) describes a similar paradox that marked the rebuilding of the Mostar Bridge, a project funded by the European Union and completed with much fanfare in 2004. Long a symbol of Bosnia's multiethnic history, the bridge had joined the largely Croatian Croat section of Mostar with its Muslim old town until Bosnian Croat forces shelled it in 1993. Despite the investment and attention given to the bridge's restoration, Mostar remains almost totally segre-gated and locals had little involvement in the ceremonies celebrating the bridge's reopening (pp. 108–110). The dilemmas of memorialization and participation that divide Croats and Muslims in Mostar or Serbs and Muslims in Srebrenica mirror the larger challenges to building a unified Bosnian state.

CONCLUSION: THE "NEW" EUROPE AND THE "NEW" RACISM

In the early 1990s, the collapse of socialism and the integration of the European Community (today the European Union) held out much promise for a peaceful and prosperous Europe in which the violence associated with nationalism, racism, and ethnicism would be just a distant memory. As we have seen, however, the violent dissolution of the former Yugoslavia has tempered optimism about a smooth transition to the "new" Europe. The cases of Bosnia and Northern Ireland explored here point to unresolved difficulties entailed by the projects of state making (past and present) and raise the question of whether the legal, administrative, and diplomatic apparatus of the "new" Europe (i.e., the European Union) can provide effective solutions. These cases also reveal the way in which the very notion of Europe itself may fuel, rather than diminish, ethnic and national divisions. The issue of what defines Europeanness and who belongs in that category has created new differentiations within contemporary Europe.

During the cold war, the internal boundary within Europe was closed from the eastern side: with the exception of Yugoslavia, socialist states sought to prevent their citizens from traveling or emigrating to Western Europe. The economic and political collapse of the socialist bloc has reversed the equation: today West European states seek to control the flows of individuals from generally poorer Eastern European countries. The wars in Yugoslavia and the opening up of impoverished states like Albania have intensified fears of a literal flood of political and economic refugees. In prosperous countries like Italy, Austria, and Germany, which border on former socialist states (some of whom are now EU members), coping with these arrivals has become a concrete, political reality. These European emigrants are increasingly joined by individuals from Asia and Africa, often from former European colonial possessions. Some Europeans now talk about how to strictly control these population movements, prompting the image of a "Fortress Europe" with open internal borders and rigid external ones.

At the state level, this has prompted intense competition among the former socialist states to officially enter into "Europe," understood as synonymous with the European Union. In practice, the label "European" has acquired a positive meaning and its opposite (whether "Oriental," "Eastern," or "Balkan") a negative one. On the one hand, "European" has become a value judgment made by those within the EU about how to understand (and whether to admit) those looking in. On the other hand, various groups within the new states of Central and Eastern Europe (e.g., in the former Yugoslavia) adopt this same rhetoric in their efforts to position themselves as more or less European; they simultaneously depict their political opponents as non-European, creating prevalent new forms of chauvinism.

Since the 1980s, many Slovenes and Croats have emphasized their Hapsburg past and Catholic identities in depicting themselves as European peoples. They contrast themselves to "Balkanic" Serbs, said to be saddled with a dual Oriental legacy from the Ottoman Empire and from Orthodox Christianity (Bakić-Hayden 1995; Bakić-Hayden and Hayden 1992). European here implies a cultural heritage of democracy and civil society. Similar distinctions came into play in the dispute between Greece and the newly independent Republic of Macedonia over the name Macedonian and the memory of Alexander the Great; Greeks view themselves as heirs of Alexander and the founders of Europe, in contrast to Balkanic Slavs who claim the name Macedonian (Danforth 1995; Herzfeld 1997; Karakasidou 1997).

In the articulation of identity, many Europeans (as well as Americans) increasingly view cultural heritage as exerting a hold akin to that which a previous generation had imagined race playing. Ironically, then, the socially acquired patterns of culture—what anthropologists like Franz Boas and Margaret Mead used to argue against the primacy of "nature" in the historic nature–nurture debate—may now appear as fixed and fatal as our genetic makeup. Scholars like Verena Stolcke (1995) and Paul Gilroy (1987) have demonstrated how, within the new Europe, this blurring of the once-distinct boundaries of culture and nature takes place. Stolcke discusses "cultural fundamentalism" and Gilroy the "new racism," but they essentially make the same point: that identity is no longer necessarily understood or described in primordial terms, such as race, but instead is often seen as culturally constructed. The trick, however, is that culture is increasingly seen as a given and inescapable, almost as if it were a genetically given or racial characteristic. Such fears suggest not that racism in Europe has disappeared but that it has assumed new forms and a new vocabulary, all the more difficult to combat because it is disguised within the language of culture.

Writing about the politics of blackness in contemporary Great Britain, for example, Gilroy examines the historic development of notions of race in relation to those of class and nation. Respect for the law proves fundamental to images of English nationality. Identified with criminality, blacks in England (particularly young males) thus appear to stand outside of and threaten the boundaries of the nation. In the 1970s, racist leader Enoch Powell went so far as to declare mugging a "racial crime." Increasingly, though, such leaders attribute supposed criminality and antiauthoritarianism to black culture rather than to any innate characteristics (Gilroy 1987:73–110). This permits such leaders to disingenuously declare, "But we're not racist!" while nonetheless putting forward racist ideas in a new form and promoting repressive measures to deal with presumed criminality. Italy, for example, has increasingly criminalized immigrants, leading anthropologist Asale Angel-Ajani to observe that in the areas of drugs and prostitution, " these 'deviant behaviors' are being characterized as being almost 'un-Italian' in nature" (2002:41). The resulting "social panic" over immigrants (p. 41) is playing out in a Europe marked by overall demographic decline (low birth rates), a phenomenon particularly marked in countries like Italy and Spain, which in the not too distant past had to export its own surplus population.

Ironically, even when the opponents of new racism recognize the commonalties between the emigrants from European countries in the past and the immigrants to European countries today, they often employ the same language of culture and community of their "racist" opponents. This reveals the conceptual and political challenges contemporary Europeans face in articulating alternative forms of multicultural identity. The ethnographic examples in this chapter have highlighted many of the key dynamics involved in refashioning identities in the "new" Europe. Whether confronting the problems of large-scale immigration for the first time, the impact of nonwhite or non-Christian refugees, or the legacies of violent partition and civil war, contemporary Europeans draw upon older understandings of race and ethnicity even as they struggle to create new forms of identity in a world characterized by increased population flows of all sorts. As we have seen, the very issue of what defines Europeanness and who belongs in this category has proven crucial to the historical development of notions of ethnicity, race, and nation in Europe. Today, the notion of Europeanness continues to constitute an ethnic and moral boundary, as well as a geographic one, highlighting both continuities and transformations of identity.

Notes

1. Those sterilized in order to avoid "lives unworthy of life" included alcoholics and poor Germans. The latter group, including prostitutes, housewives, and female servants, made up the majority of those subjected to forced sterilization (Bock 1984:281–282).

2. Intellectuals of the "Austro-Marxist" school devoted considerable attention to the "nationalities question," which dominated politics in the late Hapsburg Empire. Thinkers like Otto Bauer and Karl Renner argued for a socialist solution of the nationalities question within the bounds of empire, a proposal that differed from the more "orthodox" interpretations of Marx and Engel's writings on nationalism.

References Cited

ANDERSON, BENEDICT. 1987. *Imagined Communities*. London: Verso.

ANGEL-AJANI, ASALE. 2002. Diasporic conditions: Mapping the discourses of race and criminality in Italy. *Transforming Anthropology* 11(1):36–46.

ARETXAGA, BEGOÑ A. 1997. *Shattering Silence: Women, Nationalism and Political Subjectivity in Northern Ireland*. Princeton, NJ: Princeton University Press.

BAKIĆ;-HAYDEN, MILICA. 1992. Orientalist variations on the theme "Balkans": Symbolic geography in recent Yugoslav cultural politics. *Slavic Review* 51(1):1–15.

BAKIĆ-HAYDEN, MILICA, and ROBERT HAYDEN. 1995. Nesting orientalisms: The case of former Yugoslavia. *Slavic Review* 54(4):917–931.

BARNARD, F. M. 1965. *Herder's Social and Political Thought*. Oxford: Clarendon Press.

———. 1969. Culture and political development: Herder's suggestive insights. *American Political Science Review* 62:379–397.

BARNIER, ALAN. 2006. Titanic town: Sport, space and the re-imag(in)ing of Belfast. *City & Society* 18(2):159–179.

BOCK, GISELE. 1984. Racism and sexism in Nazi Germany: Motherhood, compulsory sterilization and the state. In *When Biology Became Destiny*. R. Bridenthal, A. Grossman, and M. Kaplan, eds. Pp. 272–288. New York: Monthly Review Press.

BRACEWELL, WENDY. 2000. Rape in Kosovo: Masculinity and Serbian nationalism. *Nations and Nationalism* 6(4):563–590.

BREUILLY, JOHN. 1985. *Nationalism and the State*. Chicago, IL: University of Chicago Press.

BRINGA, TONE. 1995. *Being Muslim the Bosnian Way*. Princeton, NJ: Princeton University Press.

BROWNING, CHRISTOPHER. 1992. *Ordinary Men: Reserve Police Battalion 101 and the Final Solution*. New York: HarperCollins.

BRUBAKER, ROGERS. 1992. *Citizenship and Nationhood in France and Germany*. Cambridge, MA: Harvard University Press.

BUNZL, MATTI. 2005. Between anti-Semitism and Islamophobia: Some thoughts on the new Europe. *American Ethnologist* 32(4):499–508.

CANNADINE, DAVID. 1983. The context, performance and meaning of ritual: The British monarchy and the "invention of tradition," c. 1820–1977. In *The Invention of Tradition*. Eric Hobsbawm and Terence Ranger, eds. Pp. 101–164. Cambridge: University of Cambridge Press.

CHABOD, FEDERICO. 1991. *Storia dell'Idea di Europa*. Bari: Laterza.

CLAVORA, FERRUCCIO. 1988. *L'Unione Emigranti Sloveni al Servizio della Propria Comunità*. Cividale: Unione Emigranti Sloveni del Friuli-Venezia Giulia.

CLAVORA, FERRUCCIO, and RICCARDO RUTTAR. 1990. *La Comunità Senza Nome: La Slavia alle Soglie del 2000*. Udine: Juliagraf di Premariacco.

COCCHIARA, GIUSEPPE. 1952. *The History of Folkore in Europe*. John N. McDaniel, trans. Philadelphia, PA: Institute for the Study of Human Issues.

COLES, KIMBERLY. 2002. Ambivalent builders: Europeanization, the production of difference, and internationals in Bosnia-Herzegovina. *POLAR* 25(1):1–18.

CONNOR, WALKER. 1984. *The National Question in Marxist-Leninist Theory and Strategy*. Princeton, NJ: Princeton University Press.

CORRIGAN, PHILIP RICHARD D., and DEREK SAYER. 1985. *The Great Arch: English State Formation as Cultural Revolution*. Oxford: Blackwell.

CURTIS, PERRY. 1971. *Apes and Angels: The Irishmen in Victorian Caricatures*. Washington, DC: Smithsonian Institution.

DANFORTH, LORING. 1995. *The Macedonian Conflict: Ethnic Nationalism in a Transnational World*. Princeton, NJ: Princeton University Press.

DAWSON, ANDREW. 2008. Post-war Settlements and the production of new illegalities: The case of Dayton and people trafficking and prostitution in Bosnia and Herzegovina. *Dialectical Anthropology* 32:123–137.

DE FELICE, RENZO. 1976. *Fascism: An Informal Introduction to Its Theory and Practice*. Michael Ledeen, ed. New Brunswick: Transaction.

DENICH, BETTE. 1994. Dismembering Yugoslavia: Nationalist ideologies and the symbolic revival of genocide. *American Ethnologist* 21(2):367–390.

DUDEN, BARBARA. 1989. Rereading Boas: A woman historian's response to Carl N. Degler. In *Culture versus Biology in the Thought of Franz Boas and Alfred L. Kroeber*. Pp. 24–28. New York: Berg.

ELLIS, JOHN. 1963. *One Fairy Story Too Many: The Brothers Grimm and Their Tales*. Chicago, IL: University of Chicago Press.

FELDMAN, ALLEN. 1991. *Formations of Violence: The Narrative of the Body and Political Terror in Northern Ireland*. Chicago, IL: University of Chicago Press.

FULTON, JOHN. 1991. *The Tragedy of Belief: Division, Politics and Religion in Ireland*. Oxford: Clarendon Press.

GAJEK, ESTHER. 1990. Christmas under the Third Reich. *Anthropology Today* 6(4):3–9.

GALLIHER, JOHN, AND JERRY DeGREGORY. 1985. *Violence in Northern Ireland: Understanding Protestant Perspectives*. Dublin: Gill & Macmillan, Holmes & Meier.

GELLNER, ERNEST. 1987. *Nations and Nationalism*. Ithaca, NY: Cornell University Press.

GILMAN, SANDER. 1985. *Difference and Pathology: Stereotypes of Sexuality, Race and Madness*. Ithaca, NY: Cornell University Press.

GILROY, PAUL. 1987. *There Ain't No Black in the Union Jack: The Cultural Politics of Race and Nation*. London: Hutchinson.

GOLDHAGEN, DANIEL. 1996. *Hitler's Willing Executioners: Ordinary Germans and the Holocaust.* New York: Knopf.

GRAHAM, BRIAN, and SARA MCDOWELL. 2007. Meaning in the Maze: The Heritage of Long Kesh. *Cultural Geographies* 14(3):343–368.

HAYDEN, ROBERT. 1994. Recounting the dead: The rediscovery and redefinition of wartime massacres in late- and post-communist Yugoslavia. In *Memory, History and Opposition under State Socialism.* Rubie Watson, ed. Santa Fe, NM: School of American Research Press.

———. 1996. Schindler's fate: Genocide, ethnic cleansing, and population transfers. *Slavic Review* 55(4):727–748.

———. 2000. *Blueprints for a House Divided.* Ann Arbor, MI: University of Michigan Press.

———. 2007. Moral vision and impaired insight: The imagining of other people's communities in Bosnia. *Current Anthropology* 48(1):105–131.

HECHTER, MICHAEL. 1975. *Internal Colonialism.* Berkeley, CA: University of California Press.

HELMS, ELISSA. 2006. Gendered transformation of state power: Masculinity, international intervention, and the Bosnian police. *Nationalities Papers* 34(3):343–361.

HERDER, JOHANN GOTTFRIED. 1966. *Outlines of a Philosophy of the History of Man.* T. Churchill, trans. New York: Bergman.

———. 1968. *Reflections on the Philosophy of the History of Mankind.* Frank E. Manuel, ed. Chicago, IL: University of Chicago Press.

HERF, JEFFREY. 1997. *Divided Memory.* Cambridge, MA: Harvard University Press.

HERZFELD, MICHAEL. 1982. *Ours Once More: Folklore, Ideology and the Making of Modern Greece.* Austin, TX: University of Texas Press.

———. 1987. *Anthropology through the Looking Glass: Critical Ethnography in the Margins of Europe.* Cambridge: Cambridge University Press.

———. 1997. *Cultural Intimacy: Social Poetics in the Nation-State.* New York: Routledge.

HOBSBAWM, ERIC. 1990. *Nations and Nationalism since 1780: Programme, Myth, Reality.* Cambridge: Cambridge University Press.

HODGEN, MARGARET. 1963. *Early Anthropology in the Sixteenth and Seventeenth Centuries.* Philadelphia, PA: University of Pennsylvania Press.

HUGHES, MICHAEL. 1994. *Ireland Divided: The Roots of the Modern Irish Problem.* New York: St. Martin's.

HUME, JOHN. 1993. A new Ireland in a new Europe. In *Northern Ireland and the Politics of Reconciliation.* Dermot Keogh and Michael Haltzel, eds. Pp. 226–233. Cambridge: Cambridge University Press.

IGNATIEFF, MICHAEL. 1993. *Blood and Belonging.* London: BBC Books.

JUST, ROGER. 1989. Triumph of the ethnos. In *History and Ethnicity.* Elizabeth Tonkin, Maryon McDonald, and Malcolm Chapman, eds. Pp. 71–88. London: Routledge.

KARAKASIDOU, ANASTASIA. 1997. *Fields of Wheat, Fields of Blood.* Chicago, IL: University of Chicago Press.

KEDOURIE, ELIE. 1993. *Nationalism.* Oxford: Blackwell.

KITROMILIDES, PASCHALIS. 1989. "Imagined communities" and the origins of the national question in the Balkans. *European History Quarterly* 19:149–194.

KLIGMAN, GAIL. 1988a. *The Wedding of the Dead: Ritual, Poetics and Popular Culture in Transylvania.* Berkeley, CA: University of California Press.

———. 1998b. *The Politics of Duplicity: Controlling Reproduction in Ceaucescu's Romania.* Berkeley, CA: University of California Press.

KOHN, HANS. 1965. *Nationalism—Its Meaning and History.* New York: Van Kreiger.

———. 1967. *The Idea of Nationalism.* New York: Macmillan.

KOON, TRACY. 1981. *Believe, Obey, Fight.* Chapel Hill, NC: University of North Carolina Press.

LENIN, V. I. 1951. *The Right of Nations to Self-Determination.* New York: International Publishers.

MALCOLM, NOEL. 1994. *Bosnia: A Short History.* London: Papermac (Macmillan).

———. 1998. *Kosovo: A Short History.* New York: New York University Press.

MCDONALD, MARYON. 1986. Celtic ethnic kinship and the problem of being English. *Current Anthropology* 27:333–341.

———. 1989. *We Are Not French! Language, Culture and Identity in Brittany.* London: Routledge.

MILLER, DAVID, ed. 1998. *Rethinking Northern Ireland: Culture, Ideology and Colonialism.* London: Longman.

MOSSE, GEORGE. 1985. *Nationalism and Sexuality.* Madison, WI: University of Wisconsin Press.

NAIRN, TOM. 1977. *The Break-Up of Britain.* London: New Left Books.

OZYÜREK, ESRA. 2005. The Politics of cultural unification, secularism, and the place of Islam in the new Europe. *American Ethnologist* 32(4):509–512.

ROWTHORN, BOB, and NAOMI WAYNE. 1988. *Northern Ireland: The Political Economy of Conflict.* Boulder, CO: Westview Press.

SHELAH, MENACHEM. 1989. The Italian rescue of Yugoslav Jews, 1941–1943. In *The Italian Refuge: Rescue of Jews during the Holocaust.* Ivo Herzer et al., eds. Pp. 205–217. Washington, DC: Catholic University of America Press.

STEINBERG, JONATHAN. 1990. *All or Nothing: The Axis and the Holocaust, 1941–1943.* London: Routledge.

STILLE, ALEXANDER. 1991. *Benevolence and Betrayal: Five Italian Jewish Families under Fascism.* New York: Summit Books.

STOLCKE, VERENA. 1995. Talking culture: New boundaries, new rhetorics of exclusion in Europe. *Current Anthropology* 36(1):1–13.

THOMPSON, EDWARD P. 1967. Time, work-discipline and industrial capitalism. *Past and Present,* 38:22–60.

TODOROV, TZVETAN. 1987. *The Conquest of America: The Question of the Other.* Richard Howard, trans. New York: Harper & Row.

VERDERY, KATHERINE. 1991. *National Ideology under Socialism.* Berkeley, CA: University of California Press.

———. 1993. Whither "nation" and "nationalism"? *Daedalus* 122(3):37–46.

———. 1996. *What Was Socialism, and What Comes Next?* Princeton, NJ: Princeton University Press.

WACHTEL, ANDREW BARUCH. 1998. *Making a Nation, Breaking a Nation.* Stanford, CA: Stanford University Press.

WAGNER, SARAH. 2008. *To Know Where he Lies: DNA Technology and the Search for Srebrenica's Missing.* Berkeley, CA: University of California Press.

WEBER, EUGEN. 1976. *Peasants into Frenchmen: The Modernization of Rural France, 1870–1914.* Stanford, CA: Stanford University Press.

WOODWARD, SUSAN. 1995. *Balkan Tragedy: Chaos and Dissolution after the Cold War.* Washington, DC: Brookings Institution.

YOUNG, JAMES. 1988. *Writing and Rewriting the Holocaust: Narrative and the Consequences of Interpretation.* Bloomington, IN: Indiana University Press.

ŽIVKOVIĆ, MARKO. 2000. The wish to be a Jew: The power of the Jewish trope in the Yugoslav conflict. *Cahiers de l'URMIS* 6:69–84.

ZUCCOTTI, SUSAN. 1987. *The Italians and the Holocaust: Persecution, Rescue, and Survival.* New York: Basic Books.

18

Canada

Norman Buchignani, *University of Lethbridge*

When they think of them at all, Americans tend to think stereotypically about their northern neighbors. Images of Mounties and hockey aside, Americans typically harbor a sense that Canada is a fairly homogeneous place; one populated with nice, if somewhat unimaginative, folk, pretty much like those next door but with a residue of British "civility." Some may be aware of Québec and of separatist sentiments there. However, few Canadians in this century, and even fewer in this generation, would have such an impression. Each in their own way, they would have sensed and experienced a country whose social diversity is now fully as great as that in the United States. This is markedly so of ethnic and 'racial' diversity. Ethnic and race relations have played a central role in shaping Canada since before the arrival of Europeans, and this role has been enduring and increasing. Today, 50 percent of individuals in both Toronto, the country's largest city, and in the Metro Toronto urban region (2006 population, 5.1 million) are foreign-born, as are 19.8 percent of all Canadians. Current annual rates of legal immigration are proportionally more than double those in the United States, and almost 4 percent of Canadians (1,200,000) identify themselves as being First Nations (native). About 5.4 percent (1.7 million) claim some degree of aboriginal origin.[1] A new northern territory (Nunavut) run by and for Inuit people was created by mutual consent only 11 years ago.

It is often said that Canada and the United States share the longest militarily undefended border in the world. They share much more than this, and many parallels can be made between the two countries. Some are the result of the border being undefended in many other respects: they are mutually dependent societies of unequal power and influence. Huge flows of goods and people move across the border every day, and with them move ideas and values.[2] Similar ecologies and historical forces have led to the evolution of broadly similar regional cultures on each side of the line, from west to east: British Columbia shares much with the Pacific Northwest, Alberta with Montana, and the Maritime provinces with New England.

Other parallels have more general sources. Both have their roots as nation-states in Protestant colonial settler societies. Both are prosperous, highly urban societies based on fairly open capitalistic economies. Both have English as a national language (although Canada has two of them), and what English has brought with it: broadly similar notions of citizenship, the individual and the role of the state in people's affairs. Both have had a long-term dependence on immigration and are home to large native populations. As a consequence, contemporary ethnic and race relations in Canada also share a number of parallels with those in the United States (Reitz and Breton 1994). For example, both societies now positively affirm ethnic and racial equality and diversity, and the pressures of assimilation and acculturation faced by immigrants are broadly similar in each.

Even so, in other important ways ethnic and race relations in Canada have always been very different, and differently framed, than those to the south. Folk and government responses have differed as well. In what follows, I purposely highlight some of the main distinctions, bringing in key similarities with the United States where appropriate.

A STRONG AND ENDURING FIRST NATIONS PRESENCE

What was to become Canada was home to an extremely diverse set of First Nations. Some of these societies were as culturally and linguistically different from each other as Chinese and English. They often *felt* different and acted accordingly. A sense of us and them that was often as strong as anything seen today was incorporated into complex relationships between members of one First Nations collectivity and another. In these senses, ethnic relations in Canada predate the arrival of Europeans by thousands of years. When they did appear,

Europeans were quickly integrated into ongoing local systems of ethnic and political relationships. Such relations thereafter were critical to the development of fledgling European colonies. Settlers, the military, and colonial administrators in New France (successfully founded in 1608) were highly dependent on the goodwill and support of some First Nations from the onset—particularly in their struggles with the English over who would control the north-eastern part of the continent. Of necessity, much everyday settler cultural practice was native derived, particularly in the area of subsistence.[3]

French settlers quickly established a form of Latin or Catholic race relations with the original inhabitants of New France and Acadia. A person's status and authority depended not only on biology (conceived of by all Europeans very differently than now) but also on one's class and culture. This logic led to the quick rise of inter-marriage and informal liaisons between settlers and natives, to the consequent creation of a large Métis (literally, mixed) population (numbering 390,000 in 2006; see Purich 1988), and to a continuum of European and First Nations lifestyles and cultural traditions on the frontier. New France was conquered by the British in 1759–1780 and amalgamated into the nascent British Empire (1763).[4] Together with indigenous people, British entrepreneurs (chiefly Scots) then quickly developed the fur trade (from which comes Canada's animal totem, the beaver). By 1820, the fur trade extended right across what is Canada today and far into the North. The fur trade was a polyethnic enterprise that tied local ethnic relations into a global economic system: Indians and Métis were the chief trappers. Métis and French Canadians were the *voyageurs* who transported the furs and trade goods back and forth to Montréal. Almost all the owners, factors (traders), and other functionaries were British.

As was intended, the fur trade led to increasing First Nations dependence on Europeans for food, tools, clothing, and weapons. In the nineteenth century this dependence was greatly increased by population losses from imported diseases, by advancing European settlement and political hegemony, and by settler resource extraction activities. The initial subordination of First Nations people was a relentless, ongoing (if rarely overtly violent) process that extended far more recently into the modern era than similar processes did in the United States. Much of the Canadian prairies (which became Alberta, Saskatchewan, and Manitoba) were only extensively settled by Europeans after 1895, and some Inuit only came under definitive European control in the 1950s.

The sole late nineteenth-century exceptions to the Canadian way of colonizing and otherwise repressing First Nations people through non-military means involved Métis settlers and Cree in what were to become Manitoba and Saskatchewan. Fearful of losing their political, cultural, and land rights in the upcoming transfer of the Red River Settlement and the rest of the North-West from the Hudson's Bay Company to the federal government, long-established Métis settlers resisted in 1869. Under the charismatic leadership of highly religious and well-educated Louis Riel, they stopped federal land surveys, seized Fort Garry, and established a provisional government. Unable to mount a swift military response, the federal government was conciliatory, and in 1870 passed legislation (the Manitoba Act) granting Métis rights to 1,400,000 acres of land and providing for a limited range of bilingual rights and services in the new province. Vilified in Ontario but seen as a hero and defender of the faith in Québec, Riel eventually fled to the United States. In 1884 he returned to Saskatchewan in response to solicitations from local Métis settlers. Within a year, Riel mounted another rebellion centered at the Métis settlement of Batoche. This time, the railway facilitated the quick arrival of Canadian troops, and the rebellion was crushed after a series of fierce engagements. Riel and a number of Métis and Cree leaders were tried for treason. Riel was convicted and hanged, thereby making him an enduring symbol of British Canadian oppression for francophones and Québec separatists to this day.

Both early French and British colonial leaders mapped European international relations practice onto their relations with native people. Some (including Samuel de Champlain, a key founder of New France) treated natives seriously as nations and established political treaties with them. This practice was continued after 1867 by the autonomous Canadian government, which legally recognized extant treaty commitments made by the British. The last comprehensive treaty was signed with a range of peoples in the North in 1921.[5] In the end, few of the provisions of these treaties were consistently honored by the government, save perhaps in regard to the establishment of a system of band lists and reserves (reservations) upon which certain First Nations people were thereafter to live. There are currently about 615 such bands sprinkled across the country, controlling roughly 2,300 reserves and 2,700,000 hectares of land.

The period 1870–1960 illustrates many parallels with the United States. Status or registered Indians (those whose names are entered on a band list, numbering 565,000 in 2006) were relegated to reserves and excluded from full participation in Canadian society. There, they functioned as a reserve army of agricultural and resource extraction labor, an economic option that, along with subsistence bush economies, evaporated after World War II. While nonstatus Indians and Métis had the same legal rights as other Canadians, status Indians (reflecting a dubious notion that they were still members of autonomous societies) could not vote. Neither could they control their own personal or community affairs, and their cultures and languages were inexorably repressed through such means as forced attendance at residential schools. Most First Nations people in the southern part of the country had to deal primarily with a negative, paternalistic stereotype of themselves as fallen Indians—in contrast to a much more positive (but highly romantic) stereotype of what Indians were like before contact. Highly individualized ideologies of good citizenship, independence, and responsibility marginalized First Nations people and were used to blame them for their own misfortunes.[6]

Since the 1960s there has been a remarkable increase in the power and influence of First Nations people. In the vanguard were a set of increasingly effective status Indian leaders and organizations (Dyck 1985, 1991). Initially, organizations such as the Assembly of First Nations pressed for and often secured a wider interpretation of government treaty responsibilities more appropriate to modern times. Almost all residential schools were disbanded by the end of the 1960s, and since the mid-1980s band councils have secured increasing control over how reserve-based services are delivered; many are now entirely provided by local native personnel (Driben 1985). These national organizations also helped local band councils to move forward on outstanding land claims—in essence, reopening or initiating new treaties to reconsider what lands and land-use rights (such as fishing and logging) continue to be the preserve of First Nations. In British Columbia, serious negotiation over land rights began for the first time (Ponting 1997).

During 1975–1978, the Inuit and Cree of northern Québec negotiated and signed major agreements with the governments of Québec Province and Canada that exchanged aboriginal title over some lands for confirming those of others, increased local sovereignty, and money (Salisbury 1986). In 1993, the federal government and the Inuit of the eastern Arctic signed an agreement to create Nunavut, a new, Inuit-run northern territory. Nunavut was established in 1999, with all the powers and responsibilities of the Yukon and Northwest Territories. Further south, these processes also led in 1999 to the comprehensive Nisga'a land claims settlement in northern British Columbia. This settlement is now looked to by many as the model for resolving the hundreds of other land claims that are still outstanding. It gives the Nisga'a many autonomous political and economic powers within the land ceded to them, powers that elsewhere would be the sole prerogative of the provincial or federal government. Recent court interpretations of British era treaties have secured important fishing and other resources-collection rights for certain Indian bands in the Maritimes.

By the 1980s, representatives of status Indian and Inuit people were sufficiently influential to demand and secure political representation at key national forums at which important Canadian constitutional issues concerning them were addressed. As a result, significant First Nations *group* rights were affirmed in the Constitution Act of 1982 (Asch 1984). Section 25 of the Canadian Charter of Rights and Freedoms (part of the Constitution) explicitly subordinates all other constitutional provisions to the treaty and other rights of First Nations. First Nations representatives also pressed to have a voice in subsequent efforts to amend the Constitution to address Québec separatism, arguing that First Nations rights would be affected by any such new arrangements. These concerns were paramount when Elija Harper, a Cree representative in the Manitoba provincial legislature, played a significant role in blocking assent to the Meech Lake Accord to amend the Constitution. Representatives from four First Nations organizations later sat with provincial and federal representatives to hammer out the unsuccessful Charlottetown Constitutional Agreement.

Most other Canadians hold radically more positive notions of natives and native cultures than were prevalent a generation ago. These changes are the result of several factors: a general moderation of prior ethnic and racial sensitivities; ideological connections made between First Nations people, ecological lifestyles, and nature; and a sense that First Nations people are actively and appropriately moving to address historical injustices. Overall, First Nations people today have a public presence and impact across Canada that they do not have in the United States. At the same time, most First Nations people continue to face many significant disabilities and disadvantages in everyday life. Some of these are ethnic and racial (and are considered later), a distinction that, as with African Americans, is somewhat arbitrary to employ regarding a population whose life chances today are profoundly affected by past inequities.

TWO PERSISTING EUROPEAN CHARTER GROUPS

Every large landmass conquered by Europeans was at some point occupied by more than one colonial power. In the United States, this included the Spanish, Dutch, British, French, and Russians. In every case this has had some impact on subsequent race and ethnic relations. Canada, therefore, is not unique in being occupied and settled by two European powers: the French in New France and Acadia and the British initially in Newfoundland. Neither is it unique that one—the British—eventually prevailed through a combination of military conquest and political negotiation.

What makes Canada atypical of the nations that arose out of European settler societies was what happened to the losers. Conquered French established in what would eventually become Canada were not reduced to an ethnic minority in the general population.[7] Such was the fate of Mexicans in the U.S. Southwest and California after their forcible incorporation into the United States. British, British immigrants, and Canadian-born people who subsequently styled themselves British Canadians did come to hold a preponderance of political, economic, and cultural power after the Conquest. Like British-origin Americans after the American Revolution, they became a *charter group*—a population whose interests, culture, and language profoundly shaped the core institutions and values of society.

But in a significant, albeit more limited, way, so did the French. The British faced a political dilemma immediately after the Conquest: how to govern and control a large and disaffected French population without an equally large number of British foot soldier–settlers. Very few British had yet immigrated to these northern regions, as compared with those who had sought a new home in the American colonies. The British government therefore strategically extended rights and privileges to the residents of former New France that were not even available to Catholics in England. Informally, and through the Québec Act (1775), the British established an early kind of indirect colonial rule in Lower Canada (later, Québec). The French-speaking inhabitants thereby preserved much local autonomy in language, culture, religion, and politics. Extant French institutions were supported and maintained, including the French language, much of the legal system, Catholic schools, and the powerful everyday role of the Catholic church.

The nominally British population of what was to become Upper Canada (Ontario), New Brunswick, and Nova Scotia first swelled with the influx of United Empire Loyalists who fled the American Revolution and its aftermath. It is interesting to note that while the Loyalists were long portrayed in Canada as epitomizing the British founders of the country, a large minority were Germans, free African Americans, and natives. British control ensured that the number of English, Scots, Irish, and 'white' Americans in subsequent generations slowly increased through immigration while French immigration was negligible.

Through the decades, tensions between French Canadians and the expanding anglophone population of Lower Canada grew episodically. These came to a head during the economically depressed mid-1830s, when local francophone patriots and politicians first tried, unsuccessfully, to secure control over provincial revenues and increase local representation. In 1837–1838 they escalated their actions to mount a disastrous insurrection. In 1841, Upper and Lower Canada were merged into a single political entity, with the British in the majority. However, high birth rates (that would be later termed the revenge of the cradle) helped to ensure French demographic continuity and selective political power. Control of the growing urban economy was almost exclusively in the hands of British Canadians, whose elite dominated Montréal.

The British North America (BNA) Act (1867), which enabled Canadian Confederation and consequent formal independence from Britain (along with subsequent federal legislation), enshrined certain French-language and (Catholic)

education rights. It also gave significant powers to the confederating political entities like Québec that thereafter became provinces. Although a numerical minority, francophones could not be ignored by federal politicians, for no one could form a government majority in Parliament without their significant support. Roughly half of all Canadian Prime Ministers have been Québec francophones, and every Prime Minister since the 1950s has been fluently bilingual.

Then as now, French-speakers in Québec (and secondarily, in New Brunswick, where francophones are roughly one-third of the population) maintained all the necessary elements for their long-term persistence—demographically, culturally, linguistically, and in regard to personal identity (Eller 1998:299–300). Most Québec francophones lived in communities with a high degree of *institutional completeness* (Breton 1964): Virtually everything in one's daily orbit of activities could be done using economic, political, religious, educational, and other parallel institutions where French was spoken and that were used by others maintaining broadly the same core ethnocultural identity. While chronically poor economic conditions generated an ongoing exodus from these communities, such losses were more than compensated for by new births. As a consequence, in 2006 5.9 million people in Québec considered French their sole mother tongue; most were the lineal descendants of the inhabitants of New France.

The francophone communities in other provinces and territories were never as institutionally complete, lacking a full range of institutions parallel to those of the anglophones that often surrounded them. In 2006 roughly 940,000 individuals claimed French as their mother tongue and lived outside Québec, 483,000 of them in Ontario and 233,000 in New Brunswick. However, francophone community institutions outside Québec, New Brunswick, and some parts of Ontario now appear to be rapidly disappearing. This does not bode well for the long-term persistence of local francophone populations outside Québec.

Confederation did little to mitigate a persistent sense of disadvantage among Québec francophones, which in turn helped maintain distinctive local identities. This discontent episodically rose to critical levels in response to British Canadian political insensitivities, as in the conscription crisis of World War I.[8] Since the formation of the first overtly separatist government in 1976, Québec politicians have used their legislative powers to ensure that francophones remain the dominant charter group in that province.

NO HISTORY OF EXTENSIVE RACIALLY GROUNDED SLAVERY

Slavery was legal and was practiced in New France, as it was during the early days of British rule. However, under neither regime was it economically viable, and so was never widespread. Perhaps 5–6,000 individuals were enslaved during the whole of New France's existence, most of whom were native people. No impediments to slave owning were introduced after the Conquest, and from then on new settlers occasionally brought African origin slaves with them; in this fashion there was a significant influx of enslaved people travelling with Loyalists refugees from the American Revolution. Even so, abolitionist sentiment was strong, and in 1793 Upper Canada passed the Act Against Slavery barring the importation of slaves and requiring their children to be freed at age 25. In 1807 the British home government banned the slave trade in British ships, and slavery was outlawed throughout the empire in 1833. Thereafter, anyone enslaved elsewhere became legally free simply by virtue of setting foot in Canada. This augmented the Underground Railway, through which an estimated 50,000 African American political refugees fled north to freedom during 1830–1865 (Dirks 1977:23). Although many returned to the United States after the Civil War, others joined a small Afro-Canadian population that had been previously established through the immigration of Loyalists and free 'blacks' from

the Caribbean and the United States. Significant 'black' immigration did not again occur until the 1960s, and then came primarily from the Caribbean. Today's Afro-Canadian population is very diverse, including a few individuals who are eighth- and ninth-generation Canadian-born, as well as immigrants from over 30 countries. However, Afro-Canadians today represent less than one-fifth the proportion of the population of African Americans in the United States: 784,000 people, or roughly 2.5 percent of all Canadians in 2006.

Because of this very different history, Canadians have not had to generate or maintain the kind of radical racial notions some Americans historically used to justify the enslavement of other Americans based on the latter's supposed biological inferiority. Neither have Canadians had to deal so directly with slavery's sorry legacy of racial thought and practice. To this day, social race—the erroneous notion that the world's people can be divided into biologically distinct, largely self-reproducing populations—does not have anything like the salience and naturalized, take-it-for-granted status it has in the United States. As a case in point, the U.S. Census routinely collects information on the race of respondents as if this is a self-evident way to categorize people; such a query would be unthinkable on the Canadian Census. Instead, since World War II both Canadians and their governments have preferred to frame intergroup relations in terms of ethnicity (i.e., to say, in terms of perceived cultural differences and attendant identities), even when they *do* have clear racial dimensions. With the priority that Canadians currently place on ethnicity typically comes an assumption of mutability: Whether or not the perceived ethnic differences of others are thought desirable, they are believed to be cultural things that can be altered by the efforts of those who practice them. Racial ideas of the sort more prevalent in the United States do not as extensively incorporate such assumptions.

This is not to suggest that racial perceptions are irrelevant. Canadians have always employed a mix of both perceived cultural and biological criteria to distinguish each other. Perceived biological difference was a significant disability for historical First Nations, Métis, and Afro-Canadian people, even when they were culturally indistinguishable from others. Asians and African Americans were the only populations that faced explicit Canadian immigration bans in the past. Almost all Japanese Canadians were interned during World War II, but few German Canadians were. Canadians have long embraced hierarchically evaluated stereotypes of ethnocultural populations that locate most of those perceived to be 'nonwhite' lower than others. Such attitudes have moderated greatly over time, and no governmental, institutional, or personal form of discrimination based on race has been legal in Canada for almost two generations. Even so, members of the culturally heterogeneous Afro-Canadian, First Nations, and Asian populations do continue to contend specifically with racial ideas and their attendant consequences for behavior.

AN ENDURING TIE WITH BRITAIN, REAL AND IMAGINED

Both Canada and the United States arose out of British colonialism and had their core institutions framed by British immigrants and their descendants. In contrast to the United States, Canada had no revolution that separated it from the mother country. The British government exerted direct control over all the entities that were to become Canada, and the explicit tie with Britain remained powerful long after Confederation led to effective political independence in 1867. Indeed, a significant British connections persisted into the 1950s. Even now, Queen Elizabeth remains the titular ruler of Canada (although with no significant powers) and her likeness can be found on some Canadian currency, stamps, and some government office walls. Until supplanted by the ethnically neutral *O Canada* in 1980, the official national anthem was *God Save the Queen*, and the de facto 'Canadian' one was *The Maple Leaf Forever*, which explicitly valorized the British. A national flag only replaced the Royal Union Flag

(the Union Jack) in 1965. Canadian citizenship did not exist until 1910, and was created then chiefly in order to regulate British immigration. Canadian citizens retained British nationality until 1948 and were British Subjects until 1977.

This enduring tie has had a profound effect on both the makeup of the country and ethnic relations. As in the United States, most immigrants (chiefly excluding those of British or generically 'white' American origin) and First Nations people historically faced profound, overt pressure to acculturate and assimilate. In Canada, even French Canadians faced such pressures. What these individuals were supposed to conform to in each country was, however, claimed to be quite different. In the United States they were under pressure to conform to an anglophone, 'white' constructed ideal of an American that, by the 1890s, had few overt ethnic or national associations. The linked ideologies of the melting pot asserted that those who were not 'colored' could consequently achieve full Americanness by abandoning their ethnicity, even if this goal was not always achievable in practice. Similar folk in Canada had to contend with an explicitly British image of the ideal Canadian—in both an ethnic and a racial sense. They faced a regime of language and cultural *anglo conformity* without even the supportive ideological fiction that by conforming they could become fully Canadian. One could not, after all, ever become 'biologically' British.

This historical conflation of Canadianness with Britishness had many other consequences. Powerful imperial ethnic and racial stereotypes were imported through the British link. For a long time, these helped justify and maintain a "vertical mosaic" of ethnic individuals, groups, and populations (Helmes-Hayes and Curtis 1998; Porter 1965), with those most closely matching the British ideal at the top, and those who were perceived to be culturally and physically the most different at the bottom. As late as the 1950s, British immigrants were numerous and benefited greatly, while other immigrants faced disabilities in rough proportion to how much they were perceived to diverge from the ideal. French

Canadians, of course, felt both threatened and marginalized by the ethnic content of this national image and by their exclusion from the nation's key symbols. This in turn directly fueled separatist sentiments.

The British tie also shaped the nature of Canadian institutions outside Québec, almost all of which were founded and developed in the image of the British charter group. One result was much *institutional discrimination*; those who differed in language and culture faced public and private institutions that did little to accommodate them. As late as 1970, immigrant children who did not know English were routinely placed into the general school population to sink or swim, without any special language training. Even in Montréal it was then common for urban francophones to have to communicate in English at work or to receive effective service in many retail businesses.

Until the 1960s this long-standing British connection also impeded the development of an all-encompassing Canadian identity. Uncertainties over what it means to be Canadian continue to be both a running joke and the subject of serious discussion. Nevertheless, since the 1960s this uncertainty has allowed a large degree of flexibility in reshaping national symbols and ideologies. It would be fair to say that in the intervening generations the explicitly British dimension of anglophone symbols and ideologies of the nation has been almost completely eliminated.

Finally, the British connection has also profoundly shaped immigration: who was desired, who came, and who stayed. Four hundred thousand Irish rendered destitute by the potato famine of the 1840s followed imperial ties to Canada (Knowles 1997:44), but the Catholics among them found British Canadian prejudices so strong that most subsequently moved on to the United States or merged into the francophone Catholic population. There were, nonetheless, more Irish than English in Canada at the time of the first national census in 1871. Anglo-conformity pressures on Irish remained so strong that while 14 percent of Canadians report some degree of Irish origins today, one sees few parallels with the strong Irish American presence.

When in 1896 the government first began to consistently use immigration as a tool for national development, its British biases were overt. It first solicited the right class of British and 'white' American agriculturalists to help settle the Prairies. When their numbers proved insufficient, agents focused on what were then perceived as the Aryan cousins of the British in Holland, Germany, and Scandinavia. Only after that did they turn reluctantly to Eastern Europe. French farmers were not solicited, and southern Europeans, African Americans, and Asians were actively discouraged.

The last British biases and preferences in immigration were eliminated in the 1960s. Nevertheless, the aftermath of this historical connection can still be seen in today's population makeup and immigration patterns. In 2006, 580,000 Canadians were immigrants from the United Kingdom, most of whom arrived before 1970. Immigrants are now extremely diverse and come from virtually every country on earth, and immigration from Britain itself is low. Even so, some of the countries that consistently send large numbers of immigrants to Canada (see Table 18–1), such as India, Pakistan, and Hong Kong, have some kind of historical British imperial connection.

A PROFOUND ROLE FOR IMMIGRATION

Few rich countries today willingly accept large numbers of immigrants and asylum seekers as part of an organized plan for national development. Some, such as the United Kingdom, Spain, Germany, and Italy, have experienced very large influxes of immigrants over the last 15 years, but primarily due to factors outside their control: either as a result of people exercising EU mobility rights, or through the arrival of asylum seekers. Among rich countries, only in Canada, the United States, and Australia has immigration intentionally played a long-term role in national development. Immigration may have played an even more significant role in shaping Canada than it has in the United States.

TABLE 18–1 Top source countries of immigrants, 1998–2007

Country of Last Permanent Residence	Number of Immigrants, 1998–2007	Percentage of All Immigrants
China, Peoples Republic of	334,428	14.7
India	255,819	11.2
Philippines	131,045	5.7
Pakistan	121,716	5.3
United States	71,516	3.1
Korea, Republic of	67,002	2.9
Iran	62,888	2.8
United Kingdom	54,905	2.4
France	45,551	2.0
Sri Lanka	46,091	2.0
Romania	46,404	2.0
Colombia	36,027	1.6
Russia	35,875	1.6
Taiwan	35,048	1.5
Hong Kong	25,552	1.1
Top 10 source countries	1,210,722	53.1
Other countries	1,068,388	46.9
Total	2,279,110	100.0

Source: Canada. Citizenship and Immigration (2007:30).

Prior to World War II, attracting European settlers to Canada was easy. Push factors motivating many Europeans to emigrate were numerous and powerful. In contrast, ensuring that they—and native-born Canadians—stayed in the country was a challenge. Until the 1930s the border between Canada and the United States was essentially open in both directions to 'white' migrants. What at least looked like superior U.S. economic opportunities attracted many Canadian residents. A huge flow of immigrants to Canada during 1851–1901 (1,892,000 people) was required simply to partially offset those leaving for the United States (2,190,000). Improved perceived prospects in Canada and more effective U.S. border control subsequently severely reduced the movement of people south. Even so, rates of legal immigration remained higher than in the United States. Initially (1947–1967) the express

purpose was to develop the urban economy, then (1968–1990) to supply specific occupational demands, and, most recently, to compensate for a population that is aging and producing few children. By the end of 2007 roughly 6.5 million of 33 million Canadians were immigrants, and about 0.75 percent of the total Canadian population arrives each year, as compared with 0.4 percent in the United States (including undocumented migrants).

Immigration to Canada over the last century can also be distinguished from that to the United States by its much more coherent and consistent use by the state as a tool for national development. In this, it is also marked by an equally long-term trend with important implications for national diversity: a pattern of decreasing the significance of ethnic, national, and racial immigration selection criteria and increasing the importance of economic and other adaptive ones. These two trends are closely linked. When the federal government set out in 1896 to develop the prairie West, it sought farmers—ideally, British and 'white' American ones. However, in the end, in order to achieve this economic objective, the government sequentially relaxed its ethnic preferences. Between 1900 and 1930 this resulted in a doubling in the proportion of Canadians who were neither British, French, nor First Nations, to about 20 percent of the population. These economic objectives also resulted in a different national mix of immigrants than were then arriving in the United States: fewer Italians and Jews but many more British, Germans, and Ukrainians. Immigration criteria based on race were not as flexible, and like their U.S. counterparts, the government of the day actively used a range of means to limit, then virtually stop, 'nonwhite' immigration. Chinese, Japanese, and Indian immigration into British Columbia was extremely controversial (as it was along the U.S. Pacific Coast), and was effectively banned during 1921–1947. After 1910, African American farmers also were informally denied entry.

Immigration policy and practice became increasingly intertwined with other national concerns after World War II. Canada came out of the war profoundly altered. Temporarily the fourth largest industrial economy in the world, it was dramatically more urban and had a much greater international presence than before. These changes were reflected in immigration patterns, and in ever-increasing ethnic diversity. A mix of economic, human rights, and political concerns soon led the government to establish a large program of refugee settlement. This program became worldwide by the 1970s, and has since brought hundreds of thousands of increasingly diverse individuals to Canada. In the 1950s a demand for urban workers led the government to expand the range of significant source countries to include Italy, Greece, and Portugal, while a mix of international and national human rights considerations led to a reduction of specifically national, ethnic, and racial immigration restrictions. A desire to tailor immigration even more

closely to the economy led to the complete elimination of such barriers in 1962, replaced chiefly by class criteria for entry. After 1967, immigrants were supposed to be selected individually, primarily on the basis of personal skills, national language proficiency, health, age, employment demand, and whether they had sponsoring relatives already in Canada. In reality, continuing means to sponsor one's overseas relatives have ensured that chain migration has been extensive and, accordingly, that very large numbers of new immigrants have come from certain countries and regions at particular times.

Immigrant source countries have dramatically shifted over time. As recently as the mid-1960s, about three-quarters of immigrants came from Europe or the United States. In contrast, of 2,300,000 immigrants who arrived during 1998–2007, 57 percent (or 1,160,000 individuals) came from Asia and the Pacific, and another 19.5 percent were from Africa or the Middle East. European countries now contribute only 17.6 percent to the total flow, and Asian countries strongly predominate among the top source countries (Table 18-1).[9]

Postwar immigration has greatly increased the ethnic diversity of the Canadian population. Exactly how diverse and how strongly felt their own ethnicity is to Canadians today are difficult to assess with any precision. If one takes an anthropological orientation toward ethnicity, what must be kept central are ethnic identities in action: what kind of individual, personally felt attachments to group, culture, population, or nationality does a person have, how central are they to self, and how often are they activated? While detailed ethnographic studies have consistently demonstrated that such identities are very significant to many individuals in certain ethnic groups and populations, anthropologists in Canada have tended to focus their attention on groups that have been strongly marked by others *as* different (now, chiefly, First Nations people, members of various Asian groups, and Afro-Canadians; see Buchignani and Letkemann 1993). They have also tended to focus on the immigrant generation, who are often marginalized by immigration itself, and as a consequence are more often aware of their ethnicity. The design-ers of the Canadian census appreciate the need for relevant identity data but consider such information uncollectable under the constraints of doing a mass census. Instead, census takers now ask Canadians a completely open-ended question about what they see as their ethnic *origins*. Respondents can fill in more than one group if they wish. Table 18–2 summarizes some of the findings of the last (2006) census; single responses presumably are the best indication of ethnic identity.

Ethnic diversity is now highly concentrated in those prosperous urban areas that currently attract most immigrants, particularly in Metro Toronto and nearby cities, Vancouver and its suburbs, Montréal, and Calgary. These and some other urban areas have been entirely transformed by immigration over the last 30 years.

Immigration has been more of a positive, ongoing symbol of the nation than it has recently been in the United States. For over a century, immigration and an idealized image of the good

TABLE 18–2   Top 25 Canadian ethnic origins, 2006

	Ethnic Origin	Total Responses	Single Responses	Multiple Responses
1	Canadian/Canadien	10,066,290	5,748,725	4,317,570
2	English	6,570,015	1,367,125	5,202,890
3	French	4,941,210	1,230,535	3,710,675
4	Scottish	4,719,850	568,515	4,151,340
5	Irish	4,354,155	491,030	3,863,125
6	German	3,179,425	670,640	2,508,785
7	Italian	1,445,335	741,045	704,285
8	Chinese	1,346,510	1,135,365	211,145
9	NA Indian	1,253,615	512,150	741,470
10	Ukrainian	1,209,085	300,590	908,495
11	Dutch	1,035,965	303,400	732,560
12	Polish	984,565	269,375	715,190
13	East Indian	962,665	780,175	182,495
14	Russian	500,600	98,245	402,355
15	Welsh	440,965	27,115	413,855
16	Filipino	436,190	321,390	114,800
17	Norwegian	432,515	44,790	387,725
18	Portuguese	410,850	262,230	148,625
19	Métis	409,065	77,295	331,770
20	British Isles	403,915	94,145	309,770
21	Swedish	334,765	28,445	306,325
22	Spanish	325,730	67,475	258,255
23	American	316,350	28,785	287,565
24	Hungarian	315,510	88,685	226,820
25	Jewish	315,120	134,045	181,070

immigrant have been tightly intertwined in national mythology (Buchignani and Indra 1999). The good immigrant has long been deemed worthy of support because he or she has helped develop the country through hard work and law-abiding enterprise. For the last 30 years federal Multiculturalism policy has helped broaden and further integrate this ideology into that of the nation. As a result, a Canadian Broadcasting Corporation and Ekos Research Associates poll in 2002 (i.e., after 9/11) showed that 59 percent of Canadians thought there were then too few or the right number of immigrants coming to Canada; only 30 percent said that too many immigrants were coming, the comparable figure for the United States being approximately 50 percent.

At the same time, episodically, certain types of immigration have been very controversial. There has never been much citizen input into the formation of immigration policy (which contributes to its partial coherence). Neither has the government spent much effort to explain its policies to those affected by it. Practical support to facilitate the integration of immigrants has increased greatly, but little has been done to help those already in Canada adjust to newcomers or to the greatly changed neighborhoods, cities, and economic structures that result. Critically, the government has not done much to dissuade resident Canadians from the notion that they and new immigrants are operating in a zero-sum competition with each other; many social psychological studies show that feeling of zero-sum competition can increase intolerance toward immigrants in general or toward specific immigrant populations (Esses et al. 2001). One consequence of all this has been periods of focused intolerance toward some newly arrived immigrant populations, typically directed toward those seen to be the most culturally and phenotypically different at a particular point in time. Another, more recent phenomenon appears to be greater zero-sum-driven concern over immigration in general, as exemplified by an increase to 35 percent in the proportion of Canadians thinking that there are too many immigrants arriving, according to a 2006 poll done for CTV and the *Globe and Mail* by the

Strategic Council; even so, 68 percent of respondents in that poll asserted that Canada should make no distinctions among source countries, and accept immigrants from all countries.

FEW ILLEGAL IMMIGRANTS, MANY REFUGEES AND ASYLUM SEEKERS

One thing that has definitely helped maintain positive support for immigration and immigrants has been the prevailing belief that the government maintains firm control over an orderly process of immigrant selection. Canadians appear to be very intolerant of illegal immigration, but they have not had to face the high levels of formally illegal immigration that typify many areas of the United States (Buchignani and Indra 1999). No attractive underground economy or quasi-legal practice of employment supports many undocumented workers. So far, few of those illegally resident in the United States have crossed the border into Canada; and the only way many can otherwise arrive in Canada is by plane, and the government controls air access through a system of visas.

In 1985, the Supreme Court of Canada (in Re: Singh and the Minister of Employment and Immigration [1985] 1 SCR 177) ruled that illegal immigrants and asylum seekers could not be detained without cause. If they were detained, they had to be promptly given the reason for their arrest and detention, had the right to counsel and habeas corpus, and could appear personally to state their case to remain in the country. It also ruled that any minimally credible in-country claim for political asylum had to be duly considered by the government. In addition, Canada is a signatory to a number of international conventions (including the 1951 UN Convention Relating to the Status of Refugees and the 1967 Protocol) which acknowledge that asylum seekers have the right of *nonrefoulement*—the right not to be returned against their will to a place in which they may be at risk. Because of these legal and policy constraints, deportation is rarely used to control undocumented immigration. Detention is much more rarely used than in the United States, even though its practice has increased over the last 10 years, with the government usually citing concerns over national security, abuse of the immigration system, or migrant criminal activities (Pratt 2005).

Since 1981, several hundred thousand individuals have tried to secure residence in Canada by claiming political asylum (Buchignani and Indra 1999; Gilad 1990). Some clearly do not meet the legal standard for being a political refugee, but the way that the government deals with them has the effect of ideologically converting these potentially illegal immigrants into a category of person that is much more acceptable to the public: asylum seekers.

Like the ideal of the good immigrant, Canadians have strongly supported an image of the ideal political refugee: a person who, through no fault of his or her own, faces oppression by government agents at home. In actuality, the circumstances of those seeking asylum are rarely so clear-cut. Nevertheless, public support for a large program of refugee settlement has persisted and grown since 186,000 displaced persons were accepted in the decade after World War II. This public support has sometimes been concrete, as when small groups of Canadians financially carried the full first-year cost of settlement for 50,000 Southeast Asian refugees during 1979–1981 (Chan and Indra 1986; Chan et al. 1988; Dorais et al. 1987). In 1986, the people of Canada received the UN's Nansen Medal in recognition of their assistance to refugees, an award previously given only to individuals. Over each of the last 25 years 10 to 20 percent of immigrants have been accepted as political refugees.

Refugee policy up to the 1970s in both Canada and the United States strongly reflected a persistent anticommunist theme in their respective foreign policies. Since then, this bias has decreased to a far greater extent in Canada than it has in the United States, with the result that currently the world distribution of refugees and asylum seekers settled in Canada is very different than it is in the United States. Moreover, that distribution now shifts rapidly with changing world conditions. By way of an illustration, during 1996–1998, refugees most often came from Bosnia-Herzegovina,

Sri Lanka, Afghanistan, Iraq, India, Somalia, and Pakistan. In 2006 refugees most often came from Afghanistan, Columbia, Ethiopia, Burma, Sudan, the Democratic Republic of Congo, Somalia, Iran, Eretria, and Iraq.

When they get the attention of the news media, direct challenges to Canada's geographic borders by small numbers of people continue to generate very negative public reactions. Public disapproval of the arrival by chartered ship of a mere 174 Sikhs in 1987 was so strong that the Prime Minister recalled Parliament to deal with the issue (Buchignani 1993). Most recently, despite generally positive Canadian attitudes toward Chinese immigrants, in 1999 there was almost no public support for 500 asylum seekers from China who arrived in British Columbia on leaky freighters. A sudden increase in Roma asylum seekers from the Czech Republic likewise generated much negative commentary during 2008–2009. Should large numbers of individuals seek residence in Canada by such means in the future it is likely to dramatically increase hostility to the national populations in question.

The impact of refugee arrivals on ethnic diversity has been far greater than that which has arisen simply through their actual numbers. Refugees often form new national and ethnic communities or else dramatically increase the number of individuals in these communities. Group-specific chain migration through normal immigration channels almost always continues to augment these populations for a long time thereafter.

ONGOING QUÉBÉCOIS NATIONALISM

The historical establishment of two unequally powerful charter groups within the Canadian state has had several important consequences for ethnic and race relations. The most noticeable of these has been the rise of a reactive form of nationalism in the 5,900,000-strong francophone population of Québec.

A curious mix of civic and ethnic nationalism prevailed across anglophone Canada from

Confederation through the 1960s. This accreting national origin myth increasingly stressed civic, nonethnic nationalism: the creation of a uniquely Canadian nation through the efforts of all its past and present citizens, whatever their ethnic origins. Even so, neither this national myth nor government policy informed by it were in fact actively inclusive of all Canadians. Almost all the key actors in the national myth were either British or else elite French politicians, and attempts to weaken the everyday power of anglo conformity were few. Federal government accommodation to the specific concerns of francophones was limited, and that of provincial governments other than Québec and New Brunswick was even more so. The Canadian economic elite remained almost monolithically British.

Even in the nineteenth century this state of affairs provided fertile ground for the development of Québec-based ethnic nationalism among clerics and other francophone intellectuals. Separated by language and religion and shut out of many avenues to economic or political success *as French*, they generated an alternative national creation myth. The Conquest was constructed as the decisive event in national history. Either before the Fall or in the rural *habitant* way of life thereafter, early nationalists evoked a lost Eden: a stable, homogeneous, pastoral way of life grounded in the French language and Catholicism—one where Québécois individuals fixed to the soil of their ancestors participated in an authentic, unique culture that could be traced back to New France or earlier (Eller 1998:313; Handler 1988). By the early twentieth century some of the explicitly Catholic elements of this national myth were being downplayed and its cultural dimensions highlighted—in part by anthropologists like Marius Barbeau using what today would be considered a timeless, overly holistic and anthropomorphic notion of Québec folk culture. These images of a past rural life were highly attractive—and nostalgic—for by the 1920s few francophone residents of Québec actually practiced anything like it. Half its population and the driving forces of its economy were already urban based, even if some cultural

elements deriving from rural life persisted, such as strong informal kinship relations (Garique 1956).

In what has come to be known as the Quiet Revolution (1955–1970), a new set of urban, well-educated francophone leaders, spokespersons, and theoreticians swept away the overtly Catholic dimensions of this nationalist vision (Gold 1975). The explicitly ethnic and racial dimensions of Québécois nationalism were backstaged, replaced by an awkwardly framed kind of civil nationalism based on protecting the rights, language, and culture of those who were French-*speaking*. This move reflected their own experiences and aspirations as cosmopolitan individuals who believed that speaking their native French was a disability, even in their own land. The federal Bilingualism and Biculturalism Commission (struck in 1963) concluded that these Québec nationalists were correct in this opinion. It found that while anti-French personal prejudices were weak, monolingual francophones across Canada faced massive institutional language discrimination, which had ramifying implications for their life chances.

One consequence of the commission's work was federal legislation (1969) creating official bilingualism and confirming both English and French as official languages. This set of programs proposed to make the federal government bureaucracy thoroughly bilingual by the solicitation of more francophones, by providing French-language training for anglophones, and by making more public federal government communications bilingual. Over the next 20 years, an increasing number of programs and powers constitutionally within the preserve of the federal government (such as tax collection, some social programs, and immigration) were partially or wholly transferred to Québec provincial government control. French immersion school programs (and entire schools) sprung up across the anglophone parts of the country. Retailers were required to provide labeling in both official languages.

These responses did little to slow the rise of separatism—a movement to make Québec an independent country. In 1976 the charismatic René Lévesque brought the Parti Québécois to power in Québec. A parliamentary majority gave the

Parti Québécois the power to make fundamental changes in the fabric of Québec society, which it immediately exercised. The new government argued that the province's 6 million francophones were an island in a sea of 300 million anglophones (anglophone Canada and the United States), and that their language would be quickly lost without vigorous compensatory state action. This was more than an argument about language. Separatists claimed that language distinctiveness had allowed Québécois to craft their own distinctive culture: lose the language, lose the everyday culture that went with it. The previous provincial government had passed legislation in 1974 making French the sole official language of Québec. The Parti Québécois government followed with a series of bills enforcing the primacy of French—chiefly Bills 101 (1977), 178 (1988), and 86 (1993). All large- and medium-sized businesses must now provide a francophone workplace and customer service in French. All outdoor public signs are to highlight French. While anglophones maintain the right to educate their children in English, allophones—meaning chiefly immigrants whose first language is neither English nor French—are required to send their children to French language schools. The provincial government moved aggressively to solicit francophone immigrants, using its own parallel immigration program.

The first Parti Québécois government also had a referendum on separation. Although what was asked for in 1980 was only a mandate to discuss "sovereignty-association" with the federal government, voters rejected the proposal 60 to 40 percent. Virtually all Québec anglophones, allophones, and First Nations people voted against it. This referendum on separation nevertheless served as a wake-up call to the national and other provincial governments, which then made several attempts to increase Québec's powers and highlight its special status. In 1982, the federal government repatriated the Canadian Constitution from Britain and rewrote it to highlight the charter status of francophones. However, because the Québec government was not part of the repatriation process, in 1987 the federal and all the provincial governments assembled at Meech Lake

in order to further address Québécois nationalist concerns. While all of the Québec government's nonnegotiable demands were met, two provincial governments subsequently changed, and refused to support the necessary constitutional amendments. Excluded from the Meech Lake process, most First Nations representatives were strongly against its passage. All the provincial governments and four First Nations organizations met in 1992 in Charlottetown, Prince Edward Island, to try yet again. A national referendum defeated the solution they proposed.

Stung by these rebuffs, in 1995 Québec voters barely sent down to defeat a much more directly worded referendum proposal. More recently, a series of minority federal governments since 2004 have depended on at least tacit support from Québec voters, who for a range of strategic reasons have voted strongly for the separatist Bloc Québécois. In response, Parliament in 2006 supported a motion by a vote of 266 to 16 stating "that this house recognize the Québécois form a nation within a united Canada." Increasing economic prosperity, francophone self-confidence, and voter concern over conventional provincial issues like budget overruns, taxes, and the provision of services seem to have put separatism on the back burner for the time being. However, it remains a central debate in Québec politics, one unlikely to disappear or abate anytime soon.

Québécois nationalism is a political movement that cannot be considered a primarily ethnic phenomenon. It nevertheless has many ethnic (and some racial) dimensions. Up to the 1960s, separatism was clearly based on a highly exclusive sense of the nation: Québécois meant almost exclusively those who lived in Québec, who still spoke French, and whose ancestors either founded New France or else had married into that population. The gloss of civic nationalism added in recent times remains problematic for both adherents and detractors. If Québécois is now meant to refer only to a movement to guarantee that those who speak French and live in Québec have full civic rights, much of the separatist rationale for national autonomy based on the historical oppression of, and threat of cultural loss to, the descendants of New France evaporates. Moreover, nationalists have not fully convinced many anglophones or allophones that one can actually do what this ideology suggests: become Québécois by virtue of becoming a francophone (Handler 1988:175–181). They argue that (like historical anglo conformity elsewhere in the country) the ethnic (and racial) dimensions of nationalism remain sufficiently powerful that even complete franco conformity does not allow full incorporation of an individual into the nation. In this, they point to the claimed difficulties in becoming Québécois faced by fluently French immigrants such as Vietnamese and Haitians. Over the last 20 years, hundreds of thousands of anglophones and allophones have found the potential trade-offs in making the attempt unrewarding and have voted with their feet by leaving the province.

Perhaps the most knotty problem of an ethnic nature currently facing Québecers concerns First Nations people. Like most ethnic nationalist movements elsewhere, that of francophones in Québec is based on a widely prevalent theory of the collective rights of peoples. So this argument goes, a people that share origins, language, history, culture, and territory ought to have the right of national self-determination. But there is no natural level at which such claims are either authentic or inauthentic. Ironically, First Nations can—and do—make at least as strong claims of this sort against the Québec government as Québécois do against the federal government. Several northern First Nations currently are actively preparing their cases for separation from Québec and reaffiliation with Canada, should Québec separate from the rest of the country (Grand Council of the Crees 1998).

René Lévesque, Parti Québécois.

MULTICULTURALISM AND MULTIRACIALISM

National ideologies in Canada and the United States have historically characterized cultural diversity quite differently. When Americans were idealizing the United States as a melting pot of cultures, out of which was cast an American, nationalist ideologues to the North spoke of a Canadian cultural "mosaic" (Foster 1924)—a nation composed of the contributions of a number of persisting, discrete cultures and groups.

This metaphor of a Canadian cultural mosaic had far less salience and impact than its U.S. counterpart until the late 1960s. By that time, some ethnocultural populations (such as Ukrainians) that had been founded or greatly expanded by immigrants during 1896–1930 had generated an articulate, educated, well-placed, middle-class elite. These were chiefly the children of immigrants. When the federal government established the Bilingualism and Biculturalism Commission, these spokespersons were able to raise an effective objection: What about the one-third of Canadians who were then neither British nor French? Where did they fit into the proposed regime of bilingualism and biculturalism? In response, the Commission hastily cobbled together another volume to its report titled *The Contributions of the Other Ethnic Groups*. Unsatisfied, spokespersons kept up the pressure, which in 1971 resulted in the promulgation of the Trudeau government's initial policy of *Multiculturalism*—coining a word that has since become ubiquitous. Some dimensions of Multiculturalism were incorporated into the (1982) Constitution Act and subsequently into the world's first Multiculturalism Act (1988).

The government initially had a very limited vision of what federal Multiculturalism was going to be. A minor cabinet portfolio was created to oversee programs having two basic goals: facilitating immigrant adaptation and integration, and securing more public and official recognition of the achievements of ethnic groups. However, ethnic group spokespersons, academics, and federal bureaucrats almost immediately established a much larger agenda for Multiculturalism. Within three years, those involved with Multiculturalism policy were committed to changing the substance and image of the Canadian nation: to be more reflective of the diversity of groups and populations in Canada, to reflect a kind of civic nationalism that did not privilege certain ethnicities, to provide positive support for the ethnic identities of Canadians, and to make Canada's laws and practices consistent with Canada's international commitments.

This entailed much social reengineering of Canada's key symbols and origin myths. In 1982, the Canadian national holiday (July 1) was converted from Dominion Day to the ethnically neutral Canada Day—a holiday now marked primarily by local and national celebrations of ethnic and regional diversity. The just retired Governor General of Canada (i.e., the British Crown's symbolic representative) is a woman born in Haiti, while her predecessor is a woman of Chinese descent who grew up in Burma. Federal government–supported research initiatives radically expanded core knowledge about, and public awareness of, ethnic group history, current situations, and contemporary achievements and difficulties.[10] Federal financial support was also extended to revise provincial school curricula and curricular materials to make them more inclusive of French Canadians, immigrant groups, and First Nations—all of whom had been almost absent from school texts earlier.

A second major objective of federal Multiculturalism programs (and provincially created similar ones) has been the provision of financial and informational support for a range of symbolically significant ethnic group activities. Here, the rationale is threefold: to support prideful, nonexclusionary ethnic identity, to support effective integration, particularly of new immigrants, and to support the positive public acceptance of ethnocultural diversity. Such financial support has facilitated the teaching of heritage languages to the children of immigrants and the establishment of heritage schools, in which students receive a bicultural and bilingual experience. Government money has also been forthcoming for a range of ethnic performances and celebrations aimed at the general population.

A third main goal extends far beyond the range of responsibilities of federal Multiculturalism, per se. This is to facilitate more effective access to social, health, educational, and other services by Canada's culturally and linguistically diverse citizenry: consider, as one example, the language-based challenges faced by some of the fully one half of all residents of the City of Toronto for whom neither English nor French is a mother tongue.

Multiculturalism has received widespread public support since its inception. At the same time, it remains controversial in some intellectual circles, attracting (chiefly anecdotally supported) charges that it divides Canadians and impedes immigrant integration (Bissoondath 1994). More rigorous analysis (e.g., by Kymlicka 1998; Bloemraad 2006) provides little support for such assertions, but this has not lessened their prevalence.

In the early 1980s the federal government responded to a series of racial incidents directed toward South Asians and Afro-Canadians with an attempt to address social race through its Multiculturalism machinery. This proved difficult, as the government wished to combat negative folk fictions about race without unintentionally adding credibility to the erroneous idea that there actually *are* biological human races. One uniquely Canadian part of the government semantic strategy was to generate the term "visible minority groups" (VMGs) to refer to those immigrant origin populations that some other Canadians who viewed themselves as white or invisible might perceive to be biologically distinct from themselves. First Nations people were excluded from this category, chiefly for political and administrative reasons. In this admittedly awkward way, the government wished to stress that in Canada, as elsewhere, race is a *perceptual*, not a biological, issue.[11] Immigrant-origin visible minorities in Canada encompass several broad categories of person, and in 2006 represented about 16 percent of all Canadians (Table 18–3).

Visible minority group is an administrative catchall, and no research evidence supports the notion that Canadians consistently view individuals of this category in racial terms, or that when they interact with VMG individuals and *do* perceive physical difference that perception has important consequences. At the same time, from a sociological point of view the exclusion of the 4 percent of Canadians who claim a First Nations identity is completely arbitrary. Combined together, VMG and First Nations–identified individuals represent roughly 20 percent of the Canadian population. While the size of specific subpopulations varies dramatically between the two countries, this overall percentage quite closely compares with that derived from 2005 census figures for "non-whites" in the United States (US Census Bureau 2005).

Federal Multiculturalism and similar provincial and municipal efforts have been quite successful, with three important qualifications. Across Canada—including among francophones in Québec—these programs have established a strong consciousness among Canadians that Canada arose out of, and has been built upon, diversity. Most Canadians today also believe that a limited degree of behavioral diversity is not

TABLE 18–3   Visible minority groups in Canada, 2006

Group	Population in 2006
South Asians	1,263,000
Chinese	1,217,000
Afro-Canadians	784,000
Filipinos	411,000
Latin Americans	304,000
Arabs	263,000
Southeast Asians	240,000
Koreans	142,000
West Asians	157,000
Japanese	81,000

inconsistent with the goal of creating a harmonious, effective society offering equal treatment to all. These have been very positive developments for the 40 to 50 percent of Canadians who may have some kind of ethnic identity. Critically, virtually all Canadians now believe that one can positively feel Canadian and ethnic at the same time without contradiction (Canada. *Multiculturalism and Citizenship Canada* 1992; Kalin and Berry 1995). Historical anglo conformity did not allow this. Today's Québec regime of franco conformity may not either.

Even so, the qualifications are significant. First of all, the spokespersons and leaders of two key populations have never accepted the premises of Multiculturalism (Bauhn et al. 1995): representatives of Québec francophones (whether separatist or not) and those of First Nations people. In each case, the leadership has accepted and strongly identifies with the rhetoric of their special, *national* character. Québécois and First Nations spokespersons feel—some theorists (Kymlicka 1998) claim with justification—that they are more than merely another ethnic group. They are also adamant that this fact should be reflected in group-specific rights and privileges and in special relations to governments and governance. In this light, some Québécois and First Nations spokespersons have viewed Multiculturalism as a federal plot to negate their national claims and reduce them to the same status as immigrant-origin ethnic groups. While this assertion is largely unfounded insofar as the subsequent policy trajectory of Multiculturalism is concerned, the overall position of Prime Minister Pierre Trudeau at its onset was to strongly affirm individual rights while deprecating ethnocultural and subnational group rights; this stance may have played some role in the policy receiving initial governmental support. Moreover, in their affirmation of Multiculturalism, immigrant-origin ethnic group spokespersons often *do* assert an equivalency among their groups, First Nations people, and Québécois. Surprisingly, public support for Multiculturalism is sometimes higher in Québec than in most other parts of the country (Mata and Hennebry 1997:6).

Second, although many ethnic group spokespersons fault it as a failing, Multiculturalism was never intended, and could not possibly have had the resources, to support the full-blown behavioral perpetuation of ethnic cultures in Canada. With very few exceptions (such as Mexican Mennonites and Russian Old Believers in rural Alberta; see Scheffel 1991), virtually all recently established Canadian ethnic groups and populations are urban based. Even in rural areas the few groups that have persisted and grown over the generations play a unique card: like communal Hutterites in the west (Bennett 1967; Hostetler and Huntington 1996), they are bound together by both cultural and religious factors. Extremely powerful acculturative pressures and desires operate on urban immigration-based populations. In a behavioral sense, recent immigrants must conform to much 'Canadian' everyday practice from the day they arrive in order to achieve their personal goals and to function effectively. Some unwanted elements of their source cultures and social systems were, of course, among the things that motivated them to immigrate in the first place. These forces of acculturation operate particularly strongly on the young. In the absence of profound discrimination or enforced ethnic separation, the second generation in most groups exhibit very selective maintenance of source country cultural practices. This does not mean that they have ceased to identify with their roots. Multiculturalism programs are designed primarily to support positive ethnic identity through *symbolic* cultural maintenance and through language training.

Third, and by extension, Multiculturalism has not been able to profoundly transform the behavioral dimensions of ethnic and race relations through direct programming. Multiculturalism programs are grounded on the thesis that one can significantly change unwanted behaviors (in this case, ethnic and racial discrimination) by changing people's beliefs and values. There is merit in this thesis when it operates slowly on a large stage, as when programming alters the general sense of what it means to be Canadian to make it more inclusive. Even so, ethnic and racial discrimination (i.e., to say, discriminatory behavior) is often most effectively combated directly, not through attitude change (Buchignani 1983). Multiculturalism's concentration on attitudes rather than behavior exemplifies the indirect way the Canadian state generally approaches the promotion of social justice issues pertaining to ethnicity and race.

AN INCREASINGLY STRONG COMMITMENT TO INDIVIDUAL HUMAN RIGHTS

Historical Canadian governments rarely placed legal constraints on ethnic and racial minorities. In the twentieth century, the most glaring exception was the discriminatory legal treatment of those First Nations people who were registered on tribal band lists. Status Indians could neither vote nor leave reserves without permission. Their children were sent to residential schools whether this was the desire of their parents or not. Perhaps the second most significant exception was the treatment of certain minorities in wartime. Germans, Ukrainians, and some other enemy aliens faced many constraints during World War I, and some were arbitrarily jailed. During World War II the Canadian and American governments coordinated efforts to incarcerate virtually every mainland resident of Japanese origin for the duration, including citizens (but ironically excluding those in the armed forces). The government then sold their property. Several thousand residents of other nationalities were also sent to camps. Some national and ethnic immigration restrictions (most notably against Chinese, Japanese, and Indians) remained in place until after World War II. Among provincial governments, only British Columbia extensively used the law to limit the rights and activities of immigrants once they had arrived in Canada. Most Chinese, Japanese, and people from India in British Columbia could not vote prior to 1947. They were also banned from provincial jobs, crown contracts, and certain professions.

These actions were legal prior to the promulgation of the Canadian Bill of Rights in 1958. So also were informal discrimination and overt expressions of prejudice. Since then, a series of legislative and court actions have rendered illegal virtually all forms of discrimination against individuals on the grounds of nationality, ethnic origin, and race; the right to protection against these forms of discrimination is overtly asserted in the Canadian Constitution and the Charter of Rights and Freedoms. Section 15.(1) of the latter states: "Every individual is equal before and under the law and has the right to the equal protection and equal benefit of the law without discrimination and, in particular, without discrimination based on race, national or ethnic origin, colour, religion, sex, age or mental or physical disability."[12] In 1977 the Canadian Human Rights Act created the Canadian Human Rights Commission and empowered it to address claims of discrimination in areas of federal jurisdiction; all 10 provinces now have parallel legislation and commissions that address complaints of discrimination through mediation and civil law. The elimination of discrimination and injustice is now a stated responsibility of Canadian citizenship.

FEW INSTITUTIONALIZED MEANS TO ADDRESS DISCRIMINATION

Whatever their objective importance, racial and ethnic discrimination in Canada have never been anything like the big public social issues they have been in the United States. As one consequence, Canadian courts have not played the same activist role in addressing or redressing discrimination that courts did in the United States, particularly during 1950–1980. In fact, the only court-mandated forms of redress of great significance have addressed the treaty and other aboriginal rights of First Nations. Even in the case of First Nations, courts have done little to address historical inequities faced by *individuals*; one exception has been as a result of a series of civil suits and criminal prosecutions relating to the treatment of children in residential schools, orphanages, and other publicly funded institutions.

This has put the issue squarely in the court of politicians and government bureaucrats, who have been reluctant to act aggressively, either to punish discriminators or to actively protect its potential victims. The main argument for affirmative action—that historical injustices have significant, lingering consequences that must be addressed by compensatory acts—has been repeatedly made by visible minority and First Nations spokespersons, but this has had few important consequences in law or government practice (Loney 1998). The federal government initiated a policy of preferentially advancing francophone employees in the 1970s, and thereafter has instituted a basic form of affirmative hiring and advancement that also covers visible minorities in the federal government workplace (through the Employment Equity Act 1986/1996). Public institutions such as universities that receive federal funds and companies that receive federal contracts are also supposed to comply but often do not (Henry et al. 1995, chapter 8). Similar provincial and municipal government efforts at affirmative action have been episodic and lackadaisical. Some metropolitan police departments have instituted targeted searches for visible minority recruits, but 2006 Census figures showed that only 6 percent of police officers were then visible minorities. A few big-city forces have liaison officers who interface with particular urban ethnocultural groups. Some large school districts have put zero tolerance antidiscriminatory policies in place. With the exception of some resource extraction companies that operate in areas primarily populated by First Nations people, few private companies have initiated any kind of affirmative action employment practices.

In addition, Canada has no effective legislation in place that criminalizes discrimination. Federal legislation has introduced hate crimes into the Criminal Code of Canada, where it is supposed to offer some redress from explicit expressions of genocide (Section 318) and the "public incitement of hatred against ethic and racial populations" (Section 319); ethnic or racial hatred can also be used as a factor in sentencing

(Section 718 2(a)(i)). Few prosecutions have been made under these provisions and almost none have been successful. Human rights legislation based on civil law has proved to be slow, cumbersome, and ineffective in materially addressing the ethnic or racial disabilities of a significant number of Canadians.

Instead of seeking to punish or otherwise directly address the actions of discriminators, the Canadian way has been to put money and effort into programs that better prepare potential victims of discrimination to succeed, to affirm the morality and legality of equality, and to support intergroup tolerance. Here, the focus has clearly been primarily on immigrant-origin visible minority groups.

CONTEMPORARY ETHNIC AND RACE RELATIONS

Canadians have become increasingly tolerant and affirming of immigrant-origin cultural diversity over the last 50 years. Not all of the factors accounting for this change are known, but the following appear to figure prominently:

• **Sequential desensitization to difference.** Over the past two generations, Canadians have been exposed to an ever greater range of cultural difference as a result of the continuously changing nature of immigrant inflows. While at times activating resident sensitivities, immigrant diversity has increased a little at a time over a very long period during which immigrants have not engendered widespread feelings of threat or competition among those already here. This has allowed the population to get comfortable with longer resident immigrant populations while newer, more diverse incoming populations arrive. Many urban Canadians of the 1950s thought of so-called DPs—displaced persons arriving from Europe—as quite strange. They did not look so strange when many thousands of Italian and Portuguese immigrants arrived a decade later. When South Asians, Jamaicans,

Chinese, and other visible minorities began coming in force in the 1970s, reservations against southern Europeans evaporated. Thereafter, urban Canadians (who, like American urbanites, make up 80 percent of the population) have resided, been educated, worked, and secured retail and government services in highly polyethnic contexts. That experience seems to have helped make people increasingly comfortable with cultural difference.

- **A perception of quick immigrant integration.** Another historical factor reducing intolerance toward immigrant-origin populations has been a general belief in their quick integration into the economic and social mainstream. For the most part, this perception was well-founded, at least up to 1990 (Kazemipur and Halli 2001). As in the United States, the Canadian middle class expanded rapidly in the two decades after World War II, a product of a dramatic increase in reasonably well paying blue- and white-collar jobs for men; this broadened out to better include woman and extended to the professions in the two decades thereafter (1965–1985). During this long period, arriving immigrants typically faced occupational dislocation and mismatches between their skills and training and available jobs, but nevertheless quickly established themselves economically. Social integration quickly followed.

- **Increasing class resources of immigrants.** European immigrants arriving in the 1950s and 1960s from some important source countries such as Italy, Greece, and Portugal typically had much less education and occupational training than resident Canadians. Upon arrival, most migrants from these countries knew neither English nor French, and while they almost all went to cities, most came from rural contexts. As the cultural and national backgrounds of immigrants broadened thereafter, so also did their class resources. Consider immigrants 15 years and older arriving in 2007: 45 percent of them claimed to have a BA or better, rising to 74 percent among primary applicants classified as "economic immigrants" (Canada. *Citizenship and Immigration Canada* 2007). Only 31 percent of immigrants in that year said that they knew neither English nor French prior to arrival, and 47 percent of those intending to work claimed professional backgrounds. At least until 1990 greater class resources helped facilitate integration and lessen perceptions of immigrant cultural difference.

- **Solidly positive views of immigrants despite mixed feelings about high rates of immigration.** Many Canadians still consider immigration rates are too high. Ever since 1977 Canadians have been asked what they thought of the negatively framed assertion that there was too much immigration to Canada, and it was only in 2000 that a majority of respondents *disagreed* (Esses et al. 2002:72).[13] What Canadians evidently do not often do is map this ambiguity over onto actual immigrants. At least three-quarters of Canadians strongly view immigrants as hardworking contributors to the nation, and fewer than 10 percent believe that Canada would be better off without them. Moreover, an AP-Ipsos survey in 2006 found Canadians are much more likely to view the contributions of immigrants as positive (75 percent) than people in the United States (52 percent), Australia (54 percent), or major Western European countries. Considered globally, neither immigration nor immigrants engender quite as strong feelings of threat or zero-sum conflict among Canadians as they have among Americans. A Pew Research Center global survey (2002:42) found 21 percent of Canadians saw immigration as a major issue compared with 30 percent of Americans, and in this study 30 percent of Americans listed ethnic conflict in their homeland as a key issue, while only 12 percent of Canadians did.

- **Increasing positive societal support for cultural diversity in general.** From its inception, Canadian Multiculturalism policy was aimed at increasing the population's appreciation of the contributions of diversity and diverse individuals to Canada's past and present. Multiculturalism's influence was widespread, and its lead was followed by many in education, provincial and municipal government, and the media. Today most Canadians strongly support both Multiculturalism (Dasko 2005) and diversity as a positive societal value (Parkin and Mendelsohn 2003). There is also much evidence that each new generation of Canadians is more accepting of diversity when they are young than the generation before them, and that tolerance instilled when young is generally maintained through life. Older Canadians tend to be more intolerant, not because they have become more so as they age, but because they always were.
- **Increasing societal disapproval of discrimination.** Nothing can legislate against individually held prejudices, but to the extent that such prejudices remain solely beliefs they are societally irrelevant. What matters deeply is when prejudices inform discriminatory behavior, particularly when the latter is aimed at individuals and populations who are ill equipped to contend with it. In Canada, immigrants and others have benefited from the establishment and validation of societal conventions and law that categorize ethnocultural discrimination as inappropriate or illegal. There is now very widespread support for equal treatment under the law and in everyday life, and it is now difficult for a person to publicly discriminate against others without some risk of sanction. This of course is not to suggest that discrimination today is unimportant—it manifestly is not (see below)—but rather that there now exists a pervasive ideology of fair treatment that confirms the extension of equal rights and equal treatment to everyone, and in so doing validates diversity.

Comprehensive national data on Canadian attitudes toward a wide range of ethnocultural and national populations have not been collected since 1991. At that time, a careful replication (Berry and Kalin 1995; Kalin and Berry 1996) of an earlier national study (Berry et al. 1977:106) found that at an aggregate level, Canadians then still continued to use perceived ethnicity and race to evaluate each other. Many of those questioned maintained a perceptual hierarchy of groups that was not radically different than was prevalent 50 years previously: the more culturally and physically different a population was seen to be, the more negatively that population was viewed. What *had* changed significantly was the range of perceived differences between groups, which seemed to have greatly decreased over time. This trend has, if anything, accelerated in the intervening years. Today's Canadians evidently do not see as large a cultural or racial difference between one ethnocultural population and another as did their parents. Indeed, younger Canadians seem to attach almost no negative attributes to any European-origin population, and profess positive views of those with origins elsewhere, and of First Nations people. As a case in point, consider intermarriage. Many social scientists view attitudes toward intermarriage as one of the most significant indicators of feeling of similarity and difference between types of people. In the mid-1970s just 55 percent of Canadians approved of "white-black" marriages. This rose to 78 percent in 1990, and to 90 percent or more in the last decade (Bibby 2007; Parkin and Mendelsohn 2003:5).

Attitudinal indications of tolerance are supported by behavioral evidence. To further consider intermarriage, according to 2001 census results, fully 43 percent of couples that included at least one "black" person were mixed (Milan and Hamm 2004:3).[14] Incidents of extreme violence toward immigrant-origin visible minorities are rare, and are national news when they occur. Nothing approaching a race riot has occurred in the last 50 years. While both visible minority and First Nations urban populations tend to be residentially concentrated, there are no immigrant-origin or First Nations urban ghettos (Fong and

Wilkes 2003). Socially, no immigrant origin group is strongly isolated from the mainstream except (like the Hutterites) through choice.

These and other positive findings should not suggest that Canada lacks significant racial and ethnic issues. Among them, addressing disadvantages faced by First Nations people stemming from historical and contemporary discrimination is clearly Canada's most serious and intractable ethnic and race relations challenge. Like their American counterparts, First Nations people in Canada faced a disabling colonial regime of subordination that devalued their ways of life and kept them out of the mainstream of society. Although the core elements of that regime were dismantled a long time ago, their consequences remain (see Brody 1975, 1988). Critically, what were once chiefly disabilities race, ethnicity, and nationality have, over time, become enduring disabilities of class.

Today, many of Canada's First Nations people face the daunting challenges, impediments, and disappointments that arise out of structural forces that continue to keep them very poor. The incomes of First Nations adults remain dramatically lower than those of any other ethnocultural population: roughly 56 percent of nonaboriginal adults in 2005 (Gionet 2009:57). At least twice as many First Nations people live in poverty as do others. True unemployment rates reach 90 percent on some isolated rural reserves, and are probably not less than 30 percent anywhere in the country. Kept outside the mainstream for so long by forces that negated and destroyed their prior ways of life, many today face uncertainties of identity and feel profoundly deprived and powerless. These factors in turn negatively affect diet, risk of accident, and patterns of substance abuse, as well as rates of criminal victimization, domestic abuse, criminality, and incarceration. The health of adults is, on average, so poor that researchers and health workers typically consider First Nations people old at age 50 (Buchignani and Armstrong-Esther 1999), and life expectancy at birth remains about seven years lower than for others. First Nations people are six to seven times more likely to be incarcerated, and three times more likely to be the victims of violent crime than nonaboriginals (Brzozowski et al. 2006:12). While most other Canadians now have very positive attitudes toward First Nations people, this is not necessarily true of those who interface with them on a daily basis. Both negative stereotypes of drunk, lazy Indians (Braroe 1975) and some historical patterns of everyday discrimination continue to persist in many of the places where First Nations people live (Henriksen 1978; Kennedy 1982; Plaice 1990; Waldram 1987). Those facing such prejudice and discrimination typically have few resources to combat them.

At the same time, the specifically ethnic and racial difficulties of First Nations people are not a high-profile public issue; they are almost never framed as such by First Nations leadership, who have other priorities, such as securing further services and advancing land claims. Health, economic, psychological, and other problems that clearly are at least partially the consequences of historical and ongoing ethnic and race relations are often addressed by specific programs but almost never directly as race or ethnic issues.

It is difficult to assess the degree to which immigrant-origin visible minority populations face ethic or racial discrimination or how well they fare in facing it. Clearly none have had to contend with the kind of historical oppression faced by First Nations people, as all these populations have expanded dramatically only in the last 40 years. Moreover, a high proportion of incoming visible minority immigrants have brought strong class resources with them (such as high levels of education and significant occupational experience) into Canadian contexts where attitudes to diversity are much more positive than they once were. At the same time, many are at once "visible" *and* immigrants, and face potential challenges *as* immigrants and new members of the workforce that are not directly tied to ethnicity or race.

Such qualifications aside, a number of statistical studies of individual income carried out over the last 10 years (such as Reitz 2001; Pendakur and Pendakur 2002) have shown a worrying pattern.[15] While immigrant men and women who are not visible minorities earn more than their native born counterparts—even controlling for factors such as education—visible minority immigrant men who have received their education abroad earn considerably less than nonimmigrants. These studies show that much of the income differential between comparable visible minority male immigrants and native born men is the result of a severe discounting of their overseas work experience, some discounting of their overseas (but not Canadian) educational qualifications, and the long-term consequences of initial employment in jobs with few prospects for training and advancement. Such studies however do typically find some residual difference that may be the result of direct ethnic or racial discrimination. In addition, since 1990 immigrants in general have found their initial economic establishment to be slower and more difficult than it was for previous immigrants, resulting in perhaps one fifth experiencing chronic low income (Picot et al. 2007:33); chronic low employment is strongly concentrated among immigrants from Asia and Africa. While perhaps 60 percent of all new immigrants currently take work outside of their prior occupational area, the rate Asian immigrants doing so is roughly twice that of immigrants from the United States, Australia, and New Zealand (Chiu 2003:30). There also is evidence that visible minority poverty rates are consistently higher than for other populations (Kazemipur and Halli 2001:234; Reitz and Banerjee 2007:494). Police statistics suggest that about 2 percent of personal (assaults, robbery, etc.) and household (vandalism, break and enter, etc.) crime is motivated in part or whole by ethnic and racial hate (Statistics Canada 2001:25).

This and other statistical information parallels what both immigrants, visible minorities, and others say. The large scale *Ethnic Diversity Study* (Statistics Canada 2003:16–18) found that 24 percent of visible minority Canadians felt uncomfortable or out of place all or most of the time—three times the rate others reported this; one in five claimed to have experienced discrimination or unfair treatment sometimes or often in the last five years, rising to one-third among "blacks." Despite their strong support for diversity themselves, 74 percent of both visible minorities and others in a recent national poll said that there was still a lot of racism in Canada; 44 percent of visible minorities and 32 percent of others thought that a visible minority job applicant would likely lose out to a similarly qualified person who was not a visible minority (Parkin and Mendelsohn 2003:6–8).

Canadian reluctance to talk race notwithstanding, several types of evidence suggest that Afro-Canadians face racial disabilities (Breton 1998; Cannon 1995; Henry and Tator 1994). Before 1950, "blacks" in the Maritimes, Ontario, and elsewhere who were longtime Canadians had full legal rights, in the narrowest sense of the term. However, they faced routine job, residential, and other forms of discrimination that were little different in character or intensity than in the northeastern United States. As in the United States, these forms of overt, specifically racial discrimination disappeared in the 1950s and 1960s. Less overt forms did not (Clairmont and Magill 1974; Henry 1973). The depth of specifically ethnic or racial prejudice and discrimination directed toward so-called African-origin immigrants (who actually came chiefly from the Caribbean) during that era is difficult to assess, as many also faced gender, class, and immigration-generated disabilities. Changes made in immigrant selection criteria in the late 1960s thereafter increased the range of nationalities and ethnicities among the Afro-Canadian population, although in the 1970s most continued to come from the Caribbean. These changes also affected the class backgrounds of 'black' immigrants. By the 1980s, the skill and educational levels of the overall Afro-Canadian population were broadly comparable to those of other Canadians. In the 1980s and 1990s, the national range of Afro-Canadians was further expanded by the arrival of refugees, asylum seekers, and other immigrants from Africa.

It is clear that American popular culture images of African Americans have long had negative consequences across the border (Indra 1979a, 1982). No other people on earth receive as much exposure to American mass-distributed electronic and print materials as do Canadians, and one result is that other Canadians now sometimes associate Afro-Canadians with media stereotypes of African Americans emphasizing criminality and poverty.[16] A number of studies show that Afro-Canadians are sensitive to the risk of racial discrimination (Dei et al. 1997; Ebanks 1996) and believe that it is prevalent.

Support for such views comes from a wide variety of sources. On the economic front, a controlled, direct test of hiring practices during the economic recession of the early 1980s showed that Afro-Canadian job candidates in Toronto were being discriminated against (Henry and Ginzberg 1985), even if a restudy in more prosperous times did not (Henry 1989). West Indian male incomes in Toronto were then roughly $3,500 lower than would be predicted on the basis of their qualifications, chiefly as a result of their lower-than-expected job statuses (Breton et al. 1990:160); by the time of the 2001 Census the difference was $4,000. A disproportionate number of Afro-Canadians today are poor.

Disabilities may exist in other areas of life as well. Afro-Canadians appear to be treated more harshly by the justice system than others, and may have a federal incarceration rate three times higher than their proportion of the overall Canadian population (Wortley 1999). Several studies suggest that the racial climate of some schools impedes the success of Afro-Canadian children and disengages them from the educational process (Dei et al. 1997; Solomon 1992).

Some other recent immigrant-origin populations are probably at some material risk. Immigrants from South Asia (India, Pakistan, etc.) were the focus of extensive stereotyping and were occasionally targets of serious, violent incidents in the late 1970s and 1980s. The frequency of attacks against South Asian individuals has decreased significantly since then (Buchignani 1993; Buchignani and Indra 1981, 1985, 1989). Even so, South Asians continue to be thought of as the most culturally different of all large immigrant-origin populations, and ideas about South Asians are still informed by negative media portrayal of India, Pakistan, and other South Asian source countries (Indra 1979b, 1982). These stereotypes are likely to negatively impact on how South Asian immigrant overseas educational and occupational records are evaluated in the workplace.

A positive stereotype of Chinese Canadians (T. Chan 1983; K. Chan 1987) has arisen over the last 30 years, one that characterizes them as "polite, economically self-sufficient, hard-working, and law abiding" (K. Chan 1987:126), strongly familial, apolitical, quickly integrating, and not socially disruptive. This has facilitated their rapid integration into Canada's urban fabric in most places. One partial exception has been in the Vancouver area. Hundreds of thousands of ethnic Chinese immigrated to Vancouver and the surrounding region during the economic boom affecting Asian Pacific Rim countries during the 1980s and early 1990s. A significant number were from Hong Kong, who established residence in Canada as insurance against what might occur when the British colony transferred back to China. Large numbers of professional and entrepreneurial-class individuals arrived thereafter from the rest of China. Both in numbers and economic power, these new Chinese residents transformed whole towns and neighborhoods without much local input; by 2001 the proportion of Chinese in many neighborhoods in the Vancouver region was over 30 percent (Hou 2006). Large shopping malls were established to cater exclusively to Chinese. Thousands who were better off knocked down older houses in desirable areas and replaced them with what were locally termed monster houses. A few others began to be associated in the media with gangs and the drug trade. This generated focused resentment toward local Chinese as the supposed cause of a wide range of societal changes and problems, from high real estate prices to the loss of established neighborhood ways of life (Cannon 1989). There are, however, no indications that this has translated into significant anti-Chinese discrimination over the long term.

Finally, groups from the Middle East continue to contend with very negative media stereotypes of Arabs and Muslims (Kashmeri

1991). To a lesser degree than in the United States, 9/11 and the subsequent Iraq and Afghanistan wars (Canada participates in the latter, but not the former) have increased public suspicions concerning local Muslims; in a national poll in 2007, 57 percent of other Canadians thought that Muslim Canadians wanted to remain separate and distinct—yet only 23 percent of Muslims polled actually felt that way; 81 percent of Muslims said that they felt satisfied with their life in Canada, a figure much higher than those reported concerning Muslims living in Western European countries (and indeed, one 20 percent higher than the Canadian population at large). Surprisingly, only 12 percent considered discrimination to be a serious problem (Adams 2007).

GLOBAL CONNECTIONS, LOCAL STRUCTURES

There are three important additional ways in which the current Canadian situation is very similar to that in the United States. One is the persistent tendency of those who feel that they share a common ethnicity or nationality to associate with each other, and by doing so, to form local communities and institutions. Enduring identity and language-based community structures have been part and parcel of Canadian minority group life from the onset. This is not solely the case for immigrant-origin populations. Community structures have been critical to the lives of francophones in and out of Québec, and to First Nations people everywhere. Today, such communities are a central source of support for identity, practical assistance, and access to goods and services. They are also often the result of, and an impetus to, further chain migration—of First Nations people moving between rural and urban contexts and of many new immigrants. In many respects, informal community structure—the overlapping networks of personal relationships between one person and another among people who see themselves as the same—is at the very center of the set of phenomena called ethnicity.

As in the United States, the persistence of ethnic and national consciousness over time continues to vary dramatically from one group to another. Two key populations appear destined to persist indefinitely: francophones in Québec and First Nations people. Both are large, effectively instill group consciousness, are institutionally and legally distinguished by the state, face interactional barriers in associating with others, and maintain a wide range of parallel institutions. Racial identification by others continues to maintain a reactive form of consciousness among many Afro-Canadians, including those who neither affiliate with any immigrant source country nor maintain any significantly different cultural practices. Such consciousness remains strong in the Afro-Canadian populations of New Brunswick and Nova Scotia, which were founded over 200 years ago.

Of all other groups and populations, only a few ethnoreligious groups—those in which religious and cultural distinctiveness have arisen together—otherwise appear to have the resources to maintain themselves successfully beyond the second generation without ongoing immigration. The most remarkable of these is undoubtedly the roughly 30,000 communal Hutterites living in the west, whose numbers are growing rapidly through natural increase and who lose fewer than 10 percent of their members in each generation. Over two generations, several Hassidic Jewish populations seem to have been equally effective in preserving a high degree of identity, and social and cultural separation from others in the challenging context of urban Montréal (although with some augmentation through immigration). Sikhs and Ismaili Muslims (Dossa 1985) appear to be able to maintain continuity of identity, religion, and some associated core cultural practices strongly into the second generation, particularly where they are members of large communities.

Immediate (often, extended) family, kinship, and informal community were vitally important to individuals from many immigrant-origin populations prior to immigration (particularly those from Asia), and almost always continue to be so afterward. This, along with very high rates of chain migration, has led to the formation of large, deeply connected communities in almost every local Asian immigrant population across the country. Most of these communities are still too new to predict how the children of immigrants will engage with them as adults. However, there are a number of indications that many children will either not participate in them beyond maintaining ties with relatives, or else will do so very selectively. This certainly has been so historically, even for large, institutionally complete communities like Italians in Toronto (Gabori 1993; Harney 1998; Jansen 1986). In such earlier cases, institutions created by and for immigrant adults proved unable to stem identity shift, acculturation, and assimilation among their children. Some measure of British (chiefly Scottish and Irish) ethnic identity persists from very early times in those parts of the country where recent levels of immigration have been low, and where notions of ethnicity and roots have become intertwined with local/regional culture, ethnic tourism, and images of local folk culture manufactured by folklorists and others (Macdonald 1988; Pocius 1991). In contrast, some immigrants like Americans do not form communities at all, and evidently do not even think of themselves in ethnic terms.

Second, most of Canada's institutions still have not extensively adapted themselves to meet the practical, everyday needs and aspirations of people whose language or core cultural values diverge from the mainstream. The barriers to a good life facing those whose knowledge of English or French is poor remain profound; and outside of major public institutions like hospitals in large cities (which now typically can access translators and cultural interpreters), the chief remedies to their plight continue to be dependence on bilingual relatives and access to ESL and FSL programs rather than institutional change. Language and cultural accommodation by the mainstream business community has been slight. Women or those who lack substantial class resources are at a particular disadvantage

(Ng 1988; van Esterik 1991). Lack of facility with one of the two official languages continues to orient people toward those who share their birth language, strengthening interpersonal community relations and ethnic identity, and building and maintaining group-specific parallel institutions (Indra 1986).

Finally, as in the United States, transportation and communication changes have dramatically altered ties between immigrants and their descendants and the rest of the world. Few of the countries from which today's immigrants come are much more than a day's travel away. As a consequence, immigrant-origin populations and their source countries are often bound together by streams of visitors going in both directions (Patel 1999). Canadians are one of the most mobile populations in the world, and experience diversity both overseas and at home. Cheap international telephone and Internet service connect Canadians to relatives in what were once thought of as remote parts of the globe. Increased ease of communications has also facilitated access to world popular culture, augmenting the multilingual television and radio stations found in most cities. Like world music, literature is not so localized as before: Nominally ethnic Canadian authors such as Michael Ondaatje and Rohinton Mistry write of their source cultures, histories, and societies for an international audience.

All these factors mean that ethnic and race relations in Canada cannot now—if they ever could—be adequately addressed solely as localized Canadian phenomena. Neither people nor ideas are as fixed in place as before. Events in a small village in rural Punjab can have immediate implications for a Sikh family in Vancouver, and vice versa. Nationalist conflicts in the former Yugoslavia can polarize what were once amicable relations between Serbs and Croats in Toronto. World ecological ideologies can and are being used by First Nations people in Canada to re-engineer a more positive public image, at the same time that Inuit sealing practices challenge the hegemony of some of these same ecological dogmas overseas.

Notes

1. Since the 1980s, First Nations has been the preferred term of reference for Canadians who claim an aboriginal (native) heritage.
2. Canada and the United States are each other's largest trading partners by far. Forty to fifty million individual transits of the border are made each year.
3. John Ralson Saul (2008) and others have recently argued that this close historical interface between First Nations people and European settlers also strongly influenced pre-Confederation Canadian political values and views of the relationship between the individual and the colectivity.
4. Population figures for 2006 are from online results from the most recent 2006 Census of Canada, unless otherwise indicated (www12.stat-can.gc.ca/census-recensement/index-eng.cfm).
5. Many First Nations people, however, are not covered by a specific treaty. This includes most of those in British Columbia and most Inuit and Indians in the North. Neither Métis nor non-status Indians are covered by treaties. The Canadian Supreme Court declared that Inuit were Indians for purposes of the British North America Act in 1939.
6. See Aihwa Ong (1996) for a similar modern U.S. reaction to Lao immigrants.
7. Canada shares this distinction with South Africa, which also has two persisting charter groups: Dutch-origin Afrikaners and British.
8. The British connection was still so strong that Canada immediately joined the war on their side. Most Québec francophones could then trace their roots in North America back more than 250 years and had no commitment to any foreign power. Many actively resisted conscription.
9. Additional information on Canadian immigration is available at Citizenship and Immigration Canada's Web site, www.cic.gc.ca.
10. See the *Canadian Ethnic Studies Journal* for the range of current research interests concerning Canadian ethnic and racial issues.
11. The federal government has not been fully consistent in its terminology, for the 1986 Employment Equity Act does employ racial terminology such as "non-white."
12. The following subsection (2) states that this provision "does not preclude any law, program or activity that has as its object the amelioration of conditions of disadvantaged individuals or groups including those that are disadvantaged because of race, national or ethnic origin, colour, religion, sex, age or mental or physical disability."
13. Responses historically have been more favorable when a more neutral question is asked that requires respondents to assess whether current immigrant is too high, about right, or too low, as noted earlier.
14. Asian Canadian intermarriage rates are much lower than this: about 8 percent in 2001. This reflects the high proportion of Asian Canadians who are either traditionally endogamous Chinese or South Asians, the endogamous effects of large local Asian populations, and the high proportion of Asian Canadians who are immigrants (Lee and Boyd 2008:317). The out marriage rate for Asian Canadians born in Canada is around 35 percent.
15. For a review of these findings and some of the controversies surrounding their interpretation, see Reitz and Banerjee (2006) and Yoshida and Smith (2008).
16. And yet about 70 percent of Canadians supported Obama for president immediately before the last U.S. presidential election, as compared with 14 percent who supported McCain.

References Cited

ADAMS, MICHAEL. 2007. *Muslims and Multiculturalism in Canada*. Toronto: Environics Research Group.

ASCH, MICHAEL. 1984. *Home and Native Land: Aboriginal Rights and the Canadian Constitution*. Toronto: Methuen.

BAUHN, PER, CHRISTER LINDBERG, and SVANTE LUNDBERG. 1995. *Multiculturalism and Nationhood in Canada: The Cases of First Nations and Québec*. Lund, Sweden: Lund University Press.

BENNETT, JOHN. 1967. *Hutterian Brethren: The Agricultural Economy of a Communal People*. Stanford, CA: Stanford University Press.

BERRY JOHN W., and RUDOLF KALIN. 1995. Multicultural and ethnic attitudes in Canada: An overview of the 1991 national survey. *Canadian Journal of Behavioural Science* 27(3):301–320.

BERRY, JOHN, RUDOLF KALIN, and D. TAYLOR. 1977. *Multiculturalism and Ethnic Attitudes in Canada*. Ottawa: Information Canada.

BIBBY, REGINALD. 2007. *Canadians More Likely Than Americans to Approve of Black-White Marriages*. Project Canada Press Release #9. Lethbridge, Alberta: University of Lethbridge.

BISSOONDATH, NEIL. 1994. *Selling Illusions: The Cult of Multiculturalism in Canada*. Toronto: Penguin.

BLOEMRAAD, IRENE. 2006. *Becoming a Citizen: Incorporating Immigrants and Refugees in the United States and Canada*. Berkeley, CA: University of California Press.

BRAROE, NIELS. 1975. *Indian and White: Self Image and Interaction in a Canadian Plains Community*. Stanford, CA: Stanford University Press.

BRETON, RAYMOND. 1964. Institutional completeness of ethnic communities and personal relations of immigrants. *American Journal of Sociology* 70(2):193–205.

———. 1998. Ethnicity and race in social organizations: Recent developments in Canadian society. In *The Vertical Mosaic Revisited*. R. Helmes-Hayes and J. Curtis, eds. Pp. 60–115. Toronto: University of Toronto Press.

BRETON, RAYMOND, WSEVOLOD ISAJIW, WARREN KALBACH, and JEFFREY REITZ. 1990. *Ethnic Identity and Equality: Varieties of Experience in a Canadian City*. Toronto: University of Toronto Press.

BRODY, HUGH. 1975. *The People's Land: Whites and the Western Arctic*. Harmondsworth, UK: Penguin.

———. 1988. *Maps and Dreams: Indians and the British Columbia Frontier*. Vancouver: Douglas & McIntyre.

BRZOZOWSKI, JODI-ANNE, ANDREA TAYLOR-BUTTS, and SARA JOHNSON. 2006. Victimization and offending among the aboriginal population in Canada. *Juristat* 26(3):1–31.

BUCHIGNANI, NORMAN. 1983. Some comments on the elimination of racism in Canada. *Canadian Ethnic Studies* 15(2):118–124.

———. 1993. Refugees and ethnic relations in Canada. In *The International Refugee Crisis: British and Canadian Responses*. Vaughn Robinson, ed. Pp. 35–56. London: Macmillan.

BUCHIGNANI, NORMAN, and CHRISTOPHER ARMSTRONG-ESTHER. 1999. Informal care and older native Canadians. *Ageing and Society* 19:3–32.

BUCHIGNANI, NORMAN, and DOREEN INDRA. 1981. Intergroup conflict and community solidarity: Sikhs and South Asian Fijians in Vancouver. *Canadian Journal of Anthropology* 1(2):149–157.

———. 1985. *Continuous Journey: A Social History of South Asians in Canada*. Toronto: McClelland and Stewart.

———. 1989. Key issues in Canadian-Sikh ethnic and race relations, and their implications for the study of the Sikh diaspora. In *The Sikh Diaspora*. N. G. Barrier and V. Dusenbery, eds. Pp. 141–184. New Delhi: Manohar.

———. 1999. Vanishing acts: Illegal immigration in Canada as a sometime social issue. In *Illegal Immigration in America: A Reference Handbook*. David Haines and Karen Rosenblum, eds. Pp. 415–450. Westport, CT: Greenwood Press.

BUCHIGNANI, NORMAN, and PAUL LETKEMANN. 1993. Ethnographic research. In *Multiculturalism in Canada*. John Berry and Jean Laponce, eds. Pp. 203–237. Toronto: University of Toronto Press.

CANADA. CITIZENSHIP AND IMMIGRATION CANADA. 2007. *Facts and Figures 2007: Immigration Overview*. Ottawa: Minister of Public Works and Government Services Canada.

CANADA. MULTICULTURALISM AND CITIZENSHIP CANADA. 1992. *Multiculturalism Attitude Survey 1991*. Ottawa: Multiculturalism and Citizenship Canada.

CANADIAN BROADCASTING CORPORATION AND EKOS RESEARCH ASSOCIATES. 2002. *Public Attitudes Toward Immigration*. Ottawa: Ekos Research Associates.

CANNON, MARGARET. 1989. *China Tide: The Revealing Story of the Hong Kong Exodus to Canada*. Toronto: Harper & Collins.

———. 1995. *The Invisible Empire: Racism in Canada*. Mississauga, ON: Random House.

CHAN, KWOK. 1987. Perceived racial discrimination and response: An analysis of Indochinese experience in Montréal. *Canadian Ethnic Studies* 19(3):125–147.

CHAN, KWOK, LOUIS J. DORAIS, and DOREEN INDRA, eds. 1988. *Ten Years Later: Indochinese Communities in Canada*. Ottawa: Canadian Asian Studies Association.

CHAN, KWOK, and DOREEN INDRA, eds. 1986. *Uprooting, Loss and Adaptation: The Resettlement of Indochinese Refugees in Canada*. Ottawa: Canadian Public Health Association.

CHAN, TONY. 1983. *Gold Mountain: The Chinese in the New World*. Vancouver: New Star Books.

CHIU, TINA. 2003. *Longitudinal Survey of Immigrants to Canada: Process, Progress and Prospects*. Ottawa: Statistics Canada.

CLAIRMONT, D. H., and D. W. MAGILL. 1974. *Africville: The Life and Death of a Canadian Black Community*. Toronto: McClelland and Stewart.

DASKO, DONNA. 2005. Public Attitudes towards Multiculturalism and Bilingualism in Canada. In *Canadian and French Perspectives on Diversity: Conference Proceedings*. M. Adsett, C. Mallandain, and S. Settner, eds. Pp. 119–25. Ottawa: Department of Canadian Heritage.

DEI, GEORGE J. S., JOSEPHINE MAZZUCA, ELIZABETH MCISAAC, and JASMIN ZINE. 1997. *Reconstructing Drop-Out: A Critical Ethnography of the Dynamics of Black Students' Disengagement from School*. Toronto: University of Toronto Press.

DIRKS, GERALD E. 1977. *Canada's Refugee Policy: Indifference or Opportunism?* Montreal: McGill-Queen's University Press.

DORAIS, LOUIS-JACQUES, L. PILON-LE, and N. HUY. 1987. *Exiles in a Cold Land: A Vietnamese Community in Canada*. New Haven, CT: Yale University Press.

DOSSA, PARIN. 1985. Ritual and daily life: Transmission and interpretation of the Ismaili tradition in Vancouver. Ph.D. dissertation, University of British Columbia.

DRIBEN, PAUL. 1985. *Aroland is Our Home: An Incomplete Victory in Applied Anthropology*. New York: AMS Press.

DYCK, NOEL, ed. 1985. *Indigenous Peoples and the Nation State: "Fourth World" Politics in Canada, Australia and Norway*. St. John's: Institute of Social and Economic Research.

DYCK, NOEL. 1991. *What Is the Indian "Problem"? Tutelage and Resistance in the Canadian Indian Administration*. St. John's: Institute of Social and Economic Research.

EBANKS, G. E. 1996. The Caribbean diaspora in Toronto: Learning to live with racism. *Canadian Ethnic Studies* 28(2):188–190.

ELLER, JACK D. 1998. *From Culture to Ethnicity to Conflict: An Anthropological Perspective on International Ethnic Conflict*. Ann Arbor, MI: University of Michigan Press.

ESSES, V. M., J. F. DOVIDIO, and G. HODSON. 2002. Public attitudes toward immigration in the United States and Canada in response to the September 11, 2001 "Attack on America" *Analyses of Social Issues and Public Policy* 2(1):69–85.

ESSES, V. M., J. F. DOVIDIO, L. M. JACKSON, and T. L. ARMSTRONG. 2001. The immigration dilemma: The role of perceived group competition, ethnic prejudice, and national identity. *Journal of Social Issues* 57(3):389–412.

FONG, ERIC, and RIMA WILKES. 2003. Racial and ethnic residential patterns in Canada. *Sociological Forum* 18(4):577–602.

FOSTER, K. A. 1924. *Our Canadian Mosaic*. Toronto: Dominion Council of the YWCA.

GABORI, SUSAN. 1993. *In Search of Paradise: The Odyssey of an Italian Family*. Montreal: McGill-Queen's University Press.

GARIQUE, P. 1956. French Canadian kinship and urban life. *American Anthropologist* 58:1090–1101.

GILAD, LISA. 1990. *The Northern Route: An Ethnography of Refugee Experiences*. St. John's: Institute of Social and Economic Research.

GIONET, LINDA. 2009. First Nations people: Selected findings of the 2006 Census. *Canadian Social Trends* (May):52–58.

GOLD, GERALD. 1975. *St. Pascal*. Toronto: Holt, Rinehart & Winston.

GRAND COUNCIL OF THE CREES (OF QUÉBEC). 1998. *Never without Consent: James Bay Crees' Stand Against Forcible Inclusion into an Independent Québec*. Toronto: ECW Press.

HANDLER, RICHARD. 1988. *Nationalism and the Politics of Culture in Québec*. Madison, WI: University of Wisconsin Press.

HARNEY, NICHOLAS D. M. 1998. *Eh, Paesan! Being Italian in Toronto*. Toronto: University of Toronto Press.

HELMES-HAYES, R., and J. CURTIS, eds. 1998. *The Vertical Mosaic Revisited*. Toronto: University of Toronto Press.

HENRIKSEN, GEORG. 1978. *Hunters in the Barrens*. St. John's: Memorial University Press.

HENRY, FRANCIS. 1973. *Forgotten Canadians: The Blacks of Nova Scotia*. Don Mills, ON: Longmans Canada.

———. 1989. *Who Gets the Work in 1989?* Ottawa: Economic Council of Canada.

HENRY, FRANCIS, and E. GINZBERG. 1985. *Who Gets the Work: A Test of Racial Discrimination in Employment*. Toronto: Urban Alliance on Race Relations.

HENRY, FRANCES, and CAROL TATOR. 1994. The ideology of racism: "Democratic racism." *Canadian Ethnic Studies* 26(2):1–14.

HENRY, FRANCES, CAROL TATOR, WINSTON MATTIS, and TIM REES. 1995. *The Colour of Democracy: Racism in Canadian Society*. Toronto: Harcourt Brace.

HOSTETLER, J. A., and G. E. HUNTINGTON. 1996. *The Hutterites in North America*. Toronto: Holt, Rinehart & Winston.

HOU, FENG. 2006. Spatial assimilation of racial minorities in Canada's immigrant gateway cities. *Urban Studies* 43(7)1191–1213.

INDRA, DOREEN. 1979a. Ethnicity, social stratification and opinion formation: An analysis of ethnic portrayal in the Vancouver newspaper press, 1905–1976. Ph.D. dissertation, Simon Fraser University.

———. 1979b. South Asian stereotypes in the Vancouver press. *Ethnic and Racial Studies* 2(2):166–189.

———. 1982. The production and legitimation of racial and ethnic stereotypes in the Vancouver press, 1905–82. In *Perspectives on Race, Education and Social Development: Emphasis on Canada.* Vincent D'Oyley, ed. Pp. 35–43. Vancouver: University of British Columbia.

———. 1986. Bureaucratic constraints, middlemen and community organization: Aspects of the political incorporation of Southeast Asians in Canada. In *Uprooting, Loss and Adaptation: The Resettlement of Indochinese Refugees in Canada.* Kwok Chan and Doreen M. Indra, eds. Pp. 147–170. Ottawa: Canadian Public Health Association.

JANSEN, C. 1986. *Italians in a Multicultural Canada.* Queenston, ON: Mellen.

KALIN, RUDOLF, and JOHN W. BERRY. 1995. Ethnic and civic self-identity in Canada: Analyses of 1974 and 1991 national surveys. *Canadian Ethnic Studies* 27(2):1–15.

———. 1996. Interethnic attitudes in Canada: Ethnocentrism, consensual hierarchy and reciprocity. *Canadian Journal of Behavioural Science* 28(4):253–261.

KASHMERI, ZUHAIR. 1991. *The Gulf Within: Canadian Arabs, Racism, and the Gulf War.* Toronto: J. Lorimer.

KAZEMIPUR, ABDOLMOHAMMAD, and SHIVA S. HALLI. 2001. The changing colour of poverty in Canada. *Canadian Review of Sociology and Anthropology* 38(2):217–238.

KENNEDY, J. 1982. *Holding the Line: Ethnic Boundaries in a Northern Labrador Community.* St. John's: Institute of Social and Economic Research.

KNOWLES, VALERIE. 1997. *Strangers at Our Gates: Canadian Immigration and Immigration Policy, 1540–1997.* Rev. edition. Toronto: Dundurn Press.

KYMLICKA, WILL. 1998. *Finding Our Way: Rethinking Ethnocultural Relations in Canada.* Toronto: Oxford University Press.

LEE, SHARON, and MONICA BOYD. 2008. Marrying out: Comparing the marital and social integration of Asians in the US and Canada. *Social Science Research* 37:311–329.

LONEY, MARTIN. 1998. *The Pursuit of Division: Race, Gender, and Preferential Hiring in Canada.* Montreal: McGill-Queen's University Press.

MACDONALD, N. 1988. Putting on the kilt: The Scottish stereotype and ethnic community survival in Cape Breton. *Canadian Ethnic Studies* 20(3):132–146.

MATA, FERNANDO, and JENNA HENNEBRY. 1997. *Public Approval of the Federal Policy of Multiculturalism in the 90s.* Ottawa: Department of Canadian Heritage.

MILAN, ANNE, and BRIAN HAMM. 2004. Mixed unions. *Canadian Social Trends* (Summer):3.

NG, R. 1988. *The Politics of Community Services: Immigrant Women, Class and State.* Toronto: Garamond Press.

ONG, AIHWA. 1996. Cultural citizenship as subject-making: Immigrants negotiate racial and cultural boundaries in the United States. *Current Anthropology* 37(5):737–762.

PATEL, DHIRU. 1999. Technology, identity and cultural change in the South Asian diasporas. Paper presented at Citizens at the Crossroads: Whose Information Society? University of Western Ontario, London, ON, October.

PARKIN, ANDREW, and MATHEW MENDELSOHN. 2003. *A New Canada: An Identity Shaped by Diversity.* Ottawa: Centre for Research and Information on Canada.

PENDAKUR, K., and R. PENDAKUR. 2002. Colour my world: Have earnings gaps for Canadian-born ethnic minorities changed over time? *Canadian Public Policy* 28:489–512.

PEW RESEARCH CENTER FOR THE PEOPLE AND THE PRESS. 2002. *How Global Publics View: Their Lives, Their Countries, The World, America.* Washington, DC: Pew Research Center.

PICOT, GARNETT, FENG HOU, and SIMON COULOMBE. 2007. *Chronic Low Income and Low-income Dynamics Among Recent Immigrants.* Ottawa: Statistics Canada.

PLAICE, E. 1990. *The Native Game: Settler Perceptions of Indian/Settler Relations in Central Labrador.* St. John's: Institute of Social and Economic Research.

POCIUS, GERALD. 1991. *A Place to Belong: Community Order and Everyday Space in Calvert, Newfoundland.* Montreal: McGill-Queen's University Press.

PONTING, J. R. 1997. *First Nations in Canada: Perspectives on Opportunity, Empowerment, and Self-Determination.* Toronto: McGraw-Hill Ryerson.

PORTER, JOHN. 1965. *The Vertical Mosaic: An Analysis of Social Class and Power in Canada.* Toronto: University of Toronto Press.

PRATT, ANNA. 2005. *Securing Borders: Detention and Deportation in Canada*. Vancouver: University of British Columbia Press.

PURICH, DONALD J. 1988. *The Métis*. Toronto: Lorimer.

REITZ, JEFFREY G. 2001. Immigrant skill utilization in the Canadian labour market: Implications of human capital research. *Journal of International Migration and Integration* 2:347–378.

REITZ, JEFFREY G., and RUPA BANERJEE. 2007. Racial inequality, social cohesion, and policy issues in Canada. In *Belonging? Diversity, Recognition and Shared Citizenship in Canada*. Thomas J. Courchene, Keith Banting, and Wanda Wuttunee, eds. Pp. 489-545. Montreal: Institute for Research on Public Policy.

REITZ, JEFFREY G., and RAYMOND BRETON. 1994. *The Illusion of Difference: Realities of Ethnicity in Canada & the United States*. Toronto: C. D. Howe Institute.

SALISBURY, RICHARD. 1986. *A Homeland for the Cree: Regional Development in James Bay, 1971–1981*. Montreal: McGill-Queen's University Press.

SAUL, JOHN RALSTON. 2008. *A Fair Country: Telling Truths about Canada*. Toronto: Penguin.

SCHEFFEL, DAVID. 1991. *In the Shadow of the Antichrist: The Old Believers of Alberta*. Peterborough: Broadview Press.

SOLOMON, ROVEL PATRICK. 1992. *Black Resistance in High School: Forging a Separatist Culture*. Albany, NY: State University of New York Press.

STATISTICS CANADA. 2001. *Hate Crime in Canada: An Overview of Issues and Data Sources*. Ottawa: Statistics Canada.

————. 2003. *Ethnic Diversity Survey: Portrait of a Multicultural Society*. Ottawa: Statistics Canada.

STRATEGIC COUNCIL. 2006. *Public Perceptions of Immigration and Terrorism*. The Strategic Council: Toronto.

US CENSUS BUREAU. 2005. *Race and Hispanic Origin in 2005*. www.census.gov/population/pop-profile/dynamic/RACEHO.pdf

VAN ESTERIK, JOHN. 1991. Communication claims in a refugee program: A case study of an anthropologist working with immigrant and refugee settlement agencies. In *Immigrants and Refugees in Canada: A National Perspective on Ethnicity, Multiculturalism, and Cross-Cultural Adjustment*. S. Sharma, A. Ervin, and D. Meintel, eds. Saskatoon: University of Saskatchewan and University of Montreal.

WALDRAM, JAMES B. 1987. Ethnostatus distinctions in the western Canadian subarctic: Implications for inter-ethnic and interpersonal relations. *Culture* 7(1):29–38.

WORTLEY, SCOT. 1999. A northern taboo: Research on race, crime, and criminal justice in Canada. *Canadian Journal of Criminology* 41(2):261–274.

YOSHIDA, YOKO, and MICHAEL R. SMITH. 2008. Measuring and mismeasuring discrimination against visible minority immigrants: The role of work experience. *Canadian Studies in Population* 35(2):311–338.

19

■ ■ ■

Conclusion

Raymond Scupin, *Lindenwood University*

This textbook has emphasized the contribution of anthropology and sociology to an understanding of race and ethnicity issues. In the first section of the text, we focused on the professionalization of the field of anthropology and sociology during the nineteenth century, and how the issues of race and ethnicity were at the center of the major research problems. Questions involving the evolution of different races and cultures throughout the world were investigated through research on fossils, artifacts, language, and cultural beliefs and practices. However, as we learned in Chapter 1, these early anthropological paradigms were based on both racist and ethnocentric beliefs that informed the theories and hypotheses that were developed in the nineteenth century. The pioneering European anthropologists reveled in the belief that their "race" and "civilizations" were superior to any others. They believed that the human species was divisible into a small, discrete number of racial categories. They assumed that these categories were fixed and immutable. These early European anthropologists also believed that an individual's behavior and a group's culture could be explained by "racial characteristics," such as skin color and head size. They believed that there was a hierarchy of races, and that the European race was at the top of this hierarchy and Africans at the bottom. Early Greek ideas and the later Christian conception of the Great Chain of Being had paved the way for the early anthropological views of race.

It wasn't until the twentieth century that a more sophisticated understanding of the relationship between race and culture was developed through the scientific and empirical research efforts of anthropologists such as Franz Boas and others. As seen in Chapters 2 and 3, on the history of scientific racism and the contemporary evidence from both fossil and genetic evidence the concept of "race" does not have any scientific validity. Contemporary anthropological and sociological research has shown that there is no precise biological basis for the separation of human beings into races, and that the idea of race is a social and political construction that has been used to justify racism during various periods of human history. Despite the fact that some scholars and scientists assume the validity of racial categories, and ascribe to them the power to explain behavioral and cultural characteristics, genetic and other research efforts in physical anthropology in the twentieth and twentieth-first centuries have shown these assumptions to be erroneous. Race began to disappear within the scientific and anthropological vocabulary as an explanatory schematic. Yet, as seen in Chapter 2, with the appearance of books such as *The Bell Curve* and of pop-sociobiological and racialistic views such as those of Phillipe Rushton, scientific racism still surfaces within our society.

Though contemporary anthropologists and sociologists have demonstrated that there are no valid biological criteria for separating humans precisely into different racial categories, and that the concept of race cannot be used as an analytic device in understanding human evolution and development or cultural behavior, there is still a proclivity to use "race" as a social construction to classify humans into different categories, and the utilization of these classifications as the basis of racism and ethnocentrism.

In Chapter 4, we focus on the characteristics of ethnicity, which emphasizes the cultural aspects of group and individual dynamics in defining human behavior and thought. With the debunking of the biological and racial explanations of human behavior and culture, modern anthropologists and sociologists have focused on the analysis of ethnicity. Both primordialist and circumstantialist views of ethnicity are used as explanatory and interpretive techniques in assessing the role of culture and human behavior. However, as shown in examples of the construction of notions such as the "one drop rule" used to classify African Americans in U.S. society, biological notions are sometimes still conflated with cultural constructions of ethnicity. As indicated in later chapters on ethnic groups in the United States and throughout the world, these misconceptions of ethnicity are often used as the foundation of ethnonationalist movements, and become the foundation of defining one's own group versus the "other." As seen in Chapter 5, some of the research within psychological anthropology and cognitive psychology indicates that humans may be predisposed to distinguish in-groups and out-groups, which become the basis of an ethnocentric syndrome. These models need to be tested further with sophisticated empirical and ethnographic research techniques to confirm or refute these findings.

In the second section of the text, we address the historical experience and contemporary conditions of various ethnic groups within the United States, based on broad historical and ethnographic research. Chapter 6 focuses on the prehistoric, historic, and contemporary conditions of the American Indians in U.S. society. Prior to European contact, these indigenous peoples made up linguistically and ethnically diverse groups throughout North America. When they encountered the Euro-American settlers these Native American Indian groups were devastated by disease, slave labor, and warfare. After the U.S. government developed treaties, removal policies, and reservations, these native peoples faced ethnocide and were eventually treated as conquered people. American Indians have been positioned within systems of inequality and ideologies of racism that have affected their destiny in U.S. society. The struggle of the contemporary Native Americans with the U.S. government continues with political and legal battles, which has promoted an ongoing emergence of new forms of ethnic and religious identity.

In Chapter 7, we begin with an assessment of the Anglo-WASPs and the various "white ethnics" that immigrated into the United States. The WASPs, or English settlers, established the linguistic, economic, political, educational, and religious foundations for U.S. culture. Later, as discussed, various white ethnic immigrants from Germany, Ireland, Italy, Poland, and other European societies encountered the nineteenth- and early twentieth-century racial hierarchy that maintained that the WASPs were at the top of this hierarchy and other white ethnic groups occupied lower positions. Many of the leading scientists and politicians of the day worried that immigrants from Europe would debase America's exalted Anglo-Saxon racial stock. Despite this racism and ethnocentrism maintained by the WASPs, over time these ethnic groups from Europe have assimilated and eventually became accepted as "white" Europeans, who were categorized and treated differently than the nonwhite populations in the United

States. These different ethnic groups have been experiencing their own "ethnogenesis," and have adopted "whiteness" as their ethnic category along with the WASPs. Chapter 8 continues this investigation of becoming "white" with the unique experience of the American Jewish community in the United States. Jewish immigrants in the United States had to overcome the barriers based on anti-Semitism erected by the WASP nativistic movements in the late nineteenth and early twentieth centuries. Eventually, Jewish Americans became accepted as other "whites" in U.S. society.

Chapters 9 presents a historical and ethnographic overview of the African American community. Beginning with the debates that influenced anthropological portrayals of black Americans, and continuing with a survey of the periods of slavery, Jim Crow segregation, and the civil rights and black power movements, we gain a sense of the conditions and struggles of African Americans in U.S. society. African Americans faced the most blatant and persistent forms of racism and discrimination. Their continuing struggle for a pluralistic, multicultural society has been remarkable and inspirational for many peoples throughout the world.

As seen in Chapters 10 through 12, on Hispanic/Latino Americans, Asian Americans, and Arab Americans, anthropologists have been actively doing ethnographic work on the processes of ethnic change and persistence within these different communities. The portrait of U.S. society that has emerged from the recent census figures has demonstrated a trend that anthropologists and sociologists have been aware of for some time: the United States has become ethnically much more diverse. The fact that the Hispanic population grew 58 percent, to almost 45 million people, since 1990, and has pulled ahead of the formerly largest minority, the African American population, reflects the new trends in immigration and globalization. In Florida, Hispanics now outnumber African Americans, and in California they make up one-third of the population. Another

fact from the recent census figures that anthropologists and sociologists were cognizant of was that many more Americans identify themselves as belonging to more than one race. Millions of people described themselves as multiracial. In addition, the white European population is a shrinking share of the country's overall numbers, dropping to 69 percent from 76 percent in 1990. Descendants of white Europeans are now a minority in California and may soon be in Texas. Most demographers predict that before 2050 the non-European ethnic groups will outnumber the white European descendants. These new patterns and configurations of an ethnically more diverse population in the United States will require more ethnographic research by anthropologists and sociologists in the future.

As seen in the third section, in the chapters on Latin America and the Caribbean, Africa, the Middle East, Asia, Europe, and Canada, the entire world is becoming more ethnically diverse with resulting problems, conflict, and change. Traditional conceptions of race and ethnicity continue to plague many regions of the world. In some instances, these traditional notions of race and ethnicity become enshrined in important scholarly studies that have an impact on common understandings of these issues. For example, the late Samuel Huntington, a political scientist at Harvard University, wrote an influential book, *The Clash of Civilizations and the Remaking of the World Order* (1996), that continues to resonate with many people in the West and other regions of the world. Huntington argued that a unitary "Western civilization and culture" is at odds with "Islamic civilization and culture," "Hindu civilization and culture," and "Confucian civilization and culture." He envisioned these primordial ethnic and regional blocs as fragmenting the world order and resulting in more conflict and instability throughout the world. Huntington's perspective has perpetuated a new cold war type of mentality that draws on images of ancient ethnic bonds and animosities.

The anthropologists and sociologists who have conducted research in the regions discussed by Huntington have produced a much different picture of ethnic relations and civilizations. Each of these regions contains tremendous internal ethnic diversity, and the voices of these many different groups are pursuing a wide range of economic-, political-, and religious-based goals and aspirations. These supposedly fixed "real" ethnic cultures and civilizations are in flux, producing plural, diverse, and continual dynamic change. Ethnic identities and civilizations are not static and stable. Processes of globalization and local-level political and economic processes are reproducing a constant tug of ethnic and national identity along with the weakening of those identities and commitments. Anthropologists and sociologists continue to develop a more comprehensive understanding and explanation of these ethnic and global processes through intensive, in-depth research.

As globalization occurs with the rapid integration of nation-states, markets, and information technology, and the management of economic and political development goes to the World Bank, the International Monetary Fund, and the United Nations, many peoples at the local level feel threatened. These globalization processes often exacerbate ethnic tensions and conflicts. We have looked at ethnic tensions and conflicts in Latin America, the Caribbean, Africa, the Middle East, Asia, Europe, and Canada. Undoubtedly, these ethnic conflicts are to some extent a result of earlier colonial policies and the new post–cold war trends in globalization. Many ethnic groups have expressed a desire to return to a more simple way of life and traditional culture and behavior. They distrust the new global managers in attending to their needs. New resurgent forms of ethnicity are reactions to these globalization tendencies. Restoring ethnic autonomy is sometimes seen as a strategy to rectify the globalization process. Anthropologists and sociologists are studying the ethnic resurgence of the Scots, Welsh, and

Irish and why they want more independence in the United Kingdom, and why some in Quebec want to separate from the rest of Canada. These local ethnic movements for autonomy and separatism are a response to the weakening of older nation-state structures, induced by globalization. Globalization is fraught with anxieties and produces uncertainties in structures and institutions as it develops in anarchic, haphazard fashions, carried along by economic, technological, and cultural imperatives. Thus, the ethnic group becomes the refuge for people who feel they have no control over these new forces.

Though the ethnic trends discussed in this text are essentially global, they also obviously affect people on the local level. Cultural anthropologists are actively recording the various dislocations of global political and ethnic processes in these societies and the ways in which people have attempted to cope with these global changes. The continuing agony of separatist, ethnic, and religious conflicts in Kosovo, the Sudan and elsewhere threatens people throughout the world. It appears that existing institutions such as the nation-state have not been able to manage this local conflict. Perhaps by understanding the specific aspirations of these different peoples, national governments and the international community will be more responsive to their diverse needs and interests.

As anthropologists and sociologists identify the cultural and ethnic variations that can block international coordination, they may help to contribute to the reduction of ethnic tensions worldwide. Future anthropologists and sociologists must continue to synthesize their local studies (the micro level) with studies of global conditions (the macro level) to identify trends that militate against international cooperation. A concerted effort must be made to understand the underlying historical and cultural motivations that contribute to ethnic conflicts. In doing so, these anthropologists and sociologists may aid in humankind's understanding of its existence and the need for cooperation in the global village.

CONTRIBUTORS

Thomas Abowd is Visiting Assistant Professor of Legal Studies at the University of Massachusetts, Amherst. Among his publications is a piece entitled "National Boundaries, Colonized Spaces: The Gendered Politics of Residential Life in Contemporary Jerusalem," and a forthcoming article entitled "7 Mile: Arab-African American Racial and Class Encounters in Contemporary Detroit" and a manuscript under review at Syracuse University Press, *Colonial Jerusalem: the Spatial Construction of Identity and Difference in a Divided City*.

Barbara Aswad is Professor Emeritus of Anthropology at Wayne State University. Her first book was *Property Control and Social Strategies: Settlers on a Middle Eastern Plain*. She is the editor of *Arabic Speaking Communities in American Cities, Family and Gender among American Muslims*, and has published numerous articles on Arab and Turkish women in the Middle East and Arab American women. She is past president of the Middle East Studies Association of North America.

Pamela Ballinger is Associate Professor in the Department of Sociology and Anthropology at Bowdoin College. She holds degrees in anthropology from Stanford University, Cambridge University, and Johns Hopkins University. She has published articles in journals including *Current Anthropology*, *Comparative Studies in Society and History*, and *Journal of Modern Italian Studies*. Her book, *History in Exile: Memory and Identity at the Borders of the Balkans*, was published by Princeton University Press in 2003 and has been translated into Italian by *Il Veltro Editrice* (2009). Her research interests include nationalism and ethnicity, memory, Italian fascism, tourism, Italy, and the former Yugoslavia.

Janet Benson is Associate Professor of Anthropology in the Department of Sociology, Anthropology, and Social Work at Kansas State University. During 1988–1990, she participated in the Ford Foundation Changing Relations Project in Garden City, Kansas, focusing on Southeast Asian refugees. Recent publications include "Undocumented Immigrants and the Meatpacking Industry in the Midwest" (2000) and "Vietnamese Refugees, Mexican Immigrants, and the Changing Character of a Community" (2001).

Ellen Bigler is Professor at Rhode Island College in Providence Rhode Island, where she holds a joint appointment in Anthropology and Educational Studies. She is the author of *American Conversations: Puerto Ricans, White Ethnics, and Multicultural Education*. She served as a consultant to the New York State Department of Education on its K-12 Latino curriculum project, *Latinos in the Making of the USA: Yesterday, Today and Tomorrow*, and was awarded a Fulbright to examine race, identity, and educational performance in public schools in Salvador Brazil.

Rachel A. Bonney, Associate Professor of Anthropology at the University of North Carolina at Charlotte, earned her Ph.D. from the University of Arizona in 1975, with a specialization in American Indian culture. In addition to American Indian studies, her interests include American ethnic groups, the anthropology of art, Native American art in miniature, and museum studies.

Donald E. Brown is Emeritus Professor, Department of Anthropology, at the University of California, Santa Barbara. He has done field research in Brunei, Bali, Mexico, and the United States. His interests include Southeast Asia, social structure, history, and ethnicity. His principal publications are *Brunei: The Structure and History of a Bornean Malay Sultanate* (Brunei Museum, 1971); *Principles of Social Structure: Southeast Asia* (Duckworth, 1976); *Hierarchy, History, and Human Nature: The Social Origins of Historical Consciousness* (University of Arizona Press, 1988); and *Human Universals* (McGraw-Hill, 1991).

Susan Love Brown is Professor of Anthropology at Florida Atlantic University in Boca Raton, where she has taught since 1993. From 2006 to 2008 she served as interim director of the Ph.D. in Comparative Studies and director of the Public Intellectuals Program. She received her master's degree in anthropology from San Diego State University and her Ph.D. in anthropology from the University of California, San Diego. She is a political and psychological anthropologist whose interests are the Caribbean and the United States. She is a coauthor of *Meeting Anthropology* (Carolina Academic Press, 2000) and editor of a volume, *Intentional Community: An Anthropological Perspective* (SUNY Press, 2002). She also teaches a course in African American anthropology.

Norman Buchignani is an Emeritus Professor in the Department of Anthropology at the University of Lethbridge, Canada. He has been involved in studies of immigration, ethnic diversity, forced migration travel discourses, and community-based systems of meaning in Canada and elsewhere for 25 years.

Sheilah Clarke-Ekong is Associate Professor and Chair of Anthropology at the University of Missouri, St. Louis. She received her Ph.D. from UCLA. She has lived and taught in universities in Ghana and Nigeria, West Africa. Her research interests include the adaptation of traditional structures and the construction of indigenous identity. She teaches a number of Africa-focused courses and works closely with the Africa study abroad program at UMSL. Currently she is teaching a number of courses cross-listed with the Institute for Women and Gender Studies. She co-authored a recent chapter entitled "Acculturation in Filial Practices Among U.S. Chinese Caregivers." *Qualitative Health Research An International, Interdisciplinary Journal.* Janice M. Morse, editor. Volume 18. Number 6, June 2008. Pp. 775–785.

Jack Glazier is Professor in the Department of Anthropology at Oberlin College. His recent publications include *Ethnicity in Michigan: Issues and People*, with Arthur W. Helweg (Michigan State University Press, 2001) and *Dispersing the Ghetto: The Relocation of Jewish Immigrants across America* (Cornell University Press, 1998). He is currently completing a book on African American life and race relations in western Kentucky.

Ronald Kephart is Associate Professor of Anthropology and Linguistics in the Department of Sociology and Anthropology at the University of North Florida, where he teaches courses on linguistics, general and cultural anthropology, and the Caribbean. His interests include the description of Caribbean Creole languages and their use in education; race and ethnicity issues; and human evolution. He is the author of *"Broken English": The Creole Language of Carriacou* (Peter Lang, 2000), and a coauthor of the introductory textbook *Meeting Anthropology Phase to Phase* (Carolina Academic Press, 2000). He has published a number of articles on the use of English Creole in literacy education, and authored nine entries on language for the *Encyclopedia of Anthropology* (Sage, 2006).

Laurie King-Irani, who holds a Ph.D. in Social Anthropology from Indiana University, Bloomington, has worked as a journalist and editor, serving as Editor of *Middle East Report* (Washington, DC) for two years, and Editor of *Al-Raida* ("The Pioneer"), the quarterly journal of the Institute for Women's Studies in the Arab World in Beirut, Lebanon. Her doctoral research comprised an ethnographic study of citizenship among Palestinian citizens of Israel in Nazareth. Currently living in Washington, D.C., she teaches at Georgetown University.

Leonard Lieberman was a former Professor of Anthropology at Central Michigan University. Born in 1925, he received his B.A. and M.A. at the University of California, Berkeley and his Ph.D. at Michigan State University. He was coeditor with Larry T. Reynolds of *Race and Other Misadventures: Essays in Honor of Ashley Montagu* (Rowman, 1996). Among his articles are "The Debate over Race" (Phylon 39:127–41, 1968) and "How 'Caucasoids' Got Such Big Crania and Why They Shrank: From Morton to

Rushton" (*Current Anthropology* 42:69–95, 2001). Professor Lieberman passed away in February 2007.

Scott MacEachern is Professor of Anthropology at Bowdoin College in Brunswick, Maine. His research interests include the prehistory of Central Africa, the study of ethnicity and ethnic group formation processes, and cultural heritage management. He has done archaeological research in Chad, Cameroon, Nigeria, Kenya, Ghana, and Canada. Recent publications include *Komé—Kribi: rescue archaeology along the Chad-Cameroon Oil Pipeline, 1999–2004/ De Komé à Kribi: archéologie preventive le long le Oléoduc Tchad-Cameroun, 1999–2004* (with Philippe Lavachery, Tchago Bouimon and Christophe Mbida. Africa Magna Verlag, Frankfurt), "Where in Africa does Africa start? Identity, genetics and African Studies from the Sahara to Darfur" (*Journal of Social Archaeology* 7(3):393–412), and "Africanist archaeology and ancient IQ: racial science and cultural evolution in the 21st century" (*World Archaeology* 38(1):72–92).

Raymond Scupin is Professor of Anthropology and International Studies at Lindenwood University. He is the director of the Center for International and Global Studies. His research interests include Asia, Islam, religion, race and ethnicity issues, and political economy. He has done ethnographic research in Thailand and among American Indians in California. Recent publications include *Cultural Anthropology: A Global Perspective, Religion and Culture: An Anthropological Focus*, and *Peoples and Cultures of Asia*, all published by Prentice Hall Press.

CREDITS

Word Choice

Me[...]s

Punctuation

Language

Index to English

Seventh Edition

Seventh Edition

Wilma R. Ebbitt

The Pennsylvania State University

David R. Ebbitt

Scott, Foresman and Company Glenview, Illinois
Dallas, Texas   Oakland, New Jersey   Palo Alto, California
Tucker, Georgia   London, England

Copyright © 1982, 1977, 1972, 1968, 1965, 1959, 1950, 1942, 1939
Scott, Foresman and Company.
All Rights Reserved.
Printed in the United States of America.

Library of Congress Cataloging in Publication Data

Ebbitt, Wilma R.
   Index to English.

   Rev. ed. of: Writer's guide and index to English.
6th ed. c1978.
    1. English language—Rhetoric. 2. English language
—Grammar—1950–   I. Ebbitt, David R., 1919–
II. Title.
PE1411.E22   1982   808'.042   81-16632
ISBN 0-673-15541-2   AACR2

Acknowledgment
Max Lerner, "On Being a Possibilist" in *Newsweek,* October 8, 1979, p. 21

   2 3 4 5 6 - VHJ - 86 85 84 83

Preface

Revision of the *Index* has produced a shorter book and, we believe, a more readable one. We deleted out-of-date usage items and those entries on grammatical and linguistics matters that were not immediately applicable to writing. We added entries on new vogue words and phrases and on words commonly confused, and we introduced new examples and illustrative quotations. Our stylistic changes throughout the text were aimed at making the information and advice more readily accessible to readers.

Like its predecessors, this new edition of *Index to English* is intended to help today's college students develop confidence and gain competence in writing. Students are faced with the problems that bedevil every writer, experienced or inexperienced—problems relating to punctuation and mechanics, syntax and choice of words, structure and style. If they are to say what they want to say in a manner that earns the attention and wins the respect of an audience that matters to them, they must keep making decisions as they plan, write, and rewrite their papers. They are more likely to make wise decisions if they have on their desks a resource book they will turn to regularly for information and advice.

So that users of this handbook can find what they want quickly and easily, we have retained from previous editions the alphabetical arrangement of articles and the extensive system of cross references. So that the treatment of usage will be immediately helpful, we have retained the simple division of standard English into formal, informal, and general. The Introduction, addressed to the student, describes the book, explains its rationale, and tells how it can be used—for course work, for individual reference, for browsing.

To help students write so that what they have to say will be understood, respected, even enjoyed by their readers, we provide them with some rules, remind them of certain conventions, and suggest some of the uses that can be made of both highly formal and decidedly informal English. Recognizing, however, that the practical functions of formal and informal are sharply limited for undergraduates, we recommend that they set out to master general American English, the variety of English that all educated Americans read and that all need to be able to write. We also consider it the variety most suitable for classroom instruction. Because general English is the English that students read both for course work and for relaxation, they can accept its rules and conventions as belonging to the real world (rather than the ozone layer) of letters. The great majority of the illustrative passages in the *Index*—whether taken from books, learned journals, popular magazines, and newspapers or from the writing of students—represent this most useful and versatile variety.

On the issue of standards, we endorse neither anarchy nor absolutism. We don't believe that college students, or college graduates, should be encouraged to think that just any rush, or gush, of words on paper necessarily has value. Nor do we believe that students should be misled into thinking that there is only one Good English—least of all the Good English that demands observance of the rules embalmed in prescriptive handbooks and guides to linguistic etiquette.

On certain specific matters, students need—and will find—unequivocal advice. In the articles keyed to the correction chart we have made the *Index* as prescriptive as honesty and realism permit. But we refuse to condemn as "wrong" failure to observe a rule that has never been observed consistently by gifted writers, and we think it a waste of time to keep deploring practices that (though anyone may choose *not* to adopt them) have long been accepted in widely esteemed periodicals. When a locution is considered wrong, or illiterate, or merely distasteful by a sizable number of educated readers, we say so. When the same locution appears regularly in publications edited by men and women of skill, taste, and intelligence, we point out that fact as well. The student can then decide whether or not to use it in a particular rhetorical situation.

The correction entries answer directly and explicitly such questions as "What mark of punctuation do I need here?" "Should this verb be singular or plural?" "What can I do to improve the continuity of this paragraph?" But they also take into account appropriateness to the writer's subject and purpose and audience, and to the writer's self. And in most of the entries relating to usage, style, and rhetorical strategies, appropriateness is the primary criterion students are urged to apply.

In usage entries, after identifying the current status of a locution—standard or nonstandard; if standard, formal, informal, or general—we often include the alternatives: the "*pretty* good time" of informal and the "*fairly* good time" of general; the formal *arising* and the general *getting up*. The student who has read the Introduction knows that the varieties overlap and that on occasion good writers deliberately shift from one variety to another. In a paper that is predominantly in general English, then, the informal *about* may be used instead of *almost* ("I was about done") as a tactic for moving a bit closer to the reader. Here and elsewhere, we neither deny students a choice nor simply list alternatives and invite them to take their pick. What we try to do is guide them toward making intelligent choices, choices that reflect their awareness of the rhetorical context in which they are writing.

Index to English does not limit application of the labels "general," "formal," "informal" to words and phrases. It applies them as well to punctuation, to sentence patterns, to transitions, and to the styles that are the end result of the countless choices that every writer makes, deliberately or intuitively. For writing—certainly good writing—is all of a piece, and even worse than the categorical separation of words into "right" words and "wrong" is the separation of usage from style and of style from rhetoric.

Nor does the *Index* limit discussion to small writing problems that can be safely detached from the context in which they occur. Many of the entries bear on the composing of whole essays—on prewriting and getting started, on the choice of details, on the means of achieving logical sequence, on the organization and development of special types of papers, on how to stop. And many entries, like those on grammar, usage, and the origin of words, introduce readers to broad areas of scholarship. From these, as well as from many of the shorter entries, references open the door to further study.

The seventh edition of *Index to English* is not simply a split-off from *Writer's Guide and Index to English*. The following entries in this book do not appear in the combined text: Analogy, Argument, Balanced sentence, Begging the question, Bibliographical form, ''Big'' words, Cause and effect, Classification and division, Comparison and contrast, Compound sentence, Compound-complex sentence, Complex sentence, Connotation, Cumulative sentence, Deduction, Definition, Denotation, Description, Dictionaries, Etymology, Euphemisms, Examples, Exposition, Fallacies, Figurative language, Forms of discourse, *ibid.,* Induction, Metaphor, Mixed metaphors, Narration, Note form, Parallelism, Periodic sentence, Paraphrase, Précis, Prewriting, Research paper, Rhetorical situation, Simple sentence, Thesis sentence, Topic sentence.

A word about editorial procedure: In order to keep the topic of each entry in sharp focus, irrelevant material has been deleted from illustrative quotations; and when what remains is grammatically a complete sentence, it is presented without opening or closing ellipsis. To protect against the frustration of blind references, or dummy entries—like *''effect, affect.* See *affect, effect''*—every entry title is followed by at least a sentence of information. If that tells the reader what he wants to know, well and good. If not, he is then referred to the main entry.

The detailed review of the sixth edition of the *Index* by Celia M. Millward of Boston University was particularly helpful to us as we prepared this seventh edition.

Wilma R. Ebbitt
David R. Ebbitt

Introduction

What do I want to say on this subject?

What am I trying to accomplish in writing about it?

Who are my readers? What sort of people are they? What are their tastes and interests, their values and prejudices?

How can I make them share what I think and feel about my subject? Should I tell them outright what my convictions are, or should I simply put before them the evidence that has impressed me and invite them to form their own opinions?

Shall I treat the subject seriously, or are my readers the kind who respond best to a humorous approach? Shall I write as if I'm addressing them from a lecture platform, or shall I try for the style and tone of an evening of good talk with old friends?

The big questions in writing are the ones you have to face up to first when you set about planning and drafting a paper, the ones you need to keep steadily in mind as you write and rewrite. Essentially they are questions of rhetoric—how to find, organize, and present your ideas so as to achieve a specific purpose as you address a specific audience on a specific topic.

But though settling on the major strategies that are the concern of rhetoric is certainly the most important job in writing, it's not always the one that gives the most trouble. Many writers find themselves puzzling longest and fretting hardest over questions of grammar, word choice, and mechanics:

Do these two ideas belong in one sentence, or should they be in two? If in one, how should they be connected? Is the relationship between them most accurately expressed by *and* or *because* or *therefore*?

If I begin my paper with *I,* will it sound egotistical? Can I use *you* without making the reader think I'm putting words in his mouth? And if I use *him* as the pronoun after *author,* will I be accused of male chauvinism? Would it be better to use *his or her* or *her/his,* or should I avoid the issue by changing everything into the plural or by rewriting the sentence in the passive voice?

Can I open a paragraph with *and?*

Should I say *among* or *between, different from* or *different than, if I was going* or *if I were going, the girl I knew* or *the girl whom I knew?*

Shall I say *flush* or *blush, request* or *ask, cannot* or *can't?*

What punctuation do I need here—a comma, a semicolon, or a colon? *It's* or *its? There* or *their? Traveled* or *travelled*—one *l* or two?

Questions like these, especially if they are considered separately as isolated items, can cause frustration and irritation. True, some of them have clear-cut answers, to be found in almost any dictionary or handbook. *It's,* the contraction for *it is,* is wrong when used as the genitive (*its,* not *it's,* color). Similarly, *their* and *there* have separate meanings which should not be confused. *Traveled* and *travelled* are both correct; American dictionaries give *traveled* as first choice. The comma has certain functions that it does not share with other marks of punctuation; the semicolon has separate functions; so has the colon.

But in some sentences either the comma or the semicolon is satisfactory, and in other sentences either the semicolon or the colon would do. There are conventions to be learned, habits to be established, alternatives to be noted, so that the right punctuation comes automatically, or so that, when there is a choice, it will be made on sensible grounds—because it fits with other choices that have been made.

What is true of punctuation is often true of diction: there is no one "right" answer to the question of which word to use. *Request* and *ask* are both correct; which word is preferable depends on the style of the paper, which in turn depends upon purpose and audience. Both *can't* and *cannot* appear regularly in print; in a specific context, one would be better—because more appropriate—than the other.

In these cases and a great many more, rhetoric and style and usage intersect; for rhetoric includes style (*how* we say *what* we say), and style is the sum of many individual choices in syntax and usage and even punctuation. It is when all these choices come together to create one prevailing manner of expression that a paper can be said to have a particular style.

If good writing depends upon skill in handling rhetorical problems, why do we spend so much time fussing about small, individual points of usage? Perhaps the situation is less paradoxical than it sounds. Seen in proper perspective—not as a series of *do*s and *don't*s—many questions of usage turn out to be questions of rhetorical strategy.

Initially, questions about usage arise because there are different varieties of English and because these varieties don't fit equally well into every social and rhetorical situation. What is appropriate in casual talk is not always appropriate on paper. What sounds natural to an audience of teenagers baffles an audience of old people. What amuses readers in one context alienates them in another. Knowing what kinds of English there are and recognizing how and why the alternatives differ puts you in a position to suit your style to your subject and to your audience and to the occasion. When you write English that is appropriate to the rhetorical situation, you're making the right use of the language. Good English is not just arbitrarily "good." It's good because it's right for the job.

The Varieties of English

There are many ways of classifying the English we use, both the spoken and the written. *Index to English* is concerned primarily with written varieties of the language in their edited form—that is, with writing that has been gone over with some care. Its purpose is to help you increase your skill and confidence in writing standard English.

Standard and nonstandard English.   Standard English is the dialect approved by the middle class, the dominant class in our society. The other cultural variety of English is nonstandard English, which includes usages from numerous regional and social dialects. In speech the distinction between standard and nonstandard hinges on a fairly small number of pronunciations, words, word forms, and grammatical constructions habitually used by people of noticeably different educational backgrounds and social standings. In writing the distinction is chiefly based on a carryover of those speech habits, with spellings taking the place of pronunciations. He et a apple; Youse guys ain't wrote us in months; She seen them kittens drownded. Nonstandard English, which appears in published writing chiefly in dialog and in other prose that attempts to reproduce nonstandard speech patterns, is inappropriate in the writing that college students are normally expected to do. (For *Index* articles on nonstandard words and forms, see the cross references in the article Nonstandard English.)

In this *Index* we divide standard English into general, formal, and informal. The labels "general," "formal," and "informal" broadly correspond to the social and rhetorical situations in which the varieties commonly occur. Since they shade into each other, with large areas of overlap, the categories should not be rigidly interpreted nor the labels rigidly applied. While some words are clearly more formal than others—*disputatious,* for example—and some more informal—like *hassle*—many can be labeled only in context. A word that stands out as inappropriately formal in one paper might, in a different one, pass as general. To say that a passage is formal, then, doesn't mean that the vocabulary and sentence structure are exclusively formal. It means that there are enough traits usually associated with that variety of the written language to give the passage a formal feel or tone even though much of it—perhaps most of it—may be general in style.

The boundaries between the varieties continue to shift, as they have been doing for hundreds of years. Today's good formal English is close to what would have been considered general English in the essays of a half century ago, while what might be called the High Formal of the 1800s has almost disappeared. General English, meanwhile, has become increasingly relaxed, taking in more and more words, phrases, and constructions from informal. Even short periods of time bring changes in the status of individual usages. A word or phrase that's looked on as informal one year may appear often enough in well-edited publications to be considered general a year later, as the verb *bug* (to plant a secret listening device) did in the early 1970s. A formal word may catch on in general English (as *charisma* and *ambience* did), enjoy a vogue, and then either return to its source or become a permanent part of the general vocabulary. Given such short-term change, the best way to keep in touch with what's going on in the language is not by relying on dictionaries and guides to usage, which are inevitably out of date, but by reading current books and newspapers and magazines and by listening to all the voices that reach your ear, directly and by way of radio and television. As you do, you'll become increasingly aware that the language is a living, changing thing; you'll expand your range of choices; and if you read and listen intelligently and critically, you'll also increase your ability to choose well.

Formal English.   Old-fashioned formal English—what we have referred to as High Formal—survives today chiefly in oratory—in some political speeches, some sermons, some eulogies and other ceremonial addresses, as at graduation time. At its best, old-fashioned formal demonstrates that the English language is a magnificent instrument that can not only disseminate information with clarity and precision but also spark the imagination, stir the emotions, lift up the heart. At its worst, it is empty verbal posturing, or arid, sleep-inducing pedantry, or a stiff parade of big words and stilted phrasings.

Formal written English is found today in some textbooks—particularly those for advanced courses—and in some learned journals. Outside academic circles it appears in books and articles addressed to well-educated audiences willing to make a greater intellectual effort than is called for by a good read. Formal is appropriate for writing on philosophy, religion, aesthetics, literature, theoretical science, and so forth. But though its subject matter may be intellectual, its tone need not be solemn. Wit and formal English have a long history of collaboration.

The vocabulary of formal English smacks of the literary, the scholarly, the philosophical. It includes words seldom used in ordinary conversation *(desultory, ubiquitous, importunate)* and a high proportion of nouns like *hiatus, resurgence, synthesis,* which generalize about experience rather than present it directly. For those familiar with them, the words are often rich in suggestion *(omen, luminous, transcend)* or have some special appeal of sound or rhythm *(immemorial, quintessence)*, while the abstract nouns and technical terms permit the exact and concise statement of ideas.

Though formal English uses short, compact sentences for emphasis, its typical sentence is fairly long, and the elements in it are carefully ordered. Here is an example of current formal English:

The children, we hear, are badly taught and cannot read, spell, or write; employers despair of finding literate clerks and typists; the professions deplore the thickening of jargon which darkens counsel and impedes action; scientists cry out in their journals that their colleagues cannot report their facts intelligibly;

and businessmen declare many bright people unemployable for lack of the ability to say what they mean in any medium.—Wilson Follett, *Modern American Usage*

Such deliberate, studied arrangement of elements in a series ("employers despair . . . ; the professions deplore . . . ; scientists cry out . . ."), as well as word choice that shows careful consideration ("the thickening of jargon which darkens counsel and impedes action"), characterizes formal writing, making its impact quite different from that of the more casual styles.

Throughout this *Index* formal preferences are regularly identified, not because formal English is called for in most college writing but because, in college and out, what you write is likely to have readers who insist that some (seldom all) of the conventions of formal English be followed.

When you set out to write a paper in a formal style, you run some risks. The bad imitations of formal English called "officialese" are prize exhibits of unreadable prose, while literary efforts are plagued by words selected more to impress than to inform and by styles so self-conscious that they divert attention from the content. And there is the problem of sustaining a formal style—not writing just one or two neatly balanced sentences but continuing to show control of phrases and clauses, mastery of the rules of close punctuation, conservative taste in usage, and a vocabulary adequate to the demands of the subject and the style. In short, writing a successful essay in formal English is a challenging undertaking. Meeting the challenge when the occasion arises is one measure of your sophistication as a writer.

Informal English.   Informal written English is the variety of standard English that most of us use naturally in letters to members of our families and to close friends, in diaries and journals, and in other kinds of personal, intimate expression. Some elements of informal are also used—sometimes appropriately, sometimes not—when writers who share no intimacy with the readers they are addressing try to reduce the distance between themselves and their audiences.

Although it actually differs a good deal from the English we use in casual, spontaneous conversation, informal written English suggests speech in several of its characteristics. It swings over a wide range, sometimes mixing vocabulary from formal English with verb forms from nonstandard. It makes free use of slang and draws on the shoptalk that develops in every occupation and the in-group vocabulary that attaches to every sport. The writer takes many syntactic shortcuts, sometimes omitting subjects, usually skipping optional relative pronouns ("I hear he's in town" instead of "I hear that he is in town"), regularly using contractions. Some of the sentences of informal are short and elliptical ("Bet I won more than you" instead of "I'll bet that I won more than you won"); others are unusually long, with asides and afterthoughts keeping the structure loose and rambling. The following passage from an autobiography keeps the feel of informal even when its vocabulary and its sentences are within the range of general English:

> A year went by. With time we got badder and cooler. I stopped counting the scores. We hit small bars. East Side, West Side, all around the paddy town. I took a room on my old block with an old lady for a few bucks a week. She was all right. I gave her a lot of hell, but she loved me like a son—she said. I believed her, so I acted like most sons do in Harlem—I paid her no mind.—Piri Thomas, *Down These Mean Streets*

In published nonfiction the extended use of informal English is mostly limited to some periodicals addressed to special audiences (rock fans, surfers, motorcyclists), to the columns of determinedly personal columnists in more general publications, and to letters from readers. Often, published informal represents the hyped-up ''Hey, there, you guys and gals'' school of artificial intimacy, but it may also echo the flatness of much ordinary speech, as in these excerpts from campus newspapers:

> I can't see why girls should be given a free ride. They're just being used as the window dressing and guys are being played for suckers.

> The hell of a nuclear explosion isn't that awful.

In small doses, however, informal English appears in a great variety of newspapers, magazines, and books, where writers of general English use informal words and phrases to move closer to their readers. The following excerpts, from a range of sources, share the feel of informal and the personal note that is one of its chief characteristics:

> When I was 10, gangs of hoods would stone us Jewish kids.—Audrey Gellis, *Ms*.

> The average Samoan makes Bubba Smith of the Colts look like a shrimp. They start out at about 300 pounds and from there they just get *wider*. They are big huge giants.—Tom Wolfe, *Radical Chic and Mau-Mauing the Flak Catchers*

> Around 3:30 in the afternoon, he'd been fooling with his hair, spraying, setting, combing, until it was perfect.—Lawrence Gonzales, *Playboy*

> Zelda's occasional accusations that Fitzgerald was homosexual have usually been put down to the fact that she was either off her rocker or, mounted on that rocker, she was eager to wound Fitzgerald. . . . In any case, Zelda managed to so bug her husband on the subject that one day in Paris . . . he suddenly let go.—Gore Vidal, *New York Review of Books*

A single outing with one dame when he was 60 later cost him a couple hundred grand in paternity suit fees.—Tony Hiss, *New York Times Book Review*

If you have a chance to write a paper in an informal style, don't make the mistake of assuming that it won't be any more of a problem than writing to your kid sister or your best friend. Your readers probably won't include your sister or your friend, but they will include your instructor and your classmates. And while no one should be applying the standards of formal written English or even the more relaxed ones of general English, all of them have a right to insist on being able to understand what you say. In a letter to family or hometown friends, you can take a lot for granted: they know local places and people and happenings you refer to without needing to have everything spelled out in detail; they know the special connotations of some of the words you use; they know your regional and social dialects. But it's certain that not everyone in your class knows these things, nor will everyone be as willing as family and friends to puzzle over what you're getting at.

So your job will be to put informal English to work for you—to preserve its easy, casual tone while ridding it of its sloppiness and vagueness. That takes some doing.

General English.   Occupying the great middle ground between formal and informal is general written English. It's the variety of standard English that educated people most often read and that they themselves most often write. The words in its vocabulary include *spacious* as well as *roomy, precipitation* as well as *rainfall, nutty* as well as *eccentric, rip off* as well as *steal;* but unless there's a special reason for using the formal or informal words, *roomy, rainfall, eccentric,* and *steal* will be its choices. Writers of general English are likely to use words that are concrete, close to experience, referring to things, people, actions, and events more than to abstractions. The turns of phrase reflect those of speech *(look into, give up, take over);* coordinating conjunctions like *and* and *so* are much more common than conjunctive adverbs like *furthermore* and *consequently.* Typical sentences are moderate in length, with few interrupting phrases or elaborate constructions.

General written English is much less conservative than formal, more controlled than informal. Though it's more likely than informal to follow strict conventions of subject-verb agreement, it doesn't do so as consistently as formal does. It often ignores formal distinctions, as between *can* and *may, raise* and *rear.* Yet it's slower than informal to accept slang. And while the writer of general English is less conservative than the writer of formal English, he may be quite as careful. Indeed, because his style is not so restricted by conventions, he has more choices to make than the formal writer does.

General English is the most versatile and the most serviceable of the three varieties of standard written English this *Index* deals with. It's the variety we use in this book, because general English can reach more people than formal or informal can. For the same reason, it's the variety you will use in most of your writing while you're in college and after you've graduated. But keep alert to the opportunities informal and formal English offer you. Mixing the varieties of English is common practice in current writing. Note the mixture as this writer recalls the *Godfather* movies:

> There was a kind of golden aura about Brando's Don Corleone, even as he was plotting to destroy half the population of Harlem. He was a luminous goon. There, but for a few wrong turns of fate, one felt, goes a real sweetie pie of an Italian poppa. One could imagine being caressed by his caring; he was the prototypical daddy of our nursery dreams—the powerful man of the world who wipes the tears from the eyes of his babies and acts always, and only, to protect his cherished family. He was, literally, the God/Father.—Barbara Grizzuti Harrison, *Off Center*

In many magazine articles, you'll find an informal phrase dropped into a passage whose predominant tone is general or formal—possibly for shock effect, possibly because the writer wants to show a new side of himself, possibly because he wants to mock his own seriousness or a view held by his audience. Or an essay that has been light and casual may move to a thoughtful, measured, formal conclusion.

Sudden shifts in style that have no discernible motive are distracting and suggest that the writer has lost control. Sometimes he has. But a good writer knows what he's doing: by calling attention to *what* he's saying by the *way* he says it, he makes shifts in style perform double duty. Even though most of your writing may be general, then, the more you acquaint yourself with the alternatives that formal and informal English offer, the better you will be able to use them when you want to achieve rhetorical effects that rely on contrasts in style.

Using *Index to English*

Index to English applies the principles of usage described in this Introduction. Because it deals with English as it exists—in publications addressed to moderately educated and to well-educated audiences, as well as in student essays—many of its articles don't offer a simple Right and Wrong, Do and Don't. Often they give both the formal choice and the general choice, sometimes the informal choice as well. When you have a particular job of writing to do, with a particular audience in mind, the relevance of the choices will come clear.

The articles in the *Index* are alphabetically arranged. They fall roughly into six categories with some overlapping:

1. Entries on particular words and constructions, like *among, between; definitely; like, as; not about to; who, whom.* Information about the standing of a locution in current usage is often supported by examples quoted from newspapers, popular magazines, scholarly journals, and books. (The fact that something is printed doesn't mean that it's recommended; bad writing may appear in respectable publications.) Read the article to see where the locution is placed among the varieties of English, and then decide whether it fits your style in the particular rhetorical situation. The titles for entries on words and phrases are the only ones that are not capitalized.

2. Entries to be used in correcting and revising papers. Signaled by abbreviations in longhand, these entries are listed in the correction charts on the inside front and back covers of this book. They offer straightforward advice—practical *do*s and *don't*s. Go to them when your corrected papers have been returned to you, but also get in the habit of consulting them *before* you submit your essays, while you're in the process of revising your first drafts. Checking what you've written against their instructions and illustrations will help you decide whether you've punctuated a sentence correctly, used the expected case of a pronoun, made clear what a modifier relates to.

3. Entries on composition, rhetoric, and style. Many of the entries in the second category also belong in this group. Prewriting, Beginning, Thesis statement, Organization, Outline form, Paragraphs, Coherence, Transition, Emphasis, Unity, and Ending—these and other entries carry you through the stages of writing a paper. Some entries deal with specific topics in rhetoric—Argument, Cause and effect, Classification and division, Comparison and contrast, Definition, Deduction, Fallacies, Induction, Logical thinking. Style is treated more directly in such entries as Abstract language, Adjectives and style, Adverbs and style, Conjunctions and style, Diction, Figures of speech, Infinitives and style, Nominalization, Parallelism and style, Periodic sentence, Phrases and style, and Prepositions and style.

4. Entries offering information and advice on a range of topics that are useful in special writing situations: Bibliographical form, Business letters, Note form, Research papers, Technical writing, and so on.

5. Entries on grammar, offering definitions and discussions of standard grammatical terms and concepts—Collective nouns, for example, and Restrictive and nonrestrictive modifiers, Relative clauses, Subjunctive mood, and the parts of speech.

6. Entries about language and language study, such as British English, Origin of words, Sexist language, and Usage.

Refer to the *Index* when you're faced with a writing assignment (see Prewriting), as you write, as you revise what you've written, and when your corrected essay is returned to you for further revision. Besides following up the cross references that most entries contain, look up any term you come upon that is new or unclear to you—*modal auxiliaries,* for example, or *deep structure*. Most such terms are explained in entries of their own.

Index to English is intended to be more than a reference work for college writers. It's meant to be browsed in and annotated. By updating the slang and vogue words and by noting changes in usage, fresh figures of speech, allusions, and turns of phrase, you can keep the *Index* alive at the same time that you keep yourself in touch with your language.

Seventh Edition

a, an

Use *a* before all words beginning with a consonant sound: a business, a *D*, a European trip, a usage. Use *an* before all words beginning with a vowel sound, including words that begin with an *h* that's not pronounced: an apple, an *F*, an uncle, an honor, an hour.

In words beginning with *h* that are not accented on the first syllable, like *histo' rian, hyster' ical*, the *h* used to be silent, so *an* preceded such words. Today, though Americans often pronounce the *h*, some still say and write "an historian," "an hysterical witness," "an habitual set of choices" (Josephine Miles, *CCC*). Even if you hurdle the *h* when you speak, *a* is the better choice in writing: The Jews had a historic task.

When you use a series of singular nouns, you may want to repeat *a* or *an* before each one in order to give emphasis to each—"a hound, a bay horse, and a turtle-dove" (Henry David Thoreau, *Walden*)—or you may run them together with *a* or *an* before only the first noun: Soon she had bought a skirt, shirt, and scarf.

See **awhile, a while; half; kind, sort 2.**

Abbreviations

Write in full the word or words inappropriately abbreviated. Or use the correct form of the abbreviation marked.

1. Appropriateness. Abbreviations are used to save space in manuals, reference books, business and legal documents, scholarly footnotes, and some other kinds of writing. You can also use them in informal writing— notes for your own use, letters to friends. In general and formal writing, use only those abbreviations that are fully established in standard usage (see **2**) or that regularly occur in discussions of a particular subject.

2. Standard abbreviations. Always use the abbreviations *Dr., Mr., Mrs.* with names. (A comparable term, *Ms.*, is technically not an abbreviation but a combination of *Miss* and *Mrs.*) A number of abbreviations, such as *St.* (see **saint**), *B.C.* and *A.D., a.m.* and *p.m., Jr.* for Junior, and initial letters for government agencies like *CIA* and *SEC*, are standard. In formal writing, titles like *Reverend, Professor, President*, and *Senator* are not abbreviated, nor are naval and military ranks. In general writing they may be abbreviated when initials or given names are used: Professor Hylander *or* Prof. G. W. Hylander (*but not* Prof. Hylander).

3. Period with abbreviations.   Where standard practice requires a pe-riod after an abbreviation, omitting it (*p* instead of *p.* for *page* in a footnote) is a careless slip. Use only one period at the end of a sentence: The abbre-viation for both *saint* and *street* is *St.*

Increasingly, periods are omitted from abbreviations that are used in place of the words they stand for *(FBI, AFL-CIO, CBS, GNP, ID, IQ, hp, kwh,* 780 *rpm)*. In addressing letters, don't use periods with the two-letter abbreviations for states adopted by the Postal Service *(PA, TX)*.

Abbreviations that are pronounced as words *(WASP, UNICEF)* are called acronyms. Dozens entered the language during World War II *(Nazi, Gestapo, radar, sonar, Wac, Wave)*, and thousands have been created since *(NATO, SALT, laser)*. The acronym *OPEC*, from Organization of Petroleum Exporting Countries, gained worldwide prominence in the 1970s.

For abbreviations of dates, see **Months.** For abbreviations in endnotes or footnotes, see **Note form.** Compare **Contractions, Numbers, Origin of words 3c.**

ability to

The idiom is *ability* plus a *to*-infinitive (ability *to do*): He has the ability to design (*not* of designing) beautiful buildings. You can often express the idea better with an adjective or a verb: He is able to (*or* He can) design beautiful buildings; He designs beautiful buildings.

able to

Avoid using a passive infinitive (like *to be done* or *to be ended*) after *able:* This was not able to be done because of lack of time. Instead write: This could not be done because of lack of time. Or: They were not able to do this because of lack of time (*or* because they didn't have time).

about

About has a variety of uses. Check the following for trouble spots:

1. about–around.   In describing physical position, *about* and *around* are nearly interchangeable, though *around* is the more common (about the tree—around the tree). In the sense of "nearly" or "approximately," *about* is more common (about 70°), but both are standard American usage. In telling time, *around* (around two o'clock) is considered more informal.

2. about–almost.   In the sense of "almost" (about finished), *about* is standard but mainly informal.

3.   at about.   In formal English *at about* is avoided on the grounds that something must be either *at* or *about*. But *about* in *at about* is being used as an adverb, and the preposition-adverb pattern is well established: at approximately noon; in about ten minutes.

4.   about to.   *About to* is a convenient idiom for "on the point of": She was about to make a third try. The negative *not about to* (an emphatic "not going to") is more informal: I'm not about to sign up for a class at that hour.

above

Using *above* as an adverb in such phrases as "the evidence cited above" and using it as an adjective (the above prices) and as a noun (the above is confirmed) are fully established as standard but are not accepted by everyone. Some careful writers avoid using *above* as an adjective; others use it: "for a comment on the above use of the word 'claims' . . ." (Theodore Bernstein, *Watch Your Language*). In many business, legal, and other technical contexts, all three uses of *above*—as adverb, adjective, and noun—would be entirely acceptable. In general and formal writing they would bother some readers.

Absolute phrases

An absolute phrase modifies all the rest of the sentence it appears in, not just a word or group of words: *The battle lost,* the army surrendered.

Absolute phrases are economical, offering a compact way of singling out details of a scene or relating parts to a whole: He came downstairs looking much the worse for wear, *eyes bloodshot, shirt rumpled, tie askew.* But their somewhat formal quality makes them seem out of place in casual writing: *The long day finally at an end,* the kids went to bed. And absolute phrases that contain auxiliaries (*being, having, having been*) may be heavy and awkward: *The description of the scene having been completed,* the stage is set for the crucial action. A dependent clause is often smoother and sometimes more precise: After the scene has been described. . . .

Some absolute phrases have been used so often that they've become fixed formulas, or idioms: all things considered, this being the case, God willing.

See **Dangling modifiers, Idiom.**

Absolutes, comparison of

Logically, absolutes like *perfect* and *final* can't be more or most, less or least. But see **Comparison of adjectives and adverbs 4.**

abst Abstract language

Make this word or passage more concrete or more specific.

Abstract words refer to emotions, qualities, concepts, relationships: *love, courage, square root, symmetry.* They contrast with concrete words like *kiss, lion, computer, hoop,* which refer to things we can see or touch or otherwise perceive with our senses.

Abstract terms are essential in communicating ideas, and abstract language can be just as precise as concrete language. But if you rely too much on abstract vocabulary, your papers may seem to lose contact with human experience. To keep your rhetorical feet on the ground, follow these suggestions:

1. Provide concrete examples. If you're writing about courage, describe a brave act, or contrast a brave act with a cowardly one. The shift from the concept to the example will make it natural to use concrete terms. Or follow an abstract statement with a concrete expression of the same idea:

> The survey's assumption that the bodily symptoms in question are indicators of psychological distress leads to the conclusion that the working class tends to somatize its emotional troubles, whereas the middle class experiences them more directly. In other words, clammy hands and upset stomach are apt to be the poor man's substitute for angst.—Charles J. Rolo, *Atlantic*

2. Replace general terms with specific ones. *General* and *abstract* are sometimes used interchangeably, and so are *specific* and *concrete*. But the match-ups are not exact. Though we can easily classify a word as concrete or abstract, we can say that a term is specific or general only if we compare it with a related term. In the series *Volvo, car, vehicle,* all the words are concrete, but judged in relation to each other, *car* is more general than *Volvo* and more specific than *vehicle*. In the series *emotion, love, lust,* all the words are abstract, but *love* is more specific than *emotion* and more general than *lust*. So a concrete term is not always specific, and an abstract term is not always general.

Prose that strikes the reader as abstract often contains a high proportion of general terms, both abstract and concrete. Instead of using the general, abstract term *immorality,* specify the kind of immoral act you have in mind *(adultery, bribery, robbery)*. Instead of the general, concrete term *lawbreakers,* use *speeders, vandals, muggers, burglars, rapists*—naming the kind of lawbreakers you're writing about.

3. Choose your abstract terms with care. What often causes trouble isn't the use of abstract terms but the particular terms chosen. If every sixth or seventh word you write is a noun ending in *-ence, -ity, -ment,* or *-tion (permanence, responsibility, management, utilization)*, your style will be abstract and heavy. Many abstract nouns are related to verbs: *intention (in-*

tend), refusal (refuse), response (respond). Given a choice between representing an action in an abstract noun or in a full verb, you'll generally write a livelier, clearer sentence if you choose the verb:

> The achievement of clarity of thought has a definite dependence on the correctness of the formulation of the problem.

> **Better:** To think clearly, you need to formulate your problem correctly.

Though neither sentence contains any concrete words, the second is a lot more direct and easier to read than the first. Its style, we say, is more concrete.

See **Description, Details, Nominalization.**

accept, except

Accept means "receive" or "say yes to." *Except*, as a verb, means "leave out," "exclude." See **except, accept.**

Accusative case

The object of a verb or a preposition is said to be in the accusative (or objective) case. Six distinctive pronoun forms are often called accusative (or objective) forms: *me, her, him, us, them, whom. (You* is both accusative and nominative.) See **Case 2; Gerunds 2; Infinitives and style 2; it's me; Objects; who, whom.**

acquiesce

If you have reason to use the formal verb *acquiesce,* be sure to follow it with the right preposition. You can agree *to* or *with* a decision, but you acquiesce *in* a decision.

Acronyms

Abbreviations pronounced as words are called acronyms *(OPEC, SALT).* See **Abbreviations 3.**

Active voice

All verbs except those consisting of a form of the verb *be* and a past participle (is cooked) are in the active voice. See **Voice.** Compare **Passive voice.**

actually

Like *basically, definitely,* and *really, actually* is seldom necessary in writing, even when it's meant literally: "My nomination for the 'most neglected book' is actually a trilogy" (Carlos Baker, *American Scholar*). (All four words are overused in conversation as fillers or as weak attempts to provide emphasis.) In revising your papers, delete every *actually, basically, definitely,* and *really* that isn't serving a useful purpose, particularly if it appears at the beginning of a sentence: [Actually] we lost the game.

ad

Ad, the clipped form of *advertisement,* is appropriate in all but formal writing. It's not an abbreviation, so it shouldn't be followed by a period.

A.D.

A.D. stands for *anno Domini,* "in the year of the Lord," and logically, therefore, should precede a year (A.D. 107) and should not label a century. But there's a strong tendency to treat *A.D.* as if it meant "after Christ" (as *B.C.* means "before Christ"), and phrases like "in the second century A.D." have appeared regularly in the works of respected writers for many years. Some conservative stylists condemn this usage. Some more liberal stylists (and Latinists) hold that *A.D.* and *B.C.* should be treated as nontranslated adverbials, applying to both years and centuries. Consider your audience.

adapt, adopt

To *adapt* is to adjust so as to fit or conform: Immigrants often have difficulty adapting their ways to American customs and values. To *adopt* is to accept, to choose, to make your own: The motion was finally adopted; The engineers adopted the third alternative; They adopted three children in two years.

Adjectivals

Phrases, clauses, and words that are not adjectives may function like adjectives. That is, they may restrict or limit a subject, object, or indirect object. When they do, they can be called *adjectivals.*

1. **Phrases and clauses used in adjectival function:**
   The man *with the hat on* is Harry.
   I like the one *on the end* best.
   Everyone *who agrees* should raise his right hand.
   That was the summer *we went to Bermuda.*
   He asked the first man *he met.*

2. Other parts of speech in adjectival function.   Participles, which are derived from verbs, function as adjectivals: a *coming* attraction, a *deserved* penalty. And one of the most characteristic traits of English is the use of nouns in the adjectival function: a *glass* jar, the *Roosevelt* administration, *adjective* modifiers, *high-school mathematics* test. But see **Adjectives and style 2.**

Adjectives

An adjective modifies—that is, restricts or limits—a subject, object, or indirect object. *Good* performs this function in the sentence "A good dancer isn't just any dancer but a dancer who's better than others."

1. Forms.   Many adjectives don't have a form that sets them off from other parts of speech *(high, civil)*. Other adjectives consist of a noun or verb plus a suffix such as *-able (bearable)* or *-ible (reversible)*, *-al (critical)*, *-ed (chilled)*, *-ful (playful)*, *-ish (childish)*, *-less (harmless)*, *-ous (joyous)*, or *-y (dreamy)*.

Many adjectives are compared by adding *-er* or *-est* to the positive, or base, form or by putting *more* or *most* before it: *warm, warmer* or *more warm, warmest* or *most warm.* See **Comparison of adjectives and adverbs.**

Proper adjectives are capitalized, like the proper nouns they're derived from: *French* restaurants, *Italian* wines, *Elizabethan* drama, *Victorian* furniture. When used frequently enough in a merely descriptive sense, a proper adjective becomes an ordinary adjective, written without a capital: *diesel* fuel, *india* ink.

2. Functions.   The main function of adjectives is to modify a subject or object, but when preceded by *a, an,* or *the,* some adjectives serve as subjects or objects; the *just,* the *rich,* a new *high.* When so used, words that are ordinarily adjectives function as nouns and can be called *nominals.* See **Adjectivals, Nominals.**

adj Adjectives and style

Reconsider your choice of the adjective marked.

The adjectives you use should make your statements more precise or more forceful.

1. Adjectives that fail.   Some adjectives are redundant. In "briny ocean," *briny* adds nothing because all salt water is briny. (Adjectivals can be similarly redundant, as in "wandering nomads.") Very general adjectives like *good, bad, beautiful, wonderful, terrible, terrific, fantastic, incredible, awful,* and so on communicate attitudes rather than specify characteristics. The reader who finds someone described as ''good'' wants to know the particular kind of goodness. Is the person agreeable? kind? virtuous? talented? generous? Many adjectives that are specific enough have been teamed so often with particular nouns (*beady* eyes, *fond* farewell) that the combinations have become trite. In writing, think twice before using any combination of adjective and noun that comes automatically to mind. See **Triteness.**

2.   Adjectives that clutter.   Sometimes in reading over what you've written, you'll find that you've piled up adjectives. Deleting most of the adjectives and adjectivals from the following passage would improve it considerably.

> My blurred, aching, stinging eyes focused not on the shiny, slippery, polished, golden oak floors that reflected the frilly-white sparkle of the neat, spandy-clean room of my long-gone childhood but on the ugly lumps of dirty, worn-out jeans, decrepit, sagging jogging shorts, and gray, smelly, mud-caked sweat socks that littered the dingy, dusty, ragged old rug.

The stylistic effect is particularly bad when the words in adjectival position are nouns. Piling nouns in front of nouns produces prose that's heavy and hard to understand. ''The chairman selection committee progress report date has been changed'' needs to be translated into ''The date for the progress report of the committee on selecting a chairman has been changed.'' A string of prepositional phrases isn't very graceful, but it's better than the rear-end collisions of a string of nouns.

3.   Adjectives that work.   Used sensibly and sensitively, adjectives reinforce meaning and improve style. If your material is technical and your audience is familiar with the technical vocabulary, you need only be careful to use the right term—*biaxial,* perhaps, or *extravascular,* or *granular.* But if you're writing on a technical subject for readers who lack the technical vocabulary, or if you're dealing with a subject that has no special vocabulary of its own, then you have to make choices. Choose your adjectives with the needs of your subject matter and your audience, as well as your purpose, in mind. Chosen well, they'll seem to fit, to belong, as in this account:

> A few miles from Southampton I saw the real sea at last, head on, a sudden end to the land, a great sweep of curved nothing rolling out to the invisible horizon and revealing more distance than I'd ever seen before. It was green, and heaved gently like the skin of a frog, and carried drowsy little ships like flies. Compared with the land, it appeared to be a huge hypnotic blank, putting everything to sleep that touched it.—Laurie Lee, *As I Walked Out One Midsummer Morning*

According to E. B. White, ''The adjective hasn't been built that can pull a weak or inaccurate verb out of a tight place.'' True enough. And Carl

Sandburg is said to have warned a writer, "Think twice before you use an adjective." This is probably sound advice for anyone who automatically attaches an adjective to every noun and so produces what has been called "adjective-benumbed prose." But adjectives can help a writer describe his subject as he sees it, and if he chooses the right ones, they'll make the reader see it too.

See **Description.** Compare **Adverbs and style.**

Adverbials

Phrases and clauses that function like adverbs can be classed as *adverbials:* He came *in the morning; After the exam* he quit; *When it was time to go,* she didn't know what to do. Words like *home* in "He went home" and *days* in "She works days" are nouns in form but can be defined as adverbials in function.

Adverbs

As a grammatical category, "adverbs" is a ragbag containing a variety of words that modify verbs, adjectives, other adverbs, and whole clauses and sentences.

1. Forms. Most adverbs are formed by adding *-ly* to adjectives or participles: *badly, deservedly, laughingly, surely.* Some have no special adverbial sign: *now, then, here, there.* A number of adverbs have the same form as adjectives, including these:

bad	doubtless	hard	much	slow
better	early	high	near	smooth
bright	even	late	new	straight
cheap	fair	loose	right	tight
close	fast	loud	rough	well
deep	first	low	sharp	wrong

Most of these unchanged adverbs are matched by forms in *-ly,* with which they may or may not be interchangeable. See **Adverbs and style.**

Most adverbs are compared, either by adding *-er* and *-est* to the positive, or base, form or by preceding it with *more* and *most.* See **Comparison of adjectives and adverbs.**

2. Functions. Adverbs are typically used in two functions:

a. To modify single words, phrases, and clauses: He left early (*early* modifies *left*); They were practically in the street (*practically* modifies *in the street*); Fortunately no one was home (*Fortunately* modifies *no one was home*). In direct and indirect questions, *when, where, why,* and *how* perform adverbial functions: *When* did he leave? Do you know *why* he left?

b. To connect separate sentences or the independent clauses of a compound sentence (see **Conjunctive adverbs**):

> We found the dormitories empty, the classrooms silent and deserted. *Nevertheless,* we continued the search.

> They agreed to call the matter closed; *however,* they were by no means convinced.

See **Adverbials.**

adv Adverbs and style

Correct the form of the adverb marked, change its position, or reconsider your choice.

1. Use the standard form of the adverb.   You can say "He sang loud" or "He sang loudly"; both are standard. The short form is often preferred in general and informal English, the *-ly* form in formal English. (Cookbook compilers, who ordinarily use general English, are nevertheless addicted to chopping finely and slicing thinly.) The choice is a matter of style. But in some situations standard English doesn't permit a choice:

a. Omitting the *-ly* ending. When adverbs are formed by adding *-ly* to the adjective *(considerably, regularly, suddenly),* the form without *-ly* is non-standard: It hurt *considerable;* He did it *regular.* Use the *-ly* ending unless your dictionary also treats the form without *-ly* as standard.

b. Adding an unnecessary *-ly.* Even when an adverb has two forms, they're not always interchangeable. Though you can say "Drive slow" or "Drive slowly," you can't replace *close* with *closely* in "That shot hit too close."

After a linking verb, use a predicate adjective, not an adverb: The breeze smelled sweet *(not* sweetly). And don't use an adverb-adjective combination when the adjective alone can do the job: Like many of that breed, her dogs were high-strung *(not* highly strung). Compare **bad, badly.**

Don't add *-ly* to a word that already ends in *-ly (kindlily* for *kindly).* To make an adverbial from an adjective ending in *-ly (leisurely, orderly, worldly),* put the adjective in a prepositional phrase ending with a noun like *way* or *manner:* He approached us *in a friendly way;* She handled the problem *in a scholarly manner.* Words in *-ly* that indicate time may function either as adjectives (an hourly schedule) or as adverbs (the bus departed hourly).

2. Placing adverbs for clarity and style.   Many adverbs can occupy different positions in a sentence:

> Tom had *never* liked pizza. Tom *never* had liked pizza.

> *Patiently* she explained. She *patiently* explained. She explained *patiently.*

When you have a choice, first of all place the adverb so that it makes your meaning clear: not "She answered the questions that the students asked patiently" but "She patiently answered the questions that the students asked"—if it was the answering and not the questioning that was patient. Other considerations are rhythm and emphasis. Some writers hesitate to insert an adverb between the parts of a verb: instead of "have easily seen," they write "have seen easily." But "have easily seen" is smoother and more idiomatic. See **only, Split infinitive**.

3. Making adverbs count. The use of adverbs should at least be precise and if possible should contribute to the impact of the sentence. Adverbs hurt rather than help when they're used unnecessarily and redundantly (Truck horns blast *threateningly;* automobiles career *wildly;* buses lumber along *heavily*), when they qualify excessively (the *seemingly* difficult problem of controlling inflation), and when they set up a flutter of *-lys* (as in this sentence). Sometimes writers use an adverb to shore up an imprecise adjective or verb when more compact expression would do the job better:

> Scholarships should be kept for *those who are academically industrious* (the studious).

> When no one was looking, I took the goggles and *swiftly made my way* (hurried) out of the store.

adverse, averse

Be careful not to confuse these two words. *Adverse* is an adjective meaning "unfavorable" or "hostile" (adverse conditions). *Averse,* also an adjective, means "opposed" (We would not be averse to such legislation). Both have a formal tone.

advise

Besides meaning "to give advice," *to advise* is used to mean "to inform, to give information." In this sense the verb is commonly used for informing that's rather formal: Reporters were advised by an administration spokesman that. . . . In all other situations simple *tell* is more appropriate: Peter tells (*not* advises) us that he won't be back next term.

affect, effect

Affect is used most often as a transitive verb meaning "influence" (This will affect the lives of thousands) or, rather formally, "put on" (He affected a stern manner). The noun *affect* is a technical term in psychology. *Effect* is most common as a noun meaning "result": The effects will be felt by thousands. But it's also a formal verb meaning "bring about": *The change was effected hurriedly.*

aggravate

In general and informal usage *aggravate* ordinarily means "annoy" or "irritate": *The higher he turned the volume, the more aggravated I got.* Formal rules still limit *aggravate* to the meaning "make worse," as to aggravate a wound or a situation: *Friction between faculty and administration was aggravated by cuts in the budget.* The same division occurs in the use of the noun *aggravation.*

 # Agreement

Make the verb or pronoun marked agree in form with the word to which it is related—its subject if it is a verb, its antecedent if it is a pronoun.

When used together, certain parts of speech agree, or correspond in form in such a way as to express relationships of number, person, or gender. This pair of sentences illustrates several instances of agreement:

> *This* habit, which in *itself is* harmless, *is* likely to lead to *others* that *are* decidedly harmful. *(This, itself,* and *is* agree with the singular *habit. Are* agrees with the plural *others.)*

> *These* habits, which in *themselves are* harmless, *are* likely to lead to *another* that *is* decidedly harmful. *(These, themselves, are,* and *are* agree with the plural *habits. Is* agrees with the singular *another.)*

In English, agreement is largely a matter of linguistic etiquette. If you used *is* after *habits* in the sentence above, your readers would have no trouble figuring out your meaning, but they'd frown at your carelessness. Understanding the causes of mistakes in agreement will alert you to what to look for when you proofread your papers and help you avoid lapses in grammatical good manners.

1. Subject and verb agree in number (Those *birds were* seen; That *bird was* seen). There are four main causes for problems in subject-verb agreement: (a) phrases or clauses between subject and verb, (b) collective nouns as subjects, (c) compound subjects, and (d) dialect differences in verb forms.

a. Most mistakes in agreement occur when a writer makes the verb agree with a word that's not the subject and that differs from the subject in number. Often the word is the noun at the end of a clause or phrase that comes between the true subject and the verb: An *analysis* of the extent to which audio-visual aids are used in schools *make* me conclude that books are no longer the chief tools of education. The singular subject *analysis* calls for the corresponding verb form *makes,* but the plural noun *schools* immediately before the verb, and perhaps also the plural *aids are,* confused the writer. The same trouble may occur in a very short sentence: "But only one in 100 patients die" *(Newsweek).* In such situations take the time to make sure what the subject of your verb is.

b.   The first question with collective nouns as subjects is whether to treat them as singular or plural. If you're thinking of what the noun names as a unit, make the verb singular: The last *couple* on the floor *was* Janet and Tom. If you're thinking instead of the individuals that make up what the noun names, use a plural verb: The *couple* next door *were* disagreeing noisily, as usual.

Once you've made this decision, be sure you use the verb and any related pronoun consistently. If the team *was* very much on edge, the reason was that *its,* not *their,* big game was only a week away. Sometimes the pronoun will determine the verb form: When we found ourselves near where the old couple *were* living, we dropped in to see *them.* "We dropped in to see *it*" would be impossible, even after *was living.* So the sentence demands the *were-them* combination. See **Collective nouns.**

c.   Problems with compound subjects sometimes arise because the writer is uncertain whether to treat the subjects as plural or singular. Some compound subjects name a unit that calls for a singular verb: Bacon and eggs *is* my favorite breakfast. Other compound subjects represent a unit to one writer, separate things to another:

Her loyalty and patriotism *was* unparalleled in the history of her people.

Her loyalty and [her] patriotism *were* unparalleled in the history of her people.

Before deciding to use a singular verb with a compound subject, be sure your readers will not only recognize your intention but accept the logic behind it. Only subjects that are closely allied *(loyalty* and *patriotism)* can reasonably be thought of as a unit. This principle rules out "Her beauty and dishonesty *was* apparent even to me," which readers would see as an error in agreement.

When both elements of a compound subject connected by the correlative conjunctions *either . . . or* or *neither . . . nor* are plural, the verb is naturally plural; and when both elements are singular, the verb is usually singular. When one subject is singular and the other plural, the traditional rule is that the verb should agree with the nearer subject:

Neither the ideas nor the style *is* satisfactory.

Neither the style nor the ideas *are* satisfactory.

Although usage varies, this is a sensible rule to follow. See **Compound subject, Correlative conjunctions.**

d. Some American dialects, notably in Black English, lack an ending in the third-person singular, so that *do* and *see,* for example, are treated like standard English *can:* he can, he do, he see). Writers for whom this is the natural grammatical pattern have a double problem when they use a variety of standard English: they must add the ending to most present-tense, third-person-singular verbs *(starts, stops, sees)* and not add it elsewhere, as in plural verbs (they *stop*) and past-tense forms (I, you, she, we, they *stopped*). See **Principal parts of verbs 2.**

2. A third-person pronoun agrees with its antecedent in number and gender. If the antecedent—the noun it refers to—is plural, the pronoun is *they, their(s),* or *them,* depending on its use in the sentence. If the antecedent is singular, the choice of pronoun is more complicated because gender enters in. Generally, if the noun refers to a male, we use *he, his,* or *him;* if to a female, *she, hers,* or *her.* Otherwise, including situations where the sex is unknown or irrelevant, we use *it(s):* The baby dropped *its* rattle; The dog was looking for *its* master.

Problems sometimes arise when the antecedent is a noun referring to a member of a group that includes both sexes (each member of the class) or when it's one of the indefinite pronouns, like *one, anyone, everyone, no one, anybody, everybody,* or *nobody.* The question of which possessive pronoun to use with an indefinite may be solved by the context: No one in the Girl Scout troop looked forward to *her* test (though *their* might be used here if everyone was taking the same test). More often both sexes are referred to (No one at the dance . . .). The problem then is whether to use *he, he or she,* or *they.* Some grammarians assert that *they,* like *you,* has both singular and plural functions and that in indefinite reference it is usually a singular pronoun. But conservatives reject *they* as a singular. Though the use of a form of *they* to refer to words like *everyone* (Everyone in the class turned in their paper) is now firmly established in informal English and is increasingly accepted in general English, it is strongly resisted in formal English, where a form of *he* (his paper) would be expected. Using a subject that's clearly plural avoids any problem: All the students handed in their papers. See **Sexist language, they.**

3. The demonstrative adjectives (or determiners) *this, that, these, those* usually agree in number with the nouns they modify: *That coat* is expensive; *These shoes* cost more than my old pair did. See **kind, sort.**

agree to, agree with

One person agrees *to* a plan and agrees *with* another person. One thing agrees *with* another. Other idioms: I agree *in* principle; We agreed *on* a plan of attack; He agreed *to* fly or *on* flying or *that he would fly.*

ain't

Though in speech millions of Americans use *ain't* regularly as a contraction for *am not, is not, are not, has not,* and *have not,* it never appears in formal writing and rarely in expository prose except when a speaker is being quoted. In general writing, use of *ain't* is almost always a deliberate attempt to suggest informality or humor or down-to-earth common sense:

> It will never reach the audience Welles might have and should have reached, because there just ain't no way.—Pauline Kael, *New Republic*

> Those tiresome people with their tiresome quotes from Socrates about the fact that youth is going to the dogs are just trying to reassure themselves that it's all just a little bit more of the same. It ain't.—John M. Culkin, *New York Times*

See **Divided usage.**

all, al-

Note the spelling of these words and phrases:

1. *all ready* (adjective phrase): At last they were all ready to begin.

2. *already* (adverb of time): They had already begun.

3. *all together* (adjective phrase): We found them all together in an old trunk.

4. *altogether* (adverb, equivalent to *wholly*): That's another matter altogether.

5. *all right* (adjective phrase): The seats seemed all right to me.

Alright now appears frequently enough to be accepted as a variant spelling in some dictionaries. Others specifically label it a misspelling, and many authorities consider it nonstandard.

Alliteration

Alliteration is repetition of the same sound, usually at the beginning of several words in a series. Besides possibly appealing to the reader's or listener's ear, alliteration binds the phrase, or sometimes a series of phrases, into a unit: "carried by wind and water and soil and seed" (John F. Kennedy). Alliteration is appropriate in some formal prose but distracting in ordinary exposition unless it helps reinforce meaning. Check your first drafts to break up any string of words that begin with the same sound for no purpose. Compare **Assonance.**

all of

In many constructions with *all of, of* can be omitted: All [of] the milk was spilled; They passed all [of] the candidates; You can't fool all [of] the people all [of] the time. Usage is divided. With personal pronouns and the relatives *who* and *which, all* may follow the pronoun (we all), or *all of* may precede it (all of us). *All of whom* and *all of which,* as subjects of relative clauses (four attempts, all of which failed), are more formal than *who all* and *which all* (four attempts, which all failed).

all that

"It wasn't all that bad" and similar uses of *all that* are informal and imprecise. See **not all that . . . , not too. . . .**

all the farther

In some parts of the country *all the farther* is common in informal and general speech (This is all the farther I'm going), but standard written English uses an *as . . . as* construction: This is as far as I'm going.

Allusion

Loosely, an allusion is a brief reference to something that's not a part of the subject under discussion. Strictly, an allusion differs from a reference in that it doesn't name the event, person, or place but mentions it indirectly. "This latter-day Paul Revere calls us to arms against home-grown revolutionaries" is a reference to Paul Revere. "His signal is always a single lantern in the church steeple" is an allusion to Revere that leaves it to the reader to make the connection through knowledge of Longfellow's poem ("One if by land, and two if by sea"). Like other aspects of style, allusions should fit the rhetorical situation.

allusion, illusion

Allusion, discussed in the preceding entry, should not be confused with *illusion,* a misapprehension or a misleading appearance (Smoking a pipe can create an illusion of wisdom).

almost

Most for *almost* is informal. See **most, almost.**

also

Also as an adverb ordinarily stands within a sentence, not at its beginning: "They also serve who only stand and wait" (John Milton). But inversion may shift an *also* to initial position: Also defeated was the party's candidate for mayor. As a loose conjuction meaning "and," *also* is a weak sentence opener:

> He subscribed to eight magazines. Also he belonged to the Book-of-the-Month Club.

In many cases the information introduced with initial *also* should be included in the preceding sentence: He subscribed to eight magazines and belonged to the Book-of-the-Month Club. See **Conjunctive adverbs, Inversion, plus.**

alternative

Alternative comes from the Latin *alter,* "the second of two." For that reason some formal writers restrict its meaning to "one of two possibilities," but the word is regularly used to mean one of several possibilities (Another alternative would be to . . .). Dictionaries record this broader meaning.

although, though

Although and *though* introduce adverbial clauses that qualify the main statement:

> Although (*or* Though) the rain kept up for almost three weeks, we managed to have a good time.

> We managed to have a good time, though (*or* although) the rain kept up for almost three weeks.

In these examples there is no distinction in meaning. The choice between the two words may be based on sentence rhythm. *Although* is slightly more formal.

Often one of two clauses connected by *but* can be turned into an *(al)though* clause for a slight change of emphasis or for sentence variety:

> We had rehearsed time and again, but we all missed our cues the first night.

> Although (*or* Though) we had rehearsed time after time, we all missed our cues the first night.

Though is also used as a less formal *however:* He did it, though.

See **but.**

alumnus, alumna

A male graduate is an *alumnus,* a female graduate an *alumna.* Two or more male graduates are *alumni,* two or more female graduates *alumnae.* The graduates of coeducational schools—males and females together—have traditionally been called *alumni,* but *graduates* itself is a satisfactory, and sexless, alternative. Also sexless is *alums,* the plural of the clipped word *alum.* See **Sexist language.**

a.m. and p.m.

These abbreviations for *ante meridiem,* "before noon," and *post meridiem,* "after noon," are most useful in tables and lists of times. They're also used in general writing for specific hours, usually with figures: from 2 to 4 p.m. (*not* I went there in the p.m.). Though *m.* is the abbreviation for noon (12 m.), *12 noon* is more common. Midnight is *12 p.m.* The twenty-four hour system used in Europe and by the U.S. military makes *a.m.* and *p.m.* redundant: 9 a.m. = 0900, 9 p.m. = 2100. See **Hours.**

amb Ambiguity

Make your meaning unmistakable.

An ambiguous word or phrase or sentence is one that can be interpreted in two or more ways. Though the context usually shows which of the possible meanings was intended, the reader is confused at least momentarily. The most common sources of confusion are these:

1.   Inexact reference of pronouns, especially in indirect discourse: He told his father he had been talking too much. Who is the second *he,* the father or the son? Rewrite as: He admitted to his father that he had been talking too much. Or as: He criticized his father for talking too much. Or recast as direct speech. See **Indirect discourse, Reference of pronouns 1.**

2.   Modifiers that can be misinterpreted.
a.   Modifiers should not be so placed that they can seem to refer to either of two words or constructions: The governor dismissed those officeholders who had opposed him ruthlessly. Does *ruthlessly* refer to the dismissal or the opposition? Rewrite as: The governor ruthlessly dismissed those officeholders who had opposed him. Or as: The governor dismissed those officeholders who had ruthlessly opposed him. See **Squinting modifier.**
b.   Modifiers should be clearly identified as restrictive or nonrestrictive. Setting off a restrictive modifier with commas or failing to set off a nonrestrictive modifier changes your meaning: Out-of-state students [,] who were delayed by the blizzard [,] will not be penalized for late registration. With

commas, the sentence means that no out-of-state students were penalized; without commas, it means that only those delayed by the storm were excused.

c. Modifiers shouldn't mislead even momentarily. In revising a first draft, be on the lookout for puzzlers like the headline "Police Repair Man Killed by Car." See **Hyphen 5.**

3. Incomplete idioms, especially in comparisons: "I liked Alice as well as Will" might mean "I liked Alice as well as Will did," "I liked Alice as well as I liked Will," or "I liked both Alice and Will."

4. Confusing coordination, as in: The movie deals with student protests against war and sexual experimentation. Repeating *with* after *and* would limit the target of the protests.

5. Ambiguous words. When a writer uses the wrong word—say *incredible* for *incredulous*—the result is confusion but usually not ambiguity. Ambiguity occurs when a writer uses a word that has the meaning he intends but another meaning as well—for example, the dialect word *cookie* for *doughnut*, or the word *rhetoric*, which has unfavorable connotations for many but favorable connotations for some. Instances of divided usage are particularly troublesome. Readers who find *disinterested* where they expect *uninterested* are likely to be not so much confused as outraged. See **censor, censure; Connotation; convince, persuade; disinterested, uninterested; Divided usage; imply, infer; incredible, incredulous; rhetoric; Wrong word.**

See also **Comma 6.**

American

Because there's no simple adjective that corresponds to the United States of America (as *Italian,* for example, corresponds to Italy), *American* is ordinarily used. It's obviously inexact, in that all the other inhabitants of the Americas have as much right to the term as we do. Many Latin Americans refer to themselves as Americans and to us as North Americans. But the use of *American* as the adjective ("the American economy" for "the economy of the United States") and as the noun for a citizen of the United States is standard.

Americanism

An Americanism is a word or construction in English that originated in the United States *(hydrant, zipper, realtor)* or was first borrowed here, as from an African language *(goober, juke, okra)* or an Indian language *(hominy, caucus, mugwump)* or from Spanish *(canyon, rodeo, lariat). Americanism* also refers to a sense of a word that was added in the United States *(campus, carpetbagger, creek).* And it may be extended to include words that have continued to be used in the United States after becoming obsolete in England *(loan* as a verb, *gotten)* or any item of usage characteristic of the United States and not of other areas of the English-speaking world. The label *American* or *chiefly U.S.* in dictionaries identifies Americanisms.

among, between

Between is used with two, *among* with more than two. But see **between, among.**

amount, number

Number is used of countable things: a number of mistakes, a number of apples. *Amount* is preferred with mass nouns: a small amount of snow, a certain amount of humor. Distinguishing between the two words often makes writing clearer. See **Mass nouns.** Compare **fewer, less.**

Ampersand

An ampersand is the & sign. Because its primary use is to save space, the ampersand belongs only where abbreviations are appropriate. Otherwise, write out *and.*

Analogy

Analogies may be either figurative or literal. A figurative analogy suggests a resemblance between things or situations that on the surface are totally unlike—a mathematical equation and a musical composition, for example, or a football team and an epidemic. There are no literal resemblances between an undefeated team and the Black Death, but both can be said to mow down what stands in their paths. The team figuratively slaughters its opponents as the plague literally killed its victims in the fourteenth century.

Literal analogies uncover relationships between two members of the same class of things or situations. Often they reveal surprising similarities between widely separated events or individuals. The attitude of young people toward marijuana laws in the 1960s was analogized to the attitude of their grandparents toward liquor laws in the 1920s.

Whether it's compressed into a phrase (the Jane Fonda of church reform) or elaborated through a long essay, an apt analogy throws new light on the subject. Presenting something unfamiliar in terms of something familiar (the earth's strata in terms of the layers of an onion) is a common

method of exposition. Here a writer relies on analogy to introduce his interpretation of changes in international relations:

> There has been a radical transformation of power. In traditional conflicts, states
> were like boiled eggs. War—the minute of truth—would reveal whether they
> were hard or soft. Today interdependence breaks all the national eggs into a
> vast omelet. Power is more difficult to measure than ever before.—Stanley
> Hoffman, *New York Times*

Analogy becomes the basis for argument when a writer tries to persuade
his audience that because two situations are alike in some respects (proposals for gun registration in the United States and gun registration in Nazi
Germany), they're alike in still another (if enacted into law, the proposals
will result in government seizure of all civilian-owned guns). Though analogies can seldom carry the full burden of proof, they can be powerful per-
suaders. If the likenesses they cite have real bearing on the point at issue
and the differences aren't fundamental, analogies have logical force as well.

Whether used to explain or to persuade, an analogy can stir the imagination and stimulate ideas. For both writer and reader, a good analogy offers
a fresh way of looking at things.

See **Comparison and contrast, Figurative language.**

Analysis

The term *analysis* is applied to a wide range of intellectual undertakings—
attempts to grasp the nature of a thing or a concept, to separate a whole into
its parts, to discover the similarities and differences between two or more
things, to investigate causes, to attribute effects. The aim of analysis is to
increase understanding of the subject. A writer may also use analysis as a
guide to action. That is, he may analyze an assignment in order to decide
how to arrange his material or what details to include or what arguments to
use. See **Cause and effect, Classification and division, Comparison and
contrast, Definition, Logical thinking, Rhetorical situation.**

and

1. Appropriate uses. *And,* the conjunction we use most frequently,
should join two or more elements of equal grammatical rank:

> *Adjectives:* a *pink* and *white* dress; a *blue, green,* and *white* flag
> *Adverbs:* He drove *very fast* and *rather carelessly.*
> *Nouns: trees* and *flowers; trees, shrubs,* and *flowers*
> *Verbs:* I *picked up* the book and *opened* it.
> *Phrases: in one ear* and *out the other*

Dependent clauses: While the children were swimming and [*while*] *the old folks were resting,* we took a walk.

Independent clauses: The first generation makes the money, and *the second spends it.*

2.   Inappropriate uses.   In careless writing, elements that are not grammatically equivalent are sometimes connected by an unnecessary *and:*

Main verbs and participles: The men *sat* on the edge of the lake with their backs to the road, [and] apparently *watching* the ducks.

Independent and dependent clauses: A contract has been let to install new copper work on the post office [and] *which will give it the facelifting it needs.*

Besides being used where no connective is needed, *and* sometimes appears where some other connective would show the logical relationship more clearly: "Shah was a founding member of the Club of Rome and [but?] while he retains his membership, he did not attend last fall's gathering in Berlin" (Elizabeth Hall, *Psychology Today*). See **Coordination 2, Shifted constructions.**

3.   To begin sentences.   In current writing of all varieties, *and* can be used to begin a sentence, signaling a link with the preceding sentence or paragraph. Used sparingly, it will also contribute to the movement and emphasis. Overused, it will damage both, as well as bore the reader.

4.   Omitted or repeated.   *And* can be omitted in a series (Cousins, uncles, [and] aunts—all the relatives were there), but if it's omitted again and again, the result is a telegraphic style that's inappropriate in general writing. *And* may also be repeated between the items in a series, as an effective way of giving emphasis to each: "I do not mean to imply that the South is simple and homogeneous and monolithic" (Robert Penn Warren, *Southern Review*).

and etc.

Etc. is the abbreviation for Latin *et cetera,* in which *et* means "and." So *and* before *etc.* is redundant. See **etc.**

and/or

And/or is used primarily in legal and business writing. Its use in general writing is objected to by some readers because *and/or* looks odd and because *and* or *or* alone is often all that's needed. But it's sometimes useful when there are three alternatives—*both* the items mentioned or *either* one of them: inflation and/or depression; "that fear and awe we all feel in the presence of greatness and/or dingbats" (Hughes Rudd, *TV Guide*).

angle

Angle means "point of view" or "aspect" (from an economic angle) in standard general English, but it carries a strong suggestion of jargon. In the sense of "scheme" or "plan" (What's his angle?), *angle* is informal. See **Jargon.**

ante-, anti-

Don't confuse *ante-* "before" (antedate) with *anti-* "against" (antipollution).

Antecedent

An antecedent is the word, clause, or sentence that a pronoun refers to. It usually stands before the word that refers to it, but not always: We did not hear their call again, and when we found the Thompsons, they were almost exhausted. (*The Thompsons* is the antecedent of the possessive pronoun *their* and of *they*.) For relations between antecedents and pronouns, see **Agreement 2, Reference of pronouns.**

Anticipatory subject

In sentences like "It was Ann who found the food stamps" and "There are more important things than graduating," *it* and *there* are anticipatory subjects. See **it; there is, there are.**

any

1. Uses. *Any* is used primarily as an adjective (Any job will do) but also as a pronoun (Any will do). The pronoun *any* takes either a singular verb (Any of them *has* a chance of winning first prize) or a plural verb (Any of them *have* a chance of ending up in the top ten), depending on the sense of the statement.

In comparisons of things in the same class, use *any other:* He shaped the university more than any other president in its history. *Any* alone is always used when different classes are compared: I like a movie better than any book.

2. Compounds with *any*. *Anybody, anyhow, anything,* and *anywhere* are always written as single words. *Any rate* is always two words: at any rate. *Anyone* is written as one word when the stress is on the *any* (Anyone would know that) and as two when the stress is on the *one* (I'd like any one of them). *Anyway* is one word when the *any* is stressed (I couldn't go anyway) and two when the stress is about equal (Any way I try, it comes out wrong). If the word *whatever* can be substituted for the *any* (Whatever way I try, it comes out wrong), *any way* should be written as two words.

3.   Pronouns referring to *anybody, anyone*.   *Anybody* and *anyone* are singular in form and take singular verbs: anybody (*or* anyone) feels bad at times. They are referred to by *he, his, him* (Anybody knows what he deserves) or, since they often apply to a person of either sex, by *he or she, his or her, him or her,* or a form of *they* with the same meaning: "It is not usually possible to achieve intimacy with anybody in the back seat of a car; you have to live with them in every sense of the phrase" (Edgar Z. Friedenberg, *New York Review of Books*). Formal usage insists on a singular pronoun. See **Agreement 2, he or she, Sexist language, they.** Compare **every.**

4.   Other forms.   *Anyways* is regional for the generally used *anyway,* and *anywheres* is nonstandard for *anywhere*. Though many object to it, *any more* now frequently appears in print as one word: "They want to protect all those traditional events whether or not they mean something anymore" (Herbert Warren Wind, *New Yorker*). *Any more* (or *anymore*) in a strictly affirmative context meaning "now" (Any more they do as they please) is a regional idiom.

   Anyplace (now usually written as one word) has become a general synonym for "anywhere": "You will hear bitter attacks on the United States for subverting Chile, but not a word about Soviet subversion in Afghanistan or anyplace else" (Jane Rosen, *New York Times Magazine*).

apos Apostrophe

Insert an apostrophe where it belongs in the word marked; or take out an apostrophe that is incorrectly used.

Typical mistakes in the use of the apostrophe are *mans* for *man's, mens'* for *men's, it's* for the possessive *its,* and *their's* for *theirs.* Review the following uses:

1.   In possessives.   The most common use of the apostrophe is in spelling the possessive case of nouns and indefinite pronouns (*anyone, nobody, someone* . . .): Dorothy's first picture, the companies' original charters, everybody's business is nobody's business, the boys' dogs. An apostrophe should be used in singular possessives (or genitives) of time and value even though they carry no idea of possession: a day's hike, this month's quota, a dollar's worth. In formal writing an apostrophe is also preferred in plural possessives of this kind (two week's work), but usage is divided (teachers college). For special examples of possessive form, see **Possessive case.**

2.   In contractions.   The apostrophe shows the omission of one or more letters in contractions: *can't, I'm, I'll, it's (it is).*

3. In plurals.   An apostrophe was formerly expected in plurals of figures and letters (three *4*'s, two *e*'s) and plurals of words being discussed as words (the first of several *that*'s), but current usage is divided. Decades in figures are often written without an apostrophe: the mid-1980s. Using an apostrophe in writing the plural of a family name is an error: the Smiths, *not* the Smith's.

4. In representing speech.   An apostrophe may be used to indicate that the speaker omits certain sounds represented in the conventional spelling: " 'Lily,' he pleaded, 'I swear t'God, you'll get it back on pay-day. You c'n meet me up at the barn if you wanna' " (I. J. Kapstein, *Something of a Hero*). Because too many apostrophes are distracting for the reader, it's better to indicate pronunciations of this sort occasionally than to try to represent all of them.

Apostrophes should not be used in the possessive forms of the personal pronouns *(his, hers, its, ours, theirs, your)* or introduced into words that don't have them *(till,* not *'till* or *'til).*

Apposition, appositives

Beside a noun or noun-equivalent in a sentence, you can put another nominal expression called an appositive: My aunts, *Mary and Agnes,* moved to Boulder in 1969. The noun and its appositive refer to the same person(s) or thing(s). Typically, the appositive is set off by commas, but sometimes no punctuation is needed: He caught so many fish that we called him Jim [ ] *the fisherman*. See **Nominals.**

Don't use appositives unnecessarily. For example, if you use the President's name, there's no need to identify him as the President, and if you refer to "the President," there's no need to tell the reader what his name is.

Arabic numerals

Arabic numerals are the ones we normally use: 1, 2, 3, etc. See **Numbers 3.**

Argument

Aside from its everyday meaning of "disagreement" or "dispute," *argument* is used in three ways. It refers to a speech or essay designed to convince an audience (a newspaper editorial, for example). Or it refers to the line of thought, the string of key propositions, that runs through a piece of writing—the argument of a book or poem. Or it specifies a reason for believing what might otherwise seem doubtful; an argument in this sense might be a single sentence. Thus in presenting his argument (first sense) to Congress, a legislator may use as his argument (second sense) the thesis that tax shelters should be eliminated, and he may offer as one of his arguments (third sense) the proposition that tax shelters favor the rich at the expense of the poor.

Argument in the first sense may make appeals that are primarily intellectual or primarily emotional. Either kind of appeal can be used well or badly, for good purposes or bad ones.

Sometimes argument is distinguished from persuasion on the basis of purpose: argument is designed to change the mind of an audience; persuasion is designed to make an audience act. But when argument is classed with description, narration, and exposition as one of the four forms of discourse, both purposes are normally included.

See **Analogy, Deduction, Fallacy, Forms of discourse, Induction, Logical thinking, Rhetorical situation, Syllogism.**

arise, rise, get up

In referring to standing up or getting out of bed, *arise* is formal and poetic, *rise* is slightly less formal, and *get up* is the general idiom.

around

Around, like *about,* can be used to mean "approximately." See **about 1; round, around.**

Articles

Traditionally *a* and *an* are known as indefinite articles, *the* as the definite article. See **a, an; Nouns 3c.**

as

Among the meanings of *as* are "while" (As we walked along, he told us stories) and "because" (His speed is amazing, as he weighs 260 pounds). *While* is preferable to *as* if the emphasis is on the time of the action (While we were walking along, he told us stories). And though *as* is used to mean "because" (or "since") in all varieties of English, many readers dislike the usage. It can easily be ambiguous. In the sentence "As we have continued responding to erratic changes in Asia, our position has inevitably become more complex," *as* can mean either "because" or "while." See **while.**

For the growing tendency to use *as* where *like* would be expected, see **like, as.**

as . . . as

1. *As I* **or** *as me.*   In a sentence like "He admires her as much as I/me," meaning determines whether the nominative *I* or the accusative *me* is used. If you mean "as much as I admire her," use *I.* If you mean "as much as he admires me," use *me.*

In a sentence like "They sent for somebody as big as I/me," the choice doesn't affect the meaning. Both nominative *I* and accusative *me* are good English.

For a third type of sentence—"He is as big as I/me"—in which there's no preceding noun or pronoun in the accusative position, usage has always been divided. The nominative *I* is preferred in formal contexts and is insisted upon by many word watchers. See **Accusative case, Nominative case.**

2. Omitted *as.*   Writers frequently omit the second *as* in a comparison of equality (as large as) when it's joined by *or* or *if not* to a comparison of inequality (larger than): It was as large or larger than last year's crowd. But many readers and writers insist that only the complete form is correct: It was as large as, or larger than, last year's crowd. Whenever possible, move the second comparison to the end of the sentence: It was as large as last year's crowd, if not larger.

3. *As . . . as* **and** *so . . . as.*   *As . . . as* is much more common than *so . . . as* in simple comparisons of degree (as small as that, as late as you like). Both *as* and *so* are used to begin the phrases "— far as I know" and "— far as that's concerned." Many handbooks have urged that *as . . . as* be used only in affirmative statements (She's as clever as any of them) and *so . . . as* in negative statements (She's not so clever as she thinks), but the distinction has never become established in practice.

as far as

In using the phrase *as* (or *so*) *far as . . . is concerned* (As far as tuition is concerned, I don't think we're getting any bargain) many speakers and some writers drop the verb: As far as tuition, I don't think we're getting any bargain. The reduced phrase makes no more sense than "As far as I" for "As far as I'm concerned." Often *as for* can be substituted for the longer phrase: As for tuition, I don't think we're getting any bargain.

as if, as though

In formal English the subjunctive mood of the verb is commonly used after *as if* and *as though:* He acted as if (*or* as though) he *were* losing his temper.

In general English the indicative mood is usual: He acted as if (*or* as though) he *was* losing his temper. See **Subjunctive mood.**

as, like

As is the conjunction (He voted as he was expected to). *Like* is the preposition (He voted like the rest). See **like, as.**

Assonance

Assonance is the repetition of vowel sounds in words having different consonant sounds, as in *brave-vain* and *lone-show*. Assonance is characteristic of verse and also occurs in prose, especially in poetic styles: "that ideal country of green, deep lanes and high green banks" (Osbert Sitwell). Like unintentional alliteration, unintentional assonance can be distracting.

as though

As though is commonly followed by a verb in the subjunctive mood in formal English but not in general English. See **as if, as though.**

as to

As to is often a clumsy substitute for a single preposition, usually *of* or *about:* Practice is the best teacher as to (*better:* in, for, of) the use of organ stops. In some locutions it should simply be omitted: [As to] whether college is worthwhile is a question we all must try to answer. But for introducing subjects, *as to* is better than more cumbersome expressions like *as regards, as concerns, in respect to:* As to the economic value of going to college, the effect on earning power is clearly established.

as well as

When an *as well as* phrase between subject and verb gives a strong impression of adding to the subject, some writers treat it as part of the subject and let it influence the number of the verb: The singer as well as four members of the outstandingly successful band were arrested in Moose Jaw. In such cases the phrase is seldom set off by commas. But according to traditional rules the phrase is parenthetical, should be enclosed in commas, and has no bearing on the verb: "This volume, as well as others, consists of a collection of basic articles" (Robert R. Wilson, *ISIS*).

at

Forget the old vogue phrase "where it's at." People and things are where they *are:* When she called home from the airport, her father wanted to know where she was (*not* where she was at).

at about

At about can be reduced to either *at* or *about.* But see **about 3.**

athletics

When the collective noun *athletics* refers to sports and games, it usually takes a plural verb and pronoun: Our athletics *include* football, basketball, and baseball. When athletics refers to a skill or activity, it usually takes a singular verb and pronoun: Athletics *is* recommended because *it* contributes to good health.

author

An author writes books. But does a writer author books? *Author* as a verb is widely used (by publishers, among others) but also widely disapproved. It may be most defensible when it's used to refer to publication by a group (the report was authored by a presidential commission) or to the participation of a celebrity in producing an autobiography "as told to" a professional writer.

Auxiliary verbs

A verb used with other verbs to form tenses or, in the case of *be,* to change the active voice to the passive is called an auxiliary verb or helping verb. The most common auxiliaries, *be* and *have,* are used in forming the progressive and perfect tenses and the passive voice: I *am* going; He *has* gone; They *were* shot. *Do* is used in questions (Do they care?) and contradictions (They do not care) and for emphasis (Yes, they *do* care). The modal auxiliaries—*can, may, shall, will, must, ought to, could, should, would,* and *might*—are used to refer to future time (*shall* and *will*) and to suggest obligation, necessity, or possibility: You *should* reply; She *must* leave; He *could* break the record. See **Modal auxiliaries, Tenses of verbs,** and entries on individual verbs.

awful

In formal English *awful* means "awesome." In informal English it's a convenient word of disapproval meaning "ugly," "shocking," "ridiculous," "very poor" (an awful movie). In informal and sometimes in general writing, the word is also used to intensify meaning: ". . . delusions that are being chosen by an awful lot [that is, a very large number] of people in preference to standard, orthodox explanations'' (Elizabeth Janeway, *Atlantic*). This use of either *awful* or *awfully* (an awfully long wait) is, of course, deplored by word worriers.

awhile, a while

Awhile is an adverb: They talked awhile. *While* is a noun: She was gone for a long while. Strictly, prepositional phrases with the noun *while* should be in at least three words (in a while), but *awhile* after a preposition is increasingly common.

B

bad, badly

Bad is ordinarily used as the adjective (a bad apple) and *badly* as the adverb (They sing badly). But though the grammatical rule calls for a predicate adjective after a linking verb, the linking verb *feel* is frequently followed by *badly* instead of *bad:* I feel badly about it. Both *feel bad* and *feel badly* are generally accepted as standard. Formal stylists prefer *bad*. Usage is divided.

    Badly meaning ''very much'' (He wanted it badly) is standard. As a group adjective, *badly off* is general: ''But we are not Satan. Fallen though we are, we are not that badly off'' (John Morris, *American Scholar*).

    Bad as an adverb (I played bad all through the game) is informal.

    See **Hypercorrectness.**

Bad grammar

Bad grammar is applied as an expression of disapproval to all sorts of locutions, from ''I ain't got none'' to supposed confusions in the use of *shall* and *will*. As criticism the label is too vague to be helpful. See **grammatical, ungrammatical.**

Balanced sentence

When parallelism in a sentence produces structures that are noticeably alike in length and movement, the sentence is said to be balanced: ''I shall do less whenever I shall believe what I am doing hurts the cause, and I shall do more whenever I shall believe doing more will help the cause'' (Abraham Lincoln, ''Open Letter to Horace Greeley'').

basically

Basically is one of many words we use in conversation without meaning much of anything: Basically it was a good course. Don't use it in writing unless you're making a contrast, either expressed or implied: [On the surface they seem carefree and irresponsible, but] basically they're very concerned about getting established in jobs with a future.

be

Be is the most common linking verb, joining a subject and a predicate noun (Jerome was the secretary) or predicate adjective (She is energetic). When it joins a subject and a pronoun, the pronoun is in the nominative case in formal written English (It was *he*), in the accusative in informal (It was *him*). "It's I" is formal for the general "It's me." See **it's me.**

When the infinitive *be* has a subject and complement, both are in the accusative case: I wanted *him* to be *me*. When the infinitive has no subject, formal usage has a nominative as the complement (I wanted to be *he*). General usage more often has an accusative (I wanted to be *him*).

Be has more forms and a greater variety of forms than any other verb in English:

> *Present:* I am, you are, he is; we, you, they are
> *Past:* I was, you were, he was; we, you, they were
> *Infinitive:* be
> *Present participle:* being
> *Past participle:* been

See **ain't, Subjunctive mood.**

because

Because introduces an adverbial clause that gives the reason for the statement in the main clause: *Because we were getting hungry,* we began to look for a restaurant. *Since* and *as* can be used to introduce such clauses, but they're less definite.

Because also is used in general-to-informal styles where a more formal style would use *for*—that is, where what is introduced is not the cause of an effect but the premise for a conclusion:

> *Formal:* Komarov clearly had some control over his ship, for he was able to orient it well enough to accomplish re-entry.—*Newsweek*

> *Less formal:* Komarov clearly had some control over his ship, because he was able to orient it. . . .

See **as, for, reason is because.** For **because of,** see **due to.**

Begging the question

Begging the question is the logical fallacy of assuming something to be true that, in fact, needs to be proved. The debater who bases his argument for reform on the assertion ''This unfair method of voting must be changed'' begs the question of the method's fairness. In a broad sense we all beg questions all the time—''Use enough evidence to prove your point'' begs the question of how much is enough—but as a deliberate tactic in argument, begging the question is notably unfair. See **Fallacies.**

beg Beginning

Revise the opening of your paper so that it will lead more directly and smoothly into your subject or so that it will do more to stir your reader's interest.

The best advice for beginning a short paper is ''Get on with it.'' An elaborate windup is silly when the pitch is no more than a straight throw in a backyard game of catch. And an opening that indulges in philosophizing (Since the days of Plato's Academy, violence and learning have been alien entities) or announces a grand strategy (In the paragraphs that follow, I shall attempt, first by analyzing and then by synthesizing, . . .) is just as silly in a two-page paper on a campus controversy.

Ordinarily, the first step is to let your reader know what you're writing about—not by telling him what you're going to discuss but by discussing it: ''We think of the drug addict as unwilling or unable to work, but he works harder to get his dope than most of us do to get our daily bread'' (*Psychology Today*). This doesn't rule out a personal approach. There may be good reason for you to tell why you've chosen your topic or how you're qualified to discuss it. It does rule out beginnings that fail to begin.

Besides getting the paper under way, the opening paragraph or two should make a reader want to continue reading. But straining for humor or excitement or cuteness or sentiment is no way to arouse interest. As imitations of the techniques used by professional journalists, such attempts are likely to fail. The humor doesn't amuse, the excitement doesn't stir, and so on. Instead of trying out gimmicks, move into the subject and treat it with the interest *you* feel. If it doesn't interest you, your chances of making it interest your readers are slim. If it does interest you, and if you write about it as honestly and directly as you know how, your readers will keep on reading.

For long papers—from five to ten pages, say—somewhat more elaborate beginnings are sometimes necessary. But getting on with the discussion remains fundamental. If you provide the historical background of the problem you're dealing with, make sure that this material contributes to the solution you propose. If you announce what you're going to do in your paper, be sure you do it.

beside, besides

Beside is used chiefly as a preposition meaning "by the side of," as in "beside the road," "beside her." It's used figuratively in a few rather formal idioms like "beside the point," "beside himself with rage." *Besides* is used as a preposition meaning "in addition to" (Besides ourselves, about a dozen students came to the meeting), and as an adverb and a conjunctive adverb (He didn't think he ought to get into the quarrel; besides, he had come to enjoy himself) meaning "in addition."

between, among

Among implies more than two objects: They distributed the provisions among the survivors. *Between* is used of two: They divided the prize between Kincaid and Thomas. But attempts to limit *between* to use only with two items have failed. When the relationship is between individual items— participants in discussions or negotiations, for example—*between* is the word to use no matter how many items there are: "This is so . . . of some part of the debate between Einstein, Bohr, Wolfgang Pauli, and Max Born" (George Steiner, *Atlantic*).

When treating a group as a collective unit, use *among:* Divide the books among the poor.

between you and me

Though *you and I* as the object of a preposition or a verb is frequently heard and has a long history in written English, those who know better are likely to regard anyone who says or writes "between you and I" as only half-educated. *Between you and me* is always correct. See **Hypercorrectness.**

bi-

Some time words beginning with *bi-* cause confusion. *Bimonthly* and *bi-weekly,* for example, may mean "every two . . . " or "twice a . . . ." *Biennial* means "every two years," but *biannual* means "twice a year." When the context doesn't make the meaning clear, it's safest to use phrases like "every two months," "twice a week," "twice a year."

Bible, bible

When it refers to the Christian Scriptures, the word is capitalized but not italicized: You'll find all that in the Bible. In the sense of an authoritative book, the word is not capitalized: *Gray's Manual* is the botanist's bible. The adjective *biblical* is seldom capitalized.

Bibliographical form

The details of bibliographical form in a research paper may differ from author to author, from publication to publication, and especially from discipline to discipline. In some sciences, for example, a list of the references cited replaces the full bibliography of the humanities, only the first word of a book title is capitalized, the title of a journal article is omitted entirely, and the name of a journal is abbreviated. Whatever the style your instructor recommends, remember that the first rule for bibliographical form, as for note form, is consistency. Follow one style of documentation throughout.

The entries in a bibliography are listed alphabetically, according to the last name of each author. When no author is given, the first important word of the title—whether of a book, of a chapter or selection in a book, or of an article in a magazine, newspaper, or encyclopedia—serves as the key word for alphabetizing *(Manual* for *A Manual of Style)*. Each entry begins at the left margin. Subsequent lines are indented five spaces.

The entries that follow conform closely to recommendations in the *MLA Handbook*. Examine each entry carefully to see what elements are included, what order they appear in, and how they are punctuated. Entries may be single-spaced, if your instructor prefers.

A book by a single author and a second book by the same author:

Hartshorn, Truman A.   Interpreting the City: An Urban Geography.

New York: Wiley, 1980.

----------.   Metropolis in Georgia: Atlanta's Rise as a Major

Transaction Center.   Cambridge, Mass.: Ballinger, 1976.

(Instead of repeating the author's name, use ten dashes followed by a period.)

A book by more than one author:

Dunning, Eric, and Kenneth Sheard.   Barbarians, Gentlemen, and Players.

New York: New York Univ. Press, 1979.

(Do not reverse the names of co-authors following the first author's name: Bryant, Barbara, William Jensen, and Ann Wagner. If there are more than three authors, substitute "et al." or "and others" for all but the first: Gorenstein, Shirley, et al.)

A book with a corporate author:

Organization for Economic Cooperation and Development.   **Adverse**

Weather, Reduced Visibility, and Road Safety.   Paris: OECD, 1976.

A work in more than one volume:

Lyons, John.   Semantics.   2 vols.   Cambridge: Cambridge Univ. Press, 1977.

(If the books in a multivolume work are published over a period of years, give the full span: 1909–49.)

An edition other than the first:

Engel, James F., Martin R. Warshaw, and Thomas C. Kinnear.

Promotional Strategy. 4th ed. Homewood, Ill.: Irwin, 1979.

An edited work:

Emerson, Ralph Waldo. Emerson's Literary Criticism. Ed. Eric W.

Carlson. Lincoln: Univ. of Nebraska Press, 1979.

A compilation:

Steinman, Michael, ed. Energy and Environmental Issues. Lexington,

Mass.: Lexington Books, 1979.

A selection, chapter, or other part of a compilation:

Dirac, P. A. M. "Developments of Einstein's Theory of Gravitation."

In On the Path of Albert Einstein. Ed. Arnold Perlmutter and

Linda F. Scott. New York: Plenum, 1979, pp. 1-13.

A translation:

Kant, Immanuel. Lectures on Ethics. Trans. Louis Infield.

Gloucester, Mass.: P. Smith, 1978.

A book that is part of a series:

Reiss, Edmund. William Dunbar. Twayne English Authors Series,

No. 257. Boston: Twayne, 1979.

A reprinted book:

Godwin, William. Life of Geoffrey Chaucer. 2nd ed. 1804; rpt.

New York: AMS, 1974.

A signed article in a newspaper:

Butterfield, Fox. "Religions Flower as China Eases Rules." New

York Times, 27 May 1980, Sec. A, p. 12, cols. 1-6.

An unsigned article in a weekly newsmagazine:

"Robots Join the Labor Force." Business Week, 9 June 1980,

pp. 62-65, 68, 73.

(All the pages on which the article appears are listed in the bibliography, not just those pages that were actually used.)

An article in a monthly magazine:

Daniel, Glyn. "Megalithic Monuments." Scientific American, July

1980, pp. 64-67, 70-76.

An article in a journal paged continuously through the annual volume:

Boone, Sherle L., and Alberto Montare. "Aggression and Family Size."

   Journal of Psychology, 103 (1979), 67-70.

(In some journals pages are numbered continuously from issue to issue throughout the year. For such journals, cite the volume number and the year of publication of the annual volume but not the number of the issue or the month of publication. Note that when the volume number is given—without "Vol."—page numbers are not preceded by "pp.")

An article in a journal with separate pagination for each issue:

Fry, Fred L. "The End of Affirmative Action." Business Horizons,

   23, No. 1 (1980), 34-40.

(For a journal that does *not* number pages continuously through the issues of each annual volume, the issue number must be given in addition to the volume number and the year.)

A signed encyclopedia article:

C[onley], C. L[ockard]. "Blood, Human." Encyclopaedia Britannica:

   Macropaedia. 1978 ed.

A book review:

Sochen, June. Rev. of Children of Fantasy: The First Rebels of

   Greenwich Village, by Robert E. Humphrey. American Historical

   Review, 84 (1979), 576-77.

An unpublished dissertation:

Teague, Frances Nicol. "Ben Jonson's Stagecraft in His Four Major

   Comedies." Diss. Univ. of Texas 1975.

A government document:

U.S. Dept. of Labor. Work Attitudes and Work Experiences: The

   Impact of Attitudes on Behavior. Washington, D.C.: GPO, 1979.

A pamphlet:

Sex Equality in Educational Materials. American Assn. of School

   Administrators Executive Handbook Series, IV. Arlington, Va.:

   AASA, n.d.

A lecture:

Ruland, Richard.   "American Literature in Europe Since World War

  II."   American Literature Section, MLA Convention, San

  Francisco.   28 Dec. 1979.

An interview:

Del Gaudio, Jean.   Writer/Editor, Technical Communications Services,

  Owens-Corning Fiberglas Corp.   Personal interview.   18 July 1980.

A TV or radio program:

Washington Week in Review.   Mod. Paul Duke.   PBS, 25 July 1980.

See **Note form, Research papers.**

"Big" words

A word is "big" if it's too formal or heavy for the subject. See **Diction 2.**

black

Since the 1960s the term *Negro* has been replaced in most writing by *black,* usually not capitalized. *Afro-American* is also used.

bloc, block

Leave off the *k* only when you're writing about a common-interest group— of senators, for example—whose members can be expected to vote the same way on legislation affecting the interest they share: The amendment was defeated by the farm bloc.

born, borne

In most senses of *bear,* the past participle is spelled with a final *-e,* but the spelling *born* is used in the sense "brought into being" in the passive voice. Thus "She has borne three children," but "Three children were born to her." *Born* is also used in the sense "determined by birth," as in "He was born to be hanged."

both

Both is used to emphasize two-ness: The twins were both there; Both Harry and his sister went. Though neither of these *boths* is necessary, each gives a legitimate emphasis. In "They both dressed alike," on the other hand, *both* adds nothing but awkwardness. "The both of them," a fairly common spoken idiom, should be avoided in writing.

both . . . and

When used as a pair (both the tire and the tube), the coordinating conjunctions *both* and *and* are called correlative conjunctions. See **Correlative conjunctions.**

Brackets

Brackets have specific uses in scholarly writing. Their main function is to enclose alterations and additions within quoted material:

> The story answers precisely . . . to that told in the third paragraph of Curll's *Key:* "But when he [Thomas Swift] had not yet gone half way, his Companion [Jonathan Swift] borrowed the Manuscript to peruse."—Robert Martin Adams, *Modern Philology*

In brackets Adams has identified for the reader the "he" and the "Companion" referred to by Curll.

Sic in brackets indicates that an error in the quoted material is being reproduced exactly: New Haven, Connecicut [sic]. Brackets may also be used to insert a correction: Cramer writes, "In April 1943 [the month was July], Jones published his first novel." And brackets function as parentheses within parentheses, particularly in legal documents and scholarly footnotes.

If your typewriter keyboard doesn't have brackets, draw them in by hand.

bring, take

Bring implies motion toward the speaker or writer (Bring it with you when you come). *Take* implies motion away from (Take it with you when you go). When the speaker or writer is doing the moving, he's glad he *brought* his camera along. When he's returned, he's glad he *took* his camera and *brought* it back. When the point of view doesn't matter, either term can be used: Potatoes were brought (*or* taken) from Ireland to France.

bring up

Bring up, like *raise,* is general usage for the more formal *rear* or *nurture* (That's the way I was brought up). It also means "to introduce" a subject: Having brought it up, he couldn't stop talking about it. See **raise, rear.**

British English

British English and American English differ noticeably in spelling. The British prefer -re to -er in ending words like *center* and *theater,* though they use both forms. They keep -our in a number of words where Americans use -or. They use x in a few words like *inflexion* where Americans use ct. They double more consonants, as in *traveller* and *waggon.* And they spell some individual words differently, including automobile *tyre* for U.S. *tire.* They use more hyphens than we do and the opposite order of double and single quotation marks. Differences like these occur just often enough to show that a book is of British rather than American origin—certainly not enough to interfere with comprehension.

The grammar of the popular levels of British and American English differs somewhat, though less than the vocabulary. Collective nouns referring to institutions are more likely to be plural in British usage (the government intend). British writers differ in small matters like the position of *only,* the proper preposition with *different,* the use of *shall,* and various idioms. It would be possible to assemble a fairly long list of such minor differences, but their importance shouldn't be exaggerated nor their occurrence allowed to obscure the fact that the resemblances far outnumber the differences and that the speech of the two countries represents two strands of the same language.

Usages that originate in Great Britain frequently become vogue expressions in the United States: *early on* and *a good read* are recent examples. These soon become tiresome, as home-grown vogue words and phrases do. But some Americans treat them with contempt as evidence of affectation. Such hostility to Briticisms represents an attitude almost as old as the Republic. So does its opposite—an eagerness to embrace all things British, including Briticisms. British attitudes toward Americanisms are similarly divided.

Broad reference

A pronoun referring to the idea of a preceding clause rather than to a particular antecedent is said to have broad reference. See **Reference of pronouns 2.**

bug

Both as a noun for an electronic listening device and as a verb for the planting of such a device (They bugged his home phone), *bug* has become established in general English.

bunch

In formal English *bunch* is limited to objects that grow together like grapes or can be fastened together like carrots or keys. Used of people, *bunch* is moving into the general vocabulary: ". . . another monumental American myth—that Washington is run by a bunch of cynical, untrustworthy fools" (Nona B. Brown, *New York Times Book Review*).

burglar, robber, thief

All three take what isn't theirs, but the robber uses violence or threats, and the burglar breaks into a building. See **rob.**

burst, bust

Burst is the unchanged past tense and past participle of the verb *burst. Bust* (with *bust* or *busted* as past tense and participle) is a nonstandard variant of *burst* in its literal meaning: dams and balloons burst, *not* bust.

In contexts where the meaning is figurative, *bust*—frequently with the adverbs *up* and *out*—is now common, though still somewhat informal: That interception busted the game wide open. Broncos and trusts and noncommissioned officers are *busted; burst* can't be substituted in these senses.

Business letters

Business letters include not only the correspondence sent out by companies and corporations but also the letters of individuals to business firms, colleges, government agencies, newspapers, civic organizations, and so forth. When you write a letter to apply for a job or a scholarship, to obtain information, to request assistance, or to register a complaint, the recipient is more likely to give it serious attention if you have done your best with the packaging as well as the content.

1. Materials and appearance.   Use good-quality white paper measuring $8^1/2$ by 11 inches. If at all possible, type your final draft. Keep a copy of every business letter you write.

Most business letters are now written in block style without indentions, as shown in the sample. Convention calls for one line of space between inside address and salutation, between salutation and body, and between body and close. Three lines of space are usually left for the signature. Other spacing depends on the length of your letter. In your drafts—and you may need to write several—work for an attractive, balanced page, with generous margins and plenty of space at top and bottom.

If you can sensibly do so, limit your letter to a single page. When you write more than one page, number the additional pages.

2. Heading.   Give your full address and the date. Unless you use the abbreviations adopted by the Postal Service (which are not followed by periods), write out the names of states. Note that there's no comma between

state and ZIP code and no punctuation at the ends of lines. If you use station-
ery with a letterhead that provides the address, type the date beneath it.

3. Inside address.   Give the name and full address of the person you're
writing to, just as it will appear on the envelope, beginning each line at the
left margin. How far down the page you start the inside address depends on
the length of your letter. For good balance, begin a short letter lower than
a longer one.

Whenever possible, direct your letter to an individual or at least to an
office (Personnel Director) or a department (Personnel Department).

4. Salutation.   When you're writing to a person you can name, the best
greeting is the simplest:

> Dear Ms. Nash:
> Dear Mr. Mahoney:

Note that a colon follows the name. When the circumstances call for special
formality, ''Dear Sir'' or ''Dear Madam'' is the right choice. If you're addressing an organization or an anonymous individual, the traditional greeting
is ''Dear Sirs'' (or ''Gentlemen'') or ''Dear Sir.'' If you're writing to a
women's organization, the plural of ''Madam'' is ''Mesdames.''

5. Body.   Your first paragraph should make the subject of your letter
clear. Let the reader know immediately why you're writing. If you're reply-
ing to a letter, answering an advertisement, or writing at the suggestion of
someone known to your reader, say so. By making your purpose clear from
the outset, you help your reader concentrate immediately on what you have
to say.

Your paragraphs will usually be much shorter than in a college paper—
often no more than two or three sentences. Use a new paragraph for each
item or each subdivision in your message, so that your reader can quickly
identify the specific requests you're making or the facts you're providing
and can refer to them in his response.

The style of a business letter should be clear, direct, and as brief as
clarity and completeness permit. The tone should be brisk without being
brusque. You don't want to waste your reader's time, but neither do you
want to insult him. And while being concise, be careful not to confuse or
mystify him. Provide all relevant information, especially if you're complain-
ing about defective merchandise, outlining a proposal, or seeking a job.

Finding just the right tone to use in your letter may require some effort,
since you'll often have little notion what sort of person your reader is. Under
such conditions, trying to make your writing seem personal may instead
make it sound insincere. On the other hand, if you make no attempt to speak
to the reader as an individual, your writing is likely to sound cold and aloof.
The best technique is to address the reader as a stranger who is intelligent,
respected, and probably short of time.

Don't make the mistake of trying to write in what you may think of as business style. The good business writer of today uses general English, avoiding both the clichés of commerce *(contact, finalize, angle, and/or)* and pretentious words like *ameliorate* for *improve, terminate* for *end*.

6. Close and signature. Begin the close at the left margin, in the middle of the page, or aligned with the heading, depending on overall balance. Follow it with a comma. For most business letters "Sincerely" or "Sincerely yours" is appropriate. If you're writing as an official—as purchasing agent for a campus co-op, for example—give your title under your typed name:

```
Leslie Archer
Purchasing Agent
```

In typing her name, a woman may or may not choose to indicate her marital status:

```
Dorothy Olson            (Mrs.) Dorothy Olson

(Ms.) Dorothy Olson      Dorothy Olson
                         (Mrs. Henry Olson)
(Miss) Dorothy Olson
```

7. Mailing. An envelope measuring 4 by $9\frac{1}{2}$ inches is best for business letters, but an envelope measuring $3\frac{1}{2}$ by $6\frac{1}{2}$ inches can be used. Repeat the inside address on the envelope, and give your own name and address in the upper left corner.

Heading

```
                                    431 University Place
                                    Madison, Wisconsin 53706
                                    November 12, 1981
```

Inside address

```
Mr. Dwight Morrison
Program Director
WSTR Television
546 Main Street
Madison, Wisconsin 53703
```

Salutation

```
Dear Mr. Morrison:
```

Body

```
Members of the Sociology Club at the University of Wisconsin
have been examining the influence of the University on the
surrounding community, and we believe that some of our find-
ings may be of interest to your viewers.

In order to assess the importance of the University to local
business, we have talked with many shop owners about the prod-
ucts they carry to attract student customers.  We have looked
into the way political opinions in some Madison neighborhoods
have changed since students began taking an active role in
local elections.  And we have found that a tutorial project
started by students has begun to change some people's atti-
tudes toward the University.

Members of the Sociology Club would like very much to discuss
with you the possibility of using our study as the basis of
a special program.  Two or three of us could arrange to meet
with you at your convenience.
```

Close

```
                          Sincerely yours,
```

Signature

Marilyn Thompson

```
                          Marilyn Thompson
                          President
                          Sociology Club
                          University of Wisconsin
```

but

But is the natural coordinating conjunction to connect two contrasted statements: He left, but she stayed. *But* is lighter than *however,* less formal than *yet,* and, unlike *(al)though,* doesn't subordinate the clause that follows it.

1. Connecting equals. The locutions connected by *but* should be of equal grammatical rank:

> **Adjectives:** not *blue* but *green*
> **Adverbs:** He worked *quickly* but *accurately.*
> **Phrases:** She finally arrived, not *at lunch time* but *in the early evening.*
> **Clauses:** *The first day we rested,* but *the second we got down to work.*
> **Sentences:** *The Rio Grande defied the best engineering minds of two countries for a century.* But *$10 million in flood-control work harnessed the treacherous stream.*

See **which 3** for comments on **but which.**

2. Connecting statements in opposition. The statements connected by *but* should be clearly opposed:

> He knows vaguely that the nation is not much good any more; he has read that the crust of the earth is shrinking rapidly and that the universe is growing steadily colder; but he does not believe that any of the three is in half as bad shape as he is.—James Thurber, *My Life and Hard Times.*

In "The blisters on my feet were killing me, but the road seemed to go on forever," there's no real opposition. What's needed is a second clause like "but somehow I hobbled the last long mile."

3. Beginning sentences. *But,* like *and,* is often used to begin a sentence. Separation emphasizes the contrast with the preceding sentence. Be careful, though, not to follow a *but* clause with another *but* (or *however*) clause, or both the contrast and a measure of sense will be lost:

> The magazine they founded lasted only four years and was a financial failure, *but* its influence was enormous. *But* that was not the only contribution they made to literary history.

4. Punctuation. Two clauses connected by *but* should ordinarily be separated by a comma. The contrast in ideas makes punctuation desirable even when the clauses are relatively short: I couldn't get the whole license number, but I know it began with AOK. Though writers frequently use a comma after an initial *but* (But [,] it was too late for the aging man to regain his lost skill), no punctuation should separate *but* from the clause it introduces.

but that, but what

But that as a subordinating conjunction after a negative is avoided in formal styles but appears often in general and informal styles: I don't doubt but that she will come. *But what* is sometimes used in the same construction. *That* alone can be substituted for either *but that* or *but what:* I don't doubt that she will come.

but which

If you write a clause that begins with "but which," be sure it's preceded in the sentence by a *which* clause. See **which 3.**

C

can, may (could, might)

1.   To express possibility, both *can* and *may* are used. *Can* is the only choice for simple ability: "I can swim" meaning "I'm able to swim." For feasibility ("I can swim today" meaning "There's nothing to prevent me from swimming today") *can* is less formal than *may:* "The Introduction only hints at the many paths the reader may follow" (Anna Benjamin, *Classical Philology*). Repeated use of *may* in this sense sounds excessively tentative or uncertain.

Could and *might* are used chiefly to convey a smaller degree of possibility than *can* and *may* or a shadow of doubt: She could be here by Saturday; I might have left it in my room. But *might* is also commonly substituted for *may,* with no difference in meaning. (*Might could* for *might be able to* is regional.)

2.   In requesting permission, *may* has a cool politeness appropriate to formal occasions: May I add one further point? Informally, *can* requests permission: Can I borrow the car next Sunday? *May* is also the formal choice in granting or denying permission. Except when the sense of institutional authority is central (Students may not attend class barefoot), *can* is more common: "After forbidding the Colonel to speak of love to her, she . . . tells him he can" (Henry Hewes, *Saturday Review*).

See **Divided usage.**

cannot, can not

Usage is divided. *Cannot* is more common.

can't hardly

Can't (or *cannot*) *hardly* should be changed to *can hardly,* since *hardly* means "probably not." See **Double negative.**

can't help but, can't seem to

Can't (or *cannot*) *help but* and *can't* (or *cannot*) *seem to* are established general idioms:

> The reader cannot help but question whether they, indeed, were so universally excellent.—Peter Walls, *Annals*

> What they can't seem to tolerate is unemployment, the feeling of being useless.—Alfred Kazin, *Saturday Review*

Even so, *cannot help but* is avoided by some conservative stylists, who prefer *cannot help* followed by a gerund: cannot help saying. In formal usage *seem unable to* is the alternative to *can't seem to.*

cap Capital letters

Capitalize the word marked.

Almost everyone uses capital letters at the beginning of sentences and proper names and for *I.* Some other uses of capitals are matters of taste. Formal English uses more capitals than general English, and newspaper style cuts them to a minimum. The best policy is to capitalize in accordance with well-established convention and not to capitalize in other situations without good reason.

1. Sentence capitals.   Capitalize the first word of a sentence.
a.   Capitalize the first word in a complete sentence that you enclose in parentheses and place between two other sentences. But don't capitalize if you insert it in parentheses within a sentence or if you set it off with a dash or dashes.
b.   Capitalize the first word in a sentence following a colon if you want to emphasize the sentence (He promised this: The moment agreement was reached, the trucks would roll).
c.   In dialog, capitalize the first word of what a speaker says but not the second part of an interrupted quoted sentence: "Well," he said, "it (*not* It) was nice to see you again." Except in dialog, don't capitalize parts of sentences that are quoted: "Stressing that legal restrictions on surveillance are few, he rallied the assembled with the intelligence that 'the challenge is wide open' " (David M. Rorvik, *Playboy*).

2. Proper names.   Capitalize proper names and abbreviations of proper names: names of people and places, months, days of the week, historical events (the Civil War, the Council of Trent, the New Deal), documents (the Emancipation Proclamation), companies and organizations, trade names, religious denominations, holidays, races and ethnic groups (but see **black**), languages, ships, named planes and trains, and nicknames. See **Course names.**

a. Capitalize *north, south,* and so on when they denote particular regions (the Southwest, the East) but not when they indicate direction (They started west in 1849).

b. Capitalize *army, navy,* and so on when they appear in full titles (the United States Army) and when they stand for the teams of the service academies. In other cases usage is divided: the American army (or Army), their navy (or Navy).

c. Capitalize *college* as part of a full title (He went to Beloit College) but not as a level of schooling (Neither of them went to college).

d. Don't capitalize proper nouns that have become common nouns: *tweed, sandwich, bohemian, plaster of paris,* and so on. Many proper adjectives in senses that no longer suggest their origins are not capitalized *(india ink, diesel engine)* but others usually are *(French cuffs, Xerox copy, Bibb lettuce).* Follow your dictionary.

e. Don't capitalize the names of the seasons except in *Fall term, Spring semester,* and so on, or for stylistic reasons.

3. Titles of books, articles, etc.   Capitalize the first word and last word (and the first word after a colon), all nouns, pronouns, verbs, adjectives, and adverbs, and all prepositions of more than five letters: *With Malice Toward Some; Social Humanism: An International Symposium; Now Don't Try to Reason with Me;* ''Biological Clocks of the Tidal Zone''; ''Computer Control of Electric-Power Systems.'' See **Titles.**

4. Titles, positions, relatives.

a. Capitalize personal titles before proper names: President Taft, Ambassador Clark, Senator Lodge, Sergeant York. ''The President'' for the President of the United States is still customary. Otherwise, usage is divided when an individual is referred to by title alone: The Colonel was there; The senator spoke at length.

b. Capitalize the names for family members when used as proper nouns: We had to get Father's consent. Don't capitalize when they are used as common nouns: My mother is a better dancer than I am.

5. Deity.   Capitalize the name of the Supreme Being *(God, Jehovah, Allah), Jesus,* and nouns such as *Savior.* With pronouns referring to God and Jesus, practice is divided: *He, Him, His* or *he, him, his.*

6. *Street, river, park,* and so on.   Capitalize such words as *street, river, park, hotel,* and *church* when they follow a proper name (Fifth Avenue,

Missouri River). Abbreviations of these words should also be capitalized: 2319 E. 100th St.

7. Abstractions. Usage is divided. Abstract nouns are likely to be capitalized in formal writing (less often in general) when the concepts they refer to are personified or when they refer to ideals or institutions: The State has nothing to do with the Church, nor the Church with the State.

8. Quoted lines of verse. Follow the poet's capitalization exactly.

Writers once used capitals as a form of emphasis, to stress certain words or call attention to them. Now when such initial capitals appear, the purpose is usually to amuse. If what you have to say isn't funny to begin with, capitals won't help.

✗   Careless mistakes

Correct the obvious mistake marked.

Careless lapses are inevitable in hurried work. But a college paper shouldn't be hurried work. Comma splices and fragments, mistakes in the forms of verbs and pronouns *(broke* for *broken, it's* for *its),* missing words, and similar slips are likely to occur if you give too little time or too little attention to the final stages of preparing a paper.

Train yourself to proofread carefully. Check your manuscript for such elementary mistakes as these:

> *Letters omitted* (the *n* of *an,* the *d* of *used to,* a final *y)*
> *End punctuation omitted* (including the closing quotation marks after a quoted passage)
> *Words run together (a/lot,* in *a/while)*
> *Words confused (affect, effect; principal, principle; quiet, quite; than, then; there, their; to, too; whether, weather; whose, who's)*

Check also for the unnecessary repetition of a preposition or a conjunction: It is only natural *that* with the sudden change in the administration *that* people are worrying about what new policies may be introduced.

If you're uncertain about the spelling of a word, consult your dictionary. If you're unsure what word, word form, construction, or punctuation to use, consult this *Index.*

Caret

The inverted *v* called a caret points to the place in a line of manuscript where something written above the line or in the margin should be inserted:

```
                                                        because
There was no reason for them not to get good grades,∧ all
they did was study.
```

This is an acceptable way to revise papers as long as the revisions are few and completely clear.

A caret used by an instructor as a correction mark indicates that something has been omitted.

Case Case

Correct the mistake in case.

The case of a noun or pronoun is one indication of its relationship to other elements in the sentence. (Another indication is word order.) The subject of a verb and the complement of a linking verb are in the nominative, or subjective, case *(Who is she?)*. The object of a verb or a preposition is in the accusative, or objective, case (I introduced *them;* He walked behind *her*). Certain modifiers of a noun are in the possessive, or genitive, case *(his* hat, the *dog's* bone).

Except for the spelling differences in the possessive singular *(dog's),* the possessive plural *(dogs'),* and the common plural *(dogs),* the case of nouns presents no problems. The same form is used in both subject and object positions: Your *dog* chased my *dog.* Pronouns have more forms— especially the pronouns we use most often. And when we're in the habit of using a few nonstandard forms in speech, the case of these pronouns may cause some problems in writing.

Most of the problems involve the six pronouns that change form to indicate all three cases: *I, he, she, we, they, who* (and its variant *whoever).* Thus: *She* sings (nominative); The song pleases *her* (accusative); It's *his* song, not *hers* (possessive). Note that four of the pronouns have a second form of the possessive, used when the pronoun doesn't precede a noun: *mine, hers, ours, theirs.* The pronouns *it* and *you* change their form only in the possessive: *its; your, yours.* These pronouns, as well as the indefinites (like *some/one, any/thing, each*), have the same form whether they are subjects or objects.

Here are the basic conventions to observe in standard written English:

1.   Use the forms *I, he, she, we, they, who(ever)*
a.   In subject position: *She* and *I* played on the same team; *He* asked *who* wrote the play (*who* is the subject of *wrote,* not the object of *asked*); *Whoever* wrote it had a good ear for dialog.
b.   In apposition to a noun or pronoun in subject position: The winning couple, Phil and *I*, got a trip to Disneyland; We, Phil and *I*, got a trip. . . .
c.   After a linking verb: It is *he* who should pay the bill. (But see **it's me.**)

2.   Use the forms *me, him, her, us, them*

a.   In object position: The song reminded Jack and *me* (object of verb) of our high-school graduation; College is harder for *him* than for *me* (object of preposition—see also **between you and me**). The object of an infinitive is often in the accusative case (I wanted to be *him*) in general writing and always in informal. But the nominative case (I always wanted to be *he*) is the rule in formal writing.

b.   In apposition to a noun or pronoun in object position: Prizes went to the top students, Mary and *me;* The prizes went to us, Mary and *me.*

3.   The special problem of *whom(ever).*   The object form *whom(ever)* is regularly used after a preposition: To *whom* was the remark addressed? But speakers and writers sometimes deliberately shift the preposition to the end of the sentence and use *who* for its object: *Who* was the remark addressed to? In general usage *who* at the beginning of a sentence is also increasingly common for the object of a verb: *Who* do we ask for advice? Even among formal stylists, usage is divided. See **who, whom.**

4.   Use the possessive case of nouns and pronouns to indicate possession and the other relationships discussed in **Possessive case 2,** except when the *of* phrase is customary (the end *of the street,* the roof *of the house*): It was the other *man's* hat, not *his;* the mixup resulted from *their* putting them on the same hook. "*Their* putting" illustrates the standard form for a pronoun that's the subject of a gerund. When a noun is the subject of a gerund, the common form is usual in informal and general English and is the choice of some formal writers: He complained about the *book* (more formal: *book's*) going out of print. See **Gerunds 2.**

   Avoid the nonstandard *hisself* for himself and *theirself* or *theirselves* for *themselves.*

   See **Pronouns 1, 4; Possessive case.**

catholic, Catholic

Written with a small *c, catholic* is a rather formal synonym for "universal or broad in sympathies or interests." In general American usage *Catholic* written with a capital *c* is taken as equivalent to *Roman Catholic,* both as a noun (She's a Catholic) and as an adjective (Catholic labor unions).

Cause and effect

Why something occurred (cause) or what will result from it (effect) often interests us as much as what happened.

1.   Signals of cause-effect relations.   Causal connections are conveyed by explicit statements (*A* caused *B; B* is the effect of *A*), by many familiar transitional words and phrases *(because* or *since, so that* or *in order that, thus* or *as a result),* and sometimes by simply placing one statement immediately after another (In March he was told he had cancer; three months later he shot himself).

2. Discovering causes.   Papers that investigate cause range from discussions of historical events and scientific experiments to arguments that assign responsibility or predict the consequences of a course of action. Almost all causal analysis has an argumentative edge to it, since the writer is always trying to win acceptance for a *probable* interpretation of facts. So he has to do more than simply state his conclusion. He must justify and support it by demonstrating, offering specific information, tying probable cause to known effect or probable results to an existing situation.

Because we all have a habit of jumping to the most obvious conclusion, in analyzing causes and effects you must discipline yourself to keep an open mind until you've collected enough evidence to make a convincing case, and you must avoid oversimplifying: most events have a number of causes, not just one. At the same time, you must resist the temptation to search out more and more remote causes. There's no need to go back to Genesis to explain the genesis of an event of current local interest. Finally, be sure you end up showing that something happened *because* of something else—the whole purpose of causal analysis—not merely that something happened *after* something else. Confusing temporal sequence with cause is a logical fallacy called *post hoc, ergo propter hoc,* "after this, therefore because of this." See **Fallacies, Logical thinking.**

censor, censure

When we *censor,* we delete or suppress. When we *censure,* we condemn or disapprove. To make things more complicated, the adjective *censorious* refers to censuring.

center around

Precisionists condemn it as illogical, but *center around* (The story centers around the theft of a necklace) is standard idiom:

> We could sometimes look out on shooting and fights that seemed to center around this saloon.—Edmund Wilson, *New Yorker*

> . . . accompanied by a propaganda war centered around her rightness and fitness for the throne.—Kerby Neil, *Modern Philology*

In some formal styles *on* or *upon* may be substituted for *around,* or *revolve* may be used instead of *center.* See **Logic in language.**

Centuries

The first century A.D. ran from the beginning of the year 1 to the end of the year 100. The present century began on January 1, 1901, and will end on December 31, 2000. Thus, to name the century correctly, add one to the number of its hundred except in the last year, when the number of the hundred is the number of the century, too. We live in the twentieth century.

For clarity, the hundred can be named, even in formal writing: Dr. Johnson lived in the seventeen hundreds. Similar practice—with and without the centuries—is standard in naming decades: the nineteen twenties, the sixties.

chauvinist

Until recently *chauvinist* was used almost exclusively to mean "superpatriot" or "jingoist." Then feminists began to use the label *male chauvinist* to describe a man whose attitudes were dominated by sexist prejudice or, more loosely, a man who was prejudiced against women. Now *chauvinist* is often used alone with this second meaning. Outside of feminist circles, the only sure way to avoid confusion is to specify what sort of chauvinist you're writing about.

Circumlocution

A circumlocution is a roundabout way of saying what could be expressed directly. See **Wordiness.**

Cities

If you refer to a city in a paper you write, locate it by state or by country only if it's a city your readers aren't familiar with or if it's not the city they might assume it is: Paris, Texas, but not Paris, France; Athens, Georgia, or Athens, Ohio, but not Athens, Greece.

claim

Used in the sense of "say" or "declare," *claim* suggests to many readers that the assertion should be regarded skeptically: He claims to be opposed to gun control. Using it as a mere variant of *say* (He claimed he was taking Chemistry 301) can therefore be misleading. See **say.**

Classification and division

Classification and division are related methods of analyzing and writing about a subject. Division is the process of separating a single object (a car) or institution (a college) or concept (communism) into its parts or constituent elements. Classification is the process of bringing together objects, institutions, or concepts that have something in common: cars, colleges, political philosophies can be sorted into groups on the basis of their resemblances. Division reveals internal structure; classification identifies family likenesses. In writing a paper on college life, you might draw on both methods, dividing the curriculum into its subject areas or campus social life into its various organizations and activities and classifying students on the basis of their attitudes toward their courses or the ways they use their leisure time or some other principle.

As the example suggests, one group can be classified in many different ways, and the same object can be divided into different collections of parts, depending on the writer's purpose or interest. That interest will determine whether the division or classification should meet strict requirements of completeness (all parts or items accounted for) and consistency (no overlapping of parts or of groups). Some groupings make no attempt to be either complete or consistent. The purpose of a paper entitled "Some Nuts on a Knotty Family Tree" would be simply to entertain. But a writer interested in trying to organize his experience—the real purpose of classifying or dividing—will work hard to make his analysis reasonably complete and consistent. And if he uses an original basis for dividing or classifying, he may offer his readers a new way of looking at things.

See **Logical thinking.**

Clauses

Each combination of a complete subject, like *he,* and a complete predicate, like *came home,* is traditionally called a clause. "He came home" is an independent clause. Grammatically it can stand alone. "When he came home" is a dependent clause. In ordinary prose a dependent clause does not stand alone as a sentence but is preceded or followed by an independent clause: When he came home, he looked for the cat.

1.   The clause structure of sentences.   The sentences that follow in **a, b, c,** and **d** both define and illustrate. Simple subjects and simple predicates are italicized. *IC* in brackets introduces an independent clause, *DC* a dependent one.

a.   [IC] A simple *sentence* (like this one) *consists* of a single independent subject-predicate combination.

b.   [IC] A compound *sentence has* two or more clauses of equal grammatical value; [IC] these *clauses are joined* by a coordinating conjunction, by a conjunctive adverb, or (as in this sentence) by a semicolon. [IC] A *writer may decide,* for reasons of emphasis or rhythm, to break a compound sentence into two separate simple sentences, [IC] and in such cases the only *difference* between the compound sentence and the separate sentences *is* punctuation.

c. [IC begun] A complex *sentence,* like the one [DC] that *you are* now *reading,* [IC continued] *has* at least one independent clause and one or more dependent, or subordinate, clauses, [DC] *which function* as nominals, adjectivals, or adverbials.

d. [DC] As the hyphenated *term indicates,* [IC] a compound-complex *sentence* (again illustrated by the sentence [DC] *you are reading) combines* the features of both compound and complex sentences: [IC] *it contains* two or more independent clauses and one or more dependent clauses.

See **Adjectivals 1, Adverbials, Noun clauses, Relative clauses.**

2. Reduced clauses.   Though the typical clause as traditionally defined has an expressed subject and a predicate with a full verb, many constructions lack one or the other of these elements and yet function in sentences as typical clauses do. Reduced clauses are of two types:

a. Elliptical clauses, in which a full verb can be reconstructed because it occurs earlier in the sentence:

> I don't *believe it* any more than you [*believe it*].
> They can *speak Russian,* and so can Bill [*speak Russian*].

b. Abridged clauses, in which the reader must rely on sense to fill in the missing subject and a form of *be:*

> While [*I* was] waiting, *I* read the newspaper.
> When [*he* was] sixteen, *he* went to work.
> Though [*she* was] a rapid reader, *she* disliked books.
> After [*they* had been] standing in line for an hour, *they* left.
> Though [*we* were] tired, *we* kept on working.

When the omitted subject isn't the same as the subject of the main clauses, the result is often a dangling modifier.

See **Complex sentence, Compound-complex sentence, Compound sentence, Dangling modifiers, Elliptical constructions, Restrictive and nonrestrictive modifiers.**

Cliché

A cliché is a worn-out word or phrase (like "white as snow"). See **Triteness.**

Clipped words

Ad[*vertisement*], *disco*[*theque*], *porn*[*ography*], and [*tele*]*phone* are clipped words. See **Origin of words 3c.**

coh Coherence

Make clear the relation between the parts of this sentence or between these sentences or these paragraphs.

Coherence—the traditional name for relationship, connection, consecutive-ness—is essential in expository writing. It's essential because you can't count on the minds of others working the same way your mind works. You must guide your readers from one idea, from one sentence, to another. To make a coherent presentation you have to arrange your ideas so that others can understand them.

Though careful planning in the prewriting stage will help you make clear the relationship of your ideas, testing for coherence must come after you've written a draft of your paper. To see if it hangs together, try to read it as your readers will—as if the content is new to you. Ask yourself if the relationship between statements is clear, if it's possible to move easily from one clause or sentence or paragraph to the next without losing the thread. For a passage like the following, all the logical connectives were probably in the writer's head, but that didn't help readers who tried to make sense of what was on paper:

> Disco isn't usually written to express a deep emotional meaning. All over the world people like a rhythm they can dance to. Sometimes they get such crowds that they have to turn people away.

There are many words and phrases that signal the relationship between sentence parts, sentences, and paragraphs. These signs, and suggestions for establishing coherence, are discussed in **Conjunctions and style, Prepositions, Reference of pronouns,** and **Transition.**

Collective nouns

A collective noun is a noun whose singular form names a group of objects or persons or acts. Here are some familiar examples:

army	couple	group	offspring
audience	dozen	herd	orchestra
class	faculty	jury	public
committee	family	majority	remainder
crowd	gang	number	team

Some collectives have regular plural forms *(army–armies)*. Some do not *(offspring)*. The plural of a collective noun signifies different groups: The *audiences* of New York and Seattle differed in their reception of the movie.

Some collectives are typically used in the singular *(committee is)* and some typically in the plural *(police are)*. Most are singular in one context, plural in a different one, depending on the way the writer thinks about the group. When it's the group as a whole, the collective noun takes a singular verb and a singular pronoun: "A *group* of the . . . stories *features* characters whose lives have become misshapen through means other than self-assertion" (Welford Dunaway Taylor, *Sherwood Anderson*).

When it's the individual units of the group that the writer has in mind, the noun takes a plural verb and plural pronoun: "Psychologists asked a *group* of young men and women what sex *they* wanted *their* first child to be" *(Psychology Today)*. With this example, compare "Now that John is back, the *group has its* old solidarity."

Trouble occurs when a writer treats a collective noun inconsistently. He begins by treating the word as a singular, and as long as the verb follows it closely, he makes the verb singular: The inner *circle has* great influence. But if a plural modifier comes between the collective noun and the verb, he thinks of the members of the group rather than of the group as a unit, and he shifts to a plural verb: This inner *circle* of ambitious men *pose* a serious threat.

A writer is also likely to be inconsistent when his way of thinking about the collective comes into conflict with the meaning of a sentence he's writing. He may want to keep a collective noun singular, but if the meaning calls for a plural construction, he'll often make the shift unconsciously, sometimes in mid-sentence:

> The entire *congregation troops* into the church, *seats itself,* and *remains* for a good two hours, while an aged curé berates *them* [consistency demands *it*] for *their* [*its*] sins.

In making your constructions consistent, you may find that it's the collective subject that needs to be changed, rather than the pronouns. In the example just given, beginning the sentence with "All members of the congregation troop into the church, seat themselves . . ." would avoid the problem.

Casual shifts in number are common in speech, but they're likely to attract unfavorable attention in general writing, and they're almost certain to in formal writing. When you read over your papers, be sure you haven't treated the same collective noun as both singular and plural.

See **Agreement 1b; each, every.**

Colloquial English

Usage that's characteristic of the way we talk is called colloquial. Though the division between spoken English and written English isn't nearly as sharp as it once was, some spoken usages may be inappropriate in all but the most informal writing *(You know? Terrific! Unreal!),* just as some features of written English are inappropriate in all but the most formal speech.

Dictionaries sometimes mark words *Colloq.* to indicate that they're more common in speech than in writing. Many readers mistakenly take the label to mean that the dictionaries' editors frown upon these words. In fact, colloquial words are often accurate and expressive and are used freely in good general writing. Because misinterpretation of *colloquial* is common, the label is avoided in this book. If a usage is more common in speech than in writing, that fact is stated. If the word or expression is standard English but rarely appears in general or formal writing, it's labeled informal.

See **Spoken and written English.**

Colon Colon

Use a colon here. Or reconsider the use of this colon.

The colon is a mark of anticipation. It indicates that what follows the mark will supplement what came before it.

1. Introductory uses.   Use a colon before a series of words, phrases, or clauses when the series is not preceded by an introductory word or phrase or when it's formally introduced by a set phrase like *as follows* or *including the following:*

> There are two modes of thinking, two poles by which one can orientate one's life: politics and religion.—H. Saddhatissa, *The Buddha's Way.*

> Classifying the poetry written from 1500 to 1900 in accordance with this distinction, we discover a sequence which runs as follows: predicative, then balanced; predicative, then balanced.—Josephine Miles, *PMLA*

Don't use a colon after less formal introductory words *(like, such as)* that make what follows a part of the clause: The shop carried a lot of ethnic recordings, like [:] West African, Moorish, Egyptian, and Arabian. And don't use a colon between a verb and its object or complement: The reason I went broke freshman week was that I had to buy [:] books, furniture, and tickets to a lot of things I knew I'd never go to; My three immediate goals are [:] to survive midyear exams, to get to Colorado, and to ski until my legs wear out.

When appropriate, use a colon to introduce quotations in factual writing, especially if they run to more than one sentence. The colon is more common in formal than in general or informal writing, and its appropriateness depends in part on the way you introduce the quotation. If it's built into the sentence, a comma is usual. If it's more formally introduced, a colon fits the context. Both situations are illustrated in this example:

> For example, the report cannot say, "It was a wonderful car," but must say something like this: "It has been driven 50,000 miles and has never required any repairs."—S. I. Hayakawa, *Language in Thought and Action*

2. Between clauses.   Particularly in a formal paper, you may decide to use a colon between the clauses of a compound sentence when the second clause illustrates, restates, or amplifies the first:

> The supposition that words are used principally to convey thoughts is one of the most elementary of possible errors: they are used mainly to proclaim emotional effects on the hearers or attitudes that will lead to practical results.— H. R. Huse, *The Illiteracy of the Literate*

This is the one use in which the colon and the semicolon are sometimes interchangeable. Never use a semicolon to introduce a series or a quotation.

3. Conventional uses.
a. After the salutation of formal letters: Dear Sir:
b. Between hours and minutes written in figures: 11:30 a.m.
c. Between Bible chapter and verse: Genesis 9:3–5.
d. In ratios and proportions when the numbers are written as figures: concrete mixed 5:3:1. Two colons are used instead of an equals sign in a full proportion: 1:2::3:6.
e. For the use of colons in bibliographies and notes, see **Bibliographical form, Note form.**

4. Stylistic use.   Sometimes you may use a construction that calls for a colon because you want to spotlight what the colon introduces: "It is a common dream: To stand beneath sun and blue sky, harvesting your own . . . fruits and vegetables" (*New York Times*). Both "A common dream is . . ." and "To stand . . . is a common dream" would be much less emphatic.

5. Capitals following.   To begin an independent clause after a colon, either a capital letter (as in the last quoted sentence with a colon) or a small letter can be used, but a small letter is much more common. (See the example in **2.**) Use a capital after a colon only when the clause is long or complicated, with internal punctuation, or when you want to give it special prominence: "Beneath the surface, however, is the less tangible question of values: Are the old truths true?" (*Newsweek*).

comma Comma

Insert or remove a comma at the place marked.

"Should there be a comma here?" is the question most often asked about punctuation. The general advice of this book is to use commas wherever established conventions demand them and to use them elsewhere if they'll help the reader. When there's a choice, your decision should be based on appropriateness: the complex structures and deliberate pace of much formal writing call for more commas than the simpler, brisker sentences of general English.

Uses of the comma

The following list of uses of the comma outlines the treatment in this article. The numbers and letters refer to sections and subsections.

1. To separate independent clauses
a. Between clauses connected by a coordinating conjunction
b. Between clauses connected by *but*
c. Between clauses connected by *for*
d. Between clauses not connected by a coordinating conjunction

2. With preceding and following elements
a. After a dependent clause or long phrase preceding the main clause
b. Before a dependent clause or long phrase following the main clause and not essential to its meaning

3. To set off nonrestrictive modifiers

4. To enclose interrupting and parenthetical elements
a. Around interrupting elements
b. Around conjunctive adverbs within clauses

5. In lists and series
a. Between units in lists and series
b. Between coordinate adjectives

6. For clarity

7. For emphasis and contrast

8. With main sentence elements
a. Subject and verb
b. Verb and object
c. Compound predicates

9. In conventional practice
a. In dates
b. In addresses
c. After salutations in all but formal letters
d. After names in direct address
e. In figures
f. With degrees and titles
g. With weak exclamations
h. To show omission

10. With other marks of punctuation
a. With parentheses
b. With dash
c. With quotation marks **(Quotation marks 4b, 4c)**

C_1

1. To separate independent clauses.
a. Use a comma before the coordinating conjunction when the clauses are rather long and when you want to emphasize their distinctness, as when they have different subjects:

> For all its impressiveness, Monks Mound is only a part of the even more impressive Cahokia group, and Cahokia in turn is only one, albeit the largest, of 10 large and small population centers and 50-odd farming villages. —Marvin L. Fowler, *Scientific American*

When the independent clauses are short and closely related in meaning, the comma is often omitted: "Who will live and who will die?" *(Time)*. But there's no rule that forbids using a comma to separate the clauses in a compound sentence, no matter what their length or relationship. Many experienced writers automatically place a comma before the coordinating conjunction and so guard against the momentary confusion that a sentence like this one invites: "A crowd of spectators lined the walkway to see him [ ] and the President, in standard fashion, passed along the crowd" *(New York Times)*.
b. Use a comma between two independent clauses joined by *but,* regardless of their length, to emphasize the contrast: "His achievements in office have been difficult to assess, but they have been formidable" (John David Hamilton, *Atlantic*).
c. Use a comma between independent clauses connected by the conjunction *for* to avoid confusion with the preposition *for:* They were obviously mistaken, for intercollegiate sports are always competitive. Without the guidance provided by the comma, a reader might stride through "They were obviously mistaken for intercollegiate sports," then stumble and have to begin all over again.
d. Use a comma in place of a coordinating conjunction when you have a good reason for doing so and when doing so won't confuse or annoy your readers. In most cases such punctuation represents a comma splice (see **Comma splice**), but under certain conditions a comma can appropriately stand between independent clauses that aren't joined by a coordinating conjunction:

> The intellect gets busy, means and methods are studied, purposes are assessed. —Gerald Warner Brace, *The Stuff of Fiction*

> This writer is not merely good, she is *wickedly* good. —John Updike, *New Yorker*

The clauses here are short, parallel in form, and closely bound together in meaning. Semicolons could be used instead of commas, but they'd slow the pace and make the style more formal.

Sentences punctuated like these are increasingly common in print. Not all of them are successful. If the clauses are neither short nor similar in structure, and if one or more of them contains internal punctuation, the reader may have a hard time grasping the meaning. In "The strongest and luckiest private constituencies win, social needs get pushed aside, as in the 50s, to explode a decade later" (Bill Moyers, *Newsweek*), a reader who assumes that the writer is building a series (The strongest and luckiest private constituencies win, social needs get pushed aside, and the gulf between haves and have-nots widens) is brought up short and forced to reread the sentence.

Between two independent clauses, then, you can put a coordinating conjunction (with or without a comma or a semicolon before it), a semicolon alone, or a comma alone. The choice is a matter of style. But you need to take convention into account. Before using a comma alone, consider your audience. Some very conservative readers invariably look on such punctuation as incorrect. If you can assume that your audience won't automatically condemn the practice, then be sure you're using the comma for a purpose. And, most important, be sure that your use of a comma alone won't make your reader's task more difficult.

See **Fused sentence, Semicolon 1.**

C_2 2.   **With preceding and following elements.**
a.   Use a comma after an introductory dependent clause or a long introductory phrase:

> Since encouraging women to spend money was the main point of magazines directed at us, they had distinctive characteristics. —*Ms.*

> Far from being a neutral instrument, the law belongs to those who have the power to define and use it. —Michael Parenti, *Democracy for the Few*

Often when the preceding phrase is short or when the dependent clause has the same subject as the independent clause, the comma is omitted:

> During my convalescence [ ] I will meditate on a few items. —Goodman Ace, *Saturday Review* (short phrase)

> Although Grant ignores such details [ ] he is shrewd not only about his colleagues but about his former colleagues. —Gore Vidal, *New York Review of Books* (subjects the same)

But some professional writers put commas after all introductory clauses and after all introductory phrases that contain verbals. In that way they establish a consistent pattern and avoid risking the confusion that may result from the absence of punctuation.

b.   Use a comma before a dependent clause or long phrase that follows the main clause if the subordinate element isn't essential to the meaning of the main clause:

> And as I said earlier, the rear ones should probably be snow tires, even if you get the truck in May.—Noel Perrin, *First Person Rural*

> Again and again they tried to start the engine, with the breeze freshening and the tide beginning to turn.

C₃

3.   To set off nonrestrictive modifiers.   Use a comma to set off word groups that don't restrict the meaning of the noun or verb or clause they modify. The italicized word groups in the following sentences are nonrestrictive:

> From where I was standing, *almost directly above the trunk,* I could see many of the articles that had been lost.

> Pigeons breed in the spring and the hen lays two eggs, *one of which usually hatches into a hen and the other into a cock.*

A modifier that restricts the reference of the word it modifies (as "that has been lost" restricts "articles" in the first of the preceding sentences) is essential to correct understanding and therefore is not set off by commas.
See **Restrictive and nonrestrictive modifiers.**

C₄

4.   To enclose interrupting and parenthetical elements.
a.   Use commas around a word, phrase, or clause that interrupts the main structure of the sentence:

Next summer, no matter what happens, I intend to go to Africa.

The joke, I suppose, seemed funny at the time.

My uncle, unfortunately, stopped for a drink on his way home from work.

Enclosing calls for two commas. Forgetting the second one can cause confusion: "If factory workers and farmers became more efficient, Soviet citizens were told this week [ ] they would get more domestic goods, food, housing, hospitals and schools" *(Newport Daily News).*

Usage is divided over setting off short parenthetical expressions like *of course.* Enclosing them in commas is more characteristic of formal than of general writing. There's often a difference in emphasis as well as tone depending on whether or not commas are used:

And of course there are those who talk about the hair of the dog. —*Providence Sunday Journal*

The question, of course, is not whether the family will "survive." —*Time*

b. Use commas around a conjunctive adverb that stands after the first phrase of its clause: It was this ridiculous proposal, however, that won majority approval. At the beginning of a sentence, conjunctive adverbs may or may not be set off: Therefore [,] I have decided to withdraw my application.

When *however* is used in the sense "no matter how," it should never be separated from the words it modifies: However [ ] strongly you feel . . .; However [ ] tired you are. . . . Similarly, *but* and other coordinating conjunctions are a part of the clauses in which they appear and should not be set off: But [ ] a solution must be found.

C₅   5. In lists and series.

a. Use commas to separate the units in lists and series: "He has read everything he could lay his hands on, manuscripts and printed, that was written during the period: plays, sermons, ballads, broadsides, letters, diaries, and, above all, court records" (Edmund S. Morgan, *New York Review of Books*).

See **Semicolon 2.**

Usage is divided over the use of a comma before the conjunction in a series: "letters, diaries, and records" or "letters, diaries and records." A comma is often a safeguard against boners: "He had small shoulders, a thick chest holding a strong heart [ ] and heavy thighs" (Richard Mandell, *Sports Illustrated*). See **Series.**

b. Use a comma between adjectives modifying the same noun. In the sentence "Though it was a hot, sticky, miserable day, Mrs. Marston looked cool in her fresh gingham dress," there are commas between *hot* and *sticky* and between *sticky* and *miserable* because each stands in the same relation to the noun *day*. "Hot *and* sticky *and* miserable" would make sense. There's no comma between *fresh* and *gingham* because *fresh* modifies *gingham dress,* not just *dress.* "Fresh *and* gingham" would not make sense.

Some writers today use no comma when only two adjectives modify the noun: a hot sticky day; the tall dark woman. There's no loss of clarity, but if you never use a comma between such adjectives, you deprive yourself of a rhetorical resource. By separating, a comma provides emphasis. Compare these two versions:

His long, greasy hair hung down to the shoulders of his worn, faded jacket.

His long greasy hair hung down to the shoulders of his worn faded jacket.

In the first, *greasy* and *faded* stand out as separate modifiers of their nouns.

C 6

6.   For clarity.   Use a comma to help a reader interpret a sentence correctly as he goes along, so that he doesn't have to go back over it to get its meaning. A comma between clauses joined by *for* makes it clear that the word is being used as a conjunction rather than as a preposition. Similarly, a comma can prevent a reader from even momentarily mistaking the subject of one verb for the object of another:

> When the boll weevil struck, the credit system collapsed and ruined both landowners and tenants. (*Not* When the boll weevil struck the credit system. . . .)

> Soon after the inspector left, the room was crowded with curious onlookers. (*Not* Soon after the inspector left the room. . . .)

> While I was surveying, the ice, which was sixteen inches thick, undulated under a slight wind like water (Henry David Thoreau, *Walden*). (*Not* While I was surveying the ice. . . .)

A comma can also make immediately clear whether a modifier goes with what precedes or with what follows: A great crowd of shoppers milled around inside, and outside hundreds more were storming the doors. (*Not* . . . milled around inside and outside. . . .)

In all the preceding examples there is justification other than clarity for using a comma. In the following sentence commas would simply make reading easier: "Another positive stop would be to require as many people as are able [,] to work for a living [,] and to find or create jobs for them," (Carll Tucker, *Saturday Review*). And a comma helps when a word is used twice in a row: What he does, does not concern me.

C 7

7.   For emphasis and contrast.   When *and* connects two words or phrases, there's no need to set them apart with a comma. But because a comma tends to keep distinct the elements it separates and to emphasize slightly the element that follows it, you may sometimes want to use commas for these purposes alone: "Savannah was a port, and a 'good town' as he remembered it" (Stanley Dance, *The World of Earl Hines*).

Here a comma is used for emphasis, and irony: "Midge Decter is disappointed, again" (Jane O'Reilly, *New York Times Book Review*).

C 8

8.   With main sentence elements.
a.   Subject and verb. Though it sometimes occurs in old-fashioned formal prose, don't use a comma between a subject and its verb: "All that democracy means [,] is as equal a participation in rights as is practicable" (James Fenimore Cooper, *The American Democrat*).
b.   Verb and object. Don't use a comma between a verb and its object.

(Words and phrases that must be set off by pairs of commas may, of course, come between subject and verb and between verb and object. See **4.**)

c. Compound predicates. Use a comma between the verbs of a compound predicate only when the sentence is so long and involved that it's difficult to read or when you feel a need for special emphasis or contrast. This is a sensible rule and one that many writers, teachers, and editors insist on, though in published prose the verbs in a compound predicate are frequently separated by a comma when no need for aid to the reader or for special emphasis or contrast is apparent: "Works by other writers in the past few months have reflected this fascination with language, but have delved deeper into the mysterious origins of words" (*Time*).

C9 **9. In conventional practice.**

a. In dates, to separate the day of the month from the year: May 26, 1981. When the day of the month isn't given, a comma may or may not be used: In September 1846 *or* In September, 1846. If a comma precedes the year, punctuation should also follow it: In September, 1846, the government fell.

b. In addresses, to separate small units from larger: Washington, D.C.; Chicago, Illinois; Hamilton, Madison County, New York; Berne, Switzerland.

c. After salutations in all but formal letters: Dear John,

d. To set off names in direct address: Spin it, Henry.

e. In figures, to separate thousands, millions, etc.: 4,672,342. In some styles no comma is used in figures with four digits: 2750. A comma should never be used in naming a year: 1812, *not* 1,812.

f. To separate degrees and titles from the names they follow: Donal O'Brien, D.V.M.; William Lamb, Viscount Melbourne. The comma before *Jr.* after a name is now sometimes omitted: Charles Evans Hughes [,] Jr.

g. After a weak exclamation like *well, why, oh:* Oh, what's the use?

h. Sometimes to show the omission of a word that's required to fill out a construction: He took the right-hand turn; I, the left.

C10 **10. With other marks of punctuation.**

a. When parentheses come at the end of a phrase or clause that's followed by a comma, put the comma after the *closing* parenthesis: After returning from Italy (in 1978), she lived in Oconomowoc.

b. Use a comma or a dash, not both.

c. For the use of commas with quotation marks, see **Quotation marks 4b, 4c.**

cs Comma splice

Revise the sentence marked by changing the comma to a semicolon or a period, or by inserting an appropriate conjunction, or by rephrasing to make a more satisfactory sentence.

A comma splice (comma blunder, comma fault) occurs when, without good reason, a comma alone is used to separate the independent clauses of a compound or a compound-complex sentence: He stared at his visitor, it was too dark to see who it was. Occasionally sentences punctuated in this way are deliberately constructed for an intended effect, like this series: "I was awed by this system, I believed in it, I respected its force" (Alfred Kazin, *A Walker in the City).* The term *comma splice* refers to uses of the comma that are not justified either by the matching structures of the clauses or by the close relationship of their content or by any rhetorical impact.

There are various ways to correct a comma splice:

1. **Replace the comma** with a period or semicolon.

He stared at his visitor, it was too dark to see who it was.

Revised: He stared at his visitor. It was too dark to see who it was.

This is the simplest remedy but not always the best one. Inserting a period in the following sentence would simply produce two weak sentences in place of one:

I think Americans should read this book, they would get a more accurate picture of problems in the Middle East.

Revised: I think Americans should read this book; they would get a more accurate picture of problems in the Middle East. (For a better revision, see **3.**)

2. **Join statements that belong together** with a conjunction that makes their relationship clear. If you choose a coordinating conjunction, you should probably keep the comma (see **Comma 1a**). If you choose a conjunctive adverb, replace the comma with a semicolon (see **Semicolon 1b**):

An increase in student fees would enable us to balance the budget, this is clearly not the time for it.

Revised: An increase in student fees would enable us to balance the budget, but this (*or* budget; however, this) is clearly not the time for it.

3. **Rewrite the sentence,** perhaps subordinating one of the clauses, perhaps making a single independent clause. Work to produce a good sentence, not just to correct the comma splice:

I think Americans should read this book, they would get a more accurate picture of problems in the Middle East.

Revised: I think Americans should read this book because it would give them a more accurate picture of problems in the Middle East.

One cell receives the stimulus from outside and transmits the impulse to the cell, this is known as the dendrite.

Revised: One part, known as the dendrite, receives the stimulus from outside and transmits the impulse to the cell.

If you can make a sure distinction between an independent clause and a dependent clause, you should find it easy to spot any comma splices in your sentences. Look first to see how many independent subject-verb combinations you have in each group of words punctuated as a single sentence. If there are two independent clauses, see if you have a connective between them. If there's no connective but only a comma, you've probably produced a comma splice. For exceptions, see **Comma 1d.** Compare **Fused sentence.**

Commands and requests

Direct commands are also called imperatives: Hurry up; Shut the door; Fill out the coupon and mail it today. Punctuate emphatic commands with an exclamation mark: Stop! Let's go! Punctuate less emphatic ones with a period: Stop at the next gas station.

Commands and requests are often expressed in the form of questions. Use question marks after those that you intend as questions: Would you be willing to take part in the program? Use periods after those you mean to be orders: Will you please report no later than 9:15.

committee

Committee is a collective noun, usually construed as singular. When the logic of the sentence makes it clear that you're not thinking of the committee as a single unit (The committee, men and women alike, were bustling around, collecting their papers and other belongings), it's better to use "the members of the committee."

Comparative form

Thinner and *more happily* are the comparative forms of *thin* and *happily*. See **Comparison of adjectives and adverbs.**

compare, contrast

Compare with *to* points out likenesses: He compared my writing to Allen's (said it was like his). *Compare* followed by *with* finds likenesses and differences: He compared my writing with Allen's (pointed out like and unlike traits). *Contrast* always points out differences.

When the things compared are of different classes, use *to:* He compared my stories to a sack of beans. In the common construction with the past participle, use either *to* or *with:* Compared with (*or* to) Allen's, mine is feeble. *In comparison* is followed by *with:* In comparison with Allen's, mine is feeble. *Contrast* ordinarily takes *with:* He contrasted my writing with Allen's. But *contrast* sometimes takes *to,* and *in contrast* usually does: In contrast to Allen's, my writing is magnificent.

Comparison and contrast

To compare and contrast is to establish the similarities and the differences between two or more objects, people, places, institutions, ideas, and so on. Comparing is a natural way of explaining. You can inform a reader about a subject that's unfamiliar to him by telling him how it's like and how it's unlike something he knows well. And you use contrast automatically in argument when you set out to prove that one thing is better than another.

To write a comparison, first select the points that are significant for your purpose. (If you're comparing makes of cars for potential purchasers of your own age, is cost a significant factor? Is safety? Fuel consumption? Speed? Color?) Then find out how your subjects (the makes you're comparing) are alike and how they differ in each of these respects. In organizing your discussion, you might treat one of your subjects *(A)* fully before taking up the corresponding points in another *(B)*. Or you might compare *A* and *B* point by point. Or you might set out all the likenesses between *A* and *B* and then all the differences, or the reverse. In any case, it's not enough to offer a collection of details about each of the subjects. You must work out the comparison, relating details about one to corresponding details about another, so that the reader understands the ways the subjects differ and the ways they're alike.

See **Logical thinking.**

Comp **Comparison of adjectives and adverbs**

Correct the fault in comparing the adjective or adverb marked.

To express degrees of what is named, adjectives and adverbs are compared—that is, their forms are changed by adding *-er* or *-est* to the root, or base, form *(long, longer, longest)* or by preceding it with *more* or *most (beautiful, more beautiful, most beautiful)* or with *less* or *least.*

1. Choosing the form. We say "a longer walk," not "a more long walk." We say "a more beautiful picture," not "a beautifuller picture."
a. To the root form (the positive degree), some adjectives and adverbs add *-er* to make the comparative degree, *-est* to make the superlative degree.

	Positive	*Comparative*	*Superlative*
Adjective	early	earlier	earliest
	hoarse	hoarser	hoarsest
	unhappy	unhappier	unhappiest
Adverb	fast	faster	fastest
	soon	sooner	soonest

b. Other adjectives make the comparative and superlative degrees by preceding the root form with *more, most.*

	Positive	*Comparative*	*Superlative*
Adjective	exquisite	more exquisite	most exquisite
	afraid	more afraid	most afraid
	pleasing	more pleasing	most pleasing
Adverb	comfortably	more comfortably	most comfortably
	hotly	more hotly	most hotly

Three-syllable adjectives and adverbs are ordinarily compared with *more* and *most,* one-syllable adjectives and adverbs with *-er* and *-est.* Two-syllable adjectives and adverbs are usually compared with *more* and *most,* but many can take either form: *able–abler, more able–ablest, most able; empty–emptier, more empty, emptiest, most empty.* When you're in doubt, *more* and *most* are the safer choices. In earlier times it was all right to use both methods of comparison at once, as in Shakespeare's "most unkindest cut of all," but double comparatives and double negatives are no longer standard English.

Some points of usage raised by irregular forms of comparison are discussed in **former, first–latter, last** and in **last, latest.**

2. Using the comparative. The comparative expresses a greater or lesser degree (It is *warmer* now) or makes specific comparison between two people or things (He was *kinder* [or *more kind*] than his brother). The things compared must be truly comparable:

Comparable: His salary was lower than a shoe clerk's (salary). *Or . . .* than that (*or* than the salary) of a shoe clerk.

Not comparable: His salary was lower than a shoe clerk.

(This rule holds true when the root form of the adjective is used: His salary was low, like a beginner's. *Not . . .* like a beginner.)

Logic calls for *other* with *any* in comparisons between a single unit and the group it belongs to: She's a better dancer than *any* of the *other* girls. But the comparative is frequently used when no actual comparison is involved: *higher education, older people, the lower depths.* In advertisements the job of providing a comparison is often left to the reader or listener: *cooler, fresher, stronger, faster, more economical*—than what?

3. Using the superlative.   In formal writing and in most general writing, the superlative is used to indicate the maximum or minimum degree of a quality among three or more people or things: She was the *calmest* one there; That's the *loudest* tie in the showcase. Informally, the superlative is common with two, and this usage isn't rare in general writing: Roy and Joe do push-ups to see who's *strongest;* Russia and China compete to see which can be *most critical* of the other's policies. Use of the superlative as a form of emphasis is also informal: She has the *loveliest* flowers; We saw the *best* show!

Don't use *other* to complete a superlative: Television won the largest audience for Shakespeare's plays that they had ever attracted in any (*not* any other) medium.

4. Comparing absolutes.   Logicians raise objections to the comparison of *black, dead, excellent, fatal, final, impossible, perfect, unique* on the grounds that there are no degrees of deadness or blackness or impossibility. But competent writers frequently compare these words: a *more equal* society, a *more complete* victory, a *more impossible* situation. And the Constitution speaks of "a more perfect union." Many absolutes are used figuratively with meanings that naturally admit comparison: This is the *deadest* town I was ever in. When applied to people, *black* and *white* are obviously not being used in a literal, absolute sense. See **Divided usage.**

Complement

In grammar, *complement* refers to the noun or adjective that completes the meaning of a linking verb and modifies the subject: He became *the real head of the business;* She was *busy.* See **Linking verbs, Predicate adjectives.**

complement, compliment

As a noun, *complement* means "that which completes or is called for" (a full complement). As a verb, it means "to make complete" or—of two things—"to fill out each other's lacks" (the scarf and blouse complemented each other perfectly). *Compliment* is the noun (He received many compliments for his work) and the verb (He complimented her on her victory) having to do with praise and congratulations.

Complex sentence

A complex sentence has one independent, or main, clause and one or more dependent clauses, ordinarily introduced by relative pronouns or subordinating conjunctions: She married the man *who* picked her up *when* she fell. See **Clauses.**

Compound-complex sentence

When one or more of the independent clauses of a compound sentence are modified by dependent clauses, the sentence is called compound-complex. Here the opening dependent clause modifies the first independent clause: "When its facilities were offered to Kansas State Teachers College, they were refused, for enrollment had already declined 500 below capacity" (John R. Silber, *Atlantic*). See **Clauses.**

Compound predicate

Two or more verbs with the same subject, together with their objects and modifiers, form a compound predicate: Ruth *wrote* and *mailed three letters.*

Compound predicates help make writing economical and can give it a brisk pace, as in this account of catching a fly ball: "I spun back to the wall, reached up, and pulled it in" (Robert H. Zieger, *Harper's*). See **Comma 8c.**

Compound sentence

A compound sentence contains two or more independent clauses.

1. With coordinating conjunction.   Usually the clauses of a compound sentence are connected by one of the coordinating conjunctions: "Lavin's stories are centered almost entirely on the lives of women, and they are informative in the most humane way" (Rosellen Brown, *Ms.*).

2. Without coordinating conjunction.   A compound sentence may have a semicolon instead of a coordinating conjunction between the clauses. Here semicolons join a series of independent clauses that are parallel in structure and closely related in meaning: "We will walk on our own feet; we will work with our own hands; we will speak our own minds" (Ralph Waldo Emerson, "The American Scholar"). For the use of a comma instead of a coordinating conjunction, see **Comma 1d.**

3. With conjunctive adverb.   The clauses of a compound sentence may be connected by a conjunctive adverb (*however, moreover, whereas, consequently, therefore,* and so on) that is preceded by a semicolon: FBI officials had proved themselves expert in publicizing the agency's successes; consequently, some local police gave FBI agents only grudging support.

See **Clauses, Conjunctive adverbs.**

Compound subject

Two or more elements standing as subjects of one verb make a compound subject: "Flake knives and scrapers, large core choppers, and one-handed grinding stones . . . characterize the tool kit'' (Dorothy K. Washburn, ''The American Southwest''). The verb following a compound subject is usually plural: Inflation and recession occurring simultaneously create stagflation. See **Agreement 1c.**

Compound words

Compound words are combinations of two or more words, usually written as one word or hyphenated: *doorknob, notwithstanding, quarter-hour, father-in-law, drugstore*. Some compounds continue to be written as separate words: *White House, high school, post office*. For the spelling of particular compound words, consult your dictionary. See **Group words, Hyphen, Plurals of nouns 5.**

comprise

Traditionally, *comprise* means ''consist of'' or ''include'': The whole comprises (*not* is comprised of) its parts. In current usage the nearly opposite senses of ''constitute,'' ''compose,'' and ''make up'' are very common: ''The four states that at one time comprised French Equatorial Africa . . . '' (Harold G. Marcus, *American Historical Review*). But many writers, editors, and teachers insist that *comprise* be used only in its traditional sense. Since it's a relatively formal word, the more general *make up* is a better choice in most contexts: The four states that at one time made up (*or* comprised) French Equatorial Africa . . . ; French Equatorial Africa was made up of (*or* comprised) what are now four separate states.

concept

Concept as a vogue word is often used where *idea* would be more appropriate, as in ''concepts for TV shows.'' See **Vogue words.**

Concrete words

Concrete words name things that can be seen and touched: *box, building*. See **Abstract language.**

Conditional clauses

A conditional clause states a condition (If she knows what she's talking about) that is necessary if what is expressed in the independent clause (there'll be more jobs next term) is to be true. Or it specifies an action (If the ransom is paid) that is necessary if what is expressed in the independent clause (the hostages will be freed) is to take place. *If, unless*, and *whether* are the subordinating conjunctions that most commonly begin conditional clauses. Somewhat more formal introductory words and phrases are *in case, provided, provided that, in the event that*.

1. For real or open conditions—statements of actual or reasonable conditions under which the main statement will hold true—use the indicative verb forms:

> *If the red light is on,* you know a train is in that block of tracks.
>
> He will be there *unless something happens to his car.*
>
> *Whether they come or not,* Kate will go just the same.

2. For hypothetical conditions—theoretical but still possible—use *should . . . would* or the past tense: *If he should offer another $100,* I would take it. Or *If he raised his offer,* I would take it.

3. For contrary-to-fact conditions—those that can't be met or are untrue—use the past tense of the verb if you're writing in a general style: If he *was* here, we would have seen him by now. In formal English, the plural form of the past tense, usually called the subjunctive, is firmly established in the first-person singular (If I *were* you . . .) and isn't uncommon in the third-person singular (If he *were* here . . .).
   See **if, whether; Subjunctive mood.**

Conjunctions

Conjunctions join words, phrases, clauses, or sentences. In this *Index* conjunctions are further defined and discussed according to their conventional classification:

> *Coordinating conjunctions* (*and, but, for,* etc.)
> *Correlative conjunctions* (*either . . . or, not only . . . but,* etc.)
> *Conjunctive adverbs* (*however, therefore, consequently,* etc.)
> *Subordinating conjunctions* (*as, because, since, so that, when,* etc.)

con͡j Conjunctions and style

Make the conjunction marked more accurate or more appropriate to the style of the passage.

1. Conjunctions and meaning. In everyday speech we get along with a relatively small number of conjunctions—*and, as, but, so, when,* and a few others—because we can indicate shades of meaning and exact relationships by pauses, tones, and gestures. In writing, we don't have these means of relating ideas, and we need to use connectives more thoughtfully.

Choose your conjunctions with care. Don't toss in *but* when there's no contrast between your statements (see **but 2**). Decide whether your meaning can be conveyed better by a coordinating conjunction or by a construction that uses the corresponding subordinating conjunction—*but* versus *though,* for example. And note distinctions between subordinating conjunctions. *As* can mean "because," but it's a weak *because* (see **as**). *While* can mean "although" or "whereas," but the core of its meaning is related to time. Sometimes, if your thinking has been logical and you've reproduced it on paper without skipping essential steps, the relationships are apparent, and a *therefore* or an *accordingly* will be unnecessary and unwelcome. See **Transition** and the articles on the particular conjunctions.

2.   Conjunctions and style.   Conjunctions should be appropriate to other traits of style. Often simple *but* is a better choice than *however:*

> The trail is easy walking as far as the canyon; from there on, however, it's no route for Sunday strollers.
>
> **Better:** . . . the canyon, but from there on. . . .

See **Conjunctive adverbs 1.**

Repeating a conjunction at the beginning of each item in a series makes each item distinct, avoids possible confusion, and gives the sentence strong rhythm and clear-cut parallelism:

> I took an old shutter and fixed a sort of porch roof on it, and nailed it to a locust tree nearby, and set the nest with the eggs carefully in it.—Wendell Berry, *The Long-Legged House*
>
> The tribal chants echoing from the seats were always fitting accompaniments to Mick's grunts and wails and hoots.—Robert Mazzocco, *New York Review of Books*

On the other hand, omitting *and* before the last element in a short series may build a strong climax:

> The most important of these, the most characteristic, the most misleading, is called *Some Glances at Current Linguistics.*—William H. Gass, *New Republic*

Or it may suggest that the series is only a sample, not a complete list:

> Many were the Northerners who, during and after the Civil War, went south to train, to educate, to rehabilitate Negro refugees and freedmen.—William H. Pease, *Journal of Southern History*

See **Conjunctive adverbs, Coordinating conjunctions, Correlative conjunctions, Subordinating conjunctions.** See also **Coordination, Subordination.**

Conjunctive adverbs

Conjunctive adverbs are used as connectives after a semicolon between independent clauses or after a period to introduce a new sentence. These are some of the most common:

accordingly	furthermore	moreover
also (see **too**)	hence	nevertheless
anyhow	however	otherwise
anyway (informal)	incidentally	still
besides	indeed	then
consequently	likewise	therefore

All these words are primarily adverbs. They become conjunctive adverbs when they join together, or provide connection:

Adverb: When they got back, he was *still* waiting.
Conjunctive adverb: The results were poor; *still,* we were not disheartened and set to work on the next batch with undiminished determination.

1.   Style.   Because conjunctive adverbs tend to be heavy connectives (*however,* for example, is much heavier than *but*), they're most appropriate in formal writing and in sentences of some length and complexity. In general writing they're more likely to serve as transitional devices between sentences than to connect clauses within a sentence. If you load your papers with conjunctive adverbs, you won't produce simple, straightforward English that's easy to read.

Note these appropriate and inappropriate uses:

The armored saurians, the dodo, and a few other extinct creatures are supposed to have become unviable through their exaggerated specialties; usually, however, such excesses are not reached.—Susanne K. Langer, *Philosophical Sketches.* (Appropriate with the formal sentence structure and vocabulary.)

In the morning I still felt sick; *nevertheless,* when the bugle sounded, I got up. (Inappropriately heavy in this simple context. Could substitute *but.* Better to rewrite as a complex sentence: Though I still felt sick the next morning, I got up when the bugle sounded.)

2.   Position.   By placing conjunctive adverbs inside their clauses instead of at the beginning, you give the initial stress to more important words. See the first example in **1.**

3.   Punctuation.   When a conjunctive adverb is placed inside a clause, it's often set off by commas. Whether it introduces or comes inside the second independent clause of a compound sentence, the two independent clauses are separated by a semicolon. See the second example in **1.**

Connotation

Connotation means the associations a word or phrase has, as distinguished from its denotation—what it refers to. Connotation makes the difference between *house* and *home,* between a *dutiful* child and an *obedient* one.

A writer needs to be conscious of what words connote as well as of what they denote. Although *flush* (in the sense "turn red") and *blush* are so close in meaning that they can often be substituted for each other, the overlap of the two words isn't complete. We say "He flushed with anger," but we don't say "He blushed with anger."

The context a word regularly occurs in, the variety of usage it belongs to, the prevailing social attitude toward what it refers to and toward the people who use it (politicians, advertisers, children) all contribute to the public connotations a word has. Beyond that are private connotations resulting from personal experiences. For one person *school* has connotations of confinement; for another, intellectual excitement; for still another, sociability.

Heavily connotative words are sometimes called slanted or loaded, and writers are sometimes urged to replace them with words that are more nearly neutral. The advice is not always sound. We use words not only to give information about things but also to express our feelings about them and to influence the attitudes of others. It's natural to describe an action we admire as *courageous* and one we deplore as *foolish* or *disgraceful*. Neutral terms are preferable only when we are in fact neutral or when the rhetorical situation calls for us to write as if we are.

See **Denotation.**

consensus

Consensus is a troublesome word. It's easy to misspell, and it tempts users to add *of opinion*. Since *consensus* means "agreement," *of opinion* simply repeats what the word already conveys. So let *consensus* (spelled with three *s*'s) do the job on its own.

Construction

A construction is a group of words that stand in some grammatical relationship to each other, like that of modifier and word modified (black cat), preposition and object (to the roof), or subject and predicate (They walked slowly). Any grammatical pattern may be spoken as of a construction.

contact

As a verb, *contact* means "get in touch with" (I was told to contact the superintendent). Like *get in touch with, contact* covers all means of communication (face-to-face, telephone, letter, cable, CB radio, etc.), and it's more economical—one word instead of four. But stylistically the word outrages some readers, perhaps because they continue to associate it with business jargon. See **Jargon.**

Context

The word *context* is used in different ways.

1. Verbal context. In writing, a sentence may provide the context for a word, a paragraph may provide the context for a sentence, and so on. The context is the setting—the combination of content and style—that gives meaning to what's being said and determines its appropriateness. Context is extremely important in conveying the sense in which a word is being used. For example, dictionaries record forty or more senses in which people use the word *check*, yet when *check* appears in specific contexts, as in the following sentences, we have no trouble understanding it:

> They were able to *check* the fire at the highway.
> The treasurer's books *check* with the vouchers.
> He drew a *check* for the entire amount.
> I like the tablecloth with the red-and-white *check*.
> He moved his bishop and shouted *"Check!"*
> She had difficulty holding her temper in *check*.
> *Check* your suitcase through to Seattle.

A great many words are used in more than one sense. To convey the particular meaning he intends, a writer must—and usually can—rely on the context. And besides establishing the denotative sense of the word (as illustrated with *check*), context gives clues to its connotation. We recognize this when we say, "By itself that remark might seem insulting, but in the context it couldn't possibly give offense."

2. The context of quotations. An honest writer makes sure that the quotations he uses are true to the context in which they originally occurred and that they accurately represent the ideas of the people who wrote or spoke them. Complaints by government officials that they've been quoted "out of context" are often justified.

3. Rhetorical context. Every piece of writing occurs in a rhetorical situation, or context, which includes the writer, the subject, the writer's purpose, and the audience. The choice of material, the organization, and the style of a good paper all reflect the writer's sense of the rhetorical context. See **Rhetorical situation.**

continual(ly), continuous(ly)

In the sense "uninterrupted," with reference to time, formal stylists prefer *continuous(ly)* (For weeks we observed the almost continuous eruption of the volcano), but *continual(ly)* is also used. In the sense "occurring rapidly and often," the situation is reversed—formal writers insist on *continual(ly)* (The governor broke his promises not just repeatedly but continually), but *continuous(ly)* too is standard.

Contractions

In writing, contractions are forms that show pronunciation, usually by the substitution of an apostrophe for one or more letters of the standard spelling: *can't, you're, I'm, don't, they've.* They occur regularly in informal usage but rarely appear in formal writing. In general usage a writer should use them or avoid them just as he makes other rhetorical choices, considering the rhythm of the particular sentence, whether the occasion calls for a relaxed or a restrained style, and how much distance he wants between himself and his readers. (In this book contractions are used, in part, to show that writing about a serious subject doesn't call for a style that keeps the audience at arm's length, if not out of reach.) Contractions are necessary in representing actual speech, as in dialog (but see **Apostrophe**). See **have 3.**

contrast, compare

Contrast points out differences; *compare to* points out likenesses; *compare with* does both. See **compare, contrast.**

controversial

Controversial (a controversial person, a controversial book) labels the subject a source of disagreement, of argument. But there can be disagreement about almost any subject, and no one needs to be told that certain subjects (abortion, capital punishment) and individuals are controversial. So use the label sparingly, and don't use it as a warning. Controversy is often what makes a subject interesting enough to write about.

convince, persuade

For a long time some uses of *convince* and *persuade* have overlapped: She persuaded (*or* convinced) me of the necessity for action; She convinced (*or* persuaded) me that I should act. *Convince* is now common in still a third context, where *persuade* is traditional:

> It must have contributed to the general merriment when later it was written
> . . . that the invasion failed because Adlai Stevenson convinced the President
> to cancel the air strikes so vital to the success of the invasion.—Ward Just,
> *New York Times Book Review*

The use of "convince . . . to" instead of "persuade . . . to" (persuaded the President to cancel) is deplored by many conservative stylists.

Coordinate

Two or more grammatically equivalent words, phrases, or clauses are said to be coordinate: *bread* and *butter; in the sink* or *on the stove; dancing, singing, laughing; When he lectured* and *when he prayed,* everyone listened; *He wrenched his back,* and *she broke her leg.*

Coordinating conjunctions

The coordinating conjunctions, *and, but, for, nor, or, so,* and *yet,* are used to connect two or more elements of equal grammatical rank:

> *Words:* books *and* papers; books, pamphlets, *or* magazines
>
> *Phrases:* in one ear *and* out the other
>
> *Dependent clauses:* She . . . wrote to young Lewis Rutherford cheerfully enough that his sister looked lovely *and* that the new baby was delightful.— R. W. B. Lewis, *Edith Wharton*
>
> *Independent clauses:* There is no evidence that Elizabeth had much taste for painting; *but* she loved pictures of herself.—Horace Walpole, *Anecdotes of Painting in England*
>
> *Sentences:* Perhaps I should wish that I had liked him better. *But* I do not wish it.—Renata Adler, *New Yorker*

See **Conjunctions and style, Coordination, Series.**

Coord Coordination

Correct the faulty coordination.

Faulty coordination is not a lapse in grammar or usage. It's a failure to make logical relationships clear. Coordination is faulty when, in a particular context, the material calls for a relationship or emphasis different from the one implied by the writer's use or arrangement of independent clauses.

1.   Faulty coordination may result from joining two statements that don't belong together: The condition of the house is deplorable, and the dining nook seats six comfortably. Revision should put the two statements in separate—and separated—sentences.

2.   Sometimes faulty coordination can be corrected by turning one of the independent clauses into a dependent clause. ''He went to France for the summer, and his novel was published'' suggests a causal relationship between his going to France and the publication of his novel. In some contexts this might make sense. But if the only relationship is a temporal one—two events happening at the same time but not otherwise related—the sentence needs to be revised: "During his summer in France, his novel was published,'' or "At the time his novel was published, he was spending the summer in France,'' or in some other way.

3.   Coordination may be confusing or misleading as in the example above. Sometimes it's simply ineffective:

> When I reached the intersection, I found a group of people gathered around a wrecked car. The left front tire had blown, and the car had gone out of control and run into a tree, and the driver was obviously dead.

The independent clause "the driver was obviously dead'' needs to be taken out of the coordinate relationship and made into a separate sentence. Left in the series, it implies that the death of the driver had no more importance than the blowout and the crash.

See **Subordination.**

Correlative conjunctions

Some coordinating conjunctions are used in pairs: *both . . . and, either . . . or, neither . . . nor, not only . . . but also, whether . . . or.* Of these correlatives, *neither . . . nor* and *not only . . . but also* show more conscious planning than is common in informal or general English: "The attack not only had left him blind, and in need of plastic surgery which would require years to complete, but also had deprived him of his sense of smell'' (Joe McGinniss, *Going to Extremes*).

Like coordinating conjunctions, correlatives normally join elements of the same grammatical rank:

> *Nouns:* He said that both *the novel* and *the play* were badly written.
>
> *Adjectives:* She must have been either *drunk* or *crazy.*
>
> *Prepositional phrases:* They can be had not only *in the usual sizes* but *in the outsizes.*
>
> *Verb phrases:* The wind scoop not only *caught the cool breezes* but also *picked up the captain's conversation.*
>
> *Clauses:* Whether *Mitch thumbed a ride through the mountains* or *Jenny made the long bus trip,* they were determined to be together during the vacation.

Like similar rules, the rule that constructions built on correlative conjunctions must be strictly parallel should be broken when it gets in the way of natural, rhythmic expression.

See **Shifted constructions.**

could(n't) care less

Formerly (and too frequently) a lack of concern was expressed by "I couldn't care less." Recently the negative has been dropped, and "I could care less" is used to mean the same thing: "kids who never heard of Little Richard and could care less" (Ellen Willis, *New Yorker*). Neither form is suited to college writing, except perhaps to point up triteness in dialog.

Count nouns

Count nouns name things that can be counted as separate units. See **Mass nouns, Nouns 3c.**

couple

The primary meaning of the collective noun *couple* is "a pair, two persons or things associated in some way," as in "a married couple." In general and informal usage *couple* is equivalent to the numeral *two* (a couple of pencils) or to *a few* (a couple of minutes). The *of* is frequently omitted in speech and informal writing and sometimes in general: "Re-established as a teacher, he brought forth a couple more essays on education" (Wallace Stegner, *The Uneasy Chair: A Biography of Bernard DeVoto*). Omission of the *of* before a noun (He wrote a couple essays) offends many more readers. See **Collective nouns.**

Course names

In general discussions, only the names of college subjects that are proper nouns or proper adjectives are capitalized. In writing a list of courses that includes one or more of these terms, all the course names may be capitalized for consistency, but usually the distinction is kept: I am taking biology, chemistry, European history, English composition, and French. Names of departments are capitalized (the Department of Psychology), and so are the names of subjects when accompanied by a course number (History 347).

credibility

In journalese, *credibility* ("believability") was joined to the vogue word *gap* to refer to public loss of faith in President Johnson's statements about the Vietnam War. In the Nixon administration the gap became a gulf, and *gap* went out of vogue. But *credibility* moved into officialese and flourished. Both writers and readers should remember that *honesty* and *credibility* are by no means synonymous. In college papers it's better to say that a person's word isn't trusted, or that he lies, than to say he lacks credibility.

criterion, criteria

Criteria is heard so often, particularly in college classrooms, that it's possible to forget the singular form *criterion*. As a result we run into references to "this criteria" or read that some criteria "is important." Base your judgment on *a criterion* or on *several criteria* (or *criterions*).

Cumulative sentence

A cumulative sentence makes its main statement at or near the beginning, usually in a short independent clause, and then goes on to add details in modifiers that are detachable. The modifiers may be more or less parallel to each other:

> *Ragtime* is a unique and beautiful work of art about American destiny, built of fact and logical fantasy, governed by music heard and sensed, responsive to cinema both as method and historical datum, shaken by a continental pulse.—Stanley Kauffman, *Saturday Review*

> . . . there are those of us for whom the best part of a baseball game is not the action, but the prelude—the rattle of the bat against the spiked shoes to remove mud clods, the pulling of caps, the peerings of pitcher and catcher, the waggles of the upraised bat as it explores the air through which the ball soon is humming, the hitching of the umpire's chest protector, the unwinding of the pitcher's body.—Heywood Hale Broun, *Travel & Leisure*

Or they may be built into each other:

> The cars have been piling into the infield by the hundreds, parking in there on the clay and the grass, every whichway, angled down and angled up, this way and that, where the ground is uneven, these beautiful blazing brand new cars with the sun exploding off the windshields and the baked enamel and the glassy lacquer, hundreds, thousands of cars stacked this way and that in the infield with the sun boiling down and no shade, none at all, just a couple of Coca-Cola stands out there.—Tom Wolfe, *Esquire*

As the last example shows, the cumulative sentence offers a way of clustering or massing details. Wolfe's sentence does the work of a dozen on the subject-verb-object pattern. Because it observes the natural order of speech—main statement first, then qualifications and particulars—a cumulative sentence can and often does give the impression of ease and naturalness. But unless the modifiers add strength or richness, or support the initial assertion, the sentence may wander off into insignificant or irrelevant detail. In itself, a cumulative sentence is neither good nor bad. What counts is the skill with which it's constructed and the effect that it produces.

Compare **Periodic sentence.**

cupfuls, cupsful

Cupfuls is usual. See **-ful, full.**

curriculum

Curriculum (the courses offered or the courses required in a field of study) has the Latin plural *curricula* and the English plural *curriculums*. The adjective is *curricular*. The compound adjective with *extra* is usually written as one word: *extracurricular*.

D

ᗞᗰ Dangling modifiers

Revise the sentence so that the expression marked is clearly related to the word it is intended to modify.

A phrase is said to dangle, or to be misrelated, if its position makes it seem to modify a word that it can't sensibly modify or if, in a context that demands an explicit relationship, it has no clear relation to any word in the sentence.

In the sentence "Looking farther to the left, we saw the spire of a church," *looking* obviously modifies *we*. If the phrase "looking farther to the left" is turned into a clause, *we* is the subject of the verb: [*We* were] looking farther to the left. That is, the reconstructed subject is identical with the subject of the main clause. When the phrase does *not* refer to the subject—that is, when the phrase has a different subject from the subject of the main clause—then the modifier dangles.

In the sentence "To get the most out of a sport, the equipment must be in perfect condition," reconstruction of the subject of the introductory phrase would produce something like "[For *someone*] to get the most out of a sport, *the equipment* must be in perfect condition." But since *someone* is different from *equipment*, it can't safely be omitted. If the sentence "At eleven, my family moved to Denver" is reconstructed, it reads "[When *I* was] eleven, *my family* moved to Denver." *I* doesn't equal *my family*, so *I* should not be left out.

In the following examples, try to reconstruct the subject of the introductory phrase:

Upon telling my story to my adviser, he stopped and thought.

Born in England in 1853, John MacDowell's seafaring activities began after he had migrated to this country.

In both the examples, the introductory phrase dangles. In the second, the phrase refers to a noun—*MacDowell*—that is represented only by its possessive form. This type of dangling modifier frequently appears in print.

Modifiers that dangle may also follow the independent clause: Many signs read "Visit Our Snake Farm," driving toward the city.

You should avoid dangling modifiers in your writing chiefly because educated readers don't expect to find them. As a rule there's no real question of the intended meaning of the sentence, and in context the dangling phrases are not apt to be conspicuously awkward or as nonsensical as they appear in isolation. But they're distracting in any writing that's meant to be read carefully. And by sometimes forcing the reader to search for or guess at the related noun, they can make a piece of writing needlessly difficult.

Such dangling constructions shouldn't be confused with absolute phrases, in which the phrase has its own subject. Here, for comparison, are an absolute phrase, a correct modifier, and a dangling modifier:

Absolute phrases: The car paid for with my last dollar, I was at last out of debt.

Correct modifier: Paid for with my last dollar, the car became my first piece of personal property.

Dangling modifier: Paid for with my last dollar, I drove the car away.

Though prepositional phrases sometimes dangle—"As an institution, he cordially detested the Spanish Church" (Scott Donaldson, *By Force of Will: The Life and Art of Ernest Hemingway*)—the phrases that cause most trouble are those that begin with participles or infinitives or that contain gerunds. So in revising your papers, examine every verbal phrase. If you continue to have trouble relating such phrases to the words they should modify, you might try giving them up and using clauses instead.

See **Absolute phrases, Gerunds, Infinitives, Participles.**

Dash

The dash—typed as two hyphens without space before or after—can be used singly to link a following word or word group to the main structure of the sentence or in pairs to enclose a word or word group that interrupts the main structure. Use enclosing dashes when you want greater separation from the core of the sentence than enclosing commas would provide but less separation—or less formality—than you'd get with parentheses.

If used sparingly, the dash suggests a definite tone, often a note of surprise or an emphasis equivalent to a mild exclamation. If used regularly in place of commas, colons, and semicolons, it loses all its distinctiveness and becomes a sloppy substitute for conventional punctuation. At its best the dash is a lively, emphatic mark.

1.   Before a kicker.   The single dash is often used to throw emphasis on what follows, which may be dramatic, ironic, humorous:

> The old nations still live in the hearts of men, and love of the European nation is not yet born—if it ever will be.—Raymond Aron, *Daedalus*

> For that matter, none of the Doyles of Chris's generation had children—including my mother.—Hugh Leonard, *Home Before Night*

2.   Before a summary or illustration.   The dash is used singly or in pairs with word groups that summarize what's just been said or provide details or examples:

> It takes a cataclysm—an invasion, a plague, or some other communal disaster—to open their eyes to the transitoriness of the "eternal order."—Eric Hoffer, *The True Believer*

> He was strongly in favor of peace—that is, he liked his wars to be fought at a distance and, if possible, in the name of God.—George Dangerfield, *The Death of Liberal England*

3.   Between independent clauses.   A dash is sometimes used to link independent clauses when the second expands, develops, completes, or makes a surprising addition to the first. In this function a dash is less formal than a colon:

> Bessie was no longer the Queen of the Blues—she was the Empress.—Chris Albertson, *Bessie*

> In one respect, Welles was unique among the Cabinet members—he did not think himself a better man than the President.—Margaret Leech, *Reveille in Washington*

4.   Enclosing interrupting elements.   Dashes are used to set off words and word groups, including complete sentences, that break with the main structure of the sentence:

> Fitzgerald's people believed in their world—it really mattered who won the Princeton-Harvard game, it really meant something to appear at the theatre or the opera—and because they believed in their world they owned it.—Frank Conroy, *Esquire*

data

Formal usage follows the Latin, treating *datum* as singular and *data* as plural. In general usage *datum* is rare, and *data* is treated as a collective noun. So used, it takes a singular verb to emphasize the whole—"Data so far available makes it seem doubtful" (John Mecklin, *Fortune*)—and a plural verb to emphasize the parts—"There were still a good many data in the 33–page report" (William H. Honan, *New York Times Magazine*).

Dates

The typical American form of writing dates is "August 19, 1983." The form "19 August 1983" prevails in British usage and American military usage and is gaining popularity in the United States. If the full date is given within a sentence, the year is usually set off by commas. If the day of the week is also given, it's separated from the month by a comma: The legislature met on Wednesday, December 13, 1905. When only month and year are given, no commas are necessary (In August 1983 he died), though formal stylists often use them.

The year is not written out in words except in formal social announcements, invitations, wills, and some other ceremonial situations and at the beginning of a sentence—and most writers manage to avoid beginning sentences with the year. Expressions like "January in the year 1885" waste words: "January 1885" is enough. In business writing and references, months having more than four or five letters are often abbreviated: Jan. 3, 1970.

In writing dates in figures only, American practice is month-day-year: 9/17/76. European practice is day-month-year, sometimes with the month in Roman numerals: 17–IX–76.

Deadwood

Words or phrases that add nothing to the meaning or effectiveness of a statement are deadwood. See **Wordiness.**

Declension

As applied to the English language, *declension* means the list or listing of the forms of nouns and pronouns to show number, gender, and case. See **Case, Gender, Inflection, Nouns, Number, Pronouns.**

Deduction

Deduction is the process of drawing a conclusion from propositions known to be true, or accepted as true, or assumed to be true. You're reasoning deductively when you notice a ring around the moon and say, "We're in for some bad weather." Your unspoken premise, based on your own experience or on what you've read or heard, is that the appearance of a ring around the moon means that bad weather is bound to follow. From two related propositions—(1) a ring around the moon forecasts bad weather and (2) there's a ring around the moon—an inevitable conclusion is drawn: the weather will be bad.

For the conclusion of a deductive train of reasoning to be both valid and true, correct inferences must be made from true premises. See **Fallacies, Logical thinking, Syllogisms.** Compare **Induction.**

Deep structure

Transformational grammarians distinguish between the surface form of a sentence and the more abstract relationships in its deep structure. In the five sentences "Bill bought Jane a stereo," "Bill bought a stereo for Jane," "Jane was bought a stereo by Bill," "A stereo was bought for Jane by Bill," and "It was a stereo that Bill bought for Jane," the surface subjects are *Bill, Bill, Jane, stereo,* and *it.* But at a deeper level all the sentences have the same subject, or agent—Bill—since Bill did the buying regardless of the form the expression of the fact is given.

Such a concept of sentences may enlarge your view of the sentences you write. You can experiment with ways of expressing the same deep grammatical relationships through different surface structures, noting the varying rhetorical effects. The sentences about Bill and Jane and the stereo offer an example. Each of these could also be embedded in a larger structure in various ways:

> When Bill bought Jane a stereo, he surprised her.
> Bill's buying Jane a stereo surprised her.
> Jane was surprised by Bill's buying her a stereo.
> That Bill bought Jane a stereo surprised her.
> For Bill to have bought Jane a stereo surprised her.
> The buying of a stereo for her by Bill surprised Jane.

These are only a few of the possibilities. Usually such considerations as focus, tone, transition between sentences, and the rhythm of the sentence in its context will help you choose between one surface structure and another.
See **Clauses 2, Grammar 3c.**

Definition

1. Types of definition.   Definitions are of two main kinds.
a.   A lexical, or dictionary, definition tells how a word is used in different contexts. Lexical definitions that appear in everyday prose often use the verb *means* or *expresses* or, when connotations are being emphasized, *suggests: expectorate* means "spit"; *hooked,* applied to drug use, suggests hopeless addiction.

b. A real definition (sometimes called a formal definition) identifies the essential characteristics of the thing the word refers to. It joins subject and predicate with a form of the verb *be* on the model of the equation

term-to-be-defined	=	*genus*	+	*differentia(e)*
A ballad	is	a song		that tells a story

Thus in "Logic is a specialized language dealing with the relationship of truth and falsity within a language" (Dwight Bolinger), *language* is the genus and the two differentiae (distinguishing characteristics) are *specialized* and *dealing with the relationship of truth and falsity within a language*.

Logicians have formulated rules for real definitions. One is that the definition must include all things designated by the term but exclude anything the term doesn't properly apply to. Thus "A bachelor is a person who is unmarried" is unsatisfactory because the genus is too broad. In "A shoe is a leather covering for the foot," one of the differentiae—*leather*—is too restrictive. Shoes can be made of various materials.

Other traditional rules are these: A definition should not be circular (Hostility is the state of being hostile). Except when loss or lack is a distinguishing characteristic (as in *baldhead* and *bastard*), a term should not be defined negatively (Liberty is the absence of restraint). A term should not be defined metaphorically (Television is the opiate of the people), nor should a term be defined by a synonym (A pail is a bucket).

These rules have all been laid down in the interest of precision, and in writing assignments that call for precision—as in answering examination questions on the special terms of a subject matter—you should observe them. But not all definitions require the rigor of formal logic, and often you'll want to say more about a term than can be compressed into the genus + differentiae formula.

2. Definition in exposition and argument.   As a writer, you'll have occasion to use both lexical and real definitions. When you do, you should make clear which kind you're using.

a. In the stipulative definition, a variety of lexical definition, the writer gives a word a special, limited sense that is necessary for his specific purpose:

> I do not use the word "myth" to imply something entirely false. Rather, I use it to connote a complex of profoundly held attitudes and values which condition the way men view the world and understand their experience.—Richard Weiss, *The American Myth of Success*

A stipulative definition shouldn't be so remote from ordinary usage that it won't be taken seriously. Most readers will go along with the writer who says, "In this paper I will use the word *teenager* to include twenty-year-olds," but they'll probably stop reading if they find, "In this paper *teenager* means everybody who knows what's really happening."

b.   An extended definition gives information about the essential nature of a thing, like the one-sentence formal definition, but it's not restricted to the processes of classification and division that yield the genus and differentiae. It may use *description,* telling what a thing looks like; *chronology,* giving its origin and development; *example,* giving instances of it; *comparison,* saying what it's like; *contrast,* saying what it's not; *causal analysis,* indicating what circumstances produced it and what consequences it has; and *testimony,* telling what authorities have said about it. Etymologies (histories of words) and synonyms may also be used to develop a definition. What the central elements are depends on what's being defined and also on where the writer's interest lies. A psychologist and a biologist define *man* in different ways.

An extended definition may be simply explanatory, with the aim of giving information about the subject in a readable, interesting essay. Or it may pave the way for further analysis. Once he's established his definition of *comedy,* a writer can go on to show that a new play or movie is, or is not, a comedy. Defining is also one way of conducting an argument. When opponents of legalized abortion argue that abortion is murder and its proponents argue that it's not, the issue is one of definition. Defining is often geared not to the purpose of explaining but to proving that a belief is sound or a policy wise.

3.   Phrasing a definition.   When a definition is presented in a separate sentence, the subject and the complement should normally be the same part of speech—noun matched by noun, adjective by adjective, and so on. In "Defining is to locate a thing in its class and then separate it from other members of the class," the meaning is clear, but the sentence would be easier to read if the two parts matched: "To define is to locate . . ." or "Defining is locating . . . and then separating. . . ."

Definitions that begin with *where* or *when* (Erosion is when rain washes away the topsoil) are objected to in formal contexts. But they occasionally occur in literary works of established reputation—in this example, metaphorically: "Morning is when I am awake and there is a dawn in me" (Henry David Thoreau, *Walden*). See **when, where.**

Degrees

Ordinarily, academic degrees are not given with a person's name except in college publications, reference works, and articles and letters where the degrees offer proof of competence in a particular field, as in a physician's comment on a medical matter. When used, the names of the degrees are abbreviated, and the abbreviations are separated from the person's name by a comma. In alumni publications they're often followed by the year in which the degrees were granted:

Harvey N. Probst, A.B. (*or* B.A.)   Harvey N. Probst, A.B. '38
Jane Thomson, Ph.D.   Jane Thomson, Ph.D. '81
Royce Walton, M.B.A., was master of ceremonies.

As a rule, except in reference lists, only the highest degree in an academic professional field is mentioned. If the institution granting the degree is named, the following form is usual: George H. Cook, A.B. (Grinnell), A.M. (Indiana), Ph.D. (Chicago).

Demonstrative adjectives and pronouns

This, that, these, and *those* are traditionally called demonstrative adjectives or demonstrative pronouns, according to their use in a sentence:

> *Adjectives: This* car is new. *Those* people never think of others.
> *Pronouns: These* cost more than *those. That*'s a good idea.

See **Determiners; kind, sort; Pronouns 6; that; this.**

Denotation

The denotation of a word is what the word refers to, as described in a dictionary definition: fuel = a substance that is burned to produce heat or power. When heating oil is in short supply or gasoline doubles in price, *fuel* takes on overtones, or shades of meaning, that go far beyond this literal definition. See **Connotation.**

Dependent clauses

A dependent, or subordinate, clause has a subject and verb but can't normally stand alone as a sentence: If he comes today. (In some contexts a dependent clause can stand as a sentence: If we had only called!) See **Clauses.**

Description

Description usually deals with the visible and tangible, telling how a thing looks or feels or tastes or smells. Abstractions can be described, too, but a writer who undertakes to produce a word picture of grief or pride or chaos is likely to find that he can best present them in terms of physical sensations. Description feeds on concrete detail.

Although most common in narration, description is used in all types of writing. Discussions of all subjects, except perhaps the most theoretical, include patches of description, for only description can help the reader visualize the subject or otherwise share the writer's sensory experience.

1. **Kinds of description.**   In describing an object or a scene, the writer may try to present what any impartial observer would see, to come as close as he can to putting into words the image a camera would record. Or he may try to present a scene as it appears to an observer whose perception is highly colored by emotion—for example, a fire in which he was temporarily trapped or a fire as he imagines it appeared to someone who was trapped in it. Thus descriptions range from the precise, informative reports of technical writing to impressionistic sketches.

2. **The function of details.**   Most descriptive passages fall somewhere between factual reporting and emotional (or imaginative) recreating. The writer tries to provide a picture of reality so clear that the actual scene or object would be immediately recognizable. In addition, he tries to make the reader aware of how the writer (or the writer's imagined observer) feels about it and understand why he feels as he does.

Such description, if successful, will make the subject particular and individual. Second Beach, in Middletown, Rhode Island, won't be described in details that apply equally well to other beaches on the Atlantic coast. Instead, the writer will search out the details which give that beach its special character and convey them in words which communicate what he feels as well as what he perceives. It's always best to make the details evoke the feelings. Outright statements of emotions (I was scared by the big surf) or judgments (The beach is best in late September) are unconvincing on their own. If the writer supplies the details that triggered the emotions or that lead to the judgments, such assertions become unnecessary. The appropriate generalization will form in the reader's mind. Good description shows; it doesn't need to tell.

3. **The selection and organization of details.**   When an observer who has looked long and hard at his subject (even in memory) begins to write about it, he has far more details than he can use. Selection is vital. A crowd of unrelated details will only bewilder the reader. The beachcomber won't name all the shore birds any more than he'll count the waves. Which birds? What details about the sea? Leo Rockas gives a clue: "The night club in Mozambique needs only be plainly presented; the corner supermarket had better be invested with novelty." As in every writing situation, then, the audience must be taken into account. What's commonplace to one group will be new and strange to another.

How details are organized in a description should be determined by the subject and the writer's purpose. Does the reader need to understand the spatial relations in order to picture the scene? The directions must be made clear through the use of indicators such as *here, there, on top, in the middle, below, to the left, on the right, beyond, in the distance, on the horizon.*

4. The language of description.   Again, selection counts. Descriptive prose should be neither flat nor overexcited. A rush of adjectives may call attention away from the scene to the writing. The language should suit the subject and the feelings the subject is intended to arouse. Details can be conveyed most directly and compellingly in language that's concrete and specific. Concrete diction gives things color, shape, and texture. Specific terms given them particularity and individuality.

See **Abstract language, Adjectives and style, Details, Point of view.**

det Details

Develop the passage or the topic more fully by giving pertinent details.

The symbol *det* is shorthand for "Give an example" or "What's your evidence?" or "Make this specific" or "Don't just *say* the house is in bad condition; make me *see* that it is." In revising a paper so marked, you need to supply particulars that will make your ideas or impressions clearer, your argument more convincing, or your essay more readable.

The details of a physical object are its parts (the *webbed feet* of a duck) or its attributes or qualities (*scorching* wind, *smooth* leather). The details of an abstraction like pride are the words and attitudes and actions that justify our saying that someone is proud. The details of a novel are specifics of plot, character, style, and so on. Thus the details of any subject are its particulars. In a good paper they fit together, making a pattern, leading to a generalization, or encouraging the reader to draw an inference. Besides giving substance to a paper, details make writing lively, so that it captures and holds the reader's interest. See **Description, Induction.**

Determiners

Some grammars apply the label *determiners* to a group of words, other than descriptive adjectives, that precede nouns. The group usually includes what traditional grammars call articles, demonstrative adjectives, and possessive pronouns (or adjectives), as well as such words as *some, few, several, many, each, both, half, first,* and *last.* In the phrase "*the first two* installments," the three italicized words are determiners.

Dialects

A dialect is the speech (sounds, forms, meanings) characteristic of a fairly definite region or group. It is speech that doesn't attract attention to itself among the inhabitants of a region (regional dialect) or among members of a group (group or class dialect) but that an outsider would notice immediately. All of us speak dialects of one sort or another.

The term *dialect* is also applied to written expression: there are written dialects as well as speech dialects. Standard written English, based on educated middle-class usage, is the appropriate dialect to use in college work.

1. Dialects and style.   Though most of the writing you do in college will follow the rules and conventions of standard written English, you shouldn't set out to rid your writing of all the words and word forms and phrases of the regional dialect or other group dialect you grew up with. The guiding principle should be appropriateness. What are you writing about? Who's your audience? If you're reminiscing about your childhood or describing your homesickness, don't resist an impulse to use dialectal expressions. If your instructor and your classmates are familiar with the dialect you grew up using, you may also use it successfully in other papers. The more formal and impersonal your topic and the broader your audience, the less appropriate dialectal usages will be. In any circumstances, avoid those that are likely to mystify your readers or strike them as simply ungrammatical. See **grammatical, ungrammatical.**

2. Dialects and standardization.   In modern times English has undergone two developments that at first seem contradictory. On the one hand, large groups of English speakers have migrated from England, and new national varieties of English have arisen in North America, Australia, New Zealand, India, and Africa. But none has diverged far enough from the parent language to be considered a separate tongue, as English itself separated from its Germanic ancestors. The reason history failed to repeat itself is the second major development in Modern English—standardization. In England a relatively uniform dialect spread to all parts of the island kingdom. In other English-speaking nations similar tendencies toward standardization have kept the separate national varieties basically alike.

American English has never diverged far from the parent language, partly because of cultural contacts, partly because of standardizing processes. Growing nationalism after the Revolution led Americans to predict, and eagerly expect, a new American language, but concern for preserving national unity checked the growth of American dialects. "A national language is a band of national union," wrote Noah Webster, and as textbook writer for the new nation, he pushed a standard of general—that is, national—custom.

American standardization has tended to concentrate on the written word and to pay more attention to grammar than to pronunciation. The country has never had an official standard of pronunciation, based on the speech of a single locale or class. Southern, Northern, and Western speakers may sound different but still speak standard American English. The same is not true of the Southerner, Northerner, or Westerner who says "He don't never do that."

Class dialects do exist in the United States. When we use the terms *standard* and *nonstandard* English, we refer to the social status of the speakers of each, not to good or bad qualities inherent in the dialects themselves. And while it's true that standard English in the United States has been flexible and tolerant of regional variation and of importations from nonstandard, dialect conflict has emerged. Heavy migration to Northern cities, particularly from the South and South-Midlands, has brought Northern and Southern speakers into close contact. Because many of the migrants have been poor and ill-educated, their speech—regional in origin—has been taken as indicative of their class. Thus in many Northern cities, Southern speech is equated with nonstandard speech. Hostility toward the new migrant, toward his class or race, attaches easily to his language. In return, the migrant may see in Webster's "general custom" only the values of an oppressive class.

d   **Diction**

Replace the word marked with one that is more exact, more appropriate, or more effective.

Diction means choice of words. Good diction is exact, appropriate, and effective. Faulty diction either doesn't convey the writer's meaning fully or accurately or in some other way fails to meet the reader's expectations.

1.   Choose the exact word.   The exact word is the one that conveys better than any other the meaning you intend. Some mistakes in word choice result from confusing two words that resemble each other in some way: *delusion* for *illusion, predominate* for *predominant.* Others result from confusing two words that, though similar in basic meaning, are not interchangeable in all contexts. We can speak of a *durable* friendship or a *lasting* friendship, but though we may describe shoes as *durable,* we don't say they're *lasting.* Idiom allows "the oldest existing manuscript" but not "the oldest living manuscript."

   In some instances, finding the exact word means looking for a more specific one (*complained* is more specific and may be a better choice than *remarked*). Often it means settling for a simpler expression. If you reach for a fancy phrase, you may come up with one that has nothing to do with your meaning: Because of pressure to do well on examinations, a *disquieting aura pervades* me even when I am relaxing. See **Connotation, Dictionaries, Idiom, Meaning, Wrong word.**

2.   Choose the appropriate word.   The words you choose should fit both your subject and your relationship with your audience. If your subject is technical, complex, serious, and if you're addressing readers who know something about it and want to learn more, you'll probably use a rather formal vocabulary. If your subject is light or humorous and if you know your readers well or want to establish a sense of intimacy with them, you'll express yourself more informally.

Though a style can certainly be too informal, probably the most common fault in college papers is inappropriate formality—"big" words selected more to impress the reader than to express meaning. "Big" words needn't be long; *deem* for *think* is as "big" as *domicile* for *house.* They're "big" in the sense of "pretentious"—too fancy for the writer or the audience or the subject. Such words as *ignominious, cantankerous, lachrymose, inscrutable, mortified,* and *chronicled* can be "big" in one context and not in another.

You can catch the "big" words in what you write by reading your papers aloud. If you've used words that you'd be unlikely to speak in or out of the classroom, reconsider them. See if you can't substitute words that are just as precise but more natural to you.

Though formal, general, and informal English overlap and are frequently mixed in print, you can seriously weaken what you write if you mix them carelessly. When informal name-calling interrupts a thoughtful paper on welfare, when high-flown poetic clichés break the mood of an honest piece of descriptive writing, when *know-how* is applied to a great artist's technique or *finalize* to a composer's efforts, readers will be distracted and disturbed. If you mix usage deliberately, have a good reason for doing so— to amuse or startle your reader, perhaps, or to emphasize the point you're making. Keep your audience in mind, and avoid overkill. If you find yourself being criticized for mixing usage, read and reread your papers before turning them in, and maybe ask a friend to read them, too, with an eye open for sore thumbs and an ear cocked for sour notes.

See **Dialects, "Fine" writing, Formal English, Informal English.**

3. Choose the effective word.   If your words convey your meaning accurately and if they're appropriate to the rhetorical situation, your diction will be competent, and it may be effective as well. But you'll probably move beyond competence only if you pay some attention to style. Effectiveness in writing factual prose nearly always means choosing words that convey your meaning directly and economically. But that isn't to say that you should always pick the shortest, plainest words you can find and use them in the simplest way. In a particular writing job you may find it effective to repeat a word or put it to a new use, or to choose a word for its sound as well as its sense.

Using words well often means using them imaginatively. The challenge is to avoid the trite and tiresome without making your prose so fancy that your reader pays less attention to what you're saying than to how you're saying it. See **Abstract language, Adjectives and style, Adverbs and style, Conjunctions and style, Euphemisms, Figurative language, Imagery, Nominalization, Repetition, Style, Triteness, Vogue words, Wordiness.** See also articles on individual words: **claim, contact, drunk, finalize, hopefully, however, massive, relate, viable,** and so on.

Dictionaries

Next to a well-stocked mind and a good ear, your dictionary is your chief resource in writing papers. Refer to it to check spelling and word division. Consult it when you're trying to choose the word that conveys what you want to say most precisely. Browse in it to increase your own word hoard.

A good dictionary tells what a word denotes in various contexts (see the several meanings of *office, cast, culture, critical* in your dictionary). It gives linguistic information about the word (its part or parts of speech, its inflections), something of its history, its synonyms and antonyms, and the idioms in which it appears. It may also suggest some of the connotations the word has. Watch for the labels that indicate restrictions on the use of a word or of some of its senses—subject labels like *chemistry,* temporal labels like *archaic,* geographical labels like *British,* and usage labels like *nonstandard.* And be sure you know what the labels mean. Some dictionaries use *colloquial* to mark words that are characteristically used in conversation and in informal writing. Others use *informal* for the same words.

Because dictionaries differ in the labels they apply and in the amount of labeling they do, determining the status of a word isn't always easy. You may be told that *plenty* as in "plenty hot" is informal or colloquial and therefore inappropriate for a formal essay, but you won't be warned that *adumbrate* is too formal and literary for general writing. A dictionary can give you a great deal of information, but it can't substitute for a good ear and good judgment. These you must develop for yourself.

The following dictionaries, listed alphabetically, are recommended for college work. Always use the latest editions.

The American Heritage Dictionary of the English Language (Houghton)

Funk & Wagnalls Standard College Dictionary (Funk)

The Random House College Dictionary (Random)

Webster's New Collegiate Dictionary (Merriam)

Webster's New World Dictionary of the American Language (Collins and World)

Each of these dictionaries has its own policies, procedures, abbreviations, restrictive labels, and order of definitions. To use your dictionary well, become familiar with the explantory notes in the opening pages.

Your college library will have unabridged dictionaries—the most recent include *Webster's Third New International Dictionary of the English Language* (Merriam), *Funk & Wagnalls New Standard Dictionary of the English Language* (Funk), and *The Random House Dictionary of the English Language* (Random)—as well as dictionaries in a variety of special subjects such as law, business, psychology, and economics.

See **Connotation, Definition 1a, Denotation, Diction.**

different from, different than

Formal usage prefers *different from:* The rich are different from you and me. General usage is divided between *different from* and *different than:* "The young TV generation has a completely different sensory life than the adult generation which grew up on hot radio and hot print" *(Newsweek).* *Different than* is especially common when the object is a clause: "The story would be different for an investigator who accepts the verdict of the court than for one who doesn't" (Meyer Shapiro, *New York Review of Books).* The formal alternative would be the longer, wordy expression: . . . verdict of the court from what it would be for one who doesn't.

dilemma

Dilemma has a range of meanings. The narrowest is "a choice between equally unpleasant alternatives." A broader meaning is "any difficult choice." And finally there's "any difficult problem." Since *dilemma* is a rather formal word, giving it so broad a meaning as this last is likely to be criticized.

Direct address

In direct address the audience being spoken to is named:

> *My friends,* I hope you will listen to me with open minds.
> What do you think about his coming home, *Doctor?*

Words in direct address are usually set off by commas. See **Indirect discourse.**

Direct objects

In "Dogs chase cats," *cats* is the direct object of the transitive verb *chase.* See **Objects 1, Transitive and intransitive verbs.**

discreet, discrete

Here's a case in which a mistake in spelling can result in a change in meaning. *Discreet* means "prudent, circumspect": They were so discreet in public that no one suspected a thing. *Discrete* means "separate, distinct": Further analysis revealed that the issue could be divided into discrete parts.

disinterested, uninterested

From its first recorded uses in the seventeenth century, *disinterested* has had two senses: "indifferent, uninterested" and "impartial, not influenced by personal interest.'' But the first meaning gradually disappeared from educated usage, and its revival in this century has met strong opposition. Restricting *disinterested* to the meaning ''impartial'' sets up a distinction between *disinterested* and *uninterested* and thereby prevents ambiguity. Ignoring the distinction creates ambiguity. So even though *disinterested* in the sense ''uninterested'' is established in general styles, a writer who uses it in that way should know that he risks upsetting some readers: ''I began to hate someone once who habitually said 'disinterested' when he should have said 'uninterested' '' (Alexander Cockburn, *New Statesman*).

Divided usage

Usage is said to be divided when two or more forms are in reputable use in the same dialect or variety of English. *Divided usage* doesn't apply to localisms, like *poke* for *sack* or *bag,* or to differences like *ain't* and *isn't,* which belong to separate varieties of the language. It applies to different practices in spelling, pronunciation, and grammatical form by people of similar educational background. In addition to hundreds of instances of divided usage in pronunciation, most dictionaries record forms like these:

> *In spelling:* *buses* or *busses, millionaire* or *millionnaire, catalog* or *catalogue*
>
> *In past tenses:* *sang* or *sung, stank* or *stunk*
>
> *In past participles:* *shown* or *showed, proved* or *proven*

The point about divided usage is that each of the alternatives is acceptable. A person who's learned to say ''It's I'' doesn't need to change to ''It's me,'' and one who says ''It's me'' needn't change to ''It's I.'' When there's a choice between variants of equal standing, choose the one that you use naturally, that's appropriate to your style, or the one that's customary among the people you want to reach. Before criticizing anyone's usage, make sure that it's not a variant as reputable as the one you prefer—which is usually the one you're used to.

The entries in this *Index* include divided usages and give fair warning when one or the other of two acceptable variants is likely to disturb some readers or listeners and arouse emotional attitudes. For examples, see **can, may; different from, different than; disinterested, uninterested; dove, dived; due to; enthuse; farther, further; like, as; Principal parts of verbs; reason is because; Sexist language; slow, slowly.**

div ## Division of words

Break the word at the end of the line between syllables.

To keep the right-hand margin of a manuscript fairly even, you have to divide some words at the end of a line with a hyphen. When you're not sure how to divide a word, consult a dictionary. Here are the basic rules:

1. Both the divided parts should be pronounceable. The break should come between conventionally recognized syllables: *mar gin, hy phen, chil dren, hi lar i ous, ad min is tra tive.* Words of one syllable *(matched, said, thought)* shouldn't be divided.

2. Double consonants are usually separable *(ef fi cient, com mit tee, daz zling, bat ted),* but they're kept together if there's no syllable break *(im pelled)* or if both belong to a root that a suffix has been added to *(stiff ly,* not *stif fly; yell ing,* not *yel ling).*

3. A single letter is never allowed to stand alone. Don't divide words like *enough.*

4. Words spelled with a hyphen *(half-brother, well-disposed)* should be divided only at the hyphen, to avoid the awkwardness of two hyphens in the same word.

dock

A few people will have conniptions if you write of tying up to a dock. A dock, they'll tell you, is the waterway between piers. But *dock* now also means the pier or wharf you tie up to.

doctoral, doctor's, doctorate

Doctoral is an adjective, *doctorate* a noun. A person who has earned a doctorate has earned a doctor's degree (a Ph.D.) in a doctoral program.

don't

Don't is the contraction of *do not.* It is universally used in conversation and is often used in writing when *do not* would be too emphatic or when the shorter form gives a more comfortable rhythm. Until about 1900 *don't* was the usual third-person singular *(he don't, it don't, that don't)* in informal speech, but that usage is now nonstandard.

Double negative

In nonstandard English two or more negatives are very often used to express a single negation: There ai*n't no*body home; Could*n't no*body find the body; I do*n't* have *no*thing to lose. But standard English insists on a single negative in such constructions. Instead of "They could*n't* find it *no*where," use "They could*n't* find it anywhere" (or possibly the formal "They could find it *no*where").

Sometimes a concealed double negative occurs with *hardly* or *scarcely.*

When *hardly* means "almost not" or "probably not" and *scarcely* means the same a little more emphatically, "There's hardly nothing in the campus paper" should read "There's hardly anything," and "For a while we couldn't scarcely breathe" should read "could scarcely breathe."

The objection to a double negative is not that "two negatives make an affirmative." They don't. In early English two negatives were used in all varieties of the language. The objection is simply that the double negative is not now in fashion among educated people.

Double prepositions

The *of* in a double preposition like *off of* is unnecessary. See **Prepositions and style 2.**

Doublespeak

Doublespeak is the use of language not to express but to obscure, disguise, or deny the truth. Dwight Bolinger has suggested that the label be applied to "jargon that is a sophisticated form of lying." Doublespeak is common in the pronouncements of governments and government agencies, corporations, and special interest groups of all kinds. In some cases doublespeak in the form of euphemisms is used to protect the feelings of the old, the poor, the mentally retarded, the crippled, or the criminal, but the inaction encouraged by bland doublespeak does more harm than hurt feelings. See **Euphemisms, Gobbledygook.**

doubt

After the verb *doubt* used negatively, a clause is introduced with *that:* I don't doubt that he meant well. After the verb *doubt* used positively, a clause is introduced by *that, whether,* or, less often, *if:*

> But there is reason to doubt that this is so.—Wayne F. LaFave, *Supreme Court Review*

> A couple of days ago, Walter Heller . . . said that he doubted whether that level could be reached.—Richard H. Rovere, *New Yorker*

> I doubt if this was ever a really important reason for his leaving London.—George Woodcock, *Esquire*

For *doubt but,* see **but that, but what.**

dove, dived

Both *dove* and *dived* are acceptable as the past tense of *dive.*

drunk

It seems to take courage to use the word *drunk*. We either go formal *(intoxicated)*, or grab at respectability through euphemism *(under the influence, indulged to excess)*, or try to be funny with one of dozens of slang expressions like *looped, bombed, smashed*. But *drunk* is the word.

due to

No one complains when *due* (followed by *to*) is used as an adjective firmly modifying a noun: "The failure was due to a conceptual oversight" (William Jaffé, *Journal of Political Economy*). But there has been strong objection to the use of *due to* in the sense "because of" to introduce prepositional phrases functioning as adverbs: Due to the coal miners' strike, a lot of stores were sold out of long underwear. Although this usage has been standard for decades, prejudice against it persists. As a result some writers hesitate to use *due to* in any context.

each

1. The pronoun. Though the pronoun *each* is singular (To each his own), we use it to individualize members of a group (each of the joggers). As a result, it attracts plural verbs and pronouns:

> Each of the stages in child development produce typical conflicts.—Selma Frailberg, *New York Review of Books*

> Each of these people undoubtedly modified Latin in accordance with their own speech habits.—Albert C. Baugh, *A History of the English Language*

In cases like these, the writers have treated *each* as a collective because the plural idea has been uppermost in their minds. The practice is common in informal English and increasing in general English. But in formal usage *each* is ordinarily singular, and conservative stylists insist that it must be: "Each of them was asserting its own individuality" (John Hingham, *American Historical Review*).

Sometimes when *each* refers to both men and women, a writer will use *they* rather than *his* as one way of avoiding sexist language: Each of the weekend guests brought their own climbing gear. See **Agreement 2, Collective nouns, every, Sexist language.**

2. The adjective.   As an adjective, *each* does not affect the number of the verb or related pronoun. When *each* follows the plural subject that it modifies, the verb and related pronoun are also plural: "The editions that have appeared since World War I each have their weak and strong points" (James McManaway, *PMLA*).

each other, one another

Some textbooks have insisted that *each other* refers to two only and *one another* to more than two, but writers regularly ignore the distinction. See **Pronouns 3.**

Echo phrases

An echo phrase calls to mind a passage in literature or a popular saying. See **Allusion.**

Editorial *we*

Traditionally the anonymous writers of editorials use *we* and *our* (We believe that . . . ; It is our recommendation that . . .) rather than *I* and *my*. This is because editorials supposedly speak not just for the individuals who write them but for the publications in which they appear. See **I, we.**

educationese

Educationese is the label applied to the jargon of professional educators by those who find many of their speeches painful to listen to and much of their writing almost impossible to read. See **Jargon.**

effect, affect

The common noun is *effect,* meaning "result." As verbs, *effect* means "bring about" (The shortage has effected a change in driving habits), and *affect* means "influence" or "put on" (She affected a Southern accent). See **affect, effect.**

e.g.

E.g. stands for the Latin words meaning "for example." The best way to avoid possible confusion with *i.e.* is to write out *for example*. See **Abbreviations 2, i.e.**

either

Though in speech a plural verb is common after *either* (I don't think either of them are going), in writing of any formality a singular verb is expected (Either of them was almost certain to reach the Pole).

either . . . or, neither . . . nor

When one element of a compound subject joined by *either . . . or* or *neither . . . nor* is singular and the other is plural, make the verb agree with the nearer subject. See **Agreement 1c.**

elder, eldest

These forms of *old* survive in references to the order of birth of members of a family—"the elder brother," "our eldest daughter"—and in some honorific senses like "elder statesman."

Ellipsis

The three periods—each preceded and followed by a space—that are used to indicate the omission of one or more words in a quotation are called an ellipsis: "Four score and seven years ago our fathers brought forth . . . a new nation . . . dedicated to the proposition that all men are created equal." When the last words in a quoted sentence are omitted, the end punctuation comes before the ellipsis—"Four score and seven years ago our fathers brought forth on this continent a new nation. . . ."—just as it does when the omission follows the sentence.

The omission of a line or more of poetry is generally indicated by a full line of spaced periods. The omission of a paragraph or more of prose is traditionally indicated in the same way, but current practice often uses only an ellipsis at the end of the paragraph preceding the omission.

Don't use ellipses when you're quoting only a phrase: It is worth asking whether we continue to be "dedicated to the proposition." (*Not* ". . . dedicated to the proposition. . . .")

In dialog an ellipsis indicates hesitation in speech. It may also be used as an end stop for a statement that's left unfinished or allowed to die away: "The town was poor then. And like so many who grew up in the Depression, we never expected we would have real jobs. There was no place for us in the world. It was depressing . . ." (John Thompson, *Harper's*).

Elliptical constructions

An elliptical construction omits a word or two that can somehow be supplied, usually from a neighboring construction: I work much harder than you [work]. The choice between longer and shorter forms is a matter of style. Formal English uses relatively few elliptical constructions. General and informal English use them freely. Compare **Clauses 2a.**

else's

In phrases with pronouns like *anyone, nobody,* and *someone, else*—not the preceding pronoun—takes the sign of the possessive: The package was left at somebody else's house.

empathy, sympathy

Both *empathy* and *sympathy* refer to a sharing of another's feelings (often of distress) or convictions. *Empathy,* the more fashionable word, suggests a particularly close identification with the other person.

emp Emphasis

Strengthen the emphasis of this passage.

Rightly used, emphasis indicates the relative importance of the points you're making, so that your reader recognizes the most important as most important, the less important as less important, the incidental as incidental. If you don't provide emphasis, you fail to guide your reader. If you place it where it doesn't belong, you mislead or confuse him.

1. Proportion. Ordinarily, allot space on the basis of importance. Give the point you want to emphasize the space and development its significance calls for. If you write a paper at the last minute, you may give the preliminaries more space, and therefore more emphasis, than they deserve and then, realizing that you're running out of time, leave your major point undeveloped and unemphatic. Budget your time so that you won't mislead your reader in these ways.

2. Position. As a general rule, the most emphatic position in a sentence, a paragraph, or a full paper is the end (hence the danger of leaving the final point undeveloped). The second most important is the beginning. Don't waste these natural positions of emphasis. In writing term papers and answering examination questions you'll often want to use both—stating your thesis in the opening paragraph and, after presenting the arguments that support it, restating it in your conclusion. In any case, don't let your major point get lost somewhere in between, and don't announce it at the beginning and then fail to get back to it. **See Beginning, Ending.**

3. Separation. To emphasize part of a sentence, lightly or heavily, set it off with a comma, a colon, or a dash. Or begin a separate sentence or a new paragraph to achieve the same purpose. See **Colon 4, Comma 7, Dash 1.**

4. Repetition. As long as you don't overdo it, you can gain emphasis by repeating significant words and by repeating ideas in different words. Repeating a structural pattern, such as a *who* clause, is an excellent device for emphasizing, especially in a series that builds to a climax. See **Parallelism, Repetition, Series.**

5. Economy. In the condensing that's a regular part of revision, pay special attention to the way you express ideas that deserve major emphasis. Strip sentences of unnecessary words that blur their clarity and blunt their impact. Emphatic statement needn't be brusque, but it must be direct and uncluttered. See **Wordiness.**

6. Mechanical devices. Using underlinings, capitals, and exclamation marks for emphasis is likely to bore, annoy, or amuse the reader. Telling him that he should be interested ("It is interesting to note") or impressed ("Here is the really important point that everyone should recognize") is likely to irritate him. "Big" words have the same effect, and the intensifiers used in speech—*terribly, extremely, incredibly*—are almost always ineffective in writing. On paper "a terribly shocking incident" turns out to be less, not more, emphatic than "a shocking incident." So earn your reader's attention. Don't try to grab it with mechanical hoots and verbal hollers.

end Ending

Revise the ending of your paper to round out the discussion.

When you reach the end of your discussion, wrap it up. Don't just stop, so that a reader wonders if the last page is missing. And don't ramble on until your audience is missing.

If your paper is long, you may want to review the ground you've covered, preferably in fresh phrasing. If the material is complex, you may need to pull together the points you've made and show how they add up and what they add up to. Short papers, as well as long ones, must add up to something.

If the reader of a paper you've written finishes the last sentence and thinks "So what?" either you've produced a paper that has no point, or—more likely—you've failed to make clear what the point is. A conclusion can't save a pointless paper by simply announcing a point, but by clarifying the essential argument, by bringing out what has only been implied, the final paragraph or two can strengthen a paper greatly.

If your paper has been a voyage of discovery in which you've tried to define your own attitudes, you may end up with something like, "What I feel now is that my parents gave too much to me without thinking enough about me." Whether such a conclusion works depends on what's gone before. If that point has been gradually emerging throughout the paper, fine. If it hasn't—if, for example, you've only told about the size of your allowance, your charge accounts, the gifts on birthdays and at Christmas—then your ending will leave the reader perplexed and dissatisfied.

Final sentences should avoid tag ends and anticlimax as well as irrelevance. They should build to a firm conclusion, not trail off into silence. They should wrap up the discussion in such a way that the reader not only recognizes its completeness but feels satisfied that the last words were the right ones.

End stop

An end stop is the mark of punctuation—usually a period, exclamation mark, or question mark—used at the end of a sentence. In writing dialog, a double dash may be used as an end stop when a speech is interrupted. An ellipsis can end a sentence that's intentionally left unfinished.

When two end stops would come at the close of a sentence, only the more emphatic or more necessary for meaning is used. Here a question comes at the end of a sentence that would normally close with a period; only the question mark is used: "When we say, for example, that Miss A plays well, only an irredeemable outsider would reply 'Plays what?' " (C. Alphonso Smith, *Studies in English Syntax*).

English language

The earliest records of English date from the seventh century A.D., two centuries after invading Germanic tribesmen from northwestern Europe—Angles, Saxons, Jutes, and Frisians—had made their homes in the British Isles, bringing with them the dialects that are the direct ancestors of the English language. Through those dialects English is connected to a prehistoric past—to an unrecorded language called Germanic, parent of the Low and High German languages, the Scandinavian languages, and English. Through Germanic, English is connected to a still more ancient and unrecorded language called Indo-European, the parent of (among others) most of the language groups on the European continent.

The history of English is often divided into three main periods: Old English (OE), c. 450–1100; Middle English (ME), c. 1100–1450; Modern English or New English (MnE or NE), c. 1450–, with this latter period sometimes subdivided into Early Modern English (EMnE), c. 1450–1700, and Modern English, c. 1700–.

See **Dialects.**

enormity, enormousness

Because *enormity* looks like a more compact way of expressing the idea of "enormousness," it's often used in that sense, as most dictionaries indicate. But this use is deplored by those who restrict *enormity* to the traditional meaning "enormously evil" or "great wickedness," as in "the enormity of the crime."

enthuse

Enthuse is a back formation (see **Origin of words 3d**) from *enthusiasm*. Though widely used in general and informal writing, the word is still not established in formal usage, and many readers object to it. The only other locutions we have for the idea are the longer *be enthusiastic over* or *be enthusiastic about*.

equally as

Though *equally as* is an established idiom (Color is equally as important as design), one of the words is always redundant. *Either* Color is as important as design *or* Color and design are equally important.

-ese

The suffix *-ese* is used to make new nouns (*journalese, educationese, bureaucratese*) that have the disparaging sense of "lingo" or "jargon": His mastery of sociologese left us impressed but uninformed.

Establishment

In the 1960s *Establishment* (sometimes not capitalized) became a vogue word for the powers-that-be:

> In the intellectuals' lexicon "the Establishment" now seems to include the federal, state, and local government, business corporations, foundations and other philanthropic organizations, Big Labor, Big Science, and the administrators of universities—Max Ways, *Fortune*.

While sometimes simply descriptive, it was more often a term of abuse, expressing discontent with the ins and sympathy with the outs. *Establishment* has remained anything but precise but continues to refer to either stuffy or sinister inner circles.

et al.

Et al. is the abbreviation for the Latin words meaning "and others." A note style may call for reducing a list of four or more authors of a single work to the first author named and *et al.* In ordinary writing, and in other note styles, use *and others.* See **Note form.**

etc.

Though sometimes a convenient way to end an incomplete list, *etc.,* the abbreviation of the Latin phrase *et cetera* ("and the rest"), belongs primarily to business and reference uses: This case is suitable for large photographs, maps, charts, etc. In most writings, *and so forth* or *and so on* is preferable when the reference is to things, and *and others* is preferable with lists of people. The fact that a list is incomplete can also be indicated by naming the category and then using an introductory phrase like *such as:* This case is suitable for graphics such as large photographs, maps, and charts.

Ethnic labels

American English has its full share of slang terms for members of racial and ethnic groups. While the terms may at times be used with no hostile intent and may even be used by members of the groups they name, our vocabularies would be healthier without them. Besides the labels for peoples of European, African, and Latin American origins, these terms should be avoided: *Asiatic* (for *Asian*), *Jap (Japanese), Chinaman* or *Chink (Chinese),* as well as words like *gook.*

Etymology

Etymology is the study of word origins. See **Origin of words 1.**

Euphemisms

A euphemism is a term used in place of one that names more explicitly something unpleasant or something regarded as not quite nice: *perspire* for *sweat, passed on* for *died, senior citizens* for *old people, lavatory* or *powder room* or *comfort facility* for *toilet.* Political, military, and promotional vocabularies offer countless examples. Occasionally euphemisms are warranted, to avoid causing pain or embarrassment, but in most cases honesty is better—and makes for better writing—than evasion.

every

1. *Every, everybody,* **and** *everyone* were originally singular and continue to take a singular verb: Every player on the team deserves our praise; Everybody loathes the mayor; Everyone takes the freeway. But for related pronouns that follow, usage is divided. The singular is perhaps more common in formal writing, but the plural appears in all varieties: "Everybody who has praised the inaugural address cannot possibly be as enthusiastic as they sound, unless they are merely reacting to its music" (James Reston, *New York Times*). The plural *they* is reasonable, since the reference is to a number of people. Instead of substituting *he* for *they*, formal written usage might replace *Everybody* with an explicit plural: All those who have praised. . . .

A plural pronoun is also used for clarity when the *every* phrase is the object of a verb with a singular subject: "The traditional leader then comes forward and thanks everyone for their attendance and invites them to lunch" (John A. Woodward, *Ethnology*). Treating the *every* words as collectives can sometimes prevent confusion and also avoid the awkward *he-or-she* problem. But some conservatives continue to insist that, in writing, related pronouns must be singular. See **he or she.**

2. *Everybody* is always written as one word. *Everyone* is usually written as one word, but when the *one* is stressed, it's written separately: Everyone knew what the end would be; Every one of us knew what the end would be.

3. *Every so often,* meaning "occasionally" (Every so often we have to get away from the city), should not be confused with *ever so often,* meaning "very frequently" (We went to the country ever so often in my childhood). You won't confuse the two if you give up using the exclamatory *ever so often.*

4. *Everyplace,* meaning "everywhere," is inappropriate in formal writing. *Everywheres* is nonstandard.

Examples

Examples are instances that illustrate general statements. They clarify explanations, confirm assertions, and provide support for arguments. See **Details, Induction.**

except, accept

Except as a verb means "leave out, exclude": In making the new assignment, the teacher excepted those who had made an honest effort on the last one. It's decidedly formal. *Excused* would often be more appropriate for the same meaning in general writing.

Accept means "receive" or "respond to affirmatively" and is slightly formal: I accept with pleasure; He accepted the position (as contrasted with "He took the job").

Exclamation mark

An exclamation mark (or point) is used after an emphatic interjection, after a phrase, clause, or sentence that's genuinely exclamatory, and after forceful commands. Clear-cut exclamations are no problem:

> Oh! Ouch! No, no, no!
> Damn those mosquitoes!
> It's the chance of a lifetime!

But many interjections are mild and deserve no more than a comma or period: "Well, well, so you're in college now." Often sentences cast in exclamatory patterns are simply statements (What a memorable experience that was), and the mark of punctuation is optional.

In deciding whether to use an exclamation mark, you should first ask yourself whether you intend to exclaim—to express strong feeling or give special emphasis. Walt Kelly said, "Using the exclamation point is like wearing padded shoulders." But when used sparingly, to signal genuine emotion, the mark can serve the writer as the raised voice or dramatic gesture serves the speaker:

> *The Sun Also Rises* is a major work, brilliantly constructed and colored—though last year I was taken aback to hear some students complain that Jake Barnes indulges himself in too much self-pity. How imperious the young can be when judging the victims of disasters they don't even trouble to learn about!—Irving Howe, *Harper's*

Exclamations

What distinguishes an exclamation from other kinds of utterance is its purpose: emphatic expression. In form, an exclamation may be a declarative sentence (She's late again!), a question (Can she be late again!), a command or request (Be ready when I call! Please be on time!), a verbless sentence (How terrible for you!), or an interjection (Ugh!). See **Exclamation mark.**

expect

In general and formal writing, *expect* is ordinarily limited to the senses "anticipate" (He expects you to be a great success) and "require as reasonable'' (Winsock, Inc., expects its employees to arrive on time). In American usage the sense ''to suppose, presume, believe'' in reference to past or present (I expect there were times when Lincoln was heartily fed up) is likely to be limited to informal contexts.

Exposition

Most of the writing required in college courses is explanatory—writing that's intended primarily to inform and enlighten the reader. *Exposition* (or *expository writing*) is the traditional term for writing of this kind. When extended to include argument, *exposition* refers to all factual prose, in contrast to fiction. See **Argument, Forms of discourse, Rhetoric.**

fact

The fact is often deadwood and should be deleted: The study demonstrates [the fact] that workers can become affluent. Sometimes phrases with *fact* can be replaced by single words: in spite of the fact = *although;* due to the fact that = *because. True fact* is redundant. Omit *true.*

factor

Windy phrases with *factor* should be deleted: Determination and imagination [were the factors that] brought the program its popularity. *Factor* itself, meaning ''something that helps produce a result,'' can often be replaced by a more precise or expressive word: A major factor (stimulus? influence? resource?) in creating the system was the artisan class. Used in the plural, it may give the reader no specific information and arouse suspicion that the writer doesn't have any: Many factors were responsible for the war (or the depression or the fuel shortage or the birth rate).

Fallacies

As the term is used in logic, a fallacy is an error in reasoning. If a college announces that it awards scholarships only to students who are needy, then we are reasoning correctly when we assume that a particular student who receives a scholarship at that institution is needy. But it would be fallacious to say, on the basis of the same announcement, that every needy student in the college is receiving scholarship aid. Similarly, a person who acts on the premise that an X-rated movie is not fit to see can't confidently assume that every movie with a different rating *is* fit to see. *Non sequitur* (''it does not follow'') is a comprehensive category covering all those errors in reasoning in which the stated conclusion doesn't follow from the premises, or starting points.

Popularly, *fallacy* is extended to include all misleading statements and errors in interpretation, intentional or unintentional. In this sense, a speaker or writer who deliberately withholds facts, slants evidence, draws an unjustified inference, or argues beside the point commits a fallacy. So does the speaker or writer who can't reach a sound conclusion because he doesn't know enough about a situation or because he makes a mistake in interpreting what he does know.

The common fallacies go by names that are almost self-explanatory. *Hasty generalizing* means basing a conclusion on inadequate evidence: The fact that two of every three students in my physics class are interested in a career in engineering indicates that engineering is the first choice of science majors these days. *Faulty generalizing* is generalizing that's based on weak or unrepresentative instances. It may take the form of *card-stacking* (using only data that support the conclusion) or *stereotyping* (applying labels to an entire group—calling all Scots stingy, for example).

Ignoring the question is the fallacy of shifting the grounds of the argument from the real issue to one that's not being debated. An *argumentum ad hominem* attacks not the issue itself but the character of those who support it. Setting up a *straw man* is arguing not against the opposing point of view but against a caricature of it. And using a *red herring* is introducing an issue that shifts the argument from its real subject. *Name-calling* is the irresponsible use of epithets and labels chosen for their connotations for particular audiences. (For some audiences, *liberal* is inflammatory; for others, *conservative* is.) *Hypostatization* is the appeal to an abstraction as an authority: ''Science tells us,'' instead of ''Heisenberg tells us in *Physics and Beyond*. . . .''

For other fallacies, see **Begging the question, Cause and effect 2.** See also **Logical thinking.**

famed

Dictionaries accept *famed* as standard English, but to some readers it smacks of journalese. *Famous* is a safer choice—though in most cases the audience doesn't need to be told that what you've called famous is. See **Journalese.**

farther, further

Some careful writers make a distinction between *farther,* referring to physical distance (Farther north there was heavy snow), and *further,* referring to more abstract relations of degree or extent (Nothing could be further removed from experience). But the distinction is not consistently maintained, even in formal English.

feel

Though one of the accepted meanings of *feel* is "think" or "believe" (I feel that Barnum was right), *feel* shouldn't replace those verbs. Readers need to be reminded now and then that a writer thinks and has convictions.

fellow

Fellow is general and informal when used to mean "man" or "boy" but formal in the sense "associate." In writing, the word is commonly used as an adjectival: his fellow sufferers, a fellow feeling ("a similar feeling" or "sympathy").

female

In current usage the noun *female* seems most appropriate in somewhat formal or technical contexts: "Each female is assigned a number of social security quarters at the beginning of the simulation" (James H. Schulz, *Yale Economic Essays*). It's usually a poor substitute for *woman*. As an adjective *female* has more usefulness but also focuses on classification by sex, whether human or nonhuman. See **Sexist language.**

fewer, less

The rule is that *fewer* refers to number among things that are counted (fewer particles) and *less* to amount or quantity among things that are measured (less energy). Formal usage ordinarily observes the distinction. In general writing *less* is applied to countables fairly often—"I suggest they sell two less tickets to the public" (Dwight Macdonald, *Esquire*)—but it grates on some readers' ears.

field

The phrase *the field of* can almost always be omitted: He has long been interested in [the field of] psychiatry.

Figurative language

We use figurative language when we transfer a word from a context in which it's literally true (a *smelly* cheese) to one in which it isn't (a *smelly* scandal). Everything we say and write is peppered with such transfers (*peppered* is an example). We *play ball* when we cooperate, *chime in* when we join in a conversation, *tax* the patience of others when we talk too much.

Many of these word transfers have been around so long that they've lost all their figurative, or image-making, power. (Who pictures an animal when he hears that someone has *weaseled* out of a situation?) Though *foot* continues to serve as the name for a part of the body, its reference has been extended to include the bottom or lowest part of a tree, a bed, a path, and a mountain, among many other things. In these uses, *foot* is a petrified, or dead, figure. (*Dead* is used here figuratively. So is *petrified.*)

A live figure is created when a word is extended to a new referent. We speak routinely of peeling an apple or a potato. Paul Auster, writing of the poet Laura Riding, speaks of her "trying somehow to peel back the skin of the world" *(New York Review of Books)*. The yoking of things not ordinarily thought of as alike or the phrasing of a perception in a fresh way can serve the double function of seizing the attention and of informing or persuading. Both functions are served by this figurative attack on loud music:

> Loud music—be it rock or disco—has become a secular religion, an aural opium. . . . One prominent bass guitarist typically stands directly in front of his mammoth speakers, glassy-eyed, body surfing on the sound waves that buffet him like gale-force winds. It's not uncommon to see kids running up onstage to bow their heads reverently right into the maw of the giant woofers; no wonder they stumble out of arenas with brains turned to sawdust, like the scarecrow in *The Wizard of Oz*.—Stephen Demorest, *Saturday Review*

Traditionally, distinctions between figures of speech are made on the basis of the way the meaning of the word or phrase is transferred. In a metaphor the transfer is often direct: loud music *becomes* a secular religion. In a simile it's made through *like* or *as: like the scarecrow,* listeners have their brains turned to sawdust. In other common figures the part stands for the whole (*wheel* for bicycle) or the whole for the part (*Navy* for a team at the Naval Academy) or the author for the works (*Shakespeare* for Shakespeare's plays). Hyperbole uses extravagant language for emphasis: I almost *died* of shame. Understatement seeks the same effect by the opposite means: Enthusiasm for the draft was *not overwhelming*.

Personification gives life to abstractions and inanimate objects. In this elaborate figure General Motors, Ford, and Chrysler, losing sales to foreign automakers, were pictured as pompous aristocrats being hard pressed by snapping dogs:

> The Auto Lords of Michigan continue to stride about the interior, making gruff and manly sounds, but their legs are beset with Saabs and Volvos, their ankles nibbled at by Datsuns and Volkswagens.—Michael Arlen, *New Yorker*

For other figures of speech, see **Analogy, Imagery, Irony, Metaphor, Oxymoron.** For figures of sound, see **Alliteration, Assonance, Onomatopoeia, Puns.** See also **Figures of speech.**

Figures

Figures are the symbols for numbers. See **Numbers**.

ƒig Figures of speech

This figure of speech is trite, inconsistent, or inappropriate. Revise the passage.

A good figure of speech can add color, humor, interest, or information and may convey meaning more economically than its literal equivalent. But literal expression is always preferable to a figure that doesn't work.

1. Replace trite figures.   Use figures of speech that represent your own perceptions. Many figures that once were fresh and vivid are now clichés: *cool as a cucumber, a ribbon of concrete, sick as a dog, fresh as a daisy, Old Man Winter*. The writer who thinks about what he's setting down on paper either avoids them or at least tries to give them a new look. "A cucumber-cool manner" might get by where "cool as a cucumber" would bore the reader. But there are dangers in trying to disguise clichés. Though "a lot of water has flowed under the bridge" takes on some new life in "all the water, and war, that had flowed under the bridge" (Karl Miller, *New York Review of Books*), some readers may feel that water and war don't mix.

Whenever possible, offer the reader an original figure, likes James Thurber's road "which seemed to be paved with old typewriters." If you can neither freshen an old figure successfully nor invent a new one that works, stick to a literal statement of your meaning.

2. Untangle mixed figures.   Sometimes, instead of coming up with no image at all, you may come up with too many:

> The noise, like an enthusiastic roar from a distant sports stadium, yet as insistent as the surge of distant surf, grew till it was galloping up the quadrangle in massive waves.

Here sports fans, the ocean, and horses create a catastrophe. To catch such incongruous mixtures before the final draft, read what you've written as objectively as you can.

More difficult to spot are the mixed figures that involve dead metaphors. Keep in mind that a figure that's dead in most contexts may revive in certain relationships, with ridiculous results. In the first of the following sentences, the student invents a figure that's apt. In the second, the word *faces,* which is regularly used to stand for "people," simply won't work with *sitting* or with suiting up:

> As we dressed, comments were tossed about the room as casually as the rolls of tape we were using to tape our ankles. The familiar faces, sitting in their usual corners, were all getting into their uniforms.

Don't just read what you've written before you turn a paper in. Think about what it *says*. When your figures of speech call up pictures of physical impossibilities or other absurdities because you've mixed images, they're likely to distract your readers from the point you're trying to make. If in speaking figuratively you seem to be speaking foolishly, your figurative language needs to be overhauled or abandoned.

3. Replace inappropriate figures.   A figure of speech may be inappropriate to the audience, to the subject, or to you as the writer. Whether used to explain or to amuse, similes, metaphors, and analogies drawn from biology or trout fishing or from the folklore of your home town won't work with readers who know nothing about these things. Describing bluegrass music with figures of speech appropriate to a discussion of Beethoven's symphonies, or vice versa, makes sense only if you're trying, rather desperately, to be funny. And using figures that don't match your own attitudes or temperament—poetic metaphors, for example, when your natural style is down-to-earth, or hard-boiled similes when you're typically gentle and thoughtful—gives them an off-key prominence that will disturb readers.

A figure of speech can be judged good or not good only in a context, a rhetorical situation. When you write your final draft, judge each of your figures by its appropriateness to the audience, the subject, and your prevailing tone. If you decide that a figure doesn't fit, replace it with a suitable figure or with the literal equivalent. But don't discard a figure simply because it startles you when you read over what you've written. In the context of your paper, "the moon crashed through the clouds" may be just right. See **Figurative language.**

finalize

Finalize has been in widespread use for more than a generation. Its near-synonyms, *finish, complete,* and *conclude,* lack the connotation "to make official" that gives *finalize* its usefulness in some contexts: "Before they finalize new guidelines they will consult listeners in East Europe to make sure the proposed changes are having the right effect" (Mary Hornaday, *Christian Science Monitor*). But no writer can afford to be ignorant of the prejudice against *finalize*. It was included in Maury Maverick's original list of gobbledygook in 1942, and some consider it gobbledygook today.

"Fine" writing

The adjective *fine* is generally applied to writing that's too pretentious for what's being said. "Fine" writing uses "big" words and strained, artificial figures of speech. If you write more to impress your readers than to express your ideas, you're likely to produce "fine" writing. See **Diction, Figures of speech.**

fix

In formal usage *fix* means "fasten in place." In general usage it means "repair" or "put into shape": The TV had to be fixed. As a noun meaning "predicament," *fix* has passed from informal to general: "In some respects economic theory is in the same fix as biology was years ago" (Henry M. Boettinger, *Harvard Business Review*).

flaunt, flout

Flaunt, to "wave, display boastfully," is frequently used with the sense "treat with contempt, scorn," the meaning traditionally assigned to *flout.* Readers aware of the traditional distinction deplore the confusion.

Folk etymology

When people are puzzled by an unfamiliar word or phrase, they sometimes try to make it more regular or more meaningful by rephrasing it from familiar elements: from *aeroplane* they made *airplane;* from Spanish *cucuracha,* English *cockroach;* from *saler,* "a salt-holder," first the redundant *salt-saler* and then *saltcellar,* which has no more to do with a cellar than the *sir-* in *sirloin* has to do with a knight (the *sir-* in the cut of beef is *sur,* "above"). See **Origin of words 1.**

folk, folks

In formal writing *folks* is uncommon. *Folk* is used in the senses "the common people" (usually of a certain region) and "people" (of a specified type). In general writing *folks* for "people," often with the connotation "ordinary, everyday," and for "relatives, parents" is carried over from informal.

Footnote form

When you use footnotes in a paper, triple-space between the text and the first footnote on each page. Single-space the footnotes, leaving a double space between them. See **Note form** for a discussion of documentation and examples of endnotes.

for

When *for* comes between clauses, it's classified as a coordinating conjunction. But coordinating *for* may mean the same as subordinating *because:* He was exhausted, for he had gone two nights without sleep. A comma is usually needed between clauses joined by *for* to keep it from being read as a preposition: The tutors must love the work, for the pay, which is only $300 a year plus room and board, can't be very attractive. The comma prevents the misreading: The tutors must love the work for the pay. As a conjunction, *for* is rather formal. See **because.**

Foreign words in English

1. Anglicizing foreign words.   English has always borrowed words and roots from other languages, and it's still borrowing (from French, *boutique* and *discotheque*). Words usually cross the threshold of English with their foreign spelling, perhaps with un-English plurals or other forms, and with no established English pronunciation. The process of anglicizing brings them more or less in line with English usage, though they may keep some of their foreign quality, like the *i* of *machine*, the silent *s* in *debris*, the *t* where we are tempted to put a *d* in *kindergarten*.

The speed and degree of anglicizing depends on how frequently the word is used, the circumstances in which it's used, and the people who use it. Formal writers and conservative editors keep the foreign spelling longer than writers and editors of general English. If the words come in through the spoken language, like those of the automobile vocabulary, they're anglicized sooner than if they come in by way of literature: *coupe, chamois, chauffeur, garage, detour.* Words that come in through and remain in literary, scholarly, or socially elite circles change more slowly, in both spelling and pronunciation: *tête-à-tête, faux pas, nouveau riche, laissez-faire.*

2. Using borrowed words.
a.   Italics. Words that have not been completely anglicized are usually printed in italics in magazines and books and should be underlined in the papers you write. Consult your dictionary. Words on the borderline will be found sometimes in italics, sometimes not. Formal writers use italics more than general writers.
b.   Accents and other marks. In books and magazines, words recently taken in from other languages are usually written with the accent marks they have in the language of their origin. After a time the accents are dropped unless they're needed to indicate pronunciation. But publications for the general public are more likely to drop accent marks (*expose, detente*) than are publications for limited, scholarly audiences (*exposé, détente*).
c.   Plurals. English usually brings borrowed words into its own system of conjugation and declension (*campuses,* not *campi*), though some words change slowly, especially those used mainly in formal writing (*syllabi* or *syllabuses*). See **Plurals of nouns 4.**

See **Origin of words 2b.**

form Formal English

The word or passage marked is too formal for the subject or for the style of the rest of the paper. Revise, making it more appropriate.

Formal written English is appropriate (though not mandatory) in discussions of ideas, in research papers and other scholarly works, in addresses to be delivered on ceremonial occasions, and in literary essays intended for well-educated readers. It's usually not appropriate in accounts of personal experience, in papers about campus issues, in comments on current books, movies, TV shows, or popular records, or in other writing intended for general readers.

The vocabulary of formal style includes many words not used in general written English. *Form* in the margin of your paper may refer to a word that's too formal for the context: For a while it looked as though the bad habits he had picked up were irremediable (*better:* could never be corrected). Or it may point to a sentence pattern that suggests the deliberate pace of formal English and therefore mixes poorly with sentences that suggest the spontaneity of speech:

> In addition to being younger than my classmates, I had retained, along with the babyish habit of sucking my thumb, a tendency to cry when I was not allowed to have my own way, thereby turning them against me.

> *Possible revision:* Besides being younger than my classmates, I still sucked my thumb. This irritated them, and I made things worse by crying when I didn't get my own way.

See **General English, Informal English, Standard English.**

former, first–latter, last

Traditionally, *former* and *latter* refer only to two units: "the former called the latter 'little prig' " (Ralph Waldo Emerson). Tradition holds for *former,* but the use of *latter* with more than two is common enough to be standard. Even so, some conservative readers would prefer "the last named" in references like this one: "The list of products . . . could include potassium, bromine, chlorine, caustic, and magnesium. The latter might become a very important lightweight metal" (Glenn T. Seaborg, *Bulletin of the Atomic Scientists*).

First and *last* refer to items in a series, usually more than two:

> The first president had set up a very informal organization.
> His last act was to advise his family on their future.

Latest refers to a series that's still continuing (the latest fashions). *Last* refers either to the final item of a completed series (their last attempt was successful) or to the most recent item of a continuing series (the last election). See **last, latest.**

Forms of discourse

For the last century or so it's been conventional to divide writing into four forms of discourse—narration, description, exposition, and argument. The classification is useful because it emphasizes purpose as the controlling element in a piece of writing, and examining the forms one by one enables the student of writing to concentrate on certain traits of content, organization, and style that are peculiar to each type. But the categories are not sharply distinct. Description contributes to the other three, particularly to narration; many papers that are primarily argumentative include stretches of exposition; and so on.

Formulas

Every language has some fixed phrases that have become customary in certain situations: Once upon a time, Ladies and gentlemen, Good morning, Best wishes, Yours truly, How do you do? Such phrases are too useful to be called clichés, and unlike most trite expressions they're not substitutes for simpler locutions. When called for, they should be used without apology. See **Idiom, Subjunctive mood 2a.**

Fractions

Fractions are written in figures when attached to other figures ($72^3/4$), in a series in figures ($^1/_2$, 1, 2, 4), or in tables or reference matter. In most running text they're written in words: In the local newspaper three fourths of the space was given to advertising, one eighth to news, and one eighth to miscellaneous matters. Hyphens may be used between the numerator and denominator if neither part itself contains a hyphen (seven-tenths), and hyphens should be used to avoid confusion: though *twenty seven eighths* probably means "twenty-seven eighths," it could mean "twenty seven-eighths." But hyphens are less common than they used to be and are now omitted when the numerator functions as an adjective, as in "He sold one half and kept the other."

Decimals are taking the place of fractions in factual writing, because they're more flexible and may be more accurate: .7; .42; 3.14159.

See **Numbers.**

frag Fragment

The construction marked is not a satisfactory sentence. Revise by joining it to a neighboring sentence, by making it grammatically complete, or by rewriting the passage.

A sentence fragment is a part of a sentence—usually a phrase or dependent clause—that's carelessly or ineffectively punctuated as if it were a whole sentence. You can usually correct a fragment by joining it to the preceding or following sentence or by otherwise making it grammatically complete. But sometimes rewriting is the best solution.

Below, with suggested revisions, are three common types of fragments.

1. A prepositional phrase punctuated as a sentence:

The northern part of the city is mainly residential. On the eastern outskirts are the oil refining plants. And to the south beaches and parks.

Revision: The northern part of the city is mainly residential. On the eastern outskirts are the oil refining plants and to the south beaches and parks.

2. A participial phrase punctuated as a sentence:

For sixteen years I did pretty much what I wanted to. Being distrustful and avoiding anyone in authority.

Revision: For sixteen years I did pretty much what I wanted to, distrusting and avoiding anyone in authority.

3. A dependent clause punctuated as a sentence:

I still remember him as the best teacher I ever had. Because right then he sat down and helped me work all the problems.

Revision: I still remember him as the best teacher I ever had, because right then he sat down and helped me work all the problems.

In an unexpectedly heavy turnout, over 80 percent of the citizens voted. A fact that shows how strongly they felt about the issue.

Revision: In an unexpectedly heavy turnout, over 80 percent of the citizens voted—a fact that shows. . . . Or: . . . voted. This fact shows. . . .

The deliberate setting off of a phrase or dependent clause for rhetorical effect is common in print. Used sparingly and skillfully, it can do good service as an organizational road sign that briskly points the reader toward the next topic—"But first, the new troops" (Lucian K. Truscott IV, *Harper's*)—or provides informal notice of the progress of the discussion—"Which brings us back to the absurdity of the backlash accusations" (Letty Cottin Pogrebin, *Ms.*). The parallel fragments in these two paragraphs point up a contrast:

The prevailing view is that all our options have narrowed. I don't believe it. There is a sense of being trapped—the feeling that nothing we do makes much difference. Which leads to frantic group pressures and single-issue politics, or to the cynical rejection of all forms of public life and to a wallowing in our egos.

Let's face it. We used up our resources, polluted our environment and laid staggering burdens on our government. Which means we must now place limits on our desires, needs, greeds. The historians call it the Age of Limits.—Max Lerner, *Newsweek*

And fragments of some length can sometimes be used effectively to pile up details in descriptive writing:

Prairie wool blue-green, spring wheat bright as new lawn, winter wheat gray-green at rest and slaty when the wind flaws it, roadside primroses as shy as prairie flowers are supposed to be, and as gentle to the eye as when in my boyhood we used to call them wild tulips, and by their coming date the beginning of summer.—Wallace Stegner, *Wolf Willow*.

See **Clauses, Phrases.**

freshman, freshmen

The modifier is *freshman,* not only before nouns with an obviously singular reference (a freshman dorm) but before plural and abstract nouns (freshman courses, freshman orientation).

-ful, full

When the adjective *full* (a full basket, a basket full of apples) is used as a suffix to nouns of measure (*basketful, spoonful*) or of feeling or quality (*peaceful, sorrowful*), it has only one *l*. The plural of nouns ending in -*ful* is usually made with -*s: spoonfuls, basketfuls*. With the adjective *full,* the noun is made plural: *full baskets, baskets full*.

further, farther

Both *further* and *farther* are used in referring to distance. See **farther, further.**

Fused sentence

Fused, or *run-on, sentence* is the name sometimes given to two grammatically complete sentences written with no mark of punctuation between them: If you ask me why I did it, I can only say that at the time it seemed the right thing to do [ ] that is my only explanation. To correct the error, begin a new sentence or insert a semicolon. Compare **Comma splice.**

Future tense

English verbs don't inflect, or change their form, to express future time. Some of the means we use to refer to the future are illustrated in these sentences: I am leaving next week; He sails tomorrow; She is to speak on Saturday; He is about to resign; When I am elected, I will make an investigation; They will try to be on time; She is going to refuse; Shall I take this to the cleaners? See **Tenses of verbs.**

G

Gender

In speaking of gender in modern English, we're usually talking about choice of pronouns—*he, she, it, who, which*—and about the meaning of the words that govern that choice. See **Agreement 2, he or she, Sexist language.**

General English

General English is the core of standard English. Spoken general English is what we hear in most talks for general audiences, in news broadcasts, and in the ordinary conversation of educated people. Written, edited general English is what we read in newspapers, magazines, and most books. The main focus of this *Index* is on writing general English. See **Formal English, Informal English, Standard English.**

Genitive case

The genitive, or possessive, case is indicated by the apostrophe, with or without *-s;* by the possessive form of the personal pronouns; and by the relative *whose.* See **Possessive case.**

Gerunds

1. Form and function. A gerund—also called a verbal noun—is the *-ing* form of a verb used as a noun. It can serve in any noun function: as subject or complement of a verb *(Seeing* is *believing)* or as object of a verb or preposition (He taught *dancing;* The odds are against your *winning*). Like a noun, a gerund can be modified by an adjective (Good *boxing* was rare) or used as a modifier (a *fishing* boat, a *living* wage). Yet, like a verb, a gerund can take a subject and an object and can be modified by an adverb:

The critic despaired of the author (subject) ever (adverb) *constructing* a really forceful play (object).

A gerund may be in the present or the perfect tense and in the active or passive voice: *seeing, having seen, being seen, having been seen.*

Though it has the same form as the present participle, the gerund is used differently:

> *Gerund: Running* a hotel appealed to him. (*Running* is the subject.)
>
> *Participle: Running* a hotel, he prospered. (The participle phrase modifies *he*.)

2. Subject of a gerund.   The subject of a gerund is sometimes in the possessive case and sometimes in the accusative, or objective (in nouns, the "common"), case. Formal writing uses the possessive more than general writing does: "Such a view leads to the metaphor's becoming a brief poem in itself" (Alex Page, *Modern Philology*). General is likely to use the common case: "The Vice President's humorous remarks about Hofstra not picking up this ball are somewhat offset . . . by the record" (Clifford Lord, *College Board Review*).

When the subject is a personal pronoun or a proper noun, the possessive is more usual than the common case in both formal and general: They wanted to discuss *my going* AWOL; We overlooked *Joe's swearing.* When the subject is a personal pronoun and begins the sentence, the possessive is required: *Our* (not *Us*) *worrying* won't solve anything; *His* (not *Him*) *lying* deceived nobody.

3. Phrases with gerunds.   Gerunds are often used in phrases that function somewhat like dependent clauses: *In coming to an agreement,* they had compromised on all points; *By refusing to sing,* she embarrassed her mother. The relation of the gerund phrase to the word it modifies should be clear. The reader shouldn't have to pause to make sure just what the writer intended:

> *Dangling: In coming to an agreement,* campaign promises were ignored.

> *Revision:* In coming to an agreement, both sides ignored their campaign promises.

> *Dangling: After sleeping sixteen hours,* my headache was finally gone.

> *Revision:* After sleeping sixteen hours, I was finally rid of my headache. *Or:* After I slept sixteen hours, my headache was finally gone.

See **Dangling modifiers, Idiom.** Compare **Infinitives, Participles.**

get up

In general English you get up when you stand up or get out of bed. See **arise, rise, get up.**

go

Go in the sense "become" is used as a linking verb in a number of idioms. While some *(go broke, go native, go straight)* are informal to general, others *(go blind, go lame)* are fully established in all varieties of usage. *Go and,* as an intensive with no actual motion implied, is common in speech and turns up in some general writing: "He has gone and made a genuine commercial film" (Joseph Morgenstern, *Newsweek*). *Going for* in the sense "working to the advantage of" is general: "when women in England didn't have much going for them" (Emily Hahn, *New York Times Book Review*). Neither *go and* nor *going for* in these senses is appropriate in formal writing. See **Idiom, try and.**

Gobbledygook

Maury Maverick, a congressman from Texas, coined the term *gobbledygook* for wordy, pompous, overweight prose that confuses and irritates more than it informs. Although government bureaus have earned their reputations as producers of gobbledygook, business, the military, the social sciences, and the humanities have shown an equal weakness for such jargon. Frequently gobbledygook serves the purpose of disguising the truth. See **Diction 2, Doublespeak, Jargon.**

good, well

Good is usually an adjective in standard English. *Well* is either an adjective or an adverb. "I feel good" and "I feel well" (adjectives) are both usual but have different meanings. *Good* implies actual bodily sensations; *well* refers merely to a state, "not ill." In nonstandard usage *good* takes the place of *well:* He played good; She sings good. Adverbial *good* is also heard in informal speech and frequently appears in printed representations of speech: "She's running good now," the mechanic said.

got, gotten

Either *got* or *gotten* is usually acceptable as the past participle of *get.* But *got*—not *gotten*—is often added to *has* or *have* to emphasize the notion of "possess" (I haven't got a cent; She's got a letter from home) or of "must" (You've got to lend me a dollar). Though seldom used in formal writing, the emphatic *got* is fairly common in general writing: "A lot of adults are bored by Bach because they haven't got the faintest idea of what music is about" (Marya Mannes, *TV Guide*). *Got married* is particularly distasteful to some formal stylists.

gourmet

A gourmet is a connoisseur of food and drink. As a vogue word, the adjective *gourmet* is regularly applied to food, restaurants, and cooking that a gourmet couldn't stomach. (It's even applied to cutlery.) If you mean "foreign," "expensive," or "fancy," use those words. To express general approval, *good* is available.

graduated

The idiom *to be graduated from* an institution has generally gone out of use except in formal and somewhat old-fashioned writing and has been replaced by *graduated from:* He graduated from high school in 1904. Omitting the *from*—She graduated college in 1980—is a common usage that causes violent reactions in some quarters: ". . . to say 'I graduated college' . . . is to be a language slob and a discredit to whatever learning factory mailed you a diploma" (William Safire, *New York Times Magazine*).

Grammar

Grammar has several different senses. Just as *history* can mean a field of study, events in the past, or the book that describes those events, so *grammar* can refer to a field of study, a set of abilities in our brains, or the book that describes those abilities.

1. Philosophers in Greece had begun speculating about language and words long before the Stoics in 300 B.C. singled out grammar as a field of study separate from rhetoric and poetics. Since then scholars have continued to study the structure of language, not only because language is the central defining characteristic of the human race but because it seems possible that the very foundation of our knowledge and thought—perhaps even perception itself—are shaped by the grammatical structures of our language. Grammar thus becomes an entry to the study of the mind.

2. *Grammar* may also refer to the ability every normal human being has to speak and understand sentences. We all have a grammar in our heads. We can all understand an indefinite number of new sentences we've never heard before. We can distinguish between grammatical and ungrammatical sentences (see **grammatical, ungrammatical 1**). We can recognize sentences that are ambiguous. We also understand that some sentences are related to others, as this sentence is related to the next two.

> That some sentences are related to others is also understood by us. It is also understood by us that some sentences are related to others.

The goal of a linguist, a scholar who studies grammatical structure, is to describe in a written grammar this internalized grammar that we all share.

3.   The history of linguistic study in the last hundred years falls very roughly into three schools.

a.   Traditional. Although this label is applied to a great variety of approaches, most traditional grammars start by describing parts of speech and the inflections associated with them: nouns are names of persons, places, and things, and so on. Once the parts of speech have been described, the grammar describes functions: subjects, predicates, objects, modifiers, and so on. The definitions are illustrated by examples. The reader of the grammar is expected to understand the labeling through the descriptions and examples and then to use his native knowledge of the language to apply the label in any new sentence that might contain the pattern. For example:

> A sentence adverb modifies a whole sentence rather than any individual word or construction. It usually stands at the beginning of the sentence, though it may occur elsewhere: *Fortunately,* he left; He is *allegedly* still here; No one cares, *obviously*.

Confronted with the sentence "Apparently, she left," you could identify *apparently* as a sentence adverb on the basis of the explanation and examples. Such descriptions require the ability of a native speaker to make them work.

b.   Structural. In the early part of this century a new approach to grammar emerged. Structural linguists tried to devise objective techniques for discovering the structure of a language without relying on the meanings of words (as traditional grammars do). They began by cataloging the sounds produced by native speakers, then identifying the smallest units that seemed to have meaning (morphemes), and then arranging these units into larger classes, not according to their meanings but according to their customary relationships with other units. Once the parts of speech were classified, sequences of different parts were identified (noun-verb, verb-noun, preposition-noun, adjective-noun, etc.) and then further described functionally (subject-predicate, verb-object, modifier-head, etc.).

c.   Generative-transformational. Through the 1940s and most of the 1950s, structural grammars were thought to be the new wave in English language education. Then in 1957 Noam Chomsky, a linguist at the Massachusetts Institute of Technology, published *Syntactic Structures* and revolutionized the study of language. Chomsky turned linguists toward a model of language that tries to account in a formal set of rules for the ability of native speakers to produce and understand an infinite range of new sentences. Grammarians of the generative-transformational school assume the existence of a grammar in the mind of the native speaker. They seek to account for what all languages have in common, as well as for the peculiarities that distinguish English, say, from German; and they try to deal with the full range of language, from sounds to meaning, in an integrated theory.

Chomsky's initial formulations of generative theory have been considerably modified and revised, and there are adherents of other theories of language description—tagmemic grammars, stratificational grammars, dependency grammars, and others. But for at least two decades the dominant models for research into the structure of English and other languages were generative-transformational.

4.   So far, we've ignored the most common meaning of *grammar*. This is grammar in the sense of ''good grammar''—making the ''right'' choice between *who* and *whom,* not using *like* for *as,* avoiding sentence fragments, and so on. It concentrates only on those areas where usage varies from one social class to another or from the way English teachers believe educated people should speak to the way their students actually do speak.

How we communicate depends on our social class, our geographical roots, the social situation we happen to be in, and our mode of communication—speaking or writing. What most schools teach as grammar are those features that allegedly distinguish written, fairly formal, supposedly upper-middle-class usage from other varieties. It's a serious mistake to assume that this form of grammar alone defines ''correct'' usage.

Thus when we use the word *grammar,* we have to distinguish a variety of senses:

Grammar is a field of scholarly inquiry dating back to ancient Greece.

Grammar is the knowledge of our language—whatever that language may be—that we all have in our heads.

Grammar is a set of rules for a language that can be written down and that will generate the sentences of that language along with a description of each sentence. The object of this grammar is to ''model'' or explain grammar in sense 2.

Grammar in the sense of ''good grammar'' is concerned with certain usages that are supposed to characterize the practice of upper-middle-class speakers and writers. A grammar of good usage consists of the prescriptions found in grammar books—usually fewer than twenty or thirty—that allow someone who wants to be a member of the ''educated'' community to speak and write as those already in that community allegedly speak and write.

This last sense of *grammar* is, unfortunately, the sense most familiar to American students. The associations that cluster around this grammar make it very difficult for linguists to communicate the excitement of discovering something about grammar (sense 2) that he can write down in a grammar (sense 3) that reveals the elegantly complex organization of human linguistic knowledge.

grammatical, ungrammatical

Sentences can be grammatical in either of two senses:

1. Sentences are grammatical when they meet the structural requirements of the grammar used by an individual speaker. "Can't nobody tell me what to do" is ungrammatical for some speakers, but it's grammatical for others, if the grammar they've incorporated into their nervous systems allows them to construct that sentence in ordinary conversation (see **Grammar 2**). "Nobody can tell me what to do" might be ungrammatical for those speakers who habitually say "Can't nobody tell me what to do" but grammatical for those who don't.

In this sense, *grammatical* simply describes the structure of a sentence that's normal for use by a particular person in ordinary speech. The made-up sentence "I know the man who and the woman left" is ungrammatical for all speakers of English.

2. In common usage and school usage, sentences are said to be grammatical when they meet the requirements set by those who are in a position to enforce standards of usage—teachers, editors, employers. In this looser sense, "Can't nobody tell me what to do" is said to be ungrammatical for everyone, and a person to whom the construction is normal and systematic with reference to an internalized grammar (see **Grammar 2**) is said to be speaking ungrammatical English.

Such usages might more accurately be termed "socially acceptable"— meaning "acceptable to those who are concerned about the rules of 'good grammar' " (see **Grammar 4**). In many cases, advice based on this sense of *grammatical* is accurate. Most educated people in this country don't say "Can't nobody tell me what to do." In writing, most make their subjects and verbs agree. Most avoid *ain't* in all but relatively informal situations. On the other hand, rules for usage that's grammatical in the "socially acceptable" sense also involve a good deal of folklore, as many of the articles in the *Index* make clear.

See **Usage.**

Group words

In English many groups of two or more words (that is, phrases) function like single words. Examples:

> *Nouns:* hay fever, back door, holding company, home run, sacrifice hit, school year, baby blue

> *Verbs:* dig in, hold off, look into, flare up, follow through, follow up, close up, show up, blow up, back water

> *Prepositions:* according to, in spite of, in opposition to, previous to, due to

In this book we usually ignore the superficial difference between a part of speech written as a single word and one that's written as a group of words. *Noun* (sometimes called *noun phrase*) or *verb* or *preposition* refers to both single words and to group words functioning as noun or verb or preposition.

guess

Formal usage limits *guess* to its sense of "conjecture, estimate, surmise": "The employers can only guess whom the victims will choose to sue" (Henry L. Woodward, *Yale Law Journal*). But in general and informal usage *guess* is common in its looser senses of "think, suppose, believe": "They were foolish, I guess, in trying to hold history still for one more hour" (Larry L. King, *Atlantic*).

H

had better

Had better is the usual idiom in giving advice or an indirect command: You had better take care of that cold; You'd better go. Running the *d* in *I'd, you'd, he'd* . . . into the *b* of *better* produces the informal construction without either *had* or *'d:* "But I better get with it if I'm going to be a TV viewer" (Goodman Ace, *Saturday Review*).

half

Though *a half* is traditionally considered the more elegant, there's little distinction between *a half* and *half a/an* in current formal and general usage. For example, both "a half century earlier" and "nearly half a century removed" occur in a single issue of the *American Historical Review*. *A half a/an* (a half an hour) is an informal redundancy.

The noun accompanying *half* or *half of* in a subject determines whether the verb is singular or plural: Half of the *book is* . . . ; Half of the *men are*. . . .

hanged, hung

In formal English people are hanged, pictures are hung. In general and informal usage *hang, hung, hung* is often used in all senses: "Of course, McCarthy hung himself at the hearing" (Isidore Silver, *New Republic*).

hardly

When *hardly* means "probably not" or "almost not," don't add another *not*. See **Double negative 2**.

have

1. Independent meaning.   As a verb of independent meaning, *have* has a range of senses *(have a good time/a fight/a baby/a cold/breakfast)*, with "own, possess," both literally and figuratively, the most common: They have a new car. Because *have* occurs so frequently as an "empty" auxiliary word, its meaning as an independent word meaning "possess" is often reinforced by *got* (see **got, gotten**).

2. Auxiliary.   *Have/had* functions as a signal of tense:

> *Perfect tense:* They have come.
> *Future perfect tense:* They will have gone by then.
> *Past perfect tense:* They had gone before we arrived.

See **Tenses of verbs 2**.

3. Contractions.   *He, she, it has* contract to *he's, she's, it's:* He's got a long beard; It's rained for a week. (The contractions with *is* are identical: *he's, she's, it's.*) *I, you, we, they have* contract to *I've, you've, we've, they've.* Omitted *'ve* (You['ve] been gone too long), a speech habit carried over into writing, is nonstandard. Both *had* and *would* contract to *'d:* They'd already spoken; She'd already be waiting.

Would have, wouldn't have are sometimes written *would of, wouldn't of,* a nonstandard transcription of what's spoken as *would've, wouldn't've.*

4. Had ought, hadn't ought.   *Had ought* (He had ought to take better care of himself) is a common nonstandard idiom, sometimes heard in informal speech. *Hadn't ought* (She hadn't ought to lie like that) is regional and informal.

For *have got,* see **got, gotten**. See also **had better**.

Headword

A headword, or head, is a word modified by another word, especially a noun modified by one or more adjectives (his first long *sleep*), a verb modified by one or more adverbs (*walk* carefully), or an adjective or adverb modified by qualifiers (very *old,* more *intelligently*). The headword of a construction is the word around which the rest of the construction is built: very old *men* in raincoats who had been waiting outside.

healthful, healthy

The distinction between *healthful* "conducive to health" (places and foods are healthful) and *healthy* "having good health" (persons, animals, and plants are healthy) is observed in formal and some general writing, but by and large *healthy* is now used for both meanings.

help but

Conservative stylists usually avoid using *can't* (or *cannot*) *help but*. See **can't help but, can't seem to.**

hence

Hence is primarily an adverb, but it's also used as a rather formal connective. See **Conjunctive adverbs.**

he or she

Traditionally, the masculine pronoun *he* is used with indefinite pronouns like *anyone* and *everybody* and with noun antecedents that may refer to either men or women: Every *student* must accept responsibility for *his* acts. But feminists find this usage a prime example of sexist language and prefer *he or she* (or *he/she* or *s/he*) and *his or her*. Sometimes antecedents make a masculine pronoun inappropriate and the double pronoun convenient: "In enabling a young man or woman to prepare for life in a shorter period of time, we direct his or her attention to other values" (Edward H. Litchfield, *Saturday Review*).

For writers and readers to whom avoiding *he* and *his* after a sexually indefinite antecedent isn't a matter of principle, *he or she* and its variants often seem unnecessarily awkward: "Any individual who is a candidate for promotion or tenure should her/himself make sure that records are complete" (Committee recommendation). When *he* or *his* is inappropriate, *they* is a frequent choice in general writing: In helping a young man or woman to prepare for life, we must direct their attention to other values. Switching to "young men and women" would avoid the problem. See **Agreement 2, Sexist language.**

himself, herself

Himself and *herself* are used in two ways, as reflexive pronouns, referring to the subject of the sentence (George has always taken himself too seriously; She looked at herself in the window) and as qualifiers, for emphasis (He told me so himself; The senator herself told me so).

historic, historical

Historic and *historical* ordinarily have quite different meanings. *Historic* usually means "important in history," "noteworthy," "famous": "a historic act: the toast to the French fleet by which the archbishop . . . urged French Catholics to abandon royalist opposition" (James E. Ward, *American Historical Review*). *Historical* is much more neutral, meaning "based on the facts of history," "having occurred in the past," "suitable for study by historians or using their methods": "This autobiography . . . provides a wide range of historical persons and events" (Heinz E. Ellersieck, *American Historical Review*).

hopefully

From an adverb with the established meaning "in a hopeful way, full of hope" (The dog waited hopefully for a handout), *hopefully* became a vogue word meaning "it is hoped": "Hopefully, they will reveal the thickness of the planet's ice cap" (Jonathan Spivak, *Wall Street Journal*). Sometimes it means no more than "with luck": Hopefully she'll be down in a minute. As long as it's kept away from the verb and set off by commas, there's little chance of real ambiguity. The *hopefully* vogue has faded, giving the violent opposition it aroused a chance to cool. The usage is standard though still unacceptable to some.

Hours

In formal writing, hours are often spelled out in words: at four o'clock, around five-fifteen. In newspapers and much other general writing, figures are used, especially if several times are mentioned and always in designations of time with *a.m.* and *p.m.*: at 4 p.m., just after 9 a.m., around 4:30 p.m., from 10 to 12.

however

However is particularly appropriate as a connective in the fully developed sentences of formal style. It is also the most common conjunctive adverb in general writing, where it typically serves to relate a sentence to what's gone before rather than to connect main clauses within the same sentence:

> Murder is usually reported, and 86 percent of all reported murders lead to arrests. Among those arrested, however, only 64 percent are prosecuted.—Ramsey Clark, *Saturday Review*

However can either introduce the clause it modifies (However, among those arrested . . .) or, as in the example, follow the words the writer wants to emphasize (Among those arrested, however, . . .). To begin a clause the simpler *but* is often the better choice.

See **Conjunctive adverbs.**

hung, hanged

In formal English, pictures are hung, people are hanged. See **hanged, hung.**

Hyperbole

We all use this very common figure of speech—obvious and extravagant overstatement—when we describe our troubles as *incredible,* our embarrassments as *horrible,* our vacations as *fabulous.* Such efforts to dramatize and intensify fail through repetition. Like other figures, hyperbole works well only when it's fresh. See **Figurative language.**

Hypercorrectness

Hypercorrect forms are used by speakers and writers who work so hard at being correct that they end up being wrong. Perhaps the most common example of hypercorrectness is the use of *I* for *me* in a compound object: It is a wonderful moment for my wife and I; They invited Bill and I; between you and I. Other common hypercorrect forms include *whom* for *who* (He is critical of the other members, whom he feels spend more time making accusations than solving problems), *as* for *like* (I always tried to behave as a gentleman), the ending *-ly* where it doesn't belong (She looks badly), some verb forms (*lie* for *lay*), and many pronunciations.

Hyphen

In *Manuscript and Proof,* stylebook of the Oxford University Press, John Benbow wrote, "If you take the hyphen seriously, you will surely go mad." To ward off madness, adopt a recent dictionary or stylebook as your guide and follow it consistently.

1. Word division.   The hyphen is always used to mark the division of a word at the end of a line (see **Division of words**). Other uses are in part a matter of style.

2. Compound words.   Some compound words are written as two words *(post office),* some as one *(notebook),* and some as a combination of words joined by hyphens *(mother-in-law).* The trend is away from hyphenation, toward one-word spelling. Even when a prefix ends and a root word begins with the same vowel, the current tendency is to write the word solid: *cooperate, reelect, preeminent.*

A number of compound adjective forms are conventionally hyphenated when they precede the noun: *clear-eyed, able-bodied, first-class.* Compounds consisting of an adverb plus a verbal are hyphenated when the adverb doesn't end in *-ly:* a well-marked trail (*but* a plainly marked trail).

3. Noun phrases.   Usage is divided on hyphenating noun phrases used as modifiers, as in "seventeenth century philosophy." A hyphen is more likely in formal styles: seventeenth-century philosophy.

4. Miscellaneous uses.   A numeral as part of a modifier (5-cent cigar, nine-inch boards) is hyphenated, and a hyphen is used between a prefix and a proper name: pre-Sputnik, pro-Doonesbury. A "suspension" hyphen may be used to hold together a spread-out modifier: the third-, fourth-, and fifth-grade rooms; both fourteenth- and fifteenth-century records.

5. To avoid ambiguity.   Occasionally a pair of modifiers is ambiguous without a hyphen. "A light yellow scarf" may be either a scarf that's light yellow or a light scarf that's yellow. *Light-yellow* makes the first meaning clear; *light, yellow* the second. Similarly, "new car-owner" and "new-car owner" prevent misunderstanding.

I

I

The notion that *I* (always capitalized) shouldn't be the first word in a sentence is groundless. *I* should be used wherever it's needed. Circumlocutions to avoid the natural use of *I* are usually awkward. "My present thinking is that nuclear power projects are unsound" is a clumsy way of saying "I think now [or "I think" or "I have come to think" or "At present I think"] that nuclear power projects are unsound." See **it's me, myself, we.**

ibid.

Ibid., an abbreviation of the Latin *ibidem* ("in the same place"), is used in the notes of some scholarly books, articles, and research papers. When it stands alone (^{2} Ibid.), it refers the reader to the preceding citation. When followed by a page number (^{2} Ibid., p. 37), it refers to a different page of the work just cited. In current styles of documentation *ibid.* has been replaced by the author's name or by the author's name followed by a shortened version of the title of the work. When *ibid.* appears, its use is often restricted to a second reference on the *same page* of the manuscript or publication. See **Note form 3.**

id Idiom

The expression marked is not standard idiom. Revise it, referring to an article in this *Index* or to a dictionary if you are not sure of the correct form.

Idioms are established phrases that are not easy to explain grammatically or logically. Some examples are "come in handy," "strike a bargain," "look up an old friend," "many's the time," "make good," "in respect to." We learn these phrases as units, and if we're native speakers, few of them cause us trouble. No native speaker is likely to say "hit a bargain" or "look down an old friend" or "the time is many." Idioms are often completely frozen. You can use thousands of different words as subjects and verbs of sentences, but you can't substitute any other adjective in the phrase "in good stead" (Her advice stood me in good stead).

We have trouble with idioms we haven't learned, and the most common trouble is choosing the right preposition. Because we know "conform to," we may be tempted to speak of a policy that's "in conformity to public opinion"; but the idiom is "in conformity with." In using the formal word *arise,* we might attach the preposition *off* instead of the *from* that idiom calls for. Because logic is no help, the prepositions must be learned in the phrases. Dictionaries sometimes show the preposition that's conventionally used with a particular word.

Some words are idiomatically followed by gerunds, others by infinitives. For example:

Gerunds	**Infinitives**
can't help *doing*	compelled *to do*
capable of *painting*	able *to paint*
the habit of *giving*	the tendency *to give*
an idea of *selling*	a wish *to sell*
enjoys *playing*	likes *to play*

With many common words, either is used: the way *of doing* something, the way *to do* something.

See **ability to; acquiesce; agree to, agree with; compare, contrast; Diction 1; different from, different than; it; Prepositions and style 1; Subjunctive mood 2a.**

i.e.

I.e. is the abbreviation for the Latin words meaning "that is." It's appropriate only in scholarly writing. See **Abbreviations 2.**

if, whether

Writers have a choice between *if* and *whether* before interrogative clauses (indirect questions) and clauses expressing doubt or uncertainty. *Whether* is almost always chosen in formal contexts: "It is appropriate to ask whether these decisions are to be considered a victory for those who champion individual right" (Wayne F. LaFave, *Supreme Court Review*). Both words are used in general writing, but *if* is more common: The survey asked people if TV had influenced their vote.

illiterate

Illiterate and *literate* are used to refer both to the ability to read and write (There were few schools, and most of the peasants were completely illiterate) and to familiarity with what's been written (Any literate person should know the name Kafka). Usage called nonstandard in this book is often loosely referred to as illiterate in the second sense—that is, uneducated. The label *illiterate* is applied most freely by those who demand that others use language precisely.

ill, sick

Ill is the less common, more formal word. See **sick, ill.**

illusion, allusion

An illusion misleads, an allusion refers. See **allusion, illusion.**

image

Image meaning a public conception or impression (He was criticized for not projecting the image of a President) has moved from the jargon of the public relations man and the advertiser into general use. Image makers are experts at doublespeak. See **Doublespeak.**

Imagery

An image is a word or group of words that makes an appeal to one of the senses: sight (*shiny, ghostly, mist, light green, thick brown hair*); hearing (*creaking, faraway shouts, the pounding of surf*); taste (*salty, dry, a pickled pear);* smell *(jasmine, fresh paint, a blown-out candle);* touch *(smooth, glassy, razor sharp, a stubbly beard);* or the muscular tension known as the kinesthetic sense *(squirm, jerky, jogging heavily along).* Though an image may appeal to more than one sense *(a rough, angry sea),* in a specific context one sense is usually dominant.

Studying the images in a writer's work will reveal what has impressed him in his experience and what appeals to him—colors, lines, odors, sounds. Your own writing will be richer and stronger if it includes images drawn from your own experience and based on your own taste. A borrowed image is likely to be a dead one. An image from personal experience is a live image; and a live image is like a good photograph: it reveals something of the photographer as well as showing what he has photographed.

See **Figurative language.**

Imperative mood

The form of the verb used for direct commands and requests is in the imperative mood: Bring the tapes when you come; Run! See **Commands and requests.**

implement

The catchall bureaucratic verb *implement,* meaning to "give effect" to policies or ideas (It's a great scenario, but who's going to implement it?), might often be replaced by *fulfill, execute, put into practice,* or *carry out,* if only for variety.

imply, infer

A writer or speaker *implies* something in his words or manner, suggesting a conclusion without stating it. A reader or listener *infers* something from what he reads or hears, drawing a conclusion from the available information. Having a word for each of these acts contributes to clear communication, and careful writers make the distinction.

But for centuries *infer* has also been used to mean "imply," and today many dictionaries recognize this meaning (as well as the traditional meaning) as standard. So when clarity is essential, the safe course is not simply to distinguish between *imply* and *infer* but to provide a context that underlines your meaning: From the President's words, I infer that he. . . .

Incoherence

Writing is incoherent when a relationship between parts (of a sentence, of a paragraph, of a whole paper) isn't apparent. The cause may be that there actually is no relationship between the parts, or it may be that the writer has failed to make the relationship clear. See **Coherence, Transition.**

Incomplete sentence

Punctuating a phrase or a dependent clause as if it were a complete sentence is often the result of carelessness. See **Fragment.**

incredible, incredulous

A story or situation is incredible (''unbelievable''); a person is incredulous (''unbelieving''). One way to avoid confusing the two is to refrain from using *incredible,* a voguish example of trite hyperbole (I'm taking this incredible course!) unless you mean it literally (His claim to have read *War and Peace* in one evening is incredible).

Indention

To indent in manuscript or printed copy is to begin the first line of a paragraph some distance to the right of the left-hand margin—an inch in handwritten copy, five spaces in typewritten copy. Hanging indention is indention of all lines below the first line, as in bibliography entries, each main section of an outline, and many newspaper headlines. If a line of poetry is too long to complete on one line, the part brought over to the second line should be indented. For indenting quotations, see **Quotation marks 1d.**

Independent clauses

An independent clause (like this one) can stand alone as a simple sentence. See **Clauses.**

Indicative mood

Verb forms that make assertions or ask questions are said to be indicative or in the indicative mood. The indicative is the mood of most verbs in English sentences: They *sat* on the porch even though it *was* late October; *Will* you *come* if you *are* invited? Compare **Imperative mood, Subjunctive mood.**

Indirect discourse (indirect quotation)

In indirect discourse a person's words are reported in paraphrase or summary instead of being quoted exactly:

   Direct: He said, ''I won't take it if they give it to me.''

   Indirect: He said he wouldn't take it if they gave it to him.

An indirect question restates a question at second hand:

> *Direct:* ''Is everyone all right?'' he asked.

> *Indirect:* He asked if everyone was all right.

See **Commands and requests, Questions, Quotation marks 2b, Tense 3b.**

Indirect objects

An indirect object names what or whom something is given, said, or shown to: She gave *him* a prize. See **Objects 2.**

Induction

The process of reasoning known as induction originates in curiosity and ends in conviction. You're reasoning inductively when, after asking your friends how they feel about a proposed change in the pass-fail policy and after listening to what's being said about the subject around campus, you decide that the student body is strongly opposed to the change. Note that you haven't polled the student body. That would be nose-counting, not inductive reasoning. Instead, at some point in your gathering of information, you've made the ''inductive leap,'' assuming that what is true of the people you've talked to and listened to is true of the whole group.

You can't be certain that your conclusion is correct. But you can have confidence in it—you can assume that it's highly probable—if the evidence you've examined has been relevant, adequate, and representative.

In serious argument induction usually takes the form of example after example offered in support of a generalization. As used in everyday life, inductive reasoning may seem to be little more than a hunch or an informed guess. In either case, it's important: only by using induction can we spot trends, make predictions, and discover causal relations.

See **Cause and effect, Deduction, Fallacies, Logical thinking.**

infer, imply

The writer or speaker implies; the reader or listener infers. See **imply, infer.**

Infinitives

Infinitive is a Latin grammatical term for a verb form expressing the general sense of the verb without restriction as to person, number, or tense. In Modern English the root form of the verb is the infinitive, often with *to* before it.

1. **The *to* infinitive and the bare infinitive.**   More often than not, an infinitive is used with the preposition *to:* He's the man *to see;* He was glad *to come;* She likes *to be visited.* But *to* is seldom or never used after the modal auxiliary verbs or after some full verbs: I can *see;* She must *carry* it; We let him *go;* They can't make her *talk;* I heard them *sing.*

2. **Functions of infinitives.**   Infinitives serve as subjects, as objects, as complements, and as modifiers. They in turn may have subjects, objects, complements, or modifiers.

> *Subject: To sit and read* was his idea of a holiday. For you *to do* that again would be a serious mistake.
> *Object:* She prefers *to wait* until Tuesday. The police tried *to hold back* the crowd.
> *Complement:* He seems *to be* happy.
> *Modifier:* My friend is the man *to see.* Jane is the person *to do* that. He was reluctant *to stay* longer. They're trying *to find out* what happened. *To avoid* colds, [you] stay out of crowds.

Infinitives and style

1. **Infinitives in a series.**   In a short, unemphatic series, there's no reason to repeat *to:* He decided to shower, shave, and dress. When the series is complex or when separate verbs deserve emphasis, *to* should be repeated: These were her goals—to escape the city, to avoid routine, and to find contentment.

2. **Case of pronoun with infinitive.**   For the pronoun after the infinitive of a linking verb that has no expressed subject, general English usually has the accusative case: I always wanted to be *him.* Formal favors the nominative: I always wanted to be *he.* But unless there's a reason for giving the pronoun prominence, another phrasing might be preferable: He was the person I always wanted to be.

3. **Dangling infinitives.**   Infinitives that function as absolute phrases (to tell the truth, to be sure) are sentence modifiers and as such present no problems. But an infinitive, like a participle or a gerund, will dangle if it seems to be related to a word that it can't sensibly modify or if, in a context that calls for an explicit relationship, it has no clear relation to any word in the sentence:

> *Dangling:* To swim well, fear of the water must be overcome.

> *Revised:* To swim well, the learner must first overcome fear of the water.

See **Absolute phrases, Dangling modifiers.**

4. Split infinitives. In a split infinitive a word or phrase (usually an adverb) comes between *to* and the verb: to actively pursue. Some infinitives shouldn't be split; some should be, because splitting them makes the sentence easier to understand and more pleasant to read. In still other contexts it's a matter of choice, with more splits occurring in general English than in formal. See **Split infinitive.**

Inflection

Inflection refers to the change of word forms to indicate grammatical relationships, like singular and plural number for nouns or past and present tense for verbs. See **Case, Comparison of adjectives and adverbs, Plurals of nouns, Pronouns, Verbs.**

Informal English

The word or passage marked is too informal for the subject or for the style of the rest of the paper. Revise, making it more appropriate.

Informal written English is appropriate (though not mandatory) in letters to close friends and to members of your family and may be the style you use in a diary or journal. Its casual, intimate tone makes it unsuitable for most college writing, though informal usages may be successfully introduced into papers written in general English if they're chosen with taste and judgment.

You'd be unlikely to use the informal *pretty* (pretty big, pretty soon, pretty old) in a chemistry report or a psychology examination, and you probably wouldn't describe Robert Frost as "a pretty good poet" in a paper for a literature course. But in writing for an audience of classmates, you might call a local hero "a pretty good quarterback." Whether or not *inf* appeared in the margin of your paper would depend on the context. If your style was relaxed and conversational, *pretty* would be appropriate. If your style placed some distance between you and your readers, *fairly* would be a better choice.

As applied to sections of papers or to whole papers, *informal* usually implies sloppiness—rambling sentences, vague references, trite slang, repetition, incoherence. If something you've written has been so marked, the best solution is to rethink what you want to say and rewrite the passage, aiming for clarity and precision.

See **Formal English, General English, Standard English.** See also **Agreement, Colloquial English, Repetition, Slang, Spoken and written English, Triteness.**

in, into, in to

In usually shows location, literal or figurative: He was in the house; He was in a stupor. *Into* usually shows direction: He came into the house; He fell into a stupor. But in informal and general usage *in* is common when direction is meant: "Twice a week we get in the car, and drive down the Parkway" (Richard Rose, *St. Louis Post-Dispatch*).

The *in* of *in to* is an adverb and the *to* a preposition (They went in to dinner) or sign of the infinitive (They went in to eat).

Intensifiers

Intensifiers are words like *very, greatly, terribly, much,* which intensify the meaning of adjectives and adverbs: He is much older than she; She ran very fast. See **Qualifiers.**

Intensive pronouns

Reflexive pronouns—the personal pronouns plus *-self* or *-selves*—may be used as intensives: We ourselves are responsible. See **myself, Pronouns 2.**

Interjections

Interjections are expressions of emotion like *oh, ow, ouch, ah.* See **Exclamations.**

Interrogative pronouns

Who, whom, whose, which, what are interrogative pronouns. See **Pronouns 5.**

Intransitive verbs

An intransitive verb takes no object: The money *vanished*. See **Transitive and intransitive verbs.**

Inversion

Inversion usually means placing the verb, or some part of the verb phrase, before its subject. This is the regular pattern in questions: Will she go? Did they enjoy it? Inversion is also used with expletive *there* and *it* (There was a man at the door) and in a few other situations: What a fool I am; Long may it wave; Here comes the thunder. In a declarative sentence, any part of the predicate may occasionally be inverted for emphasis: Cabbage I hate; Down he went; This I know; That she was brilliant we had no doubt.

Irony

Irony implies something markedly different, sometimes even the opposite, of what's actually said. Light irony is mildly humorous, as in the greeting "Lovely day!" in pouring rain. Heavy irony is usually a form of sarcasm or satire: "The most important argument for collecting taxes from the elderly is that it would lower the tax burden on helpless corporations and conglomerates who are struggling to make ends meet" (Art Buchwald, syndicated columnist).

irregardless

Irregardless is redundant: both the prefix *ir-* and the suffix *-less* are negative. The standard word is *regardless*.

Irregular verbs

Verbs that don't form their past tense and past participle by adding *-ed* are irregular. See **Principal parts of verbs.**

it

The neuter third-person singular pronoun *it* is used most commonly to refer to inanimates but sometimes refers to living things. Typically it replaces preceding neuter noun phrases: Have you seen *the neighbors' new car?* Yes, isn't *it* a mess? The antecedent may be a clause or a sentence: Some people say *that more money will solve the problem of our schools,* but I don't believe *it.* But sometimes *it* has no antecedent, as in impersonal statements about weather, time, distance, or events in general, and in many idioms:

> *It's* been three hours since *it* began to rain, and *it's* still five miles to camp.
> *It* isn't pleasant to live in Washington these days.
> Damn *it,* we'll have to play *it* by ear.

Though typically neuter, the antecedent of *it* may be an animal or a small child whose sex is unknown or irrelevant. *It* is also used with reference to collective nouns denoting persons (The faculty must decide for *it*-self) and in sentences where individuals are identified (I'm not sure who the tenor was, but *it* could have been Domingo).

The more important uses of *it* stylistically are those in which it fills the position of a subject or object that's fully expressed later in the sentence. In such sentences *it* is called the anticipatory subject or object:

> *It* is *doubtful that he should be given so much freedom.*
> He found *it* painful *living in the same house with a person whose racial attitudes he detested.*

> *It* was *Wordsworth* who called his gun a "thundering tube."

The advantages of such constructions are that they offer an alternative to lengthy separation of sentence parts that belong together (He found living in the same house with a person whose racial attitudes he detested painful) and a means of assigning emphasis: "It was Wordsworth who . . ." emphasizes *Wordsworth;* "Wordsworth called his gun a 'thundering tube' " emphasizes *thundering tube*.

See **its, it's; it's me; there is, there are.**

ital Italics

In handwritten and typewritten copy, underline words or passages to correspond to the conventions of using italic type.

In writing, words and statements that would be printed in italics are underlined. Though newspapers have generally abandoned italic type, most magazines and books use it, and in academic writing—course papers, articles in learned journals, dissertations, reference books—italics have standardized uses:

1.   To indicate titles of books, plays, motion pictures, television series, and other complete works, and to indicate titles of periodicals and newspapers. See **Titles 2.**

2.   To mark words considered as words rather than for their meaning: There is a shade of difference between *because* and *for* used as conjunctions.

3.   To mark unanglicized words from foreign languages: Good clothes were a *sine qua non*. See **Foreign words in English 2a.**

4.   To indicate words that would be stressed if spoken. This device is most appropriate in dialog.

5.   To indicate key words, phrases, or sentences in an argument or explanation. Here italics should be used sparingly. See **Emphasis 6.**

its, it's

Its is a possessive pronoun and, like the possessive pronouns *his, her, our, your,* and *their,* has no apostrophe: A car is judged by *its* performance. *It's* is the contraction for "it is" (It's a long road) and "it has" (It's been said before). Like other contractions, *it's* is more appropriate to informal and general than to formal styles.

it's me

The argument over "it's me" illustrates a conflict between theory and practice. The theory—that after a finite form of the verb *be* the nominative, or subjective, case should always be used—is consistently contradicted by the practice of educated speakers. (Except in dialog, "it's me" is a usage question writers rarely have to think about. In fact, most speakers seldom run into it.) We tend to use the nominative form of a pronoun when it's the subject and stands directly before the verb, but we're likely to use the accusative in most other positions, especially when the pronoun comes after the verb—in "object territory," as it's been called. (Compare **who, whom.**) All the major grammars of English regard "it's me" as acceptable. See **be 2.**

-ize

The formation of verbs from non-Greek nouns or adjectives by adding the Greek ending *-ize* (often *-ise* in British usage) has been going on since the sixteenth century. Some readers object to the addition of verbs in *-ize*, either because the new verbs duplicate in meaning verbs that are in common use *(fantasized, fantasied; formularize, formulate)* or because the proliferation adds to the stock of advertising jargon *(customize, personalize),* much of which is virtually meaningless, or of gobbledygook *(concretize, optimize).* See **finalize.**

J

Jargon

1. Sir Arthur Quiller-Couch popularized *jargon* as the name for verbal fuzziness of various kinds—wordiness, a high proportion of abstract words, "big" words, and words that add nothing to the meaning. *Buzzwords* is a recent term for a type of jargon. *Jargon* and *gobbledygook* are sometimes used interchangeably. Russell Baker satirizes current jargon (and current attitudes) in the following passage:

> "I could not love thee, dear, so much, lov'd I not honor more," the poet could write. Today he could only say, "I could not have so fulfilling a relationship with thee, dear, had I not an even more highly intensified mental set as regards the absurd and widely discredited concept known as honor."—*New York Times Magazine*

2. *Jargon* also means shoptalk, or the specialized language of a group—doctors, printers, sociologists, photographers, chicken farmers, and so on. So defined, jargon is appropriate in certain circumstances, as when a physicist writes for fellow physicists, but not in others, as when the physicist writes for a general audience. In many groups and many situations there's a tendency to go beyond the necessary technical jargon and create jargon in the first sense. Examples of the use of language to impress more than to inform include sociologese, psychologese, educationese, journalese, and bureaucratese.

See **Doublespeak, Gobbledygook, Shoptalk.**

job, position

Job is general English for the formal *position:* He got a job at the oil refinery. The word *position* has more dignity, though what it refers to isn't necessarily better paid. Because *position* can sound pompous, many writers use *job* for all levels of employment.

jock

The history of *jock,* now informal for "athlete" of either sex, illustrates a number of processes in the origin of words. *Jock* is the clipped form of *jockstrap,* a supporter for the male genitals worn during strenuous activity. (*Jock* is also a figure of speech in which the part—the "athletic supporter," as it was less vulgarly known—stands for the whole—the athlete.) *Jockstrap* in turn was created by combining *jock,* a slang term for the penis, and *strap.* The use of *jock* first for male athletes and then, by simple extension, for female athletes as well shows what can sometimes happen when the history of a word is not known or is ignored. See **Origin of words 1.**

Journalese

Roy Copperud defined *journalese* as "all that is bad in journalistic writing." (Journalistic writing today includes not only the writing that appears in newspapers and newsmagazines but the writing that's read to us by television and radio news reporters and commentators.) Journalese is journalistic jargon, loaded with clichés, vogue words, buzzwords, hyperboles, gobbledygook, and doublespeak and wholly lacking in character and conviction. It proves that even professional, "grammatical" writing can be awful.

just

The qualifier *just* is redundant in expressions like *just exactly* and *just perfect.* Omit it.

K

kid

The noun *kid* for "child" and the verb *kid* for "tease" are established in general usage. A problem with *kid* as a noun is that it now may mean not only someone past puberty but someone past adolescence (the kids in graduate school). So loosely used, *kid* is informal. In many contexts a more specific term is needed.

kind, sort

The words *kind* and *sort* are involved in three different problems for writers.

1. Agreement.   *Kind* and *sort* are singular pronouns with regular plurals. A problem arises only when singular *kind* or *sort* is followed by *of* and a plural noun. Then there's a strong tendency to treat the plural object of *of*, rather than *kind* or *sort*, as the headword of the construction and to use plural demonstratives and verbs: These sort of books are harmless; "Those kind of overhead expenses" (Lewis H. Lapham, *Harper's*). But though the construction is common in speech and there are numerous examples of its use by respected writers, strong objection to it continues. For one kind (or sort), then: *That kind* of book *is*. . . . For more than one: *Those kinds* of books *are*. . . .

2. *Kind (sort) of a(n)*.   *Kind of a(n)* and *sort of a(n)* are general idioms: "People just didn't trust that kind of an approach" (Charles Mohr, *Esquire*). Formal style would have "kind of approach."

3. *Kind (sort) of*.   As adverbs equivalent to imprecise qualifiers like *rather* and *somewhat* in more formal usage, *kind of* and *sort of* are informal to general: "She was kind of plump" (Claude Brown, *Commentary*); "Everything just sort of limped along" (E. J. Kahn, Jr., *New Yorker*).

know-how

Though *know-how* occurs in every variety of English, for many readers its connotations remain commercial and technical. To speak of the know-how of a great violinist, for example, would be inappropriate.

lab

The clipped form of *laboratory* is now common in all but the most formal usage.

lady

The vogue use of *lady* for *woman,* as in popular songs, is out of place in college writing. See **woman, lady, girl.**

last, latest

Both *last* and *latest* are used as superlatives of *late* (his last book; his latest book). But to avoid ambiguity, formal English uses *last* for the final item in a series (His last book was completed only weeks before his death), *latest* for the most recent of a series that may or may not be continued (His latest book shows steady improvement).

latter

The use of *latter* in referring to the last of more than two items is standard, but conservative stylists prefer "the last named." See **former, first—latter, last.**

lay, lie

In standard English *lie (lay, lain)* is intransitive: He let it lie there; She lay down for a nap; The boards have lain there for months. *Lay (laid, laid)* is transitive: You can lay it on the table; They laid the keel; She had laid it away for future reference. In much spoken English *lay* does the work of both verbs; but in most writing they are kept distinct, and in college writing they should always be. The *-ing* forms sometimes give trouble, with *laying* appearing where *lying* is meant: I spent the summer laying around the house.

learn, teach

In nonstandard English *learn* is often used to mean "teach": He learned me how to tie knots. Standard English makes the distinction: He *taught* me how to tie knots; I *learned* how to tie knots from him.

leave, let

Let, not *leave,* is standard English for "permit" or "allow." See **let, leave.**

lend, loan

In referring to material things, *lend* and *lends* are preferred to *loan* and *loans* in formal writing: "those who wished to lend" (George V. Taylor, *American Historical Review*). But the past tense and past participle *loaned* is preferred to *lent* in all varieties: "About $4 billion have been loaned" (Adolf A. Berle, *The American Economic Republic*). In general contexts, *loan* and *loans* are as common as *lend* and *lends* and are entirely acceptable.

In the sense "grant, impart, furnish" or "adapt or accommodate (itself)," *lend* and *lent* are always preferred: "America always lent itself to personification" (Norman Mailer, *Harper's*).

less, fewer

Use *fewer* for things that can be counted, *less* for things that can't be. See **fewer, less.**

let, leave

A common nonstandard idiom is the use of *leave* for "permit" or "allow," meanings that standard English assigns to *let.* Both uses are shown in this sentence by a writer making a transition between nonstandard and standard: "In high school I was cured of the practice of leaving [nonstandard] notebooks go, but I fell into the habit of letting [standard] homework slide."

In standard English the two verbs are interchangeable only with *alone* and the meaning "refrain from disturbing": Leave (*or* Let) me alone; All they asked of their government was to be let (*or* left) alone.

Lexical meaning

In linguistics a distinction is often made between grammatical or structural meaning and lexical meaning. In "Birds were killed," the information that *bird* and *kill* give us is the sort provided by a dictionary or lexicon—hence lexical meaning. The information given by the *-s* of *birds* (plural), *were* (past tense, passive voice), and the *-ed* of *killed* (past participle in this position) is the sort provided by our awareness of the grammar or structure of the language—hence grammatical or structural meaning. When we fully understand the sentence, we have grasped its total meaning.

liable

In formal writing and most general writing, *liable* followed by an infinitive is used to predict only undesirable results: The effects are liable to be disastrous. *Liable*-plus-infinitive to predict desirable results appears most often in informal and casual general contexts: "Walleyes are year-round sport and . . . they're liable to hit any time of the day or night" (Roger Latham, *Field and Stream*). *Likely* and *apt* are not restricted in this way.

lie

The transitive verb *lay* shouldn't be substituted for the intransitive *lie*. You *lie*, not *lay*, down when you're tired. You *lay*, not *laid*, down yesterday. See **lay, lie.**

life-style

One way to avoid overusing *life-style*, a term as vague as it is voguish, is to distinguish between what is truly a distinctive way of life—of attitudes and behavior—and a deviation from the norm in some specific respect. If you write about a person who sleeps all day and goes to work at night, don't refer to his life-style; say that he's on the night shift.

like, as

1. As prepositions. In all varieties of English, *like* is used as a preposition introducing a comparison: The description fits her like a plaster cast; Habit grips a person like an octopus; He took to selling like a bee to clover. *As* is increasingly common as a hypercorrect form: "Hate must run off you as water off the proverbial infield tarpaulin" (Laurence Sheehan, *Atlantic*).

2. As conjunctions. In all varieties of English, *as, as if,* and *as though* are used as conjunctions introducing clauses of comparison: They moved across the floor as skaters glide over a frozen pond; He walked as though he was hurt. *Like* as a conjunction is common in speech and appears frequently in informal and general writing: "Like a typical kid his age might do, Holden does violate some rules of grammar" (James Lundquist, *J. D. Salinger*). But opposition to *like* as a conjunction remains strong, and it should be avoided in most college writing.

3. The way. *The way* provides an escape from the *like-as* thicket for writers who think *like* is crude and *as* is prissy: "Hemingway once told Callaghan, 'Dostoevski writes like Harry Greb fights.' Unfortunately, Callaghan writes the way Hemingway fights" *(Time)*.

likely

"They'll probably be there" can also be expressed as "They'll likely be there" or "They likely will be there," though some formal stylists insist that *likely* in this usage must be preceded by a qualifier like *very* or *rather*. "They are likely to be there" is entirely acceptable but expresses a bit less likelihood.

Linguistics

Linguistics is a broad discipline incorporating several perspectives from which language may be studied systematically. Linguists study the structures of languages and the universal structure of language. They study the histories and the varieties of language. They study how language is acquired and how it is used.

Linguistics differs from other disciplines devoted to the study of language by having at its center a theory of language derived from the study of formal, regular, and recurrent patterns in the structures of human languages. Theories of language differ, and therefore schools of linguistics exist; but all linguists are empiricists, sharing a desire to be as objective as possible and rejecting conclusions not based on consistent theory and verified by significant data.

See **Grammar.**

Linking verbs

When a verb like *be* functions chiefly as a bridge between a subject and another noun or a modifier, it's called a linking, or copulative, verb. A linking verb is followed by single words, phrases, or clauses that function as adjectives or nouns and are traditionally known as predicate adjectives (This bottle was *full*) or as predicate nouns or predicate nominatives (The man was a *carpenter*). Some grammarians prefer to call them complements, or subjective complements.

Many verbs besides *be* are used as linking verbs. A few of them are italicized in the following sentences:

He *became* a doctor.	The ground *sounds* hollow.
The butter *tastes* rancid.	He *appeared* to be healthy.
She *felt* sad.	The dog *acts* old.
His story *seemed* incredible.	The weather *turned* cold.
This *looks* first-rate.	She *grew* moody.

Many verbs are used both with full meaning of their own (The tree *fell* into the water) and as linking verbs (He *fell* silent). Speakers who are not aware that the same verb can function both ways and who have been taught that verbs are modified by adverbs often make the mistake of substituting an adverb for the adjective that should follow a linking verb: "She felt sadly" for "She felt sad." Such hypercorrectness also crops up in writing.

For the most common source of difficulty in using the linking-verb pattern, see **Predicate adjectives.** See also **bad, badly; be 2; Hypercorrectness; it's me; look.**

literally

Literally means "actually, without deviating from the facts," but it's so often used to support metaphors that its literal meaning may be reversed. In statements like the following, *literally* means "figuratively" and *literal* means "figurative":

> All of this is taking place in Florida at a time when the nation is literally awash in oil.—Fred J. Cook, *Nation*

> In this struggle, women's bodies became a literal battleground.—Martin Duberman, *Nation*

> [New York City] is literally hanging by its fingernails.—Walter Cronkite, *CBS News*

Taken literally, such statements create very funny mental pictures.

literate

Literate is used to mean both "capable of reading and writing" and "acquainted with what has been written—educated." See **illiterate.**

loan

In referring to possession, *lend* is more formal than *loan* in the present tense. For the past tense, *loaned* is preferred to *lent* in all varieties of usage. See **lend, loan.**

Loan words

Loan words are words borrowed from other languages. See **Foreign words in English, Origin of words 2b.**

Localisms

A localism is a word or other expression in regular use only in a certain region, like *hoagie, submarine* (or *sub*), *hero, po' boy* for the same sort of sandwich in a roll. Though appropriate in conversation and informal writing, localisms are out of place in general and formal writing except to give a regional flavor. See **Dialects.**

Locution

Locution is a handy term for referring to a word or to a phrase or clause considered as a unit. In the preceding sentence "a handy term" is one locution.

logic Logical thinking

Reconsider the logical relationship that is expressed or implied.

At some time or other everyone has protested, "That doesn't make sense" or "That doesn't follow from what you just said." Everyone, that is, has some notion of the difference between logical and illogical thinking, and when something is said or written that doesn't make sense or fails to show a logical progression, everyone's impulse is to dismiss it.

In a college paper illogical thinking is revealed in irrelevant material, faulty organization, incoherent sentences, and words that blur or skew the meaning of what's being said. More narrowly, it shows up in the faulty relationship between ideas. Often the seeming breakdown in logic is simply the result of careless writing. In taking issue with the statement "The true university is a collection of books," a student wrote, "If I were to agree that a true university is no more than a collection of books, I would graduate well-read but not socially mature." This makes no sense, because simply agreeing or not agreeing with the statement about a true university could not determine the kind of education a particular student would receive at a particular school.

Presumably the student meant, "If a true university is no more than a collection of books, and if this is a true university, then I can expect to be well-read when I graduate but not necessarily socially mature." If he intended to base an *if . . . then* relationship on his agreeing with the original statement, he might say, "If I agreed that a true university is no more than a collection of books, then I would spend all my time in the library."

You can avoid such apparent lapses in logic by carefully reading what you write—seeing what you've *said* rather than what you *meant* to say—and revising your sentences before preparing your final draft.

Much more serious are the kinds of illogical thinking that undercut a whole paper. When you write to express an opinion, defend a point of view, argue for or against something, or persuade or convince your readers, keep these recommendations in mind:

1. Limit your generalizations to what you can support with evidence.

2. Make sure that what you offer as evidence is authoritative and has bearing on the issue.

3. Make sure that you attack the actual issue instead of skirmishing around the edges or wandering off into another conflict.

4. Make sure you omit no links in the chain of reasoning that leads to your conclusion.

In reading over what you've written, take a hard look at your generalizations. Are they sound enough to support your argument? Are they based on fact and justifiable inferences, or are they no more than unexamined assumptions or expressions of prejudice?

When you find yourself saying that *A* caused *B* or that *B* is the result of *A*, think over your reasons for saying so. Are they convincing? Are there reasons for *not* saying so that you've deliberately omitted? Are your comparisons justifiable and your analogies plausible?

After enjoying the violent language you've used in condemning those who hold an opposing point of view, and after admiring the eloquence with which you've praised those whose side you're supporting, ask yourself whether the faults of the former or the virtues of the latter have anything to do with the issue itself. Unless they have, don't mistake what you've had to say for logical argument.

See **Cause and effect, Classification and division, Deduction, Fallacies, Induction, Syllogisms.**

Logic and language

Sometimes an item of usage is objected to as being illogical—for example, "the reason is because." But when the objection to "the reason is because" is elaborated, it's usually that an adverbial clause (*because . . .*) is equated with a noun *(reason)*—a criticism that has to do with grammar rather than logic.

Idiom illustrates particularly well the lack of correspondence between logic and usage. The meanings of many idioms—"hard to come by," "hold your own," "out of order"—are not the sum of the meanings of their separate words. These show, more clearly than the general patterns and rules of English, that language is a human development, the result of millions of speech situations, not a preplanned system. Language isn't illogical; it's simply alogical.

Probably arguments from logic had an influence in establishing the double negative as nonstandard English. In Old and Middle English the more negatives there were, the stronger the negation. But arguments from logic have had few such successes, and the term *logical* applies to language only in its most general, popular sense of "more or less systematic."

See **Double negative, Idiom, reason is because.**

Long variants

Some writers are tempted to add an extra prefix or suffix to a word that already carries the meaning they intend. They write *irregardless,* though *regardless* already means "without regard to," or they write *doubtlessly* for *doubtless.* Some like to use suffixes that add nothing to the meaning, like the *-ation* in *analyzation,* which means no more than *analysis.* Some other long variants that it's wise to avoid are *certificated* for *certified, confliction* for *conflict, emotionality* when only *emotion* is meant, *hotness* for *heat, intermingle* for *mingle, orientate* for *orient, ruination* for *ruin,* and *utilize* when *use* is entirely adequate. See **Diction 2, Gobbledygook, Jargon.**

look

When used as an intransitive verb meaning "use the eyes, gaze," *look* is modified by an adverb: look longingly, look searchingly. As a linking verb, equivalent to *appear, look* is followed by an adjective that modifies the subject: He looks well (*or* healthy *or* tired *or* bad). See **Linking verbs.**

lot, lots

In the senses "much," "many," "a great deal," *a lot (of)* and *lots (of)* have an informal flavor. Both are established in general usage but not in formal:

> He tells Celine to make herself attractive and buys her a lot of new clothes.—Edmund Wilson, *New Yorker*

> There is lots of talk.—*Fortune*

A lot is two words, not one.

 Lowercase

Use a lowercase (small) letter instead of a capital.

As an alternative or supplement to *lc,* the correction may be indicated by a slant line through the capitals:

    It was a ǥreat Ɇxperience.

For the conventional use of capitals, see **Capital letters.**

M

Main clauses

Main clauses (like this one and the next) are independent clauses. They can stand alone as sentences. See **Clauses.**

majority, plurality

Technically a majority in an election is more than half the total number of votes cast, while a plurality is the largest number of votes cast for any one candidate but not more than half the total. Though the distinction is sometimes neglected, it's worth preserving for clarity.

In formal usage *majority* is applied only to groups of at least three things that can be counted. In informal and general usage *majority* is sometimes used also of the larger part of a single thing or mass: "A majority of the LP is taken up with bouncy dance tunes" (Robert Palmer, *New York Times*). *Most* is preferable.

∿∿ Manuscript form

Your manuscript is not in the proper form. Revise or rewrite as directed.

Instructors usually establish their own specifications for manuscript form at the beginning of the course. Whatever the details, the goal is a clean, legible copy that can be read easily. Use white 8½″ x 11″ paper, leave adequate margins, number the pages, make corrections neatly, and observe your instructor's directions for endorsing the paper. See **Division of words, Typewritten copy.**

massive

Used with abstract nouns, *massive* became a vogue word during the 1960s: massive retaliation, massive resistance, massive inequality, massive unemployment. This usage continues. Applying *massive* only to icebergs would be a step in the right direction.

Mass nouns

Mass nouns name masses that are not counted as separate units: food, money, health, water. See **Nouns 3c.**

may, can

In requesting or granting permission or expressing feasibility, *may* is the formal choice. *Can* expresses ability and is commonly used in place of *may* in general English. See **can, may.**

∿∿ Meaning
?

The word, phrase, or sentence marked does not make sense in this context. Replace it with one that communicates the meaning you intend.

For a reader to question the meaning of what you've written indicates a serious failure in communication. Ordinarily the problem is not simply the use of one word for another that's reasonably close to it in sound or meaning—*comprehension* for *comprehensibility,* for example. This would be marked *ww* (wrong word): the reader knows the word is wrong because he knows what the right one is. But *mng,* often followed by a question mark, means that the reader can't, or won't, make a guess at what you're trying to say. Rethinking and rewriting are in order. Compare **Ambiguity, Coherence, Wrong word.**

meaningful

Meaningful became a vogue word in the 1960s and still hangs on, particularly among educators (meaningful learning experiences) and young people (meaningful relationships). Before using it, ask yourself whether its omission would suggest that what you're referring to has no meaning—and remind yourself that many readers consider the term excessively vague or pretentious or both.

media, medium(s)

Medium and *media,* the Latin singular and plural forms, were taken directly into English, and formal usage consistently maintains the distinction in number, while recognizing the alternate plural *mediums:* ''the moral possibilities of the mediums themselves'' (Robert J. Reilly, *American Literature*). But *media,* like many other Latin plurals, has tended to become singular in American usage and is frequently so used in general writing: ''with help from an enthusiastic media'' (Edwin McDowell, *Wall Street Journal*). Many word watchers find singular *media* (with *medias* sometimes as its plural) highly objectionable.

Metaphor

Metaphor, now widely applied to any nonliteral use of language, traditionally refers to the figure of speech which implies that two things normally considered quite different are in some way identical or very much alike. When we're talking literally, we say it's people or machines that *polish,* flags that *unfurl,* liquids that *stream,* and flowers that *bloom.* But a writer can, through metaphor, put these words to new uses and so make a description of even the simplest things both fresh and pleasing:

> The wind continued to polish the grasses. And a purple finch unfurled his song. Twice, and now three times, its last sure note streamed into the sun-bloom.— Sally Carrighar, *One Day on Beetle Rock*

Metaphor can do more than please. It can provide a new view of things and so sharpen attitudes and change minds. It may create a sharp image with a single verb (White House action *defused* the demands of Congress), or it may set up instructive analogies that hold the reader's attention:

> Before prose rhythm can be sensibly considered, one must redefine reading. It cannot be a jet flight coast-to-coast. It must be a slow walk in the country, taken, as all walks should be, partly for the walking itself.—Richard A. Lanham, *Style: An Anti-Textbook*

And metaphor may amuse with what, put more bluntly, would be insulting:

> In "Execution Eve: And Other Contemporary Ballads," William F. Buckley, Jr., slithers venomously across the usual broad terrain of sacred and secular topics.—Steven R. Weisman, *New York Times Book Review*

See **Figurative language, Figures of speech, Mixed metaphors.**

Metonymy

Metonymy is a figure of speech in which the thing named suggests the thing meant, as in "guns (war) or butter (peace)." See **Figurative language.**

might, could

These two words express a slighter degree of possibility than *may, can:* I might go; They could turn up. See **can, may.**

Misrelated modifiers

The position of a misrelated modifier makes it seem to modify the wrong word in the sentence. See **Dangling modifiers.**

Mixed metaphors

Speakers frequently run two inconsistent metaphors together: The new measure has taken a firm foothold in the eye of the public; What they need on the ticket is a fresh face that hasn't been straddling the economic issue. Writers, who can reconsider their words, have less excuse for such obvious blunders and—since what they put into their final draft can be read again and again—more reason for avoiding them. But many metaphors that aren't logically consistent are run together in print without disturbing any but the most fussy readers: ". . . consider Walter Kerr, a highly visual critic steeped in the silent movies, who turned his back on the talkies to find more nourishment in, God help us, the Broadway stage" (Wilfrid Sheed, *New York Review of Books*).

Mixed usage

Indiscriminate, thoughtless mixing of vocabularies—formal with informal, poetic with technical—weakens writing. See **Diction 2.**

Modal auxiliaries

Can, could; may, might; must; ought; shall, should; will, would are called modal auxiliaries. They differ from other verbs in having no *-s* in the third-person singular, no infinitive, no participle, and therefore no compound or phrasal forms. Instead, they themselves always occur as part of verb phrases, complete or elliptical. The generally similar *dare* and *need* are also sometimes treated as modal auxiliaries. See **Elliptical constructions.**

Modifiers

Typically, a modifier limits the meaning of the word, phrase, or clause it modifies and makes it more exact (a *green* apple). In the following illustrations the words in italics modify the words in small capitals: A *cold windy* DAY; He FAILED *miserably;* She was *truly* SUPERB; *Undoubtedly* IT WAS THE CAT WHO STOLE THE BUTTERMILK; *Coming around the corner,* WE met him head on. See **Absolute phrases, Adjectives, Adverbs, Dangling modifiers, Gerunds 1, Infinitives and style, Participles 2, Phrases, Restrictive and nonrestrictive modifiers.**

Money

1. Exact sums of money are usually written in figures: 72¢, $4.98, $168.75, $42,810. Though round sums are likely to be written in words (two hundred dollars, a million dollars), figures may be used for them, too, particularly when several sums are mentioned.

2. In consecutive writing, amounts are usually spelled out when they're used as modifiers: a million-dollar project. Informally, figures are often used: a $2 seat.

3. For amounts in millions and billions, a dollar sign followed by the number followed by the word is most common: $50 billion. Instead of "three and a half million dollars" or "$3,500,000," "$3.5 million" is increasingly used.

4. A sum of money is usually thought of as a single unit: More than $9 million *was* invested in paintings.

Months

In reference matter and informal writing, the names of months with more than four or more than five letters are often abbreviated in dates: Jan. 21, 1982; Dec. 2, 1904; *but* May (June, July) 12, 1904. In formal writing the names of months are not abbreviated. When only the month is given, or only the month and year, abbreviation is rare in any style: He was born in January 1969; Every September she tries again. See **Dates.**

Mood

The mood of a verb, indicated by its form, tells whether the writer or speaker regards what he's saying as a statement of fact or a question concerning fact (indicative mood), as a wish or an expression of possibility or doubt (subjunctive mood), or as a command (imperative mood). See **Commands and requests, Imperative mood, Indicative mood, Subjunctive mood.**

more, most

Preceding the base forms of adjectives and adverbs with *more* and *most* is one way of expressing their comparative and superlative degrees. See **Comparison of adjectives and adverbs 1.**

most, almost

In speech *almost* is often reduced to *most:* A drop in prices would suit most anybody. *Most,* used thus, occasionally appears in factual prose for general audiences, but in college writing, if you can substitute *almost* for *most* in a sentence (almost always, almost everywhere), *almost* is normally the word to use.

Ms.

Ms. is a substitute for both *Miss* and *Mrs.* Its use is favored by those who believe that a woman shouldn't be labeled married or unmarried any more than a man is. If a first name is used after *Ms.* for a married woman, the name is hers, of course, not her husband's: Mrs. John Doe becomes Ms. Jane Doe.

In writing for college courses a choice between *Ms.* and *Miss* or *Mrs.* is most often necessary when the topic is a biographical or critical essay about a woman or her work—for example, a review of the poetry of Sylvia Plath. Sylvia Plath can be called Ms. Plath or Miss Plath. (As a poet, she remained Sylvia Plath during her marriage.) She can also be called Sylvia

Plath or simply Plath. The latter usage is now common in published writing about women.

must

In general English (but not in formal) *must* is accepted as a noun meaning "necessity"—"It has never been a must" (Henry Brandon, *Saturday Review*)—and an adjective modifier meaning "essential"—"This book is a must assignment for reporters" (Robert O. Blanchard, *Columbia Journalism Review*).

myself

Myself is a reflexive or an intensive pronoun referring back to *I:* I cut myself (reflexive); I saw the whole thing myself (intensive). In addition, *myself* is often used where *I* or *me* would be expected:

> The writing was then done by myself, taking perhaps fifteen days.—Hollis Alpert, *Saturday Review*

> Then the two of us, President Johnson and myself, walked out.—Malcolm Kilduff, *Columbia Journalism Review*

For the *-self* form, many stylists would substitute the regular nominative or accusative (*me* in the first example, *I* in the second). See **himself, herself; Pronouns 2; self.**

naked, nude

Naked and *nude* mean the same thing, but *nude* has classier connotations. It's "nude" in art. It's "naked" in the shower.

namely

Introductory *namely* is rarely needed in general writing: The topic was a particularly unpleasant one—[namely,] rising prices. See **that is.**

Narration

Stories (factual as well as fictional), autobiographies, biographies, and histories are all narratives. Like accounts of natural or mechanical processes and reports of laboratory experiments, they relate a sequence of events. In college papers you'll frequently be called on to narrate such sequences.

1.   Chronological order.   As a writer of narrative, you may have reasons for changing actual chronological order. To arouse interest, you may decide to begin in the middle, making the reader want to find out how a character got into a certain situation. Or you may give the ending first and then show the reader how each step led toward the final outcome. Or you may use a flashback (Six years ago we had had a similar experience) to explain causes or to draw a parallel.

Though the events in a narrative can be told in any order, the reader must finally be able to understand the order in which they actually took place. To make that order clear, use appropriate indicators of time (*then, later, after that,* and so on) and the right verb tenses (*had said* instead of *said* in a flashback, perhaps). And if the reader is to understand why an event took place or what effects it had, you need to use indicators of causal relationships *(in order to, because, as a result).*

2.   Pace.   In narration you can compress the events of a decade into a single sentence or extend the happenings of an hour through ten pages. You may slow your narrative with patches of description so that the reader can visualize the scene or gain a vivid sense of what's taking place. Or you may vary the pace by using dialog to dramatize a crucial action. You can make similar changes of pace in objective, factual reporting—of an industrial process, for example, or of a traffic accident—speeding up simpler stages and slowing down complex ones for clarity. Varying the pace is one way you can direct the attention and control the responses of your audience.

3.   Distance and point of view.   How the reader sees and interprets the events depends largely on the distance you establish between yourself and your subject and between yourself and your reader. Physically, you may be close to your subject, taking part in the action, even causing it; or you may be a remote observer, reporting and analyzing. You can present yourself as a learner and invite the reader to share that perspective, or you can assume the role of an expert—someone who knows much more than the reader does. The prevailing point of view (and it should prevail—that is, be maintained consistently) will help define the tone of what you write. See **Point of view.**

4.   The point of the narrative.   A good narrative relates a sequence of events in such a way that a point emerges. The reader grasps not only what took place but the significance of what took place. (He doesn't end up thinking "So what?") In an expository narrative the significance may be clearly stated. In other narratives—personal reminiscences, for example—a brief comment on the signficance of the action may be justified; but the better the storytelling, the less need there'll be for spelling out the so-what.

nauseous, nauseated

Nauseated traditionally means "sickened, disgusted" (I felt nauseated at the sight), and *nauseous* traditionally means "causing sickness or disgust" (The smell was nauseous). But the use of "feeling nauseous" and "getting nauseous" has become so common that dictionaries now record "nauseated" as a second meaning of *nauseous*. Those who grew up observing the distinction find this usage ambiguous. (Was he sick, or was he sickening?)

Negatives and style

When you use both negative and positive words in the same sentence, be sure the combination says clearly what you intend. "The vocational counseling office will try to increase its clients' inability to support themselves" should be rephrased either as "to increase their ability" or as "to remedy their inability."

Poor sentences often result from starting negatively what might better be put positively:

> This mob violence does not reflect the sentiment of an overwhelming majority of the students.

> **Better:** This mob violence reflects the sentiments of only a small minority of the students.

Some writers are fond of tricky negative constructions, including *litotes,* a variety of understatement in which an affirmative is expressed by the negative of its contrary: She was not unfond of him; He was not displeased. Litotes can be effective, but when overused it makes the writer sound coy, evasive, or just tiresome. See **Double negative.**

Negro

Since the 1960s *Negro* has been replaced by *black* in most general usage. See **black.**

neither

As a pronoun, *neither* is ordinarily construed as singular and followed by a singular verb. When the verb is separated from *neither* by a prepositional phrase with a plural object, a plural verb is frequently used in informal writing and sometimes in general writing: "Marx and Trotsky, neither of whom were notably gentle or vegetarian" (Dwight Macdonald, *Esquire*). But here, too, grammatical convention calls for a singular verb.

As an adjective, *neither* modifies a singular noun (neither side), and a pronoun referring to the noun should be singular (Neither side achieved *its* goal).

nice

As a word indicating mild approval (We had a nice time), *nice* is too imprecise for college writing. In formal prose *nice* is usually restricted to meanings like "subtle" or "discriminating": Kirk raises a nice point in his article on Camus.

nobody, no one

The pronouns *nobody* and *no one* take singular verbs, and, strictly speaking, a pronoun referring to either of them should be singular: No one lowered his voice. But sometimes meaning demands a plural pronoun: "No one sings; they simply listen reverently" (Ray Jenkins, *New York Times Magazine*). In formal writing the sentence might be recast: No one sings; everyone simply listens reverently.

nom Nominalization

Change the abstract nominalization into a concrete verb.

For most purposes the best writing is direct writing—writing that avoids three words where two will do, writing that represents an action in a verb and the agent of that action as its subject. The difference between indirect and direct writing is illustrated in these two sentences:

> It seems to be the case that certain individuals in attendance at this institution of higher education are in a state of anger over recent announcements on the part of the dean in regard to a necessity for greater restrictions where the consumption of alcoholic beverages is concerned.

> Some students here are angry because the dean announced that he was tightening the rules about drinking on campus.

Probably the most common source of indirect writing is the abstract nominalization, a noun that—according to transformational theory—has been derived from a full subject + verb in the deep structure of a sentence:

> Tom *paid* the money   ⟶ Tom's *payment* of the money
> The monks *reject* wealth   ⟶ The monks' *rejection* of wealth
> The students *are responsible* ⟶ The students' *responsibility*

The direct subject-verb-object or subject-*be*-adjective construction has been made indirect and accordingly less lively and forceful. If this kind of construction occurs often in your writing—say once every seven or eight words—readers are likely to find your style heavy, abstract, pretentious, and possibly dishonest.

To improve such a style, first look for nouns made out of verbs:

An investigation is being made of the causes for the decline in wheat production.

When you find them (*investigation, causes, decline, production*), ask whether the crucial action is in the main verb or in one of these abstract nouns. If it's in a noun (*investigation*), change the noun to a verb *(are investigating),* find a subject for it (*they,* referring to a specific antecedent? *scientists? agricultural chemists?*), and rewrite the sentence around the new subject-verb:

An investigation is being made of the causes for the decline in wheat production.

Agricultural chemists are investigating what has caused wheat production to decline.

Agricultural chemists are investigating why farmers are producing less wheat.

Or, if no concise subject can be stated, make a straight passive: The decline in wheat production is being investigated.

See **Abstract language, Deep structure, Passive voice 2, Subjects, Verbs 3.**

Nominals

A word, phrase, or clause that serves as subject of a verb, as complement of a linking verb, as object of a verb or a preposition, or as an appositive is functioning as a noun and can be called a *nominal.*

Nominative case

A noun or pronoun that is subject of a verb, complement of a linking verb, or an appositive to either is said to be in the nominative (or subjective) case. The form of the nominative singular is the common form of the noun, the form to which the endings for the possessive and the plural are typically added. The pronouns with distinctive nominative forms are the personals— *I, he, she, it, we, you, they*—and the relative *who.* (*You* is both nominative and accusative.) Though these are the usual forms for the nominative functions, see **it's me; who, whom.** See also **Case 1, Subjects.**

none

The use of *none* with a plural verb is still sometimes condemned, usually on the grounds that *none* means "no one" or "not one" and so must be singular. Usage is divided, but when the reference is to countables, *none* has long been used as a plural in the most reputable writing:

> Almost none [of the letters] are either thoughtful in their approach or deliberative in their style. —Louis J. Halle, *New Republic*

> None have been older than this sacramental alliance. —Sidney Hook, *New York Times Book Review*

> None of these documents afford any solid support for those historians who have viewed Pike as a tool or accomplice in the Wilkinson-Burr schemes. —Harvey L. Carter, *American Historical Review*

Nonrestrictive modifiers

A nonrestrictive modifier does not provide essential identification of the word modified and should therefore be set off by commas. See **Restrictive and nonrestrictive modifiers.**

Nonstandard English

Change the nonstandard word, form, or idiom to one in standard use.

"Nobody ain't got nothing," "theirself," "he do," "they knowed"—these are examples of nonstandard English. Among the articles that treat nonstandard words or forms are **Adverbs and style; Double negative; lay, lie; learn, teach; Principal parts of verbs.** See also **Dialects 2, Standard English.**

no place

Although *anyplace, everyplace,* and *someplace* for "anywhere," "everywhere," and "somewhere" have become common in general writing, *no place* for "nowhere" is still mainly informal: An hour of arguing got us no place. It's sometimes spelled as one word.

nor

By itself, *nor* is an emphatic negative conjunction, most commonly used at the beginning of a sentence in the sense "and . . . not": Nor was Paris (And Paris was not) the only place he visited. Before the last member of a negative series, *nor* gives an added distinctness and emphasis: "I did not see him or hear him" is less emphatic than "I did not see him nor hear him."

As a correlative conjunction, *nor* is paired with *neither*. See **Correlative conjunctions.**

not about to

Not about to is not the simple negative of *about to* but an idiom that stresses the remoteness of the suggested possibility: I'm not about to go along with their weird schemes. It occurs mainly in speech but also in writing. If used with any frequency, it quickly becomes tiresome.

not all that . . . , not too . . .

Not all that . . . is heard frequently in conversations and in weather forecasts (Tomorrow will be better but not all that sunny) and is seen increasingly in print. Sometimes *much* completes the phrase: I didn't like the movie all that much. In some cases an antecedent of a sort is provided for *that,* as in "She thought she might graduate with honors, but her grades weren't all that high"—that is, weren't high enough to qualify for honors. More often, as in this opening of a book review, there's no antecedent: "Usually, the tone of a popular novel is not all that important" *(New Yorker).*

For most college writing, *not all that* . . . is unsatisfactory if only because it invites the question "all what?"

Somewhat different is the *not too* . . . we use in speaking of ourselves and others. "I'm not feeling too good" means "I'm feeling rather poorly." "Their grades aren't too high" probably means "Their grades are mediocre." This usage, whether intended as understatement or as irony, is well established idiom and, while hardly precise, would be appropriate in informal writing and in a good deal of general writing, as long as the context made the meaning sufficiently clear.

not hardly, not scarcely

When *hardly* and *scarcely* mean "almost not," an additional *not* is redundant. See **Double negative 2.**

Note form

In any paper based on the words of others, the writer has an obligation to acknowledge the sources. This is primarily a matter of honesty and courtesy. In addition, documentation in the form of notes and bibliography invites the reader to judge for himself the evidence an assertion is based on and, if he wishes, to turn to the sources for further information.

You must acknowledge your sources not only when you reproduce a paragraph, a sentence, or even a significant phrase exactly but also when you reword or summarize. Whether you use direct quotations or not, you need to give the source of all facts, interpretations, and conclusions that aren't common knowledge and that you haven't arrived at through independent thought, experiment, or investigation. If you name in the text the original source of a quotation that you got from a secondary source, you should cite that secondary source in an endnote or footnote. To neglect to credit the authors and the works that the information and the ideas came from is plagiarism. See **Plagiarism.**

1. Placing notes.   Each note is keyed to a number in the text that is placed slightly above the line immediately after the statement or quotation. Notes, numbered consecutively throughout the paper, may appear at the foot of the page as footnotes, or they may be gathered on a separate page at the end of the paper as endnotes. The *MLA Handbook* recommends endnotes; some instructors prefer footnotes. Follow your teacher's instructions.

Endnotes are double-spaced with a double space between them. The number of the endnote is slightly raised, and there should be one space between the number and the first word.

Footnotes are single-spaced, with a double space between them. Triple-space between the text and the first footnote on each page. The number of the footnote is slightly raised, and there should be no space between the number and the first word.

2. Form for the first reference.   The first time you identify a source in a note, give complete documentation. In general, the form illustrated here is the form for endnotes recommended in the *MLA Handbook*, which shortens the names of publishers. Other styles used in the humanities differ in details, and those used in the sciences are fundamentally different from the form described in this article.

In the examples given below, examine each note carefully to see what elements are included, in what order they appear, and how they are punctuated.

A book by a single author:

[1] Truman A. Hartshorn, Interpreting the City: An Urban Geography (New York: Wiley, 1980), p. 322.

A book by more than one author:

[2] Eric Dunning and Kenneth Sheard, Barbarians, Gentlemen, and Players (New York: New York Univ. Press, 1979), p. 73.

(Use "et al." or "and others" when there are more than three authors: Mary Beth Sullivan and others, *Feeling Free.*)

A book with a corporate author:

[3] Organization for Economic Cooperation and Development, <u>Adverse Weather, Reduced Visibility, and Road Safety</u> (Paris: OECD, 1976), p. 62.

(A corporate author is an organization, legislative body, committee, or any other group that is cited as a book's author.)

A work in more than one volume:

[4] John Lyons, <u>Semantics</u> (Cambridge: Cambridge Univ. Press, 1977), I, 96.

(The Roman numeral is the volume number. When the volume number is given, page numbers are not preceded by "pp.")

An edition other than the first:

[5] James F. Engel, Martin R. Warshaw, and Thomas C. Kinnear, <u>Promotional Strategy</u>, 4th ed. (Homewood, Ill.: Irwin, 1979), pp. 19-20.

(If the city where the book was published is not well known, the name of the state or country should be included. This technique is sometimes used to avoid confusion between places with the same name: Toledo, Spain.)

An edited work:

[6] Ralph Waldo Emerson, <u>Emerson's Literary Criticism</u>, ed. Eric W. Carlson (Lincoln: Univ. of Nebraska Press, 1979), p. 205.

A compiliation:

[7] Michael Steinman, ed., <u>Energy and Environmental Issues</u> (Lexington, Mass.: Lexington Books, 1979), pp. iii-iv.

A selection, chapter, or other part of a compilation:

[8] P. A. M. Dirac, "Developments of Einstein's Theory of Gravitation," in <u>On the Path of Albert Einstein</u>, ed. Arnold Perlmutter and Linda F. Scott (New York: Plenum, 1979), p. 6.

A translation:

[9] Immanuel Kant, <u>Lectures on Ethics</u>, trans. Louis Infield (Gloucester, Mass.: P. Smith, 1978), p. 153.

A book in a series:

[10] Edmund Reiss, __William Dunbar__, Twayne's English Authors Series, No. 257 (Boston: Twayne, 1979), p. 69.

A reprinted book:

[11] William Godwin, <u>Life of Geoffrey Chaucer</u>, 2nd ed. (1894; rpt. New York: AMS, 1974), II, 271.

A signed article in a newspaper:

[12] Fox Butterfield, "Religions Flower as China Eases Rules," <u>New York Times</u>, 27 May 1980, Sec. A, p. 12, col. 1.

An unsigned article in a weekly magazine:

[13] "Robots Join the Labor Force," <u>Business Week</u>, 9 June 1980, p. 62.

An article in a monthly magazine:

[14] Glyn Daniel, "Megalithic Monuments," <u>Scientific American</u>, July 1980, pp. 75-76.

(No volume numbers are used for weekly or monthly magazines. Notice the form for citing the date of the issue.)

An article in a journal paged continuously through the annual volume:

[15] Sherle L. Boone and Alberto Montari, "Aggression and Family Size," <u>Journal of Psychology</u>, 103 (1979), 69.

(In some journals pages are numbered continuously from issue to issue throughout the year. For such journals, cite the volume number and the year of publication of the annual volume but not the number of the issue or the month of publication.)

An article in a journal with separate pagination for each issue:

[16] Fred L. Fry, "The End of Affirmative Action," <u>Business Horizons</u>, 23, No. 1 (1980), 36.

(For a journal that does *not* number pages continuously through the issues of each annual volume, the issue number must be given in addition to the volume number and the year.)

A signed encyclopedia article:

[17] C. L[ockard] C[onley], "Blood, Human," <u>Encyclopaedia Britannica: Macropaedia</u>, 1978 ed.

(When an article is only initialed, the rest of the author's name as cited in the list of contributors is placed between square brackets.)

A book review:

[18] June Sochen, rev. of <u>Children of Fantasy: The First Rebels of Greenwich Village</u>, by Robert E. Humphrey, <u>American Historical Review</u>, 84 (1979), 576-77.

An unpublished dissertation:

[19] Frances Nicol Teague, "Ben Jonson's Stagecraft in His Four Major Comedies," Diss. Univ. of Texas 1975, p. 71.

A government document:

[20] U.S. Dept. of Labor, <u>Work Attitudes and Work Experience: The Impact of Attitudes on Behavior</u> (Washington, D.C.: GPO, 1979), p. 3.

A pamphlet:

[21] <u>Sex Equality in Educational Materials</u>, American Assn. of School Administrators Executive Handbook Series, IV (Arlington, Va.: AASA, n.d.), 12.

(When citing pamphlets, imitate the form of a book citation as closely as possible, using appropriate abbreviations if facts of publication are missing. The "n.d." in this entry means "no date.")

A lecture:

[22] Richard Ruland, "American Literature in Europe Since World War II," American Literature Section, MLA Convention, San Francisco, 28 Dec. 1979.

An interview:

[23] Personal interview with Jean Del Gaudio, Writer/Editor, Technical Communications Services, Owens-Corning Fiberglas Corp., 18 July 1980.

(Begin an interview entry by designating the type of interview, personal or telephone.)

TV or radio program:

[24] <u>Washington Week in Review</u>, mod. Paul Duke, PBS, 25 July 1980.

The citation of an unusual source that doesn't fit any of the conventional forms (a phonograph record or record jacket or personal letter, for example) should conform as closely as possible to the style used for other notes:

[25] R. A. Randall, letter to the author, 23 April 1981.

Subsequent references:

26 Dirac, p. 8.

27 Lyons, p. 103.

28 "Robots Join," p. 65.

If more than one work by the same author is used, then subsequent references must include at least the key word in the title:

29 Hartshorn, Interpreting, p. 83.

30 Hartshorn, Metropolis, p. 101.

When two or more notes in order refer to the same work or even the same page, simply repeat the short form:

31 Reiss, p. 72.

32 Reiss, p. 72.

(*Ibid.*, which used to appear regularly in notes, is now out of fashion.)

Noun clauses

A noun clause is a dependent clause that fills a nominal position: it functions as a noun. Many noun clauses are introduced by *that* or *whether,* some by *what, who, whoever, whatever, why, when,* and other interrogatives.

> **Subject:** *That anyone could raise his grades by studying* had never occurred to him. *Whether or not she should go* bothered her for days. *Why sociology has been growing so rapidly* is a complicated question. (A noun clause as subject often suggests a formal style.)
> **Object of a verb:** He knew [*that*] *it would never happen again.* (When the noun clause is object of the verb, introductory *that* is often omitted in general English.)
> **Complement:** His favorites were *whoever flattered him.*
> **Object of a preposition:** The cost depends on *where we spend the night.*
> **Appositive:** The doctrine *that we must avoid entangling alliances* was first stated by Washington.

See **Relative clauses.**

Nouns

Nouns are best identified by their forms and by the positions they fill in sentences.

1. Forms. English nouns may be inflected by number and case. Many have a plural ending in *-s* or *-es: hats, kindnesses, lecturers.* These and other forms of the plural are discussed in **Plurals of nouns.**

The ending of the possessive singular is written with an apostrophe and an *s: boy's, manufacturer's.* The possessive plural adds an apostrophe to the regular spelling *(boys', manufacturers')* and apostrophe-*s* to plurals not ending in *-s (men's, sheep's).* See **Possessive case.**

Some common distinctive endings make nouns from other parts of speech. They include *-er* (buyer), *-or* (advisor), *-ness* (darkness), *-th* (warmth), *-tion* (inflation).

Some nouns in English have different forms for masculine and feminine: *actor-actress, confidant-confidante, executor-executrix.* See **Gender, Sexist language.**

Nouns may be single words or compound words written solid, as two words, or hyphenated: *bathroom, bookcase, stickup, hub cap, go-getter.* See **Group words, Hyphen.**

2. Position and function. *Dog* and *day* are nouns by their forms: they occur with plural and possessive inflections (the dog's leash, two days' work). But since they can occur in positions normally filled by adjectives (*dog* days) and adverbs (He works *days*), they can be called, in context only, adjectivals and adverbials. Thus if we call them nouns, we define them by formal characteristics; if adjectivals or adverbials, by syntactic function. If they also function as nouns syntactically, as in "The *dog* is man's best friend" or "*Day* will come eventually," then they are nouns in nominal function. See **Nominals.**

Here are examples of the chief uses of noun phrases and therefore of nouns:

> *Subject of a verb: A high wind from the east* blew for three days.
> *Object of a verb:* The wind damaged *the trees, which were loaded with ice.*
> *Object of a preposition:* In *the night,* on *a frozen pond,* fishing is no sport for *a feeble spirit.*
> *Complement:* He has become *president of the firm.*
> *Attributive: The young woman's* partner had the grace of a *baby* hippo.
> *Apposition:* The first settler, *Thomas Sanborn,* came in 1780.
> *Modifier of a verb:* He arrived *two months ago.*

3. Classes of nouns. In the traditional grouping of nouns that follows, many nouns clearly fall into more than one group:

a. Proper nouns, names of particular people and places, written with capitals and usually without *the* or *a:* Anne, Dale A. Robb, London, Georgia, France, the Bay of Naples. All other nouns are called common.

b. Concrete nouns, names of things that can be perceived by the senses: *leaf, leaves, road, trousers, intellectuals.* Concrete nouns are opposed to abstract nouns—names of qualities, actions, types, ideals, and so on: *goodness, thievery, beauty, heroism.*

c.   Mass nouns, names of masses that can be divided but not numbered as aggregates of separate units: *dirt, oxygen, wealth*. They're used with *the* (but not *a* or *an*) or without an article in the singular, and ordinarily they have no plural. Mass nouns are opposed to count nouns, which name what can be counted as separate units. Count nouns are used with both *a(n)* and *the* (but not without an article in the singular), and they have plurals: *a boy, the stick, horses*. Some words, especially abstract nouns, can be either mass or count nouns:

Wood is used in building.   Beauty is only skin-deep.

Mahogany is a valuable wood.   That boat is a beauty.

d.   Collective nouns, names of groups of things regarded as units: *fleet, army, committee, trio*. See **Collective nouns.**

nowhere near

Though in general use, *nowhere near* has an informal tone: It was a good score but nowhere near as high as we'd hoped for. Formal usage would substitute "not nearly as (*or* so) high as."

Number

Number in English grammar is the singular and plural aspect of nouns and pronouns and verbs. Number in nouns is most important, since it controls the number of verbs and pronouns. In verbs, number is indicated only in the present tense (she sings, they sing) except in the pair *was–were*. See **Plurals of nouns, Reference of pronouns, Subjects.**

number

Number, a collective noun, takes a singular verb when the group as a group is meant and a plural verb when the individual units are the writer's concern. Ordinarily "a number of" takes the plural (A number of tickets have been sold), and "the number of" takes the singular (The number of tickets left unsold is discouraging).

Numbers

1. Figures.   Figures are conventionally used in the following:
a.   Dates (June 29, 1918), except in formal social correspondence and some ceremonial contexts. See **Dates.**
b.   Hours with *a.m.* or *p.m.*: 5 p.m. (*but* five o'clock).

c. Street addresses and highway numbers: 2841 Washington Avenue, Route 99.

d. Pages and other references: p. 761; Act III, scene iv, line 28 (III.iv.28) *or* act 3, scene 4, line 28 (3.4.28).

e. Exact sums of money: $4.98, 75¢.

f. Measures expressed in the conventional abbreviations: 15 cc., 3 km, 6″, 10 lbs., 32°F.

The plural of a figure is formed by adding either -*s* or, somewhat more formally, apostrophe-*s:* six 5s *or* six 5's; the 1970s *or* the 1970's. For the possessive, the apostrophe is not usual with figures: They imported $12,000 (*not* $12,000') worth of equipment.

Except in dates, street numbers, ZIP codes, telephone numbers, and a few other regular series, a comma is used to separate thousands, millions, etc., though it may be omitted in four-digit numbers: 2,736 (*or* 2736) bushels; $4,682,981.

2. Figures or words.   Words are conventionally used for round numbers and indefinite numbers: ten million, hundreds, a dozen, a score. Words are also customary for numbers that begin sentences—''Nineteen-eighteen did not usher in the millennium'' (Henry Steele Commager, *Saturday Review*)—though the use of figures for a year in that position is not rare. Ordinal numbers like *first, second,* and *third* are normally written out, but larger ones are given in figures: the 142nd Airborne.

As a rule, newspapers use figures for numbers over ten, words for smaller numbers. Magazine and book styles (most general writing) ordinarily use figures only for numbers over one hundred that can't be written in two words: 199 *but* two hundred.

This passage illustrates a typical book style in handling numbers:

Stage coaches reached new top speeds as their horses galloped over the improved roads. It had taken four and a half days to travel the 160 miles from London to Manchester in 1754; thirty-four years later the journey had been shortened to twenty-eight hours.—T. Walter Wallbank et al., *Civilization Past and Present*

Words and figures shouldn't be mixed in a series of numbers applying to the same units. If one of the numbers is conventionally written in figures, use figures for all: from 9 (*not* nine) to 125 days. But large numbers are increasingly written in a combination of figures and words: ''$3 billion'' can be grasped more quickly than ''$3,000,000,000.''

Numbers in two words between twenty-one and ninety-nine are usually hyphenated, though the practice is declining: forty-two *or* forty two. A hyphen is used between figures to indicate a range: The prediction was based on 40–50 personal interviews and 200–300 phone calls. *To* should be used instead if the numbers are preceded by *from* or *between:* from 40 to 50 (*not* from 40–50).

3.   Arabic and Roman numerals.   Arabic numerals (1, 2, 146) are used in almost all places where numbers are not expressed in words. Roman numerals, either lowercase (i, ii, cxlvi) or capitals (I, II, CXLVI), are occasionally used to number units in a rather short series, as in outlines, chapters of books, and acts of plays, though less often now than formerly. Traditionally, Roman numerals are used for the preliminary pages in a book.

See **Fractions, Hyphen 4, Money.**

Objective case

The object forms of pronouns are said to be in the objective, or accusative, case. See **Accusative case.**

Objects

1.   Direct objects.   In the simplest kind of sentence, the direct object is a noun phrase that follows a transitive verb: Grammar puzzles *normal people;* Alice saw *the white rabbit;* The man was building *a fence.* In more complicated sentences a variety of elements can stand as direct objects: Everybody enjoys *eating steak;* Somebody said *that porpoises are smart.* The objects don't always follow their verbs: *What she meant* I'll never know. And, of course, pronouns can replace noun phrases as objects: John met *them* earlier.

Traditionally, direct objects are said to name what is affected or effected by the actions of their verbs, though this description doesn't apply in a sentence like "He received an injury in the crash" or "They experienced many humiliations."

2.   Indirect objects.   Indirect objects name the person or thing to which something is given, said, or shown—the person or thing affected, indirectly, by the verbal action: He gave *the church* a memorial window; She showed *him* the snapshot. Like direct objects, indirect objects are noun phrases or their equivalents. They follow a special set of transitive verbs, precede direct objects, and are synonymous, in corresponding sentences, with prepositional phrases introduced by *to* or *for:* He gave a memorial window *to the church.*

3.   Objects of prepositions.   The noun phrase, or equivalent, that follows a preposition is its object. The preposition indicates what relationship it has to some other element in the sentence (here, "some other element in the sentence" is the object of *to,* and "the sentence" is the object of *in*). When a relative or interrogative pronoun is the object, it may precede the preposition: *What* are you talking *about?*

Obscenity

Though the vulgar terms for the sexual and excretory body parts and functions—the so-called four-letter words—are used much more freely in print, as well as in speech, than they were fifteen years ago, in most sentences they serve either as mere fillers or as expressions of generalized emotion—most often disgust. In either case, they don't belong in college writing. See **Profanity.**

# of course

Of course should be used sparingly and fairly. It should not be used as a substitute for evidence: Of course, we all know the administration is corrupt. Nor should it be used to suggest that, for the writer, the esoteric is the everyday:

> I can name my favorite restaurant as glibly as I can name my favorite wife, country, religion, and journal of opinion. It is (I should like to say "of course," but Paone's is not widely known) Nicola Paone. . . .—William F. Buckley, Jr., *Saturday Review*

off of

The double prepositions *inside of, outside of, off of* are in general use in writing, but many formal stylists reject the *of,* particularly with *off.*

OK, O.K., okay

OK or *O.K.* or *okay* is informal and general English for "approval" (Harris gave my topic his OK), for "all right, correct" (When I checked the grounds at midnight, everything seemed to be OK), and for "endorse, approve" (If you'll OK my time sheet, I can get paid). As a verb the forms are *OK, OK'ed* or *OK'd, OK'ing* and *okay, okayed, okaying.*

one

1. The use of the impersonal *one,* referring to people in general or to an average or typical person, is formal in tone, especially if it's repeated: "the victories and defeats of one's children, the passing of elders, one's own and one's mate's'' (Benjamin DeMott, *Atlantic*); One can't be too careful, can one? Because a series of *one's* can seem pretentious, many writers refer back to *one* with forms of *he:* "One can determine his own life" (J. A. Ward, *Journal of English*). But some readers would regard *his* in this context as offensively sexist. See **Sexist language.**

A shift from *one* to impersonal *they* should be avoided in writing, and while a shift from *one* to impersonal *you* isn't rare, it would be inappropriate in formal contexts and disapproved by many readers. The *you . . . you* pattern is most common in general English. See **they, you.**

2.   *One* is often used to avoid repeating a noun in the second of two compound elements: Fred took the new copy, and I took the old one. The plural *ones* is also used this way, and logically enough, since *one* is not only a number but an indefinite pronoun: She had a yellow poncho and two red ones. But *one* as a noun substitute is often deadwood, taking emphasis away from the adjective that carries the real meaning: The plan was certainly [an] original [one].

one another

The reciprocal pronoun *one another* is used to refer to two as well as to more than two. See **each other, one another; Pronouns 3.**

one of those who

In formal English the clause following *one of those who* and similar locutions is usually plural because the relative pronoun refers to a plural antecedent:

> He is one of those people who believe in the perfectibility of man. (*Who* refers to *people*.)

> That's one of the books that make you change your ideas. (*That* refers to *books*.)

But because there's a strong tendency to regard *one* as the antecedent, a singular verb is common:

> Leslie Fiedler is one of those literary personalities who has the effect of polarizing his readers.—Peter Michelson, *New Republic*

> . . . one of those crucial questions that comes up again and again.—David Garnett, *American Scholar*

The more formal your context, the more necessary a plural verb.

only

According to the conventions of formal English, a single-word modifier should stand immediately before the element it modifies: I need only six more to have a full hundred. But usage often favors placing *only* before the verb: I only need six more to have a full hundred. The meaning is equally clear, and placing *only* with the verb is an established English idiom.

Even so, precise placement of *only* may be more satisfying to both writer and reader: "In this bicentennial year, let us only praise [*better:* let us praise only] famous men" (Gore Vidal, *New York Review of Books*). And as long as it isn't insisted on where it sounds stilted and unnatural, it can at least prevent silly statements like "He only had a face that [*better:* He had a face that only] a mother could love."

In this respect *even, ever, nearly, just, exactly,* and other such limiting adverbs are similar to *only.* They can be placed so that they spoil the emphasis: I'm tolerant about such things, but his conduct even surprises me [*better:* surprises even me].

Onomatopoeia

By their pronunciations some words suggest particular sounds: *buzz, bang, clank, swish, splash, whir, pop, clatter.* Such imitative words are well established in the English vocabulary. Using sounds that match the sense of a passage in order to intensify its meaning is a stylistic device known as onomatopoeia. Ordinarily the writer works with existing words, sometimes adapting them in the process: "The wire is cut into bullet sizes, the slippery bullets slide from the chopping block on a gangway of grease, they are slithering, skiddering, and slippering into one another" (John Sack, *Esquire*). Onomatopoeia may also inspire outright imitation of sound, as in Tom Wolfe's description of stunting motorcycles: "thraaagggh." Striving for words like *thraaagggh* can produce embarrassing results unless the writer's tongue is visibly in his cheek. See **Alliteration, Assonance, Figurative language.**

on to, onto

When *on* is an adverb and *to* a preposition in a separate phrase, they should be written as two words: The rest of us drove on to the city. The test is that *city* can't be the object of *on*. Used as a preposition, they're written solid: The team trotted onto the floor; The windows looked out onto the park. Both *floor* and *park* are objects of the compound *onto*.

on the part of

On the part of is often wordy for "by," "among," "for," and the like: The new law resulted in less wild driving on the part of (by) young people;

There has been a growing awareness of political change on the part of (among) faculty members.

or

According to conventional rules, two subjects joined by the coordinating conjunction *or* take a singular verb if each is singular, a plural verb if both are plural or if the one nearer the verb is plural:

> Cod-liver oil or halibut oil is often prescribed.

> Cod-liver oil or cod-liver oil capsules are often prescribed.

> Cod-liver oil capsules or cod-liver oil is often prescribed.

Sometimes writers use a plural verb after singular subjects joined by *or,* suggesting "either and perhaps both" rather than "not both but one or the other": Is there evidence that smoking pot or drinking beer are affecting grades? The lack of agreement would be condemned by most formal stylists. See **Correlative conjunctions.**

oral, verbal

Literally, *verbal* means "pertaining to words" and *oral* means "pertaining to the mouth." Insisting on this distinction, some writers maintain that *oral* is the one true opposite of *written*. But *verbal* is also used in the sense "unwritten" in all varieties of English: "Though written contracts were fairly often produced, a large proportion of the agreements seem to have been verbal" (Robert Sabatino Lopez, *Speculum*).

org Organization

Improve the organization of your essay by arranging the parts in an orderly sequence, or by making the movement clear through the use of appropriate signals and transitions, or both.

Every paper should have a structure that can be defined and defended. The main cause of poor organization is failure to get clear in your own mind the natural or logical divisions of your subject and the right relation of the parts of your discourse. In writing a paper, arrange the parts in an order that makes sense in terms of your purpose, and as you develop each part, take into account its place and importance in the whole scheme.

A poorly organized paper lacks direction—a logical movement from beginning to end. Or it lacks shape—proportions that do justice to the relative significance of ideas. Or it lacks unity, with irrelevant material diverting attention from the main thread of the discussion. The best way to pinpoint such structural weaknesses is to outline what you've written, reducing it to a skeleton of key statements. Then set about reorganizing and rewriting.

If rereading your paper and studying your outline leave you convinced that the organization is basically sound, examine the ways you've introduced topics and linked paragraph sequences. Even though you can justify the order of the parts of the paper, you may find you've neglected to give the reader guidance in seeing the relationships. If this is so, relatively simple repair work—improving connections and supplying transitions—should give the paper the direction, shape, and unity it *seems* to lack. Here the remedy is not drastic reworking of the entire structure but adding or rewriting sentences, particularly those at the structural joints that connect main blocks of material.

See **Coherence, Outline form, Paragraph indention, Transition, Unity.**

Originality

Original is applied to writing in two different senses. Content is original when it's gathered by the writer from his experience, from his observation of people, events, or places, or from documents like letters and newspapers. Most college papers should contain some original material. Merely rewriting a magazine article isn't a worthwhile exercise in composition. Putting together ideas taken from several such secondary sources has some value, since it requires selection and comparison. But the most useful work for improving your writing is composing papers in which a good deal of the content is original. The writing is more fun and the gain is much greater than in simply rearranging and restating what others have written. See **Plagiarism.**

Originality in expression, in style, is a different matter. The English language has been used a long time, and absolutely new words and phrases are rare. Trying too hard for originality will produce strained writing or "fine" writing, uncomfortable for writer and reader alike. Instead of trying to sound different, concentrate on telling the truth as you know it, and then, in revising what you've written, get rid of as many clichés as you can. The result should be straightforward, readable writing that carries some suggestion of your personality. When a style that deserves the label *original* appears, it's usually the by-product of an active and independent mind, not the result of a deliberate search for novelty. See **Figurative language, Figures of speech.**

Origin of words

1.   The study of the sources of words.   Every word has a history. Some words, like *chauffeur, mores, television, parapsychology,* are relatively new in English. Some, like *home, candle, go, kitchen,* have been in the language for centuries. Others have been around for some time but have acquired new meanings, like *satellite* (from a Latin word for "attendant," a term in astronomy which now probably means for most people either a dependent nation or a man-made object that orbits the earth, moon, or other celestial body). Etymology, the study of word origins, traces the changes of forms and combinations of word elements (as in *dis/service, wild/ness, bath/room, room/mate*) and follows the word or its component parts back to Old English, or to the foreign language from which it came into English, and so on to the earliest discoverable forms. Of some words, like *dude, stooge, rumpus,* earlier forms are unknown. Of others, like *blizzard,* the sources are debated. But the efforts of generations of scholars have uncovered fairly full histories for most words. These are given briefly in most dictionaries and more fully in the *Oxford English Dictionary* and in special works.

Words have arrived and are still arriving in English through two general processes—the making of new words, by either creating or borrowing them, and the compounding or clipping of words and parts of words that are already in the language. Then the usefulness of this new stock of words is increased as the words undergo changes in form.

2. New words.

a. Creation of words. Coinage, or outright creation, is rare. Even *gas,* first used by Van Helmont (1578–1644), a Belgian scientist, probably had the Greek *chaos* as well as a Dutch or Flemish word behind it. *Kodak* is a coinage, as are a good many other trade names, some familiar from advertising. Informal words like *dud* and *burble* were also creations, good-sounding words that someone made up. F. Gelett Burgess invented *blurb,* defining it as "self-praise; to make a noise like a publisher." Imitative words like *buzz, honk, swish, whiz* are attempts to translate the sounds of nature into the sounds of language. Various exclamations of surprise, pain, scorn, may have started as emotional noises—*ow, ouch, fie, phooey*—and later became regular words. Most made-up words don't stick.

b. Borrowed words. English has always borrowed words freely, from Latin, German, and French and from other languages that English-speaking people have come in contact with. Words of quite un-English form have been assimilated: *khaki* (Hindi), *tycoon* (Japanese), *ski* (Norwegian), *hors d'oeuvres* (French), *borscht* (Russian). The various words for *porch,* itself Norman French but the oldest and most English-seeming of the group, come from various languages: *piazza* (Italian), *stoop* (Dutch), *veranda* (Hindi).

Borrowing is still going on. Some words come into formal English and remain formal words: *intelligentsia, bourgeois, chef d'oeuvre, objet d'art, Zeitgeist,* and many others with political, philosophical, scientific, or literary connotations. *Sphygmograph* and many other scientific words are recent compoundings of Latin and especially of Greek words which are not otherwise in English usage, so they may be regarded as borrowings as well as compounds. Others come in as general words, especially when large numbers of people go abroad, as during a war *(camouflage, blitzkrieg)* or when a foreign invention becomes suddenly popular, as in *chauffeur, garage, chassis* of the automobile vocabulary. Some words brought by immigrants have stuck: *sauerkraut, pronto, pizza, kosher, goulash, zombie.*

Many borrowed words are dropped before they gain any general currency. The useful words are more or less adapted to English spelling and pronunciation and become true English words. See **Foreign words in English 2.**

3. Changes in form of words.
a. Word composition. Most new words are made by putting together two or more elements to create a different meaning or function. The elements may be a prefix placed before the root word *(mis-related)*, or a suffix added *(foolish-ness)*, or a combining element like *mono- (mono-syllable, monorail)*, or two independent words built together *(book-case, basket-ball, gentle-man, space-walk)*. Group words like *high school, out of town,* though not written as single words, could be included as a type of word composition.

At first a compound has no more than the meaning to be expected from its elements: *unable = not able.* But often it will develop an independent sense that can hardly be guessed at from the meanings of its elements: *cupboard, loudspeaker, meltdown.*
b. Blends. Informal English has a number of words that show the liberties users of language have always taken with their words and always will take. Some of their experiments have been added to the main English vocabulary.

One common type is blends, or portmanteau words, made by telescoping two words into one, often making a letter or syllable do double duty. *Squish* is probably a blend of *squirt* and *swish; electrocute,* of *electro-* and *execute; smog,* of *smoke* and *fog.* Blends are common in the names of many firms and products. Other examples include *motel, paratroops,* and a good many folksy efforts like *absogoshdarnlutely.*
c. Clipped words. One of the commonest types of word change is clipping—dropping one or more syllables to make a briefer form: *ad* from *advertisement, bus* from *omnibus, taxi* from *taxicab* (earlier, from *taximeter cabriolet*), *limo* from *limousine, quote* from *quotation, hifi* from *high fidelity* (a blend of clips), *stereo* from *stereophonic, auto, movie, plane, phone,* and so on. Shoptalk has many clips, like *mike* for *microphone* or *micrometer.* The speech of any closely related group is full of clips; campus vocabulary shows a full line: *econ, home ec, phys ed, grad, alum, dorm, ad building, lab, exam, gym, prof, premed,* and dozens more.
d. Back formations. *Back formation* refers to creating a new word from an older word on the assumption that the latter was derived from the former. Thus *orate* was formed by treating *oration* as if its *-tion* was a suffix that had been added to *orate* in the first place. The new word usually serves as a different part of speech, like *baby-sit* from *baby-sitter, opt* from *option, peddle* from *peddler, typewrite* from *typewriter.* Some back formations are

long established (*beg, diagnose, browse*); some are still avoided by conservative writers (*emote, enthuse, sculpt*); some are mostly for fun (*buttle, revolute*).

e.   Common nouns from proper names. Some words have come into general use because of an association with a person or place: *boycott,* from the name of an Irish land agent, Captain Boycott, who was so treated; *macadam,* from the inventor of the road surface, John L. MacAdam; *sandwich,* from the Earl of Sandwich; *jersey,* from the island of Jersey; *pasteurize,* from Louis Pasteur, who developed the process. In many cases the original proper noun has been lost in the common noun: the *jean* in *blue jeans* originally referred to Genoa, the *-nim* of *denim* to the French city of Nîmes.

f.   Playful formations. Blends and back formations are likely to have a playful note, and so do other word shifts that can't be classified. Some of these have been quite generally used: *dingus, doodad, beanery, jalopy.*

other

In comparing things of the same class, add *other* to *any:* That movie scared me more than any *other* I've seen. See **any 1.**

outl Outline form

Revise the form of your outline to observe the conventions given below.

1.   The title.   The title of the paper should stand three spaces above the outline. The heads should carry their full meaning and not refer back to the title by pronouns. See **Titles 1.**

2.   Thesis statement.   An optional practice, but a good one, is to put a sentence stating the subject and scope of the whole paper between title and first main head. See **Thesis statement.**

3.   Numbering systems.   The most widely used numbering alternates letters and figures, as shown in the example in **7.** Avoid complicated or confusing schemes of numbering.

4.   Indention.   Write the main heads flush with the left margin, and indent subheads two or three spaces from the left—enough to place them clearly in a different column.

5.   Punctuation and capitalization.   Don't use punctuation at the ends of lines in a topic outline, but in a sentence outline punctuate each sentence as you would in ordinary writing. Capitalize only the first word of a head and proper names; an outline head is not a title.

6. Heads.

a. Heads with meaning. Each head should be understandable by itself, especially if the outline is to be shown to someone for criticism or is to be submitted with the paper. The following would do as a scratch outline but wouldn't be satisfactory for other purposes:

My Vocation

   I. The work I am interested in
  II. Why I prefer this type of work
 III. What my responsibilities would be
 IV. The chances for success

b. Heads of equal importance. The main heads of an outline, those usually marked by Roman numerals, should show the main divisions of the material. Similarly, the immediate subdivisions of these heads, usually marked by capital letters, should designate logical divisions of each phase of the subject. The same principle applies to further divisions under any subhead.

Unequal headings	*Equal headings*
Books I Have Enjoyed	**Books I Have Enjoyed**
I. Adventure stories	I. Adventure stories
II. Historical novels	II. Historical novels
III. *Walden*	III. Science fiction
IV. Autobiographies	IV. Autobiographies
V. What I like most	V. Books on mysticism

c. Headings in parallel form. Equivalent heads and subheads are expressed in parallel grammatical form. In a sentence outline, use complete sentences throughout. In a topic outline, use phrase heads only. Make all heads of the same rank parallel; that is, make the heads in one series all nouns or all adjectives or all phrases, or whatever is most appropriate.

Heads not parallel	*Parallel heads*
Hitting a Forehand	**Hitting a Forehand**
I. The stance is fundamental	I. The stance
II. The grip	II. The grip
III. Watch the backswing	III. The backswing
IV. Meeting the ball	IV. The stroke
V. Follow through with care	V. The follow-through

7. Division of main points. Since a topic isn't "divided" unless there are at least two parts, a formal outline should have at least two subheads under any main head—or none at all. For every heading marked *A* there should be at least a *B*, for every *1* there should be a *2*, and so on.

Illogical single heads	*Logical subdivision*
The Tripartite System	**The Tripartite System**

I. The executive branch	I. The executive branch
A. President and Cabinet	A. President
	B. Cabinet
II. The legislative branch	II. The legislative branch
A. The House	A. The House of Representatives
B. The Senate	B. The Senate
1. Functions	1. Special functions
	2. Special privileges
III. The judicial branch	III. The judicial branch
A. The Supreme Court	A. The Supreme Court
	B. Lower courts

When a main point can't be divided, include any necessary detail in the head. For an organization in which the president has all the executive power, this heading would be satisfactory:

I.   The executive branch (the president)

8. Introduction and conclusion.   Ordinarily a paper has a beginning, a middle, and an ending (or an introduction, a body, and a conclusion), but don't use such labels in the outline. They're too general to reflect specific content, and the beginning and ending can rarely be represented by heads that are coordinate with the others. The first and last topics in an outline should be drawn from the main body of material for the paper.

over, more than

There's still some prejudice against using *over* to mean "more than" (a budget of over $5 billion), but the usage is established as standard.

Oxymoron

An oxymoron is a contradiction in terms used as a figure of speech—for example, "sweet bitterness," "loving hate," "mildly fatal," "making haste slowly," Aleksandr Solzhenitsyn's "literary illiterates." See **Figurative language.**

pair

When not preceded by a number or other plural indicator *(these, several)*, *pairs* is the preferred plural of *pair:* Pairs of figures were common in the design. Otherwise usage is divided:

> These hypotheses are confounded in two pairs.—Roselle and Campbell, *Psychological Bulletin*

> He found a car with one too many pair of skis.—*Time*

¶ Paragraph indention

Indent here for a new paragraph.

No ¶ No paragraph indention

Join this paragraph to the preceding one.

1. Indent for a new paragraph.   A paragraph symbol in the margin of your paper means that you've failed to meet your readers' expectations. From their experience with magazines and books, they're in the habit of regarding a paragraph as a series of related statements, all bearing on the action being narrated, the scene being described, or the point being argued. And they expect to be forewarned by a paragraph break of any shift in focus or any turn in the course of reasoning. When they come to a stretch of writing that drifts or leaps from one topic to another, they're confused and distracted by the lack of unity and coherence.

Your instructor may have other reasons for recommending indention. A single sentence or a short sequence of sentences that makes a significant point may demand the emphasis that being set apart as a paragraph will provide. Or a brief passage that marks a transition from one stage of the paper to another may be more helpful to the reader if it's detached from the end of a long paragraph to stand on its own. And sometimes, even if the connections in the material are close enough to justify a very long paragraph, you may be advised to break it up simply to give the reader a mental breathing spell.

Though it's not uncommon to find an 800-word paragraph in a scholarly journal where a closely reasoned argument is addressed to interested readers, most expository writing receives nothing like such close attention. Indention helps break a discussion into digestible bites. In using indention this way, be sure to look for a natural subdivision within the long paragraph. Don't divide your subject at a point that will separate two closely related sentences.

In general, the development of your topic should determine the length of your paragraphs. But take into account the kind of writing you're doing: narrative and descriptive paragraphs are likely to be shorter than paragraphs of criticism or analysis. And take into account the probable interest and attention span of your readers.

2. Join separate paragraphs.   A succession of very short paragraphs, like a succession of very long ones, makes reading difficult. An unjustified paragraph break throws the reader off the track so that he loses the connection between one idea and another. In revising, combine paragraphs in which the details or ideas are so closely related that they form a single stage in the development of the paper. In the process, make sure you provide whatever transitional words and phrases are needed to emphasize the continuity.

While a transitional paragraph that moves a paper from one phase of the topic to another may be very short—perhaps just one sentence—most paragraphs are from four to ten sentences long. If you have more than two paragraphs on a typed page of expository prose, be sure you can justify the breaks. A sequence of very short paragraphs may indicate that you're not developing your points adequately, not providing enough examples or details or comparisons. Or it may be that you've failed to recognize the close logical connections that pull your ideas together into larger units. In either case, short, choppy paragraphs suggest a collection of random observations rather than the unified development of a central idea.

See **Coherence, Transition.**

par Paragraphs

Revise or rewrite this unsatisfactory paragraph.

A paragraph is a group of related statements that a writer presents as a unit in the development of his subject. It strikes the eye as a unit because it's physically set off by indention or spacing. It will also strike the mind as a unit if the statements in it are closely related, representing a stage in the flow of the writer's thought.

Here are the most common faults in paragraphs, with suggested remedies:

1. Lack of development.   Rewrite the paragraph, including details and illustrations that will lead the reader to understand and accept its central point. See **Details.**

2. Lack of unity. Rewrite, deleting any material that doesn't contribute to the central idea, or core of meaning, of the paragraph. See **Unity 2.**

3. Lack of continuity. Revise or rewrite so that the relation between the statements that make up the paragraph is clear. Occasionally you'll find you can improve continuity simply by altering the order of sentences. Sometimes you need to supply a transition between sentences. And sometimes you must rethink and rewrite. See **Coherence, Logical thinking, Transition.**

4. Lack of transition. Begin the paragraph with a word, phrase, or sentence that links it firmly to the material that precedes it. See **Transition.**

5. Lack of a required topic sentence. Provide a topic sentence to strengthen the unity of the paragraph or to make clearer to the reader the direction your paper is taking. Not all paragraphs need topic sentences; but some do, either to present the generalization that subsequent details will support, or to pull details together into a generalization, or to introduce or sum up a stage of the discussion. See **Topic sentence.**

Parallelism

When two words or groups of words are alike grammatically and structurally, they are said to be parallel. Parallel constructions range from matching pairs of adjectives (*cold* and *wet*) to series of phrases or clauses—"Some metaphors are harmless, some are useful, some are beautiful, and some are stumbling blocks to clear thinking" (Thomas Middleton, *Saturday Review*)—to sequences of elaborately balanced sentences. The extent to which a writer should deliberately use parallelism depends on the rhetorical situation. The simple parallelism that contributes to clarity and efficiency is appropriate in all varieties of English. The exact, sustained, intricate parallelism of some balanced and periodic sentences is at home only in formal prose. See **Balanced sentence, Cumulative sentence, Parallelism and style, Periodic sentence, Rhetorical situation.**

paral Parallelism and style

//   **Use parallel structures for elements that should logically be performing the same grammatical function.**

Parallelism is one of the simplest, neatest, and most economical ways of achieving clarity. The sentence you've just read illustrates what it says. The three sentences that follow express the same idea without taking advantage of parallelism:

> Parallelism is one of the simplest ways of achieving clarity. Neatness is a major contribution made by parallelism. A sentence that uses parallel structures is more economical than one that doesn't.

Parallelism is a mode of coordination. This means that as a general rule *and, but, nor,* and *yet* should match noun (or noun equivalent) to noun, adjective to adjective, infinitive to infinitive, dependent clause to dependent clause, and so on.

1. Put into the same grammatical forms and structures those words, phrases, and clauses that are alike in purpose and related in meaning (complementary or contrasting). "He was *brilliant* but *unstable*" (predicate adjectives modifying *he*) and "He was a *brilliant* but *unstable* person" (adjectives modifying *person*) both make use of parallelism. "He was *brilliant* but an *unstable* person" does not, though the purpose of *brilliant* and *unstable* remains the same: they're still describing the subject of the sentence.

Here are some sentences that use parallelism, followed in each case by a version that doesn't:

> *Parallel nouns:* Rational thought and rational behavior rarely govern either the *formation* or the *operation* of policy.—Barbara Tuchman, *Newsweek*

> *Not parallel (noun mismatched with dependent clause):* Rational thought and rational behavior rarely govern either the *formation* of policy or *how it operates.*

> *Parallel gerunds:* Sir Percy was given to *sniffing* snuff and *prattling* foolishly as a cover for the daring Pimpernel.—Thomas Middleton, *Saturday Review*

> *Not parallel (gerund mismatched with independent clause):* Sir Percy was given to *sniffing* snuff and *he also prattled foolishly as a cover for the daring Pimpernel.*

> *Parallel pairs of adjectives:* She satisfies our secret longing to believe that those who are *good and generous* are also *stylish and beautiful.*—A. Walton Litz, *Key Reporter*

> *Not parallel (paired adjectives mismatched with adjective and verb phrase):* She satisfies our secret longing to believe that those who are *good and generous* are also *beautiful and wear the latest styles.*

Failure to use matching grammatical structures is particularly noticeable with the correlative conjunctions *both . . . and, either . . . or, neither . . . nor, not only . . . but (also).* A simple example is given in the first rewritten version above. Here's an equally common type:

> The rule is *not only* ignored by those it is directed at *but* those who are supposed to enforce it ignore it too.

It seems clear that the writer wants to emphasize how thoroughly the rule is being ignored. In revising, a good first step would be to put the verb before *not only:* The rule is being ignored. Who's ignoring it? Those who . . . and those who. . . . Then, with the correlative conjunctions added, the phrasing falls naturally into parallel form:

> The rule is being ignored *not only by those who are supposed to* observe it *but also by those who are supposed to* enforce it.

2. Do *not* make structures parallel unless the relationship of the ideas or details they express justifies parallelism. If parallelism in structure doesn't represent the logic of what's being said, the reader will be misled. The three grammatical elements that end the next sentence are not parallel:

> My year abroad taught me a lot about the way Venezuelans earn a living, spend their leisure time, and their attitudes about Americans.

Making the elements parallel (. . . and feel about Americans) would produce a smoother sentence, but as far as *meaning* goes, the change would be a mistake. In the context, the way Venezuelans feel about Americans isn't logically related to the way they earn their living or spend their leisure time. The best revision, then, would be to retain the first two elements in the series but turn the third into a separate sentence. How the new sentence would be phrased would depend on whether the writer was making a casual addition or introducing a major topic:

> My year abroad taught me a lot about the way Venezuelans earn a living and spend their leisure time. It also taught me a lot about their attitudes toward Americans. *Or:* More important, I learned a lot about. . . .

See **Parallelism, Phrases and style, Shifted constructions.** For further examples of the effective use of parallelism, see **Periodic sentence.**

Paraphrase

A paraphrase is a restatement of another writer's ideas in different words. You paraphrase when you digest the contents of a passage in a book or article in your own words, as in taking notes. Difficulties may arise in the next step—using the paraphrase in a paper of your own. First, you must acknowledge the source of the material. Second, if you include phrases or sentences from the original, you must put them in quotation marks and identify them as the original author's either in the body of your paper or in a footnote or endnote. But quoting is not paraphrasing. Nor is a paraphrase a summary. While a summary condenses the original, a paraphrase may be just as long or even longer. See **Plagiarism, Research papers.**

Parentheses

Parentheses may be used to enclose a full, independent sentence that breaks away from the main structure of the paragraph in which it appears. Like commas and dashes, they are also used within a sentence to enclose words and word groups that break away from the main structure. Of the three types of enclosing marks, parentheses indicate the most separation.

1. For additions. Within sentences, parentheses are used to enclose words and word groups that add facts to a statement without essentially altering its meaning. The additions may be illustrations (as in this book), definitions, or information thrown in for good measure:

> The few verb endings that English now retains *(-s, -ed, -ing)* are being still further reduced in ordinary speech.

> Gresham's Law (that bad money drives out good) applies as usual in this case.

> His concerts were well received in most cities (Cleveland was an exception), but he was still dissatisfied.

When overused, parentheses create clutter. If you've fallen into the habit of using them regularly, look closely at the material they enclose. Unimportant material might better be omitted. Material worth including might better be worked into the structure of the sentence in which it appears or made into a separate sentence.

2. With other marks. When a complete sentence in parentheses comes within a sentence (notice the punctuation of this one), it needs neither a capital letter nor a period. Commas and other marks of punctuation in the main sentence always *follow* the closing parenthesis (as they do here and in the preceding sentence). (A sentence in parentheses, like this one, that does not stand within another sentence has the end punctuation before the closing parenthesis.)

3. To enclose numbers or letters in an enumeration. Parentheses are sometimes used to enclose letters or figures that mark items in an enumeration: The additions may be (1) illustrations, (2) definitions, or (3) information thrown in for good measure. Parentheses give the listed items more emphasis.

See **Brackets, Dash.**

Participles

Participles are derived from verbs but can't serve as independent predicates.

1. Forms. The present participle adds *-ing* to the base form of the verb: *asking, singing.* The past participle of regular verbs adds *-ed* to the base *(asked),* and the perfect participle adds *having* to the past participle *(having asked).* In the passive, the *-ed* form is preceded by *being (being asked)* and *having been (having been asked).* Many irregular verbs have special past-participle forms: *sung, having sung, being sung, having been sung.* See **Principal parts of verbs.**

2. Functions.
a. In verb phrases. Participles enter into many verb phrases: I am asking, I am being asked, I have been asked. Though referred to as present and past, participles indicate time only in relation to the context in which they're used. See **Tenses of verbs.**
b. As modifiers. When not part of verb phrases, participles function like adjectives in that they modify nouns (a *coming* event, a *frightened* cat), like verbs in that they may take an object *(Following these clues,* he soon found her). Like both, they may be modified by adverbs *(rolling crazily).*

Compare **Gerunds.**

Participles and style

When a participle is used as an adjective, it should refer clearly to some particular noun or pronoun: Having opened the envelope, she began reading the letter *(Having opened* modifies *she).* A modifying participle is said to dangle when it seems to refer to a word the writer doesn't mean it to refer to: Kissing his wife good-bye, the door slammed behind him (technically, *kissing* modifies *the door).* Errors like this occur when the subject of the participle and the subject of the main clause aren't the same. In "[*He* was] kissing his wife good-bye, *the door* slammed behind him," *He* and *the door* aren't the same. Compare a correct modifier: [*He* was] kissing his wife good-bye, *he* let the door slam behind him. *He* in "[He was] kissing" and *he* in "he let the door slam" are the same. The first subject can be deleted. See **Dangling modifiers.**

The participle-as-adjective shouldn't be confused with the participle in an absolute phrase—a phrase that's related to the whole sentence rather than to a particular word. Some of these phrases have become formulas: Judging from her looks, she's over fifty. See **Absolute phrases, Formulas.**

Don't use a participle where a subordinate clause would read more smoothly: The train was on time, necessitating our hurrying. *Better: . . .* so we had to hurry. In revising, get rid of clumsy participial phrases like this one: The plane arriving then, we boarded it. *Better:* Then the plane arrived, and we boarded it.

For *very* with participles, see **very 2.**

Parts of speech

Parts of speech are the categories linguists set up in order to describe structures in sentences and finally sentences themselves. They group words into categories and subcategories and then describe the various patterns in which these categories may occur and the ways in which they form larger structures. Linguists working with different grammatical theories create different categories based on different sets of definitions.

Traditional schoolroom grammarians, using a system much like that developed for describing classical languages, cite eight parts of speech: nouns, verbs, adjectives, adverbs, pronouns, prepositions, conjunctions, and interjections. Nouns and verbs are defined semantically: a noun is the name of a person, place, or thing; verbs show action. The other parts of speech are defined functionally: adjectives modify nouns; adverbs modify verbs, adjectives, and other adverbs; pronouns replace nouns; and prepositions relate a noun or pronoun to some other part of the sentence.

Structural linguists use purely formal definitions. Nouns, they say, are those words that can occur with plural and possessive endings or in positions after *the* and before a verb; verbs are those words that can occur with third-person singular *-s* endings, with past-tense inflections, with perfect inflections, and with progressive *-ing* endings; adjectives are those words that can occur with comparative or superlative endings, after *more* or *most,* and in the position "The (noun) is very ————"; adverbs are those words made up of an adjective and an *-ly* ending. Structural linguists put the residue of words such as *and, in, can, very, the, not, all, therefore, because, please,* and *hello* into a large category of "indeclinable" words, or function words, which is subdivided according to where these words occur in a sentence relative to the parts of speech already identified.

Transformational grammarians are much less concerned than structuralists with devising formal tests to classify parts of speech and more concerned with the most economical and general overall description. The labels for individual words are judged "correct" only if they're necessary to describe how the words behave in the context of a sentence. Transformational grammarians assume that one part of speech may derive from another, as the verb *discover* in a deep structure like "Tom *discovered* gold" becomes, in a surface structure, the noun *discovery,* "Tom's *discovery* of gold." For transformational grammarians, it's impossible to talk about parts of speech without explaining the whole grammar of a language and without distinguishing between deep and surface structures. See **Deep structure.**

With some help from structural and transformational grammars, traditional grammar serves the purposes of this text. For descriptions of the forms and functions of the parts of speech and their stylistic uses and misuses, see the following articles:

Adjectives	**Collective nouns**
Adjectives and style	**Conjunctions**
Adverbs	**Conjunctions and style**
Adverbs and style	**Conjunctive adverbs**
Articles	**Coordinating conjunctions**
Auxiliaries	**Correlative conjunctions**

pass Passive voice

Change the verb or verbs to active voice.

1. Avoiding the passive. Using the passive voice without good reason will tend to make your sentences awkward and wordy, place emphasis where it doesn't belong, and at times leave your readers wondering who did what.

a. Don't use the passive to avoid using *I.*

Between Laredo and Austin the driving was done by me.

Revision: Between Laredo and Austin I drove. *Or:* . . . I did the driving.

b. Don't use the passive in an attempt to sound weighty or "scientific."

The proposals that were made by the administration have been received negatively by the student body.

Revision: Students disliked the administration's proposals.

c. Don't use the passive to hide or obscure the identity of the source of an action.

My roommate and I were summoned by the dean because of the waterbags that had been dropped from our windows.

Revision: The dean summoned my roommate and me for dropping waterbags from our windows.

d. Don't use the passive to vary the pattern just for the sake of varying the pattern.

After finding our way through the woods, we reached the campsite. A half-dozen trips were made to bring in our supplies. By sunset we were more than ready for a hot meal.

The shift from active to passive isn't justified. Revising the second sentence (We had to make . . .) would keep the focus consistent and make the passage easier to read.

2.   Appropriate uses of the passive.   The passive voice is appropriately used in at least three rhetorical contexts.
a.   Passives are appropriate when the agent of the action is either unknown, unimportant, or better left unidentified:

As many as a hundred notices of teaching jobs are printed each month in a newsletter best described as a "whole education" catalogue.—Jean Collins, *Change*

The grammars could not be dismissed as inferior or crude; they were simply different.—J. J. Lamberts, *A Short Introduction to English Usage*

Entry was not gained, police said, though an attempt had been made to pry open the door.

Postal rates are to be increased.

b.   Passives can be used (as in this sentence) when the subject under discussion would otherwise be the direct object: A writer can use passives when. . . . Because passives are what is being discussed in this section, the noun phrase referring to them should be the subject-topic of most of the sentences.
c.   Passives allow a writer to focus on the agent of an action by shifting the agent to the end of the sentence, where it will be stressed. This is especially desirable when the agent is represented by a fairly long and complicated noun phrase:

Active: A team bigger and tougher than any you would find outside professional football defeated us.

Passive: We were defeated by a team bigger and tougher than any you would find outside professional football.

Such a shift often makes it possible for the writer to build a tighter transition from one sentence to another. The element ending one sentence leads into the subject of the sentence that follows.
    See **Voice.**

Past tense

For past tense, regular verbs add *-ed* to the base form: *ask, asked; answer, answered*. See **Principal parts of verbs, Tenses of verbs.**

people, persons

People has long been used as a collective noun referring to a group, but as recently as the early part of this century, it was regarded as nonstandard when used with numerical quantifiers as the plural of *person,* as in "Five people are here." Though formal usage still tends to prefer *persons, people* is now thoroughly established in all plural uses. *Person* and *persons* are frequently resorted to by writers who object to using *man* or *men,* alone or in combinations like *businessman* and *policeman,* to represent both sexes, but coinages like *businessperson* have met strong resistance. Not surprisingly, *people-persons* is a case of divided usage. See **Sexist language.**

per

Per (Latin "through, by, among") is most appropriate in phrases that are still close to their Latin originals (per capita, per diem), in commercial expressions ($250 per week, $5.00 per yard), and in some technical phrases (revolutions per minute). In less specialized contexts, *a* or *every* is preferable: a dime a dozen, a thousand words every day.

percent

In informal and general writing (but not in formal) *percent* is often used instead of *percentage* or even *proportion:* Only a small percent of the class was (*or* were) present. When it's so used, the noun in the *of* phrase determines whether the verb is singular or plural. Since *class* is a collective noun, the verb could be either.

   With figures, *percent* (97.6 percent) is preferred to the percent sign (97.6%) except in technical and statistical material. *Percent* is also written as two words. It's not an abbreviation and shouldn't be followed by a period.

Perfect tense

Tenses formed with *have* and a past participle are traditionally called perfect tenses: present perfect, *has laughed;* past perfect, *had laughed;* future perfect, *will have laughed.* See **Tenses of verbs.**

Period

1.   At the end of statements.   A period is used to mark the end of every completed sentence that's not a question or an exclamation. Sometimes, when not really inquiring or exclaiming, a writer will use a period at the end of a sentence in the form of a question or exclamation: Would you be so good as to return the book at your earliest convenience. What a day.

2.   Miscellaneous conventional uses.
a.   After abbreviations: Oct.; etc.; Mr. W. Fraser, Jr.
b.   Between dollars and cents: $5.66; $0.66 (*but* 66 cents *or* 66¢)
c.   Before decimals: .6, 3.14159, 44.6 percent
d.   Sometimes between hours and minutes in giving precise time, though a colon is more usual: 2.36 p.m.

3.   With quotation marks.   When a quotation ends a sentence, most American publishers place the period inside the quotation marks whether the quotation is a complete sentence or a single word:

> "The longer you put it off," he said, "the harder it's going to be." He glared at me as he said "harder."

Periodic sentence

A periodic sentence withholds its complete meaning until its last word (as in the first sentence below) or until its last clause (as in the second and third):

> Exhaustive in its scholarship, discerning in its literary judgments, sensitive in its theorizing, it merits the adjective all biographies aspire to: *definitive.*—Robert F. Moss, *Saturday Review*

> Not so long before he died, still receiving carloads of honors as he always had, and still receiving, as also he always had, from Right and Left in turn, fanatic attacks on his social views, Mann remarked that he was a "great, unloved name."—John Thompson, *Harper's*

> The importance of disciplinary studies, the value of humanistic thinking and illumination, the urgency of facing the public with the best that the humanities can do, the clear need of bringing together the best humanists (which includes some social and natural scientists) as well as other figures such as journalists, labor leaders, businessmen, and politicians, all argue for an institution devoted to such and other ends.—Morton W. Bloomfield, *PMLA*

A great many short and simple sentences have their base structures at the end and therefore fit the definition of a periodic sentence; but rhetoricians reserve the term for sentences of some length and complexity. Because a periodic sentence keeps the reader in suspense, its resolution brings a feeling of satisfaction (or, in some cases, relief). A long periodic sentence always gives a passage a distinct touch of formality. It's necessarily a studied production, often using sustained parallelism, as in the examples above. Remaining airborne through clause and phrase as it does, it can achieve unusual dramatic emphasis when it finally returns to earth—or, if poorly done, it can end with the thud of anticlimax. Used sparingly in appropriate contexts, the periodic sentence can give a passage strength and individuality. But a succession of periodic sentences is tiring to read and creates a style too high-flown for everyday topics.

The prime example of the periodic sentence as cliché is the nominating speech. Here, a very long series of clauses beginning "a man who" or "a woman who" precedes the name of the nominee, which usually comes as a surprise to no one at all.

See **Parallelism.** Compare **Cumulative sentence.**

Person

Person as a grammatical term refers to both pronoun classification and verb inflection. Personal pronouns are in the first person, the one(s) speaking *(I, my, me, we, our, us);* second person, the one(s) spoken to *(you, your, yours);* third person, anyone or anything else *(he, his, him, she, her, hers, it, its, they, their, them).* Nouns are regarded as third person, as are most other pronouns.

Except in the verb *be (I am, you are, he is . . .),* English verbs indicate person only for the third singular of the present and perfect tenses: I see, you see, he *sees;* we see, you see, they see; I have seen, you have seen, he *has* seen; etc.

Personal pronouns

The personal pronouns are *I, we, you, he, she, it,* and *they.* See **Case, Person, Pronouns 1.**

Personification

Personification is a figure of speech in which an object or animal or quality or ideal is given some attributes of a human being. Here the mall of the Smithsonian Institution in Washington, D.C., is personified: "It was a hot summer, but the Mall carried on imperturbably, hosting event after event" (Edward Park, *Smithsonian*). Personification is less common today than formerly and less common in prose than in verse. See **Figurative language, Gender.**

persons

With numerical quantifiers, *persons* is preferred to *people* in formal usage: five persons. See **people, persons.**

phenomenon, phenomena

Phenomenon is the singular and *phenomena* (sometimes *phenomenons*) the plural: phenomena of the mind. Originally *phenomenon* meant "any observable event," but now it also means "something remarkable," and *phenomenal* is almost always used in that sense (Her speed is phenomenal). See **Hyperbole.**

Phrasal verbs

A main verb preceded by one or more auxiliaries (will go, has left, was thinking, is considered, must have been punished) is called a phrasal verb or a periphrastic verb. A verb-adverb combination is also called a phrasal verb. See **Verbs.**

Phrases

A phrase is a group of words that functions as a unit in a sentence, a clause, or another phrase. In these examples the word that determines the classification is in italics:

> *Noun phrase:* the *plumber*
> *Verb phrase:* have *gone* to the store
> *Adjective phrase:* old enough to be my father
> *Adverb phrase:* more *quickly* than usual
> *Prepositional phrase:* in the house
> *Participle or gerund phrase:* walking down the street
> *Infinitive phrase:* to go faster

Phrases may be further classified according to their function in a sentence. *The plumber* is an adjectival noun phrase in the larger noun phrase, *my friend the plumber.* In "Walking down the street, she saw the accident," *walking down the street* is a participle phrase because its function is adjectival. In "Walking down the street is dangerous," *walking down the street* is a gerund phrase because its function is nominal. *In the morning* is an adverbial prepositional phrase in "He left in the morning," an adjectival prepositional phrase in "Breakfast in the morning," a nominal prepositional phrase in "In the morning will be soon enough."

Phrases and style

The style of a passage depends in part on how the writer combines and coordinates phrases:

> His ideas
> > about the need
> > > for intellectual renewal
> > > > and
> > > spiritual reform
> > indicate the crisis
> > > faced not only
> > > > by those
> > > > > in places
> > > > > > of power
> > > but
> > > > by those
> > > > > in all walks
> > > > > > of life.

In the preceding sentence the phrases are balanced and coordinated to create a rhythm that carries the reader along smoothly to the end. In the next sentence the phrases are merely strung out one after the other, creating a heavy, bumping kind of movement that interferes with the reader's understanding of the writer's idea:

> Our situation
> > in this century
> > > of turmoil
> > > > in the cities
> > can only be alleviated
> > > by improving the living conditions
> > > > in ghettos
> > > > > in the central cities
> > which have decayed
> > > beyond the endurance
> > > > of most
> > > > to live
> > > > > in them.

When you pile phrase on phrase, make sure you also establish enough parallelism to give your sentence shape and movement.

See **Absolute phrases, Gerunds, Infinitives, Participles, Prepositional phrases.** See also **Dangling modifiers, Parallelism.**

Plagiarism

Plagiarize is defined in *Webster's New Collegiate Dictionary* as "to steal and pass off (the ideas or words of another) as one's own." Students in college courses commit plagiarism for several different reasons, including panic, dishonesty, and ignorance of what plagiarism is. Sometimes a student plagiarizes when he drifts unconsciously from paraphrasing into copying. Whatever the cause, the penalty—a failing mark on the paper and, if the cheating is chronic or flagrant, a failing mark in the course—is justified. Copying someone else's work is the most complete failure possible.

If you haven't learned how to handle material obtained from your reading, you need guidance in the fundamentals of scholarship. Anyone using published material has a twofold responsibility: first, to make the ideas part of his own thinking and, second, to give credit to the sources he's consulted. No one is *composing* when he's copying.

Digest the material you read so that you can present it in your own words (except for the brief passages you intend to quote directly). Be able to talk about what you've read before you write about it, and when you do write, name the sources of your ideas and facts, including ideas and facts you've paraphrased or summarized. This is not only courtesy but a sign of good workmanship, part of the ethics of writing. It's also part of the legality of writing, since the plagiarist who uses copyrighted material is liable to prosecution.

In an informal paper you can give credit informally, perhaps in a preliminary note: "This essay is based on. . . . " Or you can acknowledge a source in the body of the paper: "Professor Hudspeth said in a lecture . . . " or "According to an editorial in . . . " or "Here is Jackson's position as presented in last night's debate." Or you can give credit more formally in the endnotes or footnotes that are a customary part of a research paper.

Plagiarism is stealing. And besides being dishonest, it's unnecessary and unproductive. By giving credit where credit is due, you gain free and legitimate access to everything in print (though if what you write is to be printed, you must get permission to quote copyrighted material directly). And you learn to integrate the ideas of others with your own ideas. Finally, when you express what you have to say in your own words, you're not copying but composing. See **Note form, Originality, Paraphrase, Research papers**.

plenty

As a qualifier (I was plenty worried; That car is plenty fast) *plenty* is chiefly informal. In formal and general styles such established adverbs as *very (much)* and *extremely* are preferred. An *of* is expected between *plenty* and a following noun: We had plenty of time (*not* plenty time).

plurality, majority

In an election a plurality is the largest number of votes received by any one candidate but less than a majority, which is more than half of all the votes cast. See **majority, plurality**.

Plurals of nouns

The plurals of the great majority of English nouns are made by adding -*s*. Some exceptions and special cases follow.

1. Special groups in -*s* or -*es*.
a. Some plurals can be pronounced only by adding a full syllable. The spelling is -*s* if the noun already ends in a silent -*e (edges, mazes)*, otherwise -*es: birches, misses, dishes*.
b. With a few exceptions, common nouns ending in -*y* preceded by a consonant or *qu* change *y* to *i* and add -*es: beauties, bodies, soliloquies*. Words ending in -*y* preceded by a vowel add -*s: bays, boys, honeys*.
c. Nouns ending in -*o* preceded by a vowel make regular plurals with -*s: radios, studios*. Some words ending in -*o* preceded by a consonant always or nearly always take -*s: Filipinos, pianos, solos*. Some always or nearly always take -*es: echoes, potatoes, vetoes*. Some take either: *cargoes, cargos; dominoes, dominos*.
d. Some common nouns ending in -*f* or -*fe (calf, wife, half, knife, self)* use -*ves (calves, wives, halves, knives, selves)*. Some have two plurals: *hoof, hoofs/hooves; scarf, scarfs/scarves*. But many nouns ending in -*f* and -*fe* form regular plurals with -*s: beliefs, fifes*.

2. Same form for both singular and plural.   Nouns with the same form for singular and plural include names for some living creatures *(fowl, sheep)*, all words ending in -*ics (athletics, politics)*, and some common measurements *(foot, pair, ton*—though these also have different plural forms).

3. Survivals of older forms.   Survivals include plurals in -*en (brethren, children, oxen)* and plurals with changed vowels *(feet, geese, men, teeth, women)*.

4. Foreign language plurals.   Many nouns taken into English from other languages keep their foreign plurals, at least for a time. Words chiefly in scientific or foreign use keep the foreign plural longer. *Antenna*, for example, has the plural *antennae* in biology, though it's *antennas* for TV and radio. Some common words have two plurals, the foreign *(appendices, media, nuclei)* and the English *(appendixes, mediums, nucleuses)*.

5. Compound and group words. Most compound words and group words add *-s* to the end of the group, whether written as one word or as several: *high schools, cross-examinations, bookcases.* In a few the *-s* is added to the first element: *daughters-in-law* (and other *in-law* words), *passersby, courts-martial* (also *court-martials*).

6. Plurals of figures, words, letters. Usually the plural of a letter of the alphabet, of a word as a word, or of a figure is written with *-'s*: There are two *c*'s and two *m*'s in *accommodate.* But usage is divided: the plural of figures especially is often made with *-s*: three 2s.

    See **Apostrophe 3; -ful, full; Possessive case 1a**.

plus

Plus is a preposition having the sense "with the addition of." Therefore a phrase introduced by *plus* shouldn't affect the number of the verb, but it's sometimes allowed to do so, particularly when the *plus* phrase isn't set off by commas: The committee report plus some newspaper headlines *were* all that was needed. In more formal writing the *plus* would be changed to *and*, or the verb would be made singular.

    Plus as a substitute for the adverb *besides, also,* or *in addition* (The school has a good engineering department, plus its campus is beautiful) is objectionable to many readers, even in informal contexts. It becomes more objectionable when it begins a sentence. *Plus* also occurs as a noun (a plus for the new cafeteria is its lighting) and an adjective (a plus factor). Though there are rare occasions when *plus* substitutes economically for "to which is added," college writers would do well to avoid the word except in arithmetical contexts. See **Adjectives 1**.

p.m.

This abbreviation for *post meridiem,* "afternoon," should not be used as a noun. See **a.m. and p.m.**

Poetry

When verse is quoted, it should be lined off (as well as capitalized and punctuated) exactly as written. If possible the quoted lines should be centered on the page, indented according to the scheme of the original. When so spaced, lines of verse quoted in a prose passage needn't be enclosed in quotation marks. Diagonal marks, or virgules, are sometimes used to indicate line breaks when a short passage of poetry is run into the text: It was Marlowe who wrote, "I walk abroad 'a nights/And kill sick people groaning under walls."

ⲡⱱ Point of view

The shift in point of view in the passage marked is illogical or unjustified.

Your point of view in a paper is the position from which you view your subject. The position may be physical—your location in space and time—or psychological—your attitude toward your subject. The correction symbol *pv* indicates that, in the context, your change in point of view doesn't work.

1. Don't make unjustified shifts in physical point of view. When you write a description of an object, a place, a process, or an incident, the reader sees it through your eyes; and if he's to understand what he's looking *at*, he must have a clear idea of where he's looking *from*. In describing a building on campus, for example, you may begin with a head-on view and then lead the reader full circle, using such phrases as "looked at from the left," "from the rear," "on the Main Street side." Or you may begin with a view from far across campus or even a bird's eye view—how the building would look if it was approached in a helicopter. The important thing is to keep the reader oriented. A description that jumps from front steps to basement lab to clock tower to classrooms is bound to befuddle.

2. Don't make unmotivated shifts in attitude. If you set out to describe your dormitory, what you show the reader, what you show in greatest detail, and what you don't show at all will depend on your feelings about the place. Thus psychological point of view may determine physical point of view. And attitude may also lead to some role-playing. Suppose you hate your dorm and want to convince your reader that it deserves hating. Can you best accomplish your purpose by stating your attitude in the opening sentence? By being sarcastic throughout? Or by adopting an objective, analytical tone and counting on the examples and details you present to win the reader to your side? The strategy is yours to choose; but once you've made your choice, stick to it. Like an erratic change in physical point of view, a switch in tone from sympathetic to contemptuous or from hostile to nostalgic will confuse and irritate your reader.

3. Don't make confusing changes in the distance between you and your reader. Point of view—physical or psychological or both—influences your choice of a *personal* mode of narration, description, or argument, in which your presence is clearly felt, or an *impersonal* mode, in which you don't seem to be present at all. The pronouns, if any, that you use to refer to yourself will signal to the reader something about the relationship that you want to establish. Heavy reliance on the pronoun *I* (or *we*) may suggest casual intimacy or restricted but personal knowledge of the subject or real authority. Use of *you* may give the impression that you hope to engage your reader in a dialog. The third person ("If one should . . . ") may lend objectivity or imply remoteness. A completely impersonal approach focuses on what's being discussed without calling attention to either the writer or the audience. Once you've established yourself in one relation to your reader, it's unwise to adopt another without good reason.

Many problems in word choice and syntax stem from failure to maintain a consistent point of view. For related grammatical problems, see **Passive voice, Reference of pronouns, Shifted constructions, Tense, you**. See also **Description, Details**.

politics

Politics in the usual sense is treated as a singular: In almost any group, politics *is* a controversial subject. But when used in the sense of "principles," "activities," or "tactics," it may be treated as a plural: Republican politics *were* offensive to the Federalists. Avoid treating the word both ways in the same passage.

position, job

Position is the formal word for *job*. See **job, position**.

Positive degree

The positive degree of adjectives and adverbs is the base, or root, form of the adjective *(poor, high, golden)* or adverb *(slow, slowly, bitterly)*. See **Comparison of adjectives and adverbs**.

Possessive adjectives

My, your, her, his, our, their are sometimes called possessive adjectives. See **Possessive pronouns, possessive adjectives**.

Possessive case

1. **Signs of the possessive.**   The possessive, or genitive, function in English is shown in four ways:

a.   Apostrophe-*s* or apostrophe alone. Singular nouns that don't end in the sound of *s* as in *chess* or *z* as in *breeze* and plural nouns that don't end in the letter *s* add apostrophe -*s: boy's, one's, England's, men's, children's, freshmen's*. After plural nouns ending in -*s*, only an apostrophe is used: *workers' incomes, dogs' teeth, coaches' rules*.

For singular nouns ending in the *s* or *z* sound, practice varies, as do the recommendations of stylebooks, which set up rules for writers and editors to follow for the sake of consistency. The system proposed by the *Manual of Style* (University of Chicago Press) calls for an apostrophe-*s* after all singular nouns except *Jesus, Moses,* classical names ending in *-es (Socrates, Xerxes),* and words like *conscience* and *goodness* before *sake.* These exceptions take an apostrophe only.

To indicate joint possession, the apostrophe is added only to the second of two coordinate nouns: Martha and George's son. In "Mary's and Tom's bicycles," separate objects are possessed, and an apostrophe -*s* is needed for each noun.

b.   The *of* possessive. Most possessives formed with an apostrophe or apostrophe-*s* can also be formed with an *of* phrase: the dancer's performance, the performance of the dancer. (Exceptions include such idioms as "a day's work," "an hour's time.") The choice between the two will usually depend on considerations of rhythm, idiom, and what fits best with neighboring phrases and clauses. Idiom calls for "the roof of the house," not "the house's roof." The *of* possessive is easier to work with when the noun in the possessive is modified by clauses or by other possessives. For example, both "the car's tires" and "the tires of the car" are acceptable, but if *car* is modified by the clause "that John used to drive," the *of* possessive is clearer: the tires of the car that John used to drive (*not:* the car that John used to drive's tires). If we want to indicate that the car is John's, the *of* possessive avoids a succession of apostrophes: the tires of John's car (*not:* John's car's tires).

In some contexts there's a possible difference in meaning between the two forms. "Jane's picture" probably means a picture belonging to Jane, but it might mean a picture of Jane. "A picture of Jane" can only mean that Jane is represented in the picture. (The possessive doesn't always indicate possession. A picture of Jane may be owned by someone else. See **2.**)

c.   Double possessive. Using the *of* possessive and apostrophe-*s* together is an English idiom of long and respectable standing. It's especially common in locutions beginning with *this* and *that* and usually has an informal flavor: that boy of Helen's; friends of my father's; hobbies of Anne's. The double possessive is useful in avoiding the ambiguities mentioned above: the meaning of "Jane's picture" is made clear either as "that picture of Jane" or as "that picture of Jane's."

d.   Possessive of personal pronouns. The personal and relative pronouns have possessive forms without an apostrophe: *my, your, his, her, its, our, their, whose.* It's as important not to put an apostrophe in these pronouns (and in the forms used without nouns: *ours, yours, theirs, hers*) as it is to put one in a noun in the possessive. See **its, it's; Pronouns 1; which 2.**

2.   Uses of the possessive.   The most common function of the possessive is to indicate possession: the professor's house, Al's dog, my daughter. It also indicates a number of other relationships:

Description: a writer's responsibility, children's toys, suit of wool

Doer of an act: the wind's force, the force of the wind; the author's second novel; with the dean's permission, with the permission of the dean; the doctor's arrival, the arrival of the doctor

Recipient of an act: the police officer's murderer, the murderer of the police officer; the bill's defeat, the defeat of the bill

Adverb: He drops in of an evening.

See **Case, Gerunds 2.**

Possessive pronouns, possessive adjectives

The personal pronouns have the following possessive forms: *my, mine; your, yours; his; her, hers; our, ours; their, theirs;* and the relative *who* has *whose. Its* is the only one that regularly tempts writers to use an apostrophe, through confusion with *it's,* the contraction for "it is."

My, your, her, his, our, their are used as adjectives (and sometimes called possessive adjectives) before a noun: my car. *Mine, yours, his, hers, its, ours, theirs* are used without a following noun: Ours is better than yours.

precedence, precedents

The student who wrote, "Now that precedence has been set, the next move against our rights will be easier," confused *precedent,* meaning an action or decision that can be used to justify subsequent similar moves, with *precedence,* meaning priority or preference (The graduating class was granted precedence when seats were assigned). The sentence should begin, "Now that a precedent has been set."

Précis

A précis condenses the original piece of writing but retains its information, emphasis, and point of view. Rules for the formal précis prohibit direct quotation and call for a final version that's between one third and one fifth the length of the original. The writer condenses the original by substituting appositives, verbals, and series for more expansive statement and by eliminating nonessential material. To produce a précis that accomplishes all this and is also well written calls for practice, hard work, and considerable skill.

Predicate

Almost all English sentences divide into two main elements—subject and predicate. The predicate of a clause or sentence is the verb with its modifiers and objects or complements. The predicate may be a single verb (The bell *tolled*), a transitive verb and its object (She *landed the big fish*), or a linking verb and its complement (The oldest member of the family *is usually the first to go*). Two verbs depending on one subject are known as a compound predicate: The men *washed* and *wiped* the dishes in fifteen minutes.

p adj Predicate adjectives

Use an adjective here, because the verb is a linking verb.

The error of using an adverb instead of a predicate adjective (The stereo sounds loudly) results from the habit of putting adverbs after verbs. When the verb is a linking verb, adjectives, not adverbs, fill that position. In addition to *be*, about sixty verbs (*become, feel, turn, look, taste,* and so on) can perform this linking function. What follows the verb relates to or qualifies the subject, not the verb. Accordingly, an adjective—known as a predicate adjective or an adjective in the predicate position—is required, even though in its other functions the same verb is followed by an adverb. Compare "He felt *tired*" (adjective, relates to subject) and "He felt the edge of the knife *carefully*" (adverb, relates to the verb).

Adjective: She acts *tired*.	*Adverb:* She acts *brilliantly*.
Adjective: She looks *cold*.	*Adverb:* She looked at him *coldly*.

The test for a linking verb is that the appropriate form of *be* can replace it: "The story rings true" is structurally the same as "The story is true." When you've identified a verb as linking, use an adjective after it.

See **bad, badly; Linking verbs; look.** See also **Adjectives 1.**

Predicate nominative

Words and word groups that follow linking verbs and function as nouns are called predicate nominatives or complements. They include nouns, pronouns, phrases, and clauses. See **Linking verbs.**

predominant(ly)

Predominant is an adjective: a predominant sentiment, a sentiment predominant in the state. *Predominantly* is an adverb: The population is predominantly Muslim. But the verb is *predominate:* The Muslims predominate there. Not surprisingly, the spellings *predominate* and *predominately* for adjective and adverb have become common enough to be recognized by dictionaries. But the surest way to avoid criticism is to stick with *predominant* and *predominantly*.

prefer

To is ordinarily used with *prefer:* I prefer Ireland to Spain; She preferred going by train to flying. But when an infinitive is used instead of a noun or gerund, *to* is impossible, and *than* or *rather than* is used: She preferred to take the train rather than to fly (*or* rather than a plane).

Prefix

A prefix is a letter or letters that can be placed before a word or root to change its meaning or function: *un*tie, *im*mobilize. See **Origin of words 3a.** See also **Hyphen 4, Long variants.**

Prepositional phrases

A prepositional phrase consists of a preposition and its object: without hope, in a hurry, toward a better life. In sentences, prepositional phrases are used chiefly in the functions of adverbs (She arrived *at just the right time*) or adjectives (The man *in the black coat* was gone). See **Phrases.**

Prepositions

A preposition connects a noun phrase or a pronoun or a clause to some other part of the sentence. The whole phrase is usually adverbial or adjectival in function: He showed her *to her room;* He was old *in experience;* She was surprised *at what she saw;* the click *of flying wheels.* What follows a preposition is called its object. Prepositions may be word groups (in regard to, according to) as well as single words. And many words that serve as prepositions, such as *after, but, since,* also serve as adverbs and conjunctions. See **Objects 3, Prepositions and style.**

prep Prepositions and style

Change the preposition to one that is idiomatic or less conspicuous; or supply the missing preposition.

1. Use prepositions that are exact or idiomatic.   A number of words are accompanied by particular prepositions: we say "contented *with* conditions," "*in* my estimation." Some words take on different meanings with different prepositions: agree *with* (a person), agree *to* (a suggestion), agree *in* (principle).

Choosing the right preposition presents no problem with words you use often, because you learn the words by hearing or seeing them in their typical combinations. When you learn new words, learn how they're used as well as what they mean: *acquiesce in* (acquiesce in a decision) rather than just *acquiesce*. Dictionaries give the preposition appropriate to some words. This book has entries for a few idioms in which prepositions occasionally cause trouble: **ability to; agree to, agree with; all of; compare, contrast; different from, different than.** See also **Idiom.**

When coordinating two words that take different prepositions, include both prepositions: The first lesson he learned was obedience *to* and respect *for* his elders. *Not:* . . . obedience and respect for his elders. When both words take the same preposition, there's no need to use it twice: The box office refused to make any allowance [ ] or refund *for* tickets purchased from an agent.

2.   Avoid wordy group prepositions.   English has a number of group prepositions that take up too much space for the work they do. A reference to "recent complaints on the part of dissatisfied students" is weighed down by *on the part of* where *by* would do the job. Sometimes we carry over from speech the habit of using double prepositions: *(in) back of, off (of)*. See **as to; off of; on to, onto; prior to.**

3.   Don't   omit   prepositions   indiscriminately.   Prepositions aren't dropped in formal writing. Some can be dropped in general writing as well as in informal: ". . . one of the best pieces written about the United States [in] this century" (Arthur Schlesinger, *New Republic*). But expressions like "a couple [of] days later," "a different type [of] girl," and "outside [of] his interest in boxing" remain decidedly informal.

4.   When a preposition falls naturally at the end of a sentence, leave it there. There's an old "rule" that a preposition shouldn't end a sentence (She is the one I did it for). But postponing the preposition has long been a characteristic English idiom, and rhythm often demands placing the preposition at the end. Attempts to avoid putting it there may result in stilted sentences: Tell me what it is to which you object (*better:* what you object to).

Putting the preposition at the end comes so naturally that if you place it earlier in the sentence, you may end up having it in both places: He brightened the life of everyone with whom he came in contact [with].

See **Phrases 2.**

Present tense

The base form of a verb *(ask, answer, buy, say)* is its present tense. In most verbs -*s* is added in the third-person singular. See **Tenses of verbs.**

pretty

Pretty for *rather* or *fairly* gives a sentence an informal tone: "[Archibald Cox] sets pretty straight . . . the real impact of the great case of Marbury

v. Madison'' (Charles L. Black, Jr., *New York Times Book Review*). The usage is standard.

preventive, preventative

Unless you're being paid by the letter, *preventive* is preferable in every way.

Prewriting

Prewriting is the stage of thinking, worrying, and doodling that you go through before you set down even the rough form of a paper. The process is related to what's known in classical rhetoric as invention and discovery—finding out what you have to say about your subject.

People prewrite in different ways. Some scribble, apparently aimlessly, trying to find their way to a lead-in idea. Some think through the subject again and again, doing their prewriting entirely in their heads. And some look into promising sources, jot down facts, thoughts, and impressions, and try various ways of ordering their ideas to discover the points that need most emphasis.

Whether or not your exploration of your subject involves hunting up information and finding out what others have said, the end product of prewriting is not a collection of notes. It's a sure sense that you've made the subject your own. Making the subject your own means that whatever you write will be motivated by personal concern. Writing that lacks personal concern—intellectual commitment or emotional commitment or both—is very likely to be dull writing, trite and mechanical in both thought and expression. Writing that grows out of personal concern is just as likely to have some drive and freshness. It's the kind of writing that quickly wins and holds the attention of a reader.

Though there are no rules that will guarantee successful prewriting, or pump priming, one practice that helps many writers is keeping a daily journal—entering sentences and paragraphs that capture thoughts and opinions, making notes of images that match half-formed ideas. Because his journal proved so rich a source for his public writing, one author called it his savings bank. Certainly keeping a journal is worth a try. You may find that, like other prewriting techniques, it will give you a running start on writing your papers.

pp Principal parts of verbs

Change the verb form to one in standard use.

1.   The principal parts of a verb.   The principal parts are the base form or infinitive *(ask)*, the past-tense form *(asked)*, the past participle *(asked)*.

Most English verbs are "regular"—that is, their past tense and past participle are formed by adding *-ed* to the base form. A number of the most common change a vowel *(sing, sang, sung)* in making their past-tense and past-participle forms. Some *(let, cost)* remain unchanged. Some *(bend, make)* change the final consonant. And some have less common irregularities (past forms of *teach: taught, taught).*

The trend has been toward regularity. A few verbs *(broadcast, shine, speed)* have acquired regular forms in addition to their old ones: *broadcasted, shined, speeded.* A few others *(dive, fit, prove, sew)* have reversed the trend, acquiring irregularities that are either new or revivals of archaic forms: *dove, fit* (past tense), *proven, sewn.* For some verbs *(dream, plead, show, strive, thrive)* variant pairs have long existed side by side: *dreamed, dreamt; pleaded, pled; showed, shown* (as past participle); *strived, strove; thrived, throve.*

The following list includes a number of verbs with irregular past-tense and past-participle forms. The forms labeled *NS* (nonstandard) and *D* (dialect) would not ordinarily be written. When you're in doubt, consult a recent dictionary for verbs not listed here. Usage is by no means uniform, even among speakers and writers of standard English, and neither this list nor the dictionaries record all variations.

Infinitive	*Past tense*	*Past participle*
arise	arose	arisen
bear	bore	borne
bear	bore	born (given birth to)
begin	began (D: begun)	begun
bite	bit	bitten, bit
blow	blew (D: blowed)	blown (D: blowed)
break	broke	broken (NS: broke)
bring	brought (NS: brung)	brought (NS: brung)
catch	caught (chiefly D: catched)	caught (chiefly D: catched)
choose	chose	chosen
come	came (NS: come)	come
dig	dug	dug
dive	dived, dove	dived
do	did (NS: done)	done
drag	dragged (D: drug)	dragged (D: drug)
draw	drew (NS: drawed)	drawn
dream	dreamed, dreamt	dreamed, dreamt
drink	drank (D: drunk)	drunk
eat	ate (D: pronounced *et*)	eaten (D: pronounced *et*)
fall	fell	fallen
fly	flew	flown
forget	forgot	forgotten, forgot
freeze	froze (D: friz)	frozen (chiefly D: froze)
get	got	got, gotten
give	gave (NS: give)	given (NS: give)
go	went (D: goed)	gone (NS: went)
grow	grew (D: growed)	grown (D: growed)
hang	hung	hung

Infinitive	*Past tense*	*Past participle*
hang (execute)	hung, hanged	hung, hanged
hear	heard	heard
know	knew (D: knowed)	known (D: knowed)
lay	laid	laid
lead	led	led
lean	leaned	leaned
lend (loan)	lent	lent
lie (*see* **lay**)	lay	lain
lose	lost	lost
prove	proved	proved, proven
ride	rode (D: rid)	ridden (D: rid)
ring	rang, rung	rung
run	ran (NS: run)	run
see	saw (NS: seed)	seen (NS: seed, saw)
shake	shook (chiefly D: shaked)	shaken (chiefly D: shaked)
shine	shone, shined	shone, shined
show	showed	showed, shown
shrink	shrank, shrunk	shrunk
sing	sang, sung	sung
sink	sank, sunk	sunk, sunken
sit	sat (D: set)	sat (D: set)
slide	slid	slid
sneak	sneaked (chiefly D: snuck)	sneaked (chiefly D: snuck)
speak	spoke	spoken
spring	sprang, sprung	sprung
stand	stood	stood
steal	stole	stolen (chiefly D: stole)
swim	swam	swum
swing	swung	swung
take	took (D: taken)	taken (D: took)
tear	tore	torn
throw	threw (D: throwed)	thrown (D: throwed)
wear	wore	worn
write	wrote (D: writ)	written (D: wrote)

2.   Black English verbs.   Linguists investigating the patterns of some Black English dialects have found a structure that is predictable and therefore grammatical in sentences that have traditionally been called ungrammatical. An example: The teacher gone right now, but she be back soon. The lack of a *be* form in the first clause—"The teacher [is] gone"—and the apparently incorrect form of *be* in the second—"she [will] be back"—results from what grammarians call a deletion transformation. It regularly and predictably omits a form of *be* and other auxiliary verbs such as *will,* *would,* and *have* where standard English speakers contract their form of *be*. (An exception is *'m,* as in "I'm going.") This sequence represents the process:

The teacher is	gone right now, but she will be back soon.
The teacher's	gone right now, but she'll be back soon.
The teacher[	]gone right now, but she[ ]be back soon.

Where speakers of standard English can't contract a form of *be,* speakers of some dialects of Black English can't omit it:

> **Standard English:** I don't know who he is. *Not:* I don't know who's.
> **Black English:** I don't know who he be. *Not:* I don't know who he.

See **born, borne; do; got, gotten; grammatical, ungrammatical 1; hanged, hung; lay, lie; proved, proven; set, sit.**

principal, principle

Principal is either an adjective or a noun. *Principle* is a noun only. One way to remember that the adjective is spelled *principal* is to associate it with other adjectives ending in *-al: historical, political, musical.*

Principal as a noun is probably an abbreviation of a phrase in which it was originally an adjective. The principal that draws interest was once the principal sum; the principal of a school, the principal teacher; the principal in a legal action, the principal party; the principals in a play, the principal actors. These are the only common uses of *principal* as a noun.

The noun meaning "a general truth or rule of conduct" is *principle:* the principles of science, a matter of principle.

prior to

Prior to, a rather formal preposition, is most appropriate when it adds to the notion of "before" the notion of "in anticipation of": "He urged reform leaders to work prior to the convention so as to minimize the influence of Greeley's supporters" (Matthew T. Downey, *Journal of American History*). In most contexts, particularly in general styles, *before* is the better choice.

Profanity

Using profanity—that is, referring to sacred beings carelessly or irreverently—is primarily a matter of emotional release (or simply habit) rather than a matter of meaning. In writing, it often attracts more attention to itself than it deserves. Like other kinds of swearing, profanity has no place in college writing, except perhaps in dialog. See **Obscenity.**

professor

Write: Professor Moore; Prof. E. W. Moore; E. W. Moore, a professor of chemistry; *or* E. W. Moore, Professor of Chemistry.

Strictly speaking, the title *Professor* should be given only to assistant professors, associate professors, and full professors, and not to those who haven't achieved professorial rank. When the title follows the name in an *of* phrase, exact rank is usually indicated: Professor A. B. Plant, *but* A. B. Plant, Assistant Professor of English.

The informal *prof* (my math prof) is a clipped word, not an abbreviation, and is written without a period.

Pronouns

A pronoun is commonly defined as a word that replaces a noun or another word or group of words used as a noun. The word or phrase or clause that it substitutes for, as *it* substitutes for *a pronoun* in the sentence you're reading, is called its antecedent: *it* is said to refer to *a pronoun; a pronoun* is the antecedent of *it*. Not all pronouns have antecedents. What *I* and *you* refer to depends on the identity of the writer or speaker and the audience being addressed, not on the verbal context in which *I* and *you* appear.

Like nouns, pronouns can serve as subjects and objects (though not all pronouns can serve as both). Many have a possessive form, and a few have a separate plural form. Unlike nouns, pronouns are a small, closed class of words—that is, no new pronouns are being added to the language.

The traditional subclasses of pronouns are listed below.

1. Personal pronouns. The personal pronouns are those words that specifically indicate person (first, second, or third), number, and, in the third-person singular, gender.

		Nominative	*Possessive*	*Accusative*
1st-person	*singular*	I	my, mine	me
	plural	we	our, ours	us
2nd-person	*singular*	you	your, yours	you
	plural	you	your, yours	you
3rd-person	*singular*			
	masculine	he	his, his	him
	feminine	she	her, hers	her
	neuter	it	its, its	it
	genderless	one	one's, one's	one
	plural	they	their, theirs	them

Except for the relative pronoun *who (whose, whom),* only the personal pronouns—and not all of them—have different forms for the three cases. Some of the most common grammatical mistakes occur because, unlike nouns, *I, we, she, they,* and *who* have different forms in subject and object position. See **between you and me; Case; it's me; who, whom.**

In some traditional grammars, personal pronouns in the possessive case are classified separately as possessive pronouns.

2. Reflexive pronouns. The reflexives are formed by adding *-self* or *-selves* to the possessive case of personal pronouns in the first and second persons *(myself, yourself, ourselves, yourselves)* and to the accusative case in the third person *(himself, herself, itself, themselves)*. They are used when an object or a subjective complement refers to the same thing or concept or event as the preceding noun or noun phrase:

Direct object:	She hurt *herself*.
Object of preposition:	The road twisted back on *itself*.
Indirect object:	They made *themselves* caftans.
Subjective complement:	Ben isn't *himself* today.
Object of infinitive:	Jane wanted Betty to help *herself*.

As intensives, the reflexive forms are considered to be pronouns in apposition: The owner *himself* sold the car; The owner sold the car *himself*. See **Apposition, appositives.**

3. Reciprocal pronouns. The reciprocals *each other* and *one another* substitute in object position for a compound or plural subject when the action of the verb is directed by each member of the subject toward the other members: Tom and Bill looked at *each other;* The losers kidded *one another*. Like the personal pronouns, the reciprocals are freely used in the possessive: They borrowed *one another's* clothes.

4. Relative pronouns. *Who, which,* and *that* are relatives. (*Who* and *which* are also interrogatives.) Like the personal pronouns, *who* has different forms for the possessive *(whose)* and the accusative *(whom)*. *Which* and *that* are not inflected for case.

Relative pronouns introduce dependent clauses:

The student *who* submitted this paper has dropped out.
The paper *that* she submitted won an award.
Her decision to leave school, *which* caused some excitement, was never explained.

When no specific referent for the pronoun is intended, the indefinite, or expanded, form of the relative is used: *whoever, whomever, whichever, whatever*. Unexpanded *what* is also an indefinite relative pronoun:

Whoever receives this will be pleased.
I will support *whomever* you nominate.
They will believe *whatever* he says.
They will believe *what* he says.

See **Relative clauses.**

5. Interrogative pronouns. The interrogatives *who, whose, whom, which,* and *what* are used to introduce direct and indirect questions: *What* happened? He asked me *what* happened.

6. Demonstrative pronouns. *This, that, these,* and *those* are considered adjectives when they modify nouns (*this* hat, *these* books), pronouns when they function as nouns: *This* will fix it; *Those* are too large; I prefer *these.* The demonstratives discriminate between referents close at hand *(this, these)* and referents that are more remote *(that, those).*

7. Indefinite pronouns. *Some, any, every,* and *no* compounded with *one (someone), thing (everything),* and *body (nobody),* and other words like *all, any, some, each,* and *either,* have traditionally been called indefinite pronouns. When used as subjects, the compounds take singular verbs, and pronouns referring to them are usually in the singular: Everyone is expected to do his part.

Informally, *they* is also used for indefinite reference: They ought to do something about these roads. See **they.**

See **Antecedent, Determiners, Reference of pronouns.**

Proofreading

Checking the final copy of a paper for mechanical mistakes that may have slipped into the last draft is an essential part of preparing a manuscript. See **Careless mistakes, Caret, Manuscript form, Typewritten copy.**

Proper adjectives

Proper nouns that are used like adjectives are capitalized, and so are adjectives that are directly derived from proper names if they still refer to the place or person. After proper adjectives lose the reference to their origins, they become simple adjectives and are no longer capitalized: the Indian service, india ink; the Roman forum, roman type. See **Capital letters.**

proved, proven

Prove is a regular verb, forming a past tense and past participle with *-ed: proved. Proven* has been used for centuries as an alternative past participle of *prove* and is now established in all varieties of usage.

provided, providing

Both *provided* and *providing* are in standard use as connectives:

You can't even argue, much, with the picture, providing you look at it only as a clever Western.—David R. Slavitt, *Yale Review*

Anyone who can get into M.S.U. can get into Justin Morrill, provided he is willing to work.—Duncan Norton, *Fortune*

When *if* can be used in place of either form, it probably should be.

Psychologese

Psychologese, a jargon made up of words from the technical vocabulary of psychology, is used enthusiastically if inexactly by many outsiders: *instinctual* for *instinctive, operant* for *operating, motorical* for *motor*. A great many other terms from psychology—*compulsive, empathy, motivational, neurotic, paranoid, relate, traumatic*—have entered the language, become vogue words, and lost much of their technical meaning.

public

Meaning "the people as a whole," *public* is a collective noun and can be treated as either singular or plural. A plural construction is more common: The public depend on TV newscasts for most of their information. But in the sense "a group of people with a common interest," *public* is more often singular: "There is a foreign policy public that is considerably smaller than the general public" (Carl N. Degler, *American Historical Review*).

pn Punctuation

Insert necessary punctuation, or change your punctuation to conform to standard usage.

no *pn* No punctuation

Delete the unnecessary punctuation.

The basic purpose of punctuation is to mark off sentences and to link, separate, and set off elements within sentences in ways that will make the meaning clear to readers. A good rule to follow is to use all punctuation required by current convention and as much optional punctuation as you need to help your reader. Don't use unnecessary punctuation, which may make reading more difficult. And don't rely on punctuation to bail out awkwardly constructed sentences. Instead, rewrite.

1. To end sentences.   Use periods to end statements. Use question marks to end sentences that ask direct questions. Use exclamation marks to end sentences (or to follow words or phrases) that express strong emotion and demand special emphasis. See **Exclamation mark, Period, Question mark.**

2. To separate.
a.   Use a comma before the conjunction to separate independent clauses joined by *but, for,* or *so.* You can also use a comma before the other coordinating conjunctions in compound sentences. To indicate a stronger separation, use a semicolon. See **Comma 1, Semicolon 1c.**
b.   Use a comma after a long introductory phrase or dependent clause to separate it from the main clause. You can use a comma after all introductory phrases and clauses. Don't use a comma after introductory *but, and,* or other conjunction. See **Comma 2a.**
c.   Use a comma before a nonrestrictive dependent clause or phrase that follows the main clause. Don't use a comma before a restrictive modifier that follows the main clause. See **Comma 2b.**
d.   Use commas to separate the units in a series and to separate adjectives modifying the same noun. To separate the units in a series that already includes commas, use semicolons. See **Comma 5, Semicolon 2.**
e.   Don't use a comma between subject and verb, between verb and object or complement, or, in most cases, between the verbs in a compound predicate. See **Comma 8.**

3. To set off.
a.   Use paired commas to set off nonrestrictive modifiers.
b.   Use paired commas, paired dashes, or parentheses to set off interrupting elements. Commas mark the least separation, parentheses the most. Setting off short interrupters is optional. See **Comma 4a.**

4. To link.
a.   Use a semicolon between main clauses when you want to link them rather than separate them with a period. See **Semicolon 1.**
b.   Use a colon (*not* a semicolon) to link a series, a quotation, or other material to the sentence element that introduces it. See **Colon 1.**
c.   Use a dash to link to the end of a sentence a word, phrase, or clause you want to emphasize. See **Dash 1.**
d.   Use a hyphen to link syllables and words. See **Hyphen.**

5. Other uses.
a.   Use quotation marks to identify direct quotations. See **Quotation marks 2.**
b.   Use ellipses to indicate omission of words. See **Ellipsis.**
c.   Use apostrophes to indicate possession and to indicate the omission of letters in contractions. See **Apostrophe 1, 2.**

Puns

A pun is a figure of speech in which a word is simultaneously used in two different senses (the nut that holds the wheel) or substituted for another word of similar sound but different meaning (effluent society). Deliberate punning may serve serious purposes as well as humorous ones, but unintentional puns, which may get laughs you don't want, should be weeded out in revising.

Qualifiers

Qualifiers are words used not to convey meaning in themselves but to qualify—usually by intensifying—the meaning of adjectives. They include the first words in the phrases "much older," "very quiet," "too young," "somewhat sick," "rather careless," and "quite intelligent" and adverbs of degree like *slightly*. Unless they're used thoughtfully and sparingly, qualifiers will weaken writing instead of strengthening it.

Question mark

The chief conventions governing the use of the question mark are these:

1. As an end stop. The principal use of the question mark is as the end stop of a direct question: What was the real reason?

A question mark is not used after an indirect question: He wanted to know what the real reason was.

A request that's phrased as a question is usually followed by a question mark but may not be in general and informal styles. See **Period.**

2. With quotation marks. When a sentence ends with a question mark and closing quotation marks, the question mark belongs outside the quotation marks if the sentence that encloses the quotation is the question (Did you really say, "I thought you were older than that"?), inside if the quotation is the question (He asked, "Did you really say that?"). If both are questions, only the inside question mark is used: Did she ask, "How many are coming?"

3. Within sentences. Usage is divided over a question built into a sentence: Should I quit school now [ ] I ask myself. A question mark after *now* would emphasize the question; a comma would make it less emphatic. If quotation marks were used around the question, a question mark would be appropriate: "Should I quit school now?" I ask myself. "I'm trying to decide whether I should quit school now" avoids the problem.

Questions

1. Direct and indirect questions. A direct question is a question as actually asked, not just reported. It begins with a capital and ends with a question mark: Who killed Cock Robin?

An indirect question isn't a question as actually asked but a question as reported in another sentence. An indirect question doesn't begin with a capital or end with a question mark, and it's not set off by quotation marks.

> *Direct:* He asked, "Do you really understand what you have read?"
> *Indirect:* He asked us *if we really understood what we had read.*
> *Indirect:* He always asks us *whether we understand what we have read.*

2. Leading questions. A leading question is one that's phrased so as to suggest the desired answer, like "You'd like to go, wouldn't you?" (*Compare* "Do you want to go?")

3. Questions as transitions. Occasionally, but only occasionally, asking a question in a paper is a good way to introduce a new paragraph: What can we do to improve the situation?

See **Rhetorical questions.**

quot Quotation marks

" / " Make the quotation marks conform to conventional usage.

1. Methods of indicating quotations.
a. Double quotes, not single, are the usual marks in the United States.
b. For quotations within quotations, alternate double and single quotes. Use single quotes inside double quotes and so on: "'Perry's instinct,' he says, 'soundly chose the point at which to halt the extension of the term "formula"'" (Joseph Russo, *Yale Classical Studies*).
c. When a quotation is longer than one paragraph, use quotation marks at the beginning of each paragraph but at the end of the last paragraph only.
d. If you include a long quotation in a paper, you can make it a block quotation and omit quotation marks. In a paper that's typewritten double-spaced, indent the whole quotation five spaces and set it off from the text by triple-spacing. Double-space the quotation itself. In a handwritten paper, simply indent the whole quotation.

2. Principal uses of quotation marks.
a. Quotation marks are used to indicate all passages taken from another writer, whether a phrase or a page or more (except when the quotation is indented). Any change within the quotation should be indicated—omissions by ellipses, additions by brackets. The quoted matter may stand by itself or

may be worked into your own sentence. Both methods are shown in this passage, the more formal first:

> The most that can be said for Haig was said by Churchill: he "was unequal to the prodigious scale of events, but no one else was discerned as his equal or better." (Lloyd George, more succinctly, said he was "brilliant to the top of his army boots.")—Geoffrey Barraclough, *New York Review of Books*

When brief passages of conversation are introduced not for their own sake but to illustrate a point, they are usually incorporated in the paragraph:

> I am having a drink with the manager, Yves Blais. "You don't speak French," he starts off by saying, "but that is all right because you are from Ontario, which is another country. I will speak English with you. But I have no British accent. I have a pea-soup accent." Blais volunteers the obvious—that he is a separatist. "I'm glad to be. I don't care. I refused to accept a Canada council grant of $8,000. But it has nothing to do with my shows."—Jon Ruddy, *Maclean's*

b.   There are no half quotes. A sentence is either an exact quotation and therefore in quotation marks, or else it is not an exact quotation and so is not quoted. Don't present as a direct quote material containing pronouns and verb tenses that are appropriate only to indirect statements: He boasted that he "could do twice as much work as I could." The boast must have been, "I can do twice as much work as you can." The choice is between direct and indirect quotation: He boasted, "I can do twice as much work as you can"; *or* He boasted that he could do twice as much work as I could. In the second alternative the single phrase *twice as much work* could be quoted.

3.   Miscellaneous uses of quotation marks.

a.   Quotation marks enclose titles of poems, articles, stories, chapters of books, and, in most newspapers and many magazines, the titles of books themselves. See **Titles 2a.**

b.   Words that are used as words rather than for their meaning usually appear in italics in formal writing, in quotes in general writing. But usage is divided:

> There is the ugly and almost universal use of "like" for "as."—Douglas Bush, *American Scholar*

> The word *buff* is old in the English language.—Webb Garrison, *American Legion Magazine*

c.   A word from a conspicuously different variety of English is sometimes put in quotation marks, but this only calls attention to it. If you decide that such a word suits your needs, use it without apology and without quotes:

> He spurns aspirants not of his clique, thereby creating a tyranny of taste that soon will have every center of imaginative expression . . . under its cheesy [*not* "cheesy"] thrall.—Benjamin DeMott, *New American Review*

d. A word may be put in quotation marks to show that the writer is not accepting its conventional sense in the context:

> In numerous cases it is impossible to maintain on any solid ground that one pronunciation is "better" than another, as, for example, that one pronunciation of *swamp* is better than the others given.—John S. Kenyon and Thomas A. Knott, *A Pronouncing Dictionary of American English*

But putting a word in quotation marks to signal sarcasm or ridicule (The "cute" Great Dane had eaten my sweater) is on a par with putting a question mark in parentheses to get a laugh.

e. Directly quoted *yes* and *no* (sometimes capitalized, sometimes not) frequently appear without quotation marks when they're built into the sentence in which they appear: Steve said Yes, so we went to work at once. When they're not actually spoken, they shouldn't be quoted: If she had said no, I would have resigned.

4.   Quotation marks with other marks.

a. When a question mark or an exclamation mark ends a quotation, it's placed inside the quotes:

> "Don't go near that wire!" he shouted.
> Later he said, "Aren't you wondering what would have happened?"

When a question mark or exclamation mark belongs to the construction that includes the quotation, it's placed after the quotes: What is an ordinary citizen to do when he hears the words, "This is a stick-up"? See **Question mark 2.**

b. American practice is to put periods and commas within closing quotation marks, colons and semicolons after them.

c. *He said* and all its variations are normally set off by commas from the quotations they introduce:

> "History," it is said, "does not repeat itself. The historians repeat one another."—Max Beerbohm, *Works*

But the quoted phrase may be so closely built into the sentence that no comma is wanted:

> Any moron can say "I don't know who done it."—Francis Christensen, *Notes Toward a New Rhetoric*

raise, rear

Raise in the sense of bringing up a child is suitable in all varieties of usage. *Rear* is somewhat formal. See **bring up.**

reaction

Reaction has drifted from the scientific vocabulary and is now used for nearly any response, whether emotional or mental, general or specific. Try to find a more precise term or at least a different one—*response,* for instance.

real, really

Ordinarily *real* is the adjective (a real difficulty, in real life), and *really* is the adverb (a really significant improvement; I really thought so). Both are overused as qualifiers; TV commercials and talk shows could barely exist without them, and "in a real sense" is one of the most tiresome of current clichés. Adverbial *real,* as in sentences like "Write real soon" and "It's real pretty," is informal.

rear, raise

As applied to bringing up children, *rear* is the formal choice. See **raise, rear.**

reason is because

In formal writing there's a strong preference for *reason is that,* on the grounds that *reason is because* is redundant. Even in general writing, *that* is much more common when there are no intervening words after *reason* (My only reason is that I have to work tonight) or when the intervening words aren't a clause with a subject of its own (The only reason usually given for such failures in sports is that there was inadequate concentration). But when many words or a clause with a separate subject intervenes, *reason . . . is because* often occurs in both formal and general prose:

One reason why music can stand repetition so much more sturdily than correspondingly good prose is because music, of all the arts, is by its nature least suited to the psychology of information, and has remained closer to the psychology of form.—Kenneth Burke, *Psychology and Form*

And the reason the press isn't a menace, Reston says, is because it has divested itself of so much of its power.—*Newsweek*

Even though *reason is because* has a long history in literature and is regularly used by educated speakers, writers should remind themselves that to some readers it's a hobgoblin.

Reciprocal pronouns

Each other and *one another* are called reciprocal pronouns. See **each other, Pronouns 3.**

reckon

Used to mean "suppose" or "think," *reckon* is a localism. See **Localisms.**

Redundancy

In writing, words and phrases that are repetitive or simply unnecessary are redundant. See **Repetition, Wordiness.**

 ## Reference of pronouns

Change the pronoun marked (or revise the sentence) so that the reference will be clear and the pronoun appropriate to the context.

In the sentence "Because my brother loves to ski, he spent Christmas vacation in Colorado," the pronoun *he* replaces the nominal *my brother*. *My brother* is called the antecedent of *he; he* refers to the same person as *my brother*. In "He got so frostbitten I scarcely recognized him," the pronoun *I* has a referent (the speaker) but doesn't have an antecedent. Both categories of pronouns—those that have antecedents and those that don't—create some problems for writers.

1.   Clear reference.   If the meaning of a pronoun is completed by reference to an antecedent, the reference should be unmistakable. The reader shouldn't have to figure it out. Here are situations in which reference lacks the precision that college writing demands:
a.   When the pronoun seems to refer to a nearby noun that it can't sensibly refer to:

The next year he had an attack of appendicitis. *It* burst before the doctor had a chance to operate.

Revision: . . . His appendix burst. . . . (*It* can't sensibly refer to *appendicitis*. Such slips in reference are common when the pronoun is in one sentence and the antecedent in another.)

b. When there's no noun nearby:

He isn't married yet and doesn't plan on *it*.

Revision: . . . and doesn't plan to marry.

c. When the pronoun refers to a noun used as a possessive or as an adjective:

Bill was skipping stones across the swimming hole. One cut open a young girl's head *who* was swimming under water.

Revision: . . . One cut open the head of a young girl who. . . .

Nancy longed for a chinchilla coat, though she wouldn't have dreamed of killing *one*.

Revision: . . . of killing a chinchilla.

d. When two or more pronouns are crossed so that exactly what is referred to can't be readily determined:

Businessmen without regard for anyone else have exploited the mass of workers at every point, not caring whether *they* were earning a decent living but only whether *they* were making big profits.

Revision: . . . not caring whether they paid a decent wage but only whether they were making big profits. (The sentence needs complete rewriting, but this revision at least makes both *they's* refer to the same antecedent.)

2. Broad reference.   General English uses *which, that, this,* and sometimes *it* to refer not to a specific word or phrase but to the idea of a preceding clause. Formal English avoids broad reference.

General: Her friend was jealous of her clothes and money and had taken this way of showing *it*.

Formal: . . . and had taken this way of showing her feeling.

General: The recent price jumps, then, are not primarily the middleman's fault, *which* is why he is happy no longer to be fingered in the [Consumer Price] index.—William Safire, *New York Times Magazine*

Formal: . . . the middleman's fault, and this fact explains why he. . . . (More formal: . . . the fault of the middleman, and this fact explains why he. . . .)

3. Indefinite reference.   Often you'll use the pronouns *one, you, we, he, they* in your papers to refer to your readers or to people in general instead of specifically mentioned individuals. Which of these pronouns to use is a matter of style, not of grammar. Once you've settled on one of them, use it consistently: When *you* have worked a day here, *you* have earned *your* money. With *one,* a shift to *he* is standard: When *one* has worked a day here, *he* has earned *his* money. But *not:* When *one* has worked a day here, *you* have earned *your* money. See **one.**

Don't substitute indefinite *one, you, he, we,* or *they* for a definite personal pronoun:

> For *me* there is no fun in reading unless *you* can put *yourself* in the position of the characters and feel that *you* are really in the scene.
>
> *Revision:* . . . unless I can put myself in the position of the characters and feel that I am. . . .

As a common-gender pronoun meaning "he or she," *he* is traditional in formal English, *they* in informal. General usage is divided. *He* is more conventional, *they* often more practical. See **Agreement 2, Sexist language.**

4. Avoiding and misusing pronouns.   Writers who are uncertain about the reference or agreement of pronouns sometimes try to avoid them by repeating nouns. The result is usually unidiomatic or clumsy: Arrest of the woman yesterday followed several days of observation of the woman's (her) activities by the agents.

Referent

The referent of a word is the thing or event or concept the word refers to. In a specific context, "Carolyn Robb" and "the love of my life," referring to the same person, would have the same referent.

Reflexive pronouns

Myself, yourself, himself, herself, itself, ourselves, yourselves, and *themselves* are reflexive pronouns. See **myself, Pronouns 2.**

relate

In the shoptalk of psychology the verb *relate* is a convenient term meaning to "have a realistic social or intimate relationship," as in "the patient's inability to relate." This sense of *relate* has passed into everyday usage, but the relationship is usually—and preferably—specified by a *to* phrase: They find it almost impossible to relate to adults. *Relate* became a vogue word in the 1960s.

Relative clauses

Relative clauses are introduced by relative pronouns *(that, which,* or *who)* or by relative adverbs *(where, when, why).* Those introduced by relative pronouns are often referred to as adjective clauses. A relative clause stands after the noun it modifies:

> The rain *that began in the morning* kept on all night.
> The coach was abused by the alumni *who two years before had cheered him.*
> The road to the left, *which looked almost impassable,* was ours.
> The first place *where they camped* turned out to be a swamp.

In general usage, when the clause is restrictive, the introductory adverb or pronoun (if the pronoun isn't the subject of the clause) is often omitted:

> He will never forget the time *you tried to cheat him.*
>
> *More formal:* . . . the time *when you tried to cheat him.*

> The man *I met that afternoon* became my closest friend.
>
> *More formal:* The man *whom I met.* . . .

When relative clauses are introduced by indefinite relative pronouns *(who, what,* and the compounds with *-ever),* the clauses function as nouns or as adjectives:

> The stranger at the door wasn't *who we thought she was.*
> *What actually happened* was very different from *what the newspapers reported.*
> The stranger at the door was the woman *who had moved in downstairs.*

Several relative clauses in succession make for an awkward house-that-Jack-built sentence: People who buy houses *that* have been built in times *which* had conspicuous traits of architecture *which* have since been abandoned often find *that* they have to remodel their purchases completely. See **Subordination 1.**

See **Pronouns 4; Restrictive and nonrestrictive modifiers; that; which; who, whom.** Compare **Noun clauses.**

Relative pronouns

The relative pronouns are *who (whose, whom), which (of which, whose), that, what, whatever,* and *whoever (whomever):*

Somebody *who* was sitting on the other side shouted, "Put 'em out!"
The Senator, *whose* term expires next year, is already worrying.
I haven't read the same book *that* you have.

That refers to persons and things, *who* to persons. *Which* referring to animals or objects or situations and also to collective nouns, even if they refer to persons, is now standard English:

The army *which* mobilizes first has the advantage.
The Board of Directors, *which* met on Saturday. . . .
The Board of Directors, *who* are all bankers. . . .

See **Pronouns 4; Restrictive and nonrestrictive modifiers; that; which; who, whom.**

rep Repetition

Get rid of the ineffective repetition of word, meaning, sound, or sentence pattern.

Repeating words, meanings, sounds, or sentence patterns is often effective in writing, giving prose clarity and emphasis. This article reviews some kinds of repetition that ordinarily call for revision.

1. Of words and phrases.   You're bound to repeat nouns unnecessarily if you don't use pronouns:

Ann accepted the boy's challenge and proceeded to teach the boy [him] a lesson. When the boy [he] stayed at the base line, Ann [she] ran the boy [him] from one side of the court to the other. When the boy [he] charged the net, Ann [she] beat the boy [him] with passing shots.

If you write hurriedly and don't take the time to read over what you've written, you're likely to end up with careless repetition:

I'm having financial difficulties and need to *get* out of housing. So the hassle I *got* when I tried to *get* released from my dorm contract upset me.

When you use the same word in two different senses, the result may be worse:

After I fell only a few feet my left foot found footing.

I would like to find a job with a concern that shows some concern for the environment.

In cases like these, the repetition is obvious enough to be caught and corrected with little trouble—either by omitting the unnecessary repetition or by substituting synonyms. But it does call for that little trouble.

Harder for writers to spot but equally conspicuous to readers is the pet word or phrase that pops up three or four times in the course of a paper. If it's a cliché or a vogue expression, as it's likely to be, it may bother some readers on its first appearance and become increasingly irritating thereafter. In going over a first draft, then, keep an eye out for expressions that recur. Some of the repeated words and phrases will be unavoidable, some desirable. But you may also spot some pets that you've repeated simply because they're pets. Sacrifice them.

2.   Of meaning.   In reviewing what you've written, watch for words and phrases that unnecessarily repeat what you've already said. For example, a gift is free and a fact true by definition, so drop the adjective from "free gift" and from "true fact." If the setting of many TV plays is San Francisco, then San Francisco must frequently be the setting of TV plays. Writing "In many TV plays the setting very often is San Francisco" adds words but subtracts sense. So does "at 8 a.m. in the morning."

3.   Of sounds.   Jingles and rhyming words (hesitate to take the bait, a glance askance at the dance) are distracting in papers because they draw attention from sense to sound. So are noticeable repetitions of unstressed syllables, especially the -*ly* of adverbs and the endings of some abstract nouns, like -*tion*. Reading first drafts aloud is the best way to catch such unintentional repetition of sound as "Reliance on science has led to compliance. . . ." See **Adverbs and style, Alliteration, Assonance.**

4.   Of sentence patterns.   If you unintentionally use the same pattern in one sentence after another—beginning three sentences in a row with a dependent clause, for example, or writing three successive compound sentences, or using the same coordinating conjunction in a series of sentences for no rhetorical purpose—your reader is likely to begin nodding. Sometimes this sort of repetition sets up a rhythm even more distracting than the repetition of sound within sentences. Sometimes it simply begins to bore the reader; he feels that he's being led over the same route again and again. Deliberate varying of sentence patterns isn't often called for, but if you find yourself recycling a pattern, make an effort to get untracked. See **Parallelism.**

Requests

Requests are often expressed in the form of questions: Will you please cooperate? Sometimes a period takes the place of the question mark. See **Commands and requests.**

Research paper

The research paper—sometimes called the reference paper, library paper, investigative paper, or source paper—is the culminating assignment in many college courses, including Freshman English. Done well, it serves as a valuable introduction to scholarship: preparing a good paper requires resourcefulness in using the library, ingenuity in following up leads, judgment in analyzing data, and skill in organizing and writing an essay of some length and complexity. Because a research project is an ambitious undertaking, often extending over several weeks, it should be planned carefully and worked at methodically. The main steps are these:

1. Choosing a topic. The best topic is one that you know something about but want to learn much more about. The motivation to learn more gives point and direction to your research. And the motivation to learn more about *something in particular* will help keep you from taking on an impossibly broad topic. "Robert E. Lee and the Civil War" is too big. "Lee at Gettysburg" is manageable. But neither title tells what kind of reading, thinking, and writing you'll need to do. Decide early whether what you write is to be primarily a report or a thesis paper. A report assembles the material available on the subject, digging out the information and perhaps presenting it from a fresh perspective. A thesis paper shapes evidence into support for a hypothesis; it argues a point. The decision to make the paper primarily expository (a report) or primarily argumentative (a thesis paper) has some bearing on the sources you'll investigate and more on the use you'll make of what you find.

2. Preparing a working bibliography. In your initial canvassing of sources, move systematically from the card catalog to indexes of periodicals to appropriate reference books and special encyclopedias. For information about reference books in your field of interest, consult the latest edition of the *Guide to Reference Books*. For each source that looks promising, make out a bibliography card. Copy accurately on a 3" x 5" or 4" x 6" filing card the facts of publication as well as author and title (see **Bibliographical form**), and note where the source is located in the library. (You're bound to find that some of the publications you want aren't available, and the frustration will strain your patience and your temper. But that's part of research work.) Keep your working bibliography flexible. As you begin your reading, you'll discard items that looked promising but turned out to be dead ends, and you'll add items from the new sources that keep coming to your attention.

3. Taking notes on sources. In addition to making out bibliography cards that identify your sources, you'll need to take notes on what the sources have to say. Record these notes on 4" x 6" or 5" x 8" cards. These are easy to sort, discard, or rearrange. Restrict yourself to one note—fact, opinion, quotation, or summary—per card, with the author's name and the source written in the upper right corner and, in the upper left corner, an identifying word or phrase to indicate the specific subject the note is about. Before writing the note, set down the exact page on which the material was found.

As you make notes, be sure to distinguish clearly between an author's facts and his opinions, between direct quotation and summary, between what you're taking *from* the source (see **Paraphrase**) and what you're saying *about* the source. You'll find it helpful to keep a separate running log of notes to yourself—comments, questions, hunches that will remind you, when you begin to sift through and arrange your notes, of leads to be followed up, conflicting sources to be weighed, puzzles to be solved, and hypotheses to be tested.

4.   Developing an outline.   Early in the note-taking stage, sketch a tentative outline for your paper. Keep it fluid. Let it give direction to your thinking, but don't let it channel your ideas too early. Try to divide your material into logical blocks—from five to eight, perhaps—and then keep shifting these units around until you have them in the right order. Once you have the shape of the whole paper clear in your mind, you can write (and rewrite) a section at a time.

5.   Writing drafts.   Much of a research paper consists of a digest of sources that lead to, support, or elaborate on the researcher's findings or generalizations. In summarizing, interpreting, and analyzing your sources, it's important to represent them accurately and to do so in your own words. But you won't be able to free yourself of the original phrasing until you fully understand the ideas. Then you can express them in your own words. If you merely tie together a succession of direct quotations from a source, you don't show that you've mastered the material. If you use phrases and clauses from a source without putting them in quotation marks, you leave yourself open to the charge of plagiarism (see **Plagiarism**).

As you write, keep a close check on the sources you're consulting and summarizing, so that you can give accurate and adequate credit (see **Note form**). Be meticulous in reproducing direct quotations (see **Quotation marks 2b**). And when you quote, make sure that the passage bears directly on the point you're discussing, that you present it so that its relevance is immediately clear, and that you fit it smoothly into your text.

The style of a research paper should be comparatively formal and impersonal. This doesn't mean that it should be stilted or dull. Nor does it mean that you need to avoid using *I;* in some published research *I* appears regularly. It does mean that you should keep the focus on the subject and what you've managed to find out about it—not on your feelings about it. But since all good research papers reveal the writers' interest in their topics, communicating your own interest will be a natural consequence of engaging yourself fully in your subject.

6. Documenting the paper. Your readers' chief interest will be in the substance of your paper—what you've found out about your subject—and the clarity and force with which you present it. They'll also examine the documentation, the notes and the bibliography that record your journey of exploration. Check and recheck details of bibliographical form and note form for accuracy and consistency. See **Bibliographical form** and **Note form.**

rest Restrictive and nonrestrictive modifiers

If the modifier marked is restrictive, don't separate it from the word it modifies by a comma. If it is nonrestrictive, set it off by a comma or by two commas.

''Lemmon, who isn't Jewish, plays Jews who aren't Jewish either'' (Pauline Kael, *New Yorker*). The first *who* clause in the quoted sentence tells us something about Jack Lemmon, but it doesn't set him apart. It can be dropped from the sentence without destroying the meaning: Lemmon plays Jews who aren't Jewish. But the *who* clause modifying *Jews* is essential to Kael's point: the Jewishness of the characters Lemmon plays is superficial and trivial. Dropping that clause would leave us with ''Lemmon plays Jews,'' which isn't what Kael is saying. Separating the second clause from the main clause with a comma would give us ''Lemmon plays Jews, who aren't Jewish,'' which is nonsense. The first *who* clause is nonrestrictive. The second *who* clause is restrictive.

1. Restrictive modifiers. An adjective (or relative) clause or an adjective phrase is a restrictive modifier when the information it provides about something in the main clause is essential to the meaning the writer intends.

If you speak a sentence before you write it, or read it aloud after you've written it, you can usually tell whether a clause or phrase is restrictive:

> The girl *whose book I borrowed* has dropped the course.
> The books *stolen from the library* were found in that locker.

When the modifier is restrictive, you don't pause between the word modified and the clause or phrase that modifies it.

You can be quite sure a clause is restrictive if you can begin it with *that:* The year *that I dropped out* is one *that I'd be glad to forget.* And a clause is restrictive if you can omit the relative pronoun: The year [*that*] *I dropped out* is one [*that*] *I'd be glad to forget;* The people [*whom*] *we met;* The plan [*which*] *they came up with.*

2. Nonrestrictive modifiers. An adjective (or relative) clause or adjective phrase that can be dropped from a sentence without changing or blurring the meaning is nonrestrictive and should be set off by a comma or commas. The importance of the information the modifier provides is not the deciding factor. If you write, "The bullet *which came within an inch of my head* smashed my mother's favorite teacup," the content of your adjective clause would seem to be a lot more important than the destruction of the teacup. But unless you're using the clause to specify *this* bullet among a number of bullets—unless the information in the clause is essential to the meaning of *this* sentence—you should set it off with commas.

If *which* were used to launch only nonrestrictive clauses, as *that* is used to launch restrictive clauses, *which* and *that* clauses would cause few problems. But there are times when *which* seems a better choice for starting a restrictive clause: That was the bad news *which we had been given every reason to expect. (Which* avoids the repetition of *that.)* And some clauses are restrictive in one context, nonrestrictive in another. In a different context, the clause *whose book I borrowed,* used as an example of a restrictive clause in the preceding section, can be nonrestrictive: The girl, whose book I borrowed, left soon afterward with an older woman. So can the example of a restrictive phrase: The books, stolen from the library, later turned up in a secondhand store.

Your job, then, is to know what you mean. In the modifying clause or phrase, do you mean to say something that the sentence requires for its basic meaning, or do you mean to offer information which—no matter how important—can be omitted from that sentence without detracting from its central message? If the former, the modifier is restrictive—no commas. If the latter, the modifier is nonrestrictive—commas. Say the sentence out loud. Do you make a definite pause before the modifier? Then it's nonrestrictive—commas.

You may find the same advice useful in punctuating other modifiers. Traditionally, the restrictive/nonrestrictive distinction has applied to a dependent clause introduced by a relative pronoun and functioning as an adjective. Some grammarians extend the principle to all adjectival modifiers, to appositives (see **Apposition, appositives**), and to some adverbial modifiers, including final adverbial clauses (see **Comma 2b**).

rhetoric

To the ancient Greeks and Romans, rhetoric was the art of persuasion as applied to public speaking. With the invention of printing, the term was broadened to include written argument, and some modern theoreticians broaden it still further—to something like "the art of expression." What modern rhetorics have in common with classical ones is the idea of influencing an audience: the speaker or writer of rhetorical discourse aims to bring about a change in the attitudes, beliefs, habits, or actions of the audience.

Perhaps because skill in persuasion can be turned to bad uses as well as good ones, in general usage *rhetoric* has acquired connotations of manipulation, deceit, trickery, flamboyant insincerity, or empty verbiage—"just words." Currently a writer can assume that most audiences other than those that are studying, or have studied, the principles of rhetoric will regard *rhetoric* as a term of abuse.

The suggestion of empty verbiage is equally strong in most current uses of *rhetorical:* "It will be interesting to see how many men are prepared to give more than rhetorical support today to the sex from which they have, for centuries, demanded and accepted so much" (Adrienne Rich, *Chronicle of Higher Education*).

In this book the connotations of the term *rhetoric* are entirely favorable. The use of language for dishonest purposes is condemned. To be skilled in rhetoric is to write well, and the good writer never writes "just words."

Rhetorical questions

Rhetorical questions are really statements in the form of questions, since no direct answer is expected: "Who of us born before 1950 went to college burdened with the psycho-babble of the self which recurs in all three of these memoirs—'creating a supportive community' with 'people who feel comfortable with each other's needs'?" (Francine du Plessix Gray, *New York Review of Books*). As a stylistic device the rhetorical question has its dangers: the reader may reject the answer the writer intends—in the preceding example, "None of us."

Rhetorical situation

Whenever a writer asks anything of his reader—agreement, understanding, belief, action, even just a laugh—he's engaging in the art of persuasion, or rhetoric. As he writes a paper, every decision he makes, from the selection of material to the choice of a particular word, should be guided by his sense of the rhetorical situation. The chief elements in that situation are the writer, his subject, his purpose, and his audience. Each of these elements is influenced by the other three; each offers opportunities and imposes limits.

As you plan a paper, and especially as you revise it, asking yourself questions like the following will sharpen your sense of the rhetorical situation:

What do I want to say about this subject?

Do I have enough information and evidence now, or do I need to dig for more?

Who are my readers? How much do they know about this subject, and what is their attitude toward it? What are their tastes, values, fears, hopes, prejudices?

What common ground do we have? What assumptions do we share? What can I take for granted, and what do I have to explain or argue for?

How can I make my readers see what I want them to see, think the way I want them to think, do what I want them to do? Should I start by declaring what my purpose is, or would they be more responsive if I invited them to take part in an inquiry with me, if I raised problems that we would try to solve together?

How can I make my readers identify with me, share my feelings about my subject? How can I make them understand and adopt my point of view?

Will this detail, this bit of evidence, have more weight than that one? If so, should it come first or last? How can I phrase this idea so that it will be both clear and compelling? How can I make this sentence say precisely what I mean?

Will *this* word, *this* image, *this* mark of punctuation work with *this* audience? Do I need to make my style simpler, more relaxed, or does my relationship with my readers call for increased distance, greater objectivity, a style that is altogether more formal?

What side of my personality do I want to come through in this paper? How do I want my readers to see me?

As these questions suggest, you can assess the appropriateness of what you're saying and how you're saying it only in a specific rhetorical situation. The arguments you advance, the evidence you offer, the organization you adopt, the language you select—all these should be tested, as you revise your paper, for their fitness in communicating to the particular audience your thoughts and feelings about your subject.

right

The use of *right* in the senses "directly" and "immediately" before phrases of place and time (right across the street, right after the show) is avoided in most formal writing but is established in general usage. Phrases like *right here, right there, right now,* and *right then,* though similarly avoided in formal contexts, are commonplace in general ones. Idioms like *right away* and *right off* ("at once" or "now") and *right along* ("continuously" or "all the time") are slightly more informal.

In the sense of "very," *right* is a localism, in good standing in the South: We'll be right glad to see you.

rise

Rise is somewhat less formal than *arise,* more formal than *get up.* See **arise, rise, get up.**

rob

A person or place is robbed. What's taken in the robbery is stolen. *Rob* for *steal* (They're the ones who robbed the money) is an old usage considered nonstandard today. See **burglar, robber, thief.**

Roman numerals

Roman numerals may be either lower case (iii, v, x) or capitals (III, V, X). See **Numbers 3.**

round, around

Round is a preposition and adverb in its own right, often interchangeable with *around:* "an easy irony, good for a laugh the first two or three times round" (Stanley Kaufmann, *New Republic*). It should not be written with an initial apostrophe ('round).

Around for "approximately" (around 1920; a cast of around forty) is now found in all varieties of usage.

The general adjectives *all-round* and *all-around* are overused, particularly with *athlete*.

Run-on sentence

The label *run-on sentence* is applied variously to a sentence in which two independent clauses are run together with no punctuation between, to a sentence in which two independent clauses are joined with only a comma between, and to a sentence in which a series of independent clauses are joined with coordinating conjunctions. Unless a particular meaning is specified, *run-on* is more confusing than useful. See **Comma splice, Fused sentence.**

said

As a modifier (the said person, the said idea), *said* is legal language. In general writing, *that* or *this* or just *the* is the right choice.

saint

The abbreviation *St.* is commonly used in names of places (St. Albans, St. Louis) and often before the names of saints (St. Francis, St. Anthony of Padua). The plural of the abbreviation is *SS.* (SS. Peter and Paul). Occasionally the French feminine form *Sainte* is used (Sault Sainte Marie); the abbreviation is *Ste*. Spanish forms are common in the American West: San Diego, Santa Barbara. In writing a personal name beginning with *Saint* (Camille Saint-Saens) or *St.* (Louis St. Laurent), use the spelling the bearer uses or did use.

say

Say is the usual word for "speaking" and can also be used for what's written: In his journal, Gide says. . . . In dialog repetition of "he said," "she said" is almost always better than strained alternatives like *expostulated, muttered, babbled, hissed. State,* which implies a formal "saying," is a poor substitute for *say,* whether in dialog or in ordinary text: "To be able to state this of the new work of an American poet of 50 is, to state the least, unusual" (Aram Saroyan, *New York Times Book Review*). *Assert* and similar substitutes are also unsatisfactory in most contexts. See **claim.**

    Say in the sense of "approximately," "for instance," "let us say," is used in all varieties of writing: "the specialist in the literature of, say, the English eighteenth century" (Howard Mumford Jones, *Journal of the History of Ideas*).

scarcely

When *scarcely* means "almost not," adding a *not* as in "can't scarcely" is redundant. See **Double negative 2.**

scenario

Scenario became a vogue word in the 1970s and has taken on meanings having little connection with "script" or "synopsis." When you mean *plan, prediction,* or *possibility,* use that word, instead of relying on *scenario* and forcing the reader to decide which is meant.

seem

Seem is often used to qualify a statement unnecessarily: They [seem to] run with a gang that can't [seem to] keep out of trouble. Limit your use of *seem* to situations in which you must be tentative. Don't say something *seems to be* when you know it *is*. See **can't help but, can't seem to.**

self

Self as a suffix forms the reflexive and intensive pronouns *myself, yourself, himself, herself, itself, oneself, ourselves, yourselves, themselves.* These are used chiefly for emphasis (I can do that myself) or as objects identical to the subjects of their verbs (I couldn't help myself). See **himself, herself; myself; Pronouns 2.**

As a prefix, *self* is joined to the root word by a hyphen: *self-control, self-explanatory, self-made, self-respect.* When *self* is the root word, there is no hyphen: *selfhood, selfish, selfless.*

semi-

Semi- is a prefix meaning "half or approximately half" *(semicylindrical),* "twice within a certain period" *(semiweekly, semiannual),* or "partially, imperfectly" *(semicivilized, semiprofessional). Semi-* is a live element in forming new words.

Semicolon

Use a semicolon as the link between these sentence elements.

1.   To link coordinate clauses.
a.   Between clauses without connectives. Use a semicolon, especially in a rather formal context, to link two independent clauses whose relatedness you want to emphasize:

> Some years ago, a learned colleague who was old and ill complained to me that he could no longer read German; it made his legs feel queer. I know that feeling well; I have had it while trying to read Henry James.—P. B. Ballard, *Thought and Language*

> To stay warm, he jumped around and flapped his arms and meditated on the warmth of God; his companion, a shadowy, shrunken hobo, sat hunched in a corner with the patience of the ages.—Dennis McNally, *Desolate Angel*

b.   With conjunctive adverbs. Use a semicolon to link clauses connected by a conjunctive adverb such as *however, moreover, therefore* at the beginning of the second clause:

> His popularity was undiminished; however, he no longer enjoyed the work.

> Finally, despite the hopes and prophecies described before, we do not really agree on philosophical and political values; therefore the conference, moved by the same desire for survival and development as the world at large, carefully avoided exposing the ideological differences that remain.—Stanley Hoffman, *Daedalus*

A comma before *however* or *therefore* in these sentences would produce a comma splice. See **Conjunctive adverbs.**

c. With coordinating conjunctions. Consider using a semicolon between clauses connected by a coordinating conjunction *(and, but, for, or . . .)* if the clauses are long, if they contain commas, or if for some reason—perhaps for contrast—you want to indicate a more definite break than you would show with a comma:

> The War on Poverty was a *policy* that purported to cure America's gravest social ills; but while Johnson was raising millenial expectations, federal *spending* programs in fact were making inner-city problems worse.—T. D. Allman, *Harper's*

> I do not suggest that as English teachers we stop talking about planning and organization; nor am I saying that logical thought has nothing to do with the organizational process.—Robert Zoellner, *College English*

2. To separate units with internal commas. The units may consist of listed figures or words (see, for example, the cross references at the end of the first paragraph of **self**). They may be phrases or clauses. The sentences may be long or short:

> [The snow leopard] has enormous paws and a short-faced heraldic head, like a leopard of myth; it is bold and agile in the hunt, and capable of terrific leaps; and although its usual prey is the blue sheep and the ibex, it occasionally takes livestock, including young yak of several hundred pounds.—Peter Matthiessen, *New Yorker*

> Their lyrics have been for songs; Sondheim's, for scenes.—Martin Gottfried, *Saturday Review*

In the second example, the comma after *Sondheim's* makes the semicolon after *songs* necessary.

3. Semicolon and colon. Do not confuse the semicolon with the colon. Don't use a semicolon to introduce a quotation or a listing or to perform other conventional functions of the colon (see **Colon 3**). The one occasion when you have a choice between colon and semicolon is when you're punctuating independent clauses. The semicolon is the usual link. The colon is more formal and suggests that the second clause will explain or illustrate the first. Often the choice is mostly a matter of style.

4. Semicolons and style. Semicolons are usually more suitable in the longer, more complicated sentences of formal styles than in general and informal writing, except when other punctuation makes them necessary (see **2** above). In general styles commas are often used where semicolons might appear in formal writing, or else clauses that could be linked by semicolons are written as separate sentences. But this doesn't mean that, when writing general English, you should deny your prose the effects that semicolons can give it. The use of a semicolon is often as much a matter of personal choice as of correct punctuation.

Compare **Colon, Comma.**

sensual, sensuous

Both *sensual* and *sensuous* refer to the senses, but the connotations of *sensual* are more physical, of *sensuous* more aesthetic. Sensual music and sensuous music are two different things.

Sentence fragment

A sentence fragment is a part of a sentence punctuated as a complete sentence. See **Fragment.**

Sentences

1.   Classifying sentences grammatically.   On the basis of their clause structure, sentences are classified grammatically as simple, complex, compound, and compound-complex. Each of these types of sentences can be expanded by making subjects, verbs, and objects compound and by using appositives and modifiers. See **Absolute phrases, Clauses.**

2.   Analyzing sentences rhetorically.   A sentence is not only a grammatical unit but also a rhetorical unit. Rhetorical analysis of a sentence takes into account the order of elements, the repetition of grammatical structures, and the appropriateness of such ordering and repeating to the idea expressed and to the rhetorical situation. See **Balanced sentence, Cumulative sentence, Parallelism, Periodic sentence, Phrases and style.**

3.   Building sensible sentences.   Build your clauses and arrange their parts so as to bring out the natural and logical relationships in your material. When properly used, for example, subordination and parallelism clarify such relationships. Misused, they blur or distort them. If reducing clauses to phrases or single words is a way of packing more meaning into a sentence, reversing the process—converting some elements into separate sentences— can lighten an overloaded sentence and improve its unity and clarity. See **Coordination, Shifted constructions, Subordination.**

Although some structures that lack an independent subject-verb combination are rhetorically effective, most sentences have at least one such combination. Generally, faults in sentence construction result from failure to recognize the difference between a dependent clause and an independent clause or from failure to show the relation between a modifier and what it modifies. See **Comma splice, Dangling modifier, Fragment, Fused sentence.**

Sequence of tenses

In some sentences the tense of a verb in one clause is determined by the tense of a verb in another. See **Tense 3.**

Series

A succession of words, phrases, or clauses that are grammatically coordinate makes a series. Sometimes the units are simply separated by commas (apples, pears, persimmons), but usually the last unit is joined to the rest by a coordinating conjunction. Usage is divided over putting a comma before the conjunction:

> He worked in an ad agency, trained polo ponies, and did landscape gardening on a Long Island estate.—Sanford J. Smoller, *Adrift Among Geniuses*

> Another patron . . . came to see the go-go boys with her mother, her sister [ ] and her Kodak movie camera.—Jeannette Smith, *Washington Post*

Though many writers, especially in general and informal styles, omit the comma, using it helps to indicate that the units are equivalent and in some instances prevents misunderstanding (see **Comma 5**). If the units are long or have internal commas, they're often separated by semicolons (see **Semicolons 2**).

For the rhetorical effects of a series, see **Parallelism, Parallelism and style, Phrases and style.**

set, sit

In standard English, people and things *sit* (past: *sat*) or they are *set* (past: *set*)—that is "placed":

> I like to sit in a hotel lobby.
> I have sat in this same seat for three semesters.
> She set the casserole down with a flourish.
> The post was set three feet in the ground.

A hen, however, sets (on her eggs), cement sets, and the sun sets. A large dining room table sits eight, and few city people know how to sit a horse.

Sexist language

Since the revival of the movement for equality of the sexes, there has been much criticism of discrimination against women—that is, sexism—both in current usage and in the grammar of formal English. Examples of usage that patronizes or denigrates women include labels like *working girls, coed, the little woman, the weaker sex, boss lady, woman driver,* and *lady doctor* and use of the suffixes *-ess* and *-ette: poetess, Jewess, suffragette, usherette.* Similarly offensive to many is the use of first names for women where men's full names or last names are used: Before Robert Browning came to know her, Elizabeth [Barrett] was already considered a rival of Tennyson.

Then there are the words for certain occupations and offices that seem to imply that women are excluded: *policeman, businessman, chairman, Congressman.* And most galling of all to many is the use of *man* and *men* to stand for *men-and-women (manpower, the common man, man-made, free men)* and for the whole human race *(prehistoric man, mankind,* "all men are created equal," "the brotherhood of man") and the use of *he (him, his)* as the pronoun referring to a noun that doesn't specify gender or to an indefinite pronoun *(student, citizen, spectator, person, anyone, no one).*

Though some feminists attach relatively little importance to such usage, others see it as a subtle but powerful conditioner of attitudes toward the sexes from very early childhood. For those who are seriously concerned, the substitution of *-woman* for *-man* in the words for occupations and offices *(policewoman, businesswoman, chairwoman, Congresswoman)* is no solution to the problem. Like *lady driver* and *woman doctor,* it calls attention to gender where gender is not, or should not be, of any significance. (*Male nurse* belongs in the same category. Opponents of sexist language deplore terms that stereotype either men or women.)

Person(s), people, and *humans* or (better) *human beings* are common substitutes for *man, men, mankind* when both sexes are intended. An increasing number of writers now avoid the traditional use of *he* to stand for *he or she* by using the latter in its various forms: Everyone must turn in his or her theme. . . . But because the wordiness is easily compounded and awkwardness is almost inevitable (. . . if he or she wants a passing grade), there's a growing tendency to write in the plural (All students must turn in their themes . . .) or to treat *they (them, their)* as an indefinite common-gender singular (Everyone must turn in their theme . . .). See **Agreement 2, he or she, they.**

If you consider sexism in language an issue of overriding importance, then in your writing you'll try to avoid all the usages you look on as sexist, probably including the use of *man* for an individual of either sex and any age and the use of *he* for *he or she.* If you don't believe that sexism exists in the language, or don't care if it does, or applaud the masculine bias, you'll ignore the whole matter when you write. But if you belong to neither of these extremes, you have choices to make. Even if you're mainly satisfied with the language as it is, you should be aware that your readers may not be. You can easily avoid the more obtrusive sexist usages, such as descriptive terms that classify women physically when their looks have no relevance (the blonde defense attorney) or that suggest a general lack of intelligence and competence (a cute little pre-med student). You may also decide to find substitutes for the *-man* words (*police officer* for *policeman*, for example) and to cut down on your use of generic *he* in sentences like "When a young person says he is interested in helping people, his counselor tells him to become a psychiatrist."

How far you go will depend in part on your own sensitivities as a writer. If your sense of style makes you wince at *he or she* (or *he/she* or *s/he*), if the connotations of *artificial* prevent you from accepting it as a substitute for *man-made*, if *persons* and *humans* bother you at least as much as generic *man*, then you face much more difficult choices than those writers who can settle the problem to their own satisfaction with the rhetorical question, "What's more important—syntax or souls?" For those truly torn between the demands of feminist ideology and the demands of stylistic grace and flow, the only solution is to write and revise and rewrite until at last the conflicts are resolved and both ideological and aesthetic demands are satisfied.

In this book *he* is used to refer to *student* and *writer* not because of bias or obtuseness but in the interest of economy and readability.

shall, will

Since the eighteenth century some grammarians have insisted that in expressing determination in statements about the future, *will* should be used with first-person subjects (I will pass the course) and *shall* with second- and third- (They shall do as they're told). But practice has never been uniform. In current American usage *will* is much more common with all three persons. The same grammarians have tried to keep the single function of indicating the future distinct by urging that *shall* be used with first-person subjects (I shall be at a meeting that night) and *will* with second- and third- (You will arrive about Thursday, Joan says). But again, in standard usage *will* is much more commmon than *shall* in all persons. *Shall* occurs most frequently in legal language and is usually the natural choice in first-person requests for instructions: Shall I close the door? See **should, would.**

shift Shifted constructions

Avoid the unnecessary shift in construction.

Shifted constructions are needless changes in grammatical form or point of view within a sentence. In speech and in much informal writing, shifted constructions are common, but in general and formal prose they're avoided, because they trouble the reader. The many types of needless shifting include the following:

1.   Between adjective and noun: This book is interesting and an informative piece of work. *Revised:* . . . interesting and informative.

2.   Between noun and clause: The most important factors are time and temperature, careful control at every point, and the mechanical equipment must be efficient. *Revised:* . . . and efficient mechanical equipment.

3.   Between adverb phrase and adjective phrase: Along these walks are the cottages, some of which have stood since the founding but others quite recent. *Revised:* . . . but others for only a short time.

4.   Between gerund and infinitive: Carrying four courses and to hold down a job at the same time will either develop my character or kill me. *Revised:* Carrying four courses and holding down a job. . . .

5.   Between gerund and finite verb: I have heard complaints about the plot being weak and that the setting is played up too much. *Revised:* . . . and the setting being played up. . . .

6.   Between participle and finite verb: You often see a fisherman trying to get quietly to his favorite spot but instead he broadcasts warnings with his rhythmical squeak-splash, squeak-splash. *Revised:* . . . but instead broadcasting warnings. . . .

7.   Between transitive verb and copula: Anyone who has persistence or is desperate enough can get a job on a ship. *Revised:* . . . who is persistent or who is desperate enough. . . .

8.   Between past and present: The tanks bulled their way through the makeshift barricades and fan out across the enormous plaza. *Revised:* . . . and fanned out. . . .

9.   Between active and passive: The committee members disliked each other heartily, and their time was wasted in wrangling. *Revised:* . . . heartily and wasted their time in wrangling.

10. Between personal and impersonal: When one is sick, you make few plans. *Revised:* When one is sick, one (*or* he) makes. . . .

No enumeration of shifted constructions could be complete: there are too many constructions to shift.

See **Parallelism and style; Point of view; Reference of pronouns; Tense 2, 3; when, where.**

Shoptalk

Shoptalk is the words that people in the same occupation use among themselves to refer to the things they regularly concern themselves with in their work: the noun *mud* among bricklayers to mean "mortar," the verb *docket* among lawyers to mean "make an abstract."

No occupation gets along without shoptalk. All have everyday terms that may be meaningless to outsiders but are indispensable to those who practice the trade or profession. Especially convenient are short, informal substitutes for long technical terms. So a *mike* may be a microphone in a broadcasting studio, a microscope in a laboratory, a micrometer in a shop. A *hypo* is a fixing bath to a photographer, a hypodermic injection to a nurse. Many such words are metaphoric (the television *ghost*) or imitative (the radar *blip*). Much shoptalk is so specialized or colorless that it never spreads to the general vocabulary—such printshop words as *chase, em, pi, quoins,* for example.

So long as the terms from shoptalk remain narrowly specialized, they should be used only in certain contexts or technical writing. They are inappropriate in prose intended for general audiences.

See **Jargon.** See also **Gobbledygook, Psychologese, Slang.**

should, would

In indirect discourse, *should* and *would* can function as the past tenses of *shall* and *will*. "We will go" can be reported as "He announced that we would go," and "We shall go" as "He announced that we should [*or* would] go." Because *should* has a connotation of propriety or obligation that may not be intended, *would* is preferable. See **shall, will; Tense 3.**

sic

Sic, the Latin word meaning "thus," is used to indicate that what precedes it has been quoted correctly. See **Brackets.**

sick, ill

Ill is the more formal, less common word. In the United States *ill* and *sick* mean the same thing. In British usage *sick* is usually restricted to mean "nauseated": "The mere touch of the thing would make me sick or ill, or both" (Richard Jones, *The Three Suitors*). In American usage *sick* in that sense is made clear by adding a phrase: It made me sick to (at/in) my stomach. Saying that something or someone "makes me sick" is normally figurative, meaning "disgusts me."

Simile

A simile compares with *like* or *as:* He swims like a winded walrus; straight as a lodgepole pine. See **Figurative language.**

Simple sentence

A simple sentence consists of one independent subject-predicate combination. See **Clauses.**

simplistic

Don't use *simplistic*, which means "oversimplified," as a fancy form of *simple*. A simple explanation and a simplistic explanation are quite different. When you mean "oversimplified," *oversimplified* is a better choice than the voguish *simplistic.*

since

As a subordinating conjunction, *since* can have the meaning "because": Since we were already late, we didn't rush. See **because.**

sit, set

People and things *sit* or *are set.* See **set, sit.**

-size

Size is typical of a class of nouns *(age, color, height, shape, width, weight . . .)* that also function as apparent modifiers: *medium-size, standard-size, life-size, outsize, oversize.* The *-size* words are redundant in compound modifiers with adjectives that should modify the head nouns directly: not "small-size box" but "small box," and similarly with "round-shape table," "younger-age students," "dark-color hair," and so on. See **Wordiness 1.**

Slang

Drawing a line between slang and other kinds of informal English is difficult. Many people use the term *slang* too broadly, applying it to almost any informal word, and dictionaries have been too generous with the label, marking as slang many words that simply suggest spoken rather than written style. In fact, there is no fully accepted criterion for marking off the segment of the vocabulary that constitutes slang, as disagreement among and between dictionaries and handbooks makes clear.

Though some of the words labeled slang in current dictionaries—*lulu, corker, deadbeat*—have been around for generations, the central characteristic of slang comes from the motive for using it: a desire for novelty, for vivid emphasis, for being up with the times or a little ahead, for belonging—either to a particular social group or, more broadly, to an age group or, more broadly still, to the in-group that uses the current slang. These are essentially qualities of style, and the tone and connotation are as important as the meaning of the words. Other varieties of language have ways of expressing the ideas of slang words, but their tone is more conventional. Young people like novelty, and so do grown-ups with youthful ideas. Entertainers need it in their trade. In-groups, both legal and illegal, have their slang vocabularies, which often spill over into general English. Some of the slang of drug users *(fix, snort)* has wide circulation among nonusers.

Slang is made by natural linguistic processes. It's full of clipped words *(porn, natch, hood, vibes)* and compounds and derivatives of ordinary words *(screwball, sourpuss, cockeyed, put-on, rip-off)*. Many slang terms are borrowed from the shoptalk of sports and the popular arts, especially jazz and rock. And a great many are figurative extensions of general words: *nut, dope, egg* (applied to people), *heavy, hung up, turned on, plugged in, spaced out.* Sound often contributes a good deal, as in *barf, booboo, ding-a-ling, goof, kook, nerd, wimp, zap, zip, zonk.*

Because most slang words have short lives, any discussion of slang in print is bound to be out of date. *Skidoo, vamoose, beat it, scram, hit the trail, take a powder, drag out, shag out, cut out, split* succeeded each other within a short lifetime. Words for being drunk *(soused, plastered, bombed)* and words of approval *(tops, neat, the most, cool, groovy, out of sight, baddest, dynamite, intense)* and disapproval *(all wet, lousy, cruddy, gross, downer, bummer, shuck, turkey)* change from year to year—though some survive and some recur. Many slang words prove permanently useful and become a part of the informal vocabulary *(blind date, boy friend)* or the general vocabulary *(highbrow, lemon)*.

The chief objection to slang in writing, aside from its conspicuousness, is that it elbows out more exact expressions. A slang cliché is at least as boring as a cliché in standard English, and slang that names general impressions instead of specific ones is in no way better than comparable words in the general vocabulary, like *nice* and *good*. If slang expressions are appropriate to the subject matter and the audience and if they come naturally to the writer, they should be used without apology (that is, without quotation marks). If they're not appropriate—or if they've become tiresome vogue expressions, as slang words and phrases often do—they should not be used, with or without quotation marks.

slow, slowly

Slow is widely used in speech and in informal writing in place of *slowly*. In general writing its use is restricted to only a few contexts: He drove *slow;*

but He drove away *slowly.* See **Adverbs and style 1, Divided usage.** Compare **bad, badly.**

so

1. *So* and *so that*.   To introduce clauses of purpose, *so that* is ordinarily expected in formal contexts, but *so* by itself is respectable in general use:

> [The ghost of] Patroclus comes to ask Achilles to bury him quickly so that he may pass into the realm of Hades. —Anne Amory, *Yale Classical Studies*

> I might have tried . . . to give a clearer idea of the rest of the contents, so readers could gather some notion of whether or not this kind of material might interest them. —John Thompson, *New York Review of Books*

To express consequence or result, both *so* alone and *so that* are found in all varieties of usage. *Speculum: A Journal of Medieval Studies* had these two passages in the same issue:

> The old bishop was better known as a fighter than as a churchman, so we may reasonably assume that it was prudence and not cowardice which prompted him. —Herbert L. Oerter

> He quotes frequently from the Old French, so that the reader gains a very good appreciation of the style. —Alfred Foulet

2. *So* as substitute.   *So* can substitute for a whole clause: I think *I will win;* at least I hope *so.*

3. *So* as an intensive.   As an intensive, *so* is informal: They're so rich!

so . . . as

So . . . as is an alternative to *as . . . as* in negative comparisons of degree: The gateway to nirvana is not so wide as a barn door. See **as . . . as 3.**

so-called

If you have to use *so-called,* don't duplicate the idea by putting the name of the so-called object in quotes: the so-called champion; *not* the so-called ''champion.''

some

1. As a subject. *Some* as a subject takes either a singular verb (*Some* of the material *is* difficult) or a plural verb (*Some* of the tests *are* easy), depending on the context.

2. As an adverb. *Some* as a qualifier is informal: He's some older than she is. More formal usage would have *somewhat*. Informally, *some* is also used to modify verbs: The springs were squeaking some.

In formal writing the adverb *someplace* is still avoided in favor of *somewhere*, but in the last generation or so *someplace* has moved from informal to general usage: "I began to get some idea of what I came to call the Civilization of the Dialogue, a phrase I am sure I stole someplace" (Robert M. Hutchins, *Saturday Review*). *Somewheres* is nonstandard. Compare **any**.

3. As one word or two. The compounds *somebody, somehow, something, someway, somewhat, somewhere* are written as one word. *Someone* is one word (Someone is coming) unless *one* is stressed (some one of them). *Someday* is written as either one word or two. *Sometime* in "Drop in sometime" means "at some time [two words] in the future."

somebody, someone

Like *anybody* and *anyone, somebody* and *someone* are singular and take singular verbs. In formal writing they also are referred to by a singular pronoun—*he (him, his)*. In informal and general styles both words are often referred to by *they (them, their)* in the sense "he or she" ("him or her," "his or her"): If somebody dents my car in the parking lot, I expect them to leave their name. But conservative prejudice against this usage is strong.

✍ Spelling

Correct the spelling of the word marked, referring to a dictionary if necessary.

Use your dictionary, and when alternative spellings are listed, choose the one that introduces the entry. See **Apostrophe, Capital letters, Foreign words in English, Hyphen, Plurals of nouns, Principal parts of verbs.** See also **British English, Divided usage.**

Split infinitive

An infinitive is said to be split when an adverb or an adverbial element separates the *to* from its following verb: The receptionist asked them to *kindly* sit down.

Many people have been taught to avoid splitting infinitives, and sometimes there's good reason to do so. Certainly, long intervening elements are awkward: After a while he was able to, although not very accurately, distinguish good customers from disloyal ones. Such interrupters should be moved, often to the end of the sentence.

Formal writing rather consistently avoids the split infinitive, even when the adverb can't be placed at the end of the clause:

> We must have sufficient foresight and vision patiently to guide the peoples of the world along the road they have chosen to follow.—Bernard Kiernan, *American Scholar*

> The Chinese model . . . never eclipsed the local differences that made Japan always and Korea sometimes so distinct from China as properly to constitute a separate civilization.—William H. McNeill, *The Rise of the West*

But if long intervening elements are awkward, short adverbs that modify the infinitive may fit smoothly and clearly between the *to* and the verb. Split infinitives often appear in good general writing. The first of the following citations would be ambiguous if "really" were placed before "to" and unidiomatic if it were placed after "hate." In the second, "precisely to locate" might be ambiguous, and "to locate precisely enough" would invite misreading:

> To really hate the old ruling class we would have to live under it in its days of decay.—John K. Fairbank, *New Republic*

> The major mission of Apollo 10 was to precisely locate enough lunar landmarks to prevent the crewman of Apollo 11 from dropping onto terrain for which they would be unprepared.—John Lear, *Saturday Review*

When the prejudice against the split infinitive makes a writer bend over backwards to avoid it, his meaning is often bent as well:

> She had demonstrated her inability to rear properly numerous other children.

> Myrdal replied that it would be the proper function of planning constantly to strengthen nongovernmental structures.

In the first sentence the adverb "properly" can be read as if it modifies "numerous." In the second, "constantly" might modify "planning." Both would be improved by splitting the infinitives.

Often the decision to split or not to split is stylistic. It can be based on where the writer wants the emphasis to fall. If the sentence ". . . no one expected those who have been campaigning for a greater role for women in the Catholic Church in the U.S. to meekly drop their efforts'' *(Newsweek)* ended instead with ''to drop their efforts meekly,'' *meekly* would receive greater stress.

Spoken and written English

Though talking and writing are related, overlapping skills, they differ in several respects. Speech is peppered with expressions that seldom appear in writing other than dialog: ''y'know,'' ''y'see,'' ''right?'' and all the grunts and murmurs that ask for and provide feedback in conversation. When we talk, we pay far less attention to the shape of our sentences than when we write. We're more casual about pronoun reference and agreement; we let *and* and *so* do most of the work of joining statements; we rarely make the effort to build phrases and clauses in parallel series; and we hardly ever use the nonrestrictive clause. (We might write, ''Picasso, who was born in Spain, never lost his fondness for Barcelona,'' but we'd probably say, ''Picasso was born in Spain, and he always loved Barcelona.'')

The number of significantly different sounds that all of us use in speech is much larger than the number of symbols in our writing system. In talk, words are always part of a pattern involving pitch, stress, and pause, for which the marks of punctuation provide only the barest hints. Writing blurs or fails to suggest a great many speech signals, including body language— the stance, the gesture, even the slight rise of an eyebrow that may reinforce or modify the message. Whether ''more'' modifies ''competent'' or ''competent men'' in ''more competent men'' would be shown in speech by stress (heavier stress on the ''more'' that modifies ''competent men''). To make the distinction in writing, rewording might be necessary: more men who are competent; more truly competent men.

But if we can communicate some things more directly in talk than in writing, the reverse is also true. Punctuation indicates quotations efficiently, including quotations within quotations. Spelling distinguishes between some words that are generally pronounced the same way: We'll have it; We'll halve it. Capital letters identify proper nouns and proper adjectives. Because writing can be reread, it's a surer means of communicating difficult material—detailed, complicated instructions, for example. And because writing can be repeatedly revised, it can be more precise, better organized, and more economical than talk.

In spite of their differences, written English and spoken English have a close relationship. When we say someone ''talks like a book,'' we mean that his talk is uncomfortably elaborate or stiff. It's more often a compliment to say that someone ''writes the way he talks.'' For most purposes we value writing that has the flavor of good talk. But having the flavor of talk and being just like talk—even good talk—are by no means the same. Even informal written English, the written English that comes closest to casual speech, has to be far more coherent, far more selective, and far less casual than casual speech if it's to be read with ease and comprehension.

See **Colloquial English.**

spoonful, spoonfuls

Spoonfuls is the plural of *spoonful.* See **-ful, full.**

Squinting modifier

A squinting modifier looks in two directions: it may refer to the word or phrase that precedes it or to the word or phrase that follows it: Getting out of bed *often* is a nuisance; The secretary I spoke to *reluctantly* gave me an appointment.

Standard English

Standard American English is the social dialect used by the American middle class. Because the educated members of that class use it, they approve it, and because they are the dominant class in the United States, what they approve is the standard. Both spoken standard English and written standard English can be divided into formal, general, and informal, as in this book, or into different and more numerous categories. But when used appropriately, all the locutions called standard are supposed to be acceptable to all educated users of the language. In fact, there's disagreement, in dictionaries, English texts, and books on language etiquette, about a good many usages. But there's agreement on the great majority, and the chief purpose of this book is to call attention to the areas of agreement and to encourage the intelligent use of standard English. See **Nonstandard English, Usage.**

state

When you mean no more than "said," don't use *stated.* See **say.**

strata

In formal usage *stratum* is singular and *strata* plural. In general English *strata* is sometimes treated as a singular, but readers who know Latin, and some who don't, condemn the usage.

Style

Style is choice. Style consists of the choices a writer makes—choice of words, choice of sentence patterns, even choice among optional ways of punctuating. If there weren't many different ways of expressing ideas, there would be no such thing as style.

Style is character. Or, in a nonsexist version of a famous aphorism, "Style is the writer." How writers attack a problem, how they arrange their material, the manner in which they make their assertions, the "voices" they speak in—all these reveal something about their personalities, their values, their characters.

There needn't be any contradiction between these two views of style if we think of style as the sum of the choices, *conscious or unconscious,* that a writer makes among the options the language offers. Such matters as basic word order in sentences and ways of forming plurals and indicating verb tenses are part of the structure of English and therefore not stylistic. But other matters—the ways sentences are linked, their relative length and complexity, the placing of those elements that are movable, the words used and their connotations and figurative values—give a passage the distinctive features we call style. Some of these features are the result of unconscious choice, reflecting linguistic habits and ways of thought that the writer isn't aware of. Some of them are the product of deliberate calculation. To the extent that style is the result of such conscious choice, it can be improved.

A style is good or bad, effective or ineffective, to the extent that it achieves or fails to achieve the writer's purpose, wins or fails to win the response he wants from his readers. One of the best ways of improving your own style is to analyze the prose of writers you admire and try to determine how, in choosing words and shaping sentences, they won your response. The more you know about the choices the language offers, the more likely you are to write with clarity, force, and grace, qualities that are the foundation of all good styles. And if you have something to say, you will—through constant writing and rewriting—find your own style, your own voice as a writer.

Because syntax, usage, rhetoric, and style are all interrelated, the great majority of the articles in this *Index* have a bearing on style.

Subjective case

A noun or pronoun that's the subject of a verb or the complement of a linking verb is in the subjective, or nominative, case.

Subjects

1.   Definition.   The subject of a sentence can be defined in a number of ways. Here are three:

a.   The subject performs an action (The dog bit the mailman) or is in a particular state of being (The mailman was unhappy). But this doesn't explain such sentences as "These socks wear out too quickly" or "He received the condemnation of millions." Neither *socks* nor *he* is the performer of any action. Instead, both are the objects of actions.

b. The subject is the person, place, or thing that a sentence is about. This definition doesn't explain "I just heard that a car hit the mayor." The sentence is quite clearly not "about" the speaker or a car. It's about the mayor.

Both these definitions could be correct for some sentences. "The mayor defeated his opponents in three elections" is "about" the mayor, the performer of the action—defeating.

c. The subject is the word, phrase, or clause that usually stands before the verb and determines whether the verb will be singular or plural. Where the first two definitions are based on meaning, this one is based on position in the sentence or on the relationships between inflections for number in the subject and verb: The *woman is* here; The *women are* here. In a sentence in which *there* is an expletive—adding nothing to the meaning—the subject is the noun following the *be* verb that the number of the verb agrees with: There *is a woman* outside; There *are women* outside.

2. Subjects and style. In direct, vigorous writing, the subject and verb usually express the central action in a sentence, and the subject is often the topic of a paragraph. Continuing the same grammatical subject from sentence to sentence, using pronouns and synonyms for variety, helps keep the focus of a paragraph clear. See **Nominalization, Passive voice.**

See **Agreement 1, Comma 8, Compound subject, Deep structure.** For subjects of gerunds and infinitives, see **Gerunds 2, Infinitives 2.**

Subjunctive mood

Traditionally, English grammar recognizes three moods of verbs: indicative, imperative, and subjunctive. In modern English very few forms can be surely identified as subjunctives, and the use of those few is so inconsistent that definite criteria are hard to set. Generally, the subjunctive is optional, a means of setting one's language, consciously or unconsciously, a little apart from everyday usage. Though not always a trait of formal style, the subjunctive is used regularly in some formal contexts, such as resolutions.

1. Form of the simple subjunctive. The identifiable forms of the subjunctive are *be* throughout the present tense of that verb, *were* in its past-tense singular ("if she were here" instead of "if she was here"), and *s*-less forms of the third-person singular of the present tense of other verbs that normally have an *-s* ("that he see" instead of "that he sees"). Some past-tense forms with present or future reference are also subjunctives.

2. Uses of the subjunctive.
a. Formulas. The subjunctive is found in many formulas, survivals from a time when it was used freely:

| Suffice it to say | Heaven forbid | As it were |
| Long live the king | God bless you | Be that as it may |

Some of these formulas are used in all varieties of the language. Some, like "Come what may," are rather formal.

b.   *That* clauses. The subjunctive is relatively common in demands, resolutions, recommendations, and the like, usually in formal contexts. Ordinarily, alternative expressions without the subjunctive are available.

> *Formal:* I ask that the interested citizen *watch* closely the movement of these troops.
>
> *General:* I ask the interested citizen to watch the movement of these troops closely.

> *Formal:* Who gave the order that he *be* dropped?
>
> *General:* Who gave the order to drop him?

> *Formal:* It is necessary that every member *inform* himself of these rules.
>
> *General:* It is necessary that every member should inform himself. . . . *Or:* . . . for every member to inform himself. . . . *Or:* Every member must (should) inform himself. . . .

c.   Conditions. The subjunctive may be used in *if* clauses when the fulfillment of the condition is doubtful or impossible: "If one good were really as good as another, no good would be any good" (Irwin Edman, *Four Ways of Philosophy*). The subjunctive *were* isn't necessary to convey the meaning, which the past indicative *was* would convey just as well by its contrast between past form and present or future sense.

A large proportion of the conditions the subjunctive is used to express are real or open conditions, not contrary to fact:

> We set up standards and then proceed to measure each judge against these standards whether he be a sixteenth or nineteenth or twentieth century judge.—Louis L. Jaffe, *Harvard Law Review*

> Stunkard recorded each subject's stomach contractions for four hours, and at 15-minute intervals asked him if he were hungry.—Stanley Schachter, *Psychology Today*

In such conditions the writer has a choice between the subjunctive and another verb form. There's no special virtue in using the subjunctive, and it should be rejected when it gets in the way of natural, idiomatic expression. See **Conditional clauses.**

Subordinate clauses

A dependent, or subordinate, clause (when day is done) has a subject and verb but can't stand as a sentence. See **Clauses, Comma 2.**

Subordinating conjunctions

The most common subordinating conjunctions—words that relate dependent clauses to independent clauses—are these:

after	before	since	until
although	how	so that	when (whenever)
as	if	that	where (wherever)
as . . . as	in order that	though	whether
as if, as though	once	till	while
because	provided	unless	why

The relative and interrogative pronouns *who, which,* and *what* and the relative *that* also function as subordinating conjunctions. See also **for.**

sub Subordination

Correct the faulty subordination.

Faulty subordination concerns the mishandling of dependent clauses—clauses introduced by subordinating conjunctions or by relative pronouns and used in the grammatical functions of nouns, adjectives, and adverbs. Three types of faulty subordination are commonly distinguished:

1.   **Tandem, or excessive, subordination** occurs when you write a string of dependent clauses, each modifying an element in the clause before it. The weakness is in style, not grammar:

> *Tandem:* For his teachers, he had carefully selected those who taught classes that had a slant that was specifically directed toward students who intended to go into business.

> *Revised:* . . . those who slanted their courses toward students intending to go into business.

2.   **Thwarted subordination** occurs when you add *and* or *but* to a dependent clause that's already connected to the independent clause by its subordinating conjunction or relative pronoun. This is a grammatical lapse, most commonly found in the form of *and which* or *but which* (see **which 4**):

Thwarted: In the first semester of the course we used three textbooks, and which were continued for the second semester.

Revised: . . . three textbooks, which were continued. . . .

Compare the appropriate use of a coordinating conjunction to join two dependent clauses that are parallel: Tolerance is a virtue [which] all of us praise but [which] few of us practice.

3.   Upside-down, or inverted, subordination occurs when you use sub-ordination in such a way as to make the relationship between statements seem illogical. Since it's not a blunder in grammar or style, upside-down subordination is hard to illustrate in isolated sentences. Often only the con-text determines whether subordination is upside-down. In one paper, "Pearl Harbor was attacked when Roosevelt was President" would be all right. In another, "When Pearl Harbor was attacked, Roosevelt was President" might be much better. Without a context, we can't be sure which statement should be put into the independent clause and which in the dependent clause.

But the nature of some statements makes the choice relatively easy. In most contexts this sentence would sound odd: While I received a salary increase that solved my financial problems, I had to report for work five minutes earlier on Mondays. Some such statement as this would be more likely to make sense: Though I did have to report for work five minutes earlier on Mondays, I received a salary increase that solved my financial problems. Ordinarily, upside-down subordination is corrected by turning the dependent clause into an independent clause and vice versa. Often, as in the example just given, some rewriting is advisable.

See **Coordination.**

such

As an intensifier, *such* is somewhat informal (It was such a hot day; I had never seen such energetic people). In formal and most general writing the construction would usually be completed by a *that* or an *as* clause (It was such a hot day that the tar melted; I had never seen such energetic people as I saw in Ballydavid), or the basis of the comparison would be indicated elsewhere in the passage:

In spite of high winds and raging seas, they were all out in their boats before dawn. I had never seen such energetic people.

Formal usage often introduces examples with *such as,* where general usage would have *like. Such as* is preferable when the example is only loosely or nonrestrictively connected to the preceding noun: "A number of big processors, such as Campbell and Heinz, still make their own cans" (*Fortune*).

Suffix

An element that can be placed after a word or root to make a new word of different meaning or function is called a suffix: *-ize (criticize), -ish (foolish), -ful (playful), -th (warmth)*. See **Origin of words 3a.**

Superlative degree

Hottest, most pleasant, quickest, and *most surely* are examples of adjectives and adverbs in the superlative degree. See **Comparison of adjectives and adverbs 3.**

sure

Sure in standard written English is primarily an adjective (sure footing; as sure as fate; Are you sure?). As an adverb meaning "certainly," *sure* is informal to general, while *surely* is general to formal:

> It's a novel interpretation, but it sure saves oranges.—Horace Sutton, *Saturday Review*

> The Art Commission said it surely did want to honor this splendid son of Italy.—Donovan Bess, *Harper's*

The idiom *sure* (never *surely*) *enough* is in general use: "And sure enough, in all the fearful discussions about computers, the question that inevitably comes up . . ." (Robert Langbaum, *Yale Review*).

Syllabication

When you're not sure where to break a word that comes at the end of a line, consult a dictionary. For general rules, see **Division of words.**

Syllogisms

A syllogism represents deductive reasoning reduced to a pattern consisting of a major premise, a minor premise, and a conclusion. If the rules of inference (after each example below) are followed, the reasoning will be valid. Good arguments must satisfy another condition as well: the premises must be true. The rules of inference are concerned only with validity.

1. Common patterns for syllogisms.
a. Hypothetical syllogisms:

Major premise:	If P, then Q	*or*	If P, then Q
Minor premise:	P		Not Q
Conclusion:	Therefore Q		Therefore not P

Arguments that follow this pattern will not be valid if the minor premise is "not P" and the conclusion is "Therefore not Q," or if the minor premise is "Q" and the conclusion is "Therefore not P." The major premise gives no grounds for either of these inferences.

b. *Either-or* syllogisms:

	Disjunctive	*Alternative*
Major premise:	Either A or B but not both	Either A or B
Minor premise:	A	Not A
Conclusion:	Therefore not B	Therefore B

Arguments that follow the pattern of the alternative syllogism will not be valid if the minor premise is positive—that is, "A" or "B." The major premise does not exclude the possibility of both A and B. It simply requires one of the two.

c. Categorical syllogisms:

Major premise:	All M are P
Minor premise:	S is an M
Conclusion:	Therefore S is a P

Arguments that follow this pattern will be invalid if they introduce a fourth term (in addition to M, P, and S); if they shift the meaning of a term; if the middle term (M) is not distributed (that is, if one or more of the premises in which it appears fails to affirm or deny something about the whole class the term stands for); or if a term that has not been distributed in a premise is distributed in a conclusion.

2. Testing arguments.   Although a syllogism or, more likely, a series of interlocking syllogisms is the underpinning of most solid arguments, writers don't normally construct arguments by first formulating a syllogism and then looking for evidence to support the premises. Nor does a writer present his ideas in statements that fall naturally into the pattern of syllogisms. Even so, an elementary acquaintance with the rules of inference can help a writer in at least two ways.

First, it can make him aware of the premises that underlie his argument. In "It's not a poem; it doesn't rhyme," the first clause is the conclusion and the second clause the minor premise of an incomplete syllogism that has as its major premise a proposition something like "If the lines of the passage don't rhyme, the passage is not a poem" or, to put it another way,

"All poems rhyme." That unstated assertion, or hidden premise, is too controversial to be allowed to go unsupported. If the writer intends to base an argument on it, he'd better argue for it.

Acquaintance with the rules of inference can also help a writer check the validity of his line of reasoning:

> Why do colleges waste time teaching students material they can understand or skills they can learn on their own? Instead of giving courses in science fiction, they should teach double-entry bookkeeping. *That's* a skill students can't pick up on their own.

This bit of reasoning might be spelled out as three syllogisms, each of which invites the reader to raise questions about the validity of the reasoning as well as about the truth of the premises. To take just one of the syllogisms:

> If students can learn a skill on their own, a college shouldn't teach it. (If P, then Q)
>
> Students can't learn double-entry bookeeping on their own. (Not P)
>
> Therefore colleges should teach double-entry bookkeeping. (Not Q)

Quite aside from questions of truth, the reasoning is invalid. The major premise does not assert that a college should teach *all* the skills a student can't learn on his own.

See **Deduction, Fallacies, Logical thinking.**

Synecdoche

Synecdoche is a figure of speech in which the whole stands for the part (a nation adopts a policy) or a part stands for the whole (a baseball player's bat wins a game). See **Figurative language.**

Synonyms

Broadly, synonyms are words that mean the same thing. More strictly, they are words that share at least one meaning. Very few words are completely interchangeable, because no two are likely to share all their meanings and to have the same connotations. At the very least, they'll differ in sound and therefore represent different stylistic choices.

In choosing among synonyms, you need to consider both sense—connotations as well as denotations—and sound. The meaning and suggestions of the word you want must express as precisely as possible what you have to say, and the word must fit the sound pattern of your sentence.

See **Connotation.**

Syntax

Syntax refers in general to the order and relationships of the elements of sentences. That the subject of a sentence ordinarily comes before the predicate, for example, is a feature of English syntax. Words, phrases, and clauses are all syntactic elements.

T

Tandem subordination

Tying a succession of dependent clauses together produces tandem subordination. See **Subordination 1.**

teach, learn

A teaches *B,* who is taught by *A. B* learns from *A.* See **learn, teach.**

Technical writing

Good expository writing conveys information accurately, clearly, and concisely. When such writing is about specialized subject matter—in engineering, for example, or physics or chemistry—it's called technical writing. More particularly, technical writing appears in reports, articles, and manuals produced by professionals in science and technology.

Whatever the subject matter or the nature of the communication, the first obligation of the technical writer is to present his information so clearly that it can't be misunderstood by his audience. In addition to presenting information, he must often analyze data, weigh alternative solutions to problems, make predictions, argue for a course of action. In every case he needs to take into account what his readers already know and what they want to find out.

1.   The technical writer and his audience.   The technical writer is the expert on his subject. Nobody knows as much about his project as he does. When addressing his peers—professional associates at a convention, for example—he'll naturally use the specialized terms of his profession. But when writing reports for his superiors or giving directions to subordinates, he has to gauge their probable familiarity with the vocabulary that is second nature to him. (The president of a potash firm may have been chosen for his managerial ability rather than his knowledge of potash. In reporting to him, the technical writer may have to work as hard at translating shoptalk as he would if he were addressing a general reader.) Even students in Aerospace Engineering might have trouble understanding this announcement of a lecture by an expert in the field:

> He will talk about flow visualization experiments of a turbulent water jet in a confined tank modeled to simulate certain flow conditions expected in the Anechoic Chamber/Jet Noise Facility.

Though the gap between general English and technical vocabularies is often large, what makes technical writing difficult for the reader, either layman or professional, may not be so much the terminology as the tangled syntax that results when the writer relies heavily on nominalization, passive verbs, and strings of prepositional phrases (four in the sentence quoted above). Some industrial firms and professional societies have recognized this problem. The American Chemical Society, for one, gives short courses in communication skills for chemists and chemical engineers. Notes on a recent course stressed the need for directness, simplicity, and brevity and recommended the use of the active voice and, on occasion, the first-person pronoun.

2. Technical reports.   The merit of any technical report lies in its efficiency in communicating its content to its intended audience. Its format should therefore be carefully planned.

Technical reports differ visually from other expository writing. They're divided into sections, which are often numbered. They have no long stretches of consecutive sentences. They use subheads, tables, charts, diagrams. Many, though not all, present at the beginning a summary (or abstract) of the findings, results, or recommendations. In this format, everything vital is in the summary. No crucial new information is introduced as the report proceeds through its next three or four or dozen sections. Subsequent headings depend on the nature of the report, and the order in which they appear depends on the nature of the audience. One adaptable format follows:

    I.   Summary—important results, conclusions, recommendations
   II.   Introduction—background, purpose, problem being addressed, scope
  III.   Review of previous work—if short, a part of the Introduction
  IV.   Description of present study—details of apparatus used, if the investigation is experimental; derivation of equations; procedures followed
   V.   Presentation (in table or graph form) and discussion of results—comment on salient features of the data
  VI.   Conclusions and recommendations—interpretation of results; inferences; recommendation of a solution, action, or future investigation
 VII.   Appendices—supporting data, usually highly specialized

The technical writer who is preparing his report for several different audiences will choose a format that permits him to move from the simple to the complex in content and vocabulary. He'll begin with a summary phrased in nontechnical language and an introduction that's as uncomplicated as he can make it. He'll then proceed directly to conclusions and recommendations, again presenting them so that the least informed of his readers can follow them. The experimental section, the discussion of results, and subsequent sections will be increasingly technical, and the final sections will supply data likely to be understandable only to specialists. The advantage of this format, with its progression from simple to complex, is that each reader can continue until he has satisfied his interest or reached the limit of his understanding. Even the reader who is ignorant of the technicalities of procedures, operations, or calculations will be able to grasp the general purpose, scope, and results of the study.

See **Abstract language, Nominalization, Passive voice, Phrases and style, Shoptalk.**

tense Tense

Make the tense of the verb conventional in form, or make it consistent with, or in logical sequence with, other verbs in the passage.

1. Use the standard form. In general English, avoid nonstandard forms like *drawed* and *had went* and dialectal forms like *drug* (for *dragged*), *throwed,* and such double auxiliaries as *might could* and *used to could.* See **Principal parts of verbs.**

2. Make the verb consistent with others that refer to the same time. Consistency doesn't demand that you use the same tense for verbs throughout a sentence or a paragraph or a paper. Choose the verb form or verbal phrase that expresses the distinction of time you intend. In a single sentence you may refer to past, present, and future time: When I *was* ten, I *planned* to be a veterinary surgeon, but now I *know* I *will spend* my working life as an accountant. Through skillful use of verbs you can interweave particular events with habitual action:

> Summers we generally *follow* a simple routine. Every day we *travel* the fifteen miles to our lakeside cabin. We *start off* at dawn, Mother driving and the kids rubbing sleep from their eyes, and we seldom *get* home before dark. Then we *fall* into bed, tired from a day outdoors. One night last July our simple routine *was wrecked.* Just before we *turned* into the driveway, we *saw* that the lights *were* on all over the house. Since we *knew* we *had left* the lights off and the doors locked, we *were* puzzled and a little frightened. My brother *offered* to reconnoiter. When he *came* back to the car, he *said* he *had seen* . . .

But though it's natural and easy to shift tense, don't make a shift unless it serves a purpose—normally, to mark a change in time. Careless shifts like the following are distracting for the reader:

> The observers unobtrusively *slipped* in the back door while the children *were* still getting settled at their desks. The class *begins* with the teacher reading a short passage from a book about Columbus, at the end of which she *asked* for comments.

To keep the tenses consistent, *begins* should be *began*. Or, if there's a reason for doing so, all the verbs might be put in the historical present: *slips, are, begins, asks*. See **Tenses of verbs 3a.**

3. Observe the conventional sequence of tenses.   In certain contexts actual time takes second place to the conventions of tense sequence.
a. Between independent and dependent clauses. A dependent clause that's the object of a verb in the past tense is usually put in the past tense even though it refers to an existing state of affairs:

> What did you say your name *was?*
> They didn't tell me you *were looking* for an apartment.

But when the dependent clause describes a timeless state of affairs, the present tense is often used: He told me that I always *remind* him of my father. And when the point of the sentence is the current existence of the state of affairs reported in the dependent clause, the present tense is common:

> Simply observing the people and comparing them with those I had seen three decades ago, I was convinced that they are a lot better off materially than their predecessors.—Robert Shaplen, *New Yorker*

b. From direct discourse to indirect discourse. When a dependent clause reports something said, its verb is ordinarily shifted from present to past (He said, "I *am* leaving" *becomes* He said he *was* leaving) or from past to past perfect (He said, "I *did* it" *becomes* He said he *had done* it). But this formal sequence can sometimes be misleading. To report the statement "I'm optimistic about the outcome of the election" as "He said that he was optimistic . . ." doesn't make clear whether the optimism persists. "He said that he is optimistic about the outcome of the election" leaves no doubt in the reader's mind.
c. With infinitives and participles. Infinitives and participles express time in relation to the time of the main verb. Use the present infinitive to indicate time that's the same as the time of the main verb or later than the time of the main verb:

> I plan *to go* to Washington, and I expect *to see* her there.
> I planned *to go* last week and expected *to see* her today.
> I would have liked *to see* her on her last trip.

Use the perfect infinitive for action prior to the action of the main verb:

> I would like *to have seen* her on her last trip.

Use the perfect form of the participle to express time prior to the time of the main verb, the present form to express the same time as the time of the main verb:

> *Having driven* safely through the worst blizzard in local history, he slid off the edge of his own driveway and, *jamming on* the brakes too fast, overturned the car.

See **Tenses of verbs.**

Tenses of verbs

1. Time and tense.   In English there is no simple correspondence between tense and time. The term *tense* refers to inflection, or change in form. English verbs have only two tenses: present (he leaves) and past (he left). There is no single-word verb, no inflection, that applies only to the future. But we do have various ways of referring to future time. We use the present tense accompanied by an adverb (He leaves tomorrow) or an auxiliary before the uninflected verb (He will leave tomorrow). Or we say "He will be leaving" or "He is going to leave" or "By this time tomorrow he will have left." Some grammarians call *will leave, will be leaving,* and so on, the future tense.

2. Tense and auxiliaries.   If we use no auxiliaries, the only tenses we can form are present and past. But auxiliaries enable us to refer to times in the future as well as in the past extending into the present, the past not extending into the present, and the past of a certain time already past. So some grammarians speak of six tenses, which roughly translate into the six of Latin:

Present:	He eats	*Present perfect:*	He has eaten
Past:	He ate	*Past perfect:*	He had eaten
Future:	He will eat	*Future perfect:*	He will have eaten

Still more tenses emerge if we consider the uses of *do* (emphatic tense: *does eat, did eat*) and *be* (progressive tense: *is eating, was eating*). If the past of *shall* and *will* is also taken into account, we can speak of a past future (*would eat*) and even a past future perfect (*would have eaten*).

3. Special uses of simple present and past.
a.   In addition to its basic function of referring to something going on now, the present tense is used to refer to a state of affairs that is generally true,

without reference to time (Oil *floats* on water); to habitual action that continues into the present (He *writes* in his journal every day); and, when accompanied by an adverbial, to a time in the future (She *goes* to college in the fall). Other special uses of the present tense are illustrated in

> I *hear* you are going to Europe.
> He'll come if you *ask* him.
> Thoreau *urges* us to do without luxuries.
> In the 1950s all *is* buttoned down; in the 1960s there *are* rumblings of discontent.

The third example is sometimes known as the *literary present* (Thoreau died in 1862), the fourth as the *historical present*.

b. The simple past tense is normally used to refer to something that took place in the past, either a single occurrence (He *broke* his leg) or a repeated occurrence (He *skied* at Vail every Christmas). But the past tense does not refer to past time in a dependent clause that is object of the verb in the independent clause when the main verb is in the past (I *heard* that you *were* in town); in the *if* clause that refers to a hypothetical situation (If you *knew* him, you wouldn't be surprised); nor as the polite alternative in questions or requests (*Would* you send me the catalog).

See **Auxiliaries, Tense, Verbs.**

than

At its simplest level, the choice of the case of a pronoun after *than* can be illustrated by the sentences "He is taller than I" and "He is taller than me." Both are used in general writing. Conservatives favor the nominative after an intransitive or linking verb, but many writers use the objective.

When the verb before *than* takes an object, the nominative and objective cases after *than* may have different meanings: She likes him more than I [do]; She likes him more than [she likes] me. So in standard English the case of the pronoun used with *than* after a transitive verb is the case that would be used if the dependent clause were written out. Use of the nominative case where the objective case is called for, as in the following example, is hypercorrect—that is, wrong: Though the jury said we were both guilty, the judge gave my partner a lighter sentence than [he gave] I. See **Hypercorrectness.**

that

1. *That* or *which*. Writers are often urged to use *that* to introduce restrictive clauses and *which* to introduce nonrestrictive clauses, and the advice can be helpful for those who use *which* everywhere, in the belief that it's more elegant than *that*. In practice, the choice between *which* and *that* in restrictive clauses is likely to depend on rhythm, sound, emphasis, and personal taste. If *that* has already been used in the sentence, writers may shift to *which* to avoid repetition. On the other hand, when the restrictive clause is compound, *which* may be chosen as a clearer signal to the reader that the construction is being repeated: "He had an exploratory operation for cancer which the doctors were reluctant to undertake but which he was convinced he needed" (David Halberstam, *Atlantic*). *Which* normally introduces nonrestrictive clauses in all varieties of usage.

2. Redundant *that*.   When *that* introduces a noun clause in which a modifying phrase precedes the subject, there's a temptation to repeat *that* after the modifier: "It must seem to many outsiders that if there was room for honest argument [that] a reasonable doubt had to exist . . ." (Red Smith, syndicated columnist). Don't do it.

3. Clauses without *that*.   A complex sentence like "The work [that] he does shows [that] he has talent" is perfectly correct without either *that*. The dependent clauses "he does" and "he has talent" are related to the rest of the sentence clearly enough to need no explicit signs of subordination, like *that*. No writer should handicap himself by thinking a *that* must be inserted wherever it will fit. *That*-less clauses are common, and many professional writers prefer them:

> He thinks that the Italians neither approved of Fascist terror nor were really terrorized by it. He thinks [ ] they became numb, resigned, apathetic, and cynical.—Naomi Bliven, *New Yorker*

> The convention [ ] we accept unthinkingly had not as yet established itself.— William Nelson, *Journal of English Literary History*

Using *that* to stress the subordination of short clauses often robs them of their force: He knows [that] I'm sorry; I'm glad [that] you're here; Take anything [that] you want.

That is necessary when the clause comes first (That she might be hurt never occurred to us) and when a clause has no other subject (There is a moral standard that has long been accepted). When a modifier stands between two clauses, *that* is sometimes necessary to show which clause is being modified: Mr. Wrenn said [ ] after the guests were gone [ ] Mrs. Wrenn should pack her bags. Depending on the intended meaning, *that* is needed either after *said* or after *gone*.

See **this.**

that is

That is is a rather formal connective that introduces the equivalent of, or the explanation of, what precedes it. When it both follows and introduces a complete statement, it may be linked to the preceding independent clause with a semicolon: The men worked continuously for three whole weeks to complete the dam; that is, they worked twenty-four hours a day in three shifts, seven days a week. Or it may begin a new sentence. In briefer constructions a comma or dash before *that is* is adequate: They used the safest explosive for the purpose—that is, dynamite. Better yet, *that is* could be omitted: They used the safest explosive for the purpose—dynamite. See **namely.**

their

Their is the possessive of *they. Theirs* is the absolute form: This table is exactly like theirs. Except in formal usage, *their* is often used as a common-gender singular to refer to words like *somebody, anybody, everyone:*

> Almost nobody has the words to really talk about their lives.—*Time*

> It is necessary to make anyone on the streets think twice before attempting to vent their despair on you.—James Baldwin, *Show*

See **Agreement 2.**

then

Then is an adverb of time frequently used as a connective (conjunctive adverb): The next three hours we spent in sightseeing; then we settled down to the business of being delegates to a convention.

Adjectival *then* (the then President) is common in general writing, rare in formal. Some readers find it clumsy.

then, than

Don't confuse *then,* the adverb of time, with *than,* the conjunction in clauses of comparison: *Then* the whole crowd went to Louie's; It was better as a movie *than* as a novel.

there is, there are

When *there* is used as an anticipatory subject, the verb ordinarily agrees in number with the "real" subject, which follows it: "There is still occasional sniping at the 'supersquad' and there are still lazy, indifferent, homicide detectives" (Barbara Gelb, *New York Times Magazine*). When the subject is compound and the first element is singular, usage is divided. Some writers follow the rules of formal agreement and use a plural verb, while others find a plural verb awkward before a singular noun:

There are much good history, intelligent analysis of social problems, and good writing.—David Fellman, *American Historical Review*

There is no jargon, few footnotes, some repetition, few insights and little analysis.—Lewis A. Froman, *American Political Science Review*

Like repeated use of *it is . . .* , repeated use of *there is . . .* , *there are . . .* constructions robs sentences of strong subject-verb combinations. See **Subjects 2.**

Thesis statement

A thesis statement is the most explicit statement the writer can make of his purpose—what he wants to assert or prove. Whether or not it appears in the essay itself, the thesis statement must be firmly fixed in the writer's mind, at least by the time he prepares his final draft. See **Outline form 2, Topic sentence 3.**

they

They occurs in all varieties of usage with no explicit antecedent: "One thinks of Tolstoy, and the story that all day long they had to be beating omelets for him in the kitchen" (Louis Kronenberger, *New York Times Book Review*). The indefinite reference is troublesome, however, when there's a second *they* in the same sentence: Around campus *they* were saying that *they* had a plan to boycott classes. Often impersonal *there* is preferable: There were reports around campus that they had a plan to boycott classes. *Or:* Around campus they were saying that there was a plan. . . .

Regularly in informal English and often in general English, *they,* and especially *their,* is used as a singular pronoun to refer to *everyone* and similar words. See **Agreement 2, he or she.**

thing

Thing often encourages the accumulation of deadwood in writing: [The] first [thing] you [do is to] dry out your sleeping bag.

this

Though often criticized as a sign of lazy writing, *this,* like *that,* is regularly used to refer to the idea of the preceding clause or sentence: He had always had his own way at home, and this made him a poor roommate. Confusion is caused when *this* refers only to some part of the idea of a clause or sentence or to an antecedent that's not actually expressed. See **Reference of pronouns 2.**

though

Though in the sense "however," "nevertheless," "for all that" now appears in all varieties of writing: Two things are clear, though.

thus

Thus at the beginning of participial phrases tends to encourage loose modifiers. In sentences like this one there's no noun or pronoun for the participle to modify: "D. Eldred Rinehart's term on the racing commission also is expiring, thus opening up the chairmanship" *(Washington Post).* See **Dangling modifiers.**

Thwarted subordination

Subordination is said to be thwarted when a coordinating conjunction precedes the subordinating conjunction: By the end of the summer he had completed three reports, [and] which were accepted for publication. See **Subordination 2.**

till, until

In all varieties of writing, *till* and *until* are interchangeable both as prepositions (Wait till/until tomorrow) and as conjunctions (Wait till/until they get here). Most dictionaries don't recognize the spelling *'til.*

Titles

1.   Choosing a title.   Although a title that captures the reader's interest is an advantage for a paper, trying too hard for originality or impact is a mistake. If no striking title comes to mind, just name the subject of your paper as precisely as you can in a few words. Because the title is considered a separate part of the paper, it shouldn't be referred to by a pronoun in the opening sentence: not "This is an important issue today" but "The parking problem [or whatever you're writing about] is an important issue today."

2.   Referring to titles.
a.   Italics or quotation marks. For most purposes there's a simple rule of thumb: Italicize titles of long works (by underlining them) and quote titles of short works. Italics are traditional for titles of books, magazines, pamphlets, long poems, plays, movies, television series, symphonies, and operas. Quotation marks are usual for short stories, essays, short poems, songs, chapters of books, lectures, paintings, and pieces of sculpture.

b. Capitalizing. General practice is to capitalize the first and last words of titles and all intervening nouns, pronouns, verbs, adjectives, and adverbs. Some styles also capitalize prepositions and conjunctions that contain more than five letters. Examples: *Wit and Its Relation to the Unconscious; Peace through* [or *Through*] *Meditation;* "Hills like White Elephants''; "Nobody Knows You When You're Down and Out.'' Capitals are similarly used, without italics or quotation marks, in titles of unpublished works, book series, and books of the Bible.

The is capitalized and italicized or set within quotation marks only if it's part of the recognized title: *The Yale Law Review* but the *Harvard Law Review; The American Historical Review* but the *American Sociological Review; The New York Times* but the *Los Angeles Times.* In some styles initial *the* is never treated as part of the title of a newspaper or periodical. In the pamphlet entitled *The MLA Style Sheet,* that publication is referred to as "the *MLA Style Sheet.*''

c. Consistency. A writer should choose an accepted style for handling titles and stick to it. For example, the name of the city in a newspaper title may be either italicized or not italicized: the *Los Angeles Times,* the Los Angeles *Times.* Similarly, while strict formality may demand that a title be given in full each time it appears, current styles permit the use of short forms and the omission of initial articles when they would cause awkwardness: Hemingway's [*A*] *Moveable Feast* provides background for his [*The*] *Sun Also Rises.*

Many newspapers and magazines have their own rules for handling titles. Some use quotation marks around book titles and merely capitalize the names of periodicals. For the more rigid and detailed rules governing very formal writing, as in dissertations and scholarly articles, consult such treatments as Kate L. Turabian, *Manual for Writers of Term Papers, Theses, and Dissertations* (Chicago: Univ. of Chicago Press) and the *MLA Handbook.*

too

In the sense "also,'' *too* is sometimes set off by commas, sometimes not. At times commas are necessary for clarity. Without them, the sentence "Bob, too, frequently interrupted rehearsals to give advice'' could be taken to mean that Bob interrupted too often.

Though *too* is used to modify past participles after linking verbs in all varieties of usage (She was too excited; They were too concerned), conservative stylists prefer another adverb of degree between *too* and the participle: too greatly excited, too much concerned. Objection is strongest when the participle couldn't be placed before the noun or pronoun as a modifier: He is too identified with the opposition; Priests are too removed from real life. In such cases, many writers would use intervening adverbs—"too closely identified,'' "too far removed''—particularly in formal contexts.

Some formal stylists would continue to criticize both examples, on the grounds that the constructions are incomplete—"too closely identified" for what? "too far removed" for what?

See **not all that . . . , not too . . . .**

Topic sentence

Normally, the topic sentence is the broadest, most general statement in a paragraph, the one that expresses most directly the idea that the paragraph as a whole conveys. The other sentences in the paragraph develop the idea, particularize it, illustrate it, or qualify it.

1. Position. The topic sentence has no fixed position in a paragraph. Most often it's the first sentence, as it is in this paragraph, or the second sentence, coming immediately after a sentence that provides transition from the preceding paragraph. But the topic sentence sometimes stands at the end of a paragraph, pulling details and observations together into an inclusive statement. And occasionally it occurs midway through a paragraph, introduced by particulars that lead up to it and followed by further particulars that support or qualify it. In textbooks and in other types of explanation and instruction where it's vital that the reader have a firm grasp of each stage of the discussion, the writer sometimes sets forth the central idea at the start of a paragraph and restates it in a somewhat different way at the end.

2. Rhetorical use. Topic sentences keep a reader fully informed of the chief points being made. Phrasing topic sentences keeps the writer on track, too, encouraging him to stick to his subject and so maintain the unity of his essay. But in some situations—certainly in describing and narrating and also at times in arguing—he may simply supply details and impressions and leave it to the reader to recognize what the central idea is. If the writer has done his job well, the reader will come to the right conclusion.

3. Topic sentence, pointer statement, and thesis statement. If a reader asks what a paragraph adds up to, it probably needed a topic sentence. If he asks why he's suddenly in the middle of a new subject, it probably needed a pointer statement. If he asks what the purpose of the whole paper is—what it all adds up to—the writer should have formulated a thesis statement for himself.

A topic sentence sums up what a paragraph or sequence of paragraphs *says*. A pointer statement tells what the paragraph or sequence of paragraphs will *do* (or, sometimes, what it has done). "There are three kinds of joggers" is a pointer, an organizational signpost indicating that each kind of jogger will now be described. "But what do we mean by *success*?" is an implied promise to discuss the term.

An expository or argumentative paper usually has several topic sentences and perhaps a pointer or two. By contrast, it has just one thesis statement, and that statement may or may not appear in the paper. Whether or not it does, it's the writer's expression of the controlling idea of his entire paper.

See **Outline form 2, Paragraph indention, Thesis statement, Unity 2.**

🖉 *trans* Transition

Make the transition between these sentences (or paragraphs) clear and smooth.

Transitions are words or phrases or sentences that show the relationship between one statement and another, one paragraph and another, one part of a paper and another. When you write a sentence or paragraph as an isolated unit—as if nothing had preceded it and nothing is to follow it—your reader is bound to be puzzled. A lack of transition between one paragraph and another is sometimes a sign of faulty organization and sometimes simply evidence that you've neglected to provide a signpost that shows the reader where he's been and where he's going. A lack of transition between sentences usually indicates that you haven't thought through the relationship between consecutive statements.

1. Transitions as signals. The most familiar of the markers that indicate relationships and knit a piece of writing together are conjunctions and adverbs—*and, but, still, yet, for, because, then, though, while, in order that, first, second, however, moreover, therefore,* and so on.

Some of the choices available to indicate the common logical relationships are these:

a. Addition. When you want to call attention to the fact that you're adding something, *and* is the usual connector. Others that indicate equivalent, coordinate, or similar ideas are *also, again, once again, too, likewise, moreover, furthermore, then, in addition, by the same token, similarly, analogously.* You can indicate restatements with such phrases as *that is, to clarify, more simply* or by clauses like *what this means is.*

b. Contrast. When the relation is one of contrast—ranging from direct contradiction through various degrees of opposition, qualification, restriction, and concession—some of your choices are *but, yet, however, nevertheless, nonetheless, by contrast, at the same time, instead, in place of, conversely, actually, in fact, to be sure, at any rate, anyway, still, of course, on the other hand, provided that, in case.*

c. Alternatives. You can call attention to an alternative or option by using *or, nor, either, neither, alternatively, on the other hand* (often following *on the one hand*).

d. Causal relations. You can indicate a causal relationship with *for, because, since, then, as.* You can point to a result or consequence with various words and phrases, among them *so, then, therefore, thus, hence, accordingly, as a result, in consequence.*

e.   Illustration. When what follows illustrates what has come before or particularizes it in some way, some of your choices are *for example, for instance, thus, to illustrate, in particular, namely.*

f.   Sequence. When the relation is sequential, your transitions may indicate relationships of time or space in the subject itself, or they may point up the organization of the paper. Sample time indicators are *then, soon, after, now, earlier, later, ten years ago.* Sample space indicators are *here, there, on top, in the middle, below, on the left, on the right, beyond.* You can indicate sequence by transitions like *for one thing, for another; first, second, third; to begin with; in short, in brief; finally, to summarize, in conclusion, as we have seen.* Other transitions bring out the relative importance of points— *more important, less important, above and beyond.*

2.   Transitions and style.   A transition should give an accurate indication of the relationship you intend. Beyond that, the transition marker should be in keeping with the style and tone of your paper.

a.   Accurate markers. *Actually* and *incidentally* are overworked as transitions. Since *actually* often introduces a correction and *incidentally* a digression, both may be signs that revision is needed. An unwarranted transition—for example, a *therefore* when what follows is not the result of what precedes—can be seriously misleading.

b.   Apt markers. Though *first, second, third* are preferable to old-fashioned *firstly, secondly, thirdly,* they're appropriate only when the material demands emphatic division. Overuse of any of the heavier connectives (*however, nevertheless, consequently*) can clog your style. Often you can make a transition that's just as clear, less obtrusive, and stylistically more pleasing by repeating a key word from sentence to sentence, by using a synonym or a pronoun to echo or pick up the key word, and by binding sentences or parts of sentences by means of parallel structures. Whether emphatic or subtle, transitions are your chief means of giving a piece of writing coherence.

Transitive and intransitive verbs

A transitive verb is used with a direct object; an intransitive verb is not so used: The janitor put (transitive) the books on the shelf, but they soon vanished (intransitive). Many verbs are transitive in one sense and intransitive in another: He grows corn; The corn grows well. See **lay, lie; set, sit.**

trite Triteness

Replace the trite expression with one that is simpler and fresher.

The most troublesome trite expressions, or clichés, are worn-out figures of speech or phrases: picture of health, break of day, reign supreme, from the face of the earth, crack of dawn, acid test. What was once fresh and striking has become stale and boring from being used again and again with no sense of its figurativeness. But triteness is not a matter of age. Yesterday's vogue expression can be as boring to a reader as one that dates back generations. In fact, a young reader may be more familiar with a new cliché than with an old one. So if you find yourself writing down a phrase without even stopping to think about it, stop and think about it. Think twice. Trite expression is the natural vehicle for trite ideas.

This doesn't mean that you should mistrust everyday English. Often a well-established phrase, with its connotations, will express your meaning accurately and succinctly. Going out of your way to avoid an expression only because it's been used many times before may force you into awkwardness, incoherence, or absurdly "fine" writing. The important thing is to be aware of what you're putting on paper, to be conscious of your stylistic choices and rhetorical decisions.

See **Figures of speech, Formulas, Vogue words.**

try and

The standard idiom *try and*—"Neither Congress nor the Court itself seemed prepared to try and force him to resign" (*Newsweek*)—appears regularly in general and informal contexts, but formal stylists and many general stylists prefer *try to*.

-type

The use of *-type* in compound modifiers (Polaris-type missile, family-type programs) has spread in all varieties of usage but continues to irritate many readers. Most writers choose *type of* (Polaris type of missile) or, where possible, simply omit *type* (family programs). The practice of shortening *type of* and *make of* to *type* (this type letter) and *make* (that make car) is informal.

Typewritten copy

Use only one side of the sheet, leave wide margins at both left and right, keep the type clean, and change the ribbon regularly. In first drafts, using triple space and leaving extra space between paragraphs will provide room for revision. Double space the final draft.

Indent the first lines of paragraphs five spaces. For long quotations in double-spaced copy, indent each line as in a paragraph indention and single-space the quoted matter. Use no quotation marks with these block quotations.

For the figure 1 use small *l*, not capital *I*. For a dash, use two hyphens. Leave one space after all punctuation marks except at the end of sentences; there, leave two spaces.

Transposed letters should be erased and retyped or corrected with a curved line.

Strike̸o̸vers [*not* Strikevoers] are often hard to read.

Your instructor probably won't mind if you correct a few mistakes in ink, but you should retype any page that has more than a few.
See **Caret.**

U

Underlining

Underlining in manuscripts is used to mark titles that aren't quoted, words used as words, foreign expressions that haven't been anglicized, and—sparingly—words or word groups that you want to emphasize. See **Italics.**

Understatement

Understating is one means of emphasizing: Eight o'clock classes are not universally popular. See **Figurative language, Figures of speech, Negatives and style.**

uninterested

To be uninterested is to lack interest; to be disinterested is to be neutral, which is not the same thing. But see **disinterested, uninterested.**

unique

In strict formal usage *unique* means "single," "sole," "unequaled" and consequently is not compared. In general usage *unique,* like many other words that once had an absolute meaning, has become an adjective of degree. As an emphatic "unusual," "rare," or "remarkable," it's often found compared with *more* or *most:* "The more unique his language, the more peculiarly his own will be the colouring of his language" (Otto Jesperson, *Mankind, Nation and Individual from a Linguistic Point of View*). Because of this varied usage, a reader may find unqualified *unique* ambiguous. The writer of the following sentence may have been guarding against that possibility: "It is a unique festival, and there is nothing like it in the world'' (Harold C. Schonberg, *New York Times*). Though redundant by strict formal standards, the second clause is probably practical. See **Comparison of adjectives and adverbs.**

United States

Like many proper nouns, *United States* is often used as an attributive (that is, as an adjective preceding the word it modifies): "There are some who think that the United States attempt to overthrow the Castro government was an act of international immorality" (Richard H. Rovere, *New Yorker*). No apostrophe is needed. Since *United States* has no adjectival form, its use as an attributive often sounds awkward, unless it's abbreviated to *U.S.* In most contexts *American* is preferable. See **American.**

un Unity

Unify this passage.

A sentence, a paragraph, or a paper is unified when its parts fit together to make a consistent whole. You weaken the unity of what you write when you include material that stands outside—or seems to stand outside—the core of thought or feeling you want to communicate.

Your first obligation as a writer is to have a purpose in writing and a controlling idea to which everything you include in the paper contributes. Your second obligation is to build your sentences and paragraphs in such a way that your train of thought, and in the end your purpose, will be clear to your audience.

Failures in unity can be real, as when a writer introduces irrelevant material, or apparent, as when a writer doesn't make plain to his readers a relationship that's perfectly plain to him. The first is a failure in reasoning (see **Logical thinking**). The second is a failure in composition, especially in continuity (see **Coherence, Transition**). A sentence, a paragraph, or a paper may be coherent but not unified. It may also be unified but not coherent. Good writing is both coherent and unified.

Without the context—and here *context* means both the writer's thinking about his subject and his expression of his thought—deciding whether a passage lacks unity or coherence is difficult. But some hints can be given about ways of strengthening passages that have been criticized for lacking unity.

1. Unity in sentences. For a sentence that lacks unity, there are three possible remedies:
a. Delete any phrase or clause that isn't related to the central thought. In the sentence "Parking space on the campus, which is one of the most beau-

tiful in the state, has become completely inadequate, and recently the city council voted to increase bus fares again,'' delete the *which* clause.

b.   Subordinate one statement to another to show the logical relationship. Even if readers of the sentence quoted in **a** can figure out a connection between the shortage of parking space and the cost of public transportation, the coordinating *and* obscures the writer's point. A possible revision: At a time when the shortage of parking space makes commuting to campus by car almost impossible, the city council has discouraged the use of public transportation by increasing bus fares once more.

c.   Separate seemingly disconnected statements, making two sentences, and bring in material that will provide a logical link between them. Between a sentence about inadequate parking space and a sentence about increased bus fares, this sentence might be introduced: But the commuting student is not being encouraged to switch to public transportation. See **Coordination, Sentences, Subordination.**

2.   Unity in paragraphs.   As a general rule, a paragraph lacks unity when one or more of its sentences fail to contribute to its central idea. When that idea is expressed in a topic sentence, both writer and reader can see just where the discussion slides away from the main point. So it's wise to provide topic sentences when your subject is so complicated that a reader might need help in following your treatment of it. On the other hand, you can do without topic sentences if the logic of your thought, or the strength of your emotion, creates a unified topic *idea* that the paragraph gets across to your readers.

Sticking to a subject doesn't in itself guarantee unity. In a paragraph on Robert Frost, all the sentences may be about the poet, but if two of them deal with his current reputation, one with his last public appearance, one with his marriage, and three with his poem "After Apple-Picking," it's unlikely that the paragraph will have unity. Bringing together several loosely related subjects usually means that no one of them will be adequately developed and that the paragraph will have no central focus. See **Paragraph indention, Topic sentence.**

3.   Unity in papers.   Even when each paragraph is unified, the paper as a whole may not be. Each paragraph should bear on the writer's purpose (whether or not that purpose is expressed in a thesis statement), and the paragraphs should be in such an order and so linked that the reader sees the relation of each of them to the controlling idea.

A useful way of testing a paper for unity is to outline it. Questions of relevance and relatedness can be more easily answered when you've seen through the surface of what you've written to the underlying structure. Reduce each paragraph to a heading. If your paper is brief—no more than four or five paragraphs, say—each paragraph may represent a main point; but in a longer paper the paragraphs should fall into logical groups or sequences with each sequence developing a theme. Be on the lookout for a heading that doesn't logically follow the preceding heading or lead into the next one. If you find such a heading, reexamine your organization, and if there's no slot that the heading obviously fills, consider dropping the paragraph it stands for. If you find a sequence of paragraphs that strays from your central thesis, you need to do some rethinking and rewriting. See **Organization, Outline form, Thesis statement.**

until, till

Until and *till* (not *'til*) are interchangeable. See **till, until.**

Upside-down subordination

Subordination is said to be upside-down when logically the dependent clause should be independent and the independent clause should be dependent. See **Subordination 3.**

Usage

The study of usage depends on wide observation of what people say and write in various situations. This observation serves as a basis for judging the standing of particular words, forms, and constructions. Works on usage include scholarly studies of the ways language is used, and has been used, in speech, in print, in letters, and so on; polls to determine attitudes toward particular usages; and guides to usage based in large part on the authors' personal taste. Both the polls and the guides focus on disputed usages— locutions accepted by some, rejected by others—and it is this area of usage study that has most interested the general public.

Researchers have built up a picture of what educated users of American English say and, more especially, write. But for many people who are interested in usage, what *is* is not nearly so important as what *should be.* Most of the popular guides to usage are conservative—that is, they restrict ''correct'' English to usages and constructions that this *Index* associates with formal styles.

Students in particular should be aware of the influence of age on what readers accept and what they reject. In *Harper's Dictionary of Current Usage,* Walter ''Red'' Smith, member of a panel that commented on particular usages, had this to say: ''In usage I accept what I have come to accept and reject what I don't accept.'' All of us find it very easy to accept what we grew up with, but as we become older, accepting new words, new meanings, new forms of expression becomes increasingly difficult. One purpose of this book is to remind students that many of the usages they take for granted are offensive to some older readers. This doesn't mean that students should adopt the attitudes toward usage of the middle-aged—and certainly not of those who see the language in imminent danger of "destruction." It does mean that they should be conscious of their audiences whenever they write.

The reaction to *Webster's Third New International Dictionary of the English Language* in 1961 revealed the intense concern about usage felt by an articulate minority of Americans. The publishers of the dictionary had decided to apply usage labels much more sparingly than in the past, on the grounds that the primary role of a dictionary was to record usage, not evaluate it, and that it was often impossible to label with any precision words taken out of context. Praised by many scholars, the decision was attacked in newspaper editorials and magazine articles as an abandonment of standards. Dictionaries published since then have been more prescriptive than *Webster's Third,* and few of the more recent books of linguistic etiquette have been as liberal as *A Dictionary of Contemporary American Usage* by Bergen and Cornelia Evans, published in 1957.

The polling technique introduced into usage study in the 1930s has been adapted by commercial publishers of dictionaries and books on usage: panels of journalists, novelists, columnists, commentators, and others concerned in one way or another with verbal communication vote on the "acceptability" of items of usage presented to them by the editors, who select the panels and also the usage "problems" the panels consider. Majority opinion is almost invariably conservative. (Panel members are predominantly middle-aged and older.) Panelists tend to express their opinions as vehemently and emotionally as do those ordinary citizens who write letters to newspapers and magazines deploring the corruption and decline of English.

Such emotionalism reveals that while word watching can make anyone's reading more interesting and his writing both richer and more precise, it can also become an unfortunate obsession. It's bad enough when the watcher (and listener) insists on "correcting" the usage of others. It's much worse when he makes usage the criterion for judging not only their educational and social level but their intelligence and their character.

Like every user of the language, you must make your own choices. They should be intelligent choices, based on sound information. The best safeguard against avoidable bias is some principle of selection, and the principle proposed in this *Index* is appropriateness. There is also the intangible called taste. If, like most of us, you find some locutions too stuffy or too crude, you can simply not use them. No one can control the usage of others, but everyone can control his own.

utilize

Utilize means "put to use." The verb *use* is almost always a better choice.

verbal, oral

Though *verbal* is widely used to mean "spoken," many word watchers insist on *oral* for that meaning. See **oral, verbal.**

Verbals

The parts of a verb that function as nouns or adjectives are called verbals. For their various uses see **Gerunds, Infinitives, Participles.**

Verbs

1.   Forms.   If we exclude *be* and the modal auxiliaries, all verbs can add to the base form *(ask, sing, tear)* the suffix *-ing (asking),* the suffix *-s (asks),* and the suffix *-ed (asked)* or use some other change in form as the equivalent of the *-ed—sing, sings, singing, sang, sung; tear, tears, tearing, tore, torn. Be* has eight forms *(be, am, is, are, was, were, being, been); can, may, must,* and other modal auxiliaries have only one or two forms. We recognize verbs by their form and their position in a sentence even when we don't know what they mean. In "I am sure that his words will coruscate," we recognize *am* and *will* as verbs because we've already learned their forms. Even if we've never seen or heard *coruscate,* we recognize it as a verb because it depends on *will.*

Verbs fall into two classes: a closed one (no new verbs are added) whose function is primarily grammatical, and an open one (new verbs are constantly added) in which the meaning of the words is important. In "He got hurt," *got* performs the grammatical function of showing past tense and passive voice, and *hurt* carries the lexical meaning. See **Auxiliaries, Gerunds, Infinitives, Participles, Principal parts of verbs, Tenses of verbs, Voice.**

2.   Function.   Verbs, with their modifiers and any objects or complements, form the predicates of clauses, which are combinations of subjects and predicates. See **Agreement, Clauses, Linking verbs, Objects, Predicates, Transitive and intransitive verbs.**

Verbs and style

The rhetorical function of a verb is usually to comment on the topic of a sentence. Generally speaking, the important action in a sentence should be in the main verb after the topic-subject has been stated. In the sentence

"The possibility of a decision in regard to an investigation of reasons for student transfer exists," the one verb is *exists*. It states only that the very long and complicated topic-subject is there for the reader to consider. But the important action is not that a possibility exists; it's that someone may decide to investigate why students transfer: [The president?] may decide to investigate why students transfer. This sentence has two verbs—*decide* and *transfer*—and a verbal, the infinitive *to investigate*. The crucial actions in a sentence should be represented by verbs, not in the abstract nouns related to verbs. See **Absolute phrases, Conditional clauses, Nominalization, Passive voice, Subjunctive mood, Tense.**

Vernacular

Vernacular once meant "the local language as opposed to Latin." In England the word was used to refer to natural spoken English as opposed to formal literary English, and this usage gained social and political overtones in the United States. In the 1800s Mark Twain wrote stories and Walt Whitman wrote poems in styles adapted from ordinary speech. Since then it's been impossible to flatly oppose the literary language to the vernacular language, for the vernacular has been more important to American literature than the formal or academic. See **Colloquial English.**

very

1. As a qualifier. *Very* is so much used as a qualifier that some teachers and editors have tried to outlaw it. But as long as it's used sparingly, *very* is a much better choice than overblown intensifiers like *incredibly, terribly, fantastically,* and so on.

2. With past participles. Some readers complain about the use of *very* before past participles that are not established in adjectival function, on the grounds that *very* ("extremely") can't modify verbals. They insist that an adverb of degree, such as *greatly* or *much,* must stand between *very* and these participles—not "very disoriented" but "very much disoriented." In general practice some past participles regularly take *very* (very troubled), some *much* (much improved), some either (very pleased, much pleased), some neither (lighted). Let your ear be your guide.

Vogue words

Particular words and expressions are constantly enjoying great popularity in one social or professional group or another, but a true vogue word is one that's moved into general usage and there become a fad. Some begin in the slang of the black ghetto or the campus and find their way into the copy of advertising writers. Others start in the professions or the bureaucracy and become clichés through the efforts of journalists and commentators. Still others are borrowings, like the British *early on*. As P. A. Duhamel has said, "The jargon of the day can so fascinate some speakers that they will repeat it mindlessly, substituting incantation for communication" *(Boston Herald-Advertiser)*. Writers are not immune to this weakness.

Some vogue words and expressions have little specific meaning to begin with, in the contexts in which they appear. (For a time the word *like* was used in place of a grunt as a filler in conversation.) Through endless repetition other vogue words lose what force and meaning they had *(actually, basically, meaningful, relevant)*. Still others take on so many meanings in so many different contexts as to become almost meaningless *(massive, concept, scenario)*. Whether short and simple *(thrust)* or long and fancy *(counterproductive)*, all vogue words have one thing in common: they've become a bore. Writers should do their best to avoid using them.

See **Cliché, Gobbledygook, Slang, Triteness.**

Voice

Voice is a term borrowed from the grammars of the classical languages, where it usually differentiates distinctive verb endings. In English, *passive voice* refers to constructions made with the past participle and some form of the verb *be* (was killed). All other verb forms are *active*.

	Active voice	*Passive voice*
Present:	he asks (is asking)	he is asked (is being asked)
Future:	he will ask	he will be asked
Perfect:	he has asked	he has been asked
Infinitives:	to ask, to have asked	to be asked, to have been asked
Participles:	asking, having asked	being asked, asked, having been asked

Get is also used for the passive, especially in informal English: If he should get elected, we'd be lost; Our house is getting painted. See **Passive voice.**

wait on, wait for

Wait on for *wait for* (She's waiting on the mail) is regional or dialectal.

wake

English is oversupplied with verbs for waking from sleep (intransitive) and waking someone else from sleep (transitive). Most common is *wake (woke* or *waked; woke, waked,* or *woken),* to which *up* is frequently added in general English. *Awaken (awakened, awakened)* is almost as common but more formal. *Awake (awoke* or *awaked; awoke, awaked,* or *awoken)* is rather formal. *Waken (wakened, wakened)* is least used.

want

Except in the rather rare sense "have need" (They want for the bare necessities of life), *want* should not be followed by *for:* I want [for] you to go. Nor should it be followed by a *that* clause: I want that you should go.

Want for "ought," "had better" (You want to review all the notes if you're going to pass the exam) is informal.

Want in and *want out* (That dog wants out) occur in general and informal writing but not in formal.

way, ways

Way in the sense "far" is established in general writing, though not in formal: "It goes way back to his red-baiting days" (T.R.B., *New Republic*).

There's some prejudice against the use of *ways* to mean "distance," as in "a little way[s] down the road."

we

We is frequently used as an indefinite pronoun in expressions like "we find" and "we feel," to avoid passive and impersonal constructions. It's also used to mean "I and others," as in writing for a group or institution. In newspapers and magazines, editorial *we* may speak for the publication; in books it can mean "you readers and I," "all of us" (with *us* ranging from a limited group to the entire human race), or simply "I, the author." And there is the royal *we* of monarchs and popes, the corporate *we* of business letters, and, particularly since the growth of radio-television "talk" shows, the *we* that can only mean "I," as in an entertainer's "We always draw well in Vegas."

We for *I* has been taken up by some ordinary citizens, with no hint of publicity agents, teammates, or bureaucratic associates, on the peculiar grounds that it's more modest. It isn't.

See **I.**

well, good

Well is either an adjective (She looks well) or an adverb (He swam well). *Good* is an adjective (a good feeling). See **good, well.**

what

When a predicate nominative connected to a *what* clause by a linking verb is singular, the verb is singular: What I want to discuss is the responsibility of students. When the predicate nominative is plural, usage is divided:

> . . . what surprises and captures the reader is the hundreds of black-and-white photographs. . . .—*Time*

> What he wanted were people who could stimulate. . . .—Anthony Starr, *Esquire*

when, where

A *when* or *where* clause is probably the standard form for defining in informal usage and occurs often in general contexts: Welding is when (*or* where) two pieces of metal are heated and made into one. But there is strong prejudice against it. The grammatical argument is that an adverbial clause can't serve as the predicate complement of a noun, which requires as complement another noun or a noun phrase or clause: Welding is the process by which two pieces of metal are heated and made into one.

whether

Or not is required after *whether* when *whether* introduces a complete or elliptical adverbial clause: Whether [he is] right or not, he deserves a hearing. In noun clauses *or not* may be used for emphasis; but it isn't necessary and many writers prefer to omit it:

> Whether readers find him successful will depend on their patience.—Charles F. Mullet, *American Historical Review*

> If the child at home wonders whether he is loved, the pupil in school wonders whether he is a worthwhile person.—Robert Dreeben, *Harvard Educational Review*

When the alternatives are spelled out, *or not* is redundant: Whether [or not] the move is good or bad is debatable.

Repeating *whether* after *or* (Whether . . . or whether . . .) can be helpful to readers when the alternatives are long and complex, as in some formal or technical contexts.

See **Conditional clauses; if, whether.**

which

1. For broad reference. The use of *which* to refer to the whole idea of a preceding clause (They plan to tear it down, *which* is a pity) is well established, but objections are properly raised when the reference is so loose that, at first reading, the *which* seems to refer only to the preceding word: She liked the book, *which* was puzzling. Similarly, a reader shouldn't have to wrestle with two *which*'s, one of specific and one of broad reference, in a single short sentence: I worked Saturdays to earn money *which* was owed on the car, *which* pleased my parents.

2. In the possessive.   *Whose* as the possessive of *which* is older and less cumbersome than *of which* and is preferred by most writers: "a pattern whose outlines are clearly visible" rather than "a pattern the outlines of which are. . . ."

3. In parallel clauses.   When parallel relative clauses with the same antecedent are connected by a coordinating conjunction, a writer sometimes omits the relative pronoun before the first clause and then uses it before the second: "It seems to hold as much promise for American politics as the second-hand legislative reforms [ ] Sinclair propounded in his novels, and which successive Democratic administrations enacted" (Andrew Kopkind, *New York Times Book Review*). In this example, the missing *which* could be inserted, or the *which* after *and* could be dropped.

Sometimes a single adjective *which* clause is attached to a main clause by *and* or *but:* In elementary school I became interested in ballet, not a very popular art form where I lived, and which most of my classmates thought was silly. Omitting the *and* in this clumsy sentence only creates confusion, because without it the *which* doesn't seem to have any reference at all. The mixed construction can be turned into a balanced one by inserting *which was* before *not:* In elementary school I became interested in ballet, which was not a very popular art form . . . —and which most of my classmates thought was silly. See **Subordination 2.**

4. *Which* or *that*.   For the choice between *which* and *that* as relative pronouns, see **that.**

while

The central meaning of *while* is "during the time that": While the rest were playing cards, he was studying. In general English *while* is also used to mean "although" or "whereas" (While the cast is talented, the play is a bore) and to introduce the second of two clauses in place of *though* or *but* (The beagle was a thoroughbred, while the rest of the pack were mongrels). Because of the several senses, *while* can create ambiguity unless you use it with care. Among formal stylists there's some prejudice against *while* when no sense of time is involved.

who, whom

In all varieties of English, *who* is consistently used for subjects except when it's immediately followed by the subject of an interrupting clause. Then what *The New Yorker* used to call The Omnipotent Whom is common, as if the pronoun rather than its clause were the object of the interrupting clause: "children whom Taylor thinks can bend spoons by paranormal powers" (Martin Gardner, *New York Review of Books*). As subject, *who* is the right form in such constructions.

In formal styles *whom* is consistently used for objects, but informal and general styles often break the traditional rule. General usage permits *who* in questions like these:

> And who was the hard sell aimed at?—Mary McCarthy, *New York Review of Books*

> Who are they trying to impress?—Bruce Price, *Washington Post*

The reason educated writers sometimes accept *who* as object when they'd reject *I, we, he, she,* and *they* is that *who* is so often in subject territory, preceding the verb. When the pronoun functions as subject, function and position are in harmony, and *who* is the natural choice. When the pronoun functions as object, function and position are at odds. In formal contexts most writers ignore position and let function determine form. In casual conversation and casual writing, position is allowed to determine form. General usage usually favors the demands of function except when the pronoun introduces the whole sentence (Who can we turn to?). In college writing, subject *who* and object *whom* are usually the appropriate choices, unless *whom* sounds unnatural in the context.

See **one of those who.**

whose

Whose is interchangeable with *of which* and often the better choice. See **which 2.**

will, shall

Whether pointing to the future and expressing determination or simply indicating the future, *will* is more common than *shall* in all three persons. See **shall, will.**

-wise

Over a long period the suffix *-wise* was used to form a limited number of adverbs from nouns (*edgewise, lengthwise, slantwise*). Some years ago it increased in faddish use, especially in an abstract rather than a special sense *(average-wise, budget-wise, weather-wise, tax-wise)* until new *-wise* words became a joke. Now both the overuse and the ridicule have died down. When a noun has no established adjectival form, a *-wise* coinage may serve a need and save space. But often the *-wise* word lacks precision *(production-wise)*; sometimes it saves no space *(economy-wise* versus *in economy);* and it may simply duplicate an existing word *(drama-wise* for *dramatically).* Besides, tacked-on *-wise* incites some readers to violence.

woman, lady, girl

An adult human female is a woman. She may or may not be a lady, just as a man may or may not be a gentleman. Feminists oppose the use of *girl* for any human female who is no longer a child.

𝒲 Wordiness

Replace the wordy expressions with more compact and exact ones.

There are two cures for wordiness—surgery and treatment. Surgery means cutting out words. Treatment means revising or rewriting.

1. Cut out deadwood, the type of wordiness that contributes nothing but clutter:

> At [the age of] forty he was a handsome [looking] man.
> In [the case of] television commercials, stereotypes are everywhere.
> The writer is a member of a cultural minority because [of the fact that] he is a writer.
> The architecture [of the buildings] and the landscaping [of the grounds] speak of town pride.
> [It also happened that] we were the same age.
> He kept things moving in [the field of] basset breeding throughout [the entirety of] his career.

The most common deadwood consists of unnecessary phrases like "green *in color*," "seven *in number*," "rectangular *in shape*" and clichés like "in the business world" and "in the field of economics," which you may use without thinking. Good writing requires thought. When you revise a first draft, look closely at every phrase. Does "green in color" mean any more than "green"? Doesn't "in business" say everything that "in the world of business" says?

Sometimes a phrase that contributes nothing to the meaning of a sentence nevertheless fits its rhythm or has some other stylistic justification. Perhaps adding "in my life" to "for the first time" provides a desired emphasis. But as a rule simply eliminating deadwood is a step toward a compact, direct, honest prose style.

2. Compress inflated passages.   When deadwood is involved, no replacement is necessary, but loose, unfocused expression often demands rewriting:

> The reason that I'm telling all this is because I want to demonstrate in the clearest way possible that the cultural background of my family was of such a nature as to encourage my interest in the reading of books, magazines, etc.
>
> *Rewritten:* All this shows that my family background encouraged me to read.

Using unnecessary words produces flabby writing. You can often improve a first draft greatly by reducing long-winded phrases and other circumlocutions to single words that are more direct, more emphatic, and at least as clear:

Instead of		
	in this day and age	today
	at this point in time	now
	during the time that	while
	in the event that	if
	at the conclusion of	after

ⱳ **Word order**

Change the order of words or other elements to make the meaning clear or the phrasing more natural or more effective.

The placing of words and word groups in a sentence is the most important means of showing their grammatical relationships. Word order plays a major role in style, particularly in achieving emphasis.

1. Interrupted constructions.   Keep your subjects close to your verbs. When a word or words interrupt a construction, the effect is usually clumsy unless the interrupter deserves special emphasis:

> *Between subject and verb:* Newspaper headlines *in these trying and confused times* are continually intensifying our fears.
>
> *More natural:* In these trying and confused times, newspaper headlines are. . . .

2. Wandering modifiers.   Keep your modifiers close to the words they modify. When modifiers are separated from their headwords, the result is frequently awkward, sometimes misleading:

Bob recovered from exhaustion plus what apparently was a bug making the rounds following two days' bedrest.—Grace Lichtenstein, *New York Times*

Better: Following two days' bedrest, Bob. . . .

Her uncle, King Leopold, was even unable to influence her.

Better: Even her uncle. . . .

I decided that if I moved in the direction of the apple tree growing beside the fence calmly, I might make it before the bull charged.

Better: . . . moved calmly in the direction. . . .

3. Word order and emphasis. Don't change normal word order unless you have a reason for doing so. As a rule an element shifted from its usual position receives increased emphasis, as when the object is put before subject and verb:

Object first: I was surprised to find Salinger's novel on the list. *That book* I read when I was fourteen.

Predicate adjective first: Lucky are the ones who need no longer worry.

See **Ambiguity, Dangling modifiers.**

world

Inflated phrases with *world*—"the business world," "the fashion world," "the world of science" (or economics or politics or athletics)—can usually be collapsed: After graduation he went into [the world of] advertising. "Today's modern world" means "today." In other cases more specific language is preferable: This is especially true in the world of jazz [*better:* among jazz musicians]. *Area, field,* and *realm* are misused in the same way.

would, should

In indirect discourse, *shall* as well as *will* is likely to be reported as *would:* She said, "We shall see"; She said that we would see. See **should, would.**

would have, would of

Would of for *would have* is nonstandard. See **have 3.**

𝓌𝓌 Wrong word

Replace the word marked with one that says what you mean.

No word is right or wrong in itself. As a correction symbol, *ww* means that the word does not convey a meaning that makes sense in the context. In the sentence "What he said showed real comprehensibility of the problems of Asia," *comprehensibility* doesn't make sense; it's the wrong word. *Comprehension* (or *understanding*) would be the right word. In "Some people remain stagnant to the lessons of life," *stagnant* needs to be replaced—possibly by *oblivious*. In "I remember explicitly my first puff," *clearly* would be a good choice to replace *explicitly*. Errors like these occur when you use words without being sure of their meaning, when you confuse words of similar sound, or when you simply write too hurriedly and fail to proofread your work. Sometimes a spelling is so wide of the mark (*bonified* for *bona fide*) that it's marked *ww* or *mng*. See **Careless mistakes; Meaning; precedence, precedent.**

X **Correct the obvious error.**

See **Careless mistakes.**

Xmas

X is the first letter in the Greek word for *Christ*. It's been used for centuries as an abbreviation in the word *Xmas*, pronounced exactly like *Christmas*. Today, however, *Xmas* is most likely to be pronounced *eks mus,* and for many its popularity with advertisers has given it unpleasant commercial connotations. Except for purposes of irony, *Xmas* is inappropriate in serious writing.

yet

Yet is both an adverb (The books haven't come yet) and a coordinating conjunction roughly equivalent to *but:* His speech was almost unintelligible, yet I found I enjoyed it. *But* is less formal and much more common.

you

In giving instructions, as in a how-to paper, *you* is often a good stylistic choice (Then you glue the bottom strip . . .), certainly preferable to repeated use of the passive (The bottom strip is then glued . . .). As an impersonal pronoun, *you* is more common than *one* in general usage and not at all rare in formal:

> In a sense, Richard III, as Shakespeare sees him, is a little boy who has found out that God does not strike you dead when you tell a lie.—Arnold Edinborough, *Shakespeare Quarterly*

> There are at least three ways to treat any philosophical work: (1) You may inquire into its background. . . .—Frederick Sontag, *Journal of Religion*.

Writers should avoid switching back and forth between *you* and *one* and should take care that their *you, your* is clearly indefinite, not personal. "Your parents depend on alcohol and pills to get them through the day" might better be "Our parents. . . ."

See **one, they.**

youth

As a collective noun, *youth* meaning "young people in general" can be followed by either singular or plural verbs and pronouns. In American usage the singular construction is much more common: "Russian youth wants to avoid military conscription as sincerely as American youth does" (George Feifer, *New York Times Magazine*). But when *the* precedes *youth*, a plural verb is often desirable to make clear that more than a single person is meant: The increase in tuition made education too expensive for the youth who were most in need of it.

Though the collective use includes both sexes, *youth* meaning "a young person" ordinarily refers to a young man, and the usual plural is *youths*.

Youth isn't a comfortable word for either a group or an individual. *Young people, adolescents, young men and women, girls and boys, boy(s),* or *young man* (or *men*) is often a better choice.

See **kid.**

 A correction symbol indicating approval—"good idea," "well expressed," and so on.

Additional Correction Symbols

Correction Chart

To the student: When one of these correction symbols calls attention to a weakness in your paper, look up the *Index* entry that discusses the problem, and make the revision. The symbols in the chart are arranged alphabetically; page numbers for the entries follow the instructions.

ab   Write out this word. Or use the standard abbreviation.   1

abst   Make this word or passage more concrete or more specific.   4

adj   Reconsider your choice of adjective.   7

adv   Correct the form or change the position of the adverb. Or reconsider your choice of adverb.   10

agr   Make the verb agree with its subject or the pronoun with its antecedent.   12

amb   Make your meaning unmistakable.   18

apos ⩔   Insert or remove an apostrophe as required.   24

beg   Revise the beginning of your paper to make it lead more directly and smoothly into your subject or to arouse your reader's interest.   32

cap   Capitalize the word marked.   45

case   Correct the mistake in case.   48

coh   Make clear the relation between the parts of this sentence or between these sentences or paragraphs.   54

colon ⌄   Use a colon here. Or reconsider the use of this colon.   56

comma ⌃   Insert or remove comma here: C_1 between independent clauses, 59; C_2 with preceding or following elements, 60; C_3 with nonrestrictive modifiers, 61; C_4 with interrupting and parenthetical words and phrases, 61; C_5 in lists and series, 62; C_6 for clarity, 63; C_7 for emphasis, 63; C_8 with main

sentence elements, 63; C_9 in conventional practice, 64; C_{10} with other marks of punctuation, 64.

comp   Correct the fault in comparing the adjective or adverb marked.   67

conj   Make this conjunction more accurate or more appropriate to the style of the passage.   72

coord   Correct the faulty coordination.   78

cs   Revise this sentence to correct the comma splice.   64

d   Replace this word with one that is more exact, more appropriate, or more effective.   93

dm   Revise the sentence so that the expression marked is clearly related to the word it is intended to modify.   82

det   Develop this passage more fully by giving pertinent details.   91

div   Break the word at the end of this line between syllables.   97

emp   Strengthen the emphasis of this passage.   103

end   Revise the ending of your paper to round out the discussion.   104

fig   Replace this trite, inconsistent, or inappropriate figure of speech.   114

form   Make this word or passage less formal, more appropriate to your style, subject, and audience.   118

frag   Make this construction a grammatically complete sentence, or join it to a neighboring sentence.   119

gloss   See this *Index* for an entry on the word marked.

id   Replace this expression with standard idiom.   135

inf   Make this word or passage less informal, more appropriate to your style, subject, and audience.   141